# DOUGLAS COUNTY, NEBRASKA MARRIAGES 1854–1881

*Compiled by*

Greater Omaha Genealogical Society
and Friends

P.O. Box 4011
Omaha, NE 68104

CLEARFIELD

Printed for
Clearfield Company, Inc. by
Genealogical Publishing Co., Inc.
Baltimore, Maryland
2002

International Standard Book Number: 0-8063-5129-2

*Made in the United States of America*

# INTRODUCTION

The marriage records in this publication have been transcribed from the original county marriage applications and records. Microfilm copies of the marriage applications and records are available in the office of the Douglas County, Nebraska County Clerk and the Nebraska State Historical Society, 1500 R Street, Lincoln, NE 68508. Microfilm copies of only the marriage records are available at the W. Dale Clark Library, 215 South 15th Street, Omaha, NE 68102. The original marriage applications and records for this time period are now in the custody of the Historical Society of Douglas County Library/Archives Center, 30th and Fort Streets, Omaha, NE. All marriage records prior to 1909 were kept in each county.

The text includes all marriages and applications for marriages, even if the marriage did not take place. It also includes all extra information recorded on the application or license. It is noted when there is no evidence a marriage actually took place. Researchers are encouraged to check the original record. Every effort has been made to assure the accuracy of this transcription; however, gremlins creep in and cause errors. It is often difficult to read a handwritten record accurately.

Information in this publication is arranged in alphabetical order of grooms Every name is indexed except the official performing the ceremony. Occasionally a name as found in the original record is "known" to be wrong. Annotation in brackets after a name shows the "known" correct name. All versions of a name are included in the index. The index lists brides by both their married and maiden names.

To read a citation:

Name of groom [age of groom; current residence of groom; place of birth of groom; father of groom; mother of groom] *Maiden* name of bride [age of bride; current residence of bride; place of birth of bride; father of bride; mother of bride] date of marriage, place of marriage. *Official. Witness.* Unfortunately, not every record includes all of this information.

AAGAARD, Jens Joseph [20; Omaha; b: Denmark; f: Jens AAGAARD; m: Inger NIELSON] md. Petrina Maria PETERSON [17; Omaha; b: Denmark; f: Peder LARSON; m: Marie NIELSEN] on 16 Jul 1881 at Vor Frelser's Church. Off: GYDESEN. Wit: P. LARSEN, A.M. NIELSON. Age consent given by parents of the bride and guardian of the groom.

ABBOTT, Joseph [23; Omaha; b: Michigan; f: John ABBOTT; m: Catharine BROWN] md. Lizzie B. BROWN [17; Omaha; b: Missouri; f: H.M. BROWN; m: Molly WARE] on 19 May 1880. Off: JAMESON. Wit: Charles BROWN, Evangaline BROWN.

ABEL, Albert [28; Omaha; b: Prussia; f: Elias ABEL; m: Adeline CARR] md. Emma SOLOMON [18; Omaha; b: Prussia; f: Jacob SOLOMON; m: Bertha] on 1 Mar 1874. Off: PEABODY. Wit: Abraham BROWN; Adeline CARR.

ABLE, Albert [23; Douglas Co.; b: Denmark; f: Christian ABLE; m: Anna NEILSON] md. Delphine CRITCHFIELD [16; Douglas Co.; f: A.J. CRITCHFIELD; m: Sarah A. POLMANTIRE] on 18 Apr 1876 at Florence. Off: CRITCHFIELD. Wit: John STEVENSON, Florence, Maria STEVENSON, Florence. Age consent given by father of the bride.

ABNEY, James C. [32; Cheyenne, WY Territory] md. Annie WILLIAMS [19; Omaha] on 23 Feb 1869 at O'GORMAN's house. Off: O'GORMAN. Wit: Annie FLARNY, C. SLATTERY.

ABORN, Edward S. [31; Philadelphia, PA; b: Philadelphia, PA; f: William K. ABORN; m: Catherine SILL] md. Ida WOLFF [21; Philadelphia, PA; b: Germany; f: Henry WOLFF] on 22 May 1871. Off: GASSMAN. Wit: Mrs. T.G. GASSMAN; Miss C. SORENSON.

ACKERMAN, David [29; Grand Island; b: Pennsylvania; f: David ACKERMAN; m: Catherine FLICK] md. Lily M. CLARK [18 or 19; Omaha; b: Indiana; f: E.V. CLARK; m: Catherine AULT] on 15 Apr 1877. Off: PARDEE. Wit: parents of the bride, Rev. L.H. TIBBLES.

ADAMS, Alva [23; Iowa; b: Missouri; f: James ADAMS; m: Elizabeth CULVER] md. Agnes JOHNSTON 25; Iowa; b: Ohio; f: D. JOHNSTON; m: Elizabeth CASTLE] on 1 Oct 1878. Off: BARTHOLOMEW. Wit: J.A. TICE of Wisconsin, W. SAALFELD.

ADAMS, Charles [21; Omaha; b: Ohio; f: John ADAMS; m: Jane HOAG] md. May GRACE [19; Omaha; b: New York; f: Richard GRACE; m: Mary EGEN] on 3 Jan 1877. Off: PEABODY. Wit: Dunk SIMPSON, Allie GRACE.

ADAMS, Edward [27; Tama Co., IA] and Phoebe Jane MULLINIX [18; Tama Co., IA]

license issued on 17 Aug 1860. No marriage record. Off: ARMSTRONG.

ADAMS, John F. [24; Omaha] md. Catharine LEWIS [18; Omaha] on 25 Apr 1867. Off: ROSE. Wit: Samuel N. FORD. Statement under oath.

ADAMS, John [22; Omaha; b: TN; f: Charles ADAMS; m: Emly WATSON] md. Lucy L. BARNETT [27; Omaha; b: KY; f: Randolph BARNETT; m: Julia SAUNDERS] on 8 Jan 1876. Off: BRITT. Wit: Sarah BRITT, Albertha LAWSON.

ADAMS, Thomas [25; Plattsmouth; b: Indiana; f: J.Q. ADAMS; m: Semantha FRANKLIN] md. Mrs. Cecelia A. LONSDALE [34; Plattsmouth; b: Illinois; f: Wm. JAMES; m: A.P. POTTER] on 18 Mar 1874. Off: WRIGHT. Wit: Fred C. REED; George THRALL.

ADAMS, William B.M. [22; Omaha; b: Ripon, WI; f: Thomas ADAMS; m: Emma L. DUKE] md. Sarah J. RICHARDS [23; Omaha; b: WI; f: John RICHARDS; m: (Miss) A.J. HILL] on 16 Nov 1881. Off: RILEY. Wit: B.P. MATSON, J.P. SOUTHARD.

ADAMS, William J. [27; Sarpy Co.; b: IA; f: Asa ADAMS; m: Philipina CABLE] md. Dora L. BAYLEY [18; Sarpy Co.; b: NE; f: Jefferson BAYLEY; m: Mary Jane ANDERSON] on 31 Aug 1881. Off: MAXFIELD. Wit: Mrs. David MARQUETTE, E.B. WEIST.

ADAMS, William Lawson, Jr. [34; Troy NY; b: Morrisville, NY; f: William Lawson ADAMS; m: Araminta D. PLATT] md. Clara Eliza KELLOM [25; Omaha; b: Troy, PA; f: John H. KELLOM; m: Harriet N. NEWELL] on 7 Sep 1875. Off: STEWART. Wit: P.L. PERINE, P.H. ALLEN.

ADAMS, William [53; Omaha; b: Holland; f: Ceb ADAMS] md. Mary NIELSON [48; Omaha; b: Denmark; f: Nils PETERSON; m: Mary PETERSON] on 20 Jun 1870. Off: GIBSON. Wit: Richard A. THOMPSON, Cuming Co.; Ragnel OLSEN, Cuming Co.

ADDINGTON, J.L. [24; Des Moines; b: IN; f: J.L. ADDINGTON; m: Nancy FANSHER] md. Mary CRIST [22; b: WI; f: George CRIST; m: Elizabeth SELLON] on 6 Apr 1881. Off: BEANS. Wit: Marck HUNT, Mrs. Flora HUNT.

ADKINS, Piatt [28; Omaha] md. Maria ALGEO [21; Omaha] on 31 Jul 1861 at John I. REDICK's residence on Farnham St. Off: KUHNS. Wit: Mrs. REDICK, Sebastian M. ADKINS, Martin DUNHAM.

ADSIT, German [29; Omaha] md. Ann C. WELLS [29; Omaha] on 30 Sep 1862 at ARMSTRONG's residence. Off: ARMSTRONG. Wit: Mrs. Geo. ARMSTRONG, G.R. ARMSTRONG.

ADSIT, Shuble [25; Douglas Co.] md. Mary BROWN [21; Douglas Co.] on 26 Nov

1865. Off: SLAUGHTER. Wit: Mrs. A.B. SLAUGHTER, Mrs. COLE.

ADSIT, Shuble [34; Saunders Co.; b: Delaware Co., NY; f: Orra ADSIT; m: Ruth CULVER] md. Clara GILBERT [30; Saunders Co.; b: Wisconsin; f: William H. GILBERT; m: Emily JANES] on 2 Jan 1873. Off: TOWNSEND. Wit: Mary E. TOWNSEND; Christen NIELSEN.

AGARD, Julius [32; Omaha; b: Demnark; f: Peter AGARD; m: Nicholena JENSEN] md. Mrs. Anna CHRISTENSEN [30; Omaha; b: Denmark; f: James CHRISTENSEN; m: Almaria CHRISTENSEN] on 6 Dec 1869. Off: GIBSON. Wit: Charles C. CODER, S.B. RUSSELL.

AGER, Henry G., M.D. [Omaha] md. Mrs. Nancy ROUTH [Omaha] on 24 Jun 1865 aboard the steamboat Mary E. Forsyth. Off: DICKINSON. Wit: Jene CAMPBELL, Mr. CLANCY, clerk of the steamboat.

AHERN, William [29; California; b: Ireland; f: Thomas AHERN; m: Kate BARRY] md. Nora HAGGARTY [28; Chicago, IL; b: Ireland; f: Richard HAGGARTY; m: Mary MURPHY] on 21 Oct 1879. Off: McCARTHY. Wit: Mary CALLAHAN, Bart DUGGAN.

AHLQUIST, Gustav Wm. [27; Omaha; b: Sweden; f: Charles G. AHLQUIST; m: Johanna RINGSTROM] md. Louisa H. MILNER [19; Omaha; b: Pennsylvania; f: Edwin MILNER; m: Ann ROLLINGSON] on 25 Des 1877. Off: SEDGWICK. Wit: Charles G. AHLQUIST, Julius H. STEIN.

AHMANSON, Jacob A. [23; b: Denmark; f: John A. AHMANSON; m: Sophia FIELDSTED] md. Catharine T. STROUP [18; b: Michigan; f: Conrad STROUP; m: Sophia GARDNER] on 21 Sep 1878. Off: STENBERG. Wit: E.A. McCLURE, S.W. BOGGS of Missouri.

ALBERT, John [35; Omaha; b: Germany; f: John ALBERT; m: Anna GIER] md. Mrs. Matilda PARKS [34; Omaha; b: Indiana] on 26 Dec 1872. Off: BILLMAN. Wit: Thos. TUTTLE; Aug FULREIDE.

ALBERT, Valentine [26; Ashland, Saunders Co.; b: Germany; f: Joseph ALBERT; m: Catherine] md. Sophia KELSCHENBACH [22; Omaha; b: Germany; f: Philip KELSCHENBACH; m: Mary E. FISCHER] on 7 Jan 1873. Off: THURSTON. Wit: Frederick HERSKE; Mrs. Wilhelmina HERSKE.

ALDRICH, Oney [22; Douglas Co.] md. Sarah H. MICKEL [26; Douglas Co.] on 4 Feb 1869. Off: HYDE. Wit: Mrs. J.R. HYDE, Mrs. Mary CLARK. Age consent given by mother of the bride, she attended the wedding.

ALEXANDER, Isaac [30; Independence, MO; b: MO; f: Isaac ALEXANDER; m: Lucy WALDRON] and Isabella BUTLER [21; Douglas Co.; b: VA; f: William BUTLER; m: Mary COMNEY] filed an affidavit on 3 May 1876. Off: SEDGWICK.

ALEXANDER, Issac [26; Omaha; colored; b: Missouri; f: Issac ALEXANDER; m: Lucy] md. Violet MAYWEATHER [21; Omaha; colored; b: Baltimore, MD; f: David MAYWEATHER; m: Catharine] on 26 Mar 1872. Off: STEWART. Wit: P.L. PERINE; Frank SEARS.

ALEXANDER, John [colored; 28; Omaha; b: VA; f: John ALEXANDER] md. Ida CRUMP [colored; 18; Omaha; b: Omaha; f: Jerry CRUMP; m: Jane ARCADIA] on 18 Aug 1875. Off: PEABODY. Wit: G.W. SHIELDS, . E.T. COWN.

ALFORD, Henry A. [27; Indianapolis, IN; b: Indianapolis, IN; f: Thomas G. ALFORD; m: Isabella VANBALARICUM] md. Anna Margaret RAFERT [19; Omaha; Indianapolis, IN; f: Anthony F. RAFERT; m: Margaret DANIELS] on 21 Aug 1879. Off: HARSHA. Wit: Anthony F. RAFERT, F.E. BOWEN.

ALFRED, John [32; Clinton, IA; b: Liverpool, England; f: James ALFRED; m: Margaret ALFRED] md. Ella H. GIBSON [30; San Francisco, CA; b: NY; f: John GIBSON; m: Margaret HENDERSON] on 26 Aug 1876. Off: SEDGWICK. Wit: C.L. BRISTOL, M.B. KNOX.

ALLEN, Charles A. [27; Omaha; b: Wisconsin; f: William ALLEN; m: Maria ABORN] md. Augusta J. OLSEN [23; Omaha; b: Sweden; f: John OLSEN; m: Annie ANDERSON] on 18 Oct 1876. Off: SEDGWICK. Wit: Olive OLSEN, E.B. KNOX.

ALLEN, Charles D. [27; Omaha; b: New Orleans, LA; f: Thomas D. ALLEN; m: ---- PARKER] and Anna Martha WISE [21; Omaha; b: Pennsylvania; f: Jesse R. WISE; m: Julia A. SHAFFER] license issued on 3 Feb 1872. Off: TOWNSEND.

ALLEN, Ethan [39; Omaha; b: NY; f: Lyman ALLEN; m: Anna DEWELL] md. Mary E. JOHNSON [19; Omaha; b: MO; f: Geo. W. JOHNSON; m: Mary A. PENNINGTON] on 15 Mar 1875. Off: PEABODY. Wit: C.S. BRISTOL, C.D. WOODWORTH.

ALLEN, Francis M. [20; Omaha; b: Wisconsin; f: William ALLEN; m: Maria ABORNS] md. Lizzie S. BIEN [16; Omaha; b: NY; f: Bernard BIEN; m: Sophia HELM] on 2 May 1874. Off: DONNELLY. Wit: Burnett BIEN; Mrs. Emily BIEN. Age consent given by Mrs. Ada WILDER, sister of groom [parents are dead]; Age consent given by the father of the bride.

ALLEN, George W. [30; Douglas Co.; b: Illinois; f: Franklin ALLEN; m: Rebecca MYERS] md. Gertrude SMITH [20; Douglas Co.; b: IA; f: Mahew SMITH; m: Eliza GILMORE] on 2 Mar 1875. OFF: HENNEY. Wit: J.H. SMITH, Ernie HOFFMEISTER.

ALLEN, Isaac Newton [27; Clarksville, NE; b: New York; f: Horace ALLEN; m: Ann Eliza AKIN] md. Lenora GRIFFIN [20; Omaha; b: Michigan; f: Charles GRIFFIN; m: Hannah G. JORDAN] on 3 Jun 1879 at Irvington. Off: SPENCER. Wit: Esther WESTGATE and Mary GRIFFIN, both of Douglas Co.

ALLEN, Michail [32; Bryan, W(yom) T(err); b: Ireland; f: Arthur ALLEN; m: Margaret FOGERTY] md. Mary QUICK [24, Omaha; b: Dublin, Ireland; f: Andrew QUICK] on 5 Jun 1870. Off: CURTIS. Wit: Frank ROONEY; Ann O'NEIL.

ALLEN, Pompy [colored; 22; Douglas Co.] md. Martha OLDEN [colored; 23; Douglas Co.] on 22 Jul 1868. Off: FLORKEE. Wit: John JANKINS, Jackson GORDEN, Michael STEINER.

ALLING, J.H. [23; Elkhorn] md. Miss J.E. MUNGER [18; Elkhorn] on 12 Dec 1861 at the ME Church. Off: SMITH. Wit: A.F. MUNGER, Luther ABBOTT.

ALLISON, Ignatius [48; Omaha; b: New Hampshire; f: James ALLISON; m: Mary HOILT] md. Mrs. Eliza A. McNAUGHTON [40; Omaha; b: New York; f: John McNAUGHTON; m: Nancy SMITH] on 15 Sep 1880. Off: SHERILL. Wit: Wm. F. DOOLITTLE, Mrs. A.F. SHERRILL.

ALLISON, William L. [28; U.S. Army; b: Indiana; f: Henry ALLISON; m: Pauline ELROD] md. Eviline H. THOMAS [20; Douglas Co.; b: Kentucky; f: William THOMAS; m: Harriet TELLES] on 27 Feb 1871. Off: SHERRILL. Wit: Edward BURNS; Julius HOPPE.

ALLMEN, John August [27; Omaha; b: Sweden; f: John ALLMEN; m: Catharine ANDERSON] md. Emma C. APPLEGREN [19; Omaha; b: Sweden; f: John APPLEGREN; m: Mary JOHNSON] on 9 Jul 1869. Off: LARSON. Wit: Mrs. Mary B. LARSON, Mrs. Johanna C. LARSON.

ALLOWAY, Johnathan [28; Omaha; b: PA; f: Johnathan ALLOWAY; m: Elizabeth ANDERSON] md. Mrs.? Nancy C. STEWART [33; Omaha; b: OH; m: Sarah (McKINNON)? BANES] on 5 Dec 1869. Off: SHINN. Wit: B. DEMOREST, Mrs. Sarah DEMOREST.

ALLSTREND, William [29; Council Bluffs, IA; b: Sweden; f: John ALLSTREND; m: Mary DALLBORN] md. Mrs. Lucinda SWANSON [22; Council Bluffs, IA; b: Missouri; f: Louis SWANSON; m: Mary MILLER] on 14 Oct 1878. Off: BARTHOLOMEW. Wit: Max BERGMAN, M.H. REDFIELD.

ALPERS, Henrek George [35; Omaha; b: Germany; f: John F. ALPERS; m: Mary ENTELKE] md. Mary WILHELM [34; Omaha; b: Germany; f: Christopher WILHELM; m: Anna C. IMIKE] on May 1875. Off: PEABODY. Wit: Christian WITT, H.C. HADEN.

ALTHOUSE, Gerhardt [28; Omaha; b: Holland; f: Bernhart ALTHOUSE; m: Cissina] md. Christina BERGQUIST [27; Omaha; b: Sweden; f: Peter BERGQUIST; m: Nanna JOHNSON] on 8 Aug 1875. Off: BENEKE. Wit: Alexander DAEMON, Rosina DAEMON.

AMBROSIO, Henry [46; Saratoga Pct; b: Italy; f: Dennis AMBROSIO; m: Catharine BARICALLA] md. Matilda FISH [26; Saratoga Pct; b: Illinois; f: George L. FISH; m: Lucy CALL] on 7 Jul 1873. Off: TOWNSEND. Wit: John B. MANTEL; Babette MANTEL; both of Saratoga Pct, Douglas Co.

AMES, Joseph P. [36; Washington Co.; b: Ohio; f: D.P. AMES; m: Susan PEARCE] md. Mary HAWLEY [Washington Co.; b: Kentucky; f: Harris HAWLEY; m: Martha WOOD] on 27 Dec 1877. Off: TAGGART. Wit: Mrs. E.L. WEBSTER of Fillmore Co., Lucretia LIPPINCOTT of Blair.

AMSBARY, Charles [20; Plattsmouth; b: IL; f: Alansin AMSBARY; m: Sarah ROYCE] md. Mary QUINLIN [19; Omaha; b: IA; f: Daniel QUINLIN; m: Mary HALLEY] on 23 Feb 1881. Off: ENGLISH. Wit: Felix SLAVEN, Mrs. Felix SLAVEN. Age consent given by Felix SLAVEN.

AMSBARY [AMESBURY], William A. [22; Spring Valley; Douglas County] md. Angeline Harriet DIFFIN [GRIFFIN] [15 or 16; Douglas Co.] on 5 Dec 1857. Off: COLLINS. Wit: Nelson AMSBURY, Richard AMSBURY. Age consent given by step-father of bride.

AMSBARY [AMSBURY], D.W. [Florence precinct] md. Loa LEMON [Florence precinct] on 26 Mar 1865. Off: JANNEY.

ANDERSEN, Hans L. [27; Douglas Co.; b: Germany; f: C.A. ANDERSEN; m: Mary BOYSON] md. Sophia JACOBSON [20; Douglas Co.; b: Denmark; f: Lars JACOBSON; m: Karn MASSEN] on 13 Aug 1878. Off: LIPE. Wit: ---- MEYERS, Margaret MEYER.

ANDERSEN, Lars [40; Omaha; b: Denmark; f: Anders ANDERSON; m: Mary LARSEN] md. Stina FELT [29; Omaha; b: Denmark; f: Nels FELT; m: Carrie RASSMUSSEN] on 18 Sep 1881. Off: CHRISTIANSEN. Wit: Hans JENSEN, Council Bluffs, Mrs. CHRISTIANSEN, Council Bluffs.

ANDERSEN, Martin [25; Omaha; b: Denmark; f: Andreas JOHNSON; m: Anna PETERSON] md. Amalie JACKSTADT [21; Omaha; Germany; f: Gotfried JACKSTADT; m: Louise BLUBM or BENHM] on 18 Mar 1879. Off: WRIGHT. Wit: William F. FLYNN, S.C. DOREMUS.

ANDERSEN, Neils [24; Omaha; b: Denmark; f: Anders ANDERSEN; m: Mary LARSEN] md. Anna M. JOHANSEN [22; Omaha; b: Denmark; f: Johanes ANDERSEN; m: Mary ANDERSEN] on 11 Oct 1869. Off: HESSEL. Wit: Nels MARTINSON, Robert HANSEN.

ANDERSEN, R.W. [28; Omaha] b: Denmark; f: R.W. ANDERSEN; m: Margaret PETERSON] md. Caroline SMITH [20; Omaha; b: Denmark; f: Christian SMITH; m: Anna SMITH] on 30 Apr 1879. Off: LIPE. Wit: J.T. CLARK, M.A. KURTZ.

ANDERSON, Amos [colored; 25; Omaha; b: MO; f: John ANDERSON; m: Melinda] md. Rosa SCANTLIN [colored; 20; Omaha; b: SC; f: Bran SCANTLIN; m: Margaret SCANTLIN] on 3 Jan 1876. Off: BRITT. Wit: Edward RECTOR, Wilson HERON.

ANDERSON, Andrew W. [38; Omaha; b: Sweden; f: Anders OLLSON; m: Anna ANDERSON] and Olivia MEGLEY [32; Omaha; b: Sweden; f: Andrew PETERSON; m: Ellen JOHNSON] affidavit issued on 5 Jan 1874. Off: PEABODY.

ANDERSON, Andrew W. [38; Omaha; b: Sweden; f: Anders OLESON; m: Anna ANDERSON] md. Olivia NIGLEY [32; Omaha; b: Sweden; f: Andrew PETERSON; m: Ellen JOHNSON] on 5 Jan 1875. Off: PEABODY. Wit: Mary C. PEABODY, Will B.R. KILLINGSWORTH.

ANDERSON, Andrew [29; Omaha] md. Mary MATTHEWSON [MATTHIESON] [27; Omaha] on 27 Jun 1868. Off: STUCK. Wit: W.W. FOOT, H. HANSON.

ANDERSON, Andrew [50; Omaha; b: Sweden; f: Anders JENSEN; m: Mathilda ANDERSON] md. Jennette JENSEN [29; Omaha; b: Sweden; f: Jens SWENSSON; m: Hanna JENSEN] on 30 Dec 1881. Off: STENBERG. Wit: Charles SALHOLM, H.C. ELBERT.

ANDERSON, Andrew [53; Beatrice; b: Norway; f: Andrew ANDERSON; m: Anna JONSEND] md. Johanna GRINDE [34; Wisconsin; b: Norway; f: Bottolf GRINDE; m: Marsey PETERSON] on 26 Jun 1879. Off:

HILMEN. Wit: P. WEIG, Mrs. S.M. HILMEN.

ANDERSON, Anton M. [28; Howard Co.; b: Denmark; f: Andrew JORGENSON; m: Maren ANDERSON] md. Laurine M. LARSON [20; Omaha; b: Denmark; f: Mathias LARSON; m: Christena ANDERSON] on 5 Mar 1875. Off: HANSEN. Wit: Rev. J.S. BENZON, Anna Dorothea BENZON.

ANDERSON, August [35; Saunders Co.; b: Sweden; f: Andrew ANDERSON; m: Maggie OLESON] md. Augusta P. FREDRIKSON [32; Omaha; b: Sweden; f: Frederick FREDRIKSON; m: Carrie OLESON] on 7 Jul 1874. Off: BENSON. Wit: J. LIND and wife Sophia SKAGERSTROM.

ANDERSON, August [35; Saunders Co.; b: Sweden; f: John ANDERSON; m: Mary Christine] md. Johanna Mary JOHNSON [30; Omaha; b: Sweden; f: John JOHNSON] on 19 Jan 1872. Off: SUNDBORN. Wit: J. NILSSON; M. NILSSON.

ANDERSON, Bent [26; Omaha; b: Sweden; f: Anders TERVERSEN; m: Else BENSDAUGHTER] md. Cesse SWENSEN [36; Omaha; b: Sweden; f: Swen JOHNSON; m: Else LOUISDAUGHTER] on 25 Sep 1869. Off: HYDE. Wit: H.A. CHAPMAN of Florence, H. ABEL.

ANDERSON, Charles [28; Omaha; colored; b: Pittsburg, PA; f: John ANDERSON; m: Sarah HOWARD] md. Maggie PIERSON [19; Omaha; colored; b: Indianapolis, IN] on 21 Oct 1873. Off: GAINES. Wit: E.R. WILLIAMS; Mrs. J.W. ELICE.

ANDERSON, Charles [30; Omaha; b: Copenhagen, Denmark; f: Andrew JENSEN; m: Ester SIODAL] and Hansine PETERSEN [23; Omaha; b: Denmark] license issued 2 Nov 1871. Off: TOWNSEND.

ANDERSON, Christian [24; Omaha; b: Sweden; f: Andres MATTSON; m: Elsie ERICKSEN] md. Anna WALQUEST [20; Omaha; b: Sweden; f: John WALQUEST; m: Ingra MATTSON] on 11 Nov 1872. Off: TOWNSEND. Wit: William H. IJAMS; David H. PRATT.

ANDERSON, George T. [21; Omaha; b: Springfield, ILL; f: George ANDERSON; m: Jane TRUE] md. Minerva C. RUCKER [20; Omaha; b: Pittsburg, PA; f: Daniel RUCKER; m: ---- THORNTON] on 3 Feb 1873. Off: LYTLE. Wit: E. PORTER; Josephine WARNER.

ANDERSON, Gustave [26; Florence; b: Sweden; f: Anders OLSEN] md. Christine NELSON [21; Florence; b: Sweden; f: Nils ANDERSON] on 26 Dec 1870. Off: LARSON. Wit: Gunnar A. LUNDQUIST; Carl ANDERSON of Florence.

ANDERSON, H.C. [42; Omaha; b: Denmark; f: Andrew PETERSON; m: Carry ANDERSON] md. Mrs. Emilie OLESON [45;

Omaha; b: Denmark; f: Peter OLESON; m: Louise JENTZEN] on 5 Jun 1880 at Mr. JONASON's residence. Off: GYDESON. Wit: L. NIELSON, S. JONASON.

ANDERSON, Hans [23; Omaha; b: Denmark; f: Anders PETERSON; m: Mary HANSEN] md. Mary HANSEN [22; Omaha; b: Denmark; f: Hans NELSON; m: Carrie PETERSON] on 16 Aug 1870. Off: GIBSON. Wit: Charles H. BRYNE; George ARMSTRONG.

ANDERSON, Harry [30; b: Sweden; f: Nels ANDERSON; m: Ellen OLESON] md. Lillie Amanda NALSON [16; Iowa; b: Sweden; f: Peter NALSON; m: Tilda LARSON] on 9 Dec 1878. Off: BARTHOLOMEW. Wit: Max BERGMAN, M.H. REDFIELD.

ANDERSON, James [27; Omaha; b: Sweden; f: Anders NELSON] md. Betsy CHRYSEL [21; Omaha; b: Sweden; f: Peter CHRYSEL] on 4 Dec 1869. Off: OLSEN. Wit: Hans NILSON, Jeninie OLSEN.

ANDERSON, Jens C. [32; Omaha; b: Denmark; f: Nels P. ANDERSON; m: Anna KNUDSEN] md. Maria C. SMITH [34; Omaha; b: Denmark; f: Hans P. SMITH; m: Bridget KNUDSEN] on 13 Jul 1871. Off: BILLMAN. Wit: Mrs. Bella L. BILLMAN; Mrs. Wm. HUGHES; et al.

ANDERSON, John [24; Omaha; b: Sweden; f: Ole ANDERSON; m: Hannah NELSON] md. Christine JACOBSON [24; Omaha; b: Sweden; f: Nels JACOBSON; m: Mary JOHNSON] on 24 Apr 1881. Off: ANDERSON. Wit: A. SKJERDINGSTAD, Lotta SKJERDINGSTAD.

ANDERSON, John [25; Council Bluffs; b: Sweden; f: Andrew JOHNSON; m: Mary NILSON] md. Hanna JOHNSON [22; Council Bluffs; b: Denmark; f: Peter PETERSON] on 19 Feb 1871. Off: LARSEN. Wit: Gabriel PATTERSON; Martin QUICK.

ANDERSON, John [27; Omaha; b: Sweden; f: Anders CARLSON; m: Christina FLINK] md. Hanna C. JOHNSON [23; Omaha; b: Sweden; f: John JOHNSON; m: Maria CARLSON] on 5 Oct 1880. Off: STENBERG. Wit: Frank LINDBERG, Mrs. Martha LINDBERG.

ANDERSON, John [31; Washington Co.; b: Denmark; f: Nils ANDERSON; m: Dorte MUNSON] md. Grete PAULSEN [26; Washington Co.; b: Sweden; f: Paul PIERSON; m: Kerstine SWENSEN] on 3 Jan 1873. Off: TOWNSEND. Wit: Charles DEMEREST; Mary E. TOWNSEND.

ANDERSON, Louis [31; Omaha; b: Sweden; f: Andrew ANDERSON; m: Mary ANDERSON] md. Annie ANDERSON [22; Omaha; b: Sweden; f: Andrew ANDERSON; m: Elsie ERICKSEN] on 26 Mar 1877. Off: ANDERSON. Wit: E. STENBERG, C. COLLIN.

ANDERSON, Nels [25; Florence; b: Sweden; f: Carl ANDERSON; m: Hannah OLSON] md. Belle BIRD [17; Florence; b: NE; f: George (John crossed out) BIRD; m: Elizabeth THIRTLE] on 15 Oct 1881. Off: CHADWICK. Wit: E.F. SMYTHE, Home STULL (C. Wm. EDGERTON crossed out). Age consent given by sister of the bride, Missouri E. BIRD, who certified that "their parents agree to this marriage."

ANDERSON, Nels [30; Burt Co.; b: Sweden; f: Anders TRUEDSON; m: Ingrid NILSON] md. Ellen PEHRSON [28; Omaha; b: Sweden; f: Pehr ANDERSON; m: Ingrid ANDERSON] on 21 Feb 1870. Off: LARSON. Wit: Mrs. Johanna C. LARSON; Engla J. NORMAN.

ANDERSON, Niels C. [23; Omaha; b: Denmark; f: Anders ANDERSON; m: Ane LARSEN] md. Ane LARSEN [25; Omaha; b: Denmark; f: Hans LARSON; m: Maren JORGENSON] on 2 Feb 1874. Off: HALL. Wit: Sabastian BLUMELE; Neils LARSON.

ANDERSON, Nils Johann [26; Omaha; b: Sweden; f: Andrew BENSEN; m: Inger LARSDOTTER] md. Anna Sophia ANDERSON [b: Sweden; f: Anders ANDERSON; m: Anna NILSDOTTER] on 25 Aug 1881. Off: FOGELSTROM. Wit: Bengt ANDERSON, Mrs. Anna ANDERSON.

ANDERSON, Olaf [23; Omaha; b: Sweden; f: Andreas ANDERSON; m: Kare JOINSDOTTER] md. Brita SWENDOTTER [24; Omaha; b: Sweden; f: Swan JORENSON; m: Brita ALSDOTTER] on 30 Nov 1879. Off: FOGELSTROM. Wit: John LARSON, Mrs. Matilda LARSON.

ANDERSON, Oliver P. [Omaha] md. Mrs. Caroline PAULSEN [Omaha] on 1 May 1865 at the bride's residence. Off: DICKINSON. Wit: Mary PAULSEN, J.A. TOOKER, et al.

ANDERSON, P.O. [34; Omaha; b: Sweden; f: A. NEILSON; m: Martha SODERBERG] md. Ida M. JOHNSON [18; Omaha; b: Sweden; f: John JOHNSON; m: Engey STENI] on 25 Aug 1877. Wit: John JOHNSON, G.C. GRAVER. Off: BENEKE.

ANDERSON, Peter [24; Omaha; b: Sweden; f: Andrew PETERSON; m: Segra WAHLBERG] md. Anna NELSON [23; Omaha; b: Sweden; f: Nels JOHNSON; m: Anna ANDERSON] on 16 Dec 1872. Off: SWEDERS. Wit: Gustav SWANSON; Mrs. Olivia SWEDERS.

ANDERSON, Peter [26; Omaha] md. Christiana ANDERSON [minor, Omaha] on 26 Oct 1868. Off: STUCK. Wit: Martin

BOWMAN, W.C. KELLOGG. Age consent given by the guardian of the bride.

ANDERSON, Peter [28; Omaha; b: Sweden; f: Anders LARSON; m: Pernila SWANSON] md. Kate ANDERSON [27; Omaha; b: Sweden; f: Andrew JOHNSON; m: Hannah SWANSON] on 20 Mar 1874. Off: PEABODY. Wit: Nels ANDERSON; Engre ANDERSON.

ANDERSON, Peter [29; Omaha] md. Hannah YENTZ [29; Omaha] on 10 Apr 1869. Off: LARSON. Wit: Hans OLSON, John F. NORDSTROM.

ANDERSON, Peter [30; Omaha; b: Sweden] md. Carrie LINN [25; Omaha; b: Sweden] on 2 Nov 1869. Off: LARSON. Wit: Andrew CHRISTENSEN, August LARSON of Washington Co.

ANDERSON, Peter [Omaha] md. Karna ANDERSON [Omaha] on 9 Oct 1864 at DICKINSON's office. Off: DICKINSON. Wit: John AHMANSON, Henry ANDERSON, A.J. OLDS, Lars PETERSON, Annie ANDERSON.

ANDERSON, Swan Petter [29; Washington Territory; b: Sweden; f: Anders SWANSON; m: Mary MUNSON] md. Miss B.A. PAINT [28; b: Sweden; f: N.P. PAINT; m: Christina THELIN] on 21 Sep 1878. Off: BARTHOLOMEW. Wit: Isaac COE, James W. LOVE.

ANDERSON, William P. [25; Omaha; b: Ohio; f: James W. ANDERSON; m: Elizabeth McCLARY] md. Susan OVERAKER [24; Omaha; b: Illinois; f: Henry OVERAKER: m: ---- RISBY] on 4 Oct 1871. Off: KELLEY. Wit: Mrs. MASON; Geo. RIDGWAY.

ANDRE, William F. [27 or 29; Omaha] md. Dorothea HANSEN [22; Omaha] on 23 Nov 1868. Off: MULCAHY. Wit: William GENTLEMAN, Celestine THIEBAUT [THIEBEAUT].

ANDRESEN, Julius N. Chr. [22; Omaha; b: Denmark; f: Andreas N. ANDRESEN; m: Boutilla P. SCHULTZ] md. Nicoline M. NIELSEN [23; Omaha; b: Prussia; f: Niels S. NIELSEN; m: Bodil Christine] on 31 Oct 1873. Off: LIPE. Wit: John OLSEN; Mary OLSEN.

ANDREWS, William [22; New York City] md. Nellie BELMONT [19; St. Louis, MO] on 21 Dec 1865 at the Court House. Off: HASCALL. Wit: Wm. KELLOGG, Jr., W.P. SNOWDEN.

ANGEL, William W. [32; Omaha; b: Ohio; f: David ANGEL; m: Adaline PORTER] md. Kate TAYLOR [22; Saratoga Pct., Douglas Co.; b: Ohio; f: Jonah R. TAYLOR; m: Eliza Ann WARD] on 13 Feb 1872 at O'GORMAN's house. Off: O'GORMAN. Wit: Joseph SUTHER; Willie TAYLOR; Elisa TAYLOR; Magie TAYLOR all of Florence.

ANKOR, Christian [32; Saunders Co.; b: Finland; f: Emanuel ANKOR; m: Helena C.

LUNDBERG] md. Karin NELSDOTTER [28; Omaha; b: Sweden; f: Nels PETERSON; m: Anna JONSDOTTER] on 4 Feb 1871. Off: LARSON. Wit: August NYGREN, Saunders Co.; Mrs. Maria S. FALK.

APPEL, George D. [29; Omaha] md. Ida WILKE [30; Omaha] on 14 Jul 1868. Off: William H. MORRIS. Wit: Robert GRESBERGER, Maurice HOFFACHTER.

APPLEBY, John [25; Douglas Co.; b: England; f: James APPLEBY; m: Mary EVANS] md. Catharine E. SCOTT [18; Douglas Co.; b: NJ; f: Hobert SCOTT; m: Margaret VALENTINE] on 28 Jun 1869 at Elkhorn. Off: HURLBUT. Wit: Thomas WILKINSON of Elkhorn, Hobert SCOTT of Elkhorn.

APPLEBY, Thomas [29; Elk Horn City; b: England; f: James APPLEBY; m: Mary EVANS] md. Annie B. WOOD [18; Elk Horn City; b: Ohio; m: Mary E. BROWN] on 22 Dec 1878. Off: BEAR. Wit: John and C.E. APPLEBY, John BRYANT; Grace GUGIN all of Elkhorn.

ARCHIBALD, Joseph [29; Omaha; b: Scotland; f: John ARCHIBALD; m: Margaret DUNCAN] md. Hannah S. HARKINSON [29; Omaha; b: Pennsylvania; f: Charles HARKINSON; m: Sarah TIBBEN] on 1 Sep 1874. Off: LIPE. Wit: Robert JENKINSON; Mrs. JENKSINSON.

ARKWRIGHT, Daniel C. [28; Shelby Co., IA; b: Preston, Eng.; f: John ARKWRIGHT; m: Ann CRASS] md. Martha H. POTTER [30; Pottawattamie Co., IA; b: TN; f: Isaac HARMAN] on 26 Nov 1869. Off: GIBSON. Wit: Charles BYRNE, A.K. LUCUS of Council Bluffs.

ARMBRUSTER, Joseph [24; Douglas Co.; b: Germany; f: Andrew ARMBRUSTER; m: Mary A. HUNT] md. Mary ARMBRUSTER [24; Douglas Co.; b: Germany; f: Anders ARMBRUSTER; m: Matilda WISER] on 9 Jan 1871 at the German Catholic Church. Off: GROENEBAUM. Wit: Christian LARSEN; Carolina KENNER.

ARMBRUSTER, Sigmund [24; Sarpy Co.] md. Catharine TAX (TEX) [18; Sarpy Co.] on 12 Apr 1869. Off: GROENBAUM. Wit: Jacob TEX, Catharina SCHNEIDER.

ARMSTRONG, David [55; Sarpy Co.] md. Mrs. Loiza PUTNAM [42; Omaha] on 29 Oct 1868 at S. ADAIR's house. Off: SHINN. Wit: Mr. and Mrs. ADAIR.

ARMSTRONG, James S. [28; Albion, NE; Indiana; f: John H. ARMSTRONG; m: Susan BEGGS] md. Emma NYE [27; Indiana; Indiana; f: Ira C. NYE; m: Elizabeth PARDEE] on 10 Dec 1879. Off: BEANS. Wit: Wm. BROWN; W.J. McCUNE.

ARMSTRONG, James [31; b: England; f: Joseph ARMSTRONG; m: Eliza STEWART] md. Alice TURNER [23; Detroit, MI; b: Canada; f: Richard TURNER; m: Ruth VALENTINE] on 3 Dec 1878. Off: SHERRILL. Wit: Sidney E. LOCKE, James McNEELY.

ARNDT, August F. [41; Omaha; b: Prussia; f: Charles ARNDT; m: Elizabeth HERMANN] md. Katharine LEMMEL [30; Omaha; b: Alsace; f: ---- LEMMEL] on 7 Nov 1872. Off: BILLMAN. Wit: George LEMMEL, Ashland, O (Ohio?); Mrs. Bella BILLMAN.

ARNOLD, George M. [30; Omaha; NY; f: Andrew ARNOLD; m: Annie SNYDER] md. Amanda ARNOLD [20; Omaha; b: KY; f: John ARNOLD; m: Maria J. CRANE (BOARDMAN was written in and crossed out.)] on 30 Dec 1869. Off: PORTER. Wit: Charles PARKER; Rodney DUTCHER.

ARNOLD, George [22; Omaha] md. Ellen Augusta TAYLOR [20; Omaha] on 13 Aug 1868 at Col. E.B. TAYLOR's residence. Off: TAYLOR. Wit: Col. E.B. TAYLOR, father of the bride, Col. J.R. TAYLOR, Col. Jno. RITCHIE, John TAFFE, et al.

ARNOLD, John R. [26; Omaha; b: OH; f: J.N. ARNOLD; m: Mary ROBINSON] md. Mattie E. McDONALD [ 26; Omaha; b: IN; f: Moses MORANE; m: Nancy MILLER] on 28 Omaha 1875. Off: PEABODY. Wit: J.T. McCARTY, Lilly M. MOLLOTT.

ARNOLD, Joseph W. [30; Omaha; b: Pennsylvania; f: Sylvanus ARNOLD; m: Eliza BLISS] md. Emily E. PERKINS [24; Omaha; b: Michigan; f: V.G. PERKINS; m: Jane FRAZIER] on 18 Oct 1871. Off: DeLaMATYR. Wit: Byron REED; Mrs. REED.

ARNOLD, William B. [31; Cass Co.; b: New York; f: Enoch ARNOLD; m: Sybil JEFFORDS] md. Lois H. PIKE [30; Papillion Station; b: Vermont; f: Moses PIKE] on 13 Apr 1871. Off: GASMANN. Wit: Mrs. N.E. GASMANN, Schuyler; Mrs. J.G. GASMANN.

ASHBURN, Robert [21; Omaha; b: Iowa; f: Jesse ASHBURN; m: Elmira GLASS] md. Retta SHEPHERD [18; Omaha; b: Iowa; f: John SHEPHERD; m: Ann VANASDAL] on 27 Mar 1880. Off: MARQUETT. Wit: D.C. HARPER, C.R. SPIER.

ASHBURNE, Thomas J. [21; Omaha; b: Illinois; f: Barnett ASHBURNE; m: Elizabeth GLASS] md. Anna CRANEY [18; Omaha; b: Indiana; f: James CRANEY; m: Mary HAWS] on 16 Jun 1871. Off: GIBSON. Wit: G. Robt

ARMSTRONG; Mrs. Mary ONEY. Age of consent given by mother of groom.

ASHBY, William H. [37; Beatrice; b: Missouri; f: Samuel W. ASHBY; m: Mary J. PEERY] md. Zilla SHAW [18; San Francisco, CA; b: New Jersey; f: Wm. SHAW; m: Caroline REED] on 4 Jul 1879 at Brownell Hall. Off: DOHERTY. Wit: Mrs. S.H. WINDSOR, Mrs. E. DOHERTY, both of Brownell Hall.

ASHTON, John [32; Omaha; b: Philadelphia, PA; f: Anthony ASHTON; m: Cecelia TOMLINSON] and Mary CAWAN [23; Omaha; b: Canada West; f: Edward CAWAN; m: Caroline McGUIRE] license issued on 12 Mar 1871. No marriage record. Off: GIBSON.

ASTMAN, Henry [40; Omaha; b: England; f: Thomas ASTMAN; m: Anna PETOT] md. Bessie WHITLOCK [23; Omaha; b: PA (IL crossed out); f: John WHITLOCK; m: Ellen J. BORONSS] on 8 Mar 1882. Off: BENEKE. Wit: Jos. ROSE, Mrs. A. WHITLOCK. Application 3 Nov 1881.

ASTRUP, Laurence R. [33; Omaha; b: Denmark; f: R. ASTRUP; m: Karen NELSON] md. Louisa FUHRMAN [21; Omaha; b: Denmark; f: Mathias FUHRMAN; m: Minnie LARSON] on 10 Apr 1877. Off: PEABODY. Wit: D. TUENGREN, Wm. NELSON.

ATWELL, Austelette E. [33; Omaha; b: Erie Co., PA; f: Walter ATWELL; m: Clementina ROOT] md. Mrs. Annie M. MIDDLETON [35; b: Auburn, NY; f: Aaron WARREN; m: Lucie GRANCEY] on 11 Jun 1870. Off: BENNETT. Wit: A.S. TOWER; Enoch WELDEN.

ATWOOD, Nathaniel [50; Lincoln; b: Ohio ; f: Nathaniel ATWOOD; m: Hannah EDSALL] md. Mary A. MITCHELL [21; Plattsmouth; b: Kentucky] on 1 Apr 1873. Off GAYLORD. Wit: E.A. ALLEN; Georgia B. GAYLORD.

AUBRAY, John A. [24; Omaha; b: Luxemburg; f: John AUBRAY; m: Elizabeth BARNICH] md. Kate HAN [17; Omaha; b: Baden; f: Valentine HAN; m: Francisca EICHHORN] on 7 Apr 1877. Off: PIETZ. Wit: Veronica EGENBERGER of Plattsmouth, Gustav WERKBACH. Age consent given by mother of the bride, witness to signature: Wm. WERKBACH.

AUMOCK, Charles M. [29; Omaha] md. Mrs. Allice J. ALEXANDER [25; Saratoga; Douglas Co.] on 25 Oct 1857. Off: LEACH. Wit: Mr. and Mrs. GRAY of Saratoga, Isaac BRENTNELL. On back of this license is written: F.H. HARTY of Standish, MI, G.L. SPRAGUE, Marshfield, MA, both died in Omaha. Ringe LUCAN, NY, killed by lightning.

AUST, William [30; Omaha; b: Prussia; f: Gottlieb AUST] md. Emma MUHS [18;

Omaha; b: IA; f: Peter MUHS; m: Anna SCHNECKLOTH] on 12 Jun 1875. Off: PEABODY. Wit: August AUST, Edward KUPPIG.

AUSTIN, John [22; Omaha; colored; b: Virginia; f: Sanders AUSTIN] md. Francis SMITH [23; Leavenworth, KS; colored; b: Lexington, MO] on 25 Jul 1870 at the residence of Mrs. ROBERSON. Off: HUBBARD. Wit: C. CURTIS; Mrs. ROBERSON or ROBINSON.

AUSTIN, William B. [23; Omaha; b: England; f: John AUSTIN; m: Elizabeth SENTOR] md. Fanny A. SALVY [21; IA; b: IA; f: Thomas SALVY; m: Sarah J.] on 27 Nov 1875. OFF: BRITT. Wit: S.H. BRITT, Talitha BALDWIN.

AUTHES, George [23; Omaha; b: Germany; f: Christoph AUTHES; m: Margarethe DAUTH] md. Amanda GETZSCHMAN [24; Omaha; b: Germany; f: Amandus GETZSCHMAN; m: Hermine DIETRICH] on 31 Mar 1880. Off: FALK. Wit: Paul GETZSCHMAN, Julius FESTNER, Mary GETZSCHMAN.

AVERY, Sylvanus [32; Calhoun; b: Canada West; f: Charles AVERY; m: Mary PATTERSON] md. Jennie PIERCE [30; Calhoun; b: New York; f: William PIERCE; m: Hannah FLAG] on 15 Jan 1870. Off: RIPPEY. Wit: Mr. and Mrs. ARNOLD; Mrs. SHOAF; Mrs. C. BELDAN.

AXFORD, Harris W. [33; Omaha; b: England; f: John AXFORD; m: Elizabeth GAUNTLETT] md. Antoinette V. ROBINSON [26; Omaha; b: IA; f: Andrew P. ROBINSON; m: Sarah BANKS] on 11 Oct 1875. Off: BRITT. Wit: James A. BARRETT, Leo. W. CLEMONS.

AYE, John [36; Chicago Precinct; b: Germany; f: John AYE; m: Margareth RADMANN] md. Wiebke Catharine FEDDE [23; Douglas Co.; b: Germany; f: John FEDDE; m: Margareth MARTENS] on 23 Dec 1878. Off: BENEKE. Wit: John LEMKE, Christian FEDDE of Douglas Co.

AYER, Jared B. [27; Omaha; b: New York; f: Isaac T. AYER; m: Tamson BIGELOW] md. Sarah AUSTIN [17; Omaha; b: New York; f: Charles G. AUSTIN; m: Emeline A. RUMMER] on 17 Sep 1873. Off: TOWNSEND. Wit: David G. TALLENT; Annie D. TALLENT. Age of consent given by mother of the bride. Father of bride is "either dead or has abandoned ... he having left his home ... some two months ago."

AYERS, Osborne [40; Omaha; b: New York; f: Fredus AYERS; m: Permelia HALL] md. Rasaltha BRINK [31; Omaha; b; New York; f: Oscar F. BRINK; m: Adah B. DAVID] on 1 Jan 1870. Off: GIBSON. Wit: Alexander ATKINSON; Mrs. Temple ATKINSON.

BABER, Frank H. [33; Omaha; b: New York; f: Frank H. BABER; m: Jane HOWELL] md. Alice SHERKEY [23; Omaha; b: Ohio; f: Richard SHERKEY; m: Hannah OWENS] on 4 Sep 1880. Off: MILLSPAUGH. Wit: James McMICHAEL, Sister Mary HAYDEN.

BABER, Richard T. [22; Crawford, IA; b: Virginia; f: John BABER; m: Annie RIGSBY] md. Mary M. HAMMOND [16; Crawford, IA; b: Wisconsin or Michigan; f: John T. HAMMOND, deceased; m: Ann LOCKWOOD, deceased] on 9 Oct 1870. Off: GIBSON. Wit: John BOBER; Rebecca J. BOBER (from Omaha or Crawford, IA?). Age of consent given by bride - she wants no guardian appointed.

BADGLY (BAGDLY), James md. Catherine GOGGIN on 12 Jan 1858. Off: PORTER.

BAGLY (BAGLEY), James [Douglas Co.] md. Honora LOMAY [Douglas Co.] on 7 Apr 1863, both of legal age. Off: KELLY. Wit: John COLLINS, Elisabeth KINELLY.

BAGLY (BAGLEY), Michael [35; Omaha] md. Ann MAHAR [35; Florence] on 7 Apr 1861 at the Catholic Church of Omaha. Off: KELLY. Wit: John BAGLY (BAGLEY), Mary Ann CASSIDY.

BAIER, Christian [28; Omaha; b: Germany; f: Frederick BAIER; m: Elizabeth HETTINGER] md. Wilhelmina SCHULTZ [23; Omaha; b: Germany; f: Frederich SCHULTZ; m: Gustive SIEBERT] on 14 Jul 1881. Off: SMITH. Wit: C.D. RUTHER, W.G. GEHER.

BAILEY (BAILY), William T. md. Mary F. FLETCHER on 11 Jul 1865 at the Methodist Episcopal Church. Off: LEMON. Wit: George BARTLETT, Emma A. BARTLETT.

BAILEY, Francis L. [22; Omaha; b: Southampton, England; f: John BAILEY; m: Elizabeth FAVRE] md. Ann Emma HOLLAND [17; Omaha; b: Indiana; f: James HOLLAND; m: Margaret FINLEY] on 27 Jan 1873. Off: THURSTON. Wit: S.H. DREW; M.C. GUILL.

BAILEY, Frank L. [27; b: England; f: Frederick BAILEY; m: Elizabeth MANNING] md. Matilda HINES [18; Austria; f: John HINES] on 1 Dec 1878. Off: WILLIAMS. Wit: George and Mrs. BURKE [sic].

BAILEY, George M. [22; Elkhorn; of the Army of the U.S.] md. Emma J. McLAUGHLIN [17; Denver; Colorado Territory] on 15 Jun 1866 at the house of G.B. BAILEY, Elkhorn. Off: VAN ANTWERP. Wit: Mr. and Mrs. G.B. BAILEY, Inez BELDEN. Age consent given by father of the bride.

BAILEY, John B. [21; Cleveland, OH; b: Ohio; f: D.R. BAILEY; m: Emma BENNETTS] md. Alice I. HILL [17; Omaha; b: Utah; f: William HILL; m: Emma] on 28 Oct 1874. Off: PEABODY. Wit: Mary C. PEABODY; Emma HILL.

BAILEY, John B. [29; Omaha; b: England; f: Joseph BAILEY; m: Hannah HOPE] md. Lizzie LOWE (HOGAN was crossed out) [19; Omaha; b: Omaha; f: ----; m: Elizabeth (HOGAN?)] on 9 Nov 1876. Off: MULCAHY. Wit: Michael O'NEILL, Mrs. Tarina JACKSON.

BAILEY, John C. [25; Washington Co.; b: Wisconsin; f: Turner BAILEY; m: Lucy BRADFORD] md. Mrs. Clara KYLE [28; North Platte; b: Boston; f: Benjamin KYLE; m: Clara BRADFORD] on 16 Sep 1878. Off: SHERRILL. Wit: John BRADFORD, Mrs. H.R. BRADFORD.

BAILEY, John [26; Council Bluffs; b: VT; f: Eaton BAILEY; m: Mary PIKE] md. Dora SUIT [24; Council Bluffs; b: IL; f: Henry SUIT; m: Phebe HEWITT] on 31 Jul 1875. OFF: PEABAODY. Wit: A.E. SIMPSON, Mary SUIT.

BAILEY, John [42; Council Bluffs, IA; b: Devonshire, Engl.; f: Thomas BAILEY; m: Maria BEER] md. Anna CHRISTIAN [30; Council Bluffs, IA; b: Missouri; f: R.R. CHRISTIAN; m: Percila BORSTON] on 1 May 1879. Off: SHROPSHIRE. Wit: J.J. JUDSON, Joseph WOODHAM.

BAILEY, Joshua B. [26; Washington Co.] md. Catherine HALL [18; Douglas Co.] on 23 Nov 1865. Off: SLAUGHTER. Wit: Mr. and Mrs. HALL.

BAILY, Anderson [22; Mills Co., IA] md. Mary PIERCE [16; Mills Co., IA] on 20 Apr 1869. Off: HYDE. Wit: Jackson PIERCE, Telitha PIERCE. Age consent given by father of the bride, John PIERCE of Mills Co., IA.

BAKER, Alexander H. [49; West Omaha Pct; b: Livingston Co., NY; f: Samuel BAKER; m: Salome ELDRED] md. Mary J. BERLIN [30; Union Pct; b: Pittsburgh, PA; f: Jonathan BERLIN; m: Nancy WILSON] on 27 Dec 1872 at Union Pct. Off: BILLMAN. Wit: Jonathan BERLIN; Mrs. Nancy P. BERLIN.

BAKER, Charles E. [24; Omaha; b: NY; f: John BAKER; m: Elmira BURNELL] md. Clara RAMET [19; Omaha; b: MO; f: John RAMET; m: Kate BRANGHBENDEN] on 11 Oct 1881. Off: SHANK. Wit: H.M. LAUBAUCH, Edmond S. SHANK.

BAKER, Daniel W. [32; Cheyenne Co.; b: New York; f: John BAKER] md. Margaret McKEOWN [22; North Platte; b: Scotland; f: Hugh McKEOWN; m: Mary SCHROWFORD] on 16 Jul 1872. Off:

DIMMICK. Wit: Mr. and Mrs. Sylvanus WRIGHT; Mrs. Kate G. DIMMICK.

BAKER, James A. [21; Omaha; b: NY; f: James A. BAKER; m: Eliza SAINT CLAIR] md. Mary DOLAN [18; Omaha; b: IN; f: H. DOLAN; m: Eliza Anna ALLEN] on 25 Apr 1881. Off: WRIGHT. Wit: Emma SQUIRES, Henry RANDOLPH.

BAKER, William [25; Omaha; b: London, England; f: James BAKER; m: Rebecca FOX] md. Martha SCOTT [24; Omaha; b: London, ENG; f: John SCOTT; m: Mary FOGARTY] on 6 Sep 1870. Off: DeLaMATYRE. Wit: Thomas SAMPSON; Mary SCOTT.

BALCH, Edward E. [24; Omaha] md. Lizzie STEWART [17; Omaha] at 9 PM, Monday evening, 12 Oct 1868. Off: DIMMICK. Wit: Dr. MOORE, Mrs. Chas. WHITMORE, Mrs. G.M. ROBERTS, et al. Age consent given by the father of the bride.

BALDWIN, B.B. [27; Elk Horn Station, NE; b: Michigan; f: Grove BALDWIN; m: Esta WILLIS] md. Mary CHAMBERS [19; Omaha; b: Missouri; f: John CHAMBERS; m: Mary VERKIER] on 16 S ep 1879 at Trinity Cathedral, Omaha. Off: MILLSPAUGH. Wit: Martin GOULD, Mary HAYDEN.

BALDWIN, Henry [28; Omaha; b: Ireland; f: David BALDWIN; m: Margaret ROSE] md. Anna FLANAGAN [22; Omaha; b: Ireland; f: Andrew FLANAGAN; m: Anna BERMINGHAM] on 28 May 1881. Off: WILLIAMS. Wit: Mrs. H.H. PRINGLE, Hastings, MN, Mrs. John WILLIAMS. Filed 15 Aug 1882 by A.M. CHADWICK.

BALDWIN, Sherman C. [43; Council Bluffs; b: OH; f: Runey BALDWIN; m: Calistia KINGSBURRY] md. Caroline LETZIR [43; Council Bluffs; b: Germany] on 2 Oct 1876. Off: STEWART. Wit: Rev. Joshua RULE, Bellevue, Sarah A. NOLL.

BALKWELL, Charles [22; Omaha; b: England; f: Charles BALKWELL; m: Susannah KNIGHT] md. Emily J. ADAMS [27; Omaha; b: Ohio; f: James ADAMS; m: Eliza ADAMS] on 20 Apr 1877. Off: PEABODY. Wit: N.A. STURGESS, E.B. KNOX.

BALL, Elisha E. [21; Mapletown, IA; b: IA; f: Nate BALL; m: Esther WICKAM] md. Eva McCLARY [18; b: IA; f: Aaron McCLARY; m: Alice WADKINS] on 31 Oct 1881. Off: BRUNZ. Wit: Daniel BALL, Mary BALL. Affidavit signed by Daniel BALL.

BALL, Norman F. [23; Douglas Co.; b: Illinois; f: Silas S. BALL; m: Charlotte ADAIR] and Nancy ARMES [19; Douglas Co.; b: Iowa; f: David ARMES; m: Eliza FIELDS] license issued on 29 Sep 1879. No marriage record. Off: BARTHOLOMEW.

BALLARD, Osceola R. [Audubon Co., IA] md. Sarah L. LORAH [Audobon Co., IA] on 23 Mar 1864 at DICKINSON's office. Off: DICKINSON. Wit: Charles H. BROWN, Martin O'BRIEN.

BALLARD, Phillip [24; Crescent, IA] md. Nancy P. BORAN [19; Crescent, IA] on 18 Jun 1868. Off: ROBERTS. Wit: H.E. PAINE, H.L. SEWARD.

BALLARD, Thomas [32; Omaha; b: New York; f: Louis BALLARD; m: Margaret MULFORD] md. Hattie CAWEN [18; Omaha; b: Kentucky; f: Harry CAWEN; m: Hariett RASE] on 18 Jan 1870. Off: GIBSON. Wit: John B. ROBERTS; Belle CLAVER.

BALLIET, Charles H. [35; Nevada, IA; b: Pennsylvania; f: John BALLIET; m: Hannah STARVER] md. Mary F. ATKINS [31; Omaha; b; Massachusetts; f: Benjmain F. ATKINS; m: Mary T. ELWELL] on 28 Oct 1880. Off: PATERSON. Wit: Saml. A. BALLIET; Ellen E.A. SCHALLER.

BAMFORTH, Frederick F. [25; Omaha; b: England; f: S.O. Charles BAMFORTH; m: Maria STANSBY] md. Mary Ann CARR [16; Omaha b: Galena, Il; f: Timothy CARR; m: Margaret MAREN] on 8 Jan 1873. Off: TOWNSEND. Wit: William H. IJAMS; Morris W.E. PURCHASE. Age of consent given by the mother of the bride. "Timothy CARR has abandoned this affiant"; bride will be 17 on 25 Apr 1873.

BANKES, Charles [28; Omaha; b: Germany; f: Henry BANKES; m: Christine HENSE] md. Emilie HUMSTEDT [22; Omaha; b: Germany; f: Henry D. HUMSTEDT; m: Elizabeth BURGDORFF] on 22 Dec 1869. Off: KUHNS. Wit: Laura M. RUTH, Mary D. KOUNTZE.

BANKS, J.W. [31; Omaha; b: Maryland; f: J.W. BANKS; m: Margaret STUBENE] md. Jessie E. SNOWDEN [17; Omaha; b: Omaha; f: Wm. P. SNOWDEN; m: Rachel LARSON] on 1 Jun 1879. Off: INGRAM. Wit: Simon CAREY, Catharine CAREY. Age consent given by W.P. SNOWDEN, father of the bride.

BANKS, Thomas [23; Omaha; colored; b: Missouri; f: Gain BANKS] md. Ann NELSON [38; Omaha; colored; b: Kentucky] on 30 May 1870. Off: GIBSON. Wit: George M. O'BRIEN; Lewis REED.

BANKS, Thomas [Douglas Co.] md. Orpha RUBY [Douglas Co.] on 26 Sep 1865. Off: MILLER. Wit: Tho. TOBY, Sarah Ann SURBER.

BARBARO, Joseph [37; Omaha; b: Italy; f: Joseph BARBARO; m: Orsula

BRIGNONE] md. Mrs. Eliza SHAW [32; Omaha; b: Michigan; f: D.B. MEAD; m: Abigail W. WOOD] on 31 Oct 1877. Off: SEDGWICK. Wit: J.F. CLUCHARD, Frank THORNE.

BARBER, Charles J. [31; Omaha; b: Union Village, NY; f: Joshua T. BARBER; m: Mary Ann O'DELL] md. Leonora E. OSTROM [17; Omaha; b: Chautaugua Co., NY; f: Adam S. OSTROM; m: Lois WALKER] on 10 Apr 1873. Off: McKELVEY. Wit: A.S. OSTROM; Lois OSTROM. Age of consent given by father of bride.

BARBER, R.W. [29; Waterloo; b: New York; f: Charles H. BARBER; m: Rachael WASHBURN] md. Adella A. CLARK [23; Waterloo; b: Indiana; f: Elam CLARK; m: Rebecca HARMON] on 15 Nov 1880. Off: CRAWFORD. Wit: S.A. TEAL of Missouri Valley, IA , M.W.E. PURCHASE of Waterloo, NE.

BARBER, Reuben W. [24; Waterloo; b: NY; f: Charles D. BARBER; m: Rachel WASHBURN] md. Emma L. BAILEY [19; Elkhorn City; b: PA; f: Gordon B. BAILEY; m: Minerva BROWN] on 5 May 1875 at Elkhorn City. Off: FOSTER. Wit: Gordon B. BAILEY, Elkhorn City, M.W.E. PURCHASE, Waterloo.

BARBER, William [31; Red Willow Co.; b: PA; f: John BARBER; m: Sarah FOSTER] md. Ida BERRY [19; Omaha; b: IA; f: H.A. BERRY; m: Clarissa WILDERMOUTH] on 10 Sep 1881 at Saratoga. Off: PURCELL. Wit: John STONE, Fort Omaha, Ella DELLAHAM, Saratoga.

BARGAUSEN [BARSHAN], Charles [28; b: Hanover, Prusia; f: Conrad BARGHAUSON; m: Henrietta HEKNAN] md. Matilda C. PETERSON [25; Omaha; b: Sweden; f: Peter SWANSON; m: Maria HELIN] on 25 Jul 1869. Off: KUHNS. Wit: Wilhelmina KESSLER, Justus KESSLER.

BARKER, Austin P. [21; Omaha; Iowa; f: James BARKER; m: Elizabeth BULLIS] md. Mary BURNS [18; Omaha; b: Philadelphia, PA; f: John BURNS; m: Mary MAHER] on 9 Mar 1879. Off: JAMESON. Wit: Mary DOHERTY, Mrs. Emily BARKER.

BARKER, Joseph, Jr. [45; Omaha; b: England; f: Joseph BARKER; m: Frances SALT] md. Eliza E. PATRICK [45; Omaha; b: PA; f: John PATRICK; m: Matilda ERSKINE] on 23 Sep 1875 at Trinity Cathedral. Off: CLARKSON. Wit: Rev. EASTER, J.H.N. PATRICK.

BARKER, Joshua M. [22; Omaha; b: Iowa; f: James M. BARKER; m: Elizabeth M. BULLIS] md. Emily CLARK [18; Council Bluffs; b: New York; f: S.F. CLARK; m: Jenny COE] on 28 Sep 1877. Off: JAMESON. Wit: Kate RUSSELL of Council Bluffs, Mrs. Clarissa LaFOLLETTE. Application signed: James M. BARKER.

BARLOW, Bluford [Elkhorn Precinct] and Mary Ann HICKEY [under 16; Elkhorn Precinct] license issued on 11 Aug 1864. No marriage record. Off: DICKINSON. Age consent given by father of the bride.

BARLOW, Harlan [30; Omaha; b: CT; f: George BARLOW; m: Harriet MERVIN] md. Mrs. Alice LEE [21; Omaha; b: WI; f: Martin OAKSON; m: Anna ANDERSON] on 23 Nov 1881. Off: SHANK. Wit: Susie C. SHANK, Genevra A. THOMAS.

BARLOW, James H. [Omaha] md. Dolly McCORMICK [Omaha] on the morning of 7 Jan 1867 at the residence of Samuel BURNS, Esq. Off: LEMON. Wit: Samuel BURNS and wife, J.H. LACEY and wife, et al.

BARLOW, Milton T. [23; Omaha] md. Mary HAYS [19; Omaha] on 19 Dec 1867 at Trinity Church. Off: VAN ANTWERP. Wit: Hon. Geo. B. LAKE, Col. HAYS, congregation.

BARLOW, Richard [27; Council Bluffs] md. Elizabeth PILLING [18; Council Bluffs] on 15 Nov 1862. Off: ARMSTRONG.

BARNACLE, James R. [21; Omaha; b: England; f: Richard BARNACLE; m: Louisa SMITH] md. Eliza. T. JONES [24; Omaha; b: England; f: Henry JONES; m: Alice ORALL] on 27 Nov 1876. Off: JAMESON. Wit: Charles H. POOL, Lucy E. HARTRY.

BARNES, James G. [29; Omaha] md. Elizabeth KEITH [26; Omaha] on 16 Apr 1867. Off: SLAUGHTER. Wit: Martin WOOD, Mrs. WOOD.

BARNES, John J. [25; b: New York; f: John H. BARNES; m: Margaret COTTER] md. Margaret HERMES [22; b: Michigan; f: M. HERMES; m: Gracie MYERS] on 1 Jun 1878. Off: FISHER. Wit: E.E. PARKER, Ida PARKER.

BARNES, Theodore B. [22; Omaha; b: Albany, NY; f: Edmund F. BARNES; m: Caroline GRAY] md. Annie HOWARD [18; Omaha; b: Cherry Vale, KS; f: Charles F. HOWARD; m: Mary] on 7 Aug 1873. Off: WRIGHT. Wit: Charles KEITH; Jane KEITH.

BARNETT, James [25; Omaha; b: England; f: John BARNETT; m: Susan UNDERHILL] md. Mrs. Catharine Ann KNOWLES [35; Omaha; b: Canada East; f: William SOMERVILLE; m: Margaret CURRY] on 26 Feb 1873. Off: TOWNSEND. Wit: Mrs. Oley WHEELER; Horace OLMSTED.

BARON, Edward P. [35; Douglas Co.] and Bridget Agnes ATKESON [ATKINSON] [24; Douglas Co.] license issued on 14 May 1868. No marriage record. Off: STUCK.

BARR, Elias A. [34; Fremont; b: Lancaster Co., PA; f: Jacob BARR; m: Susanna BARR] md. Cynthia L. ANNIS [17; Fremont; b: London, Engl.; f: ---- CHALMERS] on 25 May 1869. Off: WESTWOOD. Wit: C.L. GARRISON, Allen KOCH. [ANNIS is bride's adodpted name. She does not know her fathers christian name or the name of her mother before marriage to Mr. CHALMER. She stated that they died when she was very young.]

BARR, Galen [21; Douglas Co.; b: WI; f: John BARR; m: Emmilie GILL] md. Maria MARSHALL [16; Douglas Co.; b: NY; f: John MARSHALL; m: Mary DAVIS] on 11 Jan 1881. Off: MARQUETTE. Wit: F.W. KILE, Miss A. MARSHALL. Age consent given by mother of the bride.

BARRATT, Jesse W. [27; Fairview, NE; b: New Jersey; f: Ebenezer D. BARRATT; m: Prudence WADDINGTON] md. Lucy CHESBROW [25; Fairview, NE; b: New York; f: Benjamin CHESBROW; m: Roady HOWARD] on 20 Feb 1878. Off: ROE. Wit: L.A. HARMON, Mrs. H.M. HARMON.

BARRET, James A. [23; Douglas Co.] md. Jane C. BARNARD [21; Douglas Co.] on 3 Oct 1860 at GAYLORD's residence. Off: GAYLORD. Wit: Mr. LUDDEN, Mrs. BARNARD.

BARRETT, Daniel S. [37; Omaha; b: New York; f: James C. BARRETT; m: Maria STRANG] md. Mary E. SMITH [18; Omaha; f: Christopher SMITH; m: Mary CLARKSON] on 28 Apr 1871. Off: SHINN. Wit: Mrs. Mary SMITH; Ella CAMPBELL.

BARRETT, John [26; Omaha; b: Ireland; f: William BARRETT; m: Margaret McCARTHY] md. Julia SHANAHAN [24; Omaha; b: Ireland; f: Daniel SHANAHAN; m: Julia FITZGERALD] on 15 Oct 1876 at the Catholic Cathedral. Off: JENNETTE. Wit: Richard MULLAN, Lizzie MASON. Marriage recorded 14 Apr 1878.

BARRETT, Patrick [25; Omaha; b: Ireland; f: Peter BARRETT; m: Ann BROWN] md. Sarah KING [22; Omaha; b: Ireland; f: Martin KING; m: Margaret CANAN] on 5 Feb 1871. Off: CURTIS. Wit: John MAGNER; Margaret SULLIVAN.

BARRETT, William [22; Council Bluffs] md. Annie NAUGHTON [19; Council Bluffs] on 27 Mar 1869. Off: O'GORMAN. Wit: Dennis O. FLAHERTY, Catharine DOYLE.

BARRETTE, Edmond [25; Douglas Co.] and Mary DOLIN [24; Douglas Co.] license issued on 11 Jan 1858. No marriage record. Off: BRIGGS.

BARRY, John [28; Douglas Co.] and Mary KELLEY [27; Douglas Co.] license issued on 5 Mar 1858. No marriage record. Off: BRIGGS.

BARRY, Michael J. [25; Washington Co.; b: Canada; f: Thomas BARRY; m: Mary KELLY] md. Mary MANEY [20; Washington Co.; b: New Jersey; f: James MANEY; m: Mary RYAN] on 11 Apr 1880, St. Philomena Church. Off: McCARTNEHY. Wit: Johanna MANEY of Blair, T.J. BARRY.

BARRY, Thomas J. [25; Omaha, 1017 Chicago Street; b: Canada; f: Michael BARRY; m: Hanora CUMINGS] md. Bridget MURRAY [21; Omaha, 6th and Marcy Streets; b: OH; f: James MURRAY; m: Bridget O'MALEY] on 16 Nov 1881 at the Catholic Cathedral. Off: (RIORDAN crossed out "by me"). Wit: Denis CARROLL, Sherman Avenue, Helena BOYLE, 20th and Davenport.

BARSTON, Sumner [34; Omaha] md. Sarah E. LEWIS [24; Omaha] on 20 Dec 1867. Off: KUHNS. Wit: Mrs. W.H. KUHNS, Minnie DAME.

BARTELS, Gustav [Sarpy Co.] md. Christine PAHLMANN [Omaha] on 12 Mar 1864 at the residence of the bride's father. Off: KUHNS. Wit: Mr. and Mrs. PAHLMANN, et al.

BARTHOLOMEW, Arthur C. [27; Omaha] md. Charlotte FLORKEE [20; Omaha] on 15 Nov 1868. Off: SLAUGHTER. Wit: A.B. SLAUGHTER, S. BURNS.

BARTHOLOMEW, Leonard B. [26; Omaha] md. Mary Ann LABAUGH [22; Omaha] on 3 Jul 1861 at Mr. BOWMAN's residence. Off: ARMSTRONG. Wit: Mr. and Mrs. BOWMAN, H.C. JUDSON.

BARTHOLOMEW, William [28; Nebraska City; b: Indiana; f: James BARTHOLOMEW, m: Ruth SMITH] md. Mattie LINDSEY [32; Nebraska City; b: Ohio; f: Wm. LINDSEY; m: Nancy THOMPSON] on 16 Jan 1877. Off: McCARTNEY. Wit: W.H. BROWN, Maria McCARTNEY.

BARTLE, Frank [25; St. Paul, NE; b: WI; f: Albert (John crossed out) BARTLE; m: Elizabeth TRUBL] md. Veronika J. KAVAN [22; Omaha; b: Austria; f: Wenzel KAVAN; m: Veronka SUCHY] on 6 Jul 1881 at the Roman Catholic Cathedral. Off: RIORDAN. Wit: John VASAK, St. Paul, Mary ZENICEK, Omaha.

BARTLETT, William H. [34; St. Joseph, MO; b: Indiana; f: David BARTLETT; m: Phebe G. ELLSWORTH] md. Cora A. BUTTS [21; Lincoln, NE; b: New York; f: Peter O. BUTTS; m: Alma WILMOT] on 8 Oct 1879. Off: LIPE. Wit: Lizzie E. LIPE, Addie W. LIPE.

BARTLETT, William Wallace [20; Omaha; b: MI; f: Wallace R. BARTLETT; m: Sarah F. TOWNE] md. Rosaline M.O. WIESE [20; Omaha; b: Russia; f: Frederick A. WIESE; m: Bertha STOLTENBERG] on 2 Feb 1881. Off: INGRAM. Wit: F. Stanton LEWIS, Orville P. CHUBB. Parents of the groom signed W.W. BARTLETT, P.O. Drawer 40.

BARTON, Robert F. [27; Papillion; b: MD; f: Thomas BARTON; m: Hannah LOWE] md. Ava SAGE [21; Sarpy Co., NE; b: IN; f: Harleight SAGE; m: Sophia KNOX] on 16 Mar 1881. Off: SMITH. Wit: Wm. L. PEABODY, Max BERGMANN.

BARTOS, Joseph [21; Omaha; b: Bohemia; f: Charles BARTOS; m: Barbara LEDER] md. Anna ESPANDE [20; Omaha; Bohemia; f: John ESPANDE; m: Anna FRIDRICH] on 11 Aug 1879. Off: BARTHOLOMEW. Wit: Andrew BEVINS, Max BERGMANN.

BASCOMB, Hubert T. [38; Omaha; b: England; f: John BASCOMB; m: Anna BASCOMB] md. Mrs. Alice SPAN [32; Omaha; b: Indiana; f: John PICKORD; m: Julia Nette SKINNER] on 9 Sep 1879. Off: PORTER. Wit: Joseph BOYER, Lucy INGERSOL.

BASSET, James H. [27; Omaha; b: Massachusetts; f: Joshua H. BASSET; m: Ellen OPENSHAW] md. Maggie OPENSHAW [22; Omaha; b: Pennsylvania; f: Henry OPENSHAW] on 29 Jan 1870. Off :McCAGUE. Wit: Danis HARMAN; Minerva ROBINSON.

BATES, Fred [23; Omaha; b: MA; f: Dexter BATES; m: Emily VOSE] md. Eva WOODS [20; Omaha; b: IL; f: Frank WOODS; m: Laura MUNGER] on 28 Nov 1881. Off: BLAYNEY. Wit: Mr. and Mrs. R.A. WILLIAMS, Mr. and Mrs. BROGLE, Jennie SHIELDS.

BATES, Selah [60; Omaha] md. Mrs. Mary E. JUSTIN [47; Omaha] on 3 Mar 1869. Off: KERMOTT. Wit: Rev. J.C. JONES, Rollin C. SMITH.

BATSFORD, Thomas [26; Omaha; b: England; f: Matthew BATSFORD; m: Caroline RADFORD] md. Ann RADFORD [20; Omaha; b: England; f: Thomas KNIGHT; m: Mary] on 11 Jun 1872. Off: GUE. Wit: Mrs. Anna B. GUE; June CARR.

BATTE, Algernon [Decatur, Burt Co.] md. Medora S. CLARK [Omaha] on 16 Jul 1863 at the residence of the bride's father, John S. CLARK. Off: DAKE. Wit: Cornelia RICHARDSON, Imogene CLARK, Mr. and Mrs. John S. CLARK, Mrs. Virginia RICHARDSON.

BAUER, Karl [31; Omaha; b: Germany; f: Gotthilf BAUER; m: Anna Maria OSTERTAG] md. Barbara GRUINER [23; Omaha; b: Austria; f: Franz GRUINER; m: Anna Maria GRUINER] on 20 Jul 1876. Off: BENEKE. Wit: Chas. KAUFMANN, Mich. ROBLING.

BAUMAN, Adam [20; Omaha] md. Barbara BOSS [25; Omaha] on 14 Nov 1868. Off: STUCK. Wit: John M. SULLIVAN, Charles SCHAKE.

BAUMAN, Jonas [26; Omaha] md. Louisa BOYER [20; Omaha] on 13 Jun 1867 at BROWN's office. Off: BROWN. Wit: Albert SWARTZLANDER, Jacob PFLUG.

BAUMANN, Joseph [Omaha] md. Wilhelmina MERTENS [Omaha] on 12 May 1863 at Frederick SCHENCK's residence. Both of legal age. Off: KUHNS. Wit: Samuel ROGERS, Frederick SCHENK, et al.

BAUMANN, Otto [31; Omaha] md. Lena ZEPF [21; Omaha] on 8 Feb 1868. Off: KUHNS. Wit: Anthony YETZER, Martina ZEPF.

BAUMEISTER, Anton [25; Omaha; b: Germany; f: Lorenz BAUMEISTER; m: Victoria STOETZEL] md. Theresa MAILANDER [19; Omaha; b: Illinois; f: Peter M. MAILANDER; m: Caroline STETMER] on 23 Nov 1880, German Catholic Church. Off: GROENBAUM. Wit: Frank WASSERMANN, Clara MAILANDER.

BAUMER, Herman [27; Washington Co.; b: Germany; f: Herman BAUMER; m: Sophia MARTIN] md. Matilda KOBS [23; Omaha; b: Prussia; f: Leopold KOBS; m: Dority STEIK] on 8 Mar 1870. Off: GIBSON. Wit: John BAUMER, Fannie GODFRY.

BAUMER, John [28; Omaha] md. Josephine GRANACHER [17; Omaha] on 7 Jan 1869. Off: GROENEBAUM. Wit: Theodore BAUMER, Catherine BERN.

BAUMER, Julius [23; Omaha; b: Prussia; f: Bernhart BAUMER; m: Clara WEIHE] md. Pauline KUPPIG [19; Omaha; b: Prussia; f: Charles KUPPIG; m: Caroline AUST] on 12 Apr 1870. Off: GIBSON. Wit: William AUST; Gustav OTTO.

BAUMER, Theodore [31; Omaha; b: Prusia; f: Hermann BAUMER; m: Sophia MARTIN] md. Adele Von WASMER [19; Bellevue; b: Schleswig; f: Wm. Von WASMER] on 25 Oct 1869. Off: KELLEY. Wit: Wm. WASMER, Mr. BAUMER.

BAUSCH [BURES], Jacob [28; Omaha[ b: Germany; f: Mathe BAUSCH [BURES]; m: Helen WEINER] md. Catharina PRIBAL [PRIBYL] [25; Omaha[ b: Bohemia; f: Joseph PRIBAL [PRIBYL]; m: Catharina PROKOP] on 6 Nov 1879. Off: BENEKE. Wit: Naigel NESTEL, Victor DREHER.

BAWES, Stephen [22; Omaha; b: Ireland; f: Nicholas BAWES; m: Margaret SMITH] md. Mary HIGGINS [20; Omaha; b: Ireland;

f: Daniel HIGGINS; m: Mary CRONIN] on 29 Jan 1870. Off: CURTIS. Wit: Miles REARDON; Catherine KANE.

BAY, John P. [21; Omaha; b: Iowa; f: John P. BAY; m: Christina McCALL] md. Mary BUSH [20; Omaha; b: Canada East; f: John BUSH; m: Bridget BUSH] on 2 Sep 1872. Off: CURTIS. Wit: S.P. PIGMAN; Jennie BUSH.

BAY, William H. [21; Omaha; b: Iowa; f: John P. BAY; m: Christine McCALL] md. Lizzie H. WHITEHOUSE [19; Omaha; b: New York; f: W.J. WHITEHOUSE; m: Jane G. GRAVES] on 15 Dec 1880. Off: WILLIAMS. Wit: Wm. H. WHITEHOUSE, William WHITEHOUSE.

BEACH, George E. [42; Omaha; b: New York f: Joseph BEACH; m: Lucy FISH] md. Mrs. Mary E. BARKER [37; Omaha; b; New Jersey; f: Geriat M. KETCHAM; m: Juliet JONES] on 24 Jul 1874. Off: WRIGHT. Wit: Josephine WEBSTER; Mary H. WRIGHT.

BEALES, Austin W. [30; Ft. Calhoun, Washington Co.] md. Hannah HALL [20; Florence] on 21 Apr 1868 at John HALL's house in Florence. Off: HERMAN.

BEALES, Robert [24; Douglas Co.; b: Illinois; f: William B. BEALES; m: Elizabeth AUSTIN] md. Priscilla F. HALL [18; Durt Co.; b: Ohio; f: John A. HALL; m: C.C. MITCHELL] on 29 Jul 1871. Off: GIBSON. Wit: George ARMSTRONG; Thomas SWOBE.

BEALL, Roger L. [27; De Soto] md. Sarah Ellen HUGUS [HUGHES] [18; Omaha] at 8 PM on Thursday, 26 Jun 1862 at the residence of Peter HUGUS [HUGHES], father of the bride. Off: DAKE. Wit: Bride's relatives, George W. DOANE and wife, E.A. ALLEN, A. PATRICK, Medora CLARK, and many others.

BEAR, John [18; b: Michigan; f: John BEAR; m: Agnes STIBEL [STIBAL]] md. Elizabeth SPRUHEM [21; b: Australia; f: James SPRUHEM; m: Mary McDERMOTT] on 1 Apr 1878. Off: BARTHOLOMEW. Wit: Wm. L. PEABODY, H.A. STURGESS. Age consent given by mother of the groom, father is dead. [Signature of the mother looks nothing like her name. It appears to be Angie?]

BECHTEL, Henry [27; Omaha Barracks; b: Ohio; f: Jacob BECHTEL; m: Elizabeth HANN] md. Julia O'NEIL [30; Omaha Barracks; b: New York; f: John O'NEIL; m: Eliza BURNS] on 19 Jul 1877. Off: SEDGWICK. Wit: C.C. SPERRY, John SHILL.

BECK, Alfred M. [30; Douglas Co.] md. Annie C. DUDLEY [23; Douglas Co.] on 3 Sep 1868. Off: KELLEY. Wit: Mrs. J.E. KELLEY, Joseph PRICE.

BECK, Theodore [24; Omaha; b: Germany; f: Martin BECK; m: Mary SELINGER] md.

Kate S. FRENZER [24; Omaha; b: Prussia; f: Nicholas FRENZER; m: Margaret SCHABBACH] on 4 Jan 1870. Off: CURTIS. Wit: Martin KLASS of Council Bluffs; Theresa MECK of Council Bluffs.

BECKER, John [25; Douglas Co.; b: Europe; f: Phillip BECKER; m: Margaret DOSE] md. Helen HAMMEL [22; Chicago, IL; b: IA; f: Henry HAMMEL; m: Helen] on 7 Jun 1876. Off: McCARTNEY. Wit: Mrs. Truman BUCK, Mrs. M.F. McCARTNEY.

BECKLEY, William E. [24; Omaha; b: Pennsylvania; f: L.B. BECKLEY; m: Catharine ENIS] md. Jennie F. STERNES [19; Keokuk, IA; b: St. Louis, MO; f: Jarmine STERNES; m: Caroline BROWN] on 17 Mar 1879. Off: BENECKE. Wit: Wm. HAMMETT, Mrs. Sarah BROWN.

BECKMAN, Charles J. [24; Omaha; b: Sweden; f: Carl J. BECKMAN; m: Brita M. AHLBORN] md. Maria E. PETERSON [24; Omaha; b: Sweden; f: Henrik P. PETERSON; m: Brita PETERSON] on 2 Nov 1881. Off: HAYLAND. Wit: Oliver BURSELL, C. CEDERBLOM.

BECKMAN, Joseph [25; Omaha; b: Germany; f: Arnold BECKMAN; m: Mary HONKOMP] md. Ida KLEFFNER [18; Omaha; b: IA; f: George KLEFFNER; m: Lena] on 21 Sep 1875 at the German Catholic Church. Off: BROENEBAUM. Wit: Joseph KOESTERS, Margartha SCHMIDT.

BECKMENN, Henry [36; Douglas Co.] and Louisa DOLL [31; Douglas Co.] license issued on 15 May 1861. No marriage record. Off: ARMSTRONG.

BECKSTEAD, E. [40; Sarpy Co.; b: Canada; f: Francis BECKSTEAD; m: Mary BECKSTEAD] md. Mrs. Adaline BECKSTEAD [32; Sarpy Co.; b: Missouri; f: Michael KYON; m: Mary GUBRON] on 24 Dec 1880. Off: BARTHOLOMEW. Wit: Max BERGMANN, G.W. AMBROSE.

BEEBE, Alfred M. [30; Omaha] and Annie C. DUDLEY [23; Omaha] license issued on 13 Jan 1869. No marriage record. Off: HYDE.

BEEBE, Cornelius [25; Dunlap, IA; b: IA; f: William BEEBE; m: Lena VAN AUSDALL] md. Mary WILLIAMS [20; IA; b: IA; f: Chauncey WILLIAMS] on 16 Aug 1881. Off: BENEKE. Wit: John RIERSON, E.A. McCLURE.

BEEBE, Isaac [52; Council Bluffs] md. Mrs. Emily RUNNION [42; Council Bluffs] on 13 Nov 1858. Off: SEELY.

BEERWINE, John Emerin [33; Omaha] and Ann FARMER [21; Omaha] license issued by ARMSTRONG on 31 Dec 1861. Certificate signed by McCARTHY on 14 Mar 1862. Off: McCARTHY.

BEERY, Samuel [35; Omaha; b: OH; f: John BEERY; m: Mary HELDY] md. Hattie DODD [28; Omaha; b: IL; f: Stephen DODD; m: Cornelia SHEERS] on 28 Feb 1881. Off: STENBERG. Wit: S.W. BOGGS, Rapid City, Christian WILLE.

BEGLEY, James [45; Sarpy Co.] md. Unity KELLY [25; Omaha] on 10 Sep 1867. Off: GROENEBAUM. Wit: John LAFERDY, Mary KELLY.

BEGLEY, John [23; Omaha; b: OH, f: John BEGLEY; m: Mary WREN] md. Mary SULLIVAN [23; Omaha; b: Canada; f: Thomas SULLIVAN; m: Margaret HARRINGTON] on 20 Apr 1875 at the Roman Catholic Cathedral. Off: MOLLOY. Wit: John MURPHY, Mary BEGLEY.

BEGLEY, Thomas [28; Omaha; b: Ireland; f: Charles BEGLEY; m: Mary DOOLEY] md. Bridget HARRINGTON [25; Omaha; b: Ireland; f: John HARRINGTON; m: Mary CARRIDOR] on 27 Jan 1872. Off: CURTIS. Wit: Michael FITZMAURICE; Bridget CASEY.

BEHM, John Fred. [27; Omaha; b: Germany; f: Charles BEHM; m: Elizabeth VOGH] md. Carrie L. NICKERSON [16; Omaha; b: Wisconsin; f: Orson NICKERSON; m: Matilda PRESTON] on 10 Oct 1874. Off: PEABODY. Wit: Sylvia E. PRESTON; Sarah SHAW.

BEHRENDT, Charles [29; Omaha; b: Germany; f: Gottfried BEHRENDT; m: Amelia KRISPIN] md. Sophia M.M. HARTING [21; Douglas Co., b: Germany; f: John F.J. HARTING; m: Elizabeth J.M.] on 12 Aug 1875. Off: DIEKCMANN. Wit: Mrs. F. DIECKMANN, George SELK. Application signed by Frank WALTER.

BEHRENNS, Henry [33; Omaha; b: Germany; f: Den BEHRENNS; m: Marie WALSER] md. Caroline LEIST [35; Omaha; b: Germany; f: Christian HIME] on 5 Jun 1869. Off: HYDE. Wit: Wm. B. CROWELL, Harry ASHBY.

BEHRENS, Hans [30; Saunders Co.; b: Germany; f: Detlef BEHRENS; m: Witke MATTHIER] md. Lena LINDE [25; Omaha; b: Germany; f: George LINDE; m: Magdalena HANSEN] on 9 Sep 1876. Off: BENECKE. Wit: Mary MATTHIER, Douglas Co., ---- KIRCHL.

BEIGHEL, Thomas D. [33; California; b: Pennsylvania; f: Henry H. BEIGHEL; m: Mary CROWELL] md. Mary CALDWELL [21; Missouri; b: missouri; f: John B. CALDWELL; m: Lizzie HAMER] on 5 Apr 1874. Off: DAVIS. Wit: J.J. STUBLES; John A. HARBACH.

BEIL, Otto [26; b: Germany; f: Edward BEIL; m: Justine LERCHNER] md. Lina WESTPHAL [22; b: Germany; f: Louis WESTPHAL; m: Bertha JODET] on 15 May 1878. Off: BENEKE. Wit: August SHIPPORST, Johann FODIET.

BEINDORFF [BIENDORFF], Louis C. [28; Omaha] md. Catherine FAHRENBACH [18; Omaha] on 31 Dec 1867. Off: KUHNS. Wit: Mr. and Mrs. Christohper SCHINDLER, et al.

BEINDROFF [BIENDORFF], Charles [27; Omaha] md. Caroline TIMME [18; Omaha] on 29 Sep 1859 at Mrs. SIPPACK's residence. Off: BRIGGS. Wit: Mrs. J. SIPPACK, Henry PUNDT.

BELICK, John [23; Omaha; b: WI; f: Adolph BELICK; m: Anna MEUER] md. Mary J. WILLBURN [24; Omaha; b: NE; f: G.W. WILLBURN; m: Elizabeth LUMPKIN] on 26 Nov 1881. Off: BRANDES. Wit: Louis HAMMER, Mattie SLIGHTOM.

BELL, Anderson [28; Omaha] md. Catherine MILLER [19; Omaha] on 2 Nov 1867 at SHEEK's office. Off: SHEEK. Wit: Henry MACK, Elizabeth WELLS. This is a double wedding with George NEWMAN and Miss Stanley HAWKINS.

BELL, Cyrus D. [colored; 23; Omaha; b: Orange Co., MS; f: Abram BELL; m: Maria---] md. Cecelia SCANTLING [colored; 17; Omaha; b: South Carolina; m: Margaret] on 3 Jun 1869. Off: KERMOTT. Wit: Mrs. A.R. KERMOTT, Wm. H. SMITH.

BELL, James [31; Omaha; b: Scotland; f: James BELL; m: Jennette MORTON] md. Matilda M. HARTRY [23; Omaha; b: Bloomington, IL; f: Edwin HARTRY; m: Caroline SHEPARD] on 7 Jun 1873. Off: STEWART. Wit: John CAMPBELL; Edwin HARTRY.

BELL, John Thomas [31; Nashville, TN; b: Illinois; f: James A. BELL; m: Nancy PAYNE] md. Isabella Sharp McCANDLISH [28; Omaha; b: Ohio; f: William McCANDLISH; m: Marie HOWELLS] on 19 Nov 1873. Off: McCANDLISH. Wit: George D. STEWART, D.D.; Mrs. John EVANS.

BELL, John W. [25; Omaha] md. Priscilla LEVY [27; Omaha] on 23 Oct 1860 at Wm. HENRY's residence. Off: ARMSTRONG. Wit: Mrs. Wm. HENRY.

BELL, John W. [30; Omaha; b: Lexington, MO; f: A.C. BELL; m: Mary Ellen ----] md. Mrs. Mary E. CARTER [27; Omaha; b; Indiana; f: Robert LOCKRIDGE; m: Sarah E. WINTERS] on 25 Jun 1879. Off: HARSHA. Wit: George M. DARROW, W.H. SHIELDS.

BELL, John W. [Council Bluffs] md. Mary I. DAVIS [Council Bluffs] on 29 Apr 1865 at KUHNS' residence. Off: KUHNS. Wit: Mrs. Rebecca DAVIS, Mrs. Margaret PAPPS.

BELL, Joseph [40; Omaha; b: PA; f: John BELL; m: Margaret BLACK] md. Ellen E.

JOHNSTON [30; (26 crossed out) Omaha; b: PA; f: Wm. JOHNSTON; m: Jane SPEER] on 5 Sep 1876. Off: McCARTNEY. Wit: P.H. SHARP, David BLACK.

BELL, W. (John) [25; Omaha] md. Sarah LARGE [16; Omaha] on 21 Sep 1857 at Mr. BELL's house. Off: SEELY. Age consent given by R. LARGE. Sarah has no parents living. She lives with R. LARGE.

BELLINGER, W.T. [24; Omaha; b: MO; f: James BELLINGER; m: Camettele MILLER] md. Maggie McNABB [17; Omaha; b: IA; f: John W. McNABB; m: Rachael HILLYER] on 4 Oct 1876 at Mr. McNABB's house. Off: GAYLORD. Wit: Daniel B. BALL, John W. McNABB. Age consent given by parents of the bride.

BELLIS, Elisha D. [27; Omaha; b: NJ; f: John L. BELLIS; m: Sarah N. DILTS] md. Cora B. WITHNELL [18; Omaha; b: Omaha; f: John WITHNELL; m: Mary Ann COMER] on 7 Oct 1875. Off: LIPE. Wit: Frank L. LEHMER, John STUBBS.

BELLOWS, Henry H. [25; Omaha; b: Canada; f: Moses B. BELLOWS; m: Fannie M. PIERCE] md. Mrs. Mary A. BENHAM [26; Omaha; b: England; f: Charles MULVY; m: Louisa COLLINS] on 27 Aug 1870. Off: KUHNS. Wit: Annie CATHERWOOD; Mrs. H.W. KUHNS.

BENDER, Ed. L. [25; Omaha; b: WV; f: Chas. H. BENDER; m: Mary SHAW] md. Alice POWERS [17; Omaha; b: MI; f: Mich. Pierce POWERS; m: Catharina POWERS] on 14 Oct 1881. Off: BENEKE. Wit: Wenzel NICTEL, Thomas DREXEL. Age consent given by parents of the bride.

BENDTSON, Nels [35; Omaha; b: Sweden; f: Bendt NELSON; m: Bul JENSDOTTER] md. Anna LAGER [27; Omaha; b: Denmark; f: Anders JACOBSON; m: Anna JACOBSON] on 22 Sep 1879. Off: STENDBERG. Wit: Peter GOW, M. TOFT.

BENGSTON, August [24; Omaha; b: Sweden; f: John BENGSTON; m: Christina PETERSON] md. Josephine ANDERSON [23; Omaha; b: Sweden; f: Anders JOHNSON; m: Maria ANDERSON] on 21 Jul 1870. Off: LARSON. Wit: Axel ENGSTROM; Mrs. Maggie HANSEN.

BENGSTON, O.G. [24; Omaha; b: Sweden; f: Bengt JENSEN; m: Cagsa LARSON] md. Carolina LARSON [23; Omaha; b: Sweden; f: Lars PEARSON; m: Stina LARSON] on 5 Nov 1881 "at their residents." Off: GYDESEN. Wit: S. HANSON, K. PETERSON.

BENGSTON, Peter [43; Omaha; b: Sweden; f: Bendt OLESON; m: Bendta JOHNSON] md. Christine ERICKSON [34; Omaha; b: Sweden; f: Errick JACOBSON; m: Anna CHARLESON] on 27 Sep 1879. Off: BJORLIC. Wit: C.T. LARSON, A.W. NILSON.

BENHAM, Alexander [34; Salt Lake, Utah Terr.; b: New York; f: Johnathan BENHAM; m: Mary A. DOUGLAS] md. H. Adelaide WILLIAMS [29; Omaha; b: Louisiana; f: David R. WADE; m: Amelia E. DeLes DERNIER] on 21 Feb 1871. Off: CURTIS. Wit: Michael J. O'NEIL; Sarah O'NEIL.

BENJAMIN, John E. [23; New York; b: London, England; f: C. BENJAMIN; m: Mary] md. Mrs. Alice ROBINSON [20; San Francisco; b: New York; f: Alfred LaMOTT; m: Franklin SMITH] on 9 Oct 1874. Off: HALD. Wit: Mrs. S.A. EDDY; H.C. KING.

BENNEMAN [BRENNAN], Jacob [25; Omaha] md. Josephine WRIGHT [20; Omaha] on 19 Jan 1869 at the bride's father's house. Off: SHINN. Wit: Mr. and Mrs. WRIGHT, parents of the bride.

BENNETT, Thomas [31; Omaha; b: Canada; f: Thomas BENNETT; m: Margaret CANNELL] md. Alice LEACH [20; Omaha; b: England] on 30 Oct 1870. Off: SHINN. Wit: Margaret HUNT; Fa___ ELIKINS.

BENNETT, Wm. J. [31; Omaha; b: England; f: Wm. BENNETT; m: Mary BRADDOCK] md. Gertrude ERICKSON [19; Omaha; b: Norway; f: Frederick ERICKSON; m: Carrie OLESON] on 6 Jan 1880. Off: MAXFIELD. Wit: John HERMAN, Mary BRADDOCK, both of Blair, NE.

BENSON, Enoch [29; Seward, NE; b: Bridgeton, NJ; f: Samuel U. BENSON; m: Harriet G. DAVIS] md. Mattie J. TOBIAS [29; b: Vermont; f: James TOBIAS; m: Semantha BRENTON] on 2 Jul 1878. Off: HARSHA. Wit: P.L. PERINE, J.A. McCLURE.

BENSON, William V. [22; Omaha; b: Illinois; f: George BENSON; m: Ellen HALLAS] md. Mary EBOLD [22; Omaha; b: New York; f: Frederick EBOLD; m: Elizabeth MILLER] on 24 Jan 1877. Off: SEDGWICK. Wit: Marcia F. SEDGWICK, Emma METCALF.

BENTON, Allen H. [24; Omaha; b: Kentucky; f: Jesse G. BENTON; m: Mary OWENS] md. Martha J. COOK [21; Omaha; b: Iowa] on 10 Feb 1871. Off: LYTLE. Wit: J.B. CHRIST; Jacob KING.

BENZON, August [31; Omaha; b: Sweden; f: B.L. ANDERSON; m: Mary C. ANDERSEN] md. Tenie L. JOHNSON [24; Omaha] b: Sweden; f: John JOHNSON; m: Ingred JONASON] on 16 Oct 1879. Off: FOGELSTROM. Wit: Peter J. JOHNSON, Sven G. JOHNSEN.

BERANEK, J.J. [28; Omaha; b: Bohemia; f: B. BERANEK; m: Katharina CIHI] md. Josephine KLAPAL [24; Omaha; b: Bohemia; f: John KLAPAL; m: Maria ----] on 3 Mar 1881. Off: STENBERG. Wit: Joe SLEZAK, E.G. LUNDQUIST.

BERBERICK, John [24; Omaha; b: New Jersey; f: Adam BERBERICK; m: Louisa GINTER] md. Ida DAVIS [18; Omaha; b: Ohio; m: Ida HUGHES] on 22 Sep 1874. Off: HENNEY. Wit: John ZIEGLER; Mattie ROBINSON.

BERG, Andrew [50; Saunders Co.; b: Sweden; f: Carl BERG; m: Kjerstin ANDERSDOTTER] md. Anna M. JACOBSDOTTER [32; Omaha; b: Sweden; f: Jacob HANSON; m: Anna JACOBSDOTTER] on 22 Oct 1870. Off: LARSON. Wit: Andrew CHRISTENSON, Saunders Co.; Mrs. Johanna LARSON.

BERG, Gustave [33; North Platte; b: Prussia; f: Michael BERG; m: Augusta REYNOLD] md. Sophia SCHULTZ [30; Omaha; b: Prussia; f: William SCHULTZ; m: Antonette HEIL] on 5 May 1870. Off: KELLEY. Wit: Peter KLURSTH; Mrs. C. KLURSTH.

BERGEN, George P. [37; Omaha] md. Mrs. Mary M. BENTLEY [28; Omaha] on 25 Aug 1857. Off: BILLINGSLEY. Wit: William Young BROWN, G.C. MONELL.

BERGGREN, August [22; Omaha; b: Sweden; f: Louis BERGGREN; m: Carrie SWANSON] md. Anna HOLM [24; Omaha; b; Sweden; f: Swen HOLM; m: Johanna CARLESON] on 13 Jan 1880. Off: MARQUETT. Wit: Chas. APPLETON, Lotta APPLETON.

BERGLUND, Andrew [27; Omaha; b: Sweden; f: Hans BERGLUND; m: Annie NELSON] md. Lousia M. EDSTROM [20; Omaha; b: Sweden; f: John P. EDSTROM; m: Louisa] on 23 Sept 1873. Off: BENSON. Wit: P.G. SANDBERG; John STEEL.

BERGQUIST, Charles W. [30; Dodge Co.; b: Sweden; f: John BERGQUIST; m: Mary SANDEL] md. Hannah OLSON [26; Dodge Co.; b: Sweden; f: Ole OLSON] on 7 Nov 1871. Off: PORTER. Wit: Gustaf ANDERSON, Dodge Co.; Edna BERGQUIST.

BERGQUIST, Peter [25; Omaha; b: Sweden; f: Bingt PARSSON; m: Anna NILSSON] md. Mrs. Emma Christina POLLOCK [40; Omaha; b: Sweden; f: John BURK; m: Christina PARSSON] on 24 Dec

1881. Off: ANDERSEN. Wit: A.T. QWARNSTROM, Ella JACOBSEN.

BERGQUIST, Philip A. [33; Omaha; b: Sweden; f: John J. BERGQUIST; m: Mary SANDELL] md. Anna C. BRATTLAND [22; Omaha; b: Sweden; f: Andrew BRATTLAND; m: Brita HENDRICKSON] on 3 Dec 1880. Off: MAXFIELD. Wit: Aug. LAFSTROM, Edward LIND.

BERGQUIST, Phillip A. [26; Omaha; b: Sweden; f: John BERGQUIST; m: Mary SANDELL] md. Hilda BURG [19; Omaha; b: Sweden; f: Claus BURG] on 1 Mar 1873. Off: SWEDERS. Wit: Oscar HARTMAN; Lydia WIBERG.

BERLIN, Herman [26; Omaha; b: Germany; f: Hans BERLIN; m: Annie WITT] md. Annie ENGEL [24; Omaha; b: Switzerland; f: Sam'l. ENGEL; m: Tilly REINHART] on 29 Nov 1881. Off: STENBERG. Wit: Wm. T. BEAL, Mrs. Wm. BEAL.

BERMINGHAM, Thomas J. [25; Omaha; b: Ireland; f: James BERMINGHAM; m: Elizabeth BREEN] md. Katharine DAWSON [18; Omaha; b: Canada; f: John DAWSON; m: Ann BRADY] on 3 Feb 1881 at Holy Family Church. Off: QUINN. Wit: George MULLER, Maggie O'KEEFE.

BERNINE, Theodore [28; Omaha; b: KY; f: Isaac BERNINE; m: Nora BINCKLY] md. Frances Ann PARMETER [24; Omaha; b: NY. f: T.J. GALT; m: Almire A. SIERCE] on 9 Dec 1881. Off: HYDE. Wit: W.G. STANTON, Nora BINCKLY. Affidavit signed by W.G. STANTON.

BERNSTEN, Joergen [34; b: Norway; f: Berut OLSEN; m: Paulina JACOB] md. Marie OLSEN [36; b: Norway; f: Ole OLESON] on 29 Apr 1878. Off: HILMEN. Wit: Ole BERNTSEN, Jonetta BERNTSEN.

BERRY, Joseph W. [24; Nebraska City; b: Bodwinham, ME; f: William M. BERRY; m: Betsey Ann GODFREY] md. Helen MULLEN [24; Omaha; b: Ireland; f: Patrick MULLEN; m: Anna MORAN] on 13 May 1873. Off: CURTIS. Wit: Patrick M. MULLEN; Brdiget DONALLEY.

BERRY, Michael [27; Omaha; b: New York; f: William BERRY; m: Cathrin LYNCH] md. Ellen SHANAHAN [25; Omaha; b: Ireland; f: David SHANAHAN; m: Mary MAHONY] on 14 May 1871. Off: CURTIS. Wit: William H. BERRY; Mary SHANAHAN.

BERRY, Thomas [24; Omaha; b: Canada; f: Thomas BERRY; m: Mary KELLEY] md. Maggie SHANE [20; Omaha; b: Ireland; f: John SHANE; m: Kate KELLEY] on 5 Sep 1875 at the Catholic Cathedral. Off: JENNETTE. Wit: Thomas BARRY, Mary KELLEY.

BERRYMAN, James H. [33; Lone Tree; b: Kentucky; f: Thomas N. BERRYMAN; m: Mary J. BELL] md. Catherine HAWSLEY [28; Omaha; b: Kentucky; f: William HAWSLEY] on 6 Aug 1871. Off: BILLMAN. Wit: Mr. and Mrs. COOPER; Mr. and Mrs. HILL; et al.

BESEN, Peter [26; b: Germany; f: Nicholas BESEN; m: Lena BESEN] md. Mrs. Olive B. RYAN [24; b: Norway; f: C. OLSON; m: Julia F. EVENSEN] on 20 Feb 1878. Off: FISHER. Wit: Christ JOHNSON, Miss Leonora OLSON.

BESEN, Peter [30; Omaha; b: Germany; f: Nicholas BESEN; m: Lena BESEN] md. Mrs. Olive B. RYAN [27; Omaha; b: Norway; f: Christoph OLESON; m: Julia F. EVENSEN] on 1 May 1881. Off: SHERRILL. Wit: Carrie F. OLSON, Lizzie OLSON.

BETHGE, Andrew F. [23; Omaha; b: Massachusetts; f: A.C. BETHGE; m: Catherine FOERSTER] md. Mary T. BURKLEY [19; Omaha; b: Nebraska; f: Vincent BURKLEY; m: Theeresa STELTZER] on 4 Nov 1880. Off: ENGLISH. Wit: Frank BURKLEY of Fort Omaha; Teresa KENNEDY.

BETLACH, Franz [26; Omaha; b: Austria; f: Franz BETLACH; m: Franziska BLASKA] md. Veronika HYNEK [23; Omaha; b: Austria; f: Franc HYNEK; m: Anna MASEK] on 23 Apr 1881. Off: BENEKE. Wit: Mary VELETA, Wm. M. KIRKLAND.

BETTS, Charles [ 24; Douglas Co., b: England; f: James BETTS; m: Elizabeth WAND] md. Weat ALBERTSON [17; Douglas Co., b: Denmark; f: Christian ALBERTSON; m: Mary GRACE] on 27 Nov 1875. Off: PEABODY. Wit: George SHIELDS, Frank P. HANLON.

BEUTEL, George [40; Omaha; b: Germany; f: Jacob BEUTEL; m: Caroline UNGELFHENE] md. Kate REYNOLDS [19; Omaha; b: Scotland; f: ---- REYNOLDS] on 23 Oct 1869. Off: McCAGUE. Wit: Max BALTSCH (BALTCH), Louisa BALTSCH (BALTCH).

BEVERAGE, Simpson [35; Fremont; b: Ohio or New York; f: Peter BEVERAGE; m: Ann WATT] md. Emma SMITH [28; Fremont; b: New York; f: S. SMITH] on 20 Oct 1877. Off: FISHER. Wit: E.M. FISHER, Kitty MORRIS.

BEVINS, George [26; Council Bluffs] and Maria BUTLER [21; Council Bluffs] license issued on 19 Oct 1860. No marriage record. Off: ARMSTRONG.

BEWS, Henry [24; Omaha; b: England; f: Henry BEWS] md. Kate METSKER [24; Omaha; b: Pennsylvania; f: Thomas METSKER; m: ---- MYERS] on 3 Jul 1872. Off: GUE. Wit: Mrs. Anna B. GUE; Miss N.J. KARR.

BEYER, Wilhelm [33, Douglas Co.; b: Germany; f: Christian BEYER; m: Maria NERN] md. Margaretha BRAUNLING [22; Omaha; b: Germany; f: George BRAUNLING; m: Babetta ROTH] on 22 Oct 1876. Off: BENECKE. Wit: Frank BARLEIGH, John FREET.

BICHEL, John [26; Omaha; b: Germany; f: Christian BICHEL; m: Margaretha THUN] md. Maria POHLMANN [23; Omaha; b: Germany; f: Henry POHLMANN; m: Anna HAHN] on 7 Sep 1881. Off: BENEKE. Wit: Henry BRUHN, Henrich HAGEDORN.

BICKETT, Charles P. [29; Omaha] and Mary Ann LABAUGH [20; Omaha] license issued on 7 Apr 1859. No marriage recorded. Off: BRIGGS.

BIEDE or BRIDE, Frederick [23; Omaha] md. Fredericke BALL [20; Omaha] on 13 Apr 1869. Off: MORRIS. Wit: T.G. HARTMAN, M. PALMTAG.

BIEL, Hans H. [25; Omaha; b: Germany; f: Jacob BIEL; m: Abel BOCK] md. Maria D. PAULSON [25; Omaha; b: Germany; f: Carsten PAULSON; m: Brigitta B. BRODERSEN] on 31 Jul 1881. Off: RILEY. Wit: Rudolph BEAL, Mrs. Jabez JENSEN.

BIELER, Fritz [28; Omaha; b: Germany; f: Jacob BIELER; m: Salome ERHARDT] md. Gertrude BUCHNER [21; Omaha; b: Germany; f: Anton BUCHNER; m: Helene FLECK] on 22 Oct 1881. Off: BENEKE. Wit: Annie NISTEL, Fritz KRAUSE. The affidavit was signed by Chas. W. EDGERTON, N.P.

BIERMAN, William [30; Omaha; b: Germany; f: Henry BIERMAN; m: Kate DEICKMAN] md. Minnie EMMERICH [26; Omaha; b: Germany; f: Bernhardt EMMERICH; m: Margareta MUNNING] on 24 Jun 1874. Off: PEABODY. Wit: Mina WIRTH; Louisa ERCK.

BIESENDORFER, Joseph [27; Iowa; b: Germany; f: Joseph BIESENDORFER; m: Lizzie SMITH] md. Mary SEIRINGER [19; Omaha; b: Germany; f: George SEIRINGER; m: Ursula SEIRINGER] on 1 Sep 1879. Off: SHROPSHIRE. Wit: Henry EHRENFFORT, Mary D. EHRENFFORT.

BILLERBECK, Ferdinand [25; Omaha] md. Agnes HERRMANN [19; Omaha] on 15 Feb 1869. Off: MEYER. Wit: Wilhelmine? BILLERBECK, Fridrick? SCNAUHER.

BILLITER, Marks J. [26; Douglas Co.] md. Rebecca M. MORRIS [15; Douglas Co.] on 9 Apr 1868 at Chicago Twp. Off: McVEY. Wit: Luther WEAVER, John MORRIS. Age consent given by the father of the bride.

BILLS, Albert [26; Oakfield, IA; b: Indiana; f: Lyman BILLS; m: Elsa ELLYTHORP] md. Rilla JONES [16; Oakfield, IA; b: Iowa; f: Norton JONES; m: Jane DAY] on 29 Oct 1880. Off: BENEKE. Wit: Sarah FRANK, G.E. CARTER.

BINZENSHAM, Frederick [33; Omaha; b: Bavaria; f: Martin BINZENSHAM; m: Barbara ZODER] md. Fredericka METZGER [26; Omaha; b: Wurtemberg; f: Peter METZGER; m: Catharine ELSASSER] on 24 Nov 1874. Off: HENNY. Wit: Ferdinand HUNN; Emiline HUNN.

BIRKETT, Charles P. [32; Omaha] md. Mrs. Mary Anna BIRCH [29; Omaha] on 11 Jan 1860 at Mr. VAMPLEW's residence. Off: ARMSTRONG. Wit: Mrs. Marian VAMPLEW, James H. McARDLE.

BIRLINMIER, Christopher [42; Washington Co.; b: Germany; f: George BIRLINMIER; m: Magdalena BENDER] md. Dorothea KAUFMAN [41; Omaha; b: Germany; f: George KAUFMAN; m: Doretha WINDER] on 17 Nov 1871. Off: HILGENDORF. Wit: John ROMETSCH; William HILGENKAMP, Belle Creek, Washington Co.

BIRMINGHAM, Francis [24; Omaha; b: Kentucky; f: Frank BIRMIINGHAM; m: Julia PENDERGEIST] md. Mary BARRY [23; Omaha; b: Nebraska; f: Thomas BARRY; m: Mary KELLEY] on 9 Jun 1880, Holy Family Church. Off: QUINN. Wit: Annie BARRY of Fort Calhoun, Peter McDERMOTT.

BIRT [BURT], Richard [24; Omaha] md. Lizzie DAVIS [19; Omaha] on 12 Apr 1866 at the house of John DAVIS. Off: VAN ANTWERP. Wit: John DAVIS, Mr. and Mrs. OTTAWAY, et al.

BITTING, James [27; Des Moines, IA; b: Pennsylvania; f: Louis BITTING; m: Eliza BITTING] md. Lucy KENYON [22; Des Moines, IA; b: Des Moines, IA; f: David P. KENYON; m: Josephine BACON] on 30 Sep 1879. Off: HARSHA. Wit: Mrs. W.J. HARSHA, Mrs. M. HOCKENHULL of Jacksonville, IL.

BIXBY, R.A. [30; North Platte; b: New York; f: Alfred BIXBY; m: Catharine MICHIGAN] md. Cleora OAKS [27; Cannon Falls, MN; b: Wisconsin; f: Lucius OAKS; m: Elsie BABCOCK] on 15 Jun 1880. Off: MARQUETTE. Wit: J.P. SMITH, L.A. HARMON.

BJORKLUND, Alfred [21; Omaha; b: Sweden; f: Peter BJORKLUND; m: Margaret HANSEN] md. Antonette ELMGREN [18; Omaha; b: Sweden; f: John P. ELMGREN] on 21 Jun 1871. OfF: BILLMAN. Wit: Mrs. HUGHES and sister Mrs. BILLMAN, et al.

BJORKMAN, Lawrence [26; Omaha; b: Sweden; f: Peter PETERSON; m: Christena ANDERSON] md. Anna S. NORSILGUS [35; Omaha; b: Sweden; f: Charles G. SUNDBORN] on 11 Mar 1871. Off: SUNDBORN. Wit: N. NELSON; J.G. BROSLING.

BLACHLY, Julius C. [35; Omaha; b: Washington Co., VA; f: Miller BLACHLY; m: Elizabeth ROUGH] md. Elizabeth SNEATH [35; Omaha; b: Alexandria, PA; f: Richard SNEATH; m: Catharine HAYMAKER] on 30 Apr 1873. Off: STEWART. Wit: John S. BRIGGS; H.H. VISSCHER.

BLACK, Alexander [23; Omaha; b: Ireland; f: Alexander BLACK; m: Jane MOORE] md. Georgia Idith SAUNDERS [18; Omaha; b: Nebraska; f: J.K. SAUNDERS; m: L.M. SAUNDERS] on 17 Nov 1880. Off: HAWES. Wit: Myrtle HOARD, Edward GORMAN.

BLACK, D.D. [37; b: Illinois; f: James BLACK; m: Elizabeth DOUGLAS] md. Emma ARMAL [27; b: Iowa; f: Thomas ARMAL; m: Alcina GARVEN] on 17 Aug 1878. Off: PORTER. Wit: Wiley B. DIXON, Charles H. FOSTER.

BLACK, Davy Crockett [38; Omaha; b: PA; f: William BLACK; m: Mary BROWN] md. Lyda McLAUGHLIN [24; Omaha; b: PA; f: John McLAUGHLIN; m: Lizzie KINSEY] on 15 Feb 1881. Off: GRAHAM. Wit: Dr. W.S. GIBBS, Joseph BELL. Affidavit signed by Dr. W.S. GIBBS.

BLACK, John W. [27; Omaha; b: Canada; f: Mathew BLACK; m: Sarah WALLACE] md. Christine ANDERSON [20; Omaha; b: Sweden; f: C.J. ANDERSON; m: Anna JOHNSON] on 14 Jan 1871. Off: LARSON. Wit: William ISAACS; Hannah ANDERSON.

BLACKMER, Matthew [49; Council Bluffs, IA; b: New York; f: Ephriam BLACKMER; m: Tursey MORLEY] md. Mrs. Elizabeth BETZ [41; Council Bluffs; b: Germany; f: Charles LISTLAND; Catharine HOP] on 1 Jan 1880. Off: WRIGHT. Wit: Charles W. EDGERTON, R.L. GREEN.

BLAKE, Joseph E. [32; Omaha; b: Canton, OH; f: George BLAKE; m: Eleanore DODANE] md. Josephine SHAW [30; Schuyler; b: NY; f: Isaac VAN HOUSEN; m: Charlotte MABEN] on 23 Oct 1876. Off: WEISS. Wit: Herman J. MEYER, Mrs. Marg. MEYER.

BLAKE, Walter A. [33; Indiana; b: Indiana; f: James BLAKE; m: Eliza SPROLE] md. Jennie H. GREEN [19; Omaha; b:

Mississippi; f: Harry GREEN; m: Fanny C. FOLKES (BRYAN is crossed out)] on 28 Sep 1874 at Skye Cottage. Off: GARRETT. Wit: Albert A. JONES; Henry M. GOFF.

BLAKE, William [30, Omaha] md. Kate CREIGHTON [30; Omaha] on 21 Jun 1862. Off: O'GORMAN. Wit: Joseph CREIGHTON, Kate CREIGHTON.

BLAKESLEY, Albert [Elkhorn City] md. Harriet LEACH [Elkhorn City] on 30 Sep 1863. Both of legal age. Off: HURLBUT.

BLAKSLEE, Charles H. [23; Omaha; b: Illinois; f: William T. BLAKSLEE; m: Harriet CARPENTER] md. Melsena JONES [21; Omaha; b: Illinois; f: Horace JONES; m: Sarah A. BARBOE] on 30 Sep 1869. Off: HYDE. Wit: Geo. D. OAKS, E. EMRY.

BLAMBERG, Andrew [27; Saunders Co.; b: Sweden; f: Jonas BLAMBERG; m: Carrie ANDERSON] md. Carrie ANDERSON [21; Omaha; b: Sweden; f: Andrew TUFVESON; m: Elsa BENGTSDOTTER] on 12 Aug 1871. Off: LARSON. Wit: Mrs. Ingri MATTSON; A.N. SWEDERS.

BLANCHARD, W.S. [27; Omaha; b: NJ; f: Martin N. BLANCHARD; m: Kathrin HERMAN] md. Bridgett FITZGERALD [24; Omaha; b: Ireland; f: Thomas FITZGERALD; m: Bridget WALSH] on 15 Nov 1881. Off: BENEKE. Wit: Jacob SWANBERGER, Katie DINAI.

BLAXIM, George [23; Council Bluffs; f: Richard BLAXIM of Shiddle Parish, Co. Galway, Irel.] md. Catherine GORMAN [21; Council Bluffs; f: William GORMAN of Jordan's Town Parish, Co. E. Meath. Irel.] on 22 Feb 1859 at BVM Church. Off: CANNON. Wit: John ZIMMERMAN, Ellen LACY.

BLAZEK, Frank [23; Omaha; b: Bohemia; f: Frank BLAZEK; m: Anna SIMROTH [SEMRAD]] md. Josephine NIEMETZ [NEMEC] [18; Omaha; b: Bohemia; f: Mathias NIEMETZ [NEMEC]; m: Barbara HOWRAK [HORAK]] on 8 Mar 1874. Off: PEABODY. Wit: Martin SVANTNA [SVACINA]; H. BERTHOLD.

BLAZEK, Joseph [19; Omaha; b: Bohemia; f: Frank BLAZEK; m: Anna SIMRAT [SEMRAD]] md. Anna RUZICKA [18; Omaha; b: Bohemia; f: Joseph RUZICKA; m: Anna KOSENICK [KOZINEK]] on 23 Dec 1872. Off: TOWNSEND. Wit: Henry BERTHOLD; Frank BLAZEK. Age of consent given by father of groom.

BLEICK, Adolph [21; Omaha] md. Margaret PETERS [21; Omaha] on 7 Mar 1868. Off: KUHNS. Wit: Carl SCHROEDER, John RICHTER, et al.

BLESSINGTON, Patrick [South Platte, Cass Co.] and Ellen KILKENNEY [South Platte, Cass Co.] license issued of 19 May 1863. Both of legal age. No marriage record. Off: DICKINSON.

BLISS, George L. [40; Rutland, VT; b: Vermont; f: Ephram H. BLISS; m: Hannah GIBBS] md. Mrs. Priscilla A. (Mrs. G.A.) CROSBY [37; Rockford, Il; b: Pennsylvania; f: Francis M. BABCOCK; m: Parnel ELY] on 16 Jun 1870. Off: SHERRILL. Wit: E.H. WASNER; Ellis BARNEY.

BLISS, Moses H. [40; b: Ohio; f: Beriah BLISS; m: Mary LEWELLYN] md. Lucinda J. KINTZ [38; b: Ohio; f: George KINTZ; m: Cecelia CONAGHAN] on 4 Apr 1878. Off: HARSHA. Wit: Saml. REES, J.M. McKOON.

BLOHM, Theodore [50; Council Blluffs; b: Germany; f: Gustav BLOHM; m: Christine BRINGE] md. Wilhelmina HACKER [39; Council Bluffs; b: Germany; f: Johann HACKER; m: Maria WENT] on 1 Nov 1881. Off: CHADWICK. Wit: Frank SWEENEY, Max BERGMAN.

BLOMBERG, Hans Peter [27; Omaha; b: Norway; f: Hans Peter BLOMBERG; m: Helena Sophie HYIEM] md. Karen ERIKSON [24; Omaha; b: Norway; f: Oleg ERIKSON; m: Caroline OLESEN] on 15 Mar 1874. Off: ERDALL. Wit: Fredrik INGEBREGTSEN; Elling ARENDTSEN.

BLOOM, Ferdinand [22; Omaha; b: Germany; f: August BLOOM; m: Doras BUCHOLZ] md. Fredericka LAMPRECHT [22; Omaha; b: Germany; f: Fred LAMPRECHT; m: Dora] on 13 Feb 1874. Off: HILGENDORF. Wit: Frederick LAMPRECHT; Dorothea LAMPRECHT.

BLOTZER, Anton [25; Omaha; b: Hungaria; f: Anton BLOTZER; m: Magdalena PRICKEL] md. Maria GLOCKNER [21; Omaha; b: Hungaria; f: Andreas GLOCKNER; m: Catharina PRICKEL] on 26 Nov 1881 at St. Mary Magdalen's Church. Off: GLAUBER. Wit: Phillip FRENZER, Eva DRUMMER.

BLUMBE, Sebastian [28; Omaha; b: Wertemberg, Germany; f: Joseph BLUMBE; m: Maglalena YALTER] md. Caroline BOWER [24; Omaha; b: Wertemberg, Germany; f: Fred BOWER; m: Margaretta FRANSWARTZ] on 25 Aug 1870. Off: LYTLE. Wit: Frank WEBER; Wilhelmine WEBER.

BLUMER, Henry [25; Douglas Co.; b: Germany; f: David BLUMER; m: Sophie OSBORN] md. Lena SPECK [20; Douglas Co.; b: Germany; f: Jacob SPECK; m: Margaretta JETZ] on 28 Mar 1877. Off: SEDGWICK. Wit: Frederick SCHROEDER of Millard Precinct, David E. BURLEY.

BOARDMAN, William F. [45; Oakland, CA; b: Salisbury, CT; f: William BOARDMAN; m: Abigal NORTH] md. Kate HOLMES [23; Salisbury, CT; b: Salisbury, CT; f: Walter R. HOLMES; m: Susan WHITNEY] on 6 Oct 1869. Off: DIMMICK. Wit: Mrs. K.G.W. DIMMICK, Mrs. F.M. DIMMICK.

BOASEN, Peter [24; Omaha; b: Denmark; f: Christian BOASEN; m: Sedsel OLESEN] md. Maggie A. CORBID [21; Omaha; b: Pennsylvania; f: John J. CORBID; m: Maggie A. HIGGINS] on 7 May 1879. Off: LIPE. Wit: Eva J. LIPE, Lizzie E. LIPE.

BOAZ, J.M. [24; Sarpy Co.; b: IA; f: E.C. BOAZ; m: Mary J. WATTS] md. Mary A. FIELD [17; Sarpy Co.; b: NE; f: Thomas FIELD] on 6 Oct 1881. Off: MARQUETT. Wit: Huldah MARQUETT, E.B. SLOTHOWER, Sarpy Co.

BOCK, Eggert [25; Douglas Co., b: Germany; f: Eggert BOCK; m: Margaretha KUHL] md. Mary BOHMSEN [24; Douglas Co.; b: Germany; f: Claus BOHMSEN; m: Anna KUHL] on 22 Apr 1875. Off: PEABODY. Wit: Henry BOCK, Peter SICH.

BOCK, Eggert [29; Douglas Co.; b: Germany; f: Eggert BOCK; m: Marguert KUHL] md. Annie C. LUEDERS [f: Mike LUEDERS; m: Wiebke DORN] on 8 Oct 1878. Off: STRASEN. Wit: Juergen PAHR [PAHL], Peter GOOS.

BOCK, Henry [23; Omaha; b: Germany; f: Jochim F. BOCK; m: Catherina DECKMANN] md. Annie QUICKENSTEDT [25; Omaha; b: Germany; f: Willhelm QUICKENSTEDT] on 14 Dec 1870. Off: GIBSON. Wit: Samuel ADAIR; Frederick BOCK.

BOCK, Henry [38; Douglas Co.; b: Germany; f: Eggart BOCK; m: Margaret KUHL] md. Margaretha EHLER [20; Douglas Co.; b: Germany; f: George EHLER; m: Katey or Margaret BORNSON] on 25 Jan 1878. Off: STRADEN. Wit: Juergen PAHR of Douglas Co., Peter GOOS.

BOEHM, Frederick [21; Omaha] md. Ella WHALAN [19; Omaha] on 20 May 1868 at St. Mark's Chapel. Off: TONGUE. Wit: A.J. GOFFE, Andrew HANNON or HARMON.

BOEHME, Charles H. [25; b: St. Louis, MO; f: L. BOEHME; m: Mathilda MILLER] md. Ida H. BENSON [22; b: Crestline, OH; f: George BENSON; m: Ellen BENSON] on 21 Nov 1878. Off: SHERRILL. Wit: Wm. V. BENSON, John LEE.

BOEKHOFF, John [25; Omaha; b: Germany; f: George A. BOEKHOFF; m: Adeline MEYER] md. Sophia SMITH [24; Omaha; b: Germany; f: John Chr. SMITH; m: W. Margaretha CORDES] on 20 Dec 1874. Off: DIECKMANN. Wit: L. BOEKHOFF; H. THOMPSON.

BOELTER, John Henry [32; Polk Co.; b: Germany; f: Jacob or Jack BOELTER; m: Henrietta MIESENDALL] md. Juliette HANS [21; Polk Co.; b: Germany; f: Christopher HANS; m: Justina STUTCKA] on 28 Nov 1877. Off: SEDGWICK. Wit: C.C. SPERRY, P.O. HAWES.

BOETEL, George [35; Millard Station; b: Germany; f: Hans BOETEL; m: Katherina GANSCH] md. Louise BUSSE [Douglas Co.; b: IA; f: John BUSSE; m: Dorathea MARWIPS] on 14 Jun 1881. Off: BRANDES. Wit: Henry SIERT, August FISCHER.

BOETTGER, C.F. [35; Omaha] md. Miss M. KIMMELL [26; Omaha] on 23 Feb 1867 at GAYLORD's residence. Off: GAYLORD. Wit: John AHMONSON, Mrs. Mary TUCKER.

BOGGET, C.C. [39; Shelby, Shelby Co., IA; b: New York; f: Joseph BOGGET; m: Nancy ELDRIDGE] md. Sarah LAURANCE [19; Shelby, IA; f: Louis LAURANCE; m: Stena LAURANCE] on 3 Sep 1880. Off: MAXFIELD. Wit: Lizzie ELCORK of Fremont, Mrs. J.B. MAXFIELD.

BOGGS, George H. [32; Omaha; b: Pennsylvania; f: John H. BOGGS; m: Catharine HOOVER] md. Ida May KENDALL [22; Omaha; b: Massachusetts; f: Daniel KENDALL; m: Roxena ARNHAM] on 5 Sep 1872. Off: SHERRILL. Wit: John Edward WILBUR; Wm. L. PEABODY.

BOGUE, Frank G. [20; Omaha; b: Iowa; f: Peter BOGUE; m: Mary GOODRICH] md. Nettie HELFIN [19; North Henderson, IL; b: Illinois; f: Louis HELFIN; m: Margaret ROGERS] on 3 Nov 1880. Off: BARTHOLOMEW. Wit: Max BERGMANN, Mary Z. LAIRD.

BOHLKIN, Fred [23; Millard Station; b: Germany; f: Henry BOHLKIN; m: Anna FOHLER] md. Katie ROLL [20; Millard Station; b: MO; f: Nicholaus ROLL; m: Dorothea KARSTEN] on 30 Jun 1881 at Millard. Off: KELSEY. Wit: Mollie MOCK, Albert MOWINKLE, both of Millard.

BOHN, Frederick [33; Douglas Co.] md. Albertina HOELM [22; Omaha] on 22 Aug 1868. Off: KELLEY. Wit: P. PORTER, G.F. MAGINN.

BOLAN, Preston [36; Omaha] md. Adaline CAMELL [33 or 37; Omaha] on 17 Dec 1868. Off: GIBSON. Wit: Nathan ELLIOTT, Mrs. DOUGLAS.

BOLAND, Mathew [Omaha] md. Catherine LYNCH [Omaha] on 1 Jun 1865 at the Roman Catholic Church of Omaha. Off:

O'GORMAN. Wit: Thomas LIDLY, Ellen CAIN.

BOLANDER, John E. [31; Omaha; b: Sweden; f: John S. BOLANDER; m: Betsey JOHNSON] md. Almita or Arminter CRAIG [21; Omaha; b: Pennsylvania; f: Thomas A. CRAIG] on 23 Feb 1877. Off: PEABODY. Wit: Mary C. PEABODY, Belle FLYNN.

BOLDEN, George [negro; 27; Douglas Co.; b: VA; f: Edward BOLDEN; m: Violet WINFIELD] md Susie E. KING [negro; 20; Douglas Co., b: MO; f: ---- KING; m: Malinda KING] on 8 Mar 1876. Off: BRAXTON. Wit: Edward RECTOR, Maria DOUGLAS. Full name of bride's father is unknown to her, he having been sold as a slave.

BOLIN, Oscar [29; Omaha; b: Sweden; f: Christian BOLIN; m: Anna JACOBSEN] md. Wilhelmina HELEN [22; Omaha; b: Sweden; f: John HELLEN; m: Margaretta JOHNSON] on 28 Jan 1872. Off: SUNDBORN. Wit: Lars OLSON; Olof WALLANDER, Saunders Co.

BOLIVER, Jacob [27; Omaha; b: OH; f: Jacob BOLIVER; m: Mary WEBER] md. Augusta ENGELKE [23; Omaha; b: Germany; f: Julius ENGELKE; m: Mathilda ZIMMERMANN] on 2 Aug 1881. Off: HULLHORST. Wit: Nil F. HARTE, Gust. STEPP, J.H. HARTE.

BOLLN, Hans [28; Omaha] md. Mary GLOYE [19; Omaha] on 5 Nov 1867 at KUHNS' residence. Off: KUHNS. Wit: ? GLOYE, Mrs. H.W. KUHNS. Double license and wedding with Henry SIERT and America KONNAGER.

BOLLN, Henry [28; Omaha; b: Germany; f: Joachim BOLLN; m: Catharina HEITMANN] md. C.C. BEEKMAN [19; Omaha; b: Germany; f: Hans BEEKMAN; m: Catharina STANGE] on 16 Sep 1875. Off: HILGENDORF. Wit: William SIEVERS, Juergen WITTMACK.

BOND, C.T. [27; Missouri; f: Henry BOND; m: Minerva BATTLE] md. Mrs. Amelia [BRANDT entered and crossed out] DASHER [28; b: Germany; f: B. DASHER; m: Alsabiah JOHNSON] on 22 Aug 1878. Off: WILLIS. Wit: George SCHMIDT, Frank KLEFFNER.

BOND, J.H. [25; b: New York; f: Rev. J. BOND; m: Catharine KURTZ] md. Mary RANKIN [19; b: England; f: Samuel S. RANKIN; m: Lilian ARMSTRONG] on 22 Jun 1878. Off: LIFRE. Wit: H.J. MEYERS, Jacob SEFUND.

BOORMAN, James W. [22; Chicago, IL (or Burlington, IA); b: IA; f: James BOORMAN; m: Elizabeth SHAW] md. Jennie STARKEY [b: Salt Lake City, UT; f: William STARKEY; m: Anna McMANNING] on 24 Jul 1881. Off: SHERRILL. Wit: H.E. WEAVER, A.H. STARKEY.

BOOS, Jacob [50; Omaha; b: Germany; f: Michael BOOS; m: Margaret WYMAN] md. Mrs. Caroline STRANGLINE [39; Omaha; b: Austria; f: Johan GIBHART; m: Annie DINELIVE] on 15 Oct 1873. Off: PORTER. Wit: Dr. L. TANNER; N.J. BURNHAM.

BOOTH, L.W. [24; Omaha; b: Ohio; f: T.C. BOOTH; m: Elizabeth YOUNG] md. Maggie MONROE [22; Omaha; b: Canada; f: David MONROE; m: Mary BROWN] on 12 May 1880. Off: JAMESON. Wit: James YOUNG, Annie LEHIGH.

BOOUSTRA, Jerrian Hermanno [29; Omaha; b: Holland; f: Gerrit W. BOOUSTRA; m: Johanna HERMANIDER] md. Bertha FECHNER [30; Omaha; b: Germany; f: Carl FECHNER; m: Juliane SEIDLER] on 1 Oct 1881. Off: BENEKE. Wit: John HINRICH, L.H. VANDERBURG.

BOQUETTE, Miller F. [21; Omaha; b: Michigan; f: Joseph BOQUETTE; m: Angeline BROWN] md. Laura SHULL [16; Omaha; b: Omaha; f: Amos SHULL; m: M.E. MOWERS] on 28 Jan 1877. Off: LIPE. Wit: Amos SHULL, Joseph BOQUETTE. Age consent given by mother of the bride, Mrs. M.E. SHULL. Witnessess to signature: Rosa SIBLEY, Tillie M. McMCULLEN.

BORDEN, F. Andrew [34; Omaha; b: Alabama; f: Thomas R. BORDEN; m: Anna M. JONES] md. Jessie B. PRESTON [18; Omaha; b: Illinois; f: William PRESTON; m: Angeline BIDWELL] on 31 Oct 1877. Off: SHERRILL. Wit: Wm. T. PRESTON, Henry C. ATKINSON.

BORGSTROM, Samuel J. [27; Omaha; b: Sweden; f: John BORGSTROM; m: Nellie JOHHSON] md. Kate H. NORTON [29; Omaha; b: Sweden; f: Olof NORTON; m: Katherine NORDIN] on 10 Aug 1875. Off: BENZON. Wit: M. YOUNGSTEDT, A. BUY and wife.

BORQUIST, John [35; Saunders Co.; b: Sweden; f: Frederick PETERSON; m: Louisa YOUNGSTETLER] md. Anna JOHNSON [36; Douglas Co.; b: Sweden; f: J.P. JOHNSON; m: Margaret JOHNSON] on 5 Jul 1876. Off: HANSEN. Wit: John N. SELINE, Nette NILSEN.

BORT, Valentine [25; Omaha; b: Germany; f: Leonhard BORT; m: Elizabeth GARISH] md. Maria COOK [21; Omaha; b: Prussia] on 28 Dec 1870. Off: MORTON. Wit: A. GEBE; Mrs. Cora GEBE.

BOSARD, Wesley [22; Omaha; b: PA; f: Joseph BOSARD; m: Kate GODSHALL] md.

Rosa BEIDELMAN [17; Omaha; b: PA; f: Eli BEIDELMAN; m: Mary Ann HOFFNER] on 15 Aug 1875. Off: PEABODY. Wit: Ellen OSMUND, Mary C. PEABODY. Age consent given by father of the bride.

BOTKIN, W.H. [23; Omaha; b: Missouri; f: C.D. BOTKIN; m: Mary PICKARD] md. Mary BROWN [20; Omaha; b: Wisconsin; f: William BROWN; m: Anna HINES] on 4 Feb 1880. Off: INGRAM. Wit: E. May INGRAM, L.J. INGRAM.

BOUKAL, Adolph [23; Omaha; b: Bohemia; f: James BOUKAL; m: Mary] md. Josephine KENSKI [18; Omaha; b: Bohemia; f: John KENSKI; m: Marie RONFIK] on 2 Oct 1873. Off: TOWNSEND. Wit: Wenzel KUCERA; Mrs. Annie KUCERA.

BOUKAL, Michael [26; Omaha; b: Bohemia; f: Ignac BOUKAL; m: Mary KLENZEK] md. Fannie KREPELA [22; IL; b: Bohemia; f: Anton KREPELA; m: Fannie RICH] on 27 Sep 1881. Off: CHADWICK. Wit: Homer STULL, Max BERGMAN.

BOULDEN, Joseph Paterson [60; Utah; b: Ohio; f: William Louis BOULDEN; m: Nancy PATERSON] md. Mary LEE [50; Iowa; b: Ohio; f: John LEE; m: Ruth PARKS] on 27 Feb 1880. Off: BRANDES. Wit: August FISCHER, Edward KUEHL.

BOUMERT, Frank [27; Cuming Co.; b: Germany; f: John BOUMERT; m: Catherine WRIGHT] md. Catherine RENNER [21; Omaha; b: Germany; f: Joseph RENNER; m: Tarrent DOLID] on 2 Feb 1871. Off: GROENEBAUM. Wit: Frank RENNER; Caroline RENNER.

BOUNEVIER, John A. [25; Omaha; f: Carl Adolph BOUNEVIER; m: Christine BREDSTROIN] md. Helene Marie LINDBERG [24; Omaha; f: Peter LINDBERG; m: Catherin PETERSEN] on 25 May 1869. Off: LARSON. Wit: Mrs. Johanna C. LARSON, Mrs. Emma POLLACK.

BOUQUET, J.W. [27; Council Bluffs; b: OH; f: Joseph BOUQUET; m: Martha LABBEDEE] md. Mattie TAYLOR [23; Council Bluffs; b: NE; f: Felix TAYLOR; m: Helen TAYLOR] on 22 Dec 1881. Off: SHANK. Wit: Mr. HOMAN, Mrs. S.C. SHANK.

BOUVIER, Samuel D. [27; Blair; b: Indiana; f: Louis BOUVIER; m: Eugenia COURVOISIER] md. Alice E. RICHARDS [20; Neola, IA; f: William RICHARDS; m: Phidelia A. GOAL] on 20 Jul 1880. Off: BARTHOLOMEW. Wit: James COSGRAVE, H.J. ZIEMAN.

BOVE, Peter [35; b: Germany; f: Andreas BOVE; m: Christine PLAEHN] md. Maria VOPEL [21; b: Germany; f: Johann VOPEL; m: Dorothea FRICKE] on 24 Oct 1878. Off: BARTHOLOMEW. Wit: Max BERGMAN, Henry SIERT.

BOWAS, Stephen [30; Omaha; b: Ireland; f: Nicholas BOWAS; m: Margret RYAN] md. Annia QUIGLY [22; Omaha; b: Ireland; f: William QUIGLY; m: Mary RYAN] on 5 Feb 1876. Off: BOBAL. Wit: Edward James McGORK, Hannah MURPHY.

BOWDEN, William [28; Omaha; b: England; f: William BOWDEN; m: ---- PREDEAUX] md. Lizzie PRYOR [30; Omaha; b: England; m: Elizabeth SANDY] on 25 Jun 1870. Off: DIMMICK. Wit: Mrs. F.P. WRIGHT; Mrs. F.M. DIMMICK.

BOWE, Peter [29; Omaha; b: Germany; f: Andrew BOWE; m: Christina PLAN] md. Margaret GEHL [22; Omaha; b: Germany; f: Asmus GEHL; m: Annie THIEA] on 30 Aug 1873. Off: PORTER. Wit: Jacob GISH; Richard KIMBALL.

BOWEN, William J. [26; Omaha; b: Iowa; f: Isaac BOWEN; m: Susan P. WILLIAMS] md. Ruth B. STRICKLAND [24; Omaha; b: Ohio; f: S. STRICKLAND; m: Emily KEYES] on 7 Oct 1869 at Mrs. STRICKLAND's home. Off: GAYLORD. Wit: Benjn. L. KEYES, Wagar W. REMINGTON.

BOWEN, William R. [Douglas Co.] md. Lila M. STORRS [Douglas Co.] on 15 Dec 1868. Off: BETTS. Wit: J. BAKER, Eloise POWELL, Mr. MILLARD.

BOWERS, Granbury L. [27; Saratoga Pct, Douglas Co,; B: Baltimore, MD; f: James W. BOWERS; m: Isabella R. GETTIER] md. Annie H. ONTZEN [23; Omaha; b: Denmark; f: Jacob F. ONTZEN] on 29 Jul 1873. Off: WRIGHT. Wit: James M. ADAIR; Mrs. Mary H. WRIGHT.

BOWERS, Louis A. [29; Omaha; b: Pennsylvania or Minneapolis, MA; f: Moses BOWERS; m: Anna LOCUM] md. Mrs. S.E. DOWNEY [29; Minneapolis, MA [sic]] on 4 Mar 1879. Off: FISHER. Wit: Michael DONOVAN, Anne DONOVAN.

BOWMAN (BOWMER), Jack [colored; 22; Omaha] md. Amanda DAVIS [colored; 31; Omaha] on 19 May 1867. Off: SLAUGHTER. Wit: J.J. McLAIN, A.B. SLAUGHTER.

BOWMAN, Andrew [23; Dodge Co.; b: Sweden; f: Andrew BOWMAN; m: Caroline MATS] md. Margaret HANSEN [21; Omaha; b: Sweden; f: Hans ANDERSON; m: Caroline OLSEN] on 14 Jul 1873. Off: TOWNSEND. Wit: Charles H. BROWN; Martin BOWMAN.

BOWMAN, Charles G. [28; Omaha; b: Sweden; f: Neils PEARSON; m: Mary PEARSON] md. Clara JOHNSON [23; Omaha; b: Sweden; f: John JOHNSON; m: Mary FADLUND] on 7 Nov 1874. Off: PEABODY. Wit: Andrew BERG; Line FUGERSON.

BOWMAN, Edward W. [28; Omaha] md. Kate CONNEL [23; Omaha] on 17 Jan 1869. Off: LARSON. Wit: Henry GRAHAM, Mrs. Mary GRAHAM.

BOWMAN, Joseph C. [33; Douglas Co.; b: Virginia; f: Isaac R. BOWMAN; m: Rebecca P. COOPER] md. Minnie WAGNER [19; Douglas Co.; b: Germany; f: Charles WAGNER] on 26 Feb 1870 at Platte Valley. Off: KERSTETTER. Wit: R.P. SELSAR, Valley Station; F.J. TORREY, Valley Station.

BOWMAN, Theodore H. [25; Elkhorn Station; b: IN; f: Milton BOWMAN; m: Eliza E. CRAWFORD] md. Adda HYNE [18; Douglas Co.; b: IA; f: Martin HYNE; m: Acena HODGE] on 5 Jul 1875 at S.W. HIGBY's residence. Off: ROBERTS. Wit: Daniel CLIFTON, Chicago Precinct, Mrs. D. CLIFTON, Chicago Precinct.

BOYD, Joseph T. [31; Golden City, CO; b: Pennsylvania; f: T.P. BOYD; m: Mary S. CLOW] md. Mary B. MARSHALL [24; Golden City, CO; b: Pennsylvania; f: R.P. MARSHALL; m: Agnes CLOW] on 16 Nov 1870. Off: SHERRILL. Wit: Mary P. TUCKER; Albert TUCKER.

BOYDEN, Charles K. [23; Omaha; b: MA; f: S.A. BOYDEN; m: Almeda TINKER] md. Augusta NELSON [20; Omaha; b: Sweden; f: Gustav NELSON; m: Johanna JACOBSON] on 11 Jul 1881. Off: SMITH. Wit: Jno. J. POINTS, H. CLEAVELAND.

BOYDEN, George W. [23; Omaha; b: ME; f: Stephen A. BOYDEN; m: Almeda S. TINKER] md. Ellen J. CRUM [28; Omaha; b: NY; f: Alex CRUM; m: Mary A. HOWE] on 29 Mar 1876. Off: SHERRILL. Wit: Mrs. C.E. YOST, Mrs. John E. WILBUR.

BOYER, Joseph [23; Omaha; b: Indiana; f: George BOYER; f: Catherine ARMEN] md. Linda W. PICKARD [18; Douglas Co.; b: Indiana; f: John PICKARD; m: Juliette SKINNER] on 27 Aug 1871 at John PICKARD's residence. Off: PICKARD. Wit: Edward H. CHAPLIN, Douglas Co.; Jerome KENNEY.

BOYER, Peter [31; Omaha; b: Denmark; f: Peder C. BOYER; m: Margaret JENSEN] md. Alida MASON [25; Omaha; b: Iowa; f: H.E. MASON; m: Ruth GOWING] on 29 May 1873. Off: SHERRILL. Wit: R.G. JENKINSON; Mrs. S.A. JENKINSON.

BOYER, William M. [31; Omaha; b: PA; f: Reuben BOYER; m: Hattie MILLER] md. Mrs. Ellen K. PERRY [25; Omaha; b: PA; f: John SHAW; m: Jane CURR] on 17 Oct 1869.

Off: KUHNS. Wit: Augustus J. KAUFFMAN, Emma CRAWFORD.

BOYLE, Terence [27; Omaha; b: Ireland; f: Michael BOYLE; m: Mary GOGGIN] md. Maggie A. DOODY [25; b: Washington, DC; f: John DOODY; m: Maggie DOWNEY] on 10 May 1881. Off: ENGLISH. Wit: Patrick CLIFFORD, Mary GOGGIN.

BOYLES, Joseph R. [27; Omaha; b: Missouri; f: David BOYLES; m: Lucinda ADAMS] md. Martha Jane SMITH [16; Omaha; b: Indiana; f: Abidiah SMITH; m: Sarah E. CHILDER] on 8 Feb 1877. Off: ANDERSON. Wit: E.H. BUCKINGHAM, Jacob GISH.

BOYS, Gipson [21;Omaha; b: England; f: William BOYS; m: Mary EASTON] md. Rohwena BUNDAY [21; Omaha; b: Iowa; f: Nelson BUNDAY; m: Hannah JACKSON] on 13 Jun 1874. Off: PEABODY. Wit: Fred K. SMITH; Susan S. SMITH.

BOYSON, Mathias [28; Omaha; b: Germany; f: Sanka BOYSON; m: Sophia TORDSON] md. Dora PETERSON [23; Omaha; b: Germany; f: John PETERSON; m: Margrethe FULLARD] on 14 Mar 1871. Off: HESSEL. Wit: Mrs. L. WEBBER; Charles WEBER.

BRACHET (BRACHETS), Joseph [24] and Christian LIPFERT [19] license issued on 3 Nov 1856. No marriage recorded. Age consent given by Henry LIPFERT.

BRACKETT, Samuel [45; Council Bluffs; b: Oxford Co., ME; f: Samuel BRACKETT; m: Susan FORSS] md. Lucy FICK [25; Council Bluffs; b: Canada West; f: John FICK; m: Mary Ann ALLEN] on 1 Mar 1873. Off: TOWNSEND. Wit: Edward C. McSHANE; Philander H. REED.

BRADBURY, F.A. [40; Omaha; b: Massachusetts; f: Eben BRADBURY; m: Mary TAPON] md. Mrs. Fanny A. LINDSTROM [36; Omaha; b: South Carolina; f: G.L. GORDON; m: Emelie MORRIS] on 4 Jun 1880. Off: PATERSON. Wit: D.M. FOSTER, M. SCOTT.

BRADFORD, Alfred A. [36; Omaha; b: Canada; f: Charles BRADFORD; m: Roxanna TENNY] md. Abbie F. HOYT [33; Omaha; b: Concord, NH; f: W.B. HOYT, Ruth C. HOPLINS] on 22 Feb 1877. Off: STEWART. Wit: Henry HICKMAN, Charity F. HICKMAN.

BRADLEY, Anthony R. [28; Arlington, TX; b: Cooper Co., MO; f: R.L. BRADLEY; m: N.E. REED] md. Grace Isabel ALLAN [21; b: Bellevue; f: James T. ALLAN; m: Elizabeth A. BUDINGTON] on 25 Apr 1878. Off: MILLSPAUGH. Wit: J.P. PECK, James T. ALLAN. Affiant: James T. ALLAN.

BRADLEY, J.E. [35; Omaha; b: New York; f: John BRADLEY; m: Mary Ann COMBE] md. Nannie M. LIDDEL [27; Omaha; b: Canada; f: James A. LIDDEL; m:

M. HANLEY] on 16 Jun 1880. Off: INGRAM. Wit: J.A. INGRAM, E. May INGRAM.

BRADLEY, William [colored; 26; Omaha; b: Ohio; f: James BRADLEY; m: Caroline BROWN] md. Anna HUNTER [colored; 26; Omaha; b: Ohio; f: Len HUNTER; m: Caroline DEAN] on 6 Oct 1869 at the A.M.E. Church. Off: HUBBARD. Wit: Mr. and Mrs. HYCHCOX, Mrs. Sally MIDDTON, Mrs. Joanna HUBBARD, Mrs. P. PERKINSON.

BRADY, James [23; Omaha; b: PA; f: Charles BRADY; m: Mary PHILLIPS] md. Mrs. Bertha DAILEY [20; Omaha; b: IA; f: Michael ALBERT; m: Mary HOFFMAN] on 25 Jul 1881. Off: RILEY. Wit: Daniel MONYHAN, Katie GRACE.

BRADY, James [24; Omaha; b; Ireland; f: John BRADY; m: Mary MURPHY] md. Teresa GREENWOOD [24; b: Canada; f: George GREENWOOD; m: Teresa JONES] on 12 Apr 1878. Off: WRIGHT. Wit: Carrie WINSOR, W.H. WINSOR.

BRAIN, Emery [25; Omaha; b: Virignia; f: John S. BRAIN; m: Joanna BONNER] md. Margaret ROSS [24; Omaha; b: Scotland; f: Joseph ROSS: m: Margaret RUFF] on 17 Jul 1874. Off: PEABODY. Wit: Rose W. PEABODY, Lynn, MA; A.S. BUXTON, Reading MA.

BRAKENFELD, Hans [28; Omaha; b: Germany; f: Jacob BRAKENFELD; m: Elizabeth KRAAK] md. Cecelia GRIMM [20; Omaha; b: Germany; f: John GRIMM; m: Catharine PLOETZ] on 1 Jan 1879. Off: BENEKE. Wit: Henry SIERT, Henry VOSS or TOFER.

BRANAGAN, John [23; Omaha; b: Ireland; f: Thomas BRANAGAN; m: Ellen HERRON] md. Honora KELLEY [22; Omaha; b: Ireland; f: James KELLEY; m: Ellen KELLEY] on 6 Nov 1873 at the Catholic Cathedral. Off: BYRNE. Wit: Jeremiah AHERNE; Elizabeth CRAGG.

BRANDT, Alexander [27; Omaha; b: Hanover, GER; f: Charles A. BRANDT; m: Sophia KERL] md. Jennie GREEN [24; McGregor City, IA; b: England; f: Joseph GREEN; m: Sarah ATEROFT] on 21 Apr 1870. Off: GIBSON. Wit: C.C. SPERRY; Jeremiah McCHEANE.

BRANDT, Carston [32; b: Germany; f: Johann BRANDT; m: Lena ROHWEDER [ROHWER]] md. Antone SINKULA [20; b: Wisconsin; f: James SINKULA; m: Mary LODEL] on 3 Sep 1878. Off: BARTHOLOMEW. Wit: Max BERGMAN, Henry LEURS.

BREESE, Francis H. [28; IA; b: NJ; f: James H. BREESE; m: Nancy DeCASTER] md. Mary ARNOLD [20; IA; b: IA; f: John ARNOLD] on 1 May 1875. Off: PEABODY. Wit: F.P. HANLON, George SHIELDS.

BREMNER, William H. [39; Omaha; b: Scotland; f: William BREMNER; m: Jane STEVENS] md. Ellen SCOTT [35; Omaha; b: Scotland; f: James SCOTT; m: Mary WHITE] on 3 Jul 1869. Off: McCAGUE. Wit: Paul HARMON, Mrs. Manerva ROBINSEN.

BRENERCAMP, Joseph [28; Omaha; b: Cincinnati, OH; f: Henry H. BRENERCAMP; m: Mary HEIDEMAN] md. Carrie V. COOPER [17; Omaha; b: New York; f: Daniel M. COOPER; m: Diana MILLER] on 2 May 1874. Off: PEABODY. Wit: Mrs. Diana SADLEE; Emma COOPER. Age of consent given by Diana SADLEE, Mother of bride. Father is dead.

BRENNAN, Albert [25; Omaha[ b: Massachusetts; f: James BRENNAN; m: Esther MAHER] md. Mary POWELL [24; Omaha; b: Nebraska; f: Charles POWELL; m: Rebecca ESKELL] on 22 oct 1879 at Florence. Off: DeLAND. Wit: Samuel SCOTT and Lewis PLANT, both of Florence. Affadavit signed by wit: Max (X) BERGMANN.

BRENNAN, Charles [23; Platte Valley Pct; b: Missouri; f: William BRENNAN; m: Elizabeth IRELAND] and Annie DAVIS [14; Platte Valley Pct; b: Washington Co.; f: John DAVIS; m: Margaret DAY] application issued on 18 Jul 1873. Off: TOWNSEND. License refused.

BRESEE, Augustas O. [41; Council Bluffs; b: NY; f: David BRESEE; m: Harriet WORKS] md. Mrs. Austina BOGAL [26; Council Bluffs; b: Germany] on 23 Nov 1881. Off: STENBERG. Wit: J.P. MANNING, Peter WIIG.

BREWER, Benn [21; Omaha; b: New York; f: William BREWER; m: Lousia BARROLL] and Ida L. HULT [16; Omaha; b: New York; f: C.L.A. HULT; m: Esther J. BROWN] license issued on 12 May 1870. Off: GIBSON. Age consent given by father of bride. "I hereby certify that the above license was delivered to me for the solemnization of marraige between the parties above named and on the evening before the marriage (14 May 1870) the said Ida L. HULT committed suicide by shooting herself with a revolver as is shown by the Coroners Record - thus releasing the said Benn BREWER from obligations implied in this license." Henry W. KUHNS, Pastor Luther Church.

BREWER, Benn [22; Omaha; b: New York; f: William BREWER; m: Louisa BORRILL] md. Maria PAULSON [16; Doulgas Co.; b: Denmark; f: Peter PAULSON] on 1 Mar 1871. Off: KUHNS. Wit: Mrs. H.W. KUHNS; Mary MATTSON.

BREWSTER, Roderick P. [23; Douglas Co.] md. Miss Frank S. THOMAS [21; Douglas Co.] on 10 Dec 1865 at the Lutheran parsonage. Off: KUHNS. Wit: Mrs. KUHNS, Mary OBERMILLER.

BREWSTER, S.C. [28; Douglas Co.] md. Sarah A. GAYLORD [22; Douglas Co.] on 17 Jul 1862 at GAYLORD's residence. Off: GAYLORD. Wit: E.P. BREWSTER, Florence JACKSON, Giles E. JACKSON of New York State.

BRICKER, F.J. [27; Omaha; b: Ohio; f: J.W. BRICKER; m: Martha ANDERSON] md. Mary SHANFELBERGER [25; Fostoria, OH; b: Pennsylvania; f: William SHANFELBERGER; m: Louise ANDRESS] on 11 Jun 1880. Off: BEANS. Wit: Mrs. R.D. HILLS, Mrs. Kate MADDOX.

BRIDE, Edward [37; Omaha; b: Ireland; f: Patrick BRIDE; m: Catharine REDMOND] md. Catharine HOURIGEN [32; Omaha; b: Ohio; f: Matthew HOURIGEN; m: Ann SKIFFINGTON] on 18 May 1880. Off: ENGLISH. Wit: Chas. HOURIGEN, Mary DOOLAN.

BRIDGES, William Allen [27; Omaha; b: Kentucky; f: John O. BRIDGES; m: Elizabeth GOODMAN] md. Emma OGDEN [16; Omaha; b: Kentucky; f: James OGDEN; m: Eliza GILLETT] on 10 Jun 1880. Off: BENEKE. Wit: James OGDEN, John OGDEN.

BRIEM, Joseph [25; Omaha; b: Germany; f: Joseph BRIEM; m: Catharine RUDMANN] md. Anna FRONDEL [22; Omaha; b: Germany; f: Landolin FRONDEL; m: Rosa HESS] on 9 Aug 1881 at the German Catholic Church. Off: GLAUBER. Wit: P.A. LYSAGHT, John M. NICK.

BRIEN, Peter [23; b: Pennsylvania; f: Matthew BRIEN; m: Catharine BRIEN] and Mary HINES [24; b: Iowa; f: William Henry HINES; m: Elizabeth McGEE] license issued on 3 Dec 1878. No marriage record. Off: BARTHOLOMEW.

BRIENNIN, William [22; Valley Station; b: Ireland] md. Eliza CLOSE [22; Valley Station; b: Ohio] on 22 Jun 1870. Off: MORRIS. Wit: Thomas J. WEATHERWAX, Valley Station; C.A. BALDWIN.

BRIGGS, C.F. [22; Statun, IA; b: Pennsylvania; f: G.W. BRIGGS; m: Ella SMITH] md. Alice COOLEY [19; Omaha; b: Iowa; f: Patrick COOLEY; m: Susan HILLARD] on 10 Nov 1879. Off: WEIS. Wit: George PARDEE of Omaha, C.F. CAMPBEL.

BRIGGS, Charles H. [30; Davenport, IA; b: Hartford, CT; f: Harvey M. BRIGGS; m: Elizabeth TATES] md. Charlotte ROBINSON [19; Omaha; b: Iowa City, IA (this was crossed out) Detroit, MI; f: William ROBINSON; m: Mary KENNARD] on 25 Jan 1872. Off: SHINN. Wit: Jas. M. BRIGGS, Davenport, IA; J.S. WRIGHT.

BRIGGS, Edward R. [31; Rockport] md. Eliza L. LEWIN [23; Omaha] on 2 Apr 1869. Off: HYDE. Wit: B.W. SMITH; D.B. COBB.

BRIGGS, John W. [39; Omaha; b: Dakota Territory; f: John BRIGGS; m: Emily (crossed out) AR-CEEH-TA] md. Mary KING [20; Omaha; b: Illinois; f: Peter KING; m: Elizabeth RILEY] on 1 Sep 1871. Off: GIBSON. Wit: H.L. SEWARD; John M. THURSTON.

BRIGGS, Levi M. [24; Omaha] md. Elizabeth WELLS [27; Omaha] on 6 Feb 1868 at the residence of Samuel BRIGGS. Off: STUCK. Wit: Nettie HUNTER, Samuel BRIGGS.

BRIGGS, Thomas B. [48; Ft. Laramie, WY; b: Rhose Island; f: Samuel BRIGGS; m: Sarah BUNN] md. Mrs. Mary R. CHAPMAN [44; Providence, RI; b: Connecticut; f: Raymond M. ARNOLD; m: Abbie DERBY] on 14 May 1874. Off: WRIGHT. Wit: Emma WHITMORE; Warren ARNOLD.

BRIGHT, Mitchell [56; Council Bluffs, IA; b: Ohio; f: Shores BRIGHT; m: Harriet BROWN] md. Mrs. Maxilnili WHALEN [50; Council Bluffs, IA; b: New York; f: Robert NICHOLS; m: Debora BUTLER] on 15 Dec. 1879. Off: BARTHOLOMEW. Wit: S.N. MELIA, J.J. POINTS.

BRIND, Frederick [25; Omaha; b: Ease India; f: James BRIND; m: Mary WALLER] md. Lizzy Julia MORROW [20; Omaha; b: PA; f: John MORROW; m: Elizabeth AMENS] on 22 May 1875. Off: McCAGUE. Wit: Mr. PETERSON, Mrs. Minerva F. SHILL.

BRINKERHOFF, Moses [25; St. Joseph, MO] md. Josephine A. RABBESON [23; Omaha] on 21 Nov 1859 at the residence of Mrs. PLAIN on Farnham St. Off: KUHNS. Wit: Mrs. Mary PLAIN, Mr. and Mrs. SELDEN, et al.

BRITEY, Charles P. [29; Omaha; b: France; f: Peter BRITEY; m: Mary FOSTER] md. Josephine A. HARRIGAN [30; Omaha; b: Ireland; f: Patrick HARRIGAN; m: Annora MURPHY] on 29 Jan 1870. Off: CURTIS. Wit: Bridget CASEY; Bridget HARRINGTON.

BRITSCH [BUTSCH], Paul [24; Omaha] md. Dorette GESIGER [24; Omaha] on 25 Oct 1868. Off: STUCK. Wit: John M. SULLIVAN, J. FRANK.

BRITTAN, William S. [21; Iron Bluffs; b: White Co., IN] md. Sarah M. BURNEY [19; Iron Bluffs; b: IN] on 31 Oct 1869 "at Mr. BURNEY." Off: FLORKEE. Wit: David JACKENSON of Platte Valley, I. DENTON of Platte Valley.

BRITTON, Charles [28; Saratoga Pct., Douglas Co.; b: Elmira, MY; f: Isaac BRITTON; m: Jane SCHULTZ] md. Mrs. Ann ALDRICH [22; Saratoga Pct., Douglas Co.; b: North Carolina; f: ---- WATKINS] on 22 Mar 1873. Off: THURSTON. Wit: C.L. BRISTOL; L.F. HALE.

BROCKMAN, Peter [30; Omaha; b: Germany; f: Michael BROCKMAN; m: Abel HUSON] md. Lena KNOBLE [26; Omaha; b: Germany; f: Caspar LUGSINGER; m: Anna ZOEPFE] on 6 Mar 1877. Off: FALK. Wit: [Mr.] Fridolin ZWEIFEL, Emil MEYER.

BROCKWAY, William [22; Tavoca, IA; b: Indiana; f: Jospeh B. BROCKWAY; m: Catharine MILLER] md. Susan FISKERS [18; Tavoca, IA; b: Indiana; f: John H. FISKERS] on 1 Apr 1874. Off: HALD. Wit: Frank MORTON; Charles BRANDES.

BRODFUEHRER, Fernand [22; Omaha; b: Prussia; f: Bernhard BRODFUEHRER; m: Barbara SCHUBARDT] md. Anna KRUSE [20; Omaha; b: Germany] on 27 Oct 1870. Off: KUHNS. Wit: Christian GIST; William H. BROWN.

BRONICK, William [39; Omaha; b: Germany; f: Martin BRONICK; m: Helena WESTERMAN] md. Kate HUGHES [18; Omaha; b: Illinois; f: Martin HUGHES; m: Bridget DONOLAN] on 21 Jan 1877, Catholic Church. Off: JENNETTE. Wit: John T. SMITH, Annie DODGE.

BROOKS, Charles [30; Omaha; colored; b: Kentucky; f: Thornton BROOKS; m: Emily PARKER] md. Mary Isabel SMITH [27; Omaha; colored; b: Missouri; f: Adison SMITH; m: Jane HOBSON] on 12 Nov 1873. Off: GAINES. Wit: Mrs. BEORD; Margaret JOHNSON.

BROPHY, James [30; Omaha; b: Ireland; f: Patrick BROPHY; m: Catharine LANAGAN] md. Mary MULLEN [20; Omaha; b: Ireland; f: Patrick MULLEN; m: Ella NOONAN] on 15 Aug 1880. Off: ENGLISH. Wit: Chas. HANLEY, Bridget MULLEN.

BROSIUS, Martin C. [22; Omaha; b: Iowa; f: Daniel BROSIUS; m: Caroline HILEMAN] md. Lizza HEOURTH [22; Omaha; b: Missouri; f: Michael HEOURTH; m: Catharine MUNTD] on 25 May 1880. Off: HAWES. Wit: Joseph H. MILLARD, Amelia M. HAWES.

BROWINING, Woodson W. [23; Douglas Co.; b: MO; f: William D. BROWNING; m: Corinthia ATKINSON] md. Jennie HANGER [19; Douglas Co.; b: MO; f: Peter HANGER; m: Charity EVANS] on 14 Oct 1875 at CARLISLE's residence. Off: CARLISLE. Wit: John HANGER, Waterloo, Jennie FINNEL, Waterloo.

BROWN, Abraham S, [38; Omaha; b: Germany; f: M.B. BROWN; m: Henrietta STEINBURG] and Babette KAHN [20; Omaha; b: Germany; f: Meyer KAHN] license issued on 27 May 1871. Off: GIBSON.

BROWN, Arthur [37; Salt Lake City, UT; b: MI; f: Asa B. BROWN; m: Sophia O. BROWN] md. Isabelle CAMERON [37; Salt Lake City, UT; b: MI; f: Alexander C. CAMERON] on 2 Feb 1881. Off: MAXFIELD. Wit: Mrs. M.M. MAXFIELD, Mary SMITH.

BROWN, Charles [24; Omaha] md. Amelia CREYS [26; Omaha] on 15 Feb 1869. Off: KUHNS. Wit: George HERZOG, Charles BEINDORFF, et al.

BROWN, Charles [colored; 26; Omaha; b: Baltimore, MD; f: Henry BROWN; m: Floretta CLARK] md. Romania GRAY [colored; 27; Omaha; b: Kentucky; f: ---- FOSTER] on 4 Jul 1869 at the A.M.E. Church. Off: HUBBARD. Wit: Betsy FOSTER, W.W. PORTER, Alfred CHURCHWILL, Pompey ALLEN.

BROWN, Charley [colored; 27; Douglas Co.] and Mrs. Romania GRAY [colored; 27; Douglas Co.] license issued on 25 Jun 1868. No marriage record. Off: STUCK.

BROWN, F.M. [28; Greeley, CO; b: Pennsylvania; f: Pliney E. BROWN; m: Elizabeth E. MITCHELL] md. Ida M. COX [20; Iowa; f: David M. COX; m: Mary E. KEM] on 12 Aug 1880. Off: RILEY. Wit: Merrick CUMMINGS, D.S.M. FRETWELL.

BROWN, Francis W. [26; Chicago, IL; b: Missouri; f: Elisha W. BROWN; m: Mary A. BRENT] md. Jennie L. BENNETT [23; Omaha; b: New York; f: Samuel BENNETT; m: Cornelia L. ROGERS] on 22 Dec 1880. Off: JAMESON. Wit: G.F. WADE, Mrs. M.L.B. WADE.

BROWN, George [38; Omaha; colored; b: Virginia; f: George BROWN; m: Amelia BROWN] md. Laura CAMPBELL [17; Omaha; colored; b: Missouri; f: Levin CAMPBELL; m: Catharine FRIDAY] on 11 Feb 1872. Off: HARRAD. Wit: Henry WILLIAMS; Preston BOLDON. Age of consent given by Catharine BOLIN, mother of the bride, father is dead.

BROWN, Harrason [40] and Anis Elizabe McCOY [21] license issued on 5 Apr 1857. No marriage recorded. Off: SCOTT. Age consent given by John McCOY.

BROWN, Harrison [52; Douglas Co.; b: Nova Scotia; f: William BROWN; m: Ann STOVER] md. Angeline BOUQUET [42; Douglas Co.; b: Canada; f: Michael LEBERDEE; m: Angeline BAUPUM] on 4 Nov 1870. Off: KUHNS. Wit: Paul BOUQUET; Angie HOLMAN.

BROWN, Henry L. [colored; 28; Omaha; b: VA; f: Amos BROWN] md. Dora RANDOLF [colored; 19; Omaha; b: Washington, DC] on 17 Sep 1881. Off: RICKETTS. Wit: Mrs. Hester VINEGAR, Mrs. Berry CRAIG.

BROWN, Henry O. [28; Omaha] and Martha E. HORD (HOARD) [22; Florence] license issued on 7 Jun 1867. No marriage record. Off: HASCALL.

BROWN, Henry [23; Douglas Co.; b: Pennsylvania; f: Henry BROWN; m: Mary OSTROM] md. Catharine JUDY [16; Wahoo, NE; b: Bohemia; f: James JUDY; m: Catharine MIMAX] on 17 Jul 1880. Off: BRANDES. Wit: Edward KUEHL??, Charles KUHLMAN.

BROWN, Isaac [34; Council Bluffs, IA; b: New York; f: Isaac BROWN] md. Mary DUFREES [24; Council Bluffs, IA; b: Germany; f: Jacob DUFREES; m: Anna LUCAS] on 23 Oct 1878. Off: BENEKE. Wit: Robert M. AULIFFE, Martin JENKINS.

BROWN, James A. [45; Denver City, CO] md. Frances E. BIGELOW [29; Chicago, IL] on 9 Dec 1865. Off: SLAUGHTER. Wit: Mr. and Mrs. LUCAS.

BROWN, James J. md. Missouri KENNEDY at midday on 1 Mar 1865 at Mrs. KENNEDY's residence in Florence. Off: DIMMICK. Wit: John H. BRACKEN, Chas. BROWN, Walter BROWN, et al.

BROWN, James J. [36; Council Bluffs] md. Mary M. RYAN [22; Council Bluffs] on 20 Jan 1868 at the Roman Catholic Church. Off: O'GORMAN. Wit: John RYAN, Mary O'BRIEN.

BROWN, Joseph [22; Omaha; b: Hungaria; f: L. BROWN, m: Hanna BROWN] md. Esther NEWMAN [19; Omaha; b: Hungaria; f: Joseph NEWMAN; m: Peppi SCHOENWETTER] on 12 Mar 1881. Off: ANDERSON. Wit: M. NEWMAN, A. BROWN.

BROWN, Myron [21; Platte Valley Pct., Douglas Co.; b: Vermont f: Amos H. BROWN; m: Lillias TORREY] md. Lucretia DAVIS [22; Platte Valley Pct., Douglas Co.; b: Illinois; f: Moses T. DAVIS; m: Jane J. TAYLOR] on 19 Jul 1873. Off: TOWNSEND. Wit: William H. IJAMS; Edward B. WILLIS.

BROWN, Nelson [20; Omaha] md. Anney JONES [18; Omaha] on Monday, 13 Apr 1857 at Harrison BROWN's house in Douglas Co. Off: GAYLORD. Age consent given by Harrison BROWN.

BROWN, Oscar H. [21; Omaha; b: New York; f: Peter J. BROWN; m: Hester] md. Annie JONES [18; Omaha; b: Missouri; f: Henry JONES] on 31 Mar 1872. Off: WATT. Wit: Henry JONES; Hester BROWN.

BROWN, Randall A. [34; Douglas Co.] md. Sarah M. VAN SYCLE [18; Douglas Co.] on 22 Dec 1862 at Mr. SWEESY's residence. Off: KUHNS. Wit: Mr. and Mrs. BRIGGS, Mr. and Mrs. VISHER, et al.

BROWN, Solomon [24; Omaha] md. Annie BROWN [22; Omaha] on 21 Jan 1869. Off: HUBBARD. Wit: John HARRIS, Mrs. HARRIS.

BROWN, William F. [35; Douglas Co.; b: Tennessee; f: A.V. BROWN; m: Jane DIXON] md. Mary E. BONE [17; Douglas Co.; b: Iowa; f: Sherrad BONE; m: Malinda SCHLAGLE] on 6 Jun 1877, at Florence. Off: CRITCHFIELD. Wit: Sherrad BONE, Martha J. PALMANTER, both of Florence.

BROWN, William H. [36; b: Pennsylvania; f: William BROWN; m: Catharine EWING] md. Mrs. Jennie ENNIS [25; b: Ohio; f: Charles REED; m: Mary Ann ROSS] on 24 Apr 1878. Off: MILLER. Wit: Joseph BELL of St. Marys Avenue, T.S. McMURRAY of Saunders Street.

BROWN, William H.F. [24; Chicago Precinct, Douglas Co.] md. Mary E. BILETER [22; Chicago Precinct, Douglas Co.] on 14 Jan 1867 at Elkhorn Station. Off: DENTON.

BROWNING, Walker [22; Omaha; colored; b: Missouri; f: John BROWNING; m: Elizabeth] md. Ruth MAYWEATHER [18; Omaha; colored; b: Kentucky; f: Nicholas MAYWEATHER; m: Jane YOUNG] on 18 Oct 1872. Off: PORTER. Wit: Wiley B. DIXON; Dr. J.B. PLUMMER.

BRUDER, Timothy [32; Omaha; b: Ireland; f: Martin BRUDER; m: Mary CALAN] md. Lizzie KELLY [22; Omaha; b: Ireland; f: Frank KELLY; m: Johannah CORDIN] on 31 Aug 1876 at the Catholic Cathedral. Off: JENNETTE. Wit: Thomas BARRY, Dorah HOGAN. Thomas BURKE signed the affidavit.

BRUDMAN, Bernard F. [28; Omaha; b: Germany; f: Henry J. BRUDMAN; m: Madaline DOSE] md. Marianna HEBENSTREIT [28; Omaha; b: Germany; f: Franz HEBENSTREIT; m: Marianna A. HEBENSTREIT] on 26 Jul 1880, German Catholic Church. Off: GROENEBAUM. Wit: Louis HENNINGS, Mary COOPER.

BRUHN, Joachim H. [29; Douglas Co.; b: Germany; f: Johann BRUHN; m: Wiebke WENNINGES] md. Anna M. LUENEBURG [28; Douglas Co.; b: Germany; f: Johann F. LUENEBURG; m: Christene STROEH] on 24 Oct 1879. Off: FRESE. Wit: Hans PETERS of Sarpy Co., Marc SIERT of Douglas Co.

BRULN, John [32; Sarpy Co.; b: Prussia; f: John BRULN] md. Wilhelmine TIMMERMAN [20; Omaha; b: Germany; f: John TIMMERMAN; m: Mary TORD] on 29 May 1874. Off: PEABODY. Wit: J.J. PONTS; Jacob WIES.

BRUNNER, Thomas C. [30; Omaha; b: PA; f: John G. BRUNNER; m: Judith ERDMAN] md. Nellie M. REED [21; Omaha; b: NY; f: Henry REED; m: Sarah VANE] on 9 May 1876. Off: PARDEE. Wit: Walter READ, Hallie DUNCAN. Marriage filed 17 Mar 1877. Marriage recorded 29 Apr 1878.

BRYANT, F.B. [39; b; New York; f: J.D. BRYANT; m: Adaline MILLARD] md. Jennie HULTZINGER [22; b: Iowa; f: Peter HULTZINGER; m: Mary HOUSEL] on 23 Sep 1878. Off: FISHER. Wit: C.H. PAUL, Alice V. PAUL.

BRYANT, John [42; Douglas Co.; b: England; f: William [John crossed out] BRYANT; m: Phillis CHANDLER] md. Catherine APPLEBY [34; Douglas Co.; b: England; f: James APPLEBY; m: Mary EVANS] on 5 Jan 1877 at Elkhorn City. Off: VAN FLEET. Wit: Wm. APPLEBY, Anna APPLEBY, both of Elkhorn City.

BRYANT, John [Elkhorn City] and Kate APPLEBY [Omaha] license issued on 22 Aug 1863. No marriage record. Both of legal age. Off: DICKINSON.

BRYCE, John [24; Bellevue; b: New York; f: Alexander BRYCE; m: Nancy WEAVER] md. Lizzie B. SEATON [17; Bellevue; b: Maryland; f: John S. SEATON; m: Mary E. RASE] on 24 Mar 1871. Off: GIBSON. Wit: John GRAY; P.H. REED. Age of consent given by mother of bride, father not in Nebraska at present time.

BUCHANAN, Alexander [25; Omaha; b: Ohio; f: Alexander BUCHANAN; m: Letitia WILDMAN] md. Sadie SCHWALENBERG [18; Omaha; b: Pennsylvania; f: Frank A. SCHWALENBERG; m: Catharine MARSHALL] on 20 Sep 1879. Off: MILLSAPUGH. Wit: J.E. BOYD, T.E. BRUNNER.

BUCHANAN, Augustus [21; Omaha] and Eleverria C. PETTS [21; Omaha] license issued on 4 May 1868. No marriage record. Off: STUCK. 5 Aug 1868: "The above license canceled at request of Miss. E.C. PETTS, as said license was obtained without the consent of the said E.C. PETTS." STUCK.

BUCHANAN, Victor [41; Washington Co., NE; b: Pennsylvania; f: Walker BUCHANAN; m: Jane YOUNG] md. Mrs. Elizabeth A. HOUSER [27; Washington Co., NE; b: Indiana; f: Samuel FREED; m: Jane YOUNG] on 20 Feb 1878. Off: BARTHOLOMEW. Wit: A.R. DUFREND, A.T. LANGE.

BUCK, August Hinrick [21; Douglas Co.; b: Germany; f: John BUCK; m: Margaret HOLTZ] md. Ann M.E. TIMMERMAN [35: Douglas Co.; b: Germany; f: John TIMMERMAN; m: Maria TODE] on 26 Jan 1874. Off: PEABODY. Wit: Henry RUSER, Douglas Co.; John WEIS, Douglas Co.

BUCK, Henry [24; Omaha; b: Germany; f: Frederick BUCK; m: Lizzetta BURNS] md. Lisetta SPONSAL [21; Omaha; b: Germany; f: Adam SPONSAL; m: Lizzetta GRENNARD] on 28 May 1881. Off: RILEY. Wit: J.J. O'CONNOR, J.W. MURPHY.

BUCKLEY, John C. [35; Omaha; b: Kentucky; f: Samuel H. BUCKLEY; m: Margaret A. CASSON] md. Ella B. IDE [23; Omaha; b: Illinois; f: John IDE; m: Lydia RICHARDS] on 24 Jun 1880. Off: INGRAM. Wit: Prof. GILLISPIE, J.A. INGRAM.

BUCKLEY, Patrick [25; Douglas Co.] md. Hannah POWERS [21; Douglas Co.] on 24 Feb 1868. Off: CURTIS. Wit: John GALLAGHER, Mary SHANNAHAN.

BUCKLEY, Peter T. [29; Stromsberg; b: Sweden; f: John BUCKLEY; m: Martha HEADSTROM] md. Tillie C. ROSS [19; Omaha; b: Nebraska City, NE; f: Julian ROSS; m: Mary WALKER] on 3 Dec 1880. Off: WILLIAMS. Wit: Mrs. DUNN, Thomas ROSS.

BUCKLEY, Stephen F. [28; Douglas Co.; b: Kentucky; f: Samuel BUCKLEY; m: Margaret FRANKLIN] md. Nannie B. CLAYTON [19; Pottawattamie Co., IA; b: Iowa; f: Henry CLAYTON; m: Laura STRONG] on 28 Aug 1879 at the Deaf and Dumb Institute. Off: INGRAM. Wit: J.S. GILLESPIE, T.E. MAYNARD.

BUCKNER, Harrison [29; Omaha; colored; b: Kentucky f: ---- BUCKNER; m: Jennie] md. Mattie EVANS [21; Omaha; colored; b: Texas; f: Leonard EVANS; m: Priscilla] on 19 Aug 1873. Off: TOWNSEND. Wit: Marcia MANNING; Mrs. Mary E. TOWNSEND.

BUISSERET, Armand E.G. [24; Chicago, IL; b: Belguim; f: Antonio BUISSERET; m: Issabella MARSHOUW] md. Lillie Esther BARRY [21; Chicago, IL; b: Wisconsin; f: Albert BARRY; m: Silvia BUTTERFIELD] on 17 Apr 1880. Off: WILLIAMS. Wit: J.H. MACK, Mira BARRY, both of Chicago, IL.

BULL, John [29; Douglas Co.; b: Prussia, Europe; f: Frederic BULL; m: Doras VITTENBERG] md. Gratia ZIMMERMAN [28; Douglas Co.; b: Holstein, Europe; f: John ZIMMERMAN] on 5 Nov 1871. Off: BILLMAN. Wit: J.N. BILLMAN; Mrs. Ira C. BILLMAN.

BUNKE, Joseph [26; Omaha; b: Germany; f: Joseph BUNKE; m: Hedwig BINGER] md. Lena KREBS [22; Omaha; b: Dubuque, IA; f: John KREBS; m: Lena SIEVERS] on 10 Jun 1879. Off: BENEKE. Wit: Claus J. SCHMIDT, Carsten HAMANN.

BUNN, Ferdinand [26; Omaha] md. Irene A. SMILEY [22; Omaha] on 23 Mar 1861 at the bride's residence on Farnham St. Off: KUHNS. Wit: Geo. LAKE, Abbie HAYS, Carie SMILEY, Annie SMILEY, et al.

BUNZ, Peter [29; Union Pct., Douglas Co.; b: Germany; f: Peter BUNZ; m: Catharine SWINN] md. Louise VOSS [23; Omaha; b: Germany; f: Hans VOSS; m: Magdalena BANIGER] on 19 Oct 1872. Off: TOWNSEND. Wit: Henry VOSS; Jacob VOSS.

BURCH, Grafton H. [27; Sarpy Co.; b: VA; f: James BURCH; m: Ann L. RUTTER] md. Nancy A. TYLER [19; Sarpy Co.; b: VA; f: William TYLER; m: Ann HUTCHINSON] on 16 Mar 1875. Off: PEABODY. Wit: James S. BROWN, John W. TYLER.

BURDISH, Richard [23; Omaha; b: PA; f: Daniel BURDISH; m: Mary GAVIN] md. Mary CONNELLEY [19; Omaha; b: PA; f: Patrick CONNELLEY; m: Celia O'HARA] on 20 Jun 1881 at St. Philomena's Church. Off: ENGLISH. Wit: Edward DONOHOE, Catherine McNAMARA.

BURES, Joseph [21; Omaha; b: Germany; f: Wenzel BURES; m: Mary MATHEWS [MATIAS]] md. Kate ROMASOVA [HROMAS] [22; Omaha; b: Germany; f: John ROMASOVA [HROMAS]; m: Mary ROMASOVA [HROMAS]] on 11 Jul 1869. Off: CURTIS. Wit: Joseph ZERLER, Jacob BORSIC [BURSIC].

BURG or BERG, Andrew [30; Omaha; b: Sweden; f: Andrew BERG; m: Mary ANDERSON] md. Lena TORGERSON [22; Omaha; b: Norway; f: Mikkel TORGERSON; m: Karen JOHANNSEN] on 6 Jul 1875. Off: HANSEN. Wit: Henry A. MOE, Samuel J. BORGSTROM.

BURGDORF, Charles W. [30; Omaha; b: Germany; f: A. BURGDORF; m: F. KREMPO] md. Annie E. NARVOY [22; Omaha; b: Pennsylvania; f: William NARVOY] on 1 May 1871. Off: BILLMAN. Wit: A. SCHULTZ; Mrs. Ira C. BILLMAN.

BURGDORF, Henry [40; Omaha; b: Germany; f: Adolph BURGDORF; m: Annie KREMPKOW] md. Christine HEINRICHS [22; Omaha; b: ----; f: John HEINRICHS; m: Catharine CARSTENS] on 29 Apr 1880. Off: BENEKE. Wit: Wm. DOLL, Carrie DOLL.

BURGESS, George F. [45; Sarpy Co.; b: New York; f: William BURGESS; m: Violetta STOCKWELL] and Kate HINTON [28; Douglas Co.; b: Wisconsin; f: Thomas HINTON; m: Lavina J. LUCAS] license issued on 26 Sep 1877. No marriage record. Off: SEDGWICK.

BURGESS, J. Curtiss [30; Omaha] md. Mrs. Mary RUSSELL [23; Omaha] on 9 Dec 1867. Off: KUHNS. Wit: Mrs. A. HAMILTON, J.W. BROWN.

BURGESS, John [30; Omaha] md. Elizabeth ASTMAN [21; Omaha] on 17 Aug 1867 at the residence of the bride's mother. Off: KUHNS. Wit: Mary E. INGRAM, Frank POLLARD.

BURGOYNE, P.E. [23; New York City; b: New York City; f: W.M. BURGOYNE; m: Margaret DUNCAN] md. Emma ROBERTS [21; Omaha; b: Illinois; f: William H. ROBERTS; m: Sarah THOMPSON] on 6 Jul 1880. Off: H.A. DILLON of Brooklyn, NY, M. GOULD.

BURK, Alexander J. [34; Omaha] md. Mrs.? Eliza RUSSELL [24; Omaha] on 23 Apr 1868. Off: ROBERTS. Wit: Tom KELLY, Wm. GRANGER.

BURK, Edward [26; Omaha] md. Julia N. BURK or BORKE [16; Omaha] on 30 Nov 1868 at the Catholic Church of Omaha. Off: O'GORMAN. Wit: Peter MALONE, Catharine SLATTERY.

BURK [BURKE], Henry F. [24; Omaha; b: Ohio; f: William BURK; m: Mary BURK] md. Julia BERRY [25; Omaha; b: Canada; f: Michael BERRY; m: Hanora CONNELL] on 15 May 1877, Catholic Cathedral. Off: JENNETTE. Wit: Thomas BARRY, Mary BARRY.

BURKANSTOCK, Charles [21; Douglas Co.; b: Germany; f: Adolph BURKANSTOCK; m: Mary GIBSON] md. Caroline DONALDSON [19; Florence; b: Sweden; f: Henry DANALSON; m: Maria ANDERSON] on 6 Jun 1870. Off: MORTON. Wit: Charles LAMMERSDORF; Mrs. DEBRESSEN.

BURKE, Alexander L. [24; Omaha; f: Wm. BURKE of Cahir Parish, Co. Tipperary, Ire.] md. Mrs. Mary McCARTHY TIERNEY? [f: Michl. McCARTHY of Co. Tipperary, Ire.] on 15 Nov 1858 or 1859 at St. Mary's Church. Off: CANNON. Wit: Luke McDERMOTT, Bridget RYAN.

BURKE, George B. [45; Omaha; b: Ireland; f: William BURKE; m: Catherine BRIGGS] md. Mary L. MURRAY [33; Omaha; b: Canada; f: James L. MURRAY; m: Gertrude ----] on 20 Dec 1876. Off: MILLSPAUGH. Wit: Robt. CALDERWOOD, Mary HEYDEN.

BURKE, Gustavus [23; Saunders Co.; b: Sweden; f: John BURKE; m: Christina ELGE] md. Matilda JOHNSON [21; Omaha; b: Sweden; f: John CARLSON; m: Johanna JOHNSON] on 1 Feb 1873. Off: SUNDBORN. Wit: Carl HOLM; Emile GRAN.

BURKE, Peter [30; Elkhorn; b: Ireland; f: Thomas BURKE; m: Ann DULING] md. Mary KENNEDY [24; Calhoun, IA; b: Ireland; f: James KENNEDY] on 4 Jan 1874. Off: GARAHAN. Wit: James KENNEDY, Elkhorn; Mary KENNEDY, Elkhorn; (witness? ---- CALHOUN, Calhoun, IA?). Confusing reference is made to Missouri Valley.

BURKET, Henry K. [27; Creston, IA; b: Illinois; f: Fred C. BURKET; m: Julia A. KENNEDY] md. Ella M. HASKELL [24; b: Illinois; f: Joseph HASCALL; m: Sylvia A. PIDGE] on 4 Sep 1878. Off: JAMESON. Wit: Joseph M. HASKELL, M.A. PINNEY.

BURKHARD, A. [45; Omaha; b: Bavaria; f: Sylvester BURKHARD; m: Rosa SCHOFF] md. Mary DORNALDT [38; Omaha; b: Germany; f: George DORNALDT; m: Sophia GEFF] on 22 May 1877. Off: BENEKE. Wit: Phil WAGNER, Anna WAGNER.

BURKHARD, Frank [20; Omaha; b: New York; f: John BURKHARD; m: Catherine RIEDEL (RUDELL?)] md. Jennie V. PISCHKE [19; Omaha; b: Prussia; f: Albert PISCHKE] on 22 Nov 1870. Off: GROENEBAUM. Wit: William OSBORNE; Mary WRIGHT. Age of consent given by John BURKHARD, brother of groom; father is dead.

BURKHARD, John [22; Omaha] md. Cecilie BURLKEY [22; Omaha] on 16 Sep 1867 at the Catholic Church of Omaha. Off: O'GORMAN. Wit: Dr. DEN, Louisa BURKLEY.

BURMEISTER, Charles E. [27; Omaha; b: Germany; f: J.F. BURMEISTER; m: Elizabeth GEITMANN] md. Mary E. MEYER [32; Omaha; b: Germany] on 20 May 1871. Off: GIBSON. Wit: Otto HILFFEREST; Abraham S. BROWN.

BURMESTER, Adolphus [33; Omaha] md. Mary R. WEHRER [20; Omaha] on 9 Jan 1866. Off: KUHNS. Wit: Charles BURMESTER, Jacob SCHNEIDER, et al.

BURNES, John G. [24; Omaha; b: Ireland; f: John BURNES; m: Ellen MAHAR] and Mary A. LOWRY [16; Omaha; b: Louisiana; f: Thomas LOWRY; m: Elizabeth MORRIS] license issued on 20 Jun 170. Off: GIBSON. Age of consent given by father of bride "in Court."

BURNETT, John [colored; 25; Omaha; b: Richmond, VA; f: John BURNETT; m: Harriet WILSON] md. Matilda WILSON [colored; 19; Omaha; b: Indiana; f: Peter WILSON; m: Elizabeth RENNELS] on 14 Jun 1869. Off: HYDE. Wit: Albert JOHNSON, Jesse H. CRAFT.

BURNEY, Herman [23; Omaha; b: Sweden; f: Gustave BURNEY; m: Susanna SALHOLM] md. Josie JOHNSON [19; Omaha; b: Missouri; f: William JOHNSON; m: Elizabeth KEELER] on 31 Dec 1879. Off: MARQUETT. Wit: William JOHNSON, Elizabeth JOHNSON.

BURNEY, John Willis [20; Douglas Col; b: IA; f: John G. BURNEY; m: Mary H. DENTON] md. Nancy J. HANEY [18; Douglas Co.; b: PA; f: Edward J. HANEY; m: Hannah FRANKS] on 28 Feb 1875 at Waterloo. Off: CORLISS. Wit: E.J. HANEY, Hannah HANEY, Waterloo. Age consent given by father of the groom. Reference, Lewis REED, County Clerk (Elkhorn Station?).

BURNHAM, Nathan J. [27; Omaha; b: PA; f: Horace B. BURNHAM; m: Ruth A. JACKSON] md. Mary Clarke MORGAN [24; Omaha; b: NY; f: Albert C. MORGAN; m: Susan SQUIRES] on 5 Oct 1875 at Trinity Cathedral. Off: EASTER. Wit: Horace B. BURNHAM, C.H. FREDERICK.

BURNS, Frank [colored; 21; Omaha; b: Hollow Springs, MS; f: William BURNS; m: Emily COPELAND] md. Mary WILLIAMS [colored; 21; Omaha; b: St. Louis, MO; f: John WILLIAMS; m: Mary ROSE] on 5 Aug 1869. Off: KUHNS. Wit: Henry N. WILLIAMS, Mrs. Emeline WILLIAMS.

BURNS, George [31; Omaha; b: Illinois; f: Patrick BURNS; m: Mary DORMER] md. Harriet E. FOX [21; Omaha; b: Illinois; f: Charles FOX; m: Julia A. GRIGSBY] on 8 Oct 1879. Off: STENBERG. Wit: De DARLING, Michael DEMPSEY.

BURNS, John [27; Omaha; b: New York; f: Francis BURNS; m: Catharine] md. Mrs. Fanny TRETLER [33; Omaha; b: Lancaster, PA] on 9 Aug 1869. Off: BETTS. Wit: Max and Louisa BALTSCH (BALTCH), Andrew J. GOFFE.

BURNS, Samuel md. Sallie McCORMICK on the evening of 13 Jul 1865 at Richard McCORMICK's residence. Off: LEMON. Wit: Richard McCORMICK and family, et al.

BURNS, Samuel [33; Omaha; b: Dungannon, Ireland; f: Joseph BURNS; m: Selina McKELL] md. Mary E. DENMAN [23; Omaha; b: Newark, NJ; f: Jacob S. DENMAN; m: Selina LYON] on 22 Feb 1872. Off: DeLaMATYR. Wit: T.B.W. LEMON; J.S. McKELL, Burlington, IA.

BURR, George C. [30; Omaha; b: New York; f: Nathaniel BURR; m: Mary Jane YEOMANS] md. Stella N. SHAW [25; Omaha; b: Michigan; f: John A. SHAW; m: Rody A. HOLLISTER] on 19 Oct 1880. Off: INGRAM. Wit: Jno. AUCHAMPROUGH of Independence, IA, David P. BURR.

BURRILL, Arnold [23; Omaha; b: OH; f: J.W. BURRILL; m: Mary J. PHILLIPS] md. Lula J. KELLEY [21; Omaha; b: NY; f: John KELLEY; m: Sarah DUNHAM] on 5 Apr 1875. Off: HENNEY. Wit. Mrs. E. LUCAS, Mrs. E. HENNEY.

BURRIS, O.P. [31; Omaha; b: IN; f: Jacob BURRIS; m: Christine HYDE] md. Mrs. Jennie SLACK [27; Omaha; b: OH; f: David SHAFER; m: Henrietta SCOFIELD] on 18 Oct 1881. Off: STENBERG. Wit: Wm. F. FLYNN, Wm. H. BROWN.

BURSIK, Albert [28; Omaha; b: Bohemia; f: Albert BURSIK; m: Veronicka HASA] md. Katy KOFKA [20; Omaha; b; Bohemia; f: John KOFKA; m: Katy THREAD] on 10 Dec 1874. Off: PEABODY. Wit: A.G. McAUSLAND; Charles HART.

BURTON, Henry [26; Omaha; b: Virginia; f: ---- FALKNER] md. Louisa JOHNSON [25; Omaha; b: Kentucky] on 17 Oct 1870. Off: GIBSON. Wit: John R. MANCHESTER; R.H. ANDREWS.

BURTON, Isaac B. [24; Douglas Co.] md. Juliet C. BRITTENDALL [18; Douglas Co.; licence says Pleasant Grove, MN] on 1 Jun 1859. Off: GILBERT. Wit: Oscar F. DAVIS, P.W. HITCHCOCK.

BUSHEY, John [21; Douglas Co.; b: Canada; f: John BUSHEY; m: Bridget BURNS] md. Julia COLBERT [20; Douglas Co.; b: Ireland; f: Michael COLBERT; m: Ellen WOLFE] on 27 Jul 1876 at the Roman Catholic Cathedral. Off: William KELLEY.

BUSHEY, Michael [21; Omaha; b: Canada; f: John BUSHEY; m: Bridget BURNS] md. Martha WAYBRIGHT [19; Omaha; v: VA; f: Nathan WAYBRIGHT; m: Leah CATAMER] on 11 Feb 1881. Off: SMITH. Wit: William H. NORTON, Mrs. Mary NORTON.

BUSHNELL, Charles C. [22; Omaha; b: Illinois; f: Chester BUSHNELL; m: Delia DAYTON] md. Lucinda M. WILLIAMS [18; Omaha; b: Iowa; f: Elijah [David written here and crossed out] WILLIAMS; m: Elizabeth WHITMORE] on 21 May 1879. Off: BARTHOLOMEW. Wit: Charles S. SMITH, Jos. QUINLAN.

BUSKAT, Gustav [24; Omaha; b: Germany; f: Carl BUSKAT; m: Louisa RINGAT] md. Minna STAGAN [22; Omaha; b: Germany; f: Fritz STAGAN; m: Minna HANDRUKAT] on 26 Mar 1881. Off: BENEKA. Wit: Chas. B. SCHROHT, S. SIMAN.

BUTLER, Edward C. [28; Omaha] md. Mary B. HARRIS [27; Omaha] on 27 Jun 1868 at Union House. Off: FLORKEE. Wit: Bertha NENON, Charlotte FLORKEE.

BUTLER, Francis Marian [25; Harrison Co., IA] md. Elizabeth BAXTER [24; Harrison Co., IA] on 4 May 1861 at ARMSTRONG's office. Off: ARMSTRONG. Wit: Byron REED, George W. FORBES, Thomas L. SUTTON.

BUTLER, William H. [36; Douglas Co.; colored; b: Virginia; f: Edward BUTLER; m: Sarah BROOKS] md. Hannah Jane LEE [21; Douglas Co.; colored; b: Virginia; f: Simon LEE] on 14 Dec 1871. Off: HARROD. Wit: Ellen STRAWS; Emma McCLINTON.

BUTLER, William Wheeler [21; Omaha; b: Ireland; f: George Wheeler BUTLER; m: Eliza ROBINSON] md. Mary C. LOY [19; Omaha; b: Decatur, IL; f: John G. LOY; m: Jane RITTNER] on 25 Mar 1872. Off: BETTS. Wit: William Thomas CLARKE; L.H. WINSLOW.

BUTTERFIELD, Frederick [21; Omaha; b: WI; f: J.B. BUTTERFIELD; m: Harriett BIGELOW] md. Amanda COON [23; Omaha; b: IL; f: William COON; m: Rachel DAVIS] on 22 Mar 1881. Off: MAXFIELD. Wit: J.B. BUTTERFIELD, Mr. WARD.

BUTTERFIELD, Henry G. [37; Omaha; b: New York; f: Benj. BUTTERFIELD; m: Adaline CHAMBERLAIN] md. Eunice R. LUND [33; Omaha; b: New Hampshire; f: Thomas SENTER, Jr.; m: Mary C. GIDDINGS] on 17 Oct 1869. Off: KUHNS. Wit: Jonas GISE, John B. DETWILER.

BYERS, John M. [23; Omaha; b: MO; f: N.A. BYERS; m: Catharine REES] md. Jenny MAY [22; Omaha; b: Canada; f: James MAY; m: Britekeck] on 28 Jan 1875 at St. Philomena's Catholic Church. Off: JENNETTE. Wit: James RAFFERTY, Jenny BYERS.

BYRNE, Charles H. [31; Plattsmouth; b: New York; f: John BYRNE; m: Mary DELMAR] md. Mrs. Camilla F. VINTON [30; Omaha; b: Alton, IL; f: Peter GOFF; m: Camilla CARPENTER] on 28 Dec 1874. Off: HAMMOND. Wit: Col. S. SMITH, USA; Thos. HOLMES.

BYRNE, John E. [21; Omaha] md. Mary E. NORTON [17; Omaha] on 3 Mar 1867. Off: SLAUGHTER. Wit: A.M. CLARK, S.E. CLARK. Age consent given by the father of the bride.

CADIEN, Charles F. [21; Massachusetts; b: Amesbury, MA; f: Charles CADIEN; m: Lois KEHEW] md. Nellie M. GOODRICH [21; North Adams, MA; b: North Adams, MA; f: Henry P. GOODRICH; m: Mary L. ATWATER] on 17 Oct 1878. Off: PORTER. Wit: Berea WILLSY, Mrs. Lucy WILLSY.

CAHILL, James M. [34; Omaha; b: OH; f: Edward CAHILL; m: Sarah ADAMS] md. Mrs. Luella KIRTLEY [b: IA; f: Albert ADAMS; m: Ellen LENNEN] on 6 Nov 1881. Off: RILEY. Wit: Charles GANDEN, Mrs. Maude GANDEN.

CAHOON, Thomas [32; Ogden UT; b: DE; f: Samuel CAHOON; m: Rebecca COUFFER] md. Elvira S. GOULD [16; Omaha; b: MN; f: Leonard GOULD; m: Elizabeth VINCENT] on 3 Feb 1875. Off: CLARKSON. Wit: Mrs. ATKINSON, Mrs. E. GOULD. Age consent given by Elizabeth GOULD, mother of the bride. Father not living in this state.

CAIN, James H. [27; Emerson, IA; b: Canada; f: James CAIN; m: Christian CRAIGIE] md. Nettie B. McKELVEY [20; Omaha; b: Ohio; f: Joseph S. McKELVEY; m: Anna OSBORN] on 10 Dec 1873 at the house of Mr. BEWS. Off: GAYLORD. Wit: J.H. HOWARD? HOUSEMAN?; E.S. TOMBLIN, Emerson, IA.

CAINE, Edward [34; Omaha; b: Ireland; f: John CAINE; m: Sarah DOYLE] md. Mary O'BRIEN [26; Omaha; b: Ireland; f: Michael O'BRIEN; m: Mary BENLEY] on 27 Apr 1871. Off: CURTIS. Wit: Peter BAILEY, San Francisco; Catharine CAINE.

CALDWELL, Ephriam K. [26; Richland Co.] md. Cynthia DYKES [23; Omaha] on 18 Mar 1869. Off: PALMER. Wit: E.H. WARNER, Jacob KING, et al.

CALDWELL, Ernest [26; Omaha; b: Indiana; b: John L. CALDWELL; m: Margaret B. CALDWELL] md. Jennie L. OSTROM [17; Omaha; b: New York; f: A.S. OSTROM; m: Louise WALKER] on 31 May 1880. Off: MAXFIELD. Wit: A.S. OSTROM, E. KENNISTON.

CALLAHAN, Dennis [30; Omaha; b: Ireland; F: Timothy CALLAHAN; m: Hannah RIORDAN] md. Eliza FOLEY [30; Omaha; b: Ireland; f: John FOLEY; m: Mary FOLEY] on 16 Nov 1871. Off: CURTIS. Wit: James DONAHUE; Mary FOLEY.

CALLAHAN, Edward [46; Omaha; b: Ireland; f: John CALLAHAN; m: Johanna BRODERICK] md. Mrs. Mary SULLIVAN [24; Omaha; b: Ireland; f: John FORD; m: Ellen CALLAHAN] on 15 Jun 1869 at the Catholic Church. Off: O'GORMAN. Wit: James CALLAHAN, Ellen FORD.

CALLAHAN, H.P. [34; Omaha; b: New York; f: Peter CALLAHAN; m: Catharine McDERMOT] md. S.B. SLAVEN [24; Omaha; b: Illinois; f: Michael SLAVEN; m: Rosanna McALLROY] on 14 Sep 1880. Off: ENGLISH. Wit: Ed EAGAN, Mary CALLAHAN.

CALLAHAN, James B. [38; Douglas Co.; b: Ireland; f: John CALLAHAN; m: Johanna BRODERICK] md. Mary DALY [30; Sarpy Co.; b: Ireland; f: Peter DALY; m: Elizabeth HUGHES] on 29 Jun 1876 at the Roman Catholic Cathedral. Off: BYRNE. Wit: Edward CASSIDY, Elizabeth F. McCARTNEY.

CALLAHAN, James B. [Douglas Co.] md. Catharine DUGGAN [Douglas Co.] on 13 Feb 1866. Both of full age. Off: O'GORMAN.

Wit: Edward CALLAHAN, Bridget MALONE.

CALLAHAN, James [24; Omaha; b: Ireland; f: Timothy CALLAHAN; m: Hannah REARDON] md. Eliza O'CONNOR [20; Omaha; b: Ireland; f: Patrick O'CONNOR; m: Mary CAVANAGH] on 27 May 1870. Off: McGOLDRECK? Wit: Daniel BURKE; Mary BURKE.

CALLAHAN, Jeremiah [24; Omaha; b: Wisconsin; f: John CALLAHAN; m: Catharine KINNEY] md. Jane DOUGHERTY [17; McCardle Precinct; b: Nebraska; f: Hugh DOUGHERTY; m: Ellen McCARDLE] on 13 Jul 1879. Off: McDERMOTT. Wit: Bernard McQUILLAN, Kate DOUGHERTY. Permission to marry given by Hugh DOUGHERTY, father of the bride, and Frank (X his mark) DOUGHERTY, brother of the bride, witnessed by M. BERGMAN.

CALLBERG, Andrew P. [38; Saunders Co.; b: Sweden; f: Peter CALLSON; m: Anna ERICKSON] md. Christina OLSON [29; Omaha; b: Sweden; f: Ole OLSON; m: Anna ANDERSON] on 14 Dec 1872. Off: TOWNSEND. Wit: Tobias OLSSON; Charles OLSON.

CALLOWAY, William T. [39; Columbus, NE; b: Missouri; f: James CALLOWAY; m: Catherine MARKHAM] md. Jennie M. ADDIS [26;Omaha; b: Illinois; f: Richard ADDIS; m: Sarah A. DAVIS] on 6 Jan 1870. Off: DeLaMATYR. Wit: Mrs. MORRISON; Mrs. MORRISON.

CALLSAN, Charles [29; Omaha; b: Germany; f: C. CALLSAN; m: Catherine C. JOHNSON] md. Sarah JOHNSON [21; Omaha; b: Denmark; f: Chris JOHNSON; m: Annie JOHNSON] on 12 Sep 1877. Off: HANSEN. Wit: Lawrence ENEWOLD, Edward PETERSON.

CAMERON, Peter [32; Pawnee Co., NE; b: Scotland; f: John CAMERON; m: Margaret RAY] md. Rachel BRAWLEY [21; Omaha; b: IL; f: Michael BRAWLEY; m: Ellen GOULDSBY] on 8 Jul 1881. Off: MARQUETT. Wit: Hulda MARQUETT, Rosa BROWLEY.

CAMMENZIND, Andrew [34; Omaha; b: Switzerland; f: Marzell CAMMENZIND; m: Frena BACSTORFF] md. Mrs. Catharine POWER SULLIVAN [38; Omaha; b: Ireland; f: Edward POWER; m: Ellen WHALEN] on 8 May 1869. Off: HYDE. Wit: Will BROWN (BROWNE), George ARMSTRONG.

CAMPBELL, Albert [43; Advan, MN; b: Connecticut; f: Harvey CAMPBELL; m: Eliza COOK] md. May G. CHILDS [20; Advan, MN; b: Iowa; f: Thos. H. CHILDS; m: Anna BILLINGSLY] on 25 Dec 1879. Off: SHERILL. Wit: James DECKNER, Jennie CRUISE.

CAMPBELL, George [22; Waterloo; Iowa; f: John CAMPBELL; m: Linda ELSTON] md.

Nellie WESTON [18; Waterloo; b: Iowa; f: John WESTON; m: Rebecca CANHORN] on 14 Sep 1879. Off: STENBERG. Wit: De DARLING, Luella McLAUGHLIN of Waterloo.

CAMPBELL, Green [24; Omaha; b: Ripley, OH; f: Willson CAMPBELL] md. Rosanna GIBSON [19; Omaha; b: St. Joseph, MO] on 25 Jun 1870. Off: PORTER. Wit: Wiley B. DIXON; Inez PORTER.

CAMPBELL, John D. [26; Douglas Co.; b: WI; f: Duncan CAMPBELL; m: Susan C. BROWN] md. Mary C. HOEL [21; Douglas Co.; b: OH; f: Aaron R. HOEL; m: Catherine M. DURHAM] on 1 May 1876. Off: LIPE. Wit: John W. McCUEN, Joel SHOPSHIRE.

CAMPBELL, Thomas [22; Dodge Co.; b: Canada East; f: John CAMPBELL; m: Nancy McEDWARD] md. Mary A. LAMPHIRE [21; Chicago, IL; b: Wisconsin; f: Joshua M.E. LAMPHIRE; m: Esther WATKINS] on 18 Aug 1869. Off: HYDE. Wit: A.S. PADDOCK, Mrs. A.S. PADDOCK.

CAMPBELL, Thomas [28; Omaha; colored; b: South Carolina; f: Thomas CAMPBELL; m: Maria] md. Mrs. Charlotte ALEXANDER [30; Omaha; colored; b: Kentucky; f: Robert WILLIAMS; m: Matilda WILLIAMS] on 31 Jul 1872. Off: HARRAD. Wit: Mrs. Elizabeth KING; Mrs. Wm . R. JONES.

CAMPBELL, Thomas [40; Omaha; b: South Carolina; f: Thomas CAMPBELL; m: unknown] md. Mrs. Sarah MADDEN [39; Omaha; b: Pennsylvania; f: ---- BLACKSON; m: unknown] on 8 Dec 1880. Off: RICKETTS. Wit: Maria BRUCE, R. ROGERS.

CAMPBELL, Wesley Williams [22; Omaha; colored; b: Kentucky; f: Mat CAMPBELL; m: Lettee BERRY] md. Maggie LUCAS [20; Omaha; b: colored; b: Kentucky; f: John LUCAS; m: Clara LUCAS] on 9 Jan 1870 at the residence of Mrs. LEE. Off: HUBBARD. Wit: Phillip CROSS; John ROBERT.

CAMPBELL, William [24; Omaha] md. Mary J. EAYRS [23; Omaha] on 20 Jul 1868. Off: PALMER. Wit: Addie M. PALMER, Lizzie S. PALMER.

CAMPBELL, William [28; Alma, NE; b: Virginia West; f: David CAMPBELL; m: Rachel MADERA] md. Kate E. MASON [24; PA; b: PA; f: D.G. MASON; m: Elizabeth DEMAIN (or WERNAIN)] on 29 Sep 1881. Off: SHERRILL. Wit: Michl. DONOHUE, James CARROLL.

CANNELL [CONNELL], Patrick [40; Omaha; b: Ireland; f: Michael CANNELL; m: Catherine CANNELL] md. Hannah RYAN [30; Omaha; b: Ireland; f: Daniel RYAN; m: Margaret GAVEN] on 20 Nov 1869. Off: CURTIS. Wit: Patrick FOLEY, Mary LEAM.

CANNING, M.P. [42; Philadelphia; b: Pennsylvania; f: George CANNING; m: Hannah HASELL] md. May MORRIS [21; Council Grove, MO; b: Weston, MO; f: J.C. MORRIS; m: Hannah LEWUHO] on 23 Apr 1879. Off: BENEKE. Wit: Werner BOEHL, Gust SANBERG.

CANNON, James L. [23; Douglas Co.; b: OH; f: Charles CANNON; m: Anna McMANAMEY] md. Mary GRIFFIN [16; Douglas Co.; b: IL; f: Michael GRIFFIN; m: Julia FARREL] on 12 Jan 1875 at St. Philomena's Church. Off: JENNETTE. Wit: Martin CANNON, Rockport, Douglas Co., Lizzie GRIFFIN, Rockport, Douglas Co.

CANZETT, Hans [29; Omaha; b: Germany; f: Andrew CANZETT; m: Lucy MINCH] md. Lizzie B. SCHITTRA [38; Omaha; b: Germany; f: Matthew SCHITTRA; m: Maria JACK] on 4 Mar 1871. Off: MORTON. Wit: John REICHARD; Catie REICHARD.

CAREY, Augustus [25; Omaha; b: NY; f: Martin [George was crossed out] CARY; m: Catharine WHEELER] md. Mrs. Del STIFFEY [26; NY; b: NY; f: T. CLEMONS; m: R. ROBERTS] on 15 Apr 1875. Off: HENNEY. Wit: C.L. HENNEY; M.W. KENNEDY.

CAREY, Henry [25; Platte Co.] and Catharine MURPHY [21; Omaha] license issued on 30 Nov 1860. No marriage record. Off: ARMSTRONG.

CAREY, T.J. [25; Fremont, NE; b: New York; f: Andrew CAREY; m: Ellen AUSTIN] md. Dellia GOODWIN [20; Fremont, NE; b: Iowa; f: Michael GOODWIN, Mary REED] on 21 Dec 1878. Off: BARTHOLOMEW. Wit: Wm. L. PEABODY, M.H. REDFIELD.

CARLEN, Patrick [28; Omaha; b: Ireland; f: Michael CARLEN; m: Bridget SMITT] md. Margaret A. McATEE [21; Omaha; b: Iowa; f: Patrick McATEE; m: Ellen GOODIN] on 4 Jan 1870. Off: CURTIS. Wit: Mathew HELMER; Julia HELMER.

CARLILE, Jacob K. [27; Omaha; b: England; f: Wm. CARLILE; m: Maggie KELLIHAN] md. Mary E. KIRK [18; Omaha; b: Ireland; f: Robert F. KIRK; m: Lucy F. LOCKWOOD] on 9 Oct 1881. Off: ANDERSEN. Wit: James H. KIRK, Theodore RIGBY.

CARLSON, A.P. [24; Omaha; b: Sweden; f: Carl JOHNSON; m: Maria JOHANSDOTTER] md. Anna PETERSON [21; Omaha; b: Sweden; f: Peter ANDERSON; m: Johanna ANDERSON] on 2 Jan 1870. Off: BENNETT. Wit: Nels J. RYBERG; Mrs. Johanna RYBERG.

CARLSON, Alfred [31; b: Sweden; f: Charles JOHNSON; m: Mattie R. SWANSON] md. Annie F. GRANSTRIM [25; b: Sweden; f: Charles GRANSTRIM; m: Sophia JOHNSON] on 16 May 1878. Off: LIPE. Wit: Mrs. J.T. CLARK, John GRANSTRIM.

CARLSON, Andrew F. [29; Omaha; b: Sweden; f: Carl ERICKSON; m: Lena ANDERSON] md. Caren Elizabeth SODERLAND [23; Omaha; b: Sweden; f: Magnus SODERLAND; m: Christena SOLENG] on Nov 1875. Off: HENNEY. Wit: Paul STEIN, F.J. WALKER.

CARLSON, James [28; Omaha; b: Denmark; f: Carl DREIER; m: Wilhelmina JENSON] md. Anna JACOBSON [30; Omaha; b: Denmark; f: Jens JACOBSON; m: Margaret NELSON] on 13 Mar 1874. Off: PEABODY. Wit: Bennett F. MASON; G.W. AMBROSE.

CARLSON, John F. [29; Omaha; b: Sweden; f: Carl ENGLEBRECKSEN; m: Eva LINDBORN] md. Hannah JOHNSON [27; Omaha; b: Sweden; f: John ANDERSON; m: Engri MANSON] on 26 Sep 1877. Off: WEDIN. Wit: A.J. EDGAR, Charles E. SEAGREN.

CARLSON, Ole [25; Omaha; b: Sweden; f: Carl G. SWENSON; m: Alner OLESDOTTER] md. Berta NELSON [22; Omaha; b: Sweden; f: Neils ANDERSON; m: Elena ANDERSON] on 23 Aug 1870. Off: LARSON. Wit: John CHRISTIAN; Ole ANDERSON.

CARLSON, Ole [30; Omaha; b: Denmark; f: Charles F. OLESON; m: Mary MASSON] md. Annie HANSEN [20; Omaha; b: Denmark; f: Hans NELSON; m: Christina JOHNSON] on 22 Jul 1873. Off: TOWNSEND. Wit: Charles M. CONNOYER; Rasmus PETERSON.

CARLTON, James [25; Omaha; b: Ireland; f: Thomas CARLTON; m: Catherine MORRIS] md. Maria CORDAN [28; Omaha; b: Ireland; f: Laurence CORDAN; m: Honora HARRINGTON] on 23 May 1871. Off: CURTIS. Wit: Owen EGAN; Bridget CASEY.

CARNES, Edmond C. [30; Seward; b: Butler, PA; f: Andrew CARNES; m: Mary E. MITCHELL] md. Margaret J. BURKE [20; Omaha; b: New York; f: John BURKE; m: Elizabeth KELLY] on 31 Mar 1880. Off: ENGLISH. Wit: J. TAYLOR, Lizzie BURKE.

CARNEY, John M. [25; Omaha; b: New York; f: John CARNEY; m: Bridget CAMPBELL] md. Anna LAWLER [25; Omaha; b: Iowa; f: David LAWLER; m: Mary HENNISEY] on 7 Apr 1880. Off: BARTHOLOMEW. Wit: Isaac COE of Nebraska City, Ignataius O'REILEY.

CARNEY, William H. [23; Omaha] md. Eliza PHELPS [18 and some months; Omaha] on 4 Jul 1866. Off: HASCALL. Wit: Mrs. Sarah PHELPS, D. PHELPS.

CARPENTER, Peter C. [24; Des Moines, IA; b: New York; f: Thomas W. CARPENTER; m: Ophilia R. WHEELER] md. Minnetta J.W. SNOW [19; Omaha; b: New York; f: Thatcher N. SNOW; m: Mercy W. ASHLEY] on 18 Aug 1874. Off: GARRETT. Wit: Thatcher N. SNOW; John A. KASSON, Des Moines, IA.

CARR, George [29; Florence; b: England; f: Benjamin CARR; m: Susanna DIXON] md. Amanda E. COLE [16; Florence; b: Nebraska; f: Zachariah COLE; m: Margaret STOGDON] on 11 Jun 1874 at Florence. Off: McKNIGHT. Wit: Samuel L. BRANDON; Joseph GILBERT.

CARR, Stephen A. [30; Council Bluffs] md. Mary E. OLEPHANT [20; Council Bluffs] on 30 Aug 1859 at Herndon House. Off: BRIGGS.

CARROLL, Frank B. [21; Omaha; b: OH; f: John CARROLL; m: Ester COLEMAN] md. Delia HENNESSEY [18; Omaha; b: Canada; f: John HENNESSEY] on 26 Aug 1876. Off: MULCAHY. Wit: James F. MORTON, L.E. SIMPSON.

CARROLL, George L. [26; Rock Port; b: Kentucky; f: John CARROLL; m: Julia Ann PROPHET] md. Eunice Malisee BOWER [16; Rock Port; b: Iowa; f: Silas BOWER; m: Mary A. TRUXELL] on 21 Feb 1871 at the residence of PECK. Off: PECK. Wit: Mrs. Sarah NEAL; Margaret F. PECK; both "my residence". Age of consent given by bride's father, witness to signature Sylvester BOWER.

CARROLL, Martin [21; Omaha] md. Louisa HEANY [18; Omaha] on 3 Jan 1869 at the Catholic Church. Off: O'GORMAN. Wit: Julia HEANY, W.W. FRISBY.

CARROLL, Patrick [40; Omaha; b: Ireland; f: Peter CARROLL; m: Mary ROONEY] md. Mrs. Anne GLEASON [37; Omaha; b: Canada; f: Thomas HAWKINS; m: Mary O'BRYNE] on 4 Nov 1874 at the Roman Catholic Cathedral. Off: BYRNE. Wit: Patrick M. MULLEN; Anne QUIGLEY.

CARSTENS, Bernard [31; Omaha; b: Germany; f: Hans CARTSTENS; m: Margaret KOCH] md. Dorothea KOBARK [18; Omaha; b: Germany; f: Henry KOBARK; m: Sophia SIEVERS] on 17 Aug 1873. Off: HIGENDORF. Wit: Henry MOELLER; August CARSTENS.

CARTER, John [22; Washington Co.] and Frances L. YOUNG [22; Washington Co.] license issued on 29 Jan 1859. No marriage record. Off: BRIGGS.

CARY, Patrick [32; Omaha; b: ME; f: Patrick CARY; m: Ann McCANNON] md. Mrs. Mary DORAN [37; Omaha; b: Ireland; f: John HUGHES; m: Mary McCORMICK] on 17 Jan 1881 at St. Philomena's Church. Off: ENGLISH. Wit: P. RYAN, Miss M. FURLONG.

CASE, James A. [22; Omaha; b: Ohio; f: Flavious CASE; m: Ellen SLOAN] md. Melinda COATES [18; Omaha; b: Boston, MA; f: McKinsey COATES; m: Melinda FRISHOUER] on 26 Mar 1872. Off: TOWNSEND. Wit: C.A. BALDWIN; V.H. COFFMAN.

CASE, William Page [30; Sidney, NE; b: New York; f: James A. CASE; m: Hannah PAGE] md. Susie H. PEASE [39; Yankton Agency, Dakota Territory; b: Ohio; f: Sylvester PEASE; m: Maria HARTTE] on 18 Sep 1879. Off: MILLSPAUGH. Wit: Mrs. Mollie HUMBELIN, Rev. Robert DOHERTY.

CASEY, Christopher [22; Omaha; b: OH; f: Stephen CASEY; m: Maggie SANNOT] and Marion PICKARD [18; Omaha; b: NE; f: Lonama W. PICKARD; m: Catie BOYER] license issued on 17 Jul 1881. No marriage record. Off: SMITH. Affidavit signed by Eugene PICKARD.

CASEY, Henry [colored; 28; Omaha; b: Pennsyvania; f: Benjamine CASEY (CASY); m: Susan ISAACS] md. Caroline DUMAN or DUMAR [colored; 28; Omaha; b: Indiana] on 1 Oct 1869. Off: KERMOTT. Wit: J.H. CURREY (CURRY); Mrs. A.R. KERMOTT.

CASEY, John (or Thomas) [28; Omaha; b: MA; f: John CASEY; m: Mary NOLAN] md. Ellen CHASE [18; Omaha; b: IA; f: Isaac CHASE; m: Mary LUDLOW] on 10 Dec 1876. Off: ANDERSON. Wit: N. KRIEBS, Geo. C. BASSETT. T.P. HANLONG, n.p. signed the affidavit. Marriage filed 20 Dec 1876.

CASEY, John [25; Omaha; b: Massachusetts; f: John CASEY; m: Margaret NOLAN] md. Ellen CHILTON [24; Omaha; b: Utah; f: Isaac CHILTON; m: Ann WATKINS] on 6 Oct 1874. Off: PEABODY. Wit: John ANDERSON; Mrs. Mattie ROBBINS.

CASEY, John [28; Omaha; b: MA; f: John CASEY; m: Mary NALAN] md. Ellen CHASE [18; Omaha; b: IA; f: J. CHASE; m: Mary J. GUARD] on 10 Dec 1876. Off: ANDERSON. Wit: N. KRIEBS, Geo. C. BASSET.

CASEY, Thomas J. [31; Omaha; b: Ireland; f: Michael CASEY; m: Margaret McCANN] md. Kate CARMODY [22; Omaha; b: Ireland; f: Stephen CARMODY;

m: Mary RYAN] on 24 Jun 1879 at Holy Family Church. Off: QUINN. Wit: Thomas MULCHAY, Kitie GENTLEMAN.

CASSIDY, Edward [24; Douglas Co.; b: Illinois; f: Philip CASSIDY; m: Margaret PHALON] and Mary POLLARD [19; Douglas Co.; b: Illinois; f: Thomas POLLARD; m: Catharine BUENS] license issued on 26 Oct 1877. No marriage record. Off: PEABODY.

CASSIDY, Henry [29; Douglas Co.] and Ann DONNELLY [26; Douglas Co.] license issued on 18 Mar 1858. No marriage record. Off: BRIGGS.

CASTLETON, William [32; Omaha; b: England; f: Joseph CASTLETON; m: Mary SMITH] md. Ellen MORRIS [21 or 24; Omaha; b: England; f: Barthomolew MORRIS; m: Rebacka GARFIELD] on 23 Jan 1871 at George MEDLOCK's residence. Off: MEDLOCK. Wit: Jesse BROADBENT; Mrs. Ellen RICHARDSON.

CASTNER, John [26; Omaha; b: Bohemia; f: Thomas CASTNER; m: Barbara BLAHOW] md. Elizabeth CILIAN [30; Omaha; b: Bohemia; f: Jacob CILIAN; m: Anna] on 14 May 1874. Off: HALD. Wit: Anton JANSEN; Christian LAVTEN.

CATLIN, Charles F. [25; Omaha] md. Josephine HOMAN [24; Omaha] on 7 Jan 1867 at G.W. HOMAN's house. Off: VAN ANTWERP. Wit: George WALLACE, J. BAKER, Gen. and Mrs. MYERS.

CATLIN, Robert [25; Omaha; colored; b: Pennsylvania; f: Philip CATLIN; m: Elizabeth TRUMAN] md. Mrs. Mary Jane GRAVES [22; Omaha; colored; b: Virginia; f: Lee CARTER; m: Alcinda PETTIS] on 12 Feb 1873. Off: TOWNSEND. Wit: Benjamin H. BARROWS; George ARMSTRONG.

CATTLE, Henry A. [30; Fremont; b: Augusta, ME; f: Charles CATTLE; m: Eliza COY] md. Rebecca KULER [27; Fremont; b: Illinois; f: Joseph KULER] on 10 Jan 1871. Off: GIBSON. Wit: W.H. CADER; Dennis LONERGAN.

CAVANAUGH, Patrick [31; Omaha; b: Ireland; f: Patrick CAVANAUGH; m: Mary WILLIAMS] md. Hannah LEARY [23; Omaha; b: Ireland; f: Patrick LEARY; m: Johanah MONDABLE] on 23 May 1870. Off: CURTIS. Wit: Patrick McELLIGOTT; Maria CORCORAN.

CAYTON, James G. [Elkhorn, Douglas Co.] md. Almeda CLARK [Elkhorn, Douglas Co.] on 8 Mar 1864 at the residence of the bride's father. Off: PICHARD, (PRICHARD). Wit: O.P. CLARK, S.S. CLARK.

CEARY, Hugh [29; Omaha; b: Ireland; f: Thomas CEARY; m: Ellen CARROL] md. Mary LEAHY [25; Omaha; b: Ireland; f: Daniel LEAHY; m: Ellen GAVEN] on 9 Aug 1876 at the Roman Catholic Cathedral. Off: JENNETTE. Wit: Edward McGUIRK, Ellen DONAGHUE.

CEDERLIND, John A. [29; Omaha; b: Sweden; f: Nels BANGSTON; m: Lena NELSON] md. Louisa A. LEION [21; Omaha; b: Sweden; f: Gustavus LEION; m: Lena ANDERSON] on 16 May 1881. Off: FOGELSTROM. Wit: N.P. NILSEN, Nelly BENSON.

CENTER, Maitland [35; Omaha] md. Maria MORRIS [27; Omaha] on 17 Mar 1868. Off: STUCK. Wit: Mathew M. HAWES, James W. MAGHER.

CESSIN, Carl [28; Omaha; b: Germany; f: F. CESSIN; m: Augusta LINDTSTED] md. Lena MELCHER [19; Omaha; b: Germany; f: Frederick MELCHER; m: Frederiki BUSH] on 16 Sep 1880. Off: BENEKE. Wit: J.H. STEIN, Wenzel NISTEL.

CHADWICK, Willis T. [29; Lincoln Co.; b: New York; f: David CHADWICK; m: Fidelia PARISH] md. Angie HOLMES [26; Mercer Co., IL; b: England; f: William HOLMES; m: Hannah LAWLEY] on 1 Jan 1877 at Grand Central Hotel. Off: PARDEE. Wit: Geo. THRALL, Hannah HOLMES.

CHALFANT, John [29; Cass Co.] md. Lena M. GANT (GANTT) [22; Omaha] on the afternoon of 19 Apr 1868 at Daniel GNAT's (GANTT) residence. Off: LEMON. Wit: Daniel GANT (GANTT) and family, Rev. Jesse L. FORT, et al.

CHALMERS, Joseph Harvey [22; North Bend, NE; b: Illinois; f: Wm. CHALMERS; m: Elvira J. MACKEY] md. Alice M. WALKER [22; Ainsworth, IA; b: Iowa; f: Thomas WALKER; m: Rosa M. COMIN] on 24 Dec 1879 at the Canfield house. Off: INCHES. Wit: H. Howard HOWE, Mrs. Geo. CANFIELD.

CHAMBERLIN, E.B. [23; Council Bluffs, IA; b: Michigan; f: S.P. CHAMBERLIN; m: Emma PARMLEY] md. Malinda RUSSELL [19; b: Nebraska; f: James RUSSELL; m: Eliza DRISCOLL] on 15 Feb 1878. Off: WILLIS. Wit: Charles SCHLANCK, Stephen N. MEALIO.

CHAMBERS, William [38; Omaha] md. Sarah GARVEY [43; Omaha] on 18 Feb 1867. Off: EGAN. Wit: James McEVOY, Honora QUINN.

CHANDLER, E.B. md. Clara D. KENNEDY [Florence] on 15 Mar 1865 at the house of the bride's father, in Florence. Off: VAN ANTWERP. Wit: Mary W. KENNEDY, Lieut. Geo. O. WILLIAMS.

CHAPMAN, A.Y.[G.] [36; Omaha] md. Nellie or Nettie BIRD [24; Omaha] on 20 Jun 1868. Off: KERMOTT. Wit: Mrs. Amanda R. KERMOTT, Frank R. KERMOTT.

CHAPMAN, Hugh [41; Omaha; b: Ireland; f: William CHAPMAN; m: Elizabeth IRELAND] md. Emily BARNACLE [19; Omaha; b: England; f: Richard BARNACLE; m: Louisa SMITH] on 25 Dec 1871. Off: LYTLE. Wit: D. MONROE; Wm. HOLIDAY.

CHAPMAN, John [22; Washington Co.] md. Martha J. WILSON [17; Washington Co.] on 5 Mar 1868 at KUHNS' residence. Off: KUHNS. Wit: William WILSON, John H. BRACKIN. Age consent, father of the bride being present.

CHAPMAN, William Laub [31; Chapman; b: Bavaria; f: Philip LAUB; m: Anna Maria GRAVE] md. Margaret (Maggie) DONOVEN [20; Chapman; b: Ireland; f: John DONOVEN; m: Jane HICKEY] on 1 Oct 1874 at the Roman Catholic Bishop's residence. Off: BYRNE. Wit: James VIEREGG, Lone Tree U.P.R.R.; Catharine RONAN, Bishop's House. (In index as CHAPMAN -- probably in error, as they are "of Chapman, Nebraska").

CHARLES, Warry I. [21; Omaha; b: China; f: Main CHARLES; m: Luida THOMAS] md. Mary E. WHITING [18; Omaha; b: Salt Lake, Utah Territory; f: William WHITING; m: Dora WHITING] on 14 Mar 1876. Off: WEIS. Wit: Julius ROEDER, L.B. ARNOLD. Park GODWIN signed the affidavit. Note: This is a chinaman, the first in the history of Nebraska married to a white woman. (There is a small, unflattering drawing of a "Chinaman.")

CHARVOZ, Louis "Lew" [22; b: Switzerland; f: John CHARVOZ; m: Anna M. BOVIN] and Mary HENRY [26; b: Kentucky; f: Robert H. HENRY; m: Bridget O. KANE] license issued on 27 Nov 1878. No marriage record. Off: HANLON.

CHASE, M.L. [39; Quincy, IL; b: Quincy, IL; f: Charles CHASE; m: Rebecca CATHER] md. E.J. READER [35; Quincy, IL; b: Quincy, IL; f: Daniel READER] on 3 Apr 1876. Off: BRITT. Wit: Mrs. S.J. BRITT, Mrs. A.J. SHEPARD.

CHASTE, Eugene [22; Omaha; b: France; f: Eugene CHASTE; m: Katie WALL] md. Mary SCHWABATA [20; Omaha; b: Bohemia; f: John SCHWABATA; m: Josephine] on 14 Oct 1875. Off: PEABODY. Wit: Dr. P. LIEBER, Lena LENBURG.

CHENEY, Charles [26; Omaha; b: VT; f: S.S. CHENEY; m: Martha FARINGTON] md. Maggie FLEMING [19; Omaha; b: Scotland; f: Mitchel FLEMING; m: Isabella BENNET] on 16 Sep 1875. Off: SHERRILL. Wit: Mitchell FLEMING, Mrs. Mary J. SHERRILL.

CHERRY, Thomas G. [21; Omaha; b: Ohio; f: Matthias H. CHERRY; m: Harriet H. BALDWIN] and Mary B. CHESSMAN [14; Omaha; b: Indiana; f: John L. CHESSMAN; m: Harriet DORAN] affidavit issued on 19 May 1873. Off: TOWNSEND.

CHEVAUX, Mari Louis Emile [26; Omaha; b: Switzerland; f: Mark CHEVAUX; m: Harriet ROULAET] md. Euphrosine BOAND, nee ALUSSY [19; Omaha; b: Switzerland; f: Francois BOAND; m: Harriet CHEVAUX] on 28 Jun 1872. Off: TOWNSEND. Wit: Albert PLAN, Sidney, NE; Andre CAMMENZIND.

CHILD, John A. [40; Portland, OR; b: England; f: John A. CHILD; m: Sarah A. CULLINS] md. Josephine C. ROBERTSON [25; Indianapolis, IN; b: IN; f: Lewis TRINKLEY; m: Caroline SCHMIDLAP] on 23 Dec 1876. Off: MILLSPAUGH. Wit: Henry GOULD, Lislie (?) Sister (?) Mary HEYDEN.

CHILD, P.C. [30; Illinois; b: Massachusetts; f: Rensler CHILD; m: Marcia MARCY] md. Martha BOEMAN [27; Busiras (Bucyrus?), OH; b: Ohio; f: John BOEMAN; m: Jemima BRADLEY] on 2 Aug 1874. Off: PEABODY. Wit: Mary C. PEABODY; Amanda J. BOEMAN, Busiras, OH.

CHOLLMAN, John [26; Omaha; b: Sweden; f: S.M. CHOLLMAN] md. Augusta ALLSINE [20; Omaha; b: Sweden; f: R.G. ALLSINE; m: Margaret OLSEN] on 30 Jul 1870. Off: GIBSON. Wit: Henry CHOLLMAN; Frank A. HULLMAN.

CHOLMAN, Henry [26; Omaha; b: Sweden; f: Marcus CHOLMAN; m: Maria PETTERSON] md. Mary OCANDEL [20; Omaha; b: Sweden; f: Gabriel OCANDEL; m: Magdaline NILSON] on 29 Nov 1873. Off: RING. Wit: John CHALMAN; Frane LINDBERG.

CHRIST, John B. [39; Sidney; b: Ohio; f: Jonathan CHRIST; m: Susanna BIEBER] md. Ellen L. LOWRY [22; Omaha; b: Iowa; f: Patrick LOWRY; m: Mary MURPHY] on 27 May 1880. Off: ENGLISH. Wit: J. LOWRY, Maggie LOWRY.

CHRISTEN, Peter [26; Omaha] md. Catharine ASENDORF [21; Omaha] on 15 Jul 1867 at the parsonage. Off: KUHNS. Wit: Mr. and Mrs. Frederick DALLONE.

CHRISTENSEN, Anders [29; Omaha] md. Sophia SORENSEN [24; Omaha] on 7 Mar 1869. Off: LARSON. Wit: Hans P. DIEDRICHSEN, Johannes SORRENSON.

CHRISTENSEN, Christian [23; Omaha; b: Denmark; f: Christian HANSEN] md. Mary POLSEN [20; Omaha; b: Denmark; f: Gens POLSEN] on 27 Nov 1869. Off: KUHNS. Wit: John AHMANSON, John HANSEN.

CHRISTENSEN, John [24; Omaha; b: Denmark; f: Christen CHRISTENSEN; m: Annie PETERSON] md. Mary ALBERTSON [19; Omaha; b: Denmark; f: Jens ALBERTSON; m: Mary BROWN] on 5 Nov 1870. Off: McCAGUE. Wit: Paul HARMAN; J.L. PATTON.

CHRISTENSEN, Julius [24; Omaha; b: Denmark; f: Christ RASMUSEN; m: Bjerde Sophia] md. Ann Christine HANSEN [20; Omaha; b: Denmark; f: Andres HANSEN] on 25 May 1869. Off: DENMURE. Wit: Peter A. HANSON, Jens HANSON.

CHRISTENSEN, Ole J. [26; Omaha; b: b: Denmark; f: Jens P. CHRISTENSEN; m: Hedevig JENSDOTTER] md. Elizabeth C. PETERSON [27; Omaha; b: Denmark; f: Pater N. RASMUSSEN; m: Agnethe LEMSDOTTER] on 23 Feb 1881. Off: GYDESEN. Wit: William ANDERSEN, Chr. HANSEN.

CHRISTENSEN, Peter Anton [23; Council Bluffs] md. Inger Catharine NIELSEN [21; Omaha] on 21 Sep 1867. Off: DAM. Wit: J.C. RASMUSSEN, N. NIELSEN.

CHRISTENSEN, Peter [28; Omaha] md. Anna Elsie MICHOLSON [20; Omaha] on 2 Oct 1867 at KUHNS' residence. Off: KUHNS. Wit: Mrs. H.W. KUHNS, Charlotte E. CLARK.

CHRISTENSEN, Stephen [26; Omaha; b: Denmark; f: Christ JENSEN; m: Karran SORENSEN] md. Mary A. SORENSEN [23; Omaha; b: Denmark; f: Soren CHRISTINSEN; m: Johanna ZIMMIRMANSON] on 13 Apr 1871. Off: LARSON. Wit: John A. ALLMEN, Saunders Co.; Mrs. Johanna C. LARSON.

CHRISTENSON, Jens Peter [37; Omaha; b: Denmark; f: Christian JENSEN; m: Maria SORENSDOTTER] md. Mrs. Clara CARLSDOTTER [40; Omaha; b: Sweden; f: Carl Peter JOHNSON; m: Catharine ANDUSDOTTER] on 11 Oct 1880. Off: STENBERG. Wit: Carl GRANDPRE, Jens HANSEN.

CHRISTENSON, Louis J. [28; Omaha] md. Anne LARSON [21; Omaha] on 30 Jul 1867. Off: DAM. Wit: N. THERKELDSON, J.V. JENSEN.

CHRISTENSON, Nels J. [23; Omaha; b: Denmark; f: Harbo CHRISTENSON; m: Maria NELSON] md. Caroline SCHOW [26; Omaha; b: Denmark; f: Hans Jenseon SCHOW; m: Thilde C. BECK] on 12 Feb 1881. Off: GYDESEN. Wit: Chr. PETERSON, James SCHOW.

CHRISTENSON, Stephen [31; Omaha; b: Denmark; f: Christian JENSON; m: Caren SORENSON] md. Anna HANSON [21; Omaha; b: Denmark; f: Hans RASMUSSEN; m: Else NELSON] on 18 Dec 1875. Off: HANSEN. Wit: J.S. BENZON, Mrs. Anna D. BENZON.

CHRISTIANSEN, Dennis Miller [25; Omaha; b: Denmark, Europe; f: Chris JENSEN; m: Mary ANDERSEN] md. Johanna Christina MONK [25; Omaha; b: Denmark, Europe; f: Soren MONK; m: Anna PETERSEN] on 3 Nov 1871. Off: ERDALL. Wit: Lars JORGENSEN; Peder MONK.

CHRISTIANSEN, James H. [26; Omaha; b: Denmark; f: Christian W. NELSON; m: Anna LARSDATTER] md. Christine M. JOHNSON [23; Omaha; b: Denmark; f: Lorence JOHNSON; m: Anna Botelle JOHNSON] on 5 Sep 1879. Off: LIPE. Wit: Lizzie E. LIPE, Nellie BAVERMAN.

CHRISTIANSEN, James [29; Washington Co.; b: Denmark; f: Christian JACOBSON; m: Margaret NELSON] md. Mary LARSON [27; Omaha; b: Denmark; f: Lars PAULSEN; m: Mary LARSON] on 30 Oct 1877. Off: PEABODY. Wit: Joseph QUINLAN, George SHIELDS.

CHRISTIANSEN, John C. [26; b: Denmark; f: C. JENSON; m: Johanna M. JENSDOTTER] md. Olive C. RASMUSSEN [22; b: Denmark; f: Andrews RASMUSSEN; m: Anna CASPERSON] on 24 Dec 1878. Off: HANSEN. Wit: Niels JENSEN, Mrs. Anna JENSEN.

CHRISTIANSEN, Peter C. [48; Douglas Co.] md. Martie PAULSEN [32; Douglas Co.] on 14 Sep 1862 at Charles P. BIRKETT's residence. Off: ARMSTRONG. Wit: Mr. and Mrs. Charles P. BIRKETT.

CHRISTIANSON, John C. [51; Omaha; b: Denmark; f: Christian CHRISTIANSON; m: Dorothea THOMAS] md. Johanna ANDERSON [33; Omaha; b: Sweden; f: Andres JOHNSON; m: Christina JOHNSDOTTER] on 20 Jan 1872. Off: TOWNSEND. Wit: Hans OLSEN; John SAMUELSON.

CHRISTIANSON, John [27; Omaha; b: Denmark; f: Paul CHRISTIANSON; m: Anna B. MORITSEN] md. Anna M. GRIESEN [20; Omaha; b: Denmark; f: Andrew GRIESEN; m: Niette LORENTSEN] on 22 Jul 1879. Off: BERTESEN. Wit: M. HANSEN, Frederik NIELSEN.

CHRISTIANSON, Niels [26; b: Denmark; f: C. CHRISTIANSON; m: Anne LARSDATER] md. Ane Maria Sophia NIELSON [26; b: Denmark; f: Niels Jenson KLINGENBERG; m: Catharine Marthe FILSUF] on 28 Sep 1878. Off: STENBERG. Wit: M. TOFT, Andrew Nelson KJEIR.

CHRISTIANSON, Peter J. [28; Omaha; b; Denmark; f: Christian OLESON; m: Anna

CHRISTIANSON] md. Anna J. ANDERSON [28; Omaha; b; Denmark; f: Andus ERICKSON; m: Johanna JENSEN] on 27 Nov 1880, Vor Frelsers Church. Off: GYDESEN. Wit: Erik ANDERSON, Niels JENSEN.

CHRISTIE, James [21; Omaha; b: Pennsylvania; f: James CHRISTIE; m: Elizabeth STOTT] md. Frances E. LOTT [19; Omaha; b: Pennsylvania; f: Charles J. LOTT; m: Elizabeth WILSON] on 13 Dec 1877. Off: JAMESON. Wit: Mrs. M[argaret] W. JAMESON, Rev. J.A. HUDSON of Plattsmouth.

CHRISTOFFERSEN, Anders [Andrew] [28; Omaha; b: Denmark; f: Christopher LARSON; m: Marren LARSON] md. Mattie M. HANSEN [24; Omaha; b: Denmark; f: Christ HANSEN; m: Sophia NELSON] on 4 Apr 1877. Off: FISHER. Wit: E.M. FISHER, Kitty MORRIS.

CHRISTOPHER, James [25; Omaha; b: Ireland; f: John CHRISTOPHER; m: Kate O'KEEFE] md. Kate M. PHELAN [22; Omaha; b: Ireland; f: John PHELAN; m: Mary RAHER] on 18 Nov 1877. Off: QUINN. Wit: J.C. LUCAS, Maggie KEEFE.

CHRISTY, Edward [21; Omaha; b: Iowa; f: Cornelius CHRISTY; m: Priscilla McKOY] md. Kate CROSS [21; Omaha; b: New York; f: Simon CROSS; f: Charlotta MILLER] on 10 Jun 1879 at Omaha. Off: WEISS. Wit: Mrs. Dora WEISS, J.M. CORWELL.

CHUMBLY, J.C. [34; Omaha; b: VA; f: Allen CHUMBLY; m: Nancy GLASCOW] md. Flora TILLMAN [24; Omaha; b: NY; f: Jacob TILLMAN; m: Maria WESTBROOK] on 17 May 1881. Off: STENBERG. Wit: Wm. H. BROWN, Mrs. Jennie BROWN.

CLAIBORNE, Charles B.E. [37; Glenwood, IA; b: England; f: Richard B. CLAIBORNE; m: Sarah WOODWORTH] md. Mrs. Rose SHEPPARDSON [33; Glenwood, IA; b: Massachusetts; f: A. THOMPSON; m: Olive GLEASON] on 2 Mar 1870. Off: KUHNS. Wit: Mrs. H.W. KUHNS; Mrs. P. CHRISTENSEN.

CLAIR, John [23; Omaha; b: Buffalo, NY; f: James CLAIR; m: Margaret FANNING] md. Mary REDDEN [21; Omaha; b: Ireland; f: John REDDEN; m: Alice DINGLE] on 21 Jan 1873. Off: CURTIS. Wit: Louis HUCK; Josephine VEZ.

CLAPP, Charles M. [23; Omaha; b: Massachusetts; f: Moody CLAPP; m: Flora GODING] md. Emma L. GOERNER [23; Omaha; b; Germany; f: Frederick GOERNER; m: Bertha J. LESIR] on 20 Nov 1880. Off: BAUGHER. Wit: Laura GOERNER, G.P. MARTIN, both of Douglas Co.

CLARE, Charles [28; Omaha; b: Kentucky; f: John CLARE; m: Elizabeth HOLT] md. Arena ALBEN [31; Omaha; b: Illinoia; f: James ALBEN; m: Margaret Ann MAY] on

10 Mar 1879. Off: BENEKE. Wit: Mrs. J.C. ETZENSPERGER, John SHEPHARD.

CLARK, Edward Mills [26; Omaha; b: New York; f: James CLARK; m: Rebecca JUDSON] md. Mrs. Sarah E. MILLS [23; Omaha; b: Indiana; f: John FISHER; m: Nancy BURK] on 6 Sep 1878. Off: ANDERSON. Wit: E.D. SPEARS, James SHEPARD.

CLARK, Edward [34; Omaha; b: England; f: Edward CLARK; m: Sarah SAGE] md. Helena LEISGE [21; Omaha; b: Germany; f: Conrad LEISGE; m: Mary PLAACK] on 24 May 1876 at St. Marks Church. Off: PATERSON. Wit: Mrs. Anna SHERLOCK, Mrs. Wm. CLEBURNE.

CLARK, Edwin J. [24; Council Bluffs] md. Kate J. DENNIS [18; Omaha] on 10 Oct 1866. Off: KNOTTS. Wit: D.B. CLARK, J.B. DENNIS.

CLARK, Edwin K. [26; Omaha; b: Cincinatti, OH; f: Justin S. CLARK; m: Mary J. MILLER] md. Mary E. TRUMBULL [23; Omaha; b: Springfield, IL; f: Benjamin TRUMBULL; m: Keziah POTTS] on 18 Jul 1871. Off: SHERRILL. Wit: James S. GIBSON; John D. PREST.

CLARK, Elam [56; b: Indiana; f: William CLARK; m: Esther JONES] md. Mrs. Lizzie M. BOWLES [35; b: Missouri; f: Martin B. BOWLES; m: Jane LAMPKIN] on 7 Nov 1878. Off: HARSHA. Wit: Sara HENDERSON, Edith E. CLARK.

CLARK, George W. [25; Omaha; b: Ohio; f: John C. CLARK; m: Margaret LYNCH] md. Elizabeth E. STUBEN [17; Omaha; b: Indiana; f: John STUBEN; m: Amelia ROAHKA] on 14 Oct 1881. Off: SHERRILL. Wit: Gussie W. BOEHME, Alvina ROSHKA.

CLARK, Henry S. [32; Baltimore, MD] md. Susan McKENNA [20; Omaha] on 21 Jan 1869. Off: HYDE. Wit: S.H. HASKINS, ---- DOUGHERTY.

CLARK, James [30; Colfax Co.; b: Ireland; f: Steven CLARK; m: Ellen WILLIAMS] md. Mary CRONAN [20; Omaha; b: Ireland; f: John CRONAN; m: Bridget RYAN] on 8 Feb 1874 at the Roman Catholic Cathedral. Off: BYRNE. Wit: Albert HEIRLZLIN; Barbara HAFNER.

CLARK, John [28; Omaha; b: Virginia; f: Josiah CLARK; m: Fannie CAMPBELL or COPBELL] md. Ellen McGUE [22; Omaha; b: Ireland; f: Terrance McGUE; m: Briget CURTIS] on 14 Jul 1870. Off: KERMOTT. Wit: Mrs. A.R. KERMOTT; H.H. CLARK.

CLARK, Joseph [27; b: CT; f: Joseph CLARK; m: Roda SWAN] md. Minnie M. HAWES [19; b: MA; f: Abram HAWES; m: Sarah A. TURNER] on 11 Oct 1876. Off: SHERRILL. Wit: A.C. KINKADE, W.F. HAWES.

CLARK, Mitchell [colored; Omaha] md. Maria GARNER [colored; Omaha] on 19 Jan 1865 at KUHNS' residence. Off: KUHNS. Wit: Eliza PATRICK, Mrs. C. POWEL, et al.

CLARK, Noah S. [27; Omaha; b: Haddam, CT; f: Joseph CLARK; m: Rhoda SWAN] md. Minnie M. HAWES [19; Omaha; b: Watertown, MA; f: Abram HAWES; m: Sarah TURNER] on 12 Oct 1876. Off: SHERRILL. Wit: A.C. KINKADE, Auburn, CA, W.T. HAWES. J.M. SPENCER signed the affidavit.

CLARK, Pierce [41; Grand Island] md. Susan SEWARD [32; Grand Island] on 30 Nov 1867 at the Catholic Cathedral. Off: O'GORMAN. Wit: Edmund CORWIN.

CLARK, Simon B. [29; Omaha; b: Pennsylvania; f: Miles J. CLARK; m: Sarah M. BROTHERLINE] md. Elizabeth BAILEY [22; Omaha; b: Illinois; f: John BAILEY; m: Josphine VERMIRE] on 26 Oct 1880. Off: WRIGHT. Wit: B.C.E. WESTERDAHL, Rodney DUTCHER.

CLARK, Thomas H. [46; PA; b: PA; f: Christopher CLARK; m: Catharine MURPHY] md. Elizabeth (Libbie) M. RILEY [36; Omaha; b: PA; f: Corneliue RILEY; m: Sarah A. LAUGHLIN] on 12 Jan 1881 at St. Philomena's Church. Off: ENGLISH. Wit: F. DELLONE, Statia DROWLEY.

CLARK, Thomas [35; Omaha] md. Christena GUNTER [27; Chicago, IL] on 8 Mar 1868. Off: KUHNS. Wit: Charles S. GUNTER, Sophia SEYLER, et al.

CLARK, W.F. [21; Omaha; b: Illinois; f: H. CLARK; m: Martha M. RISLEY] md. Mary KNAPP [16 or 17; Omaha; b: Germany; f: Simon KNAPP; m: Mary T. SCHILLINGER] on 5 Jun 1879 at West Omaha. Off: SLAUGHTER. Wit: Albert M. CLARK, W.B. SLAUGHTER, Jr. both of West Omaha. Application signed by A.M. CLARK.

CLARK, William H. [26; Council Bluffs; b: Jamestown, NY f: Samuel R. CLARK; m: Minerva COLE] md. Elizabeth BAKER [24; Council Bluffs; b: Germany; f: (Charles WAGNER, crossed out) Conrad BAKER; m: Elizabeth POPERT] on 25 Dec 1872. Off: TOWNSEND. Wit: George W. AMBROSE; William O. BARTHOLOMEW.

CLARK, William R. [22; Omaha; b: Pennsylvania; f: John CLARK; m: Minerva RIGGS] and Carolina E. VAN KEUREN [26; Omaha; b: New York; f: Benjamin VAN KEUREN] license issued on 20 Aug 1871. Off: GIBSON.

CLARK, William [22; Platte Valley Pct., Douglas Co.; b: England; f: Thomas CLARK; m: Jane GOLDSWORTH] md. Fannie GIBBS [20; Platte Valley Pct., Douglas Co.; b: England; f: Thomas GIBBS; m: Betsey BRYANT] on 4 Jul 1873 at ADAIR's residence. Off: ADAIR. Wit: Mrs. Mary A. ADAIR; Mrs. Ann RAPP.

CLASSEN, Peter [33; Douglas Co.; b: Germany; f: Peter CLASSEN; m: Metta LOHSE] md. Amelia A. SCHEIBE [25; Douglas Co.; b: Germany; f: John G. LOHMANN; m: Johanna C. MILLER] on 25 Apr 1876. Off: HILGENDORF. Wit: Julius SCHWANEBERG, Charles BROWN.

CLAUSEN, Fred [30; Elk Horn, Douglas Co., NE; b: Germany; f: Hans CLAUSEN; m: Michael ROVER] md. Rekena MUSSER in Chicago Precinct on 16 Feb 1878. Off: ROBERTS. Wit: Cyrus BALDWIN, Gustave REASONER both of Chicago Precinct. Affiant Andrew PATRICK.

CLAUSEN, Henry [28] md. Mary A. ANTHONESSEN [23; Omaha] on 9 Nov 1866 at KUHNS' residence. Off: KUHNS. Wit: Col. BAUMER, Mrs. H.W. KUHNS, et al.

CLAUSEN, Peter [25; Omaha; b: Denmark; f: Lars CLAUSEN; m: Christine LOCKSTOER] md. Mattie M. PETERSON [19; Omaha; b: Denmark; f: Christian PETERSON; m: Margarethe BINMAN] on 15 Aug 1881. Off: STENBERG. Wit: William HANSEN, Jorgen FINMANT.

CLAUSSEN, Jurgen [31; Douglas Co.; b: Holstein, Germany; f: Claus Jens CLAUSSEN; m: Hannah M. GREBE] md. Paulina C. RODEWALD [25; Douglas Co.; b: Holstein, Germany; f: John F. RODEWALD; m: Ann C. TIEDJE] on 4 Jun 1870. Off: KUHNS. Wit: Mrs. H.W. KUHNS; Anna CATHERWOOD.

CLAWSON, John H. [35; Fremont; b: Denmark; f: Erastus H. CLAWSON; m: Ann MARTINSON] md. Nellie BERGGREN [28 or 31; Fremont; b: Sweden; f: Schwenson BERGGREN; m: Johannah NELSON] on 9 Aug 1869. Off: LARSON. Wit: Swen HEDENSBERG of Saunders Co., Christian PETERSON.

CLAWSON, William [21; b: Illinois; f: W.H. CLAWSON; m: Margaret KENNEDY] md. Martha GUILL [22; b: Iowa; f: James GUILL; m: Julia DORVIS] on 23 Dec 1878. Off: WEISS. Wit: Andrew MOYER, Mrs. Mary MOYER.

CLAY, Henry [33; Council Bluffs; b: Rhode Island; f: Giles CLAY; m: Lydia

CAPWELL] md. Maggie MORSE [33; Council Bluffs; b: Illinois; f: John MORSE] on 27 May 1870. Off: MORTON. Wit: Mary A. DUNLOP; E.J. BREMER.

CLAY, William [30; Omaha] md. Mrs. Charlotte ALEXANDER [36; Omaha] on 24 Mar 1869 at GLOVER's office. Off: GLOVER. Wit: O.S. WOOD, Mrs. O.S. WOOD.

CLEARY, Edward [22; b: Ireland; f: Nicholas CLEARY; m: Margaret McDONALD] md. Ellen HEGGERTY [23; b: Ireland; f: John HEGGERTY] on 16 Jun 1878. Off: QUINN. Wit: James RYAN, Ellen SPELLMAN. Affiant signed "his mark."

CLEARY, James [28; Grand Island; b: Ireland; f: John CLEARY; m: Ann RUSSELL] md. Joanna DONAHY [26; Grand Island; b: Ireland; f: Timothy DONAHY; m: Mary SULLIVAN] on 4 May 1874 at 9th Street Cathedral. Off: BYRNE. Wit: William FRANCE; Katie O'BRIEN.

CLEARY, Michael [34 or 35; Omaha; b: Ireland; f: Nathan K. CLEARY; m: Mary KNOWLAN] md. Honora MATHER [24; Omaha; b: Ireland; f: John MATHER; m: Mary FOX] on 27 Jul 1869. Off: CURTIS. Wit: Frank NORTON, Maria COREDEN.

CLEARY, Thomas [Omaha] md. Margaret LYNCH [Omaha] on 1 Nov 1863 in the Catholic Church of Omaha. Both of legal age. Off: O'GORMAN. Wit: John C. YATES, Catharine MURRAY.

CLEGG, William [30; Sarpy Co.; b: Germany; f: John CLEGG; m: Dorothea MAVIS] md. Minnie BROCK [17; Sarpy Co.; b: Germany; f: Stephen BROCK; m: Helen STOLBORER] on 31 Oct 1875. Age consent given by father of the bride.

CLEMENS, Ashton [31; Douglas Co.] md. Philicia J. PICKARD [Douglas Co.] on 14 Oct 1868 at the residence of the bride's father. Off: KUHNS. Wit: Maggie and Mary INGALLS, Dr. PINNEY, Charles GOODRICH, et al.

CLEMMONS, William [28; Seward, NE; b: Iowa; f: Daniel CLEMMONS; m: Elizabeth McHIRRON] md. Mrs. Mary LEONARD [26; Lincoln, NE; b: Ireland; f: John MADIGAN; m: Margaret] on 1 May 1878. Off: BARTHOLOMEW. Wit: Seth COLE, F.A. HARMANN of Bloomington.

CLEMONS, George W. [34; Council Bluffs; b: Dansville, NY; f: Telemachus CLEMONS; m: Rhoda R. ROBERTS] md. Frances THORP [27; Council Bluffs; b: Illinois] on 25 Dec 1871. Off: TOWNSEND. Wit: B.E.B. KENNEDY; C.R. BOYSON, Council Bluffs.

CLIFFORD, George W. [29; Omaha] md. Elizabeth WOODING [28; Omaha] on 13 Dec 1866. Off: ROSE. Wit: Mrs. James D. WOOD, Emma ROLAND.

CLIFFORD, George W. [Douglas Co.] md. Katherine R. REMINGTON [Douglas Co.] on 24 Dec 1864 at DICKINSON's office. Off: DICKINSON. Wit: John H. KELLOM, Mrs. Jane K. SUTER.

CLIFTON, Charles [20; Douglas Co.; b: Nebraska; f: Daniel CLIFTON; m: Tabetha ALLKEIER] md. Emma CROSBY [22; Douglas Co.; b: New York; f: Thomas CROSBY; m: Lucy BIGLOW] in Chicago Precinct on 19 Aug 1878. Off: ROBERTS. Wit: P.H. BOWMAN, J.M. STEWERT. Age consent given by father of the groom, "x" his mark.

CLIFTON, Daniel [38; Chicago Pct., Douglas Co.; b: Jackson Twp, OH; f: Thomas CLIFTON; m: Nancy KIMBALL] md. Mary A. CROSBY [19; Chicago Pct., Douglas Co.; b: Racine, WI; f: Thomas CROSBY; m: Mary] on 2 Mar 1873 at Chicago, Douglas Co. Off: ROLFES. Wit: Patrick H. KEANE, Chicago, Douglas Co.; Katharine KEANE, Chicago, Douglas CO. (Bride was born 10 Jan 1854).

CLIFTON, William [21; Douglas Co.; b: Sarpy Co.; f: Daniel CLIFTON; m: Tabitha ALKIER] md. Mollie DONAHOO [17; Douglas Co.; b: Douglas Co.; f: Thomas J. DONAHOO; m: Nancy M. DIBBLE] on 17 Sep 1877 at the residence of Tom DONAHOO. Off: ROBERTS. Wit: Mr. CUNNINGHAM, Charles CLIFTON, both of Chicago Precinct. Age consent given by father of the bride.

CLINES, Michael [38; Colfax Co.; b: Ireland; f: Thomas CLINES; m: Mary RATCHFORD] md. Mrs. Jane McCOY [27; Omaha; b: Scotland; f: Archie McCOY; m: Jane FRISE] on 25 Jun 1880. Off: McCARTHY. Wit: James McCOY, Mary CASEY.

CLINTON, John [26; Omaha; b: Ireland; f: Patrick CLINTON; m: Catharine CARR] md. Hanora COLLINS [33; Omaha; b: Ireland; f: Thomas COLLINS] on 18 Oct 1869. Off: CURTIS. Wit: James BAGLEY, Elizabeth KENNELLY.

CLOSSON [CLAUSON], Emory [26; Douglas Co.] and Juliaett WILSON [Saunders Co.] license issued on 1 Mar 1869. No marriage record. Off: HYDE.

CLOWRY [CLOURY], Robert C. md. Caroline A. ESTABROOK on 29 Aug 1865 at the Lutheran Church. Off: KUHNS. Wit: Alice CLARK, Maggie INGALLS, Camie GOODWELL, Frank LEHMER, Frank MURPHY, Richard BARKELOW, et al.

COADY, Patrick [24; Omaha; b: Ireland; f: Martin COADY; m: Nancy LONG] md. Margaret HUGHES [21; Omaha; b: Ireland f: John HUGHES; m: Mary McCORMICK] on

2 Nov 1873 at the German Catholic Church. Off: GROENEBAUM. Wit: Mrs. GARETY; Mrs. KELLY.

COBB, Elisha [Monona Co., IA] md. Annie Maria McCULLOUGH [Monona Co., IA] on 2 Jun 1865 at DICKINSON's office. Off: DICKINSON. Wit: John H. KELLOM, Thos. L. SUTTON.

COBURN, William [23; Omaha] md. Savannah S. NEALY [21; Omaha] on 28 Oct 1866. Off: SLAUGHTER. Wit: John R. COX, Drusilla STEWART.

COBURN, William [31; Omaha; b: New Hampshire; f: Samuel COBURN; m: Harriet N. PETTIS] md. Annie D. SPRIGG [29; Omaha; b: Illinois; f: John C. (SPRIGG?); m: Julia A. REMANN] on 26 Nov 1874. Off: SHERRILL. Wit: L.T. SPRIGG; Belle SPRIGG.

COE, Earl B. [24; Omaha; b: NY; f: Benj. COE; m: Nancy LONSBERRY] md. Mary C. FREEMAN [23; Omaha; b: MI; f: Edward C. FREEMAN; m: Julia E. SHAW] on 28 Dec 1881. Off: SHERRILL. Wit: Gilbert N. HITCHCOCK, A.N. CHADWICK.

COFFEE, John C. [28; Omaha; b: Ireland; f: Michael COFFEE; m: Sarah MOORE] md. Bridget HURLEY [28; Omaha; b: Ireland; f: Patrick HURLEY; m: Margaret BLUM] on 3 Apr 1870. Off: CURTIS. Wit: John REIDY; Mary A. O'MARA.

COFFEIN, Charles M. [21; Omaha; b: Maine; f: William COFFEIN; m: Almira MURPHY] md. Elizabeth PETTIT [18; Omaha; b: Wisconsin; f: William PETTIT; m: Malinda DOUGLAS] on 28 Apr 1871. Off: PORTER. Wit: T.W.T. RICHARDS; J.P. BARTLETT.

COFFEY, William [24; Douglas Co.; b: Ireland f: Timothy COFFEY; m: Mary MADDEN] md. Mrs. Julia CURRAN [27; Highland Falls, Orange Co., NY; b: Ireland; f: William McGINNIS; m: Ann FITZSIMONS] on 27 Jun 1872. Off: TOWNSEND. Wit: Jacob S. SPANN; George E. PRITCHETT. (Julia CURRAN's affidavit signed by Judith COFFEY.)

COFFIN, C.M. [26; b: Maine; f: William COFFIN; m: Martha MURPHY] md. L.L. COONS [21; b: Massachusetts; f: D.B. COONS; m: Thulia THOMAS] on 21 Jun 1878. Off: STENBERG. Wit: M. TAFT, S. BURGSTROM.

COFFMAN, Franklin H. [32; Omaha; b: Ohio; f: Christin COFFMAN; m: Margaret SINER] md. Susie J. BUSHEY [18; Omaha; b: Canada; f: John BUSHEY; m: Bridget BURNES] on 4 Jul 1874 at the German Catholic Church. Off: GROENEBAUM. Wit: E. PAGE; J. BUSHEY.

COGAN, Dominick [34; Omaha; b: Ireland; f: Thomas COGAN; m: Bridget KEVLIHAN] md. Catharine SPELLMAN [22; Omaha; b: Ireland; f: John SPELLMAN; m:

Mary HELLY?] on 13 May 1880, Holy Family Church. Off: QUINN. Wit: Patrick DESMOND, Ella SPELLMAN.

COILE [KOILE], Patrick [Omaha] md. Mary GADOLA [Omaha] (1) on 15 Oct 1864 at the residence of the bride. Off: DICKINSON. Wit: Ellen RYAN, Annie NELSON, Ralf BOWMAN, Lorenzo HOBBS. They married (2) on 16 Nov 1864 at O'GORMAN's house. Off: O'GORMAN. Wit: Vincent BERKLEY, M. McCORMACK.

COKLEY, Cornelius [35; Omaha; b: Ireland; f: Patrick COKLEY; m: Catharine DRISCOLL] md. Mary LAFFIN [27; Omaha; b: Ireland; f: Patrick LAFFIN; m: Ann FRANKLIN] on 23 Nov 1879. Off: ENGLISH. Wit: J.H. FEENEY, Ellen (x) CONNORS.

COLBY, Harry [21; Exira, Audubon Co., IA; b: Beloit, WI; f: Eben COLBY; m: Mary D. POMEROY] md. Harriet LEFFINGWELL [18; Exira, Audubon Co., IA: b: Beloit, WI; f: Andrew LEFFINGWELL; m: Fannie KELLOGG] on 19 May 1873. Off: TOWNSEND. Wit: John T. ROGERS, Exira, IA; Barnabas D. BRIGGS, Exira, IA.

COLE, David [22; Omaha; b: Ireland; f: Frank COLE; m: Fanny FORBES] md. Etta E. SMITH [17; Omaha; b: Michigan; f: Newton J. SMITH; m: Susan BENEDICT] on 26 May 1880. Off: ROE of Seward. Wit: Luther A. HARMON, Mattie E. MASON.

COLE, John F. [22; Omaha; b: Pennsylvania; f: Thomas COLE; m: Mary NICHOLS] md. Norma S. MORFORD [16; Omaha; b: Pennsylvania; f: Abner T. MORFORD; m: Esther J. MAGREW] on 22 Oct 1870. Off: GIBSON. Wit: Abner T. MORFORD; James H. MORFORD, Washington Co.

COLE, John, Jr. [26; Sarpy Co.; b: Ireland; f: John COLE; m: Jane BLAIR] md. Lucilla JOHNSON [18; Sarpy Co.; b: Pennsylvania; f: John JOHNSON] on 31 Oct 1870. Off: KELLY. Wit: Geo. W. GRATH; Mr. LANCASTER, Nebraska City (or Kansas?). (COLEMAN inserted in one place, but probably error.).

COLE, Seth T. [25; Omaha] md. Justine C. MAJO [20; Omaha] on 21 Nov 1868. Off: MAY. Wit: F.W. MEYER, Mrs. C. MAY.

COLE, Zachariah [48; Florence; b: Indiana; f: Hugh COLE; m: Barbara HORNBACH] md. Mrs. Sarah NEAL [36; Florence; b: Ohio; f: Robert CLARK; m: Margaret] on 11 Jul 1874 at PECK's house. Off: PECK. Wit: A.G. BROWN, Florence; Samuel Lee BRANTON.

COLEMAN, James [40; Omaha; b: Ireland; f: Owen COLEMAN; m: Catharine NULTY] md. Bridget DUFFY [28; Omaha; b: Ireland; f: Michael DUFFY; m: Bridget EGAN] on 14 May 1873. Off: CURTIS. Wit: Michael DUFFY; Ellen BEGLEY.

COLLAMER, William N. [24; Yankton, Dakota Territory] md. Julia F. EVANS [23; Omaha] at 7:45 P.M., 3 Feb 1863 at the residence of the bride's father. Off: DIMMICK. Wit: Mr. and Mrs. Chas. B. EVANS, James BROWN, et al.

COLLETT, Austin M. [26; Omaha] md. Mary A. KRIEBS [26; Omaha] on 20 Jul 1867 at Mrs. Mary GIESLER's residence on Farnham St. Off: KUHNS. Wit: Mrs. Mary GIESLER, Mary GIESLER.

COLLINS, Edward [29; Omaha; b: Ireland; f: Patrick COLLINS; m: Mary REDDY] md. Hanorah GALVIN [23; Omaha; b: Ireland] on 30 May 1869. Off: CURTIS. Wit: John HYNES, Mary HYNES.

COLLINS, Jacob S. [43; Washington Co.] md. Hannah M. BLACKFORD [40; Washington Co.] on 11 Nov 1860. Off: SMITH. Wit: Horace SPENCER, Jane R. SMITH.

COLLINS, James L. [26; b: Philadelphia; f: James COLLINS; m: Mary SMITH] md. Mary BALLINGER [21; b: England; f: William BALLINGER; m: Elizabeth WILLIAMS] on 20 May 1878. Off: FISHER. Wit: Mr. and Mrs. DOVE.

COLLINS, Jerry [22; Omaha; b: Ireland; f: Dennis COLLINS; m: Mary CALAGAN] md. Delia CUNNINGHAM [21; Omaha; b: Ireland] on 14 Nov 1869. Off: CURTIS. Wit: James W. DRENNEN, Mary HIGGINS.

COLLINS, John S. [22; Memphis, TN; b: Emory, VA; f: Charles COLLINS; m: Harriet N. HART] md. Mary BURNHAM [21; Omaha; b: Manch Chunk?, PA; f: Horace B. BURNHAM; m: Ruth A. JACKSON] on 3 Jul 1873. Off: GARRETT. Wit: Hon. George W. DOANE; Gen. George D. RUGGLES.

COLLINS, John [22; Douglas Co.] md. J. FITZSIMONS [23; Douglas Co.] on 5 Mar 1867. Off: EGAN. Wit: Patrick BEGLEY, Mary DOWD.

COLLINS, Thomas [34; Omaha; b: Ireland; f: Thomas COLLINS; m: Catherine LANG] md. Margaret CASEY [26; Omaha; b: Ireland; f: Michael CASEY; m: Alice REGAN] on 20 Aug 1871. Off: CURTIS. Wit: Michael McDONALD; Margaret DEE.

COLLINS, Thomas [black; 21; St. Joseph, MO; b: Missouri; f: Albert COLLINS; m: Anne MUMFORD] md. Belle STITT [black; 19; St. Joseph, MO; b: Kentucky; f: James STITT; m: Fanny BISHOP] on 8 Mar 1879. Off: Bartholomew. Wit: Mrs. O.J. JOHNSON, E.M. RECTOR, both of Omaha.

COLYAR, Charles [21; Douglas Co.; b: Massachusetts; f: Daniel COLYAR; m: Mary

A. KING] md. Julia HUMPHREY [23; Douglas Co.; b: England; f: John HUMPHREY] on 2 Apr 1870. Off: GIBSON. Wit: Samuel FARRER; Charles CANOYER.

COMES, Byron [23; Omaha; b: Pennsylvania; f: H.T. COMES; m: Liddie EASTWOOD] md. Lottie WRIGHT [18; Omaha; b: Illinois; f: John WRIGHT; m: Esther BIGALOW] on 12 May 1879. Off: STENBERG. Wit; George D. APPEL, H.T. LACY.

CONGLETON, John M. [45; Omaha; b: Kentucky; f: James R. CONGLETON; m: Jane GASS] md. Francisco E. WYMAN [40; Omaha; b: Wisconsin; f: W.W. WYMAN; m: Amelia Ann TUPPER] on 28 Apr 1879. Off: SHERRILL. Wit: Geo. A. HOAGLAND, Miss Carrie E. WYMAN.

CONKLIN, D.J. [31; Audubon Co., IA; b: Ohio; f: G.H. CONKLIN; m: Ann FRANKS] md. Etta EWING [18; Audubon Co., IA; b: Iowa; f: John EWING; m: Susan BUTLER] on 8 Mar 1879. Off: WEISE. Wit: George KARLL, Alexander McCLELLAND.

CONKLIN, William B. [25; Nort Platte; b: Grand Gulf, MS; f: Elijah CONKLIN; m: Harriet WILSON] md. Bessie CLELAND [19; Omaha; b: Natchez, MS; f: T.H. CLELAND; m: Lucretia SAVAGE] on 5 Oct 1875. Off: STEWART. Wit: Col. James W. SAVAGE, Gen. Chas. F. MANDERSEN. Affidavait signed by John E. EDWARDS.

CONNELLY, James [23; Omaha; b: Canada; f: Michael CONNELLY; m: Mary O'HARA] md. Julia CORCORAN [19; Omaha; b: New York; f: John CORCORAN; m: Julia LEARY] on 30 Aug 1880. Off: HAWES. Wit: Miss McAUSLAND, Miss Amelia HAWES.

CONNELLY, Morris [28; Omaha; b: Ireland; f: Dennis CONNELLY; m: Catherine BERMINGHAM] md. Mrs. Mary COWIN [35; Omaha; b: Canada; f: Robert COWIN; m: Margaret McQUILLAN] on 18 Sep 1870. Off: CURTIS. Wit: Daniel McNAMARA; Bridget McNAMARA.

CONNER, Charles H. [31; Omaha; b: New York; f: William CONNER; m: Margaret HARKINSON] md. Sarah M. HURLEY [23; Omaha; b: Iowa; f: David HURLEY; m: Betsey WEBB] on 16 Sep 1877. Off: LIPE. Wit: David HURLEY, Betsey HURLEY.

CONNERY, John [34; Dixon Co.; b: Ireland; f: John CONNERY; m: Anna RYAN] md. Mary BURNS [24; Omaha; b: Ireland] on 13 Jun 1869. Off: CURTIS. Wit: John McMAHAN, Mary HIGGINS.

CONNOR, William C. [23 or 29; Omaha] md. Mrs. Elizabeth RECTOR [18; Omaha] on the evening of 20 Jun 1867 at the residence of C.A. EVANS. Off: DUNGAN. Wit: C.A. EVANS, F. EVANS, B.M. DAVENPERT, et al.

CONNOR, William F. [33; Elkhorn; b: PA; f: J.C.H. CONNOR; m: Susan WALTERS] md. Mary J. CRYLE [36; Elkhorn; b: IL; f: William OVERLANDER; m: Mary NEAL] on 29 Dec 1875. Off: PEABODY. Wit: Isaac COE, F.P. HANLON.

CONNOR, William [31; Evansville, IN] md. Martha E. STUDLEY [26; Omaha] on 1 Apr 1868. Off: KERMOTT. Wit: James S. TUCKER, James H. BALDWIN.

CONNOR [CONNER], John W. [26; Fort Kearney] md. Julia WALSH [19; Cincinnati, OH] on 26 Sep 1866 at St. Philomena's Church. Off: CURTIS.

CONOYER, Charles M. md. Mary HANTING on 31 Dec 1865 at Philomena's Catholic Church. Off: CURTIS. Wit: Michael KOPPES, Lilly HANTING.

CONOYER, Charles [21; Omaha] md. Mary KOPPS [16; Omaha] on 5 Oct 1862. Off: McMAHAN. Wit: B.J. BAKER, Catherine CARNAHAN.

COOK, Allan [37; Council Bluffs; b: New York; f: Aaron Cook; m: Lydia A. CULAN] md. Maria MIDLER [23; Council Bluffs; b: Pennsylvania; f: Christopher MIDLER; m: Sarah WEBB] on 12 Jan 1870. Off: SHERRILL. Wit: W.T. MIDLER; Ella BARNEY.

COOK, Charles B. [33; Omaha; b: Ohio; f: Z. COOK; m: Elizabeth BROWN] md. Mrs. D.E. REMINGTON [34; Omaha; b: New York; f: Joseph WILLIAMS; m: Calista BARNES] on 3 Apr 1879. Off: PATERSON. Wit: Arthur H. WILLIAMS; Ida REMINGTON.

COOK, H.H. [26] md. Alice WARNER [17] on 13 Aug 1867 at Mr. WARNER's house. Off: VAN ANTWERP. Wit: Mr. WARNER, Miss WHITFORD, et al. Age consent given by the parents of the bride with endorsement by SHEEKS.

COOK, Henry [21; Des Moines, IA; b: Pennsylvania; f: Simeon COOK; m: Mary RICE] md. Anna SWEENEY [20; Chicago, IL; b: Illinois; f: John SWEENEY; m: Mary Ann SWEENEY] on 25 Sep 1880. Off: McLAUGHLIN. Wit: G.T. ANDERSON of Des Moines, IA, F.H. HAIL of Nebraska City.

COOK, John P. [42; Washington Co.; b: SC; f: John COOK; m: Hannah WITTY] md. Hattie MOORE [26; Washington Co.; b: OH; f: Samuel MOORE; m: Alsina WHITTAKER] on 13 Aug 1876. Off: ROE. Wit: Frank M. MOORE, Mary H. GREER.

COOKS, Charles [29; Avoca, IA; b: Canada; f: Samuel COOKS; m: Rebecca MASON] md. Bell BUSEY [22; Omaha; b: Illinois; f: William BUSEY; m: Rebecca LUTZ] on 5 Feb 1871. Off: GIBSON. Wit: William A. KELLY; Mrs. Amanda KELLY.

COOLEY, Arthur H. [23; Omaha; b: Pennsylvania; f: John COOLEY; m: Susanah PATTERSON] md. Laura J. LEHMER [19; Omaha; b: Pennsylvania; f: William LEHMER; m: Elizabeth STOKES] on 18 Oct 1871 at the 2nd Presbyterian Church. Off: STEWART. Wit: Charles P. BYRNE; George F. LEHMER.

COONAY, Patrick [51; Omaha; b: Ireland; f: William COONAY; m: Maria BURNS] md. Mrs. Rose ROACH [39; Omaha; b: Ireland; f: James BURNS; m: Mary FARLEY] on 27 Oct 1879. Off: WEISS. Wit: L. RUF, J. (x) HEFFINGER.

COONEY, Patrick [38; Omaha; b: Ireland; f: John COONEY; m: Mary WELCH] md. Elizabeth SULLIVAN [28; Omaha; b: Ireland; f: Thomas SULLIVAN; m: Johanna McCARTHEY] on 9 Mar 1881 at St. Philomena's Church. Off: ENGLISH. Wit: Edward EGAN, Jane LYNCH.

COONS, Edward [21; Omaha; b: New York; f: Philip COONS; m: Almira SIMMONS] md. Jessie H. BULLOCK [22; Omaha; b: Canada West; f: George H. BULLOCK; m: Agnes S. FINDLEIGH] on 6 Oct 1869. Off: GASMANN. Wit: Frank WESTON, Harry RAINFORTH.

COONS, Edward [27; Omaha; b: NY; f: Philip COONS; m: Elmira SIMMONS] md. Lucy L. WILLIAMS [23; Omaha; b: MA; f: Duelley B. WILLIAMS; m: Thallia THOMAS] on 5 Aug 1875. Off: HENNEY. Wit: Charles L. WOOD, Mrs. S. MELLIS.

COOPER, Robert E. [27; Omaha; b: Pennsylvania; f: James COOPER; m: Mary MITCHELL] md. Anna C. CRUME [20; Omaha; b:Iowa; f: James B. CRUME; m: Hannah SEARS] on 25 Apr 1877. Off: WRIGHT. Wit: Levi T. PERKINS, Anna C. PERKINS.

COOPS, Henry [32; Omaha; b: Germany; f: Iler COOPS; m: Topla TAMLICK] md. Maria KARBACH [32; Omaha; b: Germany] on 12 Oct 1871 at the German Church. Off: GROENEBAUM. Wit: Anthony FANGMANN; Peter KARBACH.

COOTE, O.W. [24; Laramie City, WY; b: IL; f: Thomas COOTE; m: Anna WARREN] md. Anna PUMPHREY [20; Parsons, KS; b: WV (OH crossed out); f: H. PUMPHREY; m: E.M. MOORE] on 30 Jun 1881. Off: MAXFIELD. Wit: Mrs. E.H. ELCOCK, Van Wert, OH, Mrs. J.B. MAXFIELD.

CORBY, Joseph D. [25; Omaha] md. Lauretta LEWIS [24; Omaha] on 19 Sep 1867 at Hamilton House. Off: VAN ANTWERP.

Wit: Parents of the bride, Mr. and Mrs. ADAMS, et al.

CORDES, John Henry [29; Sarpy Co.; b: Germany; f: Peter Christoph CORDES; m: Anna KREIGER] md. Katharina M. PETERSON [22; Sarpy Co.; b: Germany; f: Henry Christoph PETERSON; m: Katharina MERMAN] on 28 Dec 1872.1 Off: TOWNSEND. Wit: Henry MOALLER; Carl JOHN.

COREY, James B. [25; Omaha; b: Connecticut; f: Charles C. COREY; m: Amey TILLINGHAST] md. Minnie E. KENNEDY [21; Omaha; b: New York; f: I.H. KENNEDY; m: Helen M. SETTLE] on 11 Sep 1877. Off: MILLSPAUGH. Wit: Rev. Dr. RUNCEY, Sister Mary HAYDEN.

CORKERELL, William [35; Papillion; b: England; f: Jabez CORKERELL; m: Susana BATES] and Mrs. Abby RAFTSMAN [51; Papillion; b: New York; f: G.B. TUNNISON; m: Prudence VOOHES] license issued on 30 Jul 1880. No marriage record. Off: BARTHOLOMEW. Wit: Hans (x) COLE.

CORKERELL, William [35; Papillion; b: England; f: Jabez CORKERELL; m: Susana BATES] md. Mrs. Abby RAFTSMAN [51; Papillion; b: New York; f: G.B. TUNNISON; m: Prudence VOORHES] on 30 Jul 1880. Off: BARTHOLOMEW. Wit: Henry COLEY, Mrs. E.J. COLEY.

CORNEILLE, George [29; b: Ireland; f: William CORNEILLE; m: Maria PIPER] md. Henrietta E.L. BECKER [19; b: Germany; f: Edward BECKER; m: Dorothea L. FONQUET] on 6 Mar 1878. Off: BENEKE. Wit: Phil DOER, Minnie BECKER.

CORNELL, George T. [26; Douglas Co.; b: West Virginia; f: Thomas CORNELL; m: Jane KEYES] md. Jennie COILE [23; Omaha; b: Missouri; f: Thomas CARROLL; m: Agnes TROY] license issued on 16 June 1870. Off: GIBSON. Wit: Patrick PARTELL; Mary CARROLL.

CORNIG [CORNEY], Peter [27; Omaha] md. Letia THORNTON [25; Omaha] on 8 Feb 1869. Off: KUHNS. Wit: Mr. and Mrs. George W. WALKER, Mrs. M.A. FESSENDEN, et al.

CORNISH, Delos [24; Omaha; b: Rome, NY; f: Bernard CORNISH; m: Louisa VREDENBURGH] md. Nora FERRIS [21; Omaha; b: Ireland; f: Thomas FERRIS; m: Johanna CANTY] on 24 Nov 1872. Off: CURTIS. Wit: Michael LYONS; Mary LEHEY.

CORNISH, George T. [26; Omaha; b: Rome, NY; f: Barnard CORNISH; m: Louisa VREEDENBERG] md. Lucy HENSMAN [18; Omaha; b: Rock Island, IL; f: Joseph HENSMAN; m: Mary Ann RICHARDSON] on 5 Sep 1869. Off: McCAGUE. Wit: Isaac CORNISH, Andrew HARMON.

CORNISH, Marcus [21; Omaha; b: Oneida Co., NY; f: Barnard CORNISH; m: Louisa FREDENBURGH] md. Mrs. Annie E. GAY [19; Omaha; f: Jeremiah PALMER; m: Susan OLIVER] on 12 Apr 1872. Off: KUHNS. Wit: George T. CORNISH; Andrew J. HARMON.

CORRICK, Thomas [24; Omaha; b: England; f: William E. CORRICK; m: Elizabeth M. MARSHAL] and Rebecca HUBIA [19; Omaha; b: England; f: John HUBIA; m: Elizabeth TWEARY] license issued on 29 Aug 1870. Off: GIBSON.

CORRIDON, Timothy [27; b: Ireland; f: Richard CORRIDON; m: Elizabeth LEARY] md. Mary RYLE [23; b: Ireland; f: Thomas RYLE; m: Mary KACY] at the Cathedral on 21 Nov 1878. Off: EMBLEN. Wit: Michael J. MAHONY, Bridget CASEY.

CORRIGAN [CARRIGAN], David [Columbus] md. Margaret LAFFERTY [Omaha] on 8 May 1864 at the Catholic Church of Omaha. Off: O'GORMAN. Wit: Thomas CLEARY, Margaret CLEARY.

COSGRAVE, James [27; Omaha; b: Ireland; f: Patrick COSGRAVE; m: Mary WELCH] md. Catherine CASEY [24; Omaha; b: Ireland; f: Michael CASEY; m: Catharine REAL] on 9 Oct 1870. Off: CURTIS. Wit: William DREIN; Mary FITZMAURICE.

COULTER, George A. [24; Omaha; b: Albany, NY; f: Christopher C. COULTER; m: Sarah F. MAXWELL] md. Susie SIDNER [23; Omaha; b: Galena, IL; f: F.B. SIDNER; m: Eveline ----] on 20 Jan 1876. Off: PRESSON. Wit: J. STEVENS, Frank DURNALL.

COULTER, George S. [25; Omaha; b: New York; f: Wm. F. COULTER; m: Elizabeth MALONY] md. M.J. WILSON [40; Omaha; b: Prussia; f: Arndt WILSON; m: ? MELIUS] on 13 Aug 1877. Off: FALK. Wit: Mrs. A.F. KNIGHT, Henry CARLTON.

COULTER, William [28; Omaha] md. Catherine GOSS [20; Omaha] on 21 Nov 1868. Off: KUHNS. Wit: Mrs. Jesse LOWE, Mrs. Elizabeth REEVES et al.

COUNTRYMAN, Charles K. [27; Omaha; b: IL; f: Isaac COUNTRYMAN; m: Amanda DeLaMATER] md. Annie E. BARTEL [19; Omaha; b: IA] on 29 May 1876. Off: SEDGWICK. Wit: Marcia F. SEDGWICK, Douglas Co., Mary EBOLD, Douglas Co.

COWAN, John [24; Omaha; b: Montreal, Canada East; f: Samuel COWAN; m: Margaret BIRRELL] md. Celia M. FAY [25; Omaha; b: Ireland; f: Edward FAY; m: Catharine CALLIGAN] on 15 Sep 1873 at the Bishop's residence. Off: BYRNE. Wit: Charles B. COOK; Molly McDEVITTE.

COWAN, Robert W. [34; Douglas Co.; b: Illinois; f: Thomas M. COWAN; m: Hannah FARNSWORTH] md. Mary E. GALLUP [32; Omaha; b: Canada; f: Simon GILBERSON; m: Anne KEARNEY] on 14 Feb 1877. Off: CRITCHFIELD. Wit: Henry RICE of Florence, Anne GALLUP.

COWLES, John [21; Florence; b: Wales; f: John COWLES; m: Penelope JENKINS] md. Louisa P. CULLEY [18; Florence; b: England; f: Edward CULLEY; m: Sarah Ann] on 19 Dec 1875. Off: PEABODY. Wit: M.J. BORLAND, James L. BORLAND.

COX, Aphelon [28 Omaha; b: IL; f: Jeremiah COX; m: Elizabeth CHRIST] md. Emelie Bell TUTTLE [17; Omaha; b: IA; f: P.M.C. TUTTLE; m: Jane LOGAN] on 17 Jul 1881. Off: INGRAM. Wit: H.E. COX, South 17 Street, Omaha, Ed FOSTER. Age consent given by parents of the bride.

COX, Charles W. [27; Omaha] md. Ermina A. KELLOGG [26; Omaha] on 24 Nov 1859 at the bride's residence on Harney St. Off: KUHNS. Wit: James VAN DUSEN, Mary J. VAN DUSEN.

COX, George [46; Saunders Co.] md. Lucrecie L. LAMB [38; Omaha] on 28 Aug 1867. Off: SHEEKS. Wit: John MALSBERRY, Philip B. BRUSH.

COX, Thomas J. [23; Omaha; b: New York; f: George P. COX; m: Mary Ann LANDER] md. Lizzie G. McDONALD [19; Omaha; b: Maryland; f: John McDONALD; m: Jane RUSSELL] on 3 Aug 1877. Off: JAMESON. Wit: Harry X. BAY, Nellie McDONALD.

COZZOLO, Ferdinand [28; Omaha] md. Frances KELLOGG or KELLEY [18; Omaha] on 17 May 1868. Off: STUCK. Wit: Mr. WESTON, Mrs. KELLOGG or KELLEY.

CRAIG, Thomas P. [27; Concord, IL; b: Morgan Co., IL; f: Moses H. CRAIG; m: Sarah HUMBLE] and Elizabeth C. PARLEIR [17; Sarpy Co.; b: Morgan Co., IL; f: John PARLEIR; m: Rebecca] application issued on 10 Mar 1873.

CRAIG, William S. [25; Tekamah, Burt Co.; b: Ohio; f: Johnson CRAIG; m: Martha THOMPSON] md. Mary L. HAYNES [21; Omaha; b: Michigan; f: James HAYNES; m: Mrs. Bella S. BILLMAN] on 27 Dec 1872. Off: BILLMAN. Wit: A.G. EBERHART; Mrs. Bella S. BILLMAN.

CRANDAL, James R. [28; Omaha] md. Catharine BARNES [26; Omaha] on 2 Nov 1867. Off: KERMOTT. Wit: Mrs. Alonzo C. DORT, Miss Mittie DORT. Note reads "Give certificate to wife in Omaha."

CRANDALL, Harvey [22; Shelby Co., IA; b: Iowa; f: Albert CRANDALL; m: Nellie HOLCOMB] md. Alice O'BANNON [18; Dunlap, b: Missouri; f: John O'BANNON; m: Emaline MOXLEY] on 31 Jan 1878. Off:

BORDEN. Wit: Geo. W. MEDLOCK, Owen SLAVEN.

CRANDELL, George T. [29; Omaha; b: Saratoga, NY; f: Otis CRANDELL; m: Ann Eliza H. LAKE] md. Ann Janette TAYLOR [23; Providence, RI; b: Smithfield, RI; f: Thomas B. TAYLOR; m: Nancy A. ROSS] on 18 Dec 1869. Off: SHERRILL. Wit: Wm. J. CONNELL, Annie D. SPRIGG.

CRANE, John T. [31; Schiawassee, MI] and Eliza J. FEE [26; Council Bluffs] license issued on 16 Apr 1866. No marriage record. Off: HASCALL.

CRANE, Van Buren [Exira, Audubon Co.] md. Mary E. BUSH [Exira, Audubon Co.] on 9 May 1863 at Empire House. Both of legal age. Off: DAKE. Wit: Crescenzia WASSERMAN, Mary A. CRANE.

CRARON, William [28; Omaha; b: Illinois; f: James CRARON; m: Ellen HAUGHEY] md. Ellen RILEY [27; Omaha; b: Wisconsin; f: John RILEY; m: Bridget DENIN] on 4 Feb 1880, Holy Family Church. Off: QUINN. Wit: Robert CRAREN, Kate RILEY.

CRAUSE, Frederick [25; Germany; f: Frederick CRAUSE; m: Henrietta WENZENER] md. Ernstine VOLZMANN [25; b: Germany; f: Carl VOLZMANN; m: Gustine STABENOW] on 2 Feb 1878. Off: BARTHOLOMEW. Wit: J.S. GIBSON, J.R. CONKLING.

CRAVENS, James [27; Omaha; b: KY; f: Squire CRAVENS; m: America WYATT] md. Belle WILLS [19; Omaha; b: MO; f: Dock WILLS; m: Mary HOLLMAN] on 10 May 1881. Off: RILEY. Wit: Duff GREEN, Margaret GREEN.

CRAVER, Theophilus B. [27; Grinell, IA; b: New Jersey; f: Samuel P. CRAVER; m: Elizabeth NELSON] md. Mary D. NOBLE [22; Montana; b: Iowa; f: D.P. NOBLE; m: Minerva PEAT] on 31 Aug 1874. Off: GATES. Wit: Thomas S. CRAVER, Grinell, IA; Miss. S.J. DAVIS, Grinell, IA.

CRAWFORD, Daniel W. [Omaha] md. Mrs. Eliza BEERS [Council Bluffs] on 1 Feb 1865 at KUHNS' residence. Off: KUHNS. Wit: Lizzie JONES, Mrs. H.W. KUHNS.

CRAWFORD, Frank J. [20; Elkhorn; b: OH; f: Geo. CRAWFORD; m: Josephine JANNEY] md. Emma M. LINK [22; Millard; b: IN; f: Harvey LINK; m: Mary ABBOTT] on 7 May 1875 at Chicago Precinct. Off: McARTHUR. Wit: G.G. BENTON, Elkhorn Station, Maria McARTHUR, Elkhorn Station. Age consent given by father of the groom. The young man is not of age quite, by a month or so.

CREIGHTON, James [48; Omaha; b: Ohio; f: John CREIGHTON; m: Mary BARRICKMAN] md. Catharine Ann McCALLUM [39; Omaha; b: Canada] on 4

May 1869. Off: CURTIS. Wit: John B. FUREY, Catharine M. FUREY.

CREIGHTON, John A. [30; Omaha] md. Sarah E. WAREHAM [25; Omaha] on 9 Jun 1868 at the Catholic Church of Omaha. Off: O'GORMAN. Wit: T. KENNY, C. DRAKE, Catherine M. THERN, Mary GRIER.

CREIGHTON, Joseph [36; Omaha] md. Catherine FURLONG [28; Omaha] on 1 Dec 1860 at the Catholic Church of Omaha. Off: KELLY. Wit: William BLAKE, Catherine CONRY.

CREMB, George E. [35; Pottawatomie Co., IA; b: Ohio; f: Nathan L. CREMB; m: Susanna ETSON] md. Mary J. HINES [26; Pottawatomie Co., IA; b: Pennsylvania; f: Michael J. HINES; m: Mary LOYD] on 16 Aug 1871. Off: WALTER. Wit: Julius ROEDER; F. STUBBENDORF.

CRESTEN, Clarence [22; Omaha; b: Albany, NY; f: Clarence CALLAHAN; m: Catharine CRESTEN] md. Emma HOOKER [21; Darlington, WI; b: Illinois; f: Solomon HOOKER; m: Elizabeth DONNAN] on 14 Jun 1872. Off: LYTLE. Wit: Michel CURREN; Clarisa STOKES.

CRIGLER, James R. [23; Omaha; b: Virginia; f: James R. CRIGLER; m: Elizabeth LEACH] md. Jennie MASON [23; Omaha; b: Iowa; f: H.E. MASON; m: Ruth GOWIN] on 12 Jul 1874 at the M.E. Parsonage. Off: ADAIR. Wit: G.B. SISCO; Mrs. M.A. ADAIR.

CRISS, George W. [25; Elkhorn Station; b: Indiana; f: George W. CRISS; m: Martha BAILEY] md. Emma KENNEDY [23; Elkhorn Station; b: Pennsylvania; f: Mathew KENNEDY; m: Lucy HYDE] on 1 Aug 1871. Off: GIBSON. Wit: George ARMSTRONG; C. WOOD.

CRITCHFIELD, Absolam W. [26; Papillion; b: Indiana; f: Jacob CRITCHFIELD; m: Harriet BOWER] md. Isabella A. REEVES [24; Florence; b: Iowa; f: William REEVES; m: Jane BRADDOCK] on 20 Sep 1878. Off: FISHER. Wit: Mrs. Sarah ROBERTS, Mrs. C.H. DEWEY.

CROMIE, William D. [26; Woodbine, IA; b: Maryland; f: James CROMIE; m: Fanny MALLOY] md. Florence DALLY [21; Woodbine, IA; b: Iowa; f: John W. DALLY; m: Ruth A. GOODRICH] on 25 Oct 1877. Off: SEDGWICK. Wit: R.H. WILBUR, D.A. Van NANCE, Sr.

CROMWELL, Herman Robert Otto [26; Omaha; b: Germany f: Fritz CROMWELL; m: Mary MEYERS] md. Mrs. Ellen LITTON [30; Omaha; b: Dublin, Ireland; f: John HYLAND; m: Margaret KENNEY] on 1 Jun 1876 at CAMP's office. Off: CAMP. Wit: James F. MORTON, B.F. PENDERY.

CRONIN, Jeremiah [28; Omaha; b: Ireland; f: Michael CRONIN; m: Mary CALLAHAN] md. Catherine MORIARTY [25; Omaha; b: Ireland; f: Michael MORIARTY; m: Mary] on 7 Feb 1875 at the Roman Catholic Cathedral. Off: BYRNE. Wit: Patrick GLYN, Mary COOPER.

CRONIN, Michael [28; Omaha; b: Ireland; f: Michael CRONIN; m: Mary CALLAHAN] md. Kate HANRAHAN [27; Omaha; b: Ireland; f: Thomas HANRAHAN; m: Elizabeth FITZMAURICE] on 16 Jan 1870. Off: CURTIS. Wit: Timothy MORIARTY; Mary FITZMAURICE.

CRONK, Albert [31; Douglas Co.; b: New York; f: O.B. CRONK; m: Sophia BROWN] md. Mrs.? Emma BROWN [29; Douglas Co.; b: Illinois; f: Hiram BROWN; m: Rebecca CHRISTIAN] on 4 Nov 1874. Off: PORTER. Wit: E.G. BARTLETT, Union Pct.; Davis SIMMONS, Union Pct.

CRONYN, William W. [27; New York City; b: Canada; f: David CRONYN; m: Anna HAWTHORNE] and Etta N. WRIGHT [18; Omaha; b: OH; f: James WRIGHT; m: Hattie SMITH] license issued on 31 Mar 1881. No marriage record. Off: SMITH.

CROOK, James D. [26; Elkhorn Station, NE; b: North Carolina; f: Joseph CROOK; m: Jane BATES] md. Hannah HOPPER [21; Elkhorn Station, NE; b: Canada; f: Wm. HOPPER; m: Dorthy FARRELL] at Elkhorn Station on 16 Dec 1878. Off: ADRIANCE. Wit: Mary J. HOPER, Frances STEWART, both of Elkhorn Station.

CROOK, Swen [28; Crawford Co., IA; b: Sweden; f: Olaf CROOK; m: Selina ANDERSON] md. Louisa LAWSON [LARSON] [25; Omaha; b: Sweden; f: Lars LARSON; m: Hannah JOHNSON] on 21 Mar 1877 at the 18th Street M.E. Church parsonage. Off: PARDEE. Wit: George A. WINCHEL, Mrs. M.L. PARDEE.

CROSMAN, Henry [22; Buffalo, NY; b: New York; f: John CROSMAN; m: Fannie STOCKFORD] md. Annie GRAVES [23; Kentucky; b: Kentucky; f: John GRAVES; m: Sallie WALKER] on 27 Dec 1878. Off: STENBERG. Wit: Michael GILLEGAN, Maggie SULLEVAN.

CROSS, William R. [28; Douglas Co.] md. Sarah Jane CHURCH [27; Douglas Co.] on 16 Oct 1868. Off: KERMOTT. Wit: J.H. NOTEWIRE, Mrs. M.A. McCALLUM.

CROSSLE, Henry W. [32; McCardle Pct., Douglas Co.; b: Ireland; f: James CROSSLE; m: Charlotte WALLER] md. Georgiana CHOULER [26; Omaha, pro tem; b: England; f: John CHOULER] on 5 Dec 1872. Off: EBERHART. Wit: Edward JOHNSON; A.G. EBERHART.

CROW, Gilbert C. [23; Atlantic, IA; b: Illinois; f: Thomas G. CROW; m: Mary L. CLAYTON] md. Ruby R. WANNEMAKER

[20; Golden, CO; b: Wisconsin; f: W.L. WANNEMAKER; m: Hannah A. CHATFIELD] on 8 Jan 1880. Off: INGRAM. Wit: O.F. STEPHENS, Mrs. Wm. STEPHENS.

CROWDER, James H. [34; Missouri Valley, IA; b: IN; f: Wm. M. CROWDER; m: Hannah C. COX] md. Ella L. BROWN [21; Douglas Co.; b: PA; f: D.F. BROWN; m: Hannah E. ANDERSON] on 4 Apr 1876. Off: BRITT. Wit: D.F. BROWN, Hannah E. BROWN.

CROWELL, Joseph W. [Omaha] md. Johannah LEWNWALL [Omaha] on 17 Sep 1864 at DICKINSON's office. Off: DICKINSON. Wit: Andrew LEWNWALL, Rebecca LEWNWALL.

CROWLEY, John W. [24; Omaha] md. Henriette BELCHER [BETSCHER] [Omaha] on 28 Jan 1869 (written 1865 in error). Off: KERMOTT. Wit: Col. J.H. NOLEWARE, Albert OSTRAM.

CROWNER, Nathaniel [33; Omaha] md. Mary HOLMES [21; Omaha] on 30 Jan 1862 at F. SAPP's house. Off: BARNES. Wit: Mr. and Mrs. SAPP, Mrs. HUNT, Mrs. HIGLEY, et al.

CROY, David [28; Omaha; b: Scotland; f: Henry CROY; m: Jane ROBERTSON] md. Annie G. CHARTERS [19; Omaha; b: Ireland; f: James CHARTERS; m: Eliza ALLEN] on 19 Mar 1873. Off: GARRETT. Wit: Thos. B. WILKES; Wm. T. FALCONER.

CRUGAN, Charles E. [24; Lincoln; b: Brighton, IA; f: Daniel CRUGAN; m: Mary A McKEE] md. Melissa A. WILLIAMS [23; Lebanon, OH; b: Lebanon, OH; f: Charles WILLIAMS; m: Lucinda] on 13 May 1872. Off: ALEXANDER. Wit: D.W. MONTGOMERY, Elkhorn; S.B. GALEY, Lincoln.

CRULEY, Charles [26; Omaha; b: Missouri; f: Michael CRULEY] md. Louisa CAVEO [19; Omaha; b: Missouri; f: Edward CAVEO] on 28 Feb 1870. Off: CURTIS. Wit: Henry FANGER; Ada PETERS.

CRUME, Nicholas M. [23; Florence; b: WI; f: John CRUME; m: Sarah CHARLICOM] md. Mary E. CHRISTIAN [16; Florence; b: Utah Territory; f: Cornelius CHRISTIAN; m: Mary E. PHELPS] on 26 Jan 1881. Off: SPENCER. Wit: Alphonzo CUTLEY, Florence and Fannie CRUME, Florence.

CRUPPER [CRUFFIER], James [32; Omaha] md. Mrs. Mary Jane CUTTING [31; Omaha] on 30 May 1868. Off: KELLY. Wit: Dr. MERCER, J. KELLY.

CRUZ, Antoino [46; Omaha] md. Mrs. Catharine McDERMOT [33; Omaha] on 11 Apr 1868. Off: STUCK. Wit: Col. James W. SAVAGE, Alexander J.BURK.

CRYER, John B. [48; Valley Pct, Douglas Co.; b: England; f: John CRYER; m: Jane SPENCER] md. Mary WAGSTAFF [28; Valley Pct, Douglas Co.; b: England; f: John WAGSTAFF; m: Sarah HIRST] on 17 Dec 1872 at Valley Station. Off: BALLOW. Wit: Everett G. BALLOW, Valley; Harriet C. BALLOW, Valley.

CUDDY, William John [24; Omaha; b: Worcester, MA; f: David CUDDY; m: Catharine HIGGINS] md. Della May NASON [18; Omaha; b: Augusta, ME; f: Charles E. NASON; m: Louisa E. STONE] on 19 Apr 1879. Off: FISHER. Wit: C.E. NASON, Willie NASON.

CULLIGAN, Edward or Edmond [30; Elkhorn; b: Ireland; f: Patrick CULLIGAN; m: Bridget GERAN] md. Mrs. Margaret CARROLL [30; Omaha; b: Ireland; f: Michael SHINN; m: Bridget CONSIDEN _?_ ] on 15 Jun 1869. Off: KELLEY. Wit: Michael GRIFFIN; Patrick KENNEY.

CULP, Hiram [27; Douglas Co.; b: Armstrong Co., PA; f: Jacob CULP] md. Mary PURCHASE [18; Washington Co.; b: New York; f: Evan PURCHASE] on 14 Nov 1871 at Elkhorn. Off: DODGE. Wit: Wm. M. RYAN, Douglas Co.; R.W. BARBER, Douglas Co.

CUMMINGS, Arthur R. [24; Omaha; b: Massachusetts; f: Calvin CUMMINGS; m: Mary FREEMAN] and Hattie HELLER [18; Omaha; b: Connecticut; f: John HELLER; m: Mary DOYLE] license issued on 10 Dec 1877. No marriage record. Off: SEDGWICK.

CUNER, Louis [28; Omaha; b: Italy; f: Passqual CUNER; m: Catherine CUNER] md. Lizzie PALMTAG [23; Douglas Co.; b: KY; f: Michael PALMTAG; m: Lizzie APELBALLER] on 10 May 1882. Off: COLANERI. Wit: John CUNER and wife. License issued on 26 Apr 1881; filed 23 Jun 1882.

CUNNINGHAM, Barney [32; Omaha; b: Ireland; f: Eugene CUNNINGHAM; m: Mary RIORDAN] md. Mary McCANN [19; Omaha; b: Illinois; f: John McCANN; m: Mary McAVOY] on 11 Aug 1874. Off: PEABODY. Wit: George WARRINGTON; Michael PARR.

CUNNINGHAM, Courtland M. [21; Omaha; b: New York; f: Porter CUNNINGHAM; m: Catharine TURPENNY] md. Kate Z. CARPENTER [17; Omaha; b: Council Bluffs, IA; f: Daniel W. CARPENTER; m: Anna B. McCULLOCH] on 29 Apr 1874 at the Trinity Cathedral. Off: GARRETT. Wit: P.J. TIERNEY; James HALLEY. Age of consent given by father of the bride.

CUNNINGHAM, Dennis [23; Omaha; b: Ireland; f: George CUNNINGHAM; m: Mary GODFREY] md. Mary E. WINDHAM [20; Omaha; b: Illinois] on 4 Jul 1869. Off: CURTIS. Wit: Thomas SPICER, Mary CONSIDINE.

CUNNINGHAM, Granville W. [Douglas Co.] md. Eliza WIRTS [Douglas Co.] on 26 May 1864 at Hamilton House. Off: DICKINSON. Wit: J.W. BURGMAN, Henry NYE, Miss THOMAS.

CUNNINGHAM, M.G. [35; Washington Co.; b: Ohio; f: John R. CUNNINGHAM; m: Annie WOLF] md. Annie CHRISTIANSON [23; Omaha; b: Missouri; f: John CHRISTIANSON; m: Annie JOHNSON] on 1 Nov 1879. Off: BARTHOLOMEW. Wit: Isaac COE of Nebraska City, J.J. MANN of San Francisco.

CUNNINGHAM, S.L. [28; Omaha; b: Indiana; f: Samuel CUNNINGHAM; m: Lydia WILSON] md. Sarah E. MOCK [23; Omaha; b: Pennsylvania; f: John D. MOCK; m: Susanna BROWN] on 25 Dec 1880. Off: MARQUETT. Wit: Arthur M. COLEMAN, S.M. COLEMAN.

CUPPY, Grenville M. [26; Avoca, IA; b: Iowa; f: Adam CUPPY; m: Christina SHAFER] md. Ella BROWN [22; Avoca, IA; b: Iowa; f: Robert BROWN; m: Mary MERLATTE] on 9 Jan 1879. Off: BARTHOLOMEW. Wit: M.D. HYDE, M.H. REDFIELD.

CURL, James R. [36; Douglas Co.; b: Indiana; f: William CURL; m: Eliza ING] md. Mrs. Mary F. ASHLEY [29; Omaha; b: Warsau, IL; f: C.C. COLE; m: Mary J. HILL] on 6 Jun 1877. Off: SHERRILL. Wit: Lathiel T. CHASE, John BURLEY.

CURLISS, John [37; Pottawattamie Co., KS?; b: Michigan; f: William CURLISS; m: Maria LEWLESS] md. Lozania LETNER [18; Omaha; b: Iowa; f: Lewis LETNER; m: Rirama ADAMS] on 5 Feb 1872. Off: BRANDES. Wit: Frank WALTER; John R. LETNER.

CURRAN, James R. [24; Council Bluffs; b: NY; f: Peter CURRAN; m: Mary SMITH] md. Louise HILLENS [18; Council Bluffs; b: NY; f: Henry HILLENS; m: Ann McGLOUGHLIN] on 19 Apr 1876. Off: SEDGWICK. Wit: F.P. HANLON, George W. SHIELDS.

CURRY, James H. [35; Omaha] md. Sarah ESTY [24; Omaha] on 23 Aug 1867 at FLORKEE's house. Off: FLORKEE. Wit: Wm. HENNECK, Wm. HENRY, W. WHITE.

CURTIS, Franklin A. [23; Omaha] md. Lucinda CLARK [18; Omaha] on 25 Jan 1869. Off: KELLEY. Wit: D.R. CLARK, Miss PRICE, Mrs. J. BALSON.

CUSHING, Michael P. [27; Leavenworth City, KS] md. Kate MURRAY [23;

Columbus, NE] on 4 Oct 1866 at St. Philomena's Church. Off: CURTIS.

CUTCHAFLE, Alfred [colored; 27; Omaha; b: Marysville, KY; f: Aaron FINCH; m: Margaret] md. Amanda WELCH [colored; 25; Omaha; b: Kentucky; f: Moses FINEY (FINNEY); m: Elizabeth NORTON] on 16 Aug 1869. Off: KUHNS. Wit: Mrs. Mary LAFOND, Ellen DRAPER.

CUTHBERTSON, Edward [30; Omaha; b: London f: John CUTHBERTSON; m: Harriet LAW] md. Augusta Harriet CROFT [19; Omaha; b: Rock Island, IL; f: John T. CROFT; m: Eliza NICHOLS] on 2 Jan 1875. Off: PEABODY. Wit: Joseph W. MAJORC, Mary MAJORS.

CUTLER, Samuel J. [26; Omaha; b: New York; f: Samuel J. CUTLER; m: Emma CULL] md. Mathilda C. HANSEN [20; Omaha; b: Denmark; f: John HANSEN; m: Margaretta NELSON] on 6 Mar 1877. Off: FISHER. Wit: Mrs. E.M. FISHER.

DAGETT, William H. [27; Council Bluffs; b: Ottawa, IL; f: Henry DAGETT; md. Louisa YORK [Council Bluffs; b: Keokuk Co., IA; f: William YORK; m: Melissa EARLE] on 5 Apr 1870. Off: GIBSON. Wit: H.F. STRONG; John R. MANCHESTER.

DAHLGREN, Andrew M. [30; Omaha] md. Annie DAHLOF [27; Omaha] on 13 April 1869. Off: HYDE. Wit: Mrs. G.P. THOMAS of Tekamah, Mrs. J.R. HYDE.

DAHLGREN, C. John [35; Omaha; b: Sweden; f: Lars JOHANSON; m: Johanna or Clara JOHANSON] md. Clara ANDERSON [29; Omaha; b: Sweden; f: Andrew NIRA; m: Christina PERSON] on 16 Jun 1877. Off: HANSEN. Wit: M.A. LARSON, Gustaf BERG.

DAHLOF, Magnus H. [30; Omaha; b: Sweden; f: John DAHLOF; m: Catharine JOHNSON] md. Sophia WENNEMO [25; Omaha; b: Sweden; f: Hugo WENNERMO; m: Caroline SHULTS] on 21 Aug 1869. Off: KUHNS. Wit: Annie B. CATHERWOOD, Mrs. W.H. KUHNS.

DAHLSTROM, Andrew G. [31; Omaha] md. Mary C. SODERBERG [24; Omaha] on 13 Apr 1868. Off: KERMOTT. Wit: Francis R. HILL, Sophia HILL.

DAHLSTROM, Nils [32; Saunders Co.; b: Sweden; f: Nils DAHLSTROM; m: Christina PETERSON] md. Matilda OLESON [28; Saunders Co,; b: Sweden; f: Ole ANDERSON; m: Christina OLESON] on 4 Nov 1872. Off: TOWNSEND. Wit: Lars M. OLESON; Tobias OLESON, Saunders Co.

DAILEY, A.W. [23; Omaha; b: Canada; f: Henry DAILEY; m: Clara DRAPER] md. Eliza J. ROBINSON [22; Omaha; b: Missouri; f: James ROBINSON; m: Margureta BANNISTER] on 15 Mar 1879. Off:

STENBERG. Wit: D. TURNGREN, Nils Kgelsberg NILSEN.

DAILEY, Dennis [24; Holt Co.; b: Ireland; f: Dennis DAILEY; m: Mary BEIRNE] md. Harriet MAXWELL [22; New York; b: Ireland; f: Johnston MAXWELL; m: Fanny GANLY] at the Cathedral on 1 Jan 1878. Off: O'BRIAN. Wit: John MURPHY of Dubuque, Kate NOLAN.

DAILEY, Patrick H. [31; Omaha; b: Ireland; f: Hugh DAILEY; m: Winnie DOYLE] md. Mrs. Annie CAREY [27; Omaha; b: Prussia; f: Fred SHELTON; m: Mary TARSON] on 31 Dec 1874. Off: PEABODY. Wit: Thomas GROSE; Maggie HALL.

DAILY [DAILEY], Patrick [25; Omaha; b: Ireland; f: Jeremiah DAILY; m: Ellen MURPHY] md. Catherine CLARK [20; Omaha; b: Ireland; f: Patrick CLARK; m. Mary O'BRIEN] on 11 Jul 1869. Off: CURTIS. Wit: John MARRINAN, Margaret FRANCES.

DAINES, Robert [29; Omaha] md. Jemima SEAMONS [20; Omaha] on 1 May 1859. Off: BRIGGS. Wit: Nelson BAKER, Joseph FOX.

DALL, Leopold [27; Douglas Co.; b: Germany; f: Fred DALL] md. Minnie WALTHER [25; Omaha; b: Germany; f: Jacob WALTHER] on 11 Apr 1871. Off: GIBSON. Wit: H. STULL; Frederick KUMPF.

DALLOW, Ebenezer [41; Omaha; b: New York; f: Samuel DALLOW; m: Anna BRADLY] and Clare BURDETTE [17; Omaha; b: New York] license issued on 13 Oct 1869. No marriage record. Off: HYDE.

DALLOW, Ebenizer [41; Omaha; b: New York; f: Samuel DALLOW; m: Hannah BRADLEY] md. Sophia AMOSS [26; Omaha; b: Bermingham, England; f: Jesse AMOSS; m: Fannie LOGAN] on 12 Jul 1870. Off: ESTABROOK. Wit: Edward WHELEHAN; Sarah B---ET.

DALLY (DALLEY), John W. [35; Magnolia, Harrison Co., IA] md. Nancy LaFERRE [LaFESSE] [24; Magnolia, IA] on 2 Dec 1865 at Douglas House. Off: KUHNS. Wit: John HIGBY, M.W. KENNARD.

DALTON, William [30; Omaha] md. Jane DOOLEY [24; Omaha] on 11 Feb 1868 at the Catholic Church of Omaha. Off: O'GORMAN. Wit: William RYAN, Margaret LENIHAN.

DALY, John [22; Omaha] and Ellen FITZGERALD [25; Omaha] license issued on 22 Mar 1858. No marriage record. Off: BRIGGS.

DAMON, Jeremiah H. [33; Omaha; b: Baring, ME; f: Seth G. DAMON; m: Nancy G. BASFORD] md. Mary Ann McCARTHY [18; Omaha; b: Quebec, CAN] on 23 Mar 1872. Off: BILLMAN. Wit: Mrs. Belle D. BILLMAN; Katie LINDVALL.

DANIEL, Christian [26; Omaha; b: Germany; f: Christian DANIEL; m: Lucy RAMM] md. Wetha HIBBLER [22; Omaha; b: Germany; f: Henry HIBBLER; m: Kate RUSKIN] on 9 Aug 1872. Off: BRANDES. Wit: T.G. MORTON; Mrs. TUMB.

DANIELS, Henry [colored; 28; Omaha] md. Mary SIMONS [colored; 23; Omaha] on 7 Apr 1867 at KUHNS' residence. Off: KUHNS. Wit: Mrs. W.H. KUHNS, Elizabeth GETSCH.

DANIELS, John M. md. Martha Jane McDOWELL on 15 Mar 1865 at the parsonage. Off: LEMON. Wit: Mrs. Margaret B. LEMON, Mr. McDOWELL, bride's brother-in-law, Mrs. McDOWELL.

DANIELSON, John A. [23; Omaha; b: Germany; f: Esmus DANIELSON; m: Catherine GALESEN] md. Christine CHRISTENSON [18; b: Germany; f: Andres CHRISTENSEN; m: Nicholena RASMUS] on 7 Mar 1871. Off: McCAGUE. Wit: Alex DAEMON; Mrs. Wilhelmina DAEMON.

DARLING, Benjamin [52; Pottawattamie Co., IA; b: VT; f: Joseph DARLING; m: Hulda PERRY] md. Mary GRIMSHAW [38; Pottawattamie Co., IA; b: Canada; f: Nelson GRIMSHAW; m: Emeline WILSON] on 25 Aug 1876. Off: SEDGWICK. Wit: F.P. HANLON, Henry HORNBERGER.

DARLING, Richard [23; Omaha; b: England; f: Thomas DARLING; m: Elisa DENILLE (or DEVILLE)] md. Cahterine MEEHAN [19; Omaha; b: Canada; f: Patrick MEEHAN; m: Mary MURRAY] on 17 Oct 1875. Off: BOBA. Wit: Micahel MEEHAN, Honora MEEHAN.

DARLING, Stephen [26; Omaha; b: NY; f: J.A. DARLING; m: Elizabeth VAN ORDER] md. Elizabeth HEART [22; Omaha; b: ME; f: William HEART; m: Elizabeth] on 24 Mar 1875. Off: PEABODY. Wit: Lewis K. MARSHALL, Elvira MARSHALL, Wyoming House.

DARSCHER, Reimer [45; Omaha; b: Denmark; f: Bernhard DARSCHER; m: Margretha E. STRUBE] md. Mrs. Catharine EBERT [42; Omaha; b: Denmark; f: Benidix KRULL, Louisa LUTJE] on 19 Nov 1879. Off: WRIGHT. Wit: C.T. BOND, D. Van ETTEN.

DAUB, Lawrence [22; Omaha; b: Erie, PA; f: John A. DAUB; m: Barbara ANTON] md. Mary or Maria HASSER [21; Omaha; b: Rochester, NY; f: Frank HASSER] on 27 Jun 1869 at the German Catholic Church. Off: GROENEBAUM. Wit: Jane LYME, John A. BATESON.

DAVIDSON, George S. [27; Omaha] md. Maggie MORGAN [19; Omaha] on 11 Oct 1861 at ARMSTRONG's office. Off: ARMSTRONG. Wit: Dudley MISNER, Ellen MULLEN, Robert S. KNOX.

DAVIDSON, George [30; Fort Kearney] md. Jenette N. SMITH [20; Zanesville, OH] on 19 Jan 1866. Off: MILLER. Wit: Judge KELLOGG, John P. MOLIBER.

DAVIES, James H. [21; Omaha; b: England; f: James DAVIES; m: Eliza PIPE] md. Dell O'NEIL [19; Omaha; b: St. Louis, MO; f: James O'NEIL; m: Delia McCARTY] on 21 Nov 1876. Off: PEABODY. Wit: Rosa RYAN, Jas. QUINLAN.

DAVIS, Charles B. [20; Omaha; b: Illinois; f: Charles M. DAVIS; m: Mary COLSEN] md. Ellen TOZER [19; Omaha; b: England; f: William TOZER; m: Sarah WIDGERY] on 8 Dec 1880. Off: PATERSON. Wit: Rev. Frank B. MILLSPAUGH, Wiss TOZER.

DAVIS, Douglas A. [23; Omaha; b: MO; f: James DAVIS; m: Elizabeth GOFF] md. Mary B. LOWARY [19; Omaha; b: MO; f: James LOWARY; m: Fannie MANN] on 11 Mar 1881. Off: STENBERG. Wit: Chas. H. AUSTIN, H.C. HARTMAN.

DAVIS, Edwin [38; Omaha; b: Canada; f: Samuel DAVIS; m: Rheumilla TILDEN] md. Elizabeth CLIFTON [26; Sarpy Co.; b: Vermillion Co., IL; f: Charles CLIFTON; m: Hannah RICE] on 24 Sep 1874. Off: WRIGHT. Wit: Emlin LEWIS; Mary H. WRIGHT.

DAVIS, Frederick E. [25; Wahoo, Saunders Co., NE; b: Jersey Co., IL; f: Andrew J. DAVIS; m: Nancy COWAN] md. Ida GIFFORD [22; Akron, IA; b: Summit Co., OH; f: George GIFFORD; m: Francis LANG] on 28 Feb 1878. Off: BARTHOLOMEW. Wit: Warren SWITZLER, Charles R. REDICK.

DAVIS, Frederick H. [23; Douglas Co.; b: IA; f: Thomas DAVIS; m: Elizabeth BENYON] md. Nellie S. CLARKSON [22; Douglas Co.; b: IL; f: Robert H. CLARKSON; m: Meliora McPHERSON] on 11 May 1876 at Trinity Cathedral. Off: CLARKSON. Wit: Thomas DAVIS and Elizabeth DAVIS, Indianapolis, Herman KOUNTZ, Meliora CLARKSON. Edward P. PECK signed the affidavit.

DAVIS, George M. [42; Valley Pct., Douglas Co.; b: Pennsylvania; f: Isaac DAVIS; m: Frances STONER] md. Mathilda J. PHELPS [36; Valley Pct., Douglas Co.; b: Louisiana] on 18 Jan 1873 at Valley Station. Off: DENTON. Wit: John DAVIS, Valley Station, Douglas Co.; William SHORT, Valley Station, Douglas Co.

DAVIS, Jacob [35; Omaha] md. Catharine MAACK [26; Omaha] on 19 Oct 1867 at KUHNS' residence. Off: KUHNS. Wit: Mr.

and Mrs. Henry CLAUSON, Mrs. W.H. KUHNS.

DAVIS, John W. [22; Florence; b: Jackson Co., IN; f: John W. DAVIS: m: Lydia WILSON] md. Mary RATLIFF [18; Wayne Co., IA; b: Iowa; f: William D. RATLIFF; m: Nancy NICHOLAS] on 4 Aug 1870. Off: GIBSON. Wit: Gidean L. PUGSLEY, Florence; Porter D. REDMAN, Florence.

DAVIS, John W. [24; Omaha; b: Illinois; f: Joseph DAVIS; m: Mary TEEPLES] md. Katie DIERKS [19; Fremont; b: Germany; f: John F. DIERKS; m: G.M. BERNS] on 21 Oct 1874. Off: PEABODY. Wit: Wm. A. THORP; Gertie E. THORP.

DAVIS, John W. [colored; 28; Omaha; b: VA; f: Andrew DAVIS; m: Henrietta GREEN] md. Marie FRANKLIN [colored; 26; Omaha; b: MO; m: Clara FERGUSON] on 17 Nov 1875. Off: BRAXTON. Wit: Mrs. Hannah MOSSET, Mrs. Matilda HOOKER.

DAVIS, Lorenzo K. [27; Lincoln; b: Ohio; f: J.W. DAVIS; m: Esther A. SHIVLEY] md. Mary A. FETHERSTONE [18; Lincoln; b: Iowa; f: Thomas FETHERSTONE; m: Matilda CARMICHEL] on 12 May 1879. Off: STENBERG. Wit: Robert GLYNN, Frank KLEFFNER.

DAVIS, Nathaniel W. [22; Elkhorn] md. Mary M. HANEY [20; Elkhorn] on 3 Mar 1867 in Elkhorn "in presence of witnesses." Off: DENTON.

DAVIS, Ole S. [26; Atlantic, IA; b: Norway; f: George DAVIS; m: Mary OLESON] md. Mary AMUNDSON [29; Atlantic, IA; b: Sweden; f: Christopher AMUNDSON; m: Catharina SIMONSON] on 6 Jan 1876. Off: HILMEN. Wit: C.H. HILGENDORF, Mrs. HILGENDORF.

DAVIS, Oscar F. [Omaha] md. Sarah F. DICKINSON [Omaha] on 22 Apr 1863 at John H. KELLOM's residence. Both of legal age. Off: DIMMICK. Wit: Harriette N. KELLOM, H. Elisabeth MILLER.

DAVIS, Thomas G. [23; Cass Co., IA] md. Amanda Jane WEST [19; Montgomery Co., IA] on 6 Jun 1861 at BIRKETT's office. Off: BIRKETT. Wit: John McCARTHY, et al.

DAVIS, U. or N. W. [21; Omaha] md. Rebecca E. SHARP [18; Omaha] on 9 Mar 1858 at Douglas House. Off: GAYLORD. Wit: Washington LEWIS, G.M. MILLS, both of Douglas Co.

DAVIS, William F. [21; Omaha; b: Defiance, OH; f: Zephania DAVIS; m: Susan LEWIS] md. Hattie L. BRIDGE [18; Omaha; b: Newark, NJ] on 2 Nov 1869. Off: KUHNS. Wit: Mr. and Mrs. D. St. GYER, Sarah SLIPE.

DAVIS, William R. [22; Omaha; b; Tennessee; f: Wm. DAVIS; m: Maria ROSE] md. E.L. CLEAVELAND [16; Omaha; b: Wisconsin; f: Edward CLEAVELAND; m: Laura THOMPSON] on 10 Sep 1877. Off: BARTHOLOMEW. Wit: Frank P. HANLON, C.C. SPERRY. Age consent given by father of the bride.

DAVIS, William [20] and Ann A. GOFF [17] license issued on 21 Feb 1857. No marriage record. Off: SCOTT. Age consent given by Amos DAVIS.

DAWLEY, A.L. [29; LeClaire, IA; b: IA; f: D.V. DAWLEY; m: Sabins CARLTON] md. Ida A. WAGNER [25; Davenport, IA; b: Germany; f: Ferdinand WAGNER; m: Ursula WURTEMBERGER] on 3 Feb 1881. Off: SHERRILL. Wit: Mrs. S.H.H. LARK, Mrs. A.F. SHERRILL.

DEAMUD, William H. [32; McArdle Precinct; b: Michigan; f: Samuel DEAMUD; m: Sarah M. MOORE] md. Mrs. Sarah B. GOSS [33; McArdle Precinct; b: Michigan; f: Micajah WILLETT; m: Phoebe GRIFFEN] on 22 Dec 1879 at the residence of Mrs. J.T. GRIFFEN. Off: INGRAM. Wit: Mrs. A.W. GRIFFEN of Omaha, Mrs. J.D. GRIFFEN of Fairview Farm.

DEAN, Henry [21; Rockport, Douglas Co.; b: Pennsylvania; f: John D. DEAN; m: Elizabeth THOMAS] md. Cynthia BAWES [16; Rockport, Douglas Co.; b: Iowa; f: Silas BAWES] on 23 Feb 1870 at PECK's residence in Florence. Off: PECK. Wit: "my wife"; France E. PECK and Margaret J. PECK, daughters "both at home in Florence"; Jane PECK, resides "near here". Age of consent given by father of bride, George L. CARROLL, witness.

DECKER, James F. [24; Elk Horn City; b: New Jersey; f: Simeon V. DECKER; m: Catharine FORBES] md. Jennie E. CRUISE [20; Omaha; b: Texas; f: Thomas CRUISE; m: Catharine CARSON] on 23 Feb 1880, Waterloo. Off: NEILSON. Wit: Mr. and Mrs. AUSTIN, Mr. and Mrs. SWEET, all of Waterloo, et al.

DECKER, Michael [25; Omaha; b: VA; f: John P. DECKER; m: Mary SMITH] md. Mrs. Katie E. FERGUSON [25; Omaha; b: IL; f: George ANDERSON; m: Eliza J. TRUE] on 16 Dec 1875. Off: BRITT. Wit: Jacob MARKEL, Robert LAING.

DEE, Michael [25; Douglas Co.] md. Catharine CONNOR [25; Douglas Co.] on 2 Feb 1862. Off: DILLON. Wit: Thomas COLLINS, Catharine COONIHAN.

DEE, Michael [34; Omaha; b: Ireland; f: John DEE: m: Mary LONG] md. Mrs. Mary ENRIGHT [34; Omaha; b: Ireland; f: Jeremiah ENRIGHT; m: Mary CARIMODY] on 31 Dec 1871 at the Catholic Church of Omaha. Off: O'GORMAN. Wit: Daniel RYAN; Ellen DEE.

DEERSON, Peter N. [34; Douglas Co.; b: Germany; f: Peter N. DEERSON; m: Hellen MILLER] md. Margaret GUTHARD [21; Douglas Co.; b: Germany; f: Hans GUTHARD] on 3 Jul 1874. Off: PEABODY. Wit: Emlen LEWIS, M.D.; Otis H. BALLOW.

DeFORREST, Con E. [26; Los Angeles, CA; b: New York; f: C.V. DeFORREST; m: Catherine RICE] md. J.E. BATES [18; New York; b: California; f: A.B. BATES] on 13 Feb 1877. Off: PATERSON. Wit: Miranda JOHNSON, Hester WRIGHT.

DEGNAN, Matthew J. [31; Omaha; b: Ireland; f: John DEGNAN; m: Mary DIVINE] md. Martha F. MURPHY [23; Omaha; b: City of New York; f: Wm. S. MURPHY; m: Bridget HARGADON] on 14 Nov 1871 at the Catholic Church of Omaha. Off: O'GORMAN. Wit: William R. MURPHY; Rosy McARDLE.

DEHMST, Peter [35; Cuming Co.; b: Baden, Germany; f: Christopher DEHMST; m: Margareta YEGER] md. Catherine MARTI [30; Omaha; b: Switzerland; f: Peter MARTI; m: Salome WUISTER] on 18 Feb 1870. Off: GIBSON. Wit: H.F. STRANG; John R. MANCHESTER.

DEHN, Markus [46; Omaha; b: Russia; f: Daniel DEHN; m: Catharine DEHN] md. Barbara JAKL [28; Omaha; b: Bohemia; f: Joseph JAKL; m: Barbara TANDEJSKOVA] on 14 Jun 1880. Off: KOCARNIK. Wit: Wenceslas FIALA, Fred. HENRY.

DEISING, George [26; Omaha; b: NJ; f: Geo. DEISING; m: Elizabeth SNYDER] md. Annie HERNICK [20; Omaha; b: IA; f: John HERNICK; m: Mary SHULER] on 27 Sep 1881. Off: BRUNS. Wit: Henry PULS, Elisabeth PULS.

DeKAY, Edwin [25; Lincoln; b: Warwich, NY; f: Thomas DeKAY; m: Sarah QUICK] md. Fannie I. FELLOWS [21; Omaha; b: Sheffield, IL; f: Ephraim FELLOWS; m: Alice W. PERKINS] on 14 Feb 1876. Off: STEWART. Wit: Emily W. STEWART, Mrs. S.H.H. CLARK.

DeLAND, James T. [26; Omaha; b: NY; f: James H. DeLAND; m: Ellen BUCKLY] md. Kate C. GUNDERSON [19; Douglas Co.; b: Norway; f: Adam GUNDERSON; m: Gussie HANSON] on 15 Mar 1876. Off: CRITCHFIELD. Wit: Albert ABLE, Delia CRITCHFIELD, Florence.

DELAND, William Henry [22; Florence; b: New York; f: James DELAND; m: Ellen BUCKLEY] md. Geneva REEVES [18; Florence; b: Nebraska; f: William REEVES; m: Mary? Jane BRADDOCK] on 18 Nov 1874 at Florence. Off: STEVENSON. Wit:

William BRACEY; John C. MEADIE, parents of the groom.

DELANEY, Jeremiah [28; Omaha; b: Ireland; f: Dennis DELAN(E)Y m: Abby KELLEY] md. Ellen SCANLAN [23; Omaha; b: Ireland; f: Edward SCANLAN; f: Honora WHELAN] on 6 Jan 1870. Off: CURTIS. Wit: Edward GORMAN; Ellen CANTY.

DELANEY, Patrick [25; Omaha] md. Mary KELLEY [24; Omaha] on 7 Feb 1869. Off: CURTIS. Wit: John CONNER, Margaret O'BRIEN.

DELANEY [DULANEY], David E. [31; Omaha] md. Sophia NELSON [21] on 12 May 1862. Off: McCARTHY. Wit: Hiram M. DICKINSON, Charles P. BIRKETT.

DELANY, Henry A. [31; La Platte; b: England; f: Patrick DELANY; m: Anne G. ROBERTS] and Fannie P. DALEY [21; La Platte; b: MD; f: Samuel DALEY; m: Frances E. ROWLES] license issued on 22 Sep 1875. No marriage recorded. Off: PEABODY. On back of application: Wit: Marion F. WOOD, Lucretia E. DALEY; also stamped date of filing: 22 Sep 1888.)

DELFEL, John [20; Omaha; b: Ohio; f: George DELFEL; m: Christine LEIHGEBER] md. Lizzie ROSS [18; Omaha; b: Washington, D.C.; f: Julius ROSS; m: Louisa F. GROUSE] on 26 Jan 1880, German M.E. Church. Off: BRUEGGER. Wit: M. BUEHLER, Mrs. C. KAISER.

DELFS, Johann C. [26; West Omaha; b: Germany; f: Max DELFS; m: Christina RAHN] md. Mrs. Margaretha PETERS [36; West Omaha; b: Germany; f: Peter WRIEDT; m: Elizabeth GRIMSMANN] on 10 Jul 1880. Off: BARTHOLOMEW. Wit: August CARSTENS, Max BERGMANN.

DELFS, John [40; b: Sarpy Co.; b: Germany; f: Marx DELFS; m: Katharina SCHMIDT] md. Margaretha BARGSTEDT [22; Sarpy Co.; b: Germany; f: Edward BARGSTEDT; m: Wiebke EHLERS] on 17 Mar 1880. Off: BENEKE. Wit: Claus SIEVERS, Gretchen SIEVERS both of Douglas Co.

DELLESTIN, James W. [28; Alloy? NY; b: New York; f: Uriah DELLESTIN; m: Maria STRATTAN] md. Mary M. McKENZIE [24; Omaha; b: New Orleans, LA; f: John McKENZIE] on 1 Aug 1871. Off: GIBSON. Wit: W.H. CADER; Maggie BROWN.

DELLON, Edward J. [45; Omaha] md. Adile SAUNIER [25; Omaha] on 18 Oct 1868. Off: William H. MORRIS. Wit: Justin P. BABEY, R.J. STUCK.

DELLONE, Frederick [27; Omaha] md. Jennetta HEANEY [20; Omaha] on 27 May 1866 at the Roman Catholic Church of Omaha. Off: O'GORMAN. Wit: Alexander DELLONE, Maria WAV__ING. See: DESLONDE.

DELSMAN, John B. [23; Columbus; b: WI; f: John B. DELSMAN; m: Dina EIMERS] md. Clara HEITKEMPER [19; IA; b: IA; f: Hermann HEITKEMPER; m: Anna] on 25 Nov 1875 at the German Catholic Church. Off: GROENBAUM. Wit: Mrs. Catharine FRENZER, Mary TEX.

DEMOREST, Peter A. [Omaha] md. Hannah M. STEWART [Omaha] on the evening of 3 May 1863 at the ME Church in presence of the congregation. Both of legal age. Off: LEMON.

DeNAYER, John B. [44; Lancaster Co.; b: Belgium; f: Edward DeNAYER; m: Marie Antoine PERRIER] md. Margaretta BARNES [38; Lancaster Co.; b: Ohio; f: Ezekia BARNES; m: Barbara BARNES] on 21 Mar 1879. Off: BENEKE. Wit: L.G. BRAGE, P.A. SANDBERG.

DENEHY, James [24; Omaha; b: Ireland; f: Daniel DENEHY; m: Elizabeth HANLON] md. Caroline LASSER [18; Omaha; b: Germany; f: Jacob LASSER; m: Amelia JOSEPH] on 24 May 1873. Off: TOWNSEND. Wit: Charles H. BYRNE; Leavitt H. BURNHAM.

DENKER, Wm. [23; b: Germany; f: H.C. DENKER; m: Christina DUEHRKOP] md. Emma SEIDLER [ 18; Papillion; b: Papillion, NE; f: Fritz SEIDLER; m: Fredricka RICHTER] on 4 Dec 1878. Off: WRIGHT. Wit: David VAN ETTEN, Robert MURDOCK.

DENNER, Louis [32; b: Italy; f: C. DENNER; m: Mary DENNER] md. Nellie F. BOWMAN [19; b: Illinois; f: John A. BOWMAN; m: Jennie R. MOIST] on 2 Feb 1878. Off: WILLIS. Wit: Mrs. Hattie PHELPS, Rodney DUTCHER. Affidavit signed "his mark."

DENNIS, Abraham [52; Douglas Co.] md. Elizabeth HARVEY [35; Douglas Co.] on 7 Sep 1862 at A.D. JONES' residence. Off: ARMSTRONG. Wit: Mr. and Mrs. A.D. JONES, Mr. and Mrs. L. LAWRENCE.

DENNIS, James H. [30; Omaha] md. Mrs. Martha M. MILLER [32; Omaha] on 6 Apr 1868. Off: KUHNS. Wit: Mrs. W.H. KUHNS, James MOHR.

DENNY, John [49; Neola, IA; b: Ireland; f: William DENNY; m: Mary MENNEN] md. Ellen HUGHES [28; Council Bluffs; b: Ireland; f: John HUGHES; m: Catherine HUGHES] on 26 Apr 1877 at the R.C.

Cathedral. Off: MARTIN. Wit: James COYLE, Sarah HUGHS, both of Council Bluffs.

DENTON, John W. [31; Douglas Co.] md. Martha G. WILLIAMS [24; Douglas Co.] on 23 May 1866 at the Court House. Off: HASCALL. Wit: Joseph A. DENTON, H.E. JACKSON, et al.

DEPUY, Thomas E. [35; Omaha; b: Orange, NJ; f: Henry B. DEPUY; m: Joan GATHARITE] md. Margaret M. MACKEI [23; Omaha; b: Canton, MO; f: Jacob MACKEI; m: Eunice SWEET] on 5 Mar 1873. Off: RUBY. Wit: Mary L. HARRIS; Jacob MACKEI.

DERMAN, William F. [22; Council Bluffs; b: MO; f: George W. DERMAN; m: Sophia KENNEDY] md. Agnes MITCHELL [26; Council Bluffs; b: PA; f: Henry MITCHELL; m: Catherine PATTERSON] on 4 May 1876. Off: DONNELLY. Wit: Edward O. SULLIVAN, George KARLE.

DESLONDE, Francis [28; Omaha] md. Helena REILY [19; Omaha] on 5 Oct 1862. Off: O'GORMAN. Wit: Frederick DESLONDE, Emma WAREHAM. See: DELLONE.

DESMOND, Patrick [30; Omaha; b: Ireland; f: William DESMOND; m: Nora LONG] md. Susan McCAHILL [24; Omaha; b: Iowa; f: John McCAHILL; m: Bridget LYNCH] on 18 Aug 1880. Off: ENGLISH. Wit: Dennis RYAN, Katie GOGGIN.

DEVENPORT, Perry F. [25; Omaha; b: MO; f: F.P. DEVENPORT; m: Louise A. HOLDEN] md. Mary M. PROTEAN [26; Omaha; b: Canada; f: Joseph PROTEAN; m: Florence BOURGET] on 10 Jul 1881. Off: MAXFIELD. Wit: Mrs. E.H. ELCOCK, Van Wert, OH, Mrs. M.M. MAXFIELD.

DEVERS [DEVUS], S.A. [27; Omaha] md. Eliza McCLAIN [21; Omaha] on 24 Aug 1868. Off: McCAGUE. Wit: Steven ROBINSON, Mrs. H(enrietta) M(atilda) McCAGUE.

DEVITT, Patrick E. [25; Omaha; b: IA; f: Edward DEVITT; m: Alice CONDON] md. Catherine McCAFFREY [23; Omaha; b: WI; f: Patrick McCAFFREY, Elizabeth DORSEY] on 15 Jun 1881. Off: ENGLISH. Wit: Mrs. TAYLOR, Ed EGAN.

DHAM, William [27; Omaha; b: Prussia; f: Charles DHAM; m: Mena MENGEL] md. Lena REAN [22; Omaha; b: Schleswig, Holstein] on 16 Jun 1872. Off: GROENEBAUM. Wit: Casimire WIRTH; Catharine PYE.

DICKERHOFF, John [34; Omaha; b: Blair Co., PA; f: John DICKERHOFF; m: Caroline HEBEUCH] md. Laura HOYE [16; Omaha; b: London, England; f: John HOYE; m: Amelia BIRCH] on 26 May 1872. Off: CLARKSON. Wit: Willis TABS; E. TABS. Age of consent given by father of the bride.

DICKERSON, Joseph [23; Douglas Co.] md. Mary Ann BAYLES (BAILES) [24; Douglas Co.] on 14 Apr 1858 at the ME Church. Off: GAYLORD. Wit: G.W. HOMAN, A.H. PALMER.

DICKINSON, Charles G. [28; Cheyenne, WY; b: Ohio; f: Elisha N. DICKINSON; m: Elizabeth M. BROWN] md. Laura C. MICHAEL [24; North Platte; b: Des Moines, IA; f: ??? MICHAEL; m: N.K. KEZARTEE] on 20 Dec 1877. Off: SHERRILL. Wit: Mrs. I.T. CLARK, Oscar CLARKE.

DICKINSON, George W. [26; Omaha; b: Ohio; f: Charles S. DICKINSON; m: Ellen CARR] md. Mrs. Ella C. TAYLOR [26; Omaha; b: New York; f: Peter B. COLE; m: Catharine HAMM] on 18 Feb 1879. Off: LIPE. Wit: William SHULL, Mattie SHULL. Affidavit signed by John P. SHIPMAN.

DICKSON, K.M. [Omaha] md. Harriet E. PERRY [Omaha] on the evening of 8 Mar 1864. Off: LEMON. Wit: Mr. and Mrs. SELDEN, et al.

DIDRICKSON, Peter [23, Douglas Co.; b: Germany; f: Dedrick DIDRICKSON; m: Celia COURT] md. Maggie PETERS [18; Douglas Co.; b: Germany; f: Theo. PETERS; m: Margret SEVERS] on 12 Jul 1876. Off: SEDGWICK. Wit: Peter GOOS, Douglas Co., F.P. HANLON, Douglas Co.

DIETERICH, Herman [21; Omaha; b: Germany; f: R.H. DIETRICH; m: Alma WIGAND] md. Anna Melisa TUCK [20; Omaha; b: Missouri; f: John TUCK; m: Susan SMITH] on 2 Apr 1874. Off: DAVIS. Wit: John W. LYTLE; Wm. SCOTT.

DIETRICHSEN, Jacob [24; Ft. Calhoun; b: Germany; f: Dietrick DIETRICHSEN; m: Anna MARTINSEN] md. Lena HANS [26; Ft. Calhoun; b: Germany; f: Peter HANS; m: Eda HOPE] on 29 Jun 1874. Off: HILGENDORF. Wit: Jno. SCHNEEDE; Peter HINS.

DILLMAN, Henry [29; b: Germany; f: Jacob DILLMAN; m: Annie M. HATZMENN] md. Katie RICHARD [20; b: Pennsylvania; f: John RICHARD; m: Sophia SENKEL] on 10 Sep 1878. Off: FALK. Wit: Adam KOCH, Henry RICHARD, Katie SCHEID, Anna WIEDERMEIER.

DINAN, Daniel [32; Omaha; b: Irelalnd; f: Timothy DINAN; m: Bridget NEIL] md. Johanna FOLEY [22; Omaha; b: Ireland; f: Timothy T. FOLEY; m: Margaret ENRIGHT] on 23 Sep 1877 at the Catholic Church. Off: JENNETTE. Wit: Thomas MURPHY, Bridget DINAN.

DINEEN, John C. [25; Omaha] md. Margaret GORMAN [23; Omaha] on 11 Apr 1861 at the Catholic Church of Omaha. Off: KELLY. Wit: John ?, Ann HEALEY.

DINGMAN, John R. [25; IA; b: Council Bluffs; f: John B. DINGMAN; m: Martha RITTER] md. Alice BICE [18; IA; b: IA; f: Charles BICE; m: Rebecca RICHMOND] on 16 Aug 1881. Off: HYDE. Wit: Dr. GRADDY, Charles POWELL.

DINNEEN, Michael [23; b: Ireland; f: Patrick DINNEEN; m: Margaret PENDERGAST] md. Honora E. KENNELLY [23; b: Nebraska; f: John KENNELLY; m: Elizabeth DEE] on 15 Jun 1878. Off: KELLY. Wit: John REAGAN, Margaret KENNELLY.

DINSDALE, Robert [39; Douglas Co.; b: England; f: George DINSDALE; m: Margaret BRELTAN] md. Johanna McALBERTSON [49; Douglas Co; b: Denmark; f: Gregis JENSEN; m: Meran PETERSDOTTER] on 15 Dec 1870. Off: GIBSON. Wit: Joseph ADAIR; William ROBERSON, Sarpy Co.

DITZEN, Henry [22; b: Germany; f: Conrad DITZEN; m: Octavia ANATONI] md. Maria FELDKAMP [18; b: Germany; f: Anton FELDKAMP; m: Caroline SCHROEDER] on 31 Dec 1878. Off: FALK. Wit: Louis SCHROEDER, Charles HORST.

DIXON, John [22; Omaha; b: Ireland; f: James DIXON; m: Mary YOUNG] md. Catherine SLATTERY [23; Omaha; b: Ireland; f: Michael SLATTERY; m: Bridget MEDDEN] on 7 Aug 1870. Off: CURTIS. Wit: Andrew MURPHY; Catherine FERRY.

DODGE, Peter C. [22; Beatrice; b: NY; f: W.E. DODGE; m: M.M. CAIN] md. Irene A. BROCK [25; Creston, IL; b: NY; f: Samuel BROCK; m: Amanda McDOWELL] on 15 Dec 1875. Off: STEWART. Wit: John CARROLL, Mrs. Emily W. STEWART.

DOFFEN, Powell [32; Omaha; b: Germany; f: Henry DOFFEN] md. Frederika RAUH [21; Omaha; b: Germany; f: John RAUH; m: Mary SEBOLT] on 19 Mar 1870. Off: GIBSON. Wit: Louis HERR; Charles DITTBERNER.

DOHERTY or DOUGHERTY, John [40; Douglas Co.] md. Grace GARVEY [28; Omaha] on 7 Jan 1868 at the Catholic Church of Omaha. Off: O'GORMAN. Wit: Hugh BRENNAN, Catherine BRENNAN.

DOHERTY, Robert [31; Omaha; b: Ireland; f: John DOHERTY; m: Isabella HARMAN] md. Emma WINDSOR [24; Omaha; b: MD; f: Henry J. WINDSOR; m: Susan H. BENSON] on 1 Aug 1876 at Trinity Cathedral. Off: CLARKSON. Wit: Mrs. Susan WINDSOR, Gilbert MEES.

DOHLE, Henry [27; Omaha; b: Germany; f: Henry DOHLE; m: Helene SCHWEITER] md. Julia STOCKHAMMER [18; Omaha; b: Germany] on 9 Jul 1869. Off: KELLEY. Wit: Patrick McGOVERN, Frederick SCHONDEN.

DOHRMANN, Henry (Hinrick) [29; Shelby Co., IA; b: Germany; f: F. DOHRMANN; m: Dora DOSE] md. Christina

EVAN [24; Avoca, IA; b: Germany; f: Evan EVANS; m: Anna PETERSON] on 21 Jul 1876. Off: SEDGWICK. Wit: Annie HANSEN, F.P. HANLON, Douglas Co.

DOLAN, John R. [34; Omaha; b: New York; f: Patrick DOLAN; m: Margrett REILY] and Ollie EVERS [22; Omaha; b: Iowa] license issued on 24 Dec 1877. No marriage record. Off: HANLON.

DOLEN, Joseph [Council Bluffs] and Mary BLOIEN [Council Bluffs] license issued on 7 May 1863. No marriage record. Both of legal age. Off: DICKINSON.

DOLL, August [47; b: Germany; f: Friedrich DOLL; m: Elizabeth KROEGER] md. Eliabeth FRIER [39; b: Germany; f: George FRIER; m: Elizabeth MOR] on 5 Dec 1878. Off: BENEKE. Wit: Conrad LEISGE, William DOLL.

DOLL, Charley [30; Douglas Co.] md. Sina MILLER [22; Douglas Co.] on 10 Mar 1868. Off: STUCK. Wit: William DOLL, Andrew MILLER, et al.

DOLL, John [29; Omaha; b: Germany; f: Fred DOLL; m: Maggie BRANDLE] md. Caroline OSWALD [21; Omaha; b: Germany; f: Charles OSWALD; m: Caroline HOUSER] on 28 Mar 1874. Off: PEABODY. Wit: Charles HART; Frank COLE.

DONAHEY, Fulton [26; St. Charles, MO] and Maria BOYLE [about 18] license issued on 5 Apr 1867. No marriage record. Off: HASCALL. Age consent given in person by the guardian of the bride.

DONALDSON, Cyrus [32; Little Sioux, IA; b: PA; f: William A. DONALDSON; m: Sarah HALL] md. Adel HALL [20; Little Sioux, IA; b: IA; f: Andrew HALL; m: Sarah Jane MOODY] on 3 Jul 1875. Off: PEABODY. Wit: Ellen OSMUND, Mabel L. PEABODY.

DONALDSON, James W. [23; DeWitt, Cuming Co.] md. Ellen A. PANCOAST [18 last Christmas; DeWitt, Cuming Co.] on 1 Jul 1866. Off: JANNEY. Wit: John PANCOAST, Sarah M. JANNEY.

DONALDSON, N.F. [29; Mills Co., IA; b: OH; f: Fielding DONALDSON; m: Caroline JONES] md. Lizzie LITTLE [21, Douglas Co.; b: PA; f: George L. LITTLE; m: Felecia or Francis WICK] on 25 May 1876. Off: LITTLE. Wit: Geo. D. STEWARD, Thos. OFFICER, Council Bluffs.

DONECKER [DORNACKER], Augustus [21; Omaha] md. Sarah BUCHANAN [21; Omaha] on 16 Dec 1866. Off: SLAUGHTER. Wit: Wm. COBURN, Savannah COBURN.

DONELLY, Thomas [25; Omaha; b: Ireland; f: John DONELLY; m: Kate AGAN] md. Mary CASEY [26; Omaha; b: Ireland; f: Patrick CASEY; m: Margaret RYAN] on 27 Jun 1870. Off: CURTIS. Wit: Patrick KELLEY; Mrs. Annie BLOCK.

DONK, Charles [ 21; Rochester, NY; b: Wayne Co., NY; f: Carl DONK; m: Hannah EICKHOFF] md. Mary ASHFORD [22; Florence; b: Fayette Co., IL; f: Jesse ASHFORD; m: Almira GLASS] on 9 Jul 1869. Off: HYDE. Wit: George SMITH, C.D. HYDE.

DONNELLY, Edward [29; Saratoga Pct., Douglas Co.; b: Ireland; f: Terrence DONNELLY; m: Fanny McGOVERN] md. Mary Ellen BURKE [18; Saratoga Pct., Douglas Co.; b: Fort Riley, KS; f: Barton BURKE; m: Mary O'CONNELL] on 13 Jan 1873. Off: THURSTON. Wit: H.W. CENNEBAUGH; Bridget MARSTON. (Bride was 18 on 22 Nov 1872.)

DONNELLY, Samuel F. [25; Omaha; b: New York; f: G.G. DONNELLY; m: Susan R. WEED] md. Julia A. GATES [22; Omaha; b: New York; f: Wm. H. GATES; m: Marietta STRONG] on 8 Dec 1877. Off: JAMESON. Wit: Dr. Geo. L. MILLER, Mrs. [H.E.] MILLER.

DONNELLY, Thaddeus Henry [28; Omaha; b: Oswego, NY; f: James DONNELLY; m: Mary J. WATSON] md. Delia McMAHAN [20; Omaha; b: Ireland; f: Michael McMAHAN; m: Ann LYNCH] on 24 Jan 1877, Catholic Cathedral. Off: FINOTTI. Wit: James DONNELLY, Bridget COLLINS.

DONNELLY, William [49; Douglas Co.; b: Ireland; f: John DONNELLY; m: Nancy MURPHY] md. Mrs. Ellen LEARY [35; Douglas Co.; b: Ireland; f: Timothy McCARTY; m: Catharine CURRAN (CRAVEN?)] on 23 Apr 1874 at Elkhorn. Off: KEENAN. Wit: Thomas O'SHEA, Council Bluffs; Mrs. Mary O'SHEA, Council Bluffs.

DONOVAN, John J. [24; Omaha; b: Ireland; f: Michiel DONOVAN; m: Ellen ALLEN] md. Mary GALVIN [20; Omaha; b: Ireland; f: James D. GALVIN; m: Ellen COLLINS] on 6 Nov 1879, filed in 1888. Off: McCARTHY. Wit: Patrick EGAN, Mary CALAHAN.

DONOVAN, Michael [33; Omaha] md. Ann McGUIRE [22; Omaha] on 12 Mar 1869 at O'GORMAN's house. Off: O'GORMAN. Wit: E.L. SHEPPARD, Margaret HALLORAN.

DOODY, Michael [21; Omaha; b: OH; f: Michael DOODY; m: Mary CAREY] md. Kate FINELY [20; Omaha; b: WI; f: James FINELY; m: Mary O'DONNELL] on 23 Oct 1876. Off: WRIGHT. Wit: James Osgood ADAMS, Mrs. E. FINLY.

DOOLY [DOOLEY], John md. Maria REDLIG on 8 Jul 1865 at the Roman Catholic Church of Omaha. Off: O'GORMAN. Wit: Patrick DELONG, Helen KERAN.

DOON, Rasmus Peterson [23; Omaha; b: Denmark; f: Rasmus PETERSON; m: Gurtie LARSON] md. Ann Stina ANDERSEN [23; Omaha; b: Denmark; f: Andres ANDERSEN; m: Marian LARSON] on 13 Jul 1872. Off: TOWNSEND. Wit: George KLEFFNER; John M. WAMBAUGH.

DORAN, Patrick [25; Willow Island (Dawson Co.?)] md. Mary HUGHES [23; Omaha] on 6 Jan 1869 at the Catholic Church. Off: O'GORMAN. Wit: James RUDY, Delia McCOY.

DORE, Patrick [29; Omaha; b: Ireland; f: Edmund DORE; m: Nora LEE] md. Annie McGLINCHY [32; Omaha; b: Ireland; f: Cornelius McGLINCHY; m: Mary COYLE] on 15 Dec 1880. Off: ENGLISH. Wit: Edward EGAN, Cresentia SCHRAFFEL.

DORMANN, August [30; Omaha; b: Germany; f: August DORMANN; m: Bertha Juliana SANGENSEFREN] md. Frederika KANENBLEY [20; Omaha; b: Jersey City, NJ; f: Frederick KANENBLEY; m: Metta MEYER] on 9 Dec 1871. Off: GASSMANN. Wit: G.F. FARMAINE; George HEIMROD.

DORN, Francis [27; Omaha; b: Austria; f: Francis DORN; m: Francisca PROKOP] md. Annie YANDA [JANDA] [20; Omaha; b: Bohemia; f: Joseph YANDA [JANDA]] on 27 Feb 1872. Off: TOWNSEND. Wit: Valentine BARTH; Frederick SOMMER.

DORN, Frank [31; Omaha; b: Germany; f: Frank DORN; m: Francisca DORN] md. Mary NEWARK [NOVAK] [25; Omaha; b: Bohemia; f: John NEWARK [NOVAK]; m: Annie NEWARK [NOVAK]] on 22 Mar 1876. Off: SEDGWICK. Wit: Thomas KASTNER, Frank P. HANLON.

DORNECKER, Nicolas [26; Omaha] md. Henrietta VALCHER [22; Omaha] on 11 Jul 1868. Off: KELLY. Wit: B. GILLETT, Fred GILLHORN.

DORR, Joseph W. [23; Omaha; b: Illinois; f: Phillip G. DORR; m: Mary A. WHILHARBOR] md. Margaret P. DURRITT [17 years 7 months; Omaha; b: New York; f: Henry DURRITT; m: Sarah H. ASCOTT of York Center, York Co.] on 15 Jul 1877. Off: SEDGWICK. Wit: Marcia F. SEDGWICK, Hans JOHNSON.

DORR, Philip G. [48; Omaha; b: Germany; f: Frederick DORR; m: Elizabeth] md. Mrs. Marie HOUSTON [32; Omaha; b: Germany; f: Herr POHLMANN; m: Theresa HUNDERLICK] on 28 Oct 1873. Off: HALE. Wit: C.C. SCHAEFFER; G. SCHAEFFER.

DORWALD, Frederick [28; Omaha] md. Augustus SALZWELD [21; Omaha] on 29 Dec 1867. Off: KELLEY. Wit: Wm. H. MORRIS, J. TOOKER, J.W. SAVAGE.

DOTY, George N. [23; Omaha; b: West Virginia; f: Ezra S. DOTY; m: Elizabeth CROSS] md. Sarah J. ELLIS [16; Omaha; b: Iowa; f: Jonathan D. ELLIS; m: Mary E. LUDDINGTON] on 18 Oct 1873. Off: TOWNSEND. Wit: Jonathan D. ELLIS; Mary E. ELLIS.

DOTY, John C. [30; New York; b: New York; f: John DOTY; m: Olive E. WALKER] md. Mrs. Susan F. BAKER [31; New York; b: New York; f: Warren FAY] on 30 Aug 1871. Off: DeLaMATYR. Wit: Mr. BARTHOLOMEW.

DOUGHERTY, Charles [21; Omaha; b: PA; f: John DOUGHERTY; m: Margaret CALL] md. Mary DUFFY [22; Omaha; b: Canada; f: James DUFFY; m: Winnefred GALLAGHER] on 9 Feb 1875 at the Roman Catholic Cathedral. Off: BYRNE. Wit: Francis DOUGHERTY, Ellen O'CONNOR.

DOUGLAS, James M. [St. Louis, MO] and F. Georgiana LEE [Omaha] license issued on 5 May 1858. No marriage record. Off: WATSON.

DOUGLAS, Robert W. [23; Elkhorn; b: New York; f: David DOUGLAS; m: May WARNICK] md. Jenny A. HANEY [21; Elkhorn; b: Pennsylvania; f: John HANEY; m: Sarah BOLIN] on 22 Feb 1871 at Elkhorn Station. Off: DODGE. Wit: Samuel B. and Mollie HANEY, Elkhorn; Clark B. HANEY, Elkhorn.

DOUGLASS, Stephen M. [27; Omaha] md. Clara B. PRINTZ [21; Cincinnati, OH] on 3 Apr 1868. Off: KUHNS. Wit: Oscar F. STEPHENS, William B. KING.

DOUTHETT, E. [26; Omaha; b: IL; f: R. DOUTHETT; m: Eliza MONTGOMERY] md. Mary DEVLIN [26; Omaha; b: Canada; f: John DEVLIN; m: Matilda BULLIS] on 15 Nov 1881. Off: STENBERG. Wit: Geo. W. PETTENGILL, J.P. MANNING.

DOW, Willard W. [26; Sarpy Co.; b: Illinois; f: Robert M. DOW; m: Ann BENNETT] md. Mary Jane JARVIS [26; Sarpy Co.; b: Canada West; f: John JARVIS; m: Mary CURTIS] on 31 Jan 1872. Off: TOWNSEND. Wit: Philander H. REED; Jerome HERTZMANN.

DOWDALL, Peter [26; Omaha; b: Ireland; f: John DOWDALL; m: Rose HALL] md. Catharine T. JUDGE [22; Omaha; b: PA; f: Paul JUDGE; m: Margaret GILMARTIN] on 19 Oct 1881. Off: SHAFFEL. Wit: John PRICE, Catherine MAHODY.

DOWLING, Michael [24; North Bend; b: New York; f: Michael DOWLING; m: Hannah McCARDLE] md. Mary E. PURCELL [23; North Bend; b: New York; f: Thomas PURCELL; m: ELiza Ann O'HARER] on 31 Dec 1870. Off: CURTIS. Wit: Albert E. SIMPSON; Mary SIMPSON.

DOWNES, John [22; Omaha] md. Margarett CONNER [23; Omaha] on 5 Apr 1869. Off: GIBSON. Wit: Nathan ELLIOTT, John MORRELL.

DOWNEY, Patrick [32; Omaha] md. Mary MURRY [20; Omaha] on 14 Jul 1867 at the Roman Catholic Church of Omaha. Off: O'GORMAN. Wit: James McCULLOUGH, Mary A. McCULLOUGH.

DOYLE, Benjamin N. [27; Omaha; b: Massachusetts; f: John N. DOYLE: m: Elizabeth E. MARSH] md. Hattie E. PALMER [19; Omaha; b: Iowa; f: George PALMER; m: Mehitabel M. DeWOLFE] on 19 May 1874. Off: PEABODY. Wit: John M. THURSTON; John E. KELLEY.

DOYLE, Edward F. [21; Council Bluffs; b: IA; f: Andrew DOYLE; m: Mary A. BACHUS] md. Dellie WELSH [18; Council Bluffs; b: WI; f: William WELSH; m: Julia CHOAT] on 5 Feb 1881. Off: ANDERSEN. Wit: Theodor GREBE, Louis GREBE.

DOYLE, James [23; Douglas Co.] md. Jane LANGDON [16; Douglas Co.] on 15 Dec 1867 at the Catholic Cathedral. Off: GROENBAUM. Wit: Michael LANGDON, Mary GELASPY. Verbal age consent given by the father of the bride.

DOYLE, William [24; Council Bluffs; b: NJ; f: Martin DOYLE; m: Sarah BODINE] md. Carrie GERSBECK [18; Council Bluffs; f: Joseph GERSBECK; m: Caroline BEELER] on 3 Mar 1875. Off: PEABODY. Wit: V.P. ERP, Council Bluffs, Sarah BODINE.

DRAKE, Flemon [27; Omaha; b: An Arbor, MI; f: Flemon DRAKE; m: Electa DEPUE] md. Hellen M. INGALLS [19; Omaha; b: Attica, NY; f: Oscar P. INGALLS; m: Kate STARING] on 18 Aug 1869. Off: BETTS. Wit: Osacr P. INGALLS, E.M. MORSEMAN.

DRAKE, Frank E. [26; Omaha; b: New Jersey; f: Eliphalet DRAKE; m: Anna M. STEWART] md. Sarah M. KOON [24; Omaha; b: New York; f: E.M. KOON; m: Sarah ----] on 11 Aug 1877. Off: HARSHA. Wit: Ida M. GOODMAN, S.C. GOODMAN.

DREHER, Victor [39; Omaha; b: Germany; f: Conrad DREHER; m: Barbara MATHANER] md. Mrs. Margaretha BAUER [39; Omaha; b: Germany; f: Johannes WEBER; m: Margaretha WOLF] on 7 Aug 1880. Off: BENEKE. Wit: Edward BURSKI, Albertine HOTTENROTH.

DRENNAN, James W. [26; Omaha Barracks; b: Ireland; f: Daniel DRENNAN; m: Mary WALLACE] md. Alice KEOWEN [18; Omaha Barracks; b: Canada East; f: Francis KEOWEN; m: Delia LYNCH] on 18 May 1873. Off: CURTIS. Wit: Jeremia COLLINS; Bridget COLLINS.

DREW, Charles L. [23; Omaha; b: Boston, MA; f: Loraine J. DREW; m: Louisa TYLER] and Cordelia C. PAGE [20; Omaha; b: Ohio; f: Charles W. PAGE; m: ---- NASH] license issued on 7 Apr 1870. Off: GIBSON.

DREW, George T. [27; Omaha; b: Michigan; f: Hiram DREW; m: Martha McNEAL] md. Carrie M. SORENSON [24; Omaha; b: Denmark; f: John SORENSON; m: Johanna ZIMMERMAN] on 9 Oct 1877. Off: SEDGWICK. Wit: H.A. STURGESS, John G. BRADISH.

DREW, Samuel H. [23; Omaha; b: Illinois; f: Sands P. DREW; m: Rebecka PERKINS] md. Ella J. HOLLAND [18; Florence; b: New York or Indiana; f: James HOLLAND; m: Margaret WEBSTER] on 15 Nov 1870 at Florence. Off: STEVENSON, PUGSLEY also signed cert. Wit: Maria KEETCH, Florence; Charl PETTERSON, Florence.

DRISCOLL, Dennis [24; US Army; b: England; f: William DRISCOLL; m: Ella JONES] md. Elizabeth F. JENNINGS [19; Omaha; b: Missouri; f: James JENNINGS; m: Mary BRYANT] on 26 Mar 1871. Off: GIBSON. Wit: J.P. DISBROW; Marietta DISBROW.

DRISCOLL, George W. [22; Omaha; b: New York; f: John DRISCOLL; m: Martha McGUIRE] md. Martha E. ELLISON [18; Omaha; b: New York; f: Wm. E. ELLISON; m: Elizabeth J. CARTER] on 1 Dec 1873. Off: PEABODY. Wit: Ira O. TUTTLE, San Francisco; Jesse F. KEIL. Age of consent given by mother of the bride, Elizabeth Jane ELLISON.

DROESSEL, Ralph [29; Omaha; b: Germany; f: Paul DROESSEL; m: Theodora SAUTER] md. Lena KLEIN [19; Omaha; b: PA; f: Fritz KLEIN; m: Elizabeth MASSION] on 12 Jun 1881. Off: FRIES. Wit: Alfred MASSION, Catharina ELSASSER.

DROST, Louis C. [23; Omaha; b: Germany; f: Frederick DROST; m: Minna SONNE] md. Mary E. McGEE [28; Florence; b: Missouri] on 9 Jul 1873 at Florence. Off: DeLANDE. Wit: Samantha CHAPMAN, Florence; Edward SPURGANS.

DROSTE, August [32; Omaha; b: Germany; f: William DROSTE; m: Julia CAPELLE] md. Emma HARTWIG [22; Omaha; b: Germany; f: William HARTWIG; m: Maria SCHMIDT] on 9 Jan 1873. Off: ESTABROOK. Wit: James C. WIEMIRS; Edward KREISSMANN.

DROSTE, Edward [29; Omaha; b: Germany; f: August DROSTE; m: Julia CAPELLE] md. Ernestine ACKERMANN [21; Omaha; b: Wisconsin; f: George ACKERMANN; m: Auguste RIECKS] on 27 Jun 1879. Off: HILEMAN. Wit: Emil ACKERMANN, Julius FESTNER.

DRUMMOND, Melville J. [22; Lincoln; b: West Virginia; f: Pelton DRUMMOND; m: Elizabeth McINTYRE] md. Jennie CLARK [24; Omaha; b: Illinois; f: Lorenzo D. CLARK; m: Rose ----] on 29 Sep 1877. Off: MULCAHY. Wit: Leonidas B. ARNOLD, Richard De DARLING.

DRURY, William [Florence] md. Elizabeth Mabell TUTTLE [Florence] on 10 Feb 1864 in Florence City. Off: TURNER.

DUCKER, Lewis [22] md. Esther THOMAS [20] on 1 Jan 1868. Off: HURLBUT.

DUEHOLM, Christian P. [27; Omaha] md. Magdelina HOLST [28; Omaha] on 7 Nov 1868. Off: KUHNS. Wit: John AHMANSON, Peter MICHELSEN.

DUFF, James M. [26; Omaha; b: Pennsylvania; f: Dennis DUFF; m: Mary A. DUGAN] md. Emily BRODERICK [19; Omaha; b: London, England; f: James BRODERICK; m: Esther WELCH] on 14 Apr 1873. Off: CURTIS. Wit: William P. HICKEY; Teresa LIES.

DUFFAK, James [25; Omaha] md. Barbara JENSEN [JANSA] [25; Omaha] on 9 Feb 1869. Off: HYDE. Wit: DeMotte HYDE, Anton JENSEN [JANSA].

DUFFEY, Martin [22; Omaha; b: Ireland; f: Patrick DUFFEY; m: Catherine McCORMICK] md. Eliza MORAN [24; Omaha; b: Ireland; f: Patrick MORAN; m: Catharine O'CONNER] on 13 Aug 1870. Off: McGOLDRICK. Wit: John FOLEY; Mary McMAHON.

DUFFY, Bernard J. [24; Omaha; b: Dublin, Ireland; f: Patrick J. DUFFY; m: Mary McCORMICK] md. Annie McGARVIN [25; Omaha; b: Ireland; f: Patrick McGARVIN; m: Ella McGARVIN] on 13 Jun 1870. Off: CURTIS. Wit: Jeremiah COLLINS; Maria CORRIGAN.

DUFFY, James [36; Omaha; b: Ireland; f: Michael DUFFY; m: Bridget EAGEN] and Mary RYAN [33; Omaha; b: Ireland; f: Thomas RYAN; m: Winefer LOWRY] license issued on 20 Oct 1879. No marriage record. Off: BARTHOLOMEW.

DUFFY, Michael [32; Omaha; b: Ireland; f: Michael DUFFY; m: Bridget EGAN] md. Margaret BAGLEY [22; Omaha; b; Ireland; f: Charles BAGLEY; m: Mary DURELEY] on 5

Nov 1877, Catholic Cathedral. Off: JENNETTE. Wit: John GUINAN, Kate CARROLL.

DUGUID, Thomas [29; Sarpy Co.; b: Scotland; f: Robert DUGUID, m: Eliabeth McDONALD] md. Annie NUSLEIN [21; b: Maryland; f: John NUSLEIN, m: Barbara BOWER] at the German Catholic Church on 20 Oct 1878. Off: GROENBAUM. Wit: Rudolph NUSLEIN, Anna UNDERMEYER.

DUKE, John James [19; Engl.; no parents or relatives in this county, active for himself for 3 years] and Anna WALKER [18; Engl.] license issued on 24 May 1860. No marriage record. Both emigrants to Utah. Off: ARMSTRONG.

DUNCAN, Alexander [39; Council Bluffs; b: Pennsylvania; f: Wm. A. DUNCAN; m: Elizabeth LICHKY] md. Emma J. KELLEY [32; Council Bluffs; b: Virginia; f: Patrick KELLEY; m: Ann NOWIKY] on 12 Mar 1874. Off: PEABODY. Wit: F.P. HANLON; Levi A. WELDEN.

DUNCAN, Lemuel [42; Saunders Co.] md. Sarah ALAWAY [33; Saunders Co.] on 10 Sep 1867. Off: SHEEKS. Wit: John MALSBURRY, Thomas SWOPE.

DUNDY, Elmer S. [31; Falls City] md. Mary H. ROBINSON [20; Omaha] on 17 Jun 1861 at the residence of the bride's parents. Off: KUHNS. Wit: Judge KELLOGG, Judge LOCKWOOD, Judge WAKELY, et al.

DUNGAN, George W. [25; Florence] and Mary Ann CASSIDY [18; Florence] license issued on 8 Oct 1861. No marriage record. Off: ARMSTRONG.

DUNHAM, Benjamin [30; Omaha; b: New Jersey; f: John DUNHAM; m: Emeline] md. Rose Ann DUFFEY [21; Omaha; b: Maryland; f: Michael DUFFEY; m: Rose A. KIRCLAHAN] on 23 Jan 1872 at O'GORMAN's house. Off: O'GORMAN. Wit: Charles HANLEY; Mary MADDEN.

DUNHAM, Martin [Omaha] md. Sarah J. WINSHIP [Omaha] on 13 Jul 1863 at the residence of the bride's mother. Both of legal age. Off: KUHNS. Wit: Samuel SWENGEL, Wm. RYAN.

DUNHAM, Samuel [31; Dunlap; IA; b: Iowa; f: Cornelius DUNHAM; m: Margaret SCOTT] md. Sophrona ROBBINS [21; Dunlap, IA; b: New York; f: Henry ROBBINS; m: Maria FRIK] on 1 Apr 1874. Off: PEABODY. Wit: Saul HENDRICKSON; A. SWARTZLANDER.

DUNK, William [58; Burt Co.; b: England; f: Richard DUNK; m: Winnie WICKS; md. Mrs. Mary TURNER [63; Douglas Co.; b: England; f: John REEVES; m: Mary KENNISTON] on 15 Nov 1876 at Florence. Off: CRITCHFIELD. Wit: William REEVES, Florence, Eliza K. MITCHELL, Florence.

DUNMORE, Louis [22; Florence; b: Michigan; f: Wm. H. DUNMORE; m: Laura SIMMONS] md. Lucy NICHOLS [22; Florence; b: Illinois; f: John NICHOLS; m: Charlotte MOSES] on 25 Oct 1870. Off: KUHNS. Wit: Louisa and Phebe NICHOLS, both of Florence.

DUNN, Elijah [25; Omaha; b: Vermont; f: William DUNN; m: Betsy E. PRATT] md. Mrs. Mary A. ROSS [25; Omaha; b: England; f: Thomas WALKER] on 11 Mar 1871. Off: DeLaMATYR. Wit: P.M. HARTSON; D. HARTSON.

DUNN, James T. [Douglas Co.] md. Ellen BARD [Douglas Co.] on 12 Sep 1865 at the Court House. Off: HASCALL. Wit: Lewis S. REED, John H. SAHLER, et al.

DUNN, Martin [31; Omaha] md. Mary BOYLE [23; Omaha] on 27 Sep 1868. Off: CURTIS. Wit: John BURKE, Catharine KENAN.

DUNN, Michael [30; Omaha] and Mary McBRIDE [24; Omaha] on 9 Apr 1860. Off: ARMSTRONG.

DUNN, R.H. [25; Hamburg, IA] md. Anna S. STREETER [23; Omaha] on 10 Nov 1868. Off: RICE.

DUNNE, George B. [32; Omaha; b: Ireland; f: John DUNNE; m: Mary BRADLEY] md. Sarah J. GARDNER [18; Council Bluffs; b: Council Bluffs, IA; f: James GARDNER; m: Sylvia COLLINS] on 17 Jun 1872. Off: TOWNSEND. Wit: George KLEFNER; John M. WAMBAUGH.

DUNNIGAN, Francis [Frank] [25; Omaha; b: Ohio; f: Thomas DUNNIGAN; m: Anne McGARRY] md. Lizzie MASON [18; Omaha; b: Pennsylvania; f: Michael MASON; m: Harriet RYAN] on 1 Dec 1877. Off: REYNOLDS. Wit: Richard MOORE, Julia BARRY.

DUNNING, Hilliard S. [39; Carson, NV; b: ME; f: Reuben DUNNING; m: Lucy HOLDNG] md. Anna L. WING [35; MA; b: ME; f: W.M. WING; m: Charlotte RUNNELS] on 21 Oct 1875. Off: BRITT. Wit: H.C. PRATT, Mary C. PRATT.

DUNNING, William H., M.D. [28; Sarpy Co.; b: England; f: Henry DUNNING; m: Elizabeth CHORD] md. Mary T. CONDON [22; Sarpy Co.; b: Illinois; f: John CONDON; m: Hannah] on 25 Feb 1874. Off: PEABODY. Wit: Jacob PALMER, Forest City; Daisy CONDON, Forest City.

DUQUEMY, Alfred F. [30; Douglas Co.; b: France; f: J.B. DUQUEMY; m: Mary COLIN] md. Mary C. LOY [21; Douglas Co.;

b: Decatur, IL] on 30 Mar 1870. Off: DIMMICK. Wit: F. EDWARDS; Annie HAUSE.

DURMANDY, Charles [25; Omaha; b: Ireland; f: Charles DURMANDY; m: Catherine ISDELL] md. Mary COYLE [22; Omaha; b: Ireland; f: Hugh COYLE; m: Catherine CLARK] on 8 Jan 1870. Off: CURTIS. Wit: Hugh COYLE; Catherine SLATTERY.

DURNALL, Ezekiel [26; Omaha; b: Fairview, OH; f: Samuel DURNALL; m: Eliza BOYD] md. Jane LATEY [22; Omaha; b: Torrington, England; f: Thomas H. LATEY; m: Jane WARREN] on 20 Nov 1870. Off: KUHNS. Wit: Samuel BURNS; Henry LATEY.

DURNALL, Samuel, Jr. [28; Sarpy Co.] md. Adelaide CHAPMAN [18; Omaha] on 27 Nov 1861 at the residence of the bride's father. Off: KUHNS. Wit: Mr. and Mrs. B.H. CHAPMAN, Miss RITCHIE, Henry DURNALL, et al.

DUTKIN [DEETKIN], Albert [29; Omaha; b: Germany; f: Leanhard DUTKIN [DEETKIN]; m: Julia BENDER] md. Clara BLEIK (BLACK) [17; Omaha; b: Germany; f: John BLEIK; m: Dorothea (Barbara written in and crossed out) SCHROEDER] on 25 Dec 1869. Off: GIBSON. Wit: John BLEIK, Mrs. Dorothea BLEIK.

DUTTON, Edward [24; Omaha; b: Delaware Co., PA; f: Nathan C. DUTTON; m: Maria BUTLER] md. Mary B. WALLACE [23; Omaha; b: Versailes, IN; f: John WALLACE; m: Hannah SWETT] on 16 Apr 1870. Off: KUHNS. Wit: Allen ROOT; Julia CARTER.

DWORAK, Joseph [26; Omaha; b: Bohemia, Europe; f: George DWORAK; m: Catherine HERPST] md. Annie SHANKA [18; Omaha; b: Bohemia, Europe; f: Mathew SHANKA; m: Mary HIGHNY [HEJNY]] on 16 Sep 1871 at the German Catholic Church. Off: GROENEBAUM. Wit: Wenzsolaus [Wenceslaus] KUCERA; Frances VANOUR [VANOUS].

DWYER, John [37; Omaha; b: Ireland; f: Thomas O. DWYER; m: Ellen BUTLER] md. Mary WHITE [27; Omaha; b: New York City; f: Alexander WHITE; m: Catherine WHITE] on 16 Jul 1881. Off: SHAFFEL. Wit: Charles WHITE, Aggie WHITE.

DWYER, William M. [30; Omaha; b: Ireland; F: Edmund DWYER; m: Mary RYAN] md. Annie SULLIVAN [25; Omaha; b: Canada; f: John SULLIVAN; m: Bridget EGAN] on 27 Feb 1872 at O'GORMAN's house. Off: O'GORMAN. Wit: Edward LUCAS; Mary KENNY.

EAMES, John [39; Cheyenne, Wyoming Terr; b: England; f: John EAMES; m: Ann BERNANT] md. Mrs. Anna LYONS [35; Omaha; b: England; f: Thomas ASTMAN; m:

Ann PETIT] on 6 Oct 1871. Off: HODGES. Wit: Henry ASTMAN; Mr. FREEMAN.

EATON, David [21; Omaha] md. Mollie ADAMS [18; Omaha] on 11 Nov 1867. Off: SLAUGHTER.

EATON, Edrick L. [30; Council Bluffs] md. Emma SALVETER [21; St. Louis, MO] on 30 May 1866. Off: ROSE. Wit: James JOHNSON, Mrs. Carrie JOHNSON.

EATOUGH, James [Omaha] md. Sarah FOOT [Omaha] on 19 Nov 1863 at the Lutheran parsonage. Both of legal age. Off: KUHNS. Wit: Mrs. KUHNS, Elizabeth BEYER.

EAYRES, Edwin Wm. [28; Omaha; b: England; f: William EAYRES; m: Rachel MEEHAN] md. Della MURPHY [20; Philadelphia; b: New Jersey; f: Barton MURPHY; m: Eliza P. THOMAS] on 24 Sep 1880. Off: WRIGHT. Wit: Rachel AINSCOW, Edward AINSCOW.

EBBISSON, James [27; Fontenelle; b: Sweden; f: Ebbi PAULSSON; m: Ellen SWENSDOTTER] md. Anna OLSDOTTER [27; Fontanelle; b: Sweden; f: Ola JAMESSON; m: Ture BENGTS(DOTTER)] on 2 Jul 1869. Off: GLOVER. Wit: Rev. W.J. KERMOTT, Arthur L. TERRY.

EBERHART, Alvin G. [21; Omaha] md. Maggie GUERIN [21; Peoria, IL] on 22 Oct 1867 at Omaha House. Off: VAN ANTWERP. Wit: H.A. LOVEWELL, Mrs. HARDING. Double endorsement given by SHEEKS. [Trinity Church records name the bride as Maggie F. GUINN.]

EBERHART, Alvin G. [24; Omaha; b: Pennsylvania; f: Uriah EBERHART; m: Catharine GIESEY] md. Mary A. GREEN [21; Omaha; b: London, England; f: John GREEN] on 10 Dec 1871. Off: James MORRIS. Wit: E. WYMAN; Mary Ann MORRIS; Wm. M. WYMAN.

EBREIGHT, Ezra [29; Douglas Co.; b: Ohio; f: David EBREIGHT; m: Hannah O'BRIEN] md. Mary LONGSBERRY [23; Douglas Co; b: Michigan; f: William LONGSBERRY; m: Mary McACARTHY] on 11 Jun 1877 at North Omaha. Off: SPENCER. Wit: Leonard AMES, Mrs. AMES, both of North Omaha.

EDDY, John M. [26; Omaha; b: Kane Co., IL; f: Spaulding EDDY; m: Mary STEVENS] md. Alda Van CAMP [20; Omaha; b: Canada; f: Ira Van CAMP; m: Phoebe BURKE] on 12 Jul 1869. Off: KUHNS. Wit: Ira Van CAMP, M.D., Mr. STEVENS.

EDDY, Ruben L. [30; Genesee Co., MI; b: Michigan; f: Jefferson EDDY; m: Mary CHAPIN] md. Maria A. MATNEY [22; Douglas Co., KS; b: Kansas; f: Charles MATNEY; m: Bethia GREEN] on 15 Jun 1878. Off: BARTHOLOMEW. Wit: Wm. L. PEABODY, Christian KAEBLER of Douglas Co.

EDEN, A.O. [40; Omaha; b: Germany; f: Onne EDEN; m: Antge M. JANSSEN] md. Henriette MAUKE [38; Omaha; b: Germany; f: Daniel MAUKE; m: Wilhelmina KNOR] on 19 Apr 1881. Off: BENEKE. Wit: Ferdinand STREITZ, Ger. BUSING.

EDHOLM, Benjamin [24; Omaha; b: Sweden; f: L.P. EDHOLM; m: J.J. PETERSON] md. Johanna ANDERSON [22; Omaha; b: Sweden; f: Anders LARSON; m: Lena SWENSON] on 25 Jan 1875. Off: PEABODY. Wit: Will B.R. KILLINGSWORTH, Mabel L. PEABODY.

EDHOLM, Nelson J. [22; Omaha; b: Sweden; f: L.P. EDHOLM; m: Johannah J. PETERSON] md. Mary A. RICE [18; Omaha; b: Pennsylvania; f: Nelson RICE; m: Adell MOORE] on 10 Feb 1880. Off: COPELAND. Wit: Mrs. J.J. EDHOLM, Mrs. A.M. RICE.

EDHOLM, Osborn [25; b: Sweden; f: L.P. EDHOLM; m: J.J. PETERSON] md. Mary Grace CHARLTON [24; b: Illinois; f: J.B. CHARLTON; m: Lucy GOW] on 6 May 1878. Off: MILLER. Wit: John McCAGUE of 23rd and Nichols Street, Mrs. S.S. CLEVELAND of Cumings Street.

EDHOLM, P.L. [23; Omaha; b; Sweden; f: L.P. EDHOLM; m: Johana J. PETERSEN] md. Mrs. Kittie SANKY [25; Omaha; b: Canada; f: John BUSHEY; m: Alice BURNS] on 1 Sep 1877. Off: CARTNEY. Wit: J.B. CHARLTON, A.G. CHARLTON.

EDLER, T. Phil [24; Omaha; b: Germany; f: Q. Phil EDLER; m: Anna Maria BAYER] md. Alice BATTON [18; Saunders Co.; b: Nebraska; f: T. BATTON; m: Liddy BAILY] on 25 Oct 1877. Off: JAMESON. Wit: R.H. NEALE, Jr., W.F. MANNING.

EDMONDSON, Ephriam [colored, 25; Omaha] md. Sarah Anna PATTERSON [colored; 25; Omaha] on 19 May 1868. Off: BETTS. Wit: Mr. and Mrs. Wm. SYDENHAM, G.C. BETTS, et al.

EDWARDS, M. Jonathan, Jr. [21; Sarpy Co.] md. Lucy S. WALKER [23; Douglas Co.] at 11 AM on 17 Oct 1867 at the residence of the bride's father, L.A. WALKER. Off: DIMMICK. Wit: Mr. and Mrs. L.A. WALKER, Jennie BROWN, Mrs. F.M. DIMMICK, et al.

EDWARDS, Mathias G. [26; Omaha; b: Cadiz, OH; f: P.T. EDWARDS; m: Elizabeth GLASS] md. Lucy A. CASDELL [20; Omaha; b: Elwood, KS; f: Charles CASDELL; f: Emma WOODRUFF] on 29 Aug 1870. Off:

BETTS. Wit: William WILKINSON; Frederick BEHM.

EDWARDS, Nicholas Norway [22; Missouri; f: Isaac EDWARDS; m: Sarah PHELPS] md. Jessie SAUNDERS [16; b: Dubuque, IA; f: John K. SAUNDERS; m: Sarah PHELPS] on 21 Sep 1878. Off: QUEALEY. Wit: J.K. SAUNDERS, S.E. YERGA. Age consent given by John K. SAUNDERS, father of the bride.

EDWARDS, William J.F. [42; Omaha; b: England; f: John W. EDWARDS; m: Ann M. COLES] md. Sarah Ann RITCHIE [28; Calhoun; b: OH; f: Andrew RITCHIE; m: Susannah O'BRIEN] on 14 My 1875. Off: HAMMOND. Wit: Ambrose RITCHIE, Calhoun Bottoms, George BIRD, Florence Precinct.

EDWARDS, William [23; Omaha; b: North Carolina; f: Isaac JOHNSON; m: Margaret ALLEN] md. Mrs. Eliza J. PLEAT [40; Omaha; b: Virginia] on 21 Jun 1870. Off: PORTER. Wit: Rodney DUTCHER; R.H. ANDREWS.

EGALAND, Andres [ 24; Omaha] and Mamie REGTROP [18; Omaha] license issued on 16 May 1859. No marriage record. Off: BRIGGS.

EGAN, Peter F. [27; St.Paul; b: Canada; f: Peter EGAN] md. Lucy McCARTHY [21; b: Canada; f: Florance McCARTHY; m: Francis McCARTHY] on 15 Jun 1878. Off: KELLY. Wit: James P. McCARTHY, Mrs. T.C. MORGAN.

EGBERT, Augustus A. [32; Omaha; b: New Jersey; f: James EGBERT; m: Mary VLIET] md. Lutheria L. GRIFFIN [Douglas Co.; b: Michigan; f: Joel T. GRIFFIN; m: Juliette C. GRIFFIN] on 24 Aug 1869. Off: KERMOTT. Wit: Joel T. GRIFFIN of Douglas Co., Juliette C. GRIFFIN of Douglas Co.

EGGE, Adolph [25; Grand Island; b: Germany; f: Peter EGGE; m: Anna RITTER] md. Otielie ROSENKRANZ [22; Omaha; b: Germany; f: Henry ROSENKRANZ; m: Mary LORENSEN] on 16 Apr 1870. Off: MORTON. Wit: Dr. Theodore BAUMER; Mrs. Adelia M.H. BAUMER.

EGGER, Joseph [23; Omaha; b: Germany; f: Joseph EGGER; m: Rosa BULAG] md. Anna FICENS [FICENEC] [20; Omaha; b: Germany; f: John FICENS [FICENEC]; m: Fanny] on 27 Oct 1874 at the German Catholic Church. Off: GROENEBAUM. Wit: Mathew SCHINKER; Mrs. C. MINIKUS.

EGGERS, Henry [25; Omaha] md. Caroline BOYE [24; Omaha] on 4 Oct 1868. Off: KUHNS. Wit: Mrs. H.W. KUHNS, Catherine GROSS.

EHLERS, Dietrich C. [27; Omaha; b; Germany; f: Carl EHLERS] md. Anna E. WARAGE [24; Omaha; b; Germany; f: Henrich WARAGE; m: Anna E. SCHWENN]

on 2 Mar 1877. Off: JAMESON. Wit: Henry ALPERS, Alice JENSEN.

EHLERS, William [32; Douglas Co.; b: Germany; f: Nicholas EHLERS; m: Mary KUMPS] md. Katherina BOGART [28; Douglas Co.; b: Germany; f: Henry RUZER; m: Kathrina SERK] on 10 Nov 1876 at STEINERT's house. Off: STEINERT. Wit: Hulda M. NOWAG, STEINERT's house, Jennie STEINERT, STEINERT's house.

EICHNER, Claus [30; Papillion, Sarpy Co.; b; Germany; f: Claus EICHNER; m: Anna NIEMANN] md. Elsabe HARMSEN [21; Papillion, Sarpy Co.; b: Germany; f: Rolf HARMSEN; m: Katrine Hawe PEPER] on 13 Mar 1878. Off: WEISE. Wit: Henry SIERT, Fred. HARMSON.

EICKE, Henry A. [22; Douglas Co.; b: NE; f: Henry EICKE; m: Elizabeth SOHL] md. Mary SIEVERS [23; Omaha; b: Germany; f: Theodore SIEVERS; m: Margaretha MAYS] on 28 Feb 1881 at McArdle Precinct. Off: BENECKE. Wit: Herman SMITH, T.H.C. CLISSMANN, McArdle Precinct.

EICKE, John [36; Sarpy Co.; b: Prussia; f: Jacob EICKE; m: Cathrine RYMAN] md. Solama RAMALA [26; Sarpy Co.; b: Pennsylvania; f: Joseph RAMALA; m: Elizabeth WORNER] on 6 Apr 1871. Off; LYTLE. Wit: Wilson RAMALIA, Sarpy Co.; Julia RAMALIA, Sarpy Co.

EIRING, William [21; b: Wisconsin; f: Henry EIRING; m: Wilhelmine MILLER] md. Elizabeth STROUP [15; b: Michigan; f: Conrad STROUP; m: Sophia GARDNER] on 16 Mar 1878. Off: BENEKE. Wit: J.A. AHMANSEON, Kate STROUP. Age consent given by Sophia (x her mark) STROUP, mother of the bride. The father is dead.

EISELE, John C. [30; Omaha; b: Germany; f: Jacob EISELE; m: Catrine FRANK] md. Katie REMINGTON [29; Omaha; b: Erie Co., PA; f: Joseph REMINGTON; m: Sarah MALORY] on 3 Jul 1869. Off: HYDE. Wit: P.C. ARMSTRONG, Wm. A. TIFFANY.

EITNER, Ernest [34; Omaha; b: Germany; f: Christian EITNER; m: Mary KASIMIR] md. Mary HOPPE [29; Omaha; b: Germany] on 27 Nov 1872. Off: BILLMAN. Wit: J.R. WALTERS; Thomas TUTTLE.

EKBERG, Nels [27; Sarpy Co.; b: Sweden; f: Andos EKBERG; m: Karna PETERSON] md. Lizel NELSON [27; Omaha; b: Sweden; f: Nelse NELSON; m: Bankda JOHANSSEN] on 20 Jul 1878. Off: STENBERG; Wit: S. BURGSTROM, Mrs. Mary PETERSEN of Sarpy Co., NE.

EKERSON, O. [31; Cass Co.; b: Sweden; f: O. EKERSON; m: Catherine SIMSON] md: Hannah PERSON [31; Cass Co., NE; b: Sweden; f: P. PERSON; m: E.N. NELSON] on 5 Jul 1881. Off: ANDERSON. Wit: L.R. WRIGHT, G.A. SIENE.

EKLUND, Anton [39; Omaha; b: Sweden; f: Christian EKLUND; m: Caroline SCHULTZE] md. Mary JOHNSON [27; Omaha; b: Sweden; f: Andrew JOHNSON; m: Anna ANDERSON] on 23 Jul 1881. Off: RILEY. Wit: Max BERGMANN, P.H. GARRIGAN.

ELBING [ELBLING], George [22; Omaha; b: Austria; f: John ELBING (ELBRING); m: Mary STOUGHTON] md. Anna KROVINEK [KRIVANEK] [22; Omaha; b: Austria; f: Wenzer KROVINEK [Wenzel KRIVANEK]; m: Therese WILLIMOVA [WILEM or VILEM]] on 20 Aug 1869. Off: HYDE. Wit: C.W. KELLOGG, Charles HENSINGER.

ELIASON, Christian [43; Omaha; b: Sweden; f: Elias TUFVESON; m: Ellen OLSON] md. Petennalla SWENSON [30; Omaha; b: Sweden; f: Swen SWENSON; m: Bettie JOHNS] on 6 Jul 1869. Off: KERMOTT. Wit: Wm. H. SMITH, Frank R. KERMOTT.

ELIESON, Ingebright S. [27; Omaha; b: Norway; f: Ole ELIESON; m: Katherine C. DEVOLD] md. Inge ACKER [21; Omaha; b: Norway; f: Jacob ACKER; m: Martha JACOBSON] on 29 Dec 1870. Off: KUHNS. Wit: James S. GIBSON; Mary M. SAHLER.

ELINGSON, Peter [28; Plattsmouth; b: Christina, Norway; f: Erling PETERSON; m: Jorjine ANDERSON] md. Josephine DAHLINE [25; Plattsmouth; b: Venisberg, Sweden; f: Sterling ANDERSON; m: Lisa PETERSEN] on 30 Oct 1880. Off: McLAUGHLIN. Wit: Charles O. AHLQUIST of Plattsmouth, Martin OLSEN.

ELLERTH, Peter [29; Fontenelle; b: Sweden; f: Nils JOHNSON; m: Hanna SWANS] md. Annie PETERSON [23; Omaha; b: Sweden; f: Peter PETERSON; m: Ellen PETERSON] on 2 Jun 1871. Off: BENNETT. Wit: J. EBBESON; T. EBBESON.

ELLICKSON, John [27; Omaha] md. Beckey LUNDVALL [20; Omaha] on 2 Jul 1868. Off: KUHNS. Wit: Mr. and Mrs. Ezra MILLARD, Mrs. CALDWELL, et al.

ELLINGWOOD, Thomas B. [32; Omaha; b: Massachusetts; f: Samuel F. ELLINGWOOD; m: Mary CLEMENTS] md. Lucy DASHER [28; Omaha; b: Pennsylvania; f: Benjamin DASHER; m: Nancy DAVIS] on 9 Nov 1870. Off: KUHNS. Wit: Joseph REDMAN; David MOUNT.

ELLIOTT, Nathan [23; Omaha] md. Camilla E. BEARD [20; Omaha] on 13 Jan 1867. Off: ROSE. Wit: Mr. and Mrs. Geo. BEARD.

ELLIS, Martin [28; Omaha; b: Sandyville, OH; f: William ELLIS; m: Eva HANELINE] md. Fanny MARKS [20; Omaha; b: Indianola, IA] on 6 Jun 1869. Off: KELLY.

ELLIS, Wm. Henry [18; Saratoga Precinct; b: Iowa; f: J.D. ELLIS; m: Mary E. LUDDINGTON] md. Nancy M. CLARK [21; Union Precinct; b: Ohio; f: Josiah CLARK; m: Nancy MAXFIELD] on 20 Dec 1879. Off: BARTHOLOMEW. Wit: John H. BRACKIN, Wm. H. WHITNEY. Age consent given by J.D. ELLIS, father of groom.

ELLSWORTH, William [30; b; England; f: John ELLSWORTH; m: Maria PROCTOR] md. Gyda THOBRO [25; b: Norway; f: Ole THOBRO; m: Olean LARSON] on 30 May 1878. Off: FISHER. Wit: S.J. LARSON, Ane Mary OSTERGAARD.

ELSASSER, Charles (Karl) [26; Omaha; b: Germany; f: Christian ELSASSER; m: Jacobine WACHER] md. Katharina HUNT [25; Omaha; b: Germany; f: Johannis HUNT; m: Johanna KERN] on 10 Sep 1881. Off: BENEKE. Wit: Peter ELSASSER, Christ ELSASSER.

ELSASSER, G.F. [20; b: Illinois; f: J.F. ELSASSER; m: Amelia WALKER] md. Elizabeth HENGEN [20; b; Omaha; f: Joseph H. HENGEN; m: Elizabeth ROEBLING] on 22 Apr 1878. Off: GROENBAUM. Wit: Morice HENGEN, Miss E. ELSASSER.

ELSASSER, Jacob [22; Omaha; b: Germany; f: Christ ELSASSER; m: Jacobine WAKER] md. Maggie KNAUBER [20; Omaha; b: Germany; f: Louis KNAUBER; m: Susie SNEIDER] on 16 Dec 1881. Off: BENEKE. Wit: Gottlieb ZIMMERMAN, Fred URLAN.

ELSASSER, Peter (Pete) [21; Omaha; b: Chicago, IL; f: G. Frederick ELSASSER; m: Emilie WACKER] md. Anna LORENZEN [19; Newton, IA; b: Germany; f: H. LORENZEN; m: Lizzie JENSEN] on 28 Sep 1881. Off: FRESE. Wit: Carl GETZSCHMANN, Catharina ELSASSER.

ELWELL, Edward W. [25; Douglas Co.; b: ME; f: Joseph ELWELL; m: Merendie REDLON] md. Addie GROSSE [20; Douglas Co.; b: AL; f: A. GROSSE; m: Armanthia WILSON] on 25 Jan 1876 at the Omaha Barracks. Off: WRIGHT. Wit: F.A. BRADBURY, USA, Omaha Barracks, Henry SUTTON, USA, Omaha BARRACKS.

ELY, Jerry [26; Atchinson Co., MO; b: VA; f: Thomas ELY; m: Eliza PALMER] md. Lucy PAYNE [23; Omaha; b: VA; f: Samuel PAYNE; m: Marie E. CRAIG] on 14 Dec 1875. Off: STEWART. Wit: John CARROLL, Cazner W. SWEEZY.

ELY, William H. [35; Douglas Co.] md. Eliza MILLER [24; Douglas Co.] on 7 May 1857. Off: GAYLORD. Wit: E.P. SMITH, Alexander MILLER.

EMERICK, John [Forest City, Sarpy Co.] md. Elizabeth JOHNSON [Iron Bluffs, Douglas Co.] on 6 Dec 1863 at Eli JOHNSON's house. Both of legal age. Off: DENTON.

EMERSON, Harrington [26; Lincoln; b: Trenton, NJ; f: Edwin EMERSON; m: Mary Louise INGHAM] md. Florence BROOKS [19; Omaha; b: Ann Arbor, MI; f: D.C. BROOKS; m: Harriette BRIER] on 24 Jun 1879. Off: HARSHA. Wit: Datus C. BROOKS, Samuel D.J. EMERSON of Milford.

EMERY, Charles [23; Omaha; b: Illinois; f: Elias L. EMERY; m: Rachael Ann LOWMAN] md. Emma WALKER [22; Omaha; b: New York; f: Alden B. WALKER; m: Mary B. DOUGLAS] on 16 Oct 1879. Off: COPELAND. Wit: Mrs. E.L. EMERY, A.B. WALKER.

EMERY, Frederick B. [46; Missouri; b: Maine; f: Joseph EMERY; m: Aliance MAYO] md. Sarah WILLIAMS [29; Missouri; b: Missouri; f: James JOHNSON; m: Elizabeth GOOD] on 22 Apr 1874. Off: HENNEY. Wit: Arlena EMERY, Pierce City, MO; Emeline EMERY, Pierce City, MO.

EMPEY, Albert T. [26; Papillion, Douglas Co.; b: Canada West; f: Thomas EMPEY; m: Ellen] md. Emma J. MOORE [19; Blair, Washington Co.; b: Ohio; f: Samuel MOORE; m: Alzina LAFFERTY] on 1 Jun 1872. Off: McKELVRY. Wit: Angelina McKELVRY; Hattie J. MOORE, Papillion. (A record, which was subsequently crossed out and reworded, shows that in Pappillion (sic), Sarpy Co., McKELVRY married this couple with Samuel MOORE and L.M. MOORE as witnesses.)

EMS, Richard [53; McArdle Pct, Douglas Co.; b: England; f: Edward EMS; m: Jane DAVIS] md. Mrs. Martha AVERY [40; McArdle Pct, Douglas Co.; b: Canada West; f: James BROWN; m: Mary STOVER] on 29 Sep 1873. Off: TOWNSEND. Wit: Hiram AVERY, McArdle Pct, Douglas Co.; Mrs. Mary A. SWEENEY.

ENDER, Christian [23; Omaha] md. Rebecca KASSELL or HUSSEY [23; Omaha] on 5 Apr 1869. Off: KELLEY. Wit: T.P. TOPHAM, John DANON.

ENDFIELD, Adam [25; Cass Co.; b: Ohio; f: Peter ENDFIELD; m: Susanna ALHOUSE] md. Louisa ENDFIELD [18; Cass Co.; b: Iowa; f: Henry ENDFIELD; m: Lucy Ann LOWER] on 20 Jun 1874. Off: PEABODY. Wit: Geo. W. AMBROSE; F. SMYTHE.

ENEWOLD, Lawrence C. [30; Omaha; b: Denmark; f: Christen R. ENEWOLD; m: Marie JENSEN] md. Maggie KLINDT [21; Omaha; b: Denmark; f: Christian KLINDT; m: Anna WESTERGAARD] on 19 Dec 1880, Danish Church. Off: GYDESEN. Wit: Chas. KLINDT, Chas. ENEWALD.

ENEWOLD, Robert C. [33; b: Denmark; f: Christian R. ENEWOLD; m: Karen M. JENSEN] md. Anna C. HENRICKSON [21; b: Denmark; f: Henrik NELSON; m: Dora HENRICKSON] on 1 May 1878. Off: HANSEN. Wit: James HENRICKSON, Hans LARSON.

ENGEL, Charles [21; Omaha] md. Mina TIMME [18; Omaha] on 8 Aug 1868. Off: William H. MORRIS. Wit: John DELANEY, Col. J.W. SAVAGE, Wm. L. PEABODY.

ENGEL, Nathanel [25; Omaha; b: Germany; f: Nicholaus ENGEL; m: Poppatabea JOHNSEN] md. Anna HAMMEL [23; Lyons; b: WI; f: Owen HAMMEL; m: Ann KING] on 28 Jun 1881 at the German Catholic Church. Off: GROENEBAUM. Wit: James COLNOW, Lizzie HENZE.

ENGLE, Clarence M. [23; Kansas City, MO; b: Ohio; f: George B. ENGLE; m: Permelia KELLOGG] md. Lida A. ROGERS [19; Omaha; b: Pennsylvania; f: T.C. ROGERS; m: Amelia BOYD] on 29 Dec 1879. Off: MAXFIELD. Wit: Henry ROGERS, Mrs. Henry? ROGERS.

ENGLER, Ephraim [29; Omaha; b: Prussia; f: Christoph ENGLER; m: Sophia RICHTER] md. Maria M. BOYE [23; Omaha; b: Holstein, Prussia; f: John Jacob BOYE; m: Wipke Christina TEKSTEN] on 9 Oct 1870. Off: KUHNS. Wit: Henry EGGERS; John MOHR.

ENGLISH, George C. [23; b: Rochester, NY; f: Nathan ENGLISH; m: Mary HOBBS] md. Jennie E. DOOLITTLE [19; b: Omaha; f: W.V. DOOLITTLE; m: Mary BUSHNELL] on 3 Jun 1878. Off: SHERRILL. Wit: Geo. W. HALL, Wm. FLEMING, Jr.

ENGSTROM, F.E. [34; Omaha; b: Sweden; f: A. ENGSTROM; m: E. SEIGEL] md. Hannah PEHRSON [22; Omaha; b; Sweden; f: Peter PEHRSON] on 14 May 1877. Off: REHNSTROM. Wit: V.A. ENGSTROM, G. COLLIN, A. ENGSTROM, P. PEHRSON.

ENGSTROM, Francis Oscar [36; Logan Creek, Dodge Co.; b: Sweden; f: Andres ENGSTROM; m: Elizabeth SIAGREN] md. Caroline KOHLER [36; Omaha; b: Sweden; f: Johan KOHLER; m: Louisa SODERQUIST] on 6 May 1873. Off: TOWNSEND. Wit:

Jerome F.L.D. HERTZMANN; Charles A. ENGSTROM.

ENOS, A.A. [55; Dodge Co., NE; b: New York; f: Flavel ENOS; m: Harriet STORER] md. Mrs. A.C. STOVER [40; Omaha; b: Pennsylvania; f: Wm. HENRY; m: Catherine SWARTZ] on 13 Jul 1879. Off: LIPE. Wit: D.S.M. FRETWELL, Mary A. FRETWELL.

ENRIGHT, David [25; Omaha; b: Ireland; f: Michael ENRIGHT; m: Ellen DILLON] md. Nora LEINHAN [22; Omaha; b: Ireland; f: Patrick LEINHAN; m: Ellen DORE] on 18 Aug 1876 at the Catholic Cathedral. Off: KELLEY. Wit: Timothy CARR, Mary SWEENEY.

ENSIGN, Theodore [26; Omaha; b: Connecticut; f: Sidney ENSIGN; m: Clarinda PRENTIS] md. Carrie F. HIGBY [20; Omaha; b: New York; f: J.C. HIGBY; m: Francis A. PADDOCK] on 25 Feb 1874. Off: STEWART. Wit: Charles C. WESTON; Sallie B. PONSFORD.

EPENETER, John [24; Omaha] md. Henrietta RUDOESKY [22; Omaha] on 15 Apr 1861 at KUHNS' residence on Douglas St. Both of legal age. Off: KUHNS. Wit: John T. PAULSON, George HARZOG.

EPPERSON, Sidney C. [30; Omaha; b: Illinois; f: Green EPPERSON; m: Thirza WOOD] md. Mary E. WHITE [22; Omaha; b: New York] on 15 May 1871. Off: GIBSON. Wit: Geo. W. EDMANDS; Mrs. Josephine EDMANDS.

ERATH, William H. [22; Omaha; b: Wisconsin; f: Max ERATH; m: Catharine SCHULTZ] md. Sophie WAGNER [20; Omaha; b: Missouri; f: Joseph WAGNER; m: Mary ----] on 10 Aug 1880. Off: BENEKEE. Wit: Auguste MENNEKE, Joseph SEGER.

ERB, Eugene W. [32; b: Germany; f: Francis C. ERB; m: ? ACHTE] md. Catharine METZGER [22; b: Germany; f: Peter METZGER; m: Catharine ELSASSER] on 29 Jun 1878. Off: BORDEN. Wit: Martin OBERST, Minna OBERST.

ERBEN [URBAN], Emanuel [24; Omaha; b: Bohemia; f: Joseph ERBEN [URBAN]; m: Kate SAMOLOK [SMOLIK]] md. Bridget GILL [18; Omaha; b: St. Louis, MO; f: John GILL; m: Maggie OATES] on 24 Feb 1879 at the Cathedral. Off: McDERMOTT. Wit: Frank VOTICAKA [VODICKA], Mary CASEY.

ERCK, John H. [27; Omaha; b: Germany; f: Henry ERCK; m: Mary DORMANN] md. Louisa W. BIERMANN [21; Omaha; b: Germany; f: Christian H. BIERMANN; m: Catharine M. PICKMAN] on 19 Jun 1869. Off: KUHNS. Wit: Adolph BURMESTER, Mrs. W.H. KUHNS.

ERFLING, Edward Charles [33; Omaha] and Frances M. SCHAEFER [36; Cincinnati, OH] license issued on 12 Jul 1867. No

marriage record. The license was filed on 28 Sep 1875. Off: HASCALL.

ERFLING, Edward Charles [33; Omaha] md. Francis M. SCHAEFER [36; Cincinnati] on 12 Jul 1875. Off: HINGENDORF. Wit: Anna WAGNER, Council Bluffs, Johanna HILGENDORF. (Evidently no affidavit or license was issued prior to letter from HILGENDORF.)

ERICKSON, A. [25; Omaha; b: Sweden. f: A. ERICKSON; m: Hannah ERKBACH] md. Clara CARLSON [25; Omaha; b: Sweden; f: Chas. CARLSON; m: Hannah RYDQUIST] on 28 Nov 1881. Off: STENBERG. Wit: J.L. WAHLSTROM, Mrs. Annie WAHLSTROM.

ERICKSON, Charles [20; Omaha; b: NE; f: John ERICKSON; m: Louisa BRADFORD] md. Elizabeth FOX [19; Omaha; b: England; f: Joseph FOX; m: Anna BARBER] on 28 Jul 1881. Off: MAXFIELD. Wit: Minnie WINSHIP, Katie WINSHIP.

ERICKSON, Chris L. [22; Omaha; b: Denmark; f: Christ N. ERICKSON; m: Stina LARSON] md. Carrie S. BROSIONS [18; Omaha; b: Iowa; f: Daniel BROSIONS; m: Caroline HEILMANN] on 21 Oct 1879. Off: BRANS. Wit: Emma LEWIS, Mrs. Caroline BROSIONS.

ERICKSON, Nels [30; Omaha; b: Denmark; f: Erik NIELSEN; m: Mette JENSEN] md. Inger POULSEN [33; Omaha; b: Denmark; f: Paul FREDERICKSON; m: Mette LAURSEN] on 30 Sep 1881 at Vor Frelser's Church. Off: GYDESEN. Wit: Fr. TOULSEN, M. ANDERSEN.

ERICKSON, Olaf F. [31; Omaha; b: Sweden; f: Pher ERICKSON; m: Maria SWENSON] md. Caroline JOHNSON [18; Omaha; b: Sweden; f: Lelzequiest JOHNSON; m: Mary NELSON] on 21 Apr 1870. Off: GIBSON. Wit: Jeremiah McCHEANE; George ARNOLD.

ERICSON, Fred [40; Omaha; b: Norway; f: Eric HANSEN; m: Jennie JOHNSON] md. Christina NELSON [29; Omaha; b: Sweden; f: Lars NELSON; m: Annie SWANSON] on 18 Sep 1877. Off: SEDGWICK. Wit: Peter BLOMBERG, Carrie BLOMBERG.

ERIKSEN, Hans P. [28; Omaha; b: Denmark; f: Erick HANSEN; m: Margaret JOHNSON] md. Hansena JOHANSON [29; Omaha; b: Denmark; f: Johan ---- and Carrie CHARLES] on 5 Jun 1872. Off: BILLMAN. Wit: Col. A.G. BRACKETT, Omaha Barracks; Lt. W.C. RAWALLE, Omaha Barracks.

ERLENBORN, Alfred G. [22; Odobolt, IA; b: IL; f: Anton ERLENBORN; m: Rosa HAEFNER] md. Ernestine W. PITSCHNER [20; Odobolt, IA; b: IA; f: Ernst PITSCHNER] on 24 Nov 1881. Off: FRESE. Wit: Charles REAM, Heinr. F. WARNECKE, both Odobolt, IA.

ERNST, Henry [25; Douglas Co.; b: Holstein, Germany; f: George ERNST; m: Anna ROHWER] md. Catherine MUMM [25; Douglas Co.; b: Schleswig, Germany; f: Detlef MUMM; m: Margurita LORENZEN] on 9 Oct 1870. Off: GIBSON. Wit: Mrs. Mary GIBSON; Detlef MUMM.

ERRICKSON, S.H. [28; b: Sweden; f: Errick NEBERG; m: Inga PETERSON] md. Carolina Wilhelmina PETERSON [27; b: Sweden; f: Per Mangnus MANGNUSON; m: Catrina Elizabeth HAGERSTROM] on 4 May 1878. Off: STENBERG. Wit: Gustaf FRISHEDT, Christina FRISHEDT.

ERRICKSON, Sivert [28; Omaha; b: Norway; f: Erik SIVERTSON; m: Karen OLSDATTER] md. Amostine MAGNUSEN [23; Omaha; b: Sweden; f: Johannes MAGNUSEN; m: Quije ANDERSDATER] on 22 Jul 1880, Von Frelser's Kirk. Off: GYDESEN. Wit: Niels PETERSON, Gusta JOHNSON.

ERSKINE, R.J. [27; Omaha; b: Canada; f: Robert ERSKINE; m: Jane WILLIAMS] and Etta WEEKS [17; Council Bluffs; b: Wisconsin; f: Charles WEEKS; m: Mary FULMER] license issued on 2 Jul 1879. No marriage record. Off: BARTHOLOMEW.

ESCHLE, William [25; Omaha; b: Germany; f: Constantine ESCHLE; m: Lena DIESCHLER] md. Lena RUDOLPH [25; Omaha; b: Germany; f: George RUDOLPH; m: Lena SPRESLER] on 19 Sep 1877. Off: SEDGWICK. Wit: Lucia M. FENTON of Syracuse, NY, Marcia F. SEDGWICK.

ESDOHR, Henry [23; Omaha; b: Germany; f: Albert ESDOHR; m: Matilda WENDT] md. Phebe Ann CORNISH [17; Omaha; b: Long Island, NY; f: Ebenezer CORNISH; m: Nancy PRATTS] on 18 May 1872. Off: BRANDES. Wit: Toney YOUNG; Mrs. Minnie HUTH. Age of consent given by Nancy GOSSMAN, mother of the bride; father is dead.

ESMER, Frederick W. [27; Millard Precinct, Douglas Co.; b: Germany; f: Frederick ESMER; m: Mary SAUER] md. Louisa KIEBING [18; Douglas Co.; b: Germany; f: ??? KIEBING; m: Elvina KIEBING] on 26 Feb 1877. Off: SEDGWICK. Wit: Herman G. KIEBING of Douglas Co.

ESTABROOK, Henry D. [24; Omaha; b: New York; f: Experience ESTABROOK; m: Caroline A. MAXWELL] md. Clara M. CAMPBELL [23; Omaha; b: Vermont; f: O.C. CAMPBELL; m: Charlotte FOSTER] on 22

Oct 1879. Off: SHERRILL. Wit: Experience ESTABROOK, John H. KELLOM.

ETTELMAN, W.R. [26; Florence, NE; b: IA; f: Daniel ETTELMAN; m: Anna BOWMAN] md. Lillie May MORTON [16; Florence; b: IA; f: Edward H. MORTON; m: Maria SPRAGUE] on 25 Jul 1881 at Florence. Off: COWAN. Wit: John ELLIOTT , Florence, Annie L. GALLOP, Florence. Age consent given by parents of the bride.

EVANS, Charles E. [27; Omaha; b: Philadelphia, PA; f: John EVANS; m: Annie M. SNELL] md. Mrs. Rachael M. DRIVER [26; Omaha; b: Indiana] on 7 Jun 1870. Off: GIBSON. Wit: Charles GREGG; Charlotte HARVEY.

EVANS, Charles T. [28; Douglas Co.] md. Mary E. KINCAID [19; Douglas Co.] on 5 Nov 1865 at Mr. KINCAID's house. Off: MILLER. Wit: Father and mother of the bride.

EVANS, Charles [27; Omaha; b: NY; f: Patrick EVANS; m: Elizabeth KELLEY] md. Sarah ASHBURN [20; Omaha; b: IL; f: Jesse ASHBURN; m: Almira GLASS] on 5 Oct 1876. Off: PEABODY. Wit: Mrs. R.M. BOYER, William C. FOX.

EVANS, Chester A. [Omaha] md. Manda FRY [Omaha] on 12 Apr 1865 at DICKINSON's office. Off: DICKINSON. Wit: Samuel M. CHANNEL, Lucy L. EVANS.

EVANS, John B. [24; Omaha; b: IL; f: John EVANS; m: Eliza P. DAVIS] md. Fannie C. DRAKE [24; Omaha; b: NJ; f: E. DRAKE] on 26 Apr 1876. Off: STEWART. Wit: S.H.H. CLARK, Frank E. DRAKE.

EVANS, John E. md. Elizabeth ASTMAN on 29 May 1865 at the residence of the bride's parents. Off: DICKINSON. Wit: Mr. and Mrs. Thos. ASTMAN, Mrs. Geo. GARDNER, Henry ASTMAN.

EVANS, Wm. M. [Davis Co., IA] md. Ellen McGEE [MAGEE] [Union Co., IA] on 9 Sep 1863 at Douglas House. Both of legal age. Off: DICKINSON. Wit: Mrs. George ARMSTRONG, Mrs. H.L. EDWARDS.

EVENS, Albert S. [22; Missouri; b: Ohio; f: Wm. T. EVENS; m: Elizabeth TILLEY or FILLEY] md. Hattie TWEED [19; Ohio; b: Ohio; f: Robert TWEED; m: Jane WAKEMAN] on 26 Dec 1874. Off: HALE. Wit: Geo. TILDEN; William DAILY.

EVENSON, Andrew [36; Omaha; b: Norway; f: Even JOHANSON; m: Bertha M. JOHNSON] md. Henrekke L.C. MORK [19; Omaha; b: Denmark; f: Peter MORK; m: Else MORK] on 25 Oct 1877. Off: HILMEN. Wit: Ole SVENSON, Mrs. MORK.

EVEREST, David [29; Nebraska City] md. Myra H. WILLARD [30; Nebraska City] on 27 Apr 1869. Off: KUHNS. Wit: David S. MACK, Lucy A. BROWN.

EVEREST, Frank L. [21; Atchison, KS; b: Minnesota; f: Aaron S. EVEREST; m: Maria

M. DARRAH] md. Belle L. RICHARDSON [21; San Francisco, CA; b: California; f: Prescott V. RICHARDSON; m: Rachel DARRAH] on 30 Jul 1880. Off: SHERILL. Wit: Geo. E. STEVENS, Mrs. A.F. SHERILL.

EVERS, Frederick [27; Sarpy Co.; b: Germany; f: Henry EVERS; m: Dorothea ZIESENIS] md. Annie SENJAN [26; Omaha; b: Germany; f: John SENJAN; m: Sarah LAMP] on 3 Jul 1873. Off: TOWNSEND. Wit: William H. LAWTON; John M. THURSTON.

EVMER, Fredrick W. [27; Douglas Co.; b: Germany; f: Fredrick EVMER; m: Mary SAUER] md. Louisa KIEBING [18; Douglas Co., b: Germany; f: ---- KIEBING; m: Elvira KIEBING] on 26 Feb 1877. Off: SEDGWICK. Wit: Hermania KIEBING, Herman KIEBING.

EWERS, Frank [27; Omaha; b: Virginia; f: Jonathan EWERS; m: Nancy TAVERNER] md. Rose J. WYLIE [22; Omaha; b: Indiana; f: I.N. WYLIE; m: Sarah Jane GITHENS] on 29 Dec 1879. Off: JAMESON. Wit: J.R. BOYCE, J.H. BURROUGHS.

EWING, Emerson [28; Omaha; b: Missouri; f: Joseph EWING] and Mrs. Nancy MILLER [31; Omaha; b: Missouri; f: Harry MARTIN; m: Louvenia MARTIN] license issued on 10 Nov 1879. No marriage record. Off: SIMERAL.

EWING, James P. [32; b: Ohio; f: David EWING; m: Anna NEAL] md. Freddie LANGHOFF [26; b: Germany; f: John LANGHOFF; m: Freddie WOLF] on 19 Dec 1878. Off: SHERRILL. Wit: Mrs. Elizabeth ROBERTS, Delia WELCH of Columbus, NE.

EYTH, Joseph [25; Omaha] md. Mary FEISER [21; Omaha] on 12 Apr 1869. Off: GROENEBAUM. Wit: Gotfried and Gertrude REBHAUSEN.

FAGAN, James [23; Omaha; b: Missouri; f: Peter FAGAN; m: Mary DAVIS] md. Bridget KENNEDY [21; Omaha; b: Illinois; f: John KENNEDY; m: Mary KENNEDY] on 15 Nov 1880. Off: ENGLISH. Wit: J. CLARE, Miss M. FAGAN.

FAGERSTJERNA, Peter Wilhelm Pouleon [45; Omaha; b; Denmark; f: Ole FAGERSTJERNA; m: Anna P. MARIA] md. Edna T. SNELL [33; Omaha; b: New York; f: Richard SNELL; m: Margaret COMSTOCK] on 17 Aug 1877. Off: ROSE. Wit: George W. ROSE of Council Bluffs, H.C. JESSEN.

FAIR, James B. [46; Omaha; b: PA; f: David FAIR; m: Rebecca McMONIGAIL] md. Adeline A. MOSHER [36, Omaha; b: NY; f: Peter WELLS; m: Margaret MONSON] on 17 Oct 1876. Off: McCARTNEY. Wit: Joseph REDMAN, Mrs. Joseph REDMAN.

FAIRMAN, Richard [29; Douglas Co.] md. Martha A. BARNES [23; Douglas Co.] on 23 Nov 1865. Off: HASCALL. Wit: Mrs. HUNT, Mrs. RICHARDS, et al.

FAIST, Louis [27; b: Germany; f: Wm. G. FAIST; m: Catharine HARRNER] md. Annie PLANE [18; b: New York; f: James PLANE; m: Margaret SULLIVAN] on 26 Jul 1878. Off: BORDEN. Wit: J.F. MORTON, Mary MORTON.

FALCONER, James [84 or 34; Omaha; b: Scotland; f: Thomas FALCONER; m: Christine DRYSDALE] md. Eliza McKITTRICK [21; Omaha; b: England; f: Thomas McKITTRICK; m: Eliza McPHERSON] on 3 May 1880. Off: COPELAND. Wit: David KNOX, Thomas LIDELL.

FALCONER, Thomas [26; Omaha; b: Scotland; f: Thomas FALCONER; m: Christina DRYSDALE] md. Maggie ALLEN [19; Omaha; b: Scotland; f: William ALLEN; m: Margaret EWING] on 10 Jun 1870. Off: DIMMICK. Wit: Mitchell and Wm. FLEMING; George ALLEN, Chicago.

FALK, Gustave [23; Omaha; b: Sweden; f: Charles FALK; m: Christine PETERSON] md. Theresa SMIRSCH [SMRZ] [22; Omaha; b: Bohemia; f: James SMIRSCH [SMRZ]; m: Francis MACA] on 15 Jan 1881. Off: STENBERG. Wit: C.J. WESTERDAHL, H. JACOBSON.

FALLER, Herman [29; Yankton, Dakota; b: Germany; f: Thomas FALLER; m: Caroline KAFER] md. Josephine FLAK [22; Omaha; b: Germany; f: Jacob FLAK; m: Elizabeth SEAMAN] on 3 Mar 1874. Off: HALL. Wit: Jacob FRANK; Fred HERZKE.

FALLIN, David A. [26; Mattoon, IL] md. Mary POLAND [20; Omaha] at 8 A.M. on 12 Jan 1869 at the residence of the bride's father. Off: DIMMICK. Wit: James J. BROWN, Mrs. M.K. BROWN, T.B. LEMON, Jr., et al.

FANNELL, John [30; Kansas] and Margaret MOLOY [27; Kansas City, MO] license issued on 14 Jun 1862. Off: ARMSTRONG.

FANNING, Patrick [28; Omaha; b: Ireland; f: Patrick FANNING; m: Bridget MURPHE] md. Annie MASTERSON [29; Omaha; f: Andrew MASTERSON; m: Bridget DIAL] on

1 May 1875 at the Roman Catholic Cathedral. Off: BYRNE. Wit: John MURPHY, Eliza RYAN.

FARM, John [22, MI; b: Sweden; f: John FARM; m: Ellen SWANSON] md. Christina JOHNSON [31; Omaha; b: Sweden; f: Jens JOHNSON; m: Hannah JOHNSON] on 14 Dec 1881. Off: FOGELSTRUN. Wit: Olaf JOHNSON, Henry NILSON.

FARQUER, Jeremiah W. [45; Omaha; b: Pennsylvania; f: John FARQUER, m: Elizabeth SMITH] md. Rebecca F. FRENCH [34; Omaha] on 2 Aug 1870. Off: KELLEY. Wit: J.S. TUCKER; Anthony BAKER.

FARREL, John [45; Omaha; b: Ireland; f: Cornelius FARRELL; m: Ellen POWERS] md. Catharine SWEENEY [30; Omaha; b: Ireland, f: Pall SWEENEY; m: Elin CRETEN] on 27 April 1875 at the Roman Catholic Cathedral. Off: BYRNE. Wit: Michael MANSFIELD, Julia SULLIVAN.

FARRELL, John [31; Omahah; b: New York; f: Patrick FARRELL; m: Margaret RILEY] md. Mary HANLON [20; Omaha; b: Connecticut; f: John HANLON; m: Julia CONNELL] on 1 May 1877, R.C. Cathedral. Off: JENNETTE. Wit: Joseph FARRELL of DeWitt, Saline Co., Kate HANLON.

FARRELL, Michael [26; Omaha; b: Pennsylvania; f: John FARRELL; m: Eliza CARROLL] md. Maria SHANNON [24; Omaha; b: Ireland; f: Michael SHANNON; m: Mary TULLEY] on 22 Nov 1880. Off: ENGLISH. Wit: Jerome COULTER, Mrs. Jerome COULTER.

FARRER, Sysander P. [31; Omaha; b: Zanesville, OH; f: Joseph FARRER; m: Isabella ELLIOTT] md. Margaret GARRIGAN [28; Omaha; b: Ireland; f: Philip GARRIGAN] on 5 Nov 1871. Off: McCAGUE. Wit: M. BERRY; J. WITHROW.

FASE, Henry [27; Sarpy Co.] md. Mary UHE [17; Sarpy Co.] on 9 May 1867 at the residence of the bride's home in Sarpy Co. Off: FLORKEE. Wit: "In presence of a large asemble," Andreas FASE. Age consent given by the bride's father.

FATE, William H.H. [37; Union Co., Dakotah; b: Ohio; f: Thomas FATE; m: Sarah HULL] and Laura BAKER [23; Idaho Territory; b: ??; f: Robert BAKER] license issued. No marriage or date recorded. Date is probably December 1877. Off: SEDGWICK.

FAY, David [29; San Mateo, CA] md. Mary A. BROWN [18 and 3 months; Ringwood, IL] on 20 May 1867. Off: HASCALL. Wit: L.E. BEAUMONT, Mrs. R. HOCUM.

FAYHTINGER [FAYTINGER], Frank [28; Omaha; b: Bohemia; f: Frank FAYHTENGER [FAYTINGER]; m: Barbara NOWOK [NOVAK]] md. Frances WOSHEKER [21; Omaha; b: Bohemia] on 29 Jun 1869. Off:

KELLEY. Wit: W.H. JOHNSON, Judge PORTER.

FEAY, Alfred T. [27; Omaha; b: Manchester, England; f: James FEAY; m: Fanny TAYLOR] md. Carrie E. SMITH [24; Omaha; b: Mesopotamia, OH; f: John J. SMITH; m: Marietta SHELDON] on 14 Jan 1871 at J. SMITH's house, Sarpy Co. Off: GAYLORD. Wit: John J. SMITH, Papillion Branch; Eliza C. HEADLY.

FEDDE, Christian [23; Douglas Co.; b: Germany; f: John FEDDE; m: Maggie MARTINS] md. Maggie GLANDT [23; Douglas Co.; b: Germany; f: ---- GLANDT] on 31 Mar 1874 at McArdle Precinct. Off: ROLFS. Wit: Mary GLANDT, McArdle Pct; Marcus GLANDT, McArdle Pct.

FEDDE, John [29; Douglas Co.; b: Germany; f: Claus FEDDE; m: Maria MULLER] md. Meto BOE (BOEGE) [24; Douglas Co.; b: Germany; f: F. BOE; m: Louise SCHWARS] on 5 Feb at Millard Pct. Off: FLORKEE. Wit: A.C. BARTHOLOMEW, Millard Pct., L.M. BARTHOLOMEW, Millard Pct.

FEE, William F. [22; Omaha; b: Cleveland, OH; f: John FEE; m: Charlotte McGUIRE] md. Mariam R. DRISKELL [20; Omaha; b: Sigourney, IA; f: Perry DRISKELL; m: Sarah Ann HOBBS] on 21 Apr 1873. Off: LYTLE. Wit: C.M. COFFREN; Geo. AYERS.

FEEDERLE [FEDRLE], Frederick [28; Omaha] md. Mary REIZ [23; Omaha] on 13 Apr 1868. Off: MORRIS. Wit: James H. HAMILTON, Mrs. J.H. HAMILTON.

FEKENSCHER, Henry H. [27; Douglas Co.; b: Germany; f: Augustus FEKENSCHER; m: Caroline VOGT] md. Mary K. HALDY [23; Omaha; b: Germany; f: George F. HALDY; m: Catherine VOUBEL] on 28 Mar 1870. Off: MAY. Wit: Augustus MEYER; Matilda STOETZEL.

FELIX, Henry [39; Omaha] md. Jane MOORE [21; Omaha] on 29 Oct 1867. Off: McCAGUE. Wit: Earnst KREBS, Froed BOETTGER.

FELL, William H. [44; Omaha] md. Mary AUMOCK [46; Omaha] on 19 Apr 1868. Off: KERMOTT. Wit: Mr. and Mrs. Henry HICKMAN.

FELLIAN, Michael [26; North Platte; b: Indiana; f: Fred FELLIAN; m: Kate BLISS] md. Hannah O'MERA [17; St. Louis; b: Galina, IA; f: Thomas O'MERA; m: Eliza BARRETT] on 1 Dec 1870. Off: CURTIS. Wit: Patrick BURKLEY, St. Louis, MO; Kate BLISS.

FELT, John M. [24; Omaha; b: Sweden; f: Gustave FELT; m: Mary PETERSON] md. Anna C. JOHNSON [39; Omaha; b: Sweden; f: John JOHNSON; m: Lizzie NELSON] on 10 Feb 1877. Off: PEABODY. Wit: Adolph BOWMAN, Anna C. CARLSON.

FENDRICH, Wenzel [32; Omaha; b: Bohemia; f: Frank FENDRICH; m: Catharine NOWAK [NOVAK]] md. Mrs. Anna HAWLINEK [HAVLINEK] [24; Omaha; b: Bohemia; f: John WOBORIL [VOBORIL]; m: Mary MASANEK] on 24 Feb 1873. Off: TOWNSEND. Wit: Joseph SKLENER, Burt Co.; Edward C. McSHANE.

FENKELL, Ernest L. [23; Omaha; b: Chagrin Falls, OH; f: Eli B. FENKELL; m: Hannah HOWELL] md. Annie E. FAY [22; Omaha; b: Mount Raggy, CT; f: Edward FAY; m: Catherine] on 27 May 1873. Off: STEWART. Wit: John H. COWIN; Celia M. FAY.

FENTON, Morris [28; Omaha; b: Ireland; f: Dan FENTON; m: Ellen FITZGERALD] md. Margaret SULLIVAN [28; Omaha; b: Ireland; f: Joseph SULLIVAN; m: Margaret DAILEY] on 7 Jan 1875 at the Roman Catholic Cathedral. Off: BYRNE. Wit: Michael McCARTHY, Catharine SWEENEY.

FENTON, Norman C. [22; Dalton, OH; b: OH; f: C.S. FENTON; m: Susin CULBERTSON] md. Ethal CUSTER [18; Dalton, OH; f: William CUSTER; m: Susin DECK] on 27 Jun 1876. Off: SEDGWICK. Wit: F.P. HANLON, Douglas Co., J.F. SWEESY, Douglas Co.

FENTON, William [27; Omaha; b: Ireland; f: Thadeus or Thomas FENTON; m: Joan O'BRIEN] md. Mary Ann KEARNEY [20; Omaha; b: Ireland; f: John KEARNEY; m: Mary McCRISKAN] on 11 Dec 1873 at the Roman Catholic Cathedral. Off: BYRNE. Wit: Patrick QUINLAN; Margaret KEARNEY.

FERGUSON, Arthur N. [34; Omaha; b: Albany, NY; f: Fenner FERGUSON; m: Helen E. UPJOHN] md. Delia L. SEARS [28; Omaha; b: Canton, NY; f: Leonard SEARS; m: Delia S. FOOTE] on 12 Apr 1879. Off: WILLIAMS. Wit: Milliard SEARS, Mrs. F. FERGUSON.

FERRIS, J.W. [27; Council Bluffs] md. Josephine WARNER [19; Council Bluffs] on 27 Jun 1868. Off: STUCK.

FERRY, Edward [24; Elkhorn Station; b: Ireland; f: James FERRY; m: Margaret DANNELLY] md. Mary BRITTON [18; Douglas Co.; b: Indiana; f: John BRITTON] on 30 Oct 1870 at Elkhorn Station. Off: LONERGAN. Wit: Phillip HALL, Elkhorn Station; Kate FERRY, Elkhorn Station.

FIALD [FIALA], Anton [27; Omaha; b: Bohemia; f: Wenzel FIALD [FIALA]; m: Kathrine SOSKA [SOUSEK]] md. Barbara WAVRA [VAVRA] [32; Omaha; b: Bohemia;

f: John WAVRA [VAVRA]; m: Marie] on 15 Feb 1874. Off: HENNEY. Wit: Joseph MICHAEL; Frank KONVALIN.

FIELDING, Patrick [29; Omaha; b: Ireland; f: John FIELDING; m: Kate MAHONEY] md. Mrs. Mary SAUNDERS [23; Omaha; b: Ohio; f: William MURRAY; m: Johanna MURRAY] on 10 Jun 1870. Off: PORTER. Wit: Wiley B. DIXON; Richard NAGLE.

FIKES, William H. [24; Omaha; b: Aurora, IL; f: Nelson FIKES: m: Elizabeth McELWAIN] md. Isabella SNELL [22; Douglas Pct., Douglas Co.; b: Quincy, IL; f: Frederick SNELL; m: Mary NEIDERAUR] on 4 Jan 1872. Off: KUHNS. Wit: Issac G. HASCALL; Frederick SNELL.

FINCH, Geo. W. [30; Atlantic, IA; b: OH; f: Geo. FINCH; m: Mary MORROW] and Mary A. BRADSHAW [24; Atlantic, IA; b: Ireland; f: Peter BRADSHAW; m: Adelia MAHAN] filed affidavit on 26 Oct 1881. No record of license or marriage. Off: BERGMANN.

FINCH, Hiram A. [28; Omaha; b: Connecticut; f: John M. FINCH; m: Louisa BRADLEY] md. Emily N. PORTER [24; Omaha; b: Illinois; f: John L. PORTER; m: Emily GILLEM] on 10 Nov 1874. Off: PEABODY. Wit: Mrs. J.M. PARKER; Mrs. E.K. BUTTERFIELD.

FINNELL, Benjamin W. [27; Waterloo; b: KY; f: Benjamin W. FINNELL; m: Eliza C. WALL] md. Mary Jane BUTLER [17; Waterloo; b: MO; f: O.P. BUTLER; m: Amanda CARROLL] on 13 Jul 1875 at the Catholic Cathedral. Off: LONERGAN. Wit: Wm. HOGAN, Elkhorn, Mary CALLALEE (or CALLAHAN), Elkhorn.

FINNEY, Geo W. [38; Douglas Co.] md. Mrs. Jennie MURPHY [24; Council Bluffs] on 2 May 1868. Off: STUCK. Wit: W.F. DEGRAFFENRIED, Charles A. MELDRUM.

FIRTH, Abram [26; Philadelphia, PA; b: England; f: Samuel FIRTH; m: Susan HAEGH] md. Clara E. BURDETTE [18; Omaha; b: England; m: Sarah AMOS] on 12 Apr 1870 at Joseph FOX's residence. Off: HURLBUT. Wit: Joseph FOX; W.C. SHERO.

FIRTH, Rowland [22; Phillipsburg, NJ; b: England; f: John FIRTH; m: Mary YARDLEY] md. Nancy Jane TOOKER [17; Omaha; b: Gloversville, NY; f: James A. TOOKER; m: Hannah SIPPERLY] on 20 Jul 1873. Off: WRIGHT. Wit: James A. TOOKER; Lucinda B. HILLS. Age of consent given by father of bride (she was 17 on 28 Mar 1873).

FISETTE, Charles H. [36; Omaha; b: Canada; f: Charles FISETTE; m: Judith BERTHROME] md. Louisa M. YOKELE [26; Omaha; b: Illinois; f: Peter YOKELE; m: Rosella DHONDT] on 17 Nov 1877. Off: PARDEE. Wit: Geo. HOMAN, Sr., Mrs. Geo. HOMAN.

FISETTE, Charles H. [36; Omaha; b: Canada; f: Chas. FISETTE; m: Judith BERTHIOME] md. Louise M. YOKEL [26; Omaha; b: IL; f: Peter YOKEL; m: Rozella DHOHRDT] on 17 Nov 1876. Off: PARDEE. Wit: Geo. HOMAN, Sr., Mrs. Geo. HOMAN. Marriage filed 2 Oct 1877.

FISHER, Albert [21; Douglas Co.; b: Germany; f: Godfrey FISHER; m: Mary DISLATT] md. Mary BISHOP [19; Douglas Co.; b: Bohemia; f: Albert FISHER; m: Anne ----] on 25 Apr 1876. Off: SEDGWICK. Wit: E.C. BROWN, Douglas Co., Marica F. SEDGWICK, Douglas Co.

FISHER, August [46; Omaha; b: Germany f: John FISHER; m: Concordia BLIER] md. Joanna HUGEL [29; Omaha; b: Germany; m: Agata BLOUM] on 25 Apr 1874. Off: HALD. Wit: Geo. A. WEGGALD; Louis DRELL.

FISHER, Bazil [22; Florence; b: Ohio; f: Christian FISHER; m: Mary E. RHODES] md. Isabel R. REEVES [19; Florence; b: Iowa (England crossed out); f: William REEVES; m: Jane BRADDOCK] on 11 Nov 1874 at Florence. Off: STEVENSON. Wit: Zack FISHER; Louisa REEVES.

FISHER, Caspar [28; Sarpy Co.] md. Amanda RINGO [24; Douglas Co.] on 7 Nov 1865 at Mr. RINGO's residence. Off: LEMON. Wit: Willard FISHER, Nancy FISHER, et al.

FISHER, Edward [34; Omaha] md. Mary A. CASTILLO [26; Omaha] on 22 Sep 1867 at the parsonage. Off: VAN ANTWERP. Wit: Mr. and Mrs. DOEHARTY, Rev. P.B. MORRISON.

FISHER, Martin [26; Omaha; b: Germany; f: Frank FISHER; m: Julia SANDER] md. Mary ALLBRIGHT [22; Omaha; b: Germany; f: John ALLBRIGHT] on 18 Mar 1873. Off: LYTLE. Wit: Joshua BUDD; J.J. STUBBS.

FISHER, Thomas [22; Omaha; b: Missouri; f: A.J. FISHER; m: Linda Jane PHILLIPS] md. Lizzie CLARK [23; Omaha; b: Tennessee; f: William CLARK; m: Fanny HARPER] on 20 Dec 1877. Off: SEDGWICK. Wit: J.W. ADAMS, T.J. COX.

FISHER, William B. [24; Omaha; b: Missouri; f: Thomas FISHER; m: Francis BLACKWELL] md. Samantha A. DAVIDSON [25; Omaha; b: Ohio; f: William DAVIDSON; m: Rebecca] on 20 Sep 1869. Off: DeLaMATYR. Wit: Alex MACKIE; John ELLIS.

FISHER, William R. [23; Omaha; b: Indiana; f: John FISHER; m: Nancy MORGAN] md. Louisa BRINLEY [22; Omaha; b: Michigan; f: William Samuel BRINLEY] on 8 Mar 1873. Off: PORTER. Wit: Nancy FISHER; Capt. J.P. KELLEY.

FISHER, William [30; Omaha; b: Germany; f: Andrew FISHER; m: Catharine HACKER] md. Mary BUETTNER [22; Omaha b: Germany; f: Andrew BUETTNER; m: Barbara] on 9 Dec 1872. Off: BANDES. Wit: Ferdinand THUM; Mrs. Emilie THUM.

FISK, Benjamin C. [23; Douglas Co.] md. Priscilla Jane CLARK [19; Douglas Co.] on 7 Oct 1867. Off: HURLBUT.

FITCH, William [22; Omaha; b: Illinois; Joel FITCH; m: Ann WAGGEY] md. Mary E. LEE [20; Omaha; b: Iowa; f: Nathan LEE; m: Catherine MORIETTA] on 16 Nov 1870. Off: GIBSON. Wit: Mrs. Mary J. GIBSON; Mrs. Mary STEPHENS.

FITCHETTE, George H. [24; Omaha; b: New York; f: Harvey M. FITCHETTE; m: Ellen MOREY] md. Eva McLAIN [17; Washington Co.; b: Ohio; m: Mary DAVIDSON] on 9 Mar 1871. Off: DANIELS. Wit: William R. MOREY; Mrs. Nellie PADDOCK. Age of consent given by mother of bride, Mrs. Mary FOSTER or (step?) father Mr. Henry FOSTER. Interpretation difficult.

FITHIAN, William H. [39; Omaha; b: Illinois; f: William FITHIAN; m: Orletha BERRY] md. Valencia E. RICE [27; Omaha; b: Kentucky; f: Wm. P. RICE; m: Olivia P. ROSS] on 6 Jul 1874. Off: PEABODY. Wit: Charles F. MANDERSON; Silas A. STRICKLAND.

FITZGERALD, Mathew [31; Elm Creek; b: Ireland; f: Patrick FITZGERALD; m: Cathrine POWER] md. Mary COFFEE [28; Troy, NY; b: Ireland; f: Michael COFFEE; m: Alice DROHAN] on 11 Sep 1871 at the Catholic Church of Omaha. Off: O'GORMAN. Wit: E.P. CUNNINGHAM; Josephine BURNET.

FITZMORRIS, Michael [24; Omaha; b: Ireland; f: Michael FITZMORRIS; m: Mary FLAHERTY] md. Ellen DEE [24; Omaha; b: Ireland; f: Michael DEE; m: Catharine HARGAN] on 16 Sep 1873 at the Catholic Cathedral. Off: O'GORMAN. Wit: Thomas FITZSIMONS; Mary FITZSIMONS.

FITZMORRIS, T.J. [26; Omaha; b: Ireland; f: Michael FITZMORRIS; m: Mary FLAHERTY] md. Mary SWIFT [21; Omaha; b: Omaha; f: Thomas SWIFT; m: Bridget DOOLING] on 25 Aug 1880. Off: ENGLISH. Wit: John SWIFT, Maggie SWIFT.

FITZPATRICK, William [30; Omaha; b: Ireland; f: Cornelius FITZPATRICK; m: Ellen SARSFIELD] and Catharine McCORMICK [32; Omaha; b: Ireland; f: Michial McCORMICK; m: Bridget FEE] license

issued on 12 Apr 1879. Off: BARTHOLOMEW.

FLANAGAN, Hugh [26; Omaha; b: Ireland; f: Cormick FLANAGAN; m: Mary McFARLAND] md. Bridget KIEFF [20; Omaha; b: Ireland; F: Patrick KIEFF; m: Mary FLINN] on 3 Jul 1870. Off: CURTIS. Wit: Patrick KIEFF; Mary WARD.

FLANAGAN, Peter [30; Fremont; b: Ireland; f: Bernard FLANAGAN; m: Mary FLANAGAN] md. Mary GLISPIE [28; Omaha; b: IL; f: Wm. GLISPIE; m: Mary THOMAS] on 17 May 1876 at the Cathedral. Off: BYRNE. Wit: James MALONEY, Bridget MALONEY.

FLANNERY, John [22; Omaha[ md. Eliza FLANIGAN [22; Omaha] on 4 Jul 1867 at the parsonage. Off: VAN ANTWERP. Wit: James B. LOCKWOOD, Mrs. C.A. VAN ANTWERP.

FLECK, Carl [36; Omaha; b: Germany; f: Johan FLECK; m: Frederika SCHMIDT] md. Johanna OLSEN [28; Omaha; b: Norway; f: Ole PETERSEN; m: Olena HANSDATAR] on 24 Sep 1873. Off: HALE. Wit: Anthony NIEDERMEYER; John GREEN.

FLEGEL [FLEGLE], John [27; Omaha; b: Bohemia, f: George FLEGEL [FLEGLE]; m: Eva BROMOL [KRUML]] md. Mary DOBRA [DOBRY] [20; Omaha; b: Bohemia; f: Michael DOBRA [DOBRY]; m: Mary HOFFEK [HOUFEK]] on 14 Aug 1873. Off: TOWNSEND. Wit: Frank M. MARESH; Wenzel KUCERA.

FLEMING, Allan M. [29; Valley; b: Ohio; f: A.W. FLEMING; m: Rebecca McCOLLIN] md. Edith E. CLARK [25; Waterloo; b: Indiana; f: Elam CLARK; m: Rebecca ----] on 1 Jun 1880 at Waterloo. Off: SHAW. Wit: Elam CLARK, Mrs. V. BARTLETT.

FLEMING, Isaac A. [30; Nebraska City] md. Mrs. Belle E. CARR [27; Nebraska City] on 16 Dec 1880. Off: BARTHOLOMEW. Wit: George W. ARBUTHNOT, Mrs. George W. ARBUTHNOT.

FLEMING, Wm. [31; Omaha; b: Scotland; f: Mitchell FLEMING; m: Isabella BENNETT] md. Ida DOOLITTLE [22; Omaha; b: Iowa; f: Wm. V. DOOLITTLE; m: Mary J. BUSHNELL] on 17 Jan 1880. Off: SHERRILL. Wit: J.H. KELLOM, Albert SNOW.

FLETCHER, A.L. [24; Omaha; b: PA; f: O.P. FLETCHER; m: Catharine ORTT] md. Eva WILLIAMS [23; Omaha; b: MI; f: John WILLIAMS; m: Lillie BRINK] on 15 Sep 1881. Off: CHADWICK. Wit: H. CLEAVELAND, H.W. THAYAR.

FLEURY [FLENRY], Charles [24; Omaha] md. Cornelia DEMAREST [23; Omaha] on 15 Jan 1868. Off: KUHNS. Wit: Mary POLAND, John S. CAULFIELD, et al.

FLINN, John [48; Omaha] md. Mrs. Martha Ann KNIGHT [50; Omaha] on 25 Apr

1868. Off: MORRIS. Wit: Michael McDERMOTT, Dr. S.D. MERCER.

FLOOD, Albert S. [39; Omaha] md. Lizzie H. EVANS [22; Omaha] on 8 Nov 1868. Off: James MORRIS. Wit: Mrs. C.H. CHANDLER, Geo. B. BASSETT.

FLORA, Elisha H. [25; Omaha; b: Virginia; f: Melrazo R. FLORA; m: Lucy Ann DUNKLY] md. Annie M. LAIRD [22; Omaha; b: Iowa; f: J.A. LAIRD; m: Amanda SAFFEL] on 19 Sep 1869. Off: Wm. H. MORRIS. Wit: Saml. ORCHARD, John SILLS or ELLIS.

FLORA, Melville R. [21; Omaha; b: Missouri; f: Melville FLORA; m: Anna DUNKLY] md. Mary Jane POLAND [18; Omaha; b: Iowa; f: John POLAND; m: Mary McCANN] on 27 Aug 1869. Off: Wm. M. MORRIS. Wit: Wm. SPENCER, Emma SPENCER.

FLYNN, Martin [Elkhorn Precinct] md. Ellen KANE [Elkhorn Precinct] on 14 May 1865 at the Catholic Church of Omaha. Off: DAXACHER.

FLYNN, Michael [38; Mercer Co., IL] md. Bridget O'BRYEN [38; Omaha] on 20 Oct 1867 at the Catholic Cathedral. Off: O'GORMAN. Wit: Thomas SWIFT, Mary SWIFT.

FLYNN, Wm. F. [37; Omaha; b: New Bruns; f: Wm. FLYNN; m: Catharine CURTIN] md. Mrs. Lettie SAUER [28; Omaha; b: Iowa; f: Jesse T. DAVIS; m: Julia HOSKINSON] on 31 May 1880. Off: SHERILL. Wit: E.D. McLAUGHLIN, Chas. W. EDGERTON.

FODREN, Nathan [25; Omaha; b: Indiana; f: Nathan FODREN; m: Hannah MACE or MARE] md. Kate PARKER [18; Omaha; b: Ohio; f: James M. PARKER] on 3 Oct 1869. Off: HYDE. Wit: John W. STOUT, Jennie PARKER.

FOGG, Charles N. [29; Omaha; b: ME; f: Benjamin S. FOGG; m: Susan FARROW] md. Jennie E. ENGLISH [22; Omaha; b: IA; f: William DOOLITTLE; m: Mary BUSHNELL] on 11 Jul 1881. Off: SHERRILL. Wit: Wm. F. DOOLITTLE, Wm. FLEMING.

FOLEY, John [29; Omaha; b: Ireland; f: Edmund FOLEY; m: Alice CONNERS] md. Johanna DUGGAN [29; Omaha; b: Ireland] on 7 Jan 1873. Off: CURTIS. Wit: William KEEF; Kate MURPHY.

FOLEY, Patrick D. [27; Omaha; b: Ireland; f: Daniel FOLEY; m: Margaret CRONIN] md. Mary BARRETT [19; Omaha; b: Omaha; f: Edward BARRETT; m: Honora LYNCH] on 12 May 1874 at 9th Street Catholic Cathedral. Off: BYRNE. Wit: Timothy FOLEY; Margaret F. GRADY.

FOLEY, Patrick [25; Omaha; b: Ireland; f: Jeremiah FOLEY; m: Ellen FOLEY] md. Eliza FOLEY [26; Omaha; b: Ireland; f: Timothy FOLEY; m: Mary FOLEY] on 24 Nov 1870. Off: CURTIS. Wit: Richard KEEFE; Mary FOLEY.

FOLEY, Patrick [27; Omaha; b: Ireland; f: John FOLEY; m: Mary FOLEY] md. Mary DALY [22; Omaha; b: Ireland; f: William DALY; m: Hannah DENAN] on 14 Aug 1870. Off: GOLDRICK. Wit: Patrick MORAN; Margaret HUNN.

FOLEY, Timothy [27; Omaha; b: Ireland; f: Timothy FOLEY; m: Margaret ENRIGHT] md. Eliza DINAN [21; Omaha; b: Ireland; f: Timothy DINAN; m: Bridget O'NEAL] on 12 Jul 1874 at the Catholic Cathedral. Off: BYRNE. Wit: Daniel DINEN; Mary BARRETT.

FOLGMAN, Friedrich [25; Omaha; b: Germany; f: Ernst FOLGMAN; m: Catharina STRBENOR] md. Louisa SCHROEDER [36; Omaha; b: Germany; f: Carl SCHROEDER; m: Marie MEYER] on 13 Dec 1881. Off: FRESE. Wit: Theodore KRAUSE, E.C. ERFLING, both of 1023 Leavenworth Street.

FOLL, Albert [23; Omaha; b: France; f: Antoine FOLL; m: Catharine SCHMEOR] md. Mary SHAFFER [22; Omaha; b: Germany; f: Baltiz SHAFFER] on 10 Dec 1874. Off: BENEKE. Wit: Wm. MACK; Dr. A. HOTTENROTH.

FOLSOM, Charles N. [29; Saunders Co., NE; b: Vermont; f: David W. FOLSOM; m: Maria SEVER] md. Pearl DAVIS [19; Saunders Co., NE; b: Indiana; f: Wm. DAVIS; m: Nancy WHITING] on 25 Mar 1878. Off: JOHNSON. Wit: Mrs. RUNYON, Mrs. Dr. MORTON, both of Wahoo.

FONTS, Wm. A. [23; Missouri Valley, IA; b: IA; f: W.N. FONTS; m: Elizabeth SMITH] md. Ella MOATS [21; Missouri Valley, IA; b: IA; f: Peter MOATS; m: Caroline STILIERBANER] on 28 Sep 1881. Off: MAXFIELD. Wit: N. FONTS, Elizabeth SMITH.

FORAN, Phillip [26; Omaha; b: NY; f: Phillip FORAN; m: Bridget DONOVAN] md. Sarah HILLAHAN [24; Omaha; b: Ireland; f: Peter HILLAHAN; m: Anastasia DOHERTY] on 11 May 1881. Off: STENBERG. Wit: John GUHEEN, Kate RILEY.

FORBES, J. Walker [28; Douglas Co.; b: New York; f: James FORBES; m: Sarah DURDICK] md. Matilda CATHERWOOD [28; Omaha; f: James CATHERWOOD; m: Elizabeth PATTERSON] on 24 Dec 1874.

Off: McCAGUE. Wit: Harvey SIDNER; H.M. McCAGUE.

FORBES, J.B. [23; Irvington; b: New York; f: James W. FORBES; m: Sarah BURDETT] md. Ella E. KNIGHT [22; Irvington; b: Massachusetts; f: J.G. KNIGHT; m: Lovinia STRAIGHT] on 1 Jan 1874 at Irvington. Off: FITCH. Wit: Hattie V. WILEY, Irvington; Henry B. WILEY, Irvington.

FORD, Andrew [30; Omaha; b: Ireland; f: Michael FORD; m: Mary DOYLE] md. Bridget A. GORMAN [24; Omaha; b: Ireland; f: Michael GORMAN; m: Ann STOKES] on 17 Jun 1873. Off: CURTIS. Wit: John TRACEY; Mary FAXAN.

FORD, James [27; Omaha] md. Emma LONGFELLOW [26; Omaha] on 25 Oct 1866. Off: HASCALL. Wit: Mr. and Mrs. STANFIELD.

FORD, John [35; Omaha; b: Ireland; f: Michael FORD; m: Mary DOYLE] md. Bridget E. CLARK [24; Omaha; b: Ireland; f: Patrick CLARK; m: Catharine LYNCH] on 4 Nov 1872. Off: CURTIS. Wit: Alveh HALL; Mary E. LOWREY.

FORD, Stephen [28; Omaha; b: New York; f: Stephen FORD; m: Pamelia STILLWELL] md. Delinda A. PRATT [17; Omaha; b: New York; f: Joel PRATT] on 17 May 1871. Off: DIMMICk. Wit: Sylvanus WRIGHT; Mrs. K.G. DIMIMCK.

FORD, William W. [30; Omaha; b: London, England; f: John FORD; m: Elizabeth FLOYD] md. Adie R. HALL [21; Omaha; b: Black Rock, NY; f: Mark HALL; m: Mary] on 30 Apr 1873. Off: MORRIS. Wit: Lizzie MORRIS; Alfred E. MORRIS.

FORDYCE, John A. [24; Omaha; b: Ohio; f: Aaron FORDYCE; m: Susan BRANDINGBURG] md. Amy M. JONES [17; Omaha; b: Illinois; f: John C. JONES; m: Susanna SAMS] on 8 Dec 1873. Off: McDONALD. Wit: John C. JONES; Susannah JONES. Age of consent given by father of bride.

FORNER, Edward [30; Dakotah; b: Germany; f: Frederick FORNER; m: Christine SCHNEIDER] md. Eva KOOSER [28; Des Moines, IA; b: Pennsylvania; f: William KOOSER] on 20 Jun 1871. Off: BILLMAN. Wit: J. AHMANSON; Mrs. Ira C. BILLMAN.

FORREST, Julius W. [30; Omaha; b: MO; f: James A. FORREST; m: Sarah E. WILSON] and Mary E. WHITING [17; Omaha; b: UT; m: Dora] license issued 12 Nov 1875. Off: PEABODY. No marriage recorded.

FORREST, William H. [21; US Army; b: New York City; f: John FORREST; m: Sarah FORREST] md. Annie HALL [24; Philadelphia, PA; f: Augustus WALTER; m: Barbara HALLET] on 26 Mar 1871. Off:

GIBSON. Wit: Mrs. Marietta DISBROW; Mrs. J.P. DISBROW.

FORSELL, Gustavis [26; Omaha; b: Sweden; f: John JOHNSON; m: Christina JOHNSDOTAR] md. Anna Sophia GRONHOLM [24; Omaha; b: Sweden; f: Peter GRONHOLM; m: Sarah PETERSEN] on 15 Jun 1872. Off: TOWNSEND. Wit: John C. CHRISTIANSEN; Augustus SWANSON.

FORST, Francis [23; Florence City; b: New York City; f: John FORST; m: Anna BROWN] md. Margaret Jane PECK [19; Florence Pct, Douglas Co.; b: Ohio] on 1 Jan 1872 at Florence Pct. Off: PECK. Wit: Mrs. Jane PARKS; Mrs. Sarah NEALE; Mrs. Eliza PECK.

FORSYTH, James [30; Omaha] md. Jennie A. BROWN [23; Omaha] at 8:30 PM on 25 Mar 1869 at James BROWN's residence. Off: DIMMICK. Wit: Mr. and Mrs. James BROWN, Mr. and Mrs. LAWTON, Frank KENNARD, Agnes McAUSLAND, et al.

FOSTER, Charles [24; Omaha; b: Illinois; f: Frankling P. FOSTER; m: Zerviah P. PORTER] md. Marion FLEMING [19; Omaha; b: Scotland; f: Mitchel FLEMING; m: Isabella BENNETT] on 13 Mar 1879. Off: SHERRILL. Wit: Mitchel FLEMING, John R. PORTER. Affidavit signed by John R. PORTER.

FOSTER, J. Lemuel [39; Yankton, Dakota] md. Nancy A. RANDALL [25; Council Bluffs] on 26 Oct 1868. Off: ALLEN. Wit: Mrs. Belle ALLEN, J.M. ALLEN.

FOSTER, John [38; Omaha] md. Mrs. Catharine O'HEARN [26; Omaha] on 11 Apr 1860. Off: BIRKETT. Wit: Edmund KELLEY.

FOSTER, John [Douglas Co.] md. Sarah GUY [Douglas Co.] on 22 Oct 1865 at Florence. Off: TURNER.

FOSTER, Mattes [22; Council Bluffs; b: Illinois; f: John FOSTER; m: Grace MYERS] md. Elizabeth J. KIRKLAND; [19; b; Canada; f: John KIRKLAND; m: Elizabeth J. McCLELLAND] on 16 Oct 1878. Off: FISHER. Wit: John BARNES, Maggy BARNES.

FOUNTAIN, Alfred [18; Osco [Kearney Co.]; b: Black Hawk Co., IA; f: Isaac FOUNTAIN; m: Belle WILSON] md. Mary GOODRO [15.5; Tippi Branch [Pawnee Co.]; Kankakee, IL; f: Joseph GOODRO; m: Louise LARRA] on 20 Dec 1879. Off: HARSHA. Wit: J.S. GILLESPIE, Fred I. REED. [Note to researchers: request a copy of the permission to marry. It is too long to print.]

FOURIE, Henry [28; Omaha; colored; b: Louisiana; f: Adolph ----; m: Rebecca] md. Emma WHITE [18; Omaha; colored; b: Missouri] on 8 Apr 1873. Off: GAINES. Wit: M.E. GAINES; E. RADNEY.

FOUTS, James N. [21; Dunlap, IA; b: Iowa; f: Eli FOUTS; m: Emeline YOUNG] md. Rena ROUNDY [18; Shelby Co.; IA; b: Iowa; f: Washington ROUNDY; m: Elvira WILLIAMS] on 19 Jul 1877. Off: SEDGWICK. Wit: Charles REED of Dunlap, IA, William COOK of Shelby Co., IA.

FOUTS [FOUST], George W. [Elkhorn] md. Lucy JOHNSON [Elkhorn] on 6 Aug 1863 at Eli JOHNSON's house. Both of legal age. Off: DENTON.

FOWLER, William J. [23; Omaha; b: New York City; f: William FOWLER; m: Katarine MENNIX] md. Katarine SCOW [16; Omaha; b: Denmark; f: Nelson SCOW; m: Ellen] on 5 May 1869. Off: HYDE. Wit: Nelson SCOW, Mrs. Ellen SCOW.

FOX, George [23; Omaha] md. Electa A. STONER [28; Omaha] on 18 Nov 1867 at SHEEKS' office. Off: SHEEKS. Wit: C.A. DOWNY, O.H. DAVIS.

FOX, Henry [Douglas Co.] md. Mary Catharine REDMAN [Douglas Co.] on 1 Jan 1865 near Omaha at the residence of the bride's father. Off: KUHNS. Wit: Daniel REDMAN, Joseph REDMAN, Jacob KUHNSMAN, et al.

FOX, Joseph [46; Omaha] md. Hannah CLARKE [46; Omaha] at 7:30 o'clock on Thursday evening, 31 May 1866 at DIMMICK's house. Off: DIMMICK. Wit: Dr. G.C. MONNELL, Albert TUCKER, et al.

FOY, Hugh [27; Omaha; b: Iowa; f: Hugh FOY; m: Mary CANNON] md. Charlotte KEARN [21; Omaha; b: Iowa; f: Matt KEARN; m: Ellen ARTHUR] on 31 Aug 1869. Off: CURTIS. Wit: James REIDY, Mary CONSIDINE.

FRAHM, Claus [30; Douglas Co.] and Margaret FRAHM [25; Douglas Co.] license issued on 25 Jun 1866. No marriage record. Off: HASCALL.

FRAHM, Henry [32; Fort Calhoun, Washington Co.] md. Dora ROHWER [23; Omaha] on 27 Nov 1860 at KUHNS' residence. Off: KUHNS. Wit: Frederick KUMP, Hans J. ROHWER.

FRAHM, John [24; Douglas Co.; b: Germany; f: Juergen FRAHM; m: Anna C. KURT] md. Ida THORNDORF [22; Douglas Co.; b: Iowa; f: Alvinder THORNDORF; m: Dora SASS] on 3 Dec 1880. Off: BARTHOLOMEW. Wit: Wm. L. PEABODY, Max BERGMANN.

FRAISSINET, Hugo [25; b: Germany; f: Gustav FRAISSINET] md. Pauline STANKE [19; b: Germany; f: Michael STANKE; m: Augusta STANKE] on 24 Jul 1878. Off: BARTHOLOMEW. Wit: Joseph ROSENSTEIN, Christopher HENSINGER.

FRANCIS, James R. [25; Douglas Co.; b: IL; f: Calvin FRANCIS; m: Milda SHARP] md. Leona SNYDER [20; Douglas Co.; b: IA; f: Azra SNYDER; m: Margaret SMITH] on 28 Mar 1881. Off: GRAHAM. Wit: Mary SNYDER, Florence, Eliza M. GRAHAM.

FRANK, Jacob [21; Omaha] md. Coelestine SEEMAN [21; Omaha] on 9 Nov 1868. Off: STUCK. Wit: John M. SULLIVAN, Christ SHULTZ.

FRANKLIN, Edward B. [colored; 23; Omaha] md. Mary J. PAINE [colored; 24; Omaha] on 18 Feb 1868. Off: SLAUGHTER. Wit: Fred KISLINGBURY, Hattie L. SLAUGHTER.

FRANKLIN, Warren B. [Washington Co.] md. Joannah McCARTY [Omaha] on 14 Jul 1864 at DICKINSON's office. Off: DICKINSON. Wit: Mr. and Mrs. Timothy KELLEY.

FRANKLIN, William [25; Omaha; colored; b: Tennessee; f: Joseph FRANKLIN; m: Clorenda THOMPSON] md. Maria PERKINSON [25; Omaha; colored; b: Missouri] on 21 Mar 1871. Off: OUSLEY. Wit: Dann'l WILLIAMSON; Mrs. Priciller LUCAS.

FRANZEL, Antone [22; Omaha; b: Germany; f: Anton FRANZEL; m: Barbara SAVISCOSKA] md. Barbara DODA [20; Omaha; b: Germany; f: James DODA; m: Mary MORISH] on 27 Jan 1877. Off: SEDGWICK. Wit: J.H. STEIN, D.E. BURLEY.

FRASER, Andrew [29; Omaha; b: Nova Scotia; f: Donald FRASER; m: Jennett McKAY] md. Louzelia KELKER [25; Omaha; b: New Castle, PA; f: Rudolph KELKER; m: Elanor RANDOLPH] on 30 Dec 1869. Off: SHERRILL. Wit: Mitchell FLEMING, William FLEMING.

FRASER, Simon [29; Omaha; b: Scotland; f: Simon FRASER; m: Anna ROSS] and Margaret CORRIGAN [19; Omaha; b: NE; f: Patrick CORRIGAN; m: Elizabeth NOLAN] filed affidavit on 22 Dec 1881. No marriage record. Off: BERGMANN.

FRAZELL, Jacob H. [34; Illinois; b: Ohio; b: Moses A. FRAZELL; m: Margaret PENCE] md. Ida J. BLAKEMAN [28; Omaha; b: Illinois; f: George BLAKEMAN; m: Melissa SCOTT] on 18 Apr 1879. Off: JAMESON. Wit: Mrs. Melissa C. BLAKEMAN, Mrs. Clarissa LA FOLLETTE, et al.

FRAZER, George [27; Washington Co.; b: Canada; f: George FRAZER; m: Elmira WOOD] md. Addie PETER [19; Omaha; b: St. Joseph, MO] on 26 Mar 1870. Off: McGURNY. Wit: Dennis BRUNO; Emma BERK.

FREDERICK, Barnard [30; Omaha; b: Germany; f: George FREDERICK; m: Johanna MASSENHELTER] md. Eliza GENKS [18; Omaha; b: Indiana; f: Jesse GENKS; m: Lucinda LATHRUM] on 20 Nov 1869. Off: GIBSON. Wit: Robert GEASEBERGER, Ida APPEL.

FREDERICKSON, Henry [31; Washington Co.; b: Germany; f: Claus FREDERICKSON; m: Christina HENRICKSON] md. Louisa HINZ [20; Omaha; b: Germany; f: Pater HINZ; m: Fredericka HOOP] on 24 May 1873. Off: TOWNSEND. Wit: Edward C. McSHANE; John HEROLD.

FREDERICKSON, Nicholas [25; Omaha; b: Germany; f: John FREDERICKSON; m: Dorothea NISSEN] md. Catharine PETTERSON [23; Omaha; b: Germany; f: Thomas PETTERSON; m: Mary LORENSON] on 28 Mar 1880 at the house of E. JEPSEN. Off: GYDESEN. Wit: E. JEPSEN, C. FREDERICKSON.

FREEMAN, Andrew [29; Omaha; b: Pennsylvania; f: Andrew FREEMAN; m: Alice ULRIC] md. Arebella ROW [19; Omaha; b: Colorado; f: George ROW; m: Annie BEATY] on 29 Mar 1879. Off: BARTHOLOMEW. Wit: Dr. J. QUINLAN, Wm. L. PEABODY.

FREEMAN, George A. [24; Omaha; b: New York; f: William FREEMAN; m: Betsy HODGES] md. Lucinda PENNEY [21; Omaha; b: Illinois; f: Jacob PENNEY; m: Matilda BROWN] on 10 Apr 1870. Off: GIBSON. Wit: Samuel ADAIR; Mary ADAIR.

FREEMAN, John M. [20; Florence; b: Iowa; f: Joseph FREEMAN; m: Mary A. PERKINS] md. Sarah CAUDLE [16; Florence; b: Iowa; f: Gervan CAUDLE; m: Martha DUNCAN] on 9 Apr 1870. Off: GIBSON. Wit: Edward TILTON, Florence; Wm. J. CONNOLL, Florence. Age of consent (8 Mar) given by Joseph FREEMAN; Gervan CAUDLE and Martha, his wife.

FREEMAN, Lewis N. (Louis W.) [22; Omaha; b: Caroline, NY; f: Gilbert G. FREEMAN; m: Emily M. SURDAN] md. Francelia G. WEEKS [22; Omaha; b: Trenton, WI; f: J.V. WEEKS; m: Imogene COOKSON] on 3 Oct 1870. Off: DeLaMATYR. Wit: J.H. HAMMOND; C.L. BRISTOL.

FREEMAN, Patrick [26; Fort Laramie, [WY]; b: Ireland; f: Joseph FREEMAN; m: Alice SPELLMAN] md. Emily MASON [21; Douglas Co.; b: Ireland; f: Michael MASON; m: Henrietta RYEN] on 4 Sep 1877 at the Cathedral. Off: REYNOLDS. Wit: Mr. WIRTH, Lizzie MASON.

FREES, Frederick [28; Chicago, IL; b: Hesse Darmstadt; f: Charles FREES; m: Elizabeth HAMMER] md. Madaline WICKERSHEIM [21; Chicago, IL; b: France; f: Michael WICKERSHEIM; m: Mary GEBHARD] on 27 Aug 1877. Off: ANDERSEN. Wit: H.T. LEAVITT, F.M. WILSON.

FRENCER (FRENCZER) [FRANCER], John md. Mary O'CONNOR on 19 Oct 1865 at the Catholic Church. Off: CURTIS.

FRENZEL, Earnest A. [29; Omaha] md. Mrs. Johannah LIPPAH (LIPPACH) [widow; 29; Omaha] on 26 Dec 1859 at the groom's residence on Farnham St. Off: KUHN. Wit: F. BUNN, Charles BIENDORF and wife.

FRENZER, Joseph [23; Omaha] md. Elizabeth BREMER [22; Omaha] on 21 Nov 1866 at St. Philomena's Church. Off: CURTIS.

FRESE, Adolph W. [32; West Point, Cuming Co,; b: Prussia; f: Henry FRESE; m: Henrietta SCHMERRSAHL] md. Barbara KAMM [24; Omaha; b: Bavaria; f: Melchior KAMM; m: Maria VOLK] on 9 Mar 1873. Off: HILGENDORF. Wit: Jno. George GOODMAN; Maria KAMM, West Point, Cuming Co.

FRICKE, William [30; Douglas Co.] md. Caroline UHE [ 21; Douglas Co.] on 6 Apr 1859 at Friedrich FRICKE's house in Douglas Co. Off: FLORKEE. Wit: Julius FRICKE, Andreas UHE, Rev. John MILLER, Elizabeth FLORKEE, Frederick FRICKE.

FRISBIE, William W. [28; Omaha] md. Irene BINGHAM [23; Omaha] on 18 Jan 1868. Off: SLAUGHTER. Wit: W.P. SMITH, H. OSBORN, Mrs. OSBORN.

FRISONI, Otto [27; Omaha; b: Germany; f: Phillip Julius FRISONI; m: Louise YOUNG] md. Marie POEHLMANN [20; Omaha; b: Germany; f: Henry POEHLMANN; m: Theresea WANDERLICH] on 2 Feb 1875. Off: HINGENDORF. Wit: Max LANDAUER, Pilipp Gottfried DORR.

FRITSCHER, Charles Lewis [28; Omaha; b: Germany; f: William FRITSCHER; m: Ernestine GERSENHEIMER] md. Mary M. SCHNEIDER [19; Omaha; b: Ohio; f: Jacob SCHNEIDER; m: Frances RICHTER] on 3 Oct 1869. Off: KUHNS. Wit: Lewis WEINSTEIN, Ella NELSON.

FRITZ, Nicholas [27; St. Marys Co., IA; b: Germany; f: John FRITZ; m: Catherine MANN] md. Mrs. Miranda CLARK [27; St. Marys Co., IA; b: New York; f: Israel BOWEN; m: Louisa DURHAM] on 31 Jan 1874. Off: PEABODY. Wit: L.B. WILLIAMS; Robert TOWNSEND.

FRITZ, William H. [27; Omaha; b: PA; f: Thomas FRITZ; m: Mary M. GRAYBILL] md. Mary E. MIDDLETON [28; Omaha; b: Canada; f: John MIDDLETON] on 15 Apr 1875. Off: PEABODY. Wit: Israil L. FRITZ, Mary C. PEABODY.

FROSHLE, William G. [31; Omaha] md. Anna SANSER [25; Omaha] on 30 Jun 1868 at Union House. Off: FLORKEE. Wit: Christian RENSCHLER, Elizabeth FLORKEE.

FROST, George [27; Elkhorn; b: England; f: William FROST; m: Charlotte MEEHAN] md. Lucy HOWLETT [26; Elkhorn; b: England; f: William HOWLETT; m: Ann ELLEY] on 7 Jul 1874. Off: PEABODY. Wit: Mary C. PEABODY; A.S. BUXTON, Reeding, MA.

FROST, Harry [25; Omaha; b: England; f: William FROST; m: Charlotte MEEHAN] md. Jane CLARK [21; Omaha; b: England; f: George CLARK; m: Sarah Ann REED] on 6 Jun 1881. Off: HARRIS. Wit: W.B. SMITH, O.S. WOOD, M.D.

FROST, Herick [25; Omaha; b: Sweden; f: Mats FROST; m: Carrie ERRICKSON] md. Becca LARSON [22; Douglas Co.; b: Sweden; f: Lars LARSON; m: Becca ANDERSON] on 15 Dec 1875. Off: PEABODY. Wit: A. POLAND, H. NEWMAN.

FROST, John V. [32; Omaha; b: Sweden; f: C.M. DALGREN; m: Mary C. LINDQUIST] md. Mrs. Eva Charlotte ANDERSON [26; Omaha; b: Sweden; f: John ANDERSON; m: Britta ANDERSON] on 4 May 1869. Off: GLOVER. Wit: Fannie A. BLAIR, Mrs. Elizabeth RICHARDSON.

FRUEHAUF, John J. [31; Omaha] md. Fanny BETZELY [25; Omaha] on 6 Mar 1869. Off: KELLEY. Wit: Adolphus BOHME or BOHER, D.B. TOPHAM.

FRY, George W. [Harrison Co., IA] md. Sarah PALMER [Harrison Co., IA] on 2 Dec 1864 at DICKINSON's office. Off: DICKINSON. Wit: Augustus MACON, George B. SMITH.

FRY, Joel [22; Harrison Co., IA] md. Sophrona PALMER [19; Harrison Co., IA] on 21 Sep [year not recorded, probably 1867]. Off: SHEEKS. Wit: M.H. PARKS, J.S. HASCALL.

FRY, Jonas A. [26; Elkhorn City; b: England; f: Samuel FRY; m: Mary Ann FORNES] md. Anna OSTLER [18; Elkhorn City; b: England; f: George OSTLER; m: Edith HANTHER] on 6 Apr 1881 at the home of the bride's father. Off: WOODMAN. Wit: G.L. MARTIN, Elkhorn City, Dr. LAW, Elkhorn City.

FUHRMANN, Charles [21; Omaha; b: Denmark; f: Matthias P. FUHRMANN; m: Mena LARSON] md. Cecilia JOHNSON [19; Omaha; b: Sweden; m: Hannah] on 14 Oct 1873. Off: PATERSON. Wit: James or Jans JOHNSON; Carrie JOHNSON.

FUHRMANN, Charles [26; Omaha; b: Denmark; f: M.P. FUHRMANN; m: Minna LARSON] md. Jossie LARSON [21; Omaha; b: Sweden; f: Lars OLSON; m: Anna LINGQUIST] on 8 May 1879. Off: HARSHA. Wit: B.B. WOLF, B.C. WESTFALL.

FULCHER, Theodore P. [29; Bellevue; b: Ohio; f: George W. FULCHER; m: Jane CLOUD] md. Mary E. MYERS [26; Bellevue; b: Pennsylvania; f: Henry MYERS; m: Johanna CROLLUS] on 3 Mar 1880. Off: LIPE. Wit: Mrs. Belle ESTELL, Mrs. Lizzie LIPE.

FULLER, John S. [22; Douglas Co.] md. Elizabeth H. DAY [25; Douglas Co.] on 19 Oct 1868 at the ME parsonage. Off: WESTWOOD. Wit: Rev. Thomas B. LEMON, Mrs. H.C. WESTWOOD. "They claimed to come from Denver, CO and stated that the gentleman was originally from Balllstonspa, KY and the lady from East Windham, MA."

FULLREID, Augustus W. [27; Omaha; b: Germany; f: Carl FULLREID; m: Caroline KRUSE] md. Lottie GRAHAM [20; Omaha; b: MO] on 22 Sep 1875. Off: LIPE. Wit: Thomas TUTTLE, Annie TUTTLE.

FULTON, Benjamin [negro; 31; Omaha; b: KY; f: Isaac FULTON] md. Mrs. Lottie GRAYER [negro; 23; Omaha; b: MO; f: ---- TUNNER; m: Julia TUNNER] on 2 Dec 1881 at the Methodist Church. Off: PICKELLY. Wit: Chas. BRYANT; Allen SYDNEY.

FUREY, John [22; Omaha; b: Canada East; f: Charles FUREY; m: Ann HUGHES] md. Bridget NOLAN [19; Omaha; b: Ohio; f: Nicholas NOLAN; m: Catharine DOYLE] on 14 Jan 1873. Off: CURTIS. Wit: Patrick CRADY; Margaret HUGHES.

GAGE, Charles L. [22; Omaha; b: Rhode Island; f: Lemuel GAGE; m: Julie A. SHERIDAN] md. Jennie R. NEELEY [18; Omaha; b: Pennsylvania; f: William NEELEY] on 29 May 1873. Off: WRIGHT. Wit: Sarah NEIHLY; Savannah COBURN.

GAHAN, Thomas [22; Omaha] md. Josephine STOCKMIRE [20; Omaha] on 21 Apr 1868 at the Omaha Cathedral. Off: KEENAN. Wit: John GENTLEMAN, Mary Ann McGILL.

GALBRETH [GALBRAITH], Richard M. [23; Platteville, WI] md. Jennie E. MANN [21; Platteville, WI] at 8 o'clock on Tuesday evening, 16 Oct 1866 at DIMMICK's house. Off: DIMMICK. Wit: Robert S. KNOX, K.G.W. DIMMICK.

GALLAGHER, Constantine V. [23; Omaha; b: Iowa; f: Constantine GALLAGHER; m: Catherine McCORMICK] md. Kate CREIGHTON [19; Omaha; b: Ohio; f: James CREIGHTON] on 12 Oct 1871 at O'GORMAN's residence. Off: O'GORMAN. Wit: Martin GRIFFIN; Ada DOHENEY, Council Bluffs.

GALLAGHER, John [26; Sarpy Co.; b: Ireland; f: Thomas GALLAGHER; m: Margaret POWERS] md. Margaret HALLEY [26; Omaha; b: Ireland; f: Nicholas HALLEY; m: Bridget CUMMINGS] on 9 Feb 1874 at the Roman Catholic Cathedral. Off: BYRNE. Wit: William Wallace MILLER; Catherine GALLAGHER.

GALLAGHER, Sylvester K. [32; Woodbury Co., IA: b: Grant Co., WI; f: James GALLAGHER; m: Jane McREYNOLDS] md. Rebecca F. SMITH [24; Woodbury Co., IA; b: Mobile, AL; f: Douglas SMITH; m: Rebecca FRANCIS] on 28 Apr 1873. Off: WRIGHT. Wit: Mrs. M.H. WRIGHT; John M. MARSTON.

GALLAGHER, Thomas Q. [22; Omaha; b: Portland, ME; f: Bryan GALLAGER; m: Mary] md. Elizabeth CAMPBELL [22; Omaha; b: New York] on 20 Jul 1869. Off: KUHNS. Wit: Mrs. T.M. SUTHERLAND, Mrs. J.B. DETWILER.

GALLETT, Andreas [39; Omaha; b: Switzerland; f: Andreas GALLETT; m: Catharine GARMANN] md. Theresia SCHROFF [22; Omaha; b: Germany; f: Charles SCHROFF; Maria FEHRLI] on 6 Dec 1879. Off: WEISS. Wit: Carl KOHLMEIER, Eva KOHLMEIER.

GALLIGAN, Peter [26; Omaha; b: Ireland; f: Peter GALLIGAN; m: Annie SMITH] md. Mary MADDEN [24; Omaha; b: Wisconsin; f: James MADDEN; m: Julia MAGINNIS] on 2 Jan 1877 at R.C. Cathedral. Off: KELLY. Wit: Patrick GALLIGAN, Katie MADDEN.

GALLIGHER, John W. [21; Omaha; b: New York; f: James M. GALLIGHER; m: Catharine McMANNIS] md. Mary A. DOUGHERTY [22; McArdle Precinct; b:

Nebraska; f: Hugh DOUGHERTY; m: Ellen McARDLE] on 28 Mar 1880. Off: ENGLISH. Wit: Pat. DOUGHERTY, Maggie DOUGHERTY.

GALLIVAN, Henry W. [33; Omaha; b: Massachusetts; f: Thomas GALLIVAN; m: Mary CAREY] md. Josephine ROLFER [20; Omaha; b: Ohio; f: Henry ROLFER] on 22 Nov 1877. Off: SWARTZ. Wit: G.P. ATCHISON, Charles MANSFIELD.

GAMBLE, William W. [25; Davais Co., MO; b. IL; f: M.W. GAMBLE; m: Elizabeth RANDOLPH] md. Nancy MORRISON [17; Sarpy Co.; b: NY; f: Daniel MORRISON; m: Matilda FENTON] on 13 Sep 1875. Off: STEWART. Wit: Mr. and Mrs. William WILLIAMS.

GANKLE [KUNKL], Charles [30; Omaha] md. Mary FOUSEK [25; Omaha] on 30 Dec 1868. Off: HYDE. Wit: Anton JANSEN [JANSA], John HULA.

GANTZ, William F. [25; Omaha; b: Pennsylvania; f: Charles GANTZ; m: Ameila SHADLOCK] md. Sarah A. PHILLIPS [21; Des Moines, IA; b: Illinois; f: Haynes PHILLIPS; m: Elizabeth STEVENS] on 31 Oct 1877. Off: PEABODY. Wit: George HINES, Jennie HINES.

GARDNER, George M. [28; Douglas Co.; b: New York; f: P.R. GARDNER; m: Jennette MUNGER] md. Sarah CAMPBELL [19; Waterloo; b: Indiana; f: John CAMPBELL; m: Laurinda ELLSTON] on 22 Nov 1874 at Waterloo. Off: HITCHCOCK. Wit: John CAMPBELL; Messrs. DENTON and LOGAN, all of Waterloo.

GARDNER, James [27; Omaha] md. Charlotte HESS [20; Omaha] on 21 May 1868. Off: KUHNS. Wit: John N. ARNOLD, Mrs. H.W. KUHNS.

GARDNER, Peyton [26; WY Territory; b: Portsmouth, NH; f: John GARDNER; m: Rebecca CLARK] md. Mrs. Mary E. McINTYRE [22; Boone Co., IA; b: Iowa; f: Darriel McINTYRE; m: Ann RAMSEY] on 25 May 1869. Off: HYDE. Wit: DeMott HYDE, G. GROSVENOR of Tekamah.

GARNSEY, Lemon T. [25; Omaha; b: Great Bend, PA; f: Lemon T. GARNSEY; m: Clora THOMAS] md. Georgia M. HILTON [17; Omaha; b: Pittsfield, MA; f: Hastings B. HILTON] on 12 Sep 1870. Off: EVERTS. Wit: Charles MOLTAN; John CURTIS. (Certificate written in Chicago).

GARRETSON, John W. [22; Omaha; b: Iowa, f: Wm. GARRETSON; m: Christine NEWCOMB] md. Mary DAUBLE [18; Omaha; b: Germany; f: Anthony DAUBLE; m: Mary HABER] on 26 Jun 1880. Off: HAWES. Wit: Frank WALTERS, J.S. WRIGHT.

GARRETT, Solomon [28; Douglas Co.; b: OH; f: Alfred E. GARRETT; m: Martha SHANON] md. Mittie (or Mattie) H. WICKHAM [24; Omaha; b: NY; f: Norman S.

WICKHAM; m: Catharine BEAR] on 15 Apr 1875. Off: HALE. Wit: Hattie WICKHAM (RITTER) crossed out, Eveline SAULSPAUGH. Application signed by J.H. SAULPAUGH.

GARRETTY, Francis [33; Omaha; b: Patterson, NJ; f: Patrick GARRETTY; m: Bridget McCRYSTAL] md. Sarah BRENNAN [27; Omaha; b: Ireland] on 17 Feb 1873. Off: KELLEHER. Wit: William GENTLEMAN; Anna ROLLS.

GARRIGAN, Philip Henry [27; Council Bluffs; b: Massachusetts; f: Philip GARRIGAN; m: Mary STICKNEY] md. Minnie LEADMAN [ 28; Council Bluffs; b: MO; f: John LEADMAN; m: Mary DANIELS] on 1 Dec 1880. Off: MAXFIELD. Wit: S. SMITH, Willie STEPHENS.

GARRISON, Charles L. [25; Omaha; b: Lebanon, OH; f: Thomas GARRISON; m: Margaret M. MAUL] and Louise HALL [20; Omaha; b: Eau Plaine, WI; f: George HALL] license issued on 22 Dec 1870. Off: GIBSON.

GARRISON, John [23; Omaha; b: Westchester Co., NY; f: Albert GARRISON; m: Mary JONES] md. Jessie HISLOP [24; Omaha; b: Scotland; f: Robert HISLOP] on 1 May 1868. Off: DIMMICK. Wit: Mr. and Mrs. J.A. CALDWELL, Mr. and Mrs. Geo. W. FINNEY.

GARRISON, Jonathan H. [29; Omaha; b: Canada West; f: John T. GARRISON; m: Rebecca BROWN] md. Susan DUCRO [18; Omaha; b: St. Louis, MO; f: Victor DUCRO] on 24 Nov 1872. Off: LYTLE. Wit: Victor DUCRO; Harry LaFOND.

GARVEY, John [25; b: Indiana; f: Michael GARVEY; m: Sarah MACK] md. Catharine RYAN [22; b: Canada; f: Thomas RYAN; m: Ann O'NEIL] on 16 May 1878. Off: O'BRIAN. Wit: Mike LEARY, Eliza RYAN.

GARVEY, Patrick [20; Douglas Co.] md. Mary RYAN [18; Douglas Co.] on 10 Jan 1866. Off: CURTIS. Wit: Daniel HOGAN, Brigget GARVEY.

GARVIN, Thomas [25; Omaha; b: Ireland; f: Daniel GARVIN; m: Peggy HEFFERNER (HEFFENER)] md. Honora SULLIVAN [23; Omaha; b: Ireland; f: Jeremiah SULLIVAN; m: Ellen CURRAN] on 19 Jun 1870. Off: CURTIS. Wit: William CUNNINGHAM; Ellen O. DERNAL (O'DERNAL).

GAVIN, Edward H. [27; Omaha; b: Ireland; f: Hugh GAVIN; m: Margaret HORN] md. Mary P. COLEMAN [22; Omaha; b: New Brunswick; f: Timothy COLEMAN; m: Mary HALEY] on 31 Aug 1870. Off: CURTIS. Wit: Thomas CORMAN; Mary GESLOSPIE.

GAY, Charles [26; Omaha] md. Annie PALMER [18; Omaha] on 2 Dec 1868. Off: KELLEY. Wit: Mrs. J.E. KELLEY, Maggie RICE.

GAY, John L. [23; Merrick Co.] md. Civilah HASTLETON [20; Omaha] on 30 Mar 1867. Off: HASCALL. Wit: G. CUNNINGHAM, E.J. CUNNINGHAM.

GAYTON, Charles [24; b: Ohio; f: Austin GAYTON; m: Celia GALLAGHER] md. Marion PICKARD [16; b: Douglas Co., NE; f: Laomei W. PICKARD, m: Catharine BOYER] on 30 Sep 1878. Off: FALK. Wit: Charles GROTHE, Mrs. Catharine GROTHE. Age consent given by Chas. GROTHE, guardian, and mother of the bride, Kate GROTHE. Age consent written on letterhead of "Omaha House," Fred WIRTH, prop., 201 and 203 Harney Street.

GAYWOOD, Theo [39; Chicago; b: Scotland; f: Fredric GAYWOOD; m: Jannett GOLDER] md. Mrs. Annie McFARLAND [42; Omaha; b: England; f: Thomas TIBBETT; m: Elizabeth LAMB] on 31 Dec 1877. Off: WRIGHT. Wit: Simeon BLOOM, David Van ETTEN.

GEDDES, James [21; Omaha; b: Nova Scotia; f: William GEDDES; m: Elizabeth BLACKY] md. Esther GEDDES [24; Omaha; b: Nova Scotia; f: John GEDDES; m: Mehitabel GOARY] on 27 Dec 1869. Off: DIMMICK. Wit: Mrs. K.G.W. DIMMICK, Lissie A. HENRY.

GEE, William W. [31; Omaha] md. Phebe A. HAYES [27; Des Moines, IA] on 27 May 1866. Off: SLAUGHTER.

GEHLE, Henry [30; Calhoun; b: Germany; f: Charles GEHLE; m: Louise PETERMEGERS] md. Louise RUGENMEISS [30; Calhoun; b: Germany; f: John RUGENMEISS; m: Louise SUELWOLD] on 22 May 1875. Off: PEABODY. Wit: Wm. ALSTADT, F.P. HANLON.

GEIST, Christ C. [24; Omaha; b: Germany; f: Hermann GEIST; m: Helena HERGERADER] md. Amelia KOEHLER [21; Omaha; b: Germany; f: Gothelf KOEHLER; m: Willhelmina KRUHER] on 14 Apr 1871. Off: KUHNS. Wit: Ferdinand V. BRODFUEHUR; William GEIST.

GELSTON, George W. [25; Douglas Co.] md. Mary WILKNAY [22; Washington Co.] on 27 Sep 1862 at Elkhorn. Off: HURLBUT.

GENSLER, Andrew [27; Omaha; b: Germany; f: John FISHER; m: Catherine GENSLER] md. Crescentia (Annie) DANEEDER [20; Omaha; b: Germany] on 19 Jan 1871 at the German Catholic Church. Off: GROENEBAUM. Wit: Michael KOPPER; Mrs. Anna KOPPER.

GENSTREN, Jacob [60; Omaha] md. Kester Sophie ANDRESSEN [60; Omaha] on 28 Feb 1866. Off: HASCALL. Wit: Mr. and Mrs. ANDRESSEN, Chas. P. BIRKETT.

GENTLEMAN, Robert [26; Columbus; b: Ireland; f: William GENTLEMAN; m: Martha SHANON] md. Mary FAGAN [22; Omaha; b: Ireland; f: Peter FAGAN; m: Mary DAVIS] on 14 Jun 1874 at the Roman Catholic Cathedral. Off: JENNETT. Wit: James FAGAN, Wm. GENTLEMAN, May T. FAGAN, Ellen DEANE.

GENTLEMAN, William [31; Omaha; b: Ireland; f: William GENTLEMAN; m: Johanna SULLIVAN] md. Ellen Maria DOYLE [25; Omaha; b: MI; f: Michael DOYLE; m: Mary LESTER] on 11 Jan 1881 at St. Philomena's Cathedral. Off: ENGLISH. Wit: Henry PAUL, Elizabeth MURPHY.

GEORGESON, Ola [19; Omaha] md. Anna HALWER [23; Omaha] on 5 Nov 1866. Off: HASCALL. Wit: S.J. HASCALL, K. NEILSON.

GEPPNER, Michael [27; Omaha; b: Ohio; f: John GEPPNER; m: Elizabeth ROOKER] md. Roina ALBIN [31; Omaha; b: Illinois; f: James ALBIN; m: Margaret Ann MAY] on 5 Oct 1879. Off: STENBERG. Wit: Mrs. Chatarine (x) DUGAN, Mrs. Mary SULLIVAN.

GERBER, Frederick [23; Omaha; b: Switzerland; f: Jacob GERBER; m: Elizabeth GYGER] md. Theresa GEIS [22; Omaha; b: Bavaria; f: Andrew GEIS; m: Catherine EDELMAN] on 4 Nov 1873 at the German Catholic Church. Off: GROENEBAUM. Wit: William GUSTHHORST; Mrs. GUSTHHORST.

GERCKE, Herman [26; Madison Co.; b: Prussia; f: Frederick GERCKE; m: Elizabeth WINKLEMAN] md. Sarah E. BUCKLEY [18; Waterloo; b: New York] on 22 Jul 1871. Off: GIBSON. Wit: James MORRISON; B. McNARRI.

GERHARD, Franz L. [24; Omaha; b: Germany; f: John GERHARD; m: Sarah AMEND] md. Margaretha KARBACH [22; Omaha; b: Germany; f: Peter KARBACH; m: Margaretha KESSLER] on 16 Nov 1880, German Catholic Church. Off: GROENEBAUM. Wit: Mr. HOFFMANN, H. KAUFMANN.

GERSPACHER, Anton [21; Council Bluffs; b: Pennsylvania; f: Julius GERSPACHER; m: Caroline ----] md. Mary O'NEILL [18; Council Bluffs; b: Illinois; f: James O'NEILL; m: Julia PERCIL] on 16 Oct 1879. Off: BARTHOLOMEW. Wit: Max BERGMAN, S.N. MEALIA.

GETTEY, William J. [27; Omaha; b: New York City; f: William J. GETTEY; m: Ann J. CARR] md. Mary M. REEVES [20; Omaha; b: Missouri; f: J.C. REEVES; m: Elizabeth EVANS] on 6 Nov 1873. Off: DONNELLY. Wit: V.M. MACKEY; A.D. JONES.

GEVREZ, Theodore [33; Omaha; b: Ohio; f: Theodore GEVREZ; m: Jane SMITHSON] md. Mrs. Mary C. McCORMICK [32; Omaha; b: Ohio; f: Rufus MAXON; m: Estina FULLER] on 31 Mar 1874. Off: PEABODY. Wit: M.G. McKOON; Mr. Emile FRENCH.

GEYER, Joseph [48; Omaha; b: Germany; f: Joseph GEYER; m: Therklee MOEYER] md. Mrs. Carolina FRANKE [45; Omaha; b: Germany] on 8 May 1869. Off: HYDE. Wit: A.R. HOEL, D.B. WALL.

GIBBONS, Henry [28; Valley, Douglas Co.; b: Ireland; f: Joshua GIBBONS; m: ---- COLGAN] md. Charlotte E. DREW [18; Valley, Douglas Co.; b: Earl, IL; f: Ezra DREW; m: ---- GREENLEAF] on 11 Aug 1872 at Valley Station. Off: BULLARD. Wit: A.T. DUFFEY, Valley; Mrs. T.J. TORREY, Valley. Theodore N. VAIL, requested by groom to make application for license.

GIBBS, Francis [30; Sarpy Co.; b: England] md. Elizabeth JONES [28; Omaha; b: England; f: John JONES; m: Mary NEEDS] on 17 Mar 1871. Off: DANIELS. Wit: C.F. TAYLOR; Madison LOVETTE.

GIBBS, John [28; Douglas Co.; b: England; f: Thomas GIBBS; m: Elizabeth BRYANT] md. Emma SHELDON [18; Douglas Co.; b: NY; f: John SHELDON; m: Sarah CAREY] on 3 Feb 1876. Off: STEWART. Wit: Mrs. Emily W. STEWART, William CLARK, Waterloo.

GIBBS, W.S. [27; Waterloo; b: ME; f: Wm. H. GIBBS; m: Martha A. SMITH] md. Mollie McLAUGHLIN [19/ Waterloo; b: PA; f: James McLAUGHLIN; m: Ida McCREADY (or McCREARY)] on 15 Feb 1875 at Waterloo. Off: CORLISS. Wit: R.W. BARBER, Waterloo, Miss S. McLAUGHLIN, Waterloo.

GIBBS, William [21; Platte Valley Pct, Douglas Co.; b: England; f: Thomas GIBBS; m: Betsey BRYANT] md. Eliza SAVAGE [20; Platte Valley Pct, Douglas Co.; b: England; f: George SAVAGE; m: Eliza BRYANT] on 4 Jul 1873 at ADAIR's residence. Off: ADAIR. Wit: Mrs. Mary A. ADAIR; Mrs. Ann RAPP.

GIBSON, George L. [37; Omaha; b: Perry, ME; f: John D. GIBSON; m: Lydia SMITT] md. Lizzie COOPER [24; Omaha; b: Central Falls, RI; f: George H. COOPER; m: M. GANNAN] on 4 Jan 1870. Off: DelaMATYR. Wit: L.B. GIBSON; Mary ADAIR.

GIBSON, Henry [27; Omaha] md. Augusta A. KEYES [22; Omaha] on 3 Jun 1867. Off: SLAUGHTER. Wit: Andrew McAUSLAND, Eugenia KEYES, et al.

GIBSON, William E. [24; Douglas Co.; b: New York; f: James GIBSON; m: Mary McCURLEY] and Juliette LUDINGTON [17; Douglas Co.; b: Iowa; f: H.L. LUDINGTON; m: Eliza CULLEN] license issued on 10 Mar 1880, Irvington. Off: BARTHOLOMEW. No marriage recorded.

GILBERT, James [31; Omaha b: England; f: David GILBERT; m. Annie CLIFFORD] md. Maria ERICKSON [21; Omaha; b: Australia; f: John ERICKSON; m: Auguste TYBELL] on 3 May 1876. Off: LIPE. Wit: John GILBERT, Frank GILBERT.

GILBERT, John [22; Council Bluffs; b: Philadelphia, PA; f: James GILBERT; m: Mary MORRIS] md. Mary INGOLDSBY [22; Omaha; b: Philadelphia, PA; f: Owen INGOLDSBY; m: Mary NARIE] on 12 May 1870. Off: GROENEBAUM. Wit: John GILBERT; Mrs. Maggie GILBERT.

GILBERT, Nathan E. [28; Sidney; b: New York; f: Morris GILBERT; m: Olive ELDRED] md. Sarah E. SPURGEON [19; Omaha; b: Ohio; f: Asa SPURGEON; m: Sarah E. LARSON] on 28 Feb 1872. Off: KUHNS. Wit: C. WOOD; E.T. SPURGEON.

GILES, Paul [21; Omaha; b: MS; f: Russell GILES; m: Jane HAYES] md. Josephine GRIGSBY [22; Omaha; b: AR; f: James GRIGSBY; m: Harriet WILLIAMS] on 2 Jan 1881. Off: RICKETTS. Wit: Thomas HARGREAVES, Dock REYNOLDS.

GILHAM, William [Kansas City, MO] md. Julia FREDERICK [Kansas City, MO] on the evening of 14 Jul 1863 at Farnham House. Both of legal age. Off: LEMON. Wit: Mr. and Mrs. NEWMAN.

GILL, James M. [27; Omaha; b: Indiana; f: Mason C. GILL; m: Mary APPLEGATE] md. Harriet NEWHOUSE [22; Omaha; b: Pennsylvania; f: Lewis NEWHOUSE] on 7 Apr 1872. Off: BRANDES. Wit: William R. CLARK; Mrs. Carrie E. CLARK.

GILLBANKS, John [Douglas Co.] md. Annie MATHEWS [Douglas Co.] on 23 Dec 1864 at DICKSON's office. Off: DICKSON. Wit: John H. KELLOM, Charles H. BROWN.

GILLE, Frederick [23; Omaha; b: Prussia; f: Andrew GILLE; m: Elizabeth FRICKE] md. Catharine (Kate SCHMIDT) SMITH [19; Omaha; b: Luxumbourg, Europe; f: Jacob SMITH; m: Eugenie JUNGERS] on 2 Dec 1871. Off: GROENEBAUM. Wit: Matthew SCHINNEN; Rosa SCHMIDT.

GILLEN, William F. [25; Omaha; b: Ireland; f: Patrick GILLEN; m: Sarah KELLEY] md. Kate FAGIN [22; Omaha; b: Ireland; f: Owen FAGIN; m: Ann HULE] on 21 Jun 1869. Off: CURTIS. Wit: John CLEAR, Mary Ann CLEAR.

GILLESPIE, David W. [32; Omaha] md. Mary E. DYER [30; Omaha] on 3 Oct 1868. Off: ALLEN. Wit: Mr. and Mrs. C.L. RODWAY.

GILLESPIE, Hugh [30; Omaha; b: OH; f: W.M. GILLESPIE; m: Mary MANERLY] md. Ora FINCH [25; Omaha; b: IL; f: John FINCH; m: Mary CRAWFORD] on 15 Mar 1883. Off: BRANDES. Wit: Walter BRANDES, Fred MEYERS. Affidavit signed by BRANDES 26 Oct 1881.

GILLESPIE, John [23; Omaha; b: England; f: Alexander GILLESPIE] md. Nellie HANIFINN [16; Omaha; b: Ireland; f: Morris HANIFINN; m: Johanna LUCID] on 10 May 1879. Off: Fr. McDERMOTT. Wit: Anthony LIEBLER; Margaret CARLTON. [Age consent given by the father of the bride, Mr. HANIFFIN, witnessed by Johanna LUCID. Taken from the records of St. Philomena Church, Rev. E.M. GLEASON, pastor. Filed 17 Feb 1938, Bryce CRAWFORD, County Judge.]

GILLIGAN, Michael T. [24; b: Massachusetts; f: Michael GILLIGAN; m: Mary CURLEY] md. Mary KILLANAN [17; b: Omaha; f: Jeremiah KILLANAN; m: Bridget TUEY] on 6 May 1878. Off: WRIGHT. Wit: James BRADY, Theresa BRADY. Age consent given by father of the bride, Jerry KILLANAN.

GILMORE, Daniel [23; Omaha] md. Elizabeth Leadbetter BECKWITH [23; Omaha] on 1 Sep 1868. Off: KERMOTT. Wit: Alfred CURCHEBAL, Charles KYLE. Another license was issued on 20 Sep 1868 to Daniel GILMORE and Elizabeth LEADBETTER. It was not returned.

GILMORE, John R. [29; Douglas Co.] md. Mary L. CONCANNON [20; Douglas Co.] on 18 Sep 1867 at Primrose, Douglas Co. Off: DENTON.

GIPSON, Franklin [22; Dunlap, IA; b: Iowa; f: Nelson GIPSON; m: Rebecca Ann] md. Sarah BUNDY [19; Dunlap, IA: b: Iowa; f: Louis BUNDY; m: Cordelia BUNDY] on 20 Sep 1870. Off: KELLEY. Wit: Wm. McCORD; I. HASKALL. William McCORD sworn to the qualification of the parties above named to enter into the marriage relation.

GIPSON, William H. [22; Omaha] md. Laura PATTEN [20; Omaha] on 13 Feb 1869 at the residence of John SANDERS. Off: SHINN. Wit: "The said SANDERS, his father and family."

GIPSON, William [24; Omaha; colored; b: Lexington, MO; f: William GIPSON; m: Sarah STEVENSON] and Ella KILLMER [22; Omaha; white; b: Syracuse, NY; f: John KILLMER; m: Jane KNOWLES] application issued on 4 Jul 1873. Off: TOWNSEND. License refused. This license is refused, things are badly mixed. Judge Hunt of the United States Supreme Court, holds that any state in the Union may regulate the suffrage by the color of the hair, or any other whim, so that the right of male negroes to make laws for elegant and cultivated but disfranchised white women, be always secured.

While on the other hand, the Supreme Court of the State of Nebraska has decided that negroes cannot be excluded from juries any more than red headed people or people five feet high. And in accordance with this decision the recent Legislature of Nebraska were asked to repeal the law forbidding the comsummation of happiness between male negro and elegant white woman, and between which man and the lady of dark complexion; but the God and Equality Legislature killed the bill.

I trust the time will soon come when "Equality" will mean equality in all things, policitically, civily, religiously, (no African M.E. Chruch), socially, and especially matrimonially.

My advice is cross over into Iowa where a Negro can marry the Governor's daughter, if she is willing, as she ought to be.

Your obient servant, Robert TOWNSEND, Probate Judge.

GISEKE, Hermann [44; Omaha; b: Germany f: Henry GISEKE; m: Mary TOHLE] md. Laura WESSEL [27; Omaha; b: Germany] on 11 Jul 1873. Off: TOWNSEND. Wit: Alfred ARNEMANN; Josephine ARNEMANN.

GISH, Jacob [31; Omaha; b: Lancaster Co., PA; f: Jacob GISH; m: Maria HOLLINGER] md. Jennie E. HORNER [28 or 23; Omaha; b: Massachusetts (crossed out); f: William HORNER; m: Rachel BEGGS] on 18 Nov 1871. Off: DeLaMATYR. Wit: Hon. G.W. HOMAN; Mr. MINER.

GIVENS, J.M. [50; Omaha; b: Indiana; f: Daniel GIVENS; m: Elizabeth TAYLOR] md. Mrs. Belle TROUPE [36; Omaha; b: Ohio; f: Samuel NYSWANER; m: Hannah YOUNG] on 24 Mar 1880. Off: BARTHOLOMEW. Wit: John F. CRONIN, Max BERGMANN.

GLADE, Henry [29; Omaha; b: Germany; f: William GLADE; m: Louise MUELLER] md. Mary NOZISKA [19; Omaha; b: Bohemia; f: John NOZISKA; m: Maria NOZISKA] on 4 Nov 1880. Off: BENEKE. Wit: D.L. NOZISKA, Louis HELLBORN.

GLADSTONE, Sam [24; Omaha; b: Hungary; f: Bernard GLADSTONE; m: Hannah "full name unknown"] md. Kitty LYTER [19; Omaha; b: Ohio; f: Charles LYTER; m: Maggie EWING] on 28 Mar 1877. Off: SEDGWICK. Wit: Marcia F. SEDGWICK, Emma MITSKUFF.

GLASS, Herman [28; Omaha] md. Lucy Ann GOODWILL [18; Omaha] on 10 May 1859. Off: WATSON. Wit: Alfred SAYER, Mrs. L.A. GOODWILL.

GLAZE, W.A. [21; Ottumwa, IA; b: Ohio; f: Benjamin GLAZE; m: Ellen CAMPBELL] md. Sadie HARLAN [22; Omaha; b: Winterset, IA; f: N.A. HARLAN; m: Ellen BARNES] on 10 Nov 1879. Off: W.K. BEANS. Wit: Mr. GLAZE and wife, Mr. GARNER and wife of Ottumwa.

GLEASON, Michael [27; Omaha] md. Ellen BROWN [19; Omaha] on 24 May 1868. Off: CURTIS. Wit: John McCABE, Mary O'BRIEN.

GLESMANN, Henry [26; Sarpy Co.; b: Germany; f: John GLESMANN; m: Elizabeth RUNNER] md. Elizabeth RONAN [18; Omaha; b: Germany; f: Christian RONAN; m: Catharina STEFFEN] on 14 Oct 1874. Off: PEABODY. Wit: Christian WILT; John GLESMAN.

GLESMANN, John D.W. [34; Sarpy Co.; b: Germany; f: John GLESMANN; m: Elizabaeth ROEURRAN] md. Anna GOETTSCH [19; Sarpy Co.; b: Germany; f: Henry GOETTSCH; m: Gretchen KUEHL] on 19 Oct 1880. Off: BARTHOLOMEW. Wit: Charles ANDERSEN, Charles WITT.

GLISSMAN, Hans. Chr. [25; Douglas Co.; b: Germany; f: James GLISSMAN; m: Dorothea KRENBZFELDT] md. Emma EICKE [18; Douglas Co.; b: Omaha; f: Henry EICKE; m: Elizabeth SOHL] on 3 Mar 1875. Off: GREGG. Wit: Herman HORIES, Douglas Co., Minna GERNDORF, Douglas Co.

GLYNN, Patrick [30; Douglas Co.; b: Ireland; f: Nicholas GLYNN; m: Bridget NAUGHTON] md. Margaret O'CONNOR [21; Douglas Co.; b: IA; f: Thomas O'CONNOR; m: Annie] on 5 Jun 1876 at the Roman Catholic Cathedral. Off: JENNETTE. Wit: Wm. GENTLEMAN, Ebbie O'CONNOR.

GOBLE, Milton H. [28; Marshall, TX; b: Baldwinsville, NY; f: Milton GOBLE; m: Catharine C. LASHER] md. Charlotte A. ALLEN [19; Omaha; b: Canada East; f: John ALLEN] on 15 May 1873 at Trinity Cathedral. Off: GARRETT. Wit: Chas. E. RICE; George PATERSON.

GOEBEL (JOEBEL), August [36; Omaha] md. Caroline JACOBI [31; Omaha] on 14 Sep 1868. Off: GROENEBAUM. Wit: Cath. FRENZER.

GOLDBLATT, B. [25; Omaha; b: Russia; f: Louis GOLDBLATT; m: Rosie GREENBEC] and Edith WOOLFS [23; Omaha; b: Russia; f: Louie WOOLFS; m: Annie ----] license issued on 1 Jun 1881. No marriage record. Off: KARN. Filed 1 Jun 1891 by SHIELDS.

GOLDSTADT, Henry Christ [29; Douglas Co.; b: Germany; f: Henry GOLDSTADT; m: Margaretha STOLTENBERG] md. Rosalie ZIPLIES [22; Omaha; b: Germany; f: Johann F. ZIPLIES; m: Maria TANTURATH] on 28 Aug 1880. Off: BENEKE. Wit: Gustav WECKBACK, Peter RAHELE.

GOODALE, Francis [Council Bluffs] md. Isabella LATTON [TATTON] [Council Bluffs] on 9 Jun 1864 at Douglas House. Off: DICKINSON. Wit: Henry CAVENAUGH, Martha WHITE, Col. Samuel SUMMERS, et al.

GOODCHILDS, Wilford [33; Omaha; colored; b: Missouri; f: Thomas GOODCHILDS; m: Emily GREEN (affidavit) or RAINY (license)] md. Mrs. Susan FOUNTAIN [30; Omaha; colored; b: Pennsylvania; f: James CREIGHTON; m: Sarah WALLS] on 11 Nov 1873. Off: GAINES. Wit: R.D. CURRY; Mr. EARLY.

GOODMAN, Francis M. [Paducah, KY] md Myra May LEWELLEN [Wappelo Co., IA] on 14 Sep 1865 at the parsonage. Off: KUHNS. Wit: Louisa J. MOREHEAD, Abraham HERSCH, et al.

GOODMAN, Robert S. [28; Omaha; b: England; f: Lewis GOODMAN; m: Julia SOLAMAN] md. Almina VLIET [29; Omaha; b: Illinois; f: John VLIET; m: Pamelia BURGESS] on 22 Dec 1879. Off: COPELAND. Wit: Lewis A. GROFF, Mrs. H.H. CHAMBERLAIN.

GOODWIN, J.T. [29; Council Bluffs, IA; b: Indiana; f: Francis GOODWIN; m: Sarah GREATHOUSE] md. Ella SWARTS [18; Glenwood, IA; b: Illinois; f: Lewis SWARTS; m: Elizabeth FOY] on 3 Dec 1879. Off: COPELAND. Wit: Mrs. H.A. CHAMBERLAIN, Lewis A. GROFF.

GOODWIN, Lawrence [19; Pottawattamie Co., IA; b: Indiana; f: William J. GOODWIN; m: Mary SIGLER] md. Sarah A. GROVE [16; Pottawattamie Co, IA; b: Iowa; f: Jacob GROVE; m: Jane GARDNER] on 15 Dec 1880. Off: BARTHOLOMEW. Wit: Max BERGMANN, William L. PEABODY.

GOODWIN, T.H. [27; Pottawattamie Co., IA; b: Indiana; f: W.J. GOODWIN; m: Mary E. SIGLER] md. Harriet E. HALL [20; Pottawattamie Co., IA; b: Iowa; f: Alcana HALL; m: Lucy A. FIELDS] on 13 Jan 1880.

Off: HARSHA. Wit: John L. SMITH, Mrs. Jennie S. SMITH.

GOODWIN, W.H. [21; Omaha; b: New York; f: John GOODWIN; m: Mary McADAM] md. Emma WULLBRANDT [21; Fairmont [Fillmore Co.]; b: Michigan; f: John WULLBRANDT; m: D.E. FISHER] on 9 Oct 1880. Off: BRANDES. Wit: Justus CAREY, Edward BUEHL.

GOOS, Peter [28; Omaha] md. Lena LAMP [17; Omaha] on 31 Mar 1868. Off: KUHNS. Wit: Henry LAMP, Mrs. H.W. KUHNS. Age consent given by the father of the bride.

GORAHM, T.O. [21; Omaha; b: IA; f: Lester GORAHM; m: Maria HOTTELING] md. Mrs. Minnie BRITTON [20; Omaha; b: KY; f: John SHACKLOT; m: Mary BARNS] on 12 Jul 1876. Off: PARDEE. Wit: Joseph CREBO, Hallie GORHAM. Marriage filed 3 May 1877.

GORDON, Charles A. [51; Omaha; b: Scotland; f: Charles A. GORDAN; m: Ellen A. FARRISH] md. Jennet SCOTT [48; Omaha; b: Scotland] on 18 Mar 1873 at Trinity Church. Off: GARRETT. Wit: Letitia GARRETT; Mary E. HAYDEN.

GORDON, George M. [22; Douglas Co.] md. Rebecca Jane BROWN [19; Douglas Co.] on 10 Nov 1858. Off: BURCH. Wit: Mary BURCH, Florence (Amelia) DOANE.

GORDON, Joseph E. [29, Keokuk, IA; b: Keokuk, IA; f: James GORDON; m: Margaret WATERS] md. Margaret (Maggie) O'DEA [24; CO; b: Memphis, TN; f: Patrick O'DEA; m: Bridget CALLIVAN] on 3 Jun 1881 at St. Philomena's Church; Off: McCARTHY. Wit: Thomas ROE, Jane LYNCH.

GORHAM, Charles [24; Rockford, Winnebago Co., IL] md. Jenette HOBERT [18; Rockford, Winnebago Co., IL] on 26 Nov 1860 at ARMSTRONG's office. Off: ARMSTRONG. Wit: Charles HOBERT, Mrs. JOHNSON.

GORMAN, Edward [22; Omaha; b: St. Louis, MO; f: Michael GORMAN; m: Julia LAUNDRIGAN] md. Ellen CANTZ [20; Omaha; b: Ireland; f: Timothy CANTZ; m: Mary LAWLER] on 11 Jan 1870. Off: CURTIS.

GORMAN, Patrick J. [29; Omaha; b: Ireland; f: Edward GORMAN; m: Margaret DONAHOE] md. Ellen WELCH [18; Omaha; b: Ireland; f: William WELCH; m: Mary] on 3 Jan 1875 at the Roman Catholic Cathedral. Off: MALLOY. Wit: John McMANUS, Katie GRASSHOPPER.

GORMAN, Patrick md. Mary McMAHON on 12 Jul 1865 at the Catholic Church of Omaha. Off: DAXACHER.[NOTE: The date 1865 is probably an error and should be 1866.]

GORMAN, Simon [54; Omaha] md. Johanna WELCH [27; Omaha] on 28 Nov 1857. Off: SEELY.

GORTON, Lewis C. [24; Omaha; b: MO; f: Elisha GORTON; m: Cornelia NOLAN] md. Ella WHITLOCK [22; Omaha; b: PA; f: John WHITLOCK; m: Ellen Jane BURROWS] on 29 Sep 1875. Off: LEMON. Wit: Mr. and Mrs. George WHITLOCK.

GOSH, J.H. [22; Omaha; b: Germany; f: James GOSH] md. Emma SNYDER [19; Omaha; b: NE; f: William SNYDER; m: Christine CUNSMAN] on 10 Jan 1881. Off: BRANDES. Wit: August FISCHIE, Hubert VERPOORTEN.

GOSS, Chester [Douglas Co.] md. Charlotte PRICE [Douglas Co.] on 28 May 1863. Off: TURNER.

GOTTSCH, Henry [23; Omaha; b: Germany; f: Henry GOTTSCH; m: Margaret KUHL] md. Augusta GLASMAN [GLISSMAN] [19; Omaha; b: Germany; f: John GLASMAN [GLISSMAN]; m: Louise RONNAN] on 1 Oct 1874. Off: PEABODY. Wit: Ch. Wilh. WITT; Henry GLASMAN.

GOUDY, Henry T. [58; Omaha; b: Wehn? Co., OH; f: William GOUDY; m: Cassandra CROFFORD] md. Mrs. Celia WILLIAMS [36; Omaha; b: Paris, France; f: Joseph BRUSHES; m: Mary KAYSER] on 30 May 1870. Off: BENNETT. Wit: Jeremiah McCHEANE; Mike McDERMOTT.

GOULD, Frank P. [25; b: New York; f: Whitney GOULD] md. Ella A. ATKINS [22; b; Pennsylvania; f: Hiram A. ATKINS; m: Susan B. FOSTER] on 21 Dec 1878. Off: LIPE. Wit: S.S. ATKINS, Mrs. Amanda ATKINS.

GOULD, John [26; Omaha; b: New York; f: George GOULD; m: Eunis NORTON] md. Mrs. Ann Van CASTLE [25; Omaha; b: Louisiana; f: John JOHNSON; m: Arminda VINE] on 14 May 1879. Off: STENBERG. Wit: E.A. McCLURE, R. De DARLING.

GOULD, Joseph W. [23; Omaha] md. Louisa J. KNIGHTS [20; Omaha] on 30 Nov 1867. Off: SLAUGHTER.

GOULD, Patrick [44; Omaha; b: Ireland; f: Thomas GOULD; m: Betsy LANE] md. Mrs. Anastasia O'BRIEN [40; Omaha; b: Ireland; f: William WELSH; m: Ellen GOULD] on 24 Feb 1875. Off: PEABODY. Wit: Rasmus PETERSON, N.O. BYRNE.

GOW, James [24; Bellevue; b: Bellevue; f: James GOW; m: Lucy M. CLEVELAND] md. Emma HIKE [18; Bellevue; b: New York; f: Henry HIKE; m: Minerva STONE] on 22 Aug 1880. Off: BARTHOLOMEW. Wit: L.H. CHASE, Mary CHASE.

GRAABE, Claus [25; Douglas Co.; b: Germany; f: John GRAABE; m: Anna KAKEN] md. Minnie RABE [25; Omaha; b: Germany; f: Hans RABE; m: Anna STICKEN] on 16 Aug 1877. Off: BARTHOLOMEW. Wit: C.C. SPERRY, H.A. STURGES.

GRABOW, Heinrich [24; Sarpy Co.; b: Germany; f: Johann GRABOW; m: Maria SHRADER] md. Anna ELHERT [22; Douglas Co.; b: Germany; f: Jacob ELHERT; m: Helena PETERS] on 23 May 1879. Off: BENEKE. Wit: Henry LEHMANN of Omaha, John GRAWBOW of Sarpy Co.

GRACE, Samuel [34; Omaha; b: New York; f: Richard GRACE; m: Mary NORTON] md. Helen RYAN [19; Omaha; b: Canada; f: Timothy or John RYAN; m: Ann or Mary DOLAN] on 14 Jul 1874 at the Roman Catholic Cathedral. Off: BYRNE. Wit: James GRACE; Alice GRACE.

GRACE, Thomas [Douglas Co.] md. Ellen KEARN [Douglas Co.] on 2 Sep 1865 at the Catholic Church of Omaha. Off: BEAN. Wit: John BRENNEN, Nancy KEARN.

GRADY, Michael [29; Omaha; b: Ireland; f: Lacky GRADY; m: Bridget MILLEY] md. Margaret FRANCIS [19; Omaha; b: Ireland; f: Robert FRANCIS; m: Mary LYNCH] on 8 Jan 1871. Off: KELLY. Wit: Patrick GORMAN; Bridget CARROLL.

GRADY, Thomas [26; Omaha] and Margaret COLEMAN [18; Omaha] license issued on 10 Nov 1861. Off: ARMSTRONG.

GRADY, William [32; Omaha; b: Ireland; f: William GRADY; m: Jane CONNOLLY] md. Charlotte O'CONNOR [22; Omaha; b: Iowa; f: Thomas O'CONNOR] on 24 Sep 1872 at the Roman Catholic Church. Off: O'GORMAN. Wit: Thos. FURLONG; H.F. LUCAS; Annie MURPHEY, Council Bluffs; H. O'CONNOR, Council Bluffs.

GRAHAM, Charles H. [28; Omaha; b: Mississippi; f: Thomas GRAHAM; m: Margaret GRAHAM] md. Mrs. Elmira Bell PERRY [25; Omaha; b: Kentucky; f: Douglas MITCHEL] on 7 Oct 1879. Off: PORTER. Wit: Henry WILSON, Mary MITCHEL.

GRAHAM, George [26; b: Germany; f: William GRAHAM; m: Ellen DEVINE] md. Bertha SCHMID [27; b: Germany; f: Sebastin SCHMID; m: Elizabeth SCHMID] on 2 Feb 1878. Off: WEISS. Wit: Chas. W. EDGERTON; A.B. SNOWDEN.

GRAHAM, George [47; Omaha; b: Cannady] md. Mrs. Kate CHRISTOPHER [40; Omaha; b: New York] on 3 Nov 1869 at Omaha Precinct No. 6. Off: ESTABROOK. Wit: Julian HOADBINE, Lizzie HOADBINE, Mary DUTTON

GRAHAM, Henry R. [28; Omaha] md. Mrs. Mary GRANT [28; Omaha] on 10 Aug 1868. Off: McCAGUE. Wit: Mr. and Mrs. ROBINSON.

GRAM, U.T. [29; b; Germany; f: H.T. GRAM; m: Karn NEILSON] md. Kirsten Schmidt BRANDRUP [18; b: Germany; f: Nielse BRANDRUP; m: Elena SCHMIDT] on 23 Aug 1878. Off: BARTHOLOMEW. Wit: John G. TAYLOR, John TUTTLE.

GRAN, Peter J. [27; Saunders Co.; b: Sweden; f: Andrew GRAN] and Emma GREN [28; Omaha; b: Sweden; f: John GREN] license issued on 29 Jul 1871. Off: GIBSON.

GRANDEN, John Arved [41; Omaha; b: Sweden; f: John P. GRANDEN; m: Ulirka MATTSEN] md. Gerda Caroline ESBERG [34; Omaha; b: Sweden; f: Claus ESBERG; m: Sarah ERICKSON] on 16 Sep 1879. Off: WILLIAMS. Wit: Mrs. Alice LEE, Emma MUCHTEY.

GRANDSBERRY, Edward L. [22; Audubon Co., IA; b: New York; f: William GRANDSBERRY; m: Louisa CLARK] md. Mrs. Julia S. PATTERSON [18; Audubon Co., IA; b: Audubon Co., IA; f: William BUSH; m: Hannah SMITH] on 20 Nov 1877. Off: ERFLING. Wit: Tom BALLARD of the corner of 10th and Marcy Streets, Dorothea MARTENS of 165 Leavenworth Street.

GRANITH, Charles [33; Omaha; b: Sweden; f: Gustave GRANITH; m: Elizabeth LAGER] md. Henrietta C. EKSTROM [20; Omaha; b: Sweden; f: Adloph FORNING; m: Henrietta C. EKSTROM] on 14 Jun 1877. Off: HANSEN. Wit: Daniel TURNGREN, John ANSTRAM.

GRANT, George H. [30; Blair; b: New York; f: William GRANT; m: Hattie BATES] md. Mrs. Mattie WILLIS [21; Blair; b: Illinois; f: C.F. OLMSTEAD; m: Laura FIELDS] on 2 Jul 1877. Off: SEDGWICK. Wit: Marcia F. SEDGWICK, Eliza PETERSON.

GRAPP, William [42] md. Mary SHULTZ [42] on 23 Apr 1869. Off: KELLEY. Wit: A. SWARTZLANDER, Fred ELSESSER.

GRATTON, Frank [27; Omaha; b: Pennsylvania; f: John GRATTON; m: Emma WEBSTER] md. Mrs. Caroline BINGHAM [27; Omaha; b: Minnesota; f: F.W. WINDSAY; m: Elizabeth FRY] on 16 Mar 1877. Off: FALK. Wit: John POPPENBERGER of Florence Lake, Mrs. Barbara POPPENBERGER, nee MERRITT, of Florence Lake.

GRAVES, C.H. [28; Omaha; b: Ohio; f: Charles GRAVES; m: Elizabeth RUPLE] md. Jennie TAYLOR [19; Council Bluffs; b: Omaha; f: George TAYLOR; m: Mary MORSE] on 12 Aug 1879. Off: HARSHA. Wit: Robert HOCKENHULL, Mrs. Wm. J. HARSHA.

GRAVES, Charles [21; Council Bluffs; b: Iowa; f: George GRAVES; m: Amelia MURRAY] md. Ella SPOOR [18; Omaha; b: Iowa; f: Allen M. SPOOR; m: Julia WICKS] on 15 Aug 1880. Off: HAWES. Wit: R. Grand DALTON, Allen M. SPOOR.

GRAY, Frederick W. [24; Omaha; b: Ireland; f: James GRAY; m: Sarah MEREDITH] md. Kate LITTLE [23; Omaha; f: George L. LITTLE; m: Felicia WICK] on 8 Oct 1874. Off: LITTLE. Wit: Rev. Geo. D. STEWART; Otis H. BALLOW.

GRAY, Henry [35; Omaha] md. Helen E. CRAWFORD [20; Omaha] on 31 Dec 1865 at the residence of the bride's father. Off: KUHNS. Wit: Mr. and Mrs. CRAWFORD, Samuel A. ORCHARD, K. SHULL, et al.

GRAY, R. Wallace [23; Omaha; b: Ireland; f: James GRAY; m: Sarah MEREDITH] md. Mrs. Maggie PENKUN [23; Omaha; b: Illinois; f: Peter ROTHHWETZ; m: Mary OSWALD] on 20 Oct 1879. Off: LITTLE. Wit: F.W. GRAY, James H. LITTLE.

GREB [GREBE], Frederick [24; Omaha; b: Germany; f: Christoph GREB [GREBE]; m: Rosa SHARR] md. Mary NOWAK [NOVAK] [18; Omaha; b: Bohemia; f: Joseph NOWAK [NOVAK]; m: Josephine] on 2 Jun 1873. Off: BRANDES. Wit: Ferdinand THUMB; Mrs. Amelia THUMB.

GREEN, Francis M. [Omaha] md. Sarah E. TOMLINSON [Omaha] on the evening of 2 Jun 1864 at Mr. TENNERY's house. Off: LEMON. Wit: Mr. and Mrs. George CROWELL, Mrs. TENNERY and family, et al.

GREEN, Isaac A. [25; Douglas Co.; b: NY; f: John H. GREEN; m: Sarah WOODS] md. Bessie TAYLOR [19; Omaha; b: England; f: John TAYLOR; m: Margaret TAYLOR] on 31 Mar 1875. Off: WRIGHT. Wit: Richard SHERLAND, Lily BONRETTE.

GREEN, James H. [23; Omaha; b: Illinois; f: Lucius C. GREEN; m: Harriet MONT__GUE] md. Annie CONNELLY [21; Omaha; b: Ireland; f: Thomas CONNELLY; m: Delia MONAGHAN] on 3 Nov 1870. Off: CURTIS. Wit: Joseph DEMPSEY; Catherine BIERS.

GREEN, John H. [Omaha] md. Mrs. Catherine HORSTMAN on 2 Jan 1864. Off: DICKINSON. Wit: Charles H. BROWN, Henry RICHTER.

GREEN, John [27; Omaha; b: Sweden; f: Pear GREEN; m: Caroline HOKENSEN] md. Jude JOHNSON [26; Omaha; b: Sweden; f: John JOHNSON; m: Anna CHRISTENSEN] on 17 May 1870. Off: BENNETT. Wit: Carl C. AHLQUIST; Caroline AHLQUIST.

GREEN, Oscar [28; Omaha; b: Sweden; f: John GREEN; m: Hannah NEILSON] md. Kate ANDERSON [19; Omaha; b: Sweden; f: L. ANDERSON] on 12 Mar 1871. Off: S.G. LARSON. Wit: William ROUCHE; Nellie PETERSON.

GREEN, Presly H. [Omaha] md. Agnes MEDLOCK [Omaha] on the evening of 16 Jun 1864. Off: LEMON. Wit: Mr. and Mrs. MEDLOCK, "parents of the Lady," et al.

GREEN, William N. [29; Council Bluffs] md. Harriet E. DEVAL [DEVOE] [25; Council Bluffs] on 15 Sep 1859 at Douglas House. Off: KUHNS. Wit: P.C. DE VOL, D.H. MOFFIT.

GREENE, John J. [28; Omaha; b: Canada; f: Thomas GREENE; m: Catharine O'DONNELL] and Nellie J. McGOVERN [23; Omaha; b: MA; f: Terence McGOVERN; m: Julia REILEY] filed affidavit on 6 Oct 1881. No marriage record. Off: BERGMANN.

GREENE, Winslow A. [35; Onawa City, IA] md. Julia A. SANFORD [19; Omaha] on 24 Dec 1868. Off: SLAUGHTER. Wit: Mrs. A.B. SLAUGHTER, Mrs. M.C. PRATT.

GREENFIELD, Henry C. [27; Omaha; b: Illinois; f: Elijah GREENFIELD; m: Mary F. WINTERS] md. Ella L. ARTZ [23; Omaha; b: Ohio; f: Simon ARTZ; m: Mary KAESEBIER] on 8 Nov 1879. Off: STENBERG. Wit: E. GREENFIELD, Mrs. Mary F. GREENFIELD.

GREENMAN, Henry [58; Florence; b: England; f: George GREENMAN; m: Martha BUTLER] md. Mrs? Mary TURNER [50; Florence; b: England; f: John REEVES; m: Mary KYRESTON] on 5 Apr 1870. Off: MAGINN. Wit: V.A. ELLIOTT; H.H. CLARK.

GREER, William Samuel [22; Douglas Co.; b: Canada West; f: Moses GREER; m: Sarah DAVIS] md. Laura CLAY [24; Douglas Co.; b: IL; f: Christian CLAY; m: Maria YATES] on 3 Aug 1876. Off: BRITT. Wit: S.J. BRITT, Sally M. OSBORN.

GREGANNS [GREGORIUS], Jacob [24; Omaha; b: Prussia; f: Michael GREGANNS [GREGORIUS]; m: Margaret MARTIN] md. Katie NIMICH [NEMECEK] [21; Omaha; b: Austria; f: Joseph NEMICH [NEMECEK]; m: Annie JELLECK [JILEK]] on 10 Jul 1871. Off: GIBSON. Wit: Henry GREBE; George ARMSTRONG.

GREGLER, Otto [35; Omaha; b: Germany; f: Bernard GREGLER; m: Mary LEUCHS] md. Maria ELAESSER [20; Omaha; b: Germany; f: Peter ELAESSER; m: Jacobine WACKER] on 11 Jun 1880. Off: FRESE. Wit: Wm. SEIVERS, Katharine LEHER.

GREGORY, James B. [24; Omaha] md. Hannah SPARROW [19; Omaha] on 18 Mar 1868 at KUHNS' residence. Off: KUHNS. Wit: Minnie CALLAHAN, Levi KRAFT.

GRENBURG, O.P. [24; Omaha; b: Sweden; f: O.F. GRENBURG; m: Anna MATTHIESON] md. Anna NELSON [20; Omaha; b: Denmark; f: Martin NELSON; m: Julia NELSON] on 18 Apr 1881. Off: BENEKE. Wit: Christine LUNE, Andrew GOULD.

GREVUR, Edward [28; Omaha; b: France; f: John GREVUR; m: Maria PHILIP (PHILLIP)] md. Annie LOUIS [18; Omaha; b: Douglas Co.; f: Walter (George?) LOUIS; m: Fannie GASTNER] on 10 Jul 1869. Off: HYDE. Wit: Adam EDLING, Margaret EDLING.

GRICE, Lycurgus [ 29; Douglas Co.] md. Lucy Ann ALLEN [16; Douglas Co.] on 30 Jun 1859 at the residence of James B. ALLEN in Douglas Co. Off: BRIGGS. Wit: Jesse REEVES, Preston REEVES.

GRIEB, August [25; Omaha; b: Germany; f: Christoph GRIEB; m: Rosina SCHARR] md. Ottilie SERBENSECK [22; Omaha; b: Bohemia; f: John SERBENSECK; m: Katharina BARTOSCH] on 26 Apr 1881. Off: BENEKE. Wit: Wenzel NISLET, Max LENZ.

GRIESHEIM, Charles [St. Louis, MO] md. Mary SCHMIDTS [Omaha] on 30 Jan 1865 at the Lutheran parsonage. Off: KUHNS. Wit: Mrs. C. STANG, Mrs. H.W. KUHNS.

GRIFFEN, Joel A. [23; Douglas Co.] md. Colinda A. PARKER [21; Douglas Co.] on 1 Jul 1866 at Jonas GISE's residence. Off: KUHNS. Wit: Mr. and Mrs. George ARMSTRONG, Mr. and Mrs. Joel T. GRIFFEN, et al.

GRIFFEN, M.D. [31; Omaha; b: Ireland; f: John GRIFFEN; m: Margaret KELLEY] md. Julia BUCKLEY [20; Omaha; b: Virginia; f: Michael BUCKLEY; m: Ellen COFFEY] on 4 Nov 1880. Off: ENGLISH. Wit: Owen BUCKLEY, Mary Ann DONOHOE.

GRIFFEN, Thomas [30; Omaha; b: Ireland; f: John GRIFFEN; m: Kate SHALLOO] md. Kate GEE [17; Omaha; b: Ireland; f: John GEE; m: Margaret FINNEN] on 26 Nov 1876 at the Catholic Cathedral. Off: JENNETTE. Wit: Richard MULLEN, Mary MULLEN. Age consent given by Wm. HENNESSY, uncle of the bride. Marriage reorded 15 Apr 1878.

GRIFFIN, Frank P. [Omaha] md. Rose S. ANDRUS [Omaha] on 2 Jan 1867. Off: SLAUGHTER.

GRIFFITH, John B. [22; Omaha; b: UT; f: Jonathan GRIFFITH; m: Margaret BURTON] md. Louise HIXON [18; Council Bluffs; b: England; f: William HIXON; m: Eliza Jane HOLT] on 27 Jan 1875. Off: PEABODY. Wit: Darwin NORTON, Council Bluffs, Will B.R. KILLINGSWORTH.

GRIFFITH, John M. [24; Omaha; b: New York; f: John M. GRIFFITH; m: Catharine W. KNICKERBOCKER] md. Mary M. KING [20; Omaha; b: Omaha; f: A.L. KING; m: Gertrude L. CLARKE] on 14 Oct 1879. Off: CLARKSON. Wit: Richard CARRIER, John A. ROSS.

GRIFFITHS, J.W. [33; David City, NE; b: New York; f: G.W. GRIFFITHS; m: Mary WILLIAMS] and Eva JORDAN [23; Omaha; b: New York City; f: Frank JORDAN; m: Eva SCOTT] license issued on 17 Aug 1879. No marriage record. Off: BARTHOLOMEW. Affiant: W.S. RAVENSCROFT.

GRIFFITHS, W.E. [23; Omaha; b: NY; f: William GRIFFITHS; m: Mary CANFIELD] md. Mary E. TYLER [18; Omaha; b: IN (or PA); f: Hiram TYLER; m: (possibly) Sarah SPRAGUE] on 11 Nov 1875. Off: HALE. Wit: Dale J. SENNETT; E.L. EMMERY.

GRIGG, Anthony D. [31; Lincoln; b: New York; f: Charles GRIGG; m: Elizabeth CHANDLER] and Harriett A. KUNE [30; Sarpy Co.; b: Massachusetts; f: August KUNE] license issued on 15 Apr 1871. Off: GIBSON.

GRIM, Albert [22; Omaha; b: Illinois; f: Mahlon GRIM; m: Elizabeth SOUDERS] md. Dora B. DICKEY [21; Omaha; b: Illinois; f: M.S. DICKEY; m: Elizabeth FRAIZER] on 14 Apr 1879. Off: BRANDES. Wit: Mary REINEKE, Lyman DICKEY.

GRING, William D. [41; Omaha; b: OH; f: William GRING; m: Margarett KOOSER] md. Mary A. McCLEES [33; Omaha; b: IA; f: Alexandre McCLEES; m: Feibie HEWELL] on 27 Nov 1876. Off: FISHER. Wit: S. HAWVER, R. LAING, J.W. TOUSLEY.

GROISBECK, Merrit H. [24; Omaha; b: New York; f: Nicholas GROISBECK; m: Annie HAYNES] md. Annie M. OSTROM [27; b: Canada West; f: Hiram H. OSTROM; m: Lavina VALLEY] on 5 Apr 1870. Off: DeLaMATYR. Wit: Henry OSTROM; Alice OSTROM.

GROMM, A.E. [33; Omaha; b: Germany; f: F.W. GROMM; m: Anna BREIER] md. Ada Lee SHANKS [18; Westport, MO (Kansas City was crossed out); b: MO; f: R.L. SHANKS; m: Mary H. HANDLEY] on 21 Apr 1881. Off: MILLSPAUGH. Wit: Patrick O. HAWES, Fritz BEIER.

GRONBAK (GROUNBAK), Adolph [32; Omaha] md. Charlotta Marie (May)

ERICKSEN [18; Omaha] on 23 Feb 1859. Off: BRIGGS. Wit: Chas. P. BECKETT, Hans Pieter DIDRICKSON.

GRONBE, William [24; Omaha; b: Pennsylvania; f: Jacob GRONBE; m: Elizabeth PURDY] md. Ella N. BEABER [19; Omaha; b: Philadelphia; f: Jeremiah BEABER; m: A. Catharine WIETZEL] on 21 Jan 1879 at the Evangelical Lutheran Church. Off: LIPE. Wit: S.M. WILCOX, A.F. NESBSITT.

GROOMS, George [24; Omaha; b: Kansas; f: James GROOMS; m: Emilie HANLEY] md. Maggie GREAR [21; Omaha; b: Canada; f: James GREAR; m: Sarah DAVIS] on 19 Jul 1879. Off: STENBERG. Wit: H.A. PARRISH, Emma GOERNER. Affidafit signed by wit: Max (x) BERGMAN.

GROSSMANN, Frank [32; b: Switzerland; f: Friederich GROSSMANN; m: Elizabeth HOFFMANN] md. Elizabeth LUCHSINGER [26; b: Switzerland; f: Casper LUCHSINGER; m: Anna Sophie] on 9 Dec 1878. Off: FALK. Wit: Emil MEYER, Peter BROCKMANN.

GROTHE, Carl F. [29; Sarpy Co.; b: Germany; f: Caspar GROTHE; m: Elizabeth WALSLEBEN] md. Mrs. Catharine PICKARD [26; Douglas Pct; f: George BOYER; m: Catharina] on 13 Apr 1873 at Douglas Pct. Off: DIECKMANN. Wit: Joseph BOYER; Fredericke GROTHE.

GROTHE, Charles F.L. [35; Omaha; b: Prussia; f: C. GROTHE; m: E. WALSLEBEN] md. S. Etta FUNK [16; Millard; Illinois; f: Joseph FUNK; m: Lavinia FUNK] on 4 Jan 1880, Millard. Off: RIALE. Wit: Joseph FUNK, Louisa FUNK, both of Millard. Consent of Joseph FUNK and Lavinia FUNK, parents of bride witnessed by Mirum BURNS. "S. Etta FUNK born in Illinois, county of Langerman [Sangamon], 9 Feb 1863, living now in Douglas Co., NE."

GROVER, Chris E. [29; Ohio; b: Ohio; f: J.W. GROVER; m: Rachel PIKE] md. Nellie E. BRADLEY [22; Ohio; b: Ohio; f: A. BRADLEY; m: Helen BURGESS] on 6 Nov 1878. Off: HARSHA. Wit: Mrs. N.J. HARSHA, Mary PROGER.

GROVER, Cornelius F. [28; North Platte; b: Columbiana Co., OH; f: William GROVER; m: Mary Ann WHEALEN] md. Elsie KING [30; North Platte; b: Perry Co., OH; f: Matthew KING; m: Mary McMULLIN] on 4 May 1873. Off: CURTIS. Wit: Oscar B. SHARPLESS; Agnes CLARK.

GROVER, J.G. [Elkhorn] md. Mary E. LEACH [Elkhorn] on 3 Dec 1868 at Elkhorn. Off: HURLBUT. Wit: Albert BLAKESLY, John KENNICUT.

GROVES, John [28; Omaha; b: Ireland; f: John GROVES; m: Mary O'HANLON] md. Marie J. WEISS [25; Omaha; b: France; f: James WEISS; m: Barbe HUERTZ] on 28 Apr

1875. Off: EASTER. Wit: Alexander J. PERRY, William HENNESY.

GROVES, William [27; Omaha] md. Eliza DUCE [21; Omaha] on 23 Dec 1862. Off: ARMSTRONG. Wit: Mr. and Mrs. Christopher ALDERSEN.

GROVES [GRAVES], Geo. A. [24; Omaha] md. Emma E. HOMAN [19; Omaha] on 14 Oct 1858. Off: SMITH. Wit: John HUGHES, G.H. HOMAN, R.J.R. SMITH, Julia BROWN.

GROVIJOHN, Charles [21; Cuming Co.] md. Mary KAUP [20; Cuming Co.] on 25 Nov 1867 at the Cathedral. Off: GROENBAUM. Wit: Anson VINEMEL, William GOEKE, Casy KAUP.

GRUBER, Johann [22; Omaha; b: Hungaria; f: Michael GRUBER; m: Anna LAND] md. Mrs. Anna WIEGER [22; Omaha; b: Hungaria; f: Paul WIEGER; m: Elizabeth WACHTLER] on 30 May 1881 at the German Catholic Church. Off: GROENEBAUM. Wit: John MEIDLINGER, Mrs. Kate MEIDLINGER.

GRUENIG, Charles [28; Omaha; b: Germany; f: George GRUENIG; m: Mary ENGEL] md. Annie PARKER [17; Omaha; b: Wisconsin; f: George PARKER; m: Hannah MILLER] on 2 Mar 1871. Off: MORTON. Wit: A. ISREAL; Mrs. STESESEN. Age of consent given by father of the bride.

GRUENING, George [23; Omaha; b: Germany; f: George GRUENING; m: Mary ENGLE] md. Enora DILLMONN [22; Omaha; b: Louisville, KY; f: Eberhardt DILLMONN] on 4 Nov 1872. Off: THURSTON. Wit: Daniel McFARLAND; Mrs. Hannah GRUENING.

GRUENWALD, August [27; Omaha; b: Germany; f: John GRUENWALD; m: Margaret BREWERS] md. Hattie YOUNG [21; Omaha; b: Wisconsin; f: Stephen YOUNG; m: Mary KANE] on 13 Aug 1879. Off: BENEKE. Wit: Louis FAIST, Annie FAIST.

GRUMBAUGH, William J. [28; Omaha; b: Ohio; f: John GRUMBAUGH; m: Elizabeth RIBLET] md. Josephine ABNEY [17; Omaha; b; Illinois; f: David ABNEY; m: Amanda KLEIN] on 21 Mar 1877. Off: ROE. Wit: William E. ARMSTRONG, Betsy MATSON. Age consent given by father of the bride.

GUELKER, Henry W. [40; Omaha; b: Germany; f: Christian GUELKER; m: Louise LOHEIDE] md. Mrs. Mary DAEMON [34; Omaha; b: France; f: Louis Amos DESBOIS; m: Louise FANERE] on 3 Jun 1879. Off: BENEKE. Wit: Emma GOERNER, Julius W. SEIVERLING.

GUILD, David [26; Omaha; b: Soctland; f: David GUILD; m: Margarèt DUNBAR] md. Nellie LESLIE [20; Omaha; b: Scotland; f: Peter LESLIE; m: Margaret STURROCK] on 11 Aug 1877. Off: HARSHA. Wit: William RANDALL, Betsey RANDALL.

GUILD, John [27; Omaha; b: Scotland; f: William GUILD; m: Elizabeth McFARLAND] md. Laura A. READ [20; Omaha; b: New York; f: Henry READ; m: Sarah VANE] on 6 Oct 1879. Off: BEANS. Wit: T.C. BRUNER, Mrs. J.M. MARSTEN.

GUINANE, Patrick [24; Omaha; b: Ireland; f: Edward GUINANE; m: Johanna GLEASON] md. Mary E. LOWRIE [20; Omaha; b: New Orleans; f: Thomas LOWRIE; m: Elizabeth MORRIS] on 4 Sep 1877. Off: ANDERSON. Wit: C.R. MANSFIELD, R.M. TAYLOR.

GUITAN, Adolph [21; Council Bluffs; b: Iowa; f: Francis GUITAN; m: Mary Ann MORGAN] md. Anna HOAKERSON [18; Council Bluffs; b: Sweden; f: Hans HOAKERSON; m: Ellen PETERSON] on 9 Aug 1874. Off: PEABODY. Wit: Mary C. PEABODY; C. PHELPS, Council Bluffs.

GUNDERSON, Julius [27; Omaha; b: Norway; f: Gunder PETERSON; m: Helena PETERSON] md. Mary JOHNSON [30; Omaha; b: Norway; f: John ERIKSON; m: Caren JOHNSON] on 26 Oct 1877. Off: HILMEN. Wit: Mr. P. WIIGS, Mrs. WIIGS.

GUSHURST, William [33; Omaha; b: (Rochester crossed out), Jefferson Co., NY: f: Frederick GUSHURST; m: Bridget HUCK] md. Mary STOCKMYRE [21; Omaha; b: Pennsylvania; f: Joseph STOCKMYRE: m: Catharine SAVILLE] on 27 May 1873. Off: GROENEBAUM. Wit: Louis HORN or HOOK; Therese GEIS.

GUSTAFSON, Frank A. [29; Omaha; b: Sweden; f: Gustave JOHANSEN; m: Margareta OBERBURG] md. Catharina JACOBSEN [29; Omaha; b: Sweden; f: Anders JACOBSEN; m: Maria CHRISTIANSON] on 25 Nov 1881. Off: FOGELSTRUN. Wit: Nils LARSON, A.M. LARSON. Affidavit signed by E.A. FOGELSTRUN.

GUSTAFSSON, Leonard [25; Omaha; b: Sweden; f: Friederich GUSTAFSSON; m: Anna M. PETERSON] md. Helma NEISTROM [22; Omaha; b: Sweden; f: Anders NEISTROM; m: Christine NEISTROM] on 27 Nov 1881. Off: FOGELSTRUN. Wit: Anders PETTERSON, Mrs. Lotta PETTERSON.

GUTCHOW [GUTSCHOW], Christian [28; Blair, Washington Co.; b: Germany; f: John Jacob GUTCHOW [GUTSCHOW]; m: Fredericka GUTCHOW [GUTSCHOW]] md. Catharine "Katy" BIFFAR [19; Omaha; b: Sullivan Co., NY; f: Francis BIFFAR; m: Barbara SAILER] on 24 Sep 1873. Off: DIECKMANN. Wit: Anton GERKE; J.M. HENRY.

GUTHARD, John [31; Douglas Co.; b: Germany; f: Hans GUTHARD; m: Anna MORTH] md. Margaretha SMIDTH [18; Omaha; b: IA; f: Jacob SMIDTH; m: Cathrine SMIDTH] on 25 Jan 1876 at the German Catholic Church. Off: GROENEBAUM. Wit: Frederic GILLE, Mrs. Kate GILLE.

GUTTKUNST, John G. [20; Omaha] md. Mary MAJO [18; Omaha] on 28 Jan 1869 at MAY's residence. Off: MAY. Wit: Seth T. COLE, Mrs. Justin T. COLE.

GUY, Elmer [28; Florence; b: England; f: Samuel G. GUY; m: Mary BRANDON] md. Frankie LAUGHLIN [18; Florence; b: Iowa; f: John C. LAUGHLIN; m: Olive Hannah THORN] on 21 Jul 1880. Off: SPENCER. Wit: George LALON, Rosa SALON, both of Florence.

GWIN, John W. [28; Omaha] md. Helen DAVIS [20; Omaha] on 16 Dec 1867. Off: KUHNS. Wit: George C. BASSET, Jennie LATEY, et al.

GWYNN, William J. [35; Omaha; b: Wales; f: Daniel GWYNN; m: Eliza THOMAS] md. Emily HALL [25; Omaha; b: England; f: Richard HALL; m: Annie BEEM] on 2 May 1881. Off: WILLIAMS. Wit: Geo. W. HILLIER, Mrs. Fannie HILLIER. Recorded 15 Aug 1882 by CHADWICK.

HAAG, George [50; Florence; b: Germany; f: Peter HAAG; m: Margaretha NEU] md. Mrs. Rebecca POWELL [48; Florence; b: IL; f: Hilard HATSELL; m: Nancy HOSKINS] on 9 Jun 1881. Off: SMITH. Wit: Mrs. Mary COLLINS, Mrs. Saline I. SHIPLEY.

HAAG, Jacob [33; Omaha; b: Switzerland; f: Mathias HAAG; m: Christina THONS] md. Mary M. ALSCLOMAN [38; Omaha; b: Switzerland; f: Andrew ALSCLOMAN; m: Elizabeth ALSCHLEBERGER] on 6 May 1875. Off: DIECKMANN. Wit: Chris SAUTTER, near Omaha; George SELK.

HAAG, Thomas [23; Omaha; b: Ohio; f: Andew HAAG; m: Catharine RUHL] md. Clara W. BOLDT [20; Omaha; b: Germany; f: Friederich BOLDT; m: Wilhelmina RIEGE] on 16 Nov 1880. Off: BREUGGER. Wit: William EUKANY, Eliza BOLDT.

HAAS, George [30; Washing Co.; b: Baden; f: Christ HAAS; m: Christina MONSA] md. Christina BAUMAN [28; Omaha; b: Germany; f: Jack BAUMAN; m: Christina BAUMAN] on 14 Nov 1881. Off: BENEKE. Wit: Louis HELLBORN, George APPEL.

HAASE, August [26; Omaha; b: Germany; f: Henry HAASE; m: Engeline WINKELMANN] md. Kate DERNRADY [19; Omaha; b: England; f: Luke DERNRADY; m: Mary DATTON] on 14 Apr 1880. Off: BENEKE. Wit: John BURKHARD, Leopold HIRSCHMANN.

HADLEY, Hiram [26; Washington Co.] md. Harriet C. ULTZ [18; Washington Co.] on 21 May 1860. Off: DAVIS. Wit: Rachel ROBISON.

HADLEY, William [18; Douglas Co.] md. Elizabeth HEELEY [18; Douglas Co.] on 10 Nov 1867 at the residence of the groom's brother. Off: FLORKEE. Wit: Hiram M. HADLEY, Catherine ULTZ. Age consent signed William HADLEY, legal guardian of the groom.

HAEGEN, Henry J. [25; Omaha; b: Wisconsin; f: John W. HAEGEN; m: Mary A. SEABENALER] md. Mary A. McCAFFERY [21; Omaha; b: Nebraska; f: Barney McCAFFERY; m: Rosa CAMPBELL] on 3 Sep 1879. Off: McCARTHY. Wit: Matthew KIRCH, Margaret CORRIGAN.

HAFFKE, William (Wilhelm) [22; Sarpy Co.; b: Germany; f: Carl HAFFKE; m: Rosalia SCHEWELIER] md. Wilhelmine PREIKSCH [24; Sarpy Co.; b: Germany; f: Martin PREIKSCH; m: Chalotte PREIKSCH] on 23 Dec 1881. Off: FRESE. Wit: William ADAMS, Sarpy Co., M. GUSLEY, Sarpy Co.

HAGAN [HAGAR], Isaac A., Rev. [Omaha] md. Helen M. LIDDARD [LIDDIARD] [Omaha] on 6 Jan 1864. Off: TALBOT. Wit: P.W. HITCHCOCK, Anna M. HITCHCOCK, Gilbert C. MONNELL, M.D., et al.

HAGE, August [36; Omaha; b: Germany; f: Christian HAGE; m: Charlotte STEINBRICKER] md. Wilhelmina SCHANER [26; West Omaha Pct; b: Germany; f: Karl SCHANER; m: Henrietta MISTRON] on 10 Aug 1872. Off: TOWNSEND. Wit: Hermann C. TIMME; John C. KACK.

HAGEMAN, Heinrich [22; Omaha; b: Germany; f: Henry HAGEMAN; m: Dorthea MOHR] md. Hannah HUCKFELDT [18; Omaha; b: Germany; f: John HUCKFELDT] on 13 Oct 1873. Off: TOWNSEND. Wit: Henry GEHLE; John HUCKFELDT.

HAGEN, Cyrus [25; Sarpy Co.; b: Norway; f: John HAGEN; m: Jenetta ANDERSEN] md. Seloma REMELIA [18; Sarpy Co.; b: PA; f: David REMELIA; m: Sarah GROVENOR] on 3 Jul 1876. Off: SEDGWICK. Wit: Carrie HAGEN, Douglas Co., John JOHNSON, Douglas Co.

HAGENNEY, Andrew J. [St. John's, IA] md. Mary FOX [Council Bluffs] on 21 Apr 1864 at the Catholic Church of Omaha. Off: O'GORMAN. Wit: Danl. MAGHER.

HAIGHT, David [57; Omaha; b: New York; f: James HAIGHT; m: Polly STECKLES] md. Martha McELAXANDER [38; Omaha; b: Ohio; f: Peter OVERKERGEN] on 13 Dec 1870. Off: GIBSON. Wit: John DAVIS; George McKENZIE.

HAINES, Eayre W. [24; Council Bluffs; b: Ohio; f: Eayre HAINES; m: Rebecca PITENGER] md. Hannah JUMAN [19; Council Bluffs; b: Iowa; f: Hiram JUMAN; m: Mary YOUNG] on 12 Jun 1872. Off: TOWNSEND. Wit: Mrs. C.L. BAGG, Council Bluffs; J.F.L.D. HERTZMANN.

HAINES, George [30; Omaha; b: New York; f: Henry HAINES; m: Sarah PORTER] md. Jenna RAING [26; Omaha; b: Virginia; f: Henry RAING; m: Betsy BENNETT] on 10 Nov 1873. Off: PEABODY. Wit: Mattie JENNING; James DAILY.

HALD, Alfred [24; Omaha; b: Denmark; f: C.H. HALD; m: Abbe CHRISTIANSON] md. Mary JENKEY [20; Omaha; b: Bohemia; f: Jacob JENKEY; m: Antiona SCHODDER] on 16 Aug 1875. Off: PEABODY. Wit: Mary C. PEABODY, George SWAHA.

HALE, George [41; Cincinnati, OH] md. Elizabeth C. SPENCER [about 30; Omaha] on 27 Sep 1866. Off: SLAUGHTER.

HALES, Henry A. [21; Omaha] md. Katey E. WANG [19; Omaha] on 24 Dec 1867. Off: SLAUGHTER.

HALEY, James O. [29; Omaha; b: Tennessee; f: Oliver H. HALEY; m: Addriane J. BROUDER] md. Louise D. SIGWART [26; Fort Omaha; b: Missouri; f: Nicholas SIGWART; m: Anna BEHRINGER] on 13 Jun 1880. Off: BARTHOLOMEW. Wit: Charles BOEHME, Mrs. Ida H. BOEHME.

HALEY, John [22; Omaha; b: Ireland; f: Daniel HALEY; m: Ellen MULCAHEY] and Mary HAGERTY [23; Omaha; f: Henry HAGERTY] license issued on 17 May 1873. Off: TOWNSEND.

HALEY, John [25; Omaha; b: Indiana; f: Patrick HALEY; m: Catherine HANLAN] md. Mary McANDREWS [21; Omaha; b: Ireland; f: Tom McANDREWS; m: Briget McANDREWS] on 24 Apr 1870. Off: CURTIS. Wit: John CROSBIEN; Catherine CASEY.

HALEY, Ora [28; Laramie, Wyoming Terr; b: Maine; f: Benjamin HALEY; m: Nancy Jane ROLLINS] md. Augusta F. PFEIFFER [23; Omaha; b: Virginia on 8 Jan 1872. Off: DeLaMATYR. Wit: Mr. FOX, Laramie, Wyoming Terr.; Mr. NORTON.

HALGREN, Carl [44; Omaha; b: Sweden; f: Erick HALGREN; m: Anna Margaretta] md. Anna Caroline GATBER [31; Omaha; b: Sweden; f: Olof GATBER] on 24 Jan 1872. Off: PORTER. Wit: A. JOHNSON; Areker SABERMAN.

HALL, Charles H. [35; Omaha] md. Hattie E. SMITH [Omaha] on 13 Jan 1868 at FLORKEE's house. Off: FLORKEE. Wit: Mrs. Harriet RUSTIN, Mrs. Carolina MAY, Mrs. Elizabeth FLORKEE.

HALL, Charles [27; Omaha; b: Valiparazo, Chile; f: Charles HALL; m: Hannah BELL] md. Eliza BALL [23; Omaha; b: Syracuse, NY; f: James BALL; m: Jane E. SANFORD] on 4 Jun 1869. Off: BETTS. Wit: Elbert E. SIMPSON, Ida HUTH.

HALL, Franklin A. [23; Omaha; b: Connecticut; f: M.L. HALL; m: Mary E. BLAKEMAN] md. Lida BURNELL [18; Omaha; b: New York; f: Wm. BURNELL; m: Elizabeth HOLLAND] on 10 Sep 1877. Off: FISHER. Wit: A.L. MORRIS, H.L. DAVIS, Kitty MORRIS, E.M. FISHER.

HALL, Frederick A. [27; Cheyenne, Wyoming Terr.; b: Maine; f: Taylor G. HALL; m: Eliza TILESTON] md. Julia C. COOK [26; Winterset, IA; b: Vermont; f: C.B. WELCH; m: Charlotte B. MEAD] on 9 Dec 1870. Off: BETTS. Wit: George W. DOANE; George D. RUGGLES.

HALL, George S. [27; Omaha; b: Hudson, NY; f: James HALL; m: Ann Eliza LOTT] md. Catharine E. FERGUSON [24; Omaha; b: Springfield, IL; f: George FERGUSON; m: Mary] on 17 May 1873. Off: WRIGHT. Wit: Mary W. ROBINSON; Maggie HENDERSON.

HALL, George T. [20] md. Sarah FORD [15] on 23 Dec 1868. Off: KERMOTT. Wit: May be these names written in pencil: "M.T. HALL, V.E. HALL." Age consent given by the parents of the groom and bride.

HALL, Harvey [26; Florence; b: PA; f: Chas. HALL; m: Catharine ERWIN] md. Annie GALLOP [16; Florence; b: New Brunswick; f: Charles GALLOP; m: Mary GARBISON] on 27 Dec 1881 at Florence. Off: COWAN. Wit: Lewis PLANT, Hattie COWAN, both of Florence. Age consent given by R.W. COWAN, stepfather and guardian of the bride.

HALL, Haskall B. [31; b; New York; f: Ira HALL; m: Julia SHATTUCK] md. Ella ECKLUND [20; b: Sweden; f: ECKLUND; m: Mary SCHROEDER] on 20 Mar 1878. Off: FISHER. Wit: Mr. EKLUND; Miss EKLUND. Warren SWITZLER, Notary Public.

HALL, Henley [27; Omaha; b: Virginia; f: Henley HALL; m: Jane MYERS] md. Carrie E. KEYS [24; Omaha; b: Ireland] on 31 Mar 1871. Off: DeLaMATYR. Wit: N.O. DeLaMATYR; Mrs. K. MADDOX.

HALL, John [26; Omaha; b: England; f: William HALL; m: Mary A. TAYLOR] md. Lillie STALEY [22; Omaha; b: Ohio; f: David STALEY; m: Susan ULLERY] on 18 Oct 1871. Off: KING. Wit: Judge L.B. GIBSON; Rev. M.F. SHINN.

HALL, John [32; Rapid City, Dakota Territory; b: Canada; f: John HALL; m: Ann ELWIN] md. Mrs. Flora C. LOVELAND [32; Omaha; b: OH; f: J.N. GRIDLEY; m: Mary BALDWIN] on 19 Nov 1881. Off: SHERRILL. Wit: Andrew VAUKURAN, James N. GRIDLEY.

HALL, Marques L. [46; Omaha; b: New York; f: Luther W. HALL; m: Polly TREADWELL] md. Mrs. Lucy W. TREADWELL [40; Omaha; b: Connecticut; f: Grandison TREADWELL; m: Eliza PAINE] on 24 Jul 1870. Off: DeLaMATYR. Wit: Annie SIMMS.

HALL, Marquis L. [52; Omaha; b: NY; f: Luther W. HALL; m: Polly TREADWELL] md. Mary Elizabeth BLAKEMAN [47; Omaha; b: CT; f: Eli BLAKEMAN; m: Polly COOK] on 23 Nov 1876. Off: STEWART. Wit: Mrs. Emily W. STEWART.

HALL, Myron W. [23; Union Precinct; b: Michigan; f: Horace R. HALL; m: Mary E. COOPER] md. Cynthia F.D. THOMAS [20; Union Precinct; b: Nebraska; f: Lewis THOMAS; m: Susan MOORE] on 29 Mar 1879. Off: MOORE and Lewis THOMAS. Wit: Benjamin BATES and Alma BURGMAN, both of Union Precinct.

HALL, Thomas [24; Grand Island; b: Ireland; f: Thomas HALL; m: Jane JOHNSON] md. Annie McINERNY [18; Grand Island; b: Ireland; f: Thomas McINERNY; m: Annce MEAS] on 12 Aug 1870. Off: CURTIS. Wit: Peter MELONE; Ellen O'DONNEL.

HALL, William H. [26; Omaha; b: New Orleans; f: E. HALL; m: Eliza STARK] md. Matilda NELSON [22; Omaha; b: Iowa; f: James P. NELSON; m: Mary CROSEN] on 25 Oct 1879. Off: ESTABROOK. Wit: Harry ANDERSON, Lilly ANDERSON.

HALL, William T. [27; Bedford, IN; b: Indiana; f: Daniel HALL; m: Ann KERN] md. Alice FAIT [21; Douglas Co., NE; f: Albert FAIT; m: Mary BOWDEN] on 25 Oct 1879 at Chicago Precinct. Off: ROBERTS. Wit: Amanda CONERLY and Rebecca ROBERTS, both of Chicago Precinct.

HALL, William [32; Omaha; b: Ohio; f: George HALL; m: Ann HALL] md. Debby C. MUNDELL [20; Smith Co., KS; b: Missouri; f: Hiram MUNDELL; m: Jane BROWN] on 18 Jul 1877. Off: PORTER. Wit: Oliver KELLY, Anna HAYNES.

HALLEN, Michael [25; Omaha; b: Ireland; f: David HALLEN; m: Mary BARRY] md. Catharine WHELAN [26; Omaha; b: Ireland; f: Murtagh WHELAN; m: Mary Ruth] on 1 May 1872. Off: CURTIS. Wit: Frank SLOPER; Catharine CONWAY.

HALLEY, Thomas C. [29; Omaha; b: Ireland; f: Nicholas HALLEY; m: Bridget CUMINGS] md. Josephine HANKE [23; Omaha; b: Germany; f: Lewis HANKE] on 25 Dec 1873 at the German Catholic Church. Off: GROENEBAUM. Wit: John FOLEY; Mrs. Johanna FOLEY.

HALLIDAY, Josiah A. [22 or 23; Omaha] md. Nora (Norah) O'NEIL [22; Omaha] on 22 Feb 1868. Off: O'GORMAN. Wit: Danl. McALISTER.

HALQUIST, Nelson M. [24; Omaha; b: Sweden; f: Nels JOHNSON; m: Betsey JOHNSON] md. Annie HAGELINE [24; Omaha; b: Sweden; f: Johnson HAGELINE; m: Mary NELSON] on 13 Jul 1872. Off: BAKSTROM. Wit: Charles E. SEAGREN; John FRICK.

HAMANN, Christian F. [27; Omaha; b: Germany; f: Christian H. HAMANN; m: Margareta D. CLEMENT] md. Johannah C. FECH [23; Omaha; b: Germany; f: Charles H. FECH; m: Maria E.C. JOHANNSEN] on 30 Oct 1871. Off: BILLMAN. Wit: Stein TAYLOR; Mrs. Ira C. BILLMAN.

HAMANN, Henry F. [26; Omaha; b: Germany; f: Christ H. HAMANN; m: Dorothea M. CLEMANT] md. Agatha M. STAHL [21; Omaha; b: Germany; f: Hans H. STAHL; m: Maren HANSEN] on 22 Aug 1874. Off: HILGENDORF. Wit: August PRINZ; Christian HAMANN.

HAMANN, Max H. [27; Omaha; b: Ho(l)stein, Germany; f: Max HAMANN; m: Kate ECKMAN] md. Margaret DANKER [23; Omaha; b: Germany; f: Henry DANKER; m: Engerburg CLAUSEN] on 1 Feb 1871. Off: GIBSON. Wit: W.H. CADER; Dennis LONERGIN.

HAMBLETON, James D. [33; San Francisco, CA; b: Maryland] md. Mary M. CLARKSON [20; Omaha; b: Chicago, IL; f: R.H. CLARKSON; m: Melissa McPHERSON] on 6 Sep 1870 at the Trinity

Church. Off: CLARKSON. Wit: Melissa CLARKSON; John G. GASMANN.

HAMILTON, Charles W. and Fannie MURPHY license issued in 1858. No marriage record. Off: BRIGGS.

HAMILTON, Edward [24; Omaha; b: Burlington, VT; f: Henry W. HAMILTON; m: Martha A. WALTERS] md. Caroline KITZENGER [18; Omaha; b: New York] on 11 Oct 1869. Off: KELLEY. Wit: Paul E. LAYET, J(eremiah) McCHANE.

HAMILTON, J.G. [27; Belleview; b: Scotland; f: John HAMILTON; m: Marion LOUDON] md. Lizzy J. DOW [18; Belleview; b: IL; f: Robert DOW; m: Emly LANE] on 15 Jan 1876. Off: SEDGWICK. Wit: F.P. HANLON, E.T. COWIN.

HAMILTON, J.W. [28; Washington Co.; b: Illinois; f: Wm. R. HAMILTON; m: Louisa DOYLE] md. Charlotte EDWARDS [20; Plymouth, IL; b: Illinois; f: Benjamin EDWARDS; m: Evaline DOYLE] on 31 Jul 1879. Off: BARTHOLOMEW. Wit: Max BERGMAN, Isaac COE.

HAMILTON, Thomas [35; West Omaha Pct, Douglas Co,; b: Canada West; f: Robert HAMILTON; m: Sarah BRAIDEN] md. Mary Jane BARKER [37; West Omaha Pct., Douglas Co.; b: England; f: Joseph BARKER; m: Frances SAULT] on 25 Dec 1872. Off: GUE. Wit: Joseph FOX; Elijah STODDARD; Joseph BARKER, Jr; all of West Omaha Pct.

HAMLET, Charles [26; Plattsmouth; b: Ohio; f: John HAMLET; m: Mary Ann ROSE] md. Mollie BAKER [20; Lincoln; b: Ohio; f: William BAKER; m: Sarah P. BRANDON] on 30 Jan 1880. Off: WRIGHT. Wit: L. PETERSON, M. CUMMINGS.

HAMMED, Conrad [28; Laramie, WY; b: Sweden; f: Jens HAMMED; m: Mary HEDERSTEDT] md. Johanna EDSTROM [24; Laramie, WY; b: Sweden; f: Andrew EDSTROM; m: Charlotte ANDERSON] on 27 May 1875. Off: PEABODY. Wit: Maratin EDSTROM, Oscar BOLIN.

HAMMER, Carl E. [47; Omaha; b: Sweden; f: John HAMMER; m: Kathrine LILGA] md. Caroline JOHNSON [35; Omaha; b: Sweden; f: John JOHNSON; m: Mary ISRAEL] on 5 Oct 1881. Off: CHADWICK. Wit: W. SIMERAL, Max BERGMAN.

HAMMERLOF, Conrad [33; Omaha; b: Sweden; f: Mathias HAMMERLOF; m: Britta HAGLAN] md. Sophie LINDSTROM [28; Omaha; b: Sweden; f: Lars LINDSTROM; m: Mary BRAW] on 25 Jan 1870. Off: LARSON. Wit: Mrs. Johanna C. LARSON; Engla J. NORMAN.

HAMMETT, William [44; Omaha; b: Pennsylvania; f: James H. HAMMETT; m: Anna CLINE] md. Dora S. BROWN [25; Omaha; b: Iowa; f: John BROWN; m: Sarah SINGLETON] on 19 Aug 1879. Off:

BENECKE. Wit: G.W. HOMAN, E.R. STRANG.

HAMMOND, Charles H. [30; Omaha] md. Lucinda BANKS [23; Omaha] on 30 Dec 1866. Off: MILLER.

HAMMOND, George [20; b: Maryland; f: Achsah S. HAMMOND; m: A.S. WARFIELD] md. Annie M. OLESON [17; b: Norway; f: Christian OLESON; m: Julia OLESON] on 29 Jan 1878. Off: JOHNSON. Wit: Miles D. HOUCK, Geo. W. SHIELDS.

HAMMOND, Harry [26; Omaha] md. Anna FAY [19; Omaha] on 9 Feb 1869 at Trinity Church. Off: BETTS. Wit: James CANDLISH, Christina CHRISTIE.

HAMMOND, Julius H. [31 Omaha; b: IL; f: Loren K. HAMMOND; m: Maria MERWIN] md. Olive A. HURLEY [29; Omaha; b: IL; f: John HURLEY; m: Martha] on 18 Oct 1876. Off: SHERRILL. Wit: E.K. LONG, Mrs. A.F. SHERRILL.

HANEMAN, Christin F. [29; Avoca, IA; b: Germany; f: C.J. HANEMAN; m: Dora WIESEMAN] md. Kate THODT [27; Davenport, IA; b: Germany; f: Claus THODT] on 28 May 1875. Off: PEABODY. Wit: Watson B. SMITH, Frank P. HANLON.

HANEY, Edward [24; Omaha; b: Wisconsin; f: Berry HANEY; m: Ann BAXTER] md. May A. PORTER [23; Omaha; b: Illinois; f: John R. PORTER; m: Jane M. DIXON] on 15 Nov 1871. Off: KUHNS. Wit: John R. PORTER; Harry P. DEUEL.

HANEY, John [31; Chicago Precinct, Douglas Co.; b: PA; f: John HANEY; m: Sarah BOLIN] and Mary HALL [27; Chicago Precinct, Douglas Co.; b: IN; f: Edward HALL; m: Sarah Eliza] license issued on 25 Jan 1876. No marriage record. Off: SEDGWICK.

HANGER, John Preston [23; Waterloo; b: Caldwell Co., MO; f: Peter HANGER; m: Charity EVANS] md. Mary Ann KEEFE [19; Waterloo; b: Iowa; f: Daniel KEEFE; m: Mary GUIGAN] at the house of Mrs. KEEFE on 3 Mar 1878. Off: LONERGAN. Wit: Timothy KEEFE of Waterloo, Ellie DONNELLY of Elkhorn Station.

HANLAN, Frederick [25; Omaha; b: Ireland; f: Michael HANLAN; m: Nancy BULLYER] md. Margaret CONREY [23; Omaha; b: Ireland; f: James CONREY] on 16 Aug 1869. Off: CURTIS. Wit: Charles HENLEY, Mary O'KEEFE, et al. "County of Lenawee" is written on the license.

HANSEN, Andres [27; Dodge Co.; b: Denmark; f: Hans N. HANSEN; m: Karoline HANSEN] md. Teresa KINGBEIL [31; b; Germany; f: Charles KINGBEIL; m: Dora SCHULTER] on 5 Oct 1878. Off: BARTHOLOMEW. Wit: Chs. SINDING, Mrs. Emma SINDING, both of Dodge Co., NE.

HANSEN, Andrew [24; Omaha; b: Denmark; f: Hans OLESON] md. Maria A. LARSEN [21; Omaha; b: Denmark; f: Lars NELSON, m: Bodel C. JENSDOTTER] on 9 Jun 1881. Off: ANDERSON. Wit: Peter LARSON, John C. CHRISTENSEN.

HANSEN, Andrew [26; Omaha; b: Denmark; f: Hans OLESON; m: Christiana RASMUSSEN] md. Dora BERTELSON [26; Omaha; b: Denmark; f: B. NELSON; m: C. JENSEN] on 5 Feb 1876. Off: SEDGWICK. Wit: M. HANSON, F.P. HANLON.

HANSEN, Andrew [29; Omaha; b: Denmark; f: Hans HANSEN] md. Mary NILSON [28; Omaha; b: Denmark; f: Nils PETERSON] on 18 Sep 1871. Off: PORTER. Wit: John HARROLD; John STEIN.

HANSEN, Christian (Chresten) [27; Omaha; b: Denmark; f: Nils HANSEN; m: Mary NICKOR] md. Emma HADLEY [20; Omaha; b: Sweden; f: John HADLEY; m: Mary JOHNSON] on 4 Jul 1874. Off: PEABODY. Wit: Mrs. R.A. HARRIS; Jennie McCOY.

HANSEN, Christian [31; Omaha; b: Denmark; f: Hans JENSEN; m: Anna JENSEN] md. Ella HAGG [26; Omaha; b: Sweden; f: Andro HAGG; m: Anna NELSON] on 3 Mar 1881. Off: GYDESEN. Wit: William GYDESEN, Omaha, 811 Leavenworth, T. HOLM.

HANSEN, Eve [27; b: Denmark; f: Hans MICKELSON; m: Maria HANSEN] md. Minnie JOHNSON [22; b: Denmark; f: John JERGSON; m: Mary JOHNSON] on 2 May 1878. Off: HANSEN. Wit: David H. NIELSEN, Joseph KRAGSKOW.

HANSEN, George F.J. [27; Omaha; b: Norway; f: Hans Jacob HANSEN; m: Anna ARNESON] md. Hannah NELSON [16; Omaha; b: Sweden; f: Sven NELSON; m: Anna LUNDBERG] on 29 Nov 1872. Off: THURSTON. Wit: Sven NELSON; Collen NELSON. Age of consent given by father of bride.

HANSEN, Hans [23; Omaha; b: Denmark; f: Andras HANSEN; m: Anna CHRISTENSEN] md. Annie M. SKERBEK [24; Omaha; b: Germany; f: Knud SKERBEK; m: Marie NELSON] on 11 Mar 1881. Off: STENBERG. Wit: Mark HANSEN, Andrew HANSEN.

HANSEN, Hans [33; Omaha; b: Denmark; f: Hans HANSEN; m: Johanna Katharina LUND] md. Christina HOLMER [22; Omaha;

b: Germany; f: Andrew J. HOLMER; m: Anna Katharina HEMPEL] on 21 Feb 1873. Off: TOWNSEND. Wit: Jacob JACOBSEN; John CHRISTOPHERSON.

HANSEN, Ingwer [33;Omaha; b: Prussia; f: Peter E. HANSEN; m: Marrgie INGELS] md. Annie GUTHARD [22; Omaha; b: Prussia; f: Hans GUTHARD] on 19 Nov 1870 at Hans GUTHARD's residence, Sarpy Co. Off: FAUST. Wit: M.F. FREIKE, Sarpy Co.; John HINSTADT, Sarpy Co.

HANSEN, John [25; Omaha; b: Denmark; f: John HANSEN; m: Caroline JOHNSON] md. Mary POULSON [PAULSON] [25; Omaha; b: Denmark; f: Peter POULSON [PAULSON]] on 7 Jun 1869. Off: DENMURE. Wit: C. JORGENSEN, Peter A. HANSEN.

HANSEN, Jurgen M. [23; Waterloo; b: Denmark; f: Hans MADSEN; m: Darthe MARKURSEN] md. Astrid RISMER [21; Waterloo; b: Denmark; f: ---- RISMER; m: Christiana RISMER] on 6 Nov 1881 at Waterloo. Off: NEILSON. Wit: Geo. JOHNSON, Waterloo, A. RISMER, Waterloo.

HANSEN, Lars [27; Omaha] md. Emma PIERSON [22; Omaha] on 9 Feb 1869. Off: KUHNS. Wit: Peter PETERSON, Eliza or Eva ANDERSON.

HANSEN, Laurs [28; Omaha; b: Denmark; f: Hans PAULSEN; m: Caren LARSEN] md. Maria ANDERSEN [28; Omaha; b: Denmark; f: Anders ANDERSON; m: Christine PETERSEN] on 23 Apr 1881 at their residence. Off: GYDESEN. Wit: H. MOLLER, S. HOLM.

HANSEN, Magnus C. [23; Omaha; b: Denmark; f: Hans CHRISTENSON; m: Mary MORTESEN] md. Biddy SWANSEN [31; Omaha; b: Sweden; f: Swen ERICKSON; m: Ellen NEILSEN] on 22 Oct 1877. Off: SEDGWICK. Wit: J.G. BRADISH, Peter NELSON.

HANSEN, Mark [25; Omaha] md. Ann NEILSON [24; Omaha] on 4 Sep 1866. Off: HASCALL. Wit: Peter MULHEDE, Cha. PETERSON.

HANSEN, Martin [25; Omaha; b: Denmark; f: Hans HANSEN; m: Mary RASMUSSEN] md. Louisa THOMPSON [16; Omaha; b: Denmark; f: John THOMPSON; m: Sine ALMEND] on Feb 1875. Off: PEABODY. Wit: C. PETERSON, Ole JENSEN. Age consent given by mother of the bride. Father is dead.

HANSEN, Martin [31; Monona Co., IA; b: Norway; f: Hans TORSON; m: Mary JOHNSON] md. Bertie OLESON [29; Monona Co., IA; b: Norway; f: Ole OLESON; m: Amelia CHRISTENSON] on 30 Dec 1873. Off: RING. Wit: Lewis NORELIUS; A.W. ANDERSON.

HANSEN, Mat [28; Platte Valley Pct., Douglas Co.; b: Denmark; f: Hans NELSON;

m: Karen JENSEN] md. Mrs. Mary J. DAVIS [27; Omaha; b: Kentucky; f: Benjamin DAVIS; m: Pamiliane WILLIAMS] on 5 Oct 1873. Off: HALE. Wit: Mrs. Annie GELAKKE; Luse STEIN.

HANSEN, Peter [26; Omaha] md. Sene JOHNSON [22; Omaha] on 2 Jan 1869. Off: HYDE. Wit: Henry ESTABROOK, DeMotte HYDE.

HANSEN, Peter [29; Omaha; b: Denmark; f: Nels HANSEN; m: Sophia BENSON] md. Regine PETERSON [28; Omaha; b: Denmark; f: Peter PETERSON; m: Anna CHRISTIANSON] on 14 Apr 1880, Danish Church. Off: GYDESEN. Wit: A. RASMUSSEN, M.C.E. GYDESEN.

HANSEN, Peter [30; Douglas Co.; b: Germany; f: Carsten HANSEN; m: Kathrina CARSTENSEN] md. Mrs. Anna HANSEN [25; Douglas Co.; b: Germany; f: Soenke NICOLAI; m: Auk HANSEN] on 24 Sep 1881. Off: BENEKE. Wit: August HANSEN, Johann HARTWIG.

HANSEN, Solomon [24; Omaha; b: Denmark; f: H.C. HANSEN; m: Anna HANSEN] md. Karen Margarethe PETERSON [b: Denmark; f: A. PETERSON; m: Maren NELSEN] on 30 Oct 1881 at "their residents." Off: GYDESEN. Wit: John P. JERRON, Erik PETERSON.

HANSEN, William [30; b: Denmark; f: Hans HANSEN; m: Henrietta ANDERSON] md. Christina HENSEN [23; b: Denmark; f: Hans ANDERSON; m: Hannah HENSEN] on 3 Sep 1878. Off: BARTHOLOMEW. Wit: James Osgood ADAMS, Max BERGMAN.

HANSON, A.E. [27; Weeping Water, Cass Co.; b: Ohio; f: E.S. HANSON; m: Debara PRAY] md. Belle BROOKINS [16; Weeping Water, Cass Co.; b: Illinois; f: Walter BROOKINS; m: Jane BARDEN] on 14 Aug 1878. Off: BARTHOLOMEW. Wit: Charles OGDEN, F.P. HANLON.

HANSON, Hans C. [33; Omaha; b: Denmark; f: Hans HANSON; m: Metta JENSEN] md. Amalia SWENSON [23; Omaha; b: Sweden; f: Swen ORRETSON; m: Bolla JEPPERSON] on 1 May 1877. Off: PEABODY. Wit: Jens HANSEN, Frank COLE.

HANSON, Jacob [37; Saunders Co.; b: Sweden; f: Hans HANSER; m: Betty Christiana LARSON] md. Christiana SWENSON [35; Omaha; b: Sweden; f: John ERIKSON; m: Christiana Gusta JOHNSON] on 17 Jan 1878. Off: NORDLING. Wit: Olaf HANSON; Johanna LANDIN.

HANSON, James P. [35; Douglas Co.; b: Denmark; f: Hans CHRISTIANSEN; m: Christene NELSON] md. Georgine M. NELSON [17; Douglas CO.; b: Denmark; f: Lars Jenson NELSON; m: Karen M. LARSON] on 19 Sep 1874. Off: PEABODY. Wit: Joel T. GRIFFEN; John M. THURSTON. Age of consent given by father of bride.

HANSON, Jens [24; Omaha; b: Denmark; f: Hans HANSON; m: Ane K. JORGENSEN] md. Marene K. RASMENSEN [18; Omaha; b: Denmark; f: Rasmus ANDERSON; m: Bodel K. GODFRED] on 8 Aug 1869. Off: LARSON. Wit: Anders FREDRICKSON, George (Jorgen) C. JORGENSEN.

HANSON, Peter [30; Omaha; b: Denmark; f: Hans HANSON; m: Dorothea LARSON] md. Hannah MORTENSEN [24; Omaha; b: Denmark; f: Morten LARSEN; m: Karen HANSEN] on 20 Aug 1880, Vor Fresloers Church. Off: GYDESEN. Wit: W. GYDESEN, M. GYDESEN.

HANTING, William [24; Omaha; b: Prussia; f: John HANTING; m: Mary FARDAN] md. Cecilia SATORIUS [21; Omaha; b: Prussia; f: Peter SATORIUS] on 6 Jan 1870 at the German Catholic Church. Off: GROENBAUM. Wit: Fred SCHU__ZE.

HANY (HANEY), William C. [24; Primrose; b: Pennsylvania; f: William HANEY; m: Mary or Margaret Rose] md. Mollie ELLIS [Primrose; b: Missouri; f: Moses or Moris ELLIS; m: Permelia STERET] on 1 Aug 1869 at Primrose. Off: DENTON. Wit: T.T. DENTON of Primorse, M. HENDERSON of Primrose.

HARBIN, William [25; Douglas Co.] md. Ann A. GOFF [25; Douglas Co.] on 12 May 1862. Off: McCARTHY. Wit: Adam DAVID, Robert McCARTY.

HARDER, John [23; Douglas Precinct; b: Germany; f: Claus HARDER; m: Margaret FREDERICKSON] md. Lena WEHEDE [24; Clear Creek, Saunders Co.; b: Germany; f: John WEHEDE; m: Margaret [Anna crossed out] GURTCH] on 27 Aug 1878. Off: BENEKE. Wit: Henry RUSER of Douglas Co., Wm. HAGEDORN.

HARDESTY, Samuel V. or John [36; Omaha; b: Ohio; f: John HARDESTY; m: Mary BELL] md. Ellen FLAHERTY [26; Omaha; b: Ireland; m: B. POLAND (female)] on 11 Apr 1871. Off: DIMMICK. Wit: Robert FLEMING; Mrs. Kate G. DIMMICK.

HARDING, Edward [30; Omaha; b: Prussia; f: Solomon HARDING; m: Minnie HAROLD] md. Mrs. Estella BENNETT [27; Omaha; b: New Orleans; f: Moses GOLDSTEIN; m: Estella LARISON] on 10 Jan 1874. Off: PORTER. Wit: Judge E. DUDLEY; William P. SNOWDEN.

HARKNESS, David [25; Douglas Co.] md. Julia M. TOWNE [19; Douglas Co.] on 7 Oct

1860 at Ira PRISBER's house in Kelly Precinct?. Off: BUTLER. Wit: Cloye PRISBER.

HARMON, Andrew [26; Omaha; b: Sweden; f: John E. HARMON; m: Chatharina PERSON] md. Otelea KJELSTROM [23; Omaha; b: Sweden; f: ---- KJELSTROM; m: Johanna ----] on 14 Aug 1880. Off: ANDERSON. Wit: Wm. P. SNOWDEN, D.S. BENTON.

HARMON, Arthur S. [20; Omaha; b: Connecticut; f: Paul HARMON; m: Lucinda H. STEARNS] md. Ida J. ATKINS [18; Omaha; b: Pennsylvania; f: Heil ATKINS; m: Susan R. FOSTER] on 12 Feb 1879. Off: P.C. JOHNSON. Wit: Mr. and Mrs. Elias ATKINS of Omaha. Age consent given by Paul HARMON, father of the groom.

HARMON, Eugene L. [23; Omaha; b: Rome, NY; f: A.J. HARMON; m: Cordelia CORNISH] md. Christi Anna HOLLENBACH [17; Omaha; b: Pennsylvania; f: D.A. HOLLENBACH; m: Mary Ann CETTELMOYER ] on 17 Feb 1879. Off: LIPE. Wit: A.J. HARMON; D.A. HOLLENBACH. Age consent given by D.A. HOLLENBACH, father of the bride.

HARMON, Richard [35; Omaha; b: Ireland; f: John HARMON; m: Johannah GRIFFIN] md. Johannah BRISNEE [30; Omaha; b: County Kerry, Ireland; f: Thomas BRISNEE; m: Kate McMAHON] on 13 Jul 1869. Off: CURTIS. Wit: Edmond BARROT, Mary BARROT.

HARMSEN, John [22; Sarpy Co.; b: Germany; f: Rolf HARMSEN; m: Kate PEPPER] md. Mary EICHER [23; Omaha; b: Germany; f: Claus EICHER; m: Anna NIMAND] on 7 Nov 1873. Off: PEABODY. Wit: David SCHWENCK; Max HARMSEN.

HARMSEN, Rolf [23; or 24; Sarpy Co.; b: Germany; f: Rolf HARMSEN; m: Kate HAGGE] md. Elsa B. THADE [20; Douglas Co.; b: Germany; f: Nicholas THADE; m: Kate SIEVERS] on 10 Oct 1877. Off: SEDGWICK. Wit: Henry SIERT, Fred LOGEMANN.

HARNISH, Benjamin [37; Omaha; b: Pennsylvania; f: Benjamin HARNISH; m: Anna KNICELY] and Amanda DARLING [19; Omaha; b: New York; f: Joseph DARLING] license on 31 Oct 1874. Off: PEABODY.

HARPER, John W. [24; Omaha; b: Yorkshire, England; f: Joseph L. HARPER; m: Caroline LUCK] md. Jane HALLEY [21; Omaha; b: Manchester, England; f: George HALLEY; m: Hannah CRAWFORD] on 5 Jul 1870. Off: KUHNS. Wit: Joseph L. HARPER; Mrs. J.B. DETWILER.

HARPSTER, Charles M. [26; Douglas Co.; b: Pennsylvania; f: John HARPSTER; m: Barbara ALLEY] md. Loretta SANDERS [18; Omaha; b: Ohio; f: William SANDRES; m:

Hannah REDMAN] on 14 Mar 1872. Off: KUHNS. Wit: Mrs. H.W. KUHNS; Miss Riekie KAMPRECHT.

HARPSTER, David [29; Douglas Co.] md. Amanda L. REDMAN [23; Douglas Co.] on 3 Jan 1861 in KUHNS' study on Douglas St. Off: KUHNS. Wit: Mrs. John McCORMICK, Mary A. WHEELER, Solon WILLEY.

HARR, Rudolph [27; Omaha; b: Germany; f: Louis HARR; m: Emilie JUNG] md. Minna FLYNN [22; Omaha; b: Wisconsin; f: Thomas FLYNN; m: Francis ROGERS] on 11 Apr 1879. Off: LIPE. Wit: Lizzie LIPE, Eva LIPE.

HARRIS, Edward E. [27; Lucas Co., IA; b: OH; f: John HARRIS; m: Lucindia EDMONDS] md. Hannah A. RICHARDS [21; Douglas Co.; b: IA; f: William RICHARDS; m: Phidelia A. GOULD] on 23 Dec 1876 at Irvington. Off: GREEN. Wit: Ira D. GILBERT, Irvington, Maria GILBERT, Irvington. C.A. BALDWIN, Notary Public.

HARRIS, Lewis D. [36; Omaha; b: NJ; f: Pierson HARRIS; m: Elizabeth CLAYPOOLE] md. Angeline McCASLIN [23; PA; b: PA; f: George B. McCASLIN; m: Eliza J. GREY] on 4 Oct 1875. Off: LIPE. Wit: Charles CHILDS, Mrs. CHILDS.

HARRIS, Peter [negro, 29; Omaha; b: Virginia; f: William HARRIS; m: Hattie HARRIS] md. Emma SEVEARE [negro; 20; Omaha; b: Virginia; f: Robert SEVEARE; m: Mary SEVEARE] on 30 Apr 1879. Off: FORICHE. Wit: J.G. PARKER, A.W. PARKER. Affidavit signed by Rufus JOHNSON.

HARRIS, William [29; Omaha; colored; b: Virginia; f: James HARRIS] md. Elizabeth KELLEY [19; Omaha; colored; b: Missouri] on 5 Mar 1870 at the AME Church. Off: HUBBARD. Wit: W.W. PORTER; Daniel WILLIAMSON.

HARRISON, Charles [30; Omaha; b: Canada; f: Wm. H. HARRISON; m: Maria DAKINS] md. Margaret A. BUSH [17; Sarpy Co.; b: KS; f: John BUSH; m: Mary STEVENS] on 30 Aug 1876 on the public highway near Mr. SANTERs. Off: HALL. Wit: Rosalia BUSH, Bellevue, Charles LOVEJOY, Bellevue.

HARRISON, Robert [28; Omaha; b: Ireland; f: Francis HARRISON; m: Annie GRAHAM] md. Nannie McMAMOR [23; Omaha; b: NY; f: P.J. McMAMOR; m: Elizabeth STEVENSON] on 3 Oct 1881. Off: MILLSPAUGH. Wit: Wm. SANDERS, Mrs. Carroll O'BRIEN.

HART, Amos A. [29; Omaha; b: IL; f: Henry A. HART; m: Mary EAVES] md. Sada POWELL [18; Omaha; b: IA; f: Able POWELL; m: Rebecca HATSELL] on 4 Jul 1881. Off: MARQUETT. Wit: Mrs. M.W. SIMPSON, Mrs. Winnifred ROBERTS. Affidavit signed by F.M. CHILDRES.

HART, Benjamin A. [24; Omaha; b: VA; f: John R. HART; m: Anna GOODWIN] md. Anna C. VIERS [27; Omaha; b: OH; f: Thos. J. VIERS; m: Maria] on 1 Nov 1876. Off: MILLSPAUGH. Wit: Lislie, Mary HUGDEN, Marie VIERS.

HART, Charles [32; Omaha; b: Germany; f: George HART; m: Ursula HEILIG] md. Mary JETTER [25; Omaha; b: Germany; f: Baltasar JETTER; m: Anna] on 26 Dec 1872. Off: TOWNSEND. Wit: George M. MILLS; Ferdinand THUM.

HART, Dominic [22; Omaha; b: Ireland; f: Anton HART; m: Margaret McKALE] and Ellen KILGALLON [20; Omaha; b: Ireland; f: Michael KILGALLON; m: Ellen MURPHY] filed affidavit on 8 Sep 1881. No marriage record. Off: CHADWICK.

HART, John [30; Omaha; b: Ireland; f: James HART; m: Julia FLYNN] md. Nora BOYLE [25; Omaha; b: Ireland; f: Michael BOYLE] on 6 Apr 1875 at the Catholic Cathedral. Off: BYRNE. Wit: Terrence BOYLE, Ellen DEE.

HART, Robert [40; Omaha; b: Pennsylvania; f: Henry HART; m: Elizabeth CLEMISON] md. Nancy FERGUSON [19; Omaha; b: Kentucky; f: Armstead O. FERGUSON; m: Martha] on 15 Jul 1872. Off: KUHNS. Wit: Prof. R.H. KINNEY; John MORRELL.

HARTE, Wm. F. [25; Omaha; b: KY; f: Fred HARTE; m: Johanna ROESINK] md. Mary H. BOLIVER [21; Omaha; b: NE; f: Jacob BOLIVER; m: Mary WEBER] on 22 Sep 1881. Off: BRUEDIERT. Wit: E.R. KLUGE, John HARTE.

HARTFORD, Elias [44; Douglas Co.] and Edisey FOUTS [40; Douglas Co.] license issued on 23 Apr 1866. No marriage record. Off: HASCALL.

HARTFORD, Jasper [24; Douglas Co.] md. Mary Jane COY [17; Douglas Co.] on 2 Feb 1868 at Elkhorn Twp. Off: McVEY. Wit: John DAVIS, Mrs. John DAVIS. Age consent given by the mother of the bride, the only parent.

HARTFORD, Thomas [40; Mills Co., IA] md. Susannah BAYLESS [28; Omaha] on 9 Nov 1861 in ARMSTRONG's office. Off: ARMSTRONG. Wit: Mary STARKS.

HARTMAN, Austo [33; Omaha] md. Francisco BUCKEN [20; Omaha] on 9 Sep 1868. Off: KELLEY. Wit: M.J. RYAN, R.J. STUCK.

HARTMAN, Oscar [31; Omaha; b: Sweden; f: John STEELBERG; m: Maria NORDMAN] md. Hannah HAGELIN [25; Omaha; b: Sweden; f: John HAGELIN; m: Maria NELSON] on 20 Dec 1874. Off: LIPE. Wit: N.M. HELQUIST; Annie HELQUIST.

HARTMANN, Christian H. [24; Omaha; b: Germany; f: Wilhelm HARTMANN; m: Anna AMELING] md. Martha G. THOMAS [19; Florence Precinct, Douglas Co.; b: Utah Territory; f: C.W. THOMAS; m: Jane THOMAS] on 7 Jul 1880. Off: BENEKE. Wit: A. GREENWALD, Hattie GREENWALD.

HARTSHORN, Clarence E. [22; Cass Co., IA; b: Illinois; f: Joshua P. HARTSHORN; m: Jane SIMINGTON] md. Minnie L. GREENLEAF [17; Blair, NE; b: Iowa; f: John GREENLEAF; m: Lena SLATER] on 25 Mar 1879. Off: JAMESON. Wit: Rev. R.V. DODGE of Chicago, Mrs. Mary Edgar RAMSEY of Omaha.

HARTSON, Darius [23; Omaha; b: Iowa; f: J.D. HARTSON; m: Louisa FORSYTH] md. Mary A. BALES [22; Omaha; b: France] on 8 Nov 1870. Off: KUHNS. Wit: Tarley M. HARSTON; Elijah DUNN.

HARTWIG, Johann [60; Omaha; b: Germany; f: Johann HARTWIG; m: Magdalena BLISECKER] md. Mrs. Catharine HANSEN [54; Douglas Co.; b: Germany; f: Jacob ANDERSON; m: Sophia JENSEN] on 19 Oct 1879 at H. EICKE's house. Off: MITCHELL. Wit: Ernest STRATMAN, Henry EICKE, both of Douglas Co.

HARVAT, Frank [26; Omaha; b: Austria; f: James HARVAT; m: Catherine PAZDIRKA] md. Annie JAHNAR [22; Omaha; b: Austria; f: Jas. JAHNAR; m: Mary KOVAR] on 2 Jun 1877. Off: WEISS. Wit: Louis KRUSA, Elina SABATA.

HARVEY, Andrew [29; Omaha; b: Scotland; f: Andrew HARVEY; m: Margaret KIRKWOOD] md. Margaret RITCHIE [23; Omaha; b: Scotland] on 16 Jul 1873. Off: PRESSON. Wit: John WILSON; James STOCKDALE.

HARVEY, S.N. [28; Moravea, IA; b: Pennsylvania; f: J.T. HARVEY; m: Ellen IRWIN] md. Mrs. J.F. HOFFMAN [36; Redoak, IA; b: Iowa; f: H. ROBERTS; m: M. MOONY] on 22 May 1879. Off: ROE. Wit: Joseph CHENOWITH of Malvern, IA, Robert LAING of Omaha.

HASKELL, Joseph W. [33; Memphis, TN; b: Boston, MA; f: N.D. HASKELL; m: Nancy DUNTHE] md. Bell TRAPP [26; Memphis, TN; b: Dayton, OH; f: John M. TRAPP] on 16 Nov 1874. Off: PEABODY. Wit: C.L. BRISTOL; Thomas SWIFT.

HASKELL, M.F. [26; Omaha; b: IA; f: M.M. HASKELL; m: Jane NORRIS] md. Mrs. Della GARARD [25; Omaha; b: IA; f: P. KETHAM; m: Unice SIMON] on 16 Feb 1881. Off: MARQUETTE. Wit: W. HASKELL, Sarpy Co., NE, George KING.

HASKELL [HASCALL], Henry A. [24; Omaha] md. Jennie L. HARDY [18; Omaha] on 30 Oct 1867 at Dr. E.C. STANGLAND's house. Off: VAN ANTWERP. Wit: Dr. E.C. STANGLAND and wife.

HASSETT, John E. [Omaha] md. Sophia QUINN [Omaha] on 1 May 1864 at the Catholic Church of Omaha. Off: O'GORMAN. Wit: Albert HODGES, Ellen KANE.

HASSON, Patrick [39; Utah; b: Ireland; f: John HASSON; m: Bridget DONNELLEY] md. Rose DEVLIN [30; Utah; b: Ireland; f: John DEVLIN; m: Rose DONNELLEY] on 22 Sep 1874. Off: BYRNE. Wit: Patrick DEVLIN; Anne HUGHES, Bishop's House.

HASTINGS, Patrick [25; Omaha; b: Ireland; f: Michael HASTINGS; m: Mary GALLAHAN] md. Mrs. Sarah Frances EBAUGH [24; Omaha; b: Williams Co., OH; f: Valentine SMITH; m: Annie PHILLIPS] on 17 Feb 1873. Off: TOWNSEND. Wit: Michael COADY; Bridget McNAMARA.

HATCH, Mason C. [28; Chicago; b: New York; f: Ira HATCH; m: Mary VILAS] md. Mary L. CHURCHILL [26; Omaha; b: New York; f: William H. CHURCHILL; m: Mary F. PEARSON] on 17 Dec 1874. Off: SHERRILL. Wit: Wm. L. PEABODY; W.J. CONNELL.

HATCH, Sylvanus S. [31;Omaha; b: Boston, MA] md. Katie KELLEY [20; Omaha; b: Cincinnati, OH; f: James KELLEY] on 18 May 1870. Off: MOSSMAN. Wit: James MILES; Catherine HALLEY.

HATHAWAY, Stephen B. [35; Omaha; b: Clyde, NY; f: Samuel B. HATHAWAY; m: Christenia HUFMAND] md. Alice DUCE [17; Omaha; b: England; f: Henry DUCE; m: Esther ICKERSON] on 3 Jul 1870. Off: KUHNS. Wit: Thomas H. PRICE; Mrs. Hannah PRICE.

HAUCK, Jacob [30; Omaha; b: Germany; f: Franz Georg HAUCK; m: Anna Maria MAHR] md. Kate H. BUCHAN [26; Omaha; b: Canada; f: Robert BUCHAN; m: Ellen HUTH] on 8 Jan 1879. Off: BENEKE. Wit: Oscar MOJEAN, Frank H. MEYER.

HAUPTMAN, Henry [26; Nebraska City] md. Wilhelmina MUHLENBROCK [22; Omaha] on 11 Nov 1862 at the bride's father's house. Off: FLORKEE. Wit: Savanah S. NEALLY, Mary H. HART.

HAVEL, John [32; Omaha; b: Bohemia; f: Rollins HAVEL; m: Maria KRUMER] md. Mrs. Anna BERANEK [31; Omaha; b: Bohemia; f: Joseph KUCERA; m: Jennie URBAN] on 30 Aug 1881. Off: RILEY. Wit: Parker KRUMMER.

HAVLEK, Frank [25; Omaha; b: Austria; f: Jacob HAVLEK; m: Mary PASHTA] md. Mrs. Barbara SUMMERS [22; Omaha; b: Austria; f: James KAVAN; m: Vernika SEDLACEK] on 19 Jul 1877. Off: DONNELLY. Wit: Frank POVENKA, Joseph SLEZAK.

HAWES, Wilbur F. [25; Omaha; b: Massachusetts; f: Abram HAWES; m: Sarah TURNER] md. Mary W. NILE [23; Omaha; b: Omaha; f: Wm. NILE; m: Carrie E. WILSON] on 2O Apr 1880. Off: BEANS. Wit: Abraham HAWES, Dr. J. Van CAMP.

HAWKINS, F.A. [24; Omaha; b: St. Louis, MO; f: Frank HAWKINS; m: Annie HAWKINS] md. Cora JONES [18; Omaha; b: Lincoln; f: Ebick JONES; m: Francis CLARK] on 13 May 1879. Off: FOUCHE. Wit: Mrs. FREEMAN, Emmanuel CLEMEAN.

HAWKINS, H.R.H. [Omaha] md. Eliza G. BROWN [Omaha] on 28 Aug 1864 at Henry KELLOGG's house. Off: DICKINSON. Wit: Mrs. Henry KELLOGG, Mary BROWN, Nelson LOWE, et al.

HAWKINS, John A. [31; Omaha; b: Norway; f: Joseph F. HAWKINS; m: Johnette ISLAND] md. Annie PETERSON [25; Omaha; b: Norway; f: John F. PETERSON; m: Anna Sophia KNOPE] on 20 Jun 1870. Off: KERMOTT. Wit: V.A. ELLIOTT; James LARNED.

HAWKINS, Tuls [35; Saunders Co.; b: Sweden; f: Hagan OLESON; m: Ela TULS] md. Johanna PERSON [30; Omaha; b: Sweden; f: Person STARK; m: Ela JANSON] on 7 Apr 1876. Off: LIPE. Wit: Lizzie LIPE, Kate GALLAGHER.

HAWKINSON, John [54; Douglas Co.; b: Sweden; f: Hawken HAWKINSON; m: Mary JOHNSON] md. Mrs. Mary J. CONNOR [41; Douglas Co.; b: IL; f: William OVERLANDER; Mary NEAL] on 3 Feb 1881. Off: ANDERSON. Wit: Hellen ANDERSON, Mrs. Bertha ODEN.

HAWVER, Samuel [32; Omaha] md. Carrie E. GOODWILL [22; Omaha] on 3 Dec 1867. Off: SLAUGHTER.

HAX, Henry [40; Omaha; b: Germany; f: Christopher HAX; m: Magdalen HEIN] md. Mrs. Mary HOFFMANN [35; Omaha; b: Germany; f: Peter GROSSMAN; m: Elizabeth GROSSMAN] on 1 Nov 1873. Off: BRANDES. Wit: John DAEMAN; Mrs. Wilhelmine DAEMAN.

HAXTHANSEN, David N. [30; Omaha; b: Denmark; f: Jonas HAXTHANSEN; m: Katherina THOMSEN] md. Mary HANSEN [20; Omaha; b: Denmark; f: Hans

ANDERSEN; m: Juliane MATTHIESEN] on 4 Jun 1881. Off: HYDE. Wit: W.B. SMITH, O.S. WOOD, M.D.

HAY, William [26; Evanston, WY; b: Canada; f: Alexander HAY; m: Dorothea MARTIN] md. Mary MANNING [19; Omaha; b: St. Louis, MO; f: Patrick MANNING; m: Annie BURNS] on 13 Feb 1877 at "their residence, 18th Street." Off: JENNETTE. Wit: Joseph SHAW, Katie WALSH.

HAYDEN, Kent Kane [23; b: Maryland; f: Bernard L. HAYDEN; m: Mary E. YATES] md. Minnie E. HAMPTON [18; b: Kentucky; f: John HAMPTON; m: Elizabeth W. HENDERSON] on 21 Oct 1878. Off: BARKALOW. Wit: Warren SWITZLER, Newton BARKALOW.

HAYDOCK, George W. [28; Omaha Barracks; b: Maine; f: John P. HAYDOCK; m: Eliza NEWHALL] md. Frances E. CARROLL [20; b: Vermont; f: Thomas CARROLL; m: Kate NERKIE] on 5 May 1878. Off: WRIGHT. Wit: J. McBell STEMBEL, Mrs. Nellie M. FRENCH, both of Omaha Barracks.

HAYES, Frank S. [26; Fremont; b: Massachusetts; f: Frank W. HAYES; m: Mary A. SHEPHARD] md. Addie N. ROWE [25; Iowa; b: New Hampshire; f: David B. ROWE; m: Mary C. McCRELLIS] on 25 Nov 1874. Off: HAMMOND. Wit: Edward W. SIMERAL; Nannie HAMMOND.

HAYES, James A. [34; Omaha; b: Ireland; f: John HAYES; m: Ellen FANING] md. Mrs. Hannah SMITH [61; Omaha; b: Denmark; f: John NICKERSON; m: Johanna HANSEN] on 21 Sep 1881. Off: STENBERG. Wit: N.P. JENSEN, Antonio E. PERFETH.

HAYES, John [29; Omaha; b: Ireland; f: John HAYES; m: Mary CRONIN] md. Sarah DOUGHERTY [19; Omaha; b: Ireland; f: William DOUGHERTY; m: Betsey BUTLER] on 15 Apr 1873. Off: CURTIS. Wit: Patrick HIGGINS, Grand Island; Mary TROY.

HAYES, Michael [45; Fillmore Co.; b: Ireland; f: Patrick HAYES; m: Mary McDONAUGH] md. Hannah SHANNON [42; b: Pennsylvania; f: Thomas SHANNON; m: Rosa FURRAY] on 6 Jul 1880, Holy Family Church. Off: QUINN. Wit: Geo. F. EINBLEN of Forest City, James B. FITZPATRICK.

HAYES, Thomas [29; Omaha; b: Ireland; f: Thomas HAYES: m: Mary MALLONEY] md. Mary T. MARTIN [18; Omaha; b: New York City; f: Peter MARTIN; m: Bridget C. RILEY] on 18 Oct 1874. Off: JENNETTE. Wit: Charles McGUILEY, Omaha Barracks; Lizzie ROCHE, Omaha Barracks.

HAYNES, H.M. [28; Omaha; b: New York; f: H.W.H. HAYNES; m: A.S. PERCY] md. Mrs. L.E. TODD [31; Omaha; b: Indiana; f: James RUSSELL; m: Eliza DRISCOLL] on

9 Apr 1874. Off: ADAIR. Wit: Seneca N. SISSON; Abigall R. SISSON.

HAYWARD, Francis [28; Omaha; b: New York; f: William G. HAYWARD; m: Catherine A. BRETT] md. Matilda PAYNE [21; Omaha; b: Illinois; f: Mr. SHAMBAUGH] on 1 Jan 1870. Off: KERMOTT. Wit: Mrs. A.R. KERMOTT; Frank R. KERMOTT.

HAYWARD, John [30; Omaha; b: England; f: Thomas HAYWARD; m: Charlotte LANGRAN] md. Mrs. Emma HEFFERMAN [22; Omaha; b: NE; f: John TAYLOR; m: Elizabeth SLAW] on 18 Apr 1881. Off: ENGLISH. Wit: Edward EGAN, Lizzie MURPHY.

HAYWARD, Thomas C. [25; Omaha; b: IA; f: Ebenezer HAYWARD; m: Mary AMES] md. Mrs. Annie CUNNINGHAM [25; Omaha; b: MO; m: Annie CHRISTIAN] on 1 Nov 1881. Off: CHADWICK. Wit: Max BERGMAN, Frank SWEENEY.

HAZARD, John K. [26; Douglas Co.] md. Ann O. FORREST [22; Douglas Co.] on 25 Dec 1861 at D. HAZARD's house in Douglas Co. Off: HART. Wit: Mr. and Mrs. TORREY (TORREZ)

HAZELTON, John [32; Omaha; b: Ireland; f: Michael HAZELTON; m: Mary SLATTERY] md. Jane CASSHIN [32; Omaha; b: Ireland; f: Hugh CASSHIN; m: Ellen KENNEDY] on 6 Jul 1873. Off: CURTIS. Wit: John FLANNERY; Catherine MULCAHEY.

HAZELTON, Solomon [colored; 25; Omaha; b: Baltimore, MD; f: Robert HAZELTON; m: Maria MERRIDETH] md. Arabella HARRIS [colored; 17; Omaha; b: Pittsburg, PA or Ohio; f: William HARRIS; m: Eliza WALL] on 23 Aug 1869. Off: HYDE. Wit: George SMITH, DeMotte HYDE.

HAZEN, Lyman P. [Bellevue] md. Sarah J. RUSSELL [Bellevue] on 22 Jan 1864. Off: BECHER and HOFFMAN. Wit: Thomas TODD, Miss MAHONE.

HAZLETT, Alfred [25; Beatrice; b: Pennsylvania; f: S.C. HAZLETT; m: Jane JACK] md. Libbie COTTON [19; DeWitt; b: Illinois; f: T.D. COTTON; m: Elizabeth ALLISON (FISHER was crossed out)] on 31 Aug 1874. Off: GARRETT. Wit: Benjamin B. BINGAY, Mobile, AL; Maria COTTON, DeWitt.

HAZZARD, John K. [40; Saratoga Precinct; b: New York; f: Hiram HAZZARD; m: Chloa KING] md. Emma A. SHIRLEY [22; Maquoketa, IA; b: Iowa; f: Ralph SHIRLEY; m: Adaline STEELE] on 20 Nov 1880. Off: BARTHOLOMEW. Wit: Max BERGMANN, D.S. BENTON.

HEARNE, Frank J. [23; Hannible, MO; b: Cambridge, MD; f: William L. HEARNE; m: Maria E. ROSS] md. Lillie LEE [21; Omaha; b: Michigan; f: Warren F. LEE; m: Eliza M. NELSON] on 22 Dec 1869 at St. Barnabas (Episcopal) Church. Off: BETTS. Wit: Charles MEAD, J.J. MILLER of Quincey, IL.

HEARTZ, Wm. P. [27; Des Moines, IA; b: Ireland [New York crossed out]; f: Joseph HEARTZ; m: Mary WARD] and Susan BRUMM [26; Des Moines, IA; b: Germany; f: L. BRUMM] license issued 17 Jul 1877. No marriage record. Off: HANLON.

HEATER, Evan [23; IA; b: IA; f: Samuel HEATER; m: Jane R. ROBINSON] md. Eva BASOM [b: IA; f: Amos BASOM, m: Sarah L. McCURDY] on 6 Apr 1875. Off: PEABODY. Wit: Charles WILKIS, David HARPSTER.

HEATH, James B. [23; Omaha; b: Tennessee; f: Harrison HEATH; m: Matilda HEATH] md. Annie OVERTON [20; Omaha; b: Iowa; f: Samuel OVERTON; m: Annie KITE] on 28 Jun 1879. Off: BARTHOLOMEW. Wit: James LOVE, Wm. FRANCE.

HEATH, Oscar [33; Omaha] md. Hannah MAHANA [23; Omaha] on 26 Apr 1869. Off: KUHNS. Wit: Mrs. G. KNAPP, Mrs. A. SPAULDING, et al.

HEBBELER, Henry [30; Omaha; b: Germany; f: John H. HEBBELER; m: Mary HEBBELER] md. Anna HARTMANN [21; Omaha; b: Germany; f: Nicholas HARTMANN; m: Trena SANN] on 13 Mar 1874. Off: HILGENDORF. Wit: Dietrick HEBBELER; Fritz DELFS.

HEBBELER, Hiram [37; Omaha; b: Germany; f: Christopher HEBBELER; m: Catherena DONNEMAN] md. Sofa ROSKAMP [27; Omaha; b: Germany; f: John ROSKAMP; m: Maria DONNEMAN] on 24 Oct 1871. Off: GIBSON. Wit: Detrick HIBBELER; Henry HIBBELER.

HECHT, Eugene [24; Omaha; b: Germany; f: Franz HECHT; m: Rosina WALDER] md. Sophia Margaritta SAN [22; Omaha; b: Germany; f: Claus SAN; m: Christina HANSEN] on 5 Feb 1872. Off: TOWNSEND. Wit: Theodore BECK; Ben NARZ.

HECKER, Frank J. [21; Omaha] md. Annie M. WILLIAMSON [19; Omaha] on 8 Jan 1868. Off: HURLBUT.

HECKER, W.F.A. [55; Washington Co.; b: Germany; f: F.C. HECKER; m: Julia SCHULTZ] md. Kate McCORMICK [38; Omaha; b: Ireland; f: Andrew McCORMICK;

m: Bridget McCORMICK] on 30 Jun 1879 at the Cathedral. Off: McDERMOTT. Wit: Fred Ebener MILLARD, Mrs. James HENDERSON.

HEDERICK, Frederick [Council Bluffs] md. Mary Jane TOWNSHEND [Council Bluffs] on 1 Dec 1864 at DICKINSON's office. Off: DICKINSON. Wit: Alex. John BIRK, James HICKEY.

HEELAN, Edward [22; Omaha; b: Chicago, IL; f: Phillip HEELAN; m: Margaret COLEMAN] md. Alice DOWNES [19; Omaha; b: Dubuque, IA; f: Joseph DOWNES; m: Elizabeth SMITH] on 15 Feb 1879. Off: BARTHOLOMEW. Wit: W.M. KIRKLAN, Jennie LARSON, both of Omaha.

HEFFINGER, John [28; b: Ohio; f: J.C. HEFFINGER; m: Elizabeth MARTI] md. Christine JOHNSON [19; b: Sweden; f: Andrew JOHNSON; m: Mary HENSON] on 5 Sep 1878. Off: BARTH. Wit: J. O'REILLY, Max BERGMAN.

HEGG, Andrew [45; Bell Creek; b: Sweden; f: Hansen HEGG; m: Sissa TRUEDSDOTTER] md. Karin NEILSON [45; Omaha; b: Sweden; f: Nelson LARS; m: Gunhilda JANSDOTTER] on 18 Oct 1869. Off: LARSON. Wit: Petronella V. LAGERSTROM, Johanna C. LARSON.

HEIRES, M.J. [25; Iowa; b: Germany; f: Peter HEIRES; m: Mary NOEL] md. Katie KUHL [19; Iowa; b: Wisconsin; f: Valentine KUHL; m: Clara KRAEMER] on 18 May 1880, German Catholic Church. Off: GROENEBAUM. Wit: Katie DURR of Pottawattamie Co., IA, Lizzie KOSTERS.

HEISA, Frederick [31; Omaha] md. Wilhelmina WEDDENBERDER [30; Omaha] on 29 Apr 1869. Off: KUHNS. Wit: Henry EICKE, W.A. BLUME, et al.

HEITMAN, Jeremiah [27; Omaha] md. Anna KALIKOWA (KARLIKOWA) [KALIK, KARLIK] [Omaha] on 12 Nov 1868. Off: GROENBAUM. Wit: Sebald SCHLESSINGER, Barbara KALIKOWA [KALIK].

HELD, Herman C. [31; Grand Island; b: Germany; f: Herman HELD; m: Angela CANTZEN] md. Marie VON WUSNER [18; Sarpy Co.; b: Germany; f: William H.L. VON WUSNER; m: Mary] on 11 Oct 1874. Off: PEABODY. Wit: Henry A. KOENIG, Grand Island; Dr. Theodore BAUMER.

HELEBRANT, John [34; Sherman Co.; b: Bohemia; f: John HELEBRANT; m: Frantiskr LYTVER] md. Josephine SLADOVNIK [25; Omaha; b: Bohemia; f: John SLADOVNIK; m: Katharine KUNES] on 30 Nov 1880. Off: KOCARNIK. Wit: Adam HAJEK, John HORA.

HELLBORN, Louis [27; Omaha; b: Germany; f: Gottlieb HELLBORN; m: Augusta SCHAUERHAMMER] md. Mary SMITH [21; Omaha; b: Germany; f: Theodore

SMITH; m: Marie HAAS] on 14 Nov 1881. Off: BENEKE. Wit: George APPEL, George HAAS.

HELLWIG, Charles [27; Omaha; b: Germany; f: Charles HELLWIG; m: Doris GRIMM] md. Mary KOVANDA [19; Omaha; b: Bohemia. f: Joseph KOVANDA; m: Anna SPIMVATSCKY] on 1 Oct 1881. Off: BENEKE. Wit: A.N. KEAR, Henry RITTER.

HELMES, William [40; St. Louis, MO] md. Mrs. Henriette DEYNIKE [30; Omaha] on 22 Dec 1868. Off: Certificate not signed, probably HYDE. Wit: George ARMSTRONG, W.J. HAUN.

HELMS, Charles [27; Omaha; colored; b: North Carolina; f: John HELMS] md. Ellen BATES [19; Omaha; colored; b: New York; f: John BATES] on 23 Aug 1870. Off: JOHNSON. Wit: Robert STORY; Emma THURMAN.

HEMENWAY, Charles E. [25; Platte Valley Pct.; b: Illinois; f: Charles HEMENWAY; m: Wealthy Lucy FAY] md. Elizabeth A. GRAHAM [26; Platte Valley Pct.; b: England; f: Samuel GRAHAM] on 4 March 1873 at Valley Station. Off: DeLaMATYR. Wit: E.J. TORREY, Valley; Isabella A. TORREY, Valley.

HEMPEL, Christian A. [30; Omaha; b: Denmark; f: Christian A. HEMPEL; m: Louisa MAAR] md. Mary JOCUMSEN [19; Omaha; b: Denmark; f: Lars JOCUMSEN] on 16 Oct 1869. Off: KUHNS. Wit: Neils OLSEN, Peter BOYER.

HENDERSON, James N. [33; Douglas Co.; b: NY; f: Wm. HENDERSON; m: Mary MALONY] md. Annie ROLLS [29; Douglas Co.; b: Canada; f: Joseph ROLLS; m: Elizabeth BURNS] on 29 Jul 1876 at the Roman Catholic Cathedral. Off: SMYTH. Wit: Francis GERRATTY, Sarah GERRATTY.

HENDERSON, John E. [24; Callaway, MO] md. K.A. BOURRET (BOURRETT) [16; Omaha] on 20 Jan 1868. Off: KERMOTT. Wit: Mr. and Mrs. J. BOURRET (BOURRETT). Age consent given by the parents of the bride.

HENDERSON, T. Marsh [31; Omaha; b: New York; f: Cornelius HENDERSON; m: Mary MARSH] md. Cassie Ray LARKIN [18; Omaha; b: Iowa; f: William LARKIN; m: Adelia B. McMILLEN] on 22 Dec 1880. Off: BANGHER. Wit: W.E. McMILLEN, Mrs. A.E. RANDALL.

HENDRICK (HENDRICKS), Robert [27; Omaha] md. Mrs. Mary MITCHELL [28; Omaha] on 24 Mar 1869. Off: KUHNS. Wit: William JONES, Andrew HENDRICK (HENDRICKS).

HENDRICKS, Andrew [26; Omaha; colored; b: Alabama; f: James HENDRICKS] md. Virginia FOSTER [22; Omaha; colored; b: North Carolina] on 15 May 1870 at the AME Church. Off: HUBBARD. Wit: W.W. PORTER; Pompey ALLEN.

HENDRICKSON, George D. [21; U.S. Army; b: Pennsylvania; f: Enoch HENDRICKSON; m: Julia A. CLUNGER] md. May J. POWELL [18; Florence; b: Missouri] on 28 Nov 1870 at Florence. Off: STEVENSON. Wit: Z. COLE, Florence; Charles SHROPSHIRE, Florence.

HENDRICKSON, Saul [21; Omaha; b: Illinois; f: John HENDRICKSON; m: Lucinda MOORE] md. Rose BELVILLE [19; Omaha; b: Ohio; f: Samuel BELVILLE: m: Jane HELMS] on 1 Apr 1874. Off: PEABODY. Wit: Mrs. Nancy WHALEY; Joseph WHALEY.

HENELY, Lawrence [22; Omaha; b: London, Eng.; f: John HENLEY; m: Minnefred DOLAN] md. Anastatia CONWAY [16; Omaha; b: New Orleans, LA; f: Robert CONWAY; m: Annie O'NEILL] on 25 Jul 1869. Off: CURTIS. Wit: Hugh FOY, Margaret CONWAY.

HENNESSEY, James [28; Omaha; b: Texas; f: James HENNESSEY; m: Elizabeth ROBISON] md. Caire WILLEFORD [18; Omaha; b: Iowa; f: J.H. WILLEFORD; m: Mary HUDSON] on 13 Jan 1880. Off: MAXFIELD. Wit: J.H. WILLEFORD, Mary WILLEFORD.

HENNESSY, William P. [30; Omaha; b: Ireland; f: William HENNESSY; m: Mary MULVILLE] md. Rose McARDLE [24; Omaha; b: Ireland; f: ---- McARDLE] on 9 Sep 1872 at the Catholic Church of Omaha. Off: O'GORMAN. Wit: John L. REIDY; Lara CASSIDY.

HENNING, Arthur Reinhard [23; b: Germany; f: Friedrich Gotthelf HENNING; m: Pauline SCHURIG] md. Anna SCLAPKOHL [25; b: Germany f: Jorgen SCLAPKOHL; m: Dorothea WIESE] on 7 Sep 1878. Off: BENEKE. Wit: Werner BOEHL, Johann Carl Heinrich RAVEN.

HENNINGS, Henry [46; Omaha; b: Germany; f: Claus HENNINGS; m: Rebecca LUEBECK] md. Mrs. Catharine SOLTERBECK [28; Douglas Co.; b: Germany; f: Asmus GEHL; m: Anna TIEDJE] on 16 Apr 1880. Off: BENEKE. Wit: Julius TREITSCHKE, Asmus GEHL.

HENNINGSEN, Henning [24; Omaha; b: Germany; f: Peter HENNINGSEN; m: Annie M. PAULSEN] md. Rose Clara SCHMIT [18; Omaha; b: Iowa; f: Jacob SCHMIT; m: Annie

YONGA] on 11 Aug 1873. Off: TOWNSEND. Wit: Jerome F.L.D. HERTZMANN; Herbert T. LEAVITT.

HENRICKSEN, Knud [35; Omaha; b: Denmark; f: Henrick CHRISTIANSEN; m: Barbara NICKELSEN] md. Ellen ESKELSON [27; Omaha; b: Denmark; f: Eskel ESKELSON; m: Mila NILSEN] on 9 Feb 1872. Off: ERDALL. Wit: P.C.F. MUNK; Mrs. Karen MUNK.

HENRICKSON, Peter [24; Omaha; b: Denmark; f: Henrick NEILSON; m: Annie M. MATTSON] md. Christina JANSEN [22; Omaha; b: Denmark; f: Jens MATTSON; m: Annie M.] on 18 Nov 1872. Off: ESTABROOK. Wit: Mr. and Mrs. Louis HENRICKSON.

HENRY, James [25; Omaha; b: Pennsylvania; f: Christopher HENRY; m: Mary CAMPBELL] md. Annie AYERS [20; Leavenworth, KS; b: Missouri; f: John AYERS; m: Elizabeth CHAPMAN] on 6 Dec 1870. Off: GIBSON. Wit: John MANCHESTER; J.J. NEELY.

HENRY, John S. [22] and Elizabeth HOLLERT [19] license issued on 29 Sep 1859. No marriage record. Off: BRIGGS.

HENRY, John [32; Omaha; b: Canada West; f: John HENRY; m: Martha McMASTER] md. Alice BUCHANAN [18 (on 30 June 1872); Omaha; b: Indiana; f: Alexander BUCHANAN; m: ---- JOHNSON] on 16 Jun 1873. Off: WRIGHT. Wit: Augustus H. DONECKER; Sarah DONECKER.

HENSEN, Julius [24; Omaha; b: Denmark; f: H.C. HENSEN; m: Dorothea C. ZACHARIASEN] md. Bertha OLSEN [21; Omaha; b: Denmark; f: Ola JENSEN; m: Juli(e)tte MADSEN] on 30 Jul 1870. Off: UHNS. Wit: A. HANSEN; John H.A. RATH.

HENSMAN, James [24; Omaha] md. Ellen FOX [23; Omaha] on 25 Jul 1866. Off: SLAUGHTER.

HERBST, William [24; Douglas Co.; b: Germany; f: D.F. HERBST; m: Lucia KAY] md. Sophia A.W. LAPTIN [21; Douglas Co.; b: Germany; f: J.P. LAPTIN; m: D.M. ROHRBERG] on 24 May 1878. Off: BARTHOLOMEW. Wit: Henry SIERT, F.P. HANLON.

HERDLICKE [HRDLICKA], Jacob [31; Omaha; b: Bohemia; f: Ferdinand HERDLICKE [HRDLICKA]; m: Annie UNCAJTCH] and Catherina DUS [25; Omaha; b: Bohemia; f: Witelea DUS; m: Mary GROFECK] license issued on 31 Jan 1876. No marriage record. Off: BOBAL. Wit: George LUDWIG, Theresa CIPERA.

HERMAN, Richard [Omaha] md. Catherine KELLY [Omaha] on 9 Aug 1864 at the Catholic Church of Omaha. Off: O'GORMAN. Wit: Honora KELLY, John KELLY.

HERMAN, William [21; Omaha] md. Mary EVERSON [21; Omaha] on 1 Sep 1860. Off: ARMSTRONG. Wit: Magnus WALLENBERG, Elisa BOEHME (BACHME?).

HERMEL, Edward [Allen's Grove, NE Territory] md. Margaret THOMAS [Omaha] on 17 Apr 1864 at Mrs. THOMAS' residence. Off: DICKINSON. Wit: Wm. E. MERRILL, Mr. and Mrs. THOMAS, et al.

HERRING, Wilson [45; Omaha; colored; b: Tennessee; f: Charles HERRING; m: Emily OWENS] md. Mrs. Alvira COLE [30; Omaha; colored; b: Virginia; f: Watt BALINGER; m: ---- WADE] on 9 Aug 1874. Off: HOPKINS. Wit: Jeremiah REED; Caroline GIRRLY; Cyrus Dix BELL.

HERRLE, Frederick [28; Omaha; b: Germany; f: Johann HERRLE; m: Caroline ROLAND] md. Mathilda BARTIG [25; Omaha; b: Germany; f: August BARTIG; m: Juliane ZELLMER] on 29 Feb 1880. Off: BENEKE. Wit: Henry DREFHOLT, Augusta BOEHME.

HERSMOND, Louis [27; Omaha; b: New York; f: Christian HERSMOND; m: Abeloni DACRIEF] and Johanna SOULDER [25; Omaha; b: Germany] license issued on 14 May 1870. Off: GIBSON.

HERTEN, Frank [25; Omaha; b: Germany; f: Michael HERTEN; m: Margaret MYER] md. Eliza FRANZ [20; Omaha; b: Germany; f: Ferdinand FRANZ; m: Dora ENK] on 13 Feb 1875. Off: PEABODY. Wit: Wm. HESTADT, Wm. KNELL.

HERUM, John [22; Omaha; b: Germany; f: Hans J. HERUM; m: Catherina M. HANSEN] md. Carrie C. HANSEN [23; Omaha; b: Denmark; f: Nels HANSEN; m: Dora BERTHESON] 26 Apr 1881 at GYDESEN's residence. Off: GYDESEN. Wit: Lars NIELSEN, Douglas Co., Johannes THOMSEN, Douglas Co.

HERZER, Franz [30; Lancaster Co.; b: Germany; f: Franz HERZER; m: Catherine S. KESSLER] md. Sophia L. MANKE [26; Omaha; b: Germany; f: Peter H. MANKE; m: Dena SASSE] on 17 Oct 1871 at groom's residence. Off: FAUST. Wit: Chas. BRUNNER; Fridericke FAUST.

HERZOG, George [48; Douglas Co.] md. Hedwig LASKE [LISKE] [15; Douglas Co.] on 17 Oct 1868. Off: KUHNS. Wit: Mr and Mrs. LASKI, Mr. and Mrs. Charles BIENDORF, et al. Age consent given by Julie and A.M. SCHALLER, guardians of the bride.

HESS, George A. [25; Omaha; b: Germany; f: Albert HESS; m: Elizabeth MUSSLER] md. Mrs. Elizabeth REEVES [33; Douglas Co.; b: Iowa] on 17 May 1874. Off: KUHNS. Wit: Fredrick HERZKE; Mrs. P. REEVES, Elkhorn.

HETRICK, Phillip M. [24; Washington Co.; b: PA; f: Adam HETRICK; m: Maria J. HETRICK] md. Evanna MOCK [23; Omaha; b: PA; f: John W. MOCK; m: Susan BROWN] on 1 Nov 1875 at Mrs. MOCK's residence. Off: TIBBLES. Wit: N.J. SMITH; Wm. BROWN.

HEWITT, W.I. [27; Atchison, KS; b: Ohio; f: Charles HEWITT; m: Susan KEYNER] md. Mrs. Minnie REYNOLDS [33; Topeka; KS; b: Pennsylvania; f: P.H. REYNOLDS; m: Minerva E. PHILLIPS] on 12 Feb 1880. Off: BARTHOLOMEW. Wit: David VAN ELTEN, W.J. CONNELL.

HGORD, Casper [24; Omaha; b: Sweden; f: Garran PETERSON; m: Christene JOHNSON] md. Emily GROND [34; Omaha; b: Sweden; f: Andrew GROND; m: Johane HERAMAN] on 13 Dec 1873. Off: SHERRILL. Wit: Mrs. C.P. STARRS; Ola MARTERSON.

HIBBELER, Dietrich [40; Omaha; b: Germany; f: Christof HIBBELER; m: Catharina DANNEMANN] md. Mary BOESE [23; Omaha; b: Germany; f: Johann BOESE; m: Catharina OLDEGS] on 10 Mar 1881. Off: SMITH. Wit: Max BERGMAN, S.N. MEALIO.

HIBBELER, Ludwig [29; Omaha; b: Germany; f: Christoffer HIBBELER; m: Catharina DENNEMANN] md. Margaretha GOSCH [25; Omaha; f: Peter GOSCH; m: Lotte MEEMES] on 12 Mar 1875. Off: PEABODY. Wit: Dedreich HIBBELER, Christ DANIEL.

HICKER, Morton [22; Omaha; b: Germany; f: Anders HICKER; m: Balana SHATZ] md. Henrietta SHULTZ [18; Omaha; b: Germany; f: Hans SHULTZ; m: Mary ENTRENSEN] on 24 Jun 1870. Off: GIBSON. Wit: Miss B. KNOTT; Marint KLOOS.

HICKEY, James [35; Omaha; father from Parish Laughlinbridge, Co. Carlow, Irel.] md. Bridget MORAN [25; Omaha; father from Parish Fairhill, Co. Galway, Irel.] on 6 Mar 1859 at the BVM Church. Off: CANNON. Wit: James McARDLE, Ellen MAHER.

HICKEY, John [36; Omaha] md. Margaraet KELLEY [35; Omaha] on 17 Jan 1867 at St. Philomenas Church. Off: CURTIS.

HICKMAN, Erastus M. [25; Jasper Co., IA] md. Elizabeth THOMAS [23; Douglas Co.] on 1 Jan 1866 at the parsonage. Off: KUHNS. Wit: Mr. and Mrs. R.P. BREWSTER, Mrs. KUHNS, Mrs. ROEDER, et al.

HICKS, Benjamin C. [36; Madison Co.; b: Hampton, ME; f: Eben HICKS; m: Eleanor BAKER] md. Amelia A. HUNT [18; Omaha; b: Iowa; f: George HUNT; m: Naomi MESNER] on 24 Dec 1871. Off: THURSTON. Wit: Thomas POMROY; James H. DENNIS.

HICKSTEIN, Fred [28; Omaha; b: Germany; f: Christ HICKSTEIN; m: Henrietta WOHLFEIL] md. Mary RONNER [21; Omaha; b: Germany; f: John RONNER; m: Catharine STEVENS] on 7 Sept 1874. Off: HALD. Wit: William KALBE; Roman OLZERSKY.

HIER, Gotlieb [31; Omaha; b: Germany; f: Gotlieb HIER; m: Catharine SCHLEIFREDT] md. Amelia M. KLAUSCH [20; Omaha; b: Germany; f: Samuel KLAUSCH; m: Catharine YUKNESS] on 12 Nov 1877. Off: SEDGWICK. Wit: C.C. SPERRY, Jerry LINAHAN.

HIGBY, Ira P. [24; Omaha; b: New York; f: John C. HIGBY; m: Francis A. PADDOCK] md. Caroline J. LANDON [21; Omaha; b: Columbus, OH; f: Calvin LANDON; m: Amanda VOGAL] on 15 Jul 1872. Off: TOWNSEND. Wit: Fred M. JEROME; John STEWART.

HIGGINS, John G. [27; Council Bluffs; b: LaSalle Co., IL] md. Annie O'CONNOR [20; Lasalle Co., IL; b: LaSalle Co., IL] on 25 Oct 1869 at the German Catholic Church. Off: GROENEBAUM. Wit: Jacob KRULT.

HIGGINS, John [36] md. Thompsien (sic) MURPHY [36; Omaha] on 6 Jun 1866. Off: CURTIS.

HIGGINSON, A.G. [22; b: Chicago, IL; f: George HIGGINSON; m: Anna TYNG] md. Celma BALCOMBE [21; b: Minnesota; f: Lt. A.D. BALCOMBE; m: Anna FOX] on 30 Oct 1878. Off: MILLSPAUGH. Wit: Lt. A.D. BALCOMBE, Lewis REED.

HILBERT, Alois [29; b: Germany; f: Benedict HILBERT; m: Marie POHL] md. Mary KUBICKY [18; b: Bohemia (Austria); f: Frank KUBICKY; m: Fanny KUBICKY] on 30 Nov 1878. Off: BENEKE. Wit: Henry RISSER, Andreas HILBERT.

HILDEBRAND, Guy H. [26; Louisville; b: Virginia; f: Thomas HILDEBRAND; m: Jane STEVENS] md. Gracie M. GLOVER [24; Plattsford, NE; b: Iowa; f: John B. GLOVER; m: Eliza CHILD] on 2 Oct 1878. Off: SHERRILL. Wit: Michael DONOVAN, H.T. WOODS.

HILDRETH, H.B. [24; Omaha; b: Wisconsin; f: H.H. HILDRETH; m: M.E. MURDOCK] md. Mrs. Anna L. WILDE [26; Omaha; b: Wisconsin; f: Edward QUINN; m: C.E. DAVIDSON] on 30 Apr 1877. Off: FISHER. Wit: A.D. MORRIS, Mrs. E.M. FISHER.

HILER, Peter [26; Douglas Co.; b: New Jersey; f: Stephen HILER; m: Catharine

WINTERS] md. Lucy TWADDELL [25; Douglas Co.; b: New York; f: Robert TWADDELL; m: Jane MARTIN] on 5 Mar 1874 at Irvington. Off: FITCH. Wit: Phebe H.P. KNIGHT, Irvington; W.F. STODDARD, Irvington.

HILGENKAMP, Henry William [Washington Co.] md. Caroline WILKENING [Washington Co.] on 19 Jan 1864 at the residence of the bride's father. Off: MUHLENBROCK. Wit: Hannah WILKENING, Rachael HILGENKAMP.

HILL, Humphrey R. [55; Omaha; colored; b: Ohio; f: Dennis R. HILL; m: Mary Ann DAY] md. Mrs. Indiana RUSSELL [55; Omaha; colored; b: Erie, PA; f: Robert McCONNELL; m: Amy SCIOIP] on 29 Jun 1873. Off: McCAGUE. Wit: Allen ROSS; Richard JOHNSON.

HILL, Robert [22; Douglas Co.; b: Iowa; f: Joseph HILL; m: Elizabeth ROBERTS] md. Iva C. PATE [16; Omaha; b: Iowa; f: L. PATE; m: Polly SAVAGE] on 13 Feb 1879. Off: WRIGHT. Wit: W.C. SAVAGE of Woodbine, IA, Nora WINCHELL of Omaha. Age consent given by Polly PATE, mother of the bride.

HILLS, R.C. [28; Missouri Valley, IA; b: New York; f: James HILLS; m: Harriet TAPPENDEN] md. Nellie E. ROCKWELL [19; Missouri Valley, IA; b: New York; f: A.H. ROCKWELL; m: Mary A. JENCKS] on 1 Oct 1879. Off: HARSHA. Wit: B.E. ROBINSON of Missouri Valley, IA, P.A. MICKEL.

HILPERT, Andrew [23; Omaha; b: Germany; f: Benedict HILPERT; m: Maria EBNER] md. Emilie SERBOUSOCK [22; Omaha; b: Bohemia; f: John SERBOUSOCK; m: Katharina BARTOSCH] on 9 Apr 1881. Off: BENEKE. Wit: August GRIEB, Otille SERBOUSOCK.

HILTNER, Martin L. [28; Omaha; b: Montgomery Co., PA; f: George HILTNER; m: Mary Ann KULP] md. Martha Ann JUKES [22; Omaha; b: Birmingham, Eng.; f: John JUKES] on 16 or 13 Jun 1869. Off: KERMOTT. Wit: Mrs. Amanda R. KERMOTT, Frank R. KERMOTT.

HINDLEY, Edwin P. [27; Washington Co.] md. Fanny FISK [22; Cincinnati, OH] on 3 Jun 1867 at Farnham House. Off: KUHNS. Wit: Mr. and Mrs. John C. HIGBY, et al.

HINEK [HYNEK], Anton [22; Omaha; b: Bohemia; f: Frank HINEK [HYNEK]; m: Anna SIMON] md. Barbara ROUBAL [21; Omaha; b: Bohemia; f: Bartholomew ROUBAL; m: Veronika NEMECEK] on 23 Dec 1880. Off: KLIMA. Wit: Peter MACA, Joseph SUSTERIC.

HINES, Daniel B. [29; Omaha; b: Ohio; f: Porter HINES; m: Margaret VAN NEST] md. Emma BIRCH [18; Omaha; b: Missouri; f: Michael BIRCH; m: Mary COMBS] on 26 Oct 1877. Off: LIPE. Wit: William JOBSON, Fanny KNAPP.

HINES, John [21; Sarpy Co.; b: Massachusetts; f: Thomas HINES; m: Mary BEATTY] md. Cornelia A. SUTLEY [20; Sarpy Co.; b: Illinois; f: Wilson SUTLEY; m: Emily J. HAMMOND] on 6 May 1872. Off: TOWNSEND. Wit: Almedia SUTLEY, Sarpy Co.; William McCARTY, Sarpy Co.

HINES, John [25; Omaha Barracks; b: Ireland; f: Wm. HINES; m: Mary LUREY] md. Nellie JONES [24; Omaha; b: England; f: Wm. JONES; m: unknown] on 21 Jun 1880. Off: STENBERG. Wit: J. ALEXANDER, Mrs. A.M. BERNSTEIN.

HINRICHS, John [27; Omaha; b: Germany; f: John HINRICHS; m: Catharina KARSTENS] md. Augusta FECHNER [25; Omaha; b: Germany; f: Carl FECHNER; m: Juliana SEILER] on 8 Oct 1881. Off: BENEKE. Wit: Henry HOESSLY, John A. THOELECKE.

HINS, Charles [25; Douglas Co.; b: Germany; f: Max HINS; m: Margaret EHLERS] md. Margaret ARMBRUST [18; Douglas Co.; b: Germany; f: John ARMBRUST; m: Aber WOLFF] on 25 Feb 1876. Off: HILGENDORF. Wit: Christ LESSMANN, Douglas Co., Emma LESSMANN, Douglas Co.

HINTZ, Christian [37; Washington Co.; b: Germany; f: Peter HINTZ; m: Fredericka MOHEN] md. Magdalena MOHR [19; Washington Co.; b: Germany; f: Claus MOHR; m: Katrina BOEGE] on 28 Feb 1878. Off: BENEKE. Wit: Frederick BURMEISTER of Calhoun, Washington Co., NE, Peter HINTZ.

HINTZ, Robert C. [23; Omaha; b: MO; f: William HINTZ; m: Alvina KLEIN] md. Lizzie BOEHM [21; Omaha; b: Germany; f: E.A. BOEHM; m: Minna BLUTH] on 28 Jul 1881. Off: FRESE. Wit: E.A. BOEHM, Minnie BOEHM.

HINZ, Peter [30; Omaha; b: Germany; f: Peter HINZ; m: Ida HOPP] md. Eliza QUAACK [28; Omaha; b: Germany; f: Fritz QUAACK; m: Margaret OELKE] on 28 Jan 1874. Off: PEABODY. Wit: Fred BEND; Mrs. Wm. L. PEABODY.

HIRSCH, George [43; Omaha] md. Catharine BOGATSY [25; Omaha] on 15 May 1867 at the Court House. Off:

HASCALL. Wit: Catharine MOSER, F. ELSEISSER.

HIRT, Adolph [25; Omaha; b: Switzerland; f: Gottfried HIRT; m: Henriette KREBS] md. Lena TSCHANTRA [20; Omaha; b: Switzerland or Sweden; f: Joact TSCHANTRA; m: Lena PAGAN] on 21 Jun 1880. Off: WRIGHT. Wit: Herman MEYER; Chas. SCHLAPLY.

HIRT, Michael [27; Omaha] md. Bridget KIRK [25; Omaha] on 23 Jul 1868. Off: GROENBAUM. Wit: Patrick FIELDING, Sarah CONSTINE.

HITCHCOCK, Charles [24; Omaha] md. Mariah L. WILLIAMS [27; Omaha] on 2 Dec 1866. Off: SLAUGHTER. Wit: Mr. BLACK, T.B. LEMON, Jr.

HITCHCOCK, D.W. [Omaha] md. Lizzie BILLINGS [Omaha] on 9 Dec 1863 at Mr. LEARNED's residence. Both of legal age. Off: KUHNS. Wit: Mr. and Mrs. LEARNED, Mrs. COX, et al.

HITCHCOCK, Jesse [21; Council Bluffs] md. Amanda SAPP [15; Council Bluffs] on 29 Oct 1860 at ARMSTRONG's office. Off: ARMSTRONG. Age witnesses: Martha McCARTHY, Henry MILES. "i give my daughter Manda SAP with a willan hand, mother Retchel SAP" (sic).

HITCHCOCK, P.W. [27; Omaha] md. Miss Annie M. MONELL [20; Omaha] on 27 Dec 1858. Off: WATSON. [Trinity Episcopal Church records say: Phineas W. HITCHCOCK md. Ann Mahlon VAN NOSTAND on 3 Dec 1858.]

HITCHCOCK, T.S. [46; Omaha; b: Massachusetts; f: Levi HITCHCOCK; m: Phoebe BAKER] md. Eliza A. KEAR [33; New York City; b: New York; f: Daniel KEAR; m: Phoebe HAMLIN] on 1 Dec 1880. Off: HARSHA. Wit: Geo. P. BEMIS, Mrs. Wm. J. HARSHA.

HITT, William P. [3rd Twp., Licking Co., OH] md. Lute E. MORGAN [3rd Twp., Licking Co., OH] on 20 May 1864 at the Lutheran parsonage. Off: KUHNS. Wit: Marilla ISHAM, Mrs. H.W. KUHNS.

HITZ, Paul [28; Des Moines, IA; b: OH; f: Fred HITZ; m: Fannie WITMER] md. Mary BARRY [25; Jackson Co., NE; b: Ireland; f: Lawrence BARRY; m: Agnes RYAN] on 25 Nov 1881. Off: STEWART. Wit: Wm. McGRIFF, Atlantic, IA, Mary G. STEWART.

HOAGLAND, George A. [Omaha] md. Iantha C. WYMAN [Omaha] on the evening of 22 May 1864 at the 1st Methodist Episcopal Church. Off: LEMON. Wit: Samuel BURNS, Tesse WYMAN, Theodore HOAGLAND, Maggie INGALS (INGALLS), and the "congregation therein assembled for divine worhsip."

HOBBIE, Henry C. [31; Omaha; b: New York; f: Uriah HOBBIE; m: Anna S. WILCOX] md. Catharine E. STEVENS [26;

Mt. Vernon, NH; b: New York City; f: William STEVENS; m: Louise DYE] on 27 Oct 1880. Off: GATES. Wit: Charles F. WILKENS, George HOBBIE.

HOBBS, Lorenzo [40; Omaha] md. Adeline DOUGLAS [23; Omaha] on 13 Apr 1868 at Trinity Church. Off: VAN ANTWERP. Wit: O.P. INGALLS and wife, the congregation.

HOBLIT, Clark L. [47; Atlantic, IA; b: OH; f: F.B. HOBLIT; m: Barbara RICCKLE] md. Mrs. Harriet V. CORRIE [23; Atlantic, IA; b: East TN; f: James W. ASH; m: E. KATES] on 9 Sep 1875. Off: PEABODY. Wit: F.P. HANLON, Mr. SIMERAL.

HOCKMAN, Samuel [30; Colorado Territory] md. Jane E. JARDINE [30; Audubon Co., IA] on 12 Mar 1866. Off: MILLER. Wit: Mr. and Mrs. A.R. HOEL, et al.

HOCTOR, Michael [25; Omaha; b: Ireland; f: Michael HOCTOR; m: Bridget CASHEN] md. Bridget GRACE [20; Omaha; b: Ireland] on 17 Oct 1869. Off: CURTIS. Wit: Thomas CAEN, Mary FITZPATRICK.

HODDER, Charles [20; Omaha; b: New Foundland; f: Richard HODDER; m: Jemina BUTLER] md. Edith PAUL [22; Omaha; b: New Foundland; f: John PAUL; m: Ann KIRBY] on 14 Jul 1881. Off: BEANS. Wit: Mrs. W.K. BEANS, Amelia BAER. Age consent given by parents of the groom.

HODGES, Earl A. [22; Mills Co., IA] md. Minnie L. STROUD [20; Mills Co., IA] on 16 Dec 1868. Off: HYDE. Wit: T. TALLON, H.T. GREEN.

HODGKINS, Sidney W. [40; Douglas Co.; b: NY; f: James HODGKINS; m: Julia JOHNSON] md. Laura A. TAYLOR [39; Douglas Co.; b: NY; f: John ALLEN; m: Mary] on 17 Apr 1876. Off: ANDERSON. Wit: W.F. HAWES, 18th & Izard, Mrs. Annie OLESON.

HOEFER, Jacob [31; Omaha] md. Johannah STARK [20; Omaha] on 22 Jan 1867 at the parsonage. Off: VAN ANTWERP. Wit: Chas. PPRESSER, Nellie KEITH, Mrs. VAN ANTWERP.

HOEY, John M. [Omaha] md. Anna M. CORRIGAN [Omaha] on 26 Nov 1864 at the Roman Catholic Church of Omaha. Off: O'GORMAN. Wit: James CALLAGHAN, Lissie HENLEY.

HOFELDT, Peter [24; Douglas Co.; b: Germany; f: Claus HOFELDT; m: Anna WOMELSTROF] md. Mary BACKHUUS [19; Douglas Co.; b: Germany; f: Claus BACKHUUS; m: Christina SIEL] on 16 Feb 1875. Off: PEABODY. Wit: Peter SECH; Christiana BACKHUUS.

HOFFMAN, Andrew [36; Omaha; b: Germany; f: George HOFFMAN ; m: Mary SMITH] md. Mary DOTTEREVEICH [53; Omaha; b: Germany; f: Valentine DOTTEREVEICH; m: Christiana ----] on 30 Oct 1877, German Catholic Church. Off: GROENEBAUM. Wit: Joseph KOESTERS, Maggie KARBACH.

HOFFMAN, George [21; Omaha; b: Bohemia; f: Conrad HOFFMAN; m: Margaret DUFEK] md. Anna CIPERA [19; Saunders Co.; b: Bohemia; f: George CIPERA; m: Josephine TACHOVA] on 22 Jun 1872. Off: TOWNSEND. Wit: Joseph DWORK [DWORAK]; Wenzel DUFEK.

HOFFMAN, Max [27; Omaha; b; Germany; f: Carl HOFFMAN; m: Wilhelmina SALZWEDEL] md. Caroline BUNS [19; Omaha; b: Germany; f: Kari BUNS; m: Louise SIEVERS] on 12 Aug 1877. Off: FALK. Wit: Edward MAURER, Louise RABOLD. Also named: Karl MERKEL, Sister Ida FRANZEN.

HOFFMANN, John [29; b: Germany; f: Christian HOFFMANN; m: Louise HOFFMANN] md. Annie LEONARD [23; b: Ireland; f: John LEONARD; m: Annie McDONOUGH] on 23 Jul 1878. Off: COLANERI. Wit: James MAYERS, Bridget PRICE. Written in pencil on the back "woman lives on Webster near 21st and belongs to Cathedral Parish."

HOFFMEIER, Charles [26; Cheyenne Agency; b: Germany; f: Charles HOFFMEIER; m: Hannah KERMAR] md. Mary KELLY [20; Leavenworth, KS; b: KS; f: John KELLY; m: Bridget WELSH] on 21 Sep 1875 at Bishop's house on 9th Street. Off: BYRNE. Wit: Mrs. A. BARRBER, Sarah LOFTUS.

HOFFMEISTER, Emil [22; b: Germany; f: H. HOFFMEISTER, m: Anna RICHELMANN] md. Mary WUNSEH [18; b: Germany; f: Rurckhard WUNSEH] on 10 Aug 1878. Off: STRASEN.

HOFICK [HOUFEK], Frank [29; Omaha; b: Bohemia; f: Frederick HOFICK [HOUFEK]; m: Magdalene CEMPAL] md. Frances TUDOR [25; Omaha; b: Bohemia; f: James TUDOR; m: Mary MARCH [MARES]] on 24 Sep 1872. Off: TOWNSEND. Wit: Andrew ROSEWATER; Joseph WALTER.

HOFMANN, Adam [39; Council Bluffs; b: Germany; f: Peter HOFMANN; m: Elizabeth TROUTWINE] md. Mrs. Emily ARMSLAN [23; Council Bluffs; b: Switzerland; m: Barbara BAUGHMAN or Barbara

STRICKLEN] on 27 May 1871. Off: LYTLE. Wit: John RICH----; Barbara RAPP.

HOFMANN, Simon [24; Omaha; b: Germany; f: Michael HOFMANN; m: Catharine HEINIKEL] md. Margaretta GERHARD [21; New York City, NY; b: Germany; f: John GERHARD; m: Catharina AHMEND] on 25 Mar 1872. Off: KELLEHER. Wit: Theodore DECKER; Timothea DECKER.

HOGAN, Cornelius [29; Omaha; b: Ireland; f: James HOGAN; m: Mary TWOMEY] md. Mrs. Emily LOWE [31; Omaha; b: England; f: George EVANS; m: Elizabeth FAULKNER] on 29 April 1872. Off: TOWNSEND. Wit: George W. DOANE; Charles P. BIRKETT.

HOGAN, Daniel [30; Omaha; b: Ireland; f: John HOGAN; m: Ellen CARMEL] md. Catherine FERRY [27; Omaha; b: Ireland; f: Matthew FERRY; m: Mary Ann DONELLY] on 9 Oct 1870. Off: O'GORMAN. Wit: Hugh McCAFFREY; Mary GELASPIE.

HOGAN, Daniel [34; Valley Station; b: Ireland; f: Thomas HOGAN; m: Ellen FOGARTY] md. Bridget CALVERT [20; Omaha; b: Ireland; f: Michael CALVERT; m: Ellen WOLF] on 26 Feb 1870. Off: CURTIS. Wit: John GARVEY; Lizzie THORSEN.

HOGAN, Daniel [34; Valley Station; b: Ireland; f: Thomas HOGAN; m: Ellen FOGERTY] and Kate MORISSEY [21; Elkhorn Station; b: Ireland; (see: Thomas O'BRIEN)] license issued on 18 Feb 1870. Off: GIBSON.

HOGAN, Martin [32; Douglas Co.] and Eliza WADE [26; Douglas Co.] license issued on 20 Oct 1868. No marriage record. Off: STUCK.

HOHMANN, S.B. [33; Lincoln, NE; b: Pennsylvania; f: F.W. HOHMANN; m: Cornelia BROWN] md. Helen M.K. CANDEE [24; California; b: Illinois; f: Wm. B. CANDEE; m: Mary LA TARUUETTEE] on 2 Jul 1878. Off: MILLSPAUGH. Wit: Jay NORTHROP, Geo. M. MYERS.

HOKE, Andrew [66; Omaha; b: Germany; f: Mathias HOKE; m: Mary Eve THIERI] md. Mrs. Catharine BAKER [34; Omaha; b: Illinois; f: William SANFORT; m: Maria STARK] on 2 Sep 1880, German Catholic Church. Off: GROENEBAUM. Wit: Morice NEUMANN, Lazare BROWN.

HOLDERNESS, Charles A. [25; Omaha] md. Emma E. LETNER [18; Omaha] on 17 Jan 1867. Off: SLAUGHTER.

HOLDREGE, George W. [31; Lincoln; b: New York City; f: Henry HOLDREGE; m: Mary R. GRINNELL] md. Francis R. KIMBALL [21; Omaha; b: Maine; f: Thomas L. KIMBALL; m: Mary P. ROGERS] on 19 Apr 1878. Off: COPELAND. Wit: T.L. KIMBALL, Mrs. H.E. PALMER of Plattsmouth.

HOLGIN, Vernavel [30; Omaha] md. Rebeckey WARNISS [27; Omaha] on 19 Feb 1869. Off: HYDE. Wit: W.C. KELLOGG, C.D. HYDE.

HOLLAND, J.E. [21; Douglas Co.] md. Mary D. GRACE [18; Douglas Co.] on 7 Dec 1868. Off: CURTIS. Wit: Thomas HOLLAND, Margaret CARROL.

HOLLAND, John [34; Omaha; b: Ireland; f: Michael HOLLAND; m: Johanna CARMODY] md. Bridget MARMION [25; Omaha; b: Ireland; f: Hugh MARMION; m: Mary CLARK] on 26 Apr 1880, St. Philomena Church. Off: KELLY. Wit: Frank P. HANLON, Mary MANNERS.

HOLLAND, Michael [32; Omaha; b: Ireland; f: James HOLLAND; m: Margaret RIORDAN] md. Susan FLINN [24; Omaha; f: Thomas FLINN; m: Nancy BROWN] on 7 Apr 1872. Off: CURTIS. Wit: Martin REIDY; Mary MORRISSEY.

HOLLENBACK, William [23; b: Pennsylvania; f: Daniel A. HOLLENBACK; m: Mary ZETTLEMOYER] md. Mamie KERBY [23; b: Cincinnati; f: Henry KERBY; m: Elizabeth JOHNSON] md. 11 Oct 1878. Off: BARTHOLOMEW. Wit: Wm. L. PEABODY, Max BERGMAN.

HOLLENBECK, J.B. [25; Belleview, sic; b: NY; f: John HOLLENBECK; m: Hannah BROWN] md. Alice HALL [22; Belleview; b: OH; f: Eliphalet W. HALL; m: Isobella PATTERSON] on 12 Nov 1875. Off: LIPE. Wit: Lizzie E. LIPE, Kate GALLAR.

HOLLIDAY, William [48; North Platte] md. Mrs. Jane GIFFORD [34; Douglas Co.] on 15 May 1868. Off: STUCK. Wit: J.C. CROSS, E.R. GREEN.

HOLLINGSWORTH, Elam [23; Florence] md. Martha KEETCH [16; Florence] on 27 Feb 1862. Off: LAMBSON. Wit: A.J. CRITCHFIELD, Alfred G. KEETCH. Age consent given by the father of the bride, who was present.

HOLLINS, Wm. G., Capt. [28; Pawnee Indian Reservation] md. Martha A. ALLIS [20; Pottawattamie Co., IA] on the evening of 4 Jul 1861 at Mat. PATRICK's residence. Off: KUHNS. Wit: Miss Lide PATRICK, Louisa GILMORE, J.N.H. PATRICK, et al.

HOLLISTER, Henry H. [40; Plattsmouth; b: NY; f: Hiram HOLLISTER; m: Almira CRANDELL] md. Mrs. Elizabeth HOWE [36; Omaha; b: NY; f: Phillip BURTON; m: Nancy QUACKENBURKE] on 12 Oct 1875. Off: PATERSON. Wit: George S. JONES, Mrs. S.J. JONES.

HOLM, Detlef [28; Douglas Co.; b: Germany; f: Detlef HOLM; m: Heinke ROHDE] md. Dorothea ALBERS [18; Douglas Co.; b: Germany; f: Jake ALBERS; m: Elsabe BESSERANY] on 3 Apr 1874 at McCardle Pct. Off: MYERS. Wit: Henry SHENPORT; Henry R. MYERS; Geo. or Jurgen CLAUSSEN; all of McARDLE Pct.

HOLM, John [27; Omaha; b: Sweden; f: Swen HOLM; m: Johanna ----] md. Alma B. ANDERSON [21; Omaha; f: Andreas JOHANSON; m: Johanna PETERSON] on 29 Nov 1879. Off: E.A. FOGELSTROM. Wit: Peter OLSON, Mrs. Amanda OLSON.

HOLMAN, Samuel [29; Omaha] md. Angie H. BRYANT [23; Omaha] on 4 Nov 1868. Off: KUHNS. Wit: Charles TURNER, Mrs. Amos SHULL, Miss M. BRYANT, et al.

HOLMES, A. [27; Omaha; b: Denmark; f: A. HOLMES; m: A.E. FRANDSEN] md. Maren JENSEN [24; Chicago; b: Denmark; f: I.S. JENSEN; m: C. LUNDE] on 15 Oct 1879. Off: HANSEN. Wit: Fred E. HEINERSKVEN, M. TOFT.

HOLMES, George [35; Omaha] md. Catherine HARRINGTON (HERRINGTON) [25; Omaha] on 3 Feb 1858. Off: PORTER.

HOLMES, Joseph S. md. Myra HYDE on 26 May 1867 at W. BRYANT's house on the Elkhorn river. Marriage license was issued on 7 or 9 1865? Off: SHINN. Wit: W. BRYANT and wife, et al.

HOLMES, Joseph [Elkhorn Precinct] and Mary GOODKNIGHT [Elkhorn Precinct] license issued on 21 Nov 1864. No marriage record. Off: DICKINSON.

HOLST, Sophus W. [28; Omaha; b: Denmark; f: N.P. HOLST; m: Sohpia B. FALK] md. Annie JENSEN [26; Racine, WI; b: Denmark; f: Jens SORENSEN; m: Sophia Maria HANSEN] on 21 Dec 1879 at C.C. THRANE's house. Off: GYDESEN. Wit: Mrs. H. SKONGAARD, C.C. THRANE.

HOLTAM, Thomas [28; Omaha] and Margaret BOYLE [19; Omaha] license issued on 26 Nov 1861. Off: ARMSTRONG.

HOLTZMAN, Frank A. [26; Omaha] md. Mary FERRIS [28; Omaha] on 25 Aug 1867. Off: KUHNS. Wit: Mrs. N.E. HAMMETT, Mrs. J.M. MIDDLETON, Mrs. M.A. LLOYD, Mrs. A.E. SHURTLEFF.

HOMAN, George W., Jr. [Omaha] md. Carrie J. MALLORY [Cleveland, OH] on 24 Jan 1865 at the parsonage. Off: LEMON. Wit: Mrs. Geo. W. HOMAN, Mrs. Julia NICHOLS, Josie HOMAN, Mrs. T.B. LEMON.

HONNEF, Paul [28; Omaha; b: Germany; f: Theodor HONNEF; m: Sibilla BREHM] md. Josie NEVERTAHL [NAVRATIL] [22; Omaha; b: Bohemia; f: Joseph NEVERTHAL [NAVRATIL]; m: Franciska TOMEK] on 27

Jun 1879. Off: BARTHOLOMEW. Wit: Jas. QUINLAN, John McCOFFREY.

HOOPER (or HUBER), Sebastian [22; Omaha; b: Germany; f: Sebastian HOOPER; m: Marie BRELA] md. Regina BO(E)HM [19; Omaha; b: Germany; f: Hafaer BO(E)HM; m: Marie] on 17 Feb 1875. Off: GROENEBAUM. Wit: Xavier KASTEL, Mrs. Barbara KASTEL.

HOOVER, Mathias [28; Omaha; b: Germany; f: Joseph HOOVER] md. Harriet MATTHEWS [30 "and over"; Omaha; b: Pickering Twp, Canada; f: Charles MATTHEWS; m: Electa BLAIR] on 17 Sep 1872. Off: GUE. Wit: Mrs. Annie B. GUE; Wm. SKINNER.

HOPF, J.F. Leopold [28; Omaha; b: Switzerland; f: Rudolph HOPF; m: Mary A. BAUERT] md. Caroline PFANNER [22; Omaha; b: Switzerland; f: Anton PFANNER; m: Anna B. PFYSTERER] on 31 Jan 1877. Off: STRASEN. Wit: John LOHRER, Alfred BAUER.

HOREIS, Herman [30; Douglas Co.; b: Germany; f: Peter HOREIS; m: Mate SCHROEDER] md. Minna GERNDORF [24; Douglas Co.; b: Germany; f: William GERNDORF; m: Josephine LIPSTREN] on 25 Mar 1875. Off: PEABODY. Wit: C.L. BRISTOL, Wilhelm GERNDORF.

HORN, Albert [25; Council Bluffs; b: Germany; f: John HORN; m: Christina LAHNAN] md. Clara SIGISMUND [18; Council Bluffs; b: Germany; f: August SIGISMUND] on 29 Apr 1870. Off: KELLEY. Wit: J.S. TUCKER; Wm. DACHTLER, Council Bluffs.

HORN, John [28; Sarpy Co.; b: Pennsylvania; f: Cornelius HORN; m: Betsie Ann SECORE] md. Ruth E. OSBORNE [19; Sarpy Co.; b: Nebraska; f: James OSBORNE; m: Rebecca BRECKENRIDGE] on 23 Dec 1880. Off: BARTHOLOMEW. Wit: Max BERGMANN, Wm. L. PEABODY.

HORNE, George M. [25; b: Canada; f: George HORNE; m: Elizabeth GEORGE] md. Aggie SARGENT [21; b: Iowa; f: John SARGENT; m: Adie RICHARDSON] on 28 Jun 1878. Off: FISHER. Wit: Bridget McDERMOTT, Henry S. MARTIN.

HORNE, George W. [24; Kansas City; Missouri; f: William HORNE; m: Lutitia WALKER] md. Grace V. OVERALL [27; Omaha; b: Illinois; f: Edwin R. OVERALL; m: Margaret BLACKBURN] on 30 Dec 1880. Off: MILLSPAUGH. Wit: Edwin OVERALL, Percy BARNES.

HORNISH, John B. [29; Omaha; b; Iowa; f: J.K. HORNISH; m: Harriet WYCOFF] md. Julia WHALEN [19; Omaha; b: Illinois; f: Eugene WHALEN; m: Wineford CONLEY] on 12 Apr 1880 at the Catholic Bishop's residence. Off: McCARTHY. Wit: Patrick

CONNELLY, Angelia CONNELLY, both of Plattsmouth.

HORNSBY, Elias N. [28; Omaha; b: OH; f: Littleton HORNSBY; m: Sarah MARSHALL] md. Ada H. DAVIS [19; Omaha; b: IL; f: F.A. DAVIS; m: H.C. BARRETT] on 14 Jul 1881 at First Methodist Church. Off: HAYNES. Wit: B.G. MANS, Mrs. J.B. MAXFIELD.

HORSKY, Antone [27; Helena, MT; b: Bohemia; f: Joseph HORSKY; m: Mary BARBA] md. Mary MOROVETZ [MORAVEC] [20; Cedar Rapids, IA; b: Bohemia; f: Solin MOROVETZ [MORAVEC]; m: Susy MOROVETZ [MORAVEC]] on 1 Jan 1880. Off: BENEKE. Wit: M. NOVAK, John F. DALLAN.

HORSTRICK, Henry [22; Cuming Co.] md. Magdalena WORTMEN [18; Cuming Co.] on 1 Dec 1867 at the Cathedral. Off: GROENEBAUM. Wit: Frederic GOOBIAN, Sophia KAUP.

HORTON, Wesley J. [22; Council Bluffs; b: Oneida Co., NY; f: John W. HORTON; m: Elizabeth GANNETT] md. Elizabeth JOHNSON [21; Ottumwa, IA: f: Henry JOHNSON] on 12 Oct 1872. Off: BILLMAN. Wit: J.W. McDONALD; Mrs. M.E. McDONALD.

HOSKINSON, Joseph W. [24; Douglas Co.; b: Iowa; f: Scott HOSKINSON; m: Sarah BLAIR] md. Mary M. GILLMORE [22; Douglas Co.; b: Iowa; f: James GILLMORE; m: Elizabeth McKASKIA] on 17 Nov 1879 at Elkhorn Precinct. Wit: D.S. PARMELEE, Samuel SUMNER, both of Elkhorn Precinct.

HOSP, Leander [27; Wyandote, KS; b: NY; f: Cornelius HOSP; m: Sophia AUERBACKER] md. Ella SEWARD [18; Omaha; b: IA; f: A.C. SEWARD; m: Nancy LUDINGTON] on 19 Oct 1876 at Brownell Hall. Off: DOHERTY. Wit: A.C. SEWARD, Nancy SEWARD, Miss L.B. LOOMIS, Brownell Hall.

HOSPE, Anton, Jr. [23; b: Ohio; f: Anton HOSPE; m: Maria L. GEBAUER] md. Jane R. NELIGH [23; b: Penensylvania; f: William NELIGH; m: Sarah YOUNT] on 12 Feb 1878. Off: FALK. Wit: Louis HOSPE, James J. CHAPMAN, Miss Quinne NELIGH.

HOUGHTON, Merritt D. [29; Omaha; b: MI; f: Rufus HOUGHTON; m: Lucy ABEL] md. Fanny APLEY [24; Omaha; b: CT] on 22 Jul 1875. Off: LEMON. Wit: Stephen ROBINSON, Xenos STEPHENS.

HOURIGAN, Charles [25; Omaha; b: Iowa; f: Matthew HOURIGAN; m: Ann Jane SHEFFINGTON] and Lizzie DOLAN [18; Omaha; b: Maryland; f: William DOLAN; m: Lizzie ZACHARY] license issued on 26 Jul 1879. No marriage record. Off: BARTHOLOMEW.

HOUSEL, Paul E. [23; Omaha; b: Mt. Pleasant, IA; f: C.C. HOUSEL; m: Maria J. PHELPS] md. Katie O'CONNOR [19; Omaha; b: Cork, Ireland; f: John O'CONNOR; m: Mary CONNELL] on 8 Dec 1877. Off: PORTER. Wit: C.C. HOUSEL, Edward D. McLAUGHLIN.

HOUSTON, Sam [28; Omaha; b: Mercer Co., OH; f: John S. HOUSTON; m: Hortense WORTHINGTON] md. Eliza Perla EVANS [24; Omaha; b: Philadelphia, PA; f: John EVANS; m: Eliza Permela DAVIS] on 4 Mar 1873. Off: McCANDLISH. Wit: Rev. George D. STEWART; Mrs. Maria McCANDLISH.

HOUSTON, William H. [28; Cheyenne, WY; b: Indiana; f: Harvey HOUSTON; m: Aurelia JULIAN] md. Mary QUIGLEY [24; Omaha; b: Wisconsin; f: Peter QUIGLEY; m: Catharine FINLEY] on 7 Apr 1880. Off: PETERSON. Wit: W.A. TEMPLETON, Miss Kate QUIGLEY.

HOWARD, Andrew J. [33; Fremont; b: Ashly, MA; f: Benjamin HOWARD; m: Phebe DAMAN] md. Ellen J. ALBERTSON [20; Schuyler; b: Michigan; f: Isaac ALBERTSON; m: Angenett TONEARY] on 23 Jan 1871. Off: KUHNS. Wit: Charles D. BOGUE; Charles L. HOWARD, Sharpsville, IN.

HOWARD, Charles [24; Omaha] md. Mary A. DURKIN [26; Omaha] on 17 Nov 1868. Off: STUCK. Wit: John M. SULLIVAN, Mrs. FINNEY.

HOWARD, George F. [27; Omaha] md. Clara KING [22; Omaha] on 17 Nov 1868 at the Trinity Cathedral. Off: BETTS. Wit: Hugh G. CLARKE, Wm. SEWARD, Richard CARRIER.

HOWE, Henry [33; Omaha; New York; f: Charles HOWE; m: Elizabeth AVERY] md. Mrs. Eva C. WISEBORN [30; Omaha; b: Germany; f: Christian SEIGLE; m: Elizabeth ALTERMAN] on 5 Mar 1870. Off: KUHNS. Wit: William GIEBER; Mrs. Caroline GIEBER.

HOWELL, Andrew [41; Omaha; b: AL; f: Isaac HOWELL; m: Sarah N. BLOODGOOD] md. Emma JOHNSON [23; Omaha; b: MO; f: William JOHNSON; m: Lizzie KEALER] on 29 Jan 1881. Off: MARQUETT. Wit: Lizzie JOHNSON, W.W. SCOTT.

HOWELL, Peter F. [25; Pottawattamie Co., IA; b: England; f: John HOWELL; m: Winfred BATE] and Fanny R. ROBINSON [20; Pottawattamie Co., IA; b: Iowa; f: George ROBINSON; m: Virginia BALLARD] license issued on 13 Mar 1877. No marriage record. Off: SEDGWICK.

HUBA, Jacob [25; Omaha; b: Germany; f: John HUBA; m: Elizabeth GRUENENWALD] md. Catherine MARTIN [30; Omaha; b: Switzerland; f: Peter MARTIN; m: Salma] on 20 Jan 1872. Off: BRANDES. Wit: Henry RITTER; Martin KELLER.

HUBBARD, Charles A. [30; Omaha; b: Middletown, CT; f: Ira HUBBARD; m: Margaret McNAIRY] md. Carrie A. BANNER [32; Omaha; b: Philadelphia, PA; f: George W. BANNER; m: Nancy A. HAGER] on 27 Oct 1870. Off: KUHNS. Wit: William E. FLETCHER; Josiah B. REDFIELD.

HUBBARD, George E. [42; Omaha; b: OH; f: Henry HUBBARD; m: Eliza Ann ROBERTSON] md. Annie LOVELADY [16; Omaha; b: MO; f: John LOVELADY; m: Mary E. McGEE] on 10 Sep 1881. Off: PATERSON. Wit: Saml. J. CUTLER, Andrew BEONIS. Age consent given by mother of the bride, Mary DROST, and witness was Max BERGMANN.

HUBER, Jeremias [23; Omaha; b: Germany; f: J. HUBER; m: Mary HUBER] md. Mrs. Dora KOHREGER [20; Omaha; b: Germany; f: H. SORGE; m: K. BATHEIS] on 25 May 1874. Off: HENNEY. Wit: William ALSTADT; John WETTKOFF.

HUBERT, John H. [32; Omaha; b: Prussia; f: John H. HUBERT; m: Elizabeth SHAUDORF] md. Mary Jane GRANGER [18; Omaha; b: Michigan; f: George GRANGER; m: Mary DAVIS] on 5 Mar 1870. Off: GIBSON. Wit: Ezra GREGG; Mr. SANE.

HUDZ [CHUDA], Joseph [22; Douglas Co.; b: Bohemia; f: John HUDZ [CHUDA]; m: Barbara JANAUSCHEK JANOUSEK]] md. Lizzie CUHEL [18; Douglas Co.; b: Bohemia; f: Antonie CUHEL; m: Rosa GOARTIC] on 22 Jul 1876. Off: SEDGWICK. Wit: J.N. PHILLIPS, J.T. GRIFFIN.

HUESTIS, Eugene D. [31; Omaha; b: Westchester Co., NY; f: Daniel HUESTIS; m: Mary DIXON] md. Ann J. BRACKIN [20; Omaha; b: Ohio; f: John H. BRACKIN; m: Rebecca BRACKIN] on 5 Mar 1873. Off: STEWART. Wit: John H. BRACKIN; Dr. George L. MILLER.

HUFF, Alexis M. [21; Potawatame (sic) Co., IA] md. Ellen J. DOREN [23; Potawatame Co.] on 16 Jul 1866. Off: HASCALL. Wit: Henrietta and Sarah J. HASCALL.

HUFFMAN, Howe [29; Omaha; b: IN; f: Henry HUFFMAN; m: Sarah HARTMAN] md. Rachel EVANS [26; Douglas Col; b: Wales; f: Roger EVANS; m: Elizabeth PARREY] on 27 Jan 1875. Off: WRIGHT. Wit: Sydney HOHNER, Catharine HENESEY.

HUGHES, Bernard [30; Omaha] md. Mary DORAN [24; Omaha] on 15 Nov 1860. Off: KELLY. Wit: James McEVOY, Margaret CASSIDY.

HUGHES, James [McCardle's Precinct] md. Harriet ROSING [McCardle's Precinct] on 13 Jan 1865 at O'GORMAN's residence. Off: O'GORMAN. Wit: Patrick McCARDLE, Josephine CRONICHER.

HUGHES, Michael E. [22; Omaha; b: Ireland; f: Martin HUGHES; m: Mary MAHONEY] md. Sarah M. CHRISTMAN [24; Omaha; b: Indianapolis, IN; f: Robert CHRISTMAN; m: Rachel LAKINS] on 20 Aug 1870. Off: KUHNS. Wit: Mrs. H.W. KUHNS; Robert WEIDENSALL.

HUGHES, P.F. [28; Iowa; b: Illinois; f: Martin HUGHES; m: Mary RYAN] md. Mary J. LAMBERT [21; Cass Co.; b: Ohio; f: M.F. LAMBERT; m: Rebecca WALKEY] on 20 May 1880. Off: BARTHOLOMEW. Wit: Geo. H. GUY, James SMITH.

HUGHES, Patrick [33; Omaha] md. Julianna FLEMING [32; Omaha] on 16 Aug 1867 at the Catholic Church of Omaha. Off: O'GORMAN. Wit: Pat QUINLAN, Sara CHARLES.

HUGHES, William B. [33; Omaha; b: England; f: Thomas HUGHES; m: Mary BOOLEY] md. Phoebe P. EVANS [18; Omaha; b: Wisconsin; f: Thomas EVANS; m: Mary WILLIAMS] on 4 Oct 1876. Off: LIPE. Wit: Thomas EVANS, Mary L. EVANS.

HUGHES, William H.S. [23; Omaha] md. Rebecca C.A. SMILEY [21; Omaha] on 21 Jan 1862 at KUHNS' residence. Off: KUHNS. Wit: Mrs. KUHNS, Alex. B. McCANDLESS, Mrs. Rachel McCANDLESS. License is dated 30 Jul 1861.

HUGHES, William H.S. [32; Omaha; b: Georgetown, DC; f: John E. HUGHES; m: Martha HEDGES] md. Margaret G. BERLIN [22; Omaha; b: East Liberty, PA; f: Jonathan BERLIN; m: Nancy P. WILSON] on 28 Dec 1870. Off: KUHNS. Wit: J.N.H. PATRICK, near Omaha; Robert WILSON.

HUGONIOT, Jules [25; Omaha; b: France; f: Peter HUGONIOT; m: Susan MEJNIEN] md. Julia Constance BRAND [19; Omaha; b: Switzerland; f: Francis BRAND; m: Henrietta CHEVAUX] on 17 Aug 1876. Off: BENEKE. Wit: L.A. ELLIS, C.A. ALTHAUR.

HUGUS, John W. [38; Fort Steele, Wyoming Terr.; b: Pittsburg, PA; f: Peter HUGUS; m: Eliza McCORMACK] md. Sarah G. CARNAN [31; Omaha; b: Vincennes, IN; f: Robert N. CARNAN; m: Louisa BONNER] on 12 Oct 1874. Off: PATERSON. Wit: E.R. BULLENS; W.H.S. HUGHES.

HUICK or HEUCK, George [25; Douglas Co.] md. Annie M. PLUMBECK [PLAMBECK] [Douglas Co.] on 18 Apr 1869 in her father's house in Douglas County. Off: FLORKEE. Wit: H. PLUMBECK, John KOLP. George PLUMBECK, John FEDDE are written in as witnesses and then crossed off.

HULTMAN, Frank Augustus [45; Des Moines, IA; b: Sweden; f: Peter HULTMAN; m: Annie G. ANDERSON] md. Jennie M. PALMGREN [24; Omaha; b: Sweden; f: Mangus PALMGREN; m: Caroline Elizabeth AHLMEN] on 14 Oct 1874. Off: BENZON. Wit: A. KALMAN and his wife; G. PATTERSON and his wife.

HUME, George [28; Omaha; b: Canada; f: William HUME; m: Elizabeth THOMAS] md. Arminta REDMAN [19; Omaha; b: Douglas Co.; f: Joseph REDMAN; m: Mary Jane FAIR] on 26 Apr 1877. Off: LIPE. Wit: David REDMAN; m: Joseph REDMAN.

HUME, Richard [26; Omaha; b: Canada; f: William HUME; m: Elizabeth THOMAS] and Sarah KIMBALL [22; Omaha; b: Illinois; f: James KIMBALL; m: Mary MOWBRAY] license issued on 28 Nov 1877. No marriage record. Off: SEDGWICK.

HUMPAL, Joseph [26; Omaha; b: Austria; f: Jacob HUMPAL; m: Mary SPINLER] md. Caroline STIBO [20; Omaha; b: Austria; f: John STIBO; m: Barbara BASIL] on 19 Aug 1879. Off: BARTHOLOMEW. Wit: Warren SWITZLER, J.W. MARECEK.

HUMPERT, Franz [36; Omaha; b: Germany; f: Casper HUMPERT; m: Regina STARKE] md. Mrs. Ludwine SCHWALENBERG [28; Omaha; b: Germany; f: Valentin HENN; m: Franziska EICKHORN] on 10 Feb 1880. Off: BARTHOLOMEW. Wit: John ANDRIT, Max BERGMANN.

HUMPHREY, H.N. [21; Dunlap, IA; ab: Iowa; f: Watson HUMPHREY; m: Emaline JOHNSON] md. Eliza BURKE [18; Shelby Co., IA; f: John BURKE; m: Mary HILL] on 3 Sep 1877 at the Bishop's house. Off: JENNETTE. Wit: Patrick JORDAN, James O'BOYLE.

HUMPHRIES, Wm. H. [32; Omaha; b: England; f: Edmund HUMPHRIES; m: Anna GORDON] md. Emma SCHACK [19; Omaha; b: Iowa; f: John SCHACK; m: Catharine RINEHART] on 31 Dec 1880. Off: WRIGHT. Wit: Robert GREENE, Edmund HUMPHRIES.

HUNDLEY, George [25; Omaha; b: KY; f: Thomas HUNDLEY; m: Julia SMITH] md. Nellie THOMAS [23; Omaha; b: MO; f: Jesse THOMAS; m: Hattie BLACKWELL] on 3 Oct 1888. Off: SHANK. Wit: Jesse THOMAS, Hattie THOMAS.

HUNT, Charles [25; Douglas Co.; b: OH, f: Asa HUNT; m: Jane M. SEAMAN] md. Gertrude H. VANDENBURGH [20; Douglas Co.; b: Holland; f: L.H. VANDENBURGH; m: Jane MILLER] on 30 Jun 1876. Off: SHERRILL. Wit: L.H. VANDENBURGH, Mrs. Asa HUNT.

HUNTER, Alexander [30; Florence] md. Jennie M. ECKFORD [22; Florence] on 8 Mar 1861 at Alexander HUNTER's house in Florence. Off: CRITCHFIELD.

HUNTER, Frank [24; Omaha] md. Mary HORD (HOARD) [18 and one half; Florence] on 15 Jun 1867. Off: SMITH. Wit: John ALLEN, Mrs. A.M. BURNHAM, A.M. BURNHAM, M.D. Certificate was filed and entered on 13 Jul 1903 by VINSONHALER.

HUNTER, Harrison M. [29;Omaha] md. Margaretta SILL [17; Omaha] on 28 Jan 1866. Off: SLAUGHTER. Wit: James QUINN, Elizabeth HUNTER. Age consent given by the father of the bride.

HUNTER, James H. [24; Saunders Co.; b: Ohio; f: Robert HUNTER; m: Laura TIBBALS] md. Louisa A. HARMON [16; Omaha; b: Omaha; b: A.J. HARMON; m: Cordelia W. CORNISH] on 3 Mar 1874. Off: McCAGUE. Wit: Harvey JONES, Saunders Co.; Paul HARMON.

HUNTER, James [41; Melville, IA; b: Ohio; f: Anthony HUNTER; m: Jane McCAMON] md. Mrs. Charlotta L. SCHROFE [35; Atlantic, IA; b: Pennsylvania; f: David BUNNELL; m: Mary OZIAH] on 27 Oct 1878. Off: BORDEN. Wit: Rosa FISCHER, Anna FISCHER.

HUNTER, T.C. [32; Omaha] md. Mary A. FORT [21; Omaha] on 5 Feb 1868 at Rev. J.L. FORT's residence. Off: LEMON. Wit: J.L. FORT and wife, Mrs. M.B. LEMON, et al.

HUNTOON, Asa Sylvester [24; Omaha] md. Columbia Helen CLEGG [22; Omaha] at 8 AM, Tuesday, 14 Jul 1868 at Isaac CLEGG's residence. Off: DIMMICK. Wit: O. LARSON, M.T. KINNEY, Presly MARTIN, et al.

HUPERT, Wilton M. [42 or 43; Omaha; b: Lancaster Co., PA; f: John HUPERT; m: Susan MALONEY] md. Mrs. Julia CUSACK [28 or 29; Omaha; b: Ireland; f: Henry WATSON] on 14 Nov 1871. Off: DeLaMATYR. Wit: N.O. DeLaMATYR; Irwin DePIGHT.

HURD, Dave [27; Douglas Co.; b: MI; f: Byron HURD; m: Saray DYE] md. Mary STETEN [18; Douglas Co.; b: NV; f: John STETEN; m: Christine CLICKLER] on 10

Sep 1881. Off: CHADWICK. Wit: J.L. THOMPSON, Douglas Co., Walter BENNETT.

HURD, Isaac W. [22; Elkhorn City] and Louisa J. DORKS [22; Elkhorn City] license issued 27 Aug 1857. No marriage record. Off: BRIGGS.

HURFORD, Oliver P. [36; Omaha] md. Louisa C. COON or CORN [20; Omaha] at 10:30 AM on 6 Feb 1867 at John R. MEREDITH's residence. Off: DIMMICK. Wit: Dr. G.C. MONELL, Thomas J. HURFORD, W.N. McCANDLISH, et al.

HURLBERT, Warren [21; Dunlap, IA; b: Wisconsin; f: Benjamin F. HURLBERT; m: Elmira J. POOL] md. Edith G. BARNUM [21; b: Canada; f: Milo S. BARNUM; m: Altha E. BARNUM] on 11 Dec 1878. Off: BEANS. Wit: Miss WALKER, Mr. BURNUM, wife and others.

HURLBUT, Everett B. [29; Fontanelle, Washington Co.] md. Cordelia E. MUNGER [29; Elkhorn City] on 1 May 1860 at Elkhorn City. Off: McCANDLISH. Wit: "many witnesses."

HURLEY, A.A. [21; Grand Island, NE; b: Iowa; f: Dowd HURLEY; m: Betsy WEBB] md. Mary NOLAN [20; Albion, MI; b: Wisconsin; f: John NOLAN; m: Anna MILLER] on 12 Jan 1879. Off: LIPE. Wit: Lizzie E. LIPE, Maggie McCARTHY.

HURLEY, Daniel [26; Omaha; b: Ireland; f: Jeremiah HURLEY; m: Ellen HURLEY] md. Mary Jane DRISCOLL [24; Omaha; b: Ireland; f: John DRISCOLL; m: Mary DRAWN] on 19 Jul 1874 at the Catholic Cathedral. Off: MALLOY. Wit: Michael LEE; Jennie GIBSON.

HURLEY, James C. [22; Des Moines; b: Saratoga Co., NY; f: Patrick HURLEY; m: Julia COCHLIN] md. Catharine A. KANE [19; Stuart, Guthrie Co., IA; b: Allegheny Co., PA; f: Thomas KANE; m: Mary RAFFERTY] on 24 Aug 1872. Off: TOWNSEND. Wit: William G. HOLLINS; J. KINSEY, Des Moines, IA.

HURM, William [22; Omaha; b: TN; f: Anton HURM; m: Louisa KENNER] md. Louisa STONESTREET [20; Omaha; b: IA; f: J.H. STONESTREET; m: Rachael OTTHOLM] on 25 Jul 1881. Off: BRANDES. Wit: Mollie GALLIGAN, J.T. MORTON.

HURST, James [27; Fremont, Dodge Co.] md. Rebecca Jane FULTON [23; Fremont, Dodge Co.] on 5 Jan 1868 at the Catholic Church of Omaha. Off: O'GORMAN. Wit: John CLIFFORD, Mary TIERNEY.

HUSS, Joseph [23; Omaha; b: Hungary; f: Franz HUSS; m: Catharine LOEB] md. Elizabeth BIERBAUM [23; Omaha; b: Hungary; f: Johann BIERBAUM; m: Theresa WUENSCHBERGER] on 23 Jan 1881 at the German Catholic Church. Off: GROENEBAUM. Wit: Charles KOHLMEYER, Mrs. Eva KOHLMEYER.

HUSS, Rudolf [36; Douglas Co.; b: Germany; f: Rudolph HUSS; m: Wilhelmina TRESCHER] md. Antonie TRAISSENETT [26 or 27; Douglas Co.; b: Germany; f: Charles TRAISSENETT] on 24 Mar 1877. Off: WEISS. Wit: W.F. RANSOM, H.S. TRAISSENETT, both of Florence.

HUSTAD, Charles [42; b: Norway; f: John HUSTAD; m: Anna STROM] md. Mary EGEN [34; b: Ireland; f: John EGEN; m: Margaret EGEN] on 11 Nov 1878. Off: COLANERI. Wit: John C. HOFSTED, Edward EGAN.

HUSTED, Christian C. [31; Omaha; b: Denmark; f: E. HUSTED; m: Anna CLAUSSEN] md. Louisa JESSEN [22; Omaha; b: Denmark; f: Hans C. JESSEN; m: Kirstina PETERSON] on 15 Mar 1877. Off: SEDGWICK. Wit: H.C. JESSEN, Mark HANSEN.

HUSTON, Wade [33; Omaha; colored; b: Tennessee; f: Burril WRIGHT; m: Betsey] md. Mrs. Martha JACKSON [22; Omaha; colored; b: Maryland] on 1 Dec 1872. Off: GAINES. Wit: Emanuel CLENLANS; Alex WILLIAMS.

HUTCHENSON, William H. [30; Omaha; b: South Carolina; f: Nathan HUTCHENSON; m: Elizabeth PRICE] md. Mary E. RIDER [18; Omaha; b: Iowa; f: Romain RIDER; m: Fidelia RANDALL] on 14 Aug 1880. Off: BENEKE. Wit: D.H. GEYER, Robert SKETCHLEG.

HUTCHINS, Henry [35; Council Bluffs] md. Ellen MOWHINIA [19; Council Bluffs] on 18 Dec 1866. Off: SLAUGHTER. Wit: A.M. CLARK, R.N. MOSHER.

HUTESON, Thomas J. [26; Douglas Co.] md. Martha DYMOND [19; Douglas Co.] on 17 Oct 1867 at Primrose, Douglas Co. Off: DENTON.

HUTTON, Thomas H. [22; Pottawattamie Co., IA] md. Lucy WILD [22; Pottawattamie Co., IA] on 27 Nov 1860 at ARMSTRONG's office. Off: ARMSTRONG. Wit: Capt. Wm. E. MOORE, Dr. T.J. BOYKIN, J.F. COFFMAN.

HYDE, Cornelius D. [26; Omaha; b: Vermont [New York crossed out]; f: Judson R. HYDE; m: Carrie V. DeMOTT] md. Mollie MACKEY [19; Omaha; b: Missouri; f: Alexander P. MACKEY; m: Mary E. MACAULEY] on 27 Sep 1877. Off: PARDEE. Wit: Charles E. MACKEY, "bride's mother."

HYDE, George W. [33; Omaha; b: New York; f: E.S. HYDE; m: Mary M. REYNOLDS] md. Mrs. Lou AIKEN [31; Omaha; b: Maryland; f: Leander REED; m: Martha SCOTT] on 9 Apr 1877. Off: WEISS. Wit: Parker AIKEN, Mary HIGGINS.

HYMAS, John [21; Douglas Co.] md. Catharine PERRY [26; Douglas Co.] on 12 May 1860 at E. DALLOW's residence. Off: BRIGGS. Wit: Elizabeth DALLOW.

HYMAS, William A. [24; Omaha] and Mary JAMES [22; Omaha] license issued on 7 May 1861. No marriage record. Off: ARMSTRONG.

HYNES, Thomas N.J. [35; O'Neil City; b: England; f: Patrick HYNES; m: Ellen DWYER] md. Ann FALLON [23; O'Neil City; b: Ireland; f: ?? FALLON] on 9 Jul 1878, St. Philomena Church. Off: MARTIN.

HYNES, Thomas N.J. [35; O'Niel City, NE; b: England; f: Patrick HYNES] md. Annie FALLON [23; O'Niel City, NE; b: Ireland] on 9 Jul 1878 at St. Philomena's Cathedral. Off: MARTIN.

ILER, Joseph D. [35; Omaha; b: Ohio; f: Conrad ILER; m: Julia STRINE] md. Georgia Maud GRAY [23; Omaha; b: New York; f: George W. GRAY; m: Susan BACKSTER] on 18 Nov 1880, Trinity Cathedral. Off: MILLSPAUGH. Wit: P. ILER, Geo. GRAY.

INGHRAM, Henry M. [24; Omaha; b: Iowa; f: Thomas INGHRAM; m: Eliza MORGAN] md. Caroline J. GILLELAND [23; Omaha; b: Danville, IN; f: Micajah GILLELAND; m: Belinda PARKER] on 26 Jun 1873. Off: WRIGHT. Wit: Henry ROE, Marie ROE.

IRA, George W. [29; Decatur; b: Washington, PA; f: George IRA; m: Mary A. HUNT] md. Mary B. HOBBS [20; Omaha; b: West Cambridge, MA; f: Lorenzo HOBBS; m: Mary M. FROST] on 21 Dec 1870. Off: BELLS. Wit: Lorenzo HOBBS; John McMURPHY.

IRVINE, Clarke [28; Oregon, Holt Co., MO] md. Ann K. JOHNSON [23; Douglas Co.] on 20 Nov 1859. Off: DAVIS. Wit: James CHAPMAN.

ISAAC, Joseph [24; Douglas Co.; b: France; f: George ISAAC; m: Regina MULLER] md. Ernestine KAHLER [29; Douglas Co.; b: Germany; f: Gottlieb KAHLER; m: Ernestine BAKER] on 7 Jul 1870. Off: KELLEY. Wit: J.S. TUCKER; James G. MAYNES.

ISAAC, William [28; Omaha; b: Sweden; f: John ISAAC] md. Clara J. GUSTAVESON [21; Omaha; b: Sweden] on 1 Apr 1871. Off: S.G. LARSON. Wit: Charles R. RICHARDS; Hanna ANDERSON.

ISAAKSON, August [32; Omaha; b: Sweden; f: Isaac JONASON; m: Ulricke HOKANSON] md. Christine PIERSON [21; Omaha; b: Sweden; f: Anders PIERSON; m: Stina JOHANNISON] on 16 Oct 1880. Off: FOGELSTLROM. Wit: John PIERSON, G. ANDERSON.

ISBERG, J.N. [34; Omaha; b: Sweden; f: Nils ISBERG; m: Carrie PEARSON] md. Emilie ANDERSON [24; Omaha; b: Sweden; f: Andrew ANDERSON; m: Christine OLAFSON] on 4 Mar 1881. Off: STENBERG. Wit: Wm. STAR, Betty ANDERSON.

ISHAM, David T. [38; Douglas Co.; b: Massachusetts; f: Daniel T. ISHAM; m: Emeline J. CADY] md. Maggie A. McNICHOL [20; Douglas Co.; b: Dunville, Canada; f: James McNICHOL; m: Mary LOGAN] on 2 Dec 1871 at Union Pct. Off: DIXON. Wit: Joseph GUES and wife, Union Pct; Anna S. DIXON, Irvington.

ITNYER, Hiram N. [32; Omaha; b: MD; f: J. ITNYER; m: Susan RHOADES] md. Martha J. CREIGHTON [23; b: OH; f: Francis H. CREIGHTON; m: Phoebe DRISCOLL] on 19 Sep 1876 at the Roman Catholic Cathedral. Off: JENNETTE. Wit: MAJIN, Martha Kate CREIGHTON.

IVERSON, Adolph J. [34; Washington Co.; b: Germany; f: John IVERSON; m: Eliza LAUSAN] md. Annie BUCK [BOCK] [26; Omaha; b: Germany; f: Hans BOCK; m: Margarita BUNDS] on 7 Mar 1871. Off: GIBSON. Wit: Datlef REPEN; Ferdinand STRUBY.

JACKSON, A.C. [29; Omaha; b: MO; f: Joseph T. JACKSON; m: Mary Ann TISDALE] md. Anna B. FISHER [21; Omaha; b: OH; f: C. FISHER; m: Hannah RHODES] on 23 Sep 1876. Off: SEDGWICK. Wit: Marcia SEDGWICK, Charles J. GREEN.

JACKSON, Charles A. [27; Omaha] md. Ennie NOLAN [16; Omaha] on 2 Oct 1868. Off: FLORKEE. Wit: John ALEXANDER, Wm. R. JONES, Miles M. HAMLEN. Age consent given by the mother of the bride. [The index indicates the bride and groom are colored.]

JACKSON, David [47; Douglas Co.; b: Ohio; f: John JACKSON; m: Betsey WARE] md. Mrs. Miranda KNAUSS [36; Douglas Co.; b: Virginia] on 12 Mar 1874 at Waterloo. Off: HANEY. Wit: Lewis W. DENTON, Waterloo; Ella DENTON, Waterloo.

JACKSON, Harry [27, Omaha; b: England; f: Mathew JACKSON; m: Ann GETLAND] md. Caroline E. TOOZER [18; Omaha; b: Wales; f: A.R. TOOZER; m: Caroline HOBBS] on 31 Jan 1876. Off: SHERRILL. Wit: Henry LIVSEY, Mrs. A.F. SHERRILL.

JACKSON, Henry E. [30; Douglas Co.] and Elizabeth COCHRAN [23; Douglas Co.] license issued on 27 Apr ---- (1867?). Off: HASCALL.

JACKSON, John W. [23; Pottawattamie Co., IA; b: Ohio; f: Henry JACKSON; m: Sarah WARD] md. Annie JANES [19; Pottawattamie Co., IA; b: Illinois; f: David JANES; m: Eunice MERRILL] on 22 Feb 1871. Off: GIBSON. Wit: Thos. SWOBE; W.H. CADER.

JACKSON, Richard [28; Omaha] md. Amanda COOK [23; Omaha] on 30 Oct 1865 at Tremont House. Off: KUHNS. Wit: Mr. and Mrs. A.R. HOELL, Nettie WHITFORD, et al.

JACKSON, Scott [negro, 25; Omaha; b: Missouri; f: Isaac JACKSON; m: Mary WOOD] md. Louise FORD [negro, 20; Omaha; b: Kansas; f: Jacob FORD; m: Lizzie ALLEN] on 27 Aug 1879 at the A.M.E. Church. Off: FOUCHE. Wit: Charles FREEMAN, Malinda JACKSON.

JACKSON, Thomas C. md. Helen KINNECUT on 19 Jul 1865 at Bell Creek?. Off: HURLBUT. Wit: John KINNECUT, David KINNICUT.

JACKSON, William H. [26; Omaha; b: Keesville, NY; f: George H. JACKSON; m: Harriet M. ALLEN] md. Mary E. GREER [23; Omaha; b: Newton Falls, OH; f: John L. GREER; m: Mary McEWEN] on 19 May 1869. Off: CLARKSON. Wit: Byron REED, W. CAMPBELL, divers and sundry persons.

JACOBSEN, Hans [40; Weston, Saunders Co., NE; b: Sweden; f: Jacob OLSON; m: Anna JACOBSON] md. Christine ANDERSON [29; Valley Station, NE; b: Sweden; f: Anders ANDERSON; m: Maria OLSDOTTER] on 12 Jun 1878. Off: HAYLAND. Wit: Andrew S. EKBERG, Nels ANDERSON, both of Valley.

JACOBSON, Anthony [27; St. Paul, NE; b: Denmark; f: Jacob BALTZARSON; m: Christine ANDERSDOTTER] md. Anna JENSEN [21; St. Paul, NE; b: Denmark; f: James ANDERSON; m: Mary NELSEN] on 22 Dec 1881 at "my res." Off: GYDESEN. Wit: P. GYDESEN, W. GYDESEN.

JACOBSON, Haydan [27; Omaha; b: Denmark; f: Simon JACOBSON; m: Christiane MUNSMAN] and Augustie S. AHMANSON [19; Omaha; b: Missouri; f: John AHMANSON] license issued on 8 Dec 1877. Off: SEDGWICK.

JACOBSON, Soren [39; Omaha; b: Denmark; f: S. JACOBSON; m: Stina JACOBSON] md. Anne CHRISTIANSEN

[26; Omaha; b: Denmark; f: Christen PETERSON; m: Ulette CHRISTENSEN] on 25 Nov 1881 at "their residents." Off: GYDESEN. Wit: Niels RASMNOFIN, Chr. C. KING.

JAEGGLE, Jacob [28; Loup City, NE; b: Switzerland; f: Martin JAEGGLE; m: Maria BERTLER] md. Augustine SCHROEDER [22; Omaha; b: Germany; f: George SCHROEDER; m: Johanna STUFT] on 15 May 1881. Off: BRANDES. Wit: Max BERGMANN, Wm. WECKBACH.

JAHN, Friederich Hermann, Rev. [29; Grand Island; b: Germany; f: Christian F. JAHN; m: Caroline REISS] md. Maria F. WETZEL [24; Grand Island; b: Germany; f: Carl E. WETZEL; m: Johanne BAUMANN] on 27 May 1878. Off: STRASEN. Wit: Fred HIRSHFELD, Henry HAMANN.

JAHNER, Frank [26; Omaha; b: Germany; f: Frank JAHNER; m: Kate KRIETESFIELD] md. Bertha MUNSTER [20; Omaha; b: Germany; f: John MUNSTER; m: Annie DORAN] on 5 Jun 1877. Off: STRASEN. Wit: Hans BRACKENFELD, Silo GRENDEN.

JAMES, Walter [25; Omaha; colored; b: Missouri; f: Thorton JAMES] md. Annie HAMILTON [20; Omaha; colored; b: Missouri; f: Alexander HAMILTON] on 4 Feb 1870. Off: SHINN. Wit: Hyram HOWARD.

JAMIESON, David F. [37; Hall Co.; b: Scotland; f: James JAMIESON; m: Hannah HODKINSON] md. Delia DUMPHY [21; Hall Co.; b: Ireland; f: James DUMPHY; m: Anastasia McGRATH] on 24 Jan 1880, St. Philomena's Church. Off: ENGLISH. Wit: Mr. M.P. DUMPHY, Mrs. P. DUMPHY.

JANEK [JANAK], John (Johan) [21; Omaha; b: Austria; f: Thomas JANEK [JANAK]; m: Anna DRAWAK [DWORAK]] md. Mary KRATOKWELL [KRATOCHVIL] [18; Omaha; b: Austria; f: Wencel KRATOKWELL [KRATOCHVIL]; m: Cady BARTOE [BARTOS]] on 22 Jan 1871 at the German Catholic Church. Off: GROENEBAUM. Wit: Gerhard ELBLING; Mathew WOPAREL [VOBORIL].

JANSA, James [25; Omaha; b: Bohemia; f: Martin JANSA; m: Anna WLACHOWA] md. Josie STUCHLIKOWA [18; Omaha; b: Bohemia; f: Martin STUCHLIKOWA; m: Barbara PESIKOWA] on 24 Jan 1875. Off: PEABODY. Wit: Frank KONDILE, Frank KRAGCEKE.

JANSEN, Andrew [22; Omaha; b: Sweden; f: Nicholas JANSEN; m: Anna WATTS] md. Ellen SAMPLES [21; Douglas Co.; b: Tennessee; f: James SAMPLES; m: Mary Ann SIMPSON] on 12 Mar 1872. Off: THURSTON. Wit: A. ADAMSKY; H.T.C. Frederickson BOSKI.

JANSEN, Jorgen Ravsn [32; Omaha] and Bertha Hanssine HANSEN [25; Omaha] license issued on 2 Jan 1869. No marriage record. Off: HYDE.

JANSEN, Soren [24; Omaha] md. Anna C. PETERSON [19; Omaha] on 27 Aug 1866. Off: MILLER. Wit: P. DICKERSON, Mrs. Dr. G.L. MILLER.

JANSEN, Soren [Douglas Co.] md. Mrs. Joanna Marie JANSEN [Douglas Co.] on Jul 1865 at DICKINSON's office. Off:DICKINSON. Wit: Charles P. BIRKETT, Peter MEILHEDE.

JANSEN [JANSA], Anton [23; Omaha] md. Anna NAMASEK [NAMESTEK] [18; Omaha] on 30 Dec 1868. Off: HYDE. Wit: John HULA, Charles GANKLE [KUNKL].

JARARD, Daniel [31; Omaha] md. Mariah MINNER [26; Omaha] on 11 Dec 1866. Off: KERMOTT. Wit: Mrs. C.M. HOELL, A.R. HOELL.

JARDINE, J.W. [24; b: Pennsylvania; f: J.B. JARDINE; m: Mary FLINTON] md. Mary GRIFFEN [24; b: Pennsylvania; f: Patrick GRIFFEN; m: Catharine NOON] on 10 Dec 1878. Off: LIPE. Wit: Lizzie E. LIPE, Thos. F. JARDINE.

JARDINE, Thomas T. [24; Omaha; b: PA; f: James D. JARDINE; m: Mary A. FLINTON] md. Kate McCARTHY [18; Omaha; b: Canada; f: Michael McCARTHY; m: Mary BOWES (both parents born Canada)] on 23 Nov 1876. Off: LIPE. Wit: J.W. JARDINE, Mary GRIFFIN. J.M. SPENCER signed the affidavit.

JARGENSEN, Jargen C. [JURGENSEN, Jurgen C.] [25; Omaha; b: Denmark; f: Jargan PETERSON; m: Else Marie] md. Mary NELSON [33; Omaha; b: Denmark; f: Nelson S. LANSON; m: Anna Marine] on 18 Jul 1869. Off: LARSON. Wit: Peder C.T. MUNK, John JENSEN.

JEFFCOAT, John [28; Florence] and Helen VEIRS [22; Florence] license issued on 22 May 1866. Off: HASCALL.

JEFFRIES, John E. [22; Council Bluffs, IA; b: Council Bluffs, IA; f: Edmund JEFFRIES; m: Mary Ann R. FORSYTH] md. Margaret KIMBALL [20; Weston, IA; b: Weston, IA; f: Caleb KIMBALL; m: Francis NIXTON] on 12 May 1879. Off: BARTHOLOMEW. Wit: John L. WEBSTER, Wm. L. PEABODY.

JELINEK, Joseph [24; Saunders Co.; b: Austria; f: Jacob JELINEK; m: Josephine PROHASKA] md. Mary HAJEK [20; Council Bluffs; b: Austria; f: Joseph HAJEK; m: Barbara HANZEL] on 3 Mar 1881 at St. Wenceslaus' Church. Off: KLIMA. Wit: Wenceslaus KOVARIK, John KOHOUT.

JENKINS, Clarence L. [29; South Boston, MA] md. Frances C. WITTING [18; Grand Rapids, MI] on 17 Nov 1867 at the residence of the bride's father. Off: KUHNS. Wit: Mary TRUMBUL, Joseph WOLF, Mr. and Mrs. WITTING, et al.

JENNESON, Henry E. [32; Omaha; b: Massachusetts; f: Flint JENNESON; m: Mary STOWE] md. Mrs. Lizzie A. HAUSE [35; Omaha; b: Massachusetts; f: William H. HONEY; m: Martha A. BROWN] on 8 Mar 1877. Off: PATERSON. Wit: John J. DICKEY, Mary S. Van BOSKERCK.

JENSEN, C.A. [26; Omaha; b: Denmark; f: Jens CHRISTENSON; m: Mary CHRISTENSON] md. Amelia NILSON [22; Omaha; b: Denmark; f: Nels C. THOMPSON; m: Mary OLESEN] on 23 Dec 1873. Off: BENZON. Wit: J.A. LUNDBERG; Anna D. BENZON.

JENSEN, Carl Frederick [25; Douglas Co.; b: Germany; f: Peter JENSEN; m: Margaret HANNER] md. Anna LASHANSKY [19; Douglas Co.; b: Germany; f: Angus LASHANSKY; m: Anna LANPHER] on 5 Oct 1876. Off: PEABODY. Wit: E.B. KNOX, Claus SCHEUMANN, Douglas Co.

JENSEN, George R. [35; Omaha; b: Denmark; f: Peter JENSEN; m: Kirsten RAHM] md. Mrs. Louise Olillie SCHULTZ [31; Omaha; b: Germany] on 31 Jul 1872. Off: THURSTON. Wit: S. JOERGENSON; N. JOHNSON.

JENSEN, Hans N. [24; Omaha; b: Denmark; f: Christian JENSEN; m: Annie JENSEN] md. Annie JENSEN [22; Omaha; b: Denmark; f: Lewis JENSEN; m: Caren M. JENSEN] on 14 Nov 1874. Off: PEABODY. Wit: Bennett Fdr. MASON; Fred HEINERIKSEN.

JENSEN, Hans Peter [29; Omaha; b: Denmark; f: Jens JENSEN; m: Karen Kirstine HANSEN] md. Harriet A. SWORT [19; Omaha; b: Canada; f: Lewis (Tunis?) B. SWORT; m: Charlota GRATIOT] on 1 Jul 1874. Off: GARRETT. Wit: Robert EVANS; Mrs. Eliza T. CLEBURN.

JENSEN, Jorgen [21; Douglas Co.; b: Germany; f: Andreas PAULSON; m: Christine SMITH] md. Anna C. GAADER [24; Douglas Co.; b: Germany; f: Peter N. GAADER; m: Anna Maria TURNER] on 11 Jun 1881 at the Danish Church. Off: GUYDESON. Wit: Thomas Jorgen DAHL, Douglas Co., N. DRAGE.

JENSEN, Lars [30; Douglas Co.; b: Denmark; f: Jens ANDERSON; m: Maria LARSON] md. Mary JOHNSON [28; Omaha; b: Norway; f: John PETERSON; m: Veldera KNUTSON] on 23 Dec 1877. Off: DAM [DAIN?]. Wit: Olivia BURSELL, A.J. CARLSON.

JEPSON, Charles [26; Omaha; b: Sweden; f: Swans JEPSON; m: Nellie PIERSON] md.

Louisa LINDEN [20; Omaha; b: Sweden; f: Swans LINDEN; m: Inga SWANSEN] on 28 Sep 1871. Off: GIBSON. Wit: Chas. H. BYRNE; Lucian F. HALE.

JEPSON, Edlef [28; Omaha; b: Germany; f: Thomas JEPSON; m: Enga CHRISTIANSON] and Nesine FREDRICKSEN [21; Omaha; b: Germany; f: John FREDRICKSEN; m: Catherine NESENE] on 6 Sep 1870. Off: MAY. Wit: Dietrich BRODERSON, Mrs. BRODERSON.

JEPSON, Edlef [28; Omaha; b: Prussia; f: Thomas JEPSON; m: Inga CHRISTIANSON] md. Christena FREDERICKSON [22; Omaha; b: Prussia; f: John FREDERICKSON; m: Dorothea NISSON] on 2 Jun 1874. Off: PEABODY. Wit: Enlen LEWIS; L.F. MAGUIN.

JEPSON, Peter [40; IA; b: Sweden; f: Andres JEPSON; m: Margaret ROSENTHAL] md. Charlotte JOHANSON [30; IA; b: Sweden; m: Swan JOHANSON; m: Johanna SEVANSEN] on 18 Sep 1881. Off: FOGELSTROM. Wit: Lars NILSON, Mrs. Anna NILSON.

JESPERSEN, Lauritz J. [32; Omaha; b: Denmark; f: Nis JESPERSEN; m: Carin LAGKJER] md. Christina SORENSEN [29; Omaha; b: Denmark; f: Christian SORENSEN; m: Anna LANIRSEN] on 9 Sep 1881. Off: STENBERG. Wit: John MAGHER, Jens F. CARSEN.

JESS, Claus [29; Omaha; b: Germany; f: Claus JESS; m: Maggie HESS] md. Katie KEEFER [21; Omaha; b: Wisconsin; f: George KEEFER; m: Magdalena DILLMAN] on 12 Dec 1877. Off: SEDGWICK. Wit: Peter BORE, Henry SIERTS.

JESSEN, Hans P. [23; Omaha; b: Denmark; f: H.C. JESSEN; m: Kirstene PETERSON] md. Kirstene SORENSON [20; Omaha; b: Denmark; f: H.P. SORENSON; m: Anna K. BACHE] on 16 Jun 1880. Off: STENBERG. Wit: Johanes OLSEN, Charles S. WAGNER.

JEWETT, Calvin [23; Bellevue, Sarpy Co.] md. Catharine RAMEY [24; Bellevue, Sarpy Co.] on 25 Mar 1869. Off: KELLEY. Wit: A. ROSEWATER of Douglas Co., Thomas SWIFT of Douglas Co.

JINK, Frank [25; Omaha; b: Bohemia; f: Jacob JINK; m: Anna SCUDDER] md. Mary JANCAK [25; Omaha; b: Bohemia; f: Thomas JANCAK; m: Anna JOROCEEK] on 22 May 1875. Off: PEABODY. Wit: Matthew MERAD, James KRAPEL.

JIPSON, Ingwert [21; Omaha; b: Germany; f: Thomas JIPSON; m: Inger CHRISTIANSON] md. Mary MILLER [18; Omaha; b: Omaha; f: Christian MILLER; m: Julia LUND] on 11 Oct 1879. Off: BEANS. Wit: Charles WESTERDAHL, Sol. PRINCE.

JOERG, Andrew [36; Omaha; b: Germany; f: Fidel JOERG; m: Christance HERRZ] md.

Kate HUMMELL [23; Omaha; b: Nebraska; f: John HUMMELL; m: Lena ----] on 20 Jul 1877, at ERFLING's residence, 1st Precinct, Douglas Co. Off: ERFLING. Wit: Wm. FENTON, Fried LEFHOLZ, both of 11th and Leavenworth Streets.

JOHANNES, John Henry [50; Columbus; b: Germany; f: Johan H. JOHANNES; m: Catharine WENDT] md. Mrs. Caroline TAGGER [51; Omaha; b: Germany] on 31 Mar 1873. Off: McKELVEY. Wit: H. TAGGER; Laurie TAGGER.

JOHANSON, Andrew [29; Omaha; b: Sweden; f: John ANDERSON; m: Helen PETERSON] md. Emma PETERSON [26; Omaha; b: Sweden; f: Peter ANDERSON; m: Dorothea OLESON] on 6 Sep 1879. Off: FOGELSTROM. Wit: Mrs. Dorotha OLSON, Mrs. Ida C. FOGELSTROM.

JOHN, Charley [28; Omaha; b: Germany; f: William JOHN; m: Frederika STRUKMAN] md. Mary REINHART [27; Omaha; b: Germany; f: Henry REINHART; m: Mary OBERMAN] on 20 Jul 1871. Off: GIBSON. Wit: Fred LEWAN; Otto WETTORFF.

JOHNS, John F. [28; Erie, PA; b: Erie, PA; f: John V. JOHNS; m: Margaret HABEL] md. Catharine M. CAHILL [21; Omaha; b: Ireland; f: Patrick CAHILL; m: Mary McCARTHY] on 18 Jul 1869. Off: KUHNS. Wit: Eneas DOUGHERTY, Kate WELSH.

JOHNSON, A.C. [23; Omaha; b: Denmark; f: John ANDERSON; m: Catharine PETERSON] md. Mary NICHOLSON [20; Omaha; b: Denmark; f: Frederick NICHOLSON; m: Christine GREGERSON] on 26 May 1879. Off: LIPE. Wit: Lizzie E. LIPE, Maggie HOWER.

JOHNSON, A.S. [39; Omaha; b: Sweden; f: J. JOHNSON; m: Cary CASTONSON] md. Emma JOHNSON [27; Omaha; b: Sweden; f: Christopher JOHNSON; m: Catharine SEMONSON] on 27 Sep 1879. Off: JAMESON. Wit: E.P. PEARSON, Kary JENSEN or Carrie JOHNSON.

JOHNSON, Alfred [21; Omaha; b: Sweden; f: Magnus JOHNSON; m: Sarah H. SAMUELSON] md. Maria E. SABELMAN [22; Omaha; b: Sweden; f: Enich SABELMAN] on 11 Jun 1871 at the 2nd Presbyterian Church. Off: STEWART. Wit: John R. MEREDITH; P.L. PERRINE.

JOHNSON, Alfrid [25; Omaha; b: Sweden; f: Magnus JOHNSON; m: Sarah SIMONSON] md. Anna S. ANDERSON [25; Omaha; b: Sweden; f: Anders M. ANDERSON; m: Anna LAWSON] on 14 Jan 1874. Off: PEABODY. Wit: Miss M.J. PETRIE; Mrs. Wm. L. PEABODY.

JOHNSON, Amos [23; Omaha; b: Denmark; f: Erasmus JOHNSON; m: Martha H. ANDERSON] md. Anna SMITH [25; Omaha; b: Denmark; f: Christian SMITH; m: Johanna VINTON] on 4 Oct 1869. Off: LARSON. Wit: August LARSON of Washington Co., Petronelle LAGERSTROM.

JOHNSON, Andrew F. [33; Omaha; b: Sweden; f: John JOHNSON; m: Anny LARSON] md. Annie SWANSON [18; Omaha; b: Sweden; f: Swan MORTONSON; m: Carrie MATSON] on 4 Mar 1874. Off: BENZON. Wit: A.G. LAWSON; Emeline LAWSON.

JOHNSON, Andrew [23; Omaha; b: Denmark; f: Nils C. JOHNSON; m: Mary THIESE] md. Annie A. LINDBORG [19; Omaha; b: Sweden; f: Peter LINDBORG; m: Catharine PEARSSON] on 8 May 1873. Off: TOWNSEND. Wit: Jens JENSEN; John A. BONNEVIER.

JOHNSON, Andrew [27; Omaha] md. Anna ERLICKSON [27; Omaha] on 15 Mar 1869. Off: HYDE. Wit: Will BROWN, Andreas ANDERSON.

JOHNSON, Andrew [30; Omaha; b: Sweden; f: John JOHNSON; m: Anna MATTSON] md. Nellie PAULSEN [22; Omaha; b: Sweden; f: Paul OLSSON; m: Ingra NELSON] on 7 Jan 1873. Off: TOWNSEND. Wit: G. ANDERSON; Ambrose ERICKSON.

JOHNSON, Andrew [32;Omaha; b: Denmark; f: Hans JOHNSON; m: Ablone JOHNSON] md. Mary C. MADSEN [32; Omaha; b: Denmark; f: Christian MADSEN; m: Hanne C. TUFT] on 13 Apr 1874. Off: PEABODY. Wit: Neils MADSEN; Mrs. Ingre MADSEN.

JOHNSON, Anton [36; Omaha; b: Denmark; f: N. JOHNSON; m: Stena LAWSON] md. Johannah NELSON [31; Omaha; b: Sweden; f: Nels MONSON; m: G. PETERSON] on 29 Apr 1876. Off: RING. Wit: John EKELEY, Marcus HANSON.

JOHNSON, August [35; Omaha; b: Sweden; f: John ANDERSON; m: Lisa DANELSON] md. Louise BENSON [31; Omaha; b: Sweden; f; Benson Emanuel JOHNSON; m: Christine LARSON] on 10 May 1879. Off: LIPE. Wit: Lizzie E. LIPE, Eva J. LIPE.

JOHNSON, Bengt [36; Omaha; b: Sweden; f: Johann JOHNSON; m: Bola BENGSTON] md. Tilda NELSON [30; Omaha; b: Sweden; f: Nels JOHNSON; m: Inger LARSON] on 30

Dec 1881. Off: BENEKE. Wit: August SCHROEDER, J.P.J. RYAN.

JOHNSON, Carl [29; Omaha; b: Denmark; f: John JOHNSON; m: Mary SCHNEMAN] md. Anna JOHNSON [23; Omaha; b: Denmark; f: John William JOHNSON; m: Mary MATTESON] on 19 Jun 1873. Off: TOWNSEND. Wit: Mark HANSEN; Anne HANSEN.

JOHNSON, Charles A. [29; Omaha; b: Sweden; f: John PETERSON; m: Ingren MOGNUS] md. Maggie OLESON [21; Omaha; b: Sweden; f: Oliver OLESON; m: Maggie JACOBSON] on 27 Mar 1875. Off: PEABODY. Wit: C.J. BONNER, Emma HABBE.

JOHNSON, Charles M. [28; Avoca, IA; b: Prince Edward Island; f: John JOHNSON; m: Margaret McDONALD] md. Mary M. KIMBALL [21; Avoca, IA; b: Illinois; m: Margaret FOWLER] on 21 Jun 1871. Off: GIBSON. Wit: Nelson T. WOOD, Atlantic, IA; Elizabeth BABB, Big Grove, IA.

JOHNSON, Charles P., Capt. [30; US Army; b: New York; f: Dr. Charles S. JOHNSON; m: Jane E. KELLOY] md. Sarah E. MANNING [22; Omaha; b: Wisconsin; f: F.G. MANNING; m: Ann K. SMITH] on 8 Jun 1871 near Omaha. Off: R.H. CLARKSON. Wit: Mrs. R.H. CLARKSON; Mr. and Mrs. F.G. MANNING; Mrs. E.S. BUTTERFIELD.

JOHNSON, Charles [24; Omaha; b: Sweden; f: Swen JOHNSON; m: Lena TRELSON] md. Hannah HANSEN [25; Omaha; b: Sweden; f: Hans JOHNSON: m: Helsey PEARSON] on 18 Mar 1871. Off: GIBSON. Wit: Jacob KING; J.S. WRIGHT.

JOHNSON, Charles [25; Omaha; b: Sweden; f: John P. JOHNSON; m: Anna DANIELSON] md. Ida SWENSEN [21; Omaha; b: Sweden; f: Daniel SWENSEN; m: Catharine MAGNUSON] on 11 Jul 1871. Off: BENNETT. Wit: Clinton BRIGGS; Emily J. BRIGGS.

JOHNSON, Charles [26; Saunders Co.; b: Sweden; f: John P. JOHNSON; m: Matilda OLSEN] md. Tinnie PETERSON [22; Omaha; b: Sweden] on 17 Jul 1873. Off: LARSON. Wit: Adolf J. EDGAR; Eric M. LARSON.

JOHNSON, Christ [26; b: Denmark; f: Henry JOHNSON; m: Mary JOHNSON] md. Leonora OLESON [26; b: Norway; f: Edward OLESON; m: Helene EVENSEN] on 20 Feb 1878. Off: FISHER. Wit: Peter BENSEN, Olive B. RYAN.

JOHNSON, Christ [32; b: Denmark; f: John C. JOHNSON; m: Mary PETERSON] md. Brigita HANSEN [24; b: Denmark; f: Hans ANDERSON; m: Julia NELSON] on 8 Oct 1878. Off: LIPE. Wit: Christ WILLARD, Mary HANSEN.

JOHNSON, Christian [33; Omaha; b: Denmark; f: Jens HENSEN or JOHNSON; m: Annie RASMUSSEN] md. Catherina HANSEN [32; Omaha; b: Denmark; f: Hans HANSEN; m: Carrie HANSEN] on 20 Nov 1869. Off: GIBSON. Wit: [Mrs.?] Cris CHRISTIANSEN, Nels LARSON.

JOHNSON, David H. [36; Omaha; b: VA; f: Humphrey JOHNSON; m: Maria BURRAL] md. Mrs. Katie COOK [28; Omaha; b: IN; f: William SPAULDIN; m: Lucy WINSTON] on 30 May 1881. Off: GREEN. Wit: Mrs. John LEWIS, Mrs. Susan A. BOLDEN, et al.

JOHNSON, Edward [24; Plattsmouth; b: New Jersey; f: John JOHNSON; m: Mary CARHART] md. Emily SMITH [22; Omaha; b: Illinois; f: M.C. SMITH; m: Eliza GILMORE] on 15 Feb 1870. Off: GIBSON. Wit: M.C. SMITH; Francis Mary CARTER, Valley Station.

JOHNSON, Eli [25; Douglas Co.; b: New York; f: Eli JOHNSON; m: Tina FREEMAN] md. Sarah A. ELSTON [18; Douglas Co.; b: Indiana; f: William ELSTON; m: Elizabeth HENRY] on 13 Dec 1877. Off: CORLISS. Wit: George CAMPBELL, Milla WESTON, both of Waterloo.

JOHNSON, Enos [23; Douglas Co.] md. Lizzie B. ROWE [17; Douglas Co.] on 11 Nov 1868. Off: KUHNS. Wit: Mr. and Mrs. Harrison JOHNSON, Mr. and Mrs. WEATHERWAX, et al. Age consent given by Mrs. Permelia ROWE, mother of the bride.

JOHNSON, Enos [24; Omaha; b: Sweden; f: John JOHNSON; m: Evalina NELSON] md. Josephina NYSTET [24; Omaha; b: Sweden; f: ---- NYSTET; m: unknown] on 27 Apr 1880. Off: ANDERSON. Wit: A. JACOBSON, A.P. ????.

JOHNSON, Frank B. [21; Council Bluffs; b: WI; f: B.F. JOHNSON; m: Sarah K. BOYCE] md. Caroline A. PONGELLEY [18; Council Bluffs; b: England; f: Edward PONGELLEY; m: Elizabeth SMITH] on 11 Mary 1875. Off: PEABODY. Wit: B.W. SHILEDS, Joseph BOOLS.

JOHNSON, Frank [25; Omaha; b: Sweden; f: Johannes HANSEN; m: Christina ANDERSON] md. Matilda JOHNSON [24; Omaha; b: Sweden; f: John JOHNSON] on 3 Oct 1873. Off: EASTABROOK. Wit: Caroline A. ESTABROOK; Edward WHITEHORN.

JOHNSON, Frank [29; Omaha; b: Sweden; f: Peter JOHNSON; m: Inga L. NILSON] md. Emily JOHNSON [20; Omaha; b: Sweden; f: Magnis JOHNSON; m: Sarah H. SAMUELSON] on 8 Aug 1871. Off: KUHNS. Wit: Mrs. William PHENIX; Mrs. H.W. KUHNS.

JOHNSON, George [23; Florence; b: Sweden; f: John JOHNSON; m: Britti JOHNSON] md. Engeback ANDERSON [29; Florence; b: Sweden; f: Anders ANDERSON; m: Carrie WILSON] on 2 Apr 1870. Off: GIBSON. Wit: Gust ANDERSON, Florence; Halvren NILSON, Florence.

JOHNSON, Harry [24; West Omaha; b: Omaha; f: Harrison JOHNSON; m: Minerva HAMBRIGHT] md. Elizabeth A. WALKER [19; West Omaha; b: Nebraska; f: A.J. WALKER; m: Hattie L. BENNER] on 29 Aug 1878. Off: LIPE. Wit: Mrs. C.A. HUBBARD, Mrs. Euphrasie AGUILERA.

JOHNSON, Henry C. [25; Omaha; b: Denmark; f: Jens Peter JENSON; m: Maria CHRISTENSEN] md. Sine Nicoline KRAGSKOW [16; Omaha; b: Utah; f: Peter C.S. KRAGSKOW; m: Christine Maria NELSON] on 16 Jan 1874. Off: PEABODY. Wit: R. MATTHEWSON; Peter S.C. KRAGSKOW. Father of bride signed the affidavit.

JOHNSON, Henry [24; Chicago Pct, Douglas Co.; b: Denmark; f: John JOHNSON; m: Mary JOHNSON] md. Olena PETERSON [23; Chicago Pct, Douglas Co.; b: Denmark; f: Peter PETERSON; m: Mary NELSON] on 13 Dec 1872. Off: PORTER. Wit: John SAVAGE; Mrs. Lovey SAVAGE.

JOHNSON, Henry [29; Omaha; b: Denmark; f: Jens JORGENSEN; m: Marian HANSON] md. Sophia MORTENSON [23; Omaha; b: Denmark; f: Jens MORTENSON; m: Marian PETERSON] on 30 Nov 1872. Off: SWEDERS. Wit: C.W.B. ODEN; Frederik JOHNSON.

JOHNSON, Henry [33; Douglas Co.; b: Denmark; f: John VEDERSTROMER; m: Marian HANSEN] md. Karen M. IVESON [27; Douglas Co.; b: Denmark; f: Ivor MATESEN; m: Martha M. ANDERSEN] on 24 Jun 1876. Off: LIPE. Wit: Gertie HANSEN, May HANSEN.

JOHNSON, Jacob [37; Omaha; b: Pennsylvania; f: Joseph JOHNSON; m: Elizabeth RAUP] md. Ellen BROPHY [24; Omaha; b: Ireland; f: Patrick BROPHY; m: Catharine LANAGARN] on 1 Sep 1870. Off: CURTIS. Wit: William WELLER; Catherine MURRAY.

JOHNSON, James C. [23; Omaha; b: Denmark; f: James JOHNSON; m: Annie NELSON] md. Annie E. OLESON [23; Omaha; b: Norway; f: Nels OLESON; m: Annie JOHNSON] on 10 Oct 1872. Off:

TOWNSEND. Wit: William P. HENNESSY; Jerome HERTZMANN.

JOHNSON, John A. [25; Omaha; b: Sweden; f: Johsen JOHANESON; m: Stina PETERSON] md. Anna PETERSON [25; Omaha; b: Sweden; f: Pehr PEHRSON; m: Inga JONSDOTTER] on 14 Sep 1881. Off: STENBERG. Wit: John MEAGHER, Thomas H. TERRY.

JOHNSON, John E. [21; Omaha; b: Sweden; f: Herrick JOHNSON; m: Sarah E. ANDERSON] md. Caroline BECK [20; Omaha; b: Sweden; f: Nels Peter BECK; m: Helena NELSON] on 5 Nov 1873. Off: PEABODY. Wit: Fred HANSEN; Matilda SALTHER.

JOHNSON, John W. [Omaha] md. Mrs. Hannah MESSEL [Omaha] on 13 Jul 1864 at DICKINSON's office. Off: DICKINSON. Wit: Lawrence RAINS, Mr. and Mrs. Levi MAXTED, et al.

JOHNSON, John [22; Omaha; b: Sweden; f: John BENSON; m: Margaret BILLINGRIN] md. Edna BERGQUIST [21; Omaha; b: Sweden; f: John BERGQUIST; m: Mary SANDEL] on 10 Feb 1872. Off: PORTER. Wit: Gustave ANDERSEN; Hellen ANDERSEN.

JOHNSON, John [25; Elkhorn Pct, Douglas Co.; b: Sweden] md. Emily C. HARTFORD [17; Elkhorn Pct, Douglas Co.; b: Sangamon Co., IL; f: Harrison HARTFORD; m: Elizabeth HAMILTON] on 17 Mar 1873 at Elkhorn Pct. Off: HANEY. Wit: James L. STEPHENS, Valley Pct; Elias HARTFORD, Valley Pct. Age of consent given by father of bride.

JOHNSON, John [37; b: Ireland; f: Richard JOHNSON; m: Margaret DRUHENE] md. Elizabeth KING [27; B: Ohio; f: Jeremiah KING; m: Hannah MURPHY] on 17 Jul 1878. Off: KELLY. Wit: W.H. MULCAHY, A.S.P. PALMER.

JOHNSON, Lars [22; Omaha; b: Norway; f: John RASMUSSEN; m: Johanna OLSDOTTER] md. Beret Martha OLSDOTTER [21; Omaha; b: Norway; f: Ole KNUDSON; m: Eli OLSDOTTER] on 24 Sep 1870. Off: LARSON. Wit: Andrew ANDERSON; Elling ARNETTSEN.

JOHNSON, Lewis [29; Saunders Co.; b: Sweden; f: John JOHNSON; m: Louis PIERSON] md. Carrie JOHNSON [24; Omaha; b: Sweden; f: George JOHNSON; m: Ellen JOHNSON] on 8 Jul 1874. Off: PEABODY. Wit: M.T. ANDERSON; Ann JOHNSON.

JOHNSON, Martin [24; Omaha] md. Betta NEALSON [24; Omaha] on 17 Apr 1869. Off: HYDE. Wit: T.S. NASH, C.S. HEWITT.

JOHNSON, Nels J. [25; Douglas Co.; b: Denmark; f: Jim ANDERSON; m: Dorthia ANDERSON] md. Hannah JOHNSON [30; Douglas Co.; b: Sweden; f: John PETERSEN;

m: Ellen WATSON] on 5 Jun 1876. Off: SEDGWICK. Wit: J.W. DAVIS, Douglas Co., F.P. HANLON, Douglas Co.

JOHNSON, Nels [33; Saunders Co.; b: Sweden; f: John OLSEN; m: Karen KOLN] md. Johanna PEDERSEN [25; Omaha; b: Sweden; f: Erick PEDERSEN; m: Melissa HENDERSON] on 25 Apr 1873. Off: TOWNSEND. Wit: Peter OLSEN; Martin CHRISTIANSEN.

JOHNSON, Nicklas [36; Omaha; b: Sweden; f: Gons NELSON; m: Ingborg GONS] md. Elsse JOHNSON [27; Omaha; b: Sweden; f: John OLSEN; m: Tgersten NEILSON] on 4 Nov 1873. Off: PEABODY. Wit: Robert TOWNSEND; Wm. JACKSON; Fountain, IN.

JOHNSON, Niels [34; Omaha; b: Denmark; f: Jens PAULSON; m: Ellen KNUDSON] md. Sarah OLESON [29; Omaha; b: Norway; f: Ole JACOBSON; m: Velbor LARSON] on 15 Mar 1881. Off: FOGELSTROM. Wit: Mr. and Mrs. William PETERSON, Ellen KNUDSON.

JOHNSON, Nilse [22; Sarpy Co.; b: Denmark; f: John JOHNSON; m: Annie NELSON] md. Mary HENSEN [18: Omaha; b: Denmark; f: Neils HANSEN; m: Catherine JORGENSON] on 23 Aug 1875. Off: PEABODY. Wit: F.P. HANLON, George W. SHIELDS.

JOHNSON, Oscar [31; Saunders Co.; b: Sweden; f: Charles JOHNSON; m: Christina GRINQUEST] md. Elizabeth OCANDER [18; Omaha; b: Sweden; f: Gabriel OCANDER; m: Lene NELSON] on 22 Jun 1874. Off: KING. Wit: Henry CHALMAN; Maria CHALMAN or CHOLMAN.

JOHNSON, Otto [26; Omaha; b: Demnark; f: Christian JOHNSON; m: Karen ANDERSON] md. Mary May AMERSON [18; Omaha; b: Omaha; f: William AMERSON; m: Mary McCUNE] on 23 Feb 1879. Off: STENBERG. Wit: Herman CROMWELL, Ellena CROMWELL.

JOHNSON, P.J. [28; Omaha; b: Sweden; f: John PETERSON; m: Ingrid JOHNSON] md. Emma C. PETERSON [20; Omaha; b: Sweden; f: Swan PETERSON; m: Anna JOHNSON] on 10 Mar 1881. Off: FOGELSTROM. Wit: S.G. JOHNSON, B.J. BENZON.

JOHNSON, Peter [24; Plattsmouth; b: Denmark; f: James JOHNSON; m: Mary SMITH] md. Elmire METEER [28; Plattsmouth; b: PA; f: Robert METEER; m: Cloey ANDRES] on 14 Sep 1881. Off: CHADWICK. Wit: B.R. FIELD, Plattsmouth, M.J. METEER.

JOHNSON, Peter [26; Omaha; b: Denmark; f: John NELSON; m: Mette K. PEDERSDOTTER] md. Inger W. HANSEN [26; Omaha; b: Denmark; f: Hans HANSEN; m: Marie THROULSON] on 5 Dec 1881 at "their res." Off: GYDESEN. Wit: Niels JOHNSON, N. BERTELSEN.

JOHNSON, Peter [28; Omaha; b; Denmark; f: Christ JOHNSON; m: Annie LARSON] md. Mary PETERSON [20; Omaha; b: Utah Territory; f: P.C. CHRISTIANSON; m: Martha THUN] on 5 Jan 1877. Off: HANSEN. Wit: Peder C. CUTHENSSEN [CHRISTIANSON?], of Lucabyar?, Martha THUN.

JOHNSON, Petter [28; Omaha; b: Sweden; f: John JOHNSON; m: Carrie NEILSON] md. Augusta PETERSON [19; Omaha; b: Sweden; f: Pete PETERSON; m: Hellen JACOBSON] on 25 Jul 1877. Off: ANDERSON. Wit: W.M. KNOTTS, E. HENBERG.

JOHNSON, Rufus [negro; 22; Douglas Co.; b: AL; f: Benjamin JOHNSON; m: Dafnay] md. Fanny RICHARDSON [negro; 20; Douglas Co.; b: MO; f: Charles RICHARDSON; m: Fannie RICHARDSON] on 22 Jun 1876. Off: BRITT. Wit: S.J. BRITT, Maggie VANDEFORD.

JOHNSON, T.C. [26; Council Bluffs; b: Denmark; f: James THOMPSON; m: Anna M. THOMPSON] md. Mrs. Mary SOUTHWELL [38; Council Bluffs; b: IA; f: Robert STEPHENSON; m: Elizabeth HUNSACKER] on 15 Jan 1881. Off: BARTHOLOMEW. Wit: Max BERGMAN.

JOHNSON, Thomas [26; Omaha; b: Denmark; f: Johnathan JOHNSON; m: ---- HOLMAN] md. Annie OLSON [20; Omaha; b: Norway; f: John OLSON; m: Annie BRYNIELSON] on 30 Apr 1870. Off: KUHNS. Wit: Morris MORISON; Mrs. Annie JOHNSON.

JOHNSON, W.R. [26; Omaha; b: Maryland; f: Noah JOHNSON; m: Rachel BAILEY] md. Jennie M. ALLAN [23; Omaha; b: Nebraska; f: James T. ALLAN; m: Elizabeth A. BUDDINGTON] on 11 Jun 1879. Off: MILLSPAUGH. Wit: Lyman RICHARDSON, James ALLAN.

JOHNSON, William B. [36; Valley Station; b: Ohio; f: William JOHNSON; m: Margaret RUSSELL] md. Esther J. DIMAND [19; Valley Station; b: Pennsylvania; f: Sylvester DIMAND; m: Emma TAYLOR] on 3 Jan 1870. Off: GIBSON. Wit: Mrs. Nancy C. JOHNSON, Valley Station; A.H. LANPHERE.

JOHNSON, William E. [28; Omaha; b: England; f: Samuel JOHNSON; m: Mary Anne DALLOW] md. Annie SMITH [25; Omaha; b: England; f: Charles EDMONSON; m: Elizabeth PARKINSON] on 26 Feb 1877. Off: JAMESON. Wit: William VANDUSEN, William EDMONSON.

JOHNSON, William or Wilhelm [30; Jefferson Precinct; b: Germany; f: Detleff JOHNSON; m: Wilhelmina STORK] md. Dora SCHWEEL [24; Fort Calhoun; b: Germany; f: James SCHWEEL; m: Anna STAENDER] on 17 Jun 1879. Off: BARTHOLOMEW. Wit: Fritz RIEPEN, Charles F. GOETTSCH of Jefferson Precinct.

JOHNSON, William [26; Omaha] md. Anna NELSON [24; Omaha] on 22 Mar 1868. Off: STUCK. Wit: Bernard DROST, Mary JACOBSON.

JOHNSON, William [30; Council Bluffs] md. A. LeGEE [35; Council Bluffs] at 6:30 PM on 1 Sep 1868 at DIMMICK's house. Off: DIMMICK. Wit: Mr. and Mrs. Joseph FOX.

JOHNSON, William [37; Lincoln Co.] md. Catharine E. ANDERSON [25; Otoe Co.] on 31 Jan 1867. Off: HASCALL. Wit: D.M. ANDERSON, J.G. GRAVES.

JONAS, R.E. [24; Cameron, MO; b: England; f: Simeon JONAS; m: Martha COLES] md. Alice J. McLAIN [21; Omaha; b: NE; f: J.J. McLAIN; m: Mary FALES] on 17 May 1881. Off: MAXFIELD. Wit: J.J. McLAIN, Frank CUTLER.

JONASEN, Soren [26; b: Denmark; f: Jonas PETERSON; m: Karin SORENSON] md. Guerine N.P.C. NELSON [22; b: Denmark; f: Nelse NELSON; m: Emelia Cat OLESEN] on 9 Oct 1878 at Mrs. NILSEN's, Omaha. Off: HILMEN. Wit: Mr. HUSTED, Mrs. E. NILSEN.

JONES, F.E. [24; Omaha; b: Indiana; f: Benjamin JONES; m: Isabel CORN] md. Sarah RUNYON [20; Omaha; b: Illinois; f: Alexander RUNYON; m: Mary Ann WILKIN] on 7 Nov 1879. Off: BARTHOLOMEW. Wit: J.R. SPENCER, F.P. SPENCER.

JONES, George B. [30; Omaha; b: Canada; f: John JONES; m: Caroline BREAKENRIDGE] md. Lucy E. CHASE [25; Omaha; b: Canada; f: Enoch M. CHASE; m: Elmina ALLEN] on 3 Oct 1881. Off: HARSHA. Wit: Mrs. John L. SMITH, Rena ROSS.

JONES, George [38; Omaha; b: New York State; f: William JONES; m: Maria LISH] and Mrs. Catherine McCRANEY [30; b: MS; f: L.T. COATS; m: Emily SINSEY] license issued on 12 Apr 1881. No marriage record. Off: SMITH.

JONES, Harley H. [21; Council Bluffs; b: Iowa; f: Samuel JONES; m: Mattie GOODRICH] md. Ada GUILTOR [18; Council Bluffs; b: Iowa; f: Francis GUILTOR; m: Mary MORGAN] on 23 Nov 1877. Off: PEABODY. Wit: Frank P. HANLON, James AMEY.

JONES, Harrison [55; Omaha] md. Mrs. Mary A. MATHER [47; Omaha] on 13 Mar 1868. Off: KELLEY. Wit: John WOOD, P. MURPHY.

JONES, Henry [58; Omaha; b: Wales; f: Walter JONES; m: Lavinia JONES] md. Mrs. Jane MILLER [58; Omaha; b: New York; f: John HOLDEN; m: Patience MILLER] on 23 Nov 1879. Off: MAXFIELD. Wit: Mrs. J.B. MAXFIELD, Flora D. OVERMAN.

JONES, Henry [colored; 21; Omaha] md. Matilda BRADFORD [colored; 20; Omaha] on 21 May 1868. Off: SLAUGHTER. Wit: Joseph WRIGHT, Harriet JONES.

JONES, Hiram [38; Douglas Co.] md. Mrs. Sarah Jane MORGAN [31; Douglas Co.] on 3 Aug 1868. Off: STUCK. Wit: S.D. MERCER, L.F. MAGINN.

JONES, James A. [28; Omaha] md. Margaretta (Margrata) SHELDEN [18; Omaha] on 2 Sep 1857. Off: WATSON.

JONES, James N. [27; Waterloo; b: Indiana; f: James JONES; m: Cynthia FERGUSON] md. Katie S. STOUT [18; Waterloo; b: Iowa; f: E.S. STOUT; m: Priscilla BRYANT] on 15 May 1880 at Waterloo. Off: NEISON. Wit: Mr. and Mrs. E.S. STOUT, Frank CLARK.

JONES, Martin [31; Silver City, ID; b: New York; f: Berry JONES; m: Eve ARMSTRONG] md. Mrs. Julia BURNHAM [20; Omaha; b: Rochester, NY; f: David KNOWLAND; m: Mary TURNER] on 25 Dec 1870. Off: BETTS. Wit: Oscar P. INGALLS; Herman DRAKE.

JONES, Patrick [27; Omaha; b: Ireland; f: Patrick JONES; m: Margaret KANEELY] md. Mary FLAHAV [FLAHEY] [22; Omaha; b: Ireland; f: Michael FLAHIV (FLAHIVE); m: Mary SWEENY] on 11 Jul 1869. Off: CURTIS. Wit: Thomas FLAHEV, Bridget GRIFFIN.

JONES, Richard H. [38; Sarpy Co.; b: Pennsylvania; f: Morris M. JONES; m: Mary M. PRICE] md. Josephine SUTTON [22; Omaha; b: Iowa; f: Joniah SUTTON; m: A.M. BAXTER] on 11 Apr 1874. Off: ADAIR. Wit: N.J. SMITH; Mrs. M.A. ADAIR.

JONES, Samuel B. [30; Omaha; b: NY; f: John C. JONES m: Hannah L. REED] md. Mary CHAMBERS [21; Omaha; b: NY; f: Wm. CHAMBERS; m: Jeannette KIDDER] on 17 Oct 1876. Off: SHERRILL. Wit: Major Wm. CHAMBERS, John E. WILBUR.

JONES, W.R. [26; Douglas Co.; b: New York; f: James JONES; m: Anna ROYSTON] md. Emily MARTIN [22; Omaha; b: Ohio; f: Welcome MARTIN; m: Margaret JOHNSON] on 10 Dec 1880. Off: MAXFIELD. Wit: G.L. GASCOIGNE, Mrs. K.M. GASCOIGNE.

JONES, William H. [Omaha] md. Lydia C. SULLIVAN [Omaha] on 7 Sep 1863 at Mr. LEMON's residence. Both of legal age. Off: LEMON. Wit: Mrs. LEMON, et al.

JONES, William M. [20; Douglas Co.] md. Sarah Ann ROSS [16; Douglas Co.] on 15 Jan 1868 at STUCK's office. Off: STUCK. Wit: Alexander JONES, Margaret A. JONES. Verbal age consent given by the parents of the groom. Written age consent given by Deborahan HUNTER of Rockport, mother of the bride.

JONES, William [21+; Omaha; colored] and Ellen STEVENSON [18+; Omaha; white] application issued on 17 Jun 1872. Off: TOWNSEND. "said Ellen STEVENSON is a white person, and that said William JONES is of full negro blood..."

JONGSTRIM [IONGSTIN], Nelsen [35; Omaha] md. Ann Catherine PETERSON [38; Omaha] on 9 Apr 1859 at BRIGGS' office. Off: BRIGGS. Wit: Adolf GRENBACK, John DICKINSON.

JORDAN, Daniel T. [26; Valley Station; b: Illinois; f: Walter JORDAN; m: Susan DENNEY] md. Mary J. THOMPSON [21; Valley Station; b: Illinois; f: Isaac THOMPSON; m: Susan DAVIS] on 23 Apr 1870 at Platte Valley or Omaha. Off: KERSTETTER. Wit: Geo. PARKS; Charles KELLY; both of Platte Valley or Omaha?.

JORGENSEN, Christian [27; Omaha; b: Denmark; f: Christian JORGENSEN; m: Anna Katrina LARSON] md. Eliza May JENSEN [18; Omaha; b: Wisconsin; f: Orthmand JENSEN] on 25 Nov 1871. Off: SUNDBORN. Wit: A. Gust. DAHLSTROM; Mary C. DAHLSTROM.

JORGENSEN, Jeppe [31; Douglas Co.; b: Denmark; f: Yorgen RASMUSSEN; m: Kirsten ANDERSEN] md. Charlotte N. NIELSEN [31; Douglas Co.; b: Denmark; f: Niels THOGERSEN; m: Ann Marie HANSEN] on 8 June 1872. Off: TOWNSEND. Wit: John JOHNSON; Lars JORGENSEN.

JORGENSEN, Lars [23; Omaha; b: Denmark; f: Jorgen RASMUSEN; m: Kristin ANDERSDOTTER] md. Anna Maria OLSEN [28; Omaha; b: Denmark; f: Ole PEDERSON; m: Anna Elizabeth KNUTSDOTTER] on 19 Aug 1871. Off: BENNETT. Wit: Jeppe JORGENSEN; Barmus JORGENSEN.

JORGENSEN, Soren [24; Omaha] md. Helen THOMPSON [24; Omaha] on 20 Feb 1869. Off: KELLY. Wit: Andrew WEIUGUVEST*, John CULERBERG.

JUDD, M.H. [43; Council Bluffs; b: Virginia; f: Merritt JUDD; m: Anna A. MEAD] md. Mary A. BUSHEL [22; Council Bluffs; b: Wisconsin; f: Casper BUSHEL; m: Julia KELCH] on 28 Jan 1877. Off: SHERRILL. Wit: Wm. L. PEABODY, Geo. W. HALL.

JUDGE, Anthony [30; Omaha; b: Ireland; f: John JUDGE; m: Margaret RUHANE] md. Bridget PRICE [26; Omaha; b: Ireland; f: Harry PRICE; m: Margaret JUDGE] on 9 Nov 1880. Off: ENGLISH. Wit: John PRICE, Mary BOLAN.

JUDSON, Henry M. [46; Omaha; b: NY; f: Philo JUDSON; m: Charity BRADLEY] md. Mary A. WALLS [26; Omaha; b: DE; f: Abram WALLS; m: Louisa WARNER] on 21 Jun 1985. Off: PEABODY. Wit: H.G. BUTTERFIELD; Mary C. PEABODY.

JUSTESEN, S. Peter [29; Omaha; b: Denmark; f: Just SORENSEN; m: Anna K. NIELSON] md. Ellen K. ANDERSON [23; Omaha; b: Denmark; f: Andrew FREDERICKSON; m: Karen LARSON] on 26 Mar 1881. Off: GYDESIN. Wit: Andrew Petrus THOMSON, FREDERICKSON.

KAASCH, F.J. [25; Omaha; b: Wisconsin; f: Fritz KAASCH; m: Maria LIPPKE] md. Pollie JHANS [18; Omaha; b: Germany; f: August JHANS; m: Hennie HICKSTEIN] on 9 Dec 1879. Off: FRESE. Wit: Fr. BUSCH, Mrs. Agnes KROOL.

KACK, John [42; Omaha; b: Wertemberg; f: John C. KACK; m: Barbara] md. Lizzie SCHNELLER [24; Omaha] b: Castle Marburg, Germany; f: Peter SCHNELLER; m: Margaret OCHS] on 13 Aug 1869. Off: KUHNS. Wit: Mrs. W.H. KUHNS, Ellen DRAPER.

KADLECEK, Vacslav [Vaclav] [38; Burt Co.; b: Germany] md. Mrs.? Caroline WASOWSKY [31; b: Germany] on 17 May 1869 at the German Catholic church. Off: GROENEBAUM. Wit: Gustave SOHILL.

KAESSNER, Gustav [25; Douglas Co.; b: Germany; f: Carl KAESSNER; m: Mary KAECHEL] md. Sophie CLAUSIN [24; Douglas Co.; b: Germany; f: Hans CLAUSIN; m: Cathrina RORER [ROHWER]] on 19 Feb 1876. Off: HILGENDORF. Wit: Martin THEDENS, Douglas Co., Henry SCHORMANN, Douglas Co.

KAISER, Anton [27; Omaha; b: Germany; f: John KAISER; m: Lena MEYER] md. O. Lina ELLSBORG [32; Omaha; b: Germany; f: Christian ELLSBORG; m: Margaret BROWN] on 10 Aug 1880, German Catholic Church. Off: GROENBAUM. Wit: Andrew NIESSENKEAR, John MAY.

KAISER, August [25; Omaha; b: Germany; f: Ferdenand KAISER; m: Ernestene BOBBIN] md. Caroline SPRAKTES [18; Omaha; b: Germany; f: Wilhelm SPRAKTES; m: Erkmuth BARROFSKY] on 27 Feb 1879.

Off: BRUEGGER. Wit: Michael BUEHLER, Chr. KECK.

KAISER, August [27; Omaha; b: Germany; f: Frederick KAISER; m: Ernestine BOBIN] md. Augustine BIKOVIS 15; Omaha; b: Germany; f: William BIKOVIS; m: Wilhelmina MAKIES] 16 Apr 1881. Off: SMITH. Wit: Christoph RANDZUS, August MUSKAT. Age consent given by mother of the bride, Wilhelmina LENKOSE.

KAISER, Mathias [31; Douglas Co.] and Anna STRAUS [24; Douglas Co.] license issued on 31 Oct 1868. No marriage record. Off: STUCK.

KAISER, Mathias [31; Omaha; b: Germany; f: John KAISER; m: Mary] md. Anna THANS [23; Omaha; b: Peter THANS; m: Anna] on 18 May 1869. Off: GROENEBAUM. Wit: Peder LANSER.

KAISER, Mathias [42; Omaha; b: Luxemburg; f: Clemens KAISER; m: Anna HUSS] md. Mrs. Sarah E. DAVIS [39; Omaha; b: New York; f: George KEEFER; m: Caroline SEELY] at the German Catholic Church on 13 Nov 1879. Off: GROENEBAUM. Wit: John GREEN, Peter HART.

KAISER, Peter [31; Omaha; b: Germany; f: Jacob KAISER; m: Sophia GOTTSTEIN] md. Victoria ALEXANDRIA [19; Omaha; b: OH; f: James ALEXANDRIA; m: Martha] on 28 Oct 1876. Off: BENEKE. Wit: Chas. WEBER, R. CLAYSEN.

KAMMERLING, Frederick A. [45; Omaha; b: Saxony; f: Benjamin KAMMERLING] md. Margaret KECHELE [23; Omaha; b: Leipsic; f: Anton KECHELE; m: Margaret] on 9 May 1874. Off: PORTER. Wit: S. MADDEN; Emele BURMESTER.

KANE, Daniel [26; Dodge Co.] md. Sarah C. HASHSBURGER [18; Platte Co.] on 3 Nov 1866. Off: HASCALL. Wit: Chas. H. BROWN, Ben SHEEK.

KANE, Jermiah [29; Saratoga Pct, Douglas Co.; b: Middleborough, MA; f: Jeremiah KANE; m: Margaret SMITH] and Emily E. SNYDER [16; Saratoga Pct, Douglas Co.; b: Mechanicsburg, PA; f: William SNYDER; m: Elizabeth EVINGER] license issued on 3 Jul 1873. Off: TOWNSEND.

KANE, Nicholas [58; Chicago Pct, Douglas Co.; b: Ireland; f: Patrick KANE: m: Ellen CAVANAUGH] md. Mrs. Catharine ANDERSON [52; Chicago Pct, Douglas Co.; b: Sweden] on 1 Jul 1872 at Elkhorn Station. Off: LONERGAN. Wit: Patrick CONNELL; Mrs. P. CONNELL.

KANE, Peter [28; Omaha; b: Ireland; f: Michael KANE; m: Margaret GALLARY] md. Mary CURRY [15; Omaha; b: Ireland; f: Thomas CURRY; m: Mary McMANNIS] on 25 Nov 1870. Off: GIBSON. Wit: J.R. O'BRIEN; Sarah McAVIN. [NOTE: At this time the bride is underage and does not have parental approval.]

KANE, Peter [31; Omaha; b: Ireland; f: Michael KANE; m: Margaret GALLERY] md. Mary CURRY [21; Omaha; b: Ireland; f: Thomas CURRY; m: Mary McMANUS] on 6 Jan 1874 at Bishop's House. Off: MALLOY. Wit: Peter MALONE, Bishop's House; Catharine ROWAN, Bishop's House.

KANE, Thomas [25; Sidney; b: New York; f: Edward KANE; m: Mary HARRINGTON] md. Mary C. LOWREY [18; Sidney; b: New Orleans; f: Edmond LOWREY; m: Ann CUSHION] on 6 Oct 1874 at the Roman Catholic Cathedral. Off: BYRNE. Wit: Thomas LOWRY; Ellen LOWRY.

KANSCHEIT, Charles A. [27; Omaha; b: Germany; f: G. KANSCHEIT; m: Johannah NOUTSCH] md. Caroline Margrolat KAISER [29; Omaha; b: Germany; f: F. KAISER; m: O. KINGING] on 31 Aug 1876. Off: STRASEN. Wit: Jacob SCHIPPOREIT, Mary SCHIPPOREIT.

KARBACH, Charles J. [25] md. Wilhelmina HAGAEDORN [HAGEDORN] [24] on 9 May 1860. Off: ARMSTRONG. Wit: Joseph KARBACH, Caroline HAGAEDORN [HAGEDORN].

KARBACH, Peter J. [27; Omaha] md. Grete LAMP [21; Omaha] on 29 Nov 1867. Off: KUHNS. Wit: Charles KARBACH, Frederick KUMPF, et al.

KARLL, George [33; Omaha; b: Germany; f: Herman KARLL; m: Henrietta GRAACK] md. Ida WEST [23; Omaha; b: Vermont; f: Tehemia WEST; m: Mary CULVER] on 20 Jun 1879. Off: BENECKE. Wit: John B. LORD, G. BURKE.

KARSCH, Emil [34; Omaha; b: Germany; f: David KARSCH; m: Elizabeth PRANCH] md. Frederika KNOLLMILLER [26; Omaha; b: Germany; f: Larenel KNOLMILLER; m: Catharine MOLFINTER] on 11 Nov 1875. Off: DIECKMANN. Wit: Catherine KNOLLMUELLER, Fr. DIECKMANN.

KAS(T)NER, James [22; Omaha; b: Bohemia; f: Thomas KAS(T)NER; m: Barbra BLAPOVA] md. Barbara TUPY [21; Omaha; b: Bohemia; f: Frank TUPY; m: Catharine SCHUNKOVA] on 30 Jan 1875. Off:

PEABODY. Wit: Louis SEIVON, John PITZ. Groom signed application "Kasner James."

KASSER, Charles [28; Omaha; b: Prusia; f: Christopher KASSER; m: Anna HEUBOCK] md. Ida HEYBEAY [HERZBERG] [27; Omaha; b: Prusia; f: Ernest HEYBEAY [HERZBERG]; m: Fredericka JEISLER] on 27 Jul 1869. Off: HYDE. Wit: Geo. ARMSTRONG, L.H. BORDWELL.

KAUCKY, John [49; Omaha; b: Bohemia; f: John KAUCKY; m: Mary DANESH] md. Catharine PALIK [25; Omaha; b: Moravia; f: Martin PALIK; m: Mary SHVEHLA [SVEHLA]] on 26 May 1873. Off: TOWNSEND. Wit: Wenzel SKOUMAL; Francis MARESH [MARES].

KAUFMANN, Charles [22; Omaha; b: Germany; f: Gotfried KAUFMANN; m: Elizabeth STRACK] md. Annie FICENEC [18; Omaha; b: Austria; f: George FICENEC; m: Barbara KOSCHEREK] on 3 Jul 1871. Off: GIBSON. Wit: Jacob GREGARIUS; Henry GREBE.

KAUFMANN, Henry [27; Omaha; b: Germany; f: Gottfried KAUFMANN; m: Agnes WEBBER] md. Mary KARBACH [18; Omaha; b: Germany; f: Peter KARBACH] on 14 Nov 1872. Off: GROENEBAUM. Wit: Peter KARBACH; Henry COOPER.

KAUFMANN, Julius [23; Omaha; b: Prussia; f: Gottfred KAUFMANN; m: Elizabeth STRACK] md. Mary SHAWLICK [20; Omaha; b: Bohemia; f: John SHAWLICK; m: Martha BORT] on 28 Jun 1870. Off: GIBSON. Wit: Jacob GREGARIUS; John RAMGE.

KAUP, Joseph [50; West Point, Cuming Co.] and Catharine JUKA [JAKA] [45; West Point, Cuming Co.] license issued on 28 Jun 1866. No marriage record. Off: HASCALL.

KAYSER, Constantine [27; Douglas Co.; b: Germany; f: Frederick KAYSER; m: Sophie FREZER] md. Martha HANSEN [20; Douglas Co.; b: Germany; f: Christ HANSEN; m: Sophie] on 25 Sep 1875. Off: PEABODY. Wit: William UMPHERSON, Leila M. MAKIN.

KEAN, Patrick H. [24; Elkhorn Station; b: Canada; f: Michael S. KEAN; m: Winifred KINSLA [KINSELLA]] md. Mary LUCAS [22; Omaha; b: Ireland; b: John LUCAS; m: Ellen BYRNE] on 20 Dec 1870 at the Catholic Church of Omaha. Off: O'GORMAN. Wit: James BURNS; Mary GRIFFIN; Dr. GARDNER; Lizzy LATHAN; et al.

KEAR, Andrew N. [23; Omaha; b: Germany; f: Hans N. KEAR; m: Anna NELSON] md. Christiana SMIDT [26; Omaha; b: Germany; f: Andrew SMIDT; m: Mary] on 17 Dec 1875. Off: HANSEN. Wit: Peter PETERSON; Delf PETERSON.

KEARNEY, Joseph [27; Omaha; b: Ireland; f: Francis KEARNEY; m: Catharine

McEVOY] md. Mary ROSSMAN [26; Omaha; b: Germany; f: Chris ROSSMAN; m: May HANSON] on 10 Apr 1872. Off: BILLMAN. Wit: Mrs. Bella D. BILLMAN; Jac WIDENSALL; et al.

KEARNEY, M.J. [31; Omaha; b: Ohio; f: James KEARNEY; m: Ann KELLEY] md. Mrs. Mary E. RINADO [31; Omaha; b: Boston, MA; f: Timothy LYNCH; m: Mary READ] on 10 Feb 1879. Off: BARTHOLOMEW. Wit: James W. GRAFF of Delevan, IL, Max BERGMAN of Omaha.

KEATING, Edward [28; Elk Horn Station; b: New York; f: James KEATING; m: Mary ----] and Elizabeth McCALL [20; Elk Horn Station; b: Nebraska; f: Hugh McCALL; m: Mary ----] license issued on 5 Jun 1880. No marriage recorded. Off: BARTHOLOMEW.

KEATING, Owen [30; Traintown (Omaha)] md. Mrs. Sarah E. ADAMS [26; Omaha] on 23 Jun 1868. Off: MULCAHEY. Wit: W. ELDRIDGE, Harry McGREGOR.

KEENE, Samuel [23; Douglas Co.; b: Massachusetts; f: Augustus B. KEENE; m: Prudence WOODS] md. Mrs. Catharine HARPER [22; Omaha; b: England; f: Walter CURLE; m: Mary HENDERSON] on 23 Dec 1871. Off: TOWNSEND. Wit: William H. IJAMS; WIlliam J. HAHN.

KEENE, William W. [30; Brownville; b: Illinois; f: James C. KEENE; m: Eunice PATTERSON] md. Libbie HICKS [20; Joliet, IL; b: New York; f: Obediah HICKS; m: Ann RICHARDS] on 11 Oct 1877. Off: SEDGWICK. Wit: Cassius M. WATSON of Davenport, IA, Wm. SIMIRAL.

KEEP, William W. [22; Douglas Co.] and Amanda M. RUSSELL [22; Douglas Co.] license dated 17 April 1858. Marriage recorded without a date. Off: FORGEY.

KEETCH [KUTCH], Charles G. [23; Omaha] and Mercy F__th BARKER [26; Omaha] license issued on 24 Dec 1860. No marriage record. Off: ARMSTRONG.

KEETON, Thomas F. [27; North Bend; b: New York; f: John KEETON; m: Sarah BUCKLE] md. Georgianna O. YOUNG [16; North Bend; b: Illinois; f: George YOUNG; m: Ann MILLER] on 8 Sep 1869. Off: Wm. H. MORRIS. Wit: Dr. Wm. H.H. SISSONS, Mrs. Emma E. MORRIS.

KEGLER, Julius [29; Blair; b: Berlin; f: Charles KEGLER; m: Emily PARTAL] md. A. Minna LEY [23; Omaha; b: Saxony; f: Karl (LEY?); m: Caroline KOENLER] on 28 Jul 1874. Off: DIECKMANN. Wit: H. HORNBERGER; Emily KEGLER, Blair.

KEHL, Henry [27; Douglas Co.; b: Philadelphia, PA; f: William KEHL; m: Julianna HILDERBRANDT] md. Margaret MOORE [21; Douglas Co.; b: Cleveland, OH; f: Thomas MOORE; m: Elizabeth O'BRIEN] on 29 Feb 1876. Off: MULCAHY. Wit: Lewis TAIT, Annie PLANE.

KELLEHER, Dennis M. [28; Omaha] md. Jane McGRATH [19; Omaha] on 14 Sep 1868. Off: CURTIS. Wit: John RUSH, Annie RUSH.

KELLEY (KELLY), J. Emmet [30; Omaha] md. Mary Agnes CAREFOOT [25; Omaha] on 19 Nov 1867 at the Catholic Cathedral. Off: EGAN.

KELLEY, Frank M. [22; Red Oak, IA] md. Adah H. JOHNSON [22; Omaha] on 8 Sep 1868. Off: James MORRIS. Wit: J.G. JOHNSON, Amanda R. KERMOTT.

KELLEY, H.B. [22] and Sarah ONG [18] license issued on 16 Feb 1857. No marriage record. Off: SCOTT. Age consent given by George GARDNER.

KELLEY, John E. [33; Omaha; b: Sweden; f: Jan Jansen E. KELLEY; m: Ingred NILSON] md. Hedwig Mathilda WENNGREN [25; Omaha; b: Sweden; f: Carl John WENNGREN; m: Mari Margaretha BJORKMAN] on 15 Aug 1876. Off: RING. Wit: L.C. ABRAHAMSON, E.L. OBERG.

KELLEY, John [22; Omaha; b: Ireland; f: John KELLEY; m: Anna WELLS] md. Maria CORCORAN [23; Omaha; b: Ireland; f: Martin CORCORAN; m: Catharine HOGAN] on 28 Jul 1870. Off: McGOLDRECK. Wit: Michael LEAKY; Annie FENTAN.

KELLEY, John [Omaha] md. Esther DUCE [Omaha] on 17 Jan 1864. Off: DICKINSON. Wit: Charles H. BROWN, Wesley DAPLY____?.

KELLEY, Timothy [35; Omaha] and Ellen GORGIN [23; Omaha] license issued on 10 Feb 1863. No marriage record. Off: DICKINSON.

KELLEY, William A. [30; Omaha; b: Delaware; f: Lolan KELLEY; m: Mary MITCHEL] md. Amanda E. BUSEY [20; Omaha; b: Missouri; f: William BUSEY; m: Rebecca LUTZ] on 6 Aug 1870. Off: GIBSON. Wit: Henry O'NEAL; Mrs. Mary GIBSON.

KELLEY, Wm. Albert [24; b: Canada; f: John H. KELLEY; m: Mary Ann DEALY] md. Katharine FOLEY [21; b: New Jersey; f: Timothy FOLEY; m: Mary FOLEY] on 30 May 1878. Off: SHAFFEL. Wit: Th. J. FITZMORRIS, Mary FOLEY.

KELLNER, Moritz [33; b: Austria; f: Bernhard KELLNER; m: Sone GLUCK] md. Charlotte FREEDMAN [19; b: Austria; f: Samuel FREEDMAN; m: Rebecca FELD] on 6 Nov 1878. Off: BARTHOLOMEW. Wit: Adolph MEYER, Simeon BLOOM.

KELLOGG, Henry [Omaha] md. Abby BROWN [Omaha] on 12 May 1863 at Mrs. Elizabeth WHALEN's residence. Both of legal age. Off: KUHNS. Wit: Sarah MELLUS, Charles WHALEN, et al.

KELLY, Edmund [42; Omaha] md. Esther DELANY [26; Omaha] on 3 Nov 1863. Off: McMAHAN. Wit: Patrick BEGLEY, Dora M. DELANY.

KELLY, James D. [37; Chicago, IL; b: New York; f: James KELLY; m: Jennette BUCHAMAN] md. Nettie L. KENYON [29; San Francisco, CA; b: New York; f: John KENYON; m: Mary BRAINARD] on 27 Mar 1879. Off: BARTHOLOMEW. Wit: Max BERGMAN, M.E. McKOON.

KELLY, John M. [27; Douglas Co.] md. Henrietta E.S. BEEKS [17; Douglas Co.] on 8 Feb 1859 at the house of the bride's father in Florence. Off: BARNES.

KELLY, John [27; Omaha] and Miss J. KELLY [21; Omaha] license issued on 26 Feb 1858. No marriage record. Off: BRIGGS.

KELLY, Patrick [31; Omaha; b: Ireland; f: Daniel KELLY; m: Elizabeth FOX] md. Fannie BURNS [30; Omaha; b: New York] on 28 Nov 1871. Off: O'GORMAN. Wit: John OWEN; Anna SULIVAN.

KELLY, Patrick [35; Omaha; b: Ireland; f: Thomas KELLY; m: Mary GREEN] md. Elizabeth GREEN [35; Omaha; b: Ireland] on 30 Jul 1869. Off: HYDE.

KELLY, Thomas [22; Douglas Co.] md. Ellen MULLEN [23; Douglas Co.] on 15 Feb 1866. Off: HASCALL. Wit: James SLIGHTEN, Margaret FITZGERALD, et al.

KELLY, William A. [38; b: Delaware; f: Colam KELLY; m: Mary MITCHELL] md. Mrs. Nannie E. GRANT [24; b: Pennsylvania; f: George H. FYE; m: S.H. CLAPSHAW] on 19 Mar 1878. Off: STENBERG. Wit: E.H. ROOTH, Ella TAYLOR.

KELMAN, David [26; Rock Island, IL; b: Scotland; f: Alexander KELMAN; m: Elizabeth McKENZIE] md. Leah Caroline MARKEL [20; Omaha; b: Canton, MO; f: Jacob MARKEL; m: Eunice SWEET] on 18 Feb 1873. Off: RUBY. Wit: J.E. MARKEL; J. MARKEL.

KELSEY, Charles R. [23; Omaha; B: NY; f: M.B. KELSEY; m: Phebe GALUSKA] md. Altha Belle HOUCK [21; Omaha; b: PA; f: Dorsey B. HOUCK; m: Nancy SCHOENFELD] on 1 Jan 1881. Off: WILLIAMS. Wit: Dorsey B. HOUCK, Nancy S. HOUCK.

KELSEY, Robert [29; b: Ireland; f: Daniel KELSEY; m: Ellen CAREY] md. Mary RILEY [29; b: New York; f: John RILEY; m: Bridgett DEVANEY] on 17 Mar 1878. Off: KELLY. Wit: Morris HENGEN, Nellie RILEY.

KEMPF, August [23; Omaha; b: Germany; f: Augustin KEMPF; m: Christina

WETDERER] md. Elizabeth MILLER [18; Omaha; b: Germany; f: John MILLER] on 4 Jan 1877. Off: STRASEN. Wit: Arnold JAEGGI, Elizabeth KECK.

KENDOLL, Henry C. [23; Douglas Co.; b: New Hampshire] and Francis JACKET [28; Douglas Co.; b: North Carolina; f: Brozel CENTER; m: Jane BAUTHE] license issued on 22 Jul 1870. Off: GIBSON.

KENNEDY, John J. [30; Omaha; b: Illinois; f: John KENNEDY; m: Mary MOONEY] md. Bridget MALONEY [24; Omaha; b: Illinois; f: Michael MALONEY; m: Mary ROONEY] on 12 Jul 1880. Off: ENGLISH. Wit: Jas. MALONEY, Lizzie CAVANAUGH.

KENNEDY, Joseph [44; Piedmont, Wyoming Territory; b: Ireland; f: William KENNEDY; m: Catharine DELENY] md. Mrs. Katharine WHELAN [40; Omaha; b: Ireland; f: James RYAN; m: Margaret CAVANA] on 4 Apr 1881. Off: ENGLISH. Wit: Hugh MALLEN, Jane LYNCH.

KENNEDY, Loren [24; Council Bluffs] md. Mary A. KNOWLEN [24; Council Bluffs] on 3 Jan 1869. Off: HYDE. Wit: Mrs. J.R. HYDE, DeMotte HYDE.

KENNEDY, Martin W. [32; Omaha; b: Ireland; f: John KENNEDY; m: Julia CARROLL] md. Belle DWYER [26; Omaha; b: New York; f: Jeremiah DWYER; m: Fanny WILKESON] on 3 Aug 1880. Off: ENGLISH. Wit: Thomas TALLON, Mary DWYER.

KENNEDY, Michael [26; Omaha Barracks; b: NY; f: James KENNEDY; m: Nora MANY] md. Mary DOYLE [24; b: NY; f: Joseph DOYLE; m: Elizabeth FENODAH] on 21 Feb 1876. Off: SEDGWICK. Wit: Benjaman HARNISH, Amanda HARNISH.

KENNEDY, Royal [50; Laporte City, IA; b: Ohio; f: John KENNEDY; m: Rachel KENNEDY] md. Mrs. Amelia F. BARTOW [36; Dacotah, WI; b: New York; f: Henry KREBS; m: Aletta HIGBY] on 11 May 1872. Off: TOWNSEND. Wit: A.M. BRINKERHOFF, Laporte City, IA; John GUTHRIE, Colfax, IA. (inserted in application: "... affiant has been informed and verily believes that her former husband perished by drowning.")

KENNEDY, Thomas [26; Washington Co.; b: Ireland; f: James KENNEDY; m: Mary BURK] md. Cynthis HARDIE [26; Washington Co.; b: IL; f: John HARDIE; m: Sallie SCOTT] on 12 Aug 1876. Off: DONNELLY. Wit: Ed O'SULLIVAN, Jessie OSTERHOUST.

KENNELLY, James [26; Omaha; b: Ireland; f: Martin KENNELLY; m: Bridget KESSAN] md. Margaret BEGLEY [20; Omaha; b: Indiana; f: John BEGLEY; m: Mary RAINEY] on 16 Jun 1874 at the Cathedral. Off: MALLOY. Wit: John BEGLEY; Ellen BEGLEY.

KENNELY, John [23; Omaha; b: Ireland; f: Martin KENNELY; m: Bridget KISSENE] md. Mary RYAN [19; Florence; b: Canada West; f: John RYAN; m: Mary DEE] on 26 Feb 1870. Off: CURTIS. Wit: Jeremiah DEE; Johanna KENNELY.

KENNEY, Edward C. [25; Oberlin, OH; b: Oberlin, OH; f: Daniel B. KENNEY; m: Betsy MATHEWS] and Hattie A. LEWIS [San Jose, CA; b: Minnesota] license issued on 19 Nov 1870. Off: GIBSON.

KENNEY, Horace [23; Omaha; colored; b: Virginia; f: Lewis KENNEY; m: Linda] md. Mary Jane BATES [16; Omaha; colored; b: Missouri; f: Henry BATES; m: Fannie JOHNSON] on 3 Dec 1871. Off: HARROD. Wit: Joseph TAYLOR; Maria CAMPBELL. Age of consent given by Fannie JEFFERSON, mother of bride.

KENNEY, James [23; Omaha; b: New York; f: Thomas KENNEY; m: Anna McNULTY] md. Rose CALLAHAN [23; Omaha; b: Wisconsin; f: Peter CALLAHAN; m: Catharine McDERMOTT] at St. Philomena's Church on 14 Jun 1879. Off: McCARTHY. Wit: T.D. KINNEY, Ellen RILEY.

KENNEY, Michael [28; Omaha; b: Ireland; f: Thomas KENNEY; m: Bridget FAHEY] md. Anna WHALEN [26; Omaha; b: Ireland; f: John WHALEN; m: Catharine MORAN] on 8 Jul 1874 at the Roman Catholic Cathedral. Off: BYRNE. Wit: John DOLAN; Margaret ONEIL.

KENNICOTT, Alfred [68; Saunders Co.; b: New York; f: John KENNICOTT; m: Betsey REYNOLDS] md. Mrs. Mary L. THOMAS [58; Waterloo; b: North Carolina; f: Isreal MENDENHAAM; m: Mary LOW] on 30 Dec 1874 at Waterloo. Off: BALLOW. Wit: John H. LOGAN, Waterloo; Hannah LOGAN, Waterloo.

KENNISTON, Ernest C. [24; Omaha; b: Maine; f: Daniel KENNISTON; m: Sarah BRACKET] md. Carrie F. OSTROM [18; Omaha; b: New York; f: A.S. OSTROM] on 31 Dec 1877. Off: FISHER. Wit: John MORELL, Mrs. MORELL.

KENSCHER, Edward Frederick [Omaha] md. Eliza Louisa R. LORENSEN [Omaha] on 1 Oct 1863 at KUHNS' residence. Both of legal age. Off: KUHNS. Wit: Joseph GRANACHER, Frederick DOHRNANN.

KEPLER, Edward B. [24; Omaha] md. Kate MARTIN [22; Belleview (sic)] on 20 Apr 1866. Off: KUHNS. Wit: Louisa MARTIN, John HUNTER, et al.

KERN, Daniel [26; Valley Station; b: Ohio; f: John M. KERN; m: Christina RUFF] md. Sarah Ann CONNOR [20; Valley Station; b: Ohio; f: Henry CONNOR; m: Mary TRUEAUX] on 12 Jan 1870. Off: KERSTETTER. Wit: William BRINNAN, Valley Station; Isaac L. THOMAS, Platte Valley.

KETCHUM, Charles F. [33; Omaha; b: NY; f: John F. KETCHUM; m: Margret McNEIL] md. Frances WHIPPLE [22; Omaha; b: WI; f: Ira WHIPPLE; m: Lucy HAZEN] on 11 Oct 1875. Off: PEABODY. Wit: N.W. COPPOCK, Mary COPPOCK.

KETTLE, Joseph [25; Omaha] md. Lena SCHULTZ [18; Omaha] on 6 Mar 1869. Off: HYDE. Wit: Will BROWN (BROWNE), C.D. HYDE, A. CAMMINZIND.

KEY, Charles Ward [42; Sarpy Co.; b: England; f: James KEY; m: Susan WARD] md. Lizzie GARD [26; Omaha; b: Iowa; f: Isaac GARD; m: Elizabeth WILLEY] on 11 Aug 1872. Off: KUHNS. Wit: Mrs. H.W. KUHNS; Mary EMERSON. Affidavit signed by Samuel D. MERCER.

KEYES, Clarence E. [23; Sarpy Co.; b: Spencer, MA; f: Edward KEYES; m: Rachel M. MOORE] md. Annie HODGE [21; Omaha; b: Scotland] on 5 Oct 1873. Off: PRESSON. Wit: Chas. McLEAN; Alice McLEAN.

KEYES, Thomas [35; Omaha] md. Hariet L. HUTCHINSON [28; Omaha] on 1 Dec 1867. Marriage certificate recorded 8 Feb 1868. Off: KERMOTT. Wit: Mrs. Henry HICKMAN, Mrs. A.R. KERMOTT.

KEYES, Thomas [40; Omaha; b: Ireland; f: Thomas KEYES; m: Sarah TOOLE] md. Lucine PRATT [36; Omaha; b: New York; f: Elisha PRATT; m: Wealthy] on 30 Dec 1872. Off: BILLMAN. Wit: E.T. PAGE; Mrs. L.J. PAGE.

KIANDER, Alexander [47; Omaha; b: Finland; f: August KIANDER; m: Maria KIANDER] md. Mrs. Wilamina KAPPENHORN [46; Omaha; b: Hamburg, Germany; f: Johann KUKLISS; m: Elizabeth O. WITT] on 28 Apr 1880. Off: BENEKE. Wit: H. TANGON, A.R. HEUNIG.

KIDDER, Merick E. [27; Douglas Co.] and Anne MCINTYRE [16; Douglas Co.] license issued on 10 Aug 1859. No marriage record. Off: GILBERT. Wit: Oscar F. DAVIS, P.W. HITCHCOCK, both of Douglas Co. Age consent given by mother of the bride, Sarah McINTYRE.

KIER, Claus [24; Omaha; b: Denmark; f: Nels KIER; m: Joanna NELSON] md. Mary THOMPSON [18; Omaha; b: Denmark; f: James THOMPSON; m: Mary ANDERSON] on 2 Apr 1874. Off: PEABODY. Wit: Mrs. N. NELSON; Mrs. Mary C. PEABODY.

KILFEATHER, John [29; Douglas Co.; b: New York; f: Michael KILFEATHER; m: Mary HART] md. Catharine GALLAGHER [28; Douglas Co.; b: Iowa; f: William GALLAGHER; m: Mary DEVINE] on 14 Jul 1879. Off: KOCARNIK. Wit: James NEMEC, Marg. GALLAGHER.

KILKENNY, Patrick [27; Plattsmouth; b: Ireland; f: James KILKENNY; m: Mary GROGHAN] md. Catharine MURPHY [25; Omaha; b: Ireland; f: Martin MURPHY; m: Mary SWORDS] on 14 Jan 1873. Off: CURTIS. Wit: Michael J. EGAN; Bridget MURPHY.

KILKER, Augustus F. [27; Omaha; b: Prussia; f: John B. KILKER; m: Willhelmina BASALER] md. Elizabeth REED [20; Omaha; b: New Jersey; f: Aaron REED; m: Susan F. LAFETRE] on 8 Aug 1870. Off: KUHNS. Wit: Mrs. Susan F. REED; Austin REED.

KILL, Peter [36; Omaha] md. Hannah HIT [26; Omaha] on 20 Jun 1867. Off: GROENEBAUM.

KILMER, John H. [32; Sarpy Co.] md. Emma HODSON [21; Harrison Co., IA] on 19 Sep 1868. Off: KUHNS. Wit: Ellen TORRANCE, Mrs. H.W. KUHNS.

KIMBERLAND, Daniel [27; Lincoln Co.; b: WV; f: Henry KIMBERLAND; m: Mary LUCAS] md. Amanda MERRYMAN [26; OH; b: OH; f: William MERRYMAN; m: Joanna DeARMON] on 24 Nov 1875. Off: STEWART. Wit: W.T. KELLEY, Mrs. Emily W. STEWART.

KINDLE, Carr W. [24; Omaha; b: Illinois; f: Caley (Carey?) KINDLE; m: Narcissa COE (CAL?)] md. Rosa G. ROBERTS [23; Cedar Rapids, IA; b: France, f: John] on 7 Jul 1874. Off: PEABODY. Wit: E.M. STEVENS; Rose W. PEABODY, Lynn, MA.

KING, Albert L. [25; Omaha] md. Gertrude CLARK (CLARKE) [19; Omaha] on 16 Dec 1857. Off: WATSON.

KING, Frank M. [25; Florence] md. Margaret R. FORGEY [20; Florence] on 22 Nov 1866. Off: GALLIDAY. Wit: Mary FORGEY of Florence, Samuel FORGEY of Florence.

KING, Jacob and Christian C. CHRISSENSENNE [20] license issued on 23 May 1857. No marriage record. Off: SCOTT. Age consent given by Richard DARLING.

KING, James 35; Omaha; b: Ireland; f: Owen KING; m: Ann O'NIEL] md. Hannah REGAN [27; Omaha; b: Ireland] on 10 Oct 1869. Off: CURTIS. Wit: Stephen SULLIVAN, Louisa or Joanna MOORE.

KING, Jerry [27; Dodge Co.] md. Maria SIMPKINS [24; Dodge Co.] on 18 Mar 1869. Off: KELLEY. Wit: S.B. DAVIS, S.H. RICE.

KING, John [24; Omaha; b: Illinois; f: Joseph KING; m: Lavina FATH] md. Carrie SHEETS [23; Omaha; b: Illinois; f: John SHEETS; m: Maggie BROWN] on 12 Sep 1880. Off: STENBERG. Wit: Mrs. Nellie THOMPSON, W.W. POND.

KING, Phillip [39; Omaha; colored; b: Virginia; f: Liberty KING; m: Virginia ----] md. Mrs. Elizabeth McDONALD [26; Omaha; colored; b: Illinois; f: Barnard SMITH; m: Agnes MOSLEY] on 12 May 1870. Off: KUHNS. Wit: Casper LARY; Caroline WARICKS.

KING, William H. [22; Omaha; b: MA; f: Richard H. KING; m: Helen M. WILSON] md. Florence J. CARLTON [19; Omaha; b: IL; f: George CARLTON; m: Nancie BACKUS] on 30 Oct 1876. Off: JAMESON. Wit: Frank EVERS, Minerva BEAMAN, et al.

KINGHAM, George H. [29; Boone Co.; b: England; f: George KINGHAM; m: Elizabeth DONSE] md. Annie SKINNER [28; Boone Co.; b: England; f: Charles SKINNER; m: Caroline WOOTON] on 18 Nov 1874. Off: PEABODY. Wit: Frank P. HANLON; G.W. SHIELDS.

KINGSBURY, T.B. [28; b: New York; f: Daniel KINGSBURY; m: May J. LOBDILL] md. Nancy J. BATY [18; b: Illinois; f: William BATY; m: Sarah J. BURDICK] on 16 Nov 1878. Off: BARTHOLOMEW. Wit: F.P. HANLON, M.H. REDFIELD.

KINNEAR, James [21; Florence] md. Hattie TURNER [18 and 10 months; Florence] on 21 May 1867. Off: MILLER. Wit: Mrs. Georgietta M. JOHNSON, Mrs. Catharine M. POWEL.

KINNEY, Jerome [24; Omaha; b: Connecticut; f: Francis H. KINNEY; m: Lucy NEWELL] md. Lucy PICKARD [26; Omaha; b: Ohio; f: John PICKARD; m: Juliette? SKINNER] on 8 Apr 1871. Off: DeLaMATYR. Wit: J. HARDESTY; Eillone FLARHETY or O'NIEL.

KINNEY, Martin [27; Omaha; b: Ireland; f: Thomas KINNEY; m: Bridget FAHEY] md. Margaret CASEY [19; Omaha; b: Ireland; f: Peter CASEY; m: Mary ELWOOD] on 26 Jun 1872 at the Catholic Church of Omaha. Off: O'GORMAN. Wit: Michael KINNEY; Hanagh WHELAN.

KINNEY, Michael T. [31; Omaha] md. Stella BAILEY [20; Omaha] on 14 Oct 1868 at O'GORMAN's residence. Off:

O'GORMAN. Wit: C.E. DOWNEY, Emma BAILEY.

KINSELLA, James [26; Dunlap, IA; b: Connecticut; f: P. KINSELLA; m: Margaret KINSELLA] md. Ida GRAVES [19; Dunlap, IA; b: Iowa; f: T.H. GRAVES; m: Emmiline WETZEL] on 8 Apr 1880. Off: SHERILL. Wit: Mrs. L.H. JONES, Mrs. Mary J. SHERILL.

KIRKHART, Joseph F. [35; Osceola, IA; b: Ohio; f: Joseph KIRKHART; m: Mary DUFF] md. Kate C. McKENNA [30; Omaha; b: Ohio; f: William KcKENNA; m: Charity BURGOUN] on 21 Oct 1874. Off: PEABODY. Wit: Mrs. Caroline LARGE; Marie Sophie HORTING.

KIRLEY, Peter [32; Iowa; b: Ireland; f: Peter KIRLEY; m: Catharine CARR] and Nora MANLY [30; Omaha; b: Ireland; f: ---- MANLY] license issued on 11 Apr 1874. Off: PEABODY.

KIRLIN [KISLIN], George [Harrison Co., IA] md. Mary McSWIGGEN [Harrison Co., IA] on 21 Sep 1865. Off: CURTIS.

KIRNER, Joseph [25; Omaha; b: Germany; f: Ellis KIRNER; m: Mary R. CLECK] md. Mary C. JOHNSON [24; Omaha; b: Sweden; f: John M. JACOBS; m: Mary NELSON] on 22 Feb 1874. Off: PEABODY. Wit: A. MINSSKI; John STEEL.

KIRWAN, Edward [23; Omaha; b: Ireland; f: Edward KIRWAN; m: Katharine CALNA] md. Bridget HEAVER [23; Omaha; b: Ireland; f: Patrick HEAVER; m: Catharine KELLY] on 26 Jul 1874 at the Roman Catholic Cathedral. Off: BYRNE. Wit: Richard MULLIN; Honora BOYLE.

KITCHEN, Waleton B. [27; Douglas Co.] md. Sarah HARTFORD [18; Douglas Co.] on 15 Jul 1867. Off: HASCALL. Wit: H.D. JOHNSON, Gen. E. ESTABROOK.

KLAAS, Martin [28; Blair City; b: Hessia, Germany; f: Martin KLAAS; m: Clara KRAMER] md. Caroline WIESNER [23; Blair City; b: Austria; f: Joseph WIESNER; m: Maria A. RICHTER] on 23 May 1870. Off: GIBSON. Wit: Henry COOPS; F.J. WIESNER, Blair City.

KLATTE, Charles [43; Omaha; b: Prussia; f: Charles KLATTE; m: Henrietta LEHMAN] md. Candis SMITH [23; Omaha; b: IA; f: M.T. SMITH; m: Eliza GILMORE] on 2 Feb 1875. Off: ESTABROOK. Wit: C.S. BRISTOL, D.S. PARMELEE.

KLEE, Fritz [39; Douglas Co.; b: Germany; f: Henry KLEE; m: Mary RITTER] md. Frederick FRALICH [33; Douglas Co.; b: Germany; f: ---- FRALICH; m: ---- SCHUBERT] on 27 Apr 1876. Off: HILGENDORF. Wit: Albert EDEN, Henry DUNKER.

KLEEB, William [29; Douglas Co.; b: Wisconsin; f: John KLEEB; m: Barbara SPAHR] md. Miss J.F. WHEELER [24;

Pewaukee, WI; f: Monroe WHEELER; m: Eliza WASHBURN] on 2 Oct 1879. Off: BEANS. Wit: Mrs. W.K. BEANS, Mrs. Kate MADDOX.

KLEFNER, Frank [Douglas Co.] md. Elizabeth HAGEDORN [Douglas Co.] on 22 Sep 1865 at John PAULSON's residence near Omaha. Off: KUHNS. Wit: Charles KARBACH, Frederick KUMPF, et al.

KLEIN, Emmanuel [25; Omaha; b: Germany; f: Joseph KLEIN; m: Johanna FUERST] md. Jennie JACOBS [24; Omaha; b: OH; f: Samuel JACOBS; m: Hattie BENKENDORFF] on 16 Jan 1881. Off: ANDERSON. Wit: Lewis BRASH, Marx RYPINSKI.

KLEIN, Jacob [24; Omaha; b: Germany; f: Jacob KLEIN; m: Josephine WELDE] md. Amalie BUCHER [21; Omaha; b: Germany; f: Frede SEYFRIED; m: Marie BUCHER] on 19 May 1880. Off: BENEKE. Wit: Wenzel NISTEL, Théodore BEDESSEM.

KLENCK, Henry [24; Omaha; b: NY; f: Peter KLENCK; m: Barbara KEIL] md. Josie MADDEN [18; Omaha; b: PA; f: James MADDEN; m: Mary MEEHAN] on 24 Apr 1881. Off: FRESE. Wit: Ad GIMBEL, Mrs. Clara GIMBEL.

KLEPPER, Charles [25; Wyoming; b: Germany; f: Mathias KLEPPER; m: Appolona FIKE] md. Mrs. Sophia MUNSON [21; Omaha; b: Illinois; f: Christ SPONEMAN] on 5 Mar 1870. Off: MORRIS. Wit: Charles BILIMEK or BILIMECK; Joseph BILIMEK or BILIMECK.

KLINDT, Peter [34; Washington Co.] md. Trina ASP [33; Washington Co.] on 23 Aug 1866. Off: HASCALL. Wit: Henry VESEY, C. BECKMAN.

KLINDT, William [30; Washington Co.; b: Germany; f: Hans KLINDT; m: Lenke ARP] md. Lena SOLL [18; Washington Co.; b: Germany; f: Fritz SOLL; m: Elizabeth GOSCH] on 21 Sep 1881. Off: BENEKE. Wit: Peter SOLL, George SOLL.

KLINE, William [Fontanelle] md. Mrs. Emmeline RICHARDSON [Omaha] on 28 Feb 1865 at DAKE's residence. Off: DAKE. Wit: Rev. Wm. H. VAN ANTWERP, Mrs. O.C. DAKE, et al.

KLINES, Eggert [26; Ft. Calhoun, NE; b: Germany; f: Hans KLINES; m: Lena ABT] md. Lena STOTHENBERG [21; Ft. Calhoun, NE; b: Germany; f: Peter STOTHENBERG; m: Maggie STOTHENBERG] on 3 Dec 1878. Off: WRIGHT. Wit: Rodney DUTCHER, Wm. F. FLYNN.

KLONINGER, Charles [22; Omaha; b: Germany; f: John KLONINGER; m: Auguste BAEDERLOW] md. Elizabeth DRUBA [21; Omaha; b: Pennsylvania; f: Charles DRUBA; m: Elizabeth VOLTZS] on 3 Jun 1879. Off: BRUEGEN. Wit: J.A. GILLISPIE, Wm. SAALFIELD.

KLOPP, Charles H. [26; b: Illinois; f: Isaac KLOPP; m: Mary KREAMER] md. Flora GOVE [22; Bluffton, IN; b: Indiana, Pennsylvania [both states given]; f: J.A. GOVE; m: Henrietta A. REINEMAN] on 2 Oct 1878. Off: PATERSON. Wit: Mrs. Mary HAYDEN, Lizzie SHARKEY.

KLOTZ, George [29; Omaha; b: MI; f: Bartholomo KLOTZ; m: Katharina GARDENER] md. Anna C. THRANE [22; Omaha; b: Denmark; f: C.C. THRANE; m: Bena J. RASMUSSEN] on 20 Dec 1881. Off: BENEKE. Wit: C.C. THRANE, Addie KLOTZ.

KLUTH, Albert [27; Omaha; b: Germany; f: Albert KLUTH; m: Mary LUPKA] md. Lydia SCHINKE [19; Omaha; b: Germany or Canada; f: John SCHINKE; m: Charlotte LITKE] on 26 May 1870. Off: GIBSON. Wit: William AUST; Augusta ROGGIN.

KMENT, Mike [Marcus] [a; b: Bohemia; f: Thomas KMENT; m: Annie MENDEL] md. Frances KAHOUN [23; Omaha; b: Bohemia; f: John KAHOUN; m: Katie REZEK] on 22 Mar 1879. Off: BARTHOLOMEW. Wit: F.P. HANLON, W.J. CUDDY.

KNAPP, James M. [21 or 22; Omaha] md. Renhanna McCREA [18; Omaha] on 24 Dec 1868. Off: GIBSON. Wit: Mr. McCREA, Nathan ELLIOTT.

KNEELAND, John [32; Marshalltown, IA; b: WI; f: William KNEELAND; m: Mary WILLIAMS] md. Irene HENDERSON [22; Denver; b: IA; f: George HENDERSON; m: Sophia MALTHWAIDE] on 31 Mar 1881. Off: SHERRILL. Wit: Fred MOORE and Mrs. Ella MOORE, both of Ford, Holt Co. NE.

KNIGHT, James [22; Omaha; b: Nebraska; f: William KNIGHT; m: Johanna KENNELLEY] md. Kate HALEY [21; Omaha; b: Ireland; f: Patrick HALEY; m: Anna BRANNIN] on 17 Nov 1880. Off: HAWES. Wit: J.L. WRIGHT; Mrs. A.W. HAWES.

KNIGHT, John [21; Omaha] md. Susan BROWN [19; Omaha] on 27 Mar 1869. Off: KELLEY. Wit: Mrs. F.M. KNIGHT, S. ADDIS.

KNOBEL, Abraham [30; Omaha; b: Switzerland; f: Peter KNOBEL; m: Lena STEINMAN] md. Lena LUHSINGER [20; Omaha; b: Switzerland; f: Caspar LUHSINGER; m: Anna ZOPFI] on 30 Nov 1872. Off: BRANDES. Wit: Edward WITTIG; William HEREMANN.

KNUDSON, Hans [Omaha] md. Mary Sophia JENSON [Omaha] on 29 Jul 1863 at

Charles P. BIRKETT's residence. Both of legal age. Off: DICKINSON. Wit: Mr. and Mrs. Charles P. BIRKETT, et al.

KNUTSON, Samuel [46; Omaha; b: Sweden; f: Peter KNUTSON; m: Anna C. LARSEN] md. Emma C. STENBERG [43; Omaha; b: Sweden; f: John STENBERG; m: Helena LARSEN] on 5 Sep 1881. Off: HAYLAND. Wit: N. MARTEN, S.M. PETERSON. Witness for affidavit was Max BERGMANN.

KNUTZEN, Peter Marquardt [32; Omaha; b: Germany; f: Hans KNUTZEN; m: Anna S. EVERSON] md. Sophia C. THOMSEN [26; Omaha ; b: Germany; f: Asmus THOMSEN; m: Anna JENSEN] on 14 Feb 1875. Off: HILGENDORF. Wit: Asmus THOMSEN, Christian PETERSON.

KOBS, Albert [28; Douglas Co.; b: Prussia; f: Leopold KOBS] md. Henrietta LOBS [21; Douglas Co.; b: Prussia] on 15 Jul 1870. Off: MAY. Wit: Aug SOHL, Douglas Co.; John LOBS, Douglas Co.

KOCH, Paul [28; Omaha; b: Germany; f: Ludwig KOCH; m: Caroline HARSTIG] md. Lena RICHTER [22; Omaha; b: Germany; f: Christian RICHTER; m: Sophia KLEEBLATT] on 20 Jun 1871. Off: FAUST. Wit: Chas. BRIMNER; Elizabeth F. FAUST.

KOCHEN, Peter [23; Douglas Co.; b: Germany; f: Paskall KOCHEN; m: Margaretha ROEHRIG] md. Mrs. Mary WEISER [28; Douglas Co.; b: Germany; f: Nicholaus EIFFLER] on 29 Aug 1881. Off: DAXACHERFF. Wit: Mathias WEIR, Douglas Co., Cath. WAGNER, Douglas Co.

KOCHLER, Charles [22; Decatur, IL; b: Illinois; f: John W. KOCHLER] and Ellen CASE [18; Omaha; b: Ireland; f: Michael CASE] license issued on 19 Sep 1871. Off: GIBSON.

KOENIG, Charles W. [30; Omaha] md. Marie Elenore BECHER [20; Omaha] on 20 Aug 1862 at PUNDT's residence. Off: KUHNS. Wit: Mr. and Mrs. PUNDT, Mr. BECHER, Dr. A. ROEDER, et al.

KOESTERS, Henry [27; Douglas Co.; b: Germany; f: Henry KOESTERS: m: Doress SHOULSE] md. Magrata WAGMAN [22; Omaha; b: Germany; f: Peter or John H. WAGMAN; m: Mary BANZA] on 16 Oct 1870 at Henry KOESTERS' residence. Off: DODGE. Wit: George PLUMBECK, Douglas Co.; John LIMKE, Douglas Co.

KOHREGER, Gustavus [25; Omaha; b: Prussia; f: Henry KOHREGER; m: Amelia CIEPFORT] md. Dora LORGE [18; Omaha; b: Hanover, Germany; f: Henry LORGE; m: Elizabeth BATTLES] on 1 Oct 1870. Off: KUHNS. Wit: Paul KOCK; Charls GEIST.

KOHUT, James [22; Omaha; b: Germany; f: John KOHUT; m: Annie SELIGECK] md. Annie TEHALSCHENCH [19; Omaha; b: Germany; f: John TEHALSCHENCH] on 7

Oct 1876. Off: SEDGWICK. Wit: John HOFFMAN, J.D. HAYES.

KOLBE, William [33; Omaha; b: Germany; f: Carl Heinrich KOLBE; m: Carolina KUNTZE] md. Catharine AYE [25; Omaha; b: Germany; f: John AYE; b: Margareta ROCKMANN] on 10 Jan 1878. Off: BENEKE. Wit: Dorothea MARTENS, Frederick HICKSTEIN.

KOLLS, Gustavis [29; Omaha; b: Germany; f: Gustavis KOLLS; m: Korotheas MOSS] md. Matilda ROEDER [19; Omaha; f: Augustus ROEDER; m: Clara] on 3 Jun 1873. Off: STEWART. Wit: Louis WEINSTEIN; Julius ROEDER.

KONDELE, Frank [25; Omaha; b: Bohemia; f: Martin KONDELE; m: Annie PESHIKOVA [PESEK]] md. Frances VANOUS [20; Omaha; b: Bohemia; f: John VANOUS; m: Annie FISHER] on 5 Jun 1873. Off: TOWNSEND. Wit: Thomas RILEY; Joseph DWORK [DWORAK].

KONVALLEN [KONVALIN], John [21; Omaha; b: Bohemia; f: Frank KONVALLEN [KONVALIN]; m: Barbara BJEHAUNEK [BEHOUNEK]] md. Lizzie KUNASH [KUNES] [18; Omaha; b: Bohemia; f: Joseph KUNASH [KUNES]; m: Barbara SHAVLIK] on 14 Apr 1880. Off: CARNIK. Wit: John RUZICKA, Joseph NEMEC.

KOONS, George B. [29; Omaha; b: Lockport, NY; f: William KOONS; m: Ann TANLENSON] md. Emma L. ALLOWAY [21; Omaha; b: Indiana; f: Alfred ALLOWAY] on 27 Sep 1870. Off: MORTON. Wit: G.M. MILLER; J.D. KIDD.

KOPP, Stephen A. [20; Primrose, Douglas Co.] md. Flora I. MOON [17; Primrose, Douglas Co.] on 25 May 1868. Off: STUCK. Wit: Ira K. MOON, A.F. CHAPMAN.

KORHOUT [KOHOUT], Wenzel [28; Omaha; b: Austria; f: Joseph KORHOUT [KOHOUT]; m: Annie HONLEH] md. Annie NEIHOUSE [19; Omaha; b: Ohio: f: Frank NEIHOUSE; m: Josephine ZERGER] on 1 Jun 1880. Off: HAWES. Wit: Minnie HAYDEN, Mary HAYDEN.

KORSGREN, Jacob William [25; Mo. Valley Junction, IA; b: Sweden; f: Jacob KORSGREN; m: Annie DOLL] md. Clara PETERSON [24; Omaha; b: Sweden; f: John PETERSON; m: Catharine] on 14 Nov 1872. Off: SUNDBORN. Wit: F.W. BONNEVIER; J.A. BONNEVIER.

KOSTERS, Charles M. [24; Omaha; b: NE; f: H.A. KOSTERS; m: Margaret WOLL] md. Emma LEWIS [24; Omaha; b: CA; f: J.R. LEWIS; m: Margaret GRAHAM] on 25 Apr 1881; Off: ENGLISH; Wit: Emanuel CAHN, Mary PROTEAN.

KOTTERMAN, Charles [27; Douglas Co.; b: Germany; f: William KOTTERMAN; m: Wilhelmine KRUEGER] md. Anna KANENBLEY [26; Omaha; b: NJ; f: Friederich KANENBLEY; m: Martha MEIER] on 19 Oct 1881. Off: FRESE. Wit: Mrs. Mathilde FRESE, Mrs. Henriette FRESE.

KOTTRAS, Henry [30; Dodge Co.; b: Prussia; f: Barney KOTTRAS; m: Mary ONIG] md. Kate LEWON [25; Illinois; b: Prussia; f: John LEWON] on 24 Apr 1870 at the German Catholic Church. Off: GROENEBAUM. Wit: R. ROLFEN; Franx RUBHAUSEN.

KOTYZA, Frank [25; Omaha; b: Bohemia; f: Frank KOTYZA; m: Franciska KYSELA] md. Alvoisia POSPISEL [19; Omaha; b: Bohemia; f: Matthew POSPISEL; m: Anna MARTINEK] on 17 Jan 1881. Off: KLIMA. Wit: Matthew NERAD, Joseph VRANA.

KOUGH, Joseph F. [24; Omaha; b: Pennsylvania; f: Jacob KOUGH; m: Catharine ENYEART] md. E. Estella BARR [20; Omaha; b; Wisconsin; f: John BARR; m: Emily C. GUILD] on 7 Sep 1879. Off: LIPE. Wit: John BARR, Emily C. BARR.

KOUNTZE, Herman [Omaha] md. Elizabeth DAVIS [Omaha] on 10 May 1864 at Thos. DAVIS' house. Off: VAN ANTWERP. Wit: Mr. and Mrs. Augustus KOUNTZE.

KOUSKI, Maximillian Marcin [28; Omaha] and Margaret O'BRIEN [22; Omaha] license issued on 18 May 1860. No marriage record. Off: ARMSTRONG.

KOUTCERA [KUCERA], Fred [28; Douglas Co.; b: Germany; f: Anton KOUTCERA [KUCERA; m: Fanny BARET] md. Maggie LASCHANSKY [18; Douglas Co.; b: Germany; f: August LASCHANSKY; m: Catharine LEMPFER] on 15 Jun 1880. Off: BARTHOLOMEW. Wit: Max BERGMANN, Wm. L. PEABODY.

KOUTNICK, Frank [24; Omaha; b: Bohemia; f: Matias KOUTNICK; m: Antonia SVANDOVA] md. Victoria PENKOS [18 and 6 months; Omaha; b: Bohemia; f: Peter PENKOS; m: Maria SONKEDNIK] on 6 Feb 1881 at St. Wenceslaus' Church. Off: KLIMA. Wit: Joseph MEJSTRICK, Frank SPEVAK.

KRAGSKOW, Joseph S. [20; Omaha; b: Denmark; f: Peter C. KRAGSKOW; m: Christine M. NELSON] md. Caroline KNUDSON [18; Omaha; b: Denmark; f: Knude C. KNUDSON; m: Caroline PHILLIPS] on 12 Feb 1874. Off: PEABODY. Wit: C.B. RUSTIN; John CHRISTOPHERSON.

KRAIL, William [33; Omaha; b: Germany; f: Drederick KRAIL; m: Caroline SYTHZ] md. Fredrica KNOLL-MILLER [22; Omaha; b: Germany; f: Laurace KNOLL-MILLER; m: Catherine] on 15 Nov 1870. Off: BENNETT. Wit: Rasmus RASMUSEN; Otto WELLDORFF.

KRAMARIC, Joseph [38; Omaha; b: Austria; f: Mattheas KRAMARIC; m: Barbara PETRIK] md. Mrs. Anna RANACKI [31; Omaha; b: Germany; f: Gustave KOSENTKI; m: Katharina KOSUTKA] on 12 Jun 1881 at St. Wenceslaus' Church. Off: KLIMA. Wit: John TSCHATONIC, John DOLAK.

KRAMER, Baldac [30; Douglas Co.] md. Catharine SCHITE [26; Douglas Co.] on 23 Dec 1861 at ARMSTRONG's office. Off: ARMSTRONG. Wit: L. RUF, Bladac SCHITE?, George GANTZ.

KRAMER, Peter [28; Omaha; b: Germany; f: Claus KRAMER; m: Kate KLINE] md. Hannah LEBBERT [21; Omaha; b: Germany; f: John J. LEBBERT; m: Anna E. OFT] on 30 Nov 1873. Off: HILGENDORF. Wit: Henry THIE, Union Pct; John STANDER, Douglas Co.

KRANK [FRANK], John [25; b: Bohemia; f: James [FRANK] KRANK; m: Fanny ROSS] md. Mrs. Augusta KRANK [21; b: Bohemia; f: Jacob RUESS; m: Blacka Maria [Maria BLAHA]] on 14 May 1878. Off: BARTHOLOMEW. Wit: William V. MORSE, George W. GRATTAN.

KRAUS, Christian [28; Omaha] md. Maria SCHORNBERG [34; Omaha] on 12 Oct 1867. Off: SHEEKS. Wit: Jonas BAUMAN, Cornelius SMITH.

KRAUS, Jacob I [23; Cleveland, OH?; b: Ohio; f: Peter KRAUS; m: Mary A. MEYER] md. Ruth Anna GIFFORD [17; Sioux City, IA; b: Iowa; f: Simon GIFFORD; m: Jane HERAS] on 7 Jun 1871. Off: KELLEY. Wit: Mrs. J.E. KELLEY; Mrs. KENNEDY. Age of consent given by Jane GIFFORD, Souix City, IA, mother of the bride.

KRAUSE, George [31; Omaha; b: Germany; f: Johann Wilhelm KRAUSE; m: Maria RUDLOFF] md. Marie Johanne KRUELL [24; Omaha; b: Germany; f: Andrew KRUELL; m: Louisa HANTSCHKE] on 29 Jul 1876. Off: BENEKE. Wit: Emil FRANZEN, Frederick WIRTH.

KRAUSE, Martin F.A. [29; Omaha; b: Germany; f: Friederich KRAUSE; m: Henriette WAEGNER] md. Caroline HUBER [27; Louisville, NE; b: OH; f: Frederick HUBER] on 26 Nov 1881. Off: BRUNS. Wit: H. HOFMEISTER; Annie HOFMEISTER.

KRAUSE, Theodor [21; Omaha; b: Germany; f: William KRAUSE; m: Mary RUTHUFF] md. Annie JERKEY [21; Omaha; b: Iowa; f: Frank JERKEY; m: Katharine PEFFERT] on 12 Mar 1879. Off: FALK. Wit: Abraham CASSLER, Mrs. Anna CASSLER.

KRAUSMAN, Henry [Chicago, IL] md. Elisabeth COHRENGER [Omaha] on 1 Jun 1863 at the Catholic Church of Omaha. Both of legal age. Off: O'GORMAN. Wit: Vincent BERKLEY, Cicilia BERKLEY.

KREBS, Charles [25; Omaha; b: Switzerland; f: John KREBS; m: Anna FULLER] md. Barbara SHAWLICK [20; Omaha; b: Bohemia; f: John SHAWLICK; m: Margaret OFMAN] on 21 May 1873. Off: KENNEDY. Wit: Mrs. J.E. KELLEY; Mrs. KENNEDY.

KREGBAUM [KRIGBAUM], Stanislaus K. [25; Omaha; b: Maryland; f: Henry KREGBAUM; m: Frances ARNOLD] md. Maria CASSADY [21; Omaha; b: Illiois; f: Philip CASSADY; m: Margaret PHELEN] on 18 Oct 1869 at the Cathedral. Off: DILWORTH. Wit: Frances P. DAILEY, Jane CASSADY.

KRENSIG, George [25; Douglas Co.; b: Germany; f: Frederick August KRENSIG; m: Augusta VAN WITTERN] md. Jane BLEASDALE [21; Douglas Co.; b: England; f: Robert BLEASDALE] on 8 Jan 1872. Off: BRANDES. Wit: Bernhardt LAWE; Antonie LAWE.

KREPEL, Wencel [22; Omaha; b: Bohemia; f: John KREPEL; m: Barbara KONES [KANES]] md. Josephine TUMA [17; Omaha; b: Bohemia; f: John TUMA; m: Anna KRIZ] on 21 Oct 1872. Off: TOWNSEND. Wit: Joseph DWORK [DWORAK]; Jerome F.L.D. HERTZMANN.

KRISTOFFERSON, Fritz S. [24; Omaha; b: Denmark; f: Peter KRISTOFFERSON; m: Karen Maria KNUSEN] md. Stine KRISTOFFERSON [22; Omaha; b: Denmark; f: Rasmuss KRISTOFFERSON; m: Friedericke KRISTSEON] on 4 Dec 1881. Off: FOGELSTRUN. Wit: Aug. NILSEN, Nils KRISTMANN.

KROMBECK [KRAMBECK], Detlef [32; Douglas Co.; b: Germany; f: Claus F. KROMBECK [KRAMBECK]; m: Christine KUEHL] md. Katharine ARFF [ARP] [25; Douglas Co.; b: Germany; f: Henry ARFF [ARP]; m: Katharina PAHR [PAHL]] on 11 Dec 1880, Millard. Off: KELSEY.

KROPP, Edward [24; Omaha; b: Germany; f: Louis KROPP; m: Helene HESSE] md. Caroline WULFF [24; Omaha; b: Germany; f: Charles WULFF; m: Sophie BRINKMAN] on 9 Mar 1871. Off: BENNET. Wit: Fred FATH; Mary FATH.

KROULIK, Joseph [22; Omaha; b: Bohemia; f: Joseph KROULIK; m: Anna KADLIK] md. Josephine BRED [19; Omaha; b: Bohemia; f: Frank BRED; m: Katherine VAVRIN] on 26 May 1881. Off: BENEKE. Wit: Joseph VANOUS, Mary RUZICKA.

KRUGER, John [37; Fort Omaha; b: Germany; f: Henry KRUGER; m: Maria BURGHOLZ] md. Mrs. Ann WILSON [25; Omaha; b: Kentucky; f: William CUNNINGHAM; m: Mary RICHARDSON] on 5 Nov 1880. Off: HAWES. Wit: C.J. WESTERDAHL, Mrs. A.M. HAWES.

KRUGER, William md. Hannah HILGENKAMP on 15 Apr 1863. Both of legal age. License gives residence of both as Douglas Co. Certificate gives residence of both as Washington Co. Off: MUHLENBROCK. Wit: H. WILKENNING, Caroline WILKENNING.

KRULL, Wilhelm [28; Omaha; b: Germany; f: Wilhelm KRULL; m: Maria PETTRE] md. Agnes HATTEN (HERTEN?) [19; Omaha; b: Germany; f: Michael HERTEN; m: Margareta MEYER] on 19 Jan 1871 at the Fifth Ward house. Off: HEUEGELE. Wit: Katy RICHARD; John F. METZ.

KRUSE, Conrad [30; Omaha; b: Germany; f: Jacob KRUSE; m: Margarita OLSEN] md. Mary A. O'MARA [26; Omaha] on 12 Mar 1871. Off: MAGINN. Wit: A.B. HUBERMAN; Amelia HUBERMAN.

KRUSE, Henry md. Mine ANDERSEN on 11 Jun 1865 at the Lutheran Church. Off: KUHNS. Wit: John MELENSON, Wm. BLACK, et al.

KRUSE, Henry [30; Omaha] md. Mary GULK [25; Omaha] on 6 Apr 1869. Off: KUHNS. Wit: John MOHR, Mrs. Mary LAFOND.

KRUSE, William [31; Calhoun; b: Germany; f: Johann KRUSE; m: rothea STRUVE] md. Minna STOLTENBERG [20; Douglas Co.; b: NE; f: Paul STOLTENBERG; m: Sophia IVERS] on 13 Apr 1881. Off: BENEKE. Wit: Peter GOOS, Lena GOOS.

KSANTNER, John [30; Crow Creek] md. Cerzeny WEISHATINGER [36; Crow Creek] on 1 Apr 1869. Off: HYDE. Wit: Sybrant HALL of Tekamah, William KIPP.

KUBOVEC, Frank [25; Omaha; b: Bohemia; f: James KUBOVEC; m: Elizabeth LUX] md. Fannie JEBAIR [20; Omaha; b: Bohemia; f: Anton JEBAIR; m: Mary ----] on 24 Sep 1881. at St. Wenceslaus' Church. Off: KLIMA. Wit: John SVACINA, John JAROS.

KUECHEN, William J. [30; Omaha; b: New York; f: George KUECHEN; m: Dorthea KAISER] md. Mrs. Rosalie CZESINSKI CZAJKOWSKI [35; Omaha; b: Prussia; f: Frank CZAJKOWSKI; m: Catharine WERNARORKA] on 11 Nov 1879. Off: KOCARNIK. Wit: Norman SMITH, M. John CZAJKOWSKI.

KUEHL, Peter [26; Douglas Co., NE; b: Germany; f: Hans H. KUEHL, m: Weibke HOLLER] md. Sophie PLUECKHAHN [20; Douglas Co., NE; b: Germany; f: Fritz PLUECKHAHN; m: Gretchen PETERS] on 15 Feb 1879. Off: BARTHOLOMEW. Wit: Wm. L. PEABODY, H.P. DEVALON.

KUEHN, August [27; Cass Co.; Prussia; f: Christian KUEHN; m: Augusta LEROTH] md. Anna MUELLER [23; Omaha; b: Prussia; f: Karl MUELLER; m: Minnie SCHARTOW] on 28 Mar 1877. Off: BRAUER. Wit: Charles MILLER, E. MUELLELER, Mary JANSSEN.

KUELL, John E. [27; Omaha; b: Sweden; f: John BENGTSON; m: Permilla SUNESSON] md. Ingre THORSSON [23; Omaha; b: Sweden; f: Thore JOHNSON; m: Bengta ANDERSON] on 23 Feb 1874. Off: PEABODY. Wit: Jacob SAMLER; Conrad RENSCH.

KUHL, Fred H. [21; Douglas Co.; b: Germany; f: Paul KUHL; m: Charlotte MOHR] md. Annie SICH [21; Douglas Co.; b: Germany; f: George SICH; m: Magdalene BRUGH] on 17 Dec 1881. Off: FRESE. Wit: August PRINZ, Sarpy Co., Juergen PAHL, Douglas Co.

KUHLMAN, Charles [26; Omaha; b: Denmark; f: Henry KUHLMAN; m: Mary AUKERSTIERM] md. Mrs. Elizabeth LOWER [28; Omaha; b: Germany; f: Henry SORGER; m: Elizabeth MAYNARD] on 16 Sep 1881. Off: BRANDES. Wit: A. FISCHER, Peter JOHNSON, Plattsmouth. "Sworn" on printed form was crossed out and the word "affirmed" was substituted.

KUHLTHAN, Edward [23; Omaha; b: Bavaria; f: Phillip Wm. KUHLTHAM; m: Ottilie RICHTER] md. Clara CRANDELL [22; Omaha; b: WI; f: Abram CRANDELL; m: Stratira EVERETT] on 18 Jun 1875. Off: BENEKE. Wit: Max LIEBLER, Frederick WIRTH.

KUHN, Frederick [29; Omaha] md. Joanna GANSBERG [24; Omaha] on 29 May 1869. Off: KUHNS. Wit: Mrs. Mary LAFOND, Mary BJORSETH.

KUHN, John F. [25; Centralia, IL; b: Baden; f: John KUHN; m: Babette GARNIER or GAINER] md. Annie GSANTNER [23; Omaha; b: Baden; f: John GSANTNER; m: Magdalina HARTMANN] on 27 Sep 1869. Off: KUHNS. Wit: Lenah GSANTER, O.T. WILDE.

KUHN, John [41; Sarpy Co.; b: Pennsylvania; f: Jacob KUHN; m: Rosanna ELLIS] md. Georgiana WHITTINGTON [29; Sarpy Co.; b: Maryland; f: William WHITTINGTON; m: Anna] on 10 May 1877. Off: PEABODY. Wit: G.W. RINGO; Mary A. RINGO.

KUHNE, Lewis [23; Omaha; b: Illinois; f: Peter KUHNE; m: Date BURKHART] md. Mary TREITZSCHKE [22; Omaha; b: Germany; f: William TREITZSCHKE; m: Henrietta WILDY] on 4 Oct 1874. Off: PEABODY. Wit: Julius TREITSCHKE; Otto J. WILDE.

KUMPF, Frederick [24; Omaha] and Christina ROHWER [22; Omaha] license issued 8 Dec 1859. Marriage recorded without a date. Off: KUHNS. Wit: Dorah ROHWER, Catherine ROHWER, Mrs. HANSOM.

KUMPF, Frederick [34; Omaha; b: Germany; f: Michael KUMPF; m: Magdalena SCHULL] md. Kate E. ROHWER [36; Omaha; b: Germany; f: Timothy ROHWER; m: Christina E. SIMONSEN] on 24 Mar 1870. Off: KUHNS. Wit: Anna SIMONSEN; Margaret SIMONSEN.

KUNDE, Herman [26; Omaha; b: Germany; f: August KUNDE; m: Caroline LOSCH] md. Frederike L. KRELLE [21; Omaha; b: Germany; f: George A. KRELLE; m: Louise HENSCHKE] on 27 Jan 1881. Off: FRESE. Wit: Carl SCHNITZENBERGER, Miss Math. WINDHEIM.

KUONIG, John B. and Ragia MAAG license issued on 13 Jul 1856. No marriage record. Off: SCOTT.

KUONY, Eugene [38; Omaha; b: Germany; f: John KUONY; m: Agatha SCHEIBEL] md. Christina MEHRING [22; Omaha; b: Germany; f: Bernhard H. MEHRING; m: Anna Mary PETERS] on 27 Jul 1881 at the German Catholic Church in Omaha. Off: GLAUBER. Wit: John BAUMER, Hubert JACOBERGER.

KUPPIG, Edward [28; Omaha; b: Germany; f: Gottlieb KUPPIG; m: Caroline SCHULTZE] md. Adeline MUHS [22; Omaha; b: IA; f: Peter MUHS; m: Anna SCHNEECLOTH] on 23 Jul 1881. Off: BENEKE. Wit: J.H. GAST, John DISBROW.

KUTELEK, Mike [22; Omaha; b: Bohemia; f: Mike KUTELEK; m: Anna DEBELKA] md. Anna POLALECAK [23; Omaha; b: Bohemia; f: James POLALECAK; m: Barbara TROGAN] on 25 May 1875. Off: PEABODY. Wit: James JOBLECNIK, James POLALECAK.

LACEY, Thomas M. [36; Omaha; b: Virginia; f: James T. LACEY; m: Martha F. FINLAY] md. May RICE [23; Omaha; b: Kentucky; f: James A. RICE; m: Ellen STEVENSON] on 27 Dec 1872. Off: BILLMAN. Wit: Jas. McLAUGHLIN; Martha SNOWDEN.

LaCHAPELLE, Enseba [59; Omaha; b: Canada; f: Charles LaCHAPELLE; m: Angelique BEAUSOLIEL] md. Hannah F. NIEDIECK [47; Omaha; b: Germany; f: John H. NIEDIECK; m: Isabella ESSELLAMANN] on 12 May 1880. Off: BRUEGGER. Wit: G.L. GREEN, D.C. LA CHAFRELLE.

LaCHAPELLE, Eusedi [60; Omaha; b: Canada; f: Charles LaCHAPELLE; m: Egeligne BANSOHELLE] md. Leonore CHARTIER [54; Omaha; b: Canada; f: Antoine BARON; m: Brigite LAPRE] on 15 Sep 1881. Off: BRANDES Wit: Alexander LaCHAPELLE, Thomas ROSSITER. Affidavit signed with "X" and witnessed by BERGMAN.

LACHNER, William [39; Council Bluffs; b: New York; f: Joseph LACHNER; m: Polly Ann PUTNAM] and Mrs. Thana COLSON [39; Council Bluffs; b: Illinois; b: Samuel COBURN; m: Elizabeth MASON] license issued on 2 Mar 1872. Off: TWONSEND.

LACHRER, John [24; Omaha; b: Switzerland; f: Ferdinand LACHRER; m: Elizabeth EGGER] md. Mina VOGT [31; Omaha; b: Prussia; f: Charles VOGT; m: Frederike MANGKY] on 25 Jan 1871. off: GIBSON. Wit: Robert GUS__GER; Elizabeth GIFNER or GRIFFIN.

LACKERMAN [LOCKERMAN], Henry W. [24; Omaha] md. Lottie [SLOVER] GLOVER [24; Omaha] on 21 Oct 1867 at Mr. BOWMAN's house. Off: FLORKEE. Wit: Joseph BURNS, Charlotte FLORKEE, Mrs. BOWMAN.

LAFFER, H.B. [31; Avoca, IA; b: Ohio; f: John LAFFER; m: Elizabeth BOYD] md. Susan MORGAN [30; Avoca, IA; b: Virginia; f: Nathan MORGAN; m: Hannah CROSS] on 21 Apr 1879. Off: WRIGHT. Wit: Rodney DUTCHER, Wm. T. FLYNN.

LAGE, P.R. [25; Omaha; b: Denmark; f: Rasmus LAGE; m: Karen JOHANNSON] md. Maria JOHANNSON [23; Omaha; b: Denmark; f: Johann Peter PETERSON; m: Maria CHRISTIANSON] on 29 Aug 1880, Vor Frelsers Church. Off: GYDESEN. Wit: H. JOHNSON, L. JOHNSON, both of Elk Horn Station.

LAGE, Rasmuss [51; Omaha; b: Denmark; f: Peter LAGE; m: Antje HUSEN] md. Mrs. Jennie HUBBARD [40; Omaha; b: New Jersey; f: George HOVEY; m: Maria LYONS] at the residence of J. LARSEN on 29 Nov 1879. Off: GYDESON. Wit: Peter Rasmus LAGE, Henrik LAGE.

LAIBLE, Leonard [28; Omaha; b: Germany; f: George LAIBLE; m: Mary or Margaret UNSELT] md. Emilie ELSASSER [20; Omaha; b: Germany; f: Christian ELSASSER; m: Anna WACKER; on 15 Jan 1876. Off: HEISS. Wit: Gottlob ZIMMERMANN, Jacob ELSASSER.

LAKE, George B. [33; Omaha] md. Abbie G. HAYS [19; Omaha] on 8 Sep 1861 at the residence of the bride's father in South Omaha. Off: KUHNS. Wit: Mr. and Mrs. HAYS, Mr. and Mrs. BUNN, G.I. GILBERT, et al.

LAKIN, Charles [27; North Platte; b: England; f: James LAKIN; m: Sarah BRINDLEY] md. Maria WHITEHEAD [25; England; b: England; f: Thomas WHITEHEAD] on 18 Oct 1872. Off: GUE. Wit: S. Dwight PADOCK, Seward; J. PASHELY.

LAMB, Andrew [33; Omaha; b: Germany; f: Quirene LAMB; m: Elizabeth STRUTT] md. Katy KING [26; Omaha; b: Wisconsin; f: Franz KOENIG; m: ? PETERS] on 2 Aug 1874. Off: DIECKMAN. Wit: Joseph BECKMAN; Eliza SCHWARZ.

LAMB, Charles W. [28; Omaha] and Elizabeth VAN SYCKLE [23; Omaha] license issued on 8 Feb 1860. Off: ARMSTRONG.

LAMM, Charles L. [29; Douglas Co.; b: Germany; f: Peter LAMM; m: Scholestick SECHMEN] md. Johanna STICH [30; Omaha; b: Switzerland; f: Moeritz STICH; m: Johannah BORER] on 8 Nov 1870?. Off: GROENEBAUM. Wit: Mr. and Mrs. MERGEN.

LaMONTAINE, Israel [22; Omaha; b: NY; f: John LaMONTAINE; m: Laura FULTON] md. Katie LESTER [18; Omaha; b: Baltimore; f: William LESTER; m: Rebecca LESTER] on 20 Sep 1876. Off: STEVESON. Wit: A.M. SIMPSON, Newton E. BARKELOW.

LAMOTTE, Herman [28; Omaha; b: Germany; f: Frederick LAMOTTE; m: Lena EFFERS] md. Caroline SLITTER [28; Omaha; b: Germany; f: Christian SLITTER; m: Frederike HERING] on 26 Oct 1875. Off: HENNEY. Wit: Paul STEIN, Ferdinand SCHROEDER.

LAMP, Hans A. [24; Washington Co.; b: Germany; f: Henry LAMP; m: Celia LAGE] md. Margaret SUVERKRUBBE [24; Washington Co.; b: Germany; f: James P. SUVERKRUBBE; m: Annie STEFFEN] on 18 Oct 1873. Off: TOWNSEND. Wit: Adolph STEFFEN, Washington Co.; Carl STEFFEN, Washington Co.

LAMPHER, George [32; Omaha] md. Lucia LANNING [24; Omaha] at 1 PM on Wednesday, 28 Oct 1868 at J.H. KELLOM's residence. Off: DIMMICK. Wit: Mrs. J.H. KELLOM, Mrs. O.F. DAVIS, Mrs. S. WRIGHT, Mrs. K.G.W. DIMMICK, et al.

LAMPLUGH [LAMPLEIGH], Quinby [26; North Platte; b: Newport, DE; f: Thomas LAMPLUGH [LAMPLEIGH]; m: Margaret WALKER] md. Martha DAY [19; North Platte; b: Patterson, NJ; f: David DAY; m: Anna OWENS] on 11 Sep 1869. Off: KUHNS. Wit: John E. WIGMAN, Catharine WIGMAN.

LAND, Charles R. [24; Council Bluffs; b: Illinois; f: Wm. P. LAND; m: Priscilla SIMS] md. Charlotte SMITH [17; Boomer Twp, [Pottawattamie Co.,] IA; b: Iowa; f: A.B. SMITH; m: Emma WRIGHT] on 2 Jan 1880. Off: BARTHOLOMEW. Wit: Jas. B. BRUNNER, J.J. POINTS.

LANDECKER, Clay [26; Omaha; b: OH; f: Lawrence LANDECKER; m: Malinea SLAGO] md. Annie SMITH [18; Shelby Co., IA; b: IA; f: Harvey SMITH; m: Martha MATHER] on 8 Nov 1881. Off: CHADWICK. Wit: Chas. W. EDGERTON, E.W. SIMERAL.

LANDON, Milton A. [23; Omaha; b: Erie Co., NY; f: Luther LANDON; m: Cynthias PIERCE] md. Elizabeth P. WATKINS [23; Omaha; b: New York; f: Dr. WATKINS; m: Phrania P. CHESBROUGH] on 11 Feb 1873. Off: SHERRILL. Wit: R.M. MARSHALL; James WOODARD.

LANDROCK, Charles [29; Omaha; b: Bethlehem, OH; f: Carl G. LANDROCK; m: Willmina EICHNER] md. Mrs. Marion M. PAGE [25; Omaha; b: Waltham, MA; f: Ezekiel T. PAGE; m: Elizabeth W. JOHNSON] on 2 Nov 1869. Off: KUHNS. Wit: Mr. and Mrs. Ezekiel T. PAGE, Joseph W. ARNOLD.

LANE, Dennis W. [21; Omaha; b: Ohio; f: Dennis D. LANE; m: Mary C. YOUNG] md. Mary E. McDEVITT [20; Omaha; b: Pennsylvania; f: Charles McDEVITT: m: Ellen BIGLAN] on 10 Jun 1874 at the German Catholic Church. Off: GROENEBAUM. Wit: Nellie SULLIVAN; John GARVEY.

LANE, Thomas J. [29; Omaha; b: Pittsburgh, PA; f: Jefferson LANE; m: Margaret M. HOLDER] md. Jennie P. MORAN [18; Omaha; b: Pittston, PA; f: James H. MORAN] on 8 Aug 1875. Off: PEABODY. Wit: Maggie MORAN, Katie MADDEN. Application notarized by C.A. BALDWIN.

LANER, Leonard [31; Huney Creek Station, IA; b: Missouri; f: Isaac LANER] md. Bridget FOLEY [30; Huney Creek Station, IA; b: Ireland; f: Alexander CANABEY; m: Mary BRENARD] on 19 Oct 1871. Off: GIBSON. Wit: J.S. SPAUN; A. FRAZIER, Huney Creek Station, IA.

LANG, William [29; Omaha; b: England] md. Mary WILEY [29; Omaha; b: Ohio] on 9 Jan 1871. Off: KELLEY. Wit: Barnett ASHBURN; James H. DENNIS.

LANGDON, Anthony J. [29; Sarpy Co.; b: Illinois; f: Patrick LANGDON; m: Catherine THOMAS] md. Margaret E. HERON [26; Douglas Co.; b: Michigan; f: Thomas HERON; m: Mary HORRIGAN] on 6 Feb 1877. Off: JENNETTO. Wit: Martin LANGDON, Anne HERON.

LANGDON, John J. [28; Forrest City, NE; b: Illinois; f: P.J. LANGDON; m: Catharine THOMAS] md. Francis G. HERRON [18; Omaha; b: Wisconsin; f: John HERRON; m: Mary HOURIGAN] at the Catholic Cathedral on 6 Nov 1879. Off: KELLY. Wit: P.J. LANGDON of Forrest City, Terresa HERRON.

LANGE, August [31; Omaha; b: Germany; f: Frederick LANGE; m: Wilhelmine HODEN] md. Mrs. Anne LEYET [25; Omaha; b: Baltimore, MD; f: Joseph KITCENGEL; m: Rosa WOLF] on 15 May 1874. Off: BARTLETT. Wit: Carrie KITZINGER; Henry STULL.

LANGE, Otto [28; Omaha; b: Germany; f: Gottlieb LANGE; m: Emilie KNAPPE] md. Mary KORTING [21; Omaha; b: Germany; f: Charles KORTING; m: Maggie LANGE] on 22 May 1880. Off: FRESE. Wit: Julius FESTNER, William HARTING.

LANPHER, Alonzo H. [22; Omaha; b: Monmoth, IL; f: Orrin LANPHER; m: Malinda POST] md. Mattie J. MARTIN [22; Omaha; b: Illinois] on 10 Sep 1870. Off: GIBSON. Wit: W.T. BAKER; Mrs. Mary GIBSON.

LANSENT, Henry [31; Omaha] md. Margaret SLEMMER [21; Omaha] on 25 Sep 1866. Off: MILLER. Wit: D.S. HUTCHINSON, Edward SHICK.

LANSING, Charles M. [26; Omaha; b: New York; f: Henry L. LANSING; m: Catharine O. GIBSON]; md. Mrs. Eliza M. ROGERS [24; New York; b: New York; f: Guy H. GOODRICH; m: Nancy MATTHEWS] on 1 Sep 1869. Off: GASSMAN. Wit: Rev. J. PATERSON of Nebraska City, G.C. BETTS, Rev. Thos. BETTS of Rulo.

LANSING, Jno. B. [24; Omaha; b: IL; f: Cornelius LANSING; m: Eliza GOODHUE] md. Eliza LAMB [18; Omaha; b: Salt Lake City, UT; f: Abel LAMB; m: Lizzie EVANS] on 24 Jun 1875. Off: HENNEY. Wit: J.C. BLACHLY, Mrs. McDONALD.

LARAWAY, William F. [20; Lewis, IA; b: Lowell, OH; f: Peter B. LARAWAY; m: Susannah STARLINE] md. Adah HUNT [18; Lewis, IA; b: Nebraska City; f: Moses HUNT; m: Adalaide FENELL (FENNELL)] on 25 May 1869. Off: MORRIS. Wit: Samuel B. SHAW, Mrs. Aggie C. FIELD.

LARKIN, Danford S. or Danforth [37; Omaha] md. Melissa REED [20; Omaha] on 4 Mar 1869 at the parsonage of the First ME Church. Off: WESTWOOD. Wit: F.R. DELAWARE, Henni WENTWORTH, Parker REED, John W. TOUSLEY, et al.

LaROCHE, Robert [35; Omaha; b: Prussia; f: Charles LaROCHE; m: Rosalie V. DAVIER] md. Mary J. GRAHAM [21; Omaha; b: New York; f: Guy GRAHAM; m: Bessie GRAHAM] on 15 Mar 1877. Off: PEABODY. Wit: Mabel PEABODY, Alice PEABODY.

LARSEN, Abraham [42; Omaha; b: Denmark; f: Lars SWENSON; m: Kate M. IVERSEN] md. Ann M. RASMUSSEN [29; Omaha; b: Denmark; f: John ANDERSON; m: Johanna NELSON] on 15 Jul 1874. Off: PEABODY. Wit: Sylvanus WRIGHT; P.S. SMITH.

LARSEN, Erik [26; Omaha; b: Denmark; f: Lars ERICKSON; m: Kirsten NIELSDOTTER] md. Eliza FECH [21; Omaha; b: Denmark; f: Jacob FECH; m: Johanna JEPPERSON] on 30 Dec 1881 at Vor Frelser's Church. Off: GYDESEN. Wit: Fred FREDERIKSON, K. CHRISTENSON.

LARSEN, Hans [26; Omaha; b: Denmark; f: Ole THORKILDSEN; m: Annie Marie CHRISTENSEN] md. Elsi Matine Frederika JENSEN [18; Omaha; b: Denmark; f: Christian JENSEN; m: Hulda E.A. HILFLING] on 27 Sep 1872. Off: ERDALL. Wit: Nils LARSON; H.P.C. FREDERIKSEN.

LARSEN, John Peter [35; Omaha; b: Sweden; F: Lars NELSON; m: Lizzie SWENSON] md. Louise CARLSON [22; Omaha; b: Sweden; f: Carl Gustav CARLSON; m: Gertrude HINRICKSON] on 19 Nov 1881. Off: FOGELSTROM. Wit: Emma LARSEN, Alma FOGELSTROM.

LARSEN, N.C. [35; Omaha; b: Denmark; f: Lars JENSEN; m: A. NELSON] md. Hillia C. HOLM [27; Omaha; b: Denmark; f: C. HOLM] on 30 Aug 1876. Off: unsigned, but probably SEDGWICK. Wit: Soren JORGENSON, Niels Christian NIELSEN.

LARSEN, Nils [24; Omaha; b: Denmark; f: Lars NILSON; m: Caroline HENSEN] md. Sophia CHRISTENSEN [21; Omaha; b: Denmark; f: Christian ANDERSEN; m: Carrie Mary NELSEN] on 7 Jan 1870. Off: LARSON. Wit: Mrs. Johanna C. LARSON; Engla J. NORMAN.

LARSEN, Nils [28; Omaha; b: Denmark; f: Lars GODFERSON; m: Bergette TAMASDOTTE(R)] md. Christine

CHRISTENSEN [24; Omaha; b: Denmark; f: Christian CHRISTIANSEN; m: Christine NILSTOTTER] on 14 Feb 1870. Off: GIBSON. Wit: John ORCHARD; Delas BEARD.

LARSON, Abraham [49; Omaha; b: Denmark; f: Lars SWENSON; m: Margaret IVERSEN] md. Mrs. Cathrina DITTUS [40; Omaha; b: Germany; f: Henry SCHAFFLED; m: Anna LINK] on 28 Oct 1881. Off: STENBERG. Wit: Eric PEDERSON, Mrs. Christina THUMM.

LARSON, Andrew G. [25; Omaha; b: Sweden; f: Lars LARSON; m: Johann JOHNSON] md. Caroline JOHNSON [23; Omaha; b: Sweden; f: Jonas JOHNSON; m: Anna LARSDOTTER] on 15 Jan 1872. Off: LARSON. Wit: John LIND; Matts THOMSON.

LARSON, August [28; Washington Co.; b: Sweden] md. Wilhelmina P. LAGERSTROM [31; Omaha; b: Sweden] on 2 Nov 1869. Off: LARSON. Wit: A. CHRISTENSON, Mrs. Johanna CHRISTENSEN.

LARSON, Christian Peter [20; Irvington, NE; b: Denmark; f: Lars P. JENSEN; m: Anna M. PETERSON] md. Mrs. Anna MUNN [28; Irvington; b: Germany; f: Joseph BEHRENS; m: Anna ROHWER] on 4 Oct 1878. Off: STENBERG. Wit: A.N. KEAR, Anton LARSON. Age consent given by Anton LARSON, brother of the groom.

LARSON, Christian [23; Omaha; b: Denmark; f: Axel LARSON; m: Annie PALSEN] md. Sophia C. JENSEN [25; Omaha; b: Denmark; f: J. JENSEN; m: Christina LARSON] on 16 Apr 1870. Off: KUHNS. Wit: Augustus KOUNTZE; Mrs. Kate KOUNTZE.

LARSON, Christian [27; Omaha; b: Denmark; f: Lars CHRISTIANSEN; m: Christina PETERSON] md. Anna Christina BENSON [28; Omaha; b: Denmark; f: Jens BENSON; m: Bodil Marie ANDRESDOTTER] on 6 Feb 1873. Off: PORTER. Wit: Charles RASTMUSON; A. SORENSON.

LARSON, Christian [28; Omaha; b: Denmark; f: Larson CHRISTINSEN; m: Bertha ANDERSON] and Clara LINDBERG [24; Omaha; b: Sweden; f: Charles LINDBERG] license issued on 22 Jul 1871. Off: GIBSON.

LARSON, Johan F. [26; Omaha; b: Denmark; f: Mads LARSON; m: Elizabeth AMMUNDSEN] md. Anna E. HENRICKSON [33; Omaha; b: Denmark; f: Henrik NELSON; m: Anna M. MADSEN] on 28 Jul 1874. Off: HALD. Wit: Louis HENRIKSEN; Niels PETERSON.

LARSON, John [37; Saunders Co.; b: Sweden; f: Jacob LARSON; m: Mary JOHNSON] md. Catharine CARLSON [22; Omaha; b: Sweden; f: Charles CARLSON; m: Mary JACOBSEN] on 11 Oct 1872. Off: SUNDBORN. Wit: Oscar BOLIN; Nils OLSON, Saunders Co.

LARSON, L.P. [22; Saunders Co.; b: Sweden; f: Lars OLESON; m: Annie LINDQUEST] md. Anna L. NELSON [25 Douglas Co.; b: Sweden; f: Nels DANIELSON; m: Mary SWANSEN] on 19 Aug 1876. Off: SEDGWICK. Wit: F.P. HANLON, Samuel NELSON.

LARSON, Lars C. [31; Omaha; b: Denmark; f: Nels LARSON; m: Metty CHRISTIANSON] md. Karen ANDERSON [28; Omaha; b: Denmark; f: Anders PETERSON; m: Christina] on 12 Nov 1875 at his residence. Off: JOHNSON. Wit: Anthan C. LARSEN, Soren LARSEN.

LARSON, Lawrence [22; Saunders Co.; b: Sweden; f: Lawrence LARSON; m: Mary CHRISTIANSEN] md. Lizzie GADERBURG [20; Omaha; b: Sweden; f: Peter GADERBERG; m: Lizzie JOHNSON] on 11 Mar 1873. Off: SWEDERS. Wit: G.P. SANDERS; Carl OCKANDER.

LARSON, Louis P. [21; Omaha; b: Sweden; f: Lars NELSON] md. Allthea E. GRANATH [25; Omaha; b: Sweden; f: Per G. GRANATH; m: Hedwig A. LAGER] on 13 Mar 1873. Off: SWEDERS. Wit: Gustaf SWANSON; Carl Gustaf GRANATH.

LARSON, Marten [32; Omaha; b: Sweden; f: Lars JONSON; m: Elsa MARTENSDOTTER] md. Elna SVENSDOTTER [36; Omaha; b: Sweden; f: Swen SWENSEN; m: Elna ERICKSON] on 20 Jul 1870. Off: BENNETT. Wit: Gustav ANDERSON; Alexander LINDBLOM.

LARSON, Nelson [25; Omaha; b: Sweden; f: Lars NELSON; m: Bertha BRITKEISER] md. Annie JOHNSON [25; Omaha; b: Sweden; f: John JOHNSON; m: Mary] on 8 May 1872. Off: THURSTON. Wit: J.B. PLUMMER; A. ADAMSKY.

LARSON, Oliver [22; Omaha] md. Anna OLSON [18 and 6 months; Omaha] on 5 Jul 1866. Off: HASCALL. Wit: Mr. and Mrs. LUND.

LARSON, Peter Jensen [21; Omaha; b: Denmark; f: Lars NIELSON; m: Bohl Christina JENSEN] md. Else Christina JENSEN [19; Omaha; b: Denmark; f: Jens PETERSON; m: Patre PETERSON] on 9 Apr

1881. Off: ANDERSON. Wit: John C. CHRISTENSON, Anders ANDERSON.

LARSON, Simon [30; Washington Co.; b: Denmark; f: Lars ANDERSEN; m: Kirsten SIMINSDOTAR] md. Marion Christina RASMUSSEN [23; Washington Co.; b: Denmark; f: Rasmus KNUDSEN; m: Eliza Christina JOHNSON] on 10 Apr 1872. Off: BRANDES. Wit: Thomas MULCHAY; Peter LARSON, Washington Co.

LARSON, Turner [25; Omaha; b: Denmark; f: Lars SORENSON; m: Christine SORENSON] md. Sina B. BROWN [21; Omaha; b: Denmark; f: James BROWN; m: Christine NELSON] on 28 Jan 1879. Off: LIPE. Wit: M. WIRTH, Mrs. J.T. CLARK.

LASBY, William [24; Omaha] md. Essie RYAN [23; Omaha] on 5 Jul 1868. Off: CURTIS. Wit: Michael LEHEY, Hannah CALLAGHAN.

LaSEUR, William [ 27; Preparation, IA; b: NY; f: Amasa LaSEUR; m: Pauline] md. Sarah HENDRICKSON [18; Preparation, IA; b: CO; f: James HENDRICKSON; m: Jane LANGLEY] on 25 May 1875. Off: PEABODY. Wit: E.T. COWIN, J.W. WILLIAMS.

LATEY, Henry L. [31; Omaha; b: England; f: Thomas H. LATEY; m: Jane WARREN] md. Mary E. SPOOR [16; Omaha; b: Council Bluffs, IA; f: Nelson O. SPOOR; m: Eunice L. ROBBINS] on 2 Jan 1870. Off: KUHNS. Wit: Thomas H. LATEY; Nelson O. SPOOR.

LATHROP, Louis S. [23 Douglas Co.; b: IA; f: N. LATHROP; m: Clara FOLBRE] md. Annie E. LECKENBY [21; Omaha; b: MO; f: James LECKENBY; m: Margaret BOYD] on 10 Aug 1876. Off: SEDGWICK. Wit: C.P. WOOLWORTH, T.S. SANFORD.

LAW, Franklin M. [37; Omaha; b: Michigan; f: Joseph F. LAW; m: Eliza A. MILLINGTON] md. Mrs. Daisy A. BURNS [23; Omaha; b: Ohio; f: William BURNS; m: Sarah E. TRUEX] on 24 Jul 1880. Off: STENBERG. Wit: William ERATH, Hattie S. WAGNER.

LAWRANCE, George A. [22; Adrian, MI; b: Andover, MA; f: Orrin LAWRANCE; m: Jane P. BLODGETT] md. Ida B. SHULL [19; Omaha; b; Pennsylvania; f: Jacob SHULL; m: Susan CROFT] on 4 May 1870. Off: KUHNS. Wit: John McPHERSON; Mrs. Amos SHULL.

LAWRENCE, William [23; Omaha] md. Kate M. SHULL [22; Omaha] on 5 May 1868 at the Lutheran Church. Off: KUHNS. Wit: Daniel SHULL, Maggie STEVENS, et al.

LAWS, John [35; Waterloo; b: Ohio; f: M. LAWS; m: L.T. BIRDSLEY] md. Mrs. Elizabeth ELLWOOD [23; Elk Horn Station; b: Wales; f: Samuel FRY; m: Mary Ann FLORENCE] on 14 Apr 1880 at Jefferson, Douglas Co. Off: TIMME. Wit: Charles MARTIN, Mary OSTLY, both of Elkhorn.

LAWSON, Andrew [37; Douglas Co.; b: Sweden; f: Martin LAWSON; m: Bengta LAWSON] md. Nettie NELSON [40; Omaha; b: Sweden; f: Nels SWENSON; m: Ingre NELSON] on 7 Apr 1880. Off: BARTHOLOMEW. Wit: Max BERGMANN, Rosa KINNEY.

LAWSON, Augustus D. [22; Sarpy Co.; b: Sweden; f: L. ANDERSON; m: Margaretha LAWSON] md. Mathilda LINDBERG [22; Sarpy Co.; b: Sweden; f: Alexander LINDBERG; m: Gustava ABRAHAMSON] on 28 Sep 1880. Off: DAHLSHDT. Wit: John LINDBLAD, Mrs. John LINDBLAD.

LAWSON, J.E. [30; Shelby Co., IA; b: New York; f: John D. LAWSON; m: Paruna KNAPP] md. Zelda FOSTER [28; McGregor, IA; b: New Hampshire; f: McKager FOSTER; m: Betsy TUCKER] on 22 Jan 1880. Off: MAXFIELD. Wit: John E. MILLER, Mrs. Belle M. MILLER.

LAWSON, Lucius C. [24; Council Bluffs; b: PA; f: H.B. LAWSON; m: Maria STEWART] md. Marion BAUDEN [23; Council Bluffs; b: MI; f: George BAUDER; m: Mary A. LYMAN] on 19 Apr 1875. Off: PEABODY. Wit: J.C. COWIN, J. Phipps ROE.

LAYET, Paul E. [28; Omaha; b: New Orleans, LA; f: John E. LAYET; m: Hortense BEAUREGAURD] md. Anna KITZENGER [19; Omaha; b: New York] on 11 Oct 1869. Off: KELLEY. Wit: Edward HAMILTON, Jeremiah McCHANE.

LAYTON, Frank [23; Douglas Precinct, Douglas Co.; b: Michigan; f: C.D. LAYTON; m: Maria PIKARD] md. Mary CONWAY [27; Douglas Precinct; f: Patrick CONWAY; m: Annie NEEDHAM] on 13 Dec 1880. Off: ENGLISH. Wit: James McCAFFREY of Douglas Precinct, Mary TONER of Douglas Co.

LEARY, Cornelius A. [26; Omaha; b: New York; f: Patrick LEARY; m: Nellie COTTER] md. Louisa BURKLEY [19; Omaha; b: Ohio; f: Vincent BURKLEY; m: Thersia STELTZER] on 18 Oct 1870 at the Catholic Church of Omaha. Off: O'GORMAN. Wit: Mary WHAREHAM; Patrick LEARY.

LEARY, James [28; Elkhorn Pct; b: Ireland; f: Dennis LEARY; m: Mary CARDIN] md. Mary MAHONEY [19; Omaha; b: Ireland; f: John MAHONEY; m: Johanna SULIVAN] on 28 Dec 1873 at the 9th St. Cathedral. Off: BYRNE. Wit: Michael MAHONEY; Mary HEALEY.

LEARY, Jeremiah [30; Omaha; b: Ireland; f: Dennis LEARY; m: Ann SULLIVAN] md. Margaret LINAHAN [24; Omaha; b; Ireland; f: Patrick LINAHAN] on 8 May 1870. Off: CURTIS. Wit: John SWEENEY; Johanna SWEENEY.

LEARY, Martin [44; Omaha; b: Ireland; f: James LEARY; m: Mary MORRISEY] md. Mrs. Mary Ann LEARY [27; Omaha; b: Ireland; f: Dennis LEARY; m: Mary DUFFY] on 4 Aug 1880. Off: STEENBERG. Wit: Samuel WOOLF, Aug. ISAKSON.

LEARY, Michael [24; Omaha; b: Ireland; f: Patrick LEARY; m: Johanna MANDEVILLE] md. Mary MORAN [21; Omaha; b: Ireland; f: Patrick MORAN; m: Catharine O'CONNELL] on 29 Apr at the Catholic Cathedral. Off: COLANER. Wit: Charles FLOOD, Nellie POWERS.

LEARY, P.H. [31; b: New York; f: P.H. LEARY; m: Ellen COTTER] md. Kate GRAPHOFF [28; b: Iowa; f: Henry GRAPHOFF] on 12 Dec 1878. Off: FISHER. Wit: Genl. Geo. H. CROOK, U.S.A, Mrs. CROOK.

LEARY, Patrick H. [27; Omaha; b: New York; f: Patrick LEARY; m: Ellen CUTTER] md. Mrs. Jennie M. BAYELL [26; Omaha; b: Canada; f: John SHELLINGLORE; m: Mary J.] on 15 Apr 1874. Off: LIPE. Wit: Mrs. Milton ROGERS; Mrs. Henry LATY.

LEASE, R.W., M.D. [28; Tekaman; b: Illinois; f: Henry LEASE; m: Eliza BURNHAM] md. Gracie JOHNSON [15; Hulls, IL; b: Massachusetts; f: L. JOHNSON, ---- STERTEVANT] on 1 Dec 1880. Off: MORGAN. Wit: Alex DAEMON, Lena DAEMON.

LEAVITT, H.F. [27; b: Saco, ME; f: Thomas LEAVITT; m: Hannah WATERHOUSE] md. Mrs. Florence N. MANN [22; Blair; b: Providence, RI; f: Nathan BUCHANAN; m: Jennie BROWN] on 17 Dec 1878. Off: SHERRILL. Wit: Mrs. Nealia CROWE, Richard JONES, both of 18th and Douglas Streets. This record filed 5 Aug 1879.

LEBBERT, Hans [23; b: Germany; f: John Jacob LEBBERT; m: Anna OFT] md. Henriette KAISER [17; b: Germany; f: Ferdinand KAISER; m: Ernestine RUBIN] on 25 May 1878. Off: STRASEN. Wit: August KAISER, Charles BUBIN. Age consent given by Ferdinand KAISER, father of the bride. Max BERGMAN, witness.

LeBOURVEAN, Benjamin [31; Iowa; b: Canada; f: Benjamin LeBOURVEAN; m: Eliza LABAREE] md. Mrs. Anna SNYDER [33; Omaha; b: Kentucky; f: Wm. E. CARTER; m: Thursa JOHNSON] on 14 Aug 1879. Off: BARTHOLOMEW. Wit: E.S. WARNER, Mrs. Minnie WARNER.

LEDEN, Olaf [30; Red Oak, IA; b: Sweden; f: Peter LEDEN; m: Catharine

ANDERSON] md. Augusta ANDERSON [19; Des Moines, IA; b: Des Moines, IA; f: P. ANDERSON; m: Christine NELSON] on 19 Jun 1879. Off: STENBERG. Wit: Albert R. PETERSON, Anna L. PETERSON.

LEE, Harry [32; Omaha; b: Boston, MA; f: Lonzo LEE] md. Rosa HOVEY [21; Omaha; b: VT; f: Charles HOVEY; m: Ann MARTIN] on 15 Aug 1881. Off: BEANS. Wit: Mrs. E.A. BEANS, Amelia BAER.

LEE, John A. [26; Omaha; b: Boston, MA; f: John A. LEE; m: Phoebe E. CLOUGHS] md. Alice HOCANSON [18; Omaha; b: Sweden; f: Martin HOCANSON; m: Annie NELSON] on 28 Oct 1876. Off: LIPE. Wit: James DONNELLY, Miss E. MORAN.

LEE, Peter M. [30; Omaha; b: Illinois; f: Ichabod LEE; m: Catharine MARIETTE] md. Sarah J. CRAVEN [20; Washington Co.; b: New York; f: William CRAVEN; m: Sarah McBRIDE] on 7 Nov 1880, Holy Family Church. Off: QUINN. Wit: Miss CRAVEN of Blair, Washington Co., Patrick SWEENY.

LEEDER, Augustus [30; Omaha; b: St. Louis, MO; f: Henry LEEDER; m: Caroline KLEEDUM] md. Mrs. Elizabeth WEBER [26; Omaha; b: Baton, Germany; f: Sebastian SMITH; m: Elizabeth SMITH] on 16 Apr 1873. Off: BRANDES. Wit: Peter CLARK; Isabelle CLARK.

LEEDER, Edward [23; Omaha; b: Illinois; f: Thomas LEEDER; m: Caroline BLEIDOM] md. Catharine BYERS [19; Omaha; b: Wisconsin; f: Peter BYERS; m: Margaret OLEWEIG] on 2 May 1872. Off: CURTIS. Wit: Edward LUCAS; Mary FAXON.

LEEDER, Louis [24; Omaha; b: Germany; f: Henry LEEDER; m: Caroline PLEDUING] md. Christine CHRISTY [19; Omaha; b; Scotland; f: James CHRISTY; m: Elizabeth STEWARD] on 28 May 1870. Off: KUHNS. Wit: James CHRISTIE; Charles LEEDER.

LEEHY, Morris [21; Omaha; b: Ireland; f: Morris LEEHY; m: Margaret CANNIS] md. Bridget GRIFFIN [20; Omaha; b: Ireland] on 8 Jan 1871. Off: Wiliam KELLY. Wit: Patrick McDONNELL; Ellen DEAN.

LEEMAN, W.H. [23; Omaha; b: NY; f: John LEEMAN; m: Belle MEEKER] md. Minnie A. JOHNSON [18; Douglas Co.; b: Omaha; f: Harrison JOHNSON; m: Minerva HAMBRIGHT] on 25 Dec 1876 at Harrison JOHNSON's. Off: FISHER.

LEFEVRE, Hamilton, Jr. [35; Omaha; b: MD; f: Hamilton LEFEVRE; m: Sarah Jane STREETT] md. Mary L. GREEN [21; Omaha; b: MS; f: Harry W. GREEN; m: Fanny C. FOLKES] on 26 Apr 1875. Off: EASTER. Wit: Mr. GOFF; Mrs. J.W. DAVIS.

LEFFERT, Frank [Omaha] md. Sophie HERMAN [Omaha] on 18 Aug 1864 at Mrs. HERMAN's residence. Off: DICKINSON. Wit: Mrs. HERMAN, Wm. HERMAN, E. PETERSON, William SEBEILERT.

LEGER, George [31; Grand Island; f: Russia; f: Edward LEGER; m: Dorothea WANSCHEIDT] md. Margaret IVERS [16; Omaha; b: Springfield, IL; f: Cornelius IVERS; m: Rebecca REIMERS] on 20 Jun 1872. Off: BRANDES. Wit: Cornelius IVERS; Minna METZ. Age of consent given by father of bride.

LEGROS, Frank [24; Omaha] md. Josephine St. CLAIR [19; Omaha] on 18 Aug 1861 at Mr. LEARNED's residence. Off: ARMSTRONG. Wit: Mrs. LEARNED, Mrs. Charles COX.

LEHEY, Michael [25; Omaha; b: Ireland; f: Daniel LEHEY; m: Honora GARVEN] md. Ellen DRISCOL [24; Omaha; b: Ireland; f: James DRISCOL; m: Ellen REIDY] on 28 Oct 1871. Off: CURTIS. Wit: Timothy RYAN; Mary LEHEY.

LEHMAN, William [20; Omaha; b: Germany; f: Peter LEHMAN; m: Kate ARP] md. Celia LAGGE [21; Omaha; b: Germany; f: Eggert LAGGE; m: Kate STOLLENBERG] on 8 Feb 1876. Off: SEDGWICK. Wit: Howard KENNEDY, F.P. HANLON.

LEHMANN, Henry [22; Omaha; b: Holstien, Germany; f: Peter LEHMANN; m: Catherine ARP] md. Catharine GROTMACK [23; Omaha; b: Germany; f: Claus GROTMACK; Lenah SMITH] on 21 Aug 1870. Off: KUHNS. Wit: Mrs. E.A. MALL; John C. LEHMANN.

LEHMANN, John [27; Omaha; b: Germany; f: Peter LEHMANN; m: Catharine ARP] md. Dora DUNKER [20; Omaha; b: Germany; f: Henry DUNKER; m: Perlina CLAUSSEN] on 16 Aug 1873. Off: TOWNSEND. Wit: Mrs. Thankful H. HALE; John V. CREIGHTON.

LEHR, William [35; Omaha; b: Germany; f: Wm. LEHR; m: Barbara PRUISEN] md. Annie JETTER [26; Omaha; b: Germany; f: Baldus JETTER; m: Katharina] on 12 Oct 1876. Off: STRASEN. Wit: Balthas JETTER, Christian SAUTTER.

LEIBERT, John [30; Douglas Co.] and Frances NEIDERMIER [22; Douglas Co.] license issued on 7 Oct 1868. No marriage record. Off: STUCK.

LEIMBERT, John E. [27; Omaha; b: Holland; f: Frederick J. LANEBERT (LEIMBERT); m: Agnes RITTMAN] md. Mary RASMUSSEN [19; Omaha; b: Denmark; f: Malinus RASMUSSEN; m: Nicholine MOLLER] on 7 Dec 1873. Off: LIPE. Wit: Hamlet ORUM; Catherine ORUM.

LEIN, James F. [27; Omaha] md. Catharine VAUGHN [19; Omaha] on 23 Oct 1867. Off: PALMER. Wit: Mrs. E.S. PALMER, Mrs. J.H. SAHLER, et al.

LEISGE, Henry [25; Omaha; b: Germany; f: Conrad LEISGE; m: Mary BLAAK] md. Bertha BLOTZ [20; Omaha; b: Michigan; f: Anton BLOTZ; m: Clara] on 20 Apr 1873. Off: SHERRILL. Wit: J.H. HAMMOND; Conrad LEISGE.

LEMING, L.T. [30; Omaha; b: Indiana; f: C.C. LEMING; m: Anna POTTER] md. Mary T. MILLER [22; Omaha; b: Iowa; f: Jacob MILLER; m: Sophia LOWEN] on 12 Dec 1879. Off: MARQUETTE. Wit: C.C. LEMING, H.L. LEMING.

LEMKE, John [25; Douglas Co.] md. Margaret AIE [26; Omaha] on 8 Apr 1868 at MAY's residence. Off: MAY. Wit: W. TANNENBERGER, Mrs. E. FLORKEE.

LEMME, Charles [31; Omaha; b: Missouri; f: Frederick LEMME; m: Wilhelmina HAHN] md. Maria LUEHR [29; Omaha; b: Germany; f: Henry LUEHR; m: Maria BLUHM] on 9 May 1880. Off: BENEKE. Wit: August SCHULTZ, Henry BURGDORFF.

LEMON, John R. [26; Omaha; b: Ohio; f: Samuel LEMON; m: Nancy ROBINSON] md. Elizabeth PICKELS [19; Omaha; b: Missouri; f: John PICKELS; m: Mary WITHNELL] on 22 Nov 1870. Off: KUHNS. Wit: Madison LOVETT; Charlotte E. WITHNELL.

LEMON, William [30; Douglas Co.; b: Germany; f: Henry LEMON; m: Magdalena DECKMAN] md. Christina M.D. BEITZEL [20; Omaha; b: Germany; f: Charles BEITZEL; m: ? WEIPKE] on 21 Dec 1874 at McArdle Pct. Off: MYERS. Wit: Frederick LEMON, McArdle Pct; William WOLLBURG, McArdle Pct.

LENDAIMER [TENDEMIES], Jacob [26; Omaha] md. Mrs. Mary HOFFMAN [25; Omaha] on 1 Dec 1868. Off: GIBSON. Wit: John MINIKUS, S.B. BOSWORTH.

LENDQUEST, Olof [31; Omaha; b: Sweden; f: Olof OLESON; m: Christine MATSON] md. Anna PETERSON [23; Omaha; b: Sweden; f: Peter PETERSON; m: Anna OLESON] on 31 Mar 1879. Off: BARTHOLOMEW. Wit: George SHIELDS, C.J. GREEN.

LENIHAN, Thomas md. Margaret FITZGERALD on 3 Mar 1867 at the Catholic Church. Off: EGAN. Wit: Michael CLEARY, Mrs. ROACH.

LENTELL, Junius V. [25; Valley Station; b: Massachusetts; f: J.V. LENTELL; m: Louisa BURROUGHS] md. Thaiza WILLIAMS [19; Valley Station; b: Wisconsin; f: J.M. WILLIAMS; m: Francis ESMAY] on 18 Nov 1880, Valley Station. Off: NEILSON. Wit: Mr. and Mrs. J.M. WILLIAMS, Mr. and Mrs. Jas. GAFFIN, all of Valley Station.

LEONARD, James [24; Omaha; b: Michigan; f: Patrick LEONARD; m: Ann HICKEY] md. Mary A. LEONARD [25; Omaha; b: Michigan; f: Peter LEONARD; m: Bridget CARPENTER] on 7 Jun 1879. Off: POWELL. Wit: Archie C. POWELL, S.B. LOOMIS.

LEONARD, John [25; Omaha; b: Ireland; f: William LEONARD; m: Mary CANNER] md. Esther CANNELL [20; Omaha; b: Ireland; f: Edward CANNELL; m: Mary RECRAFT] on 25 Nov 1869. Off: CURTIS. Wit: Patrick QUALEY, Bridget QUALEY.

LEPPEN, Joseph A. [29; Omaha; b: Hungary; f: Joseph A. LEPPEN; m: Amelia DI ZRINY] md. Harriet C. KRAUSE [19; Omaha; b: Poland; f: Augustus KRAUSE; m: Harriet C. KLOSE] on 25 May 1869. Off: HYDE. Wit: Dominick ST. GEYER, G. GROSVENOR of Tekamah.

LEPPER, William [37; Omaha; b: Germany; f: Henry G. LEPPER; m: Ersiala HUME] md. Helen E. HEYDE [19 Douglas Co.; b: NY; f: Frederick HEYDE; m: Adelle SAGO] on 18 Dec 1876. Off: SEDGWICK. Wit: Fred R.D. HEYDE, O.R.D. HEYDE.

LERCH, John [23; Omaha; b: Germany; f: John LERCH; m: Henrietta UTECH] md. Annie KRENEK [21; Omaha; b: Bohemia; f: Louis KRENEK; m: Augusta] on 28 Oct 1873. Off: HILGENDORF. Wit: Charles KAERSTEN; Gustav LERCH.

LERNED, Frederick T. [35; Philadelphia, PA; b: MA; f: Thos. P. LERNED; m: Elsie KENDALL] md. Etta E. STOOKAY [22; Philadelphia, PA; b: PA; f: George STOOKAY, m: Catherine HEFELDTRAGER] on 16 Oct 1876 at Trinity Cathedral. Off: MILLSPAUGH. Wit: Ellis L. BIERBOWER, Sister (?) Mary HAGDEN.

LESSENTINE, Frederick W. [34; Germany; f: Ernst LESSENTIN; m: Albertine DUMMER] md. Mrs. Jane Hedden CAMERON [43; Omaha; b: England; f: John LAMPLUGH] on 11 Jan 1878. Off: WILLIAMS. Wit: Mrs. GILLMORE, Mrs. BLAIR.

LETEL, John [26; Omaha] and Anna THOMAS [16; IA] license issued on 12 Aug 1862. Off: ARMSTRONG. Age consent given by the mother of the bride who was present, father dead.

LEUTSCHER, Jacob B. [36; Omaha; b: Holland; f: Bernerd LEUTSCHER; m: Bouwdwina OSTERBANN] md. Ida Matilda

ANDERSEN [18; Omaha; b: Sweden; f: Johan ANDERSEN; m: Christina PETERSON] on 18 Nov 1872. Off: TOWNSEND. Wit: Lewis J. THOMPSON, Harlan Co.; William KRAIL.

LEVY, David [24; Omaha; b: New York City; f: M.H. LEVY; m: Esther BEHRENDT] md. Margaret WELLS [19; Omaha; b: IL; f: Conrad WELLS; m: Elizabeth WELLS] on 21 Jun 1881. Off: BRANDES. Wit: Sary WILKINS, Mrs. A. PETERSON.

LEWARK, John [23; Douglas Co.] md. Lusetta LEWARK [19; Douglas Co.] on 11 Jun 1859 at BRIGGS' office. Off: BRIGGS. Wit: John SKEPLET, James HAZEN.

LEWIN, Washington [42; Douglas Co.] md. Mrs. Maria EUBANKS [38; Douglas Co.] on 13 Jan 1861. Off: BRIGGS. Wit: Mrs. BOWMAN, et al.

LEWIN, Washington [Omaha] md. Gracia CRAIN [Omaha] on 29 Jan 1865 at P. BRAMHALL's residence. Off: DICKINSON. Wit: Mr. and Mrs. V.W. SMITH, Mr. and Mrs. P. BRAMHALL, Mrs. Susan WALTON, Mr. and Mrs. Wm. R. BROWN, et al.

LEWIS, Allen [38; Gage Co., NE; b: Ohio; f: James LEWIS; m: Mahala SIMON] md. Caroline CNARR [22; Omaha; b: Ohio; f: James CNARR; m: Jane CRAIG] on 15 Jan 1879. Off: BORDEN. Wit: Samuel KISS, Sarah KISS.

LEWIS, J.F. [29; Evanston, Wyoming Territory; b: NY; f: Samuel LEWIS; m: Mary A. LEONARD] md. Lizzie A. POTTER [24; Omaha; b: NY; f: Hiram POTTER; m: Maria VAN ORRUM] on 9 Aug 1881. Off: MAFIELD. Wit: Addison JONES, Mrs. Mary C. JONES.

LEWIS, James H. [28; Pottawattamie Co., IA] md. Sarah A. EDWARDS [21; Pottawattamie Co., IA] on 13 Oct 1862 at HART's residence. Off: HART. Wit: M.E. HART, M.H. HART.

LEWIS, John [37; Omaha] md. Mrs. Charity TURNER [38; Omaha] on 21 Nov 1868. Off: STUCK. Wit: John M. SULLIVAN, John CRITTENDEN. The index indicates the bride and groom are colored.

LEWIS, Joseph [35; Omaha] md. Mrs. Ann PITMAN [35; Omaha] on 1 May 1859 at BRIGGS' office. Off: BRIGGS. Wit: Nelson BAKER, Joseph FOX.

LEWIS, Richard [25; Omaha; b: MN; f: Cornelius LEWIS; m: Sarah NEWBERRY] md. Belle REICHARD [20; Omaha; b: MN; f: Swan REICHARD; m: Cillia HAWKIN] on 17 May 1881. Off: BRANDES Wit: Alex DAEMON, Thom. BALLARD.

LEWIS, Walter [44; Douglas Co.; ] md. Mrs. Hellen MEEKER [37; Douglas Co.] on 17 Mar 1869 in Florence. Off: STEVENSON. Wit: William DREWRY, Mrs. DREWRY.

LEWON, Frederick [42; Douglas Co.; b: Germany; f: Henry LEWON; m: Magdalena ECKMANN] md. Elsabeth OTTE [22; Omaha; b: Germany; f: Claus OTTE; m: Mary WIEBKE] on 22 Mar 1881; Off: BENEKE. Wit: Wilhelm LEWON, Douglas Co., Eggert OTTE, Douglas Co.

LEY, William [46; Omaha; b: Germany; f: John George LEY; m: Anna Maria EMONS] md. Mrs. Anna SARP [30; Omaha; b: Bohemia; f: James GEHAL; m: Josephine KURE] on 16 Dec 1876. Off: ERFLING. Wit: Chas. BANER, Fred LEPHOLZ.

LEYFERTH, Edward [32; North Platte; b: Germany; f: Thankmar LEYFIRTH; m: Annie BURKHART] md. Annie HATTEN [20; Omaha; b: Germany; f: Michael HATTEN; m: Margaret HATTEN] on 19 Aug 1872. Off: BRANDES. Wit: Joseph MANDELBEIN; Agnes KROLL.

LIBBY, L.J. [50; Omaha; b: New Hampshire; f: Josiah LIBBY; m: Mary LEAVETT] md. Betsy BAUVAIS [22; Omaha; b: Canada East; f: Louis BAUVAIS; m: Mary A. RAMIA] on 17 Jul 1870. Off: GIBSON. Wit: F.A. CURTIS; Chas. H. BYRNE.

LIDDELL, John Craig [Florence] md. Kate PYPER [Florence] on 15 Sep 1863 at W.M. PYPER's residence in Florence. Both of legal age. Off: KUHNS. Wit: Mr. and Mrs. W.M. PYPER, Mrs. ROBISON (ROBINSON), et al.

LIEBER, Max [28; Omaha; b: Germany; f: Adam LIEBER; m: Clara MANTEL] md. Mary BOEHME [20; Omaha; b: IL; f: Louis BOEHME; m: Mary] on 20 Dec 1875. Off: DIECKMANN. Wit: Louis BOEHME, Mary BOEHME.

LIEVER, Nicholas [25; Mills Co., IA; b: Germany; f: Matthias LIEVER; m: Gertrude LOCH] md. Catharine FINKAN [17; Mills Co, IA; b: at sea; f: Matthias FINKAN; m: Catharine GANS] on 4 Aug 1872. Off: GROENBAUM. Wit: Joseph NULLUT, Mills Co., IA; Catharine NULLET, Mills Co., IA. Age of consent given by father of the bride.

LIGHTNER, Charles H. [26; Omaha] md. Eva BRUCE [21; Omaha] on 12 Dec 1868. Off: KERMOTT. Wit: J.A. BRUCE and wife.

LILIENCRON, Alexander N.C.G. [29; Bellevue, Sarpy Co.; b: Germany; f: Andreas LILIENCRON; m: Augusta STRUBE] md. Yart Louisa Francisca PETERSEN [26; Bellevue, Sarpy Co.; b: Denmark; f: Adolph PETERSEN; m: Anna KRUGER] on 8 Jun 1872. Off: BRANDES. Wit: Thomas BARBER, Bellevue; Michael PALMTAG, Bellevue.

LILLEY, John [colored; 24; Omaha] md. Hattie TINSLEY [colored; 25; Omaha] on 13 Jun 1867 at O'GORMAN's residence. Off: O'GORMAN. Wit: Margaret WITHERS.

LILLIE, Jerome A. [35; Omaha] md. Caroline PARMETER [35; Omaha] on 11 Jun 1867. Off: SLAUGHTER.

LINDE, George [28; Douglas Co.] md. Eliza LAWON [21; Douglas Co.] on 1 Aug 1868. Off: KELLEY. Wit: J. NICKENDECKER, G. GILLEHOUSER.

LINDE, George [42; Omaha; b: Germany (or Russia); f: Max LINDE; m: Helene HANSEN] md. Mrs. Minnie A. KINKEL [27; Omaha; b: IL; f: William LUTHER; m: Dorathea HICKERHAAS] on 24 Mar 1881. Off: FRESE. Wit: John BOEKHOFF, Mrs. Caroline BEINDORF.

LINDEMAN, Joseph P. [23; Omaha; b: IN; f: M. LINDEMAN; m: Elizabeth E. BOCKOVER] md. Effie D. HAZARD [20; Douglas Co.; b: NE; f: David HAZARD; m: McKENZIE] on 1 Jan 1881. Off: WRIGHT. Wit: George HAZARD, David HAZARD.

LINDEN, William [30; Council Bluffs; b: Sweden; f: Magnus ANDERSON; m: Engamyer SWENSDOTTER] md. Johanna G. HEDLUND [27; Council Bluffs; b: Sweden; f: Carl G. HEDLUND; m: Johanna KOBERG] on 7 Jul 1870. Off: LARSON. Wit: Carl L. BACKSTROM; Mrs. Johanna C. LARSON.

LINDGREN, Ole [25; Platte Valley Pct, Douglas Co.; b: Sweden; f: Nils ANDERSON; m: Elnah ANDERSEN] md. Mary Jane CLINE [19; Platte Valley PCt, Douglas Co.; b: Indiana; f: Aleck CLINE; m: ELizabeth F. COTHRIL] on 2 Sep 1872. Off: TOWNSEND. Wit: Oscar C. PRATT; John D. HOWE.

LINDLOFF, John [26; Omaha; b: Germany; f: William LINDLOFF; m: Mary SCHRODER] md. Amalia WENDELL [21; Omaha; b: Germany; f: Henry WENDELL] on 11 Nov 1876. Off: WEISS.

LINDQUEST, Nils Peter [28; b: Sweden; f: John PEARSON; m: Sara Stina JOHNDATER] md. Carry PAISKER [24; b: Germany; f: John PAISKER; m: Rosa CHALS] on 6 Mar 1878. Off: WILLIS. Wit: Mary WILLIS, Emma V. SPENCER.

LINDSAY, John [37; Omaha] md. Ellen KEARNEY [21; Omaha] on 7 Nov 1868. Off: KUHNS. Wit: Mr. and Mrs. Wm. C. LINDSAY, Mr. and Mrs. Joseph CREIGHTON.

LINDSTROM, John [26; Omaha; b: Sweden; f: Lars LINDSTROM; m: Mary BROF] md. Emma BORK [23; Omaha; b: Sweden; f: John BORK] on 16 Sep 1871. Off: SUNDBORN. Wit: G. SUNDBORN; A. SELINE.

LINGNER, John C. [Douglas Co.] md. Mary E. IRISH [Douglas Co.] on 15 Oct 1865 at Fredk. DREXEL's residence near Omaha. Off: KUHNS. Wit: Mr. and Mrs. Fred DREXEL, Geo. ZWEIBEL, Mrs. L.A. WALKER, et al.

LINGREN, Peter M. [35; Saunders Co.; b: Sweden; f: Mangus JOHNSON ; m: Stenlesa PETERSON] md. Louisa JOHNSON [28; Saunders Co.; b: Sweden; f: Jonas P. ANDERSON; m: Greta YOGON] on 18 May 1874. Off: LIPE. Wit: Caroline PETERSON; Lizzie E. LIPE.

LINQUEST, Gunnar A. [25; Omaha; b: Sweden; f: Anders NELSON; m: Mary GUSTAFERSON] md. Christine BEYERSTAN or BRYENTESAN [25; Omaha; b: Sweden; f: Brynt OLSEN; m: Carrie GUNNERSON] on 1 Aug 1871. Off: BILLMAN. Wit: Mrs. Ira C. BILLMAN; Ida DEMAREST.

LINQUEST, O. [29; Omaha; b: Sweden; f: O. OLSON; m: Christiana MATSON] md. Christiana JOHNSON [20; Omaha; b: Sweden; f: John JOHNSON; m: Celiea JOHNSON] on 26 Feb 1877. Off: PORTER. Wit: Ole OLSON, Edwin HANY.

LINSTROM, Adolph Albert [23; Omaha; b: Sweden; f: Adolph Frederick HABBE; m: Lena Stna JOHNSON] md. Emily Sophia JOHNSON [22; Omaha; b: Sweden; f: John ---; m: Anna Sophia] on 7 Dec 1872. Off: LARSON. Wit: Lawrence B. ODEN; Samuel NELSON.

LIPPE, Dennis [29; Omaha; b: Germany; f: Mathias LIPPE; m: Mary MOLTINGER] md. Annie RAMM [34; Omaha; b: Germany; f: Jouchin RAMM; m: Wipke ENGEL] on 2 Apr 1877. Off: SEDGWICK. Wit: E.B. KNOX.

LIPPIRT, Peter [43; Omaha; b: Germany; f: Philip LIPPIRT; m: Katrina BEROT] md. Anna DRESON (DREESSON) [31; Omaha; b: Germany] on 28 Nov 1871. Off: GROENBAUM. Wit: William STREVER; Peter BUGGER.

LIPSEY, William M. [25; West Point, Cuming Co.; b: Salem, OH; f: Edwin LIPSEY; m: Sarah HAYNES] md. Ann M. JONES [23; Omaha; f: Henry JONES: m: Sarah] on 26 Jun 1873. Off: SHERRILL. Wit: Wm. Henry JONES: C.T. TAYLOR.

LITER, John [24; Omaha] md. Hannah M. RAMSEY [24; Omaha] on 9 Mar 1869. Off: GIBSON. Wit: Edward C. HUGHES of Council Bluffs, James M. KNAPP.

LIVINGSTON, Frank R. [27; Omaha; b: New York; f: George H. LIVINGSTON; m: Martha RODGERS] md. Mary WILBURN [19; Omaha; b: Nebraska; f: George WILBURN; m: Elizabeth] on 22 Jun 1874. Off: PRESSON. Wit: John NYE; Maggie PRESSON.

LIVINGSTONE, R.L. [42; Washington Co.; b: Illinois; f: Lucien LIVINGSTONE; m: Jane LEECH] md. Ida May REEVES [21; Douglas Co.; b: Nebraska; f: Jesse REEVES; m: Elizabeth BARLOW] on 26 Aug 1880. Off: BRISTOL. Wit: Lucia E. BRISTOL, Rellie BRISTOL.

LIYPOLDT, John G. [24; Omaha; b: Germany; f: Jacob F. LIYPOLDT; m: Catharine OSWALD] md. Clara HOUCK [18; Omaha; b: Pennsylvania; f: D.B. HOUCK; m: Nancy SHINEFELT] on 18 Oct 1870. Off: KUHNS. Wit: Mary E. WRIGHT; William OSBORN.

LLEWELLYN, W.H.H. [26; Omaha; b: Wisconsin; f: Joseph LLEWELLYN; m: Louisa FAY] md. Ida M. SMITH [18; Omaha; b: Iowa; f: Isaac LITTLE; m: June CUMMINGS] on 8 Jun 1877. Off: SEDGWICK. Wit: Edward WILSON; Charles G. BALLUND.

LLOYDE, Warren [45; Omaha; b: NY; f: Henry J. LLOYDE; m: Sarah TUBBS] md. Helen DONAHUE [38; OH, b: Ireland; f: Cornelius DONAHUE; m: Mary McCAULIFF] on 27 Jul 1876. Off: SEDGWICK. Wit: T.S. SANFORD, Cleveland, OH, Emmett KNOX.

LOCKARD, Andrew J. [28; Wyoming Territory; b: Springfield, IL; f: Andrew J. LOCKARD; m: Mary NASH] md. Mary E. JONES [21; Sangamon Co., IL; b: Sangamon Co., IL; f: James JONES; m: Virginia WEBSTER] on 27 May 1869. Off: HYDE. Wit: George SMITH, C.D. HYDE.

LOCKLIN, Henry F. [43; Omaha] md. Harriet E. COTTON [38; Omaha] on 21 Sep 1867 at KUHNS' residence. Off: KUHNS. Wit: Mrs. A.D. JONES, Mrs. H.W. KUHNS.

LOCKLING, Orson W. [Harrison Co., IA] md. Charlotte MAULE [Harrison Co., IA] on 1 Dec 1863 in DICKINSON's office. Off: DICKINSON. Wit: Wm. MAULE, L. DYKEMAN.

LOGAN, John H. [Chicago] md. Harmantha H. THOMAS [Chicago] on 30 Oct 1864 at J.R. THOMAS' house. Off: DENTON. Wit: J.R. THOMAS, Ellen KEIN, et al.

LOGEMAN, Henry or Harry [30; Douglas Co.; b: Germany; f: Wm. LAGEMAN; m: Mary Hak EMEYER] md. Lizzie REX [17; Douglas Co.; b: Germany; f: Turgen REX] at the house of F. LOGEMAN on 29 Dec 1877. Off: STEINERT. Wit: Hulda M. NOWAG, Mr. J. STEINERT. Age consent given by the father of the bride of Millard Station, Douglas Co. Witness to his signature Henry BRUHN, Julius SCHRODER.

LOGEMANN, Fred [30; Douglas Co.; b: Germany; f: John W. LOGEMANN; m: Mary HOCKMEIER] md. Lena MARTINS [18; Douglas Co.; b: Germany; f: John MARTINS; m: Gretta REIKEN] on 24 Nov 1878 in Jefferson Precinct. Off: CRONEMEYER. Wit: Justus STIENERT of McAfdle Precinct, Henry LOGEMAN of Jefferson Precinct.

LOGES, Peter [37; Elkhorn City; b: Germany; f: John LOGES; m: Kate SYLVESTER] and Mrs. Mary SVENSON [26; Omaha; b: Germany; f: Herman CHASE; m: Margareta RUNNER] on 28 May 1874. Off: PEABODY. (Application and license only).

LOMBARDY, R.K. [28; Omaha; b: Italy; f: B.C. LOMBARDY; m: Mailan FELICI] md. Matilda C. SCHRIBNER [37; Saratoga, NE; b: England; f: Thomas TAYLOR; m: Anna HEBDEN] on 26 May 1877. Off: WRIGHT. Wit: George O'BRIERS, M. McBRIDGE.

LONERGAN, Thomas [22; Fremont; b: Ireland; f: William LONERGAN; m: Ellen SUBY] md. Mrs. Mary A. THOMAS [30; Forest City, Sarpy Co.; b: Ohio; f: Thomas McCOY; m: Catherine McCOY] on 19 Feb 1871 at the German Catholic Church. Off: GROENEBAUM. Wit: John THOMAS, Forest City; Mary Anne CONNOR, Forest City.

LONG, Warren [Iowa Co.] md. Ellen B. SWITZER [Poweshiek Co., IA] on 17 Jun 1865 in DICKINSON's office. Off: DICKINSON. Wit: Charles H. BROWN, Lizzie SWITZER, Mr. SWITZER.

LONG, William [25; Omaha; b: Germany; f: Stephen LONG: m: Elizabeth BLACK] md. Ella WHALEN [25; Omaha; b: New York; f: Hugh WHALEN] on 12 Aug 1874. Off: PEABODY. Wit: M.G. EDWARDS; P.T. EDWARDS.

LONGHREN, James R. [23; Fremont, NE; b: Canada; f: Thomas LONGHREN; m: Elizabeth A. MORROW] md. Maggie FOLEY [22; Omaha; b: New Jersey; f: Timothy FOLEY; m: Mary FOLEY] on 9 Apr 1877. Off: JENNETTO. Wit: Michael DINAU, Catherine FOLEY.

LOOKER, William H. [24; Omaha; b: PA; f: Henry LOOKER; m: Louise HATCH] md. Nellie DOW [18; Belleview; b: NE; f: Robert DOW; m: Mary ----] ON 22 Dec 1881. Off: CHADWICK. Wit: Max BERGMANN, Frank McWINNIE.

LORENZEN, William F. [24; Newton, IA; b: Germany; f: H. LORENZEN; m: Mary JENSEN] md. Anna SCHNOOR [26; Omaha; b: Germany; f: Claus SCHNOOR; m: Anna McG. STUELL] on 13 Jun 1877. Off: STRASEN. Wit: William HAGEDORN, Catharina ERASSHOF.

LORING, David R. [35; Omaha; b: Union Ville, OH; f: Nathan LORING; m: Mary POTTER] md. Mrs. Eliza J. BRYANT [35; Omaha; b: New York City; f: George W. HOMAN; m: Amy COLES] on 18 Nov 1869. Off: DE LA MATYR. Wit: George W. HOMAN, Samuel BURNES.

LOVEJOY, Eugene E. [28; Omaha Barracks; b: Connecticut; f: Francis C. LOVEJOY; m: Jerusha WHITMORE] md. Bridget E. LUCEY [22; Omaha; b: Iowa; f: Jeremiah LUCEY; m: Bridget DOYLE] on 8 Jan 1874. Off: PEABODY. Wit: Andrew J. O'LEARY; Mrs. Mary E. O'LEARY.

LOVELAND, Albert E. [26; Omaha; b: Farmington, OH; f: Edwin LOVELAND; m: Harriet BENTON] md. Flora C. GRIDLEY [21; Omaha; b: Parkman, OH; f: James U. GRIDLEY; m: Mary BALDWIN] on 23 Nov 1870. Off: SHERRILL. Wit: Edward LOVELAND; James U. GRIDLEY.

LOVETT, Henry [24; Omaha] md. Mary E. LEE [17; Omaha] on 21 Nov 1867 at the residence of the bride's mother. Off: SHEEKS. Wit: Catharine JOHNSON, Harvey DUFFIELD. Age consent given by the bride's mother, the bride "having no father."

LOWBER, Frederick [33; Omaha] md. Louisa SCHMOLD [23; Omaha] on 29 Nov 1866 at Joseph GRANACHER's residence. Off: KUHNS. Wit: Mr. and Mrs. Joseph GRANACHER, Henry LAURENT, et al.

LOWE, Benjamin K. or R. [25; Lindfield, MA] md. Helen A. NEWHALL [21; Lindfield, MA] on 25 Apr 1859 at the "Farnham House." Off: GAYLORD. Wit: Thomas F. STEWART, O.C. BURNHAM.

LOWE, James A. [30; Adair Co., IA; b: Indiana; f: John LOWE; m: Mary VAUGHN] md. Belle CUSTER [20; Omaha; b: Iowa; f: William CUSTER; m: Ruth RATHBURN] on 21 Oct 1874. Off: PEABODY. Wit: G.R. RATHBURN; C. SIMPSON.

LOWE, Thomas [40; colored] md. Celia WHEELER [22; colored] on 17 Sep 1862. Off: SMITH. Wit: Mrs. Dr. LOWE, Mrs. Col. LOWE.

LOWER, William H. [28; Omaha] md. Anna E. WICKERSHAM [21; Philadelphia, PA] on 18 Aug 1866 at Jesse LOWE's house. Off: VAN ANTWERP. Wit: Dr. and Mrs. Enos LOWE, Mr. and Mrs. Jesse LOWE, Col. and Mrs. LOWE, Miss C.A. VAN ANTWERP.

LOYDE, Fredrick M. [26; Washington, D.C.; b: NY; f: Thomas LOYDE; m: Catherine E. LOVELACE] md. Jennie BEAUCHEY [21; Douglas Co.; b: Ohio; f: John BEAUCHEY; m: Margret MALLET-DEVINE] on 27 Jan 1877. Off: ANDERSON. Wit: George LOVELACE, J.O. TALMAGE.

LUBENS, Hans [31; Elkhorn Station; b: Germany; f: Hans LUBENS; m: Martha GOSCH] md. Catherine ARPS [30; Elkhorn Station; b: Germany; f: John ARPS] on 14 Aug 1871. Off: LYTLE. Wit: Joshua BUDD; August SCHULTZ.

LUCAS, Anthony [Omaha] md. Mary M. DOUGLAS [Omaha] on 8 Jun 1865 at Dr. E. LOWE;s residence. Off: KUHNS. Wit: Dr. and Mrs. E. LOWE, et al.

LUCAS, John A. [22; Douglas Co.] md. Rachael A. TURNER [20; Douglas Co.] on 28 Nov 1868. Off: MANHALL.

LUCI, Patrick [25; Omaha; b: Ireland; f: Michael LUCI; m: Catherine DARLTON] md. Johanna BROWN [25; Omaha; b: Ireland; f: Patrick BROWN] on 28 Nov 1869. Off: CURTIS. Wit: David LYONS, Mary FITZGIBBON.

LUCKEY, Edward [24; Omaha] md. Mina KLINKE [18; Omaha] on 26 Jun 1868. Off: KUHNS. Wit: Mr. and Mrs. Edward SCHLICK, Mrs. H.W. KUHNS, et al.

LUDLOW, Oliver C. [30; Omaha] md. Mrs. Mary J. CHASE [26 or 28; Independence, IA] on 21 Dec 1868. Off: KUHNS. Wit: Mrs. H.W. KUHNS, Mary BURKET.

LUHENS, Henry [28; Omaha; b: Germany; f: J.H. LUHENS; m: Lotte LENTS] md. Anna RASMUNSEN [32; Omaha; b: Germany; f: Henry RASMUNSEN; m: Anna MARKS] on 15 Jul 1869. Off: HYDE. Wit: J.S. SPAWN, E.G. FLOYE.

LUMLEY, James R. [32; Carisbrook, Furnas Co.; b: East Indies; f: James R. LUMLEY; m: Arabella WILKINSON] md. Emily J. FELL [29; Omaha; b: England; f: John B. FELL; m: Emily] on 3 May 1873. Off: PRESSON. Wit: Maggie PRESSON; Geo. LUMLEY.

LUND, Larson [24; Omaha] md. Catharine LUND [18 and 9 months; Omaha] on 28 Apr 1866. Off: MILLER. Wit: Elizabeth E. MILLER, Sarah DAVIS.

LUND, Lewis E. [26; Saunders Co.; b: Sweden; f: Peter LUND; m: Catharine ANDERSON] md. Annie B. JOHNSON [31; Omaha; b: Sweden; f: John Peter JOHNSON] on 26 Oct 1872. Off: SUNDBORN. Wit: John EKELEY; Mrs. Inga Chri EKELEY.

LUNDBECK, Fritz [37; Omaha; b: Denmark; f: Fritz LUNDBECK; m: Lena JOERGENSEN] md. Magdalena ELLEGAARD [39; Omaha; b: Denmark; f: Christian ELLEGAARD; m: Maire KORKHOLM] on 6 Feb 1880. Off:

BARTHOLOMEW. Wit: Mrs. HOLST, George PETERSON.

LUNDWALL, Martin [26; Omaha] md. Hannah LARSEN [23; Omaha] on 27 Feb 1869. Off: HYDE. Wit: C.D. HYDE, Will BROWNE.

LUNENBORG, Henry [27; Millard Station; b: Germany; f: Bernhard LUENENBORG; m: Gertrud SURMANN] md. Christine ARFF [ARPP] [22; Millard Station; b: Germany; f: Johann ARFF [ARPP]] on 6 Sep 1881 at Millard. Off: KELSEY. Wit: Mollie MOCK, Millard, Henry HEIGHTOLD, Millard.

LUNT, Andrew J. [28, Omaha; b: Denmark; f: C.J. LUNT; m: Mary JASPERSON] md. Louisa SORENSON [23; Omaha; b: Denmark; f: Chris SORENSON; m: Anna LOUIE] on 7 Mar 1876. Off: HANSEN. Wit: Nick P. BECK, Nellie PERSON.

LYMAN, C.B. [21; Dunlap, IA; b: New York; f: T.A. LYMAN; m: Mary PATTERSON] md. Jennie SHEA [20; Dunlap, IA; b: Ireland; f: Henry MALONEY; m: Anna SHEA?] on 8 Sep 1880. Off: BEANS. Wit: Mrs. W.K. BEANS, Mrs. R.D. HILLS.

LYMAN, Charles W. [27; Omaha; b: New York; f: Hiram LYMAN; m: Abigail STODDARD] md. Nellie BELDEN [19; Omaha; b: Ohio; m: Rebecca PFOUTZ] on 6 Oct 1869 at Trinity Church. Off: CLARKSON. Wit: Charles D. SHERMAN of Cheyenne, WY, John G. GASMANN, George C. BETTS, and many others.

LYNCH, Humphrey [28; Omaha; b: Ireland; f: Humphrey LYNCH; m: Margaret O'LEARY] md. Mary O'GORMAN [20; Omaha; b: Ireland; f: John O'GORMAN; m: Mary FITZ GIBBONS] on 17 Feb 1874 at the Catholic Church. Off: MALLOY. Wit: Andrew DWORAZ, Catherine CARMODY.

LYNCH, Mathew [26; Omaha; b: Ireland; f: Patrick LYNCH; m: Margaret FINLEY] md. Caroline GRANT [16; Omaha; b: New York; f: Theodore GRANT; m: Eva FINN] on 17 Oct 1870. Off: GRAHAM. With L.G. TAYLOR; Andrew McWHINNEY. Age of consent given by mother of bride, father is dead.

LYNCH, Patrick W. [23; Omaha; b: Ireland; f: James LYNCH; m: Mary HANRAHAN] md. Ellen FITZPATRICK [20; Omaha; b: Ireland; f: John FITZPATRICK; m: Hanora HANDREHAN] on 7 Aug 1873. Off: CURTIS. Wit: Patrick FOLEY; Josephine CADOLA.

LYNCH, Patrick [25; Omaha; b: Ireland; f: John LYNCH; m: Margaret MALONEY] md. Ellen QUINLAN [18; Omaha; b: Omaha (Ireland crossed out); f: Patrick QUINLAN; m: Johanna GOGGIN] on 29 Apr 1873. Off: CURTIS. Wit: Patrick DESMOND; Bridget HARRINGTON.

LYNCH, Patrick [27; Omaha] md. Catherine SULLIVAN [29; Omaha] on 7 Feb 1869. Off: KERMOTT. Wit: W.H. CLOUD, E.N. GLOVER.

LYON, Nils [31; Omaha; b: Sweden; f: Nils LYON; m: Caroline PAULSEN] md. Mary BONNEVIER [27; Omaha; b: Sweden; f: Charles BONNEVIER; m: Christine BREDSSTROM] on 4 Sep 1873. Off: STEWART. Wit: John JOHNSON; J.A. BONNEVIER.

LYONS, Edward J. [25; Belle Creek, NE [now Arlington, Washington Co.]; b: Ohio; f: John LYONS; m: Matilda MILLER] md. Jennie DYER [20; Waterloo; b: Platte Co., MO; f: John DYER; m: Malinda THORN] on 1 Jan 1880, Waterloo. Off: ROBERTS. Wit: L.W. DENTON, W. EVANS, both of Waterloo.

LYONS, William [23; San Francisco; b: Sacramento City, CA; f: Julius LYONS; m: Adel NEWTON] md. Josephine HEUSTON [22; Jefferson, KS; b: Jefferson, KS; f: L. HEUSTON; m: Hattie KING] on 24 Nov 1875. Off: HALE. Wit: Ben MURPHY, Molly NOLEMS.

LYTLE, John W. [30; Omaha] md. Anna B. LA FOLLETT [20; Omaha] on 3 Oct 1866. Off: KERMOTT. Wit: Thompson OVERTON, Mrs. C. LA FOLLETT.

MAACK, John H. [31; Douglas Co.] md. Ann MUHS (MUHES) [33; Douglas Co.] on 23 Jan 1867. Off: MILLER. Wit: Louis SHIELDS, George FISHER.

MAACK, Nicholas [22; Omaha] md. Helena GORGENSEN [28; Omaha] on 23 Nov 1868. Off: MULCAHY. Wit: William GENTLEMAN, Celestine THIEBAUT.

MAAS, Henry [26; Omaha; b: Germany; f: Christian MAAS; m: Cathrina SCHLUTER] md. Margareta EHLERS [19; Omaha; b: Germany] on 11 Feb 1871. Off: GIBSON. Wit: Henry CLAUSSEN; Claus H. MUNDT.

MABERGERE, John E. [40; Omaha; b: Sweden; f: Erick PERSON; m: Catherine MOBAEK] and Elizabeth MOBINE [22; Omaha; b: Sweden; f: Car. ----; m: Elizabeth PETERSON]. License issued Apr 1877. Off: SEDGWICK. No marriage recorded.

MABLOY, William [21; Omaha; b: Peoria, IL; f: William MABLOY; m: Mary SWEENY] and Annie CORLEY [20; Omaha; b: Boone, IA] license issued on 24 Aug 1869. No marriage record. Off: HYDE.

MacCARTHY, Michael [27; Omaha; b: Ireland; f: Patrick MacCARTHY; m: Catharine FORRISEY] and Katie M. O'BRIEN [26; Omaha; b: Ireland; f: Patrick O'BRIEN; m: Mary MANSFIELD] license issued on 6 Jun 1879. No marriage record. Off: BARTHOLOMEW.

MACE [MARE], Louis [33] md. Mrs. Eliza Jane FERRY [32] on 16 Apr 1869. Off: Wm. H. MORRIS. Wit: Mrs. Emma E. MORRIS, John P. BARTLETT.

MACH, John [25; Omaha; b: Bohemia; f: Frank MACH; m: Annie KRIZOVA [KRIZ]] md. Josephine MISORA [MIZERA] [18; Omaha; b: Bohemia] on 3 Jul 1872. Off: LYTLE. Wit: D.D. VODICKA; Mrs. Barbara SOMER [SOMR].

MACK, Frederick [28; Omaha; b: Germany; f: Conrad MACK; m: Anna KOEHLER] md. Charlotte FRANKE [22; Omaha; b: Germany] on 11 Aug 1870. Off: GIBSON. Wit: William MACK; Gottlob ZIMMERMANN.

MACK, Henry [negro; 36; Omaha; b: AL; f: Ed. COLLINS] md. Mrs. Martha GREEN [negro; 33; Omaha; b: MO; f: Harvey BROOKS] on 25 Sep 1881. Off: ALLEN. Wit: Thomas PHILLIPS, Eliza Jane ALLEN. Affidavit witnessed by CHADWICK.

MACK, John [33; b: Germany; f: Marcus MACK; m: Anna GRUBER] md. Anna FISHER [21; b: Germany; f: Gotlieb FISHER; m: Fannie SIEFERT] on 26 Aug 1878 at the German Catholic Church. Off: GROENBAUM. Wit: Charles KOHLMEYER, Laura FISHER.

MACK, Tobias [36; Stanton Co.; b: Germany; f: Thobias MACK; m: Annie HETTER] md. Josephine ROTTLER [38; Stanton Co.; b: Germany; f: Lawrance ROTTLER] on 29 Mar 1870. Off: KELLEY. Wit: J.S. TUCKER; H.?. LAMASTER.

MACKEY, Sid [22; Omaha] md. Emma HOWLETT [20; Omaha] on 6 Oct 1867 at SHINN's residence. Off: SHINN. Wit: A.B. SMITH, Doct. MATHEWS' wife, et al.

MACKEY, Van M. or McKEY, Wm. Van M. [24; St. Joseph, MO] md. Lizzie JONES [18; Omaha] on 15 Apr 1868. Off: KERMOTT. Wit: Grace McKEY, Mrs. J.C. McKEY.

MADDEN, F.L. [24; Omaha; b: New York; f: John MADDEN; m: Mary TRACY] md. Alice MEANEY [20; Omaha; b: Ohio; f: Patrick MEANEY; m: Helen STANLEY] on 2 Jun 1880. Off: GRAHAM. Wit: Simon H. KENNEDY, Mary CLEAVELAND.

MADDEN, John [30; Rockford, IA] md. Bridget MADDEN [30; Rockford, IA] on 10 May 1868 at the Catholic Church. Off: KEENAN. Wit: John MURRY, Catherine SLATTERY.

MADSON, Niels [26; Omaha; b: Denmark; f: Christian MADSON; m: Hannah CHRISTIAN] md. Ingri ANDERSON [29; Omaha; b: Sweden; f: Anders TUASON; m: Elsa BANGTSON] on 1 Apr 1870. Off: SHERRILL. Wit: G.A. WESHGREN; Ella BARNEY.

MADSON, Olla [47; Sweden] md. Karna MONSON [30; Sweden] on 8 Apr 1860. Off: NIELSON. Wit: Andrew HENDRICKSON, Elizabeth HENDRICKSON, et al.

MAELLER, Henry [25; Omaha; b: Germany; f: Detlef MAELLER; m: Magdalene REPEN] md. Annie GLAE [24; Omaha; b: Germany; f: Max GLAE; m: Dora] on 5 Dec 1874. Off: PEABODY. Wit: Christian MOELLER; Claus STOLTENBERG.

MAGEE, Frank M. [21; Douglas Co.; b: PA; f: R.B. MAGEE; m: Hannah J. MACORSIN] md. Elizabeth C. THOMAS [21; Douglas Co.; b: OH; f: Lewis THOMAS; m: Susan MOORE] on 25 Dec 1875 at Union Precinct. Off: GREEN. Wit: Lewis THOMAS, Union Precinct, Susan THOMAS, Union Precinct.

MAGEE, Harry [40; Omaha; b: Pennsylvania; f: Barnett MAGEE; m: Catherine MEGARY] md. Mary E. WARREN [22; Omaha; b: Ohio; f: Barney MOON; m: Mary MOON] on 13 Feb 1877. Off: WEISS. Wit: COLLIN.

MAGINN, L.F. [32; Omaha; b: NY; f: James MAGINN; m: Mary CLARK] md. Jenine L. BLATCHLEY [23; Omaha; b: IN; f: Miller BLATCHLEY; m: Elizabeth ROWE] on 27 May 1875. Off: STEWART. Wit: P.L. PERINE, Joseph LEHMER.

MAGNUSON, Charles M. [30; Burt Co.; b: Sweden; f: Magnus NELSON; m: Mary SWANSEN] md. Mary Justiva CRONLAND [28; Burt Co.; b: Sweden; f: John P. CRONLAND; m: Mary E. ALLEN] on 13 May 1869. Off: HYDE. Wit: Sylvanus WRIGHT, A.R. HOEL.

MAHANNAH, Frank [28; Omaha; b: Pennsylvania; f: John MAHANNAH; m: Mary RAMSEY] md. Sarah V. BRADFORD [20; Omaha; b: Maine] on 19 Aug 1870. Off: McCAGUE. Wit: Mrs. McCAGUE; Geo. G. EARLE.

MAHER, John [27; Council Bluffs; Thomas MAHER of Parish Ballen, County Carlow, Irel.] md. Bridget McNAMARRA [25; Council Bluffs; John McNAMARRA of Parish Dow, County Clare, Irel.] on 8 Mar 1859 at the BVM Church. Off: CANNON. Wit: James HICKEY, Ellen MAHER.

MAHONEY, Con. [28; Council Bluffs, IA; b: Iowa; f: Cornelius MAHONEY; m: Mary WALLACE] md. Mrs. Caroline ENGEL [35; Council Bluffs, IA; b: Germany; f: Frederick SCHLOUTZ; m: Catharine SCHOULTZ] on 5 Jul 1879. Off: BARTHOLEMEW. Wit: J.G. MAHONEY, Jas. QUINLAN.

MAHONEY, Michael [29; Omaha; b: Ireland; f: John MAHONEY; m: Johanna SULLIVAN] md. Mary HALEY [33; Omaha; b: Ireland; f: Patrick HALEY; m: Kate HANDRAHEN] on 31 Mar 1872. Off: CURTIS. Wit: James COSGRAVE; Bridget DOHERTEY.

MAHONEY, T.P. [27; Omaha; b: IN; f: Jerry MAHONEY; m: Mary SHANAHAN] md. Ellen POWERS [22; Omaha; b: IL; f: Edmund POWERS; m: Margaret BURNE] on 14 Jun 1881. Off: ENGLISH. Wit: Edward EGAN, Miss M. POWERS.

MAILER, James C. [27; Omaha; b: Scotland; f: John MAILER; m: Mary THOMPSON] md. Margaret F. ROBB [21; Omaha; b: Scotland; f: John S. ROBB; m: Margrate VERR] on 31 Mar 1873. Off: SHERRILL. Wit: John S. ROBB: C.J. TYLER.

MAJO, Gideon [47; Omaha; b: Canada] md. Mrs. Sarah E. BOGGS [37; Omaha; b: Illinois] on 23 July 1870. Off: MAY. Wit: S.J. COLE; Mrs. J.C. COLE.

MAJOR, Joseph W. [34; Omaha] md. Mary GIBBONS [27; Omaha] on 23 Jun 1868. Off: KERMOTT. Wit: Mrs. A.R. KERMOTT, Frank R. KERMOTT.

MALCHO, Christian [40; Douglas Co.; b; Germany; f: Joachim MALCHO; m: Doretea SCHROEDER] md. Mrs. Augusta OBERMEITE [35; b: Germany; f: Otto BEIL; m: Augusta LERCHNER] on 7 Jul 1878. Off: BRUEGGEN. Wit: Otto BEIL, Jr., Michael BUHLER.

MALIN, Hugh [33; Omaha; b: Ireland; f: Charles MALIN; m: Ann DONAHOE] md. Margaret McKIHAL [24; Des Moines, IA; b: Ireland; f: Thomas McKAHIL; m: Bridget LYNCH] on 15 Jun 1874 at the Cathedral. Off: LYNCH. Wit: John HALL; Bridget KINGLY.

MALLET, John [30; Omaha; b: England; f: William MALLET; m: Anna LAWN] md. Mrs. Catharine HUBERT [26; Detroit, MI; b: Michigan; f: Michael QUINN; m: Mary Q. KENNEDY] on 2 Aug 1879. Off: McCARTHY. Wit: Thomas SHANNON, Catharine SHANNON.

MALLEY, John V. [27; Omaha; b: Canada West; f: Patrick MALLEY; m: Annie MURPHY] md. Julia HANEY [18; Omaha; b: Carroll Co., IL; b: Patrick HANEY; m: Catharine SHERRY] on 16 Nov 1872. Off: CURTIS. Wit: T.C. RYAN; Anastatia CROWLEY.

MALLORY, Charles L. [30; Omaha; b: New York; f: Barnam MALLORY; m: Ann HENDERSON] md. Jennie M. PALMER [17; Omaha; b: Illinois; f: Thos. PALMER; m: Clarissa COOLEY] on 7 Jan 1871. Off: KUHNS. Wit: Mr. and Mrs. Thomas PALMER. Age of consent given by Thos. & Clarissa PALMER, parents of the bride.

MALLORY, Lorence F. [24; Douglas Co.] md. Ella A. BAILEY [18; St. Louis, MO] on 8 Mar 1868. Off: SLAUGHTER. Wit: Henry A. HALES, Katy E. HALES.

MALMBORY, Olof [40; Omaha; b: Sweden; f: Mons SWENSON; m: Elna PEERSON] md. Nellie L. NELSON [25; Omaha; b: Sweden; f: Lars NELSON; m: Anne E. MALMQUIS] on 21 Mar 1881. Off: STENBERG. Wit: J.T. LAGERGREN, John MATTSON.

MALONEY, E. (or Michael) [22; Omaha; b: IL; f: Michael MALONEY; m: Catherine SULLIVAN] md. Nellie SULLIVAN [19; Omaha; b: NE; f: ---- SULLIVAN; m: Miss POWERS] on 7 Nov 1881. Off: SHAFFEL. Wit: Richard FLEMING, Catherine SULLIVAN.

MANEY, George P. [28; Sarpy Co.; b: New York; f: Marian MANEY; m: Mary GRADY] md. Amy D. FISHER [22; Sarpy Co.; b: New York; f: Orin H. FISHER; m: Olive ABBY] on 29 May 1871. Off: GIBSON. Wit: Willard FISHER, Sarpy Co.; Mrs. Christiana FISHER, Sarpy Co.

MANGER, Fred A. [20; Omaha; b: England; f: H.D. MANGER; m: Sarah HALL] md. Alice A. ORCHARD [19; Omaha; b: NE; f: Andres R. ORCHARD; m: Amanda HELLM] on 4 January 1881. Off: JAMIESON. Wit: L. SWARTZ, Minnie G. KENDRICK.

MANGOLD, Peter [22; Millard Station; b: Iowa; f: Michael MANGOLD; m: Barbara SCHWARTS] md. Mary GLANDT [21; Millard Precinct; b: Nebraska; Peter GLANDT; m: Lena LANDTAN] on 27 Feb 1878. Off: BARTHOLOMEW. Wit: Thomas F. HALL, Wm. L. PEABODY.

MANGUIRE, John [22; Omaha; b: Michigan; f: Nicholas MANGUIRE; m: Theresa KERN] md. Nora DEVITT [19; Omaha; b: Ireland; f: Edmund DEVITT; m: Kate CUMMINGS] on 5 Jun 1871. Off: CURTIS. Wit: Peter BESCEN; Mary DEVITT.

MANNING, Andrew [33; Omaha; b: Ireland; f: Dennis MANNING; m: Margaret MULLHOLLAN] md. Jane McNERLY (McNERLEY) [22; Omaha; b: Ireland] on 15 Aug 1869. Off: CURTIS. Wit: Thomas KING, Ellen BROPHY.

MANNING, Lawrence [27; Omaha] md. Sarah KELLEY [Omaha] on 22 Nov 1868. Off: CURTIS. Wit: William McGLEN, Bridget McGLEN.

MANNING, Patrick [33; Douglas Co.; b: Ireland; f: Dennis MANNING; m: Margaret DONNELLY] md. Jane F. CASSIDY [23 Douglas Co.; b: IL; f: Phillip CASSIDY] on 27 Apr 1876. Off: BYRNE. Wit: Edward CASSIDY, Mary SMITH.

MANNING, William F. [31; Omaha; b: Massachusetts; f: Albert C. MANNING; m: Eliza Ann HOLBROOK] md. Lillie V. GRAY [22; Omaha; b: Nebraska; f: William L. GRAY; m: Catharine B. PRUCE] on 19 Oct 1880. Off: JAMESON. Wit: R.H.N. KELLEY, Mrs. Emma C. KELLEY.

MANNING, William J. [39, Toledo, OH; b: NY; f: Willsie MANNING; m: Amanda M. SIMPSON] md. Mary TAYLOR [25; Leavenworth, KS; b: IN; f: Daniel B. TAYLOR; m: Francis A. BURLIN] on 10 Jan 1881. Off: GRAHAM. Wit: J. Frank LARIMUR (or DARIMUR), Mrs. Francis A. NORTON, Leavenworth, KS.

MANS, B.G. [27; Pennsylvania; f: John MANS; m: Rebecca GREY] md. Susan DAVIS [19; b: Illinois; f: Frank DAVIS; m: Harriett BARRETT] on 16 Jun 1878. Off: BENEKE. Wit: Mrs. E.A. HINES, Addie DAVIS.

MANSFIELD, Charles R. [34; Omaha; b: Vevay, IN; f: Ward MANSFIELD; m: Zelda COX] md. Mrs. Love COUSINS [24; Omaha; b: Athens, OH; f: Benjamin COUSINS; m: Jane] on 7 Nov 1872. Off: ESTABROOK. Wit: H.D. ESTABROOK; Mathilda MEISEL.

MANSON, Norris E. [27; Omaha; b: Sweden; f: Errick MANSON; m: Helena NELSON] md. Natalie Alida BILSTED [26; Omaha; b: Denmark; f: Niels BILSTED; m: Gustina GRAT] on 30 Mar 1874. Off: BENZON. Wit: Mrs. Anna BENZON; Severina JOHNSON.

MANSS, Christ [30; Omaha; b: Germany; f: John MANSS; m: Margaret WEIMER] md. Margaret BRUNING [22; Omaha; b: Missouri; f: Henry BRUNING; m: Maragaret FOSTER] on 30 Oct 1880. Off: BENEKE. Wit: Frederick MANSS, William BRUENING.

MARBLE, Joel L. [32; Omaha; b: IL; f: B.W. MARBLE; m: Hopestie KATCHUM] md. Lizzie DENT [34; Omaha; b: Ireland; f: William VOGAN; m: Jane MORTON] on 10 Oct 1881. Off: POWELL. Wit: Florence E. DENT, William DENT.

MARCH, Wm. T. [Douglas Co.] and Emma L. MICKLE [Douglas Co.] license issued on 21 Oct 1865. No marriage record. Off: HASCALL.

MARCY, Stephen B. [57; Omaha; b: New York; f: Stephen MARCY; m: Axey HAWE] md. Mrs. Catherine JOHNSON [52; Omaha; b: Ohio; f: Aaron COOPER; m: Elizabeth FLEUKEY] on 10 Jan 1871. Off: GIBSON. Wit: W.H. CADER; C.P. PAULSEN.

MARES, Charles [24; b: Bohemia; f: Mack MARES; m: Mary BOWER] md. Mary NEMECEK [23; b: Bohemia; f: Antoine NEMECEK; m: Anna HENZL] on 12 Nov 1878. Off: KOCARNIK. Wit: Joseph SLEZAK, Wenceslas KUCERA.

MARES, Francis [21; Omaha; b: Bohemia; f: John MARES; m: Mary BORCK] md. Leona VODICKA [18; Omaha; b: Bohemia; f: Joseph VODICKA; m: Anna HOLUB] on 24 Jan 1872. Off: TOWNSEND. Wit: Joseph DWORK [DWORAK]; Joseph KOZICH [KOZIC].

MARK, Peter J. [29; Dodge Co.] and Eliza EISENHANER [25; Omaha] license issued on 4 Jan 1863. No marriage record. Off: ARMSTRONG.

MARKEL, Jacob E. [24; Omaha] md. Henrietta H. CORBIN [18; Omaha] on 4 Aug 1868. Off: WESTWOOD. Wit: Mr. and Mrs. T.M. CONPROPST, Mrs. H.C. WESTWOOD.

MARKEL, Solomon [57; Page Co., IA; b: PA; f: Henry MARKEL; m: Elizabeth KILLDON] md. Mrs. Anna M. LARKIN [40; Omaha; b: OH; f: Archibald McDONALD; m: Margaret E. MOORE] on 15 Mar 1881. Off: STENBERG. Wit: Archie FLOYD, Augusta ANDERSON.

MARKIN, Michael [28; Des Moines, IA; b: Ireland; f: John MARKIN; m: Bridget QUINLAN] md. Nancy COULIHAN [19; Des Moines, IA; b: VT; f: Patrick COULIHAN] on 16 Jun 1876. Off: MULCAHY. Wit: James F. MORTON, Joseph H. HOLMES.

MARKLE, James W. [24; Omaha; b: Canada; f: Alexander MARKLE; m: Elizabeth BUCKHAM] md. Julia PERKINS [20; Omaha; b: Michigan; f: Leroy PERKINS; m: Kate HOFFMAN] on 4 Jul 1874. Off: PEABODY. Wit: Like C. REDFIELD; Mrs. Phebe A. REDFIELD.

MARLEY, Charles [26; Omaha; b: England; f: Thomas MARLEY; m: Ann LEWORTHY] and Minnie DAVISAN [28] license issued on 24 Sep 1870. Off: GIBSON.

MARLEY, Charles [32; Omaha; b: England; f: Thomas MARLEY; m: Ann LEWORTHY] md. Mary J. LEACH [30; Omaha; b: England; f: Sanuel C. LEACH; m: Jane LEAKE] on 19 Oct 1875. Off: PARDEE. Wit: John STEFFEN, Rosetta STEFFEN.

MARSHALL, George W. [32; Iron Blufs] md. Mrs. Sarah J. THOMPSON [25; Iron Bluffs] on 11 Mar 1866 at the residence of the bride's father in Fontanelle, NE. Off: JANNEY.

MARSHALL, John L. [32; Medina, NY; b: New York] md. Caroline M. FROST [24; Omaha; b: Waltham, MA; f: George W. FROST; m: Abbie P. PICKERING] on 21 Nov 1872. Off: DeLaMATYR. Wit: J.S. COLLINS; George P. BEMIS.

MARSHALL, Lewis K. [22; Yankton, SD; b: IA; f: Martin A. MARSHALL; m: Elizabeth MUNSELL] md. Mrs. Elvira SCOTT [22; Dubuque, IA; b: OH; f: John W. DUNCAN; m: Filure] on 18 Jan 1875. Off: PEABODY. Wit: George W. SHIELDS, Virginia DANSLOW.

MARSHALL, Pardon [22; Douglas Co.] and Mary Jane KOPP [16; Douglas Co.] license issued 29 Nov 1859. No marriage recorded. Off: ARMSTRONG. Allen MARSHALL and Pardon MARSHALL were sworn and testified to legal ability...and that consent of parents were given.

MARSHALL, Pardon [Elkhorn Precinct] md. Annie Elizabeth KAY [Elkhorn Precinct] on 11 Apr 1865 at Lewis W. DENTON's residence in Chicago Precinct. Off: CROOKS. Wit: Mr. and Mrs. Allen MARSHALL, et al.

MARSTON, J.M. [33; Omaha] md. Mrs. Elizabeth ABERCROMBIE [36; Omaha] on 1 Mar 1868. Off: SLAUGHTER. Wit: A.M. CLARK, S.E. CLARK.

MARTENS, J.F. [29; Douglas Co; b: Germany; f: Bohne MARTENS; m: Christine CHRISTIANSON] md. Caroline HANSEN [23; Douglas Co.; b: Germany; f: Carsten HANSEN; m: Christine CARSTENS] on 12 Jun 1880. Off: BENEKE. Wit: Bernard THOMSEN, Johann HARTWIG, both of Douglas Co.

MARTENSON, Olof [35; Omaha; b: Sweden; f: Martin SENSEN; m: Annie NIELSDOTTER] md. Annie SWENSDOTTER [25; Omaha; b: Sweden; f: Swen JOHNSON; m: Johanna LARSDOTTER] on 27 Sep 1871. Off: BENNETT. Wit: Charles BIRKETT; G. ANDERSON.

MARTIN, Charles F. [23; Elkhorn City; b: IL; f: F.S. MARTIN; m: Betsey PECK] md. Mary OSTLER [22; Elkhorn City; b: England; f: George OSTLER; m: Edith HANTHER] on 6 Apr 1881 at the home of the bride's father. Off: WOODMAN. Wit: Samuel FRY, Elkhorn Station, Mary A. FRY, Elkhorn Station.

MARTIN, John [colored; 22; Omaha; b: Viriginia; f: Edmund MARTIN; m: Martha MARTIN] md. Ellen STEVENS [colored; 16; Omaha; b: Missouri] on 21 Oct 1869. Off: KERMOTT. Wit: Mrs. A.R. KERMOTT, Mrs. Howard COSSLEY.

MARTIN, Robert E. [29; Douglas Co.; b: Missouri; f: William S. MARTIN; m: Elizabeth MERRILL] md. Sophrona E. REEVES [18; Omaha; b: Iowa; f: Jesse REEVES; m: Elizabeth BARLOW] on 29 Nov 1870. Off: KUHNS. Wit: A.D. JONES; V.M. MACKEY.

MARTIN, Samuel P. [45; Bellevue; b: Indiana; f: Moses S. MARTIN; m: Frank R. REED] md. Henrietta JULIAN [19; Bellevue; b: England; f: Jacob JULIAN; m: Elizabeth ALLEN] on 27 Mar 1878. Off: BARTHOLOMEW. Wit: Jos. QUINLAN, Thomas MULCHAY.

MARTINS, Fritz C. [30; Omaha; b: Germany; f: Henning MARTINS; m: Anna SCHLOMER] md. Anna SIEMONSEN [25; Omaha; b: Germany] on 23 Jan 1872. Off: BILLMAN. Wit: Louis SCHROEDER; Mrs. M. SIMONSON.

MARTINSON, Marsh [30; Omaha; b: Denmark; f: Morten MARTINSON; m: Annie MATSON] md. Mrs. Annie JOHNSON [22; Omaha; b: Denmark; f: Klemen MORRISON] on 18 Oct 1873. Off: AXLING. Wit: Nelse MORRISON; N.A. CHRISTENSEN.

MARTINSON, Martin [32; Omaha; b: Denmark; f: Adolph MARTINSON; m: Caroline PETERSON] md. Caroline PETERSON [37; Omaha; b: Denmark; f: Nels PETERSON; m: Mary THISE] on 2 Jan 1875. Off: PEABODY. Wit: A. JENSEN, Nils Nilson KYELSBERG.

MARTIS, John Peter [33; Omaha] md. Terissa DISH [30; Omaha] on 3 Jan 1869. Off: GROENBAUM. Wit: Mathias SHANKER, Kate SMITH.

MASER, Julius F. [25; b: Missouri; f: Theodore MASER; m: Anna MAYFIELD] md. Alice E. BARTON [24; b: New York; f: Charles C.C. BARTON; m: Eliza RUSSELL] on 20 May 1878. Off: STENBERG. Wit: Hugh THOMSON of Omaha Barracks, Mrs. Agnes HUGHES.

MASON, H.P. [34; Omaha; b: New York; f: H.E. MASON; m: Ruth GOWEN] md. Emma L. KIDDER [24; Omaha; b: Illinois; f: Geo. F. KIDDER; m: Clarisa CHANDLER] on 15 Feb 1874. Off: McCAGUE. Wit: Peter BOYER; Luther H. HARMON.

MASON, Harry [26; b: Iowa; f: Ira MASON; m: Sarah J. HUNTLEY] md. Josephine KNIGHT [19; b: Omaha] on 6 May 1878. Off: PORTER. Wit: Wellington RUDD, Martha RUDD.

MASON, Henry C. [25; Omaha] md. Milla S. BUTLER [18; Omaha] on 11 Jul 1867 at the parsonage. Off: KUHNS. Wit: Mrs. H.W. KUHNS, Rachel A. KUHNS, et al.

MASON, Joseph H. [27; Dodge Co.; b: Philadelphia, PA; f: Joseph H. MASON; m: Rachel WRIGHT] md. Cora TALCOTT [21; Fremont; b: Wisconsin; f: Moses O. TALCOTT; m: Jane GRAY] on 23 Jul 1880. Off: MCLAUGHLIN. Wit: D.S. BENTON, A.W. FERGUSON.

MASON, William [30; Omaha] md. Emma May FORBES [19; Omaha] on 16 Apr 1869.

Off: KERMOTT. Wit: Mrs. Amanda R. KERMOTT, Frank R. KERMOTT.

MASTERS, Samuel [22; Nodway Co., MO; b: Illinois; f: George MASTERS; m: Sarah FISHER] md. Catharine GARNETT [18; Sarpy Co., NE; b: Iowa; f: William GARNETT; m: Puss[?] STONE] on 17 Oct 1879. Off: LIPE. Wit: Alexand. DAEMON, F.M. LAWSON.

MATA, Lee [28; Omaha; b: Mexico; f: Peter MATA] md. Catherine RILEY [33; Omaha; b: Ireland; f: Patrick RILEY; m: Catherine McDERMOTT] on 30 May 1870. Off: MORTON. Wit: Thos. MULCAHEY; Mary A. McBAY.

MATHEWS, Archie [28; Ashland; b: Virginia; f: Samuel MATHEWS; m: Elizabeth SPENCER] md. Cordelia (Cora) BINGMAN [19; Omaha; b: Iowa; f: William BINGMAN; m: Mary] on 21 Feb 1874. Off: GARRETT. Wit: W.J. YATES; Thomas McCORMICK.

MATHEWS, Clark L. [25; Douglas Co.] md. C. VANCE [17; Douglas Co.] on 15 May 1858. Off: SEELY. She has no parents or guardian within territory.

MATHEWS, John M. [26; Omaha; b: Scotland; f: William MATHEWS; m: Ellen PRYOR] md. Nancy J. FIELDING [25; Omaha; b: Pennsylvania; f: George FIELDING; m: Jane PHILLIPS] on 22 Jun 1870. Off: GIBSON. Wit: H.F. STRONG; C. WOOD.

MATHEWSON, Charles P. [25; Norfolk; b: Pomfret, CT; f: Charles MATHEWSON; m: Mary G. GROSVENOR] md. Henrietta M. COON [19; Omaha; f: Archibald F. COON] on 10 Apr 1873. Off: DeLaMATYR. Wit: Watson B. SMITH; L.M. BENNETT.

MATHEWSON, Nels [31; Omaha; b: Denmark; f: Mathias LARSEN; m: Anna Katharina PETERSON] md. Anna Hansen LYNGSTADT [28; Omaha; b: Norway; f: Hans Anderson LYNGSTADT; m: Johanna PETERSON] on 6 Apr 1881. Off: ANDERSEN. Wit: Wm. PETERSEN, Stina FELT.

MATHEWSON, Robert [38; Omaha; b: West Virginia; f: Moses C. MATHEWSON; m: Margaret S. McCURDY] md. Sadie A. MASON [28; Omaha; b: New York; f: W.P. or H.P. MASON; m: Ruth GARVAN] on 7 Apr 1870. Off: DeLaMATYR. Wit: Otis E. MASON; R.G. JENKENSON.

MATHIS, Edwin R. [28; Omaha; b: Delaware, f: Enoch J. MATHIS; m: Esther REEVES] md. Jennie LOCKRIDGE [20; Chicago Pct, Douglas Co.; b: Indiana; f: Robert LOCKRIDGE; m: Sarah WINTER] on 25 Jun 1873 at Elkhorn. Off: SHERRILL. Wit: R.G. CARTER, Elkhorn; P.H. KEAN, Elkhorn.

MATHIS, William R. [32; Omaha; b: NJ; f: Enoch J. MATHIS; m: Ester REEVE] md. Selina JONES [19; Omaha; b: NY; f: Henry JONES; m: Alice ORRILL] on 22 Jun 1875. Off: CONGER. Wit: Bride's parents, Mrs. CONGER, Nettie and Amelia PHELPS, many neighbors.

MATHISON, Matthew [31; Omaha; b: Norway; f: Chris MATHISON; m: Ann Marie ERICKSON] md. Bertha OLSON [23; Omaha; b: Norway; f: Ole CHRISTOPHERSON; m: Lena DEHL] on 10 Jul 1872. Off: KUHNS. Wit: Mrs. H.W. KUHNS; Mrs. George DEBOLT.

MATSON, Peter [26; Omaha; b: Denmark; f: Mads PETERSON; m: Margaret FREDERICKSON] md. Sophia PETERSON [30; Omaha; b: Denmark; f: Peter JOHNSON; m: Mary NELSON] on 18 Oct 1875. Off: HANSEN. Wit: Anton JENSEN, Prod NIELSON.

MATTESON, Peter D. [26; Omaha; b: Sweden; f: Matt SWENSEN] md. Emma ANDERSON [19; Omaha; b: Sweden; f: Lars ANDERSON; m: Hanna] on 3 Jul 1871. Off: LARSON. Wit: Samuel J. WIDEN; Andrew NELSON.

MATTHIES, Claus [27; Omaha; b: Germany; f: Thomas MATTHIES; m: Margaretta SCHULTZ] md. Mary WAGNER [22; Omaha; b: Germany; f: Henry WAGNER] on 11 Sep 1872. Off: LYTLE. Wit: Nicholas MERGEN; Johan SCHULTZ, Ashland.

MATTIES, George [21; Omaha; f: Henry MATTIES; m: Elizabeth] md. Josephine BLAKELY [22; St. Louis; b: Ireland; f: Martin BLAKELY; m: Margaret] on 10 May 1870. Off: KELLEY. Wit: J.S. TUCKER; G.N. HOLLINS.

MATTINGLY, Peter [27; Douglas Co.] md. Margret A. CASSADY [20; Douglas Co.] on 6 Jan 1866. Off: CURTIS. Wit: Samuel I. MATTINGLY, Maria CASSADY.

MATTSON, Nels [25; Omaha; b: Denmark; f: Mathias HANSEN; m: Caroline PETERSON] md. Caroline NELSON [23; b: Denmark; f: Nils ANDERSON] on 12 Jun 1871. Off: GIBSON. Wit: Levi H. BORDWELL; Bennett F. MASON.

MATZA, Peter [25; Omaha; b: WI; f: Thomas MATZA; m: Catharine PRANGAR] md. Josie HYNEK [19; Omaha; b: Germany; f: Frank HYNEK; m: Annie MITATEK] on 15 Sep 1881. Off: BENEKE. Wit: Anton HYNEK, Wenzel NISTEL.

MAURETZEN, Theodor Alfr. [22; Omaha; b: Norway; f: Alfred MAURITZEN; m: Tillie ATZEN] md. Lena Marie ADAMS [20; Omaha; b: Norway; f: John ADAMS] on 15 Jul 1876. Off: HANSEN. Wit: K. KNUDSENS, John CLINESTARSEN.

MAURITZEN, John C. [26; Omaha; b: Denmark; f: Mauritz JOHNSON: m: Trine NELSON] md. Thora A.E. WIPPERT [24; Omaha; b: Denmark; f: Johannes WIPPERT; m: Caroline G. PETERSON] on 28 May 1874. Off: MARSSEN. Wit: Sorn Chr. PEDERSEN; J.A. THORRY. (Filed 2 Oct 1884, J.H. McCULLOCH).

MAUSS, Vic [35; Douglas Co.; b: Germany; f: Johannes MAUSS; m: Catharina SCHEIDT] md. Nina FELZMANN [25; Douglas Co.; b: Germany; f: Ernest FELZMANN, m: Auguste FELZMANN] on 12 Apr 1878. Off: BENEKE. Wit: George C. GRAVES, Bernhard LACHSE?, both of Douglas Co.

MAWAS, Charles [21; Omaha; b: Germany; f: Ludwig MAWAS; m: Mary BLOEK] md. Mary LAMPRECHT [21; Omaha; b: Germany; f: Fred LAMPRECHT; m: Dora] on 13 Feb 1874. Off: HILGENDORF. Wit: Frederick LAMPRECHT; Dorotheas LAMPRECHT.

MAXFIELD, Abram W. [Council Bluffs] md. Clara CLINTON [Council Bluffs] on 23 Jan 1865 at VAN ANTWERP's boarding place. Off: VAN ANTWERP. Wit: Mrs. VAN ANTWERP, Miss PARMETER.

MAXTED, Levi [Omaha] md. Mary MESSEL [15; Omaha] on 7 Jul 1864 at DICKINSON's office. Off: DICKINSON. Wit: Mrs. Hannah MESSEL, Lawrence RAINS, et al. Age consent by mother of the bride, no father living.

MAXWELL, Charles A. [24; Colorado Territory] md. Julia M. LOCKE [20; Geneva, WI] on Thursday, 1 Nov 1866 at Gen. E. ESTABROOK's house. Off: VAN ANTWERP. Wit: Gen. and Mrs. E. ESTABROOK, Elicie MINTON.

MAYBURY, John [28; Antelope Co.; b: Ireland; f: Richard MAYBURY; m: Nora O'SULLIVAN] md. Frances TOPHAN [23; b: New York; f: John R. TOPHAN; m: Eva HAWKS] on 23 Jun 1878. Off: BARTHOLOMEW. Wit: Charles P. NEEDHAM, John G. JACOBS.

MAYS, Charles L. [30; Omaha; b: Virginia; f: Thomas MAYS; m: Elizabeth WELCHER] md. Amada KEEPS [35; Omaha; b: Philadelphia, PA; f: Peter FRIES; m: Mae MULLEN] on 31 Jan 1871. Off: DeLaMATYR. Wit: James BARKER, Military Bridge; Jennie KEEPS, 11th between Cass & Chicago St.

McALLISTER, Ralph [30; Omaha; b: Maine; f: Alfred McALLISTER; m: Waity Ellen FOSTER] md. Elizbeth C. HOBBY [22; Omaha; b: New York; f: Uriah HOBBY; m: Ann S. WILCOX] on 17 Jul 1872. Off: KUHNS. Wit: Uriah HOBBY; Henry C. HOBBY.

McANSLAND, Robert R. [26; Omaha; b: New Foundland; f: Alexander McANSLAND; m: Agnes RITCHIE] md. Mary E. LANNSBERRY [18; Omaha; b: Connecticut; f: Daniel W. LANNSBERRY; m: Emeline WOOD] on 9 May 1877. Off: Fisher. Wit: Mrs. McANSLAND, Joseph M. MILLARD.

McARDLE, John [32; Omaha; b: Canada; f: Patrick McARDLE; m: Catharine BOURKE] md. Emma M. JOHNSON [20; Omaha; b: Sweden; f: Anderson JOHNSON; m: Eliza JOHNSON] on 21 Jan 1875. Off: PUTNAM. Wit: Vera GOULD, J.C. WILKINSON.

McARDLE, Patrick [28; Douglas Co.] md. Catherine CONNERY [28; Douglas Co.] on 5 Jun 1861 at the Catholic Church of Omaha. Off: KELLY. Wit: Hugh DOUGHERTY, Mary KELLY.

McARTHUR, Archie [23; Omaha; b: Canada; f: Archie McARTHUR; m: Catharine SMITH] md. Mary FREDERICKSON [22; Omaha; b: Denmark; f: Johann FREDERICKSON; m: Johanna JENSEN] on 16 May 1880. Off: HAWES. Wit: Henry HALL, Matilda HALL.

McAUSLAND, A.G. [22; Omaha] md. Eugenia KEYES [21; Omaha] on 4 Dec 1867. Off: SLAUGHTER.

McBAY [McBRAY], George N. [31; Omaha; b: Pennsylvania; f: Robert McBAY; m: Margaret BARNES] md. Mary Ann HUBBARD [30; Omaha; b: Cincinnati, OH; f: George HUBBARD] on 13 Oct 1869. Off: DE LA MATYR. Wit: Charles DUNLAP, Mary A. DUNLAP.

McBRIDE, John [26; b: Illinois; f: Thomas McBRIDE; m: Rebecca ROBINSON] md. Kate or Kitty Cora DOWNEY [23; b: Illinois; f: John DOWNEY; m: Mary O. MEARS] on 18 Sep 1878. Off: McDERMOTT. Wit: Eugene RHULLIES, A. Mary COLANERI.

McBRIDE, John [27; Omaha] md. Bridget DOYLE [24; Omaha] on 1 May 1861 at the Catholic Church of Omaha. Off: KELLY. Wit: Michael DUNN, Bridget McKEOWN.

McCABE, Joseph W. [38; Keokuk, IA; b: IA; f: Joshua McCABE; m: Susan HUDSON] md. Mrs. Nancy Jane GOSSAGE [25; Keokuk, IA; b: IA; f: Warrington Cary POPE; m: Lucy MOORE] on 12 Nov 1881. Off: CHADWICK. Wit: Max BERGMANN, Wm. K. MILLER.

McCAFFREY, Owen [26; Omaha; b: Ireland; f: Hugh McCAFFREY; m: Susan McDERMOTT] md. Therese KENNEDY [20; Omaha; b: OH; f: John KENNEDY; m: Julia CARROL] on 29 Feb 1881. Off: ENGLISH. Wit: Joseph McCAFFREY, Ellen KENNEDY.

McCAIG, John K. [31; Omaha; b: Canada; f: William McCAIG; m: Catharine CONNOLLY] md. Sarah WISEMAN [34; Omaha; b: Illinois; f: Jacob WISEMAN; m: Catherine SHOAF] on 12 Aug 1879. Off: STENBERG. Wit: Frank D. KENT, Sophia (x) HASSETT.

McCALLUM, John [54; Council Bluffs, IA; b: Canada; f: Archibald McCALLUM; m: Mary THOMPSON] md. Mrs. Carrie SEAMAN [26; Council Bluffs, IA; b: IL; f: A.D. SIMONS; m: Mary WITT] on 13 Aug 1881. Off: SMITH. Wit: H. HOCHSTETTER, Max BERGMANN.

McCAMLEY, James [27; Sarpy Co.; b: New York City; f: William McCAMLEY] md. Katie SERSION [CISAR] [24; Omaha; b: Bohemia; f: Anthony SERSION [CISAR]] on 26 Mar 1870. Off: McCANDLISH. Wit: Romain PALMER; M. McCANDLISH.

McCANDLISH, R.C. [21; Creston, Platte Co., NE; b: Quincy, IL; f: William McCANDLISH; m: Maria H. HOWELLS] md. Mollie S. MARKEL [22; Omaha; b: Canton, MO; f: Jacob MARKEL; m: Eunice SWEET] on 1 May 1879. Off: McCANDLISH. Wit: J.R. MEREDITH, Wm. Justin HARSHA.

McCANN, John H. [22; Douglas Co.; b: NY; f: David McCANN; m: Sarah DECKER] md. Minnie GODRIGE [18; Omaha; b: Chicago; f: Charles H. GODRIGE; m: Mary] on 22 Apr 1875. Off: PEABODY. Wit: W.E. WELSH, Sarah ALLISON.

McCARDLE, John [27; Douglas Co.] and Ann GUNUP [GUMP] [25; Douglas Co.] on 24 Nov 1860. Off: ARMSTRONG.

McCARTHY, Charles [30; Omaha; b: Ireland; f: Charles McCARTHY; m: Margaret BUCKLEY] md. Jane McGARVEY [30; Omaha; b: Ireland; f: Hugh McGARVEY; m: Kate FRILL] on 16 Oct 1875. Off: BYRNE. Wit: Cornelius O'DONNELL, Ellen HEGARTY.

McCARTY, Henry [35; Omaha; b: Ireland; f: Henry McCARTY; m: Mary CARR] md. Eliza Jane CARR [26; Omaha; b: Canada; f: Christopher CARR] on 28 Mar 1873. Off: McKELVEY. Wit: A.H. DORECKAN; Angie McKELVEY.

McCARTY, John R. [22; Sarpy Co.; b: Iowa; f: Robert McCARTY; m: Judy Ann REMER] md. Charlotte Jane SEXTON [18; Avoca, IA; b: Iowa; f: Isaac SEXTON] on 21 Jan 1874. Off: PEABODY. Wit: A.W. TENNANT; Mrs. E.A. TENNANT.

McCARTY, Martin [27; Omaha; b: Ireland; f: Michael McCARTY; m: Ellen DRISCOLE] md. Hannoraha McCARTY [21; Omaha; b: Ireland; f: Michael McCARTY; m: Johanna RYAN] on 13 Feb 1877. Off: JENNETO. Wit: Peter O'MALLEY, Margaret McCARTHY.

McCARTY, Robert A. [26; Sarpy Co.; b: IA; f: Enoch McCARTY; m: Amy SEXTON] md. Louise KALENBACH [15; Omaha; b: Germany; f: Christ KALENBACH; m: Mary GUTEKNUST] on 8 Feb 1881. Off: BANGTER. Wit: G.P. MARTIN, Jennie E. McCARTY. Age consent given by parents of the bride.

McCAWLEY, James [27; of Harrison Co., IA; f: Patk. or Peter McCAWLEY of Parish Killesher, County Fermanaugh, Irel.] md. Elizabeth MORROW [20; Harrison Co., IA; f: Patk. MORROW, County Antrim, Irel.] on 11 Sep 1859 at St. Mary's Church. Off: CANNON. Wit: William KERRIGAN, Johanna QUINN.

McCLELLAN, Henry C. [35; Fort Omaha; b: IN; f: Uriah McCLELLAN; m: Elizabeth ENGLAND] md. Mrs. Bridget ROBERTS [31; Fort Omaha; b: Ireland; f: Thomas RAFTER; m: Mary DONNALLY] on 4 Sep 1881 at Fort Omaha. Off: MILLSPAUGH. Wit: Michael CODY, Fort Omaha, James GREEN, Fort Omaha.

McCLELLAND, Adam [38; Omaha Barracks; b: Ireland; f: Robert McCLELLAND; m: Anne HAMILTON] md. Susan RILEY [35; Douglas Co.; b: Ireland; f: Thomas RILEY; m: Daphney RILEY] on 25 Sep 1872. Off: PORTER. Wit: Mrs. H.L. SEWARD; Edwin HANEY.

McCLELLAND, Dr. William [40; Omaha] md. Florence ROGERS [21; Omaha] on 26 Feb 1869. Off: KUHNS. Wit: Hon. G.W. DOAN (DOANE) and wife, Dr. COFFMAN, Capt. A. PATRICK, et al.

McCONNELL, Fred R. [27; Salt Lake; b: Albany, NY; f: Robert McCONNELL; m: Anna L. WARDELL] md. Bertha M. ISAACS [b: Burlington, IA; f: N.P. ISAACS; m: Maria D. WORDEN] on 24 Aug 1881. Off: MURESH. Wit: Chris. ISAACS, Lizzie ISAACS.

McCONNELL, Robert J. [30; Evanston, WY; b: New York; f: Robert McCONNELL; m: Amea WARDELL] md. Mattie E. STORRS [21; Omaha; b: Nebraska; f: Charles P. STORRS; m: Elizabeth W. FRENCH] on 8 Apr 1880. Off: SHERILL. Wit: Wm. R. BOWEN, Chas. P. STORRS.

McCORMICK, James [22; Omaha; b: Peoria, IL; f: John McCORMICK; m: Elizabeth BERGADOLL] md. Elizabeth HAMILTON [24; Omaha; b: Peoria, IL; f: James HAMILTON] on 12 May 1869. Off: KELLEY. Wit: M. SULLIVAN, P. MURPHY.

McCORMICK, Josiah L. [Douglas Co.] md. Margaret or Anna Magdalina G. MILLS [Douglas Co.] on 29 Jan 1863 at Geo. M. MILLS' house. Off: DAKE. Wit: Mr. and Mrs. Geo. M. MILLS, Jesse LACEY, Harriet KEITH.

McCORMICK, Robert [38; Elkhorn; b: Ireland; f: Robert McCORMICK; m: Ann PLUNKETT] md. Mary O'BRIEN [26; Omaha; b: Ireland; f: Theodore O'BRIEN; m: Mary HANLON] on 26 Sep 1869. Off: CURTIS. Wit: James H. STAPLETON, Catherine McCORMICK.

McCORMICK, Thomas [49; Omaha] md. Winnifred SHEA [38; Omaha] on 28 Oct 1860 at the Catholic Church of Omaha. Off: KELLY. Wit: John DUNCAN.

McCOURT, Francis [30; Douglas Co.; b: Ireland; f: John McCOURT; m: Catherine GALLAGHER] md. Ellen McHUGH [22; Omaha; b: Ireland; f: Thomas McHUGH; m: Mary KELLEY] on 7 Aug 1870. Off: CURTIS. Wit: Arthur H. ROBINSON; Anastasia CROWLEY.

McCOY, Alonzo A. [28; Omaha] md. Anna Laura PRUETT [23; Omaha] on 12 May 1867. Off: CHIVINGTON. Wit: Mrs. PRUETT, Miss PRUETT, et al.

McCOY, Prestin [40] and Rebca Jane BROWN [19] license issued on 21 Mar 1857. No marriage record. Off: SCOTT. Age consent given by Nelson BROWN.

McCRAY, James [34; Omaha; b: Pennsylvania; f: Samuel McCRAY; m: Eliza J. SCOTT] md. Mrs. Mary F. DONK [28; Omaha; b: Illinois; f: Jesse ASHBURN; m: Almira GLASS] on 17 Jan 1874. Off: PEABODY. Wit: Samantha McNEIL; Sarah ASHBURN.

McCREADY, John [34, Omaha; b: England; f: George McCREADY; m: Wilmina STEWARD] md. Amelia LONG [18 or 20; Omaha; b: Germany; f: John LONG; m: Amelia POWALTZ] on 23 Oct 1876. Off: SEDGWICK; Wit: George T. CONNELL, Elizabeth NAUGHTON.

McCREARY, John [26; Pace Co., IA] md. Mary E. CREIGHTON [25; Page Co.?] on 25 Nov 1858 at St. Mary's Church. Certificate says both from Ohio. Off: CANNON. Wit: Joseph CREIGHTON, Catherine CREIGHTON.

McCUEN, G.H. [23; Cass Co., IA; b: OH; f: J.R. McCUEN; m: Elizabeth HAYES] md. Minnie BEAR [18, Cass Co., IA; b: IA; f: John C. BEAR; m: Helen WALMER] on 28 Dec 1881. Off: INGRAM. Wit: H.D. MOSER, Mrs. H.L. MOSER both of Marne, IA.

McCULLOUGH, S.H. [33; Colfax Co., IA; b: PA; f: John McCULLOUGH; m: Esther A. FERGUSON] md. Lucea B. SAUNDERS [26; Cortland, NY; b: NY; f: P. SAUNDERS] on 31 Dec 1881. Off: STEWART. Wit: M. DONOVAN, Ellen DIFFBY.

McCUNE, John W. [28; Omaha] md. Anna DORSEY [26; Omaha] on 13 Jun 1867. Off: SLAUGHTER.

McCUNE, Joseph M. [31; Omaha; b: Pennsylvania; f: Seth R. McCUNE; m: Julia A. WILSON] md. Lydia ELLENGWOOD [26; Omaha; b: Massachusetts; f: Samuel ELLENGWOOD; m: Mary CLEMENTS] on 22 Jun 1871 at the 2nd Presbyterian Church. Off: STEWART. Wit: George A. KENNARD; E. Pearl EVANS.

McCURDY, Samuel C. [24; Council Bluffs; b: Iowa; f: J.R. McCURDY; m: Mary EPPERSON] md. Annie DOLAN [29; Glenwood, IA; b: Massachusetts; f: John DOLAN; m: Mary GLYNN] on 29 Dec 1874. Off: PEABODY. Wit: Wm. B.R. KILLINGSWORTH; Talmage E. BEEBE.

McCUTCHEN, J.H. [24; Omaha; b: Indiana; f: George McCUTCHEN; m: Emelia LERCHES] md. Fredericka ZAH [18; Omaha; b: Illinois; f: John ZAH; m: Catharine SMITH] on 3 Nov 1880. Off: INGRAM. Wit: G.J. HUNT, Lettie J. INGRAM.

McDERMOTT, Charles M. [28; Omaha] md. Mary A. HARTNETT [22; Omaha] on 23 May 1868. Off: CURTIS. Wit: T.B. PRICE, Nora HOLLIDAY.

McDERMOTT, Charles [32; b: Ireland; f: Tom McDERMOTT; m: Mary SMITH] md. Katie KEEVENS [25; b: Ireland; f: Patrick KEEVENS; m: Ann RINNELS] on 17 May 1878. Off: KELLEY. Wit: James WESTON, Mary BURCKLY.

McDERMOTT, John [24; Omaha; b: Ireland; f: Patrick McDERMOTT; m: Norah RUSH] md. Mrs. Christiana Jane LLOYDJOINS [29; Omaha; b: England; f: John William ROGERS; m: Jane BEARD] on 30 Jun 1881. Off: INGRAM. Wit: John W. ROGERS, Saul J. BEDDIS.

McDERMOTT, Michael [36; Omaha; b: Ireland; f: Patrick McDERMOTT; m: Catherine BRANNAN] md. Rosey CASSIDY [27; Omaha; b: Scotland; f: Patrick CASSEDY] on 3 Jun 1870. Off: GOLDRICH. Wit: Patrick MALONE; James RODNEY.

McDONALD, Charles [31; Richardson Co.] md. Ora B. HENRY [18; Omaha] on 14 Oct 1858. Off: SMITH. Wit: Anna HENRY, John McCAMPBELL, Mr. BOYD.

McDONALD, Frank L. [26; Omaha] md. Drusilla K. STEWART [22; Omaha] on 4 Mar 1869 at the bride's residence. Off: WESTWOOD. Wit: the bride's mother, Charles PIGMAN, et al.

McDONALD, James [29; Columbus, NE; b: Canada; f: Alexander McDONALD; m: Flora FRAZIER] md. Eva NORRIS [23; Columbus, NE; b: Michigan; f: George NORRIS; m: Laura HOXIE] on 26 May 1879. Off: FROST. Wit: R. LAING, Lena F. LAING.

McDONALD, John W. [22; Omaha; b: Ohio; f: William McDONALD; m: Mary PAINTER] md. Martha E. HENDERSON [21; Omaha; b: Missouri; f: Daniel HENDERSON] on 15 Mar 1870. Off: KELLEY. Wit: Mrs. ROSS; Miss ROSS.

McDONALD, John [27; Omaha; b: Scotland; f: John McDONALD; m: Jane RUSSELL] md. Alice KING [20; Omaha; b: IA; f: Wm. KING; m: Aster EDWARDS] on 22 Nov 1881. Off: HARRIS. Wit: Joseph CARNABY, George ELLIOTT.

McDONELL, C.D. [23; Omaha; b: Illinois; f: John McDONELL; m: Helen McLAREN] md. Emma FOREMAN [18; Omaha; b: Denmark; f: Peter FOREMAN; m: E. JOHNSON] on 23 Dec 1879. Off: SHERRILL. Wit: James DECKER, Jennie CRUISE.

McDOUGALL, Archibald [34; Sarpy Co.] md. Mary CURRY [28; Sarpy Co.] on 6 Jan 1869. Off: KUHNS. Wit: Mrs. M.E. WEATHERWAX, Mrs. B. GANTZ, Nancy SNOWDEN, et al.

McELROY, William [30; Omaha; b: New York; f: John McELROY; m: Catharine HART] md. Mary M. O'BRIEN [19; Omaha; b: Wisconsin; f: George M. O'BRIEN; m: Kate E. CARROLL] on 19 Dec 1871. Off: O'GORMAN. Wit: P.P. SHELBY; Catharine O'BRIEN.

McELWAIN, James S. [24; Omaha] md. Emily A. BROWN [20; Omaha] on 19 Sep 1867. Off: SLAUGHTER. Wit: A.B. SLAUGHTER, H.L. SLAUGHTER.

McENTEE, John [25; St. Mary's, Wyoming Terr.; b: Ireland; f: John McENTEE; m: Ellen RILEY] md. Rose McENTEE [20; Omaha; b: Ireland; f: Terrence McENTEE; m: Mary DUNN] on 20 Nov 1872. Off: CURTIS. Wit: Peter MALONE; Mary MORAN.

McEVOY, James [Douglas Co.] md. Bridget D. FITZPATRICK [Douglas Co.] on 30 May 1864 at the Catholic Church of Omaha. Off: O'GORMAN. Wit: Patrick McEVOY, Margaret A. CASSIDY.

McEVOY, Patrick [26; Douglas Co.; b: Ireland; f: James McEVOY; m: Mary PHALAN] md. Joanna KENELLEY [22; Douglas Co.; b: Ireland; f: Martin KENELLEY; m: Bridget KISCINE (KESSAN)] on 28 Sep 1870. Off: CURTIS. Wit: James KENELLEY; Honora KENELLEY.

McFALL, Andrew J. [28; Brownville; b: Lancaster, PA; f: James A. McFALL; m: Eliza SPROUL] md. Ellen KAVANAUGH [24; Brownville; b: New Orleans, LA; f: John KAVANAUGH; m: Mary] on 23 Jun 1869.

Off: CLARKSON. Wit: Mrs. BELDEN, R.W. FURNASS of Brownville.

McGARVEY, Thomas [50; Douglas Co.; b: Ireland; f: Michael McGARVEY; m: Margaret McNALLY] md. Margaret McCRARY [37; b: Ireland; f: Lawrence McCRAREY; m: Mary DARBOY] on 30 Dec 1869. Off: CURTIS. Wit: John FRENZER; Jane McCRAREY.

McGAVOCK, William J. [30; Memphis, TN, b: Ireland; f: Alexander McGAVOCK; m: Sarah DEVELIN] md. Mary F. ARNOLD [21; Douglas Co.; b: England; f: John N. ARNOLD; m: Mary ROBINSON] on 26 Jul 1876 at the Roman Catholic Cathedral. Off: BYRNE. Wit: James Charles TOBIN, Lizzie MURPHY.

McGEE, Thomas C. [24; Omaha; b: Maryland; f: D.K. McGEE; m: Mary WETZEL] and Rachel C. LEION [18; Omaha; b: Dakota; f: Henry LEION; m: Sarah WILTZ] license issued on 29 Jun 1874. Off: PEABODY.

McGINN, Mathew A. [31; Burlington, IA; b: Pennsylvania; f: Mathew McGINN; m: Mary DOUGHERTY] md. Kate CREIGHTON [28; Omaha; b: Ohio; f: Francis CREIGHTON; m: Phoebe DRISCOLL] on 12 Jun 1877. Off: JENNETTO. Wit: Frank O'BRIEN, Mary F. CREIGHTON.

McGLINN, William [36; Douglas Co.] md. Bridget WALDREN [30; Douglas Co.] on 2 Nov 1867. Off: O'GORMAN. Wit: Wright DONELLY, Mrs. KING.

McGOVERN, John [22; Omaha; b: Nebraska; f: Patrick McGOVERN; m: Alice McGERTY] md. Therese GRACE [17; Omaha; b: Iowa; f: Martin GRACE; m: Elizabeth McNALLY] on 7 Sep 1880. Off: ENGLISH. Wit: E.C. MOORE, Philomena GRACE.

McGRATH, Roderick [28; Omaha; b: Canada; f: Roger McGRATH; m: Jane GREEN] md. Theresa GLEASON [21; Omaha; b: Canada; f: William GLEASON; m: Ann HAWKINS] on 16 Feb 1881. Off: ENGLISH. Wit: Maggie DALTON, James GREEN.

McHALE, David [31; Omaha; b: Ireland; f: John McHALE; m: Ann LYONS] md. Mary MULLONEY [23; Omaha; b: Ireland; f: Samuel MULLONEY; m: Bridget McDONAGH] on 27 Jan 1873. Off: CURTIS. Wit: Peter AUSBRO; Bridget WARD.

McHUGH, Patrick [24; Omaha; b: Bangor, ME; f: Patrick McHUGH; m: Elizabeth JAMES] md. Maggie McDEVETT [19; Omaha; b: Bangor, ME; f: William McDEVETT; m: Mary BRADLEY] on 14 Nov 1870. Off: CURTIS. Wit: Benjamin F. PETTINGLEY; Statia CROWLEY.

McHUGH, Patrick [26; Omaha; b: Canada West; f: Patrick McHUGH; m: Ann WALKER] md. Rosa K. WELCH [19; Omaha; b: Maine; f: Christopher WELCH; m: Mary CONNELS] on 30 Jun 1872. Off: CURTIS. Wit: Warren REED; Mary REED.

McHUGH, Thomas P. [23; Omaha; b: PA; f: Michael McHUGH; m: Ellen NELAN] md. Maria BOHAN [19; Omaha; b: Ireland; f: James BOHAN; m: Bridget CASEY] on 30 Oct 1881. Off: STENBERG. Wit: Edward WOODS, Mrs. Ellen DILLON.

McILWREITH, Hamilton H. [30; Omaha; b: Soctland; f: John McILWREITH; m: Jesse H. HOWAT] md. Mrs. Alice HURKET [33; Omaha; b: England; f: George LESTER; m: Martha CROCKETT] on 16 Jan 1880. Off: JAMESON. Wit: C.W. SMITH, Amelia ALLENSPAUGH.

McINROE, Patrick [50; Omaha b: Ireland; f: Owen McINROE; m: Catharine KAY] md. Ellen O'CONNER [45; Omaha; b: Ireland; f: Michael O'CONNOR; m: Margaret ROONEY] on 28 Nov 1875. Off: BOBAL. Wit: Peter O'ROURKE, Maggie GORDON.

McINTIRE, Robert [27; Florence] md. Florilla CAMRON [21; Florence] on 26 Jul 1867 at Florence. Off: ADRIANCE. Wit: R.E. LAWRENCE, Mrs. M. DAVIDSON.

McINTOSH, James J. [19; Omaha; b: Canada; f: James McINTOSH; m: Bridget CONNORS] md. Mary HELAN [20; Omaha; b: Ireland; f: Thomas HELAN; m: Ellen TOBIN] on 23 May 1870. Off: CURTIS. Wit: Thomas HELAN, Lincoln City; Catherine SLATTERY.

McINTOSH, James R. [28; Harvard, NE; b: New York City; f: James McINTOSH; m: Ann DERGEN] md. Azelia ALBRO [27; Columbus, PA; b: Pennsylvania; f: George ALBRO; m: Roba CARR] on 5 Oct 1878. Off: JAMESON. Wit: Gilmore KING, Mrs. Ida L. KING, both of Union City, PA.

McINTYRE, Richard P. [34; Omaha; b: Ireland; f: Owen McINTYRE; m: Elizabeth NICHOLS] md. Bridget HALL [26; Omaha; b: Ireland; f: James HALL] on 25 May 1875. Off: BYRNE. Wit: John HALL, Mary O'RILEY.

McINTYRE, Stephen F. [34; Douglas Co.] md. Mary C. WHIPP [34; Douglas Co.] on 5 Oct 1868. Off: ALLEN. Wit: S.D. MERCER, M.D., Mrs. Belle ALLEN.

McKAIG, Walter W. [47; Chicago, IL; b: Ohio; f: Silas McKAIG; m: Elizabeth WRIGHT] md. Hariffa NASH [23; California; b: Wisconsin; f: Samuel NASH; m: Anna ELLIS] on 24 Sep 1874. Off: PEABODY. Wit: Mrs. C.F. TOWNSEND; Eugene A. THOMAS.

McKAIN [McKANE], Jas. [23; Harrison, IA] md. Mary LACY [22; Harrison Co., IA] on 12 Sep 1859 at St. Mary's Church. Off: CANNON. Wit: Thomas MOHAN, Honorah DOLAN.

McKEE, A. [37; Omaha; b: Ireland; f: Henry McKEE; m: unknown] md. Nancy Jane MORRIS [19; Douglas Co.; b: Iowa; f: Richard MORRIS; m: Diana HARRIS] on 23 Dec 1880. Off: GERSTON. Wit: John APLEBY, Wilan APLEBY, both of Elkhorn City.

McKEE, John A. [32; Omaha; b: PA; f: Thomas McKEE; m: Elizabeth ANDRE] md. Mary MATSON [19; Omaha; b: Sweden] on 3 Dec 1875. Off: PEABODY. Wit: Mabel L. PEABODY, Charles H. NICHOLS.

McKEE, Scipio P. [45; Omaha; colored; b: North Carolina; f: Cicero PREUARD; m: Harriet MURRELL] md. Mrs. Jane MERRIWEATHER [42; Omaha; colored; b: Kentucky; m: Maria HUNT] on 29 Mar 1873. Off: PORTER. Wit: E.G. DUDLEY; Wm. P. SNOWDEN.

McKENNA, James [57; Dakota Co.; b: Ireland; f: Lawrence McKENNA; m: Mary MONTAGUE] md. Mrs. Susan LEACH [44; Dakota Co.; b: England; f: ---- EDWARDS] on 27 Jun 1873. Off: CURTIS. Wit: Francis J. KELLEHER; Susan RONAN.

McKENZEY [McKINZEY], Mendice B. [24; Douglas Co.] and N. Caroline BRECKENRIDGE [16; Douglas Co.] license issued on 10 Dec 1857. No marriage record. Off: SEELY. Age consent given by father.

McKENZIE, Alexander [30; b: Scotland; f: Alexander McKENZIE; m: Clementine McKENZIE] md. Emma N. BROWN [21; b: Omaha; f: William BROWN; m: Martha Ann PATTERSON] on 9 Nov 1878. Off: MILLSPAUGH. Wit: W.O. LANDERS, A. SORENSON.

McKEY, Garten H. [40; Omaha; b: MO; f: Walter McKEY; m: Sarah GARTIN] md. Anna LEHIGH [25; Omaha; b: Canada; f: John LEHIGH; m: Jane DACK] on 18 Jan 1881. Off: MAXFIELD. Wit: Mr. and Mrs. PRENTISS.

McKINNEY, James [negro; 28; b: Kentucky; f: Peter McKINNEY; m: Anna MONJOYE] md. Laura HANSEL [negro; 18; b: Missouri; f: George HANSEL; m: Sarah HANSEL] on 6 Sep 1878. Off: WEISS. Wit: John WILSON.

McKINSTRY, Horace K. [53] md. Catherine M. HODGSON [40] on 13 Sep 1867 at H.K. McKINSTRY's house. Off: VAN ANTWERP. Wit: Mrs. Addie WINJALL, Miss Eleacy S. HODGSON.

McKNIGHT, George E. [28; Fremont] md. Ellen TALCOTT [19; Omaha] on 25 Dec 1867 at STUCK's office. Off: STUCK. Wit: Patrick DONNELLY, Timothy KELLY.

McLAIN, Charles F. [23; b: Ohio; f: J.J. McLAIN; m: Mary E. FALES] md. Ora M. CHESWELL [20; b: Boston, MA; f: Wm. H. CHESWELL; m: Eliza E. MEADER] on 24 Sep 1878. Off: FISHER. Wit: Alice McLAIN, James WOODARD.

McLAUGHLIN, Daniel [31; Dakota City, Dakota Co.] md. Ellen McCUNE [26; Keokuk, IA] on 28 Nov 1861 at the Catholic Church of Omaha. Off: O'GORMAN. Wit: Vincent BERKLEY, Johanna O'BRIEN.

McLUCAS, J.M. [26; North Platte; b: York Co., ME; f: Abraham McLUCAS; m: Jane NAISON] md. Bell HEMPHILL [18; Omaha; b: Indiana; f: J.C. HEMPHILL; m: Hester A. ROGERS] on 4 Jun 1872. Off: STEWART. Wit: J.M. WATSON; Helen E. WATSON.

McMAHON, James [34; b: England; f: James McMAHON; m: Margaret TAYLOR] md. Henrietta HASCALL [21; b: Kansas; f: Isaac S. HASCALL; m: Sarah HARRISON] on 29 Sep 1878. Off: LIPE. Wit: I.S. HASCALL, Mrs. C.F. GOODMAN.

McMAHON, Michael J. [25; Omaha; b: Ireland; f: Patrick McMAHON; m: Kate FOGERTY] md. Abby FENTON [27; Omaha; b: Ireland; f: Roger FENTON; m: Mary FOLEY] on 7 Jan 1873. Off: KELLEHER. Wit: P.O. MALLEY; Jane BIRMINGHAM.

McMANNIS, James C. [27; b: Ireland; f: John McMANNIS; m: Catharine SLOWIE] and Anna N. HAMMOND [19; b: Missouri; f: George HAMMOND; m: A. WARFIELD] license issued on 11 Feb 1878. No marriage record. Off: BARTHOLOMEW.

McMEANS, Rollin L. [28; Omaha; b: Indiana; f: N.S. McMEANS; m: Martha LYBROOK] md. Mary Jane WHITTLOCK [23; Omaha; b: New Jersey; f: E.R. WHITTLOCK; m: C.A. CLEAMAN] on 24 May 1877. Off: SEDGWICK. Wit: Mr. and Mrs. ALLEN.

McMILLEN, Daniel [Douglas Precinct] md. Bridget L. McCUNE [Omaha] on 8 Oct 1864. Off: O'GORMAN. Wit: Duncan McMILLEN, John McCUNE.

McMULLEN, William H. [29; Omaha; b: New Jersey; f: Hugh McMULLEN; m: Ester HALL] md. Emma HATTEROTH [18; Omaha; b: Illinois; f: John HATTEROTH; m: Mary E. CLARK] on 7 Apr 1877. Off: PARDEE. Wit: John ARMSTRONG, G. WINCHELL.

McMURRAY, Richard M. [36; Omaha] md. Marietta JOHNSON [18; Omaha] on 25 Nov 1861 at Hadley JOHNSON's house. Off: HART. Wit: Hadley JOHNSON, Mrs. H. JOHNSON.

McNALL, Wilber [24; Douglas Co.] md. Mary E. JACKSON [18; Douglas Co.] on 17 Oct 1867 at Primrose, Douglas Co. Off: DENTON.

McNAMARA, Matthew A. [29; Omaha; b: Ireland; f: Patrick McNAMARA; m: Mary NOLAN] md. Ellen SULLIVAN [18; Omaha; b: Boston, MA; f: Patrick R. SULLIVAN; m: Catharine BOWEN] on 25 Feb 1873. Off: CURTIS. Wit: Henry Joseph LUCAS; Hannah SULLIVAN.

McNAMEE, William J. [28; Omaha; b: Ireland; f: Joseph McNAMEE; m: Mary Ann McKENNA] md. Hannah DONAVAN [28; Omaha; b: OH; m: Mary ----] on 3 Jan 1875 at the Roman Catholic Cathedral. Off: BYRNE. Wit: Peter MALONE, Bishop's House, Mary DONOVAN, Metropolitan Hotel.

McNANY, Hugh [31; Buffalo, NY; b: New York; f: Hugh McNANY; m: Sarah JOHNSON] md. Nellie TILLIE [20; Minneapolis, MN; b: Minnesota; f: John TILLIE; m: Catharine HENNEY] on 28 Jul 1880. Off: STENBERG. Wit: Jack NUGENT, Ella BROADHEAD.

McNAULTY, James S. [27; Omaha; b: Pennsylvania; f: James McNAULTY; m: Eliza DEVINE] md. Kate NOLAN [24; Omaha; b: Ireland; f: Charles NOLAN; m: Mary SCANALL] on 23 Jul 1879. Off: McCARTHY. Wit: Michael DWYER, Brigetta E. FORD.

McNEELY, Francis M. [25; Blair; b: IA; f: Hugh McNEELY; m: Emilie CARR] md. Wilimine FIBE [21; Blair; b: OH; f: Edward FIBE; m: Martha FIBE] on 5 Nov 1881. Off: STEWART. Wit: H.M. BOWEN, M.G. STEWART.

McNEIL, Patrick [23; Omaha; b: Providence, RI; f: James McNEIL; m: Ann NOLAN] md. Samantha ASHBURN [18; Florence; b: Illinois; f: Jesse ASHBURN; m: Almira GLASS] on 20 May 1870 at Florence. Off: STEPHENSEN. Wit: James HOLLAND, Florence; Charles DONK, Florence.

McNEIL, R.F. [23; Omaha; b: MI; f: Sylvester McNEIL; m: Benina MOOR] md. Maggie HOWER [19; Omaha; b: NE; f: Peter HOWER; m: Phoebe LOW] on 20 Jul 1881. Off: INGRAM. Wit: T. SUDBOROUGH, Eva M. INGRAM.

McNELEIGH, Willis S. [25; Omaha] md. Mary J. O'GRADY [15; Omaha] on 4 Jun 1868. Off: SLAUGHTER. Wit: Mrs. ALDERSEN, Mrs. A.B. SLAUGHTER. Age consent given by the father of the bride.

McNERNY, Daniel [25; Douglas Co.] md. Margret WALSH [23; Douglas Co.] on 6 Jan 1866. Off: CURTIS. Wit: John CLIFFORD, Briget GARVEY.

McNULTY, John [26; Omaha] and Hanora QUINN [22; Omaha] license issued on 12 Oct 1867. No marriage record. Off: SHEEKS.

McPHERSON, Damost [28; DeSoto, Washington Co.; b: Canada East; f: William McPHERSON; m: Mathilde LeDUC] md. Adaline BEAVERS [21; DeSoto, Washington Co.; b: New York; f: Louis BEAVERS; Eugenie COURVISEE] on 26 Dec 1871. Off: TOWNSEND. Wit: A. McNEIL; James BELL.

McPHERSON, J.P. [25; Omaha] md. Mrs. Susannah SHULL [widow; Omaha] on 7 Aug 1861 at KUHNS' residence on Douglas St. Off: KUHNS. Wit: Mr. and Mrs. Joseph SHEELY, Mrs. H.W. KUHNS.

McQUADE, Felix [33; Omaha; b: Ireland; f: Patrick McQUADE; m: Rosa TRANNOR] md. Catharine HOUGH [26; Omaha; b: Ireland; f: Bernard HOUGH; m: Catharine FOLHAN] at St. Philomena's Church on 26 Oct 1879. Off: KELLY. Wit: William FITZPATRICK, Mary WILLIAMS.

McQUARRIE, John [32; Blair; b: Ireland; f: Charles McQUARRIE; m: Mary MATHEWSON] md. Maggie HIGGINS [20; Blair; b: Ireland; f: Theophilus HIGGINS; m: Caroline McCLEAN] on 17 May 1880. Off: BARTHOLOMEW. Wit: Max BERGMANN, John J. POUITS.

McSHANE, F.T. [25; Omaha; b: Ohio; f: Thomas McSHANE; m: Alice CREIGHTON] and Agnes O'CONNER [ 20; Omaha; b; Ireland; f: Charles O'CONNER; m: Johanna FLYNN] license issued on 21 Apr 1879. No marriage record. Off: BARTHOLOMEW.

McSHANE, John A. [25; Douglas Co.; b: OH, f: Thomas McSHANE; m: Alice CREIGHTON] md. Mary M. LEE [20; Douglas Co.; b: NY; f: John G. LEE; m: Margaret MANNAGAN] on 25 Arp 1876 at the Roman Catholic Cathedral. Off: BYRNE. Wit: Mathew McGINN, Burlington, IA, Alice CREIGHTON.

McWATERS, William H. [24; Omaha; b: Iowa; f: Charles H. McWATERS; m: Sarah ALBROW] md. Louise CEMMENSTEONE [20; Omaha; b: Illinois; f: Henry CEMMENSTEONE; m: Sarah N. RADAWAY] on 6 Jul 1880. Off: STENBERG. Wit: Wm. P. SNOWDEN, Mrs. Nellie HARRIS.

McWHINNEY, William [38; Douglas Co.; b: IA, f: William McWHINNEY; m: Elizabeth McDOWELL or McDOWD] and Mary E. GIBBONS [21; Douglas Co.; b: PA; f: Michael GIBBONS; m: Mary E.] license issued on 13 Mar 1876. No marriage record. Off: SEDGWICK.

McWINNIE, Frank [35; Omaha; b: Ireland; f: Michael McWINNIE; m: Mary DELANEY] and Mrs. Anna W. HUBBARD [40; Omaha; b: NY; f: Terence (Thomas crossed out); m: Ellen DOWN] license issued on 27 Jun 1881. No marriage record. Off: SMITH. Application signed by Max BERGMANN, N.P.

MEAD, J.W. [22; Sarpy Co.; b: IL; f: Augustus MEAD; m: Phebe E. WILLIAMSON] md. Mary J. MONAHAN [22; Sarpy Co.; b: NE; f: Bernard MONAHAN; m: Margaret HOWE] on 21 Feb 1881. Off: ENGLISH. Wit: Louis LESIEND, Papillion, Rose DORAN, Papillion.

MEANEY, Michael [23; Omaha] md. Bridget GARVEY [19; Omaha] on 16 Aug 1867. Off: O'GORMAN. Wit: John SULLIVAN, Honora QUINN.

MEANEY, Patrick B. [35; Omaha; b: Ireland; f: John MEANEY; m: Alice BUTLER] md. Mary HENSMAN [19; Omaha; b: England; f: George C. HENSMAN; m: Mercy WILCOX] on 25 Nov 1873. Off: PEABODY. Wit: Mrs. Mercy HENSMAN; Bernard DOYLE.

MECKGRAFF, Lewis [33; Douglas Co.] md. Catharina CLARK [28; Douglas Co.] on 23 Aug 1860. Off: ARMSTRONG. Wit: F. COUNT, John T. REDICK, Mr. SHEFIELD, et al.

MEDLOCK, George W. [21; Omaha; b: England; f: George MEDLOCK; m: Charlotte SHAFTERR] md. Susa GOLDEN [18; Omaha; b: Iowa; f: Joel GOLDEN; m: Elizabeth HENRY] on 1 Jun 1874. Off: STEWART. Wit: Mrs. Emily W. STEWART; Mrs. B.S. WALKER.

MEDSON, Frederick [29; Omaha; b: Denmark; f: Mads OLSEN; m: Hannah C. CHRISTIANSEN] md. Mary HANSEN [29; Omaha; b: Denmark; f: Hans ANDERSON; m: Mary HANSEN] on 24 Feb 1870. Off: GIBSON. Wit: Mrs. Fannie GODFREY; H.F. STRONG.

MEEHAN, Michael M. [23; Omaha; b: Canada; f: Patrick MEEHAN; m: Mary MURRY] md. Ellen D. ENRIGHT [20; Omaha; b: Ireland; f: Michael ENRIGHT; m: Ellen DILLON] on 4 Jun 1876 at the Roman Catholic Cathedral. Off: JENNETTE. Wit: Louis STENSEN, Mary MEEHAN.

MEEHAN, Patrick [35; Springfield, MA; b: Ireland; f: Patrick MEEHAN; m: Mary FLYNN] md. Catharine O'GRADY [30; Brooklyn, NY; b: Ireland; f: James O'GRADY; m: Margaret MEEHAN] on 26 July 1872. Off: CURTIS. Wit: James ROACH; Omaha, pro tem; Mary QUINLAN, Omaha, pro tem.

MEEKER, Augustus [25; Tioga Co., NY] md. Kitty TURNER [18; Omaha] on 29 Apr 1869 at Trinity Church. Off: CLARKSON. Wit: Jesse TURNER, Mrs. TURNER, O.P. HURLBUT, et al.

MEEKS, Thomas J. [28; Omaha; b: Albany, NY; f: James MEEKS] md. Annie PFEIFFER [19; Omaha; b: St. Louis, MO; f: Francis PFEIFFER; m: Susan MADDOX] on 28 Jan 1871. Off: KUHNS. Wit: Dr. Theodore BAUMER; Max MEYER.

MEERHOLZ, Herman [42; Omaha Barracks; b: Germany; f: Bernard MEERHOLZ; m: Eva MAINZ] md. Mrs. Eliza MOYLAN [40; Omaha Barracks; b: Ireland; f: B. CANAVAN] on 28 Mar 1878. Off: HARSHA. Wit: Mrs. W.J. HARSHA, Matildla MURRY (her mark).

MEGEATH, Samuel A. [26; Omaha] md. Judith W. CARTER [23; Omaha] on 19 Apr 1859. Off: WATSON. Wit: Wm. FRICKE.

MEHREN, Charles [25; Omaha; b: Germany; f: Henry MEHREN; m: Mary Ann ROHRIG] md. Elizabeth GURNEY [23; Omaha; b: England; f: George GURNEY; m: Annie RIEDEL] on 9 Oct 1873. Off: PORTER. Wit: Julius MEYER; Hugo HATT.

MEIDLINGER, Johann [22; Omaha; b: Hungary; f: Matthias MEIDLINGER; m: Theresia OSWALD; md. Katharina SCHUSTER [19; Omaha; b: Hungary; f: Matthias SCHUSTER; m: Theresia KRASI] on 22 May 1881 in the German Catholic Church. Off: GROENEBAUM. Wit: Charles KOHLMEYER, Mrs. Eva KOHLMEYER.

MEIDLINGER, John [24; Omaha; b: Hungary; f: Paul MEIDLINGER; m: Maria] md. Julia BERTENLEHNER [20; Omaha; b: Hungary. f: Albert BERTENLEHNER; m: Theresa WACHTER] on 30 Oct 1881 at St. Mary Magdalene's Church. Off: GLAUBER. Wit: Charles KOHLMEYER, Eva KOHLMEYER.

MEIS, Joseph [32; Omaha] md. Elizabeth ENENBAG [19; Omaha] on 4 Feb 1867. Off: HASCALL. Wit: Frank MURPHY, Ben SHEEKS.

MELDRUM, Thomas [25; Omaha] md. Jenny H.P. FLEMING [16; Omaha] on 24 Apr 1868. Off: PALMER. Wit: William FLEMING, Miss M. McALLEN, Mrs. M.B. PALMER, et al. Age consent given by the father of the bride.

MELIA, Michael [21; Sarpy Co.] md. Kate McCANNEY [18, Omaha] on 2 Jul 1864 at FACKLER's residence in Sarpy Co. Off: FACKLER. Wit: Thomas WILSON of Sarpy Co., Mrs. Jacob FACKLER of Sarpy Co.

MELLONE, Thomas [27; Omaha; b: Ireland; f: Michael MELLONE; m: Ellen RILEY] md. Mary MURRAY [23; Omaha; b: Canada; f: James MURRAY; m: Bridget FITGERALD] on 29 Oct 1879. Off:

McCARTHY. Wit: Thomas BRENNAN, Susan McHALE.

MELLUS, Richart T. [28; Omaha; b: Maine; f: John MELLUS; m: Emily AVERELL] md. Anna BLACKWOOD [19; Omaha; b: St. Louis, MO; f: Joseph BLACKWOOD; m: Hannah COLLINS] on 28 May 1872. Off: McCAGUE. Wit: E.M. SHIPMAN; Mrs. Sarah MELLUS.

MELQUIST, John A. [37; Omaha; b: Sweden; f: Anders ANDERSON; m: Eva ANDERSON] md. Christine J. SANDBERG [27; Omaha; b: Sweden; f: P. SANDBERG; m: Josephine SANDBERG] on 24 Nov 1881. Off: PETERSON. Wit: J.P. LNYGG, Henry OAK.

MENGEL, George [22; Omaha; b: Prussia; f: Jacob MENGEL; m: Mary MAURER] md. Annie BITTNER [22; Omaha; b: Prussia; f: William BITTNER] on 16 Sep 1870. Off: LARSON. Wit: Otis E. MASON; Martin PETTER.

MENTER, Charles J. [25; Omaha; b: New York; f: Chester MENTER; m: Wealthy COVEY] md. Martha E. McELHANY [28; Omaha; b: Ohio] on 3 Oct 1872. Off: GUE. Wit: Mrs. Ann E. WITHROW, Canton, OH; Mrs. Eliza WITHROW.

MENTZ, George [30; Omaha Barracks; b: Germany; m: Anna] md. Hattie E. MACHIN [21; Boone County; b: Iowa; f: Joseph MACHIN; m: Martha E. MACHIN] on 16 Jul 1878. Off: HICKOX. Wit: J.R. WHEELER, G.W. HICKOX.

MERCER, William [24; Douglas Co.] md. Martha COY [18; Douglas Co.] on 24 Apr 1868 at Primrose. Off: DENTON.

MERGEN, John [26; Council Bluffs] md. Catharine KEIRCH [23; Council Blufs] on 2 Nov 1866. Off: HASCALL. Wit: Nicholas MERGEN, P. MERGEN.

MERGEN, Nicholas [Omaha] md. Bridget DISCH [Omaha] on 17 Jan 1865 at the Catholic Church of Omaha. Off: DAXACHER.

MERGEN, Philip [27; Omaha; b: Luxembourgh, GER; f: Peter MERGEN; m: Mary SAGRE] md. Waldburga DECH on 4 Nov 1871 (German Catholic Church crossed out). Off: GROENEBAUM. Wit: John MERGEN, Council Bluffs; Ellen KIVSOHT, Council Bluffs.

MERRIAM, Lewis, Jr. [32; Halton, ME; b: Halton, ME; f: Lewis MERRIAM; m: Mary A. FOSS] md. Annie BURNHAM [22; Douglas Co.; b: PA; f: Horace B. BURNHAM; m: Ruth A. JACKSON] on 7 Aug 1876. Off: CLARKSON. Wit: Horace B. BURNHAM, Frederick H. DAVIS.

MERRILL, Richard H. [25; Omaha; b: Ireland; f: Edmund MERRILL; m: Bridget SHIELDS] md. Mary McHUGH [23; Omaha; b: Ireland] on 13 Jun 1870. Off: CLARKSON. Wit: Mrs? Elizabeth BUTTERFIELD; Miss

S.E. VAN PATTEN; Rev. Dr. A.W. CHASE, Nebraska City; Mrs. R.H. CLARKSON.

MERRITT, John [40: Omaha; b: London, England; f: Samuel MERRITT; m: Phoebe ARMSTRONG] md. Caroline ROSENTHAL [23; Omaha; b: Germany; f: Jacob ROSENTHAL; m: Dena GOODMAN] on 12 Nov 1874. Off: SHERRILL. Wit: Samuel REICHENBERG; Fanny REICHENBERG.

MERTON, J.H. [27; Omaha; b: Ohio; f: Oliver O. MERTON; m: Chloe Ann BECKETT] md. Ellen GOLDEN [18; Omaha; b: Iowa; f: George GOLDEN; m: Eliza WILLIAMS] on 22 Mar 1880. Off: BARTHOLOMEW. Wit: Max BERGMANN, Osso or Odso RITTER.

MERTSHEIMER, Frederick [27; Omaha; b: Ohio; f: Frederick MERTSHEIMER; m: Margaret GAES] md. Marion L. BALDWIN [23; Omaha; b: Ohio; f: Charles A. BALDWIN; m: Marion GRIDLEY] on 12 Nov 1874. Off: SHERRILL. Wit: C.A. BALDWIN; Champion S. CHASE.

MERZ, Adam [26; Omaha; b: Germany; f: Peter MERZ; m: M. GRAF] md. Elisa MARTI [35; Omaha; b: Switzerland; f: U. BRIEDERMAN; m: Magdalena BRICHBITHAL] on 22 May 1877. Off: WEISS. Wit: Fred SCHIESS.

MESSERSMITH, Earnest [25; Omaha; b: Germany; f: Henry MESSERSMITH; m: Augusta BENEWAYS] md. Josephine MESSERSMITH [21; Omaha; b: Wisconsin; f: George MESSERSMITH; m: Engle HELMKE] on 22 Mar 1873. Off: LYTLE. Wit: Henry MESSERSMITH; M.L. PECK, Florence.

METCALF, John N. [26; Omaha; b: Iowa; f: Henry O. METCALF; m: Mary FLEMING] md. Julia E. MAGUIRE [19; Omaha; b: Wisconsin; f: Patrick MAGUIRE; m: Katy MAGRATH] on 11 Feb 1872 at O'GORMAN's house. Off: O'GORMAN. Wit: Patrick McCLUNE; Mary L. KINEL.

METCALF, John N. [32; Omaha; b: Iowa; f: H.O. METCALF; m: Mary A. FLEMING] md. Kate B. CALDWELL [18; Omaha; b: Iowa; f: John CALDWELL; m: Matilda McCRILLIS] on 8 Jul 1877. Off: WEISS. Wit: J. BOYD, Jennie CALDWELL.

METCALF, Zachary T. [24; Omaha; b: Bloomington, Il; f: John S. METCALF; m: Emily FLETCHER] and Mary LITTLE [18 (on 17 Apr 1873); Omaha; b: Chicago, IL; f: George LITTLE; m: Annie ARMROD] license issued on 27 Oct 1873. Off: TOWNSEND.

METZ, Phillip [Omaha] md. Josephine BECHER [Omaha] on 25 May 1864. Off: HOFFMAN. Wit: Gustavus BECHER, William DOLL.

METZGER, Edward [46; Omaha; b: Switzerland; f: Adrian METZGER; m: Josepha LICET] md. Naomi A. HIENT [39; Omaha; b: Ohio; f: Enish MATSON; m: Mary DEALEY] on 6 Jan 1870. Off: GIBSON. Wit: Seward B. DAVIS; Nicholas DANECKER.

METZLER, Alvin [27; Omaha; b: Pennsylvania; f: John METZLER; m: Jennie HEILMANN] and Mary PROGER [23; Omaha; b: Council Bluffs, IA; f: William PROGER; m: Lizzie CHIPLEY] license issued on 18 Aug 1879. No marriage record. Off: PEABODY.

MEYER, Arthur [24; Washington Co.; b: Switzerland; f: Jacob MEYER; m: Elizabeth FLUGEL] md. Elizabeth MUELLER [19; Washington Co.; b: Switzerland; f: Jacob MUELLER; m: Mary STRASSER] on 8 Jan 1881. Off: ANDERSON. Wit: Hermann J. MEYER, Emil MEYER.

MEYER, Henry [24; Omaha] md. Emma NEIGHLY [17; Omaha] on 9 Feb 1861 at the residence of the bride's parents. Off: MUHLENBROCK. Wit: Elizabeth FLUKY?, Henry REITZE, et al. Age consent given by Wm. NEIGHLY, father of the bride.

MEYER, Hermann J. [31; Omaha; b: Switzerland; f: Jacob MEYER; m: Alice FLUGEL] md. Margaretta JOCUMSEN [19; Douglas Co.; b: Denmark; f: Lars JOCUMSEN; m: Karen MADSEN] on 29 Jun 1872. Off: KUHNS. Wit: William T. SEAMAN; George DUVERNOY.

MEYER, Jacob [22; Omaha; b: Switzerland; f: Jacob MEYER; m: Barbara Von GUNTER] md. Fanny FISHER [20; Omaha; b: Wisconsin; f: John FISHER; m: Francisca SIEVERT] on 8 Dec 1879. Off: WEISE. Wit: Charles FISHER, Laura FISHER.

MEYER, Joseph [37; Omaha; b: Ohio; f: Anthony MEYER; m: Barbara GATES] md. Bertha HERRING [30; Omaha; b: Germany; f: Ferdinand HERRING; m: Augusta POHL] on 15 Sep 1874. Off: PEABODY. Wit: E.F. SMYTHE; John D. HANE.

MEYER, Louis C. [25; Omaha; b: Germany; f: Conrad MEYER; m: Elizabeth K A N I M E Y E R] m d. Margaret TROWBRIDGE [20; Omaha; b: WV; f: David B. TROWBRIDGE; m: Mary SNYDER] on 20 Aug 1876. Off: BENEKE. Wit: Gust WECKBACH, Adolph BUELER.

MEYERS, Emanuel [54; Omaha; b: MD; f: Peter E. MEYERS; m: Elizabeth ERB] md. Mrs. Sarah Ann SNYDER [31; Omaha; b: MD; f: Samuel SHILT; m: Mary Ann YEGELEIN] on 18 Jan 1875. Off: DIECKMANN. Wit: Fr. DIECKMANN, Bertha FECHNER.

MEYERS, Jacob [36; Douglas Co.] md. Mrs. Mary MILLER [35; Omaha] on 31 Aug 1868. Off: KELLEY. Wit: R.J. STUCK, J.A. TOOKER.

MICHEL, Francis [27] md. Elizabeth ROBERTS [20] on 20 or 29 Jan 1857 at the house of James ROBERTS. Off: MITCHEL. Age consent given by Samuel L. DIGGELS.

MICHEL, Heinrich [26; Omaha; b: Germany; f: Johann MICHEL; m: Anna Katharina TORDTE] md. Louise SCHULZ [26; b: Germany; f: Friederich SCHULZ; m: Ernestine SIEBERT] on 23 Mar 1881. Off: BENEKE. Wit: Lina RAY, E. RAUSCH.

MICHELL, John [50; Burt Co.] md. Joanne Christina Friederike CASTDORF [34 or 39; Burt Co.] on 30 Aug 1867 at KUHNS residence. Off: KUHNS. Wit: Mr. and Mrs. John BLEICK, et al.

MICHELSEN, Charles O. [24; Omaha; b: Denmark; f: John MICHELSEN; m: Christine DUVALL] md. Minnie E. LYNCH [23; Omaha; b: New York; f: James H. LYNCH; m: Mary HANRAHAN] on 14 Nov 1880. Off: ENGLISH. Wit: J.H. LYNCH, Susan LYNCH.

MICHELSON, Anton [24; Omaha; b: Denmark; f: Michal FRANSON; m: Christina LENSEN] md. Elizabeth HUNTER [22; Omaha; b: Scotland; f: William HUNTER; m: Margaret WEDDLE] on 23 Jul 1870. Off: KUHNS. Wit: Minnie CALLAHAN; Peter MICHELSEN.

MICHELSON, Peter [40; Omaha; b: Denmark; f: Michael FRANDSEN; m: Christine NELSON] md. Emelie DANIELSEN [27; Omaha; b: Denmark; f: Peter DANIELSEN; m: Christianna JOHANNSON] on 18 Mar 1880. Off: GYDESEN. Wit: P. NIELSEN, C. LYSHOULDS.

MIDGLEY, Charles [40; Omaha; b: England; f: John MIDGLEY; m: Rebbaca] md. Elizabeth BERGO [24; Omaha; b: NY; f: Peter BERGO; m: Adeline BRENALL] on 8 Feb 1876. Off: SHERRILL. Wit: Mrs. A.F. SHERRILL, Mr. MINER.

MIES, Peter [30; Omaha; b: Prussia; f: Gottfred MIES; m: Lizzie SHEITZ] md. Elizabeth MILLER [25; Omaha; b: Prussia; f: John MILLER; m: Jedrid KNETTFRED] on 30 Apr 1870 at the German Catholic Church. Off: GROENEBAUM. Wit: Gottfred RUBHAUSEN; Mrs. Gertrud RUBHAUSEN.

MIKKELSON, Jens Larson [28; Omaha; b: Denmark; f: Michael J. MIKKELSON; m: Dorothia M. LARSON] md. Anna Botilda MIKKELSON [19; Omaha; b: Denmark; f: Casper MIKKELSON; m: Maria C. LORENSON] on 26 Nov 1870. Off: KUHNS. Wit: Peter C. CHRISTENSON; Paul THOMPSON.

MILBURN, Ralph J. [21; St. Joseph, MO] md. Margaret GOODMAN [22: Omaha] on 2

Feb 1868. Off: KELLEY. Wit: B.F. FRANKLIN, Ida MARTIN.

MILHUUS, Michael [35; Missouri Valley, IA; b: Norway; f: John MILHUUS; m: Marit SKARHEM] md. Mary KNUTSEN [26; Douglas Co.; b: Norway; f: Knud KNUTSEN; m: Kari JORGENSEN] on 11 Mar 1876. Off: SEDGWICK. Wit: O.S. WOOD, Douglas Co., Mary KNUTSEN, Douglas Co.

MILIANI, Giacomo [35; Omaha; b: Italy; f: Giacomo MILIANI; m: Katarina] md. Victoria WILBORN [22; Omaha; b: Missouri; f: George WILBORN; m: Elizabeth] on 21 Jan 1872. Off: BILLMAN. Wit: Mrs. Charles BILL(MILL?)MAN, et al; Mr. and Mrs. DENNIS.

MILIUS, Frederick [35; Omaha] md. Ida J.M. TREITSCHKE [24; Omaha] on 20 Mar 1869. Off: KUHNS. Wit: O.J. WILDE, John B. DETWILER, et al.

MILLER, Alexander [24; Omaha] md. Rose Hannah Mary DICKERSON [22; Omaha] on 7 Apr 1860 at BRIGGS' house. Off: BRIGGS. Wit: E.J. BRIGGS.

MILLER, Charles P. [22; Omaha; b: NY; f: T.F. MILLER; m: Jane P. HOLDEN] md. Nellie L. MORSE [22; Omaha; b: NH; f: C.C. MORSE; m: Lydia T. GOULD] on 23 Mar 1875. Off: PEABODY. Wit: O.F. DAVIS, Jas. M. WATSON.

MILLER, Chester [22; Omaha; b: Vermont; f: P. MILLER; m: Saloma LAROCK] md. Alberta OWENS [24; Omaha; b: Missouri; f: Young OWENS; m: Ann Elizabeth TRIVILLA] on 14 Oct 1880. Off: SHERRILL. Wit: Francis COLTON of Galesburg, Mrs. S.H.H. CLARK.

MILLER, Christian [30; Omaha; b: Germany; f: Detlef MILLER; m: Carolina RIEKEN] md. Wilhelmina GORTS [22; Omaha; b: Germany; f: Christian GORTS; m: Augusta BOWER] on 14 Nov 1870. Off: GIBSON. Wit: Charles N. RIEKEN; Christian RIEKEN.

MILLER, Eber S. [24; Omaha; b: Illinois; f: Bethuel MILLER; m: Amantha JORDAN] md. Mrs. Mahala ROBENSON, widow [24; Omaha; b: Kansas; f: John BANKS; m: Mariah BANKS] on 7 Nov 1873. Off: MEDLOCK. Wit: ---- MILLER; Mary P. DORK.

MILLER, Frederick [24; Elkhorn City; b: Germany; f: Frederick MILLER; m: Sophia REECE] md. Rachel BRANDUD [22; Elkhorn City; b: Germany; f: William BRANDUD] on 26 Feb 1870. Off: MORTON. Wit: G.M. McBAY; Mary Ann McBAY.

MILLER, George A. [23; Omaha] md. Mary N. WILLIAMSON [17; Omaha] at 7 A.M., Saturday, 19 Sep 1868 at OATHWAIT's residence. Off: DIMMICK. Wit: Mr. and Mrs. F.J. HECKER, Mr. and Mrs. Milton OATHWAIT, et al. Age consent given by the guardian of the bride.

MILLER, George [negro; 32; b: Missouri; f: Merrill MILLER] md. Maggie CRAIG [negro; 26; b: Missouri] on 25 Dec 1878. Off: PORTER. Wit: Jane WRIGHT, Emma HARRIS.

MILLER, H.F. [22; b: Illinois; f: Henry MILLER; m: Sophia STENKEL] md. Ella B. KENNELL [25; b: Ohio; f: Valentine KENNELL; m: Mary DOHN] on 13 Sep 1878. Off: BARTHOLOMEW. Wit: C. WARNER, Anna NICHOLS.

MILLER, Harry F. [26; Omaha; b: Illinois; f: John H. MILLER; m: Sophia STUENKEL] md. Mollie CAPPENHAN [29; Omaha; b: Germany; f: Ludwig CAPPENHAN; m: Wilhelmina KOKOLEES] on 27 Oct 1880. Off: BENEKE. Wit: Henry RAND, Emma MILLER.

MILLER, Harry L. [28; Omaha; b: New York City; f: Harry MILLER; m: Frances GORDON] md. Mattie A. SCOTT [22; Omaha; b: Luttson, MO; f: David SCOTT; m: Malinda JONES] on 19 May 1869. Off: KUHNS. Wit: James LESTER, Mary FORD.

MILLER, Henry H. [19; Douglas Co.] md. Nancy A. BUTTER [16; Douglas Co.] on 1 May 1867. Off: HASCALL. Wit: W.J. IRELAND, Harriet BURNHAM.

MILLER, Henry William [26; Douglas Co.; b: Milwaukee, WI; f: John MILLER; m: Sophia M. JOHNSON] md. Catharine McFARLAND [26; Nebraska City; b: Ireland; f: Andrew McFARLAND; m: Catharine McFARLAND] on 18 Jan 1872. Off: McCAGUE. Wit: Paul HARMAN; John McFARLAND, Nebraska City.

MILLER, James [39; Douglas Co.; b: Canada; f: Donald MILLER; m: Mary YORK] md. Mrs. Sarah FRULLER [30; Douglas Co.; b: Ohio; f: Henry KLINE; m: Elizabeth LEWIS] on 24 Jun 1880, Jefferson Precinct. Off: ----. Wit: Elmer E. SPENCER, of Irvington.

MILLER, John W. [23; b: Illinois; f: John H. MILLER; m: Mary BROWN] md. Mrs. Catherine CLARK [29; b: Missouri; f: George CLARK; m: Dora ROBINSON] on 4 Mar 1878. Off: MILLSPAUGH. Wit: Wm. SMITH, Mary HAYDEN.

MILLER, John [30; Omaha] md. Anna HUGHES [23; Omaha] on 16 Apr 1868. Off: KELLY. Wit: D. KULGHER, P. KEEFE.

MILLER, John [40; Omaha; b: Sweden; f: John JOHNSON; m: Carrie JOHNSON] md. Cecelia ANDERSON [28; Omaha; b: Sweden; f: Andrew SWANSON; m: Christine PETERSON] on 30 Jul 1881. Off:

STENBERG. Wit: Frank LINDBERG, Mrs. Martha LINDBERG.

MILLER, John [53; Greenwood Co., KS; b: IN; f: John MILLER; m: Abby NATHY] md. Mrs. Mildred S. FULLER [39; Woodford Co., KS; b: TN; f: Thomas H. PAYNE; m: Sarah PEAY] on 2 Oct 1876. Off: SEDGWICK. Wit: Alexander McCLELLAN, Lizzie PAGE.

MILLER, Joseph J. [25; Valley; b: PA; f: Alexander MILLER; m: Charlotte FINLAW] md. Maggie MITCHEL [22; Omaha; b: Ireland; f: James MITCHEL; m: Anna Bella CALHOUN] on 28 Jan 1875. Off: FITCH. Wit: Henry W. CROSSLE, Papillion View House, Henry KRUSE, Papillion.

MILLER, Peter Christian [40; Omaha; b: Denmark; m: Katria KERTMANN] md. Julia Augusta LUND [29; Omaha; b: Denmark; f: Ever Peter LUND: m: Mary E. FREDERICKSON] on 11 Apr 1872. Off: TOWNSEND. Wit: George ARMSTRONG; Chas. H. BYRNE.

MILLER, Ruches C. [28; Omaha; b: New York; f: Israel MILLER; m: Elizabeth MILLER] md. Ina L. BAKER [28; Omaha; b: Maine; f: Seba WHITCOME; m: Darras PIERCE] on 25 Sep 1869. Off: Wm. H. MORRIS. Wit: D.T. KIDD, Jas. W. SAVAGE.

MILLER, S.G. [35; Douglas Co.; b: Illinois; f: L. MILLER; m: E.E. CANNON] md. Mary J. MARTIN [35; Douglas Col; b: Missouri; f: Preston WORLEY; m: Sarah CAMES] on 4 Jun 1877. Off: PEABODY. Wit: Emmett B. KNOX, Hiram A. STRUGES.

MILLER, Samuel B. [27; Omaha] md. Cordelia M. JOHNSTON [31; Omaha] on 18 Aug 1867. Off: SHEEKS. Wit: James B. WILLIAMS, Eliza HAWKINS.

MILLER, Townsend H. [21; Glenwood, IA; b: Glenwood, IA; f: Michael MILLER; m: Martha A. JOHNSON] md. Lethe EDMUNDSON [22; Glenwood, IA; b: Glenwood, IA; f: James EDMUNDSON; m: Mary Ann TUMBLESON] on 29 Jan 1874. Off: ADAIR. Wit: Samuel H. SHEPARD; Mrs. J.M. ADAIR.

MILLER, William H. [26; Omaha; b: MI; f: John MILLER; m: Annie WACKER] md. Mary E. MADDEN [22; Omaha; b: Ireland; f: Michael MADDEN] on 33 Apr 1876 at the Bishop's House. Off: BOBAL. Wit: John MADDEN, Miss WHITESIDE.

MILLER, William [Omaha] and Catharine DAILY [Omaha] license issued on 4 Apr 1863. Both of legal age. Off: DICKINSON.

MILLS, Alex [40; Omaha; b: OH; f: Peter MILLS; m: Mary McLAIN] md. Sarah J. COCHAN [18; Omaha; b: IA; f: David FISHER; m: Nancy MORGAN] on 23 Dec 1875. Off: PEABODY. Wit: C.H. NICHOLS, Miner W. BRUCE, Creighton.

MILLS, Henry [27; Springfield, IL; b: NY; f: William H. MILLS; m: Adeline A. CUMMINGS] md. Mary FAWCETT [26; Omaha; b: Ireland; f: William FAWCETT; m: Eliza RODGERS] on 14 Jan 1875 at Mrs. FAWCETT's. Off: LEMON. Wit: Eliza FAWCETT, William FAWCETT.

MILLS, Morris [23; Laramie, WY; b: New York; f: William A. MILLS; m: Alice BROOKS] md. Florence M. BRACKIN [20; Omaha; b: Nebraska; f: John H. BRACKIN; m: Rebecca BRACKIN] on 3 Apr 1877. Off: SHERRILL. Wit: S. GIBSON, George MILLER.

MILLSPAUGH, Frank R. [33; Omaha; b: NY; f: Cornelius MILLSPAUGH; m: Elvira ROSEBROOK] md. Mrs. Mary HAMILTON [30; Omaha; b: IL; f: Robert CLARKSON; m: Meliora McPHERSON] on 20 Oct 1881. Off: CLARKSON. Wit: Mrs. Meliora CLARKSON, Joseph R. CLARKSON, Kirby MILLSPAUGH, Brainard, MN.

MILLUS [MILLER], Daniel C. [25; Omaha] and Sarah WISEMAN [16; Omaha] license issued on 3 May 1858. No marriage record. Off: PORTER. Age consent given by John MILLUS, guardian, for "miner (sic) above the age of 16 years)."

MINCH [WINCH], Christian md. Catherine HADEN on 16 Sep 1858. Off: PORTER.

MINOGUE, John [28; Omaha; b: Ireland; f: John MINOGUE; m: Margaret MAHAN] md. Hannah CAREY [19; Omaha; b: Illinois; f: Michael CAREY; m: Ellen SULLIVAN] on 17 Jul 1879. Off: McDERMOTT. Wit: Dominic COGAN, Annie LAWLOR.

MITCHEL, William H.H. [20; Omaha] md. Eliza Jane SHOEMAKER [18; Omaha] on 22 Nov 1860 at Mr. McGAVERN's residence on Harney St. Off: KUHNS. Wit: Robert MITCHEL, Ellen BROWN, et al. Age consent given by Robert MITCHEL, father of the groom.

MITCHELL, Charles [21; Omaha; b: OH; f: Benjamin MITCHELL; m: Mary THOMPSON] md. Carrie M. WOOD [23; Omaha; b: IL; f: David WOOD; m: Mary] on 22 Nov 1875. Off: DONNELLY. Wit: Jessie OSTERHAUS, Julia TIFFEY.

MITCHELL, Henry [colored; 26; Omaha] md. Amy ROBISON [colored; 27; Omaha] on 9 Dec 1866 in the colored church. Off: FLORKEE. Wit: the whole congregation.

MITCHELL, John [father from Irel.] md. Ellen MAHER [father from Irel.] on 26 Apr 1859 at St. Mary's Church. Off: CANNON. Wit: James HICKEY, Bridget HICKEY.

MITCHELL, Lawrence [23; Omaha] md. Mary RICE [17; Omaha] at 9:30 PM on 1 Apr 1866 at Chas. McGUIRE's residence. Off: DIMMICK. Wit: Mr. and Mrs. Robert MITCHELL, Mr. and Mrs. Charles McGUIRE, et al. Age consent given by the father of the bride.

MITES, Abraham Israel [26; Omaha; b: Poland; f: Israel MITES; m: Freda MITES] md. Cecelia ADLER [24; Omaha; b: Bohemia; f: M. ADLER; m: Lotta GOLDSCHEDEN] on 5 Dec 1870. Off: MORTON. Wit: Mrs. Lena GREAUBAUM; Mrs? Morris GREAUBAUM.

MIX, Eugene B. [36; Aurora, IL; b: Aurora, IL; f: Russel C. MIX; m: Sophronia EWELL] md. Fannie E. WOODWORTH [21; Aurora, IL; b: Aurora, IL; f: Lyman WOODWORTH; m: Latetia TANNER] on 7 Jul 1881. Off: SHERRILL. Wit: J.C. JONES, Mollie GALLAGHER.

MIZERA, Frank [22; Saunders Co.; b: Bohemia; f: Michael MIZERA; m: Josephine FRANA] md. Mary ANESOVCKY [Mary Anna SUCHY] [19; Saunders Co,; b: Bohemia; f: James ANESOVCKY [SUCHY]; m: Barbara] on 7 Jan 1873. Off: TOWNSEND. Wit: John MACH; Martin SVATNA [SVACINA].

MOBLEY, Seth P. [27; Grand Island; b: Washington Co., OH; f: John B. MOBLEY; m: Lucy A. PRATT] md. Mrs. Maggie T.G. EBERHART [23 or 24; Grand Island; b: Ireland; f: Daniel GUERIN; m: Maggie O'BRIEN] on 9 Dec 1871. Off: GASSMANN. Wit: Col. C.S. CHASE; Gov. Alvin SAUNDERS.

MOBURY, William [22; Bellevue, Sarpy Co.] md. Fanny E. STEPHENSON [21; Bellevue, Sarpy Co.] on 12 Jun 1868. Off: KUHNS. Wit: Mrs. H.W. KUHNS, Fanny BUTTERFIELD.

MOCKBEE, Charles E. [27; Omaha; b: IL; f: Richard MOCKBEE; m: Delia A. WHITNEY] md. Joanna DWIER [22; Omaha; b: In; f: John DWIER; m: Mary DEWIRE] on 21 Apr 1875. Off: BYRNE. Wit: Andrew BODEN, Katie HARNETTE.

MOCKELMANN, Andrew [29; Elkhorn Station, Douglas Co.; b: Germany; f: Nicholas MOCKELMANN; m: Maria HAGEMANN] md. Barbara MILLER [17; Elkhorn Station, Douglas Co.; b: Germany; f: Andrew MILLER; m: Johana GERBER] on 11 Mar 1878. Off: BENEKE. Wit: Wilhelm DOLL, George SCHMID. Age consent for bride given by Andrew MILLER.

MOE, Charles N. [34; Douglas Co.] md. Ellen HART [20; Douglas Co.] on 22 Nov 1861 at George W. CROWELL's residence. Off: ARMSTRONG. Wit: Mr. and Mrs. George W. CROWELL, Mrs. Henry CROWELL.

MOE, Hans Andreas [34; Omaha; b: Norway; f: Gulbran MOE; m: Annie NELSON] md. Annie JOHNSON [27; Omaha; b: Sweden; f: Jonas JOHNSON; m: Ingrid JOHANSON] on 18 Nov 1875. Off: HILMEN. Wit: R. BING, P.J. JOHNSON.

MOELLER, Fred (Fritz) [29; Douglas Co.; b: Germany; f: Charles MOELLER; m: Catharina BUELK] md. Katharina SCHEEL [19; Omaha; b: Germany; f: Joachim SCHEEL; m: Anna STENDER] on 23 Jul 1881. Off: BENEKE. Wit: Hans SCHERAGER, Washingon Co., Peter GOOS.

MOFFAT, John D. [29; Omaha] md. Mrs. Myra HILL [30; Omaha] on 21 Jan 1868. Off: KUHNS. Wit: Mrs. Rebecca TAYLOR, Mrs. H.W. KUHNS.

MOGENSEN, Soren Peter [23; Omaha; b: Denmark; f: Mogens SORENSEN; m: Maren RASMUSSEN] md. Anna LAURSEN [24; Omaha; b: Denmark; f: Laurs SORENSEN; m: Marek JOHANSEN] on 21 Mar 1873. Off: PORTER. Wit: Frederick CHRISTIANSEN; James H. THRANE.

MOHAN [MAHAN], Thomas [23; Council Bluffs] md. Honorah DOLAN [24; Council Bluffs] on 12 Sep 1859 at St. Mary's Church. Off: CANNON. Wit: James McKAIN, Mary LACY.

MOHR, Bernard M. [26; Blair; b: Germany; f: Jacob MOHR; m: Mathilda OLAND] md. Louisa C.M. MEYER [20; Blair; b: Germany; f: John MEYER; m: Caroline LOCKNER] on 15 May 1874. Off: PEABODY. Wit: Henry ROLLA; Julius KEYLER, Blair.

MOHR, Henry [28; Omaha; b: Germany; f: Frederick MOHR; m: Annie TIEDERMANS] md. Elizabeth PRENZ [29; Omaha; b: Germany; f: Charles PRENZ] on 22 Jul 1870. Off: KUHNS. Wit: Mrs. H.W. KUHNS; Annie CATHERWOOD.

MONAHAN, Hugh [38; Fremont Co, IA; b: Ireland; f: Timothy MONAHAN; m: Catharine DONOVAN] md. Elizabeth CRAIG [38; Omaha; b: Ireland; f: John CRAIG; m: Bridget GARAHAR] on 6 Feb 1876. Off: BOBAL. Wit: Patrick O'BYRNE, Kate O'BYRNE.

MONK, John S. [27; Onawa, IA; b: Kane Co., IL; f: Hugh MONK; m: Catherine SHERWIN] md. Ella M. SANFORD [17; Omaha; b: Illinois; f: S.H. SANFORD] on 11 May 1870. Off: RIPPEY. Wit: Mrs. and Mrs. S.H. SANFORD. Written age of consent given by father of the bride.

MONK, Peter C.F. [28; Omaha; b: Denmark; f: Sern MONK; m: Annie PETERSON] md. Kate Ann MOSSON [27; Omaha; b: Denmark; f: Mads NESSON; m: Enga M. PETERSEN] on 22 Oct 1870. Off: LARSON. Wit: Andrew STEPHENSEN; Dinis MULLER.

MONRO, John [29; Omaha; b: Scotland; f: John MUNRO; m: Marian STEVENSON] md. Mary E. MILLER [18; Omaha; b: Cincinnatti, OH; f: John MILLER; m: Margaret] on 15 Apr 1870. Off: KUHNS. Wit: W.H. FLORIDA; Mrs. Jane E. FLORIDA.

MONTAGUE, John [29; Omaha] md. Mary DORSEY [36; Omaha] on 3 Jan 1867 at the Catholic Church of Omaha. Off: O'GORMAN. Wit: Peter MALONE, Mary STRAIN.

MOON, Edwin [27; Council Bluffs] md. Margaret MORE [27; Council Bluffs] on 1 Aug 1867. Off: HASCALL. Wit: H.J. RUNNELLS, Angeline SMITH.

MOON, George [40; Omaha; b: Alabama; f: Hill MOON] md. Sarah EMERY [30; Omaha; b: Missouri] on 21 Jun 1870. Off: PORTER. Wit: J.T. GOVE; Charles PARKER.

MOORE, C.A. [35; Omaha; b: New York; f: Clayton MOORE; m: Mary CLARK] md. Kate SEWARD [24; Omaha; b: Ohio; f: Albert SEWARD; m: Mary CREMER] on 12 Nov 1880. Off: MAXFIELD. Wit: M. RIGGS, Cyrus ROSE.

MOORE, Edward C. [23; Omaha; b: Davenport, IA; f: Patrick MOORE; m: Mary McLAUGHLIN] md. Elizabeth TONER [23; Omaha; b: Ireland; f: Francis TONER; m: Anna HUGHES] on 28 Apr 1881 at First Philomena's Church. Off: ENGLISH. Wit: Patrick TONER, Anna MOORE. Filed 12 Jun 1882 by CHADWICK.

MOORE, Fred [30; Ford, Holt Co., NE; b: NY; f: Linus MOORE; m: Jane DOREMUS] md. Ella A. HUNTER [23; Oil City, PA; b: PA; f: James M. HUNTER; m: Mary STOUGHTON] on 30 Mar 1881. Off: JAMESON. Wit: P.A. LARGEY, Montana, Miss M. CREIGHTON.

MOORE, George P. [25; Omaha; b: New York; f: Russell MOORE; m: Hannah WEBB] md. Anna L. RILEY [20; Omaha; b: Missouri; f: J.E. RILEY; m: Rachel BUCKLEY] on 21 Jul 1880. Off: MILLSPAUGH. Wit: J.E. RILEY, Rachel RILEY.

MOORE, Hugh [37; Newport, KY; b: England; f: Robert MOORE; m: Helene WHITE] md. Lavinia HAINSWORTH [29 (35 crossed out); Omaha; b: England; f: James HAINSWORTH; m: Mary HURST] on 22 Nov 1881. Off: MILLSPAUGH. Wit: M. BECKLE, Minnie HAINSWORTH.

MOORE, J.R. [38; Union Precinct; b: Ohio; f: James B. MOORE; m: Margaret SPRECHER] md. Grace M. BURGMAN [16; Union Precinct; b: Nebraska; f: J.W. BURGMAN; m: Nancy M. THOMAS] on 15 Oct 1879. Off: BARTHOLOMEW. Wit: F.R. WOOLEY, C.E. WOOLEY, both of Union Precinct. Age consent given by J.W. BURGMAN, father of the bride.

MOORE, Richard [27; b: Ireland; f: John MOORE; m: Ellen BURNS] md. Mary TOYE [22; b: Canada; f: Thomas TOYE; m: Julia LYONS] on 30 May 1878. Off: SHAFFEL. Wit: Thomas TOYE, Agnes RYAN.

MORAN, Michael [35; Omaha; b: Ireland; f: James MORAN; m: Nappy KELLEY] md. Delia McINERNEY [22; Omaha; b: Ireland; f: Michael McINERNEY; m: Eliza BURKE] on 30 May 1875. Off: MALLOY. Wit: M.C. CAPPOCK, Nellie CREW.

MORE, George [24; Omaha] and Sarah CARTER [20; Omaha] license issued on 29 Mar 1861. No marriage record. Off: ARMSTRONG.

MORE, Jacob [Kelly Precinct?, Douglas Co.] md. Lydia THOMAS [Kelly Precinct?, Douglas Co.] on 23 Mar 1865 at Farnham House. Off: DICKINSON. Wit: Henry NYE, Esther THOMAS, et al.

MORFORD, James H. [22; Washington Co.; b: Pennsylvania; f: A.T. MORFORD; m: Jane McGREW] md. Mary E. HARRISON [20; Washington Co.; b: Canada] on 6 Nov 1869. Off: GIBSON. Wit: Charles HASKINS, W.J. McLEAN of Blair.

MORFORD, William N. [21; b: Pennsylvania; f: Abner T. MORFORD; m: Esther J. McGREW] md. Martha E. OGDEN [17; b: Kentucky; f: James OGDEN; m: Eliza E. JILLETTE] on 21 Feb 1878. Off: BARTHOLOMEW. Wit: James OGDEN. Age consent given by James OGDEN, father of the bride.

MORGAN, Patrick C. [35; Omaha] md. Ellen MOONEY [23; Omaha] on 5 Jun 1868 at the Catholic Church. Off: O'GORMAN. Wit: John RUSH, Mary MOONEY.

MORIARTY, Timothy [27; Omaha; b: Ireland; f: Michael MORIARTY; m: Mary MALONEY] md. Margaret BOYLE [26; Omaha; b: Ireland; f: Michael BOYLE; Mary ERGGEN] on 28 Oct 1872. Off: CURTIS. Wit: Jeremiah CRONAN; Nora BOYLE.

MORITZ, Anton [31; Omaha; b: Germany; f: Jacob MORITZ; m: Louise MEIER] md. Louise PFLEIDARER [30; Omaha; b: Germany; f: Jacob PFLEIDARER; m: Anna FRODEL] on 19 Nov 1881. Off: BENEKE. Wit: Paul PLATZ, Jos. BIESENDORFER.

MORITZ, John [30; Omaha; b: Germany; f: Casper MORITZ; m: Mary LODZ] md. Mrs. Mary IECHELL [30; Omaha; b: Germany; f: Heinrich SCHWAB; m: Rosina M. BOHN] on 22 Jul 1875. Off: BENEKE. Wit: Henry VOFR, Henry HEINIECKE.

MORLEY, George [49; Lincoln; b: Canada; f: Nathaniel MORELY; m: Sarah KINGSHOT] md. Mrs. Charlotte STEWART [38; Lincoln; b: England; f: Daniel PARRY; m: Margaret EADEN] on 20 Aug 1874. Off: PEABODY. Wit: Charles C. PARRY; Joseph E. PARRY, Seward Co.

MORLEY, Patrick [28; Omaha] md. Elizabeth DOULAUGHTY [32; Omaha] on 10 Jan 1869. Off: HYDE. Wit: Andrew ROSEWATER, C.D. HYDE.

MORLEY, William R. [25; New Mexico Terr.; b: Massachusetts; f: Francis A. MORLEY; m: Dorcas S. SMITH] md. Ada McPHERSON [19; Council Bluffs; b: Iowa; f: Marquis S. McPHERSON; m: Mary TIBBALLS] on 26 Jan 1872. Off: BRESEE. Wit: Dr. Joseph CUNNINGHAM, Council Bluffs; Mary HANKINSON, Council Bluffs.

MORONEY (MORONY), Edward [33; Omaha; b: Ireland; f: Edward MORONEY (MORONY); m: Christiana OSBORNE] md. Isabella Wilhelmina SWART [18; Omaha; b: London, Canada West; f: Thomas SWART; m: Charlotte GRATIOT] on 22 Feb 1870 at St. Mark's Church. Off: RIPPEY. Wit: Mr. and Mrs. James ROSE. Age of consent, "James ROSE and Elizabeth ROSE give consent for our sister Isabella Wilhelmina SWART... at present under our control and guardianship", witness, H.G. CLARK.

MORONEY, John [25; Omaha; b: Ireland; f: Stephen MORONEY; m: Margaret NAGLE] md. Annie RILEY [23; Omaha; b: Ireland; f: Brien RILEY; m: Mary] on 20 May 1872 at St. Philomena Church. Off: KELLEHER. Wit: Michael LEAHEY; Anna LEAHEY.

MORONEY, William [28; Omaha; b: Ireland; f: Stephen MORONEY; m: Margaret NAGLE] md. Margaret L. O'SULLIVAN [22; Omaha; b: New York] on 13 Jun 1872 at the Catholic Church of Omaha. Off: O'GORMAN. Wit: Martin KENNY; Bridget MALONEY.

MORRELL, John [32; Omaha; b: Maine; f: Levi MORRELL; m: Lois DEERING] md. Florence OSTROM [18; Omaha; b: New York; f: A.S. OSTROM; m: Lois WEIBKE] on 29 Feb 1872 at the 2nd M.E. Church. Off: SHINN. Wit: Ella CAMPBELL; M.G. McKOON.

MORRIS, A.D. [32; Omaha; b: OH; f: Joseph MORRIS; m: Maria PIERSON] md. Kitty BROFEE [22; Omaha; b: MI; f: James BROFEE; m: Cordelia A. LACEY] on 19 Dec 1876. Off: FISHER. Wit: W.R. BARTLETT, Sarah F. BARTLETT.

MORRIS, Abraham [27; Omaha; b: Poland; f: Moses MORRIS] md. Cecelia LAVINE [26; Omaha; b: Germany; f: Isaac LAVINE] on 29 May 1876 at CAMP's office.

Off: CAMP. Wit: J.F. MORTON, Dr. B.F. PENDRY.

MORRIS, John H. [44; Douglas Co.; b: Kentucky; f: Garry MORRIS; m: Eliabeth ORSBORN] md. Mrs. Sarah KITCHEL [22; Douglas Co.; b: Illinois; f: Elias HARTFORD; m: Rachel LAMB] on 17 Jul 1871 at Iron Bluffs School House. Off: ADRIANCE. Wit: William MORRIS, Douglas Co.; Sophia MORRIS, Douglas Co.

MORRIS, John [40; Page Co., IA] and Mary WELSH [27; Page Co., IA] license issued on 24 Nov 1859. Off: ARMSTRONG.

MORRISON, Hector F. [45; Cleveland, OH; b: Scotland; f: Roderick MORRISON; m: Ann FRASER] md. Ann McLEAN [30; Cleveland, OH; b: Scotland; f: Laughlin McLEAN; m: Barbara McLEAN] on 22 Oct 1870. Off: GIBSON. Wit: W.I. BAKER; W.H. CADER.

MORRISON, J.W. [35; Omaha; b: Maryland; f: Elijah S. MORRISON; m: Angeline STANSBURY] md. Anna M. ROGERS [24; Omaha; b: Iowa; f: Samuel ROGERS; m: Fanny KNIGHT] on 14 Oct 1880. Off: MAXFIELD. Wit: W.A. MORRISON, Mary GETSCHMANN.

MORRISON, John P. [32; Traer, IA; b: Canada; f: James MORRISON; m: Christina SMILEY] md. Williamina A. COPELAND [26; Oakland, CA; b: Canada; f: Alexabder COPELAND; m: Anna ANDERSON] on 23 Dec 1875. Off: STEWART. Wit: Mrs. Emily W. STUART, Mary MEEHAN.

MORRISON, Morris [24; Omaha] md. Linnie OLSEN [17; Omaha] on 14 Jan 1869. Off: KUHNS. Wit: Andrew BURG, Ola OLSEN, et al.

MORRISON, William [46; Sarpy Co.; b: Ireland; f: John MORRISON; m: Elizabeth KELLEY] md. Emily PETERSON [18; Sarpy Co.; b: Utah Territory; f: Bert PETERSON; m: Mary EVERSON] on 20 Sep 1880. Off: BARTHOLOMEW. Wit: Wm. L. PEABODY, Wm. J. CONNELL.

MORRISSEY, Patrick H. [33; Omaha; b: Ireland; f: John MORRISSEY; m: Mary HUSSEY] md. Mrs. Amanda KEEP [41; Omaha; b: Philadelphia, PA; f: Peter FREEZE; m: Jane McMULLEN] on 5 Sep 1874. Off: PEABODY. Wit: Maria FEE; Amanda DARLING.

MORROW, James [30; Iowa; b: Pennsylvania; f: Hugh MORROW; m: Ellen BLOCH] md. Emely PALMER [18; Iowa; b: Iowa; f: Elisha PALMER; m: Nancy HILL] on 6 Dec 1870. Off: GIBSON. Wit: J.S. SPAUM; Thomas MULCAHY.

MORROW, Patrick [25; Omaha; b: Ohio; f: Michael MORROW; m: Ann CONNORS] md. Rachel BROMAAN or Regina BROMENN [22; Omaha; b: Canada; f: Ignatius BROMAAN] on 19 Nov 1874 at the German Catholic Church. Off: GROENEBAUM. Wit: John EDGAR; John BYERS.

MORSE, Herman [65; Buchannan, IA: b: Massachusetts; f: Herman MORSE; m: Susan BARDWELL] md. Mrs. Betsey N. HATCH [52; Buchannan, IA; b: Woodstock, VT; f: Levi BILLINGS; m: Ruth SHERMAN] on 1 Nov 1873. Off: McDONALD. Wit: W.H. BROWN; Walter NOTEWARE.

MORSE, William V. [27; Omaha; b: Nova Scotia; f: C.C. MORSE; m: Francis SANGSTER] md. Emma R. LEHMER [24; Omaha; b: Pennsylvania; f: Wm. LEHMER; m: Elizabeth STOKES] on 4 Feb 1874. Off: STEWART. Wit: William LEHMER; G.F. LEHMER.

MORTLEY, James A. [27; Utica, NY; b: Utica, NY; f: James A. MORTLEY; m: Orphia H. ALLEN] md. Monellah JACKSON [22; Des Moines, IA; b: Illinois; f: John JACKSON; m: Sophia] on 28 Apr 1877. Off: WEISS. Wit: OSTERLUND.

MORTON, Charles [24; Ogallala; b: Denmark; f: Jens Peter MORTON; m: Birgitt HOFF] md. Hannah JOHNSON [23; Omaha; b: Denmark; f: Henry JOHNSON; m: Johanna Maria JEPSEN] on 12 Nov 1873. Off: LIPE. Wit: John MAY; Emma HANSON.

MORTON, Frank S. [25; Omaha; b: Newfoundland; f: John T. MORTON; m: Elizabeth MEENEY] md. Mrs. Elizabeth WILLIAMS [23; Omaha; b: Tennessee; f: Perry DOUGHERTY; m: Mary BROADY] on 26 Mar 1872. Off: ESTABROOK. Wit: J.H. SMITH; Harriet SMITH.

MORTON, James F. [53; Omaha; b: Ohio; f: Thomas MORTON; m: Sarah CLARK] md. Mary G. RUSSELL [49; Omaha; b: Maine; f: David DYER; m: Abigail GRENDALL] on 1 Jul 1877. Off: SHERRILL. Wit: E.D. McLAUGHLIN, Thomas MULCAHY.

MORTON, Joy [24; Chicago; b: Michigan; f: J. Sterling MORTON m: Caroline JOY] md. Carrie J. LAKE [23; Omaha; b: Michigan; f: George B. LAKE; m: Jane POPPLETON] on 23 Sep 1880, Trinity Cathedral. Off: CLARKSON. Wit: Hon. Geo. B. LAKE and wife, Hon. J. Sterling MORTON and wife, of Nebraska City.

MORWINKEL [MOWINKEL], John [27; Sarpy Co.; b: Germany; f: Henry MORWINKEL [MOWINKEL]; m: unknown] md. Anna JOHNSON [16; Sarpy Co.; b: Pennsylvania; f: John JOHNSON; m: Mary GIBS] on 22 Dec 1880. Off: BARTHOLOMEW. Wit: Max BERGMANN, Wm. L. PEABODY.

MOSCRIP, Robert J. [29; Belleview; b: Canada; f: Robert MOSCRIP; m: Eliza FAIRFIELD] md. Emma SLIGHTAM [19; Belleview; b: Wisconsin; f: William SLIGHTAM; m: Emma C. ELCOCK] on 28 Mar 1874. Off: HENNEY. Wit: Hattie MOSCRIP; William CALLAWAY.

MOTLEY, John F. [Council Bluffs] md. Ellen M. WITTUM [Council Bluffs] on 8 Sep 1864 at Frank LEFFERT's residence. Off: DICKINSON. Wit: Mr. and Mrs. Frank LEFFERT, Mrs. Herman LEFFERT.

MOUNT, David T. [Omaha] md. Lizzie A. WINSHIP [Omaha] on 31 Jan 1865 at the Lutheran parsonage. Off: KUHNS. Wit: Mrs. H.W. KUHNS, Mrs. A.D. JONES.

MOUNTAIN, James H. [34; Omaha; b: PA; f: James MOUNTAIN; m: Savilla MADDEN] md. Anna O'ROURKE [22; Omaha; b: OH; f: Michael O'ROURKE; m: Catharine HUNT] on 5 Jan 1875. Off: GATES. Wit: J.H. BRACKEN, E.D. HUSTES.

MOUNTAIN, Moses [27; Sarpy Co., NE; b: Illinois; f: John MOUNTAIN; m: Lizzie FAGUE] md. Josephine DALE [22; Sarpy Co., NE; b: Missouri; f: John DALE] on 31 May 1877. Off: PEABODY. Wit: Mary TUCKER; Mabel PEABODY.

MOURER, Nicholas [26; Harrison Co., IA] md. Elizabeth BABB [17; Harrison Co., IA] on 20 Jan 1869. Off: KELLEY. Wit: D.B. TOPHAM, M. HELLMAN.

MOWERS, Ira (Jacob) [26; Saunders Co.; b: New York; f: Jacob MOWERS; m: Ruth LIVINGSTON] md. Emma A. CLEGG [22; Omaha; b: Virginia; f: Isaac CLEGG; m: Susan C. RUSSELL] on 6 Feb 1871. Off: STEWART. Wit: Isaac CLEGG and wife, Ida CLEGG; et al.

MOXHAM, Benjamin [24; Omaha; b: England; f: Samuel MOXHAM; m: Jane] md. Lizzie Ann McGEE [19; Omaha; b: Maryland; f: Daniel K. McGEE: m: Ann] on 27 Jun 1874. Off: PEABODY.

MOXHAM, Benjamin [28; b: England; f: Samuel MOXHAM; m: Jane MANNING] md. Louisa MORRIS [20; b: Illinois; f: Ben. MORRIS; m: Emma STILTS] on 6 Feb 1878. Off: JAMESON. Wit: Sam M. MOXHAM, S.A. ROBERSON.

MOXHAM, Samuel [27; Omaha; b: England; f: Samuel MOXHAM; m: Jane ANNING] md. Ellen M. ROBERSON [19; Omaha; b: IA; f: William ROBERSON; m: Roxena CLINKENBEARD] on 6 May 1875. Off: WRIGHT. Wit: Sylvester ROBERSON, Josephine ROBERSON.

MUCKLEY, John [34; Omaha; b: England; f: John MUCKLEY; m: Sarah FOSTER] md. Molly JOHNSON [34; Omaha; b: England; f: William JOHNSON] on 17 Feb 1871. Off: KELLEY. Wit: W.H. LAWTON; J.H. WEBBER.

MUELLER, Carl F.A. [30; 0maha; b: Germany; f: Friedrich MUELLER; m: Sophie REINBOHT] md. Emma LIEFFERS [23; Omaha; b: Germany; f: Johann LIEFFERS; m: Johanne Doris RODEMANN] on 12 Aug 1879. Off: FRESE. Wit: F.C. FESTNER, Mrs. Pauline HIENTZE.

MUELLER, Johann [24; Ogden, Boone Co., IA; b: Germany; f: Johann MUELLER; m: Maria NEVE] md. Catharine BOETEL [24; Douglas Co.; b: Germany; f: Hans BOETEL; m: Catharine GOSCH] on 24 Aug 1880. Off: BARTHOLOMEW. Wit: Claus SIEVERS, Hans ROHWER, both of Douglas Co.

MUELLER, Joseph F. [32; Omaha; b: Germany; f: Lorenz MUELLER; m: Christine BANGET] md. Melvina KRIEBS [26; Omaha; b: IA; f: John KRIEBS; m: Lena SMITH] on 15 Jan 1881. Off: GROENEBAUM. Wit: William FLEMM, Mrs. Catharine SCHREINER.

MULBURN, Robert J. [29; Douglas Co.] and Annie McDONALD [18; Douglas Co.] license issued on 17 Jan 1868. Off: STUCK.

MULCAHY, Patrick B. [30; Council Bluffs; b: Maryland; f: John MULCAHY; m: Bridget LAFFING] md. Mary McDONALD [21; McKee Co., IA; b: Ireland; f: Randall McDONALD; m: Catherine GIBBONS] on 19 Feb 1873. Off: CURTIS. Wit: Patrick CODEY; Alice COLLINS, Council Bluffs.

MULCAHY, T.H. [28; Omaha; b: Maryland; f: A.J. MULCAHY; m: Margaret LAFEIN] md. Ella GUAINE [25; Omaha; b: Ireland; f: Edward GUAINE; m: Johanna GLEASON] on 24 Oct 1880. Off: ENGLISH. Wit: John SHAY, Johanana GUNAINE.

MULL, John [44; Omaha] md. Ingre JOHNSON [45; Omaha] on 3 Jun 1867 at KUHNS' residence. Off: KUHNS. Wit: Mrs. H.W. KUHNS, Rachel A. KUHNS. "...in the bonds of holy Dedlock."

MULLEN, Jeremiah (Jerry) [27; Omaha; b: WI; f: John MULLEN; m: Bridget KEEFE] md. Mary DAVEY [28; Omaha; b: Ireland; f: John DAVEY; m: Ellen MORAN] on 31 Dec 1880. Off: ENGLISH. Wit: Wm. MULLEN, Ellen DOUGLAS.

MULLEN, William [21; Omaha; b: IA; f: John MULLEN; m: Bridget KEEFE] md. Sarah JOHNSON [21; Omaha; b: New York State; f: G.J. JOHNSON; m: Mary FOLEY] on 26 Jun 1881. Off: ENGLISH. Wit: J.H. BURKE, Margaret KEEFE.

MULLER, John [25; Omaha] md. Melissa A. GRAHAM [20; Omaha] on 10 Feb 1868. Off: STUCK. Wit: W.H. MORRIS, J.A. TOOKER, Dr. S.D. MERCER.

MULLIGAN, Patrick [30; Sarpy Co.; b: Ireland; f: Michael MULLIGAN; m: Mary DUFFEY] md. Mary GALLAGHER [20; Sarpy Co.; b: Ireland; f: Thomas GALLAGHER; m: Catherine POWER] on 7 Jan 1871. Off: CURTIS. Wit: John KEILY; Catherine GALLAGHER, Papillion.

MULLIGAN, William J. [27; Omaha; b: Ireland; f: John MULLIGAN; m: Sarah STEPHENSEN] md. Mary O'HARRA [20; Omaha; b: New Mexico; f: John O'HARRA; m: Margrete MANT] on 12 Mar 1870. Off: BENNETT. Wit: James KELLY; Patrick PUARTELL.

MULLIN, P.M. [24; Omaha; b: Ireland; f: P.M. MULLIN; m: Ann MORAN] md. Bridget DONNELLEY [21; Omaha; b: Ireland; f: William DONNELLEY; m: Bridget FALLON] on 15 Jan 1875. Off: BYRNE. Wit: Peter MALONG, Annie HUGHES.

MULLINGER, William R. [49; Omaha; b: England; f: George MULLINGER; m: Mary STANLEY] md. Mrs. Elizabeth VEACH [30; Omaha; b: MO; f: Charles POWELL; m: Rebecca CONGER] on 7 Jul 1881. Off: RILEY. Wit: John S. PUTMAN, Elizabeth PUTMAN.

MULLOY, James G. [26; Timberville; b: Ohio; f: Thomas MULLOY; m: Harriet ULAN] md. Mary E. NORRIS [26; Clermont Co., OH; b: Ohio; f: William NORRIS; m: Harriet ULAN] on 16 Mar 1871. Off: GIBSON. Wit: Thomas L. NORRIS, Timberville, (NE); Mrs. Adda T. NORRIS, Timberville, (NE).

MULLOY, Thomas F. [42; Salt Lake City, Utah; b: England; f: Thomas MULLOY; m: Ann PHILLIPS] and Mrs. Annie E. ELLSWORTH [26; Culumbus, WI; b: Munroe, MI; f: A.L. HATHAWAY; m: Annie E. ASHLEY] on 10 May 1872. Off: TOWNSEND. License and application only.

MULVIHILL, John [24; b: New York; f: John MULVIHILL; m: Johanna MAHONEY] md. Delia DALTON [17; Bellevue; b: Bellevue; f: Wm. DALTON; m: Mary MAXWELL] on 17 Jun 1878 at the Catholic Church of Omaha. Off: KELLY. Wit: Margaret DALTON of Bellevue, Jeremiah MULVIHILL.

MUMM, Jorgen [30; Omaha; b: Germany; f: Karsten MUMM; m: Elsiba THOEMING] md. Wiebke SIEVERS [21; Omaha; b: Germany; f: John SIEVERS; m: Lena WICK] on 27 Apr 1872. Off: BILLMAN. Wit: Augustus FULREID; Mrs. Bell S. BILLMAN.

MUNDSCHENK, Peter [31; Omaha; b: Germany; f: Peter MUNDSCHENK; m: Katrine KELLER] md. Augustine J. BOUND [27; Omaha; b: Switzerland; f: John F.S. BOUND; m: Louise H. CHEVAUX] on 19 Jan 1878. Off: BENEKE. Wit: John PETZ, Mark BOND.

MUNHOVEN, Anthony [29; Omaha; b: Germany; f: John MUNHOVEN; m: Susan THILLEN] md. Susanna HURT [26; Omaha; b: Germany; f: Melher HURT] on 18 Oct 1869 at the German Catholic Church. Off: GROENBAUM. Wit: Mathias KAISER.

MUNSON, John B. [25; Omaha; b: Connecticut; f: O.A. MUNSON; m: M. DENNING] md. Julia A. WALKER [32; Omaha; b: Iowa; f: R. DIERCELL; m: ---- McDONALD] on 7 Mar 1877. Off: PARDEE. Wit: W.W. HILDRETH, George A. WINCHELL.

MUNSON, Samuel [37; Howard Co.; b: East Indies; f: Samuel MUNSON; m: Abbie J. JOHNSON] md. Evelyn Grace O'CONNELL [19; Saratoga Pct, Douglas Co.; b: New York City, NY; f: John O'CONNELL, m: Alice] on 2 Oct 1873 at Trinity Cathedral. Off: GARRETT. Wit: John O'CONNELL, Saratoga Pct.; Mrs. Alice O'CONNELL, Saratoga Pct.

MURBACH, Simon [31; Medicine Bow, Wyoming Terr.; b: Switzerland; f: Ulrich MURBACH; m: Maggie GESLER] md. Lena OBERLE [24; Omaha; b: Baden, Germany; m: Maggie OBERLE] on 10 Jul 1871. Off: GIBSON. Wit: Robert GETSBERGER; Frederick THEIS.

MURPHEY, David [30; Omaha; b: Ireland; f: Patrick MURPHEY; m: Margaret RAGAN] md. Ellen LINNEHAN [28; Omaha; b: Ireland; f: Jermiah LINNEHAN; m: Betty COKE] on 5 Dec 1873 at the German Catholic Church. Off: GROENEBAUM. Wit: Miss BARRETT; Frank KOESTERS.

MURPHY, Andrew [22; Omaha] and Mary McGRATH [22; Omaha] license issued on 22 Jan 1869. No marriage record. Off: HYDE.

MURPHY, Anthony [27; Chicago Pct, Douglas Co.; b: Ireland; f: Robert MURPHY; m: Catharine SHENEHAN] and Mrs. Nancy Jane FLATBUSH [28; Platte Valley Pct, Douglas Co.; b: Indiana; f: Benjamin BACON; m: Sylvia BACON] license issued on 1 Feb 1873. Off: TOWNSEND.

MURPHY, Dennis [30; Council Bluffs; f: Patk. MURPHY of Parish Rathcomel, Co. Westmeath, Irel.] md. Mary MALONE [25; Council Bluffs; f: Thomas MALONE of Parish Crochen, King's Co., Irel.] on 29 Oct 1859 at BVM Church. Off: CANNON. Wit: Patrick LENAN, Ellen LENAN.

MURPHY, Edward [24; Omaha] and Mary FALLON [20; Omaha] license issued on 7 Apr 1861. No marriage record. Off: ARMSTRONG.

MURPHY, Hugh [29; Omaha; b: Elgin, IL; f: John MURPHY; m: Mary GARVEY] md. Nellie McGRATH [28; Chicago, IL; b: IL; f: Owen McGRATH; m: Mary CLARY] on 2 Aug 1881. Off: RIORDAN. Wit: Thomas

LANERY (or LOWRY), Margareta LANERY (or LOWRY).

MURPHY, James [34; b: New York; f: James MURPHY; m: Johanna Matilda BANNISTER] md. Mrs. Catharine CONNERS [42; b: Ohio; f: Jacob LANCE; m: Mary WHEELER] on 6 Dec 1878. Off: ANDERSON. Wit: John LANG, Emma R. LANG.

MURPHY, John [27; Omaha] md. Johanna KEEFE [25; Omaha] on 17 Feb 1867 at the Catholic Church. Off: EGAN. Wit: Thomas LENIHAN, Ellen CASEY.

MURPHY, John [28; Omaha; b: Ireland; f: James MURPHY; m: Betty DOYLE] md. Maggie KENNEDY [21; Omaha; b: Ireland; f: Daniel KENNEDY; m: Mary FITZGERALD] on 7 Nov 1875. Off: BOBAL. Wit: James DONOGHUE, Mary McNULTY.

MURPHY, Martin D. [28; Omaha; b: Ireland; f: James MURPHY; m: Eliza HICKEY] md. Bridget M. DOUGHERTY [22; Omaha; b: Ireland; f: John DOUGHERTY; m: Margaret COLL] on 9 Aug 1873. Off: TOWNSEND. Wit: Thomas MURRAY; Jared AYER.

MURPHY, Martin [30; Omaha; b: Ireland; f: Daniel MURPHEY; m: Bridget SHERIDEN] md. Mary McANDREW [24; Omaha; b: Ireland; f: Mike McANDREW; m: Mary HOOKS] on 10 Jan 1875 at the Roman Catholic Cathedral. Off: BYRNE. Wit: Richard MULLIN, Mary HAGAN.

MURPHY, William F. [22; Evanston, Wyoming Terr.; b: Ireland; f: William MURPHY; m: Ellen DELANEY] md. Mary A. CALLAHAN [18; Omaha; b: Illinois; f: John CALLAHAN; m: Mary GEARY] on 16 Nov 1871 at the Catholic Church of Omaha. Off: O'GORMAN. Wit: Martin GRIFFIN; Julia CALLAHAN.

MURPHY, William L., Jr. [23; Laramie City, Wyoming Territory; f: William L. MURPHY] md. Mary A. HANNIGAN [ 18; Omaha; b: Omaha; f: Edward HANNIGAN; m: Cathrine CORCORAN] on 16 Sep 1875. Off: JENNETTE. Wit: John CLARE, Lizzie McARTNEY.

MURRAY, George W. [Omaha] md. Nancy S. WILSON [Omaha] on 21 Nov 1864 at Mrs. Patrick COILE's residence, known as the Farmers' Home. Off: DICKINSON. Wit: W.L. BILLITER, Mrs. Patrick COILE, et al.

MURRAY, Henry B. [31; Salt Lake City, UT; b: New York; f: Samuel MURRAY; m: Mary SCOTT] md. Mrs. Francis M. CARPENTER [31; Salt Lake City, UT; b: Vermont; f: C.K. MUNGER; m: Eliza MARSH] on 24 Oct 1874. Off: PEABODY. Wit: Mary C. PEABODY; Harry CARPENTER.

MURRAY, Michael [29; Iowa] md. Luella ELLIS [23; Iowa] on 2 Apr 1869 at O'GORMAN's house. Off: O'GORMAN. Wit: John MURRAY, Mary DALY.

MURRAY, Patrick [27; Omaha; b: Ireland; f: Thomas MURRAY; m: Mary COLLINS] md. Ellen CONNER [26; Omaha; b: Ireland; f: Patrick CONNER; m: Margaret O'NEIL] on 13 Jun 1869. Off: CURTIS. Wit: James SHANNON, Bridget GRIFFINS.

MURRAY, Thomas [22; Omaha; b: Ireland; f: Patrick MURRAY; m: Ann FARLEY] md. Rose Ann PEPPER [22; Omaha; b: Ireland; f: Patrick DANNELLY; m: Elizabeth GREEN] on 25 Nov 1869. Off: CURTIS. Wit: Hugh MURRAY, Mary GIBBINS.

MURRAY, Thomas [35; Sarpy Co.; b: Ireland; f: Michael MURRAY; m: May COYN] md. Hannah MURPHY [22; Omaha; b: Ireland; f: John MURPHY; m: ---- McCANTZ] on 14 Jan 1877. Off: JENNETTO. Wit: Dommick CAJAU, Margaret BOYLE.

MURTAGH, John [22; Omaha; b: Ireland; f: Peter MURTAGH; m: Mary SMITH] md. Mary RAINEY [25; Omaha; b: Ireland; f: Archie RAINEY; m: Agnes] on 11 Sep 1874. Off: STEWART. Wit: Mrs. Emily W. STEWART; B.S. WALKER.

MUTART, John A. [25; Council Bluffs] md. Sarah B. FLEMING [20; Council Bluffs] on 18 Sep 1867. Off: SLAUGHTER. Wit: A.B. SLAUGHTER, S.B. SHAW.

MYERS, Charles [28; Omaha; b: Sweden; f: Gustafson MYERS; m: Mary MYERS] md. Emma SEXANER [24; Omaha; b: NE; f: Wm. SEXANER; m: Emily WOOSTER] on 24 Nov 1881. Off: STELLING. Wit: The bride's parents, the Misses Ida and Nellie SEXANER.

MYERS, Henry L. [24; Omaha] md. Molly NASH [20; Omaha] on 31 Oct 1865. Off: HASCALL. Wit: Thos. L. SUTTON, Mr. ORCHARD.

MYERS, Henry R. [44; Douglas Co.; b: Pennsylvania; f: Samuel MYERS; m: Mary Christine] md. Mrs. Catharine M. O'MALLEY [32; Douglas Co.; b: Ireland; f: James LARKINS; Elizabeth GOVELIE] on 23

May 1878. Off: BARTHOLOMEW. Wit: Wm. F. HEINS, Henry EICKE.

MYERS, William [30; Omaha; b: Pennsylvania; f: John MYERS; m: Eliza EDMUNDSON] md. Margaret LUDWIGSEN [26; Douglas Pct, Douglas Co.; b: Germany; f: Jens LUDWIGSEN; Chaterina MUHS] on 8 Feb 1872. Off: STEWART. Wit: Mrs. J.W. WARNER; Mrs. H.H. COOK.

MYLANDER, Claes [25; North Platte; b: Sweden; f: Magnus MYLANDER] md. Hannah PETERSON [26; Chicago, IL; b: Sweden; f: Peter MANSSON; m: Maria Chatharina ROLIG] on 3 Sep 1870. Off: LARSON. Wit: Johan HELM; Olof J. WALLIN.

NABES, Joseph J. [26; Council Bluffs; b: England; f: Richard NABES; m: ---- RODGERS] md. Lottie OSTLER [19; Omaha; b: England; f: George OSTLER; m: Edith HODDER] on 26 Apr 1870. Off: KERMOTT. Wit: Mrs. A.R. KERMOTT; Frank R. KERMOTT.

NASH, Francis B. [62; Falls City; b: MA; f: Ebenezer NASH; m: Persis BINGHAM] md. Carrie D. ROBINSON [ 42; Omaha; b: NY; f: Daniel ROBINSON; m: Carrie M. CROPSEY] on 5 Aug 1875 at Trinity Cathedral. Off: CLARKSON. Wit: Rev. James PATERSON, Rev. John D. EASTER, D.D.

NASH, Frederick A [25; Golden City, CO; b: Akron, OH; f: Frederick A. NASH; m: Mary H. WATERS] md. Elina BARBAN [23; Omaha; b: St. Francis, Canada; f: Lewis BARBAN; m: Margaret] on 26 May 1873. Off: CURTIS. Wit: Edward W. NASH; Catherine NASH.

NASON, Abner W. [29; b: New York; f: Jesse NASON; m: Clara ROUSE] and Jennie V. BARNEY [19; b: Vermont; f: John M. BARNEY; m: Ellen MYERS] license issued on 25 Oct 1878. No marriage record. Off: BARTHOLOMEW.

NAST, Albert [29; Virginia City, Montana Territory] md. Creszentia WASSERMAN [25; Omaha] on 31 May 1866 at the Lutheran Church. Off: KUHNS. Wit: Andrew WASSERMAN, Charles NAST.

NAST, Charlie [39; Omaha; b: Germany; f: Christian NAST; m: Friedericka STEDELMEIER] md. Mrs. Anna SEISER [36; Omaha; b: Germany; f: Matthias FRIEDERICH; m: Francisca DELBOR] on 16 Sep 1880. Off: FRESE. Wit: G.F. ELSASSER, Mrs. Henrietta BURLAGE.

NEAL, Harrison D. [19; Douglas Co.; b: IA; f: John NEAL; m: Abigail LISK] md. Isabel LAUMAN [17; Appanoose Co., IA; b: Appanoose Co., IA; f: James LAUMAN; m: Sally SUMNER] on 2 Apr 1876. Off: CORLISS. Wit: Reuben LAUMAN, Waterloo, Eliza A. CORLISS, Waterloo. Age consent

given by father of the groom and father of the bride.

NEALE, Stephen F. [Washington Co.] md. Sarah CLARK [Douglas Co.] on 21 Jun 1865. Off: HERMANN.

NEBER, Charles or Carl [41; Omaha; b: Germany; f: Jacob NEBER; m: Phillipine ZAFF] md. Elizabeth HOFKE [34; Omaha; b: Germany; f: Friederich HOFKE; m: Charlotta BACHARD] on 28 Nov 1879. Off: ANDERSON. Wit: Edward D. McLAUGHLIN, Frederick SCNHELL of Douglas Co.

NECKEL, Wilhelm [58; Omaha; b: Germany; f: Friederich NECKEL; m: Lena DREWS] md. Mrs. Elizabeth CASTNER [ 39; Omaha; b: Bohemia; f: Jacob CILIAM; m: Anna MUSIKA] on 21 Jun 1879. Off: KOCARNIK. Wit: Marten SPOETLE; John PROCHASKA.

NECKEL, William [ 54; Omaha; b: Germany; f: Frederick NECKLE; m: Lena DRINES] md. Wilhelmine WITTORFF [44; Omaha; b: Germany[ f: John WITTORFF; m: Martholina ECKMANN] on 15 Aug 1875. Off: PEABODY. Wit: George LINDE, Fred LEWON.

NEFF, Pius [25; Dakota City or County] md. Mary KENNEY (KANNEY) [25; Dakota City or County] on 2 Jun 1861 at the Catholic Church of Omaha. Off: KELLY. Wit: John McBRIDE, Dora DELANY (DELANEY).

NEIBY, George [21; Omaha; b: Pennsylvania; f: Valentine NEIBY; m: Mary HORSTING] md. Cora HENDER [18; Omaha; b: Chicago; f: Hildreth HENDER; m: Lanona EATON] on 15 Feb 1880. Off: INGRAM. Wit: Mr. and Mrs. E.B. HUBBARD.

NEILSEN, Anton [39; Grundy Co., IA; b: Denmark; f: Andrew NEILSON; m: Anna FREDERICKSON] md. Maren RONNING [35; Council Bluffs; b: Denmark; f: Peter RONNING; m: Catharine RONNING] on 10 Feb 1874. Off: PORTER. Wit: George CLEFNER; Joseph MAJORS.

NEILSON [NELSEN], David H. [28; Omaha] md. Mary KRAYSKOW [SKRAYSKOW] [16; Omaha] on 3 or 30 Jan 1869. Off: ADAIR. Age consent given by the father of the bride.

NELIGH, John D. [28] md. Catharine PROBST [24; Douglas Co.] on 13 Mar 1860 in KUHNS' study on Farnham. Off: KUHNS. Wit: Dorah ROHWER, John C. HILEMAN.

NELLIS, C.W. [27; Missouri Valley, IA; b: New York; f: Warner NELLIS; m: Emma BARNES] md. Anna M. MILLER [19; Missouri Valley, IA; b: Ohio; f: William MILLER; m: Anna HADE] on 29 Jul 1878. Off: FALK. Wit: Lena DUMSER of Pekin, IL, Anna MEERMANN.

NELSON, Andrew (Anders) [22; Florence; b: Sweden; f: Peter NELSON; m: Christina ANDERSON] md. Caroline PETERSON [26; Florence; b: Sweden; f: Peter ERICKSON; m: Caroline OLSEN] on 30 Oct 1872. Off: TOWNSEND. Wit: Charles H. BYRNE; Ausust OLSEN, Florence.

NELSON, Andrew C. [32; b: Denmark; f: Nels LAWSON; m: Mary FRIEDERIECHSON] md. Mary RASSMUSSEN [19; b: Denmark; f: Martin RASSMUSSEN; m: Christine PETERSON] on 26 May 1878. Off: MEDLOCK. Wit: Peter J. BROWN of West Omaha, Lars T. NELSON.

NELSON, Andrew [21; Omaha; b: Sweden "in Europe"; f: Nels NELSON] md. Betsey JOHNSON [21; Omaha; b: Sweden "in Europe"; f: John JOHNSON] on 31 Oct 1871. Off: SUNDBORN. Wit: A. EKLUND; Johan HEGLUND.

NELSON, Andrew [33; Omaha; b: Denmark; f: Sorenson NELSON; m: Bodel Christina] md. Caroline NELSON [27; Omaha; b: Denmark; f: Tue NELSON; m: Anne M. NELSON] on 7 Mar 1874. Off: PEABODY. Wit: Christen NELSON; Tyogen Christena NELSSEN.

NELSON, August [35; Douglas Co.; b: Sweden; f: Peter NELSON; m: Cory ANDERSON] md. Mrs. Annie PAULSON [30; Douglas Co.; b: Sweden; f: Volin PAULSON; m: Mary NELSON] on 25 Sep 1881. Off: JOHNSON. Wit: Wilhelm NELSON, Britta Kajsa NELSON.

NELSON, Charles A. [24; Lincoln; b: Sweden; f: Nels G. MAGNUSON; m: Betty LINDSTROM] md. Louisa ANDERSON [25; b: Sweden; f: Andrew MICKELSON; m: Christine SWENSON] on 26 Dec 1878. Off: STRASEN. Wit: Christopher JENSON, S.G. HAGSTROM.

NELSON, Charles [35; NY; b: NY; f: R.P.P. NELSON; m: Sarah WARREN] md. Sarah E. JEFFREY [26; Omaha; b: Quebec, Canada; f: John JEFFREY; m: Mary Ann JEFFREY] on 12 Dec 1875. Off: PEABODY. Wit: Charles H. NICHOLS, Richard JOHNSON.

NELSON, Christian [28; Omaha; b: Denmark; f: Nelse RASSMUSSEN; m: Christine NELSON] md. Gina RASSMUSSEN [22; Omaha; b: Denmark; f: Andrew RASSMUSSEN; m: Mary ANDERSEN] on 13 Oct 1879. Off: ANDERSON. Wit: E.D. SPEARS, D.S. BENTON.

NELSON, E. [Douglas Co.] md. Katie GRIFFITH [Douglas Co.] on 28 Jun 1863 at the Lutheran Church. Both of legal age. Off: KUHNS. Wit: Mrs. H.B. SACKET, Mrs. W.H.S. HUGHES.

NELSON, Halvar [29; Florence; b: Norway; f: Nils ANDERSON; m: Sofa NILSON] md. Julia ANDERSON [25; Florence; b: Norway; f: Anders BERGERSON; m: Ella BERGERSON] on 23 Jan 1871. Off: GIBSON. Wit: Marcus NELSON, Florence; Casper NELSON, Florence.

NELSON, Hans [22; Omaha; b: Denmark; f: Nels HANSEN; m: Bodil RASMUSSEN] md. Mary MATTSON [25; Omaha; b: Sweden; f: Rulof MATTSON; m: Kristina NIELSON] on 16 Aug 1872. Off: TOWNSEND. Wit: E.B. WILLIS; Jerome F.L.D. HERTZMANN.

NELSON, James J. [31; Douglas Co.; b: Demnark; f: Nils HANSEN; m: Anna Sophia JENSEN] md. Cora Sophia PETERSON [21; Douglas Co.; b: Denmark; f: Jens PETERSON; m: Cora JENSEN] on 18 Jun 1880 at L. JENSEN's residence. Off: GYDESEN. Wit: Lars JENSEN, Hans NIELSEN, both of Millard, Douglas Co.

NELSON, John C. [35; Omaha; b: Glasgow, Scotland; f: William NELSON] md. Annie DONAVAN [19; Omaha; b: Wheeling, WV; f: William DONAVAN; m: Jane LYTLE] on 16 Aug 1870. Off: CURTIS. Wit: John F. DONAVAN; Susan DONAVAN.

NELSON, John P. [34; Burt Co.; b: Sweden; f: Nels JOHNSON; m: Anna SAMPSON] md. Mary NELSON [29; Omaha; b: Sweden; f: Peter NELSON; m: Mary Christina JOHNSON] on 22 Apr 1873. Off: SUNDBORN. Wit: Jacob HANSON; Hilda OLSON.

NELSON, Larson [26; Omaha; b: Sweden; f: Nils JONSSON; m: Hanna SKONBERG] md. Anna JOHANSEN [22; Omaha; b: Malmo, Sweden; f: Johanes SWENSSON; m: Johana JONSSON] on 20 Aug 1881. Off: ANDERSON. Wit: Lewis LARSON, Jerome P. PENTZAL.

NELSON, Marcus [31; Florence; b: Norway; f: Nils SIPREANSEN; m: Ale JOHNSON] md. Boletta JOHNSON [20; Florence; b: Norway; f: John HANSEN; m: Mary BRENGLESON] on 23 Jan 1871. Off: GIBSON. Wit: Halver NELSON, Florence; Casper NELSON, Florence.

NELSON, N.W. [34; Omaha; b: Sweden; f: Nels LARSON; m: Carry NELSON] md. Mary NELSON [19; Omaha; b: Sweden; f: Bent NELSON; m: Bettie NELSON] on 30 Sep 1880. Off: ANDERSON. Wit: G.A. LINDQUEST, A.C. TROUP.

NELSON, Nels [29; Omaha; b: Denmark; f: Nils NELSON; m: Sedsel NELSON] md. Sarah Maria CARLSON [27; Omaha; b:

Sweden; f: Carl JOHNSON; m: Maria ANDERSDOTTER] on 1 Oct 1870. Off: HESSEL. Wit: John ROSSLING; Lovisa HOLMBERG.

NELSON, Olaf Rye [27; Omaha; b: Denmark; f: Soren NELSON m: Jacobine JACOBSEN] md. Amalia G. SCHAEFFER [17; Omaha; b: Laport, IN; f: Charles SCHAEFFER; m: Caroline MEYER] on 29 Sep 1876. Off: LIPE. Wit: Christian B. NELSON, Mrs. Kunigunde JANKOWSKIE. C.L. BRISTOL, Notary Public.

NELSON, Olaf [26; Omaha] md. Anna ANDERSON [24; Omaha] on 22 Aug 1868. Off: KERMOTT. Wit: Andrew C. DAHLSTROM, Mary C. DAHLSTROM.

NELSON, Olaf [28; Omaha; b: Sweden; f: Inman NELSON; m: Christine TRULSON] md. Celia BENGTON [25; Omaha; b: Sweden; f: Bengt NELSON] on 22 Jun 1872. Off: SUNDBORN. Wit: John MATTSON; E. STROME.

NELSON, Olaf [28; Wahoo; b: Sweden; f: Nels OLESON; m: Mary OLESON] md. Sophia SKORGERSTROM [28; Omaha; b: Sweden; f: Charles SKORGERSTROM; m: Mary] on 28 Jun 1875. Off: LIPE. Wit: Jacob HANSCOM, Louisa NELSON.

NELSON, Olaf [35; Omaha] md. Anna ANDERSON [35; Omaha] on 16 Aug 1868. Off: STUCK. Wit: Mr. and Mrs. William JOHNSON.

NELSON, Peter [24; Omaha; b: Sweden; f: Nels OLSON; m: Nellie SWANSON] md. Hilda C. OLSON [24; Omaha; b: Sweden; f: Olagus MANISON; m: Anna C. NELSON] on 30 Jun 1873. Off: SUNDBORN. Wit: N.E. AXLING; Christina WIBERG.

NELSON, Peter [28; Omaha; b: Denmark; f: Nels JENSEN; m: Christine McGRADY] md. Agathe Christine JENSON [29; Omaha; b: Denmark; f: Peter JENSON; m: Else Christene PETERSON] on 20 Sep 1879. Off: HANSEN. Wit: Peter RASMUSSEN, Nils CHRISTANSEN.

NELSON, Peter [30; Omaha; b: Denmark; f: Nils CHRISTENSEN; m: Mary THOMPSON] md. Minna JOHNSON [22; Omaha; b: Denmark; f: Nelson JOHNSON; m: Margaret LARSON] on 22 Oct 1870. Off: GIBSON. Wit: Eleazer HALE; Hector F. MORRISON, Cleveland, OH.

NELSON, R.P. [29; Omaha; b: Denmark; f: Nels NELSON; m: Mary MORTENSEN] md. Sophia HANSON [26; Omaha; b: Denmark; f: Christian HANSON; m: Enger B. MICKELSON] on 29 Nov 1879. Off: STENBERG. Wit: C.C. THRANE, Peter OLSEN.

NELSON, Robert [30; Omaha; b: England; f: John NELSON; m: Sarah DAVIS] md. Elisa CHERRY [25; Omaha; b: Canada; f: Richard CHERRY; m: Mary THOMPSON] on 3 Feb 1870. Off: KUHNS. Wit: Annie CATHERWOOD; Mary BURKHART.

NELSON, Samuel Peter [27; Omaha; b: Sweden; f: Nels Otto DONALSON; m: Mary SWENSON] md. Josephina ODMAN [22; Omaha; b: Sweden; f: Lars ODMAN; m: Dora OLESON] on 16 Mar 1875. Off: LEMON. Wit: Jacob AMEN, A. PETERSON.

NELSON, Swan [27; Omaha; b: Sweden; f: Nels TYKSON; m: Bolla ANDERSON] md. Hannah PETERSON [29; Omaha; b: Sweden; f: Peter NELSON] on 22 Feb 1873. Off: SWEDERS. Wit: Andrew JOHNSON; A. NORGREN.

NELSON, William [30; Omaha; b: Denmark; f: Soren NELSON; m: Jacobina JACOBSEN] md. Carolina RASMUSSEN [22; Omaha; Denmark; f: Jeno RASMUSSEN; m: Caroline SORENSEN] on 3 Mar 1877. Off: LIFRE. Wit: Soren NELSON, Jeno RASMUSSEN.

NEMEC, N.D. [26; b: Bohemia; f: Mike NEMEC; m: Josephine LEBENSKA [LIBENSKY]] md. Josephine "Josie" JOHNSON [JANSA] [28; b: Bohemia; f: James JOHNSON [JANSA]; m: Katie KOWISKA] on 26 May 1878 at Bohemian Town [South Omaha]. Off: KOCARNIK. Wit: George HOFFMANN, Francis SPEVAK.

NESBIT, Joseph H. [38; Nebraska City] md. Josephine BOSWORTH [19; Nebraska City] on 3 Jan 1867. Off: HASCALL. Wit: Calvin BRING, Mrs. BOSWORTH, mother of the bride.

NESTOR, Henry [23; Omaha; b: Germany; f: Henry NESTOR; m: Emma HILLNER] md. Bertha STANGE [18; Omaha; b: Chicago, IL; f: Charles STANGE; m: Emma GROSSE] on 3 Feb 1873. Off: MYERS. Wit: Charles HERBERTZ; Gustavus KOLLS.

NEUMAN, Morris [31; Council Bluffs; b: Hungaria; f: Julius NEUMAN; m: Lena BROWN] md. Rosa BROWN [20; Omaha; b: Hungaria; f: Lazar BROWN; m: Anna BROWN] on 12 Feb 1876. Off: SEDGWICK. Wit: Marica F. SEDGWICK, Douglas Co., Mary EBOLD, Douglas Co.

NEVE, Carl Frederik Wilhelm [21; Omaha; b: Denmark; f: Eberhart D. NEVE; m: Christina NELSON] md. Anna J. JORGENSEN [22; Omaha; b: Denmark; f: John JORGENSEN; m: Christina HORNSLETH] on 14 Nov 1874. Off: PEABODY. Wit: H.P. JENSEN; E.D. NEVE.

NEVILLE, James [32; Omaha; b: Illinois; f: Harvey NEVILLE; m: Alley HERIMAN] md. Annie E. RAMSDELL [35; Omaha; b: New York] on 12 Dec 1871. Off: DIMMICK. Wit: Mr. and Mrs. Sylvanus WRIGHT; Mrs. F.M. DIMMICK.

NEVITT, Thomas J. [Omaha] md. Bloomey Jane OTIS [Omaha] on 24 Apr 1860 at Mr. LOGAN's house. Off: BARNES. Wit: Mr. LOGAN, David RICHARDS, Joseph MEGEATH, et al.

NEWBERRY, Joseph C. [36; Cass Co.; b: PA; f: Theroa NEWBERRY; m: Elizabeth CHAMPLIN] md. Sophrona CLEMENT [26; Omaha; b: IL; f: Gilbert M. CLEMENT; m: Lucy A. BARTON] on 26 Dec 1876. Off: SEDGWICK. Wit: John SCHILL, George W. SHIELDS.

NEWBURN, Walter [57; Omaha; b: Ireland; f: John NEWBURN; m: Mary GIBSON] md. Mrs. Matilda UNDERWOOD [36; Omaha; b: Ireland; f: John GIBSON; m: Eliza JOHNSON] on 15 Dec 1875. Off: PEABODY. Wit: George W. SHIELDS, H.A. STURGIS.

NEWMAN, August [26; Jefferson Precinct, Douglas Co.; b: Germany; f: Ferdinand NEWMAN; m: Mine KLEUDER] md. Matilda HAASS [19; Jefferson Precinct, Douglas Co.; b: Germany; f: John HAASS; m: Hanna KOBS] on 21 Apr 1878. Off: STRASEN. Wit: Albert KOBS, Mrs. KOBS.

NEWMAN, George F.H. [23; Omaha; b: Mexico] and Susan A. HENNING [20; Omaha; b: Iowa; f: John HENNING; m: Adeline FARR] license issued on 25 Jun 1870. Off: GIBSON.

NEWMAN, George [24; Omaha] md. Stanley (female) HAWKINS [19; Omaha] on 2 Nov 1867 at SHEEKS' office. Off: SHEEKS. Wit: Henry MACK, Elizabeth WELLS. This is a double wedding with Anderson BELL and Catherine MILLER.

NEWMAN, Henry [29; Omaha; b: Hungary; f: Julius NEWMAN; m: Lena BROWN] md. Rose MOSS [24; Omaha; b: Prussia; f: Frederick MOSS; m: Malea SHOLLAN] on 21 Dec 1879. Off: WRIGHT. Wit: Rudolph BROWN, Joseph BROWN.

NEWMAN, Horace C. [Douglas Co.] md. Lydia FORBES [Douglas Co.] on the evening of 30 Oct 1864 at the Methodist Episcopal Church. Off: LEMON. Wit: Samuel BURNS, I.W. LOWSLEY, congregation.

NEWMAN, Jesse [22; Omaha; b: Mississippi; f: David NEWMAN; m: ----] md. Hattie COWDEN [18; Omaha; b: Missouri; f: William COWDEN; m: Eliza NOTHERLAND] on 16 Sep 1880. Off: MILLSPAUGH. Wit: Frank BELLERSAY, Hampton WATSON.

NEWMEISTER, Edward [27; Omaha; b: Germany; f: Frederick NEWMEISTER; m: Rozena LOCH] md. Kate DIPPEL [23; Omaha; b: Germany; f: Henry DIPPEL; m: Harmena SCHUMAKER] on 10 Jul 1870. Off: KERMOTT. Wit: Henry H. CLARKE; Mrs. A.R. KERMOTT.

NEWSHAM, James [32; Omaha; b: England; f: James NEWSHAM; m: Nancy PARKINSON] md. Maggie WHELAN [25; Omaha; b: Canada East; f: Martin WHELAN; m: Mary DELANY] on 19 Jan 1870. Off: BENNETT. Wit: Mathew LYNCH; Clara HAUCK.

NEWTON, John [30; Leavenworth, KS; b: New York; f: Michael NEWTON; m: Mary CLARK] md. Nellie M. BURDEN [21; Springfield, MO; b: Missouri; f: Wade BURDEN; m: Mary Louise MADISON] on 6 Sep 1880, Trinity Church. Off: MILLSPAUGH. Wit: Chaplain ENGLAND of Fort Omaha, E.D. THOMAS, U.S.A.

NICHOLS, Charles E. [28; Omaha; b: New York; f: Edmund NICHOLS; m: Anna MATTISON] md. Eloise B. POWELL [27; Omaha; b: Michigan; f: Charles POWELL; m: Mary A. BACON] on 5 Aug 1872. Off: CLARKSON. Wit: Geo. W. DOANE; E. WAKELY.

NICHOLS, J.M. [25; Omaha; b: PA; f: T.A. NICHOLS; m: Helena KUERR] md. Mary NELSON [23; Omaha; b: IA; f: Nels NELSON; m: Carrie OLESON] on 13 Apr 1881. Off: BEANS. Wit: Mrs. W.K. BEANS, Mrs. Anna NELSON.

NICHOLS, Jeremiah V. [52; Wahoo; Saunders Co.; b: Renseler Co., NY; f: George NICHOLS; m: Eunice VINCENT] md. Mrs. Sarah E. ALEXANDER [38; Wahoo; b: Indiana; f: Wm. DAVIS; m: Nancy WHITING] on 25 Mar 1878. Off: JOHNSON. Wit: Mrs. ALLEN, Mrs. PHELPS, both of Wahoo.

NICHOLS, Stephen R. [Omaha] md. Julia S. HOMAN [Omaha] on 18 Aug 1864 at G.W. HOMAN's residence. Off: LEMON. Wit: G.W. HOMAN and lady, Samuel BURNS, Lt. WILLIAMS, Josie HOMAN, et al.

NICHOLSON, Charles P. [47; Omaha; b: NY; f: John NICHOLSON; m: Margaret McMULLEN] md. Ellen OLIVER [28; Omaha; b: OH; f: David OLIVER; m: Elizabeth NICHOLS] on 4 Jul 1881. Off: BRANDES. Wit: Edward KUELL, P. PENNER. Affidavit signed by Charles BRANDES.

NICHOLSON, James Henry [31; Omaha; b: New York; f: James NICHOLSON; m: Mary A. LARKIN] md. Caroline MUELLER [21; Omaha; b: New York; f: Alois MUELLER; m: Crezenia HANKE] on 9 Jan 1874. Off: PEABODY. Wit: C.H. GUIOU; F.P. HANLON.

NICKELS, Claus M. [24; Omaha; b: Germany; f: Claus M. NICKLES; m: Catharine ROWERT] md. Regina ROSE [26; Omaha; b: Prussia; f: Jacob ROSE; m: Henrietta ROSENBERG] on 5 Jun 1875. Off: PEABODY. Wit: John G. BRADISH, Wm. H. CHURCHILL.

NIELSEN, Casper [26; Dixon Co.; b: Norway; f: Nels JOHNSON; m: Anna CHRISTOPHERSON] md. Mary GUNDERSON [17 on 10 May 1872; Florence; b: Norway; f: Gunder ADAMSON, also known as Adam GUNDERSON; m: Gundil HANSON] on 19 Mar 1873. Off: TOWNSEND. Wit: William O. BARTHOLOMEW; Gust BERG, Florence.

NIELSEN, Christen [26; Omaha; b: Prussia; f: Niels S. NIELSEN; m: Bodel C.N. TAUSEN] and Maren JENSEN [22; Omaha; b: Prussia; f: Laust JENSEN; m: Bodel HINSEN] license issued on 22 Apr 1871. Off: GIBSON.

NIELSEN, Hans [24; Omaha; b: Denmark; f: Johan H. NIELSEN; m: Ellen Marie SIMONSEN] md. Meta K. JOHANSEN [21; Omaha; b: Denmark; f: Peter H. JOHANSEN; m: Anna Maria JOHANSEN] on 23 Apr 1879. Off: HILMEN. Wit: Mr. A.N. KJAER, Mrs. A.N. KJAER.

NIELSEN, Jens P. [26; Fremont; b: Denmark; f: Nels FRENDSEN; m: Ingaborg ANDERSON] md. Egidia HANSEN [22; Washington Co.; b: Denmark; f: H.P. MADSEN; m: Karen KNUDSEN] on 30 Mar 1871. Off: LARSON. Wit: Peter SORENSEN; O. OLSEN.

NIELSEN, Peter [35; Omaha; b: Denmark; f: Nils C. PETERSON; m: Berti M. MATISEN] md. Sanne NILSEN [26; Omaha; b: Denmark; f: Nils J. LARSEN; m: ---- PETERSON] on 15 May 1876. Off: HANSEN. Wit: N.M. ANDERSEN, Mrs. N.M. ANDERSEN.

NIELSON, Andres [22; Omaha; b: Denmark; f: Niels MADSEN; m: Eva C. JOHNSON] md. Kiersti ANDERSON [26; Omaha; b: Sweden; f: Anders TYFVESEN; m: Elsie BANKSSON] on 18 Nov 1872. Off:

TOWNSEND. Wit: Niels MADSEN; Mrs. Ingra MATTSON.

NIELSON, Charles F.M. [31; Omaha; b: Baltimore, MD; f: Thomas NIELSON; m: Caroline DAWSON] md. Emily C. BAUCHETTE [26; Omaha; b: Canada; f: Joseph BAUCHETTE; m: Margery FRAZER] on 14 Jan 1870. Off: DeLaMATYR. Wit: Mr. HART; Mrs. HART.

NIELSON, Christian B. [30; Omaha] md. Caroline PRIES [FRIES] [24; Omaha] on 20 Sep 1867. Off: DAM. Wit: John RATH, Morris MORRISON.

NIELSON, John [23; Omaha; b: Norway; f: Gurt HIGGEN; m: Anna CHRISTENSON] and Lena JOHNSON [23; Omaha; b: Sweden; f: John B. BERGERSON; m: Brita S. NELSON] license issued on 16 Oct 1871. Off: GIBSON.

NIELSON, John [31; Omaha; b: England; f: George NIELSON; m: Mary SYKES] md. Annie FLAHERTY [26; Omaha; b: Ireland; f: Patrick FLAHERTY; m: Bridget PULTIN] on 23 Nov 1870. Off: KUHNS. Wit: Davis ROBISON; Mary FLAHERTY.

NIKLAUSEN, Gustave [27; Washington Territory; b: Sweden; f: Nicolas PETERSON, m: Carsse PETERSON] md. Christina HANSEN [25; b: Sweden; f: Hans JENSEN; m: Else OLSON] on 21 Sep 1878. Off: BARTHOLOMEW. Wit: Isaac COE of Nebraska City, James W. LOVE.

NILADON, Joseph [25; Omaha; b: Bohemia; f: Frank NILADON; m: Anna PLATEKA] and Antonie SPAGAK [28; Omaha; b: Bohemia; f: John SPAGAK; m: Antonie POLAK] license issued on 11 Mar 1875. No record of marriage. Off: PEABODY.

NILSEN, Jacob [23; Omaha; b: Norway; f: Nils SAMUELSEN; m: Anna JACOBSEN] md. Lizzie EDLING [23; Omaha; b: Sweden; f: John EDLING; m: Brita JOHNSON] on 8 May 1871. Off: BENNETT. Wit: Jonas ADLING; C.J. MARTINELL.

NILSON, Jacob N. [27; Omaha; Wit: f: Christian NILSON; m: Caroline J. JACOBSON] md. Anna M. HARTMAN [23; Omaha; b: Sweden; f: Olof F. HARTMAN; m: Annie MATTSON] on 2 Nov 1881. Off: HAYLAND. Wit: Chas. ERICKSSON, C. CEDERBLOM.

NILSON, Nils [NIELSON, Niels] [Omaha] md. Mary CHRISTIANSEN [Omaha] on 27 Jul 1864 at C.P. BIRKETT's residence. Off: DICKINSON. Wit: Mr. and Mrs. C.P. BIRKETT, Christian LINBERG.

NINDEL, Christian N. P[aul] [31; Omaha; b: Germany; f: Johann C. NINDEL; m: Carolina LOHSE] md. F. C[lara] W. MILDNER [20; Germany; b: Germany; f: Herman MILDNER; m: Auguste MEIER] on 15 Jun 1880 at Douglas Precinct. Off:

BENEKE. Wit: John SCHWENK, Catharina SCHWENK, both of Douglas Precinct.

NJVARY, Paul [36; Omaha; b: Austria; f: Martin NJVARY; m: Juliana SCHNABLE] md. Elizabeth REIS [30; Omaha; b: Prussia; f: Eli REIS] on 22 Sep 1873. Off: WITTE. Wit: John REINHARTS; Dr. Philipp LIEBER.

NOBLE, John H. [31; Omaha; b: England; f: William NOBLE; m: Mary SPENCER] md. Mary SCOTT [30; Omaha; b: London, ENG; f: John SCOTT; m: Mary BANDEY] on 18 Jan 1873. Off: GARRETT. Wit: Mrs. Letitia GARRETT; Mrs. M.E. HAYDEN.

NOCK, Valentine [26; Omaha; b: Germany; f: John NOCK; m: Mary FIX] md. Susannah SHANK [23; Omaha; b: Maryland; f: Conrad SHANK; m: Catharine KEISER] on 14 Sep 1869. Off: KUHNS. Wit: Mr. and Mrs. Frederick BITTEROLF, Mrs. Sarah DEMOREST.

NODLEIBLER, Haver [32; Omaha; b: Germany; f: Haver NODLEIBLER; m: Magdalena POLSTER] md. Mrs. Mary K. WASSERMAN [40; Omaha; b: Germany; f: Frank BAUMEISTER; m: Marguerita CERTS] on 7 Jan 1874 at the German Catholic Church. Off: GROENEBAUM. Wit: Mr. and Mrs. NAST.

NOLAN, John [24; Omaha; b: Ireland; f: Simon NOLAN; m: Bridget DOYLE] md. Rosa McMAHON [21; Omaha; b: Ireland; f: Phillip McMAHON; m: Juda COLLINS] on 14 Oct 1870. Off: CURTIS. Wit: Peter McMAHON; Emelia McMAHON.

NOLAN, Thomas [26; Omaha; b: Ireland; f: Charles NOLAN; m: Mary SCANNELL] md. Mary BOYLE [19; Omaha; b: Ireland; f: Michael BOYLE; m: Mary G__PIN] on 20 Sep 1870. Off: CURTIS. Wit: John FITZGERALD; Margaret BOYLE.

NOLAN, William [28; Blair; b: Ireland; f: John NOLAN; m: Mary KERNS] md. Mary Agnes McKINLEY [22; Blair; b: Ireland; f: John McKINLEY; m: Bridget CAREY] on 7 May 1871. Off: CURTIS. Wit: Edward McKINLEY; Jane MORAN.

NORD, Peter N. [23; Omaha; b: Sweden; f: N.L. NORD; m: Baingata NELSON] md. Annie STAR [22; Omaha; b: IL; f: C.J. STAR] on 24 Dec 1875. Off: PEABODY. Wit: F.M. GREGG, Christine STAR.

NOREEN, Albert O. [26; Omaha; b: Sweden; f: Olof MATSON; m: Magt LARSON] md. Minnie JOHNSON [21; Omaha; b: Sweden; f: John HOLDSTDT; m: Annie M. JOHNSON] on 2 Nov 1875. Off: PEABODY. Wit: Emma HABBE, Robert STEIN.

NORLANDER, William [38; Omaha; b: Sweden; f: Swan NORLANDER; m: Augusta FINNSTROM] md. Matilda JOHNSON [28; Omaha; b: Sweden] on 22 Feb 1872. Off: McCAGUE. Wit: Paul HARMON; Mrs. Matilda McCAGUE.

NORMAN, August E. [23; Omaha; b: Sweden; f: H. NORMAN; m: Christine NELSON] md: Miss M.E. THOMAS [23; Omaha; b: Scotland. f: John J. THOMAS; m: Eliza Jane DUNN] on 27 Aug 1881. Off: RILEY. Wit: David VAN ETTEN, J.P. SOUTHARD.

NORMAN, John F. [28; DeCalb Co., MO; b: Sweden; f: Niels NORD] md. Christina ANDERSON [22; Omaha; b: Sweden; f: Andrew ANDERSON; m: Margaret ANDERSON] on 7 Jul 1870. Off: KUHNS. Wit: E.B. TAYLOR; E.A. ARNOLD.

NORTH, Moroni [37; Council Bluffs; b: New York; f: Alva NORTH; m: Almira HATCH] md. Mrs. Julia BUSHEL [40; Council Bluffs; b: France; f: Joseph KALCH; m: Margaret SMITH] on 15 Mar 1874. OfF: PEABODY. Wit: Miss M.J. PETRIE; O.P. KILLINGSWORTH.

NORTON, Augustus [21; Omaha; b: IL; f: Phillip NORTON; m: Elizabeth SHELDON] md. Madoria FERGISON [18; Omaha; b: IA; f: John FERGISON; m: Elizabeth HOPKINS] on 28 Sep 1876. Off: ANDERSEN. Wit: W.P. SNOWDEN, D.E. BURLEY.

NORTON, Charles [33; Omaha; b: Louisiana; f: Justin NORTON; m: Laura FISH] md. Mary JOHNSON [30; Omaha; b: Copenhagen, Den.; f: Jens JOHNSON] on 13 Nov 1869. Off: GIBSON. Wit: J.W. SAVAGE, John VIEHMANN.

NORTON, James A. [22; Omaha; b: MA; f: Phillip NORTON; m: Eliza SHELDON] md. LewElla HOARD [16; Omaha; b: MI; f: P.B. HOARD; m: Emiline RICHARD] on 25 Jan 1876. Off: SEDGWICK. Wit: Alfred HARPY, Douglas Co., Ellen KELLEY, Douglas Co. Age Consent given by father of the bride.

NORTON, William H. [21; Omaha; b: Illinois; f: Phillip NORTON; m: Eliza SHELDON] md. Mary WAYBRIGHT [17; Omaha; b: Virginia; f: Nathan WAYBRIGHT; m: Leah KETTERMAN] on 2 Jul 1879. Off: BARTHOLOMEW. Wit: F. Lee FOREMAN, Michael BUSHEY. Age consent given by Leah (x) WAYBRIGHT, mother of the bride.

NOTE TO PROOFREADER: Check this entry against original. It looks peculiar.

BODING, Andrew A. [27; Saunders Co.; b: Sweden; f: Anders PEARSON; m: Martha C. LARSON] md. Lina JOHNSON [27; Omaha; b: Sweden; f: John SWANSON; m: Martha CARLSON] on 4 Sep 1875. Off: PEABODY. Wit: Anders PERSON, Martha CARLSON.

NUZUM, Thomas J. [24; Weston, Pottawattamie Co., IA; b: Pennsylvania; f: George NUZUM; m: Eliza FORNER] md. Eliza KIMBALL [20; Weston, Pottawattamie Co., IA; f: Caleb KIMBALL; m: Fanny NIXON] on 6 Aug 1878. Off: BARTHOLOMEW. Wit: M.H. REDFIELD, F.P. HANLON.

NYE, John P. [24; Essex, IA; b: NY; f: Thomas NYE; m: Julia E. GATES] md. Lucy B. HOEL [19; Douglas Co.; b: Douglas Co.; f: Aaron R. HOEL; m: Catherine M. DURHAM] on 24 Apr 1876. Off: LIPE. Wit: J.W. McCUEN, Joel SHOPSHIRE.

NYGREN, Nels [32; Omaha; b: Sweden; f: Nels PETERSON; m: Allen (?) (Alice?) NELSON] md. Caroline NELSON [21; Douglas Co.; b: Sweden; f: Larson NELSON; m: Carrie ANDERSON] on 5 Apr 1876. Off: LIPE. Wit: Lizzie E. LIPE, Kate GALLAGHER.

O'BRIEN, James [33; Omaha; b: Canada; f: Michael O'BRIEN; m: Lizzie McDONALD] md. Margaret O'NEIL [26; Omaha; b: Ireland; f: Hugh O'NEIL; m: Lizzie O'HERN] on 28 Sep 1879. Off: BRANDES. Wit: Henry FISHER of Council Bluffs, Ch. MEYERS.

O'BRIEN, John [23; Omaha; b: England; f: John O'BRIEN; m: Susan MALLOY] md. Elizabeth A. BARR [29; Omaha; b: NY; f: John BARR; m: Annie M. JOHNSON] on 2 Nov 1875. Off: PEABODY. Wit: Benjamin HARRIS, Amanda (HARRIS?).

O'BRIEN, John [28; Omaha] md. Catharine SWEENEY [25; Omaha] on 24 Nov 1866 at St. Philomena's Church. Off: CURTIS.

O'BRIEN, Martin or Morgan [27; Omaha; b: Ireland; f: Bryan O'BRIEN; m: Johanna CARNAY] md. Margaret CORRELL (CARROLL) [17; Omaha; b: Ireland; f: Timothy CORRELL; m: Catherine HARMON] on 6 Jan 1870. Off: CURTIS. Wit: James SULLIVAN; Ellen SULLIVAN. Age of consent, "I Mrs. CORRELL is well pleased to give my daughter in marriage to Morgan O'BRIEN of Omaha I say Margeet CORRELL is 17 years of age. X.".

O'BRIEN, Matthew [22] md. Phoeba CHAPMAN [19; Wood River Station] on 14 Jun 1867 at the parsonage. Off: KUHNS. Wit: Mrs. W.H. KUHNS, Rachel A. KUHNS.

O'BRIEN, Michael [26; Ireland; b: Ireland; f: William O'BRIEN; m: Bridget KIEFFE] md. Catherine FOLEY [22; Ireland; b: Ireland; f: Patrick FOLEY] on 9 Apr 1871. OfF: CURTIS. Wit: Peter MALONE; Lizzie PRENDERGAST.

O'BRIEN, Michael [Elkhorn] md. Elisabeth O'CONNOR [Elkhorn] on 5 Jul 1865 at the Roman Catholic Church of Omaha. Off: O'GORMAN. Wit: Thomas O'CONNOR, Margaret O'CONNOR.

O'BRIEN, P.J. [35; b: Ireland; f: Patrick O'BRIEN; m: Julia SCHEECHEN] md. Elizabeth DIGGAN [30; b: Ireland; f: John DIGGAN; m: Bridget DIGGAN] on 21 Nov 1878 at the cathedral. Off: EMBLEN. Wit: John LYNCH, Mary LYNCH.

O'BRIEN, Peter [25; Omaha; b: New Jersey; f: James O'BRIEN; m: Catharine RYNE] md. Margaret EVERGREEN [22; Omaha; b: Maryland; f: Robert EVERGREEN] on 16 Jul 1879. Off: McCARTHY. Wit: Martin KELLEY, Mary SCEELLY. Affidavit signed by wit: Max (x) BERGMAN.

O'BRIEN, Thomas [23; Douglas Co.; b: Ireland; f: Patrick O'BRIEN; m: Bridget MORRESSEY] md. Kate MORRESSEY [21; Omaha; b: Ireland; f: John MORRESSEY; m: Honor SHE--HAN] on 21 Feb 1870. Off: CURTIS. Wit: Simon MACK, Valley Station; Ellen VELLEY.

O'CONNER, Andrew [30; Ponca; b: Ireland; f: Thomas O'CONNOR; m: Mary GREEN] md. Mary McCARTY [26; Omaha; b: Ireland; f: Timothy McCARTY; m: Catharine HOGAN] on 17 Jun 1869. Off: CURTIS. Wit: Peter MALONE, Hannah McCARTY.

O'CONNOR, Jeremiah [21; Omaha] md. Mary KELLY (KELLEY) [18; Omaha] on 2 Nov 1868. Off: CURTIS. Wit: Hugh McCLEAN, Bridget McCLEAN.

O'CONNOR, John [24; Omaha; b: England; f: Morris O'CONNOR; m: Ellen FORD] md. Ann MURPHY [22; Omaha; b: Ireland; f: Luke MURPHY; m: Mary SEWARD] on 25 Jan 1870. Off: CURTIS. Wit: Eugene POWERS; Catherine MURPHY.

O'DEA, John [27; Omaha] and Miss J. GOGGAN [24; Omaha] license issued on 4 Mar 1858. No marriage record. Off: BRIGGS.

O'DONAHUE, James [28; Omaha; b: Ireland; f: Michael O'DONAHUE; m: Johannah DOOYER] md. Ellen J. FLEMINGS [21; Omaha; b: Illinois; f: James FLEMINGS; m: Ellen McDONALD] on 17 Apr 1871. Off: CURTIS. Wit: H.S. CHRISTIE; Catharine McSHANE.

O'DONELL, Thomas [24; Omaha; b: Ireland; f: Thomas O'DONELL; m: Bridget HALEY] md. Margaret ROCHFORD [24; Omaha; b: Ireland; f: John ROCHFORD; m: Honora CLOON] on 11 Jul 1869. Off: CURTIS. Wit: Thomas ROCHFORD, Ellen DRISCOLL.

O'DONNEL or O'DONAHUE, Patrick [27; Douglas Co.] md. Eliza THOMPSON or PALMERSTON [25; Douglas Co.] on 6 Dec 1868 at St. Philomena Church. Off: PALMERSTON. Wit: John FOGARTY, Honora BOYD.

O'DONNELL (DONNELL), William G. [23; Douglas Co.] md. Sarah A. LATHAM [19; Douglas Co.] on 10 Dec 1867. Off: KELLEY. Wit: J.R. COX, P. KELLY.

O'DONNELL, Daniel [27; Holt Co., NE; b: Ireland; f: Daniel O'DONNELL; m: Kate McDAVITT] md. Sarah BOYLE [22; Philadelphia, PA; b: Ireland; f: Patrick BOYLE; m: Bridgett COLL] on 27 Oct 1879. Off: ENGLISH. Wit: M. DONAVAN, Mrs. M. DONAVAN.

O'DONNELL, Edward W. [24; St. Louis, MO; b: St. Louis, MO; f: James O'DONNELL; m: Lavina ZEGRINO] md. Mary DANNER [21; Omaha; b: Columbus, OH; f: John DANNER; m: Martha TAYLOR] on 12 Mar 1873. Off: TOWNSEND. Wit: James CARR; Lizzie WILLIAMS.

O'DONOGHUE, Dennis [24; Omaha; b: Ireland; f: Michael O'DONOGHUE; m: Julia CRANE] md. Mary A. SPILANE [20; Omaha; b: Ireland; f: John SPILANE; m: Mary SPILANE] on 25 Aug 1870. Off: CURTIS. Wit: David BERSLOUX; Annie BERSLOUX.

O'DONOGHUE, J.B. [33; Omaha; b: Valentia, Ireland; f: Patrick O'DONOGHUE; m: Bridget BUTLER] md. Jannie E. STAFFORD [35; Omaha; ab: Macon, GA; f: John STAFFORD; m: Elizabeth SMITH] on 9 May 1875. Off: EASTER. Wit: May GIBBONS, John RUSH.

O'DONOHOE, John [29; Omaha; b: Ireland; f: James O'DONOHOE; m: Mary LOUGHLIN] md. Nellie McNULTY [19; Omaha; b: Illinois; f: Hugh McNULTY; m: Bridget HURLEY] on 18 Oct 1880, St. Philomena's Church. Off: McCARTHY. Wit: Daniel MOYNEHAN, Marsella GOFF.

O'DONOUGH [DONOUGH], Michael [Douglas Co.] md. Mary COLLINS [Omaha] on 4 Jan 1858. Off: PORTER.

O'FLANNIGAN, John [60, Omaha] md. Julia Frances THOMAS [38; Omaha] on 20 Apr 1864. Off: GAYLORD. Wit: Wm. H. BLACK, J.M. DOSIER.

O'GRADY, Jeremiah [27; Omaha; b: Ireland; f: Thomas O'GRADY; m: Mary SHEA] md. Mrs. Margaret POWERS [24; Omaha; b: Ireland; f: Morris HARRIGAN; m: Mary QUINLAN] at St. Philomena Church on 16 Sep 1879. Off: KELLY. Wit: Patrick FOLEY, Bridget CASE.

O'HEARN, Michael [24; Douglas Co.; b: Ireland; f: Michael O'HEARN; m: Bridget CODY] md. Kate McCORMICK [28; Douglas Co.; b: Ireland; f: Robert McCORMICK] on 7 Jan 1872. Off:

LONERGAN. Wit: Jos. MOCKLER, Fremont; Kate FERRY, Elk Horn.

O'KEEFFE, John [26; Omaha; b: Ireland; f: James O'KEEFFE; m: Ellen DORAN] md. Ellen MURPHY [17; Omaha; b: Ohio; f: Thomas MURPHY; m: Rose Ann PYNEN] on 27 Oct 1873 at Thomas MURPHY's res. Off: BYRNE. Wit: Thomas FALLON; Elizabeth MURPHY.

O'KEEFFE, William [22; Omaha; b: Australia; f: John O'KEEFFE; m: Catherine CANNING] md. Bell BISHOP [29; Evansville, IN; b: Lexington, KY; f: Wesley BISHOP; m: Lucasey HIGGINS] on 28 Oct 1870. Off: GIBSON. Wit: Mrs. Mary J. GIBSON; David CLARK.

O'MALLEY, Peter [26; Omaha; b: Ireland; f: James O'MALLEY; m: Winnifred O'MALLEY] md. Ellen GENTLEMAN [17; Omaha; b: Canada; f: Nicholas GENTLEMAN; m: Mary GARVEY] on 21 Jul 1874 at the Cathedral. Off: MALLOY. Wit: William GENTLEMAN; P. McDONALD; Nellie DEAN; Mary FAGAN.

O'NEAL, Henry [26; Omaha; b: England; f: Phoenix O'NEAL; m: Rachel SMITH] md. Mary MAHER [23; b: Ireland] on 12 Aug 1869. Off: GIBSON. Wit: C.C. TICE, George L. GIBSON.

O'NEIL, J.W. [27; Omaha; b: Ireland; f: Patrick O'NEIL; m: Catharine WHALEN] md. Ellen LOVELLY [26; Omaha; b: Canada; f: Edward LOVELLY; m: Bridget DONNOLLON] on 15 Apr 1880, St. Philomena Church. Off: KELLY. Wit: Edward LOVELY [sic], Elizabeth POUND.

O'NEIL, Thomas [28; Kearney City] md. Winniford GORMLEY [Winniford COLLINS, alias GORMLEY; 23; Kearney City] on 6 Nov 1866 at St. Philomena's Church. Off: CURTIS.

O'NEIL, William P. [42] md. Lucretia O'NEIL [50] on 21 Nov 1865 at Mr. WHELAN's house. Off: HASCALL. Wit: T.E. DUNN, Mary E. TRUMAN.

O'NEILL, Edward [23; Council Bluffs] md. Hellen Man McNEAL [19; Elk Horn City] on 17 Sep 1860. Off: ARMSTRONG. Wit: Mrs. BLAIR, Miss GOODRICH.

O'NEILL, Michael J. [29; Omaha; b: Ireland; f: Paul O'NEILL; m: Rosana DUGGAN] md. Sadie E. McCRISTAL [21; Omaha; b: Ohio; f: Daniel McCRISTAL; m: Susan LYNCH] on 19 Jan 1871. Off: O'GORMAN. Wit: Kate CREIGHTON; W.E. McELROY; C.V. GALAGHER; Mary Ann O'BRIEN.

O'NEILL, Patrick [25; Omaha; b: Ireland; f: Hugh O'NEILL; m: Alice HURREA] md. Annie McDONALD [20; Omaha; b: Ireland; f: Charles McDONALD; m: Annie O'NEILL] on 19 Sep 1869. Off: CURTIS. Wit: Bernard BRADLEY, Annie MORAN.

O'REILLY, Joseph [29; Omaha; b: Alabama; f: John O'REILLY; m: Francis MURPHY] md. Addie LECKENBY [18; Omaha; b: Nebraska City; f: James LECKENBY; m: Margaret CLINTON] on 16 Jan 1877. Off: WEISS. Wit: Jennie PERRY, William RANDOLPH.

O'REILY (O'REILEY, O'RILEY), Michael [21; Omaha, f: Bartholomew O'REILEY of Parish Tralee, Co. Kerry, Irel.] md. Mary HEALY [20; Omaha; f; Patrick HEALY of Parish Tralee, Co. Kerry, Irel.] on 14 Feb 1859 at St. Mary's Church. Off: CANNON. Wit: Michl. LENEHAN, Ann O'REILY.

O'ROURKE, Peter [35; Omaha; b: Ireland; f: Farron O'ROURKE; m: Abby McGORMAN] md. Mary J. DEVIN [27; Omaha; b: Wisconsin; f: Hugh DEVIN; m: Ann KEW] on 11 Apr 1877. Off: W.K. Wit: Henry BINKE, Julia BARRY.

O'SULLIVAN, James [30; Omaha] md. Ellen BRENNAN [21; Omaha] on 4 Sep 1866 at the Catholic Church of Omaha. Off: O'GORMAN. Wit: John McMAHON, Ellen BRENNAN.

OAKLEY, Nelson A. [21; Onawa, IA; b: Erie Co., NY; f: Robert OAKLEY; m: Lucinda COLBURN] md. Lorena J. PETERSON [21; Omaha; b: Indiana; f: Samuel PETERSON; m: Almira DAVIS] on 13 Apr 1872. Off: BILLMAN. Wit: Mrs. Bella D. BILLMAN; Mrs. ANNIS, et al.

OAKS, John F. [31; Omaha; b: New York; f: George OAKS; m: Mary Ann RONGUEY] md. Mrs. Annie Maud FANNING [25; West Point, NE; b: New York; f: Whitney SICKER; m: Elmira DERBY] on 7 Sep 1880. Off: BEANS. Wit: Mrs. W.K. BEANS, Mrs. Kate MADDOX.

OBERG, Richard [30; Douglas Co.] md. Frederica STIEGHORST [23; Washington Co.] on 20 Feb 1869 at Union House. Off: FLORKEE. Wit: A. BARTHOLOMEW, Fred MUELLER.

OBERST, Martin [37; Sarpy Co.; b: Germany; f: Jacob OBERST; m: Elizabeth ROLAND] md. Mrs. Minna SCHLUMPH [33; North Platte; b: Germany; f: Fred. MEYER; m: Sophie BUCHARD] on 31 Aug 1878. Off: BOFDEN. Wit: Eugene W. ERB, Katharine METZGER.

OCANDER, Oscar [25; Omaha; b: Sweden; f: Gabreal OCANDER; m: Sophia LARSSON] md. Emma OSTWALD [19; Omaha; b: Sweden; f: Johan OSTWALD; m: Catharine MORTENSSON] on 29 Oct 1881. Off: ANDERSON. Wit: Oliver BURSELL, Sarah Elisabeth BURSELL.

OCHSE, Conrad [51; Omaha; b: Germany; f: Conrad OCHSE] md. Wilhelmina STORDA [31; Omaha; b: Germany; f: John H. STORDA; m: Margreta ROHVEDDER] on 22 Mar 1875. Off: PEABODY. Wit: F.P. HANLON, Robert P. CHURCHILL.

OCHSENBEIN, George W. [24; Omaha; b: Ohio; f: Samuel OCHSENBEIN; m: Elizabeth STIGER] md. Betty ANDERSON [19; Omaha; b: Sweden; f: Andrew ANDERSON; m: Mayastina] on 8 Aug 1873. Off: WRIGHT. Wit: Andrew PETERSON, Mary HANSTON.

ODEN, Charles [30; IA; b: OH; f: Charles ODEN; m: Eliza HODGES] md. Eva VINCENT [19; IA; b: IA; f: James VINCENT; m: Mary McCALL] on 28 Sep 1881. Off: GRAHAM. Wit: E.M. GRAHAM, Esther WESTGATE.

ODEN, Laurence B. [25; Burt Co.; b: Sweden; f: E.G.B. ODEN; m: Anna BLOMBERG] md. Nellie NELSON [21; Omaha; b: Sweden; f: Nels BENGTSON; m: Anna ANDERSON] on 18 Apr 1874. Off: BENZON. Wit: N. MALMSTON; C.W.B. ODEN and wife.

OFT, Claus [29; Jefferson Precinct; b: Germany; f: Hans OFT; m: Catharine CURT] md. Mrs. Antje KRAMER [26; Jefferson Precinct; b: Germany; f: Johan LEBBERT; m: Anna OFT] on 11 Aug 1878. Off: STRASEN. Wit: Hans LEBBERT, Henry SIERT.

OGBURN, Charles H. [25; Omaha; b: Wisconsin; f: Henry A. OGBURN; m: Caroline DEBORDE] md. Carrie C. SMITH [25; Omaha; b: London, England; f: Justin SMITH; m: Caroline SMITH] on 17 Dec 1871. Off: KUHNS. Wit: Ambrose E. STEVENS; Thomas T. CROFT.

OGDEN, Robert T. [24; Omaha; b: KY; f: James OGDEN; m: Flora GILLETT] md. Ella WROTH [25; Omaha; b: MO; f: A.B. WROTH; m: Martha M. UNVOCAY] on 13 Oct 1881. Off: BENEKE. Wit: J.J.L.C. JEVETT, James OGDEN.

OGLEBY, Joseph N. [25; Douglas Co.; b: Pennsylvania; f: E.B. OGLEBY; m: Mary W. NAYLOR] and Gussie N. HANSON [24; Douglas Co.; b: Nebraska; f: E.B. HANSON; m: M.B. WILSON] license issued on 21 Oct 1878. No marriage record.

OHME, Frank [29; McCardle Pct, Douglas Co.; b: Germany; f: Charles OHME; m: Mary MENIKE] md. Lena SMITH [27; Omaha; b: Germany; f: Claus SMITH; m: Mary WALDER] on 15 Mar 1873. Off: MEYERS. Wit: Henry EICKE, McCardle Pct; F. PETERSEN, Sarpy Co.

OLDEWAGE, Henry [29; Omaha; b: Germany; f: Fred OLDEWAGE; m: Minnie HOLDHIES] and Louise TIEHMANN [20; Omaha; b: Germany; f: Henry TIEHMANN; m: Sophia COOK] filed an affidavit on 13 Jul 1876. No marriage recorded. Off: SEDGWICK.

OLESEN, James [21; Omaha; b: Denmark; f: Ole JENSEN; m: Judide MASEN] md. Mary LARSON [22; Omaha; b: Sweden; f: Lars LARSON; m: Mary JACOBSEN] on 12 Nov 1873. Off: LIPE. Wit: Julius HANSEN; Andrew HANSEN.

OLESON, John [29; Omaha; b: Sweden; f: Ole ANDERSON; m: Joanna ANDERSON] md. Joanna HOLLEN [27; Omaha; b: Sweden; f: Lars HOLLEN; m: Margaret ANDERSON] on 22 Nov 1874. Off: RING. Wit: Oscar BALIN; A.W. ANDERSON.

OLESON, Samuel [28; Omaha; b: Sweden; f: Ole SWENSON; m: Carrie ANDERSON] md. Matilda PETERSON [24; Omaha; b: Sweden; f: John PETERSON; m: Annie JOHNSON] on 16 May 1874. Off: HALD. Wit: Michel BRESTKRENTZ; William SCHMIDTH.

OLESON, William [23; Omaha; b: Norway; f: George OLESON; m: Anne BRYNJULS] md. Nelly JOHNSON [22; Omaha; b: Norway; f: John JOHNSON; m: Johanna OLSON] on 29 Mar 1877. Off: SEDGWICK. Wit: Morris MORRISON, Ole OLSON.

OLIVER, George T. [23; Pittsburg, PA; b: Ireland; f: Henry W. OLIVER; m: Margaret BROWN] md. Mary D. KOUNTZE [19; Omaha; b: Ohio; f: Christian KOUNTZE; m: Margaret ZERBE] on 19 Dec 1871. Off: KUHNS. Wit: Augustus KOUNTZ; James B. OLIVE, Pittsburg, PA.

OLIVER, John H. [23; Omaha] md. Julia A. CARPENTER [25; Omaha] on 16 Feb 1869. Off: HYDE. Wit: O.P. INGALLS, Mrs. WILSON.

OLSEN, Andrew [29; Florence; b: Sweden; f: Ole OLSEN; m: Carrie HOLVERD] md. Elisa ANDERSON [30; Florence; b: Sweden; f: Andrew ANDERSON; m: Carrie NELSON] on 3 Feb 1870. Off: GIBSON. Wit: N. NELSON, Florence; Carrie NELSON, Florence.

OLSEN, Charles [32; Omaha] md. Mary or Marie STEEL [25; Omaha] on 23 Mar 1868. Off: FYRANDO.

OLSEN, Hans [32; Omaha; b: Denmark; f: Ole JOHNSON; m: Mary HANSON] md. Susan JOHNSON [22; Omaha; b: Denmark; f: John KENOSIN (?); m: Martha PETERSON] on 6 Oct 1876. Off: DONNELLY. Wit: Mary J. DONNELLY, B.V. DONNELLY.

OLSEN, Hans [42; Omaha] md. Ellen LARSEN [37; Omaha] on 15 Sep 1868. Off: KELLEY. Wit: James ANDERSEN, A. ABESON.

OLSEN, Hans [47; FLorence; b: Sweden; f: Olof OLSEN; m: Carrie JOHNSON] md. Betsey JOHNSON [36; Florence; b: Sweden; f: John NILSSON; m: Kestina NILSDOTTER] on 13 Feb 1870 at Florence. Off: DELAND. Wit: Peter HANSEN; James H. DELAND, Florence.

OLSEN, James [27; Omaha; b: Denmark; f: Ole HANSEN; m: Carrie M. MARQUIS] md. Anna M. JOHANSON [27; Omaha; b: Denmark; f: Rasmus JOHANSON; m: Meta Alena ANDERSON] on 25 Jul 1870. Off: KUHNS. Wit: Nils LAWSON; Mrs. Carrie L. LAWSON.

OLSEN, Jens [23; Omaha; b: Denmark; f: Ole ENGLEMAN; m: Margareeta HANSEN] md. Mary NELSON [24; Omaha; b: Prussia; f: Sorensen NELSON; m: Christina NELSON] on 24 Aug 1872. Off: BILLMAN. Wit: Julius ANDRESEN; Miss Line NELSON.

OLSEN, Johanes [25; Omaha; b: Denmark; f: B.C. OLSEN; m: Petrina BORCH] md. Christine CHRISTENSEN [19; Omaha; b: Denmark; f: Jens CHRISTENSEN; m: Anna M. CHRISTENSEN] on 16 Jun 1880. Off: STENBERG. Wit: Hans P. JENSEN; Charles S. WAGNER.

OLSEN, John [25; Omaha; b: Sweden; f: Olof WESTERBERG; m: Johanna SWESON] md. Mary NELSON [26; Omaha; b: Sweden; f: Nels NELSON; m: Caisa ANDERSON] on 10 May 1881. Off: STENBERG. Wit: Peter GOW, D.M. McKNIGHT.

OLSEN, Martin [27; Omaha; b: Norway; f: Ole ANDERSEN; m: Gurnil HELVERSON] md. Amelia MILSKOW [34; Omaha; b: Norway; f: Erick MILSKOW] on 13 Jan 1870. Off: LARSON. Wit: Mrs. Johanna C. LARSON; Engla J. NORMAN.

OLSEN, Thorwald [32; Omaha; b: Copenhagen, DEN; f: Christian OLSEN; m: Marie ROSENJELM] md. Anna Keiser JOHNSON [27; Omaha; b: Sweden; f: Johannes ERICKSON; m: Martha OLSON] on 14 Jan 1872. Off: LARSON. Wit: Frank A. HULTMAN; Mrs. Annette HULTMAN.

OLSON, Anders [26; Omaha; b: Norway; f: Ola ANDERSON; m: Caren ARTUSON] md. Ollena JOHNSON [24; Omaha; b: Norway; f: John LARSON; m: Joanna OLSON] on 1 May 1875. Off: BENZON. Wit: John CHALLMAN, Mere JOHNSON.

OLSON, Andrew [28; North Platte; b: Sweden; f: Henry OLSON; m: Ala ANDERSON] md. Sophrona VAUGHAN [20; North Platte; b: Canada; f: Thomas VAUGHAN] on 21 May 1870. Off: DIMMICK. Wit: Mr. and Mrs. E.F. COOK, Mrs. F.M. DIMMICK.

OLSON, Lars [35; Omaha; b: Sweden; f: Ola HANSON; m: Benta LARS] md. Chatarina BOLIN [29; Omaha; b: Sweden; f: Christian BOLIN; m: Anna JACOBSON] on 13 Jul 1869. Off: HYDE. Wit: G.J. KIP (KIPP), C.D. HYDE.

OLSON, Ole [29; Omaha] md. Ane Mesine JENSEN [20; Omaha] on 24 Aug 1867. Off: SHEEKS. Wit: Knude NEILSON, G.G. RILEY.

OLSON, Paul C. [35; b: Denmark; f: Ola CHRISTINSON; m: Elsa M. PAULSON] md. Mary M. LARSON [26; b: Denmark; f: Lars HANSON; m: Boeld HANSON] on 9 Dec 1878. Off: WEISS. Wit: Andrew CAMENZIND, Emil MEYER.

OLSON, Swan [25; Elkhorn Pct, Douglas Co.; b: Sweden; f: Olof SWANSON; m: Marie Catharina JOHNSON] md. Christina JOHNSON [24; Elkhorn Pct, Douglas Co.; b: Sweden; f: John JOHNSON] on 7 Feb 1873. Off: SWEDERS. Wit: A.G. ASKWIG, Elkhorn Pct; John ASKWIG, Mills Co., IA.

OLSSON, John [24; Omaha; b: Denmark; f: Ole JOHNSON; m: Carrie RASSMUSSEN] md. Dora JOHNSON [22; Omaha; b: Denmark; f: Christ JOHNSON; m: Annie LARSON] on 20 Nov 1881 at Vor Frelser's Church. Off: GYDESEN. Wit: Georg JOHNSON, Chr. LARSON.

OLSSON, Lars [27; Dodge Co.; b: Sweden; f: Ole OLSSON; m: Kari LARS] md. Kari OLSDOTAR [19; Omaha; b: Sweden; f: Oliver ANDERSEN] on 25 Dec 1871. Off: TOWNSEND. Wit: Ambrose ERICKSON; Olufreer CHAPMAN.

OLSZENSKY, Raman [30; Omaha; b: Germany; f: John OLSZENSKY; m: Rosalia KARGA] md. Sophie SELIGMAN [23; Omaha; b: Germany; f: John SELIGMAN; m: Dorothea ROUNAN] on 26 Nov 1875. Off: PEABODY. Wit: Frederick HICKSTEIN, Mary C. PEABODY.

OMAN, Gabriel [35; Omaha; b: Sweden; f: Lars OMAN; m: Dora JOHNSON] md: Hannah NELSON [22; Omaha; b: Sweden; f: Nils NELSON; m: Mary SWANSEN] on 22 Oct 1881. Off: WRIGHT. Wit: Joanna C. WRIGHT, Lulu KING.

OMAN, Jacob [26; Omaha; b: Sweden; f: Louis OMAN; m: Dorothea] md. Mary JOHNSON [24; Omaha; b: Sweden; f: John JOHNSON; m: Anna GERETTA] on 1 Apr 1872. Off: TOWNSEND. Wit: Jerome F.L.D. HERTZMANN; L. JOHNSON.

OMAN, Jacob [28; Omaha; b: Sweden; f: Lars OMAN; m: Dorthea OLESON] md. Catharine OLESON [27; Omaha; b: Sweden; f: Peter OLESON; m: Anna OLESON] on 21 Feb 1874. Off: BENZON. Wit: J. LANDEN; Maria LANDEN; Gabriell OMAN; J. OMAN.

ONELL, Charles [27; b: Sweden; f: Andrew SAMUELSON; m: Christina NIELSON] md. Jenny HECKENSON [20; b:

Sweden; f: John HECKENSON; m: Mary PETERSON] on 4 May 1878. Off: STENBERG. Wit: Gustaf FRISHEDT, Christina FRISHEDT.

ONHE, William [24; Papillion Pct, Sarpy Co.; b: Germany; f: Andrew ONHE; m: Rachel BAUMGARDEN] md. Agnes HAUG [20; Omaha; b: Germany] on 25 Sep 1872 at Wm. FLORKEE's house, Chicago Pct. Off: FLORKEE. Wit: J.M. ADAIR; Elisabeth FLORKEE, Chicago Pct.

ORCHARD, John [21; Douglas Co.] md. Anna GUY [20; Douglas Co.] at 8 PM on 5 Feb 1867 at DIMMICK's house. Off: DIMMICK. Wit: Sylvanus WRIGHT, Elmer D. DIMMICK, et al.

ORCHARD, Samuel A. [30; Omaha] md. Eliza A. CRAWFORD [23; Omaha] about 8 P.M. on 3 Jan 1866 at the residence of the bride's father. Off: DIMMICK. Wit: Mr. and Mrs. ORCHARD, Theo and Henry GRAY, Lieut. VALENTINE, et al.

ORCHARD, Samuel A. [38; Omaha; b: Kentucky; f: A.R. ORCHARD; m: Amanda HELLEM] md. Mattie S. DUNCAN [24; Omaha; b: Kentucky; f: Peter DUNCAN; m: Marie HAM] on 2 May 1877. Off: PARDEE. Wit: James WOODLAND, Hattie DUNCAN.

ORTON [OSTON], L.L. [28; White Cloud, KS] md. Louisa N. DELAWARE [29; Omaha] on 6 Jul 1868. Off: KUHNS. Wit: Mr. DELAWARE, J.B. DETWILER, R. WIDENSALL, et all.

ORWIG, George W. [26; Omaha; b: Pennsylvania; f: Samuel ORWIG; m: Lydia HARTMAN] md. Elizabeth R. WILBORN [22 or 23; Omaha; b: Virginia (West); f: George WILBORN; m: Elizabeth LUMKINS] on 4 Jul 1870. Off: KUHNS. Wit: George W. WILBORN; Mrs. Mary J. WILBORN.

OSBORN, Luther W. [31; Blair; b: New York; f: John OSBORN; m: Julia HEATH] md. Maggie A. ROGERS [20; Omaha; b: Kentucky; f: Peter ROGERS; m: Sarah WRIGHT] on 16 Dec 1874. Off: GARRETT. Wit: Wm. McCLELLAND; Alexander ROGERS.

OSBORN, Troy C. [25; Madison Co.; b: Virgina; f: Enoch B. OSBORN; m: Irene COX] md. Mary LYON [18; Platte Valley Pct, Douglas Co.; b: Minnesota; f: Charles LYON] on 15 Mar 1873. Off: ROLFS. Wit: John LYONS, Platte Valley Pct; Bethey PARKER, Platte Valley Pct.

OSBORN, William [21; Omaha; b: Iowa; f: Abraham OSBORN; m: Mary A. SMITH] md. Mary E. WRIGHT [17; Omaha; b: Missouri; f: Thos. K. WRIGHT; m: Jane KELLY] on 11 Dec 1870. Off: DeLaMATYR. Wit: Thomas J. WRIGHT; Mrs. Jane WRIGHT.

OSBORN, William [22; Omaha] md. Elizabeth WYSEL [22; Omaha] on 22 Aug

1866. Off: MILLER. Wit: Clara KELLOM, Mrs. G.L. MILLER, Mrs. J.H. KELLOM.

OSBORNE, Jefferson [28; Omaha] md. Jenny JOHNSON [26; Omaha] on 10 Apr 1861. Off: BIRKETT. Wit: Harrison JOHNSON, Thomas J. WEATHERWAX.

OSBURN, John L. [24; Kane, IA; b: VA; f: George OSBURN; m: Eliza GRANT] md. Eliza or Ellenor MAGRUDER [28; Kane, IA; b: VA; f: D.A. MAGRUDER; m: Margaret GOSBURN] on 18 Jan 1876. Off: EASTER. Wit: D.N. MAGRUDER, Kane, IA, W.H. KING, Kane, IA.

OSTERMAN, Henry [Fontanelle] md. Tracie TEMBEL [Fontanelle] on 15 Aug 1863. Both of legal age. Off: MUHLENBROCK. Wit: Charlotte FLORKEE, Charles OSTERMAN.

OSTRUM, Harvey J. [26; Omaha] md. Alice DWYER [18 years and 2 months; Omaha] on 1 Jul 1867 at BROWN's office. Off: BROWN. Wit: Patrick HEALY, C. LYNCH.

OTIS, Frank L. [33; Omaha; b: New Hampshire; f: Rufus OTIS; m: Ada PERKINS] md. Therese M. SIX [22; Omaha; b: Germany; f: John SIX; m: Theresa DEIRINGER] on 11 Oct 1880. Off: BEANS. Wit: Earne DETWILER, Anna HANSON.

OTTEN, John A. [24; Douglas Co.; b: MD; f: Albert OTTEN; m: Ellen PEAK] md. Bertie P. LONG [18; Blair; b: Germany; f: John LONG; m: Amelia PROVISE] 6 May 1875. Off: PEABODY. Wit: Benjamin HARNISH, Amanda HARNISH.

OTTOWAY, Charles R. [25; Omaha] md. E. Jane CHIVINGTON [16; Omaha] on 6 Apr 1858. Off: SHILMAN. Wit: Jacob ADRIANCE, John BARKER.

OVERGARD, Anders Christensen [41; Washington Co.; b: Denmark; f: Christian A. OVERGARD; m: Anna CHRISTIANSEN] md. Mrs. Dorothea JANSEN [41; Washington Co.; b: Denmark; f: Jens JENSEN; m: Mary JENSEN] on 25 Jul 1874. Off: PEABODY. Wit: Willie R.B. KILLINGSWORTH; Mary C. PEABODY.

OVERMIRE, William H. [22; Omaha; b: "on ship Yankee on the ocean between England and America"; f: George B. OVERMIRE; m: Elizabeth FICKLE] md. Mary LELAND [22; Omaha; b: Ohio; f: George LELAND; m: Elizabeth HILL] on 1 Oct 1874. Off: HANSEN. Wit: Thos. W. GARDNER; George H. St. CLAIR.

OWEN, Otis [44; Council Bluffs; b: Indiana; f: Samuel OWEN; m: Rachel SPEAR] md. Mattie McCLAIN [25; Council Bluffs; b: Nebraska; f: James McCLAIN; m: Nancy J. McCLAIN] on 21 Jul 1879. Off: BARTHOLOMEW. Wit: Wm. L. PEABODY, Max BERGMAN.

OWENS, John and Mary McGAVEY license issued on 17 Nov 1856. No marriage record. Off: SCOTT. Age consent given by Mr. DOUGHERTY.

OWENS, Phil B. [28; Omaha; b: Maryland; f: Loring OWENS; m: Anna TRAVILLA] md. Flora M. ROGERS [19; Omaha; b: Iowa; f: Samuel ROGERS; m: Fanny KNIGHT] on 24 Dec 1879. Off: LIPE. Wit: Ella OWENS, Alberta OWENS.

OWENS, Richard [27; Omaha; b: New York; f: Richard OWENS; m: Jane EDWARDS] md. May M. HAWLEY [18; Dunlap, IA; b: Illinois; f: Josephus HAWLEY; m: Lura EDDY] on 16 Jan 1872. Off: DeLaMATYR. Wit: N.O. DeLaMATYR; Hattie DELIGHT.

OWENS, William [23; Waterloo; b: Pennsylvania; f: John W. OWENS; m: Mary E. MELLBURNE] md. Mary Ellen CURRENCE [18; Omaha; b: Nebraska; f: A.J. CURRENCE; m: Anna J. NELSEN] on 18 Nov 1880. Off: HAWES. Wit: A.E.J. CURRENCE, Maud EMERY.

OWNEY, Bedford [23; Douglas Co.] md. Mary M. ASHBURN [18; Douglas Co.] on 10 Nov 1867. Off: SHEEKS. Wit: James W. SAVAGE, Barnes ASHBURN.

PAASCH, Charles [22; Douglas Co.; Germany; f: Frederick PAASCH; m: Lottie PETERSON] md. Lena SCHNEIDER [23; Douglas Co.; b: Germany; f: Peter SCHNEIDER; m: Maggie] on 30 Jan 1875 at FLORKEE's house. Off: FLORKEE. Wit: A.C. BARTHOLOMEW, Millard Precinct, L.M. BARTHOLOMEW, Millard Precinct.

PABIAN, John [22; Omaha; b: Bohemia; f: John PABIAN; m: Theresa SPEDL] md. Barbara BARTAS [20; Omaha; b: Bohemia; f: Charles BARTAS; m: Barbara LEDR] on 15 Feb 1881 at the Bohemian Church. Off: KLIMA. Wit: Charles BARTAS, Joseph VRANA.

PACKEISER, Leopold [ 32; Omaha; b: Germany; f: Leopold PACKEISER; m: Wilhelmine BARTIGKETT] md: Henriette BROSH [22; Omaha; b: Germany; f: Ferdinand BROSH; m: Carolina JANETZKO] on 14 Apr 1881. Off: BENEKE. Wit: August STRUSPAIT, Fred WILLUHN.

PADDOCK, Algernon Sydney [29; Omaha] md. Emma L. MACK [20; Omaha] on 22 Dec 1859. Off: WATSON. Wit: J.M. PADDOCK, Susan PADDOCK, John A. PARKER, Jr., Louisa GILMORE.

PAGE, John S. [36; Omaha; b: Ohio; f: John E. PAGE; m: Larane SEVENS] md.

Elizabeth C. WINCHESTER [29; Burlington, IL; b: Canada; f: Royal WINCHESTER; m: Serenia CHURCH] on 4 May 1871. Off: GIBSON. Wit: John RICHARD; Mrs. J. RICHARD.

PAILING, James [45; Plattsmouth; b: England; f: James PAILING; m: Henrietta F. GRAY] md. Mrs. Catharine WILLIAMS [42; Union Pct, Douglas Co.; b: Indiana; f: Henry LUDDINGTON; m: Juliette TARPENNING] on 8 May 1873. Off: TOWNSEND. Wit: Benjamin E.B. KENNEDY; Cornelius WILLIAMS of Union Pct., NE.

PAINTER, James M. [28; Omaha] md. Elizabeth ABERCROMBIE [27; Omaha] on 8 Feb 1867. Off: HASCALL. Wit: Tho. K. WRIGHT, W.S. HOWENSTIEN.

PAIST, Charles E. [23; Elkhorn Station; b: Dayleshaven, PA; f: D. Bradshaw PAIST; m: Mary A. WEST] md. Nellie E. DOWLING [16; Elkhorn Station; b: Cincinnati, OH; f: William DOWLING; m: Sarah J. MILLER] on 21 Sep 1870 at Elkhorn Station. Off: DODGE. Wit: Mrs. Sarah J. DOWLING, Elkhorn Station; Mrs. Matilda P. LYONS, Elkhorn Station.

PALMER, William [25; Harrison Co., IA] and Mary BOWES [32; Harrison Co., IA] license issued on 29 Sep 1859. No marriage record. Off: BRIGGS.

PALMQUIST, Adolf [22; Omaha; b: Sweden; f: John PALMQUIST; m: Mary Christine] md. Christine WENBERG [27; Omaha; b: Sweden; f: Andrew WENBERG; m: Mary WENBERG] on 29 May 1869. Off: KERMOTT. Wit: Mrs. A.R. KERMOTT, Frank R. KERMOTT.

PAMP, Carl E. [24; Douglas Co.; b: Sweden; f: Nels P. PAMP; m: Anna Christina TELEN] md. Annie JOHNSON [24; Omaha; b: Sweden; f: John PERSEN; m: Elsie MUNSEN] on 20 Jan 1872. Off: TOWNSEND. Wit: William H. IJAMS; Jerome HIRTZMANN.

PAPE, Hermann [40; Omaha; b: Prussia; f: Frederick PAPE; m: Dorothea TEASING] md. Sophia DEIRKS [19; Omaha; b: Holstein, Germany; f: Detleff DEIRKS; m: Augusta HANSON] on 23 Aug 1879. Off: BRANDES. Wit: Mrs. Ida KAISER, A. KNUTH.

PAPEZ, Joseph [27; Omaha; b: Bohemia; f: John PAPEZ; m: Barbara GANAS] md. Josephine VODICKA [21; Omaha; b: Bohemia; f: Jacob VODICKA] on 29 Jan 1870. Off: KELLEY (KELLY). Wit: F.D. COOPER; J.S. TUCKER.

PARCEL, Charles E. [28; Omaha] md. Henrietta WHITFORD [24; Omaha] on 4 Aug 1868 at the Lutheran Church. Off: KUHNS. Wit: Mr. and Mrs. James SKINNER, et al.

PARCELL, William T. [24] and Marian Ann AMSBARY [19] license issued on 5 May 1860. No marriage record. Off: ARMSTRONG.

PARCELS, Frank G. [22; Omaha] md. Irene SHINN [20; Omaha] on 3 Jan 1867 at M.F. SHINN's residence. Off: LEMON. Wit: Moses F. SHINN, Nancy SHINN, et al.

PARK, Gilbert G. [Plattford, Sarpy Co.] and Sarah J. PRESTON [Plattford, Sarpy Co.] license issued on 11 May 1864. No marriage record. Off: DICKINSON.

PARKER, A.W. [23; Omaha; b: Virginia; md. Augusta BYNG [19; Philadelphia, PA; b: South Carolina; f: George BYNG; m: Sarah BYNG] on 4 Oct 1879. Off: JAMESON. Wit: Jesse NEWMAN, Hattie COWDEN.

PARKER, Charles [25; Omaha; b: England; f: Richard PARKER; m: Ann MASTERS] md. Catharine STREETER [25; Omaha; b: England; f: John STREETER; m: Ann FRAZER] on 25 Sep 1872. Off: ESTABROOK. Wit: H.D. ESTABROOK; Phillip STREETER.

PARKER, Francis M. ]23; Missouri Valley Junction, IA; b: Buchanan Co., MO; f: Stephen H. PARKER; m: Eliza SCRUGGS] md. Annie E. PENNY [18; Elkhorn Station; b: Illinois; f: Jacob PENNY] on 3 Apr 1871 at SHINN's res. Off: SHINN. Wit: Miss? C. CAMPBELL, Iowa?; A. STEWART, near Elkhorn?; et al.

PARKER, Frank H. [25; Beatrice; f: H.W. PARKER; m: Almira DOLL] md. Cora M. PLACE [22; Satan Cruiz, CO; b: Illinois; f: George W. PLACE; m: Harriet L. BILLINGS] on 21 May 1880. Off: BRISTOL. Wit: Lucien E. BRISTOL, Bellie BRISTOL.

PARKER, S.G., Jr. [25; Des Moines, IA; b: Illinois; f: S.G. PARKER; m: Mary MITCHELL] md. Matey E. COFFEY [21; Omaha; b: Ohio; f: John COFFEY; m: Maria STAGE] on 20 Jul 1878. Off: BARTHOLOMEW. Wit: Wm. L. PEABODY, Joel T. GRIFFEN.

PARKER, William [35; Omaha; b: PA; f: Roger PARKER; m: Alice BLEASDALE] md. Mrs. Harriet E. LOCKLIN [36; Omaha; b: IL; f: William M. ALLEN; m: Maria ABORN] on 30 Apr 1881 at Trinity Rectory. Off: PETERSON. Wit: H. LENNING, Florence LEMING. Filed 29 May 1889 by SHIELDS.

PARKINS, Thomas C. [26; Omaha; b: Washington, D.C.; f: Joseph E. PARKINS; m: Charlotte CUTHBERT] md. Anna N. BUCHANAN [21; Palmyra, NE; b: Indiana; f: Alexander BUCHANAN; m: Matilda RICE] on 14 Jun 1880. Off: INGRAM. Wit: G.W. WILLARD, Alexander BUCHANAN.

PARKINSON, Francis [28; Omaha] md. Margaret BRENNAN [25; Omaha] on 17 Jun 1861. Off: KELLY. Wit: Wm. BLAKE. "Correct record"...as appears in church record typed and stamped 13 Dec 1913, Off: STENSON.

PARKS, S.A. [30; b: Pennsylvania; f: James PARKS; m: Mary H. HANLEY] md. Mary THOMAS [24; b: Iowa; f: John THOMAS] on 15 May 1878. Off: BECKLEY. Wit: Frank A. MAGEE, John C. McCARTY.

PARKS, Thomas H. [42; Douglas Co.; b: IL; f: T.S. PARKS; m: Ann MILLER] md. Mrs. Margaret M. WILLIAMS [34; Omaha; b: MO; f: Elias BROWN; m: Rebecca WATTS] on 2 Dec 1875. Off: STEWART. Wit: Silas A. STRICKLAND, Henry M. BROWN.

PARMELY, Edward A. [28; Omaha; b: Washington, DC; f: Dan S. PARMELY; m: Mary A. BARBOUR] md. Sarah K. COON [22; Omaha; b: Pittsburg, PA; f: Archibald F. COON] on 10 Apr 1873. Off: DeLaMATYR. Wit: Watson B. SMITH; L.M. BENNETT.

PARMLEE, Lemuel [29; Omaha; b: IA; f: Dennis PARMLEE; m: Cynthe LEWIS] md. Mary ALBERTSON [18; Omaha; b: OH; f: Andrew (Benjamin crossed out) J. ALBERTSON; m: Sophia WAGNER] on 17 Aug 1881. Off: MAXFIELD. Wit: Geo. EVISON, Mrs. Geo. EVISON.

PARR, Michael [32; Omaha; b: Ohio; f: John A. PARR: m: Elizabeth MEINHART] md. Hellen Laura McINTOSH [32; Omaha; b: Michigan; f: James McINTOSH; m: Laura RAWSON] on 9 Dec 1873. Off: WRIGHT. Wit: Henry R. BENJAMIN; Mary H. WRIGHT.

PARRISH, Henry A. [21; Omaha; b: Virginia; f: John G. PARRISH; m: Susan G. FARRAR] md. Addie O. DUNCAN [20; Omaha; b: Illinois; f: Charles DUNCAN; m: Odyssa SANDS] on 15 Sep 1880. Off: LIPE. Wit: Chas. HIGGINS, Chas. DUNCAN.

PARSHALL, Glasgow [50; Mercer Co., IL; b: Pennsylvania; f: Caleb PARSHALL; m: Nancy MATHEWS] md. Sarah K. KINNEY [30; Omaha; b: Ohio; f: John KINNEY; m: Margaret BROWN] on 27 Nov 1873. Off: STEWART. Wit: Mrs. F.O. BEHM; Jeremiah BEHM.

PASCH, Henry [28; Douglas Co.; b: Germany; f: Fred PASCH; m: Lotte PETERSON] md. Elsabe ROHWER [22; Douglas Co.; b: Germany; f: Jurgen ROHWER; m: Elsabeth THODE] on 6 Oct 1874. Off: PEABODY. Wit: Gen. C.F. MANDERSON; Claus SIEVERS.

PASHLEY, John [54; Omaha; b: England; f: John PASHLEY; m: Mary] md. Mrs. Hannah SPENCER [40; Omaha; b: England; f: ---- CHAMBERS] on 1 Jan 1873. Off: SHERRILL. Wit: Chas. T. TAYLOR; E.C. STANGLAND.

PATRICK, Charles B. [22; Corning, MO; b: Jackson, MI; f: Samuel PATRICK; m: Jane MARTIN] md. Mary JORDAN [18; Galesburg, IL; f: ---- JORDAN; m: Catherine CLARKE] on 10 Dec 1870. Off: DANIELS. Wit: W.D. CRESAP; H.C. WALLACE.

PATTERSON, Arthur [28; Richardson Co.] md. Emily A. HOOPER [26; Clinton, IA] at 12 o'clock, Thursday, 25 Feb 1869 at DIMMICK's house. Off: DIMMICK. Wit: Mrs. F.P. WRIGHT, Mrs. K.G. DIMMICK.

PATTERSON, Ashbell [30; Omaha; b: NY; f: Uri H. PATTERSON; m: Amelia BUTLER] md. Annie C. HAYDEN [22; Omaha; b: NY; f: Bernard S. HAYDEN; m: Mary E. YATES] on 19 Jul 1881. Off: MILLSPAUGH. Wit: Dr. James PEABODY, Ruel K. HAYDEN. Affidavit signed by Willis M. YATES.

PATTERSON, Gabriel [29; Omaha; b: Sweden; f: Carl PETERSON; m: Christina ANDERSDOTTER] md. Karin EDLING [17; Omaha; b: Sweden; f: John EDLING; m: Brita JOHANSDOTTER] on 28 Jan 1872. Off: LARSON. Wit: Frank A. HULTMAN; Charles J. MARTINELL.

PATTERSON, George [29; Omaha] md. Mrs. Kate SMITH [25; Omaha] on 4 Nov 1868. Off: MULCHAY. Wit: L.M. HERBERT of St. Louis, MO, Martin GRIFFIN, James F. MORTON.

PATTINSONGILL, Richard [21; Montreal, Canada; b: London, ENG; f: Col. R. PATTINSONGILL; m: Mary Ann MOORE] md. Antonia Maria IRELAND [18; Chatham, Canada; b: Chatham, Canada; f: Thos. A. IRELAND; m: Ellen LABADIE] on 19 Aug 1871 at O'GORMAN's house. Off: O'GORMAN. Wit: Peter MALONE; Mary DOWD.

PATTON, William J. [21; Omaha; b: Missouri; f: D.A. PATTON; m: Margaret PEELER] md. Nellie DEE [21; Omaha; b: Omaha; f: Jeremiah DEE; m: Julia COSON] on 25 Sep 1879. Off: STENBERG. Wit: Mrs. E. Estella KOUGH, Jose S. KOUGH.

PAUL, Cornelius H. [27; Omaha; b: New York; f: Caleb J. PAUL; m: Emeline LANE] md. Alice V. PHELPS [20; Omaha; b: Winchester, OH; f: Horace W. PHELPS] on 10 Nov 1870. Off: DeLaMATYR. Wit: C.C. HONSEL; Marion J. HONSEL.

PAUL, James I. [27; Omaha] md. Anna L. ROBINSON [27; Omaha] on 7 Dec 1866. Off: KERMOTT. Wit: Mr. and Mrs. A.R. HOELL.

PAULSEN, Charles P. [28; Omaha; b: Denmark; f: Jurgen PAULSEN; m: Carolina WINTER] md. Augusta M. BARNEY [20; Omaha; b: Sweden; f: Frederick BARNEY] on 12 Aug 1870. Off: GIBSON. Wit: A.A. EKELUND; Mrs. Anna EKELUND.

PAULSEN, Johannes Theodore [23; Omaha] md. Anne Caroline HAGEDORN [23; Omaha] on 30 Mar 1861 at KUHNS' residence on Douglas St. Off: KUHNS. Wit: Mrs. H.W. KUHNS, Henry RICHTER, John EPENETER.

PAULSEN, Peter [34; Omaha; b: Denmark; f: Paul PETERSON; m: Mary NELSON] md. Elida ANDERSON [24; Omaha; b: Sweden; f: Lars ANDERSON; m: Christina LEIBER] on 24 May 1876. Off: SEDGWICK. Wit: John STEELE, Douglas Co., Hannah STEELE, Douglas Co.

PAVER, Robert L. [22; Omaha; b: OH; f: William H. PAVER; m: Sarah A. LORD] md. Mary J. HAMILTON [18; Omaha; b: Chicago, IL; f: James HAMILTON; m: Ellen TEARAL] on 20 Jul 1875. Off: PATTERSON. Wit: P.A. GUSHWIST, Anna BOLANDER.

PAXTON, Charles T. [23; Detroit, MI; b: Detriot, MI; f: John W. PAXTON; m: Mary BALDOCK] md. Johanna ARNDT [18; Omaha; b: Germany; f: August ARNDT; m: Wilhelmina TEADKA] on 6 Jun 1872. Off: TOWNSEND. Wit: William H. IJAMS; Charles H. BYRNE.

PAXTON, Stephen S. [41; Rawlings, WY; b: New York; f: James PAXTON; m: Anna Van CAMP] md. Mrs. Rebecca R. MORROW [27; Akron, OH; b: Ohio; f: Hugh J. GIBBONS; m: Amy GOSS] on 14 May 1880. Off: MAXFIELD. Wit: Mrs. CANFIELD, Mrs. MILLER.

PAYNE, William Augustus [29; Douglas Co.; b: Wayne Co., PA; f: Homer R. PAYNE; m: Louisa GREELY] md. Mrs. Margaret BLACK [28; Douglas Co.; b: Montgomery Co., OH; f: Henry BLACK; m: Mariah RICE] on 20 Jun 1869 at John CARTER's in Valley Station. Off: DENTON. Wit: John CARTER of Valley Station, Wm. BLACK of Valley Station.

PAYTON, W.B. [44; Omaha; b: Virginia; f: Andrew PAYTON; m: Mary MILLS] md. Mrs. Anora CORNISH [35; Omaha; b: Indiana; f: Augustus TURNER; m: Triphenia GRAFFORD] on 16 Jan 1879. Off: FRANCKE, pastor of the First M.E. Church. Wit: Chas. W. EDGERTEN, John LEWIS.

PEABODY, James H. [33; Omaha] md. Eliza J.D. YATES [30; Omaha] on 21 Nov 1867. Off: VAN ANTWERP. Wit: Victor H. COFFMAN, M.D., Miss Lida PATRICK, Wm. J. YATES, et al. Double endorsement given by SHEEKS. [Trinity Church records give the bride's name as Eliza Jane Delaplane GATES.]

PEACOCK, Charles [36; Omaha] md. Martha WOOD [28; Omaha] on 21 Dec 1868. Off: KELLEY. Wit: J.B. MOORE, John SMITH, D.B. TOPHAM.

PEACOCK, Charles [37; Omaha; b: North Elba, NY; f: James PEACOCK; m: Sarah MOTT] md. Jemima BAVENZER [27; Omaha; b: Cleveland, OH; f: George RAGAN; m: Jemima McPHARLAN] on 22 or 24 Oct 1869. Off: KERMOTT. Wit: Mrs. Abigal A. FULLER, Mrs. A.F. KERMOTT.

PEAK, Julius [46; Washington Co.; b: Ohio; f: Daniel PEAK; m: Clarissa TORREY] md. Mrs. Viola SIMONDS [25; Douglas Co.; b: Indiana; f: Harvey THOMPSON; m: Elizabeth ROLLINS] on 5 Feb 1879. Off: JOHNSON. Wit: N.J. SMITH, J.P. SMITH.

PEARSON, Charles R. [28; Omaha] md. Maria SHALENBURGER [21; Omaha] on 30 Nov 1866. Off: HASCALL. Wit: Mr. and Mrs. Horace LOMBARD.

PEARSON, John J. [32; Fulton, WI; b: OH; f: John J. PEARSON; m: Eveline POMEROY] md. Mrs. Sarah G. POMEROY [35; Suffield, CT; b: CT; f: Paul HARMON; m: Abagail GILLETT] on 12 May 1875. Off: McCAGUE. Wit: Paul and A.J. HARMON, George C. MERICLE.

PEARSSON, John [24; Omaha; b: Sweden; f: Andrew PEARSSON; m: Christina YANSDOTER] md. Johanna BRUSA [19; Omaha; b: Sweden; f: Ole BRUSA; m: Mary SAMUELSDOTER] on 26 Apr 1872. Off: TOWNSEND. Wit: Charles H. BROWN; John P. BARTLETT.

PEASE, Alfred L. [24; Burt Co., NE; b: Michigan; f: H.C. PEASE; m: Louisa TURNER] md. Mamie A. BROWN [19; Burt Co., NE; f: Harrison BROWN; m: ---- McCOY] on 8 Feb 1877. Off: PARDEE. Wit: W.P. COOLEY, Abbie A. COOLEY.

PEASLEY, Charles [24; Richmond, VA; b: Virginia; f: James PEASLEY; m: Mary JOHNSON] and Amelia HURT [20; Hamburg, IA; b: Iowa; f: George HURT; m: Jane ROGERS] license issued on 14 Feb 1872. Off: TOWNSEND.

PECK, Albert James [31; Florence; b: OH; f: Simeon PECK; m: Christiana HILLINSHEAD] md. Amanda Z. ORCHARD [25; Omaha; b: IN; f: A.R. ORCHARD; m: Amanda M. HELM] on 11 Sep 1875. Off: PECK. Wit: Mr. and Mrs. A.R. ORCHARD, Fannie G. PECK, Florence.

PECK, Edward P. [21; Omaha; b: OH; f: J.P. PECK; m: E.H. AMES] md. Mary E.

BISHOP [21; Omaha; b: IL; f: James E. BISHOP; m: C.L. WILSON] on 18 Sep 1876. Off: CLARKSON. Wit: J.P. PECK, James E. BISHOP.

PECK, George Wm. [19; Douglas Co.] md. Elizabeth TRISLER [19; Douglas Co.] on 7 Mar 1861. Off: PECK. Wit: John K. SMITH, Mary A. SMITH. Age consent given by Simon PECK, father of the groom.

PECK, Martin Luther [Douglas Co.] md. Melissa Jane SHIPLEY [18; Washington Co.] on 23 Aug 1863. Off: PECK. Wit: Eliza PECK. Age consent given by bride's father.

PEDERSEN, Jens (James) [36; Omaha; b: Denmark; f: Peter JENSEN; m: Ingra Catharina JENSEN] md. Mrs. Louisa Charlotte ADSTROM [42; Omaha; b: Sweden] on 9 Jan 1873. Off: JOHNSSON. Wit: Jesse BROADBENT; John CHRISTENSON.

PEETS, Frederick [29; Douglas Co.; b: Germany; f: Gottlieb PEETS; m: Margaret] md. Mary EIFFLIE [21; Omaha; b: Germany] on 28 Apr 1872 at West Omaha Precinct. Off: MYERS. Wit: Henry EICKE, McArdle Pct; Fritz LEVON, McArdle Pct.

PEETZ, Fritz [24; Douglas Co.; b: Germany; f: Gottlieb PEETZ; m: Johanna ENGEL] md: Marie SANER [18; Douglas Co.; b: NE; f: Conrad SANER; m: Catharina BLUMENAN] on 6 Mar 1881 at Millard Precinct. Off: BENEKE. Wit: Lavina MANGOLD, Millard Precinct, Hans HOLLING, Millard Precinct.

PELLANT, Frank [30; b: Bohemia; f: Martin PELLANT; m: Mary FRILETZ] md. Antonia THOTKA [23; b: Bohemia; f: Wenzel THOTKA; m: Annie THOTKA] on 1 Jul 1878. Off: KOCARNIK. Wit: Aloysius SIMON, Frank BELOVIC.

PEMBROOKE, John C. [22; Illinois; b: Illinois; f: Michael PEMBROOKE; m: Ellen O'CONNER] md. Bridget McDONALD [22; St. Paul, OR; b: St. Paul, OR; f: Mills McDONALD] on 9 Dec 1878 at the cathedral, Omaha. Off: McDERMOTTL Wit: Edward EAGAN, and other witnesses. This record was filed on 10 Oct 1888.

PENDERY, Abram S., Dr. [33; Omaha; b: Hamilton Co., OH; f: William D. PENDERY; m: Mary Ann SKILLMAN] md. Eva J. LIPE [16; Omaha; b: Illinois; f: W.A. LIPE; m: Lizzie E. BROWN] on 18 Sep 1879. Off: LIPE. Wit: Mrs. Nellie BOORMAN, Mrs. Lizzie E. LIPE. Age consent given by W.A. LIPE, father of the bride.

PENDY, Patrick [25; Omaha] md. Mary DIGGIN [25; Omaha] on 24 Apr 1869. Off: CURTIS. Wit: Peter MALONE, Bridget HARRINGTON.

PENKUN, F.W. [22; Omaha; b: Germany; f: Frederick PENKUN; m: Dora SEEBACH] md. Maggie ROTHOLTZ [18; Peoria, IL; b: Peoria, IL; f: Peter ROTHOLTZ; m: Mary

OSWALD] on 9 Jan 1874. Off: STEWART. Wit: W.N. NASON; E.H. SAGE.

PENNEY, Theodore [23; Douglas Co., b: Ohio; f: R.M. PENNEY; m: Jane STROUGH] md. Ellen DECKER [19; Douglas Co.; b: Ohio; f: S. DECKER; m: Katey FORBES] on 6 Mar 1877. Off: Douglas Co. Justice of the Peace. Wit: James DECKER, C. LEWIS.

PENNY, John W. [Omaha] md. Lucy L. EVANS [Omaha] on 31 Aug 1865. Off: MILLER. Wit: Mr. and Mrs. EVANS, parents of the bride.

PERKINS, C.E. [29; Omaha; b: VT; f: Benjamin R. PERKINS; m: Alice PEARSONS] md. Sallie V. HICKMAN [26; Omaha; b: IL; f: Wm. W. HICKMAN; m: Elvira PROUD] on 23 Jun 1881. Off: HARSHA. Wit: W.T. SEAMAN, James NEVILLE.

PERKINS, George W. [29; Blair; b: Canada; f: John PERKINS; m: Rosella CORBIN] md. Mary M. WESTON [31; Omaha; b: Iowa; f: John WESTON; m: Lucy STONE] on 12 Aug 1869. Off: HYDE. Wit: Mortimer or DeMotte HYDE, S.S. PRICE of Missouri.

PERRINE, Upton [23; Montgomery, AL; b: Pennsylvania; f: Reden PERRINE; m: Catherine RIDDLE] md. Sadie E. CAFFERTY [24; Omaha; b: New Jersey; f: James CAFFERTY] on 12 Jul 1871. Off: KING. Wit: Mrs. C.A. KING; Lizzie SIMONS.

PERSON, Anders [26; Douglas Co.; b: Sweden; f: Par NELSON; m: Elna JOERNSEN] md. Bengta NELSON [28; Douglas Co.; b: Sweden; f: Nels OLESON; m: Hannah PERSSON] on 26 Aug 1881. Off: FOGELSTROM. Wit: Elin JOHNSON, Mrs. I.P. ELMGRIN.

PERSON, Pete [26; Saunders Co.; b: Sweden; f: Truls PERSON; m: Hannah SWANSON] md. Ellen JOHNSON [17; b: Sweden; f: Christof JOHNSON; m: Louisa LONVIN] on 22 Jun 1878, Off: HANSEN. Wit: Swan Johan HAGSTRAM; Frederik JOHNSON. Age consent given by Christopher JOHNSON, father of the bride.

PETERS, Claus [25; Saunders Co.; b: Germany; f: Peter PETERS; m: Elizabeth RODE] md. Louise A. RHEIN [19; Omaha; b: Pennsylvania; f: Frederick RHEIN; m: Anna Maria STEIN] on 19 Aug 1880. Off: FREDE. Wit: Mrs. Mina PETERS of Saunders Co., Mrs. Cacilie TROSSING.

PETERS, Detlef [27; Saunders Co., NE; b: Germany; f: Peter PETERS; m: Elsbeth RHODE] md. J.W.M. SCHEMBER [26; Omaha; b: Germany; f: H.W. SCHEMBER; m: Maria B. HENKEL] on 21 Feb 1879. Off: FALK. Wit: Mrs. Cecelia DROSSIN, Mr. R. DROSSIN, Messrs. Claus MARTEN and H. BERTHOLD.

PETERS, Frank [39; Omaha; b: Germany; f: John J.F. PETERS; m: Maria M. KOHN] md. Caroline GSANDNER [29; Omaha; b: Germany; f: John GSANDNER; m: Magdalena HARTMAN] on 27 Sep 1873. Off: BRANDES. Wit: Ferdinand PETERSON; Anton GSANDNER.

PETERS, J.W. [29; Belleview, Sarpy Co.] md. A.E. GOW [25; Belleview] on 9 Sep 1868 at LEMON's residence. Off: LEMON. Wit: Mrs. M.B. LEMON and family.

PETERS, Peter [23; Omaha] md. Mary LARSON [19; Omaha] on 27 Jul 1868. Off: STUCK. Wit: Max MATTESON, W.F. DeGRAFFENRIED.

PETERSEN, Adolph [28; Sarpy Co.; b: Germany; f: Henry PETERSON; m: Elizabeth SIMPSON] md. Alice DINER [18; Otoe Co.; b: PA; f: John DINER; m: Matilda FRESLER] on 16 Feb 1875. Off: PEABODY. Wit: C.L. BRISTOL, Margaret GOSES.

PETERSEN, Andrew [24; Omaha; b: Sweden; f: Peter BENSON; m: Hannah JOHNSON] md. Caroline OLSON [25; Omaha; b: Sweden; f: Martin OLSON; m: Christine PETERSEN] md. 28 Apr 1872. Off: LARSON. Wit: Nels SWANSON; Mrs. Clara SWANSON.

PETERSEN, Nels Chr. [22; Omaha; b: Denmark; f: Christian PETERSEN; m: Marianne NELSEN] md. Christine MADSON [19; Omaha; b: Denmark; f: Mads SORENSEN; m: Marianne CHRISTENSEN] on 24 May 1881 at Vor Frelser's Church. Off: GYDESEN. Wit: Peter CHRISTENSEN, Robert NEILSEN.

PETERSEN, Olof [26; Omaha; b: Sweden; f: Peter OLSON; m: Annie PETERSEN] md. Johanna PETERSEN [23; Omaha; b: Sweden; f: Erick PETERSEN; m: Mary HENDERSON] on 4 Jun 1872. Off: BRANDES. Wit: Charles ANDERSON; John JOHNSON.

PETERSEN, Peter C. [33; Omaha; b: Denmark; f: Peter PETERSON; m: Catharine CHRISTIANSEN] md. Dora M. JACOBSEN [27; Omaha; b: Denmark; f: Jacob JACOBSEN; m: Anna Maria CLAUSON] on 5 May 1873. Off: TOWNSEND. Wit: Christian CHRISTIANSEN; William P. HENNESSEY.

PETERSEN, Peter [25; Omaha; b: Denmark; f: Peter JENSEN; m: Annie MATTSEN] md. Lena ANDERSEN [18; Omaha; b: Rio de Janeiro, Brazil; f: Christian ANDERSEN; m: Dorah MOLT] on 2 Nov

1870. Off: KUHNS. Wit: Christian ANDERSEN; Dorah ANDERSEN.

PETERSEN, Soren T. [29; Omaha; b: Denmark; f: Peter GIBSON; m: Gunemaria HANSEN] md. Micaeline C. JORGENSEN [20; Omaha; b: Denmark; f: Jorgen JORGENSEN; m: Annie M. THOMPSON] on 16 Sep 1873. Off: TOWNSEND. Wit: John W. LYTLE; George J. GILBERT.

PETERSEN, Soren T. [33; Douglas Co.; b: Denmark f: Peter JEPSEN; m: Gunne Maria HANSEN] md. Maria Magrethe THOMSEN [22; Douglas Co.; b: Denmark; f: Hans THOMSEN; m: Ane Maria CHRISTENSEN] on 29 Sep 1876. Off: LIPE. Wit: Fred SCHAEFFER, Mrs. Mary ELLIOT.

PETERSON, Albert R. [28; Omaha; b: Denmark; f: F.L. PETERSON; m: Mary OTZEN] md. Anna L. PETERSON [19; Omaha; b: Sweden; f: Swen PETERSON; m: Catharine JOHNSON] on 19 May 1879. Off: STENBERG. Wit: E.A. McCLURE, R. De DARLING.

PETERSON, Andrew [22; Omaha; b: Denmark; f: Peter WILLIAMSON; m: Catharine ANDERSON] md. Louisa M. HARDEN [19; Omaha; b: Fayette Co., PA; f: William HARDEN; m: Sarah WYLY (WYLEY)] on 24 Aug 1869. Off: KUHNS. Wit: M.T. PATRICK, Lyda PATRICK.

PETERSON, Andrew [27; Omaha; b: Sweden; f: Peter ANDERSON; m: Bride JONSON] md. Lizzie ANDERSON [30; Omaha; b: Sweden; f: Hans JOHNSON; m: Mary OLESON] on 2 Feb 1874. Off: PEABODY. Wit: Emily BUTTERFIELD; David L. KEYES.

PETERSON, Andrew [28; Omaha; b: Sweden; f: Peter BENSON; m: Jennie JOHNSON] md. Emily C. FRODMAN [22; Omaha; b: Sweden; f: Charles Uldric FRODMAN; m: Sophia Fredericka PARSON] on 19 Oct 1876. Off: PEABODY. Wit: S.J. LARSON, Mrs. Emma HOBBEY.

PETERSON, Anton [25; Omaha; b: Denmark; f: Peter CHRISTENSON; m: Mathilde ANDERSEN] md. Marie CHRISTENSON [22; Omaha; b: Denmark; f: Peter CHRISTENSON; m: Christine ANDERSON] on 9 May 1881 at "their res." Off: GYDESEN. Wit: Peter CHRISTENSON, Niels Chr. PETERSEN.

PETERSON, Byrngel [35; Omaha; b: Sweden; f: Peter ANDERSON] md. Keyerstin OLSDOTTER [23; Omaha; b: Sweden; f: Olof SEGELSON] on 12 Dec 1869. Off: LARSON. Wit: Gunnar A. LINDQUIST, Ingeborg OLSON.

PETERSON, Charles [28; Omaha] md. Lena SCHRODER [27; Omaha] on 22 Jul 1878. Off: BARTHOLOMEW. Wit: Wm. L. PEABODY, Wm. SIMIRAL. [The certificate states 1878 and it was recorded then, but the license was issued 29 Jun 1868.]

PETERSON, Charly [25; Florence; b: Sweden; f: Peter PETERSON; m: Helen SANDBERG] and Johanne OLSON [24; Omaha; b: Sweden; f: Ole ANDERSON; m: Karin NIELSEN] license issued on 2 Mar 1871. Off: GIBSON.

PETERSON, Christian [24; Omaha; b: Prussia; f: Peter PETERSON; m: Catherine SCHNEHEIRN] md. Marian MATSEN [19; Omaha; b: Denmark; f: Christian MATSEN; m: Anna JOHNSON] on 5 Mar 1870. Off: KUHNS. Wit: Minnie STEWART; Carl T. RATH.

PETERSON, Christian [29; Omaha] md. Mary WILSON [18; Omaha] on 19 Jan 1867. Off: HASCALL. Wit: D.C. CHRISTENSON, Christina PETERSON.

PETERSON, Edward [34; Sarpy Co.] md. Caroline BEARBEEN [24; Sarpy Co.] on 19 Feb 1869. Off: HYDE. Wit: L.H. BORDWELL, Wm. J. HAHN.

PETERSON, Erick [31; Omaha; b: Sweden; f: Peter HANSON; m: Hellen] md. Mary A. ALEXANDER [31; Omaha; b: Ithaca, NY; f: Robert ALEXANDER; m: Christeen SNYDER] on 17 Sep 1869. Off: KUHNS. Wit: Mrs. H.W. KUHNS, Annie CATHERWOOD.

PETERSON, James [25; Omaha; b: Denmark; f: C.C. UTRUT; m: Anna LARSON] md. Anna C. PETERSON [22; Omaha (Shelby Co., IA, crossed out); b: Denmark; f: Peter HALM; m: Anna M. PETERSON] on 7 Aug 1875. Off: CONGER. Wit: Henry WILSON, Mrs. E. CONGER.

PETERSON, Jan [Omaha] md. Albertina DANELSON [Omaha] on 7 Nov 1868. Off: STUCK. Wit: John M. SULLIVAN.

PETERSON, John M. [27; b: Sweden; f: Petter COLSON; m: Annie SOLMERSON] md. Nellie JOHNSON [19; b: Sweden; f: Peter JOHNSON; m: Betsy ANDERSON] on 5 Apr 1878. Off: LIPE. Wit: Nels MADSON, Trige MADSON.

PETERSON, Lars [33; Valley Station, NE; b: Denmark; f: Peter JORGANSON; m: Christine ANDERSON] md. Betty NELSON [20; Valley Station, NE; b: Sweden; f: Peter NELSON; m: Anna HANSON] on 29 Dec 1878. Off: HAYLAND. Wit: Niels PETERSON of Valley Station, Andrew ANDERSON and wife.

PETERSON, Lars [Omaha] md. Annie ANDERSON [Omaha] on 9 Oct 1864 at DICKINSON's office. Off: DICKINSON. Wit: John AHMANSON, Henry ANDERSON, A.J. OLDS, Mr. and Mrs. Peter ANDERSON.

PETERSON, Lorentz Christian [22; Omaha; b: Copenhagen; f: Claus Frederick PETERSON (PETTERSON); m: Morentze Sophia GINSON] md. Hulda Marie OLSEN [19; Omaha; b: Norway; f: Frederick OLSEN; m: Maren HANSON] on 22 May 1869. Off: HYDE. Wit: John H.A. RATH, Henry V. GROLSTED.

PETERSON, Nels [25; Omaha; b: Norway; f: Peter BORGENSEN; m: Mary OLSON] md. Annie OLSON [18; Omaha; b: Norway; f: Ole OLSON; m: Mgar MARTAR] on 16 Dec 1881 at Ole OLSON's residence. Off: HENDRICKSON. Wit: Lars LARSEN, Oluf OLSEN.

PETERSON, Nels [27; Douglas Co.; b: Denmark; f: Peter NELSON; m: Maron HANSON] md. Mary OLESON [18; Douglas Co.; b: Sweden; f: L.P. OLESON; m: Anna LINDQUEST] on 18 July 1879 at Valley. Off: HAYLAND. Wit: L. PETERSON, L.P. LARSON both of Valley.

PETERSON, Peter C. [37; Omaha; b: Denmark; f: Peter PETERSON; m: Katherine KRUSTENSON] md. Mette J.J. PLATZ [23; Omaha; b: Denmark; f: Jens Hensen PLATZ; m: Matte J.J. PAULSON] on 17 Oct 1876. Off: SEDGWICK. Wit: Jacob JACOBSON, Charles J. GREEN.

PETERSON, Peter [31; Omaha; b: Norway; f: Peter LARSON; m: Bert GENSEN] md. Eva ANDERSON [23; Omaha; b: Sweden; f: E. ANDERSON; m: Marie BRYNTESEN] on 27 Jun 1870 at MAY's res. Off: MAY. Wit: Mrs. T. SUFHEN; Miss A. HEISER.

PETERSON, Soren C. [26; Omaha; b: Denmark; f: Peter PETERSON; m: Christian SORENSEN] md. Mary JOHNSON [25; Omaha; b: Denmark; f: Nels JOHNSON; m: Sophia NELSON] on 31 Mar 1877. Off: HANSEN. Wit: Sophia NELSON, Nels JOHNSON.

PETERSON, Swen M. [34; Omaha; b: Sweden; f: Peter NELSON; m: Christine ANDERSON] md: Maria JOHNSON [34; Omaha; b: Sweden; f: John ERICKSON; m: Christine CARLSON] on 5 Sep 1881. Off: HAYLAND. Wit: N. MARTEN, S. KNUTSON.

PETERSON, William [34; Omaha; b: Denmark; f: Peter WILLIAMSON; m: Anna C. PETERSON] md. Mary PETERSON [26; Omaha; b: Denmark; f: Peter EVERSON; m: Mary PETERSON] on 14 Sep 1875. Off: HANSON. Wit: Rasmis NIELSON, Peter NIELSON.

PETTEGREW, David A. [25; Florence; b: Iowa; f: David A. PETTEGREW; m: Lydia SHAW] md. Melissie BARNES [16; Florence; b: Iowa; f: Aaron T. BARNES; m: Martha WILSON] on 10 Mar 1870. Off: KUHNS. Wit: John C. LINGNER; Mrs. Lidie PETTEGREW. Age of consent, J.C.

LINGNER and E. LINGNER his wife, guardians. (David A. PETTEGREW, witness to signature of guardians).

PETTY, John W. [32; Omaha; b: Missouri; f: Solomon PETTY; m: Mary FRANCE] md. Mary Frances DOLAN [23; Dallas Co., IA: b: Ireland; f: John DOLAN; m: Mary DALY] on 20 Jul 1872. Off: LYTLE. Wit: N.F. REAVIS; John A. HORBACH.

PEYCKE, Ernest [29; Omaha; b: Germany; f: John H. PEYCKE; m: Caroline M. REIFORT] md. Julia L. Von BORRIES [22; Omaha; b; Michigan; f: Henry Von BORRIES; m: Susanne Maria SONFRON] on 14 May 1879. Off: SHERRILL. Wit: Max MEYER; Albert WELLER.

PFEIFER, Frank [22; Omaha; b: Germany; f: George PFEIFER; m: Francisca WEISER] md. Barbara RADLER [21; Omaha; b: Germany] on 7 Jan 1873. Off: GROENEBAUM. Wit: Jos. KOESTERS; Elizabeth RUBHANAN.

PFLUG, Frederick [27; Douglas Co.] md. Grettchen BRANT [20; Douglas Co.] on 30 Mar 1862 at Mr. KIRCH's residence on Farnham St. Off: KUHNS. Wit: Mr. and Mrs. KIRCH, Mr. and Mrs. DOLL.

PFOUTZ, Ira [29; Omaha; b: Ohio; f: Jesse PFOUTZ; m: Rebecca KENZIE] md. Mrs. Mary F. WHITE [23; Omaha; b: Maryland; f: Joseph HARTMAN; m: Margaret BROWN] on 21 Mar 1870. Off: KUHNS. Wit: Mr. and Mrs. Joseph H. MILLARD.

PHAAB, Neils P. [31; Omaha; b: Denmark; f: Hans P. PHAAB; m: Mary RASMUSSEN] md. Kierstine M. SORENSEN [26; Washington Co.; b: Denmark; f: Peter M. SORENSEN; m: Anna JOHNSON] on 2 Mar 1871. Off: KUHNS. Wit: Peter SORENSEN; Hans P. SORENSEN.

PHELAN, Albert [22; Omaha] md. Mary DOLAN [21; Omaha] on 19 Aug 1868 at the Catholic Church. Off: O'GORMAN. Wit: F. McEVOY, Peter MALONE.

PHELAN, Patrick [38; Omaha; b: Ireland; f: William PHELAN; m: M. CAVY] md. Mary COLLOPY [27; Omaha; b: Pennsylvania; f: John COLLOPY; m: M. BROUGHTON] on 12 Jun 1877. Off: JENNETTO. Wit: Patrick CARROLL, Mary J. BIRIMIGHAM.

PHELPS, Frank [30; Omaha; b: New York; f: A.W. PHELPS; m: Emily PRICHARD] md. Jennie KRIEBS [22; Omaha; b: Iowa; f: Nicholas KRIEBS; m: Mary REESE] on 16 Feb 1880. Off: BRUECHERT. Wit: "Their parents above names."

PHELPS, George W. [27; Omaha; b: IA: f: C.J. PHELPS; m: Saray SEYDELL] md. Alice BAY [21; Omaha; b: IA; f: John P. BAY; m: Christine McCALL] on 30 Jan 1875. Off: FROST. Wit: Nola PHELPS, J.O. McCART.

PHELPS, John C. [27; Omaha; b: Niagara Falls, NY; f: John PHELPS; m: Hannah GRINNELL] md. Mrs. Catherine KANE [27; Omaha; b: Ireland; f: James KELLEY; m: Sibby CANAN] on 25 Apr 1870. Off: CURTIS. Wit: Henry O'NEIL; Catherine TIERNEY.

PHELPS, John E. [27; Omaha; b: IA; f: Oliver J. PHELPS; m: Sarah SIDELL] md. Anna M. NELSON [21; Omaha; b: Denmark; f: Ferdinand NELSON; m: Anna LARSEN] on 17 Aug 1881. Off: BEANS. Wit: Soren LARSEN, Viola M. PHELPS.

PHELPS, Timothy G. [22; Omaha; b; Iowa; f: O.J. PHELPS; m: Sarah SEDELL] md. Margaret DAWSON [20; Omaha; b: Canada; f: John DAWSON; m: Ann BRADY] at Holy Family Church on 21 Aug 1879. Off: QUINN. Wit: Patrick CARROLL, Kate DAWSON. P.J. CARROLL witness to signature (X).

PHELPS, Walter [29; Omaha; b: Canada; f: Alfred PHELPS; m: Emily PRITCHARD] md. Eliza MORRIS [28; Omaha; b: England; f: James MORRIS; m: Mary Ann MORRIS] on 22 Nov 1881. Off: HARRIS. Wit: James MORRIS, Frank PHELPS.

PHILBROOK, B.F. [26; Dunlap, IA; b: Maine; f: Lube PHILBROOK; m: Lucinda SMITH] md. Lucy E. HARTRY [24; Omaha; b: Illinois; f: Edwin HARTRY; m: Caroline SHEPHERD] on 4 Nov 1879. Off: JAMESON. Wit: Harry C. HARTRY, Mrs. Tillie BELL.

PHILLIPS, Geo. S. [42; Longmont, CA; b: VT; f: Seth PHILLIPS; m: Hannah WILLIAMS] md. Eliza BISSELL [34; Grand Rapids, MI; b: VT; f: Peter BISSELL; m: Betsey MUNCY] on 24 Oct 1881. Off: MARQUETT. Wit: Mrs. O. BIRD, Mrs. H. MARQUETT.

PHILLIPS, Joseph [25; Douglas Co.] and Catherine SCOLLARD [20; Douglas Co.] license issued on 27 Nov 1868. No marriage record. Off: STUCK.

PHIPPS, Charles A. [29; Omaha] md. Nora VAN DEUSEN [19; Omaha] on 27 Mar 1868. Off: KERMOTT. Wit: Mrs. M. HUNT, Charles HUNT.

PHOENIX, Richard [35; Omaha; b: NY; f: Richard PHOENIX; m: Anna KEEN] md. Jennie HOOD [24; New York City; b: NY; f: James HOOD; m: Jane Ann MOOK] on 28 May 1881. Off: PETERSON. Wit: Otis H. BALLOU, Patrick O. HAWES. Filed 29 May 1889 by P.W. SHIELDS, Co. Judge.

PICKARD, Eugene [24; Douglas Co.; b: Ohio; f: Reuben PICKARD; m: Julia McANDRES] md. Nancy BOYER [21; Douglas Co.; b: Ohio; f: George BOYER; m: Catherine ARMEN] on 22 Aug 1871. Off: KUHNS. Wit: Joseph BOYER, Douglas Co.; Mrs? Linda PICKARD, Douglas Co.

PICKARD, Frank [28; Medicine Bow, Wyoming Territory; b: Indiana; f: John PICKARD; m: Juliette SCINNER] md. Laura BELL [17; Douglas Co.; b: Ohio; f: Hiram BELL] on 20 Nov 1879. Off: JAMESON. Wit: Oscar J. PICKARD, Lucy INGERSOLL. Age consent for the bride "who is now in my charge" given by R.H. PICKARD.

PICKARD, Orin W. [19; Douglas Co.; b: NE; f: James W. PICKARD; m: Jane SCOTT] md. Emma BROCK [16; Douglas Co.; b: Germany; f: Stephen BROCK; m: Lena PHENNIG] on 17 Feb 1881 at the house of Mrs. J. PICKARD. Off: GRAHAM. Wit: Oscar J. PICKARD, Ella BOWERS. Age consent given by mother of the groom and signed by Oscar J. PICKARD. The father had died. Age consent given by parents of the bride. Witness was A. CLEMENS.

PICKARD, Oscar J. [23; Douglas Co.; b: NE; f: James PICKARD; m: Jane SCOTT] md. Ellen A. BOWERS [18; Douglas Co.; b: PA; f: Gabriel BOWERS; m: Lydia BOYER] on 8 Oct 1881. Off: SHERRILL. Wit: Ben MICHAEL, Rev. Amos CRESSER, Red Willow.

PICKETT, William [Douglas Co.] md. Ann COLEMAN [Douglas Co.] on 15 Nov 1863. Off: LAWRENCE. This was recorded in 1864 and the date changed to 1863.

PIER, William H. [40; Omaha; b: Kentucky; f: Mathew PIER; m: Rebecca KIMBALL] md. Mary A. HEFLIN [31; Omaha; b: Illinois; f: John HEFLIN] on 12 Jul 1871. Off: GIBSON. Wit: Annie C. FISHER; Harry BARLOW.

PIERCE, Doran [34; Omaha] md. Susan MELDRUM [34; Omaha] on 19 Jun 1867 at the parsonage. Off: VAN ANTWERP. Wit: Mrs. C.A. VAN ANTWERP.

PIERCE, Frank [26; Shelby, IA; b: Clide, OH; f: Daniel PIERCE; m: Julia RICHARDS] md. Helen LAWSON [23; b: Shelby, IA; f: John LAWSON; m: Carna KNAPP] on 20 Oct 1874. Off: WRIGHT. Wit: Joseph G. PIERCE, Shelby, IA; Alice PIERCE, Shelby, IA.

PIERCE, Isaac N. [32; Omaha; b; Kentucky; f: Cornelius PIERCE; m: Cynthia H. NICKELS] md. Mrs. Julia K. JOHNSON [22; Omaha; b: New Jersey; f: Washington MARSH; m: Phoebe I. BALL] on 28 Apr 1879. Off: FISHER. Wit: J.A. LESTER, Mrs. Chas. E. STUBBS.

PIERCE, W.B. [40; Omaha; b: NY; f: Peter PIERCE; m: Mary ROBINSON] md. Mrs. Helen N. BEEMER [36; Omaha; b: NY; f:

Lucius KELSEY; m: Clara MAY] on 30 Dec 1881. Off: BEANS; Wit: Mrs. W.K. BEANS, Anna HANSEN.

PIERCE, William [25; Valley Pct, Douglas Co.; b: Missouri; f: James PIERCE; m: Elizabeth] md. Mrs. Anna Maria LEWIS [30; Valley Pct., Douglas Co.; b: New York; f: Samuel HAWKINS; m: Catherine] on 10 Jan 1872 at Waterloo. Off: DENTON. Wit: L.J. DENTON; M.J. DENTON; et al, all of Waterloo; L.W. COURTER, Fort Carny.

PIERCEY, M. James [32; Omaha; b: England; f: Moses PIERCEY; m: Anna W. FLETCHER] md. Addie F. COLBY [19; Omaha; b: San Francisco, CA; f: Orrin P. COLBY; m: Emeline DUIGIN] at the First Baptist Church on 8 Jan 1879. Off: August BECK, Lilian J. COLBY.

PIERCY, David A. [37; Douglas Co.; b: NY; f: Alexander PIERCY; m: Elizabeth McCULLOCH] md. S. Libbie STOUT [32; Douglas Co.; b: NY; m: Agnes (HINDE) STOUT] on 26 Jun 1876. Off: LIPE. Wit: D.M. MILLER, G.T. BEMIS.

PIHLKJER, William [28; Omaha; b: Denmark; f: Jens PIHLKJER; m: Christine JACOBSDOTTER] md. Anna MICHAELSEN [23; Omaha; b: Denmark; f: Michael LARSON; m: Catherine PETERSON] on 13 Apr 1870. Off: BENNETT. Wit: Jeremiah McCHAENE; Rodney DUTCHER (DUCHER).

PIKE, Brigham [Sarpy Co.] md. Martha WRIGHT [Sarpy Co.] on 4 Mar 1865 at Herndon House. Off: DICKINSON. Wit: Mrs. E.T. PAGE, G.S. RAYMOND.

PILES, Issac [26; Yankton, Dakota Terr.; b: Ohio; f: James PILES; m: Margaret ENGLISH] md. Florence A. KING [20; Council Bluffs; b: Pennsylvania] on 21 Sep 1873. Off: HAMMOND. Wit: Capt. John WARD; Mrs. T.P. HAMMOND.

PILGRIM, James M. [Omaha] and Emma ALLEN [Omaha] on 20 Aug 1866. Off: HASCALL. Wit: Etta and S.J. HASCALL.

PILLSTER, Charles F. [22; Douglas Co.; b: Germany; f: Joseph PILLSTER; m: Catherine RICHOUT] md. Bertha SMITH [20; Omaha; b: Germany; f: Sebastian SMITH; m: Elizabeth SMITH] on 7 Mar 1871. Off: KELLEY. Wit: Jacob WEBBER; Elizabeth WEBBER.

PINE, James A. [34; Saratoga Pct, Douglas Co.; b: New York City; f: James PINE; m: Julia ASHTON] md. Mary J. PEARCE [21; Omaha; b: Squaw Village, NJ; f: William N. PEARCE; m: Martha HARRIS] on 7 May 1873. Off: WRIGHT. Wit: James SKINNER; Mary SKINNER.

PITTS, Charles [24; Omaha; colored; b: Ohio; f: Joseph PITTS; m: Mary] md. Mrs. Virginia WATSON [25; Omaha; colored; b: Virginia; m: Priscilla] on 8 Oct 1873. Off:

GAINES. Wit: J. ALEXANDER; W.W. PORTER.

PIVONKA, Frederick [28; Creston, IA; b: Bohemia; f: James PIVONKA; m: Anna KOLAR] md. Magdalena MARESH [22; Omaha; b: Bohemia; f: Matthew MARESH; m: Anna ROUBAL] on 20 Nov 1871. Off: TOWNSEND. Wit: Joseph DWORAK; John FICENEC.

PJIRRON, John F. [22; Omaha; b: Sweden; f: Magnus F. PJIRRON; m: Christine OSTROM] md. Esther ROBINSON [23; Omaha; b: Scotland; f: Archy ROBINSON; m: Mary McMILLAN] on 5 Mar 1881. Off: PATERSON. Wit: Charles ROBINSON, Emma C. PJIRRON.

PLAMBECK, Jochim [30; Douglas Co.] md. Anna Elizabeth WAGEMANN [18; Douglas Co.] on 3 Jul 1868 at Union House. Off: FLORKEE. Wit: George PLAMBECK, John H. WAGEMAN, Elizabeth FLORKEE.

PLEASENT, J.H. [28; Williamstown, MO] md. Ettie MARKEL [19; Williamstown, MO] on 2 Sep 1868. Off: ALLEN. Wit: J.E. MARKEL, Hattie H. MARKEL.

PLESTED, James [Florence] md. Judith PERRIN [Florence] on 15 Aug 1863. Both of legal age. Off: DICKINSON. Wit: Thomas L. SUTTON, Chas. F. BROWN.

PLEULER, Frederick [27; Omaha; b: Germany; f: George PLEULER; m: Annie ANGLER] md. Mary BOETTNER [20; Omaha; b: Germany; f: Gotlieb BOETTNER; m: Annie WENT] on 11 Mar 1871. Off: MORTON. Wit: George MULDOON; Henry SUHENS or LUKENS.

PLUMLEIGH, Charles [27; Illinois; b: Illinois; f: Thos. PLUMLEIGH; m: Eliza C. HERMAN] md. Ella M. BRADFORD [17; Dakota Terr.; b: Connecticut; f: Daniel P. BRADFORD; m: Harriet N. RICE] on 9 Apr 1871. Off: McCAGUE. Wit: Daniel P. BRADFORD, Dakota Terr.; Mrs. Emma J. SWOBE.

PLUMMER, Thomas G. [37; Omaha; b: Kentucky; f: Samuel PLUMMER; m: Susan GOLLADAY] md. Sarah A. BEEZLEY [22; Omaha; b: Indiana; f: Sylvester BEEZLEY; m: Francena KINDRED] on 6 Oct 1880. Off: BRANDES. Wit: M.R. KINDRED, Mrs. Martha BERDELL.

POINTS, Charles N. [28; Omaha; b: IN; f: T.R. POINTS; m: Telitha GUTHRIE] md. Josie A. SOLOMON [23; Omaha; b: OH; f: N.I.D. SOLOMON; m: Maggie V. KINNEAR] on 27 Feb 1875. Off: LIPE. Wit: W.S. WALTER, Mrs. Lizzie E. LIPE. Application signed by John J. POINTS.

POINTS, Zebdee [24; Missouri Valley, IA; b: Iowa; f: John POINTS; m: Mary JUMP] md. Emma PRUETT [18; Missouri Valley, IA; b: Iowa; f: Marten PRUETT; m: Eliza BABER] on 2 Oct 1879. Off: BARTHOLOMEW. Wit: S.N. MEALIA, Max (X) BERGMANN.

POLLAND, James [27; Omaha] md. Fanny KAY [19; Omaha] on 1 Jan 1869. Off: BETTS. Wit: Mr. and Mrs. KAY, "a large company."

POLLARD, Charles [21; Omaha] md. Sophia JONES [21; Omaha] on 2 Mar 1869. Off: KERMOTT. Wit: Mrs. M.A. McCALLUM, Wm. H. SMITH.

POLLARD, Frank [31; Omaha] md. Mary E. INGRAM [25; Omaha] on 13 Feb 1869. Off: KELLEY. Wit: G. SMITH, E. RYAN.

POLLOCK, Samuel S. [34; Omaha] md. Emma KNIGHT [21; Omaha] on 6 Sep 1868. Off: WESTWOOD. Wit: Mr. BUTTERFIELD, J. Frank HESS, Mr. POLLOCK's brother.

POLSON, Swen [24; Omaha; b: Sweden; f: Paul OLSEN; m: Ingrid NIELSDOTTER] md. Hannah PETERSON [25; Omaha; b: Sweden; f: Peter SWENSEN] on 7 Jan 1871. Off: LARSON. Wit: Andrew POLSON; Johannah POLLACK.

POMROY, Hiram [45; Omaha; b: Vermont; f: Sylvanus POMROY; m: Mary BAGLEY] md. Mrs. Eliza E. HAMPLETON [38; Omaha; b: Connecticut; f: George H. WALKER; m: Chloe DART] on 30 Sep 1879. Off: JAMESON. Wit: Rev. I.W. READ, Rev. S.D. BADGER of Illinois.

POPPE, John [27; Cincinnati, OH; b: OH; f: William POPPE; m: Elizabeth MORRIS] md. Sadie WHITRIDGE [25; Clyde, NY; b: NY; f: William NEWMAN; m: Jane Harriet GUILD] on 10 Aug 1881. Off: SMITH. Wit: Max BERGMANN, H. HOCKSTETTER.

PORATH, John [37; Douglas Co.; b: Germany; f: Henry PORATH; m: Sophie SCHUHR] md. Lisette NEICKEL [37; Douglas Co.; b: Mecklenberg, Germany; f: Frederick NEICKEL; m: Magdalene DREWS] on 3 Feb 1876. Off: SEDGWICK. Wit: Aaron R. HOEL, W. NEICKEL.

PORTER, Edward [23; Omaha; b: Cincinnati, OH; f: Robert PORTER; m: Martha] md. Sabina WARNER [21; Council Bluffs; b: Indiana; f: George WARNER; m: Marie WALTERS] on 11 Feb 1873. Off: TOWNSEND. Wit: George T. ANDERSON; Minerva C. ANDERSON.

PORTER, Josiah [28; Omaha; b: England; f: Josiah PORTER; m: Jane GRACE] md. Margaret J. SCHALKENBACH [18; Omaha; b: Chicago, IL; f: Joseph SCHALKENBACH; m: Minna WECKBACH] on 15 Mar 1879 at Fort Omaha by A. WRIGHT, Post Chaplin, U.S.A. Wit: Michael CODY, Ord. Sergt.

U.S.A. and Nellie ROACH both of Fort Omaha.

PORTER, Wallace W. [36; Omaha; colored; b: Tennessee; f: Moses PORTER; m: Lucinda GUTHRIE] md. Georgiana RUCKER [21; Omaha; b: colored; b: Missouri; f: George or Adam RUCKER; m: Cassander REDEN] on 21 Jul 1874. Off: GAINES. Wit: Adam RUCKER; E.S. CLENLONS.

PORTER, Washington [21; Council Bluffs] md. Helen WADSWORTH [18; Council Bluffs] on 14 Oct 1867. Off: SHEEKS. Wit: Jas. W. SAVAGE, Frank GRIFFIN.

PORTERFIELD, W.D. [37; Omaha; b: Ohio; f: William PORTERFIELD; m: Maria HAHN] md. Viola COFFIN [27; Ashland, CO; b: Indiana; f: Isaac COFFIN; m: Sarah LIUTHECUM] on 2 Mar 1880. Off: BARTHOLOMEW. Wit: Jno. A. LADD of St. Louis, Richard KITCHEN.

PORTERFIELD [POTTERFIELD], James [30; Council Bluffs] md. Mary COFFIN [22; Omaha] on 7 Sep 1859 at Douglas House. Off: KUHNS. Wit: Mr. and Mrs. NUTT.

POSENSKI, Barnard [42; Omaha] md. Mrs. Mary GALACHEN [26; Omaha] on 15 Jan 1869. Off: KELLEY. Wit: John DELANY, D.B. TOPHAM, et al.

POST, John [23 (34 on affidavit); Douglas Co.; b: OH; f: David POST; m: Elizabeth BURGEHASER] md. Maggie MORAN [17; Douglas Co.; b: Douglas Co.; f: James H. MORAN; m: Bridget BRADY] on 16 Apr 1876 at the Bishop's House. Off: BYRNE. Wit: Peter MOLONE, Teresa GLEESON. Age consent given by parents of the bride.

POTTENGER, Sanford [55; Desoto; b: Prebble Co.; OH; f: Robert POTTENGER; m: Francis GEE] md. Amanda PHELPS [57; Florence; b: New York; f: James WEBB; m: Hannah GRISWALD] on 11 Apr 1870. Off: GIBSON. Wit: L.H. BORDWELL; H.F. STRING.

POTTER, Clark [36] md. Mary Jane VINCENT [28] on 10 Jan 1861 at Jesse REEVES' house in Douglas Co. Off: BIRKETT. Wit: A.D. JONES, Harrison JOHNSON.

POTTER, George, Jr. [21; Omaha; b: NY; f: George POTTER; m: Jane MONTANA] md. Mary BATY [23; Omaha; b: IL; f: William BATY; m: Sarah BURGET] on 6 Oct 1875. Off: ESTABROOK. Wit: Wm. BARTHOLOMEW, Nellie BATY.

POWELL, Albert M. [39; Omaha; b: Virginia; f: Jacob L. POWELL; m: Jane AULD] md. Emma HANN [27; Omaha; b: England; f: James HANN; m: Ann MELBOURNE] on 1 Oct 1874. Off: WRIGHT. Wit: Cicero L. BRISTOL; Mary J. BRISTOL.

POWELL, Charles W. [25; Douglas Co.; b: IA; f: Able POWELL; m: Rebbaca HATSEL] md. Flora J. PAGE [20; Douglas Co.; b: IN; f:

Charles PAGE; m: Martha J. GIBBS] on 4 Dec 1876. Off: SEDGWICK. Wit: Belle POWELL, Douglas Co., Geo. W. PAGE, Douglas Co.

POWELL, John V. [28; Omaha; b: Indiana; f: Sylvester POWELL; m: Sarah Anne EARLY] md. Allice WISE [18; Omaha; b: Pennsylvania; f: Jesse WISE; m: Julia A. SHAFFER] on 31 Oct 1870. Off: GRAHAM. Wit: A.B. CALLAHAN; Mrs. M.A. DWYER.

POWER, John [29; b: Ireland; f: Nicholas POWER; m: Mary POWER] md. Mary QUINLAN [23; b: Massachusetts; f: Patrick QUINLAN; m: Mary KEARNEY] on 28 Sep 1878 at the Catholic Cathedral, Omaha. Off: COLANERI. Wit: James BROPHY, Maggie SHANAHAN.

POWERS, Eugene [29; Omaha; b: Ireland; f: Patrick POWERS; m: Brdiget HUSSEY] md. Margaret HORIGAN [19; Omaha; b: Ireland; f: Morris HORIGAN; m: Mary QUINLAN] on 8 Oct 1872. Off: CURTIS. Wit: Martin REIDY; Ellen DEE.

POWERS, Horace E. [30; Omaha; b: IL; f: N.H. POWERS; m: Catharine HART] md. Nellie B. PORTER [23; Omaha; b: IL; f: J.D. PORTER; m: Sarah BASCOM] on 22 Jul 1881. Off: SHERRILL. Wit: Mrs. Sarah C. GOODMAN, J.W. LOUISBERRY.

PRACHER, Wilhelm [31; Omaha; b: Germany; f: Alexander PRACHER; m: Francisca SCHROTTENBERG] md. Susanna TRIMMER [19; Omaha; b: KS; f: John TRIMMER; m: Mary Ann KNIGHT] on 13 Apr 1881. Off: LAING. Wit: John TRIMMER, P.J. QUEALEY.

PRATT, Edward B. [24; Sidney; b: VA; f: H.C. PRATT] md. Kate E. COPELAND [20; Omaha; b: OH (MA crossed out); f: Wm. W. COPELAND; m: Mary L. ROBINSON] on 25 Oct 1876. Off: MILLSPAUGH. Wit: Wm. W. COPELAND, Mary L. COPELAND.

PRATT, George W. [34; b: Massachusetts; f: David PRATT; m: Susan MONTGOMERY] md. Margaret BROWN [21; Creston, IA; b: Illinois; f: James B. BROWN; m: Sarah BENNETT] on 25 Feb 1878. Off: WRIGHT. Wit: Edward AINSCOW, Rachel AINSCOW.

PRATT, Henry E. [Omaha] md. Mrs. Louisia Jane HURD [Omaha] on 25 Aug 1863 in Justice's Court. Both of legal age. Off: McCARTHY.

PRESTON, Cornelius K. [28; Sarpy Co.; b: Norwich, NY; f: James PRESTON; m: Catherine KENNEDY] md. Minnie S. JONES [21; Douglas Co.; b: England; f: Daniel JONES; m: Ann WILLIAMS] on 18 Jul 1869. Off: GLOVER. Wit: Nathan FODREN of Douglas Co., Sarah JONES of Douglas Co.

PRESTON, John B. [35; Sarpy Co.; b: New York; f: James H. PRESTON; m: Catherine KENNEDY] md. Mary DYKES [19; Omaha; b: Missouri] on 29 Sep 1870. Off: ESTABROOK. Wit: Jacob KING; Christene KING.

PRESTON, William [31; Omaha] md. Emily Victoria ORCHARD [22; Omaha] at 7 PM, 28 Mar 1866 at A.R. ORCHARD's residence. Off: DIMMICK. Wit: S.A. ORCHARD, Albert TUCKER, et al.

PRICE, John [28; Omaha; b: Ireland; f: Henry PRICE; m: Cisley JUDGE] and Bridget McCANDRY [25; Omaha; b: Ireland; f: Michael McCANDRY; m: Mary HOOKS] license issued on 15 Apr 1879. No marriage record. Off: PEABODY.

PRICE, Robert F. [29; Omaha; b: Germany; f: George PRICE; m: Mary] md. Mary L.C. ZIEMANN [23; Omaha; b: Germany; f: Michael F. ZIEMANN; m: Mary C. BERENDT] on 1 Aug 1875. Off: HILGENDORF. Wit: Charles TIETZ, John CANE.

PRICE, Thomas H. [22; Omaha; b: Canada; f: Thomas K. PRICE; m: Sarah A. BAILEY] md. Hannah EDMUNDS [18; Omaha; b: Wales; f: Nathaniel EDMUNDS; m: Charlotte JONES] on 3 Mar 1870. Off: DeLaMATYR. Wit: T.C. DeLaMATYR; Bell HALL.

PRICHARD, Joseph G. [21; Vermont; f: Joseph A. PRICHARD; m: Mary A. BAXTER] md. Minnie P. SPAULDING [18; b: Illinois; f: Charles SPAULDING; m: Mary McALLISTER] on 23 Jul 1878 at Irvington. Off: SPENCER. Wit: Walace BRUCE, Miss M.V. GOODWIN.

PRINZ, August [31; Omaha; b: Germany; f: Charles PRINZ; m: Mary SCHEIDT] md. Henrietta STAHL [25; Omaha; b: Germany; f: Henry STAHL; m: Mary HANSEN] on 31 Aug 1873. Off: HILGENDORF. Wit: Henry MOHR; Hans PETERS.

PRITCHETT, Goerge E. [35; Omaha; b: New York; f: Edward C. PRITCHETT; m: Sophia LAWSON] md. Harriet G. HANSCOM [23; Omaha; b: Council Bluffs, IA; f: Andrew J. HANSCOM; m: Catharine Ann YOUNG] on 4 Apr 1877. Off: SEDGWICK. Wit: Ben WOOD.

PROCHNOW, August [21; Douglas Co.; b: Germany; f: Ferdinand PROCHNOW; m: Henrietta BIUNKE] md. Caroline LABS [18; Douglas Co.; b: Germany; f: Ferdinand LABS; m: Henriette KLABUNDE] on 13 Feb 1880.

Off: FRESE. Wit: Fritz PROCHNOW, Joh. LABS.

PROCHNOW, Frederick [26; Omaha; b: Germany; f: Ferdinand PROCHNOW; m: Fredericka] md. Erstine HAKS [20; Omaha; b: Germany; f: John HAKS; m: Johanna KOBS] on 9 May 1875. Off: HILGENDORF. Wit: Herman BAEMER, Mathilda BAEUMER.

PROCTOR, George Wesley [22; Omaha; b: MA; f: Alfred H. PROCTOR; m: Mary A. BLODGETT] md. Harriet M. HOOVER [19; Omaha; b: PA; f: John W. HOOVER; m: Margaret HANSON] on 8 May 1876. Off: BRITT. Wit: S.J. BRITT, Ellen BURKE.

PROCTOR, Richard A. [24; Omaha; b: Wasnington, D.C.; f: Richard PROCTOR; m: Mary O'DONNELL] md. Maggie JARVIS [19; Laramie, WY; b: Utah; f: Charles JARVIS; m: Amilia THOMAS] on 24 Mar 1877. Off: SEDGWICK. Wit: Marcia SEDGWICK, Hans JOHNSON.

PROCTOR, Thomas [35; b: England; f: Thomas PROCTOR; m: Sarah MINETT] md. Mrs. Doratty H. PEACOCK [32; b: England; f: John COCKFIELD; m: Jane HADLEY] on 16 Oct 1878. Off: MILLSPAUGH. Wit: Archie EAK, James STOCKDALE.

PROPST, George F. [23; Grinnel, IA; b: IA; f: W.A. PROPST; m: Elizabeth A. CUNNINGHAM] md. Luellia EDMUNDSON [20; Meriden, IA; b: IA; f: Frank EDMUNDSON; m: Julia GREESON] on 27 Apr 1881. Off: RILEY. Wit: John A. HAAS, Mrs. Francis DAILEY.

PRUCHA, Joseph [22; Omaha; b: Bohemia; f: John PRUCHA; m: Mary BABEZE] md. Anna KODSA [18; Omaha; b: Bohemia; f: Joseph KODSA; m: Anna KESERA] on 11 Oct 1881 at St. Wenzeslaus' Church. Off: KLIMA. Wit: Wenceslaus SCHAVLIK, Wenceslaus MATCHA.

PUGH, Richard [38; Omaha; b: Wales; f: Richard PUGH; m: Jane EDWARDS] md. Mary L. COOPER [20; Omaha; b: New York; f: Daniel M. COOPER; m: Dianna MILLER] on 30 Nov 1873. Off: STEWART. Wit: Frank M. WILSON; Carrie L. HEWITT.

PUGSLEY, Charles H. [24; Florence; b: Connecticut; f: Joseph F. PUGSLEY; m: Margaret WORDEN] md. Minnie STEVENSON [17; Florence; b: England; f: Alexander STEVENSON; m: Magdalene PATERSON] on 5 Dec 1871. Off: STEVENSON. Wit: G.L. PUGSLEY, Florence; John STEVENSON, Florence. Age of consent given by father of the bride, signature witness, W.J. HAHN.

PUGSLEY, Gidean L. ]24; Florence; b: Connecticut; f: Joseph F. PUGSLEY; m: Margaret WORDEN] md. Julia E. CAMERON [18; Florence; b: Ohio; f: J.L. CAMERON; m: Julia BOLAND] on 5 Mar 1870. Off: MORTON. Wit: George M.

McBAY; Mary Ann McBAY. Age of consent given by bride, she signed and said she was of age.

PULS, Julius A. [22; Omaha; b: Germany; f: Carl PULS; m: Lucy STURL] md. Albinie RASHKE [18; Omaha; b: Indiana; f: August RASHKE; m: Rose KRAUS] on 25 Dec 1880. Off: BENEKE. Wit: Gustav WECKBACH, Otto STUBEN.

PULS, Thomas [26; Douglas Co.; b: Germany; f: Henry PULS; m: Luzia STUHL] md. Matthilde GROTHE [29; Douglas Co.; b: Germany; f: Frederick GROTHE; m: Johanna C.W. LESKE] on 11 Jun 1881. Off: SMITH. Wit: Johann WEHDE, Douglas Co., Katharina WEHDE, Douglas Co.

PURCHASE, M.W.E. [31] md. Miss E.A. BARBER on 25 Dec 1861 at Wm. RYAN's house. Off: HART. Wit: Wm. M. RYAN, Dr. G. SMITH.

PURCHASE, Thomas J. [25; Belle Creek Pct., Washington Co.; b: New York; f: Evlan PURCHASE; m: Mary BOHEE] md. Emma BENTON [20; Belle Creek Pct., Washington Co.; b: Michigan; f: A.A. BENTON; m: Almira WATSON] on 9 Mar 1873 at Elkhorn Station. Off: ROLFS. Wit: Vallentien SCHMECK, Elkhorn Station; James PARKINHAN, Elkhorn Station.

PURINTON, T.E. [28; Waterloo, IN; b: Michigan; f: D.B. PURINTON; m: D.C. HOWE] md. Emejean WALLACE [19; Waterloo, IN; b: Indiana; f: Thomas WALLACE; m: Fidelia M. STRAIGHT] on 9 Jul 1880. Off: BARTHOLOMEW. Wit: A.P. BURHUS, F.M. BURHUS, both of Atlantic, IA.

PURTELL, Patrick [31; Omaha Barracks; b: Ireland; f: Patrick PURTELL; m: Margaret FITZGERALD] md. Alvira SAUER [28; Omaha, Barracks; b: Prussia; f: John F. SAUER; m: Annie REINHARDT] on 17 Apr 1872. Off: DIMMICK. Wit: Mrs. Kate G. DIMMICK; William FREDERICKS.

PUSSER, Charles [31; Omaha] md. Caroline SEIFFERT [18; Omaha] on 23 Mar 1868. Off: STUCK. Wit: John DAVIS, G.F. BABCOCK.

PUTNAM, W.E. [37; Omaha; b: New York; f: John PUTNAM; m: Nancy SMITH] md. Susanna Day MANGER [23; Omaha; b: New York; f: Henry Day MANGER; m: Sarah Ann HALL] on 13 Dec 1880. Off: INGRAM. Wit: O.F. STEPHENS, John MOTT.

PYLE, Hartwell [29; Oskaloosa, IA; b: OH; f: Aaron PYLE; m: Lydia A. WILLIAMSON] md. Jennie MOATS [30; Missouri Valley, IA; b: OH; f: Peter MOATS; m: Caroline STILIERBANER] on 28 Sep 1881. Off: MAXFIELD. Wit: Lizzie ELCOCK, Mrs. J.B. MAXFIELD.

QUADE, Heinrich "Henry" [27; b: Germany; f: Henry QUADE; m: Dora RUST] md. Louisa KEPPENHAHN [19; b: Germany; f: Louis KEPPENHAHN; m: Wilhelmine KUKLIS] on 9 Jun 1878. Off: BRUEGGER. Wit: Michael BUEHLER, William SAALFIELD.

QUANN, Edmund [42; b: Ireland; f: John QUANN; m: Mary QUINLAN] md. Mrs. Mary ALLEN [30; b: Ireland; f: Patrick QUIRKE; m: Mary O'CONNOR] at the Catholic Cathedral of Omaha on 3 Oct 1878. Off: COLANERI. Wit: Thomas T. ALLAN, Carrie J. MARKS.

QUICK, Martin [25; Omaha; b: Sweden; f: Erick MARTINSON; m: Gonela SWANSON] md. Lena OLSON [22; Omaha; b: Norway; f: Ole LARSEN; m: Ingeborg JOHNSON] on 12 Jan 1872. Off: ERDAHL. Wit: Mrs. M. CHRISTIANSEN; Ellen OLSON.

QUICK, Tunis P. [42; Lincoln; b: NJ; f: John P. QUICK; m: Elizabeth BELLIS] md. Libbie B. THAYER [20; Lincoln; b: MN; m: Ardelia GIBERSON] on 12 Nov 1876. Off: PORTER. Wit: Charles H. FOSTER, Mrs. Inez HANEY.

QUINLAN, Michael [38; Omaha; b: Ireland; f: John QUINLAN; m: Ellen LYONS] md. Bridget RYAN [33; Connecticut; b: Ireland; f: Michael RYAN; m: Johanna LINAHAN] at the cathedral on 22 Feb 1879. Off: McDERMOTT. Wit: Patrick QUINLAN, Mary RYAN. Affidavit signed by John QUINLAN.

QUINLAN, Patrick [31; Omaha; b: Ireland; f: John QUINLAN; m: Ellen LYONS] md. Margaret HOWELL [27; Omaha; b: Pennsylvania; f: Thomas HOWELL; m: Ann TOPPER] on 29 Aug 1869. Off: CURTIS. Wit: William FENTON, Mary VOGLE or BOYLE.

QUINLIN, Patrick [30; Omaha] and Margaret BLESSINGTON [30; Omaha] license issued on 21 Jun 1861. No marriage record. Off: ARMSTRONG. Date written as 1861 but recorded in 1862.

QUINN, Daniel [26; Blackhawk, CO; b: Ireland; f: Daniel QUINN; m: Hanorah BOLAN] md. Mary QUINN [22; Elkhorn, Douglas Co.; b: IL; f: John QUINN; m: Margaret CARRAGG] on 15 October 1876 at the Elkhorn Catholic Church. Off: LONEGAN. Wit: John H. QUINN, Elkhorn, Lizzie NASON, Valley Station.

QUINN, Henry [25; Omaha; b: CA; f: James QUINN; m: Catherine CALLAHAN] md. Maggie NAGLE [18; Omaha; b: Canada;

f: James NAGLE; m: Mary McGOVERN] on 25 May 1881. Off: MAXFIELD. Wit: Thomas ELCOCK, Van West, OH, Mrs. M. MAXFIELD.

QUINN, John [32; Wyoming Terr.; b: Ireland; f: John QUINN; m: Catharine MURREY] md. Bridget DALTON [22; Omaha; b: Ireland; f: Maurice DALTON; m: Margaret BOOK] on 6 Apr 1870. Off: CURTIS. Wit: Peter O'ROURKE; Mary SIBERT.

QVISTGARD, A.J. [30; Omaha; b: Denmark; f: Jens QVISTGARD; m: Maren CHRISTINSON] md. Minna PAGEL [20; Omaha; b: Chicago; f: John PAGEL; m: Minna CHRISTEN] on 30 Jan 1879. Off: HANSEN. Wit: E. ANDRES, Philip ANDRES both of 555 Thirteenth Street, Omaha.

QWARNSTRON, A.P. [27; Omaha; b: Sweden; f: A. QWARNSTRON; m: Annie PERSON] md. Matilda D. JOHNSON [27; Omaha; b: Sweden; f: John JOHNSON; m: Agusta ANDERSEN] on 11 Jan 1877. Off: SEDGWICK. Wit: John EKWALL, Frank HANLOU.

RAABE, Henry [33; Douglas Co.; b: Germany; f: Henry RAABE; m: Margaretha SCHRAMM] md. Nellie STUHR [21; Douglas Co.; b: Iowa; f: Marx STUHR; m: Gretchen ARP] on 14 Feb 1880. Off: BENEKE. Wit: John DOOSE, Jochim STUHR, both of Douglas Co.

RAASCH, August [22; Omaha] md. Alice K. BROWN [19; Omaha] on 6 Dec 1866 at the parsonage of Trinity Church. Off: VAN ANTWERP. Wit: Mrs. VAN ANTWERP, Johanna STARK.

RABE, Charles H. [31; Omaha; b: IL; f: William RABE; m: Mary KNIGGE] md. Dora RAGENDORF [20; Omaha; b: MN; f: John RAGENDORF; m: Mina MAHLMANN] on 30 Apr 1881. Off: FRESE. Wit: Wilhelm SCHMIDT, Adam GIMBEL.

RABE, Henry (Hinrich) [23; Douglas Co.; b: Germany; f: Hans RABE; m: Anna STICK] md. Sophia Dorothea Wilhelmina NEIKELL [19; Douglas Co.; b: Germany; f: Mr. NEIKELL; m: Christine Ulrike Lisette NEIKELL] on 21 Sep 1879 at McArdle Precinct. Off: BENEKE. Wit: William LEWON, Claus GRABBE, both of Douglas Co.

RACEK, Mathew [22; Saunders Co.; b: Bohemia, Austria; f: Matthew RACEK; m: Annie SUCHE] md. Annie KAVAN [21; Omaha; b: Bohemia, Austria; f: Wenser (Hensen?) KAVAN; m: Flora ROUSICK (ROUSIK)]. Off: KELLEY. Wit: Peter FRENZER; D. CLARK.

RAMGE, Frank J. [24; Omaha] md. Carrie E. YOUNGER [22; Council Bluffs] on 12 Mar 1866 at KUHNS' residence. Off:

KUHNS. Wit: Mrs. H.W. KUHNS, Henry SHULL.

RAMSEY, Oberlin N. [31; Omaha; b: New Hampshire; f: G.P. RAMSEY; m: V.G. MORRELL] md. Mary EDGAR [24; Omaha; b: Tennessee; f: John T. EDGAR; m: Francis Russell SMITH] on 5 Feb 1874. Off: SHERRILL. Wit: John T. EDGAR; O.P. HOSFORD or HURFORD.

RANCH, Franklin P. [24; Harrisburg, PA; b: Harrisburg, PA; f: John RANCH; m: Levina KAYNOR] md. Jennie FLORKEE [19; b: Omaha; f: William FLORKEE; m: Elizabeth WOLF] on 21 Mar 1878 at the home of Mrs. Elizabeth FLORKEE. Off: ADAIR. Wit: A.C. BARTHOLOMEW, Lottie BARTHOLOMEW, both of Millard Precinct.

RANCHER, Christian [27; Sarpy Co.] md. Barbara BROWN [21; Sarpy Co.] on 11 Sep 1867 at FLORKEE's house. Off: FLORKEE. Wit: John SAUTTER, Elizabeth FLORKEE.

RANDALL, A.G. [22; Omaha; b: Michigan; f: B. RANDALL; m: Esther RUST] md. Alice E. START [17; Omaha; b: Iowa; f: George G. START; m: Phelina LARKIN] on 20 May 1877. Off: LIFRE. Wit: John CLARK, Ellen CLARK.

RANK, Peter [24; Omaha] md. Mary KHILLIAN [KILLIAN] [18; Omaha] on 15 Apr 1868. Off: CURTIS. Wit: Antony LIPROZ, Alice LIPROZ

RANKIN, William [23; Omaha; b: Ireland; f: S.S. RANKIN; m: Sarah E. ARMSTRONG] md. Sophia MARCHAN [19; Omaha; b: France; f: George MARCHAN; m: Sarah MARCHAN] on 10 Nov 1880. Off: BAUGHER. Wit: Mr. and Mrs. J.H. BOND.

RANNIE, James N. [ 34; North Platte; b: England; f: Edward RANNIE; m: Elizabeth MORLAND] md. Anna PARKER [23; Fremont, NE; b: Pennsylvania; f: Uriah PARKER; m: Sarah THOMAS] on 29 Dec 1880. Off: BARTHOLOMEW. Wit: Max BERGMAN, C.A. BALDWIN.

RANSON, Frank [37; Douglas Co.; b: France; f: John RANSON; m: Rasalind GRAU] md. Mary MORIARTY [30; Omaha; b: Ireland; f: Michael MORIARTY; m: Margraet MALONEY] on 28 Jan 1875 at the Roman Catholic Cathedral. Off: BYRNE. Wit: Patrick NAUGHTON, Omaha Barracks, Anne MORIARTY.

RASER, Charles O. [21; Council Bluffs; b: Wheeling, WV; f: Conrad RASER: m: Catharine HEARTZOG] and Evangeline WILLIAMS [18; Council Bluffs; f: Augustus M. WILLIAMS; m: Elizabeth BRYANT] application issued on 5 Aug 1873. Off: TOWNSEND.

RASMUSSEN, Charles [29; Omaha; b: Denmark; f: Rasmus HANSEN; m: Margaret HANSEN] md. Matilda NIELSON [22; Omaha; b: Sweden; f: J. NELSON; m: Johana JACOBSON] on 1 Jun 1872. Off: BILLMAN. Wit: Hans JONSON; John OLSEN.

RASMUSSEN, Charles [32; Omaha; b: Denmark; f: Rasmus HANSEN; m: Margaret HANSEN] md. Ellen NELSON [22; Omaha; b: Sweden; f: Swan NELSON; m: Anna SANBERG] on 19 Aug 1874. Off: PEABODY. Wit: E.G. BOREMAN; Clara JOHNSON.

RASMUSSEN, Erick [26; Douglas Co.; b: Denmark; f: Rasmus HANSEN; m: Ellen ERICKSON] md. Caroline SCHMIDT [30; Douglas Co.; b: Germany; f: Hans SCHMIDT; m: Rebecca C. STALD] on 5 Jun 1880, Danish Church. Off: GYDESIN. Wit: Robert DINSDALE, J.M. GREGERSEN.

RASMUSSEN, Hans [28; Douglas Co.; b: Germany; f: Henry RASMUSSEN; m: Maggie INGLE] md. Maggie HANSEN [23; Douglas Co.; b: Germany; f: Henry HANSEN; m: Maggie SIERKS] on 8 Aug 1876 at McArdle Precinct. Off: CROSSLE. Wit: H. Bernard THOMPSEN, McArdle Precinct, Georgina E. CROSSLE, McCardle Precinct.

RASMUSSEN, J.C. [23; Davenport, IA; b: Germany; f: August RASMUSSEN; m: Anna M. STADE] md. Nora F. HOYE [21; Omaha; b: Massachusetts; f: Patrick HOYE; m: Mary S. INGOLDSLY] on 6 Nov 1879. Off: ENGLISH. Wit: J.D. WARREN, Mollie DORSEY.

RASMUSSEN, John P. [52; Omaha; b: Denmark; f: John P. RASMUSSEN; m: Christina LARSEN] md. Mrs. Annie M. JOHNSON [27; Omaha; b: Denmark; f: John P. ANDERSEN; m: Johanna NIELSEN] on 24 Mar 1872. Off: LARSON. Wit: H.P. SMITH; S.P. SMITH.

RASMUSSEN, Lars [36; Omaha; b: Denmark; f: R. JENSEN; m: Ellen LARSEN] md. Esther Margrether BOYSEN [28; Omaha; b: Denmark; f: A. BOYSON; m: Sophia BOYSON] on 22 Jul 1876. Off: SEDGWICK. Wit: C.P. PAULSEN, Henry LAGE.

RASMUSSEN, Ludwig Wilhelm [24; Omaha; b: Denmark; f: Rasmuss HENSON; m: Henrietta C. HENSON] md. Ingre Christen NELSON [29; Omaha; b: Denmark; f: Nils JENSON; m: Anna M. PETERSON] on 15 Jan 1876. Off: HANSEN. Wit: J.S. BENZON, Dorathea BENZON.

RASMUSSEN, Mathias [27; Omaha; b: Germany; f: Christian RASMUSSEN; m: Sophia GIBSON] md. Annie LARSON [27; Omaha; b: Sweden; f: Lars LARSON; m: Dorothea] on 14 Jan 1873. Off: BILLMAN. Wit: Fred RASMUSON; Julia RASMUSON.

RASMUSSEN, Nels [40; Omaha; b; Denmark; f: Rasmus NELSON; m: Mary CHRISTIANSEN] md. Christina JORGENSEN [30; Omaha; b: Denmark; f: Jorgen CHRISTIANSEN; m: Mary HANSEN] on 4 Nov 1871. Off: BILLMAN. Wit: Mr. NELSON; Mrs. NELSON.

RASSMUSSEN, Peter [33; Omaha; b: Denmark; f: Rasums JENSEN; m: Meta M. HANSEN] md. Fredericka K. NELSEN [22; Omaha; b: Denmark; f: Nels J. NELSEN; m: Magrada K. SANDFUS] on 4 Jan 1879. Off: STENBERG. Wit: M. MORTENSON, August NEILJEN or NIELSEN.

RATHMAN, Christian [41; Ft. Calhoun; b: Germany; f: John D. RATHMAN; m: Kate ROHWER] md. Sophia HARSTMAN [20; Omaha; b: Germany; f: Frank HARSTMAN; m: Kate RICHTER] on 10 Jun 1874. Off: PEABODY. Wit: John H. GREEN; Rose W. PEABODY.

RATLIFF, Daviss [25; Council Bluffs; b: Virginia; f: David RATLIFF; m: Sarah Jane FERGUSON] md. George Annie JOHNSON [16; Council Bluffs; b: Iowa; f: James BILLETER; m: Lydia JOHNSON] on 17 Jul 1880. Off: ANDERSON. Wit: A.M. CHADWICK, W.P. SNOWDEN.

RAYMOND, Eugene Kincaid [30; Omaha] md. Julia CARPENTER [20; New York City] on 30 Jun 1868. Off: KERMOTT. Wit: Rev. E.J. SCOTT of Brookfield, MO, W.H. SMITH.

RAYMOND, George S. [32; Omaha] md. Susan N. McCLELLAND [22; Omaha] on 30 Oct 1865 at KUHNS' residence. Off: KUHNS. Wit: Mrs. KUHNS, Mary OBERMILLER.

RAYMOND, Winthrop [28; Virginia, MT; b: OH; f: Daniel RAYMOND; m: D. MATLICK] md. Ella H. BATEMAN [21; Omaha; b: MI; f: R.P. BATEMAN; m: Hannah E. POPPLETON] on 28 Feb 1876. Off: CLARKSON. Wit: A.J. POPPLETON, John CREIGHTON.

READ, T. Walter [26; b: England; f: Henry READ; m: Sarah VANE] md. Josephine LITZEN [18; b: Iowa; f: Jacob LITZEN; m: Caroline REHN] on 4 Mar 1878. Off: JOHNSON. Wit: Mr. GUILD, Laura READ.

READING, George W. [28; Douglas Co.] md. Mary E. KERSTOTTER [Douglas Co.] on 15 Aug 1868. Off: MANHALL.

REAVIS, Isaac [Omaha] md. Elizabeth LEWIS [Omaha] on 22 Feb 1863 at the Lutheran parsonage. Off: KUHNS. Wit: M.L. OVERTON, Mrs. KUHNS.

RECORD, William L. or S. [23; Omaha; b: Missouri; f: Alexander RECORD; m: Helen

JACKSON] md. Matilda McKELVEY [18; Omaha; b: Indiana; f: Joseph McKELVEY; m: Ann OSBURN] on 11 Nov 1869. Off: ELLIS. Wit: Sarah WINLUS, A. BAKER, J.F. ELLIS, Nettie McKELVEY.

REDD, James A. [28; Omaha; b: Ohio; f: Nathaniel REDD; m: Sarah Ann FARRAR] md. Alice BENNETT [21; Omaha; b: Iowa; f: James BENNETT; m: Catharine GRANGER] on 29 Jul 1873. Off: TOWNSEND. Wit: George T. ANDERSON; Minirva C. ANDERSON.

REDFIELD, Josiah B. [38; Omaha] md. Margaret Ellen LOYD [30; Omaha] on 23 Oct 1867 at the parsonage. Off: KUHNS. Wit: Mrs. W.H. KUHNS, Olive C. ALLEN.

REDFIELD, Melvin H. [21; Omaha; b: Wawpaca, WI; f: Josiah B. REDFIELD; m: Susan BROWN] md. Frankie Rosella SMITH [20; Omaha; b: MI; f: Newton Jasper SMITH; m: Susana BENEDICT] on 21 Jul 1881 at Valley Station. Off: GRAFFIN. Wit: W.G. WHITMORE, Valley, Mrs. W.G. WHITMORE, Valley. Age consent given by parents of the groom.

REDICK, John I. [37; Omaha] md. Mary A.E. MAY [19; Omaha] on 8 Oct 1866 at Trinity Church. Off: VAN ANTWERP. Wit: The Congregation.

REDMAN, George L. [20; Omaha; b: Pennsylvania; f: Joseph REDMAN; m: Mary J. THAYER] md. Martha Ann OLMSTED [13; Omaha; b: Michigan; f: Horace OLMSTED; m: ELlen COLLINS] on 22 May 1874. Off: PEABODY. Wit: Emlen LEWIS; Horace OLMSTED. Age of consent given by parents of groom and bride.

REDMOND, Henry [29; Omaha; b: Maryland; f: Henry REDMOND; m: Bridget McCORMICK] md. Hattie McMILLAN [18; Omaha; b: Detroit, MI; f: ---- McMILLAN; m: Sarah BARBER] on 15 May 1870 at St. Barnabas Church. Off: BETTS. Wit: Michael DELAHUNT; Mary A. COSTELLO.

REED, Byron [32; Omaha] md. Mary M. PERKINS [18; Omaha] on 26 Apr 1862 at Allan ROOT's residence. Off: GAYLORD. Wit: Allan ROOT, John CAMPBELL.

REED, John E. [26, Douglas Co.; b: IA, f: Wm. E. REED; m: Charlott BIVEN] md. Lillie C. EVANS [17; Douglas Co.; b: IA; f: E.D. EVANS; m: Lorinda PECKENPAW] on 10 Nov 1976 at Waterloo. Off: CORLISS. Wit: Matilda LYONS, Waterloo, Wm. EVANS, Waterloo. Age consent given by parents of the bride.

REED, Jonathan [21; Florence] md. Emma KEETCH [17; Florence] on 27 Mar 1862 at Andrew J. CRITCHFIELD's house in Florence. Off: LAMBSON. Wit: Andrew J. CRITCHFIELD, E. HOLLINGSWORTH. Age consent given by the father of the bride.

REED, Joseph [28; Canton, OH] and Amanda J. RAFF [22; Omaha] license issued 28 Apr 1858. No marriage record. Off: BRIGGS.

REED, Peter [30; Birmingham, CT; b: Ireland; f: Peter REED: m: Catharine McALARNEY] md. Catherine GUILFOYLE [21; Birmingham, CT; b: Ireland; f: Lawrence GUILFOYLE; m: Catharine HANNON] on 18 Aug 1873. Off: CURTIS. Wit: Rev. Francis J. KELLEHER; Louisa CRAWFORD.

REED, Samuel G. [24; Omaha; b: Covington, KY; f: T.L. REED; m: Mary E. COOPER] md. Annie WALKER [24; Omaha; b: Lebanon, OH; f: William WALKER; m: Catherine DENNIS] on 3 Feb 1876. Off: BRITT. Wit: Helen McKOON, Sarah J. DEWEY.

REESE, Franklin Pierce [26; Omaha; b: Ohio; f: Daniel REESE; m: Angeline BUTORFF] md. Lucy N. ELDRIEDGE [21; Omaha; b: Illinois; f: Samuel S. ELDRIEDGE; m: Luna MECHEM] on 20 Jan 1879. Off: BARTHOLOMEW. Wit: M.H. REDFIELD, W.J. CUDDY.

REESE, William J.J. [22; b: Iowa; f: John F. REESE; m: Clara PANECKA] md. Addie KNOX [19; b: New York; f: ---- KNOX; m: --- - TAGGER] on 28 Apr 1878. Off: QUINN. Wit: George A. COULTER, Susie M. COULTER.

REESE, Wm. [23; Omaha; b: Ohio; f: Choxley REESE; m: Almira Van TRESS] md. Laura FISHER [18; Omaha; b: Ohio; f: John FISHER; m: Fanny SEIBERT] on 10 Jan 1880. Off: WRIGHT. Wit: Charles FISHER, Barbara ROBAR.

REEVES, Edward [41; Florence] and Sarah Ann PUNCHER [30; Florence] license issued in 1862. [No day or month given, appears between 14 Jul and 7 Aug.] No marriage record. Off: ARMSTRONG.

REEVES, George J. [26; Douglas Co.] md. Victoria WILBORN [18; Douglas Co.] on 5 Jul 1866. Off: TURNER. Wit: William REEVES, George W. WILBORN, et al.

REEVES, George [35; Douglas Co., b: England; f: William REEVES; m: Jane BRADDOCKS] md. Hulda M. RICKER [21; Douglas Co.; b: Maine; f: W.H. RICKER; m: Abigail SPAULDING] on 5 Apr 1877. Off: FISHER. Wit: Elizabeth FISHER, J.W. TOUSLEY.

REEVES, John [22; Omaha; b: Canada; f: Henry REEVES; m: Alice BATRAN] and Barbia KOTREC [21; Omaha; b: Bohemia; f: A. KOTREC] filed an affidavit on 29 Aug

1876. No marriage recorded. Off: SEDGWICK.

REEVES, William N. [23; Omaha; b: Omaha; f: Jesse REEVES; m: Elizabeth BARLOW] md. Elizabeth (Bettie) SUMNER [17; Douglas Co.; b: Iowa; Guardian: James LYMAN] on 7 Jan 1877. Off: ROBERTS. Wit: Joseph D. CROOK, Charles T. CHIFTON.

REFEL, Maurice [35; Omaha; b: France; f: Hersh REFEL] md. Elizabeth McLAUGHLIN [26; b: Scotland; f: John McLAUGHLIN; m: Jane PATTERSON] on 19 Sep 1870. Off: GIBSON. Wit: S.A. ORCHARD; C.C. HANSEL.

REGAN, Michael [30; Omaha; b: Ireland; f: Thomas REGAN; m: Honora COOKE] md. Johanna DEE [30; Omaha; b: Ireland; f: Thomas DEE; m: Johanna KERN] on 2 Feb 1875. Off: BYRNE. Wit: Denis SHANAHAN, Mary CARMODY.

REGAN, Michael [34; Omaha; b: Ireland; f: Thomas REGAN; m: Hanora COOK] md. Hanora KELLEY [35; Omaha; b: Ireland; f: Patrick KELLEY; m: Honora GANEY] on 11 Feb 1873. Off: CURTIS. Wit: John HENNESSEY; Mary DOWD.

REGNISHECK [REZNICEK], John [22; Omaha; b: New York; f: Joseph REGNISHECK [REZNICEK]; m: Anna BUBEK] and Lotta WASSKU [VASKU] [18; Omaha; b: Missouri; f: Joseph WASSKU [VASKU]; m: Mary DOSTAL] license issued on 29 Oct 1880. No marriage record. Off: BARTHOLOMEW.

REICHENBERG, Samuel [27; Omaha; b: Germany; f: Lob REICHENBERG; m: Brendel GUDMAN] md. Fanny ROSENDALE [25; Omaha; b: Germany; f: Jacob ROSENDALE; m: Dina GUDMAN] on 2 Oct 1869. Off: Wm. H. MORRIS. Wit: D. DAVIDSON, D.T. KIDD.

REICHERN, Nicholas [Omaha] md. Catherine TEITGEN [Omaha] on 15 Dec 1868. Off: KELLEY. Wit: F. MURRY, E. KELLY.

REID, William J.I. [33; Brooklyn, NY; b: Toronto, Canada; f: Hugh REID; m: Elizabeth DOUGLAS] md. Mary N. SMITH [30; Omaha; b: Vermont; f: Rollin C. SMITH; m: Mary A. BERCHORD] on 15 Sep 1870. Off: EVERTS. Wit: J.R. MEREDETH; O.P. HURFORD.

REILY [RILEY], Patrick [27; Buchanan Co., MO; father from Parish Radh., Co. Clare, Irel.] md. Catherine MULLONE [26; Omaha; father from Parish Radh, Co. Clare, Irel.] on 23 Nov 1858 at St. Mary's Church. Off: CANNON. Wit: Patrick CLIFFORD, Margaret GORMAN.

REIMERS, John [28] md. Botilde THOMPSON [24] on 5 Apr 1869. Off: KUHNS. Wit: Henry CLAWSON, Mrs. Mary LAPORT.

REINEKE, Ernest H.L. [25; Omaha; b: Hamburg, Germany; f: Ernest REINEKE; m: Margaret RATGINS] md. Mary GISIGER [22; Omaha; b: Switzerland; f: George GISIGER; m: Mary LEMMER] on 9 Jul 1870. Off: KUHNS. Wit: Charles LEMME; Mrs. Anne LEMME.

REINING, Paul [24; Omaha; b: Germany; f: Peter REINING; m: Theresa BOS] md. Louisa WINTER [23; St. Louis, MO; b: Germany; f: Conrad WINTER; m: Augusta TECH] on 8 Dec 1874. Off: PEABODY. Wit: Thomas F. HALL; John D. HOWE.

REITER, John [22; Omaha; b: Austria; f: Simeon REITER; m: Anna DORSCHER] md. Anna MILLER [21; Omaha; b: Germany; f: Christopher MILLER; m: Maria MEIER] on 17 Aug 1881. Off: RILEY. Wit: Geo. WAGONER, Gotleib SORENSEN.

REKINGER, John [25; Omaha] md. Lucy SMITH [26; Omaha] on 4 Mar 1866 at the bride's residence. Off: KUHNS. Wit: Dina SCOT, Mrs. M. ROGERS, et al.

REMI, Charles [38; Fort Omaha; b: Germany; f: Max REMI; m: Eleonore RUHOFF] md. Wilhelmine SPARKTIES [24; Omaha; b: Germany; f: Carl SPARKTIES; m: Irkmud BARROWSKI] on 17 Jan 1881. Off: BENEKE. Wit: Lichnei SPARKTIES, Wenzel NISTEL.

REMINGTON, Wager H. [29; Omaha; b: Hudson, NY; f: Richard M. REMINGTON; m: Jane H. MORSE] md. Catharine SULLIVAN [19 or 21; b: New York City; f: Eugene SULLIVAN; m: Elnor FRINELL] on 15 Jul 1869. Off: KUHNS. Wit: Ruth B. STRICKLAND, Wm. J. BOWEN.

REMINGTON, Walter E. [23; Neola, IA; b: Iowa; f: W. REMINGTON; m: Eliza NORTON] md. Hannah WILLIAMS [22; Council Bluffs, IA; b: Iowa; f: William WILLIAMS; m: Mary JONES] on 25 Oct 1879. Off: JAMESON. Wit: H.A. JAMESON, Ella CLARKE.

RENTSHLER, Jacob [36; Omaha; b: Germany; f: G. RENTSHLER; m: M. GISSLER] md. Caroline BRACHT [19; Sarpy Co.; b: Iowa; f: Joseph BRACHT; m: Louisa WALTER] on 3 Apr 1877. Off: FALK. Wit: C. GRUNING; Joseph HAHN.

REPASS, Ellis [24; Douglas Co.; b: Pennsylvania; f: Jacob REPASS; m: Rebecca] md. Mary JOHNSON [19; Douglas Co.; f: Eli JOHNSON; m: Lucy TRUMAN] on 20 Dec 1874 at BALLOW's res. Off: BALLOW. Wit: Everett G. BALLOW, Valley Pct.; Susie P. BALLOW, Valley Pct.

REPROBLE, John [27; Council Bluffs; b: Indiana; f: George REPROBLE; m: Sarah F. GROSNICLE] md. Mary E. EDWARDS [24; Council Bluffs; b: Arkansas; f: Wm. EDWARDS; m: Martha WILKINSON] on 15 Jun 1869. Off: HYDE. Wit: DeMott HYDE, J.C. FARLEY of Council Bluffs.

REULAND, Peter [27; Plattsmouth; b: Germany; f: John REULAND; m: Annie LAST] md. Catherine MAUTTERNASH [25; Waterloo, IA; b: Germany; f: Nicholas MAUTTERNASH; m: Mary FABER] on 21 Feb 1871 at German Catholic Church. Off: GROENEBAUM. Wit: Mr. and Mrs. Michael KOPPES.

REVER, Alexander [45; Omaha; b: France; f: Alexander REVER; m: Clara LaPOINT] md. Mrs. Mary NEWHOUSE [23; Omaha] on 17 May 1869. Off: HYDE. Wit: Mrs. O.P. INGALLS, J.W. CALDWELL.

REYNOLDS, James [35; Omaha; b: Ireland; f: John REYNOLDS; m: Bridget DEGNAN] md. Elizabeth SULLIVAN [25; Omaha; b: Canada; f: John SULLIVAN; m: Bridget EGAN] on 29 Jun 1871. Off: CURTIS. Wit: Mathew A. McNAMARA; Annie SULLIVAN.

REYNOLDS, Zachariah Taylor [26; Omaha; b: SC; f: James REYNOLDS; m: Francis C. KELLY] md. Mrs. Mary TOBANA [28; Omaha; b: KY; f: John CAMERON; m: Julia DONALD] on 26 Feb 1875. Off: McCROSKY. Wit: Mrs. A. HARKINS, Mercer Street, Mrs. A. NORMAN, Mercer Street.

RHODES, Edward [26; St. Joseph, MO; b: Illinois; f: John S. RHODES; m: Susan CULVER] md. Artie BILLINGS [19; Council Bluffs; b: Iowa; f: William BILLINGS; m: Martha WORDMAN] on 4 Nov 1874. Off: PEABODY. Wit: Julius ROSENFIELD; John N. FISHER.

RHODES, Henry F. [23; Omaha; b: New York; f: Frederick RHODES; m: Lorena A. GEORGIA] md. Cora B. REEVES [18; Chicago Precinct; b: Nebraska; f: Preston REEVES; m: Permelia STERRITT] at Chicago Precinct on 14 Oct 1879. Off: HARSHA. Wit: A.W. ALBRO of Illinois, J.B. PIPER.

RICE, James [22; Council Bluffs; b: Buchanan Co., IA; f: John RICE; m: Melvina DAVIS] md. Margaret FOREMAN [19; Pottawattamie Co., IA; b: Pottawattamie Co., IA; f: Mason FOREMAN; m: Sarah ROGERS] on 7 Jan 1878. Off: BARTHOLOMEW. Wit: George L. SHIELDS, J.G. BRADDISH.

RICE, Joseph T. [30; Omaha] md. Abbie BROWN [21; Omaha] on 22 Oct 1868. Off: KUHNS. Wit: John GRETZINGER, Frances A. KELLEY, Nancy E. HAMMETT.

RICE, William F. [25; Omaha; b: Ohio; f: Charles RICE; m: Minnie FRANKLIN] md.

Emilie ELSAESSER [18; Omaha; b: Illinois; f: G.F. ELSAESSER; m: Emilie WALKER] on 7 Oct 1880. Off: LIPE. Wit: A.S. PENDERY, Md., Mrs. E.J. PENDERY.

RICH, Andrew [45; Omaha; b: Austria; f: Jacob RICH; m: Mary Ann AHLER] md. Mrs. Barbara KUNES [37; Omaha; b: Bohemia; f: Jacob SMITH; m: Anna SIMON] on 18 Nov 1875. Off: BOBAL. Wit: Alois SIMON, Anne PETRICEK.

RICH, Julius [28; Omaha; b: Berlin, Prussia; f: Kaufman RICH; m: Amelia or Almina HERSCHFELDT (HERSCHFELD)] md. Cecelia MYERS [23; Omaha; b: Berlin, Prussia] on 15 Mar 1870. Off: PORTER. Wit: Emanuel SIMON; Julius REINHART.

RICHARDS, David F. [25] md. Mrs. Louisa C. TAPPING (TAPPEN) [22] on 22 Dec 1859 or 24 Dec 1860. Off: BARNES. Wit: Mrs. HIGBY (HIGLEY), Jack WISENALL, Mrs. HUNT.

RICHARDS, Thomas W.T. [27; Omaha; b: Virginia; f: Jesse RICHARDS; m: Eleanor JENKINS] md. Fannie Ella TOWNES [19; Omaha; b; Kentucky; f: John A. TOWNES; m: Margaret UTTERBACK] on 2 Feb 1870. Off: KUHNS. Wit: Mr. and Mrs. Burr H. RICHARDS, Baltimore, MD; Mr. and Mrs. William STEPHENS.

RICHARDS, William H. [26; Douglas Co.; b: OH; f: Wm. H. RICHARDS; m: Fidelia GOOLD] md. Mary MOREL [16; Florence Precinct, Douglas Co.; b: Utah Territory; f: Paul Henri MOREL; m: Elise OBERT] on 30 Oct 1876. Off: SEDGWICK. Wit: Paul H. MOREL, Douglas Co., David E. BURLEY. Age consent given by father of the bride.

RICHARDSON, Benjamin [22; Omaha; colored; b: Nashville, TN; f: John RICHARDSON; m: Nancy DUKE] md. Lucy MARYWEATHERS [19; Omaha; colored; b: Kentucky; f: James N. MARYWEATHERS] on 6 Jul 1870. Off: KERMOTT. Wit: Joseph LAHANAHA; Jane MARYWEATHERS.

RICHARDSON, Lyman [26; Omaha] md. Virginia Harrison CLARK [24; Omaha] on 27 Sep 1860 at John M. CLARK's house. Off: GAYLORD. Wit: O.D. RICHARDSON, John M. CLARK.

RICHARDSON, Theodore W. [25; Douglas Co.] md. Adeline HILL [18; Douglas Co.] on 19 Oct 1866 at Elkhorn. Off: DENTON. Wit: Mr. and Mrs. James STATIN.

RICHARDSON, Trad [26; West Virginia; b: Warren Co., PA; f: Edwin P. RICHARDSON; m: Emeline HUTCHINSON] md. Mrs. Jennie W. CARTER [41; Richmond, VA; b: Richmond, VA; f: William EDWARDS; m: Harriet ENGLISH] on 4 May 1869. Off: HYDE. Wit: H.C.B. NERRDE, E. ESTABROOK.

RICHELEU, Edward [28; Omaha] md. Mary Ann WADHAM [30; Omaha] on 24 Apr

1869. Off: HYDE. Wit: George SMITH, Mortimer HYDE.

RICHTER, Henry [24; Omaha] md. Joanna IVERSON [20; Omaha] on 17 May 1862. Off: GRANT. Wit: Henry KEONIG, Theodore PAULSON.

RICKARD, A.N. [31; Omaha; b: Iowa; f: Adam RICKARD; m: Amanda WOODWARD] md. Minnie ROLFER [23; Omaha; b: Iowa; f: Henry ROLFER; m: Mary BERGENSTEIN] on 7 Oct 1879. Off: LIPE. Wit: John M. NICHOLS, Lida C. CRAWFORD.

RICKARD, Thomas [26; Omaha Barracks; b: Brooklyn, NY; f: John RICKARD; m: Catharine McGUINNESS] md. Marth CANNARY [18 on 1 May 1873; Princeton, MO; b: Princeton, MO; f: Robert W. CANNARY; m: Charlotte BURCH] affidavit issued on 22 May 1873. Off: TOWNSEND.

RICKLEFSEN, Oscar [30; Omaha; b: Germany; f: Oscar RICKLEFSEN; m: Henrietta DELFS] md. Mary STISCOLA [26; Omaha; b; Germany; f: Detlef STISCOLA; m: Mary ANDRESEN] on 27 Jun 1872. Off: BRANDES. Wit: Ludwig ANDRESEN; Oscar VOIGHTLANDER.

RIDDIFORD, Henry [23; Omaha; b: England; f: Erin RIDDIFORD; m: Eliza PEARCE] md. Kate EHLERS [19; Omaha; b: Germany; f: Richard EHLERS; m: Damin KIESER] on 7 Apr 1876. Off: BRITT. Wit: H.L. DAVIS, S.J. BRITT.

RIDINGS, Henry [colored; 26; Omaha] md. Mrs. Ginnie PATTERSON [colored; 24; Omaha] on 20 May 1868 "in his house." Off: FLORKEE. Wit: Dr. TROPER.

RIEDEL, William [25; Douglas Co.; b: Germany; f: George RIEDEL; m: Mary BUSSE] md. Lena PASCH [21; Douglas Co.; b: Germany; f: Claus PASCH; m: Julia SCHMIDT] on 21 Mar 1881. Off: SMITH. Wit: Max BERGMANN, Peter GOOS.

RIEDT, Carl [24; Omaha; b: Germany; f: Christoph RIEDT; m: Annie YOUNG] md. Annie C. HEUBEL [23; Omaha; b: Germany; f: Valentine HEUBEL; m: Angelie REITZ] on 18 Sep 1870. Off: KERMOTT. Wit: J.L. WOOD, M.D.; S.C. KING.

RIEPEL, Joseph [20; Omaha; b: Germany; f: Johann RIEPEL; m: Catharine NEWBERGER] md. Maria BALACH [18; Omaha; b: Germany; f: Johann BALACH; m: Maria KRUDEL [KROUTIL]] on 21 Nov 1880, German Catholic Church. Off: GROENEBAUM. Wit: Charles KOHLMEYER, Mrs. Eva KOHLMEHER.

RIEPEN, Fredirick [22; Omaha; b: Germany; f: Detlef RIEPEN; f: Henrietta HAHN] md. Margaret RONFELDT [21; Omaha; b: Germany; f: Andrew RONFELDT; m: Annie MUHL] on 18 Apr 1872. Off: BILLMAN. Wit: Mrs. Bella D. BILLMAN; Mrs. ANNIS; et al.

RIESTERER, Benedict [36; Omaha; b: Germany; f: Joseph RIESTERER; m: Carolina RIESTERER] md. Augusta PFEFFERER [33; Omaha; b: Germany; f: Joseph PFEFFERER; m: Johanna KOCH] on 19 March 1881. Off: BENECKE. Wit: V. VANCHURA, W. NISTEL.

RIGBY, Theodore F. [27; Omaha; b: OH; f: Henry RIGBY; m: Ruth A. SCHNEEDECKER] md. Ada O. KIRK [21; Omaha; b: IA; f: Robert KIRK; m: Lucy F. LOCKWOOD] on 21 Aug 1881. Off: ANDERSON. Wit: Wm. H. KIRK, Jacob K. COSLILE.

RILEY, James [28; Omaha] and Mary Jane FLANIGAN [24; Omaha] license issued on 31 Aug 1867. No marriage record. Off: SHEEKS.

RILEY, John and Mary MURPHY license issued on 2 Jul 1864. No marriage record. Off: DICKINSON.

RILEY, Thomas [23] and Anna Theresa RILEY [20] license issued on 21 Apr 1860. No marriage record. Off: ARMSTRONG.

RING, George E. [22; Omaha; b: New York; f: John B. RING; m: Pernie WARREN] md. Anna L. BENSON [21; Omaha; b: Sweden; f: Lewis BENSON; m: Ella LARSON] on 2 Jun 1877. Off: SEDGWICK. Wit: Avery WILKINS, M. BUTTERFIELD.

RING, Nelson M. [32; Omaha] md. Anna M. PETERSON [21; Omaha] on 3 Aug 1867. Off: DAM. Wit: Neils JENSEN, C.C. WESTERGARD. This is a double wedding with Peter C. ROLD and Karen JENSEN.

RIORDAN, J.J. [28; b: Massachusetts; f: Cornelius RIORDAN; m: Mary WINTER] and A.C. THOMAS [28; b: Ohio; f: Louis THOMAS; m: Calistia THOMAS] license issued on 31 Dec 1878. No marriage record. Off: SIMERAL.

RISDON, Marcella Reuben [39; Omaha; b: Warrensville, Cuyahoga Co., OH; f: Thaddeus J. RISDON; m: Alta FREEMAN] md. Fannie Amelia BURNHAM [31; Douglas Co.; b: Princeton, IL; f: Noah BURNHAM; m: Mary MORSE] on 23 Aug 1881 at Elkhorn. Off: BEANS. Wit: Mrs. Mary M. BURNHAM, Elkhorn, Mary E. BURNHAM.

RISING, D.T. [40; Sac Co., IA] md. Ruth JOHNSON [30; Sac Co., IA] on 11 Sep 1860. Off: ARMSTRONG. Wit: Wm. CRAMER, D.T. RISING, Jonas SEELY, John T. REDICK.

RITCHEY, Granville md. Adeline G. BROWN [17; Florence] on 28 May 1865 at Florence. Off: TURNER. Wit: Edward

REEVES, Mary Ellen BROWN. Age consent given by father of the bride.

RITCHIE, James [22; b: Scotland; f: James RITCHIE; m: Ann BURNS] md. Hannah Sophie BURGESS [24; b: New Jersey; f: Louis BURGESS; m: Elizabeth HURBITT] on 30 Oct 1877. Off: MILLER. Wit: Murdock McKINZIE, Ida S. BURGESS.

RITENBURG, Albert [34; Omaha; b: New York; f: Wm. M. RITENBURG; m: Helena HENDRICKSON] md. Rohama BUNDAY [27; Omaha; b: Burlington, IA; f: Nelson BUNDAY; m: Hannah JACKSON] on 10 Mar 1879. Off: PORTER. Wit: Charles MANSFIELD, Charles POWELL. Affidavit signed by the bride.

RITNER, Henry N. [25; Omaha; b: Glasgow, Scotland; f: John A. RITNER; m: Annie C. WEAVER] md. Harriet A. WISE [17; Omaha; b: Iowa; f: Jesse R. WISE; m: Julia Ann SHAFFER] on 6 Sep 1873. Off: PRESSON. Wit: Maggie PRESSON; Anna PRESSON.

RIX, Detlef [35; Omaha; b: Germany; f: John RIX; m: Lucy MATHESEN] md. Mrs. Maria STEUBEN [36; Omaha; b: Germany; f: Hans PAULSON; m: Catharine HANSEN] on 30 May 1874. Off: DIECKMANN. Wit: Mrs. Friederick DIECKMAN; Margaretha BECKMAN.

ROACH, James [34; Springfield, MA; b: Ireland; f: Michael ROACH; m: Margaret MEEHAN] md. Mary QUINLIVAN [24; Springfield, MA; b: Ireland; f: Patrick QUINLIVAN; m: Eliza FLYNN] on 26 Jul 1872. Off: CURTIS. Wit: Patrick QUINLIVAN; Catharine O'GRADY.

ROACH, John [22; Omaha] md. Mary SHEA [23; Omaha] on 8 Feb 1863 at the Catholic Church of Omaha. Off: McMAHON. Wit: Luis RUFF, Anne KANE.

ROACH, Thomas [21; Omaha; b: Illinois; f: John ROACH; m: Rosa BURNS] md. Jennie DAVIS [19; Omaha; b: Missouri; f: William DAVIS; m: Maria ROSA] on 11 Jun 1880. Off: BARTHOLOMEW. Wit: Charles J. BARBER, Max BERGMANN.

ROBBE, Dietrick(h) [21; Omaha; b: Germany; f: Henry ROBBE; m: Mary KESTERY] and Weyelmine SHMIDT [18; Council Bluffs; b: Prussia; f: Charles SHMIDT] license issued on 10 Feb 1870. Off: GIBSON.

ROBENSON, Joseph [28; Wyoming Territory; b: Canada; f: Thomas ROBENSON; m: Ellen BERRY] md. Catherine FINN [25; Omaha; b: NJ; f: John FINN; m: Bridget MADDEN] on 9 Jan 1876. Off: BOBAL. Wit: Thomas McCLANE, Omaha Barracks, Mrs. Anna McCLANE, Omaha BARRACKS.

ROBERSON, Sylvester A. [26; Omaha; b: Illinois; f: William ROBERSON; m: Roxey CLINKENBEARD] md. Louisa C. SCHNEIDER [16; Omaha; f: Jacob

SCHNEIDER; m: Francis REISTHER] on 2 Jul 1874. Off: McCAGUE. Wit: Samuel MIXHAM; Nellie ROBINSON. Age of Consent given by father of the bride.

ROBERTS, Henry [24; Omaha; b: Ohio; f: John ROBERTS; m: Eliza BRYANT] md. Sarah DAVIS [23; Omaha; b: Iowa; f: John DAVIS; m: Anna TWINE] on 24 Jul 1880. Off: HAWES. Wit: Mrs. Amelia M. HAWES, Josephine JACKSON.

ROBERTS, John [colored; 30; Omaha; b: Orange Co., IN; f: Elias ROBERTS; m: Nancy ARCKEY] md. Emma WILSON (WILLSON) [colored; 20; Omaha; b: Wayne Co., IN; f: William WILSON (WILLSON); m: Sharlott SHUERYLT] at 2 P.M. on 1 Jul 1869 at HUBBARD's residence. Off: HUBBARD. Wit: Emma JOHNSON, Elizabeth UMPRY, Joanna HUBBARD.

ROBERTS, Rufus [26; Douglas Co.; b: NY; f: Rufus ROBERTS; m: Mary] md. Rebecca FATE [26; Douglas Co.; b: IN; f: Francis FATE; m: Mary BELDEN] on 8 Nov 1876. Off: SEDGWICK. Wit: C.J. GREEN, E.H. BUCKINGHAM.

ROBERTS, William V. [38; Fort Omaha; b: Canada; f: Robert ROBERTS; m: Mary REYNOLDS] md. Elizabeth HATTON [30; Omaha; b: Canada; f: Thomas HATTON; m: Margaret CONNELY] on 7 May 1881. Off: PATERSON. Wit: Clark WOODMAN, Mary E. DAY. Recorded 29 May 1889. Filed by P.M. SHIELD.

ROBERTS, William [31; Omaha; b: New York; f: Thomas ROBERTS; m: Mary INGRAM] md. Elizabeth DALMAS [34; Omaha; b: Paris, France; f: William DALMAS; m: Annie CARR] on 24 Mar 1874. Off: PEABODY. Wit: Silas A. STRICKLAND; Edward ROSEWATER.

ROBERTSON, A.B. [25; b: Massachusetts; f: John C. ROBERTSON; m: Sarah F. CRAFTS] md. Elizabeth F. MEGEATH [22; b: Virginia; f: J.G. MEGEATH; m: E.V. CARTER] on 19 Feb 1878 at Trinity Church. Off: MILLSPAUGH. Wit: W.S. SCHUYLER, Lieut. FOOT.

ROBERTSON, E.L. [24; Omaha; b: Kentucky; f: Edward W. ROBERTSON; m: Martha MANNEN] md. Martha LEACH [20; Omaha; b: Chicago, IL; f: Edward LEACH; m: Mary Ann KEY] on 3 Jan 1878. Off: FISHER. Wit: Mrs. BENNETT, Miss BENNETT.

ROBESON, Henry [54; Omaha; b: Richmond, VA; f: Anthony ROBESON; m: Kate ROBESON] md. Mrs. Martha Ann MARTEN [44; Omaha; b: Kentucky; f: William YEAGER; m: Nancy Ann YEAGER] on 16 Oct 1879. Off: WEISS. Wit: George KLOTZ, Pierce GARDENER.

ROBINETTE, John L. [27; Omaha; b: Philadelphia, PA; f: Allan M. ROBINETTE; m: Elizabeth LOWER] md. Lettie J. CHARLES [26; Omaha; b: Pennsylvania; f: Henry CHARLES; m: Sadie E. REDMAN] on 8 Dec 1880. Off: BAUGHER. Wit: Edwin EAYERS, Mrs. Edwin EAYERS.

ROBINS, John B. [32; b: England; f: John ROBINS; m: Elizabeth BARNICOAT] md. Sadie WILLIS [27; b: Pittsburg, PA; f: Isaak A. WILLIS; m: Martha RUNOLDS] on 28 May 1878. Off: FISHER. Wit: E.M. FISHER, Isaac WILLIS.

ROBINSON, Charles [23; Fremont; b: Pennsylvania; f: Thomas ROBINSON; m: Sarah HALE] md. Sarah CASSELL [18; Fremont; b: Illinois; f: John CASSELL; m: Fanny GREEN] on 18 Aug 1873. Off: TOWNSEND. Wit: Thomas JOHNSON, Fremont; Nettie CASSELL, Fremont.

ROBINSON, Francis A. [34; Douglas Co.; b: Sweden; f: Leonard ROBINSON; m: Mary PETERSON] md. Christina NELSON [31; Douglas Co.; b: Sweden; f: Lars NELSON; m: Anna SWENSON] on 6 Mary 1875 at Omaha Barracks. Off:WRIGHT. Wit: Brig. Gen. E.O.C. ORD, Omaha Barracks, Capt. WHEATON, 23rd. Inf.

ROBINSON, George W. [29; Omaha; b: Virginia; f: Moore ROBINSON; m: Catharine ROBINSON] md. Annie M.C. JOHANSEN [24; Omaha; b: Sweden; f: Joahannes JOHANSEN; m: Maria Christena PETERSON] on 25 Nov 1873. Off: STEWART. Wit: Mrs. Mary W. BROWN.

ROBINSON, Harrison L. [48; Council Bluffs; b: Dunham, Canada; f: Jacob D. ROBINSON; m: Olive LUCAS] md. Mrs. Mary SMITH [45; Council Bluffs; b: England; f: Robert E. URWIN; m: Elizabeth] on 4 Sep 1873. Off: HALE. Wit: John L. WEBSTER; W.H. SMITH, Council Bluffs.

ROBINSON, Harvey [21; Douglas Co; b: Virginia; f: Harvey ROBINSON; m: Catharine McGUIRE] md. Mattie AVERY [21; Douglas Co.; b: Pennsylvania; f: Norman AVERY; m: Catharine WILLIAMS] on 8 Apr 1874. Off: STEWART. Wit: Mrs. Emily W. STEWART; B.S. WALKER.

ROBINSON, Henry G. [42; Douglas Co.] md. Angeline CLICKNER [22; Douglas Co.] on 11 Dec 1865. Off: MILLER. Wit: Susan C. ROBINSON, Mrs. MILLER.

ROBINSON, Lewis E. [23; Douglas Co.; b: Virginia; f: John M. ROBINSON; m: Elizabeth MORRIS] md. Sarah F. COMONS [19; Douglas Co.; b: Iowa; f: Robert

COMONS; m: Sophia BOYED] on 6 Mar 1874. Off: PEABODY. Wit: M.G. McKOON; James NEVILLE.

ROBINSON, Thomas F. [24; Omaha; b: England; f: Robert ROBINSON; m: Lucy J. WARBURTON] md. Mary MAHER [24; Omaha; b: Ireland; f: Patrick MAHER; m: Mary E.] on 6 Apr 1872. Off: BETTS. Wit: Wm. Thos. CLARKE; Julia FISK.

ROBINSON, W.G.T.H. [negro; 30; b: North Carolina; f: T.H. ROBINSON; m: Mary A. DEMORY] md. Mary A. TAYLOR [negro; 19; b: Brittish America; f: Hillird TAYLOR; m: Thirza TAYLOR] on 13 Aug 1878. Off: McNAMARA. Wit: H.B. TAYLOR, Mary E. HAYDEN.

ROBINSON, William G. [32; Douglas Co.] md. Mary E. MILLER [21; Douglas Co.] on 6 Feb 1862 at Mrs. Margaret TURNER's residence in Fremont. Off: HEATON. Wit: Mrs. Margaret TURNER. Age consent given by Russell MILLER, father of the bride.

ROBINSON, William G. consent to marry Mary E. MILLER, by father, Russell MILLER. [No reference or details given.]

ROBINSON, William T. [26; Council Bluffs; b: Pennsylvania; f: John ROBINSON; m: unknown] md. Mattie BUFFINGTON [18; Omaha; b: Pennsylvania; f: Harry BUFFINGTON; m: Barbara NEWSYNGER] on 15 Nov 1880. Off: BEANS. Wit: Mrs. H.K. BUFFINGTON, Mrs. W.K. BEANS.

ROBINSON, William [24; Omaha; colored; b: St. Louis, MO; f: Redick ROBINSON] md. Martha THOMPSON [22; Omaha; colored; b: Alabama; m: Harriet JENKINS] on 25 Aug 1873. Off: PORTER. Wit: William PICKETT; James J. NELIGH.

ROBISON, A.L. [29; Omaha; b: Pennsylvania; f: John K. ROBISON; m: Isabella C. McKENNEY] md. Alma V. NYMAN [26; Boonsboro, MD; b: Boonsboro, MD; f: Daniel G. NYMAN; m: Eliza W. STEPHENS] on 9 Nov 1880. Off: HARSHA. Wit: C.A. RINGER, R.C. STEELE.

ROCHE, Jeremiah J. [33; Ft. Worth, TX; b: Ireland; f: Maurice ROCHE; m: Honoria O'CONNOR] md. Margaret O'CONNOR [32; Omaha; b: Ireland; f: Charles O'CONNOR; m: Johanna FLYNN] on 21 Feb 1881. Off: ENGLISH. Wit: Chas. McDONALD, Norah O'CONNOR who lives at North Platte.

RODDY, Patrick [27; Omaha; b: Ireland; f: Michael RODDY; m: Ann CARMICK] md. Mary HENZIE [22; Omaha; b: Ireland; f: Daniel HENZIE; m: Catharine DELANY] on 9 Jan 1870. Off: CURTIS. Wit: Michael MEHAN, Council Bluffs; Johanna MORE.

RODEBANK, J.W. [31; Omaha] md. Emma M. SPRINGER [19; Omaha] on 29 Oct 1868. Off: KUHNS. Wit: Mr. and Mrs. PREBBLE.

RODGERS [ROGERS], Alexander B. [47; Omaha; b: VT; f: Thomas B. RODGERS

[ROGERS]; m: Mary BARNES] md. Mrs. Ruth E. NEWTON [37; Omaha; b: PA; f: Abraham TURNER; m: Mary SLAWSON] on 7 Mar 1881. Off: COPELAND. Wit: Charles GOODRICH, Mrs. W.E. COPELAND.

ROE, Henry [37; b: New York; f: William ROE; m: Maria WHALIN] md. Rosena FISHER [19; b: Ohio; f: Charles FISHER; m: Catharine AULTHAUS] on 6 Nov 1878. Off: STRASEN. Wit: H.G. ROSS, Anna FISHER.

ROEKGER, H.P.C. Fredrickson [27; Omaha] md. Betty SWANSON [24; Omaha] on 1 Oct 1868. Off: KUHNS. Wit: Mrs. H.W. KUHNS, Catherine GROSS.

ROEMER, Simon [21; Omaha; b: Germany; f: John ROEMER; m: Victoria Essig KRUG] md. Augusta PROPLESCH [20; Omaha; b: Germany; f: Christoff PROPLESCH; m: Charlotte REICH] on 23 Dec 1881. Off: FRESE. Wit: Paul WAAK, Mathias HASOWI.

ROENFELD, Andrew [35; Omaha; b: Germany; f: Andrew ROENFELD; m: Anna MUEHL] md. Anna ELLENHUSEN [30; Omaha; b: Germany; f: John RUSCAMP; m: Mary DANNEMANN] on 16 Jun 1877. Off: STRASEN. Wit: Dietrich HEPPLER, Claus SCHMIDT.

ROENFELDT, Henry [25; b: Germany; f: Andreas ROENFELDT; m: Anna MUHL] md. Katie HOLST [17; b: Germany; f: Henry HOLST; m: Engal TIBKE] on 26 May 1878. Off: STRASEN. Wit: Fred FIEPEN, Mrs. EHLEN.

ROESINK; John [38; Sarpy Co.; b: Holland; f: Henry ROESINK; m: Henricke] md. Mary GROTMACK [26; Omaha; b: Holstein] on 17 Oct 1875. Off: DIECKMANN. Wit: Leopold JAEGGI, George SELK.

ROGERS, Alexr. T. [42; Omaha; b: KY; f: Peter ROGERS; m: Sarah WRIGHT] md. Clara WHITMEN [37; Omaha; b: Germany; f: Joseph WHITMEN; m: Barbara WEISS] on 12 Apr 1881 at Trinity Rectory. Off: PATERSON. Wit: Hannah DENEN, Wm. E. PUTNUM.

ROGERS, Edwin J. [28; Omaha; b: Pennsylvania; f: John H. ROGERS: m: Eliza SPENCER] md. Theresa MEYERS [27; Omaha; b: Germany] on 21 Nov 1870. Off: ESTABROOK. Wit: C.D. LAYTON; Geo. A. ROGERS.

ROGERS, Ezekiel R. [22; Shelby Co., IA] md. Mrs. Marshia R. GENTRY [27; Shelby Co., IA] on 31 Mar 1868. Off: STUCK. Wit: J.P. PORTER, W.W. FOOT.

ROGERS, Isaac M. [20; b: Iowa; f: Samuel ROGERS; m: Fanny KNIGHT] md. Lena BENSON [17; b: Sweden; f: John BENSON; m: Margaret BILLENGREGG] on 11 Feb 1878. Off: PORTER. Wit: Charles W. EDGERTON, Mrs. E.G. FLOYD. "These parties were in extremis and the license was issued without the consent of parents."

ROGERS, John W. [33; Omaha; b: England; f: John ROGERS; m: Jane BEARD] md. Mrs. Tirza JOHNSON [35; Omaha; b: England; f: William BEDDIS; m: Susan CHARLES] on 7 May 1881. Off: WILLIAMS. Wit: John BOWYER, Lloyd JONES. Signed 20 Jul 1882; filed 15 Aug 1882 by CHADWICK.

ROGERS, John [23; Omaha; b: Prussia; f: Bernard ROGERS; m: Anna KUHN] md. Mrs. Clarissa STOKES [25; Omaha; b: Ohio, Michigan; f: Thomas JONES; m: Catherine] on 15 Jan 1873. Off: GARRETT. Wit: William ROBERTS; Mrs. C. ROBERTS.

ROGERS, Joshua P. [Ottaway, IL] md. Sarah Maria WYMAN [Omaha] on 25 Feb 1863 at the house of the bride's father, W.W. WYMAN. Off: DAKE. Wit: W.W. WYMAN, George T. HOAGLAND, Ianthe C. WYMAN, et al.

ROGERS, T.J. [24; Omaha; b: IA; f: Milton ROGERS; m: Jane S. SPOOR] md. Ella J. SPOOR [21; Omaha; b: IA; f: N.T. SPOOR; m: Eunice ROBINS] on 15 Jun 1881. Off: HARSHA. Wit: Miss Alice ROGERS, Milton ROGERS.

ROHWER, Carsten [33; McArdle Precinct; b: Germany; f: German ROHWER; m: Ann (Anna) HODERS] md. Anna THOMPSON [17; McArdle Precinct; b: Germany; f: Bernhart THOMPSON; m: Catherine THOMPSON] on 28 Aug 1869. Off: HYDE. Wit: Bernhart THOMPSON of McArdle Precinct, Geo. M. O'BRIEN.

ROHWER, Charles [23; Chicago Precinct; b: Germany; f: Joergen ROHWER; m: Elsabe THODE] md. Annie HOLLING [23; Chicago Precinct; b: Germany; f: Ekert HOLLING; m: Cecelia MARTENS] on 27 Apr 1879. Off: STRANSEN. Wit: Claus SIEVERS of McCardle Precinct, Douglas Co., Henry ROHWER.

ROHWER, Hans [34; Douglas Co.; b: Germany; f: Jurgen ROHWER; m: Anna HARDER] md. Elizabeth BUESEL [31 or 33; Douglas Co.; b: Germany; f: Hans BUESEL; m: Catharine GOSH] on 27 Mar 1874. Off: PEABODY. Wit: Hans PETERS, Douglas Co.; Jurgen BOSEL, Douglas Co.

ROLD, Peter C. [23; Omaha] md. Karen JENSEN [23; Omaha] on 3 Aug 1867. Off: DAM. Wit: Neils JENSEN, C.C.

WESTERGARD. This is a double wedding with Nelson M. RING and Anna M. PETERSON.

ROLF, Henry [27; Douglas Co.; b: Germany; f: James ROLF; m: Catherine Able BUSHIE] md. Sophia KAELBER [18; Millard; b: Kansas; f: Christian KAELBER; m: Anna Clara PETZINE] on 21 Nov 1880, Millard. Off: KELSEY. Wit: Fred SEIP, Nellie KELSEY, both of Millard.

ROLL, George [22; Douglas Co.; b: IN; f: Nicholas ROLL; m: Catherine CASTON] md. Johanna PAASCH [22; Douglas Co.; b: Germany; f: Henry PAASCH] on 30 Nov 1876. Off: MEYERS. Wit: John LEMPKE, Chicago · Precinct, Henry TRUELSEN, Millard Precinct.

ROMANS, Lewis [25; Harrison Co., IA; b: OH; f: Elisha ROMANS; m: Elizabeth KNIGHT] md. Minnie HOWLAND [18; Harrison Co., IA; b: Harrison Co., IA; f: Charles HOWLAND; m: Sarah STRAIGHT] on 23 Aug 1876. Off: SEDGWICK. Wit: M.B. KNOX, Joseph QUINLAN.

ROLLI, Christian [26; Willow Station; b: Switzerland; f: Samuel RALLI; m: Elizabeth GUILKER] md. Varene VAUTHRECH [VUTHRICH] [21; Willow Station; b: Switzerland; f: Ulrach VAUTHRECH; m: Mayealona ZOUGY] on 7 Aug 1869. Off: KUHNS. Wit: Rev. M. OFFICER of Fredricksberg, OH, Mrs. H.W. KUHNS.

ROODE, Orange A. [25; Jefferson Co., NE; b: MI; f: Albert R. ROODE; m: Amina EMMONS] md. Marion EGBERT [20; Omaha; b: Brazil, South America; f: George J. CLARK; m: "unknown to this affiant and she has made diligent inquiries to learn the same and cannot learn it."] on 7 Jul 1881. Off: SHERRILL. Wit: Ida SIMONS, C.I. LAWTON, 216 N. 16 Street--Dodge between 16th and 17th.

ROONEY, Franklin [29; Omaha; b: Belfast, Ireland; f: William H. ROONEY; m: Martha THOMPSON] md. Alice BUTTERFIELD [22; Omaha; b: England; f: John BUTTERFIELD; m: Hester NICHOLSON] on 22 Oct 1870. Off: BETTS. Wit: Thomas B. SMITH; Teresa GIES.

ROONEY, Joseph [23; Cottonwood Springs; b: Ireland; f: James ROONEY; m: Ellen CASEY] md. Elizabeth CURAN [28; Omaha; b: Ireland; f: John CURAN; m: Ann MURRAY] on 22 Aug 1870. Off: CURTIS. Wit: Peter MALONE; Ellen O'DONNEL.

ROOT, Allen [28 or 30; Omaha] md. J. Adelaide GOODWILL [20; Omaha] on 1 Sep 1857 at the residence of Mrs. T.G. GOODWILL. Off: SKINNER. Wit: Wm. Young BROWN, Wm. E. MOORE.

ROPER, Thomas E. [50; Laramie, WY; b: England; f: John ROPER; m: Jane HANKINS] md. Sophia C. KAPP [32; Sandusky, OH; b:

Germany; m: Christine ----] on 18 May 1875. Off: PEABODY. Wit: Mrs. J.H. BRAZIER, D.A. VAN NANCEL, Jr.

ROSACKER, John H. [28; Sarpy Co.; b: Germany; f: Chris ROSACKER; m: Annie KRUSE] md. Kate OTTE [20; Sarpy Co.; b: Germany; f: Nick OTTE; m: Kate RUSHMAN] on 9 Jul 1875. Off: PEABODY. Wit: Mrs. Hadelia BOYD, E.A. ALLEN.

ROSE, Cyrus [28; Omaha] md. Mary J. STINSON [28; Omaha] on 10 Nov 1867 at the M.E. Church. Off: SLAUGHTER. Wit: Albert ROSE, A. McAUSLAND, the congregation.

ROSE, Ebenezer [45; Ft. Calhoun; b: Rhode Island; f: Thomas ROSE; m: Betsey ADAMS] md. Mrs. Lucritia GRANDY [36; Ft. Calhoun; b: Gennesse Co, NY; f: Nathan BANNISTER; m: Lucretia LILLY] on 3 Oct 1872. Off: THOWNSEND. Wit: John I. REDICK; James G. MEGEATH.

ROSE, Joseph [36; Canton, MO; b: Germany; f: Charles A. ROSE; m: Gertrude KREVET] md. Barbara OSWOLD [37; Omaha; b: Germany; f: John OSWOLD; m: Caroline HANSER] on 5 Mar 1881. Off: RILEY. Wit: John DOLL, Caroline DOLL.

ROSELL, James H. [colored; 29; Omaha] md. Anna ANTONY [colored; 19; Omaha] on 8 Oct 1868. Off: MULCAHY. Wit: Napoleon JOHNSON, colored, Harrison JOHNSON, colored.

ROSENBERY, Abram [23; Douglas Co.] md. Mimie WRIGHT [18 and some months; Douglas Co.] on 1 Jul 1866. Off: SLAUGHTER. Wit: James WRIGHT, Harriet WRIGHT.

ROSENFELDT, Charles [30; Douglas Co.; b: OH; f: Henry ROSENFELDT; m: Eliza BROWN] md. Louise McCLURE [31; Omaha; b: MI; f: George McCLURE; m: Henrietta GRAY] on 19 Jan 1875. Off: PEABODY. Wit: J.R. CONKLING, F.P. HANLON.

ROSENKRANZ, Charles [21; Omaha; b: Denmark; f: Peter A. ROSENKRANZ; m: Mary LANKILDE] md. Mary PETERSON [21; Omaha; b: Denmark; f: Peter CHRISTENSEN; m: Mathilda ANDERSON] on 22 Dec 1881 at "their residents." Off: GYDESEN. Wit: And. CHRISTIANSON, Peter CHRISTENSEN.

ROSENSTEIN, Joseph [35; Omaha; b: Germany; f: Jacob ROSENSTEIN; m: Adelaide HERZ] md. Henrietta ROSENTHAL [19; Omaha; b: Germany; f: Jacob ROSENTHAL; m: Dine GUTTMANN] on 26 Apr 1874. Off: HALD. Wit: Joseph BLAIK; Frederick MEHREN.

ROSENSTRANCE, Siegfried [29; Douglas Co.; b: Germany; f: Mathias ROSENSTRANCE; m: Margaret SCHARMOVEKER] md. Carolina SCHARNWEBER [19; Omaha; b: Germany; f: Hans J. SCHARNWEBER; m: Anna RUMPF] on 30 Dec 1876. Off: BENEKE. Wit: Anton WILMING, John Peter MERTER. Marriage filed 29 Jan 1877.

ROSENZWEIG, Herman [22; Omaha; b: Burlington, IA; f: John ROSENZWEIG; m: Fanny JAEGLE] md. Nellie FRANK [18; Omaha; b: New York; f: John FRANK; m: Sarah ROOT] on 26 Aug 1879. Off: LIPE. Wit: John ROSENZWEIG, John FRANK.

ROSICKY, John [28; Crete; b: Bohemia; f: John ROSICKY; m: Josephine MALLAT] md. Mary BAYER [20; Chicago, IL; b: Bohemia; f: Joseph BAYER; m: Barbara URBAN] md. 30 Sep 1874. Off: PEABODY. Wit: Frank J. SOULEK; Edward ROSEWATER.

ROSS, Richard [25; Omaha; b: Maryland; f: Richard L. ROSS; m: Lucina TAYLOR] md. Mary Ann O'BYRNE [17; Omaha; b: Brooklyn, NY; f: Patrick O'BYRNE; m: Elizabeth GARAHAN] on 21 Jan 1872. Off: CURTIS. Wit: George T. ROSS; Mary COFFE. Age of consent given by father of bride.

ROST, Carl August [33; Douglas Co.; b: Germany; f: Friederick Wilhelm ROST; m: Wilhemine HELBIG] md. Christene GRIB [21; Douglas Co.; b: Germany] on 5 Nov 1879. Off: FRESE. Wit: John CHESCHGER of Harrison Co., IA, Laura GORNER of Sarpy Co.

ROUSSE, Peter [28; Omaha] md. Mrs.? Malita HATCH [30; Omaha] on 2 Mar 1868. Off: KELLEY. Wit: Mr. TUTTLE, Mary TUTTLE.

ROWE, Harvey Vinton [21; Douglas Co.; b: IA; f: James ROWE; m: Kasar PURLOCK] md. Ettie KNAUSS [30; Harrison Co., IA; b: PA; f: Samuel KNAUSS; m: Susana VANNER] on 22 Aug 1876. Off: ANDERSON. Wit: Chris HARTMAN, J.S. WRIGHT.

ROWE, W.P. [legal age, Omaha] md. E. TEASDEL [legal age, Omaha] on 10 Nov 1863 at the Lutheran parsonage. Off: KUHNS. Wit: Mrs. KUHNS, Elizabeth BEYER.

ROWELL, Henry C. [41; Omaha] md. Catharine HYMAS [32; Omaha] on 7 Aug 1862 "at their residence." Off: HART. Wit: J.O. GATES, James BAKER.

ROWLES, Joseph [24; Omaha; b: England; f: George ROWLES; m: Mary ASTMAN] md. Sadie SPILLETT [19; Omaha; b: England; f: Daniel SPILLETT; m: Sarah BRAMBLE] on 16 Jul 1879. Off: JAMESON. Wit: James O'BRIEN, Minnie VANDENBURG. Affidavit signed by Charles ROWLES.

ROWLEY, Andrew, Jr. [24; Omaha; b: New York; f: Andrew ROWLEY; m: Elenora STEWART] md. Maggie O'BRYAN [17; Omaha; b: Wisconsin; f: Maurice O'BRYAN; m: Mary DAVIS] on 25 Jul 1879. Off: McCARTHY. Wit: Edward PANETT, Johanna BEGLEY. Age consent given by Maurice O'BRYAN, father of the bride.

ROWLEY, Charles [26; b: New York; f: Andrew ROWLEY; m: Eleanor STEWART] md. Mrs. Fannie LAWRENCE [24; Fort Calhoun; b: Nebraska; f: Wm. RUNYON; m: Angeline GILBERT] on 14 Dec 1878. Off: BEANS. Wit: Richard ROWLEY of 20th Street, Wm. ROWLEY.

ROYE, Henry [21; Omaha; b: Missouri; f: Nelson ROYE; m: Harriett COWDEN] md. Mrs. Julia POTETE [20; Omaha] on 21 Jun 1870. Off: PORTER. Wit: Charles PARKER; Charles PAULSON.

RUBY, Orvill C. [39; Washington Co.] md. Melissa GRANGER [32; Washington Co.] on 1 Oct 1867. Off: SHEEKS. Wit: Thomas RUBY, Martha A. WEST.

RUDD, Willington [29; b: New York; f: Bradley RUDD; m: Lorinda BALCOLM] md. Martha McKENNY [28; b: Iowa; f: Robert McKENNY; m: Nancy ----] on 6 May 1878. Off: PORTER. Wit: Henry MASON, Josephine MASON.

RUDELINS, Alex Frederick [30; Omaha; b: Sweden; f: Per Daniel RUDELINS m: Augusta Eloisa WIDMARK] md. Hulda Charlotte NORSTEDT [20; Omaha; b: Sweden; f: David NORSTEDT; m: Hedwig JOHNSON] on 20 Feb 1873. Off: SWEDERS. Wit: John STEEN; Carl Gabriel HERLITZ.

RUDEN, Olaf [35; Florence; b: Sweden; f: Olof RUDEN; m: Carrie NELSON] md. Christine ANDERSON [25; Florence; b: Sweden; f: Anders ANDERSON; m: Carrie NILSON] on 15 Jun 1870. Off: GIBSON. Wit: Hans OLSEN, Florence; Gunnar A. LINDQUIST.

RUDSTRUM, John [21; Omaha; b: Sweden; f: John RUDSTRUM; m: Caslin OLESON] md. Mary JOHNSON [21; Omaha; b: Sweden; f: Jens LAWSON; m: Brita ANDERSON] on 28 Sep 1870. Off: GIBSON. Wit: John MANCHESTER; Elizabeth ERICKSON.

RUEDY, Andrew [22; Fremont; b: Switzerland; f: John RUEDY; m: Margaret MILLER] md. Elizabeth GIELSER [22; Plattsmouth; b: Germany] on 3 Oct 1869. Off: MAY. Wit: H. MEYER, Matilda STOUZAL.

RUEF, Edward L. [21; Omaha; b: NJ; f: John E. RUEF; m: Annie E. PHILLIPS] md. Sarah CUMMINGS [20; Omaha; b: NY; f: Thomas CUMMINGS; m: Mary BOLIN] on 24 May 1881. Off: BAUGHER. Wit: John RUEF, Thomas CUMMINGS.

RUF, Louis F. [23; Omaha] md. Emma WALKER [18, lacking one day written on the license on 3 Aug; Omaha] at 8:30 o'clock Monday evening, 6 Aug 1866 at the house of the bride's father. Off: DIMMICK. Wit: L.C. HUNTINGTON, W.N. WHITNEY, Harry WALKER, Thos. D. WALKER. Age consent given by the bride's father.

RUHLAND, Frank [25; Douglas Co.; b: Prussia; f: Morrice RUHLAND; m: Caroline VOGEL] md. Helena HASERODT [18; Douglas Co.; b: Prussia; f: Charles HASERODT; m: Frederica ROTH] on 26 Nov 1870. Off: GIBSON. Wit: Frederica HASERODT, Douglas Co.; Reinhard CLAUSSEN:

RULKOWSKI, Frank J. [29; Omaha; b: Poland; f: Adam RULKOWSKI; m: Bogmula MAICZROWIC] md. Helena HASERODT [22; Omaha; b: Germany; f: Charles HASERODT; m: Fredicka MAUF] on 31 Jan 1877. Off: WEISS. Wit: Benjamin BROW, Mrs. WARD.

RUMEL, William M. [25; Douglas Co.; b: PA; f: Nicholas RUMEL; m: Amanda PATER] md. Louisa SYLVESTER [22; Douglas Co.; b: MO; f: George SYLVESTER; m: Mary FARLEY] on 27 Dec 1876. Off: CAFALL. Wit: Mr. and Mrs. SYLVESTER, Mr. and Mrs. RUMMEL, et al.

RUPERT, William [26; Dodge Co.; b: Canada; f: Henry RUPERT; m: Catharine SHAFER] md. Menna UHLING [17; Dodge Co.; b: Wisconsin; m: Margaret UHLING] on 22 Sep 1869. Off: HYDE. Wit: Henry HAHLBERK of Logan Creek, W.J. HAHN.

RUSH, John [22; Omaha] md. Anna E. FERRY [19; Douglas Co.] on 1 Mar 1868 at the Catholic Church. Off: CURTIS. Wit: Patrick MORGAN, Lizzie BURNS.

RUSHLAU, P.J. [23; Omaha; b: MI; f: Joseph RUSHLAU; m: Mathilda JAMBOAH] md. Mary A. SMITH [19; Omaha; b: IN; f: N.P. SMITH; m: Mary WHITE] on 6 Aug 1881. Off: STENBERG. Wit: S.J. LARSON, J. MEAGHER.

RUSSELL, Joseph B. [24; North Ridgeville, OH, b: North Ridgeville, OH; f: William RUSSELL; m: Lydia A. COLE] md. Esther L. HOWARD [21; Omaha; b: Clerzy, NY; f: Isaac HOWARD] on 31 Mar 1876. Off: SHERRILL. Wit: Prof. R.D. KINNEY, Mrs. Sarah THOMPSON.

RUSSELL, William H. [41; Douglas Co.] md. Sarah E. TRISSLER [22; Douglas Co.] on 26 Nov 1865 at the Lutheran Church. Off: KUHNS. Wit: Augustus KOUNTZE, John McCORMACK, et al.

RUTAN, William H. [29; Des Moines, IA; b: Ohio; f: William RUTAN; m: Hannah CLARK] md. Medora WILEY [19; Des Moines, IA; b: Ohio; f: Jacob WILEY; m: May L. WOODFORD] on 11 Jun 1872. Off: TOWNSEND. Wit: J.F.L.D. HERTZMANN; Otho C. JEWETT, Iowa City, IA.

RUTH, L.J. [24; Omaha] md. Augusta D. SMILEY [18; Omaha] on 16 Mar 1862 at William HUGHES' residence on Farnham St. Off: KUHNS. Wit: Augustus KOUNTZE, William HUGHES, William RUTH, et al.

RUTHERFORD, John[23; Omaha; b: Scotland; f: James RUTHERFORD; m: Sarah McMASTERS] md. Isabella MACKIE [22; Omaha; b: Scotland; f: James F. MACKIE; m: Catharine GALLOWAY] on 8 Jul 1869. Off: McCAGUE. Wit: Mrs. Catharine MACKIE, Mary McLANE.

RUZICKA, John [23; Omaha; b: Austria; f: John RUZICKA; m: Anna TOMISKA] md. Josephine NOHEJL [20; Omaha; b: Austria; f: Joseph NOHEJL; m: Katie PETRICEK] on 22 Apr 1878 at "Bohemian town Omaha". Off: KOCARNIK. Wit: Mr. Fr. VRBA, Joe PETRICEK, both of Bohemian town.

RUZICKA, Joseph [22; Omaha; b: Bohemia; f: Joseph RUZICKA; m: Catharine HORAK] md. Mary SOLINKA [ZELENKA] [18; Omaha; b: Bohemia; f: Frank SOLINKA [ZELENKA]; m: Catharine VITKOVA [VITEK]] on 21 Jun 1873. Off: TOWNSEND. Wit: Joseph DWORAK; Frank SEMERAD.

RYAN, Dennis [22; b: Ireland; f: Wm. RYAN; m: Mary McDONALD] md. Margaret BOYLE [25; b: Ireland; f: Hugh BOYLE; m: Margaret McMILLIN] on 31 Jan 1878 at the Catholic Cathedral of Omaha. Off: REYNOLDS. Wit: George GRAHAM, Esther ROBERTS.

RYAN, James C. [27; Omaha; b: Ireland; f: John I. RYAN; m: Mary CALAHAN] md. Maggie CASEY [22; Omaha; b: Ireland; f: Michael CASEY; m: Kate REALE] on 10 May 1870 at the Catholic Church of Omaha. Off: MASORMAN. Wit: John HEALY; Bridget CASEY.

RYAN, James M. ]40; Ryans Junction, MT; b: Ireland; f: John RYAN; m: Jane MARTIN] md. Catharine McCRISTAL [20; Omaha; b: St. Joseph, OH; f: Daniel McCRISTAL; m: Susannah LYNCH] on 12

Apr 1873. Off: CURTIS. Wit: Henry J. LUCAS; Catharine ORD.

RYAN, John [22; Omaha; b: Canada; f: Thomas RYAN; m: Ann O'NEIL] md. Margaret CARR (HALL crossed out) [17; Omaha; b: MO; f: Timothy CARR; m: Margaret MAREN] on 19 Oct 1875. Off: BOBAL. Wit: John CORVIN, Catharine RYAN.

RYAN, Michael [22; Pottawattamie Co., IA; b: IL; f: John RYAN; m: Johana FLOOD] md. Mary Alice RAND [18; Pottawattamie Co., IA; f: James RAND; m: Carrie HOWARD] on 9 Jun 1875. Off: PEABODY. Wit: Aurora THRALLS, George WEST.

RYAN, Timothy T. [25; Saunders Co.; b: Ireland; f: Daniel RYAN; m: Mary KERWAN] md. Bridget POWERS [28; Saunders Co.; b: Ireland; f: Jeffrey POWERS; m: Mary KERWAN] on 19 Apr 1870. Off: CURTIS. Wit: Nicholas POWERS, Ashland, Saunders Co.; Bridget POWERS, ELkhorn.

RYAN, William [22; Omaha] md. Bridget BRENNAN [23; Omaha] on 24 Jan 1869. Off: CURTIS. Wit: Richard HOLLENS, Mary RYAN.

RYAN, William [23; Council Bluffs; b: IL; f: Patrick RYAN; m: Hanora O'NEIL] and Rosa COWLES [23; Douglas Co.; b: WI; f: James COWLES] filed an affidavit on 16 Oct 1876. No marriage recorded. Off: SEDGWICK.

FITCH, C.P. [29; Douglas Co.; b: IL; f: Joel FITCH; m: Ann WAGEY] and Levella M. CROWELL [22; Douglas Co.; b: OH; f: Wm. CROWELL; m: Mary HOEL] filed an affidavit on 10 Oct 1876. No marriage recorded. Off: SEDGWICK.

RYBERG, Nels G. [24; Omaha] md. Johanna ANDERSON [24; Omaha] on 12 Nov 1868. Off: KUHNS. Wit: Andrew WINQUIST, Lizzie O'BRIEN, et al.

RYLEY, Edward G. [30; Omaha] md. Fredricka C. KENZEL [20; Omaha] on 30 May 1868. Off: KUHNS. Wit: Mr. and Mrs. James M. WINSHIP, et al.

SAALFELD, Christoph [28; Omaha; b: Germany; f: Christoph SAALFELD; m: Emme PERTUCH] and Christine KELSCHENBACH [21; Omaha; b: Germany; f: Philip KELSCHENBACH; m: Marie FISHER] license issued on6 Mar 1875. No marriage recorded. Off: PEABODY.

SAALFELDT, Gustav [20; Omaha; b: Germany; f: William SAALFELDT; m: Friederike OTTO] md. Sophia DUNKER [22; Omaha; b: Germany; f: Steffen H. DUNKER; m: Pauline CLAUSSEN] on 26 Apr 1881. Off: BRUEGGER. Wit: William SAALFELDT, Dorothea LEBMANN.

SABIN, Arthur C. [26; Omaha; b: Vermont; f: Henry S. SABIN; m: Zadai VERNOL] md. Florence D. VAUGHN [19;

Omaha; b: Wisconsin; f: John M. VAUGHN; m: Deana HANDY] on 5 Apr 1871. Off: CHESSHIRE. Wit: Mr. and Mrs. DORT; Mr. and Mrs. VAUGHN, parents of bride.

SACHS, John C. [24; Omaha; b: Maryland; f: John SACHS; m: Fredericke LANG] md. Elizabeth FORSEYTH [24; Omaha; b: Iowa; f: William FORSEYTH; m: Mary PETERS] on 22 Jun 1874. Off: PEABODY. Wit: Rose W. PEABODY, Lyn, MA; Mrs. Mary C. PEABODY.

SADERLUND, Andrew [26; Omaha; b: Sweden; f: Lars LARSON; m: Martha ANDERSON] md. Anna ISAKSON [18; Omaha; b: Sweden; f: Isac ABRAHAMSON; m: Carin ANDERSDOTTER] on 15 Jan 1871. Off: HESSEL. Wit: William NELSON; Gustaf ANDERSON.

SADLER, William [30; Missouri Valley, IA; b: Pennsylvania; f: Levi SADLER; m: Sarah RUSSELL] md. Mrs. Diana COOPER [36; Missouri Valley, IA; b: New York; f: Harvey MILLER; m: Mary BUTLER] on 23 Apr 1872. Off: TOWNSEND. Wit: E.S. ARMSTRONG; G. Robt. ARMSTRONG. (Sadler is under L in marriage book index.)

SAIDE, Jerry [29; Des Moines; b; Canada; f: Zepherino SAIDE; m: Margaret CALLAGHAN] md. Catharine DOUGHERTY [24; Omaha; b: Omaha; f: Hugh DOUGHERTY; m: Ellen McARDLE] on 30 Dec 1879. Off: ENGLISH. Wit: Harry O'BRIEN, Mary DOUGHERTY.

SAINT CLAIR, George H. [23; Omaha; b: New York; f: Samuel J. SAINT CLAIR; m: Eliza BENNETT] md. Hattie NOBLE [22; Omaha; b: Michigan; f: Daniel NOBLE; m: Annie BENEDICT] on 1 Oct 1874. Off: HANSEN. Wit: Thos. W. GARDNER; William H. OVERMYER.

SAINT FELIX, Prudens D. [37; Canada; b: Canada; f: Peter D. SAINT FELIX; m: Marie M. LAROSCHEL] md. Sarah E. GROAT [21; Omaha; b: Canada; f: George GROAT; m: Harriet GROAT] on 14 Nov 1875. Off: BOBAL. Wit: Patrick McGAVOCK, Mary Anne GAVOCK.

SALLANDER, Gustaf [23; Omaha; b: Sweden; f: Arvid SALLANDER; m: Louise ASPELIN] md. Alexandra SWANSON [19; Omaha; b: Sweden; f: C.A. SWANSON; m: Anna KINDMAN] on 15 Jul 1880. Off: FOGELSTROM. Wit: Gust W. SWAN, C.F. JOHNSON.

SALLY, James [45; Omaha; b: Ireland; f: Francis SALLY; m: Catharine COLLIN] md. Elizabeth LYNCH [38; Omaha; b: Ireland; f: Thomas LYNCH; m: Susan SMITH] on 27 Jan 1880, St. Philomena's Church. Off: ENGLISH. Wit: Jas. TONER, Mrs. Susan MULLEGAN.

SAMPSON, William R. [58; Saunder? Co.; b: England; f: Samuel SAMPSON; m: Ann ROSE] md. Mary M. HARMON [37; Omaha; b: Connecticut; f: Paul HARMON; m: Abigal GELLETT] on 7 Jun 1870. Off: WESTOVER. Wit: P. HARMON; A.J. HARMON.

SAMSON, Andrew [32; Omaha; b: Sweden; f: Samuel SAMSON; m: Sessa PERSON] md. Anna JOHNSON [24; Omaha; b: Sweden; f: Andrew JOHNSON; m: Mary JOHNSON] on 15 May 1872. Off: TOWNSEND. Wit: Ferdinand STREITA; Peter PAULSON.

SAMSON, Oscar [24; Oakland; b: Sweden; f: Johannes SAMSON; m: Christine ANDERSON] md. Caroline NYGREN [24; Omaha; b: Sweden; f: Magnus ANDERSON; m: Ingred SAMUELSON] on 27 Dec 1873. Off: BENZON. Wit: P. NYGREN; Caroline PATTESON; Tilda SAMSON; G. PATTESON.

SANDERS, Thomas H. [33; Omaha; b: Massachusetts; f: B.C. SANDERS; m: Lucinda TEMPLE] md. Alvina S. McCLURE [26; Chicago, IL; b: Ireland] on 29 Jul 1871 at GAYLORD's home. Off: GAYLORD. Wit: Edmund BARRET; Mary BARRET.

SANDERS, William [30; Ft. Kearney] md. Louisa GRAVES [28; Omaha] on 25 Apr 1861. Off: BIRKETT. Wit: James SEMPLE, Thomas ?.

SANDERSON, John [24] and Josephen KORNES [19] license issued 12 Feb 1857. No marriage record. Off: SCOTT. Age consent given by Marcus SHAW.

SANDMEYER, John Henry [35; Fremont; b: Switzerland; f: Jacob SANDMEYER; m: Marie HUMBEL] md. Anna STRAUMANN [16; Omaha; b: Switzerland; f: Henry STRAUMANN; m: Anna GENNY] on 2 Apr 1875. Off: BENEKE. Wit: G.C. GRAVES, Will LEIFFE.

SANDS, Abel J. [29; Decatur, Burt Co.] md. Ellen ANDREWS [35; Decatur, Burt Co.] on 20 Jan 1866. Off: GAYLORD. Wit: George H. SANDS of Decatur, Ralph E. GAYLORD.

SANFORD, Elliott B. [26; Omaha] md. Elmira A. COREY [30; Omaha] on 28 Nov 1867 at the Trinity Church. Off: VAN ANTWERP. Wit: Miss MORRISON, Mr. JORDAN, Mr. LACEY, the congregation.

SANQUEST, John [35; Logan Creek; b: Sweden; f: John ANDERSON; m: Eva MAGNES] md. Lena DANIELSON [25; Logan Creek; b: Sweden; f: Daniel SWANSEN; m: Anna MAGNUSON] on 27 Jul 1869. Off: LARSON. Wit: Mrs. Johanna LARSON, Ida M. SWENSEN.

SASSTROM, Frank [26; Omaha; b: Sweden; f: Lars FRANSON; m: Mary NICHOLSON] md. Lina GUSTOFSON [23; Omaha; b: Sweden; f: Peter LARSON; m: Lina C. PETERSON] on 31 May 1873. Off: SUNDBORN. Wit: Oscar HARTMAN; Hanna HAGLIN.

SATHER, Anthony Olsen [25; Omaha; b: Norway; f: Ule OLSEN; m: Olia OLSEN] md. Matilda Christine RODEN [22; Omaha; b: Sweden; f: Neils F. RODEN; m: Sarah C. JOHNSON] on 20 Oct 1869. Off: LARSON. Wit: Sara Maria CARLSON, Mrs. Johanna C. LARSON.

SATTERFIELD, Wm. M. [34; Sarpy Co.] md. Rachel A. JONES [22; Douglas Co.] on Monday, 15 Sep 1862 at Mrs. Ann JONES' house. Off: GAYLORD. Wit: Mrs. Ann JONES, Daniel JONES.

SATTLER, George [22; Omaha; b: Hungary; f: Johann SATTLER; m: Eva SIDEL] md. Maria SPIELMANN [17; Omaha; b: Hungary; f: Michael SPIELMANN; m: Theresa LADISCH] on 24 Jul 1881 at the German Catholic Cathedral. Off: GLANBER. Wit: Lawrence NEUBERGER, Lawrence KLEIDASTY. Age consent given by guardian of the bride, Chas. KOHLMEYER.

SAUER, A.K. [27; Omaha; b: Michigan; f: Jacob SAUER; m: Margaret PFLUG] md. Alice M. Van AERNAM [21; Omaha; b: New York; f: John B. Van AERNAM; m: Cordelia M. SHELDON] on 13 Nov 1879. Off: INGRAM. Wit: L.B. WILLIAMS, Will J. Van AERNAM.

SAUER, Henry [24; Omaha; b: Germany; f: John SAUER; m: Mary REAL] md. Elizabeth LARGEN [20; Omaha; b: Germany] on 16 Jan 1871. Off: PORTER. Wit: Charles PARKER; Inez A. PORTER.

SAULPAUGH, John A. [45; Omaha; b: NY; f: Henry M. SAULPAUGH; m: Maria WEEKS] md. Mrs. Eveline COONEY [40; Omaha; b: England; f: Lorenzo MORTIMER; m: Eveline C. MORTON] on 28 Mar 1875. Off: PEABODY. Wit: Chas. K. MANSFIELD, Chas. U. EDGERTON.

SAUNDERS, Albert P. [35; Omaha; b: Virginia; f: Albern SAUNDERS; m: Lucinda POWELL] md. Mrs. Marion B. VAN PLEW [32; Omaha; b: England] on 28 Aug 1869. Off: PORTER. Wit: Wiley B. DIXON, R.S. KNOX.

SAUNDERS, Thomas [30; Ashland; b: Ohio; f: George SAUNDERS; m: Ellen BENNETT] md. Elizabeth AUSTIN [28; Ashland; b: New York] on 21 Dec 1871. Off: BRANDES. Wit: J.F. MORTON; Mrs. THUMB.

SAUSE, Daniel A. [27; Omaha; b: Dubuque, IA; f: Michael SAUSE; m: Ann MAGRAW] md. Mrs. Matilda J. MYERS [29; Omaha; b: Louise Co.; IA; f: Riley DRISCOLL; m: Mabel LEWIN] on 15 Feb 1873. Off: TOWNSEND. Wit: Patrick W. LYNCH; Frank W. SCHULTE.

SAUTTER, John [28; Sarpy Co.] md. Anna LEHNER [22; Sarpy Co.] on 20 May 1860 at F. DREXEL's house. Off: KUHNS. Wit: Mr. and Mrs. Louis WALKER, Agness SMILEY, et al.

SAVLICK, Vaclav [23; Omaha; b: Bohemia; f: John SAVLICK; m: Margaret HOFFMAN] md. Anna HAJEK [20; Omaha; b: Bohemia; f: John VAVERKA; m: Mary VAVERKA] on 24 Nov 1881. Off: TURK. Wit: Joseph ROSE, Francis HAJEK.

SCHAEFFER, Charles C. [30; Omaha] md. Margaret POEHLMANN [20; Omaha] on 16 Mar 1867 at KUHNS' residence. Off: KUHNS. Wit: Mrs. H.W. KUHNS, Elizabeth GETSCH.

SCHAIBOLD, Robert [29; Omaha; b: Germany; f: George SCHAIBOLD; m: Anna Mary HIRT] md. Anastasia MATTES [20; Washington Co.; b: Germany; f: John MATTES; m: Mary MATTES] on 15 Jan 1872. Off: GROENEBAUM. Wit: John BAUMER; Anna SCHMIDT, Washington Co.

SCHANLAN, Louis B. [33; West Point; b: Germany; f: Gasper SCHANLAN; m: Threasea BRUNS] md. Lena SCHMIDT [22; Prussia; f: Charles SCHMIDT; m: Caroline MILLER] on 28 Sep 1870. Off: BENNETT. Wit: D.O. ROOT; Gustavis KARKAW.

SCHARNWEBAR, Christ [36, Nancy Co.; b: Germany; f: Jacob SCHARNWEBAR; m: Mary SCHULTZ] md. Mrs. Exilde GOODROW [36; Omaha; b: Canada; f: Tusa RENAN; m: Exilda LaPORTE] on 10 Dec 1881. Off: ANDERSON. Wit: Louis SIEMIN, William SCHARNWEBAR.

SCHARNWEBER, John William Daniel [34; Omaha; b: Germany; f: John SCHARNWEBER; m: Alena SCHOUTZ] md. Wilhelmine C.M. STEMM [29; Omaha; b: Germany; f: Boye STEMM; m: Elene HEIDEBEHN] on 14 Mar 1874. Off: HILGRENDORF. Wit: John SCHARNWEBER; Cecelia STEMM.

SCHATZ, Frederick [26; Douglas Co.; b: Germany; f: Charles SCHATZ; m: Minna RADAS] md. Maggie ARFF [ARP] [22; Douglas Co.; b: Germany; f: Henry ARFF [ARP]; m: Catharine PAHL] on 30 Apr 1880 in Millard. Off: KELSEY. Wit: Henry HEITOLD, Molly MOCK, both of Millard.

SCHERL, Frederick [21; Omaha; b: Austria; f: Anton SCHERL; m: Elizabeth RUDIGIERIN] md. Amalia NIEWALD [15; Omaha; b: Germany; f: Toens NIEWALD; m: Minna WHITE] on 26 Feb 1880. Off: WITTE. Wit: C.B.W. HANN, Barbara BITTELIE.

SCHILTZ, Henry [24; Omaha] and Anni KITZINGER [19; Omaha] license issued on 9 Mar 1869. No marriage record. Off: HYDE.

SCHIMMELPFENNIG, Carl August [35; Douglas Co.; b: Germany; f: Carl Wm. SCHIMMELPFENNIG; m: Charlotte ROEMER] md. Mrs. Elizabeth MEYLE [24; Douglas Co.; b: Canada; f: John HAWMAN; m: Eliza GODTREE] on 11 Jan 1881. Off: BARTHOLOMEW. Wit: Max BERGMANN, Henry DOHLE.

SCHINKER, Matthias [28; Omaha; b: Prussia; f: John SCHINKER; m: Antoinette QUINTZ] md. Maggie ROEDINK [25; Omaha; b: Holland; f: John ROEDINK; m: Christina HASPAN] on 13 Sep 1875. Off: PEABODY. Wit: Henry TIMM, Mary BOLINER.

SCHLANK, Charles [27; Omaha; b: Austria; f: Aleck SCHLANK; m: Leah LORZA] md. Babette ROSENTHALL [22; Omaha; b: Germany; f: Jacob ROSENTHAL; m: Dina R. GUTMAN] on 12 Sep 1875. Off: PORTER. Wit: Joseph ROSENSTINE, John MERRITT.

SCHLECHT, Jacob [30; Omaha] md. Magdalena HOSNER [HAUSNER] [21; Omaha] on 7 Apr 1867 at KUHNS' residence. Off: KUHNS. Wit: Frederick KONIG, John KONIG.

SCHLESSINGER, Sebold V. md. Hannah CHRISTOPHERSON on the evening of 5 Sep 1865 at the District Parsonage. Off: LEMON. Wit: Mr. and Mrs. T.A. FOSTER, et al.

SCHLIEN, Carl [21; Omaha; b: Prussia; f: Valentine SCHLIEN; m: Charlotta KRUEGER] md. Maria PREUSS [23; Omaha; b: Prussia; f: Christoph PRUESS; m: Carolina LUSCHKAT] on 9 May 1875. Off: HILGENDORF. Wit: Christine ADAM, Henrietta LUSCHKAT. Application signed by J. HILGENDORF.

SCHLINGMANN, William [27; Omaha; b: Germany; f: Friederich SCHLINGMANN; m: Elisa ELLERMANN] md. Augusta GAMEHN [21; Omaha; b: Germany; f: Carl GAMEHN; m: Ester SCHIPPOREIT] on 17 Nov 1881. Off: FRESE. Wit: August SCHIPPOREIT, Dorothea BAWEHN.

SCHMIDT, Charles [25; Omaha; b: Germany; f: John SCHMIDT; m: Dorotheas AUPPERLE] and Mary FLAHERTY [26; Omaha; b: Ireland; f: Patrick FLAHERTY; m: Bridget] license issued on 10 Jun 1873. Off: TOWNSEND.

SCHMIDT, Claus J. [28; Omaha; b: Germany; f: Henry SCHMIDT; m: Kate BROCKMAN] md. Lena ILARS [25; Omaha;

b: Germany; f: John ILARS; m: Annie OELARENG] on 20 May 1876. Off: STEINERT. Wit: John BICHEL, Jennie STEINERT, McArdle Precinct.

SCHMIDT, Hans Peter [61; Omaha; b: Denmark; f: Peter H. SCHMIDT; m: Annie E. SOHL] md. Mrs. Johanna NIELSEN [49; Omaha; b: Denmark; f: Nils PETERSON; m: Anna NEWHOUSE] on 7 Jul 1870. Off: KUHNS. Wit: Mrs. A.S. PADDOCK; Mrs. J.S. SPAUN.

SCHMIDT, Henry [25] md. Dora HAGEDORN [21] on 30 Nov 1865 at John T. PAULSON's residence near Omaha. Off: KUHNS. Wit: J.T. PAULSON, Henry FRAHM; et al.

SCHMIDT, John A.J. [28; Omaha; b: Germany; f: Jacob SCHMIDT; m: Catharine STEFFEN] md. Sophia SEIDLER [22; Omaha; b: Germany; f: Frederick SEIDLER; m: Fredericke RICHTER] on 2 Jul 1874. Off: DEICKMANN. Wit: Pauline FECHNER; Bertha FECHNER.

SCHMIDT, Joseph [26; Douglas Co.] md. Mrs. Vichtor BAUMESTER [32; Douglas Co.] on 19 May 1868. Off: STUCK. Wit: Charles LAMMERSDORF, W.F. deGRAFFENRIED.

SCHMIDT, Peter [27; Omaha; b: Germany; f: A.C. SCHMIDT; m: Maren FROESIG] md. Line MADSEN [22; Omaha; b: Demnark; f: Mads VODDER; m: Ane JOHNSON] on 25 Apr 1880, Vor Frelsers Church. Off: GYDESEN. Wit: Christ. PETERSON, Ande KJAR.

SCHMIDT, Wm. C.H. [28; Chicago Precinct; b: Germany; f: Wm. SCHMIDT; m: Louise ZIMMERMANN] md. Maria HOCHE [19; Millard Precinct; b: Germany; f: Max HOCHE; m: Lina HARTING] on 23 Dec 1878. Off: STRASEN. Wit: Hans RATHMANN of Chicago Precinct, Douglas Co., Hans BREKENFELD.

SCHNECK, Abram [32; Columbus; b: Switzerland; f: Abram SCHNECK; m: Elizabeth SPRINGER] md. Emma HUERNER [20; Omaha; b: Switzerland; f: Jacob HUERNER; m: Anna MOSER] on 17 Oct 1875. Off: DIECKMANN. Wit: John HARTE, George SELK.

SCHNEEKLOTH, Hans [37; Douglas Co.; b: Holstein, Germany; f: James SCHNEEKLOTH; m: Celia RURSER] md. Annie KUHL [30; Omaha; b: Germany; f: Peter KUHL; m: Annie STEFFEN] on 31 Mar 1876. Off: PEABODY. Wit: J.F. SWEESY, F.P. HANLONG.

SCHNEIDER, John [44; Salt Lake City, UT; b: Germany; f: Wienant SCHNEIDER; m: Mary Eve MARTEN] md. Catharine DAEMON [21; Omaha; b: Germany; f: John DAEMON; m: Catharine ALTHAUS] on 28 Mar 1872. Off: BRANDES. Wit: John DAEMON; Mrs. Wilhelmia DAEMON.

SCHNEIDER, Nicholas D. [33; Omaha; b: Germany; f: John P.D. SCHNEIDER; m: Mary ADAMS] md. Magdalene RABELER [28; Omaha; b: Germany; f: John P. REICHMAN] on 7 Jul 1869. Off: HYDE. Wit: J. REESE, C.P. BURKETT.

SCHNESSEL, Hans Jurgen [38; McArdle Precinct, b: Germany; f: Claus SCHNESSEL; m: Catharine LUHER] md. Wilhelmina A. HORNS [35; McArdle Precinct; b: Germany; f: Hans Jacob HORNS; m: Wilhelmine A. POTTLICH] on 3 Jul 1879. Off: BARTHOLOMEW. Wit: Peter GOOS, Max BERGMANN.

SCHNETZ, Frank H. [23; Omaha; b: Germany; f: George SCHNETZ; m: Elizabeth KATZEMIRE] md. Christina REEPER [20; Omaha; b: Germany; f: Detlev REEPER; m: Henrietta HAHN] on 17 Apr 1875. Off: PEABODY. Wit: Fritz REEPER, Martin TEBKE.

SCHOEB; William [27; Omaha] md. Mary S. OTT [18; Omaha] on 15 Jun 1861 at Mr. SCHOEB's house. Off: BIRKETT. Wit: Mr. and Mrs. SCHOEB, brother of the groom.

SCHONBOIN, Leopold [29; Oxford, IA; b: Hungaria; f: Joseph SCHONBOIN; m: Catharine BANER] md. Jennie SHEELY [22; Douglas Co.; b: Omaha; f: John M. SHEELY; m: Wilhelmine GREENWOOD] on 10 Sep 1879. Off: LIPE. Wit: Joseph SHEELY, John SHEELY.

SCHRADER, Louis [41; Omaha; b: Germany; f: Louis SCHRADER; m: Maria STOLL] md. Mrs. Mary FLECKDECKER [38; Omaha; b: Switzerland; f: Andrew FLECKDECKER; m: Maria STEINER] on 19 Aug 1881. Off: BRANDES. Wit: Frederick FOAMBERG, John MANICH.

SCHRAMM, William [26; Omaha; b: Ohio; f: John G. SCHRAMM; m: Amaena LOEWEL] md. Christiana M. JENSEN [19; Omaha; f: James JENSEN; m: Carrie HANSEN] on 11 Dec 1869. Off: McCAGUE. Wit: David H. NEILSON; Mary NEILSON.

SCHREB, Henry [34; Omaha; b: Germany; f: Henry SCHREB; m: Fredrica ERN] md. Amelia LAMANN [19; Omaha; b: Germany; f: Fred LAMANN; m: Amelia MILLER] on 5 Dec 1870. Off: GIBSON. Wit: Dennia LONERGAN; Frederick BELBROLF.

SCHREINER, Wolfgang F. [29; Camp ROBISON; b: Austria; f: Francis SCHREINER; m: Barbara MAIER] md. Magdalena ABLE [28; Camp Robison; b: OH; f: George ABLE; m: Magdalena STRAUS] on 27 Aug 1876 at the Catholic Cathedral. Off: JENNETT. Wit: Rev. Jas. M.K. MARTIN, Edward BURKE.

SCHRINER, H.L. [34; Omaha; b: NY; f: Henry SCHRINER; m: Resufa SCOTT] md. Mrs. Sarah EVANS [36; Omaha; b: NY; f: Jesse ASHBURN; m: Mira GLASS] on 8 Dec 1881. Off: WRIGHT. Wit: David McCREA, G.W. WILLIAMSON.

SCHROEDER, Alfred [23; Omaha; b: France; f: Jacob SCHROEDER; m: Elizabeth EXTERMANN] md. Maggie LIEBER [17; Omaha; b: IA; f: Philip LIEBER; m: Margaret] on 13 Dec 1875 at Dr. LIEBER's residence. Off: WALTER. Wit: August KLEIN, John LINGENFELDER.

SCHROEDER, Louis [29; Omaha; b: Prussia; f: J.H. SCHROEDER; m: Marie NIEBER] md. Margaret SIMONSON [24; Omaha; b: Holstein, Germany; f: Eckhardt SIMONSON; m: Margaret VOSS] on 13 Oct 1871. Off: BILLMAN. Wit: Frederick MARTEN; Annie SIMONSON.

SCHROEDER, William [21; Union Pct.; b: Pennsylvania; f: Joseph SCHROEDER; m: Franie HICKMON] md. Lorinda WILBORN [18; Omaha; b: Illinois; f: George W. WILBORN; m: Elizabeth LUMPKINS] on 31 Dec 1872. Off: TOWNSEND. Wit: John WILLIAMS, Union Pct; Francis WILLIAMS.

SCHROF, Joseph [30; Omaha; b: Germany; f: William SCHROF; m: Christine SPAE] md. Minnie ELLEN [25; Omaha; b: Germany; f: Carl ELLEN; m: Carolina ACKERMAN] on 24 Jul 1869. Off: KUHNS. Wit: Michael KOPPES, George ARMSTRONG.

SCHROTH, Charles B. [37; b: Germany; f: Peter SCHROTH; m: Marianne BISCHOFF] and Maria DAMBROSKI [43; b: Germany; f: Ludwig DAMBROSKI; m: Elizabeth ROSS] on 18 Nov 1878. Off: BENEKE. Wit: Paul TERTSCH or FERTSCH, Joseph HASSEN.

SCHUB, Francis J. [40; Omaha] md. Levina PETTS [20; Omaha] on 6 Oct 1868. Off: KUHNS. Wit: Mrs. Thomas LATEY, Mrs. Henry LATEY, et al.

SCHUBERT, Christian [24; Omaha; b: Germany; f: Cyriacus SCHUBERT; m: Kate SMITH] md. Barbara HAHN [18; Omaha; b: Rochchester, NY; f: Adolph HAHN; m: Johanna M. JAEL] on 23 Aug 1870. Off: GIBSON. Wit: Johanna M. JAEL; Margaret SCHAFER.

SCHUCK, John P. [28; US Army; b: Germany; f: Tobias SCHUCK; m: Annie M. SCHERER] md. Mrs. Kate DANEN [22; Omaha; b: Michigan; f: William McMILLEN; m: Sarah J. BARBER] on 28 Nov 1870. Off:

GIBSON. Wit: W.H. CADER; George SOMMERS.

SCHULTZ, C.D. [35; Douglas Co.; b: NY; f: John D. SCHULTZ; m: Catherine TAYLOR] md. Annie PULS [21; Douglas Co.; b: NY; f: Augustus PULS; m: Julia KASCHAN] on 14 Jun 1876. Off: LIPE. Wit: F. BRUHN, Mary BOLIVER.

SCHULZ, Carl [27; Omaha; b: Germany; f: Gottlieb SCHULZ; m: Rosalie BAIN (or BERN)] md. Elsie OTTERBIEN [21; Omaha; b: Germany; f: Christof OTTERBIEN; m: Marie Catharine WESJOHANN (Louise OTTERBIEN crossed out)] on 12 Sep 1875. Off: BENEKE. Wit: A. WERTHEIM, Otto WIEFELS.

SCHUMACHER, Adam L. [24; Omaha; b: Prussia; f: John SCHUMACHER; m: Gertrude WEINHACH] md. Kate O'GORMAN [21; Omaha; b: Ireland; f: Michael O'GORMAN; m: Julia WHALEN] on 18 Jul 1869. Off: CURTIS. Wit: C.G. FISHER, Hannah COONEY.

SCHUMANN, Claus [21; Omaha; b: Germany; f: Christian SCHUMANN; m: Margarett SCHAFER] md. Maria LESCHANSKY [LASCHANSKY] [24; Omaha; b: Germany; f: August LESCHANSKY [LASCHANSKY]; m: Annie LANFER] on 12 Feb 1871. Off: KUHNS. Wit: John MOHR; Henry EGGERS.

SCHWANEBERG, Julius [42; Omaha; b: Germany; f: Andreus SCHWANEBERG; m: Wilheimne WARTNER] md. Mrs. Caroline BEHRENS [37; Omaha; b: Germany; f: Christopher HEIM; m: Dorothea HEIM] on 10 Jan 1874. Off: LIPE. Wit: Fred BITTEROFF; Rebekah BITTEROFF.

SCHWEICKERT, Frank [23; Omaha; b: Germany; f: Augustin SCHWEICKERT, m: Mary Anna SCHMIT] md. Mena DURRER [23; Omaha; b: Germany; f: Frank DURRER; m: Theresa ANDERMAT] on 13 Nov 1875. Off: PEABODY. Wit: Wm. N. WALKER, James A. FRASER.

SCKNEKLOTH, Hans [30; Douglas Co.] md. Lena BOLWELT [27; Douglas Co.] on 6 Mar 1869. Off: HYDE. Wit: John H. MERRICK, Peter N. DEERSON.

SCOTT, Charles M. [23; Omaha; colored; b: Illinois; f: John SCOTT] md. Mary GRAVES [24; Omaha; colored; b: Cincinnati, OH; f: John GRAVES; m: Martha A. McAFFEE] on 22 Jun 1870. Off: GRAHAM. Wit: George C. KIDDER; J. McCHEANE.

SCOTT, George [21; Omaha; b: New York; f: George SCOTT; m: Mary GARDNER] md. Eva SHELDON [19; Omaha; b: Minnesota; f: Henry SHELDON; m: Ellen HOLTON] on 23 Aug 1880. Off: BENEKE. Wit: John BAUMER, Henry RITTER.

SCOTT, John F. [27; Florence] md. Deana N. EDWARDS [23; Florence] on 16 Mar 1858. Off: FORGEY.

SCOTT, John T. [25; Holton, KS; b: IN; f: William T. SCOTT; m: Sarah A. SELLERS] md. Flora H. WILLIAMS [17; Omaha; b: MO; f: N.H. WILLIAMS; m: Sarah STARK] on 3 Nov 1875. Off: LIPE. Wit: Mark KURTZ, Mrs. TAYLOR. Age consent given by father of the bride.

SCOTT, John [30; Omaha; b: Scotland; f: William SCOTT; m: Jennett TAYLOR] md. Eliza ROSS [35; Omaha; b: Ireland; f: Patrick DUFFEY; m: Bessy DUFFEY] on 25 Jan 1871. Off: BENNET. Wit: Robert HARRIGAN; Francis X. READERER.

SCOTT, William W. [26; Omaha; b: OH; f: Wm. SCOTT; m: Jane E. THOMPSON] md. Lizzie JOHNSON [19; Omaha; b: MO; f: William JOHNSON; m: Elizabeth KEELER] on 10 Aug 1881. Off: MARQUETT. Wit: Andrew HOWELL, Emma HOWELL.

SCOTT, Wm. H. [22; Tekamah; b: New York; f: Robert SCOTT; m: Hannah SMART] md. Mary M. RUST [21; b: New Jersey; f: Wm. E. RUST; m: Mary E. ROYCE] on 10 Jun 1878. Off: HARSHA. Wit: James K. SCOTT of Tekamah, Sara HENDERSON.

SCRANAGE, Franklin [21; Bellverson, PA] md. Sarah PANNELL [25; Pittsburg, PA] on 14 May 1861 at ARMSTRONG's residence. Off: ARMSTRONG. Wit: Mrs. George ARMSTRONG.

SEAMAN, Charles F. [22; Omaha; b: Germany; f: Michael SEAMAN; m: Christina BERNDT] md. Anna BEINDORFF [18; Omaha; b: Denmark; f: Knud BEINDORFF; m: Katrina RASMUSSON] on 8 Jan 1878. Off: BENEKE. Wit: Robert PRICE, Frank WALTER.

SEARLE, Edwin N. [21; Alkali] md. Eliza J. GIFFORD [16; Alkali] on 24 Dec 1868. Off: KUHNS. Wit: John A. PARKER, John HIGBY, et al. Age consent given by the mother of the bride.

SEBOLD, George Friedrich [26; Omaha; b; Germany; f: Jacob SEBOLD; m: Margaret BAUMEISTER] md. Adelia A. BARTIG [27; Omaha; b: Germany; f: August BARTIG; m: Juliana ZELLMAR] on 1 Apr 1879. Off: STRASEN. Wit: H. DRIEFHOLD, F.V. GATTZ (crossed out), Mrs. Auguste DRIEFHOLD.

SEBRING, William D.W. [45; Omaha; b: NJ; f: Cornelius SEBRING; m: Hester WALDRON] md. Mrs. Louise D. AMES [30; Omaha; b: PA; f: Heron MAHON; m: Manirva CROW] on 15 Feb 1881. Off: SMITH. Wit: William L. PEABODY, Max BERGMANN.

SEDERBLOM, Charles [29; Omaha; b: Sweden; f: Anders SEDERBLOM; m: Gustave ANDERSDOTTER] md. Augusta ANDERSON [21; Omaha; b: Sweden; f: Andrew ANDERSON; m: Karen MANSDOTTER] on 11 Jun 1881. Off: RING. Wit: Oliver BURSELL, Oscar OCANDER.

SEDLACEK, Jacob [29; Omaha; b: Bohemia; f: John SEDLACEK; m: Mary MILARIK [MLYNARIK]] md. Mary PIVONKA [19; Omaha; b: Bohemia; f: James PIVONKA; m: Anna KOLAR] on 6 Mar 1880. Off: STENBERG. Wit: James PIVONKA, Charles MARES.

SEEKOTTER [LEEKOTTER], William [32; Omaha] md. Mary MULHED [31; Omaha] on 4 Aug 1866 at Mr. KRUSE's residence. Off: FLORKEE. Wit: Peter FRENZER, Peter MULHED, Anna MULHED.

SEELEY, Walter E. [23; Ashland; b: Cape Breton Island; f: Austin SEELEY; m: Lucy VAUGHN] md. Lucia E. SWAFFORD [16; Ashland; b: Madison Co, IA; f: M.D. SWAFFORD; m: Mary J. WILSON] on 24 Nov 1873. Off: PEABODY. Wit: J.G. PARKER; William McHUGH. Age of consent given by father of the bride.

SEELY, Jonas [26; Omaha] md. Cornelia YOUNG [23; Omaha] on 5 Oct 1857. Off: WATSON.

SEGELKE, Wilhelm H.T. [32; Omaha; b: Germany; f: Christoph SEGELKE; m: Elenore KRACKE] md. Anna SCHMID [22; Omaha; b: Germany; f: George SCHMID; m: Anna DELLER] on 5 Feb 1880. Off: BENEKE. Wit: Charles HERBERTZ of Chicago, George SCHMID.

SEGER, Joseph F. [26; Omaha; b: Germany; f: Bernhard SEGER; m: Josephine BOPST] md. Augusta MENNEKE [19; Omaha; b: IA; f: Frederick (Wm. crossed out) MENNEKE; m: Sophie KRACHT] on 24 Nov 1881. Off: SHERRILL. Wit: Samuel BINDER, Mrs. L.H. JONNES.

SEIEROE, Nels [27; Omaha; b: Denmark; f: Magens SEIEROE; m: Louisa WHINTHER] md. Eliza SCHNELL [19; Omaha; b: Burlington, IA; f: Fritz SCHNELL; m: Maria NEADERANE] on 15 Dec 1870. Off: S.G. LARSON. Wit: Frederick SCHNELL, West Omaha; Lar HANSEN.

SEIVERS, George H.W. [30; Omaha; b: Germany; f: George H. SEIVERS; m: Fredericka DE LANGUILLETTE] md. Dorothea J.L. MOHR [25; Omaha; b: Germany; f: Jacob MOHR; m: Matilda D.J.

OLANDT] on 18 Feb 1880. Off: LIPE. Wit: Mr. and Mrs. Henry BOLLIN.

SEKERA, John [33; Omaha; b: Bohemia; f: John SEKERA; m: Barbara ZELENA] md. Mary NOVAK [32; Omaha; b: Bohemia; f: Frank VAVRA; m: Maria PISKACKOVA] on 10 Jan 1878. Off: WILLIS. Wit: F.V. KRATKY, Jesse OSTERHAUT.

SELBIG, Benjamin F. [23; Omaha; b: Rochester, NY; f: Lawrence SELBIG; m: Hannah CASPER] md. Jennie BURROUGHS [18; Omaha; b: Beaver Dam, WI; f: John H. BURROUGHS; m: Chretia MERRILL] on 6 Mar 1881. Off: HARRIS. Wit: A. RICHARDS, Ellen M. WHITE.

SELDEN, Perry [26 or 27] md. Lida M. NEWELL [24 or 25] on 13 Apr 1869 at the North Omaha Lodge of Good Templars. Off: SHINN. Wit: Acting Worthy Chief William LAWTON and members.

SELK, Jurgen [22; Omaha; b: Germany; f: Jacob SELK; m: Christina EMBKA] md. Frederika GROTHE [24; Omaha; b: Germany; f: Caspar GROTHE; m: Elizabeth WALSLEMM] on 21 Jul 1873. Off: DIECKMANN. Wit: Charly GROTHE, Sarpy Co.; Mrs. Friedericka DIECKMANN.

SELLECK, Charles [38; Omaha] md. Mary Louisa PASHLY [Omaha] on 17 Dec 1868. Off: KUHNS. Wit: John PASHLY, Mrs. H.W. KUHNS.

SELZLE, Anthony [42; Omaha; b: Germany; f: Antony SELZLE; m: Anna PLUMELEY] md. Mrs. Anna NOVACEK [30; Omaha; b: Bohemia; f: Wenceslaus JANSA; m: Anna] on 2 Feb 1874. Off: HALL. Wit: A. JANSA; Sebastian BLUMELE.

SEMS, John [23; Omaha] md. Taressa SCHAUNBURG [18; Omaha] at 3 PM, 29 Sep 1866 in DIMMICK's study. Off: DIMMICK. Wit: Edward BEAUMONT, J.A. LILLIE, Mrs. F.M. DIMMICK.

SERBOUSECK, Frank [43; Omaha; b: Bohemia; f: Frank SERBOUSECK; m: Franciska ZAHRADNIK] md. Mrs. Barbara BARTOS [38; Omaha; b: Bohemia; f: Joseph LEDERER; m: Anna SLANINA] on 19 Apr 1881. Off: RILEY. Wit: Joseph BARTOS, Joseph KAVAN.

SESEMANN, Gustav [23; Omaha; b: Germany; f: Gustave SESEMANN; m: Wilhelmine DEISSE] md. Minnie A. HEIS [21; Omaha; b: Germany; f: Ludwig HEIS; m: Wilhellmine KLEINSCHMIDT] on 20 Apr 1875. Off: HILGENDORF. Wit: Ernst Carl SESEMANN, Francis Meta ERFLING.

SESSEMANN, C.E. [30; Omaha; b: Germany; f: Gustav SESSEMANN; m: Minna DIES] md. Emma ANDERSON [27; Omaha; b: Sweden; f: Peter ANDERSON; m: Paulene SWANSON] on 4 Nov 1879. Off: HARSHA. Wit: Mrs. Isabella KEYES, Mrs. Maria MUNGER.

SESSEMANN [LESSMAN], Charles [22; Omaha; b: Germany; f: Augustus SESSEMANN; m: Willemina TEIS] md. Mary B. KREEN [23; Omaha; b: Germany; f: Federman KREEN] on 24 Nov 1869. Off: KELLEY. Wit: J.C. LEMONIES, Wm. LINDLEY.

SESSIONS, Lyman W. [32; Omaha] md. Catharine REMMINGTON [32; Omaha] on 4 Nov 1866 at S.E. JENSEN's residence. Off: KUHNS. Wit: Mr. and Mrs. Francis SUTER, Mr. and Mrs. JENSEN, Mr. and Mrs. John C. LINGEL, Minerva BARNES, et al.

SEVERSON, Engebert [24; Omaha; b: Norway; f: Severt PETERSON; m: Engeburt RUDENSEN] md. Mary EVENSEN [26; Omaha; b: Norway; f: Iver GULICKSON; m: Sunnar SEVERSON] on 24 Mar 1875. Off: ERDALL. Wit: Hellek SOVORSON, Ritel SOVORSON.

SEVEY, George [27; Glenwood, IA; b: MI; f: Moses M. SEVEY; m: Charlotte STEPHENS] md. Mrs. Clara E. CHOLL [29; Glenwood, IA; b: CT; f: Henry SUTLIFF; m: Lous E. WEBSTER] on 1 Dec 1875. Off: STEWART. Wit: Mrs. Emily W. STEWART, Mary MEEHAN.

SEWARD, Horatio L. [32; Omaha] md. Ella A. BUDDINGTON [22; Omaha] on 23 Apr 1866 at Trinity Church. Off: VAN ANTWERP. Wit: Wm. H. MARSHALL, Miss E.A. PADDOCK, et al.

SEWARD, W.H. [21; Omaha; b: New York; f: S.B. SEWARD; m: Anna E. BENTLEY] and Clara L. HAHN [19; Omaha; b: Pennsylvania; f: Joseph HAHN; m: Caroline MILLER] license issued on 8 Mar 1880. No marriage recorded. Off: BARTHOLOMEW.

SEYMOUR, James W. [26; Omaha] and Jane A. STRENG [20; Omaha] license issued on 9 Nov 1858. No marriage record. Off: BRIGGS.

SEYMOUR, William [Platte Valley] md. Emma METCALF [Elkhorn] on 9 Apr 1863 at Trinity Church. Both of legal age. Off: DAKE. Wit: P.W. HITCHCOCK, Mrs. POPPLETON, Mr. HERBERT, Mrs. R.C. JORDAN, Mrs. V. VAN NOSRAND, Harriet KEITH.

SHADBOLT, Williard A. [22; Omaha; b: New York; f: Theodore C. SHADBOLT] md. Madara GARDNER [18; Omaha; b: Glenwood, IA; f: James GARDNER; m: Harriet A. BUCK] on 13 Jan 1870. Off: GIBSON. Wit: Frederick W. BEST; John E. BYRNE.

SHAFFER, Otto [21; Omaha; b: Ohio; f: William F. SHAFFER; m: Caroline NOBAUM] md. Alice PARKER [20; Omaha; b: Ohio; f: James M. PARKER; m: Mary EMMICK] on 17 Sep 1873. Off: TOWNSEND. Wit: Joseph BOYER; Jennie PARKER.

SHALL, Carle [29; Omaha; b: Prussia; f: Johan SHALL; m: Mary LORCHEN] md. Barbara FOYED [20; Omaha; b: Germany] on 14 Dec 1869. Off: MORTON. Wit: Mr. and Mrs. Geo. N. McBAY.

SHANAHAN, Dennis [27; Douglas Co.; b: Ireland; f: John SHANAHAN; m: Nora SULLIVAN] md. Bridget HARRINGTON [19; Douglas Co.; b: Ireland; f: John HARRINGTON; m: Mary CARROLL] on 27 Jun 1876 at the Roman Catholic Cathedral. Off: BYRNE. Wit: John MAHONEY, Johanna LYNCH.

SHANNON, James [25; Omaha; b: Ireland; f: Michael SHANNON; m: Mary McDERMOTT] md. Annie CLARK [19; Omaha; b: Ireland; f: Patrick CLARK; m: Mary O'BRIEN] on 26 May 1873. Off: CURTIS. Wit: Michael KINNEY; Bridget HEAVER.

SHANNON, Perry [22; Omaha; b: Butler Co., IA; f: G.W. SHANNON; m: Eliza EDWARDS] and Louisa TOMBLESON [18; Omaha; b: Tennessee; f: Henry TOMBLESON; m: Sarah M. GENTRY] license issued on 10 Jul 1879. No marriage record. Off: BARTHOLOMEW.

SHARP, Adam [27; Dowville, IA; b: Scotland; f: William SHARP; m: Agnes STEWART] md. Sarah MANN [27; Woodbine, IA; b: Scotland; f: John MANN; m: Sarah EADIE] on 8 Feb 1879. Off: BARTHOLOMEW. Wit: Wm. L. PEABODY, George H. BETHARD.

SHARP, Eneas [Douglas Co.] md. Carrie LATY [Douglas Co.] on 2 Jul 1863 at the residence of the bride's father. Both of legal age. Off: KUHNS. Wit: Mr. and Mrs. T. LATY, H. LATY, et al.

SHARP, John [32; Missouri Valley, IA; b: Pennsylvania; f: John SHARP; m: Mary Ann COFFMAN] md. Mrs. Allta THOMAS [Missouri Valley, IA; b: Illinois; f: Alvan BUTTERFIELD; m: Ilena PHIPPS] on 28 Jul 1874. Off: PEABODY. Wit: Emlen LEWIS, M.D.; Mrs. Abbie M. LEWIS.

SHARPE, George G. [27; Valley Pct, Douglas Co.; b: Canada East; f: George G. SHARPE; m: Susannah BENEDICT] md. Margaret L. HANEY [16; Valley Pct, Douglas Co.; b: 27 March 1856, Fayette Co., PA; f: William HANEY (deceased); m: ROSE (surname?)] on 23 Oct 1872 at Waterloo. Off: DENTON. Wit: Lewis W. JACKSON; J.W. DENTON; S.J. FREEMAN; all of Waterloo. Age of consent given by Margaret HANEY, mother of the bride.

SHARPE, Willis A. [21; b: Iowa; f: E.S. SHARPE; m: Harriet A. COATES] md. Etta PEYTON [19; b: Omaha; f: A. PEYTON; m: Elizabeth COURTNEY] on 31 Aug 1878. Off: JAMESON. Wit: A. WEAVER, Jennie PAYTON.

SHARPNECK, E.L. [26; Blair; b: VA; f: Sam'l. SHARPNECK; m: Lucretia LONG] md. Mary C. THOMPSON [22; IA; b: PA; f: Richard THOMPSON; m: Mary THOMPSON] on 5 Nov 1881. Off: STEWART. Wit: H.N. BOWEN, M.G. STEWART.

SHARRON, Charles B. [26; Omaha; b: Ohio; f: Charles SHARRON; m: Mary STODDARD] md. Kate CONNELLEY [18; Omaha; b: Canada; f: Michael CONNELLEY] on 13 Aug 1870. Off: MORTON. Wit: Amos PEACOCK, Cheyenne; Miss MULCAHY.

SHAW, Charles [28; Omaha; b: Germany; f: Abe SHAW; m: Ricke ABRAHAMS] md. Bertha ROSENTHAL [20; Omaha; b: Wurtemburg; f: Jacob ROSENTHAL; m: Dina GUTMANN] on 30 Apr 1880. Off: ANDERSON. Wit: Morris ELGUTTER, Sol PRUICE.

SHAW, James S. [29; Omaha] md. Virginia STEWART [30; Omaha] on 19 Sep 1867. Off: KERMOTT. Wit: Mrs. Chas. LANG; Francis HARDING.

SHAW, James [24; Omaha; b: Ireland; f: John SHAW; m: Eliza KEOUGH] md. Abbie DUSEY [23; Omaha; b; Ireland; f: John DUSEY; m: Abbie KELLY] on 15 Oct 1879 at St. Philomena's Church. Off: KELLY. Wit: Denis CUNNINGHAM, Mary CUNNINGHAM.

SHAW, Samuel B. [28; Omaha] md. Susie FIELD [30; Omaha] on 22 Sep 1867. Off: SLAUGHTER. Wit: H.W. FIELD, Mrs. FIELD.

SHEA, Thomas F. [29; Omaha] md. Mary ROACH [25; Omaha] on 28 Aug 1867. Off: O'GORMAN. Wit: John SULLIVAN, Ellen CURRAN.

SHEAHAN, John [27; Omaha; b: Ireland; f: John SHEAHAN; m: Catharine KELLEY] and Ellen BEGLEY [24; Omaha; b: NE; f: John BEGLEY; m: Mary BEGLEY] filed affidavit on 21 Nov 1881. No marriage record. Off: BERGMAN.

SHEEHAN, James [34, of St. Joseph, MO] md. Ann CLEARY [25; St. Joseph, MO] on 10 May 1861 at the Catholic Church of Omaha. Off: KELLY. Wit: William BLAKE.

SHEEHAN, John [23; b: Pennsylvania; f: Dennis SHEEHAN; m: Mary FOLLY] md. Katharine GANNON [21; b: Ireland; f: Patrick GANNON; m: Margaret MORTON] on 23 Sep 1878. Off: KELLY. Wit: James O'BOYLE, Ann McNALLY.

SHELBY, John P. [22; Omaha; b: Painesville, OH; f: Thomas SHELBY; m: Winefred TIGHT] md. Mary B. CREIGHTON [19; Omaha; b: Omaha; f: Joseph CREIGHTON; m: Catharine FURLONG] on 7 Feb 1881 at St. Philomena's Church. Off: ENGLISH. Wit: Thos. SHELBY, Jennie CREIGHTON.

SHEPARD, Samuel H. [27; Omaha; b: PA; f: Ervin SHEPARD; m: Sarah A. HARRIS] md. Sarah E. CUMMINGS [15; Omaha; b: IA; f: Ebenezer CUMMINGS; m: Sarah A. STEWART] on 21 Dec 1876 at Sarah A. CUMMINGS' home. Off: MULLIS. Wit: Wm. CUMMINGS, Sarah A. CUMMINGS, W.E. GREEN. Age consent given by mother of the bride; father is dead. W.A. CUMMINGS signed the affidavit.

SHEPHERD, Abram L. [28; Omaha] md. Mary A. RYAN [18; Omaha] on 1 Oct 1868. Off: SLAUGHTER.

SHEPHERD, Judson E. [32; Douglas Co.] md. Lauretta GRANDY [30; Douglas Co.] on 24 Feb 1866 at the Court House. Off: HASCALL. Wit: J. McHEANE, C. WILSON.

SHEPHERD, Judson E. [36; Douglas Co.; b: Vermont; f: Joseph SHEPHERD; m: Lucinda MILLER] md. Sarah TIMPERLEY [19; Douglas Co.; b: Illinois; f: John TIMPERLEY] on 11 May 1871. Off: HURLBUT. Wit: John TIMPERLEY, Union Pct; John TIMPERLEY, Jr., 2 miles NW of Union Pct.

SHEPPARD, John W. [23 or 29; Omaha; b: Boston, MA; f: Charles A. SHEPPARD; m: Mary E. SWANSEY] md. Minnie SAGNER [25; Omaha; b: Germany; f: Fredk. SAGNER; m: Christine PHOVE] on 2 Oct 1871. Off: MORTON. No witnesses listed.

SHEPPARD, William [32; Douglas Co.; b: New York] md. Hattie POOL [35; Omaha; b: England; f: William BRYANT; m: Mary WOODS] on 12 Feb 1871. Off: DANIELS. No witnesses listed. Affidavit signed by Hattie POOL's mark.

SHERIDAN, Cornelius C. [22; Omaha; b: Ohio; f: Soloman SHERIDAN; m: Sabina WORLEY] md. Mrs. Allie McDONALD [24; Omaha] on 1 Feb 1871. Off: DeLaMATYR. Wit: ---- MADDOX; N.C. DeLaMATYR.

SHERIDAN, John [35; Omaha; b: Ireland; f: Patrick SHERIDAN; m: Mandy McKUGH] md. Bridgett MURPHEY [28; Omaha; b: Ireland; f: Daniel MURPHEY; m: Bridget SHERIDAN] on 3 May 1874 at the 9th St Cathedral. Off: BYRNE. Wit: Thomas PADDEN; Annie HUGHES, 9th Street.

SHERLOCK, James J. [21; Kentucky; f: James SHERLOCK; m: Anna CLEBURNE] md. Catharine MAHANNA [19; b: Iowa; f: John S. MAHANNA; m: Mary RAMSAY] on 10 Sep 1878. Off: PATTERSON. Wit: Elof NELSON, Geo. Morgan O'BRIEN.

SHERLOCK, William [22; Iowa Co., IA; b: OH; f: Thomas SHERLOCK; m: Emma DONCASTER] md. Hermine SCHONBORN [22; Douglas Co.; b: Germany; f: John SCHONBORN; m: Catherine BOWER] on 26 Jun 1876. Off: STEVENSON. Wit: L. SCHONBORN, Douglas Co., Louis SCHONBORN, Douglas Co.

SHERRILL, A.F. [31; Omaha; b: Canada; f: Edwin J. SHERRILL; m: Sarah FOOT] md. Mary S. JONES [28; Omaha; b: New York; f: J.C. JONES; m: H. Loretta REED] on 5 Feb 1874. Off: CLARKSON. Wit: John WILBUR; George L. MILLER; W.L. PEABODY and wife; Mrs. I.C. HALL; Lucinda LEWIS, et al.

SHERWOOD, Robert P. [22; Omaha] md. Mary E. MASON [20; Omaha] on 22 or 13 Apr 1868. Off: MORRIS. Wit: William SPENCER, Emma DAVIS.

SHERWOOD, Wm. B. [25; Elkhorn City; b: NY; f: Wm. B. SHERWOOD; m: Martha Jane BESSEY] and Addie PRIDEY [22; Elkhorn City; f: NY; f: William PRIDEY; m: Phebe ANDREWS] filed affidavit on 3 Dec 1881. No marriage record. Off: BERGMANN.

SHIELDS, David [21; Omaha; b: Scotland; f: James SHIELDS; m: Jennie ROBERTSON] md. Mathilda B. HAMMOND [18; Omaha; b: MD; f: Mathias HAMMOND; m: Aschsa WARFIELD] on 22 Jan 1881. Off: ANDERSEN. Wit: G.S. SHIELDS, A.S. HAMMOND.

SHIELDS, George W. [25; Omaha; b: Scotland; f: James SHIELDS; m: Jennie ROBERTSON] md. Eva N. BEARD [20; Omaha; b: Iowa; f: George W. BEARD; m: Martha REED] on 19 Apr 1880. Off: COPELAND. Wit: James SHIELDS, George W. BEARD.

SHIELDS, George [24; Omaha; b: MO; f: Walter SHEILDS; m: Elisa PARKER] md. Annie ANDERSON [19; Omaha; b: Sweden; f: Andrew ANDERSON; m: Buliah HENSON] on 3 Apr 1876. Off: SEDGWICK. Wit: Edward GORMAN, Douglas Co., Carrie ANDERSON, Douglas Co.

SHIELDS, John C. [28; Saline Co.; b: Pennsylvania; f: John H. SHIELDS; m: Margaret E. SPEERS] md. Caroline JOYCE [24; Benton, IA; b: Ohio; f: Jacob JOYCE; m: Rebecca DONALD] on 28 Feb 1872. Off: TOWNSEND. Wit: Herbert THAYER; Nettie M. HIGBY.

SHIELDS, M.J. [39; Sarpy Co.] md. Mrs. Catharine McINTEE [28; Sarpy Co.] on 22 Jan 1868 at the Roman Catholic Church. Off: O'GORMAN. Wit: John THOMAS.

SHIMANEK [SIMANEK], George [28; Omaha; b: Germany; f: George SHIMANEK; m: Mary HERMACH] md. Barbara BLAHA [18; Omaha; b: Germany; f: Wenzel BLAHA; m: Katherine VLCK [VLACH]] on 19 Jul 1869. Off: HYDE. Wit: B.E.B. KENNEDY, C.D. HYDE.

SHINN, Frank [21; b: Illinois; f: Amos SHINN; m: Mary A. Van DYKE] md. Mrs. Julia MORTENSON [24; b: Denmark; f: Christian JEPSEN; m: Bine KETTELSEN] on 2 May 1878. Off: BARTHOLOMEW. Wit: George SAVAGE, J.R. CONKLIN.

SHINN, Moses F. [66; Omaha; b: Ohio; f: George SHINN; m: Elizabeth WOODROW] md. Mary Jane WEBB [25; Omaha; b: Illinois (Michigan crossed out); f: Aaron T. WEBB; m: Minerva McGRAW] on 23 Nov 1874 at C.J. TYLOR's residence. Off: LEMON. Wit: C.J. TYLOR, Esq, Cass St; Elizabeth G. TYLOR, Cass St.

SHINN, Stephen D. [24; Omaha] md. Harriet A. MORRIS [20; Omaha] on 8 Nov 1860. Off: SMITH. Wit: John RITCHIE, M.F. SHINN, A.D. JONES.

SHINROCK, Frederick [28; b: Ohio; f: F. SHINROCK; m: Mary JARRETT] md. Edith STEWART [22; b: Wisconsin; f: Walter STEWART; m: Maria GILPIN] on 20 Aug 1878. Off: JAMESON. Wit: Dean McCARTY, Mrs. Maria STEWART.

SHIPLEY, David V. [28; Washington Co.; b: Iowa; f: William SHIPLEY; m: Mary BEAR] md. Selina Isabell POWELL [18; Florence; b: Missouri; f: Abel POWELL; m: Rebecca Ann HATSELL] on 30 Sep 1878. Off: BARTHOLOMEW. Wit: Wm. L. PEABODY, Hiram A. STURGES.

SHIPLEY, Enoch M. [21; Douglas Co.] md. Nancy M. SWIGART [18; Douglas Co.] on 8 Sep 1866. Off: SLAUGHTER. Wit: Albert M. CLARK, Albert ROSE.

SHIPLEY, J.E. [37; Calhoun Precinct, Washington Co.; b: Iowa; f: Wm. SHIPLEY; m: Mary BEAR] md. Mary S. WOOLSEY [18; Calhoun Precinct; b: Iowa; f: Richard WOOLSEY; m: Ellen RUSSELL] on 12 Jul 1879. Off: BARTHOLOMEW. Wit: Moses H. STURMAN, Ralph E. GAYLORD.

SHIPLEY, John Alexander [25; Washington, Co.; b: IA; f: William SHIPLEY; m: Mary BEAR] md. Alice WATERMAN [19; Douglas Co.; b: England; adopted daughter of James WATERMAN and Mary] on 24 Mar 1876. Off: SEDGWICK. Wit: William SHIPLEY, Washington Co, Chas. A. BALDWIN, Douglas Co.

SHIPMAN, Benjamin F. [28; Douglas Co.; b: MI; f: Ira SHIPMAN; m: E.J. BEACH] md. Lusinda BOYD [28; Douglas Co.; b: IL; f: Valentine BOYD; m: Sarah GROOM] on 4 Apr 1876. Off: SEDGWICK. Wit: Marcia F. SEDGWICK, Douglas Co., Mary A. ABOLD, Douglas Co.

SHIPMAN, Edward M. [25; Omaha; b: Michigan; f: Ira SHIPMAN; m: Emergene BEECH] md. Lydia MILLER [25; b: Ohio; f: Sydney MILLER; m: Esther C. HALL] on 26 Mar 1870. Off: McCAGUE. Wit: C.H. BREWER; W.M. BREWER.

SHIPMAN, John P. [28; b: New Jersey; f: John P. SHIPMAN; m: Mary RITTER] md. Ada V. McCOY [23; b: Ohio; f: George A. McCOY; m: Ada CROWELL] on 3 Jun 1878. Off: JOHNSON. Wit: Mr. and Mrs. R.A. HARRIS, Wm. E. GRATTON.

SHIVERICK, Charles [31; Omaha; b: MA; f: Asa SHIVERICK; m: Mary SEARS] md. Mary Ella CRARY [24; Omaha; b: MI; f: B.D. CRARY; m: Anna A. LITTLEJOHN] on 21 Feb 1876. Off: CLARKSON. Wit: B.D. CRARY, Mrs. Anna A. CRARY. D.C. ADAMS signed the affidavit.

SHIVERS, Jacob L. [37; Omaha; b: Virginia; f: John SHIVERS; m: Margaret OATS] md. Mrs. Elizabeth FLANDERS [37; Omaha; b: Michigan; f: John SQUIRES; m: Lucinda FRISHEY] on 27 Nov 1879. Off: FISHER. Wit: Rosina WILEY, Margaret DOAN.

SHOAF, George [28; Omaha; b: Pennsylvania; f: Frank SHOAF; m: Elizabeth COON] md. Annie WILBUR [23; Omaha; b: Liverpool, England] on 2 Nov 1870. Off: BENNETT. Wit: Charles HOWARD; Mrs. Francis HUGHFIELD.

SHOAF, Randall [24; Omaha] md. Sarah Elizabeth HALL [16; Omaha] on 8 Feb 1863. Off: DAKE. Wit: Mr. and Mrs. William LYFORD, John SHOAF, George SHOAF, et al. Age consent given by Wm. LYFORD for his step-daughter.

SHOAF, Simon [21; Omaha] md. Minnie DAVIS [21; Omaha] on 28 Aug 1868. Off: MULCAHY. Wit: George M. O'BRIEN, James SLAUGHTER.

SHOEBRIDGE, Edward S. [49; Florence] md. Mary MICKLE [45; Florence] on 26 Feb 1866. Off: MARTIN. Wit: Mr. and Mrs. HODGES, Mr. and Mrs. WILBER, Mr. and Mrs. SMITH.

SHOEMAKER, W.S. [35; Logan, IA; b: Ohio; f: Alexander SHOEMAKER; m: Elizabeth HARMON] md. Eva C. DuBOIS [23; Omaha; b: Michigan; f: P.B. DuBOIS; m: Celista MOORE] on 13 Nov 1879. Off: COPELAND. Wit: Mrs. P.B. DuBOIS, Mr. EATON.

SHOGREN, Charles (Charley) [31; Elkhorn, NE; b: Sweden; f: John SHOGREN; m: Ingrid Katharina JOHANSON] md. Elizabeth P. RANDOLPH [b: KS; f: Daniel RANDOLPH; m: Lucy MINSTEAD] on 9 Aug 1881. Off: BEANS. Wit: Mary WILBORN, Mrs. E.A. BEANS.

SHORROCK, Robert [21; Omaha; b: England; f: Ralph SHORROCK; m: Sarah SHORROCK] md. Mary M. WEBB [19; Omaha; b: Illinois; f: James E. WEBB; m: Mary A. McMAHON] on 24 Dec 1874. Off: CLARKSON. Wit: James E. WEBB; Mary A. WEBB.

SHORT, Joseph [35; Omaha] md. Mrs. J. DOWNS [30; Omaha] on 24 Aug 1868. Off: KELLEY. Wit: R.J. STUCK. Joseph DOUGHERTY.

SHORT, Thomas C. [32; Sidney; b: St.Lawrence Co., NY; f: Thomas SHORT; m: Mary ALLISON] md. Susan DENNEY [20; Omaha; b: Eau Claire Co., WI; f: John DENNEY] on 29 Oct 1872. Off: CURTIS. Wit: H.B. REDDINGTON, Sydney; Elizabeth REDDINGTON, Sydney.

SHORT, William [23; Douglas Co.] md. Achsah Ann THOMAS [17; Douglas Co.] on 25 Dec 1859 at the residence of Mrs. THOMAS near Iron Bluffs City, Douglas Co. Off: BIRKITT. Wit: James H. McARDLE, John ENGLISH.

SHORTER, Robert [24; Omaha] md. Catharine CURRAN on 27 Jul 1867 at O'GORMAN's residence. Off: O'GORMAN. Wit: Martin and Bridget CURRIN.

SHRODER, John C. [29; Omaha; b: Germany; f: Christ SHRODER; m: Ilza KERZEL] md. Hannah CROPENHOFF [17; Omaha; b: Germany; f: Henry CROPENHOFF; m: Minnie KRUIG] on 27 Mar 1871. Off: GIBSON. Wit: Henry CROPENHOFF; Austin GORDON.

SHULL, Amos [40; Omaha; b: Gettysburgh, PA; f: John SHULL; m: Lavina STEWART] md. Mrs. Marietta SHULL [32; Council Bluffs; b: New York; f: Jacob MOWERS] on 25 Feb 1873. Off: TOWNSEND. Wit: Henry D. SHULL; Wiley B. DIXON.

SHULL, Daniel W. [28; Omaha; b: Pennsylvania; f: Jacob SHULL; m: Susan CROFT] md. Maggie STEVENSON [24; Omaha; b: Scotland; f: Elick STEVENSON; Magdaline PATTERSON] on 6 Jan 1870. Off: KUHNS. Wit: Ida B. SHULL; A.H. LANPHERE.

SHULL, Henry D. [32; Omaha; b: Pennsylvania; f: Jacob SHULL; m: Susannah CROFT] md. Mattie McNAUGHTON [17; Omaha; b: Kalamazoo, MI; f: John S. McNAUGHTON; m: Eliza INGALLS] on 31 Dec 1872. Off: BILLMAN. Wit: Jno. T. CLARK; Jno. S. McNAUGHTON. Age of consent given by father of the bride.

SHUTE, Charles W. [24; Omaha] md. Alice H. HADLEY [20; Omaha] on 3 Jun 1858 at the house of Henry CHAPMAN. Off: BRIGGS. Wit: Adeline CHAPMAN.

SIBERT, Andrew S. [29; Primrose; b: Pennsylvania; f: John SIBERT; m: Mary ROSE?] md. Margarett I. ROBINSON [18; Primrose; b; Virginia; f: John M. ROBINSON; m: Elizabeth MORRIS] on 7 Nov 1869. Off: DENTON. Wit: G.W. CHRIST of Primrose, M. HANY of Primrose.

SIEBEIN, Joseph [33; Omaha; b: Germany; f: Joseph SIEBEIN; m: Maria STHWEIGER] md. Allette JACOBSON [26; Omaha; b: Denmark; f: Jacob JACOBSON; m: Marian ---] on 18 Sep 1880. Off: HAWES. Wit: Mrs. Amelia M. HAWES, Mrs. MANCHESTER.

SIEBELIST, Frederick W. [41; Omaha] md. Bertha COLWAY (COLEWAY) [30; Omaha] on 9 Jun 1867 at Frederick KRUG's residence. Off: KUHNS. Wit: Mr. and Mrs. F. KRUG, et al.

SIERT, Henry [25; Omaha] md. America KONNAGER [24; Omaha] on 5 Nov 1867 at KUHNS' residence. Off: KUHNS. Wit: "each other", ? GLOYE, Mrs. H.W. KUHNS. This is a double license and wedding with Hans BOLLIN and Mary GLOYE.

SIERT, Henry [26; Omaha] and Anna SATORIUS [18; Omaha] license issued on 5 Dec 1868. No marriage record. Off: STUCK. Written on the reverse: Julius ROSS, John RUTHERFORD, at probate office; H.L. SEWARD, W.H. BENEDICT, witnesses.

SIEVERS, Ferdinand T. [26; Omaha; b: Germany; f: Peter SIEVERS; m: Margaret ROWEDER] md. Catherina SIERCK [26; Omaha; b: Germany; f: Jurgin SIERCK; m: Margarita PAPP] on 6 Apr 1871. Off: GIBSON. Wit: Henry SIEVERS; John SCHNEIDER.

SIEVERS, John Origen [34; Omaha; b: Sweden; f: Origen S. SWANSON; m: Margreet PETTERSON] md. Ida Christine HOLST [21; Omaha; b: Sweden; f: Jonas Frederic HOLST; m: Louise LINDEBORG] on 9 Dec 1880. Off: STENBERG. Wit: Charles J. WESTERDAHL, Frank SASSTROM.

SIEVERS, William [26; Omaha; b: Germany; f: Henry SIEVERS m: Fredericka DE LANGUELETTE] md. Ida MEYER [24; Omaha; b: Germany; f: Claus J. MEYER; m: Caroline LOCHNER] on 28 Nov 1876. Off: LIPE. Wit: Edw. PEYCKE, Theodore SIEVERS.

SIGWART, A.T. [26; Omaha; b: MO; f: Nicholas SIGWART; m: Anna BEHRINGER] md. Antonette TERRILL [19; Omaha; b: WI; f: John TERRILL; m: Margaret HAWTHORNE] on 25 Feb 1881. Off: MAXFIELD. Wit: John W. CARPEHR, G.N. SIGWART.

SIGWART, G.W. [21; Omaha; b: MO; f: Nicholas SIGWART; m: Annetta BEHRINGEN] md. Gussie BOEHME [18; Omaha; b: IL; f: Lewis BOEHME; m: Mathilda MUELLER] on 9 Jun 1881. Off: MAXFIELD. Wit: D.S. MOORE, Mrs. S.J. MOORE.

SILK, James [23; Omaha] md. Mary CUMMINGS [21; Omaha] on 23 Feb 1868 at the Catholic Church. Off: O'GORMAN. David LONERGAN, Ellen BROWN.

SILVER, Emil [25; Omaha; b: Germany; f: Christian SILVER; m: Barbara RUTHE] md. Rosa OBERLENDER [24; Omaha; b: Germany; f: John OBERLENDER; m: Mary FISHER] on 6 May 1874. Off: HELD. Wit: Herman TENKLE; Max NEEP.

SIMANEK, Jacob [24; Omaha] md. Maria BURIS [BURES] [23; Omaha] on 19 May 1868 at the Catholic Church. Off: O'GORMAN. Wit: Sablad SCHLESSINGER. "Both Bohemians...now of Omaha."

SIMMONDS, Charles [25; Omaha; b: England; f: Jole SIMMONDS; m: Sarah FILLMORE] md. Mary TAYLOR [20; Omaha; b: England; f: James TAYLOR; m: Esther DUEST] on 31 Jul 1874. Off: STEWART. Wit: Mrs. B.L. WALKER; Mrs. Emily W. STEWARD.

SIMMONS, James M. [36; Hillsborough, IL; b: Illinois; f: Samuel SIMMONS; m: Martha MILES] md. Annie E. KORNES [27; Green Co., IL; b: Michigan] on 12 Jan 1870. Off: GIBSON. Wit: John R. MANSFIELD; E.S. SEYMOUR.

SIMMONS, John [45; Omaha; b: England; f: H. SIMMONS; m: Eliza HAMMOND] md. Anna C. THOMSEN [42; Omaha; b: Germany; f: Asmus THOMSEN; m: Anna JENSEN] on 9 Dec 1881. Off: FRESE. Wit: William R. SHOTBOLT, Asmus THOMSEN.

SIMONTON, Seward [44; Dodge Co.; b: Maine; f: John SIMONTON; m: Eliza RICHARDS] md. Maria JENSEN [44; Omaha; b: Denmark] on 22 Feb 1872. Off: ESTABROOK. Wit: Horace W. BARNUM; James N. PHILLIPS.

SIMPSON, Albert E. [24; Omaha; b: Watertown, New York; f: John H. SIMPSON; m: Sarah NORTON] md. Mary BURKE [20; Omaha; b: Binghamton, New York; f: John BURKE] on 9 May 1870. Off: CURTIS. Wit: William DEVEREAUX; Margaret PRICE.

SIMPSON, D.T. [27; Omaha; b: Price Edward Island; f: David SIMPSON; m: Mary McKINZIE] md. Catharine McCARTHY [24; Omaha; b: Indiana; f: Timothy McCARTHY; m: Mary COSTILO] on 15 Jul 1880. Off: ENGLISH. Wit: William DOYLE, Norah DEEMUN.

SIMPSON, James F. [22; Rosemund, IL; b: Ohio; f: James SIMPSON; m: Mary NOBLE] md. Lee A. HILBERT [22; Omaha; b: Ohio; f: David HILBERT; m: Mary ATKINSON] on 9 Sep 1869. Off: KUHNS. Wit: Levi J. KENNARD, Mrs. Sarah M. KENNARD.

SIMPSON, James M. [25; Omaha; b: Iowa; f: Thomas SIMPSON; m: Mary MADDEN] md. Mary E. PRICE [26; Omaha; b: Indiana; f: Peter PRICE; m: Evaline PENDROY] on 9 Aug 1880. Off: RILEY. Wit: Merrick CUMMINGS, Harry B. MYERS.

SIMPSON, John R. [23; Omaha; colored; b: North Carolina; f: Isaac SIMPSON; m: Ann BUTLER] md. Julia BRADSHAW [23; Omaha; colored; b: Missouri; f: BRADSHAW] on 31 Mar 1874. Off: MARSHALL. Wit: Mrs. Margaret STEWART, Harney Street.

SIMPSON, Lewis E. [23, Foorence, NE; b: TN; f: John SIMPSON; m: Elizabeth WOODSON] md. Nancy E. LESLEY [16; Florence; b: IA; f: Nicholas LESLEY; m: Mary JARVIS] on 20 Mar 1881 at the residence of Mr. MATTON, Douglas Co.. Off: COWAN, Justice of Peace. Wit: John SIMPSON, Sr., Florence SIMPSON, Florence. Age consent given by the mother of the bride, Mary VOSE and signed by John SIMPSON.

SIMPSON, Perry [25; Omaha] md. Nancy FRANCIS [26; Omaha] on 19 Nov 1866 at Daniel CLIFTON's house. Off: DENTON. Wit: Daniel CLIFTON, Clarke POTTER.

SIMPSON, Peter [25; Germany; f: John NELSON; m: Ellen M. SIMPSON] md. Lillian J. BESSEY [18; Elkhorn City; b: New York; f: Lemuel BESSEY; m: Esther PURCHASE] on 17 Feb 1878. Off: Van FLEET. Wit: Fred J. SMITH, Miss Ida V.O. WILKINSON both of Elkhorn City.

SIMS, William H. [28; St. Louis, MO; b: Wheeling, VA; f: James SIMS; m: Martha Ann WRIGHT] md. Louisa J. WARD [24; St. Louis, MO; b: Arkansas; f: Peter WARD; m: Elizabeth LISTER] on 2 Jun 1869. Off: KELLEY. Wit: D.K. WELLINGTON, Lorenzo GUIO.

SINDING, Niels C. [27; Omaha; b: Denmark; f: Barthel SINDING; m: Anna Gertrue S. HOILIEN] md. Emma KLENBIEL [24; Omaha; b: Germany; f: Charles KLENBIEL] on 20 Mar 1873. OfF: LYTLE. Wit: J. FRANK; L.F. MAGINN.

SINJEN, Claus H. [30; Omaha; b: Prussia; f: Jogim SINJEN; m: Silke LAMP] md. Katrina JESS [22; Omaha; b: Prussia; f: Claus JESS] on 13 Sep 1873. Off: TOWNSEND. Wit: Charles H. BYRNE; Charles M. CONOYER.

SINNOTT, Joseph [22; Omaha; b: Ireland; f: Moses SINNOTT; m: Mary POOR] md. Mary GIBNEY [26; Omaha; b: Ireland; f: Simon GEBNEY; m: Lisha SHANDLY] on 3 Aug 1870. Off: MORTON. Wit: James SARAN; Bride HUGHES.

SINTON, William K. [26; Council Bluffs; b: Buffalo, NY; f: Joseph SINTON; m: Purden KELLEY] md. Nena GROOM [18; Council Bluffs; b: Ottumway [sic], IA; f: David GROOM; m: Mary A. JONES] on 5 Apr 1880. Off: ANDERSON. Wit: John H. BUTLER, P.E. PETERSON.

SIPP, James [59; Sarpy Co.; b: New Jersey; f: John SIPP] md. Mrs. Henriette H. ROBISON [40; Sarpy Co; b: Ohio; f: Joseph IRWIN; m: Rebecca SMITH] on 18 Sep 1880. Off: BARTHOLOMEW. Wit: B.E.B. KENNEDY, Charles R. REDICK.

SISSON, F.W. [26; Harlan, IA; b: Ohio; f: L.G. SISSON; m: Elizabeth W. WARNER] md. Stella DICKINSON [19; Omaha; b: New York; f: Norris DICKINSON; m: Harriet ASHMAN] on 26 Feb 1879. Off: BARTHOLOMEW. Wit: Charles C. SWEESY, Harry ARMSTRONG.

SISSON, Seneca N. [25; Omaha; b: Michigan; f: James N. SISSON; m: Abby GRIFFEN] md. Minerva BEMAN [34; Ypsilanti, MI; b: New York; f: Alva BEMAN; m: Eliza SMITH] on 31 Dec 1879. Off: JAMESON. Wit: William HUDSON, Mrs. Clarissa LAFOLLETTE.

SISSON, William H.H. [30; Omaha; b: New Bedford, MA; f: Daniel W. SISSON; m: Charlotte BEALS] md. Mrs. Carlotta E. COSWELL [27; Omaha; b: Williamsburgh, NY; f: Luther B. WHITMORE; m: Harriet M. HARRIS] on 10 Jan 1873. Off: MORRIS. Wit: Mr. and Mrs. Henry HICKMAN.

SJOGREN, Charles E. [29; Omaha; b: Sweden; f: Jacob SJOREN; m: Mary LINBLAT] md. Eliza FRICK [29; Omaha; b: Sweden; f: I.M. FRICK; m: Anna Stina PETERSEN] on 19 Jun 1869. Off: WESTERGREN. Wit: Elias CHRISTIANSON, Mary SWEINESON.

SKALA, Joseph [38; Omaha] md. Catharine SEVER [30; Omaha] on 15 Apr 1869. Off: HYDE. Wit: A. ROSEWATER, John POSPISCHEL.

SKEELS, Jesse [27; Omaha; b: England; f: William SKEELS; m: Susan SCOTT] md. Alice DELANEY [27; Omaha; b: Canada; f: Cornelius DELANEY; m: Ann BRIDGES] on 22 Mar 1880. Off: BARTHOLOMEW. Wit: Alfred R. DUFRENE, Max BERGMANN.

SKILLAN, William [22; Omaha] md. Mary McGREGH [19; Omaha] on 8 Jun 1858. Off: PORTER.

SKINNER, Alvah L. [22; Council Bluffs; b: Canada East; f: Samuel SKINNER; m: Sarah HENRY] and E. FAIRBANK [26; Council Bluffs; b: New York] license issued on 22 Jun 1871. Off: GIBSON.

SKINNER, Charles K. [24; Woodbine, IA; b: New York; f: S.M. SKINNER: m: Catharine H. KNAP] md. Abbie H. BURGESS [23; Woodbine, IA: b: Ohio; f: Robert BURGESS; m: Eliza BRACKIN] on 17 Jan 1872 at St. Barnabas Church. Off: CLARKSON. Wit: Mrs. R.H. CLARKSON; Mrs. J.M. WOOLWORTH; et al.

SKINNER, James F. [22; Omaha] md. Mary KENYON [21; Omaha] on 4 Aug 1868. Off: KERMOTT. Wit: Dr. O.L. MOODY, Mrs. A.R. KERMOTT.

SKINNER, Wm. J. [39; Omaha; b Canada; f: Chauncey SKINNER; m: Elizabeth BLAIR] md. Mary J. MAGUIRE [32; Omaha; b: Virginia] on 11 Feb 1874. Off: PEABODY. Wit: S.A. KELLEY; Mat HARNER.

SKLENAR, Joseph [28; Burt Co.; b: Bohemia; f: Joseph SKLENAR; m: Anna KUBIK] md. Barbara OUREDNIK [18; Cuming Co.; b: Bohemia; f: John OUREDNIK; m: Fanny JANDA] on 22 Feb 1873. Off: TOWNSEND. Wit: Henry GREBE; Charles H. BYRNE.

SKOGLUND, John P. [38; Omaha] md. Matilda SCOTMAN [21; Omaha] on 23 May 1867. Off: BROWN. Wit: Albert SWARTZLANDER, W.S. BREWSTER, Jerry McCHEANE.

SKOW, Hans N. [25; Omaha; b: Denmark; f: Hans J. SKOW; m: Mathilde K. BECK] md. Martine C. JOHNSON [29; Omaha; b: Denmark; f: Martin JOHNSON; m: Margaretha MARTINSEN] on 5 May 1881. Off: SMITH. Wit: Peter CHRISTIANSON, Joes BARSBALLE.

SKOW, J.J. [27; Omaha; b: Schleswig; f: N. SKOW; m: Carrie JENSEN] md. Sine MADSEN [29; Omaha; b: Denmark; f: Christ MADSEN; m: Helena ----] on 2 Nov 1881 at Vor Frelser's Church. Off: GYDESEN. Wit: R. PETERSON, S. SORENSEN.

SLATER, Thomas [34; Omaha; b: Albany, NY; f: Levi SLATER; m: Mary LUDLOW] md. Nettie BAKER [18; Omaha; b: Cherry Creek, NY; f: James N. BAKER; m: Eliza COOPER] on 6 Mar 1879. Off: BENECKE. Wit: Millio R. RANDOLPH, Mrs. Fannie PERRY.

SLATTER, J.O. [34; Omaha; b: Canada; f: Charles SLATTER; m: Anne OSBORNE] md. Anna C. McGUE [25; Omaha; b: MI; f: Tarrance McGUE; m: Mary CURTIS] on 25 Jan 1876. Off: CONGER. Wit: Thos. BANNER or BARNES, Henry SEAMAN.

SLATTERY, James [29; Omaha] and Kate MURPHY [24; Omaha] license issued on 8 May 1858. No marriage record. Off: BRIGGS.

SLATTERY, John B. [32; Shreveport, LA; b: NY; f: John SLATTERY; m: Ellen RYAN] md. Mary F. HERRON [22; Omaha; b: Madison, WI; f: Thomas HERRON; m: Mary HORRIGAN] on 19 Sep 1876 at the Roman Catholic Cathedral. Off: JENNETTE. Wit: Edward RYAN, Madison, WI, Margaret HERRON.

SLAUGHTER, Winfield S. [28; Jasper Co., IA; b: Iowa; f: Joseph SLAUGHTER; m: Melinda MYERS] md. Carolina RITCHIE [24; Jasper Co., IA; b: Iowa; f: Michael RITCHIE; m: Elizabeth MITZ] on 14 Apr 1877. Off: SEDGWICK. Wit: E.B. KNOX, H.S. STURGER.

SLETRE, John [28; Omaha] md. Annie WOYLLACK [26; Omaha] on 2 Feb 1869. Off: GROENBAUM. Wit: Wensel SCHMIDT, Wensel SCHIELLA.

SLIGHTARN [SLIGHTHAM], Henry [19; Douglas Co.] md. Elizabeth WILBORN [16; Douglas Co.] on 30 Dec 1862. Off: ARMSTRONG. Wit: Mrs. German ADSIT. Age consent given by the guardian of the groom and the bride's father, George WILBORN.

SLIGHTARN [SLIGHTHAM], James [21; Douglas Co.] md. Ellen SHANAHAN [18; Douglas Co.] on 10 Aug 1862 at the Catholic Church of Omaha. Off: McMAHON. Wit: Patrick GARVEY, Catherine CANE.

SLOAN, Joseph [24; Douglas Co.; b: Ireland; f: William SLOAN; m: Jane GREGG] md. Catharine ROBINSON [19; b: Ireland; f: Archie ROBINSON; m: Mary McMULLEN] on 25 Feb 1878. Off: PATERSON. Wit: Denis RYAN, Mrs. Denis RYAN.

SLOCKBOWER W.T. [23; Elkhorn City; b: NJ; f: Francis SLOCKBOWER; m: Elizabeth F. TURNER] md. Maggie PETERSON [21; Elkhorn City; b: Denmark; f: Peter PETERSON; m: Mary DEWEY] on 24 Jan 1881. Off: CHARLES. Wit: W. TURNER, Elkhorn City, M.B. TURNER, Elkhorn City.

SLOSS, John [22; Dodge Co.] md. Susan KELLEY [22; Douglas Co.] on 25 Oct 1859 at the home of the birde's father on the Little Papillion. Off: BARNES. Wit: Mrs. B. KELLY (KELLEY), Mrs. BARNES, John KELLY (KELLEY), et al.

SMAHA, George [24; Omaha; b: Bohemia; f: Joseph SMAHA; m: Francis HULLMAN] md. Frantisa BARTOS [19; Omaha; b: Bohemia; f: Anton BARTOS; m: Frantiska

KRISMON] on 17 Apr 1875. Off: PEABODY. Wit: Frank KONDELE, Charles H. BROWN.

SMIDT, William [28; Omaha; b: Germany; f: John SMIDT; m: Gertrude SMIDT] md. Matilda JACOBS [18; Omaha; b: Germany; f: Nicholas JACOBS; m: Margaret KRUSE] on 18 Jun 1873. Off: BRANDES. Wit: Gerhard ALTHAUSE; Frederica SCHULTER.

SMILEY, John A. [Douglas Co.] md. Anna M.J. BOWEN [Washington Co.] on 9 Jan 1865 at Elkhorn City. Off: HURLBUT.

SMILEY, John B. [30; b: Wisconsin; f: George SMILEY; m: Diana DROUGHT] md. Libbie P. ANDERS [24; b: New York; f: Thomas ANDERS; m: Emma SLATTER] on 18 Feb 1878. Off: FISHER. Wit: A.G. BUCHANAN, Marion FLEMING.

SMITH (SCHMID), Albert [35; Omaha; b: Switzerland; f: Henry SMITH; m: Elizabeth Bett SCHULTIS] md. Mrs. D.W.F. MARTIN [40; Omaha; b: Germany; f: Hans AUTTENSEN; m: Mary M. CRISGANSEN] on 16 Sep 1881. Off: BENEKE. Wit: Heinrich CLAUSSEN, Hilda CLAUSSEN, both of Madison Co.

SMITH, Adam [21; Platte Co.] and Margratte MURRY [20; Douglas Co.] license issued on 12 Feb 1858. No marriage record. Off: BRIGGS.

SMITH, Addison R. [24; Chicago, Douglas Co.] md. Mary M. THOMAS [21; Chicago, Douglas Co.] at 4 o'clock, 24 Jun 1866 at Eliza THOMAS' house. Off: DENTON. Wit: William SHORT, et al.

SMITH, Arthur B.G. [27; Omaha; b: Ohio; f: Eli SMITH] md. Sophia MASON [23; Omaha; b: Scott Co., IA; f: Hezekiah MASON; m: Ruth GOWING] on 12 May 1870. Off: DeLaMATYR. Wit: Bill HALL; Mr. Luna HALL.

SMITH, Charles H. [25; Omaha; b: New York; f: Henry SMITH; m: Catharine MILLER] md. Lotta BEDFORD [17; Omaha; b: Detroit; f: Peter BEDFORD; m: Caroline] on 28 Aug 1869. Off: PORTER. Wit: J.P. BARTLETT, Pat O. HAWS.

SMITH, Charles H. [30; b; New York; f: George W. SMITH; m: Eliza McMURRAY] md. Bertha G. NOWAG [19; b: Pennsylvania; f: Frank NOWAG; m: Teresa HOFFMAN] on 11 Jun 1878. Off: MILLSPAUGH. Wit: Wm. CLEBURNE and wife.

SMITH, Charles [28; Omaha; b: NY; f: Edward SMITH; m: Phebe HUNT] md. Fanny GOULD [20; Omaha; b: MN: f: Leonard GOULD; m: Elizabeth VINCENT] on 25 Aug 1875. Off: PATERSON. Wit: George W. YEAGER, Mr. G.W. DUNCAN.

SMITH, Cornelius [45; b: Ireland; f: Patrick SMITH; m: Mary KELLEY] and Esther DELANEY [45; b: Ireland] license issued on 4 Mar 1878. No marriage record. Off: BARTHOLOMEW.

SMITH, Daniel H. [26; Omaha; b: Virginia; f: Daniel H. SMITH; m: Amanda F. BULL] md. Susan FITZGEROLD [30; Omaha; b: Tennessee] on 25 Aug 1869. Off: KELLEY. Wit: Thomas BAKER, M.B. LEAVITT.

SMITH, David G. [26; Omaha; b: Germany; f: David G. SMITH] md. Matilda SHRAY [22; Omaha; b: Germany; f: Jacob F. SHRAY; m: Fredricka MEYER] on 17 Feb 1870. Off: KUHNS. Wit: Jacob F. SHRAY; Charles LAMMERSDORF.

SMITH, Delos S. [24; Brownville; b: IL; f: George SMITH; m: Melissa TISDALE] md. Mary E. HOLLADAY [ 22; Brownville; b: Brownville; f: A.S. HOLLADAY; m: Louisa PROUTZ] on 22 Dec 1875. Off: EASTER. Wit: Mary C. LYMAN, C.W. LYMAN.

SMITH, Frank [32; Kansas City, MO; f: John SMITH; m: Maud ROLAND] and Fannie THOMPSON [30; Kansas City, MO; b: MO; f: Thomas THOMPSON; m: Mary FRENCH] license issued on 7 Jun 1881. No marriage record. Off: SMITH. Affidavit signed by Henry JONES.

SMITH, Franklin D. [25; Omaha; b: Cincinnati, OH; f: Daniel SMITH; m: Ellen JONES] md. Mary SMITH [22; Omaha; b: New York] on 16 Nov 1870. Off: JOHNSON. Wit: Hary R. LUCAS; Ellen LUCAS.

SMITH, Franklin D. [28; Omaha; colored; b: Mississippi; f: Daniel W. SMITH; m: Ellen J. MILLS] md. Nancy Belle STEWART [18; Omaha; colored; b: Missouri; m: Sophia] on 14 Jan 1873. Off: GAINES. Wit: John THOMPSON; Jordan THOMPSON, both 11 & Chicago Sts.

SMITH, Fred K. [25; Omaha; b: Germany; f: Fred W. SMITH; m: Susan SHARA] md. Susan E. WILLIAMS [18; Iowa; b: Iowa; f: D.B. WILLIAMS; m: Thalia W. THOMAS] on 13 Jun 1874. Off: PEABODY. Wit: Gipson BOYS; Rohwena BOYS.

SMITH, Frederick W. [31; Omaha; b: Germany; f: Frederick W. SMITH; m: Susanna SCHERA] md. Auguste STUPIED [18; Omaha; b: Germany; f: William STUPIED; m: Dora MEIER] on 3 Dec 1879. Off: BRANDES. Wit: Mollie KLENELD, Marie STUPIED.

SMITH, Frederick [Omaha] md. Mrs. Mary C. JOHNSTON [Omaha] on 5 Feb 1865 at the bride's residence. Off: DICKINSON. Wit: Mr. and Mrs. Jas. G. MEGEATH, Mr. and Mrs. Ron WILLIAMS, et al.

SMITH, Fuller [23; Omaha; b: Canada; f: George SMITH] md. Elizabeth BUCKLER [20; Omaha; b: St. Louis, MO; f: Cornelius BUCKLER; m: Annie MURPHY] on 8 Sep 1870. Off: CURTIS. Wit: A.M. VAUN; Ellen GIBBONS.

SMITH, Geo. H. [23; Sarpy Co.; b: NE; f: Wm. H. SMITH; m: Emiline BROWN] md. Luella Mary JARMAN [21; Sarpy Co.; b: IL; f: Wm. JARMAN; m: Sarah JONES] on 2 Oct 1881. Off: PATERSON. Wit: H.B. SMITH, M.A. SMITH.

SMITH, George E. [25; Omaha; b: MA; f: John SMITH; m: Adeline BROWN] md. Ida LITTLE [18; Oamaha; b: IA; f: Isaac LITTLE; m: Jane CUMMINGS] on 20 Jul 1875. Off: CONGER. Wit: J.C. MORROW, Minnie WILSON.

SMITH, George V. [Elkhorn Precinct] and Annie E. McCLURE [Elkhorn Precinct] license issued on 29 Jul 1864. No marriage record. Off: DICKINSON.

SMITH, George W. [19; Florence; b: Iowa; f: John S. SMITH; m: Bridget DOWNS] md. Ella MEADE [16; Florence; b: Michigan; f: C.E. MEADE; m: Polly P. HOLBROOK] on 23 Feb 1880. Off: STENBERG. Wit: J.M. WALTMEYER of Florence, Edith WALTMEYER.

SMITH, George W. [23; Omaha; b: Ohio; f: John B. SMITH; m: Ann E. FURGESON] md. Amanda DUCROS [19; Omaha; b: Missouri; f: Victor DUCROS; m: Ellen GIBEAUX] on 25 Dec 1869. Off: GIBSON. Wit: Louis LEADER, Christina CHRISTIE.

SMITH, George [35; Omaha] md. Sarah M. CONVERSE [23; Omaha] on 28 Jan 1862 at M.H. CLARK's house. Off: BARNES. Wit: Mr. and Mrs M.H. CLARK, George RUST, et al.

SMITH, Henry [27; Douglas Co.] md. Mary FRANK [25; Douglas Co.] on 12 Jan 1869. Off: GROENEBAUM. Wit: Wenzel SCHMIDT.

SMITH, Herman [31; Omaha; b: Germany; f: Louis SMITH; m: Margaret KULENKAMP] md. Anna GOSCH [25; Omaha; b: Germany; f: Peter GOSCH; m: Charlotte MESS] on 13 Jan 1881. Off: BENEKE. Wit: Gusta V. WEAKBACH, Peter GOSCH.

SMITH, Ira W. [32; Omaha; b: GA; f: Alfred B. SMITH; m: Sarah Jane PRICE] md. Maria STUPIED [18; Omaha; b: Germany; f: William STUPIED; m: Caroline MUELLER] on 17 Feb 1881. Off: BRANDES. Wit: Sigmond BASS, Helena Magdalena STUPIED.

SMITH, Irvine [31; b: New Jersey; f: William SMITH; m: Permelia SEBRING] md.

Catharine W. DAVIS [25; New Jersey; b: New Jersey; f: Ephriam DAVIS; m: Elizabeth LEIDY] on 20 Nov 1878. Off: HARSHA. Wit: John C. DAVIS, Mrs. W.J. HARSHA.

SMITH, J.M. [33; Omaha; b: France; f: J.M. SMITH; m: Elizabeth MILLER] md. Anna WIESE [23; Omaha; b: Virginia; f: Julius WIESE; m: Catharine TRASK] on 11 Sep 1880. Off: STENBERG. Wit: H.C. ANDERSON, Lewis SANBY.

SMITH, Jacob J. [27; North Platte; b: IL; f: John SMITH; m: Elizabeth ANDERSON] and Annie NOLAN [20; Wood River, NE; b: WI; f: Wm. NOLAN; m: Ann SMITH] filed affidavit on 28 Dec 1881. No marriage record. Off: CHADWICK.

SMITH, Jacob [27; Omaha; b: Ohio; f: Tillman SMITH] md. Hariet ONEY [26; Omaha; b: Iowa; f: Wm. ONEY; m: Jane MOORE] on 11 Nov 1869. Off: GIBSON. Wit: F.A. BEALES, A.M. HENRY.

SMITH, James C. [29; Nevada; b: Ohio; f: Joseph SMITH; m: Nancy CHAMBERLAIN] and Anna ROMBERG [24; Omaha; b: Germany] license issued on 20 Nov 1869. No marriage record. Off: GIBSON.

SMITH, James E. [22; Omaha; b: Massachusetts; f: James H. SMITH; m: Harriet SAWYER] and Augusta BROSINS [18; Omaha; b: New York; f: Daniel BROSINS; m: Carolina HAELMAN] license issued on 27 Jul 1874. Off: PEABODY.

SMITH, James [25; Des Moines, IA; b: Austria; f: Albin SMITH; m: Maria RINSKE] md. Aloizije NEMETZ [NEMEC] [22; Omaha; b: Austria; f: Mike NEMETZ [NEMEC]; m: Barbara LIBINSKA] on 21 Nov 1874. Off: BEHM. Wit: Frank PIVONKA; Frank LZECOAK.

SMITH, Jarad J. [22; b: Iowa; f: J.K. SMITH; m: M.A. SHEARER] md. Carrie O. PATRICK [19; b: Omaha; f: Edwin PATRICK; m: Octa GOODWILL] on 23 Apr 1878. Off: MILLSPAUGH. Wit: Edwin PATRICK, Mrs. M.A. SMITH.

SMITH, John E. [29; Omaha; b: Providence, RI; f: J.E. SMITH; m: Mary J. PEABODY] md. Judith E. SCOTT [30; Omaha; b: Illinois; f: John SCOTT; m: Mary FERGUSON] on 28 May 1897. Off: BEANS. Wit: Mrs. W.K. BEANS, Lorenzo W. BEANS.

SMITH, Melville [21; Omaha; b: Massachusetts; f: James H. SMITH; m: Harriet SAWYER] md. Emma MEDLOCK [17; b: England; f: George MEDLOCK; m: Charlotte SHAFTON] on 15 Jun 1871. Off: BILLMAN. Wit: Mr. and Mrs. MEDLOCK; Mr. and Mrs. GREEN, Douglas Co.

SMITH, Michael [28; Monroe Co.] and Mary FRANCIS [25; Omaha] license issued on 11 Mar 1860. No marriage record. Off: ARMSTRONG.

SMITH, Paul [32; Marshall, IA] md. Susan A. STRAIGHT [27; Marshall, IA] on 23 Nov 1866. Off: HASCALL. Wit: John G. WALDSON, Frank MURPHY.

SMITH, Peter J. [32; Dodge Co.; b: Germany; f: J.J. SMITH; m: Mary HANSEN] md. Beata GILBERG [43; b: Sweden; f: Nicholas GILBERG; m: Annie ANDERSON] on 28 Dec 1878. Off: LIPE. Wit: A.H. ANDERSON, Mrs. Carolina ANDERSON.

SMITH, Peter S. [27; Omaha; b: Denmark; f: Samuel SMITH; m: Mary ANDERSON] md. Matilda SMITH [27; Omaha; b: Denmark; f: H.P. SMITH; m: Mary CNUDSON] on 4 Jun 1873. Off: BALLON. Wit: H.P. SMITH; Peter OLESON.

SMITH, Peter [30; Omaha; b: Germany; f: Frederick SMITH; m: Mary MATHESON (MATHEWSON)] md. Christina M.C. SCHMIDT [20; Omaha; b: Germany; f: M.G. SCHMIDT; m: Anna M.M. HANSEN] on 17 Oct 1869. Off: KUHNS. Wit: Morris GREENBAUM, Mrs. H.W. KUHNS.

SMITH, Samuel C. [29; Beatrice; b: CT; f: Henry SMITH; m: Mary A. BURT] md. Hellen McD HIGBY [24; Omaha; b: NY; f: John C. HIGBY; m: Francis A. PADDOCK] on 10 Aug 1875. Off: SMITH. Wit: Beecher HIGBY, M. Abbie SMITH, Beatrice.

SMITH, Samuel [24; Douglas Co.; b: Iowa; f: Samuel H. SMITH; m: Jane STEVENS] md. Ann Zuella LOCKWOOD [17; Douglas Co.; b: Illinois; f: C.L. LOCKWOOD; m: Emmarilla EVLYN] on 6 Jul 1874 at Saratoga Pct. Off: McCOY. Wit: Jennie McCOY, Saratoga; Maggie FORBES, Saratoga. Age of consent given by Emmarilla LOCKWOOD, mother of the bride. Affidavit signed by George McCANN.

SMITH, Thomas A. [33; Omaha] md. Mariah GORHAM [30; Omaha] on 17 Oct 1866. Off: ROSE. Wit: Mrs. Lizzie C. ROSE, Jennie FLEMING.

SMITH, Thomas H.F. [23; Omaha; b: England; f: H.F. SMITH; m: Mary GATHERGOOD] md. Sophia L. HAWKINS [21; Omaha; b: Sweden; f: Wm. HAWKINS; m: Sophia STRANG] on 16 Oct 1881. Off: SHERRILL. Wit: Mrs. J.E. JONES, Mabel G. ORCHARD.

SMITH, Thomas W.B. [23; Omaha] md. Annie EDMONDSON [17; Omaha] on 13 May 1868. Off: KUHNS. Wit: The bride's parents, et al. Age consent given by the father of the bride.

SMITH, Volney W. [Omaha] md. Nancy Elizabeth LEWIN [Omaha] on 26 Jan 1865 at the residence of the bride's father. Off: DICKINSON. Wit: Washington LEWIN, Mr. and Mrs. Wm. R. BROWN.

SMITH, Watson B. [32; Omaha; b: Vermont; f: Rollin C. SMITH; m: M.A. BIRCHARD] md. Fannie R. COON [25; Omaha; b: Pennsylvania; f: A.F. COON; m: Rebecca MEREDITH] on 15 Dec 1869. Off: DE LA MATYR. Wit: Mr. and Mrs. HURFORD.

SMITH, William H. [28; Omaha; b; Hector, NY; f: Edward SMITH; m: Caroline ELY] md. Frances E. COVELL [27; Omaha; b: Connecticut crossed out, Albany, NY; f: Lemuel COVELL; m: Lorana CHURCHILL] on 13 Oct 1869. Off: COVELL. Wit: Edward BRAISLIN, Mary CHURCHILL.

SMITH, William L. [28; California; b: Baltimore, MD; f: James SMITH; m: Caroline L. WRIGLEY] md. Emma A. ELLIOTT [21; Baltimore, MD; b: Baltimore, MD; f: George ELLIOTT] on 1 Aug 1870. Off: DeLaMATYR. Wit: Nettie O. DeLaMATYR.

SMITH, William L. [34; San Francisco, CA; b: Canada; f: Henry SMITH; m: Hannah TOMAU] md. Rebecca S. VANDYKE [35; Omaha; b: Ohio; f: Gilbert HANKINS; m: Mary VIOLET] on 29 Jun 1877. Off: SEDGWICK. Wit: Ernest P. LEWIS, J.G. McNULTRY.

SMITH, William [33; Omaha; b: Scotland; f: John SMITH; m: Elspet LUDINGHAM] md. Margaret HARTNEY [27; Omaha; b: Ireland; f: James HARTNEY; m: Mary HERAGAN] on 2 Nov 1873 at the Cathedral. Off: LYNCH. Wit: Allen MENTKLER; Maggie CARRIDEN.

SMYTH, William H. [22; Audubon, IA; b: OH; f: Wm. SMYTH; m: Nancy BROWN] md. Hattie May MUNDWEILER [18; Audubon, IA; b: IL; f: Christian MUNDWEILER; m: Alice NEED] on 18 Oct 1881. Off: RILEY. Wit: Paul STEIN, David VAN ETTEN.

SMYTHE, Edwin F. [26; Omaha; b: Kingston, NH; f: O.W. SMYTHE, m: Mary P. BURNAP] md. Charlotte A. LOWE [16; Omaha; b: Omaha; f: Jesse LOWE; m: Sophia HOPPIN] on 19 Dec 1875 at Trinity Cathedral. Off: CLARKSON. Wit: Dr. Enos LOWE, Mrs. Sophia LOWE. Age consent given by mother of the bride and signed in presence of T.B. LOWE.

SNEAD, John B. [48; Omaha; b: Tennessee; f: Mumford S. SNEAD; m: Susan DAY] md. Mary J. LATTA [30; Burt Co.; b: Ohio; f: Louis LATTA; m: Rebecca SWINNEY] on 26 Jan 1880. Off: INGRAM. Wit: Sarah A. MADGE, Julia A. INGRAM.

SNOOK, George G. [45; Omaha; b: England; f: James SNOOK; m: Mary GIBBS] md. Mrs. Thana LACHNER [39; Omaha; b:

Illinois; f: Samuel COBURN; m: Elizabeth MASON] on 28 Nov 1874. Off: PEABODY. Wit: J.W. ARNOLD; G.B. SHIELDS.

SNOW, J.D. [Douglas Co.] md. Lydia C. ARBAUGH [Douglas Co.] on 10 Sep 1863 at Jacob ARBAUGH's residence in Douglas Co. Both of legal age. Off: LEMON. Wit: N.P. ISAACS, Jacob ARBAUGH, et al.

SNOW, Solomon A. [24; Omaha] md. Anna R. HARNED or HOWARD [18; Omaha] on 8 Oct 1868. Off: KERMOTT. Wit: Wm. H. CLARK, Louisa PASHLEY.

SNYDER, John Adam [32; Omaha; b: MD; f: Adam SNYDER; m: Maria HORNING] md. Louisa HILLMER [22; Omaha; b: Germany; f: Henry HILLMER; m: Theodora or Dorathea PEILS] on 25 Nov 1876. Off: BENEKE. Wit: Mary MANGELROAT, Gottlich WILLIAMS.

SNYDER, John F. [22; Omaha] md. R. Annie RITCHIE [16; Omaha] on 15 Sep 1867. Off: KERMOTT. Wit: Rev. G.J. JOHNSON, Darius PEARCE. Signed age consent by Mr. and Mrs. (Carrie) Martin MUSNANE, parents of the bride.

SODERGREN, Lars [26; Omaha; b: Sweden; f: Johan SODERGREN; b: Britta GOTPEMANN] md. Louiza CARLSON [23; Omaha; b: Sweden; f: Carl DANIELSSON; m: Johanna NILSSON] on 17 Dec 1881. Off: ANDERSON. Wit: Oscar OCANDER, Emma OCANDER.

SODERHOLM, L.P. [30; Omaha; b: Sweden; f: Peter HANSEN; m: Ellen TUPVE] md. Matilda PETERSEN [22; Omaha; b: Sweden; f: John PETERSEN; m: Helen COLSON] on 28 Jun 1877. Off: SEDGWICK. Wit: Joseph QUINLAN, H.P. HANLON.

SOHL, August [28; Douglas Co.] and Frederica KOPS [25; Douglas Co.] license issued on 9 Nov 1867. No marriage record. Off: SHEEKS.

SOHL, Conrad [21 or 22; Douglas Co.] md. Catharine BLOOMAUER (BLUMENAUER) [20 or 22; Douglas Co.] on 16 Dec 1860 at STEVENS' residence. Off: STEVENS. Wit: Mary C. STEVENS of Douglas Co., L. BARATA of Douglas Co.

SOHRAUER, Jospeh [29; b: Prussia; f: Ephriam SOHRAUER; m: Amalie NEUMAN] md. Annie SINCERE [21; b: Hungaria, Austria; f: Henry SINCERE; m: Fannie TEITLEBAUM] on 25 Nov 1878. Off: ANDERSON. Wit: E. SIMON, B. KELLNER.

SOLHOLEN, Charles [19; Omaha; b: Sweden; f: John FRISH; m: Eliza SOLHOLEN] md. Augusta WALLINSTEIN [21; Omaha; b: Sweden; f: S.P. WALLINSTEIN] on 31 May 1871. Off: SUNDBORN. Wit: Genl. C.C. AUGER; J.H. LACEY. Age of consent given by Eliza SOLHOLEN, mother of the groom. Signature witnesses, Peter LARSSON; Niles SWANSON; Mrs. C. SWANSON.

SOLLENGER, Henry [32; US Army; b: Baden, Germany (or Bavaria); f: John SOLLENGER; m: Margaretha WISE] md. Caroline BURGHORT [22; Omaha; b: Baden, Germany] on 16 Jan 1871. Off: MORTON. Wit: Berg STINER; John BERKETT.

SOLOMAN, Jacob [31; Omaha; b: Prussia; f: Simon SOLOMAN] md. Louisa McGLOPHIN [24; Omaha; b: Denmark] on 15 Feb 1871. Off: W.H. MORRIS. Wit: Louis BRAST; Herman KOUNTZ.

SOLTERBECK, Nicholas [32; Omaha; b: Germany; f: Nicholas SOLTERBECK; m: Anna SIEH] md. Catherine GEHL [20; Omaha; b: Germany; f: Asmus GEHL; m: Anna TETE] on 20 Jun 1873. Off: PORTER. Wit: David TALLENT; Anna TALLENT.

SOMES, Wright E. [30; Omaha; b: New York; f: William SOMES: m: Betsey NUGENT] md. Carrie SHRATER [18; Omaha; b: Wisconsin; f: John SHRATER] on 26 Feb 1874. Off: PEABODY. Wit: Mary C. PEABODY; Matty NOBERG.

SOMMER, Frederick [26; Omaha; b: Germany; f: Bernhard SOMMER; m: Minnie SCHMIDT] md. Barbara KAVAN [20; Omaha; b: Bohemia; f: Wenzel KAVAN; m: Veronika CELACHEK [SEDLACEK]] on 10 Jan 1872. Off: PORTER. Wit: Chas. KAUFAMANN; Emile KARSCH.

SOMMER, Paul [29; Omaha; b: Germany; f: Charles SOMMER; m: Mary HINE] md. Anna Mary HANSEN [24; Omaha; b: Germany; f: Michael HANSEN; m: Christina GEIER] on 6 Dec 1871. Off: BRANDES. Wit: John DEAMON; Mrs. WIlhelmine DEAMON.

SOMMERCAMP, Louis H. [30; Omaha; b: Ohio; f: Caspar H. SOMMERCAMP; m: Louisa LUEHRMANN] md. Josie McCORMICK [20; Omaha; b: New Orleans; f: John McCORMICK; m: Mary McCORMICK] on 26 Dec 1880. Off: BRANDES. Wit: Mrs. Ellen HEINS, Conrad WIEDEMAN.

SONGUEST, Gustave [26; Oakland, Burt Co.; b: Sweden; f: John SONGUEST; m: Eva FREID] md. Eva BLANGUEST [20; Omaha; b: Sweden; f: Johannes BLANGUEST; m: Christina PETERSON] on 26 May 1873. Off: SUNDBORN. Wit: Andrew OLSON; N.P. NYGREN.

SORANSON, Peter [27; Omaha] md. Annie M. SORANSON [27; Omaha] on 14 Apr 1869. Off: HYDE. Wit: Mr. and Mrs. H.P. SORANSON.

SORENSEN, Andreas [29; Omaha; b: Germany; f: Giss SORENSEN; m: Katrina BEIER] md. Elsabe THOMSEN [18; Douglas Co.; b: Germany; f: Bernhardt THOMSEN; m: Katrina THOMSEN] on 4 Jun 1872. Off: FAUST. Wit: Henry BACKEN, Fremont; Mrs. F.E. FAUST.

SORENSEN, Christian [24; Omaha; b: Denmark; f: Jens SORENSEN; m: Marguerite JOHNSON] md. Sophia PETERSEN [24; Omaha; b: Denmark; f: Peter CHRISTIANSON] on 17 Oct 1873. Off: BENSON. Wit: G. LINDAL; Anna BENSON.

SORENSEN, Johannes [30; Omaha; b: Denmark; f: Nils SORENSEN; m: Christine JOHANNESDOTTER] and Else C. PETERSON [30; Omaha; b: Denmark; f: Folgesen PETERSON] license issued on 23 Jun 1871. Off: GIBSON.

SORENSEN, Lars Christian [40; Omaha; b: Denmark; f: Soeren JOERKSON; m: Johanna LARSEN] md. Anna JENSEN [29; Omaha; b: Denmark; f: Jens OLESON; m: Birgitte Maria MICKELSON] on 16 Jul 1881 at "my residents." Off: GYDESON. Wit: C. JENSEN, K.R. FILDT. Affidavit signed by BERGMANN.

SORENSEN, Lars [36; Omaha] md. Lena NELSON [31 or 32; Omaha] on 26 Mar 1869. Off: LARSON. Wit: John A. LAGERQUIST (LARGERQUIST), Henry C. NELSON.

SORENSEN, Soren [31; Omaha] and Frederikie JOHNSON [36; Omaha] license issued on 4 Feb 1869. No marriage record. Off: HYDE.

SORENSON, Alfred [24; Omaha; b: WI; f: Martin F. SORENSON; m: Caroline GASMAN] mdl Mary R. BROWNE [20; Omaha; b: Council Bluffs; f: W.D. BROWNE; m: Martha PATTERSON] on 15 Apr 1875. Off: LIPE. Wit: W.S. WALTER, Lizzie E. LIPE.

SORENSON, Hans [31; Omaha] md. Catharine RASMUSSEN [27; Omaha] on 1 May 1868. Off: STUCK. Wit: J.G. SPIVY, H. RASMUSSEN.

SORENSON, Joe [24; Omaha; b: Denmark; f: Peter SORENSON; m: Annie JENSEN] md. Thea MADSEN [25; Omaha; b: Denmark; f: Christ MADSEN; m: Helene BACK] on 16 Dec 1881 at "their residents." Off: GYDESEN. Wit: J. SKOW, W. ANDERSEN.

SORENSON, John H. [30; Omaha; b: Denmark; f: Soren JENSON; m: Louise JOHNSON] md. Johanna C. JOHNSON [20; Douglas Co.; b: Denmark; f: Peter JOHNSON; m: Mary CHRISTIANSON] on 12 Jun 1880, Vos Frelsers Church. Off:

GYDESEN. Wit: M. MORTENSON, H. MONFELDT.

SORENSON, Morten [36; Omaha; b: Denmark; f: Soren JOHNSON; m: Carina MORTENSON] md. Anna NIELSON [31; Omaha; b: Denmark; f: Nils ANDERSON; m: Anna Maria GORANSON] on 30 Mar 1875. Off: BENZON. Wit: Gabriel PATTERSON, Carrie PATTERSON. application signed by John S. BENZON.

SORENSON, Peter Christi [28; Fremont; b: Denmark; f: Soren PETERSON; m: Anna JENSON] md. Anna M. PETERSEN [22; Fremont; f: Denmark; f: Peter C. NELSON; m: Helena CHRISTIANSON] on 6 Feb 1874. Off: PEABODY. Wit: John W. LYTLE; F.P. HANLON.

SORENSON, Peter [22; b: Denmark; f: S. ANDERSON; m: Cena HANSEN] md. Christina OLESON [23; b: Denmark; f: John OLESON; m: Anna NEILSON] on 26 Mar 1878. Off: HANSEN. Wit: John OLSEN, Christine CHRISTENSEN.

SOUTHGATE, Walter [28; Omaha; b: Lexington, KY; f: Henry W. SOUTHGATE; m: Mary Jane CHITTENDEN] md. Alma Elizabeth HENDEE [20; Omaha; b: Mechanicsburg, OH; f: S.W. HENDEE; m: Mary E. MATHEWS] on 13 May 1875. Off: HALE. Wit: Silas A. STRICKLAND, Chas. H. EDGERTON, Hattie SHERWOOD.

SPAETH, Frank [29; Omaha; b: Germany; f: David SPAETH; m: Charlotte GWINLIEN] md. Louisa KONWALIN [18; Omaha; b: Bohemia; f: Frank KONWALIN; m: Barbara BELOWS] on 5 Sep 1876. Off: WRIGHT. Wit: Milly ROSS, Charles GRUENING.

SPAETH, Franz G. [33; Omaha; b: Germany; f: Daniel SPAETH; m: Charlotte KROENLEIN] md. Katharina D. SEHEER [50; Omaha; b: Germany; f: Johannis SEHEER; m: Anna K. ELSAESSER] on 10 Feb 1881. Off: BENEKE. Wit: Otto GUGLER, Marie GUGLER.

SPANGLER, George [40; Lincoln, NE; b: OH; f: Reuben SPANGLER; m: Susanne NOLAND] md. Jennie CARLYLE [26; DeSota, WI; b: Canada; f: Adam CARLYLE; m: Catherine E. COOK] on 21 May 1881. Off: SHERRILL. Wit: Michael DONOVAN, Anna CARLYLE, DeSota, MN.

SPANN, Henry V. [24; Omaha; b: Buffalo, NY; f: Henry SPANN; m: Matilda BEITTER] md. Mrs. Alice LEIGH [22; Omaha; b: St. Charles, IL; f: John PICKARD; m: Juliaette SKINNER] on 31 Aug 1869. Off: PICKARD. Wit: L.W. PICKARD of Little Papillion, Alfred Taylor FEAY.

SPANOGLE, James W. [36; Omaha; b: Ohio; f: Joshua SPANOGLE; m: Jane CESSNE] md. Mrs. Tabitha SKELTON [30; Omaha; f: John CASE; m: Sarah COLNELL] on 4 Jan 1870. Off: DeLaMATYR. Wit: Mrs. RIGNAL: Mr. RIGNAL.

SPARROW, Charles A. [37; Omaha; b: New York; f: John SPARROW; m: Elizabeth EVERTON] md. Caroline E. MOORE [24; Omaha; b: Ohio; f: Daniel MOORE; m: Mercia M. ROWE] on 12 May 1871. Off: DeLaMATYR. Wit: J.L. GOODWIN; Mary BROWN.

SPATZ, Anton [24; Omaha; b: Austria; f: Martin SPATZ; m: Lena HAZLE] md. Josepha WOARTZEL [19; Omaha; b: Austria] on 22 Oct 1871 at the German Catholic Church. Off: GROENEBAUM. Wit: Stephan GEIS; Miss GEIS.

SPAULDING, L.B. [27; Omaha; b: ME; f: Danial SPAULDING; m: Lydia CHANDLER] md. Mrs. Maggie LANDON [24; Omaha; b: IL; f: Thomas LEONARD; m: Mary BRENNING] on 12 Jan 1876. Off: WRIGHT. Wit: Mrs. Carrie J. HANCHETTE, Mrs. Johanna E. WRIGHT.

SPEARMAN, Charles [23; Sarpy Co.; b: Iowa; f: J.D. SPEARMAN; m: Sarah E. SIMONS] md. Josephine MEYERS [17; Sarpy Co.; b: Nebraska; f: Frank MEYERS; m: Josephine WALTER] on 26 Nov 1880. Off: STENBERG. Wit: Nelly or Nellie BEAM, Mrs. J.D. SPEARMAN, both of Sarpy Co.

SPEARMAN, William T. [43; Mt. Pleasant, IA; b: Kentucky; f: James D. SPEARMAN; m: Cynthia FROGE] md. Harriet (Hattie) BAKER [36; Omahas; b: Illinois] on 25 Jan 1871. Off: DANIELS. Wit: Dr. BABCOCK and wife, corner of Cass & 16th Streets.

SPELLERBERG, Wilhelm [34; Omaha; b: Germany; f: Johann SPELLERBERG; m: Justine LUTTER] md. Karolina LEHNERT [32; Omaha; b: Germany; f: Leopold LEHNERT; m: Karolina PATSCH] on 23 Apr 1881. Off: BENECKE. Wit: Elizabeth EICKE, McCardle Precinct, Lena GOOS.

SPENCER, Eugene [28; Omaha; b: Illinois; f: James SPENCER; m: ? CURTIS] md. Ellen DANE [18; Omaha; b: England; f: Joseph DANE] on 27 Dec 1869. Off: DE LA MATYR. Wit: A.J. McENEN, Clara McENEN.

SPENCER, Frank H. [22; Omaha; b: Scranton, PA; f: Samuel SPENCER; m: Louisa BABCOCK] md. Sarah C. WOODS [21; Omaha; b: Pekin, IL] on 15 May 1873. Off: WRIGHT. Wit: Dr. Lyman Frank BABCOCK; Mrs. Mary V. BABCOCK.

SPENCER, George A. [27; Lincoln, NE; b: New York; f: J.D. SPENCER; m: Agnes BIVRY] md. Mary J. YOUNG [20; Illinois; b: Wisconsin; f: John YOUNG; m: Kate WARD] on 1 Mar 1877. Off: STEWART. Wit: John C. SHUMWAY, Emily W. STEWART.

SPENCER, James H. [33; Omaha; b: Massachusetts; f: John SPENCER; m: Mary ROTHWELL] md. Lucy C. JACOBSON [26; Omaha; b: Boston, MA; f: Charles JACOBSON; m: Susan BRIDGE] on 16 Apr 1877. Off: MILLSPAUGH. Wit: E.B. ROBINSON, L. Mary HAYDEN.

SPENCER, William [22; Omaha] md. Emma V. DAVIS [18; Omaha] on 22 or 13 Apr 1868. Off: MORRIS. Wit: Robert P. SHERWOOD, Mary E. SHERWOOD.

SPERRY, John [22; Douglas Co.] md. Juliett SMITH [15; Douglas Co.] on 26 Nov 1867 at SHEEKS' office. Off: SHEEKS. Wit: Philip SMITH, John DeLANEY. Age consent given by Philip SMITH, father of the bride.

SPETMANN, Jochim H. [25; Omaha; b: Germany; f: Henry SPETMANN; m: Anna ELLIS] md. Augusta HENSINGER [28; Omaha; b: Germany] on 8 Aug 1869. Off: KUHNS. Wit: Charles HENSINGER, Charles WEYMULLER.

SPICER, Ephriam R. [23; Omaha; b: NY; f: Richard SPICER; m: Elizabeth HATHAWAY] md. Lena LOCKNER [23; Columbus; b: Germany; f: Adam LOCKNER; m: Josephine FLICKER] on 4 Oct 1875. Off: PEABODY. Wit: J.R. CONKLING, Ellie DER FORD.

SPIKER, William M. [22; Omaha] md. Malinda BARNES [19; Omaha] on 23 Dec 1866 at John C. LINGNER's residence. Off: KUHNS. Wit: Mr. and Mrs. LINGNER, Minerva BARNES, et al.

SPILMAN, J.H. [21; Marietta, GA; b: Nebraska; f: J. SPILMAN; m: Esther HANCOCK] md. Georgia B. GAYLORD [25; Fontanelle; b; Omaha; f: William BRIDGES; m: ----] on 3 Sep 1880. Off: MAXFIELD. Wit: Mrs. M.W. GAYLORD of Fontanelle, R.E. GAYLORD.

SPOOR, Allen [21; Council Bluffs] md. Julia WICKS [18; Council Bluffs] on 16 Jun 1861 at Kieltes Hotel. Off: ARMSTRONG. Wit: Elias G. SEARS, Harry P. DEUEL (DUEL).

SPRAGUE, James K. md. Emma FIRIENGA (FRIENGA) on 12 Jul 1857. Off: WALLCOK.

SPRATLEN, Edward H. [22; Omaha; b: Nebraska; f: William H. SPRATLEN; m: Susan E. DENNIS] md. Belle Francis MURSINNA [16; Omaha; b: Indiana; f: Frank E. MURSINNA; m: Annie CARTER] on 12 Oct 1880. OfF: MAXFIELD. Wit: J.J. NELIGH, C.R. KELSEY.

SPRING, Jerimiah C. [24] and Mary R. ONG [19] license issued on 5 Mar 1857. No marriage record. Age consent given by A.C. PYPER. Off. SCOTT.

SPRINGER, John [21; Wisconsin] md. Celestia M. CLARK [18; Wisconsin] on 14 Sep 1860 at Gen. ESTABROOK's house. Off: BARNES. Wit: General ESTABROOK, wife and daughter.

SPRINGER, William [25; Douglas Co.] md. Anna M. ENDLY [23; New Lisbon, OH] on 22 Mar 1868 at the residence of Henry MYERS. Off: DIMMICK. Wit: Mr. and Mrs. Henry MYERS, Sarah M. SKINNER, Mrs. K.G.W. DIMMICK.

SPRINGMEYER, G.H. [21; Omaha] md. Hattie TURNER [19; Omaha] on 20 Jul 1868. Off: KELLEY. Wit: Dr. J. VAN CAMP, W.F. DEGRAFFENRIED.

SPROUL, Michael D. [27; Omaha; b: PA; f: James SPROUL; m: Nancy SHOUP] md. Cicilia A. STEMM [23; Omaha; b: Germany; f: Boye STEMM, m: Helene HEIDEBEHM] on 4 Jul 1876. Off: LIPE. Wit: John POWERS, Miss BEGLY.

SQUIRES, Charles E. [32; Omaha; b: IA; f: N. SQUIRES; m: Eliza A. LOGAN] md. Ella J. COLE [22; Omaha; b: NY; f: M.G. COLE; m: Eliza BEELAMY] on 17 Feb 1875. Off: SHERRILL. Wit: George G. SQUIRES, Chas. V. COUTANT. Filed 27 Sep 1875.

ST. CLAIR, C.H. [26; Omaha; b: West Virginia; f: Thomas ST. CLAIR; m: Mary LLITZ] md. Anna KELLEY [19; Omaha; b: Iowa; f: James KELLEY; m: Harriet BLANCHARD] on 28 Aug 1880. Off: STENBERG. Wit: M. TOFT, Edward OLSEN.

ST. CLAIR, William H. [Council Bluffs] md. Vina KELSEY [Council Bluffs] on 29 Apr 1864 at Douglas House. Off: DICKINSON. Wit: James D. TURNER, Tiney KELSEY, et al.

ST. GERMIN, Joseph [21; Omaha; b: Canada; f: Nelson ST. GERMIN; m: Eliza GRIGWARE] md. Ella MILLER [21; Omaha; b: Illinois; f: George J. MILLER; m: Annie MARTIN] on 22 May 1879. Off: WRIGHT. Wit: C.T. BOND, Rodney DUTHCER.

STACEY, Nathanial [40; Omaha; b: Boston, MA; f: George STACEY; m: Elizabeth HASKINS] md. Elizabeth B. STOUDER [22; Omaha; b: NY; f: Frederick STOUDER; m: Margaret HALONER] on 11 Jan 1876. Off: SHERRILL. Wit: Wm. L. PEABODY, Mrs. W.L. PEABODY.

STADE, John [25; Omaha; b: Germany; f: George STADE; m: Margaret ROHWEDDER] md. Mary TIETJENS [21; Omaha; b: Germany; f: Marx TIETJENS; m: Anna JORGENSEN] on 16 Oct 1873. Off: TOWNSEND. Wit: Gustav BOHLMANN; Edward NIEHAUS.

STAFFORD, J.M. [29; Seward; b: West Virginia; f: Elisha STAFFORD; m: Nancy WHITE] md. Lotta A. PARKINS [21; Omaha;

b: Wisconsin; f: Joseph PARKINS; m: Charlotta CUTHBERT] on 8 Nov 1880. Off: HARSHA. Wit: G.W. WILLARD, P.S. PARKER.

STANARD, William [29; Omaha; b: England; f: James W. STANARD; m: Catharine HANNAH] md. Catharine SQUIRES [15; Omaha; b: Ohio; f: Jesse SQUIRES; m: Catharine McMANAGAL] on 25 Dec 1879. Off: PORTER. Wit: Jesse SQUIRES, Alfred SQUIRES. Age consent of bride by Jesse T. SQUIRES (x). Witness to mark: Albert SWARTZLANDER.

STANDEN, Horace [25; Elkhorn, NE; b: England; f: John STANDEN; m: Betsy HAPS] and Mary Jane BUTLER [22; Waterloo, NE; b: MO; f: Freeman BUTLER; m: Amanda BUTLER] license issued on 1 Jul 1881. No marriage record. Off: SMITH.

STANDEN, Richard [24; Douglas Co.; b: England; f: John STANDEN; m: Betsy APPS] md. Mary Anna ERNAY [18; Douglas Co.; b: MN; f: Ezra ERNAY; m: Charlotte GARDNER] on 4 Apr 1875 at Waterloo. Off: FOSTER. Wit: Alfred STANDEN, Elkhorn, Melissa STANDEN, Elkhorn.

STANDER, Martin J.F. [29; Douglas Co.; b: Germany; f: Frederick C. STANDER; m: Fredericke HINE] md. Margaret BROCK or Margaretha BRAACK [19; Omaha; b: Germany; f: Christian BROCK; m: Williamena SIPKE] on 28 Dec 1873. Off: HILGENDORF. Wit: Steffen BRAACK; Henry A. STANDER, Douglas Co.

STANFIELD, Levi S. [22; Omaha] md. Martha McCRACKEN [22; Council Bluffs] on the evening of 22 Aug 1866 at Wm. OVERTON's residence. Off: LEMON. Wit: Mr. OVERTON's family, et al.

STANG, Ernest [28; Omaha; b: WI; f: Charles STANG; m: Emma GROSS] md. Mrs. Augusta WESTPHAL [20; Omaha; b: Germany; f: Henry KOBARY; m: Mattie REIF] on 17 Feb 1881. Off: BENEKE. Wit: Byron STANBERG, Charles SCHMITZBERGER.

STANTON, Edwin [26] md. Margret VAN CICLE [22] on 21 Sep 1856 at the GAYLORD residence. Off: GAYLORD. Wit: Mrs. G.S. ARTHUR, Mrs. James W. SEYMOUR.

STAPENHORST, Theodore [35; Omaha; b: Germany; f: Henry STAPENHORST; m: Josephine TIEMANN] md. Fredericke BUEHLER [24; Omaha; b: Germany; f: Charles BUEHLER; m: Johanna TIEMANN] on 12 Oct 1874. Off: PEABODY. Wit: E.L. SMYTHE; Chas. SIMPSON.

STAPLETON, James [22; Omaha; b: Illinois; f: Richard STAPLETON; m: Mary JOHNSON] md. Samirah WARRACK [19; Omaha; b: Indiana; f: Amasa WARRACK] on 18 Oct 1870. Off: GIBSON. Wit: Lillie BEARD; William K. GOULD, Blair.

STAPLETON, Peter [32; Omaha; b: Ireland; f: James STAPLETON; m: Margaret DWYER] md. Jane O'BYRNE [18; Omaha; b: Wisconsin; f: Nicholas O'BYRNE] on 5 Dec 1872. Off: BILLMAN. Wit: Mr. and Mrs. Nicholas O'BYRNE.

STARK, Hermann [29; Fontenelle, Dodge Co.] md. Rachel HILGENKAMP [25; Fontenelle, Dodge Co.] on 14 Feb 1868 at KUHNS' residence. Off: KUHNS. Wit: Henry HILGENKAMP, Mrs. H.W. KUHNS, et al.

STARK, W.H. [Douglas Co.] md. Mary Anne SALISBURY [Douglas Co.] on 4 Aug 1857 at Willet House in Florence. Off: ADAMS. Age consent given by Michael MURPHY. Filed 24 Apr 1894, Irving F. BAXTER.

STARKEY, John F. [26; Douglas Co.; b: Canada; f: William STARKEY; m: Mary A. GIFFORD] md. Ellen RYAN [18; Douglas Co.; b: Canada; f: William RYAN; m: Bridget DOCHENY] on 24 Apr 1870. Off: CURTIS. Wit: Michael MELIA; Catherine MELIA.

STARKIE, A.H. [21; Omaha; b: PA; f: A.H. STARKIE; m: Ann DONOVAN] md. Ella LAVILLE [18; Omaha; b: PA; f: Patrick LAVILLE; m: Bridget COLEMAN] on 27 Oct 1881. Off: HYDE. Wit: L.B. GRADDY, Peter WALLESCHEEK.

STEBBINS, Asa H. [27; Boston, MA] md. Alice U. SKINNER [21; Omaha] on 30 Oct 1867 at Trinity Church. Off: VAN ANTWERP. Wit: Mrs. J.S.C. JEWETT, ---- SYDENKAM, et al. Double endorsement by SHEEKS.

STEBBINS, Harry [25; Omaha] md. Alice HANNAN [22; Omaha] on 7 Apr 1868 at Casement House. Off: MORRIS. Wit: Mrs. HUESTIS, Julia HUESTIS.

STEBBINS, Monte John [38; Omaha; b: England; f: Monta John STEBBINS; m: Mary WILSON] md. Mrs Mary M. (John) GREEK [42; Omaha; b: NY; f: Thomas BRYANT; m: Charity MILLS] on 28 Sep 1875. Off: PEABODY. Wit: F.P. HANLON, Wm. O. BARTHOLOMEW.

STEEL, John [24; Omaha; b: Sweden; f: Magnus STEEL; m: Ingrid NELSON] md. Hannah PERSSON [24; Omaha; b: Sweden; f: Orid PERSSON; m: Annie SVENSSON] on

29 Apr 1872. Off: SUNDBORN. Wit: Oscar HARTMAN; F. JOHNSON.

STEELE, James [28; Omaha] md. Elizabeth HENSMAN [19; Omaha] on 30 Oct 1866. Off: SLAUGHTER.

STEELE, L.A. [42; Omaha; b: New York; f: Adna STEELE; m: Elizabeth HINKLEY] md. Mrs. Sarah M. COATES [29; Omaha; b: New York; f: Wm. C. HUNT; m: Mary Jane BALLARD] on 30 Sep 1880. Off: HARSHA. Wit: Zena JOY, Addie KING.

STEFAN, Joseph [25; Omaha; b: Bohemia; f: John STEFAN; m: Anna TACHNICKA] md. Mary MUSIR [22; Omaha; b: Bohemia; f: Frank MUSIR; m: Mary (Anna crossed out) LEOPOLD] on 28 Dec 1876. Off: BENEKE. Wit: Anthony TETTGLE, Wenzel HOLST.

STEFFEN, John [25; Omaha; b: New Orleans, LA; f: Henry STEFFEN; m: Mary DREWN] md. Rosetta FARNSWORTH [19; Omaha; b: Cleveland, OH; f: Thomas FARNSWORTH] on 1 Apr 1873 at Trinity Cathedral. Off: GARRETT. Wit: John CAMERON; Maggie CONNER.

STEFFENSON, Anders [33; Omaha; b: Denmark; f: Stephen PETERSON; m: Katrina ANDERSON] md. Mary MATSON [26; Omaha; b: Denmark; f: Mats NILSON; m: Mary PETERSON] on 29 Sep 1873. Off: TOWNSEND. Wit: Lars JORGENSEN; Christian BACH.

STEIDEL, William [23; Omaha; b: Missouri; f: John STEIDEL; m: Barbara DOANE] md. Emma FRANK [20; St. Joseph, MO; b: Germany; f: Charles FRANK; m: Mary FRANK] on 16 Feb 1880. Off: INGRAM. Wit: B.E. MILLER, W.F. MILLER.

STEIN, Frederick E. [31; Omaha; b: Germany; f: Frederick C. STEIN; m: Frederica VEIDLEIG] md. Wilhelmina H. SEFFLER [LEFFLER] [31; Omaha; b: Prussia; f: August SEFFLER [LEFFLER]; m: Anna E. FEST] on 14 May 1870. Off: GIBSON. Wit: H.F. STRANG; C.C. GREGG.

STEIN, Julius H. [30; Omaha] md. Mrs. Selma YARSTON [28; Omaha] at 8:15 PM on 6 Feb 1867 "at the residence of the parties." Off: DIMMICK. Wit: Frank J. RAMGE, Mrs. C.E. RAMGE, M. RAMGE.

STEIN, Paul [24; Omaha; b: Germany; f: Ferdinand STEIN; m: Ada LIENENGER] md. Augusta PFUFFER [19; Omaha; b: Germany; f: August PFUFFER; m: Fredericka FREVOLT] on 3 Feb 1870. Off: GIBSON. Wit: T. Martin KLOOS; Henrietta SCHULZ.

STEIN, Robert E. [24; Omaha; b: Saxony; f: G.F. STEIN; m: Wilhelmenia WAGNER] md. Hannah PETERSON [22; Omaha; b: Denmark; f: Matz PETERSON; m: Cecilia JENSEN] on 27 Feb 1876. Off: LIPE. Wit: Fred STEIN, Alette JACOPSON.

STEINER, Michael [24; Omaha] md. Susan F. ROBERTSON [19; Omaha] on 6

May 1866 at John SHEELY's residence. Off: FROST. Wit: Mr. and Mrs. John SHEELY.

STEINERT, Justus [21; Douglas Co.; b: Germany; f: Matthias STEINERT; m: Catharine E.] md. Martha Jane TAYLOR [19; Douglas Co.; f: Amborse TAYLOR] on 7 Jul 1872 at Oakdale Farms. Off: MYERS. Wit: John SCHULTZ, Oakdale Farms; Mrs. Evelina MYERS, Oakdale Farms.

STEMBERG, Oscar C.F. [25; Omaha; b: Stockholm, Sweden; f: Charles F. STEMBERG; m: Maria C. LIBZELL] md. Johanna JOHNSON [21; Omaha; b: Sweden] on 2 Apr 1870. Off: BENNETT. Wit: John W. LYON; Bengti LYON.

STEMM, Louis [24; Omaha; b: Germany; f: Boye STEMM; m: Helene HEIDEHEHUN] md. Katie THIEMAN [21; Omaha; b: Minnesota; f: Charles THIEMAN; m: Maria MEIERDIERKE] on 10 Apr 1880. Off: JAMESON. Wit: C.A. THIEMAN, Louis BEINDORFF.

STENDER, John [37; Sarpy Co.; b: Germany; f: Frederich STENDER; m: Fredericka HEIN] md. Mrs. Sophia LOEPTIN [23; Sarpy Co.; b: Germany; f: Peter LOEPTIN; m: Magdalene ROHRBERG] on 27 May 1880. Off: BARTHOLOMEW. Wit: Max BERGMANN, Ralph GAYLORD.

STENGLEIN, Adam [28; Waterloo; b: Bavaria, Germany; f: Adam STENGLEIN; m: Maggie Mary] md. Johanna EMMERIK [22; Omaha; b: Hanover, Germany; f: G. EMMERIK] on 14 Apr 1874. Off: HILGENDORF. Wit: Frederick WIRTH; Mina EMMERIK.

STEPHENS, Charles R. [27; North Platte; b: MO; f: Thomas N. STEPHENS; m: Mary A. SWINDELL] md. Ida F. DEMARIST [20; Omaha; b: NY; f: William R. DEMARIST; m: Mary COX] on 12 Oct 1875. Off: LIPE. Wit: F. LEHMER, E.D. BELLIS. Affidavit signed by Oscar F. STEPHENS.

STEPHENS, Isaac W. [22; Omaha; b: Indiana; f: Isaac STEPHENS; m: Mary J. WILLIAMS] md. Mary L. BOWEN [20; Omaha; b: Iowa; f: Daniel BOWEN] on 23 Jul 1870. Off: DeLaMATYR. Wit: Drew BOWEN; Julia BOWEN.

STEPHENSON, Charles [26; Douglas Co.] md. Martha FARRAL [18; Douglas Co.] on 14 May 1868. Off: KUHNS. Wit: Mrs. H.W. KUHNS, Catharine GROSS.

STEPP, Gustav [25; Omaha; b: Germany; f: August Ferdinand STEPP; m: Johannah MIETHKE] md. Emilie ENGELKE [21; Omaha; b: Germany; f: Julius ENGELKE; m: Matilda ZIMMERMAN] on 13 Feb 1880. Off: FRESE. Wit: Jacob BOHRLEBER, Mary PULS.

STEPPLER, Charles [40; Fort Calhoun; b: Germany; f: Frederick STEPPLER; m: Catharine FISHER] md. Mrs. Margaretha JOHNSON [41; Fort Calhoun; b: Germany; f: Frederick JIPP; m: Charlotte MUELLHAGEN] on 15 Sep 1880. Off: FRESE. Wit: Charles NEBER, Mrs. Henrietta BURLAGE.

STERRICKER, Ed. [38; Omaha; b: New York; f: James STERRICKER; m: Margaret BAKER] md. Martha S. HOLMAN [28; Omaha; b: Wisconsin; f: S.A. HOLMAN; m: Johanna ARNE] on 4 Nov 1879. Off: LIPE. Wit: C.S. CHASE, Mrs. C.S. CHASE.

STERRICKER, Thomas E. [22; b: Illinois; f: James STERRICKER; m: Margaret BAKER] md. Helen K. ROBERTS [18; b: England; f: Samuel ROBERTS; m: Catharine LLOYD] on 4 Apr 1878. Off: PORTER. Wit: Mary E. WEATHERWAX, Harry Dan STILES.

STEUERNAGEL, William [33; Omaha; b: Germany; f: Rudolph STEUERNAGEL; m: Dorothea BANZER] md. Elizabeth MARTI [33; Omaha; b: Switzerland; f: John BRUDERMANN; m: Mary BRECHBRIEHL] on Dec 1875. Off: PEABODY. Wit:

STEVENS, Ambrose E. [26; OMaha; b: Connecticut; f: George E. STEVENS; m: Sarah RICHARDS] md. Flora NEWTON [24; Omaha; b: Ohio] on 14 Feb 1871. Off: DeLaMATYR. Wit: T.T. CROFT; L.J. GREBE.

STEVENS, Edwin [26; Omaha; b: Vermont; f: James R. STEVENS; m: Susan FIELD] md. Minnie I. FLETCHER [27; Hartford, VT; b: New York; f: Samuel FLETCHER; m: Clerinda FERGUSON] on 28 Jan 1880. Off: SHERILL. Wit: Mrs. A.F. SHERILL, Mrs. J.C. JONES.

STEVENS, George F. [27; Douglas Co.] md. Mary C. KOFAN [19; Douglas Co.] on 3 Jul 1858 at the residence of John HOEL. Off: BRIGGS. Wit: John HOEL, Aaron R. HOEL.

STEVENS, Lewis L. [32; Waterloo; b: Missouri; f: Thomas F. STEVENS; m: Mary A. SWINDLE] md. Hattie A. CONCANNON [21; Valley; b: Indiana; f: Thomas CONCANNON; m: Rhoda HATHAWAY] on 12 Nov 1874 at Mrs. CONCANNON's house. Off: BALLOW. Wit: Joseph C. WILLIAMS, Valley Pct., Doulgas Co.; Harriet C. BALLOW, Valley Pct., Douglas Co.

STEVENS, Zenas [34; Omaha; b: Strikersville, NY; f: Ira STEVENS; m: Percy HOTCHKISS] md. Mary E. SIDNER [23; Omaha; b: Galena, IL] on 12 Jun 1870. Off:

DeLaMATYR. Wit: L.B. GIBSON; Mary ADAIR.

STEVENSON, John [27; Florence; b: Scotland; f: Alexander STEVENSON; m: Magdaline PALERSON] md. Ann Mariah KEETCH [17; Florence; b: England; f: William K. KEETCH; m: Ann GREENWOOD] on 25 Mar 1871 at Florence. Off: STEVENS. Wit: C.H. PUGSLEY, Florence; Minnie STEVENSON, Florence.

STEWARD, John [colored; 27; Omaha; b: Clinton, MS; f: Duncan STEWARD; m: Harriet] md. Margaret MAYWETHERS [colored; 21; Omaha; b: Kentucky; f: Nicholas MAYWETHERS] on 22 Jul 1869. Off: KERMOTT. Wit: Mrs. Anna JOHNSON, Sylvester BURNS.

STEWART, Allan [21; Omaha; b: PA; f: William STEWART; m: Martha ALLEN] md. Susan DUCROS [20; Omaha; b: MO; f: Victor DUCROS; m: Ellen GETO] on 5 Sep 1875. Off: PEABODY. Wit: Victor DUCROS, T.C. McGEE.

STEWART, Edward B. [26; Omaha] md. Mary O'DONNELL [24; Omaha] on 9 Feb 1869. Off: O'GORMAN. Wit: Lisey BYRNS, Mathew WILSON or WELDON.

STEWART, George P. [28; Omaha; b: OH; f: Wm. STEWART; m: Phoebe PRICE] md. Jennie BYERS [19; Omaha; b: MO; f: John BYERS; m: Catherine REESE] on 14 Nov 1876. Off: McCARTNEY. Wit: Mrs. Annie MONTIETH, Mrs. Maria McCARTNEY.

STEWART, Thomas J. [35; Omaha] md. Anna RITCHIE [18; Omaha] on 21 Aug 1861 at GAYLORD's residence. Off: GAYLORD. Wit: M. DUNHAM, Thomas ALSOP.

STIBOR, Frank [23; b: Bohemia; f: Joseph STIBOR; m: Mary RYANT] md. Mary TICHACEK [18; b: Bohemia; f: Vaclav TICHACEK; m: Magdalaena LISKA] on 23 Apr 1878. Off: BARTHOLOMEW. Wit: Max BERGMAN, Gust HILLBORN.

STIFFLER, John N. [26; Douglas Co.] md. Mary E. FUNK [18; Douglas Co.] on 7 Sep 1868. Off: MANHALL.

STINCHCOMBE, William A. [25; Omaha; b: Ohio; f: James STINCHCOMBE; m: S.S. SHAW] md. Gwinnie NELIGH [22; Omaha; b: Pennsylvania; f: Wm. NELIGH; m: Sarah LOUNT] on 5 Nov 1879. Off: FROST. Wit: Evan WYMAN, Minerva WYMAN.

STIRMAN, Charles F. [23; Omaha] and Miss L.M. WILSON [22; Omaha] license issued on 9 Apr 1880. No marriage record. Off: BARTHOLOMEW.

STITT, Albert W. [26; Omaha; b: OH; f: William STITT; m: Delia PENNINGTON] md. Barbara WHITE [18; Omaha; b: TN; f: Thomas WHITE; m: Mary] on 15 Mar 1875. Off: LIPE. Wit: E.R. KNIGHT, Maria STITT.

STITT, Charles F. (21; Douglas Co.; b: IL; f: Henry STITT] and Flora B. SHAW [19; Douglas Co.; b: KY; f: Samuel SHAW; m:

Julia HUNGER] filed an affidavit on 23 Jul 1876. No marriage recorded. Off: SEDGWICK.

STITT, Henry S. [32; Omaha] md. Mariah L. KERNS [28; Omaha] on 4 Sep 1868 at Trinity Cathedral. Off: BETTS. Wit: Henry C.B. NORRIS, John A. FIELD, et al.

STITT, Lee [22; Omaha; b: OH; f: William STITT; m: Delila JONES] md. Eliza J. REDDEN [16; Omaha; b: Canada; f: John REDDEN; m: Kate KANE] on 19 Nov 1876 at the Catholic Cathedral. Off: JENNETTE. Wit: B.H. McDONALD, Lizzy F. McARTNEY. No affidavit filed. Marriage filed 21 Mar 1878.

STOCKMAN, Edward [21; Omaha] md. Amanda M. JONES [21; Omaha] on 3 Aug 1868. Off: STUCK. Wit: C.F. PALMER, C.B. GRIFFIN.

STOKES, James C. [29; Omaha; b: Bradford Co., PA; f: John STOKES; m: Sarah COLBURN] md. Nancy A. HALL [23; Omaha; b: Iowa; f: John L. BALLARD; m: Elizabeth GOODWIN] on 19 Sep 1869. Off: KUHNS. Wit: Mr. and Mrs. Henry FOX, Mr. and Mrs. Joseph PENNY.

STOLL, Adolph [25; Omaha; b: Germany; f: Johann STOLL; m: Kathrina MINHOLD] md. Louise ISTLER [23; Omaha; b: Germany; f: K. ISTLER; m: Marie KLEIN] on 21 Aug 1881. Off: BENEKE. Wit: John BOCKHOFF, Friedrick WEISSMAN.

STOLTENBERG, Henry [28; Washington Co.; b: Germany; f: Peter STOLTENBERG; m: Margaret STOLTENBERG] md. Mary MECKELSON [18; Washington Co.; b: Germany; f: Claus MECKELSON; m: Margaret SCHWAGER] on 19 Jun 1880. Off: WRIGHT. Wit: Claus MICHEELS, Egert GLINDT.

STONE, John [23, Fort Omaha; b: PA; f: William STONE; m: Mary Ann PHEIFER] md. Mrs. Ella DELLAHUM [24; Douglas Co.; b: OH; f: H.J. BERRY; m: Alarisa Ann WILDERMUTH] on 3 Sep 1881 at Saratoga. Off: PURCELL. Wit: Ernest MORSE, Fort Omaha, Ida BERRY.

STONES, Frederick A. [24; Saratoga Pct, Douglas Co.; b: Greene Co., NY; f: Frederick STONES; m: Mary ALLEN] md. Matilda GRAHAM [23; Saratoga Pct, Douglas Co.; b: Georgia; f: Albert GRAHAM; m: Mary Ann] on 16 Jan 1873. Off: McKELVEY. Wit: M.F. SHINN; Angie McKELVEY.

STORM, Hans [28; Douglas Co.; b: Germany; f: Jacob STORM; m: Catherine MILLER] md. Sophia WAGEMAN [18; Douglas Co.; b: Germany; f: John WAGEMAN; m: Catherine BANZER] on 9 Mar 1870 at Wm. FLORKEE's residence. Off: FLORKEE. Wit: George PLAMBECK; Jochim PLAMBECK; Mrs. ELizabeth FLORKEE: Charley FLORKEE.

STORY, John N. [24; Washington Co.] md. Rebecca BEUBAKER [22; Louisa Co., IA] on 14 Aug 1868. Off: STUCK. Wit: W.F. DEGRAFFENRIED, W.W. FOOT.

STOTLAN, Nathan C. [38; Omaha] md. Rebecca BETZ [37; Omaha] on 6 Nov 1868. Off: KELLEY. Wit: J.H. CLARK, O.A. ABBOTT.

STOUT, Wilbur F. [32; Pontiac, MI; b: Michigan; f: J.L. STOUT; m: Olevia P. APPEY] md. Delia E. HOLDEN [20; Idaho Territory; b: Idaho; f: D.C. HOLDEN; m: Eliza I. SMITH] on 15 Mar 1878. Off: SHERRILL. Wit: Zephaniah KNIGHT, Mrs. C.P. STORRS.

STRAHL, Rolan C. [22; Iowa; b: Ohio; f: Colbert STRAHL; m: Drusilla WILLIAMS] md. Eldora A. LEWIS [18; Iowa; b: Iowa; f: Shelton LEWIS; m: Josephine KALER] on 28 Dec 1874. Off: PEABODY. Wit: Charles HASERALTT; Thomas A. ADAMS.

STRANDBERG, John W. [36; Omaha; b: Sweden; f: Jacob STRANDBERG; m: Annie HENDRICKSON] md. Mary E. BERQUIST [32; Omaha; ba; Sweden; f: John BERQUIST; m: Christina ANDERSON] on 17 Jan 1877. Off: HANSEN. Wit: Mrs. HULTMAN, Mrs. FEISOBSEN.

STRANDQUIST, Sven A. [35; Omaha; b: Sweden; f: Anders NILSON; m: Anna SVENSON] md. Christina LUNGREN [22; Omaha; b: Sweden; f: Oli LUNGREN] on 14 Oct 1870. Off: GIBSON. Wit: Mary GIBSON; R.H. ANDRES.

STRANG, John [31; Douglas Co.; b: Germany; f: John STRANG; m: Anna NEIGLE] md. Mrs. Minnie STODEL [34; Omaha; b: Germany; f: John STODEL; m: Gustina GUSHORT] on 5 Jul 1881. Off: WRIGHT. Wit: Rodney DUTCHER; Gotleib HOYE.

STRANGLIN, John [22; Omaha; b: Germany; f: Joseph STRANGLIN; m: Kunignude BUTTNER] md. Mary NORVACEK [NOVAK] [19; Omaha; b: Bohemia; f: Joseph NORVACEK [NOVAK]] on 25 Aug 1879. Off: BENEKE. Wit: [impossible to read names].

STRASBURG, Henry [31; Omaha; b: Prussia; f: Henry STRASBURG; m: Rosa SCHINDLER] md. Elise HOCKET [25; Omaha; b: Louisville, KY] on 21 Aug 1873. Off: BALLON. Wit: C. SCHAFFER; A. BURKHART.

STRATTON, Robert M. [25; Omaha; b: Port Hope, Canada; f: Samuel STRATTON; m: Sarah McALDIN] md. Ada E. FESSENDEN [19; Ohio; b: Twinsburgh; f: John W. FESSENDEN; m: Amanda NICHOLS] on 16 May 1869. Off: WESTWOOD. Wit: L.P. FARRAR, B.D. SLAUGHTER.

STRATTON, Wm. H.J. [38; b: New York; f: Platt STRATTON; m: Elizabeth J. JONES] md. Vina WHITE [21; Massachusetts; f: Edward A. WHITE; m: Alvina S. SIMMONS] on 24 Jul 1878. Off: WILLIAMS. Wit: Kitty GILMORE; Mrs. GILMORE.

STREITZ, Henry C. [23; Papillion; b: WI; f: Ferdinand STREITZ; m: Fredricka FEST] md. Lizzie E. FLORKEE [19; Omaha; b: NE. f: William FLORKEE; m: Elizabeth WOLF] on 30 Jun 1881. Off: MAXFIELD. Wit: Mrs. Peter DOWN, Mrs. J.B. MAXFIELD.

STREITZ, William [29; Douglas Co.; b: WI; f: Ferdinand STREITZ; m: Friederika FEST] md. Anna ZOBEL [24; Douglas Co.; b: Germany; f: Frederick ZOBEL; m: Augusta FEST] on 17 May 1881. Off: BENEKE. Wit: Ferdinand STREITZ, Friederika FEST.

STRICKLAND, James K. [33; Omaha; b: Ohio; f: Samuel STRICKLAND; m: Emily KEYES] and Sarah RIDLE [32; Mount Hope, OH; b: Ohio] license issued on 30 Oct 1874. Off: PEABODY.

STRONG, Milo (Milow) [27; Omaha] md. Anna ROSE [15; Omaha] on 24 Oct 1868. Off: KERMOTT. Wit: Mrs. A.M. McCALLUM, Mrs. Darius PIERCE or PRICE. Age consent given by Eliza DUNLAP, mother of the bride.

STRUTHMEIER, Jacob [22; Council Bluffs; b: Germany; f: Henry STRUTHMEIER; m: Margaretta SEEBECK] md. Mary BANDOLE [BENDA] [18; Omaha; b: Bohemia; f: Frank BANDOLE [BENDA]; m: ---- RATH] on 7 Oct 1872. Off: BRANDES. Wit: Mrs. Rebecca STALEY; Ed REED.

STUART, Donald [30; Omaha; b: Scotland; f: Robert STUART; m: Ellen GRANT] md. Eliza Ann ADAM [17 (on 24 Jun 1873); b: Illinois; f: Alexander ADAM; m: Margaret MAIN] on 1 Sep 1873 at O'GORMAN's house. Off: O'GORMAN. Wit: Alexander ADAM, Pottawattamie Co., IA; Margaretta MAIN, Pottawattamie Co., IA.

STUBEN, John [39; Omaha; b: Germany; f: Claus STUBEN] md. Bertha RASCHKA [19; Omaha; b: IN; f: August RASCHKA] on 16 Dec 1876. Off: PEABODY. Wit: John T. PAULSON, Lizzie STUBEN.

STUBEN, Peter Henry [28; Grand Island] md. Lucia Mary PAULSEN [22; Omaha] on 28 Mar 1860 in KUHNS study on Farnham St. Off: KUHNS. Wit: John T. PAULSEN, Thomas PAULSEN.

STUHLMILLER, Henry [24; Adair Co, IA; b: Germany; f: Jacob STUHLMILLER; m: Christina DANZHLER] md. Emma SCHONBORN [19; Johnson Co., IA; b: Johnson Co., IA; f: Joseph SCHONBORN; m: Cathrina BOWER] on 9 Mar 1876. Off: BRITT. Wit: Leopold SCHONBORN, Johnson Co., IA, Minnie SCHONBORN, Johnson Co., IA.

STUHR, Peter [38; Hall Co.] md. Anna SCHEEL [26; Hall Co.] on 31 Aug 1867. Off: BROWN. Wit: Joseph GRANICHER, Josephine GRANICHER.

STUHR, Peter [Hall Co.] md. Trina SCHEEL [Hall Co.] on 6 Jun 1864 at Henry RICHTER's residence. Off: DICKINSON. Wit: James STUHR, C. STOLTENBERG, Mrs. RICHTER.

STUHT, Ernest [25; Omaha] md. Maria MATSON [20; Omaha] on 13 Feb 1869. Off: KUHNS. Wit: John H.A. RATH, Andrew NELSON, et al.

SUCHY, Frank [27; Omaha; b: Bohemia; f: John SUCHY; m: Barbara DORAK [DWORAK]] md. Barbara JANBOR [JAMBOR] [25; Omaha; b: Bohemia] on 21 Oct 1880. Off: BENEKE. Wit: Joseph WASSKIR [VASKU]; Wenzel NISTEL.

SUDAN, Adolph [26; Omaha; b: Germany; f: Gustav Adolph SUDAN; m: Ottilia WINSKOWSKY] md. Agnes UDENHOFER [21; Milwaukee, WI; b: Wisconsin; f: Herman UDENHOFER; m: Mary MUELLER] on 30 Sep 1880. Off: BENEKE. Wit: Belle TONER, Eugene P. MESSIE.

SUHL [SOHL], Nicholas [29; Omaha; b: Germany; f: Casper SUHL [SOHL]; m: Maria HINE] md. Maria NEUHAUS [18; Omaha; b: Germany; f: Frederick NEUHAUS; m: Sophia SCHROEDER] on 21 Jan 1873. Off: TOWNSEND. Wit: Frederick NEUHAUS; George KLEFFNER.

SULLIVAN, Bartholomew [35; Omaha; b: Ireland; f: John SULLIVAN; m: Catherine CONNERY] md. Mrs. Mary CHRISTY [40; Omaha; b: Ireland; f: James LANGON; m: Catherine GRADY] on 31 May 1874 at the Roman Catholic Cathederal. Off: BYRNE. Wit: Michael TROY; Ellen COLCHERT.

SULLIVAN, Eugene [23; Omaha] md. Hanora MURPHY [22; Omaha] on 3 May 1868 at the Catholic Church. Off: O'GORMAN. Wit: Maurice SULLIVAN, Mary DOWD.

SULLIVAN, John M. [25; Omaha] md. Ellen CURRAN [19; Omaha] on 30 Nov 1867. Off: MOSSMAN. Wit: James O. SULLIVAN (O'SULLIVAN), Bridget BRENNAN.

SULLIVAN, Maurice [33; Omaha; b: Ireland; f: Eugene SULLIVAN; m: Julia FINN] md. Sarah KENNEDY [22; Omaha; b: Ohio; f: John KENNEDY; m: Julia CARROLL] on 30 Jul 1873. Off: CURTIS. Wit: Martin W. KENNEDY; Theresa KENNEDY.

SULLIVAN, Timothy [25; Omaha] md. Catharine CUISICK [24; Omaha] on 27 Mar 1869. Off: O'GORMAN. Wit: William W. WELLER, Catharine MURRAY.

SULLY, Thomas [21; Omaha; b: New York City; f: Daniel SULLY; m: Mary BURNES] md. Fanny VEAR [19; Omaha; b: New York City; f: ? KING] on 15 Nov 1869. Off: PORTER. Wit: Col. F.A. HANFORD, Charles A. PARKER.

SUMMER, John [21; Elkhorn Station; b: Iowa; f: Luther SUMMER; m: Hulda Van DEVER] md. Mary WOLLEN [18; Elkhorn Station; b: Iowa; f: Truston WOLLEN; m: Myra POLLARD] at Jefferson Precinct on 11 Apr 1879. Off: ROBERTS. Wit: W. WOLLEN of Jefferson Precinct, Douglas Co., Truxton WOLLEN.

SUMNER, Ed. H. [26; Cheyenne, WY; b: WI; f: E.R. SUMNER; m: Mary RESER] md. Lena McDONALD [19; Chicago, IL; b: NY (IL crossed out); f: Alexander McDONALD; m: Hellen FULLER] on 10 Nov 1881. Off: INGRAM. Wit: W.F. BROWN, Chicago, Geo. H. BLOOMHART, NY.

SUMNER, John H. [29; Florence; b: Boston, MA; f: Samuel SUMNER; m: Jerusha NASH] md. Annie B. FISHER [17; Florence; b: Wheeling, VA] on 21 Mar 1870 at Florence. Off: DELAND. Wit: Mother and family, Zackeriah and Vastia FISHER.

SUMNER, Samuel T. [23; Douglas Co.; b: Iowa; f: Ephrian SUMNER; m: Mary DOTSON] md. Sophronia GILLMORE [18; Douglas Co.; b: Iowa; f: James GILLMORE; m: Elizabeth McCASCEY] on 23 Mar 1880, Elk Horn. Off: WILSON. Wit: Dolly SUMNER, E. LONOMON, John SUMNER all of Douglas County.

SUNDBLAD, Charles R. [26; Omaha; b: Sweden; f: William SUNDBLAD; m: Sophia ARWIDSON] md. Augusta J. ANDERSON [19; Omaha; b: Sweden; f: L. ANDERSON; m: Christina LIBERG] on 12 Mar 1875. Off: PEABODY. Wit: Geo. W. DOANE, Robert P. CHURCHILL.

SUNDBORN, Peter W. [25; Omaha; b: Sweden; f: Charles G. SUNDBORN; m: Catherine JENSEN] md. Charlotte BOLIN [24; Omaha; b: Sweden; f: Christian BOLIN; m: Anna JACOBSON] on 12 Jul 1869. Off: KERMOTT. Wit: Nels ANDERSON or NELSON, Nels MARTINSON.

SUNDBORN, Peter W. [29; Omaha; b: Sweden; f: Charles SUNDBORN; m: Catharine JOHNSON] md. Edla Maria WENNGREN [26; Omaha; b: Sweden; f: Charles WENNGREN; m: Maria] on 12 Aug 1873. Off: AXLING. Wit: Oscar HARTMAN; John RING.

SUNDEL, Gust [45; Omaha; b: Sweden; f: Ander ANDERSON; m: Annakassa OLAFSDOTTER] md. Emily (Emmelia) CAGERSTROM (or STAGERSTROM) [25; Omaha; b: Sweden; f: Charles CARLSON; m: Bretter BERGSON] on 10 Apr 1875. Off: BENZON. Wit: Mr. and Mrs. J. WESTBERG.

SUNDERWALL, Charles [25; Fremont; b: Sweden; f: Fred SUNDERWALL; m: Charlotte GRAPENGIEFSER] md. Sally GRIMSHAW [18; Council Bluffs; b: NY; f: Nelson GRIMSHAW; m: Emiline NILSON] on 27 Nov 1875. Off: PEABODY. Wit: A.E. SIMPSON, C.H. SEDGWICK.

SUNDUN, August [44, Elkhorn Station; b: Sweden; f: Nelson ASTRAND; m: Margaret C. AUGUSTEEN] md; Engrid LARSEN [47; Elkhorn Station; b: Sweden; f: Lars JOHNSON; m: Anne C. AUSTROM] on 17 Oct 1881 at Elkhorn Station. Off: SMITH. Wit: Oleg WARREN, Friedrich JANSON, both of Elkhorn.

SURPRENENT, Nacriss [42; Douglas Co.; b: Canada; f: P.S. SURPRENENT; m: Josette TROMBLE] md. Mrs. Marceline DUMAS [44; b: Canada; f: Jeremie GOYETTE; Emily HETER] on 8 May 1878. Off: SHAFFEL. Wit: John J.B. VIEN of North Platte, NE, Mary COVION.

SUTPHEN, Enoch W.N. [26; Omaha; b: Wilmington, DE; f: James SUTPHEN; m: Sarah SILCOZ] md. Maggie SKINNER [27; Omaha] on 7 May 1870. Off: KERMOTT. Wit: Henry TAGGERT; Mrs. Laura TAGGERT.

SUTTON, A.W. [24; Omaha; b: Canada; f: Jacob SUTTON; m: Catharine GEDDES] md. Edna C. BURCHARD [19; Omaha; b: IL; f: Mr. BURCHARD; m: Mrs. HILLOCK] on 10 Nov 1881. Off: RILEY. Wit: C.N. HILLOCK, Mrs. Hattie CAPRON.

SUTTON, Henry [28; Omaha; b: Connecticut; f: John SUTTON; m: Mary VERNON] md. Margaret M. HONEY [28; Omaha; b: Connecticut; f: William HONEY; m: Sarah WILLIAMS] on 17 Sep 1874 at St. Barnabas Church. Off: FUSSE. Wit: Miss M.J. DAVIS; Patrick CAIN; Thomas HOLMES; et al.

SVACINA, Jacob [23; Omaha; b: Bohemia; f: Martin SVACINA; m: Mary SLAMA] md. Barbara HAJEK [20; Omaha; b: Bohemia; f: George HAJEK; m: Annie KOHOUT] on 8 Jun 1872. Off: TOWNSEND. Wit: Charles H. BYRNE; Joseph DWORK.

SVACINA, John [23; Omaha; b: Bohemia; f: Martin SVACINA; m: Mary SLAMA] md. Mary KRAJCIK [18; Omaha; b: Bohemia] on 10 Jun 1875. Off: BOBAL. Wit: John ROSICKY, Joseph KREJCI.

SVACINA, Peter [23; Omaha; b: Bohemia; f: Martin SVACINA; m: Mary SLAMA] md. Katy INTERHOLZINGER [21; Omaha; b: Bohemia, f: James INTERHOLZINGER; m: Maggie STANPERKOVA] on 13 Jan 1879. Off: KOCARNIK. Wit: Joseph ANDRLE, John FLUEGER.

SWACKHAMER, Edgar [23; Harrison Co., IA; b: Ohio; f: Elija SWACKHAMER; m: Caroline BATES] md. Ellen BARNUM [18; Harrison Co., IA; b: Harrison Co., IA; f: David BARNUM; m: Levina PALMER] on 15 Jul 1878. Off: BARTHOLOMEW. Wit: J.W. HUPP of Harrison Co., IA, F.P. HANLON.

SWACKHAMER, Samuel Oscar [21; Omaha] md. Clara Electa DODGE [18; Omaha] on 9 Oct 1862. Off: SMITH. Wit: George RITCHIE, M. PRICHARD.

SWAIN, Elmer P. [26; Sarpy CO.; b: Vermont; f: John F. SWAIN; m: Lydia DAVIS] md. Emma J. GREEN [22; Sarpy Co.; b: New York; f: Zacheus GREEN; m: Polly GILE] on 19 Aug 1874. Off: PRESSON. Wit: D.A. HARMON; Mary H. HARMON.

SWAN, Ande [30; Omaha; b: Sweden; f: Swon ANDERSON; m: Anna JENSEN] md. Henrika JOHNSON [28; Omaha; b: Sweden; f: John HENDRICKSON; m: Anna JENSEN] on 7 Nov 1872. Off: SWEDERS. Wit: Charles Peter SWANSON; Ella SWANSON.

SWAN, Charlie P. [29; Omaha; b: Sweden; f: Swan ANDERSON; m: Annie NELSON] md. Martha NOBERG [23; Omaha; b: Sweden; f: Lars NORBERG; m: Christine NELSON] on 30 Apr 1875. Off: PEABODY. Wit: A.F. SWAN, Nellie TRUESONN. (Pencil notation on back of application: "9th bet. Dodge S.C. Ave East 565. Sunday evening, 8 o'clock".)

SWANEY, A.C. [24; Shelby Co., IA; b: MN; f: Jerry SWANEY; m: Ophy KETCHEL] md. Essie M. GROUNDS [18; Shelby Co., IA; b: IL; f: James GROUNDS; m: Anna VANSICKLE] on 13 Oct 1881. Off: INGRAM. Wit: Charles BINKLEY, Nora BINKLEY.

SWANSEN, Nels [32; Saunders Co., NE; b: Sweden; f: Swan ERKESON; m: Johanna ERLANSON] md. Christine PALLMER [30; Omaha; b: Sweden; f: John ANDERSON; m: Sarah LARSEN] on 30 Dec 1880. Off: FOGELSTROM. Wit: Mrs. Ida C. FOGELSTROM, Anna C. HOLMQUIST.

SWANSON (SVENSON), John [35; Bell, Washington Co.; b: Sweden; f: Swan JOHNSON; m: Ellen JOHNSON] md. Batilda SWANSON [36; Bell, Washington Co.; b: Sweden; f: Swan MONSON; m: Mary JOHNSON] on 21 Dec 1873. Off: BENZON. Wit: Jenny PALMGREN; Mrs. Anna BENZON.

SWANSON, Andrew [30; Omaha; b: Sweden; f: Swen ANDERSEN; m: Catherine ANDERSEN] md. Lena ANDERSON [26; Omaha; b: Sweden; f: Andreas LARSON; m: Miristina MAGNUSSON] on 19 Oct 1872. Off: TOWNSEND. Wit: Truman BUCK; Enoch HENNEY.

SWANSON, Nels [26; Omaha] md. Clara SWANSON [22; Omaha] on 7 Aug 1868. Off: KERMOTT. Wit: Mr. and Mrs. B.J. MATSON.

SWARTZ, George L. [30; Omaha; b: PA; f: Richard SWARTZ; m: Catharine LEITH] md. Sarah A. MANGER [20; Omaha; b: England; f: Henry C. MANGER; m: Sarah A. HALL] on 29 Oct 1881. Off: HARRIS. Wit: Mrs. J.W. HARRIS, 1916 Chicago Street.

SWARTZLANDER, Albert [34; b: Bucks Co., PA; f: Joseph SWARTZLANDER; m: Abigail RANKIN] md. Stella MAY [26; b: Pittsburg, PA; f: James MAY; m: Agnes LOWE] on 12 Nov 1878. Off: O'CONNOR. Wit: John REDDICK, Mrs. Jno. REDDICK.

SWARTZLANDER, Jacob [37; Omaha] md. Bella E. BRUNER [28; Omaha] on 8 Oct 1867 at Uriah BRUNER's residence near Omaha city. Off: KUHNS. Wit: Uriah BRUNER, Charles E. BRUNER, et al.

SWEATT, Henry J. [23; Harlan, Shelby Co., IA; b: Shelby Co., IA; f: A.R. SWEATT; m: J. TINSLEY] md. Lizzie E. CULVER [18; Harlan, Shelby Co., IA; b: Cedar Co., IA; f: James CULVER; m: Ellen SMITH] on 28 Apr 1879. Off: BENEKE. Wit: Samuel M. ELDER, Perry A. ELDER, both of Pittsburgh, PA.

SWEDERS, Andrew N. [25; Omaha; b: Sweden; f: Nils NILSSON; m: Charstina PEARSON] md. Olia TROIL [19; Omaha; b: Sweden; f: TROIL; m: Johanna] on 14 Oct 1872. Off: LARSON. Wit: Rev. John S. BENZON, Moline, IL; Mary TROIL.

SWEENEY, James A. [24; Omaha; b: New York; f: John SWEENEY; m: Libbie BUTLER] md. Rosana BECKER [24; Omaha; b: Canada; f: Edmund BECKER; m: Melinda STAPLES] on 22 Mar 1977. Off: SEDGWICK. Wit: Frank SLOSSON, E.B. KNOX.

SWEENEY, William [35; Omaha; b: Buffalo, NY; f: James SWEENEY; m: Micah VANDERVOORT] md. Mary Ann EMS [19; Douglas Co.; b: England; f: Richard EMS; m: Rosa A. COZZENS] on 29 Jan 1872. Off: ESTABROOK. Wit: Sarah DEACON; Desire HANDBINE.

SWEENY, John [24; Omaha] and Mary FENTON [23; Omaha] license issued on 6 Apr 1869. No marriage record. Wit: HYDE.

SWEENY, John [26; Omaha] md. Abby FOLEY [18; Omaha] on 10 Jan 1869. Off: CURTIS. Wit: Lawrence SCANLON, Eliza FOLEY.

SWEET, Marian T. [36; Douglas Co.; b: Ohio; f: David or Daniel SWEET; m: Antilla THOMPSON] md. Mrs. Jennie R. SMITH [29; Douglas Co.; b: Pennsylvania; f: Wm. HANEY; m: Margaret ROSE] on 23 Sep 1869 at Primrose. Off: DENTON. Wit: L.J. DENTON of Primrose, M. HENDERSON of Primrose.

SWEETMAN, Thomas [25; Papillion, Sarpy Co.; b: Ireland; f: Thoms SWEETMAN; m: Catharine SWEETMAN] and Amelia McMAHON [29; Papillion, Sarpy Co.; b: Ireland; f: Philip McMAHON; m: Susan] license issued on 21 Feb 1873. Off: TOWNSEND.

SWENDLY, Andrew H. [23; Omaha; b: Norway; f: Hans SWENDLY; m: Berke OLSEN] md. Randina VANWIG [23; Omaha; b: Norway; f: Peter VANWIG; m: Caroline FALK] on 16 May 1870. Off: KUHNS. Wit: John A. LUND; Jonas T. TVANWIG.

SWENEY, James [25; Kearney Co.] md. Julia Ann SOVREN [24; Omaha] on 25 Dec 1860. Off: BRIGGS. Wit: James BENNET, et al.

SWENSON, Anton Ludwick [25; Omaha; b: Celeskrone, Sweden] md. Caroline BRUCE [24; Omaha; b: Sweden] on 1 Nov 1869. Off: LARSON. Wit: Eric BERGQUIST of Washington Co., August LARSON of Washington Co.

SWENSON, Gustav [29; Omaha; b: Sweden; f: Swen BRUNTSON; m: Martha PETERSON] md. Brita OLSON [26; Omaha; b: Sweden; f: Ole MANSON; m: Bertha PETERSON] on 10 Aug 1870. Off: BENNETT. Wit: C.G. or C.H. AHLQUIST; Nils RYBERT.

SWICKARD, Albert F. [22; Omaha; b: Ohio; f: Elias SWICKARD; m: Elmira CAMP] md. Meldora DAVIS [19; Omaha; b: Iowa; f: James DAVIS; m: Mary COLSON] on

19 Mar 1874. Off: PORTER. Wit: John BRADLEY; Martin SKELTON.

SWOBE, Thomas [25; Omaha] md. Alzina SCOTT [21; Omaha] on 26 Nov 1868. Off: KUHNS. Wit: Mr. and Mrs. Milton ROGERS, Mr. and Mrs. Andrew McCAUSLAND, et al.

SWOBODA, Frank Joseph [21; Omaha; b: Bohemia; f: Frank WANICKE; m: Amalie SWOBODA] md. Filipina SWOBODA [19; Omaha; b; Bohemia; f: Joseph SWOBODA; m: Josephine DOBIAS] on 26 Jun 1879. Off: KOCARNIK. Wit: Wenceslas KAVAN, Joseph PRUSHA.

SYLVESTER, Ethan E. [21; Omaha; b: St. Louis, MO; f: George SYLVESTER; m: Mary Ann FARLEY] md. Catharine L. MORRISON [21; Omaha; b: Boston, MA; f: William P. MORRISON; m: Mary CARTER] on 27 Oct 1872. Off: ESTABROOK. Wit: Henry MEISEL; Johanna MEISEL.

SYLVESTER, George, Jr. [31; Omaha; b: England; f: George SYLVESTER; m: Mary A. FARLEY] md. Sarah A. STARKEY [21; Omaha; b: Connecticut; f: William STARKEY; m: Ann McMANNERS] on 30 Sep 1874. Off: HUDSON. Wit: William M. RUMEL; Louisa SYLVESTER.

SYLVESTER, Samuel [23; Omaha; b: St. Louis, MO; f: George SYLVESTER: m: Mary Ann FARLEY] md. Emma L. HILL [17; Omaha; b: London, England; f: William HILL; m: Emma PAGE] on 26 May 1872. Off: KUHNS. Wit: Frank M. WILSON, Belle ROBINSON. Age of consent given by father of the bride.

SYMONDS, James J. [28; Omaha; b: Minnesota; f: Charles SYMONDS; m: Jemina JOHNSTON] md. Mrs. Ella F. FREEMAN [24; Burt Co.; b: New York; f: John C. BALDWIN; m: Lucy M. GARY] on 7 Dec 1880. Off: BEANS. Wit: Thomas GROCOX, Mrs. Ethel A. BEANS.

TABER, Albert H. [28; Florence] md. Parasetta GUILL [18; Florence] on Sunday, 15 Jul 1866 at TURNER's office. Off: TURNER. Wit: Thomas GUILL, Mary TURNER.

TABOR, Joseph [26; Neola, IA; b: Illinois; f: John TABOR; m: Ann SLY] md. Kate SISSON [19; Woodbine, IA; b: New York; f: Lemuel SISSON; m: Harriet WHEATON] on 19 Feb 1880. Off: ANDERSON. Wit: A.M. CHADWICK, D.S. BENTON.

TAFFE, John [31; Dakota Co.] md. Clara A. RITCHIE [20; Omaha] on 16 Jan 1862. Off: SMITH. Wit: Horace SPENSER, David L. COLLIER, A.S. PADDOCK.

TAGGART, Charley F. [23; Hamilton, NE; b: Ohio; f: A. TAGGART; m: M.C. COANJN] md. Cecelia F. FURAY [23; Omaha; b: Ohio; f: C. FURAY; m: May McGLINCY] on 15 Jan 1877. Off: Pastor from Church of Holy Family. Wit: Felix McSHARE, Catharine CRIPHTON.

TAGGART, James A. [23; Douglas Co.] md. Malinda SCOTT [16; Douglas Co.] on 21 Aug 1856 at the house of Judge SCOTT. Off: GAYLORD. Wit: James PICKARD, Jessee SHOMAKER (SHOEMAKER). [This is the first marriage recorded in Douglas Co., NE.]

TAGGER, Henry [21; Omaha] md. Laura HILL [18; Omaha] on 29 Apr 1869. Off: KERMOTT. Wit: W.T. SEAMAN, Mrs. A.R. KERMOTT.

TALLINE, John [23; Burt Co.; b: Sweden; f: Peter TALLINE; m: Carie ERIKSON] md. Ida PETERSON [23; Douglas Co.; b: Sweden; f: Peter PETERSON; m: Caroline EIKEMAN] on 23 Dec 1876. Off: ANDERSON. Wit: Adolph BOWMAN, L.E. BRAGE.

TALT, John [27; Baltimore, MD; b: Baltimore, MD; f: Patrick TALT; m: Susan HUGHES] md. Annie HUGHES [22; West Point; b: Bedford Co., PA; f: Michael HUGHES; m: Mary HITE] on 31 Aug 1872 at the Catholic Church of Omaha. Off: GORMAN. Wit: Michael HUGHES, West Point; Patrick TALT and Susan HUGHES.

TAYLOR, B.M. [52; Omaha; b: Nova Scotia; f: Eleazer TAYLOR; m: Briah JENKS] md. Mrs. A.M.L. HUTCHINS [39; Omaha; b: Maine; f: George W. FURBUSH; m: Mary STUBBS] on 2 Sep 1879. Off: STENBERG. Wit: E.A. McCLURE, R. De DARLING.

TAYLOR, Charles Tupper [31; Omaha; b: Nova Scotia; f: Samuel TAYLOR; m: Frances TAIT] md. Catharine (Kate) BOYD [21; Omaha; b: Ohio; f: Joseph BOYD; m: Margaret McNIECE] on 17 Nov 1874. Off: GARRETT. Wit: James E. BOYD; Jesse H. LACEY.

TAYLOR, Edward A. [23; Omaha; b: Ohio; f: E.B. TAYLOR; m: Jane McCLURE] md. Mary A. McCAFFREY [22; Omaha; b: Iowa; f: Patrick McCAFFREY; m: Elizabeth DORSEY] on 31 Aug 1880. Off: ENGLISH. Wit: P. DIVITT, Mary A. McCAFFREY.

TAYLOR, Edward [22; Sandy Hill, NY] md. Sarah A. WELLIVER [18; Rock Bluffs, Nebraska Territory] on 5 Apr 1866 at Florence. Off: TURNER.

TAYLOR, Henry [32; Omaha; b: Pennsylvania; f: Thomas TAYLOR; m: Katrina MULLIS] md. Caroline STRICKLAND [21; Omaha; b: Germany; f: Augustus STRICKLAND; m: Katrina GAEBHARDT] on 23 Jan 1872. Off: TOWNSEND. Wit: William H. IJAMS; William H. LAWLER.

TAYLOR, Hiram [44; Marine, CO; b: New Jersey; f: Hiram TAYLOR; m: Mary F. THOMPSON] md. Christine B. STOWELL [38; New Bedford, MA; b: Massachusetts; f: Columbus STOWELL; m: Nancy R. CHASE] on 15 Jan 1880. Off: BARTHOLOMEW. Wit: Isaac N. CONGDON, A.C. TROUP.

TAYLOR, J.M. [25; Douglas Co.; b: Ohio; f: James TAYLOR; m: Maria PRIZER] md. Eliza GILMORE [20; Douglas Co.; b: Iowa; f: James GILLMORE; m: Elizabeth McCASCAY] on 23 Mar 1880, Elk Horn Station. Off: WILSON. Wit: Duby SUMNER, E. LONMON, John SUMNER all of Douglas Co.

TAYLOR, Joseph W. [Omaha] md. Melissa J. SULLIVAN [Omaha] on 23 Dec 1863. Both of legal age. Off: KUHNS. Wit: Mr. and Mrs. W. JONES, Mr. and Mrs. LEMON, et al.

TAYLOR, Joseph [35; Omaha; b: Missouri; f: Willis JONES; m: Maheely ----] md. Mathilda PAINE [40; Omaha; b: Missouri; f: John PAIN- [sic]; m: Lucy ANDERSON] on 1 Mar 1880. Off: STENBERG. Wit: Lucy PAINE, Martha ROBINSON.

TAYLOR, Robert M. [34; Omaha; b: Virginia; f: Dr. S.T. TAYLOR; m: Elvira M. LEARNED] md. Elizabeth BURKE [22; Omaha; b: New York; f: John BURKE; m: Elizabeth KELLY] on 6 Jul 1880. Off: ENGLISH. Wit: Mr. TAYLOR, Mrs. O'REILLY.

TAYLOR, Stephen [21; Omaha; b: Iowa; f: Ambrose TAYLOR; m: Nancy or Fanny TRIP] md. Fanny WYHLEDADL [19; Omaha; b: Bohemia; f: John WYHLEDADL; m: Fanny COUFAL] on 27 Jun 1879. Off: BARTHOLOMEW. Wit: Max BERGMANN, Jas. QUINLAN.

TAYLOR, Wiley [23; Douglas Co.; b: MO; f: George TAYLOR; m: Scynthia BROWN] md. Mary TEMPERLEY [22; Douglas Co.; b: IL; f: John TIMPERLEY; m: Mary] on 29 Apr 1875 at Mr. TIMPERLEY's. house. Off: GAYLORD. Wit: J.E. SHEPPERD, Union Precinct, John TIMPERLEY, Union Precinct.

TAYLOR, Wm. O. [27; Omaha; b: Rhode Island; f: J.D. TAYLOR; m: Lydia TAFT] md. Fannie L. McCONNELL [22; Omaha; b: Illinois; f: Robert McCONNELL; m: Annie L. WARDELL] on 18 Sep 1880. Off: SHERRILL. Wit: Sidney E. LOCKE, Robert C. STEELE.

TEAHON, Joseph [34; Omaha; b: Canada; f: William TEAHON; m: Ester BRNE] md. Sarah CASSIDY [20; Omaha; b: Omaha; f: Phillip CASSIDY] on 8 Jun 1875 at the Roman Catholic Cathedral. Off: MALLOY. Wit: Patrick FLYNN, Belle DWYRE.

TEASDALE (TEASDOLL), Martin [46; Omaha] md. Mrs. Kina DAVIS [45; Omaha] on 20 Aug 1859 at BRIGGS' office. Off:

BRIGGS. Wit: Harriet HOWTEN, Mary Ann MILLER.

TEGELBORG, Lars [31; Omaha; b: Sweden; f: Peter LARSON; m: Christine] md. Maria ANDERSON [33; Omaha; b: Sweden; f: Lars ANDERSON; m: Botilda LARSON] on 16 Aug 1869. Off: LARSON. Wit: Petronella LAGERSTROM, Charla S. LARSON.

TELLON [TELLER], John [Harrison Co., IA] md. Elizabeth OAKES [Harrison Co., IA] on 26 Jan 1865 at O'GORMAN's private chapel. Off: O'GORMAN. Wit: Peter MALONE.

TEMPLE, Samuel [37; Franklin Co., KY; b: Franklin Co., KY; f: Josiah TEMPLE; m: Mary TOMLINSON] md. Martha DRINKHARD [37; Franklin Co., KY; b: Franklin Co., KY; f: Joshua DRINKHARD; m: Polly CREGG] on 5 Sep 1874. Off: STEWART. Wit: Charles D. BRYNE; D.A. VAN NAMEE, Jr.

TENNERY, Edwin S. [49; Omaha; b: KY; f: Sylvester TENNERY; m: Mary JACOBS] md. Mrs. Luch A. LAWRENCE [29; Omaha; b: OH; f: E. LAWRENCE; m: Dorthula CAMPBELL] on 12 Jun 1881. Off: MAXFIELD. Wit: Mrs. S.J. DEWY, Mrs. Carrie STEVENS.

TERHELLEN, Christian [39; St. Louis, MO; b: Germany; f: Joseph TERHELLEN; m: Frederika LOTTEN] md. Rosa HAUSHAELTER [26; St. Louis, MO.; b: Germany; f: Frederick HAUSHAELTER; m: Henrietta SPENHART] on 8 Jun 1876. Off: BENEKE. Wit: Frederick WIRTH, Jacob HAUCK.

TERRILL, Walter [21; Council Bluffs, IA; b: WI; f: John TERRILL; m: Margaret HAWTHORNE] md. Lida CRAWFORD [19; Council Bluffs, IA; f: David CRAWFORD; m: Nancy Jane McGREW] on 13 Jun 1881. Off: ANDERSON. Wit: C.A. BALDWIN, David VAN ETTEN.

TEST, Edward F. [30; Omaha; b: Alabama; f: Edward F. TEST; m: Emma F. GOODMAN] md. Rosetta DUNHAM [20; Omaha; b: Connecticut; f: William DUNHAM; m: Sophia ELLWOOD] on 8 Feb 1877. Off: LARKIN. Wit: L.W. MONER, W.P. VONENG.

TEX, Joseph [21; Omaha] md. Mary PEARL [19; Omaha] on 17 Feb 1863 at the Catholic Church of Omaha. Off: McMAHON. Wit: George KLEFFNER, Annie O'BRIEN.

TEX, Michall [29; Omaha; b: Prussia; f: John TEX; m: Angela MEYER] md. Lizzie RUBHAUSEN [19; Omaha; b: Omaha; f: Gottfried RUBHAUSEN; m: Gertrude FENSER] on 18 Nov 1875 at the German Catholic Church. Off: GROENBAUM. Wit: Frank RUBHAUSEN, Cuming Co., Josephine HEROLD.

THELEN, Edmund [28; Rising, NE; b: Prussia; f: H. Ambrose THELEN; m: Theresa HERHAHN] md. Fanny J. BAYRHOFFER [23; Lasalle, IL; b: Wisconsin; f: Charles Th. BAYRHOFFER; m: Charlotte BAYRHOFFER] on 3 Jan 1880. Off: WEISS. Wit: George KARLL, E.F. SMYTHE.

THELLER, Arnold [42; Omaha] md. Mrs. Sarah F. PERRY or PEENEY [33; Omaha] on 18 Mar 1869. Off: KUHNS. Wit: Mrs. H.W. KUHNS, Matilda JONSON.

THIEBAUT, Celestine [33; Omaha] md. Maggie DALARD [21; Omaha] on 11 Feb 1868 at the Catholic Church. Off: O'GORMAN. Wit: E. BEASON, Ann HUGHES.

THIEDE, Julius [26; Omaha; b: Germany; f: Gotlieb THIEDE; m: Fredrica ROSENCRANZ] md. Agnes SARTORIUS [17; Omaha; b: Germany; f: Peter SARTORIUS; m: Gertrude SALLED] on 22 Jun 1870. Off: GIBSON. Wit: John E. BYRNE; J.H. HAMMOND. Age of consent given in open court by Celia HANTING, the person having charge of Agnes SARTORIUS.

THOMAS, Charles [35; Omaha; colored; b: Louisville, KY; f: Charles THOMAS; m: Agnes JOHNSON] md. Mary Isabella SMITH [25; St. Louis, MO; colored; b: St. Louis, MO; f: Addison SMITH; m: Jane HOPSON] on 8 Jun 1872. Off: LYTLE. Wit: Josua BUDD; J.J. STUBBS.

THOMAS, Frank L. [25; Omaha; b: Pennsylvania; f: David THOMAS; m: Catharine EVANS] md. Ellen KEGAN [21; Omaha; b: New Jersey; f: John KEGAN; m: Mary KALLARY] on 14 Feb 1880. Off: ENGLISH. Wit: D.B. HOUCK, Miss Brid. KENNEDY.

THOMAS, G.W. [24; Douglas Co.; b: OH; f: G.W. THOMAS; m: Elizabeth REED] md. Mary R. SPRECHER [31; Douglas Co.; b: OH; f: George SPRECHER; m: Sarah A. RENSHAW] on 22 Jan 1876 at Irvington. Off: GREEN. Wit: William WILSON, Union Precinct, Margaret WILSON, Union Precinct.

THOMAS, George H. [33; Omaha; colored; b: Alabama; f: Enoch THOMAS; m: Sarah HORN] md. Eva Jane BERRYHILL [18; Omaha; colored; b: Missouri; f: Silas BERRYHILL; m: Mary Jane] on 12 Nov 1872 at GAINE's residence. Off: GAINES. Wit: Isaac ALEXANDER; Alfred KIRCHAFALE.

THOMAS, Henry M. [21; Council Bluffs; b: Canada; f: Thomas THOMAS; m: Mary J. METCALF] md. Mary J. BARNES [20;

Council Bluffs; b: Atlantic, IA; f: William BARNES] on 8 Sep 1870. Off: GIBSON. Wit: Maggie JOHNSON, Council Bluffs; Edward CADIS, Council Bluffs.

THOMAS, John D. [52; Omaha; b: Prussia; f: Peter THOMAS; m: Mary SIMON] md. Sylvia E. PRESTON [36; Omaha; b: Canada West; f: Rufus PRESTON; m: Ermina HAWKINS] on 1 Sep 1875. Off: PEABODY. Wit: Fred BEHM, Mrs. Carrie BEHM.

THOMAS, John [25; Union Precinct, Douglas Co.] md. Jennie M. HUNT [19; Omaha] on 22 Sep 1868. Off: KUHNS. Wit: Mr. and Mrs. John ROBB, Mrs. A. HUNT, et al.

THOMAS, John [26; Omaha; b: England; f: Edward THOMAS; m: Jane RASEWORN] md. Annie PERKINS [30; Omaha; b: Illinois] on 20 May 1871. Off: ESTABROOK. Wit: Mattie CONNOR; Jane RUSSELL.

THOMAS, John [30, Washington Co.] md. Mary HOUSE [19; Washington Co.] on 18 Feb 1859 at BRIGGS' home. Off: BRIGGS. Wit: Manie or Morris ROBLANGEL; Catherine HOUSE.

THOMAS, John [48; Omaha; b: Purssia; f: Peter THOMAS; m: Mary SIMON?] md. Mrs. Elizabeth ROBLING [50; Omaha; b: Prussia; f: John FRIGELS; m: Mary SIMON?] on 11 July 1872. Off: TOWNSEND. Wit: Joseph ROSENSTEIN; George KLEFFNER.

THOMAS, Jordan [26; Omaha; colored; b: North Carolina; f: Stephen THOMAS; m: Harriet RUFFIN] md. Sarah DAVIS [19; Omaha; colored; b: Kentucky; f: Henry DAVIS; m: Amanda HENDRICKS] on 13 Feb 1873. Off: PORTER. Wit: Gustave ANDERSON; Julia ROY.

THOMAS, Samuel E. [29; Omaha; b: Philadelphia; f: William THOMAS; m: Margaret EVANS] md. Mrs. Sarah WEBBER [--; ----; b: Des Moines, IA; f: Samuel PERKINS; m: Mary A. WILLIAMS] on 19 Mar 1880. Off: BENEKE. Wit: Peter DE PIESE, Wenzel VIRTEL.

THOMAS, Valentine H. [24; Douglas Co.] md. Nancy Jane SNOWDEN [20; Omaha] on 27 Jan 1869 at the residence of the bride's father. Off: ALLEN. Wit: J.B. ALLEN, Wm. SNOWDEN.

THOMAS, William F. [20; Omaha; b: Plympton, MA; f: Henry L. THOMAS; m: Clarisa L. STANDISH] md. Emily F. KEENE [27; Omaha; b: West Roxbury, MA; f: Augustus B. KEENE; m: Prudence W. WOODS] on 2 Jun 1872. Off: KUHNS. Wit: William H. KEENE; Loyd KNIGHT, Holidaysburgh, PA. Age of consent given by William H. KEENE, guardian of groom; father is dead and mother is remarried.

THOMAS, William M. [colored; 26; Omaha; b: Charleston, SC; f: Morris THOMAS; m: Ann VAUGHN] md. Emma WATTS [colored; 24; Omaha; b: Charleston,

SC; f: Brown SCANTLIN (SCANTLING); m: Margaret LAWTON] on 12 Aug 1869. Off: KUHNS. Wit: Cyrus D. BELL, Mrs. Margaret SCANTLING.

THOMAS, Winfield S. [26; Omaha; b: Pennsylvania; f: William THOMAS; m: Laura NORRIS] md. Josephine NEWLAND [18; Omaha; b: Ohio; f: Joseph NEWLAND: m: Mary KELLY] on 28 Oct 1870. Off: GIBSON. Wit: Henry A. FITCH; Ellen HUTCHENSON.

THOMPSON, Charles [24; Omaha; b: NY; f: Wm. T. THOMPSON; m: Catherine FOOT] md. Jennie WEAVER [18; Omaha; b: IL; f: Jacob WEAVER; m: Mary ANDREWS] on 29 Apr 1875. Off: PEABODY. Wit: C.H. FREDERICK, E.T. COWIN.

THOMPSON, Daniel H. [29; Omaha; b: New York; f: Luman THOMPSON; m: Lauretta BUTTON] md. Nora COOK [18; Omaha; b: Brownsville; f: James COOK] on 25 Aug 1869. Off: SHINN. Wit: R.W. GARNER, A.A. STANLEY of Blair.

THOMPSON, Edmund F. [23 or 25; Omaha; b: New York City; f: Cephas G. THOMPSON; m: Mary G. OGDEN] md. Clara A. BISBEE [22; Omaha; b: Rhode Island; f: William O. BISBEE; m: Hariet Marian BALLON] on 2 Dec 1869. Off: GASMANN. Wit: William H. BISBEE, Catherine S. BISBEE.

THOMPSON, Edward C. [27; Marne, IA; b: IL; f: John THOMPSON; m: Jane SWANEY] md. Ella SPANGLER [23; Omaha; b: IL; f: Jacob SPANGLER; m: Jane CLARK] on 29 Dec 1881. Off: SHERRILL. Wit: J.T. CLARK, Oscar CLARK.

THOMPSON, Ervin [52; Missouri Valley Junction, IA; b: Missouri; f: Ephraim THOMPSON; m: Sarah CURREY] md. Harriet C. VESSEL [30; Omaha; b: South Carolina; f: L.B. CLARK; m: Hannah V. JACKSON] on 26 Feb 1870. Off: GIBSON. Wit: Thomas M. MURPHY; Mrs. Sarah E. MURPHY.

THOMPSON, George I. [22; Sarpy Co.] md. Melissa C. HUFF [18; Sarpy Co.] on 11 Jul 1866 at the Court House. Off: HASKELL. Wit: S.E. GRAVES, E. SHATTUCK, et al.

THOMPSON, George W. [28; Omaha; b: NY; f: Joseph THOMPSON; m: Martha FARREN] md. Oliva B. VICKROY [18: Douglas Co.; b: IL; f: Orin VICKROY; m: Ann HEANEY] on 11 Nov 1876. Off: DONNELLY. Wit: Henry TRAYNOR, Mary E. TRAYNOR.

THOMPSON, Granville [Douglas Co.] md. Ellen THOMAS [Douglas Co.] on 13 Aug 1865. Off: HASCALL. Wit: Joseph A. GOINGS, A. COFFEE, ? COFFEE, et al.

THOMPSON, James W. [28; Omaha; b: Wisconsin; f: William THOMPSON; m: Jane M. WILSON] md. Elizabeth A. LAFFERTY [18; Omaha; b: Iowa; f: James LAFFERTY; m: Mary A. ERWIN] on 4 Jan 1879. Off: BARTHOLOMEW. Wit: Chas. C. WESTON, W. SIMERAL.

THOMPSON, John [26; Plattsmouth; b: Ireland; f: Henry THOMPSON; m: Margaret BURK] and Nora QUIRCK [QUICK] [24; Omaha; b: Ireland] license issued on 2 Oct 1869. No marriage record. Off: HYDE.

THOMPSON, Richard A. [40; Cuming Co.; b: Norway; f: Thomas THOMPSON; m: Ellen GUNDERSON] md. Ragnel OLSEN [43; Cuming Co.; b: Norway; f: Ole OLSEN; m: Carrie LARSON] on 20 Jun 1870. Off: GIBSON. Wit: William ADAMS; Mary NIELSON.

THOMPSON, Theodore [25] and Eliza LEWCUS [26] license issued on 23 Sep 1856. No marriage record. Age consent given by Y.R. LEWCUS. Off: SCOTT.

THOMPSON, Thomas J. [22; Garden Prairie, IL; b: Vermillion, IL; f: Josiah THOMPSON; m: Elizabeth C. ERWIN] md. Sarah J. BUSSEL [25; Grand Island; b: Lancashire, England; f: John BUSSEL; m: Jane TUCKER] on 8 Feb 1876. Off: BRITT. Wit: S.J. BRITT, Carrie WOOD.

THOMSEN, Andreas [29; Omaha; b: Germany; f: Thomas THOMSEN; m: Elsabe OTZEN] md. Anna TIBBKE [25; Omaha; b: Germany; f: Martin TIBBKE; m: Johanna ENGLEMEIER] on 23 Dec 1872. Off: DIECKMANN. Wit: Frederick DIECKMANN; Fredericke DIECKMANN.

THOMSEN, Hans [24; Papillion, Sarpy Co.; b: Germany; f: Frederick THOMSEN; m: Anna EICHNER] md. Regina BEICEL [19; Millard Precinct; b: Germany; f: Rudolph BEICEL; m: Wibke SCHLOEMER] on 13 Mar 1878. Off: WEISS. Wit: Henry SIERT, Fred HARMSEN.

THOMSEN, Hans [29; Omaha; b: Denmark; f: Peter THOMSEN; m: Sophie GIDDENFELD] md. Martina HANSEN [22; Omaha; b: Denmark; f: John HANSEN; m: Mary NELSON] on 16 Jun 1877. Off: SEDGWICK. Wit: Jacob JACOBSEN, M. MARTENSON.

THOMSEN, Rasmus J.H. [29; Omaha; b: Germany; f: Rasmus THOMSEN; m: Anna

JENSEN] md. Lucie M. DUHRENDORFF [b: Germany; f: Fred DUHRENDORFF; m: Lucy M. RIXEN] on 30 Nov 1875. Off: HILGENDORFF. Wit: Harrold THOMSEN, Anna THOMSEN, Washington Co.

THOMSON (TOMSON), Henry [22; Omaha; b: Denmark; f: John THOMSON; m: Hansena J. HANSEN] md. Mary LARSON [21; Omaha; b: Denmark; f: Lars HANSEN; m: Bodil HANSEN] on 27 Jun 1873. Off: TOWNSEND. Wit: Mark HANSEN; Ole JOHNSON.

THOMSON, Hugh [28; Omaha Barracks; b: Scotland; f: James THOMSON; m: Jane LOWRIE] md. Agnes HUGHES [21; b: West Virginia; f: William HUGHES; m: Mary PATTERSON] on 13 May 1878. Off: STENBERG. Wit: Alice BARTON, Walentin ADAMS.

THOMSON, James C. [41; Plattsmouth; b: Canada; f: James C. THOMSON; m: Louisa CUTENAR] md. Mrs. Mary RISCH [40; Plattsmouth; b: Germany; f: Johann KAUFMEYER; m: Christine FISCHER] on 30 Mar 1880. Off: BENEKE. Wit: August WEISS, Sam. BEATTY.

THOMSON, James [26; Elkhorn City, NE; b: Indiana; f: George THOMSON; m: Sarah LISTEN] md. Sarah Ann GUGIN [16; Elkhorn City, NE; b: Missouri; f: James N. GUGIN; m: Grace NOBLE] on 15 Sep 1878. Off: Van FLEET. Wit: H.A. GRAY, Thom. BOYER both of Elkhorn City. Age consent given by parents of the bride.

THOMSON, John [22; Omaha; b: Denmark; f: Thomas NELSON; m: Sarah HANSEN] md. Mary HANSEN [24; Omaha; b: Denmark; f: Hans CHRISTIANSEN] on 12 Dec 1874. Off: PEABODY. Wit: S.C. PEDERSON; Ole Chris THOMSON.

THORN, Frank [32; Omaha; b: IA; f: Francis THORN; m: Harriet INGHAM] md. Mrs. Annie B. CARPENTER [[32; Omaha; b: PA; f: Samuel McCULLOUGH; m: Melvira PICKET] on 12 May 1875. Off: LIPE. Wit: C.M. CUNNINGHAM, Mrs. CUNNINGHAM.

THORNBURGH, Thomas T. [28; 2nd Army USA; b: Tennessee; f: M. THORNBURGH; m: Olivia A. DYER] md. Lida CLARK [20; Omaha; b: Pennsylvania; f: Robert CLARK] on 26 Dec 1870. Off: GASMAN. Wit: Gent or Geret ALVOFD; Mrs. C.C. AUGER. Affidavit signed W.P. CLARK, 1st Lt. and Adj. 2nd Cavalry.

THORSON, Charles [24; Saunder Co.; b: Sweden; f: Thore JOHNSON; m: Ellen SWENSEN] md. Gustava L. JOHNSON [20; Omaha; b: Sweden; f: John JOHNSON m: Everlena PEERSON] on 21 Nov 1870. Off: LARSON. Wit: John JOHNSON; Jens THORSON, Saunders Co.

THORSON, Martin [25; Saunders Co.; b: Sweden; f: Thore JOHNSON; m: Eleanor

SWENSON] md. Augusta JOHNSON [19; Omaha; b: Sweden; f: John JOHNSON; m: Eva NILSON] on 7 Aug 1874. Off: PEABODY. Wit: John E. KNOLL; Thomas HOLMES.

THUM, Ferdinand [35; Omaha; b: Germany; f: Frederick THUM; m: Rebecca SMITH] md. Mrs. Amelia ELSASSER [37; Omaha; b: Germany; f: Johan WACKER; m: Thorothea BINDER] on 19 Sep 1871. Off: MORTON. Wit: Gotlieb ZIMMERMAN; Catherine ZIMMERMAN.

THUMA, John [26; Omaha; b: Germany; f: John THUMA; m: Anna SPRAEL] md. Kate SWOBODA [21; Omaha; b: Austria; f: Anton SWOBODA; m: Kate ANDER] on 18 May 1874. Off: PEABODY. Wit: O.S. WOOD; E. LEWIS.

THURSTON, John M. [25; Omaha; b: Montpelier, VT; f: Daniel S. THURSTON; m: Ruth MELLEN] md. Mattie L. POLAND [23; Omaha; b: Montpelier, VT; f: Luther POLAND, Jr.; m: Clara M. BENNETT] on 25 Dec 1872. Off: GUE. Wit: L. POLAND; D. NEUMAN, Lincoln.

TIBBALS, G.W. [40; Omaha; b: CT; f: Charles TIBBALS; m: Elizabeth BRISTOL] md. Mary H. MERWIN [35; Omaha; b: CT; f: Charles MERWIN; m: Martha STODDARD] on 9 Sep 1881. Off: HARSHA. Wit: P.L. PERINE, Mrs. J.R. MEREDITH.

TIBBITS, Abraham [24 or 25; Douglas Co.] md. Hannah SOWLE [26 or 28; Douglas Co.] on 1 Jan 1858. Off: BRIGGS. Wit: John CHRISMAN, Mrs. Mary W. GAYLORD.

TIBKE, Martin [26; Omaha; b: Germany; f: Martin TIBKE; m: Engel MEYER] md. Dora REEBER [23; Omaha; b: Germany] on 21 Jun 1871. Off: GIBSON. Wit: Frederick RIEBER; Rodney DULCHER.

TIERNEY, Luke D. [Cass Co., IA] md. Ann BLAKE [Cass Co., IA] on 28 Apr 1865 at the Catholic Church. Off: DAXACHER.

TILDEN, Charles H. [25; Hazelton; b: Ellington, CT; f: Austin TILDEN; m: Julia GRIGGS] md. Roella E. POTWIN [22; Hazelton; b: East Windsor, CT; f: John POTWIN; m: Sop(h)ronie BELLNAP] on 29 Sep 1870. Off: KUHNS. Wit: Mrs. H.W. KUHNS; George C. POTWIN, Hazelton.

TILDEN, George [31; Omaha; b: New York; f: Josiah TILDEN; m: Mary B. WILLIAMS] md. Ida V. CLEGG [21; Omaha; b: Virginia; f: Isaac CLEGG; m: Susan] on 28 Apr 1874. Off: STEWART. Wit: Mrs. Isaac CLEGG; Mrs. A.S. HUNTOON.

TILLOTSON, Francis [28; Omaha] md. Margaret J. NASH [22; Omaha] on 6 Dec 1866. Off: HASCALL. Wit: Henry M. NASH, C.D. LAYTON.

TIMM, Henry [30; Omaha; b: Germany; f: Geo. TIMM; m: Mary BIGIRMAN] md. Louisa KUNAS [18; Omaha; b: Germany; f: Peter KUNAS; m: Christina CRISTINSIN] on 11 Jan 1876. Off: HILGENDORF. Wit: Gustav WILKE, Margaretha PETERS.

TIMMONS, James [37; Wyoming Territory; b: Ireland; f: Patrick TIMMONS; m: Ann MULLEN] and Lizzie BURNS [28; Omaha; b: Ireland] license issued on 6 Oct 1869. No marriage record. Off: HYDE.

TIMPERLY, John P. [24; Douglas Co.] md. Rebecca A. WERTZ [24; Douglas Co.] on 21 Feb 1869 at Little Papillion. Off: HURLBUT. Wit: William CUNNINGHAM, Jessie EBRIGHT.

TIMPKE, Heinrich [Grand Island, Hall Co.] md. Helena OBERMULLER on 29 May 1865 at DICKINSON's office. Off: DICKINSON. Wit: Hans OBERMULLER, George PLAMBECK, Charles H. BROWN, C.S. DICKINSON.

TIPTON, James [30; Wyandotte, KS; colored; b: Lafayette Co., MO; f: George EWING] md. Mrs. Mary GRAHAM [25; Omaha; colored; b: Illinois; m: Louisa McCLAINE] on 5 July 1870 at Richard JOHNSON's residence. Off: HUBBARD. Wit: Richard JOHNSON; Laura JOHNSON.

TISHER, Zack [25; b: Ohio; f: Christian TISHER; m: Mary Ellen RHOADES] md. Leota Viella ROSS [17; b: Rochell, IL; f: Wm. ROSS; m: Sadie KOKER] on 15 Sep 1878. Off: HARSHA. Wit: L.S. RATHBUN, Sam HENDERSON. Age consent given by Mrs. Sadie RATHBUN, mother of the bride.

TITUS, William [colored, Omaha] md. Sarah KELLY [colored, Omaha] on 18 Dec 1866 at Thomas DAVIS' residence. Off: KUHNS. Wit: Thomas DAVIS, Herman KOUNTZE, et al.

TIZARD, Richard [28; Omaha; b: England; f: Richard TIZARD; m: Edith BOW] md. Kate O'NEILL [19; Omaha; b: Canada; f: Michael O'NEILL; m: Anastasia HANIGAN] on 15 July 1874 at Bishop's House. Off: BYRNE. Wit: John O'NEIL; Josephine HENNESSY.

TOBANNAH, Joseph [25; Omaha] md. Mary CARRIGAN [21; Omaha] on 4 Jul 1868 at the dwelling of Mr. WOODS. Off: FLORKEE. Wit: Mary KUEON, Kartine BUTTER, Mattie WOOD, Elisa FOULLER.

TOBIAS, Carston [29; Omaha] md. Ann Catharine JOHNSON [24; Omaha] on 27 Apr 1869. Off: DENMURE. Wit: Peter NELSON, Nelson MARTINSON.

TOENSFELDT, George [26; Douglas Co.; b: Germany; f: Henry TOENSFELDT; m: Elizabeth OTT] md. Margarret SCHOENER [24; Douglas Co.; b: Germany; f: Henry SCHOENER; m: Wiebke SIEVERS] on 12 Jan 1881. Off: FRESE. Wit: Hans THOMSEN, Douglas Co., Eggert OTTE, Douglas Co.

TOFT, John H. [33; Omaha] md. Mary MILLER [24; Omaha] on 19 Dec 1867. Off: KUHNS. Wit: Mrs. Mary NELSON, Christian Nelson.

TOLAND, William [27; Omaha] md. Elizabeth WHELAN [17; Omaha] on 24 Feb 1862. Off: O'GORMAN. Wit: Emma WILLIAMS, Mrs. WHELAN.

TOLIVER, Dalton R. [21; Jefferson, IA; b: Illinois; f: Isam TOLIVER; m: Matilda RUNNELS] md. Sarah or Maggie MOSTILLER [17; Jefferson, IA; b: Indiana; f: Peter MOSTILLER; m: Ruth A. CHAD] on 24 Mar 1871. Off: GIBSON. Wit: John GRAY; R. Burns DURALL. Age of consent, Peter MOSTILLER and Miss? Ruthan MOSTILLER, "lawful patents of Maggie", age 16.

TOMBRINCK, Herman [32; b: Germany; f: Martin TOMBRINCK; m: Catharine HOCHS] md. Katharina CISEINER [CISAR] [24; b: Bohemia; f: John CISEINER [CISAR]; m: Franciska HVEZDA] on 2 Jun 1878. Off: SHAFFEL. Wit: Antonie VEDESHAL, Michael MAILANDT.

TOMNEY, Patrick [39; Douglas Co.] md. Elizabeth A. BURTON [23; Douglas Co.] on 30 Jan 1866 at the Court House. Off: HASCALL. Wit: Frank MURPHY, A. CROOKS.

TOMPSETT, Isaac [24: Douglas Co.; b: Canada; f: George TOMPSETT; m: Philadelphus POWELL] md. Elizabeth A. RICH [20; Douglas Co.; b: Canada; f: Thomas RICH; m: Susan COLERIDGE] on 11 Jul 1876. Off: CLARKSON. Wit: Thomas RICH, Jason RICH.

TOMPSON, John [31; Omaha] md. Rachael STEWART [18; Omaha] on 31 Oct 1867. Off: KUHNS. Wit Ennis SYPHAX, Susan WYNN, et al.

TONAR, Terrence [23; b: Ireland; f: Redman TONAR; m: Elizabeth QUEEN] md. Mary McDONALD [23; b: Ireland; f: Thomas McDONALD; m: Mary KINLEN] on 3 Sep 1878. Off: COLANERI. Wit: Jennie BROWN, W.J. HANRAHAN.

TONDER, Peter Peterson [24; Omaha; b: Denmark; f: Nels Nelson TANDER; m: Anna NELSON] md. Dorothea M. NELSON [28; Omaha; b: Denmark; f: Jeppea NELSON; m: Sarah S. NELSON] on 5 Oct 1875. Off: HANSEN. Wit: A. NELSON, Maran NIELSON.

TOPE, Sylvester P. [26; Douglas Co.; b: OH: f: James TOPE; m: Eliza MURRAY] md. Jennie B. TIMPERLY [21; Douglas Co.; b: NE; f: John TIMPERLY; m: Mary TIMPERLY] on 31 Jul 1881 at John TIMPERLY's. Off: SPENCER. Wit: Augustus

WEAKS, Douglas Co., Alice TIMPERLY, Douglas Co.

TORMEY, Thomas [28, Douglas Co.; b: Ireland; f: Barney TORMEY; m: Mary DYER] md. Mary CONVEY [18; Sarpy Co.; b: Ireland; f: Patrick CONVEY; m: Bridget WALSH] on 7 Dec 1874 at the Cathedral. Off: MALLOY. Wit: Peter MALONE; Annie HUGHES.

TOUHY, Patrick [30; Grand Island; b: Ireland; f: Michael TOUHY; m: Mary MALONEY] md. Kate SLOAN [28; Ashland Co, OH; b: Ashland Co., OH: f: John B. SLOAN] on 4 Oct 1870. Off: GIBSON. Wit: Henry F. BAND; Eleazer HALE.

TOUSLEY, Jason W. [23; Omaha; b: NY; f: J.W. TOUSLEY; m: Samantha E. WELLS] md. Ella E. BURLINGHAM [21; Omaha; m: Mary ----] on 31 Jan 1875. Off: WRIGHT. Wit: J.W. TOUSLEY, John H. TOUSLEY.

TOVEY, Thomas [24; Omaha] md. Mariah BANKS [19; Omaha] on 29 Mar 1868. Off: STUCK. Wit: John DAVIS, Frank MURPHY.

TOWLE, Albert L. [30; Omaha; b: Salem, MA; f: Abraham TOWLE; m: Mary WILSON] md. Mary W. HARRIS [18; Omaha; b: Des Moines, IA; f: George HARRIS; m: Mary CROSE] on 9 Oct 1869. Off: BETTS. Wit: Rev. Jno. R. RIPPEY, Mr. MEEKER.

TOWN, George S. [23; Omaha; b: MN; f: Saylon TOWN; m: Louisa REED] md. Emily E. PACE [18; Omaha; b: OH; f: Edward PACE; m: Mahoea LONG] on 22 Jun 1881. Off: BENEKE. Wit: J.C. GREEN, John B. CHIPMAN.

TOWSLEY, John H. [23; Saratoga Pct., Douglas Co.; b: Columbia Co, NY; f: John W. TOWSLEY; m: Eunice S. WELLS] md. Ellen M. CAMPBELL [20; Omaha; b: Walworth Co., OH: f: Duncan CAMPBELL; m: Susannah BROWN] on 4 June 1872. Off: SHINN. Wit: J.P. COCHRAN; John D. CAMPBELL.

TOY, Thomas [23; Omaha; b: Canada; f: John TOY; m: Elizabeth JOHNSON] md. Agnes RYAN [16; Douglas Co.; b: Douglas Co.; f: Thomas RYAN; m: Ann McCABE] at the Catholic Cathedral of Omaha on 9 Feb 1879. Off: COLANERI. Wit: John J. O'ROURKE, Margaret TOY. Age consent given by Thomas RYAN, father of the bride.

TRACY, John [27; Omaha; b: Ireland; f: Christopher TRACY; m: Ann FARLY] md. Bridget FARRELL [34; Omaha; b: Ireland; f: Phillip FARRELL; m: Margaret DIGNAM] on 24 Jan 1875 at St. Philomena's Cathedral. Off: JENNETTE. Wit: James DUFFY, Kate POWER.

TRACY, William [24; Omaha; b: Scotland; f: Timothy TRACY; m: Jane WATT] md. Mary BAGLEY [21; Omaha; b: Omaha; f: John BAGLEY; m: Mary WREN] at the Catholic Cathedral of Omaha on 2 Feb 1879. Off: COLENERI. Wit: Mary BAGLEY, Michael CLAREY.

TRAELSON, Andrew [31; Omaha; b: Denmark; f: Traels RASMUSSEN; m: Kirsten PETERSON] md. Hanne M. SORENSEN [24; Omaha; b: Denmark; f: Soren MADSEN; m: Maren HANSEN] on 3 Jan 1880, Vor Frelsers Church. Off: EYDESEN. Wit: M. PETERSON, S. MADSEN.

TRAILL, David B. [37; b: Scotland; f: David TRAILL; m: Isabelle BOWMAN] md. Agnes M. FRANCE [30; b: New York; f: James FRANCE; m: Annie MILL] on 8 Nov 1878. Off: HARSHA. Wit: Wm. FRANCE, J.S. FRANCE.

TRANGER, Newberry B. [29; Fort Omaha; b: Pennsylvania; f: Frederick TRANGER; m: Maria BRUNNER] md. Ellen Helena ROACH [20; Fort Omaha; b: London, England; f: William ROACH; m: Margaret MURPHEY] on 24 Nov 1880, Holy Family Church. Off: QUINN. Wit: Edward McGURK, Hanna DONEHUE, both of Fort Omaha.

TRAVER, John R. [45] and Marth HURLEY [36] license issued on 1 Apr 1857. No marriage record. Off: SCOTT. Age consent by Jessee SHOEMAKER.

TREACY, John [26; Omaha; b: Scotland; f: Timothy TREACY; m: Jane WATT] md. Margret BREW [19; Omaha; b: Scotland; f: John BREW; m: Violat HAMILTON] on 1 May 1876 at the Bishop's House. Off: BYRNE. Wit: William GENTLEMAN, Elizabeth TRACY.

TREAT, George S. [23; Atlantic, IA; b: PA; f: Jason A. TREAT; m: Mary Ann SAWYER] md. Dencie A. NILES [20; Schyler; b: PA; f: Arthur G. NILES; m: Sally WILMARTH] on 15 Dec 1875. Off: PARDEE. No witnesses given. (License issued 13 Dec 1875. Certificate dated Dec 1876. Recorded 12 Sep 1876.)

TREAT, George S. [23; Atlantic, IA; b: PA; f: Jason A. TREAT; m: Mary Ann SAWYER] and Dencil A. NILES [20, Schuyler; b: PA; f: Arther G. NILES; m: Sally WILMOOTH] license issued on 15 Dec 1876. No marriage record. Off: PEABODY.

TREITSCHKE [FRITSCHE], Julius [24; Omaha; b: Germany; f: August TRIETSCHKE [FRITSCHE]; m: Henrietta WILDER] md. Mrs. Katharina DREXEL [28; Omaha; b: Missouri] on 22 Dec 1872. Off: DIECKMANN. Wit: F. MILIUS; Julius WILDE.

TRENKLE, Hermann [21; Omaha; b: Germany; f: Joseph TRENKLE; m: Leva KLUUSMAN] md. Annie OBERUNDER [19;

Omaha; b: Germany; f: John OBERUNDER; m: Mary YAGLER] on 25 Dec 1871. Off: TOWNSEND. Wit: William AUST; Rosa OBERUNDER.

TRESLER, John L. [22] md. Mary E. WILSON [18] on 10 Apr 1867 at the Court House. Off: HASCALL. Wit: W. WILSON, Judge BRIGGS.

TREYNOR, William H. [23; Council Bluffs; b: Iowa; f: Thomas P. TREYNOR; m: Mary T. SMITH] md. Lizzie B. TROUT [19; Omaha; b: Pennsylvania; f: Russell M. TROUT; m: Sarah J. SILVERS] on 25 Jan 1879. Off: BEANS. Wit: Sam'l. BURNS and wife, Russell M. TROUT and wife.

TRIMMER, John [47; Omaha; b: York Co., PA; f: David TRIMMER; m: Katie MILLER] md. Mrs. Malvina JEFFERS [34; Omaha; b: Connecticut; f: John BLISS; m: Malvina BANKRUFT] on 5 Jun 1869. Off: HYDE. Wit: J.R. MANCHESTER, Lewis REED.

TRISIER, Emanuel [31; Mills Co., IA; b: Ohio; f: Isaac TRISIER; m: Nancy WILLIAMS] md. Susan SPRAUWL [27; Wyoming, NY; b: Wyoming, NY; f: Samel SPRAUWL; m: Sarah CRAWFORD] on 6 Jun 1870. Off: DelaMATYR. Wit: Mr. and Mrs. TRISLER.

TRISLER, James M. [22; Florence; b: Indiana; f: Isaac TRISLER] and Hilda RICKER [20; Maine; b: Maine; f: Hubbard RICKER] license issued on 3 Jan 1870. Off: GIBSON.

TRITELY, Lorenz [24: Douglas Co.; b: Bohemia; f: Frank TRITELY; m: Anna SCHLIZINGER] md. Mary ULBORN [22; Douglas Co.; b: Bohemia; f: Jim ULBORN; m: Mary COREL] on 22 Jul 1876. Off: SEDGWICK. Wit: J.N. PHILLIPS, J.T. GRIFFIN.

TROTT, Ferdinand [23; b: Wisconsin; f: August TROTT; m: Catharine STOCK] md. Louisa GEWINNER [21; b: Boston; f: George GEWINNER; m: Victoria SCHNEIDER] on 12 Dec 1878. Off: LIPE. Wit: Otto GEWINNER, Gennie M. HUNT.

TROUT, J.W. [32; Omaha; b: Virginia; f: John TROUT; m: E. MASON] md. Martha A. SKELTON [20; Omaha; b: Iowa; f: James SKELTON; m: Bertha CASE] on 12 Jun 1877. Off: FISHER.

TRUELSEN, Thomas [23; Omaha; b: Germany; f: Thomas TRUELSEN; m: Margaret HAGGE] md. Margaret DIERKS [22; Omaha; b: Germany; f: Joh DIERKS; m: Elsabe SCHERNER] on 25 Aug 1874. Off: PEABODY. Wit: Hans HAGGERS; Henry TRUELSEN, Millard.

TRUEMAN, Gardner C. [Omaha] md. Mary Elizabeth McKENNA [17; Omaha] on 27 Dec 1864. Off: O'GORMAN. Wit: John WHELAN, step-father of the bride, Catherine

HAPETTOR. Age consent given by step-father and mother of the bride.

TRUMBULL, William [30; Omaha; b: IL; f: R.M. TRUMBULL; m: K.E. POTTS] md. Eva HUBBARD [22; Omaha; b: MI; f: E. HUBBARD; m: Emma ROE] on 2 Mar 1876. Off: GAYLORD. Wit: Emma NEWCOMB, Mrs. Mary W. GAYLORD.

TSCHONIDSCH, John [38; Omaha; b: Austria; f: George TSCHONIDSCH; m: Barbara SVETASCH [SVITAK]] md. Anna DLOUHY [27; Omaha; b: Bohemia; f: Joseph DLOUHY; m: Rosa VINCUC] on 26 Mar 1880. Off: BARTHOLOMEW. Wit: Adolph BOUKL, Frank HARIVIORT [HARVAT].

TUCKELSON, Nils [44; Omaha; b: Denmark; f: Tuckelson JOHNSON; m: Ann M. HANSEN] md. Ann M. CHRISTENSEN [28; Omaha; b: Denmark; f: Christian CHRISTIANSEN; m: Annie K. NELSON] on 11 Jan 1870. Off: GIBSON. Wit: N. LARSON; Thos. SWOBE.

TUCKER, Albert [30; Omaha] md. Margery M. ORCHARD [23; Omaha] at 8 PM, 1 Jan 1863 at DIMMICK's residence. Off: DIMMICK. Wit: Mr. and Mrs. A.R. ORCHARD.

TUCKER, Charles S. [50; Chicago; b: Boston, MA; f: William TUCKER; m: Mary Ann KIRBY] md. Emma F. KENNEDY [30; Omaha; b: Milton, MA; f: Jason F. KENNEDY; m: Jane Doggett CAMPBELL] on 22 Jan 1874 at Col. BURNHAM's house. Off: GAYLORD. Wit: Lyman RICHARDSON; Mrs. Martha PARMELEE.

TUCKER, James [23; Florence] and Betsey LERWILL [21; Florence] license issued on 26 May 1860. No marriage record. Off: ARMSTRONG.

TUCKER, Joseph [25; Omaha; b: Germany; f: August TUCKER; m: Mary STOPFFEL] md. Caroline STRICKLINE [23; Omaha; b: Germany] on 9 June 1873. Off: BRANDES. Wit: Henry LANER; Mrs. Agnes KROLL.

TUCKER, Reginald [30; Custer Co., NE; b: Bermuda; f: W.T. TUCKER; m: Elizabeth HIGINBOTHOM] md. Sophia B. MILLS [25; Joplin, MO; b: Kansas; f: James MILLS; m: Sarah BOOTH or BOONE] on 19 Jan 1878 at St. Marks Church, Omaha. Off: PETERSON. Wit: William Tudor TUCKER, Hettie L. TUCKER.

TUCKER, W. Tudor [72; Omaha; b: Bermuda Island; f: William TUCKER; m: Hesta TUCKER] md. Rosalie MASTERS [32; Omaha; b: Bermuda Island; f: William MASTERS; m: Maria BLUCK] on 24 May 1880, St. Mark's Church. Off: PATERSON. Wit: Mrs. Louis WAMBSGANS, E.C. COOPER.

TUCKER, Wm. H. [33; Custer Co., NE; b: Bermuda; f: W.T. TUCKER; m: Elizabeth HIGINBOTHOM] md. Cecelia A. MASTERS [29; b: Bermuda; f: W.L. MASTERS; m: Maria BLUCK] on 6 Jul 1878. Off: WILLIAMS. Wit: Mrs. HIGGS, Hetty TUCKER.

TUNISON, David O. [41; Sarpy Co.; b: NY; f: Garret B. TUNISON; m: Prudence VORHEES] md. Bertha CASE [36; Douglas Co.; b: IN; f: John CASE; m: Sarah CALDWELL] on 24 Feb 1876. Off: PARDEE. Wit: C.R. MANSFIELD, Mrs. A.W. FULLRIEDE.

TUNNELL, Albert M. [31; b: Virginia; f: George TUNNELL; m: Hannah G. NICHOLSON] md. Harriet M. THOMPSON [24; b: Canada; f: John E. THOMPSON; m: Harriett M. SIMMONS] on 4 Apr 1878 at the residence of A.L. GIBSON. Off: CLARKSON. Wit: S.I. HOWELL, M.F. SPEARS.

TURMAN, Z.B. [40; Fontanelle, Dodge Co.] md. Catherine A. GUSTINE [22; Omaha] on 1 Mar 1860. Off: SMITH. Wit: Jacob ADRIANCE, H.L. DAVIS.

TURNER, Arthur [colored; about 28; Omaha] md. Sarah TODD [colored; 18; Omaha] on 26 Dec 1866 at Mr. LEWIS' house. Off: FLORKEE. Wit: Jeremiah THOMPSON, Gospel LANEY.

TURNER, James [25; Omaha; colored; b: Georgia; f: Robert TURNER; m: Filius TURNER] md. Mary DAVIS [23; Omaha; colored; b: Virginia; f: Champ GILBERT; m: Louisa] on 19 Aug 1873. Off: BALLON. Wit: Henry WALKER; Elisabeth WALKER.

TURNER, James [31; b: Georgia; f: Robert REED; m: Fillis TURNER] md. Eliza FOSTER [18; b: Missouri; f: ----- FOSTER; m: Romania BROWN] on 17 Sep 1878. Off: WATSON. Wit: Birde's family and others, John SIMPSON, Thomas CAMBEL, Ada HOOK, Eliza NELSON.

TURNER, William R. [36; Elkhorn City; b: New Jersey; f: Emanuel TURNER; m: Isabel ROSS] md. Jennie WILCOX [24; Elkhorn City; b: New York; f: Dudley WILCOX; m: Kezia TOWNSEND] on 24 Nov 1870 at Elkhorn City. Off: ADRIANCE. Wit: L.H. WILCOX, Elkhorn City; Addie R. WILCOX, Elkhorn City.

TURTLE, William [45; Omaha; b: England; f: William TURTLE; m: Jane CLABROUGH] md. Mrs. Annie EVERETT [39; Omaha; b: Ireland; f: John COLLINS; m: Johanna MAHONEY] on 15 Dec 1881. Off: MILLSPAUGH. Wit: John TURTLE; Mary TURTLE.

TUTTLE, James [19; Omaha; b: MO; f: Preston M.C. TUTTLE; m: Sarah J. LOGAN] md. Sarah WHITE [17; Omaha; b: IL; f: William WHITE; m: Ruth A. SCOVELL] on 19 Sep 1875 at 410 Farnham Street. Off: GAYLORD. Wit: R.E. GAYLORD, Harry WHITE. Age consent given by father of the groom and father of the bride.

TUTTLE, John M. [20; Omaha; b: Missouri; f: P.M.C. TUTTLE; m: Sarah LOGAN] md. Louisa RIPLEY [18; Omaha; b: Ohio; f: John RIPLEY; m: Agnes WEBER] on 22 Sep 1879. Off: LIPE. Wit: Jennie McNIEL, Nellie McNIEL. Age consent given by P.M.C. TUTTLE, father of the groom.

TUTTLE, Peter M. [20; Omaha; b: MO; f: P.M.C. TUTTLE; m: Sarah J. LOGAN] md. Lizzie B. KECK [19; Omaha; b: PA; f: John C. KECK; m: Elizabeth SCHALLEN] on 2 May 1881. Off: MILLSPAUGH. Wit: John PALMER, Lizzie TUTTLE. Age consent given by father of the groom.

TUTTLE, Thomas T. [27; Omaha; b: Missouri; f: P.M.C. TUTTLE; m: Sarah LOGAN] md. Jennie H. DuBOIS [20; Omaha; b: Michigan; f: P.B. DuBOIS; m: Celista MOORE] on 2 Jul 1879. Off: LIPE. Wit: E.L. EATON, Mrs. EATON.

TUTTLE, Walter [24; Saratoga, Douglas Co.] md. Elizabeth MICCLE or Elizabeth M. TOWN [18, Florence, Douglas Co.] on 13 Jun 1858. Off: BURCH. Wit: Francis TUTTLE of Saratoga, Julia M. TOWN of Florence.

TWINE, George [25; Omaha; b: Virgina; f: William TWINE; m: Louisa] md. Amanda HAYNES [37; Omaha; b: Ohio; f: William HAYNES] on 18 Oct 1874. Off: WRIGHT. Wit: Joseph M. RICHARDS; Mary H. WRIGHT.

TYLER, George [29; Omaha; b: England; f: George TYLER; m: Jane PRICE] md. JOHN [29; Omaha; b: England; f: Thomas JOHN; m: Sarah COZZENS] on 13 Nov 1872. Off: TOWNSEND. Wit: William H. IJAMS; Mrs. Mary IJAMS.

TYLER, William Henry [23; Omaha; b: England; f: George TYLER; m: Jane PRICE] md. Sarah Ann MORGAN [22; Omaha; b: England; f: Walter MORGAN; m: Mary GEORGE] on 13 Nov 1872. Off: TOWNSEND. Wit: William H. IJAMS; Mrs. Mary IJAMS.

TYRREL, A.C. [35; Madison, NE; b: MA; f: Franklin Y. TYRREL; m: Ann Maria] md. Josie SUMPTION [31; Ridgeville, IN; b: IN; f: Robert H. SUMPTION; m: Berilla WARD] on 5 Oct 1881. Off: CHADWICK. Wit: F.P. GABB, Eugenia KINGMAN.

UHLIG, Otto [26; Sidney; b: Germany; f: C.A. UHLIG; m: Johanna] md. Louisa JOHANSON [21; Omaha; b: Sweden] on 3 Feb 1875. Off: PUTNAM. Wit: F.W. HIRST, H.C. DEAR.

UHLMAN, Rudolph [Douglas Co.] and Lisette DOLL [Douglas Co.] license issued on 27 Jun 1863. No marriage record. Both of legal age. Off: DICKINSON.

UMATHIM, Sephen [22; Omaha; b: Hungary; f: Joseph UMATHIM; m: Mary KOLLNAKER] md. Mary ZIMMERMAN [18; Omaha; b: Hungary; f: Powell ZIMMERMAN; m: Magdalena SMITH] on 22 Sep 1881 at the German Catholic Church; Off: GLAUBER; Wit: Charles KOHLMEYER, Eva KOHLMEYER.

URLAN, Frederick Wm. [29; Omaha] md. Catharine CAPPIUS or CAPPINS [19; Omaha] on 18 May 1867. Off: BROWN. Wit: Frederick W. BODINGER, Otto CHRISTMAN, Mrs. Catherine CLAY.

UTERMAN, Jurgen [33; Washington Co., NE; b: Germany; f: Hinrich UTERMAN; m: Magaretha SCHROEDER] md. Magdalena HAGGE [23; Omaha; b: Germany; f: Marx HAGGE; m: Magdalena HARTE] on 27 Nov 1879. Off: BENEKE. Wit: Henry SIERT, N.C. RIECKEN.

VALENTINE, Edward K. [22; Omaha] md. Frances A. CRAWFORD [18; Omaha] on 1 Mar 1866. Off: SLAUGHTER. Wit: Mr. and Mrs. CRAWFORD, parents of the bride.

Van CAMP, Albert E. [29; Omaha; b: Canada; f: Ira Van CAMP; m: Phoebe L. BURKE] md. Helen or Ellen BROWN [32; Omaha; b: Iowa; f: Wm. BROWN; m: Martha A. PATTERSON] on 25 May 1897. Off: JAMESON. Wit: Abel JOHNSON, Mrs. Sarah S. JOHNSON, both of Bluffton, OH.

VAN CAMP, Ira [42; Omaha; b: Darlington, Canada West; f: Jesse VAN CAMP; m: Clarasa PRICE] md. Mrs. Sara Virginia COWAN [36; Omaha; b: Cambridge, OH; f: Joseph BUTE; m: Mary SMITH] on 5 Jul 1870. Off: DIMMICK. Wit: Mrs. J.R. PORTER; Mrs. F.M. DIMMICK.

VANDERVEER, Charles E. [24; Omaha; b: New Jersey; f: William B. VAN DERVEER; m: Sarah WEISE] md. Charlotte BOYLES [21; Omaha; b: Wisconsin; f: Squire BOYLES; m: Millie BYERS] on 1 July 1870. Off: KUHNS; Wit: Mrs. Frank E. BROWN; Mrs. H.W. KUHNS.

VAN DUSUR, William [26; Omaha; b: New York; f: Robert VAN DUSUR; m: Hepsabeth FOX] md. Alice EMONDSON [21; Omaha; b: England; f: Charles EMONDSON; m: Elizabeth PARKINSON] on 19 Apr 1877. Off: ANDERSON. Wit: C.B. MANSFIELD, E. STEINBERG.

VAN DYKE, Marcus [26; Grand Island; b: Ohio; f: Abijah Van DYKE; m: Silvia LAURENCE] md. Maria A. JEROME [30; Grand Island; b: Ohio; f: Charles JEROME; m: Sally OWENS] on 28 Oct 1874. Off: PEABODY. Wit: C.L. BRISTOL; E.B. KNOX.

VAN HORN, James J. [38; Mt. Gilead, OH; b: Mt. Gilead, OH; f: Craven O. VAN HORN; m: Mary EMERSON] md. Margaret E. WILSON [21; Omaha; b: Weston, MO; f: Robert WILSON; m: Mary E. HARRIS] on 18 April 1873 at St. Barnabas Church. Off: HAMMOND. Wit: Rob WILSON; Mrs. HOLMES; Chas. T. CRARY; Gen. Geo. D. RUGGLES; "and many others".

VAN KURAN, Andrea S. [29; Omaha; b: Rochester, NY; f: Isaac VAN KURAN; m: Cynthia M. CARPENTER] md. Carrie LOVELAND [21; Omaha; b: Farmington, OH; f: Edwin LOVELAND; m: Harriet C. BENTON] on 29 Aug 1873. Off: SHERRILL. Wit: John H. KELLOM; Charles A. BALDWIN.

VAN LANINGHAM, Cyrus J. [40; Douglas Co.] md. Kate KELLY [22; Douglas Co.] on 17 Dec 1867. Off: KUHNS. Wit: R.N. MORROW, L.C. LEEDS, et al.

VAN NOY, William H. [22; Omaha; b: Indiana; f: Henry A. VAN NOY; m: Melinda C. MOONEY] md. Isabella SHEEHEY [18; Omaha; b: Canada; f: Christopher SHEEHEY; m: Mary] on 17 July 1873. Off: CURTIS. Wit: James O'BRIEN; Jenny MAY.

VanCAMP, Charles L. [28; Omaha; b: Canada; f: Levi VanCAMP; m: Sarah BURK] md. Grace L. BRADLEY [29; Omaha; b: OH; f: J.H. BRADLEY; m: Grace RUSH] on 25 Sep 1876. Off: A. WRIGHT. Wit: Edwin PATRICK, Dr. I. VanCAMP.

VanCAMP, Ham B. [21; Douglas Co.; b: Canada West; f: Ira VanCAMP; m: Phoebe BURK] md. Maggie HENNESEY [18; Douglas Co.; b: Canada West; f: John HENNESEY; m: Ellen KELLEY] on 27 Aug 1876. Off: ANDERSON. Wit: C.C. SPERRY, Mrs. SIMPSON. Albert VanCAMP signed the affidavit.

VANDANECKER, James B. [23; Omaha; b: Baltimore, MD; f: George VANDANECKER] md. Mary DUGAN [19; Omaha] on 14 July 1870. Off: PORTER. Wit: A.C. TRUE; Mary O. BRIAN or O'BRIAN.

VanDANIKER, James B. [30; Deadwood, Dakota Territory; b: Baltimore, MD; f: Geo. W. VanDANIKER; m: Maggie S. BERNARD] md. Celia PIERSON [26;

Omaha; b: Sweden; f: Gabrial PIERSON; m: Ella NELSON] on 9 Nov 1876. Off: STEWART. Wit: H.R. LUCAS, John McARDLE.

VANDENBURG, L.H. [45; Omaha; b: Holland; f: G. VANDENBURG; m: Rikja LAMMERTSEN] md. Mrs. Margaret HUNT [49; Omaha; b: Canada; f: Andrew BERRELL; m: Elespoi FORSYTH] on 18 Sep 1876. Off: JAMESON. Wit: Charles HUNT; Mrs. G. HUNT.

VANDENBURGH, John A., M.D. [23; Omaha; b: Netherlands; f: L.H. VANDENBURGH; m: Jane MILLER] md. May DORT [20; Omaha; b: Omaha; f: A.C. DORT; m: Jane PARKS] on 11 May 1876. Off: MORGAN. Wit: L.H. VANDENBURGH, A.C. DORT.

VANDERFORD, Joseph [31; Omaha; b: Ohio; f: Alexander VANDERFORD; m: Nancy DIXON] md. Rosana BUSHEA [24; Douglas Co.; b: Iowa; f: Joseph BUSHEA; m: Mary BUSHEA] on 10 Jul 1879. Off: FISHER. Wit: Joseph NICHOLS, Jorelian RICE.

VANDERFORD, William [30; Omaha; b: OH; f: Alexander VANDERFORD; m: Nancy DIXON] md. Tillie JOHNSON [242; Omaha; b: Sweden; f: John JOHNSON; m: Mary CARLSON] on 25 Nov 1875. Off: PEABODY. Wit: C.H. NICHOLS, Mabel L. PEABODY.

VanKURAN, Arthur J. [28; Omaha; b: MA; f: Isaac VanKURAN; m: Cynthia M. CARPENTER] md. Amelia J. PHELPS [b: Canada; f: Alfred W. PHELPS; m: Emily PRITCHARD] on 29 Dec 1881. Off: HARRIS. Wit: Mr. and Mrs. Isaac VanKURAN, Mr. and Mrs. Alfred PHELPS.

VanORMAN, Oristen U. [25; Omaha; b: Ohio; f: Oliver O. VanORMAN; m: Chloe A. BECKET] md. Deuce A. NILES [24; Omaha; b: Pennsylvania; f: A.G. NILES; m: Sarah WILMARTH] on 19 Nov 1880. Off: JAMESON. Wit: Joseph F. HORAN, Emma R. NILES.

VANOUS, Joseph, Jr. [23; Omaha; b: Bohemia; f: Joseph VANOUS; m: Mary WAVRIN] md. Mary RUZICKA [20; Omaha; b: Bohemia; f: Joseph RUZICKA; m: Katharina HORAK] on 6 Jun 1881. Off: BENEKE. Wit: Wenzel SMITH, Mary VANOUS.

VANSCOY, Noah D. [21; Rockville; b: WV; f: John VANSCOY; m: Emily SLAGLE] md. Rose WEBSTER [20; Jasper Co., IA; f: Charles WEBSTER; m: Mary FLEMING] on 22 May 1876. Off: SEDGWICK. Wit: J.G. BRADISH, Douglas Co., F.A. SACKETT, Douglas Co.

VARNA, Mathew [24; Omaha; b: Bohemia, Austria; f: Thomas VARNA; m: Barbara MELACEK [MILACEK]] md. Annie KADIS [20; Omaha; b: Bohemia, Austria; f:

Joseph KADIS; m: Annie ULIHRACH] on 28 Sep 1870. Off: KUHNS. Wit: Mathew NERAD; Frank BOKAK [BOHAC].

VARNER, Ollavis [22; Douglas Co.] md. Mrs. Sophia LARSON [37; Douglas Co.] on 18 Jan 1868 at STUCK's office. Off: STUCK. Wit: Knudt NELSON, Ben SHEEKS.

VAUCHMA, W. [25; Omaha; b: Bohemia; f: John VAUCHMA; m: Anna URBANEK] md. Francis SMIRSH [20; Omaha; b: Bohemia; f: Jacob SMIRSH; m: Francis MACA] on 15 Mar 1881. Off: BENEKE. Wit: F.J. SMIRSH, Gust FALK.

VEIL, Joseph [26; Omaha] md. Theresia BUNTRICK [18; Omaha] on 22 Feb 1869. Off: MEYER. Wit: H. LANGLOTZ, Frederica LANGLOTZ.

VEIRS, Brice [35; Douglas Co.; b: Virginia; f: Daniel VEIRS; m: Harriet SLINGLAND] md. Ellen F. WEBBER [21; Omaha; b: New Hampshire; f: Alfred T. WEBBER; m: Mary A. WEBBER] on 20 Sep 1871. Off: KUHNS. Wit: Samuel MORE, Douglas Co.; Thomas B. ELLINGWOOD.

VELETA, Albert [19; b: Bohemia; f: Vencil VELETA; m: Mary VELETA] md. Mary BOWER [18; Wahoo; b: Bohemia; f: Jon BOWER; m. Anna NOVAC] on 27 Apr 1878. Off: BARTHOLOMEW. Wit: Wm. L. PEABODY, Wm. J. CONNELL.

VERMILLIAN, William P. [30; Omaha; b: Ohio; f: Charles VERMILLIAN; m: Ann KING] md. Mrs. Sarah A. LANGSTAFF [22; Omaha; b: Illinois; f: Wileus HEWIT; m: Sarah A. ROBESON] on 1 Feb 1870. Off; GIBSON. Wit: George M. O'BRIEN; Wm. TRAHER.

VESTEEG, Arie [22] and Jane MEYER [16] license issued on 4 Feb 1869. No marriage record. Off: HYDE. Written age consent given by the mother because the father is dead.

VEZY, William [27; Pottawattamie Co., IA; b: McLain Co., IL; f: John VEZY; m: Nancy McINTYRE] md. Minnie E. WIGHTMAN [17; Pottawattamie Co., IA: b: Lacelle Co., IL; f: David Edward WIGHTMAN; m: Amanda MILLIKEN] on 4 Apr 1878. Off: BARTHOLOMEW. Wit: Nellie WARE of Illinois, A.N. FERGUSON.

VICKEY (VICKERY), John L. [21; Park Co., IN; b: North Carolina; f: Anderson VICKEY (VICKERY); m: Nancy SWAIN] md. Ruhanna McCOLLUM [18; Guthrie Co., IA; b: North Carolina; f: William McCOLLUM; m: Susie LAMB] on 19 Jul 1869. Off: KELLEY. Wit: Joseph LIES, D.B. TOPHAM.

VICTOR, Alexander [21; Dunlap, IA; b: Missouri; f: C.C. VICTOR; m: Elizabeth CARRY] md. Madalein HOMER [18; Dunlap, IA; b: Iowa; f: Ben. HOMER; m: Patience BENTLEY] on 30 Sep 1878. Off: WEISS. Wit: J.C. BOYD, J. McCLELLAN.

VINCENT, Thomas J. [24; Douglas Co.; b: Missouri; f: John VINCENT; m: Mary Jane EVANS] md. Mary E. ARNOLD [18; Doulgas Co.; b: Illinois; f: Evans ARNOLD; m: Matilda SWAGER] on 27 Sep 1874 at Elkhorn Station. Off: McARTHUR. Off: Geo. E. SHARPE, Valley Pct.; Mrs. James McARTHUR, Elkhorn Sta.

VISSCHER, Henry H. [36; Omaha] md. Mrs. Nancy REYNOLDS [27; Omaha] on Tuesday, 18 Oct 1859. Off: DAVIS. Wit: Clinton BRIGGS.

VISSCHER, Will L. [33; Omaha; b: KY; f: F. VISSCHER; m: E.W. LIGHTFOOT] md. Emma B. MASON [22; Omaha; b: MA; f: ---- MASON; m: ---- MANTZE] on 15 Mar 1876 at Trinity Cathedral. Off: CLARKSON. Wit: Dr. Geo. L. MILLER, Alfred SORENSON.

VLNA, Frank [23; Omaha; b: Bohemia; f: John VLNA; m: Rosaria KLEKA] md. Mary KAVAN [18; Omaha; b: Bohemia; f: Frank KAVAN; m: Theresia VELEBA] on 19 Apr 1879. Off: KOCARNIK. Wit: Wm. KAVAN, Joseph NEMEC.

VODICKA, Vaclav L. [28; Omaha; b: Bohemia; f: Jacob VODICKA; m: Anna MUNCHNA [MACHOVA]] md. Mary NEMETZ [NEMEC] [23; Saunders Co.; b: Bohemia; f: Joseph NEMETZ [NEMEC]; m: Mary] on 12 Dec 1872. Off: TOWNSEND. Wit: William H. IJAMS; John MACH.

VOGEL, Herman [56; Pottawattamie Co., IA; b: Germany; f: William VOGEL; m: Louise REINICKE] md. Ernestine BERNDT [23; Pottawattamie Co.; b: Germany; f: Carl BERNDT; m: Christiana KNOBLOCH] on 18 Oct 1880. Off: BARTHOLOMEW. Wit: Max BERGMANN, George W. DOANE.

VOLK, Barnhard [25; Addison Co., IA; b: Germany; f: Grist VOLK] md. Anna FISHER [19; b: Sioux City, IA; f: Joseph FISHER; m: Betsy MUCK] on 20 Mar 1878. Off: BARTHOLOMEW. Wit: Warren SWITZLER; Gustave BENEKE.

VOLKMAN, Jacob [Douglas Co.] and Catherine MISLER [Douglas Co.] license issued on 26 Jun 1863. No marriage record. Both of legal age. Off: DICKINSON.

VOLKNEIER, Ernst [34; Omaha; b: Germany; f: Gottfried VOLKNEIER; m: Eliza

DANIELS] md. Sarah CAMPBELL [26; Omaha; b: Ireland; f: John CAMPBELL; m: Sarah RAY] on 14 Oct 1879. Off: ENGLISH. Wit: Fred ZIPZ, Margaret RYAN.

VOLSTEDT, Henry [45; Omaha; b: Germany; f: Carsten VOLSTEDT; m: Wibke HOEFT] md. Teovile TRONOVSKA [26; Omaha; b: Germany; f: Andrew TRONOVSKA; m: Pauline FUNCK] on 20 Mar 1880. Off: BENEKE. Wit: Henry SIERT, B. LANGE.

Von TROTT, Albert [21; Omaha; b: Wisconsin; f: Augustus Von TROTT; m: Catharine STORK] md. Bertha ENGSTROM [20; Omaha; b: Sweden; f: C.A. ENGSTROM; m: Mathilda HAGLUNDH] on 18 May 1880. Off: BRISTOL. Wit: Willie WHITEHOUSE, Anna TROTT.

Von WINDHEIM, George P. [21; Omaha; b: Chicago, IL; f: Augustus Von WINDHEIM; m: Sudnah JONES] md. Josephine HENGEN [18; Omaha; b: Omaha; f: Joseph H. HENGEN; m: Elizabeth FREICHELS] on 31 Dec 1879 at the German Catholic Church. Off: GROENEBAUM. Wit: James CLAIR, Mrs. E. ELSAASER.

VON DORN [VAN DORN], Theodore L. [28; Omaha; b: Chester, NJ; f: Abraham VON DORN; m: Sarah HEATH] md. Huldah J. RENECKER [15; Omaha; b: Covington, KY; f: Andrew J. RENECKER; m: Elizabeth B. SMITH] on 5 Sep 1869. Off: KUHNS. Wit: Mrs. H.W. KUHNS, Annie CATHERWOOD.

VON KROSIGK, Heinrich G.F. [32; Douglas Co.; b: Germany; f: Anton VON KROSIGK; m: Emma VON DER MARIVITZ] md. A.M. JOHNSON [23; Omaha; b: Sweden; f: F. JOHNSON; m: A. ANDERSON] on 16 Aug 1881. Off: BENEKE. Wit: Guitar BENDORFF, Douglas Co., Dorn WIEFEER, Douglas Co.

VON WASMER, Charles S. [24; Grand Island; b: Prussia; f: William VON WASMER; m: Mary WOLLER] md. Elizabeth B. SEXAUER [19; Omaha; b: Pennsylvania; f: William SEXAUER; m: Rosalia WOOSTER] on 27 Sep 1871. Off: KUHNS. Wit: William SEXAUER; Henry LIVESEY.

VON WINDHEIM, Philipp [40; Omaha] md. Emma STANG [30; Omaha] on 5 Mar 1866 at the bride's residence. Off: KUHNS. Wit: Mrs. W.H. HUGHES, Mrs. A. SMITH; et al.

VonSTERNFELS, Oskar N. [27; Omaha; b: Russia; f: Franz J. VonSTERNFELS; m: Olga VonMAKAROFF] md. Jany JELINEK [21; Saline Co., NE; b: Wisconsin; f: Frank JELINEK; m: Antonie SPINNER] on 20 Jan 1880. Off: BARTHOLOMEW. Wit: U.L. VODICKA, John ROSICKY.

VORIS, William A. [22; Omaha; b: PA; f: E.C. VORIS; m: Julia TROXELL] and Nettie

PHELPS [19; Omaha; b: NE; f: George PHELPS; m: Anna HONSELL] license issued 9 Jul 1881. No marriage record. Off: SMITH. Affidavit signed by BERMAN.

VOSS, Henry, Jr. [29; Omaha; b: Germany; f: Henry VOSS; m: Wilhelmina K. PETERSON] md. Wilhelmina LEHMANN [19; Omaha; b: Germany; f: Peter LEHMANN; m: Katharina ARP] on 22 Oct 1881. Off: BENEKE. Wit: Henry TOSSEN, Charles LEHMANN.

VOSS, William [21; Omaha; b: Germany; f: Henry VOSS; m: Wilhelmina PETERSON] md. Bertha LEHMAN [22; Omaha; b: Germany; f: Peter LEHMAN; m: Catharine ARP] on 23 Oct 1879. Off: BENEKE. Wit: Henry VOSS, Wilhelmine VOSS.

VOWINKLE [MOWINKLE], Charles [30; Omaha; b: Germany; f: Charles VOWINKLE [MOWINKLE]; m: Rosine GOETZ] md. Pauline ROEDER [20; Omaha; b: Belleville, IL; f: Augustus ROEDER] on 20 Nov 1871. Off: BILLMAN. Wit: Aaron CAHN; C.E. BURMESTER; et al.

VREELAND, J.P. [29; Omaha; b: Kentucky; f: Geo. W. VREELAND: m: Roxanna PARKER] md. Rachael HANSOM [21; Omaha; b: Norway; f: Paul HANSOM; m: Isobel ERICKSON] on 10 Feb 1874. Off: PRESSON. Wit: Woods DUNCAN; Maggie PRESSON.

WACKHAUS, Martin [22; Pottawattamie Co., IA; b: Germany; f: Conrad WACKHAUS; m: Catharine RUERICH] md. Carry BLUMENSTEIN [16; Council Bluffs; b: Germany; f: Matheas BLUMENSTEIN; m: Elizabeth LUDWIG] on 8 Mar 1880. Off: BARTHOLOMEW. Wit: James MORRIS, Wm. J. CONNELL.

WADE, George F. [36; Cambridge, MA; b: Massachusetts; f: Rufus WADE; m: Emily A. RAND] md. Mary L. BENNETT [27; Omaha; b: New York; f: Samuel F. BENNETT; m: Cornelia S. ROGERS] on 17 Nov 1880. Off: JAMESON. Wit: W.R. BENNETT of Cambridge, MA, Sarah M. BURNS, L.F. BENNETT.

WAEGERT, Christ [32; Millard Precinct; b: Germany; f: Job WAEGERT; m: Mary PETERSON] md. Anna HARTING [22; Elk Horn Precinct; b: Germany; f: Thomas HARTING; m: Katharina PAULSON] on 17 Dec 1880. Off: BENEKE. Wit: John LEMKE, Henry SIERT.

WAGECK, Frederick [29; Omaha; b: Germany; f: Jacob WAGECK; m: Susannah LENZ] md. Margaaret MILLER [36; Omaha; b: Germany; f: Joseph MILLER; m: Margaret FOGEL] on 11 Aug 1873. Off: PORTER. Wit: Alex DAMON; Mrs. Rosena DAMON.

WAGNER, Friedrich Wilhelm [61; Douglas Co.; b: Germany; f: Johann WAGNER; m: Marie RADEMANN] md. Mrs. Christine HASEBROCK [62; Douglas Co.; b: Germany; f: Albert HASEBROCK; m: Christine BOLLN] on 17 Jan 1880, Saratoga Precinct. Off: BENEKE. Wit: Cornelius VER BEIST, H. VER BEIST both of Saratoga Precinct.

WAGNER, Henry [29; Omaha; b: Germany; f: George WAGNER; m: Anna PATTERSON] md. Eleanor PATTERSON [19; Omaha; b: Germany; f: John PATTERSON] on 7 Feb 1872. Off: BRANDES. Wit: Gerhard ALTHAUS; Maggie RUTHENG.

WAGNER, Henry [colored; 21; Omaha; b: Nashville, TN; f: Henderson YAUBRA; m: Rosetta WAGNER] md. Amanda WOODS [colored; 18; Omaha; b: Columbia, MO; f: Henry DUNCAN; m: Margaret WOODS] on 17 Aug 1869. Off: KUHNS. Wit: Mrs. H.W. KUHNS, Mrs. A. FINKE.

WAGNER, Jacob [29; Muscatine, IA] md. Emeline J. BOWER [18 and 6 months; Douglas Co.] on 5 Jul 1866 at TURNER's Florence office. Off: TURNER. Wit: Silvester BOWER, Elizabeth HANDY.

WAGNER, Julius [41; Council Bluffs; b: Prussia; f: Christian WAGNER; m: Anna BUNDESMAN] md. Anna SCHAEFER [26; Omaha; b: Germany; f: George SCHAEFER; m: Caroline LUDTENWARK] on 27 Nov 1869. Off: CURTIS. Wit: John LONERGAN of Elkhorn, Frances ERFLING.

WAGNER, Matthias [35; Omaha; b: Germany; f: Robert WAGNER; m: M. HOWE] md. Mary SAND [ 25; Omaha; b: Missouri] on 10 Apr 1877. Off: TIENTZ. Wit: Nicolaus SCHINNERT, Aemilia SAND.

WAGONER, John [29; Omaha; b: Germany; f: Hobert WAGONER; m: Margaret HAIR] md. Leeda HORST [20; Omaha; b: Germany; f: John HORST; m: Aleda ALLSMYER] on 19 Oct 1871. Off: GIBSON. Wit: Chas. M. CONOYER; Peter KILL.

WAHL, John [40; Saunders Co.] md. Maria LUDA [LOUDA] [38; Omaha] on 15 Feb 1869. Off: MEYER. Wit: Wenzel MAUSHARK [MARUSAK], Katarina MAUSHARK [MARUSAK].

WAHLBERG, John [32; Omaha; b: Sweden; f: John WAHLBERG; m: Annie ANDERSEN] md. Martha ANDERSEN [24; Omaha; b: Sweden; f: Andrew ANDERSEN; m: Bertha ANDERSEN] on 27 Mar 1872. Off: SUNDBORN. Wit: J.P.A. MUHR; A. SODERLUND.

WAHLGREN, Carl [30; Omaha; b: Sweden; f: Eric WAHLGREN; m: Christina POLM] md. Ulrica Charlotta TUDDEN [27; Omaha; b: Sweden; f: John TUDDEN; m: Fredrika BJORKLAND] on 23 Oct 1870. Off: SUNDERLAND. Wit: Martin OHLSON; Peter W. SUNDBORN.

WAHLSTROM, John L. [23; Omaha; b: Sweden; f: J. WAHLSTROM; m: Louise LAMSON] md. Anna O. BOHMAN [18; Omaha; b: IL; f: Gustav BOHMAN] on 6 Nov 1881. Off: FOGELSTRUM. Wit: Nils LARSON, Emma LARSON.

WAHTLER, George [25; Omaha; b: Hungary; f: By WAHTLER; m: Theresa RIPPEL] md. Elizabeth BARAK [28; Omaha; b: Hungary; f: John BARAK; m: Maria KRUDEL] on 7 Nov 1880, German Catholic Church. Off: GROENBAUM. Wit: Mr. KOHLMEYER, Mrs. KOHLMEYER.

WALCH, Joseph [27; Omaha; b: Germany; f: Michael WALCH; m: Mary PITCHER] md. Mary WECHELL [26; Omaha; b: Germany; f: Henry SCHAB; m: Rosena BANE] on 26 Nov 1870. Off: GIBSON. Wit: Gustav WINDHAM; Louis WEINSTEIN.

WALKER, Adam [colored, Omaha] md. Manda JAMES [colored, Omaha] on 9 Sep 1863. Both of legal age. Off: LEMON. Wit: Col. John RITCHIE, Mrs. Col. JAFFE, et al.

WALKER, Andrew [24; Platte Co.; b: Canada West; f: James WALKER; m: Ann BENNETT] md. Catharine O'BOYLE [22; Riverside, Cook Co., IL; b: Canada West; f: James O'BOYLE; m: Catharine McGLINN] on 31 May 1872. OFF: TOWNSEND. Wit: Frank WALKER; Catherine BOYLE.

WALKER, Edwin H. [24; Omaha; b: England; f: Thomas D. WALKER; m: Sarah HENTON] md. Elizabeth BALLINGER [19; Omaha; b: England; f: William BALLINGER; m: Elizabeth WILLIAMS] on 25 Dec 1870. Off: DIMMICK. Wit: Thomas D. WALKER; Louis F. RUF.

WALKER, George M.P. [28; Omaha; b: ME; f: A.B. WALKER; m: Mary B. DOUGLAS] md. Margaret A. GORMAN [19; Omaha; b: IN; f: Patrick GORMAN; m: Bridget GORMAN] on 25 May 1881 at St. Philomena's Church. Off: ENGLISH. Wit: Edward A. HEARON, Mary A. GORMAN.

WALKER, Henry [46; Omaha; colored; b: Winchester, VA; f: Emanuel WALKER; m: Ara Ellen MAGRUDER] md. Mrs. Elizabeth STEWART [24; Omaha; colored; b: Ohio; f: Joh HOLLY; m: Elizabeth] on 21 Apr 1873. Off:LYTLE. Wit: Joshua BUDD; John T. HOLTZMAN.

WALKER, John [27; Omaha; b: Canada West; f: James WALKER; m: Ann BENNETT] md. Eunice PRATT [24; Omaha; b: Canada West; f: John BENNETT; m: Martha CUNNINGHAM] on 15 Feb 1872.

Off: BILLMAN. Wit: A.B. NOBLE; H.S. SHELTON.

WALKER, Lanncelot [55; Omaha; b: England; f: Joseph WALKER; m: Mary S. WALKER] md. Mrs. Charlotte WALKER [41; PA; b: PA; f: Robert WALKER; m: Catharine McGUIRE] on 5 Oct 1881. Off: MAXFIELD. Wit: G.T. WALKER, Mary S. WALKER.

WALKER, Walter [25; Douglas Co.] and Rachel VIERS [24; Douglas Co.] license issued on 20 Feb 1866. No marriage record. Off: HASCALL.

WALKER, William S. [30; Denver, CO Territory] md. Mary Jane PATRICK [21; Omaha] on 16 Oct 1862 at Col. A.R. GILMORE's residence. Off: KUHNS. Wit: A.R. GILMORE, M.L. GILMORE, R.W. WILSON, J.N.H. PATRICK, et al.

WALL, Andrew [33; Omaha] md. Rosa SMALL [25; Omaha] on 2 Feb 1868. Off: KELLEY. Wit: Judge Ben SHEEKS, Thomas SWOBE.

WALL, Francis [23; Omaha; b: England; f: Patrick WALL; m: Mary HOPKINS] md. Emma FREEMAN [18; Omaha; b: England; f: Joseph FREEMAN; m: Martha ASTHMAN] on 6 Sep 1871. Off: MORRIS. Wit: S.F. GILLEN; J.M. THURSTON.

WALLACE, George Y. [23; Omaha] md. Inez C. BELDIN [20; Omaha] on 9 Jan 1868 at Trinity Church. Off: VAN ANTWERP. Wit: O.P. HURFORD, the congregation.

WALLACE, W.L. [25; Omaha; b: Texas; f: Thomas WALLACE; m: ---- FRASIER] md. Alice May DUNCAN [15; Omaha; b: Illinois; f: Charles DUNCAN; m: Odyssa SANDS] on 29 Sep 1880. Off: LIPE. Wit: Henry PARRISH, Mrs. O. ENGLE.

WALLER, F.C.B. [40; Omaha; b: England; f: George WALLER; m: Ann BECKLEY] md. Mrs. Carrie SHADLEY [40; Omaha; b: Kentucky; f: John TAYLOR; m: Mary Jane SHOEMAKER] on 26 Apr 1879. Off: FISHER. Wit: Mrs. E.M. FISHER, Mrs. Lucy SWAN.

WALLIN, Victor [46; Omaha; b: Sweden; f: Lars WALLIN; m: Johanna KAMPE] md. Carolina LILJA [23; Omaha; b: Sweden; f: Anders LILJA; m: Cajsa JOHANSON] on 16 May 1881. Off: BRANDES. Wit: E.D. McLAUGHLIN, August FISCHER.

WALLINGTON, George [26; Omaha; b: Washington, DC; f: George WALLINGTON; m: Rachel DIGGS] md. Mary HICKS [27; Omaha; b: MO (KY crossed out); f: Allen TURNER; m: Rachael CASEY] on 30 Jul 1881. Off: GREEN. Wit: John LEWIS, Alfred LEWIS.

WALLSTROM, Charles W. [22; Omaha; b: Sweden; f: A.O. PETERSON; m: Johanna C. SANDBERG] md. Charlotte W. SANDELL [25; Omaha; b: Sweden; f: Carl Gustav SANDELL; m: Anna B. PETERSON] on 19 Mar 1881. Off: FOGELSTROM. Wit: August PETERSON, Emma G. ANDERSON.

WALSH, Edward [27; Omaha; b: MO; f: Thomas WALSH; m: Ann MULDOON] md. Electa CRANE [27; Omaha; b: NJ; f: Abram CRANE; m: Margaret AYRES] on 25 Oct 1881 at the Roman Catholic Cathedral. Off: RIORDAN. Wit: Bridget J. CONNOR, Delia CLABBY.

WALSH, Edward [33; b: Ireland; f: Stephen WALSH; m: Margaret WHITE] md. Mary Jane DOAK [33; b: Philadelphia; f: Henry DOAK; m: Maria STUMP] on 8 May 1878. Off: O'BRIAN. Wit: James GALLIGAN, Teresa PURCHETT.

WALSH, Joseph [25; Omaha] md. Emilie SCHOLLE [18; Omaha] on 21 Mar 1868. Off: ROBERTS. Wit: J.C. MYER, F.W. BODINGER.

WALTER, Frank [28; Omaha] md. Louisa JUNGSTROM [22 or 23; Omaha] on 24 Dec 1868. Off: MULCAHY. Wit: Albert NELSON or NIXON, Nils or Nilson JUNGSTROM, J.F. MORTON.

WALTER, Jesse [24; Council Bluffs; b: Iowa; f: George WALTER; m: Helen CUNIS] md. Fanny HUGE [19; Council Bluffs; b: Indiana; f: J.T. HUGE; m: Mary MANDEHOUL] on 23 Jan 1880. Off: BENEKE. Wit: W.H. BROWN, J.F. YOUNG, both of Council Bluffs.

WALTER, Sanford [21; Douglas Co.; b: IA; f: Isaac WALTER; m: Reeny WILLIAMS] and Ida BARTON [19; Douglas Co.; b: IA; f: James BARTON; m: Rebba C. WHITE] license issued on 13 Jan 1876. No marriage record. Off: SEDGWICK.

WALTERS, Charles [24; Union Pct, Douglas Co.; b: Pennsylvania; f: Henry WALTERS; m: Mary FISHER] md. Jennie LUTES [18; Lincoln, Lancaster Co.; b: Pennsylvania; f: James LUTES; m: Mary WILSON] on 8 Apr 1872. Off: THURSTON. Wit: E.G. BARTLETT, Douglas Co.; J.H.L. WILLIAMS, Doulgas Co.

WALTHORN, C.H. [27; b: Michigan; f: William WALTHORN; m: Eliza THOMPSON] md. Sarah DUBOIS [24; b: Missouri; f: William DUBOIS; m: Sarah WILLIAMS] on 12 Nov 1878. Off: WRIGHT. Wit: Jennie YOUNG, Jennie KEEFE.

WALTON, Carl [33; Omaha; colored; b: Tennessee; f: Mack WALTAN; m: Francis LYANS] md. Mollie SEVENS [34; Omaha; colored] on 6 Mar 1870. Off: MORRIS. Wit: Solomon BROWN; Michael MURPHY.

WALTON, Carl [colored; 29; Omaha] md. Emma ALTON [colored [19; Omaha] on "Sunday evening before preaching", 8 Apr 1866 at WILLIAMSON's room. Off: FLORKEE. Wit: Daniel WILLIAMSON, Rev. Henry BRINGMEIER, Henney WILLIAMS.

WALTON, Charles [33; Omaha; b: Tennessee; f: Mack WALTAN; m: Francis LYONS] and Manerva REIKEN [19;Omaha; b: St. Louis, MO] license issued on 5 Feb 1870. Off: GIBSON.

WAMPLER, Christopher W. [24; Omaha; b: Philadelphia, PA; f: Michael WAMPLER; m: Sarah GANTER] md. Mar E. SNOWDEN [20; Omaha; b: Missouri; f: William P. SNOWDEN; m: Rachel LARRISON] on 22 Aug 1870. Off: KUHNS. Wit: Mrs. Martha A. BROWN; Mrs. Catherine MITCHELL.

WANDEL, George [31; Columbus; b: Germany; f: George WANDEL; m: Lizzie BERG] md. Delia WELCH [29; Columbus; b: Illinois; f: Michael WELCH; m: ----] on 7 Feb 1880, Trinity Rectory. Off: MILLSPAPUGH. Wit: Sister Mary HAYDEN, G.F. MAYOR.

WANGBERG, Peter [24; Omaha] md. Anna Christena HANSEN [20; Omaha] on 1 Aug 1867. Off: HASCALL. Wit: Edward CALLAHAN, J.H. KELLOM.

WANGBERG, Peter [27; Burt Co.; b: Norway; f: John C. WANGBERG; m: Annie PETERSON] md. Emely C. OLANDER [18; Burt Co.; b: Sweden; f: Nels OLANDER] on 1 Nov 1870. OFf: GIBSON. Wit: Samuel ADAIR; William R. TURNER, Elkhorn City.

WANTQUEST, Charles [31; Valley; b: Sweden; f: Andrew ANDERSON; m: Annie NIELSON] md. Christina OLSON [23; Valley; b: Sweden; f: L.P. OLSON; m: Annie LINDQUEST] on 20 Nov 1881 at Valley. Off: HAYLAND. Wit: Lars PETERSEN, Valley, A. ANDERSON, Valley.

WANVIG, Jonas Peter [24; Omaha; b: Norway; f: John Peter WANVIG; m: Caroline FALK] md. Selja NELSON [21; Omaha; b: Sweden; f: Ingman NELSON; m: Anna MATTSON] on 15 Mar 1873. Off: SWEDERS. Wit: Olaf NELSON; Caroline TROIL.

WARD, John L. [30; Omaha] md. Margaret M. MUSGROVE [18; Omaha] on 26 Jul 1861. Off: ARMSTRONG. Wit: Lieut. PROVOST and lady, Lieut. STRICKLAND, et al.

WARD, William M. [31; Cheyenne, WY; b: MO; f: Alexander WARD; m: Margaret MASTERSON] md. Elizabeth R. HASERODT [19; Omaha; b: PA; f: Chas.

HASERODT] on 31 Oct 1875. Off: GATES. Wit: Homer STULL, Chas. HASERODT.

WARE, Henry B. [21; Villisca, IA; b: Iowa; f: James B. WARE; m: Charlotta M. BURNETT] md. Ella M. ENGLISH [22; Villisca, IA; b: Illinois; f: Edward ENGLISH; m: Anna H. HEDLEY] on 13 Aug 1878. Off: JAMESON. Wit: Mrs. JAMESON.

WARE, Lyman Eugene [30; Omaha; b: Maryland; f: Lyman Casy WARE; m: Esther Ann HURD] md. Harriet D. McCLOUD [31; Omaha; b: Massachusetts; f: Mathew McCLOUD; m: Martha Ann REED] on 20 Apr 1880. Off: SHERILL. Wit: Myron WARE, Walter WARE.

WARING, Joseph H. [39; Omaha; b: Washington, DC; f: Joseph H. WARING; m: Martha H. MINOR] md. Annie P. STEWART [28; Omaha; b: St. Joseph, MO] on 25 Feb 1873. Off: LYTLE. Wit: Mrs. Rose GRAY; Mrs. Catherine POMEROY.

WARKENER, Nicholas [Omaha] md. Sally MISCHLER [Omaha] on 27 Apr 1864 at DICKINSON's office. Off: DICKINSON. Wit: George HARTMAN, Charles H. BROWN.

WARNER, Erastus H. [29; Washington Co.] md. Frances E.M. SEYMORE [23; Douglas Co.] on 3 Dec 1862 at Emerson SEYMORE's residence in Saratoga. Off: KUHNS. Wit: Randall A. BROWN, Sallie VAN SYCLE, Henry GRAY, Cornelia RICHARDSON, et al.

WARNER, Erastus H. [36; Omaha; b: New York; f: Hyman WARNER; m: Sarah RICHARDS] md. Ella N. BARNEY [21; Omaha; b: Maine; f: Henry BARNEY; m: Lucy WERKES] on 31 Aug 1870. Off: SHERRILL. Wit: Albert TUCKER; E.S. SEYMOUR.

WARNER, George A. [26; Omaha; b: IN; f: Alexander WARNER; m: Permilia FARRINGTON] md. Nancy McNUTT [22; Independence, KS; b: MO; f: James McNUTT; m: Eliza HAWK] on 10 Mar 1881. Off: RILEY. Wit: Amos GOTHORN, Maggie SWANSON.

WARREN, David [24; Douglas Co.] md. Sarah HANZER [17; Douglas Co.] on 29 Oct 1866. Off: ADRIANCE, of Fremont. Wit: Thos. DONAHO, John WESTON.

WARREN, George E. [26; Elkhorn City; b: New York; f: William WARREN; m: Nettie CARY] md. Jane OSTLER [19; Elkhorn City; b: England; f: George OSTLER; Edith H. ADDER] on 13 Mar 1871. Off: DANIELS. Wit: Mrs. Eliza BONNER; Mrs. Esther M. DANIELS.

WARWICK, Robert [27; Omaha; b: Pennsylvania; f: William WARWICK; m: Margaret HOLTEN] md. Bessie McNEIL [24; Omaha; b: New York; f: Sylvester McNEIL; m: Binina MOORE] on 9 Jun 1880. Off: INGRAM. Wit: J.A. INGRAM, Lettie J. INGRAM.

WASHBURN, Charles D.M. [Waukeshaw Co., WI] md. Mary J. MARTIN [Nebraska Territory] on 19 Oct 1865 at Hamilton House. Off: KUHNS. Wit: Henry COPPOCK, Mrs. Ellen BOUGHTON, Mr. and Mrs. WINDSLOW, et al.

WASHBURN, Wm. G. 29; Beatrice; b: Maine; f: George WASHBURN; m: Eliza GILLMORE] md. Flora E. WIGHT [26; b: Boston; b: Maine; f: Daniel WIGHT; m: Julia A. PEABODY] on 15 Apr 1880. Off: HARSHA. Wit: Mrs. Wm. J. HARSHA, Mrs. J.L. SMITH.

WASMER, William [Sarpy Co.] md. Dora KUHL [Sarpy Co.] on 24 Oct 1865. Off: HASCALL. Wit: Christian WASMER, Henry KOENIG.

WATERMAN, Joseph R. [25; Boston, MA; b: Roxbury, MA; f: Melzar C. WATERMAN; m: Augusta GLINES] md. Helen F. DECATUR [18; Boston; b: Roxbury, MA; f: George W. DECATUR; m: Mary RICHARDS] on 7 Jan 1880. Off: JAMESON. Wit: Mrs. JAMESON, Hattie CAMPBELL.

WATERS, Randolph H. [31; Omaha; b: IA; f: Charles R. WATERS; m: Sarah ALBROS] md. Julia Ann RICHARDSON [28; Omaha; b: IL; f: David RICHARDSON; m: Mary BURGESS] on 17 Jul 1876. Off: SEDGWICK. Wit: D.E. BURLEY, Marcia F. SEDGWICK.

WATSON, David B. [41; Omaha; b: PA; f: Thomas WATSON; m: Susan DAVIS] md. Anna Elizabeth LONG [40; Omaha; b: OH; f: Eric LONG; m: Martha JOHNSON] on 25 Apr 1881. Off: STENBERG. Wit: George A. HARRINGTON, Frank D. DOYLE.

WATSON, Gilbert P. [28; Sarpy Co.; b: MI; f: Eli WATSON; m: Betsey E. GILBERT] md. Anna McCARRAGHER [29; Washington Co.; b: Ireland (Scotland crossed out); f: Joseph McCARRAGHER; m: ---- NELSON] on 8 Mar 1876. Off: STEWART. Wit: Mrs. Emily W. STEWART, Jennie McCARRAGHER, Washington Co.

WATTS, Henry [24; Nebraska City] md. Emma SCANTLING [20; Leavenworth, KS] on 10 Sep 1867 at John ALLIAS' residence. Off: FLORKEE. Wit: Pompey ALLEN, Henry SMITH.

WEAVER, Andrew [27; Omaha; b: Pennsylvania; f: J.J. WEAVER; m: Malinda SUTLEY] md. Jennie M. HUNT [25; Omaha; b: Ohio; f: A.S.A. HUNT; m: Jane M. SEAMAN] on 1 Jul 1879. Off: JAMSEON. Wit: Sadie SPILLETT, Gertrude W. JAMESON.

WEAVER, John A. [23; Douglas Pct, Douglas Co.; b: Freeport, IL; f: John M. WEAVER; m: Rose CHADWICK] md. Clara PICKARD [21; Douglas Pct, Doulgas Co; b: Bloomington, IL; f: James W. PICKARD; m: Jane SCHOTT] on 15 Jan 1873 at Douglas Pct. Off: SHERRILL. Wit: A. CLEMENS, Douglas Pct; J.E. ROBARTS, Douglas Pct.

WEAVER, John [32; Ogden, UT; b: Pennsylvania; f: Charles WEAVER; m: Eliza HILEMAN] md. Lottie WHEELER [26; Lawrence, MA; b: England; f: John WHEELER; m: Maria WEBB] on 9 Jan 1879 at the First M.E. Church. Off: FISHER. Wit: J.A. WILLES, Mrs. E.M. FISHER.

WEBER, Adam [21; Omaha; b: Bohemia; f: Adam WEBER; m: Catherine SMITH [SMIT]] md. Kate NEMECHE [NEMECEK] [20; Omaha; b: Bohemia; f: Joseph NEMECHE [NEMECEK]; m: Anna GUILICK [KULIK]] on 13 Jul 1869. Off: HYDE. Wit: A.R. HOEL, Wm. KIP.

WEBER, Emil [18; Florence; b: Illinois; f: Jacob WEBER; m: Amelia ROTTLER] md. Mary BOLINGER [18; Florence; f: Wim BOLINGER; m: Elizabeth (Mary Ann crossed out) WILLIAMS] on 28 Nov 1874. Off: STEVENSON. Wit: Thomas D. WALKER, Florence; Hannah T. CUBLEY, Florence; parents of bride. Age of consent given by father of groom.

WEBER, Jacob [34; Douglas Co.; b: France; f: John G. WEBER; m: Mary Ann RESLINGER] md. Mary O'HARA [29; Douglas Co.; b: Canada; f: Patrick O'HARA; m: Bridget MONLEY] on 6 Feb 1881 at Holy Family Church. Off: COLANERI. Wit: Alexander JOLY, Mary BOLAN.

WEBSTER, George O. [27; US Army; b: Litchfield, CT; f: E.B. WEBSTER; m: Ann E. BELDAN] md. Charlotte L. COX [29; New York; b: New York; f: Richard COX] on 24 Nov 1870. Off: GASMAN. Wit: Lt. W. COX, Ft. Laramie; Mrs. J.G. GASMAN.

WEBSTER, Luman H. [23; Omaha] md. Nellie LEWIS [22; Omaha] on 20 Nov 1866. Off: ROSE. Wit: Mr. and Mrs. E.D. LEWIS, Andrew McAUSLAND, Jennie KEYES, Mrs. Dr. VAN CAMP.

WEEKS, Charles [23; Omaha; b: IL; f: Thomas B. WEEKS; m: Ellen MOORE] md. Mrs. Mollie OATMAN [21; Omaha; b: Mt. Pleasant, IA; f: Roddley COATS; m: Henriette BOWEN] on 4 Feb 1881. Off: J.R. RICKETTS. Wit: Mrs. Betsy FOSTER, Josiah WADDLE.

WEEKS, John [23; Omaha] md. Emma H. WISE [17; Omaha] on 26 Feb 1869. Off: KERMOTT.

WEEKS, Thomas E. [25; Council Bluffs; b: Ohio; f: J.B. WEEKS; m: Emily SMILEY] md. Mary L. TANNIHILL [22; Omaha; b: Ohio; f: Lewis K. TANNIHILL; m: Lodemia EGLADDEN] on 13 Feb 1879. Off:

INGRAM. Wit: T.M. GOWDY, Nellie ROCKWELL, both of Council Bluffs.

WEEKS, Willis [25; Big Grove, IA; b: Iowa; f: Studley E. WEEKS; m: Catharine MULLER] md. Caroline FOLTHIZER [24; Big Grove, IA; b: Indiana; f: Frederick FOLTHIZER; m: Barbara POL] on 16 Feb 1874. Off: PEABODY. Wit: Allen SPOOR, Big Grove, IA; Julia A. SPOOR, Big Grove, IA.

WEHNEST, George [25; Omaha; b: Hanover, Germany; f: Charles C. WEHNEST; m: Elizabeth KOTHE] md. Annie CROSS [21; Omaha; b: Berlin, Prussia; f: William CROSS; m: Bertha MILLER] on 27 Jan 1870. Off: GIBSON. Wit: Albert CROSS; Julius BAUMER.

WEHRER, J. Louis [24; West Omaha; b: Germany; f: John WEHRER; m: Magdelena WAGNER] md. Mary THETENS [17; West Omaha; b: Germany; f: Theodore THETENS; m: Dora KRUSE] on 13 Jul 1878. Off: STRASEN. Wit: Adolph BURMESTER, Charles WEBER both of West Omaha. Age consent given by Theodore THETENS, father of the bride.

WEHRER, William [30; Cheyenne, WY Territory; b: Germany; f: John WEHRER; m: Magdalena WAGNER] md. Caroline HOFFMAN [19; b: Germany; f: Peter HOFFMAN; m: Rosa SCHMIDT] on 3 Oct 1878. Off: BARTHOLOMEW. Wit: Adolph BURMESTER, Louis WEHRER.

WEIDERKER, Andrew [26; Douglas Co.] md. Ann Elizabeth RENFER [26; Douglas Co.] on 22 Mar 1868 at MAY's residence. Off: MAY. Wit: J.M. FORRER, B.G. McCONAUGHEY.

WEINHAGEN, Paul [28; Omaha; b: Germany; f: Julius WEINHAGEN; m: Augusta MAYWALD] md. Anna STROETZEL [23; Omaha; b: Germany; f: Friederick E. STROETZEL; m: Anna L.H. HEIN] on 26 Jan 1881. Off: BENEKE. Wit: Mrs. C.C. SCHAEFFER, Louis W. HABERCOM.

WEIS, John [28; Douglas Co.; b: Germany; f: Peter WEIS; m: Ceceilia EDMOLDS] md. Annie TIMMERMANN [22; Omaha; b: Germany; f: Joachim TIMMERMANN; m: Lean] on 12 Mar 1872. Off: KUHNS. Wit: Henry NEEJER; Lewis BEINDORF.

WEIS, Philipp [St. Joseph, MO] md. Catharine S?CHICKETAINS [Council Bluffs] on 14 Aug 1865. Off: HASCALL. Wit: John S?CHICKETAINS, John EPENETER.

WEISER, Joseph [43; b: Germany; f: John WEISER; m: Maria DROLL] md. Mrs. Maria EIFLER [28; McCardle Precinct: b: Germany; f: Nicholas EIFLER; m: Maria WELLENMLCHER] on 17 Feb 1878 at the German Catholic Church. Off: GROENBAUM. Wit: Mr. LYSRINGER, Mathias NEW.

WEISS, Herman [33; Sarpy Co.] and Miss Theodore UHE [20; Douglas Co.] license issued on 27 Mar 1861. No marriage record. Off: ARMSTRONG.

WELCH, Michael [24; Omaha; b: PA; f: Patrick WELCH; m: Mary McMAHAN] md. Frances BRADLEY [21; Iowa City, IA; b: Iowa City, IA; f: Philip BRADLEY; m: Maria THOMPSON] on 29 Aug 1881. Off: WRIGHT. Wit: J.T. NESBITT, Wm. H. HOLSIZER.

WELCH, Thomas [25;Omaha; b: Ireland; f: James WELCH; m: Margaret McGRETCH] md. Bridget WARD [19; Omaha; b: Ireland; f: Michael WARD; m: Ane KELLEY] on 14 May 1874 at the Roman Catholic Cathedral. Off: LYNCH. Wit: Michael NOLAN, Council Bluffs; Mary O'KEEF.

WELDEN, Mathew [30; Omaha; b: Ireland; f: James WELDEN; m: Margaret MADDEN] md. Catherine SKULLY [24; Omaha; b: Ireland; f: Martin SCULLY; m: Ann DOYLE] on 26 Jun 1870. Off: CURTIS. Wit: Chancey W. REED; Catharine CONNELLY.

WELLER, Jacob [30; Omaha; b: Ohio; f: David WELLER; m: Lydia RITTER] and Mary ONG [28; Omaha; b: Indiana] license issued on 8 Jun 1871. Off: GIBSON.

WELLING, James M. [30; Omaha; b: Ohio; f: William H. WELLING: m: Rebecca CONNELLY] md. Mary E. COFFEY [20; Omaha; b: New York] on 20 Feb 1873. Off: STEWART. Wit: Homer FARRELL; Mrs. Emma FARRELL.

WELLINGHAM, John B. [24; Douglas Co.] md. Catharine SCHRODER [17; Douglas Co.] on 14 Jan 1868. Off: KELLEY. Wit: Mrs. Catharine WILLIAMS, John WILLIAMS, Joseph SCHRODER. Age consent given by, Joseph SCHRODER, Sr., father of the bride.

WELLMAN, Charles K. md. Irene WATKINS on 2 Jun 1863. "Both pilgrims bound for California," of legal age. Off: DICKINSON. Wit: Wm. H. WELLMAN, Charles H. BROWN, et al.

WELLS, George G. [28; Fairfield, IA; b: OH; f: Thomas WELLS; m: Mary GREGG] md. Mary S. HUNTZINGER [27; Omaha; b: PA; f: Chas. HUNTZINGER; m: Amanda KITCHEN] on 6 Sep 1881. Affidavit signed by Nicholas ITTNER and witnessed by A.M. CHADWICK, County Judge. Off: MAXFIELD. Wit: Mr. and Mrs. ITTNER.

WELLS, John B. [35; Douglas Co.] md. Mrs. Christina R. BAKER [34; Columbus] on 13 May 1868. Off: KUHNS. Wit: Mrs. H.W. KUHNS, Catharine GROSS.

WELLS, Samuel [23; Council Bluffs, IA; b: Iowa; f: William WELLS; m: Eliza MILLER] md. Louise SHAFER [22; Iowa; b: New York City; f: Hiram SHAFER; m: Margaret BERDAN] on 6 Aug 1878. Off: BARTHOLOMEW. Wit: M.H. REDFIELD, F.P. HANLON.

WELSH, Isaac [24; Sarpy Co.] and Mary Ann MELIA [16; Sarpy Co.] license issued on 12 Jul 1862. No marriage record. Off: ARMSTRONG. Age consent given by father and mother of the bride, Michael MELIA and Brighet MELIA, signed "X".

WELSH, John D. [21; Omaha; b: St. Louis; f: Edward WELSH; m: Mary MALOY] md. Mary ROLFER [22; Omaha; b: OH; f: Henry ROLFER; m: Catharine LAFERTY] on 25 Sep 1875. Off: PEABODY. Wit: George ARMSTRONG, William McPHERSON.

WELSH, William E. [27; Douglas Co.; b: MD; f: Edward WELSH; m: Mary GOLDSBOROUGH] and Sarah ALLISON [25; Omaha; b: MI; f: Daniel DORAN; m: Sarah RUTNER] license issued on 22 Apr 1875. No record of marriage. Off: PEABODY.

WENDT, Henry [27; Washington Co.; b: Germany; f: William WENDT; m: Louise FELMAR] md. Margret SCHUMACHER [18; Washington Co.; b: Germany; f: Henry SCHUMACHER; m: Dorethea BRENNER] on 6 Apr 1876. Off: SEDGWICK. Wit: Joseph ZAEFFLER, Douglas Co., S.H. RICE, Douglas Co.

WENHOLTZ, Alfred C. [30; b: Pennsylvania; f: William WENHOLTZ; m: Elizabeth BRUNER] md. Hattie FRANCE [26; Omaha; b: Iowa; f: J. FRANCE] on 15 Mar 1871. Off: DeLaMATYR. Wit: Charles DOELAR; Ellen CASEY.

WERNER, Theodore J. [31; North Bend; b: Philadelphia, PA; f: Theodore W. WERNER; m: Sarah LAVELL] md. Mary Ann HARING [31; Omaha; b; Patterson, NJ; f: David HARING] on 21 Oct 1869. Off: KERMOTT. Wit: Mrs. Amanda R. KERMOTT, Mrs. Howard COSSLEY.

WEST, Charles [24; Omaha; b: Germany; f: John J. WEST; m: Johanna PERSERLER] md. Christina PETERSON [24; Germany; b: Germany; f: Christian PETERSON; m: Johanna HANSEN] on 27 Jul 1880. Off: BARTHOLOMEW. Wit: C.A. BALDWIN, H.J. ZIEMANN.

WEST, George W. [24; Omaha] md. Adelila A. JANVIRIN [Great Falls, NH] on 19 Sep 1868. Off: PALMER. Wit: Mrs. M.B. PALMER, Addie M. PALMER.

WEST, James [24; Omaha] md. Mrs. Lucinda N. RAMSEY [25; Omaha] on 25 Dec 1867. Off: BROWN. Wit: Charles MITCHELL, Mary E. RUSSELL.

WEST, Joseph B. [32; Omaha; b: Delaware; f: James WEST; m: Rachel DAVIS] md. Marion E. BRIDGE [23; Omaha; b: England; f: Robert BRIDGE; m: Elizabeth BENTELY] on 14 Sep 1869. Off: KUHNS. Wit: C.L. FRITSCHER, Mary A. WEST.

WESTALL, William G. [23; Elkhorn Sta.; b: Philadelphia, PA; f: William WESTALL; m: Mary TWITTY] md. Anna (Annie) BUTLER [16; Elkhorn Sta; b: Missouri; f: John BUTLER; m: Amanda CAREL] on 14 Feb 1870 at Elkhorn Church. Off: LONERGAN. Wit: Andrew CAIN, Elkhorn Station; Catherine FERRY, Elkhorn Station. Age of consent given by John and Mrs. Amanda MAGUIRE.

WESTEN, Henry [22; North Platte; b: Sweden; f: Christman WESTON; m: Martha CARLSDOTTER] md. Eva ANDERSON [19; Minneapolis, MN; b: Sweden; f: Andrew ANDERSEN; m: Christine ANDERSON] on 12 Jun 1871. Off: GIBSON.

WESTERDAHL, Berndt C.E. [24; Omaha; b: Sweden; f: Ulof WESTERDAHL; m: Joanna SJOBERG] md. Hannah Carolina YUNGSTROM [24; Omaha; b: Sweden; f: N. YUNGSTROM; m: P. ----] on 18 Mar 1875. Off: HANSEN. Wit: Francis GARRETTE, 254 Douglas St., C.J. WESTRDAHL.

WESTERGREN, Swen A. [Raulings, WY Territory; b: Sweden; f: Hans WESTERGREN; m: Sicilia ANDRESEN] md. Carrie MATSON [19; Omaha; b: Sweden; f: Mats MATSON; m: Christina OLSEN] on 9 Sep 1873. Off: TOWNSEND. Wit: Solomon P. STODDARD; Mary SAISPAIR.

WESTERLIN, Nils P. [35; Dodge Co.; b: Sweden; f: Pehr ANDERSON; m: Karna SWENSON] md. Kirstin NELSON [30; Douglas Co.; b: Sweden; f: Nils NILSON; m: Elna LARSON] on 29 Sep 1871. Off: BENNETT. Wit: S.M. NELSON; Henrietta HANSEN.

WESTERMAN, Joseph A. [31; Omaha; b: Ohio; f: Jacob WESTERMAN; m: Catharine ROHN] md. Mary C. KLINCH [19; Omaha; b: Pennsylvania; f: John W. KLINCH; m: Mary C. SCHUCK] on 9 Mar 1880. Off: LIPE. Wit: Mr. And Mrs. Alexander DAEMON.

WESTPHAL, George [28; Omaha; b: Prussia; f: Jacob WESTPHAL; m: Johanna FRANK] md. Auguste KOBARG [19; Omaha; b: Prussia; f: Henry KOBARG; m: Martha KIND] on 22 Feb 1879. Off: BRANDES. Wit: Gustave WILKE, Caroline WILKE.

WESTPHAL, Vilhelm Carl [21; Omaha; b: Denmark; f: George WESTPHAL; m: Henriette MELCHIOR] md. Laura H. MICHELSON [22; Omaha; b: Denmark; f: John MICHELSON] on 30 Apr 1874. Off: PEABODY. Wit: J. MICHELSON; James M. BORGLUM.

WETMORE, Frank H. [21; Walnut, IA; b: IL; f: Geo. H. WETMORE; m: Mary ELLIS] md. Lizzie C. ELLIS [19; Adair, IA; b: Canada; f: Joseph ELLIS; m: Louise BOND] on 20 Oct 1881. Off: CHADWICK. Wit: Seth H. CLAY, York, NE, Chas W. EDGERTON.

WHALEN, James [28; Plattsmouth; b: Ireland; f: Timothy WHALEN; m: Nora CARROLL] and Mary McKEVITT [27; Omaha; b: Canada; f: Timothy McKEVITT; m: Bridgett CARROLL] license issued on 14 Feb 1879. No marriage recorded. Off: BARTHOLOMEW.

WHALEN, Jeremiah A. [32; Omaha; b: Ireland; f: Patrick WHALEN; m: Johanna RYAN] md. Catharine McNALLY [24; Omaha; b: Illinois; f: Bernard McNALLY; m: Bridget WINTERS] on 20 Apr 1880, Holy Family Church. Off: QUINN. Wit: James LAWLESS, Miss BOWERS.

WHALEY, Charles H. [Pawnee Reservation] md. Lizzie C. RICKETS [Pawnee Reservation] on the evening of 5 May 1863 at Douglas House. Both of legal age. Off: DAKE. Wit: Aurelius BOWEN of Nebraska City, Wm. MOORE of the Pawnee Reservation, Abby Catharine WILBUR.

WHEELER, George H. [21; Finnemore, WI] md. Emily A. MURDOCK [22; Omaha] on 2 Jul 1868. Off: KUHNS. Wit: Mr. and Mrs. MAYMARD, et al.

WHEELER, George R. [33; Council Bluffs; b: Vermont; f: Samuel S. WHEELER; m: Jane FENTON] md. Lois E. HORTON [18; Council Bluffs; b: Michigan; f: Edwin HORTON; m: Matilda] on 6 July 1872. Off: TOWNSEND. Wit: Robert ARMSTRONG; William J. CONNELL.

WHEELER, James C. [29; b: New York; f: T.M. WHEELER; m: Candace THURBER] md. Annie M. ROBISON [23; Jamaica, NY; b: New Brunswick; f: Henry B. ROBISON; m: Caroline BETTS] on 4 Oct 1878 at Trinity Rectory. Off: PATERSON. Wit: Lizzie SHARKEY, J.M. ROBINSON brother of the bride, of New York.

WHEELER, James H. [40; Douglas Co.] md. Adah WATE [21; Douglas Co.] on 14 Dec 1867. Off: KELLY. Wit: Rosa GREEN, Thomas GREEN.

WHEELER, John [colored; 28; Omaha; b: St. Louis, MO; f: A. WHEELER; m: Mary SISCO] md. Mrs. Johnna McFARLAND [colored; 28; Omaha; b: Zenia, OH; f: Evans MACKLAND; m: Eliza THOMAS] on 17 Jun 1869. Off: KUHNS. Wit: Docia GREEN, Mattie GOENS.

WHITAKER, Charles [57; Stratford, IA; b: Pennsylvania; f: James WHITAKER; m: Sarah SCOTT] md. Margaret M. BURCKER [55; Washington, D.C.; b: Pennsylvania; f: Henry BURCKER; m: Margaret EYSTER] on 10 Nov 1880. Off: MILLSPUAGH. Wit: Henry GIBSON, Kate E. O'BRIEN.

WHITCOMB, Burchard [21; Council Bluffs] md. Mrs. Melissa M. JOHNSON [23; Council Bluffs] on 17 Dec 1868. Off: KUHNS. Wit: William H. HARRISON, Mrs. H.W. KUHNS.

WHITE, Arthur M. [22; Valparaiso; b: Wisconsin; f: John WHITE; m: Elizabeth SNOOK] md. Lillian BITHER [22; Sun Prairie, WI; b: Wisconsin; f: Dean BITHER; m: Almaretta WILKINS] on 17 Mar 1880. Off: BEANS. Wit: Mrs. Kate MADDOX, Mrs. W.K. BEANS.

WHITE, Charles K. [29; Omaha; b: OH; f: G.W. WHITE; m: Hannah A. BARBER] md. Hattie LEIDY [22; Omaha; b: MN; f: Samuel LEIDY; m: H. WYNCKOOP] on 10 Sep 1881. Affidavit signed by John C. DREXEL. Off: MARQUETT. Wit: Fred JENKINSON, Mrs. H. MARQUETT.

WHITE, H.E. [25; Omaha; b: Ohio; f: Abraham C. WHITE; m: Harriett DOWD] md. Elizabeth E. GEARY [18; Omaha; b: England; f: George GEARY; m: Eliza WALRICH] on 13 Feb 1879. Off: JAMESON. Wit: Sadie GEARY of Calhoun, Robert R. BALIMAN.

WHITE, James L. and Anne E. LOZIER license issued on 5 Feb 1857. No marriage record. Off: SCOTT. Age consent given by E.S. LOZIER.

WHITE, James L. [35; Omaha; b: Chicago, IL; f: Thomas WHITE; m: Bridget MULLADY] md. Anna JONES [26; Omaha; b: Belleville, Canada West; f: James JONES; m: Jane McMASTER] on 27 Feb 1872. Off: BILLMAN. Wit: Chas. N. BURGDORF; Frederick LAPASH.

WHITE, James [27; Omaha; b: New York City; f: William WHITE; m: Mary ELLISON] md. Albina LEGRO [18; Omaha; b: Bohemia; f: Henry LEGRO] on 2 Jun 1870. Off: GIBSON. Wit: Jacob GISH; Jacob L. BAKER.

WHITE, Thomas [40; Omaha; b: Ireland; f: Patrick WHITE; m: Kate LEEN] md. Ellen KELLY [35; Omaha; b: Irelalnd; f: Patrick KELLY; m: Ann GALLAGHER] on 15 Aug 1869. Off: CURTIS. Wit: James BAGLEY of near Omaha, Honora BAGLEY of near Omaha.

WHITE, Thomas [41; Omaha; b: Ireland; f: William WHITE: m: Sophia WEBSTER] md. Mary CUDMORE [27; Omaha; b: Jefferson City, MO; f: William CUDMORE; m: Martha GANNAN] on 20 Feb 1871. Off: GIBSON. Wit: Luke USHER; William TRAHER.

WHITE, William O. [23; Omaha; b: Canada; f: Oliver WHITE; m: Agnes STEVENSON] md. Alice FREEMAN [19; Omaha; b: IN; f: Lindsay FREEMAN; m: Mary MOORE] on 28 Jul 1881. Off: MAXFIELD. Wit: Mrs. Mary MAXFIELD, Lizzie ELCOCK.

WHITEHEAD, Alexander [26; Creston, IA; b: Illinois; f: J.S. WHITEHEAD; m: Helan BAIN] md. Susie RICHMOND [22; Oceola, NE; b: Canada; f: William RICHMOND; m: Elizabeth BLEWETT] on 22 Oct 1879. Off: BARTHOLOMEW.

WHITEHORN, Edward [Omaha] md. Fanny DALLOW [Omaha] on 18 Dec 1863 at the bride's residence. Both of legal age. Off: DICKINSON. Wit: Ebenezer DALLOW, Marian BRIDGE.

WHITLOCK, Edward [28; Clay Co., NE; b: Connecticut; f: Henry WHITLOCK; m: Sarah BEECHER] md. Jennie SHAW [25; Clay Co., NE; b: New York; f: Charles SHAW; m: Isabell URE] on 29 May 1878. Off: FISHER. Wit: Jesse WARD, T. KENNETT or KERMOTT.

WHITLOCK, George C. [27; Omaha] md. Emily ROWLAND [24; Omaha] on 21 Jan 1869 at Trinity Church. Off: BETTS. Wit: Mr. and Mrs. M.R. WOOD, Miss WALLACE.

WHITLOCK, George [28; Omaha; b: Pennsylvania; f: John WHITLOCK; m: Ellen J. BURROWS] md. Lizzie CARLTON [20; Omaha; b: New York; f: George L. CARLTON; m: Nancy BACKUS] on 24 Dec 1874. Off: LEMON. Wit: George L. CARLTON; Nancy B. CARLTON.

WHITMORE, Charles [31; Omaha; b: Baltimore, MD; f: John P. WHITMORE; m: Jane DAVIS] md. Mary BROWN [20; Omaha; b: Illinois; f: John BROWN; m: Elizabeth] on 25 May 1872. Off: TOWNSEND. Wit: Wm. JOHNSON; John MAY.

WHITMORE, Frank [25; Valley, NE; b: Massachusetts; f: Charles WHITMORE; m: Julia CLAP] md. Mary GARDNER [29; Malone, NY; b: Scotland; f: James GARDNER; m: Jane GUY] on 12 Jun 1879. Off: CRAWFORD. Wit: J.R. HUNTER, Mrs. E.A. HUNTER, both of Denver, CO.

WHITNEY, Charles F. [21; Omaha; b: New York; f: Wm. N. WHITNEY; m: Harriet LUCKEY] md. Emma L. LOGAN [21; Omaha; b: Illinois; f: John LOGAN; m: Roxana KELLOGG] on 3 Apr 1870. Off: SHERRILL. Wit: Martha A. BARAN; James SKINNER.

WHITNEY, Charles F. [29; Des Moines, IA; b: Ohio; f: Oliver W. WHITNEY; m: Esther A. RISING and Sarah E. CURTIS [24; Bridgeport, CT; b: Connecticut; f: Burr CURTIS; m: Eunice T. GRAY] on 6 May 1872. Off: TOWNSEND. (License and application only, no marriage recorded.)

WHITNEY, Daniel [32; Omaha] md. Mary A. PERRIN [26; Omaha] on 19 Dec 1866. Off: FROST.

WICKLIFFE, William A. [30; Douglas Co.] md. Mrs. Margaret HUNT [36; Douglas Co.] on 8 May 1866. Off: ROSE. Wit: Mrs. Lizzie C. ROSE, Eliza LEWIN.

WICKWIRE, Charles [27; Omaha; b: Connecticut; f: Edward WICKWIRE; m: Nancy L. WHITNEY] md. Olivia FORD [19; Omaha; b: New York; f: Ambrose FORD; m: Mary LUCKEY] on 19 Feb 1877. Off: FISCHER. Wit: W.H. WHITNEY, Mrs. WHITNEY.

WIDGERY, James [24; Omaha; b: England; f: Isaac WIDGERY; m: Elizabeth TOZER] md. Julia BUCKNOLE [24; Omaha; b: England; f: Edward BUCKNOLE; m: Susan BARGER] on 2 Apr 1874. Off: PEABODY. Wit: Hendrick E. PAINE; Mrs. Sarah A. PAINE.

WIDSTRAND, N.J. [44; Dodge Co.; b: Sweden; f: John JOHNSON; m: Permelia METZ] md. Amelia WENNGREN [19; Omaha; b: Sweden; f: Charles WENNGREN; m: Mary JENSEN] on 16 Mar 1876. Off: SEDGWICK. Wit: Eric L. OBERG, Hedwig M. WENNGREN.

WIEMERS, James C. [29; Omaha; b: Germany; f: Henry W. WIEMERS; m: Franda Christine HELMBOLD] md. Emilie DROSTE [23; Omaha; b: Germany; f: William DROSTE; m: Julia CAPELLE] on 23 May 1872. Off: BILLMAN. Wit: Arnold PEYCKE; L.O. WEINSTEIN.

WIIG, Christopher [20; Sarpy Co.; b: Norway; f: Johan WIIG; m: Jonetta CHRISTOPHERSEN] md. Cordy JORGENSEN [29; Sarpy Co.; b: Norway; f: Jorgen SWENSEN; m: Gundhild OLSEN] on 29 Jun 1872. Off: TOWNSEND. Wit: Peter WIIG, Sarpy Co.; John D. CAMPBELL. Age of consent, Peter WIIG, over 23, brother of groom, says Christopher will be 21 on 18 Oct 1872. Parents live in Norway. Legal age there is 15.

WIIG, Peter [27; Omaha; b: Norway; f: John WIIG, Bellevue; m: Anca (Auca) JERROLD] md. Gurine WORNES [25; Omaha; b: Norway; f: Peter WORNES; m:

Mary PETERSON] on 16 Apr 1876. Off: HILMEN. Wit: Christopher WIIG, Anna S. JERVOLD.

WILBUR, John E. [23; Omaha; b: Bridgeport, CT; f: Martin WILBUR; m: Mary WHITE] md. Charlotte L. JONES [24; Omaha; b: New York, NY; f: John Calvin JONES; m: Hannah L. REED] on 9 Sep 1873. Off: SHERRILL. Wit: Mrs. Edward F. COOK; Col. Reuben H. WILBUR.

WILBURN, George W. [24; Florence] md. Mary J. REEVES [18; Florence] on 29 Apr 1866 at William REEVES' house in Florence. "...the interesting ceremony took place in the presence of and with the consent of the father and mother of the beautiful bride..." Off: TURNER. Wit: Mary TURNER, Aranetta REEVES, et al.

WILCOX, Charles H. [29; Omaha; b: Bristol, CT; f: William WILCOX; m: Sarah A. YALE] md. Sarah LONG [36; Omaha; b: Maumie, OH; f: Eric LONG; m: Martha JOHNSON] on 8 Feb 1876. Off: SEDGWICK. Wit: Frank PONN, Douglas Co., Newton WEATHERFORD, Douglas Co.

WILCOX, E. Lemuel [49; Omaha; b: Oneida Co., NY; f: Lemuel WILCOX; m: Rhoda PATTERSON] md. Lucy BRIGGS [35; Omaha; b: Connecticut; f: William BRIGGS] on 26 Aug 1869. Off: GIBSON. Wit: Pat O. HAWS, Mrs. Louisa SELLECK.

WILCOX, Jeremiah C. [32; Douglas Co.] md. Perlia J. SAUNDERS [19; Douglas Co.] on 25 Apr 1866 near Elkhorn. Off: HURLBUT.

WILCOX, Melville S. [28; Elkhorn Pct., Douglas Co.; b: Oneida Co., NY; f: Dudley WILCOX; m: Keziah TOWNSEND] md. Mary THRUSH [26; Elkhorn Pct, Douglas Co.; b: Lee Co., IA] on 26 Sep 1872 at Elkhorn City. Off: WHITE. Wit: Wm. R. TURNER, Elkhorn City; T.M. BOYER, Elkhorn City.

WILCOX, R.T. [26; Omaha; b: MI; f: F. WILCOX; m: Oliva THOMS] md. Flora ROBINSON [20; Omaha; b: IL; f: J. ROBINSON; m: Mary GORDON] on 23 Jan 1876 at CAMP's home. Off: CAMP. Wit: William CAMP, Sarah CAMP.

WILCOX, Trueman W. [28; Omaha] md. Mrs. Amanda LUELLIN [25; Omaha] on 6 Sep 1868 at Trinity Cathedral. Off: BETTS. Wit: Mrs. SMITH, Mrs. JOHNSON, the whole congregation.

WILCOX, William S. [25; Omaha; b: Michigan; f: Guy C. WILCOX; m: Nancy WEATHERBY] md. Annie HULIN [23; Omaha; b: Texas] on 28 Jun 1871. Off: DANIELS. Wit: Wm. J. HOLLINGS; T.J. LANE.

WILDE, E.R. [27; Douglas Co.; b: WI; f: C.H. WILDE; m: Emelie KENT] md. Martha HARDING [25; Harrison Co., IA; b: OH; f: James T. HARDING; m: Jane CONNER] on

22 May 1881 in West Omaha Precinct. Off: MITCHELL. Wit: W.D. EASLEY, West Omaha, Mary C. EASLEY, West Omaha.

WILEY, H.B. [23; Irvington; b: Illinois; f: A.C. WILEY; m: Maria HAMMOND] md. Hattie V. WILLIAMS [20; Irvington; b: Ohio; f: Franklin WILLIAMS; m: Catharine VERNON] on 21 Dec 1873 at Irvington. Off: FITCH. Wit: C.M. GREGORY; Halsey V. FITCH, Irvington.

WILEY, William [23; Omaha; b: Mount Vernon, OH; f: William WILEY; m: Mary REED] md. Hattie MASCRIPE [18; Omaha; b: Belleview; f: Robert MASCRIPE; m: Sarah FAIRFIELD] on 2 Jul 1875. Off: PEABODY. Wit: Will J. GATTY, Byron D. CLARK.

WILKEY, John [34; Omaha; b: IA: f: John WILKEY; m: Elizabeth CARTREL] md. Catharine WILLIAMS [44; Omaha; b: IN; f: H.S. LUDINGTON; m: Julyett] on 3 Nov 1876. Off: PEABODY. Wit: Christina BENGSTEN, Wesley or Harley M. WILLIAMS.

WILKEY, John [37; b: Ohio; f: John WILKEY; m: Elizabeth COTTER] md. Mrs. M.J. PLANE [34; b: Massachusetts; f: Richard SULLIVAN; m: Chrine LAHAL] on 28 Sep 1878. Off: WEISS. Wit: Mrs. Dora WEISS, Mrs. F. RETTY.

WILKINS, J. Wesley [29; Omaha; b: Boston, MA; f: Daniel WILKINS; m: Louisa BROWN] md. Salina BRAINLEY [27; Indianapolis, IN; b: England; f: John BRAINLEY; m: Rebecca HOLMES] on 27 Mar 1879. Off: MILLSPAUGH. Wit: Rev. Robert OLIVER of Nebraska City, Rev. James PATTERSON.

WILKINS, Walter B. [24; b: Massachusetts; f: Charles WILKINS; m: Mary Anne BUNCHER] md. Lena M. WILKINS [24; b: New Hampshire; f: Lucien WILKINS; m: Mary MILLS] on 30 Apr 1878. Off: SHERRILL. Wit: Charles WILKINS, Mrs. A.F. SHERILL.

WILKINSON, Peter [26; Oakdale, Antelope Co.; b: Indiana; f: David WILKINSON; m: Phebe LIVINGSTON] md. Nancy Jane SAFFELL [20; Jefferson Co., IA; b: Iowa; f: WIlliam SAFFELL] on 7 May 1873. Off: BALLON. Wit: D.L. THOMAS; John W. LYTLE.

WILLARD, G.W. [26; Omaha; b: Missouri; f: G.W. WILLARD; m: Mary A. JACKSON] md. N.E. PARKINS [23; Omaha; b: Wisconsin; f: J.E. PARKINS; m: Charlotte CUTHBERT] on 30 Jun 1879. Off: HARSHA. Wit: Martha VESS, W.P. WEBSTER.

WILLARD, Joseph A. [27; Genoa, NE; b: NH; f: Paul WILLARD; m: Nancy F. FOLLETT] md. Minnie WILLSON [27; Genoa, NE; b: Sweden; f: Fredrick WILLSON; m: Elizabeth ANDERSON] on 2 Jul 1881. Off: SMITH. Wit: Homer STEELL, Douglas Co., Max BERGMAN, Douglas Co.

WILLE, Christian [24; Omaha; b: Germany; f: Nicholas WILLE; m: Margaret KORTEL] md. Anna KRULOCHOGLER [18; Omaha; b: Bohemia; f: John KRULOCHOGLER; m: Anna] on 1 Aug 1874. Off: PEABODY. Wit: Wm. ALLSTADT; Charles HART.

WILLEBROOK, Jacob [33; Omaha; b: Holland; f: C. WILLEBROOK; m: C. VANSLAUS] md. Wilhelmina ENKEN [21; Douglas Co.; b: Germany; f: William ENKEN; m: Johanna HOLZEGER] on 12 Jan 1877. Off: SEDGWICK. Wit: August SUSH, John QUINLAN.

WILLIAMS, A.C. [24; Douglas Co.; b: Wisconsin; f: J.M. WILLIAMS; m: F.A. ESSMEY] md. Miss C.J. BYARS [19; Omaha; b: Missouri; f: Harold BYARS; m: Kate SANDERS] on 23 Mar 1880, Valley. Off: NEILSON. Wit: Mr. and Mrs. J.M. WILLIAMS, Mr. and Mrs. BYARS, et al, all of Valley.

WILLIAMS, Alexander [23; colored; b: Montgomery, AL; f: William WILLIAMS; m: Susan McCAW] md. Mrs? Hattie ALTON [23; colored; b: Tennessee; f: Alford ALTON; m: Matilda FRY] on 23 May 1870. Off: GIBSON. Wit: George M. ARNOLD; John E. BYRNE.

WILLIAMS, C.P.R. [26; Grand Island; b: Pennsylvania; f: Nathan WILLIAMS; m: Hannah R. FULSE] md. Mrs. Amy E. HALL [28; Omaha; b: Pennsylvania; f: George STERNE; m: Ann TAYLER] on 12 Nov 1873. Off: GARRETT. Wit: Mrs. J.M. PARKER; F.E. SMITH.

WILLIAMS, David R. [28; Omaha; b: OH; f: D.B. WILLIAMS; m: Hannah CAFFEE] md. Ellen D. FALCONER [23; Omaha; b: Scotland; f: Thomas FALCONER; m: Christina DRYSDALE] on 2 Nov 1876. Off: McCARTNEY. Wit: James FALKNER, W. HARCOMBE.

WILLIAMS, Edgar B. [21; Omaha; b: NY; f: L.B. WILLIAMS; m: Ellen VAN AERNAM] md. Hattie L. JOHNSON [19; Omaha; b: NE; f: Saul R. JOHNSON; m: Martha E. SPRATLIN] on 27 Sep 1881. Off: HARSHA. Wit: L.B. WILLIAMS, Saul R. JOHNSON.

WILLIAMS, Edmon A. [24; Muscatine, IA] md. Nancy M. PETERSON [20; Omaha] on 8 Jul 1867. Off: KERMOTT. Wit: Amanda R. KERMOTT, Mrs. Darius PEARCE.

WILLIAMS, Eli [24; Stockton, CA] md. Isabel SHEPHERD [18; Cass Co., IA] on 28 May 1862 on the creek near Forrest Retreat.

Off: SHINN. Wit: Moses HETTAND, William SHEPHERD.

WILLIAMS, George [32; Omaha] md. Mary HAWKINS [19; Omaha] on 14 Oct 1867. Off: McCAGUE. Wit: Mrs. P. HARMAN (HARMANS), Geo. MERICLE, et al.

WILLIAMS, George [35; Omaha; b: New Jersey; f: Henry WILLIAMS; m: Phebe MASON] md. Mrs. Sarah JOHNSON [32; Omaha; b: Iowa] on 2 Dec 1869. Off: GIBSON. Wit: Mrs. Elizabeth KELLEY, Patrick KELLEY.

WILLIAMS, Henry C. [22; Omaha] md. Lucy JONES [23; Omaha] on 2 Nov 1867. Off: KUHNS. Wit: John HOLLAND, Anna L. HOLLAND.

WILLIAMS, John E. [32; b: Wales; f: Daniel WILLIAMS; m: Margaret EVANS] md. Josephine PETERSON [18; Pottawattamie Co., IA; b: Council Bluffs, IA; f: Nelson PETERSON] on 7 Dec 1872. Off: BRANDES. Wit: J.F. MORTON; L.P. VAN HOOSEN.

WILLIAMS, John H. [colored; 21; Omaha] md. Martha JACKSON [colored; 20; Omaha] on 22 Aug 1866 at Dr. LOWE's residence. Off: FLORKEE. Wit: Dr. LOWE and family, Wilson POTER, Sara KELLY.

WILLIAMS, John H.L. [19; Douglas Co.] md. Loretta SHRODER [19; Douglas Co.] on 28 Nov 1867. Off: SHEEKS. Wit: William KIP, Enos WILLIAMS, fathers of the bride and groom present.

WILLIAMS, John W. [Douglas Co.] md. Mariah BLACK [Douglas Co.] on 27 Aug 1865 at John CARTER's residence. Off: KUHNS. Wit: Mr. and Mrs. J. CARTER, Mrs. COOPER, Mrs. BLACK, et al.

WILLIAMS, John [37; Platt Co., MO; b: MO; f: Wilson W. WILLIAMS; m: Catharine LUDDINGTON] md. Josephine REEVES [17; Omaha; b: Omaha; f: Cameron REEVES; m: Elizabeth EVANS] on 25 Mar 1875. Off: PEABODY. Wit: L. BURNHAM, F.P. HANLON.

WILLIAMS, Louis [24; Omaha; b: Illinois; f: John WILLIAMS; m: Sarah DARLING] md. Louisa PROVAST [18; Omaha; b: Kansas] on 11 Jan 1877. Off: LIFRE. Wit: Lee SCHORNBORN, Miss McCLASKY.

WILLIAMS, Robert [26; Omaha; colored; b: North Carolina; f: Sandy WILLIAMS: m: Matilda] md. Mrs. Elizabeth WILLIAMSON [25; Omaha; colored; b: Missouri; f: Joseph GARNER; m: Jane GREEN] on 16 May 1872. Off: TOWNSEND. Wit: J.F.S.D. HIRTZMANN; A. McNEIL.

WILLIAMS, Rollo A. [21; Omaha; b: MA; f: Louis F. WILLIAMS; m: Huldy D. HADLEY] md. Lizzie SHIELDS [20; Omaha; b: MO; f: Louis SHIELDS; m: Doralty BECK] on 17 Sep 1881. Off: GRAHAM. Wit: Fred BATES, Jennie SHIELDS.

WILLIAMS, Simon [negro; 32; Omaha; b: Missouri] md. Eliza NELSON [negro; 21; Omaha; b: Missouri; f: Charles CLARK; m: Annie CLARK] on 11 Dec 1879. Off: FOUCHEE. Wit: Taylor REYNOLDS, Jessie NEWMAN.

WILLIAMS, Willard [36; Ashland, NE; b: NY; f: Stephen WILLIAMS; m: ---- EATON] md. Mrs. Maggie GALLIGAN [35; Omaha; b: OH; f: Henry GALLIGAN; m: Adelia DOLAND] on 17 Feb 1881. Off: ANDERSON. Wit: W.P. SNOWDEN, Jacob KING.

WILLIAMS, Wylie [colored; 27; Omaha] md. Sarah PACE [colored; 21; Omaha] on 11 Jul 1868. Off: STUCK.

WILLIAMSON, Daniel [25; Douglas Co.] md. Julia BELL [21; Douglas Co.] on 6 Jan 1866 at the Lutheran parsonage. Off: KUHNS. Wit: Mr. and Mrs. D.T. MOUNT, et al.

WILLIAMSON, Harvey [colored; 35; Omaha; b: Ann Arbor, MI; f: Ephriam WILLIAMSON; m: Charlotte PRITCHET] and Bell GREEN [colored; 20; Omaha; b: Pittsburg, PA; f: William GREEN] license issued on 12 Jun 1869. No marriage record. Off: HYDE.

WILLIAMSON, Robert B. [42; Omaha] md. Clara H. INGHAM [37; Omaha] on 22 Feb 1868. Off: SLAUGHTER. Wit: Mrs. A.B. SLAUGHTER, Fred KISLINGBURY.

WILLIE, Christian [32; Omaha Barracks; b: Germany; f: George WILLIE: m: Lizzie WAISE] md. Louisa SEAMAN [25; Omaha Barracks; b: Germany; f: Michael SEAMAN; m: Christena BAREN] on 6 Nov 1873. Off: PEABODY. Wit: Charles TIETZE; Justine TIETZE.

WILLIS, E.A. [21; Omaha; b: Pennsylvania; f: Isaac A. WILLIS; m: Martha SMITH] md. Mary HANAVAN [22; Omaha; b: Ireland; f: Morris HANAVAN; m: ----] on 28 Mar 1880. Off: ENGLISH. Wit: Chas. P. McKEU, Maggie CORCORAN.

WILLIS, John H. [33; Omaha; b: England; f: John WILLIS; m: Ellenor HESELTINE] md. Margaret DENT [25; Omaha; b: England; f: John DENT; m: Mary A. HERD] on 16 Apr 1870. Off: BETTS. Wit: Robert RECHELIEU; Elizabeth RECHELIEU.

WILLIT, Micajah [53; McArdle Pct, Douglas Co.; b: New York; f: Richard WILLIT; m: Rachel BIRDSALL] md. Mrs. Susan F. REED [45; Omaha; b: New Jersey; f: Asher LAFETRE; m: Elizabeth] on 4 Mar 1872. Off: KUHNS. Wit: Mrs. Mary WATERMAN; Austin W. REED.

WILLTIN, James R. [24; Omaha; b: Texas; f: Perry J. WILLTIN; m: ELiza FALKNER] md. Mary A. GAULT [16; Omaha; b: Illinois; f: Moses GAULT; m: Mary J. OVERLAND] on 28 Jan 1874. Off: PEABODY. Wit: F.P. HANLON; H.T. LEAVITT.

WILLUHN, Samuel [46; Douglas Co.; b: Germany; f: Samuel WILLUHN; m: Christine AVUSUZYS] md. Mrs. Agnes METZ [42; Omaha; b: Germany; f: John WEBER, Mary WEBER] on 19 Mar 1881. Off: SMITH. Wit: Max BERGMANN, John M. TUTTLE.

WILMARTH, Stephen [37; Omaha] md. Mrs. Doria JURGENSEN [42; Omaha] on 19 Jan 1869. Off: KELLEY. Wit: D.B. TOPHAM, W. SMITH.

WILSON, A.L. [32; Omaha] md. Sarah K. ADAIR [20; Omaha] on Monday between 4 and 5 PM, 24 Dec 1866 at DIMMICK's house. Off: DIMMICK. Wit: Sylvanus WRIGHT, Fanny P. WRIGHT.

WILSON, Aaron [24; Logan Co., OH] md. Margaret OLINGER [20; Burt Co., NE] on the evening of 30 May 1866 at Marshall KENNARD's residence. Off: LEMON. Wit: Mr. and Mrs. Marshall KENNARD.

WILSON, C.H. [25; Omaha; b: Illinois; f: Alexander WILSON; m: Sarah GREGORY] md. Mrs. Emeleia SPERLING [24; Omaha; b: New York; f: John SPERLING; m: Mary THOMAS] on 27 Aug 1880. Off: MAXFIELD. Wit: Mrs. Manne MAXFIELD.

WILSON, Charles Forsyth [24; Denver; b: Canada; f: Benjamin F. WILSON; m: Agnes FORSYTH] md. Hattie M.E. WARNER [23; Syracuse, NY; b: New York; f: Marshall D. WARNER; m: Sally A. FOSTER] on 14 Aug 1880. Off: BRISTOL. Wit: Jos. A. BRISTOL, Rellie BRISTOL.

WILSON, Charles N. [colored; 24; Omaha; b: Alabama] md. Julia DAVIS [colored; 21; Omaha] on 13 Jun 1869. Off: KERMOTT. Wit: Mrs. A.R. KERMOTT, Maud Scott KERMOTT, W.T. SEAMAN.

WILSON, Charles W. [21; Omaha; b; Indiana; f; Charles WILSON; m: Ruth M. BURR] md. Mary OVERTON [18; Omaha; b: Indiana; f: Robert OVERTON; m: Margaret YANTS] on 16 Sep 1869. Off: HYDE. Wit: Barbara WILSON of Douglas Co., Thomas J. WILSON of Douglas Co.

WILSON, Gustave [30; Genoa; b: Sweden; f: Frederick WILSON; m: Elizabeth ANDERSON] md. Mary CROSS [20; Genoa; b: MI; f: R.D. CROSS; m: Mary WANNS] on 12 Sep 1881. Off: SHERRILL. Wit: A.F. SHERRILL, Mrs. Chas. WILKINS, Jr.

WILSON, Henry [32; Omaha; b: Virginia; f: Robert WILSON; m: Clerry SEWARD] md. Fanny WILKINS [21; Omaha; b: Philadelphia; f: James WILKINS; m: Fanny COBBLE] on 3 Feb 1874. Off: GAINES. Wit: E.S. CLEMENS or CLENLAUS; W.H. BUTLER.

WILSON, Henry [negro; 34; Omaha; b: VA; f: Robert WILSON; m: Cherry REINES] md. Mrs. Stanton SPARKS [negro; 31; Omaha; b: MO; f: George LONG; m: Patsy LONG] on 30 Jul 1881. Off: WRIGHT. Wit: Rodney DUTCHER, Amelia WELLS. Affidavit signed with an "X" and witnessed by Herm. HOCHSTETTER.

WILSON, John C. [35; Omaha; b: Glasgow, SCOT; f: William WILSON] md. Annie DONOVAN [19; Omaha] on 16 Aug 1870. Off: CURTIS. Wit: John F. DONOVAN; Susan DONOVAN.

WILSON, John S. [25; North Platte] md. Ellen WESTON [16; Elkhorn] on 16 Dec 1867. Off: PALMER. Wit: Platt SAUNDERS, J.C. WILCOX, et al. Signed age consent by George B. WESTON, father of the bride.

WILSON, John [38; Omaha; b: Scotland; f: John WILSON; m: Jean CLARK] md. Matilda KRENZER [23; Omaha; b: IL; f: John KRENZER; m: Lizzie HOFNEY] on 24 May 1881. Off: WILLIAMS. Wit: John KRENZER, Mrs. John KRENZER. Filed 15 Aug 1882 by CHADWICK.

WILSON, William [27; Douglas Co.; b: IA; f: Benjamin WILSON; m: Mary RITCHIE] md. Margaret E. THOMAS [21; Douglas Co.; b: OH; f: Lewis THOMAS; m: Susan MOORE] on 25 Dec 1875 at Union Precinct. Off: GREEN. Wit: Lewis THOMAS, Union Precinct, Susan THOMAS, Union Precinct.

WILSON, Wm. A. [25; Ohio; b: Ohio; f: James WILSON; m: Michal GILLEM] md. Mary E. PETTIT [21; Omaha; b: Wisconsin; f: Wm. F. PETTIT; m: Melinda DOUGLAS] on 20 Feb 1874. Off: PORTER. Wit: Nathan J. BURHAM; William B. KEEF.

WINKELMAN, F.E. [26; Grand Island, NE; b: PA; f: Lawrence WINKELMAN; m: Jane CHAPMAN] md. Ina B. JENNEY [21; Omaha; b: VT; f: M. JENNEY; m: Louisa C. WALBRIDGE] on 30 Nov 1881. Off: INGRAM. Wit: Mrs. F.A. McELROY, Mrs. E.F. ROLLINS, both of Grand Island.

WINKLER, Allen [27; b: Ohio; f: Orange WINKLER; m: Anna HILL] md. Kate HAUAFAN [18; b: Ireland; f: Morris HAUAFAN; m: Johanna LUCID] on 2 Feb 1878 at the Episcopal residence. Off: O'BRIAN. Wit: Wm. SMITH, Mrs. SMITH.

WINKLER, August [22; Omaha; b: Bremen, Germany; f: John Wilhelm WINKLER; m: Anne WIAMS] md. Mrs. Barbara SLAPNICKE [21; Omaha; b: near Baronne, Bohemia; f: James SKLA; m: Fanny BENZEL] on 2 Jul 1879. Off: POWELL. Wit: Mrs. E.B. NICHOLS, Miss S.B. LOOMIS.

WINQUIST, Claus [23; Omaha; b: Sweden; f: John WINQUIST; m: Christine PIERSON] md. Charlotte ENGLUND [25; Omaha; b: Sweden] on 16 May 1871. Off: SUNDBORN. Wit: Andrew SODERLUND; Peter NELSON.

WINSLADE, John E. [27; Omaha; b: Wisconsin; f: John WINSLADE; m: Elizabeth KERTHELTZ] md. Sadie E. WOLFE [21; Omaha; b: Germany; f: Thomas WOLFE; m: ELizabeth] on 18 May 1874. Off: WRIGHT. Wit: William SEXAUER; Henry LIVESY.

WINSLOW, Andrew P. [23; Saline Co.; b: Maine; f: Nathaniel WINSLOW; m: Eliza HOWARD] md. Lucy L. HAWKINS [21; Omaha; b: Keighsburgh, Henderson Co. IL; f: John J. HAWKINS; m: Maria E. WORDEN] on 21 Mar 1873. Off: TOWNSEND. Wit: David P. REDMAN, Saratoga Pct; Jerome F.L.D. HERTZMANN.

WINSLOW, Lorenzo H. [22; Omaha; b: New York; f: P. WINSLOW; m: Mary HAVENS] md. Mary FALLON [22; Omaha; b: Iowa; f: George FALLON; m: Nellie COLLINS] on 11 May 1874. Off: McDONALD. Wit: James GILL; Hattie GILL.

WINSPEAR, James H. [26; Omaha] md. Emeline L. CRONEMEYER [22; Omaha] on 17 Apr 1869. Off: GIBSON. Wit: S.H. ELLIOTT, H.P. ELLIOTT.

WIRTH, J.C. [25; Omaha; b: Austria; f: Johan WIRTH; m: Matilda M. KUENZEL [KUNCL]] md. Meta MENKE [22; Omaha; b: Germany; f: Hendrick MENKE; m: Meta SHROEDER] on 23 Jan 1878. Off: BENEKE. Wit: Adelina JOHN, Alice CASPER.

WISE, George W. [22; Omaha] md. Mary A.J. DURANT [19; Omaha] on 15 Aug 1866. Off: KERMOTT. Wit: Henry HICKMAN, Amanda R. KERMOT.

WISE, George W. [Cambridge, Henry Co., IL] md. Chastina LEEPER [Cambridge, IL] on 19 May 1864 at DICKINSON's office. Off: DICKINSON. Wit: Amanda WISE, John H. BRACKEN.

WISSMAN, Frederick [30; Omaha; b: Germany; f: Frederick WISSMAN; m: Ezetta PIPER] md. Annie HIBBELER [32; Omaha; b: Germany; f: Christian HIBBELER; m: Christina DANAMAN] on 3 June 1873. Off: TOWNSEND. Wit: Dedrich HIBBILER; Christian DANIEL.

WISTERGAARD, James C. [25; Omaha; b: Denmark; f: Christian WISTERGAARD; m: Annie C. JOHNSON] md. Mary HOLST [22; Omaha; b: Denmark; f: Peter HOLST] on 18 Feb 1871. Off: GIBSON. Wit: H.L. DODGE, Douglas Co.; Luke USHER.

WITT, John H. [32; Omaha] md. Sophia MEEWES [24; Omaha] on 16 May 1868. Off: KUHNS. Wit: Mrs. H.W. KUHNS, Catharine GROSS.

WITTE, Charles [23; Douglas Co.; b: IA; f: August WITTE; m: Sophia QUITSOW] md. Mary J. HOPPER [22; Douglas Co.; b: Canada; f: William HOPPER; m: Dorothy FARRELL] on 12 Jun 1881 at William HOPPER's residence. Off: WOODMAN. Wit: Wm. HOPPER, Elkhorn Station, Dorothy HOPPER, Elkhorn Station.

WITTENAN, William [28; Fort Omaha; b: Germany; f: Ernest WITTENAN; m: Charlotte NEANDER] md. Miss Georgie A. YOUNG [31; Omaha; b: VA; f: Thomas YOUNG; m: Jane YOUNG] on 24 Oct 1881. Off: BENEKE. Wit: J.J.C.L. JEWETT, J.J. GALLIGAN.

WITTMAAK, George [25; Douglas Co.; b: Germany; f: George WITTMAAK; m: Catharina STANGE] md. Malvina FICK [20; Douglas Co.; b: Germany; f: Charles FICK; m: Christina VOIGHT] on 3 Mar 1876. Off: SEDGWICK. Wit: Charles FICK, Douglas Co., Hans BECKMAN, Douglas Co.

WODIC, Emanuel [25; Pvt. in Co. K, U.S. Inf.] md. Catharine WOTIZ [21; Douglas Co.] on 22 Oct 1862 at Farnham House. Off: ARMSTRONG. Wit: Lt. and Mrs. John GOODRICH, et al.

WOLCOTT, Frederick B. [25; Rose Creek; b: Athens, PA; f: John P. WOLCOTT; m: Rebecca B. RODGER] md. Hannah CALLAHAN [17; Omaha; b: Ireland; f: Timothy CALLAHAN; m: Hannah RIORDAN] on 4 Sep 1870. Off: MAY. Wit: Mary GUTEHUNET; Delia MAJO. Age of consent given by father of bride. Wit: Edwin J. ROGERS.

WOLDRIG, Theodore [30; b: Germany; f: John WOLDRIG; m: Maria BLUM] md. Minna LEY [20; b: Germany; f: Charles LEY; m: Caroline KOEHLER] on 14 Jun 1878. Off: BENEKE. Wit: Charles GRABBERT, Wilhelm SCHMIDT.

WOLF, Henry [22; Washington Co.; b: Germany; f: Joachim WOLF; m: Zilke MULLER] md. Lizzie SOLL [19; Washington Co.; b: Germany; f: Fritz SOLL; m: Friederika GUSCH] on 11 Mar 1880. Off: BENEKE. Wit: Peter F. SOLL of Douglas Co., Christian P. SOLL of Washington Co.

WOLFEL, John C. [40; Omaha; b: Pennsylvania; f: Joseph WOLFEL; m: Christine LUST] and Mrs. Ellen SPENCER [28; Omaha; b: England; f: Joseph DOVE; m: Mary SHELTON] license issued on 21 May 1879. No marriage record. Off: BARTHOLOMEW.

WOLFER, William [37; Peru, IL; b: MD; f: Christian WOLFER; m: Dora SMITH] md. Kate KINNEY [27; Omaha; b: IL; f: Peter KINNEY; m: Kate BURKHARD] on 22 Sep 1875. Off: PEABODY. Wit: Chas. HOHLFELT, Rosa KINNEY.

WOLFF, Alfred F. [29; Omaha; b: Denmark; f: Ferdinand WOLFF; m: Eliza FRENCHEN] md. Emma M. LYON [18; Omaha; b: Sweden; f: Peter H. LYON; m: Carrie PEARSON] on 14 Jul 1880. Off: STENBERG. Wit: Otto WOLFF, Julius WOLFF.

WOLFF, Julius [53; Dodge Co.; b: Germany; f: August WOLFF; m: Fredericka SCHMIDT] md. Catherine BRETENSTEIN [36; Washington Co.; b: Germany; f: John BRETENSTEIN; m: Elizabeth WEBER] on 10 Mar 1877. Off: LIFRE. Wit: Lizzie LIFRE, Helen McTECKHAM.

WOLFF, Otto [26; Omaha; b: Denmark; f: Ferdinand WOLFF; m: Eliza FRENCHEN] md. Amelia HOLEN [23; Omaha; b: Denmark; f: Carl HOLM; m: Johanna M. PETERSON] on 31 Jul 1880. Off: STENBERG. Wit: P. BOISEN, A. BOISEN.

WOLFF, Victor [26; Omaha; b: Germany; f: Joseph WOLFF; m: Katharine KRAFFT] md. Emma KLEFFNER [19; Omaha; b: Omaha; f: George KLEFFNER; m: Helena ZIMMERMANN] on 29 Jun 1879. Off: BENEKE. Wit: Catharine KOLHE, Wm. KOLHE.

WOLGAMOTT, John [25; Peoria, IL; b: Indiana; f: Washginton WOLGAMOTT; m: Nancy DAWSON] md. Albina BENNETT [18 (on 19 Oct 1872); Peoria; IL; b: Canada; f: James BENNETT; m: Anna BYE] on 11 June 1873. Off: MORRIS. Wit: Mrs. A.B. LORING, Boston; Mrs. M.B. SWITZER.

WOLLESEN, Thomas [25; Douglas Co.; b: Germany; f: Hans WOLLESEN] md. Catharina Maria KLINDER (or KLINKER) [21; Douglas Co.; b: Germany; f: John KLINKER; m: Catharina Maria TRULS] on 9 Feb 1875. Off: PEABODY. Wit: Edward U. SIMERAL, F.P. HANLON.

WOOD, Charles [29; Omaha; b: North Carolina; f: Berry WOOD; m: Rebecca SMITH] md. Anna NIEDERMEYER [21; Omaha; b: New Jersey; f: Anton NIEDERMEYER; m: Louisa HELBLUCK] on 26 Apr 1880, German Catholic Church. Off: GROENEBAUM. Wit: E.N. PAINE, Carrie NIEDERMEYER.

WOOD, Nelson T. [23; Atlantic, IA; b: New York; f: Sheldon L. WOOD; m: Eliza MARTIN] md. Elizabeth BABB [22; Big Grove, IA; b: Iowa; f: William BABB; m: Julia OGLEBY] on 21 June 1871. Off: GIBSON. Wit: Charles M. JOHNSON, Avoca, IA; Mary M. KIMBALL, Avoca, IA.

WOODARD, James I. [27; Omaha; b: Michigan; f: Sylvender WOODARD; m: Rhoda WALTON] and Adaline BARBARA [23; Omaha; b: Canada; f: Louis BARBARA; m: Catharine O'BRIEN] license issued on 28 Jul 1879. No marriage record. Off: BARTHOLOMEW.

WOODS, George H. [28; b: Vermont; f: Willard WOODS; m: Emmarancy MATSON] md. Anna M. HAPEN [28; b: Germany; f: John HAPEN; m: Selony CURTIS] on 10 Sep 1878. Off: STENBERG. Wit: Gust BENEKE, S.W. BOGGS.

WOODS, Nathaniel l[colored; 21; Omaha] md. Mathis (Mattie) TOLLES [colored; 18; Omaha] on 22 May 1868 at TAYLOR's home. Off: FLORKEE. Wit: Mr. TAYLOR and his wife.

WOODWORTH, James [23; Washington Co.; b: Michigan; f: Perry WOODWORTH; m: Esther NORTON] md. Helena MORANEY [27; Omaha; b: Ireland; f: Michael MORANEY; m: Hellena MORANEY] on 19 Jan 1871. Off: GIBSON. Wit: H.C. CAGE; Mrs. Ann WALLACE.

WOOLLEY, Frederick R. [24; Seward Co; b: Cincinnati, Oh; f: Stites WOOLLEY; m: Mary Ann STEVENSON] md. Celia E. BURGMAN [16 (In Mar 1872); Union Pct, Douglas Co.; b: Scott Co., IA; f: Isaac W. BURGMAN; m: Nancy A. THOMAS] on 26 Feb 1873 at Irvington. Off: DIXON. Wit: Rev. E.B. HURLBUT, Irvington; Geo. BURGMAN, Union Pct.

WORKMAN, (no first name given) [22] and Elizabeth PORTER [16] license issued on 30 Mar 1857. No marriage record. Off: SCOTT. Age consent given by H.B. PORTER.

WORLEY, H.A. [28; Omaha; b: Ohio; f: Philip H. WORLEY; m: Justina M. BURKE] md. Eliza H. BERLIN [26; Douglas Co.; b: Pennsylvania; f: Jonathan BERLIN; m: Ann WILSON] on 22 Oct 1879. Off: SHERRILL. Wit: Mrs. J.N.H. PATRICK, Mrs. W.H.S. HUGHES.

WORTHINGTON, Charles [23; Omaha; b: Iowa; f: Irving WORTHINGTON; m: Caroline BREWER] md. Callie WILLEFORD [15; Omaha; b: Iowa; f: James WILLEFORD; m: Mary HUDSON] on 8 Sep 1880. Off: STENBERG. Wit: Theodore DAUGHERTY, Carrie WILLEFORD.

WRAGE, Henry [25; Washington Co.; b: Germany; f: Henry WRAGE; m: Anna SWAN] md. Bessie McARRAGHER [18; Washington Co.; b: Ireland; f: Joseph McARRAGHER; m: Jane NELSON] on 1 Feb 1881. Off: SMITH. Wit: William DOLL, D.C. EHLERS.

WRASSE, Johan [20; Douglas Co.; b: Germany; f: Carl WRASSE; m: Albertine ZWEMCKE] md. Johanna PAGEL [17; Douglas Co.; b: Germany; f: Christof PAGEL; m: Johanna BAERWALDE] on 22 Mar 1881. Off: FRESE. Wit: Johann LABS, Douglas Co., Albert KOBS, Douglas Co. Age consent for the groom given by "my friend, Johann WRASSE," and witnessed by FRESE. Age consent given by Wilhelmine BAERWALDE for her niece J. PAGEL.

WREN, Thadeus [25; Omaha; b: Ireland; f: John WREN; m: Catharine MALONE] md. Hattie C. WILKINS [18; Omaha; b: Iowa; f: Samuel WILKINS; m: Mary AMOS] on 11 Sep 1869. Off: KUHNS. Wit: Annie CATHERWOOD, Mrs. H.W. KUHNS.

WRIGHT, Augustus S. [42; Omaha] md. Mrs. Helen C. DORING [20; Omaha] on Thursday after the 22nd Sunday after Trinity, 12 Nov 1868 at Trinity Church. Off: BETTS. Wit: Mr. WRIGHT, Sr., Francis M. DIMMICK, Mrs. BARNEY, the congregation.

WRIGHT, Charles A. Spencer [21; Omaha; b: NY; f: Charles H. WRIGHT; m: Mary C. KETCHAM] md. Sarah E. ROBERTS [19: Omaha; b: IA; f: John ROBERTS; m: Sarah A. McKEE] on 8 May 1876. Off: BRITT. Wit: Charles H. WRIGHT, NY, John ROBERTS.

WRIGHT, Joseph [colored, 22; Omaha] md. Mrs. Harriet JONES [colored; 24; Omaha] on 21 May 1868. Off: SLAUGHTER. Wit: Henry JONES, Matilda BRADFORD.

WRIGHT, Silas [23; Omaha; b: Illinois; f: Thomas K. WRIGHT; m: Jane KELLEY] md. Sadie M. LEE [19; Omaha; b: Iowa; f: John LEE; m: Mary A. SMITH] on 26 Feb 1874. Off: WRIGHT. Wit: Mrs? Ira LEE; Mrs. M.H. WRIGHT.

WYETH, Edward [24; Omaha; b: Germany; f: Johan WYETH] and Rosina SAMMER [22; Omaha; b: Germany; f: Nicholas SAMMER] license issued on 19 June 1871. Off: GIBSON.

WYMAN, Albert U. [26; Omaha] md. Harriet C. FAKE [21; Omaha] on 23 Nov 1859. Off: WATSON. Wit: Mr. and Mrs. WYMAN, Mr. and Mrs. FAKE, D.H. MOFFAT, Jr.

WYMAN, Evan [31; Omaha; b: Pennsylvania; f: Joseph WYMAN; m: Hannah KEITH] md. Minervia C. NEIGHLY [20; Omaha; b: Pennsylvania; f: William NEIGHLY] on 10 Jun 1871. Off: DeLaMATYR. Wit: Mr. COLVIN; Mrs. COLVIN.

YATES, Willis M. [31; b: Missouri; f: Joseph I. YATES; m: Julia Ann NORRIS] md. Idalyn H. GUYER [GWYER] [23; b: Wilmington, NC; f: Wm. A. GUYER [GWYER]; m: Sarah HALL] on 2 Jul 1878. Off: MILLSPAUGH. Wit: Kent HAYDEN, Rev. Robert DOHERTY.

YAW, Franklin M. [37; Omaha; b: MI; f: Joseph F. YAW; m: Eliza MILLINGTON] md. Mattie APPLEBY [27; Omaha; b: IA; f: George APPLEBY; m: Catharine GREEN] on 27 Dec 1881. Off: CHADWICK. Wit: Max BERGMANN, Chas. L. THOMAS.

YEATES, William [26; Omaha; b: England; f: George YEATES; m: Jane HALL] md. Isophean BOULTON [30; Omaha; b: Missouri; f: William BOULTON; m: Anna BAKER] on 28 Sep 1874. Off: PEABODY. Wit: Emlen LEWIS; J.M. BORGLUM.

YEATS, Daniel [29; Omaha; b: IL; f: Alexander YEATS; m: Margaret CLUBB] md. Mary C. RICH [23; Omaha; b: Canada; f: Thomas RICH; m: Susan COLERIGE] on 19 Apr 1881. Off: MILLSPAUGH. Wit: A.J. SIMPSON, Nelson J. EDHOLM.

YERGA, John M. [43; Omaha; b: PA; f: David YERGA; m: Susan SECHRIST] md. Sarah E. GETTINGS [24; Omaha; b: MO; f: Isaac EDWARDS; m: Sarah J. PHELPS] on 21 Mar 1876. Off: GAYLORD. Wit: R.E. GAYLORD, Mrs. Mary W. GAYLORD.

YETTER, Balthas [26; Douglas Precinct, Douglas Co., NE; b: Germany; f: Balthas YETTER; m: Katharine HEUGSLER] md. Bertha WINKLER [20; b: Wisconsin; f: Gotthelf WINKLER; m: Charlotte MILLER] on 7 Jul 1878. Off: STRASEN. Wit: John YETTER, Christian SAUTTER.

YING, Charley [34; Omaha; b: China; f: Foo YING; m: Liddie QUOO] md. Emma TRIPLETT [22; Omaha; b: Buenos Ayres, South America; f: ---- PARISH] on 15 Sep 1881. Off: CHADWICK. Wit: C.W. METTITT, Mrs. THOMAS.

YONLEY, Thomas D.W. [28; Omaha] md. Margarett Ann LESURE [Omaha] on 13 Sep 1857 at the house of N. LESURE. Off: SHINN.

YOSTE, Martin [26; Omaha; b: Germany; f: Frederick YOSTE; m: Margareta WEBER] md. Gusta KETCHMIRE [21; Omaha; f: John KETCHMIRE; m: Minnie STONE] on 23 Dec 1874. Off: LIPE. Wit: T.H. SLATTER; Ellen LEONARD.

YOUNG, Andrew [27; Logan Creek] md. Louisa FORSLAND [24; Logan Creek] on 24 Apr 1869. Off: HYDE. Wit: George SMITH, H.C.D. TRUIDE.

YOUNG, Frank H. [29; McKinley (changed from Custer Co.); b: ME; f: M.F. YOUNG; m: Mary A. WOODS] md. Clara D. ALBERTSON [25; Fremont; b: IN (or MI); f: Isaac ALBERTSON; m: Anngenette TONCRAY] on 20 Jun 1881. Off: SMITH. Wit: H. CLEAVELAND, Max BERGMANN.

YOUNG, George [36; North Bend; b: Scotland; f: James YOUNG; m: Georgiana ORRICK] md. Mrs. Jennete (Jennette) MORRISON [38; Montreal, Canada; b: Scotland; f: John SUMMERS; m:

Catherine RUTHVEN] on 22 Nov 1869. Off: HYDE. Wit: Thos. MELDRUM, Mrs. Isabella FLEMING.

YOUNG, H.W. [37; Carroll, IA; b: Massachusetts; f: H.W. YOUNG; m: Eliza Jane REGAN] md. Marietta SMITH [27; Douglas Co.; b: Iowa; f: John SMITH; m: Mary A. SHEARER] on 20 Oct 1880 at Florence Precinct. Off: MAXFIELD. Wit: Grace CLARK of Calhoun, Mrs. Geo. PECK.

YOUNG, Hans [25; Omaha; b: Germany; f: C.H. YOUNG; m: Maria PAULSEN] md. Auguste RANDON [22; Omaha; b: Germany; f: August RANDON; m: Hedwig LORENZ] on 5 Mar 1881. Off: BENEKE. Wit: Valentin DUMPERTH, Henry VOSS.

YOUNG, J.H. [22; Omaha] and Orpha HENRY [17; Omaha] license issued on 15 Oct 1857. No marriage record. Off: BRIGGS. Age consent given by father.

YOUNG, Peter A. [30; Oakland, Burt Co.; b: Sweden; f: Peter NILSON; m: Charlotte SWANSON] md. Christina OSBERG [25; Omaha; b: Sweden; f: Nils M. OSBERG; m: Christina OLSON] on 14 June 1873. Off: AXLING. Wit: C.W.B. ODEN; Charles E. MALMSTEN, Oakland, Burt Co.

YOUNG, Shepard [62; Chicago, IL; b: Erie Co, PA; f: Ira YOUNG; m: Mary T. TALLBEE] md. Mrs. Frances M. WARD [39; Chicago, IL; b: Vermont; f: Elijah STEVENS; m: Fanny] on 20 May 1873. Off: BRANDES. Wit: James F. MORTON; Dr. L.P. VAN HOOSEN.

YOUNG, Toney [24;Omaha; b: New Orleans, LA; f: Toney YOUNG; m: Elizabeth EULER] md. Minnie HUTH [18; Omaha; b: Germany; f: Frederick HUTH; m: Louisa BECKER] on 16 Apr 1872. Off: BRANDES. Wit: John DAEMON; Mrs. Wilhelmina DAEMON.

YOX, Joseph [23; Omaha; b: Chicago, IL; f: Peter YOX] md. Matilda C. PERRY [24; Omaha; b: Ohio; f: Peter C. PERRY] on 15 Aug 1870. Off: DeLaMATYR. Wit: N.O. DeLaMATYR; Jennie HELDRETH.

ZEHNER, John W. [30; Central City, Colorado Territory] md. Eliza McKEE [25; Omaha] on Thursday evening at 8:30 P.M., 11 Feb 1869 at Wm. MILLER's residence. Off: DIMMICK. Wit: Mr. and Mrs. William MILLER, Mr. and Mrs. Richman McKEE, Daniel ALLEN, et al.

ZIMMERMAN, Andrew [22; Omaha; b: Switzerland; f: Andrew ZIMMERMAN] md. Anne EDMONSON [20; Omaha; b: England; f: William EDMONSON; m: Elizabeth PARKINSON] on 21 Jun 1869. Off: BETTS. Wit: Charles SKINNER, William Francis GILLEN.

ZIMMERMAN, Gottlieb [24; Omaha; b: Germany; f: William F. ZIMMERMAN; m: Louise BUCHLER] md. Catherine ELSSASER [18; Omaha; b: Germany; f: Fred ELSSASER; m: Jacobine WALKER] on 29 Sep 1870. Off: MORTON. Wit: William SANDERS; Cornelius IVERS.

ZIMMERMAN, John [27; Sarpy Co.; b: Germany; f: John ZIMMERMAN; m: Katrina STUCK] md. Katrina WEISS [21; Omaha; b: Germany; f: Peter WEISS; m: Celia EMALD] on 4 Oct 1873. Off: PORTER. Wit: C.H. CINGEN (SINGEN); John WEISS.

ZINK, John [21; Omaha; b: Germany; f: John ZINK; m: Louisa BOWERS] md. Rosa BERNARD [18; Omaha; b: France; f: Ferdinand BERNARD; m: Margaret ANDREW] on 6 Jun 1869. Off: CURTIS. Wit: Thomas COEN, Mary MOONEY.

ZISKOVSKY, Anton [34; Omaha; b: Austria; f: Josef ZISKOVSKY; m: Mary BRUSEK] md. Mrs. Annie REICH [33; Omaha; b: Austria; f: Josef ERBEN [URBAN]; m: Katharina SAMELIK] on 13 Nov 1880. Off: BENEKE. Wit: Wenzel NISTEL, F. DEAHEK.

ZOTZMAN, Frederick [31; Omaha; b: Prussia; f: Charles ZOTZMAN; m: Dorothea SEEGER] md. Julia RASMUSSEN [23; Omaha; b: Denmark; f: Christian RASMUSSEN; m: Sophia GIBSON] on 20 Mar 1873. Off: WERFIELD. Wit: Martin RASMUSSEN; Christiana PETERS.

AAGAARD
Inger NIELSON 1
Jens 1
Jens Joseph 1
Petrina Maria
  PETERSON 1
ABBOTT
Catharine BROWN 1
John 1
Joseph 1
Lizzie B. BROWN 1
Luther 2
Mary 31
O.A. 150
ABBY
Olive 96
ABEL
Adeline CARR 1
Albert 1
Elias 1
Emma SOLOMON 1
H. 3
Lucy 70
ABERCROMBIE
Elizabeth 118
Elizabeth, Mrs. 97
ABESON
A. 116
ABLE
Albert 1, 35
Anna NEILSON 1
Christian 1
Delphine
  CRITCHFIELD 1
George 137
Magdalena 137
Magdalena STRAUS
  137
ABNEY
Amanda KLEIN 57
Annie WILLIAMS 1
David 57
James C. 1
Josephine 57
ABOLD
Mary A. 140
ABORN
Catherine SILL 1
Edward S. 1
Ida WOLFF 1
Maria 2, 118
William K. 1
ABORNS
Maria 2
ABRAHAMS
Ricke 139
ABRAHAMSON
Carin
  ANDERSDOTTER
  134
Gustava 89
Isac 134
L.C. 81
ABT
Lena 83
ACHTE
? 43
ACKER
Inge 42
Jacob 42
Martha JACOBSON 42
ACKERMAN
Carolina 137
Catherine FLICK 1
David 1

Lily M. CLARK 1
ACKERMANN
Auguste RIECKS 39
Emil 39
Ernestine 39
George 39
ADAIR
Charlotte 7
J.M. 117
J.M., Mrs. 105
James M. 15
Joseph 37
M.A., Mrs. 31, 78
Mary 49, 53, 149
Mary A., Mrs. 27, 52
Mr. and Mrs. 4
S. 4
Samuel 14, 49, 162
Sarah K. 168
ADAM
Alexander 150
Christine 136
Eliza Ann 150
Margaret MAIN 150
ADAMS
Agnes JOHNSTON 1
Albert 21
Alva 1
Araminta D. PLATT 1
Asa 1
Betsey 132
Catharine LEWIS 1
Ceb 1
Cecelia A. JAMES 1
Charles 1
Clara Eliza KELLOM 1
D.C. 140
Dora L. BAYLEY 1
Edward 1
Eliza 6
Elizabeth CULVER 1
Ellen LENNEN 21
Emily J. 6
Emly WATSON 1
Emma L. DUKE 1
J.Q. 1
J.W. 46
James 1, 6
James Osgood 38, 61
Jane HOAG 1
John 1, 98
John F. 1
Lena Marie 98
Lucinda 16
Lucy L. BARNETT 1
Luella 21
Mary 136
Mary NIELSON 1
May GRACE 1
Mollie 40
Mr. and Mrs. 30
Philipina CABLE 1
Rirama 33
Sarah 21
Sarah E., Mrs. 80
Sarah J. RICHARDS 1
Semantha FRANKLIN 1
Thomas 1
Thomas A. 150
Walentin 155
William 1, 58, 155
William B.M. 1
William J. 1
William Lawson, Jr. 1

ADAMSKY
A. 74, 89
ADAMSON
Gunder 113
ADDER
Edith H. 162
ADDINGTON
J.L. 1
Mary CRIST 1
Nancy FANSHER 1
ADDIS
Jennie M. 22
Richard 22
S. 84
Sarah DAVIS 22
ADKINS
Maria ALGEO 1
Piatt 1
Sebastian M. 1
ADLER
Cecelia 106
Lotta GOLDSCHEDEN
  106
M. 106
ADLING
Jonas 113
ADRIANCE
Jacob 117, 158
ADSIT
Ann C. WELLS 1
Clara GILBERT 1
German 1
German, Mrs. 143
Mary BROWN 1
Orra 1
Ruth CULVER 1
Shuble 1
ADSTROM
Louisa Charlotte 120
AGAN
Kate 37
AGARD
Anna CHRISTENSEN 1
Julius 1
Nicholena JENSEN 1
Peter 1
AGER
Henry G., M.D. 1
Nancy ROUTH 1
AGUILERA
Euphrasie 77
AHERN
Kate BARRY 1
Nora HAGGARTY 1
Thomas 1
William 1
AHERNE
Jeremiah 16
AHLBORN
Brita M. 9
AHLER
Mary Ann 129
AHLMEN
Caroline Elizabeth 72
AHLQUIST
C.G. 152
C.H. 152
Carl C. 56
Caroline 56
Charles G. 1
Charles O. 42
Gustav Wm. 1
Johanna RINGSTROM
  1
Louisa H. MILNER 1

AHMANSEON
J.A. 41
AHMANSON
Augustie S. 74
Catharine T. STROUP 1
J. 48
Jacob A. 1
John 4, 25, 39, 74, 121
John A. 1
Sophia FIELDSTED 1
AHMEND
Catharina 69
AHMONSON
John 14
AIE
Margaret 91
AIKEN
Lou REED 73
Parker 73
AINSCOW
Edward 40, 124
Rachel 40, 124
AKIN
Ann Eliza 2
ALAWAY
Sarah 39
ALBEN
James 26
Margaret Ann MAY 26
ALBERS
Dorothea 70
Elsabe BESSERANY 70
Jake 70
ALBERT
Anna GIER 1
Bertha 16
Catherine 1
John 1
Joseph 1
Mary HOFFMAN 16
Matilda PARKS, Mrs. 1
Michael 16
Sophia
  KELSCHENBACH 1
Valentine 1
ALBERTSON
Andrew J. 119
Angenett TONEARY 71
Anngenette TONCRAY
  170
Benjamin J. 119
Christian 12
Clara D. 170
Ellen J. 71
Isaac 71, 170
Jens 25
Mary 25, 119
Mary BROWN 25
Mary GRACE 12
Sophia WAGNER 119
Weat 12
ALBIN
James 52
Margaret Ann MAY 52
Roina 52
ALBRO
A.W. 129
Azelia 101
George 101
Roba CARR 101
ALBROS
Sarah 163
ALBROW
Sarah 102

ALDERSEN
Christopher, Mr. and
  Mrs. 57
Mrs. 102
ALDRICH
Ann WATKINS 18
Oney 2
Sarah H. MICKEL 2
ALEXANDER
Allice J., Mrs. 5
Charlotte WILLIAMS
  22
Charlotte, Mrs. 27
Christeen SNYDER 121
Ida CRUMP 2
Isaac 2, 154
J. 68, 123
John 2, 73
Lucy 2
Lucy WALDRON 2
Mary A. 121
Robert 121
Sarah E. DAVIS 112
Violet MAYWEATHER
  2
ALEXANDRIA
James 79
Martha 79
Victoria 79
ALFORD
Anna Margaret RAFERT
  2
Henry A. 2
Isabella
  VANBALARICUM 2
Thomas G. 2
ALFRED
Ella H. GIBSON 2
James 2
John 2
Margaret 2
ALGEO
Maria 1
ALHOUSE
Susanna 43
ALKIER
Tabitha 28
ALLAN
Elizabeth A.
  BUDDINGTON 78
Elizabeth A.
  BUDINGTON 16
Grace Isabel 16
James 78
James T. 16, 78
Jennie M. 78
Thomas T. 126
ALLBRIGHT
John 46
Mary 46
ALLEN
---- PARKER 2
Ada 2
Ann Eliza AKIN 2
Anna DEWELL 2
Arthur 2
Augusta J. OLSEN 2
Belle, Mrs. 48, 101
Charles A. 2
Charles D. 2
Charlotte A. 54
Daniel 170
E.A. 5, 9, 132
Eliza 32
Eliza Anna 6

ALLEN, cont.
Eliza Jane 95
Elizabeth 97
Ellen 37
Elmina 78
Emma 123
Ethan 2
Francis M. 2
Franklin 2
George 45
George W. 2
Gertrude SMITH 2
Harriet E. 118
Harriet M. 74
Horace 2
Isaac Newton 2
J.B. 154
J.M. 48
James B. 56
John 54, 68, 72
Laura A. 68
Lenora GRIFFIN 2
Lizzie 74
Lizzie S. BIEN 2
Lucy Ann 56
Lyman 2
Maggie 45
Margaret 41
Margaret EWING 45
Margaret FOGERTY 2
Maria ABORN 2, 118
Maria ABORNS 2
Martha 149
Martha OLDEN 2
Mary 68, 150
Mary Ann 16
Mary E. 95
Mary E. JOHNSON 2
Mary QUICK 2
Mary QUIRKE 126
Michail 2
Mr. 101
Mrs. 101, 112
Olive C. 127
Orphia H. 108
P.H. 1
Pompey 18, 66, 163
Pompy 2
Rebecca MYERS 2
Thomas D. 2
William 2, 45
William M. 118
ALLENSPAUGH
Amelia 101
ALLEY
Barbara 62
ALLIAS
John 163
ALLING
J.E. MUNGER 2
J.H. 2
ALLIS
Martha A. 69
ALLISON
Eliza A.
McNAUGHTON 2
Elizabeth 64
Eviline H. THOMAS 2
Henry 2
Igantius 153
Ignatius 2
James 2
Mary 141
Mary HOILT 2
Pauline ELROD 2
Sarah 99

William L. 2
ALLKEIER
Tabetha 28
ALLMEN
Catharine ANDERSON
2
Emma C. APPLEGREN
2
John 2
John A. 25
John August 2
ALLOWAY
Alfred 84
Elizabeth ANDERSON
2
Emma L. 84
Johnathan 2
Nancy C. STEWART 2
ALLSINE
Augusta 25
Margaret OLSEN 25
R.G. 25
ALLSMYER
Aleda 161
ALLSTADT
Wm. 167
ALLSTREND
John 2
Lucinda SWANSON 2
Mary DALLBORN 2
William 2
ALMEND
Sine 61
ALPERS
Henrek George 2
Henry 41
John F. 2
Mary ENTELKE 2
Mary WILHELM 2
ALSCHLEBERGER
Elizabeth 58
ALSCLOMAN
Andrew 58
Elizabeth
ALSCHEBERGER
58
Mary M. 58
ALSDOTTER
Brita 4
ALSOP
Thomas 149
ALSTADT
William 71
Wm. 52
ALTERMAN
Elizabeth 71
ALTHAUR
C.A. 71
ALTHAUS
Catharine 136
Gerhard 161
ALTHAUSE
Gerhard 143
ALTHOUSE
Bernhart 2
Christina BERGQUIST
2
Cissina 2
Gerhardt 2
ALTON
Alford 167
Emma 162
Hattie 167
Matilda FRY 167
ALUSSY
Euphrosine 25

ALVOFD
Gent 155
Geret 155
AMBROSE
G.W. 9, 23
Geo. W. 43
George W. 27
AMBROSIO
Catharine BARICALLA
2
Dennis 2
Henry 2
Matilda FISH 2
AMELING
Anna 63
AMEN
Jacob 112
AMEND
Sarah 52
AMENS
Elizabeth 17
AMERSON
Mary May 77
Mary McCUNE 77
William 77
AMES
D.P. 2
E.H. 120
Joseph P. 2
Leonard 40
Louise D. MAHON 138
Mary 64
Mary HAWLEY 2
Mrs. 40
Susan PEARCE 2
AMESBURY
Angeline Harriet DIFFIN
2
see: AMSBARY 2
William A. 2
AMEY
James 78
AMMUNDSEN
Elizabeth 89
AMOS
Mary 170
Sarah 46
AMOSS
Fannie LOGAN 33
Jesse 33
Sophia 33
AMSBARY
Alansin 2
Angeline Harriet DIFFIN
2
Charles 2
D.W. 2
Loa LEMON 2
Marian Ann 118
Mary QUINLIN 2
Sarah ROYCE 2
William A. 2
AMSBURY
D.W. 2
Loa LEMON 2
Nelson 2
Richard 2
see: AMSBARY 2
AMUNDSON
Catharina SIMONSON
34
Christopher 34
Mary 34
ANATONI
Octavia 37

ANDER
Kate 155
ANDERMAT
Theresa 137
ANDERS
Emma SLATTER 143
Libbie P. 143
Thomas 143
ANDERSDATER
Quije 44
ANDERSDOTTER
Carin 134
Christina 119
Christine 74
Gustave 138
Kjerstin 11
Kristin 79
Maria 111
ANDERSEN
Agusta 126
Amalie JACKSTADT 3
Anders 3
Andres 38
Andrew 161, 164
Ann Stina 38
Anna M. JOHANSEN 3
Annie 4, 161
Annie M. 127
Bertha 161
C.A. 2
Caroline SMITH 3
Carrie Mary NELSEN
88
Catherine 152
Charles 54
Christian 88, 121
Christina PETERSON
91
Christine ANDERSON
164
Dorah 121
Dorah MOLT 121
Elnah 92
Gurnil HELVERSON
116
Gustave 77
Hans 64
Hans L. 2
Hellen 77
Ida Matilda 91
James 116
Jenetta 59
Johan 91
Johanes 3
Johanna NIELSEN 127
John P. 127
Juliane MATTHIESEN
64
Kirsten 79
Kirsten SIMINSDOTAR
89
Lars 3, 89
Lena 121
M. 43
Margaret PETERSON 3
Maria 61
Marian LARSON 38
Martha 161
Martha. 77
Martin 3
Mary 3, 26, 111
Mary BOYSON 2
Mary C. 11
Mary LARSEN 3
Mathilde 121
Mine 86

N.M. 113
N.M., Mrs. 113
Neils 3
Ole 116
Oliver 117
R.W. 3
Sophia JACOBSON 2
Stina FELT 3
Swen 152
W. 146
William 25
ANDERSON
A. 160, 162
A.H. 144
A.W. 61, 116
Ala 116
Alma B. 70
Amos 3
Ander 151
Anders 3, 4, 61, 74, 77,
89, 103, 133
Anders M. 76
Andreas 4, 76
Andrew 3, 4, 73, 77,
114, 116, 121, 138,
140, 162
Andrew W. 3
Andrew, Mrs. 121
Ane LARSEN 4
Anna 3, 4, 7, 22, 42,
107, 111, 116
Anna J. 26
Anna JENSEN 151
Anna JOHNSON 13
Anna JONSEND 3
Anna KNUDSEN 3
Anna LAWSON 76
Anna Maria
GORANSON 146
Anna NELSON 4
Anna NILSDOTTER 4
Anna S. 76
Anna Sophia 4
Anna Sophia
ANDERSON 4
Anna WALQUEST 3
Annie 2, 4, 121, 140,
144
Annie G. 72
Annie NELSON 151
Annie NIELSON 162
Anton M. 3
August 3
Augusta 90, 96, 138
Augusta J. 151
Augusta P.
FREDRIKSON 3
B.A. PAINT 4
B.L. 11
Barbara 61
Becca 50
Belle BIRD 4
Bengt 4
Bengta 86
Bent 3
Bertha 88
Betsy 121
Betsy CHRYSEL 3
Betty 73, 116
Bodel K. GODFRED 62
Bolla 112
Botilda LARSON 153
Bride JONSON 121
Brita 133
Brita SWENSDOTTER
4

BABB
Elizabeth 76, 108, 169
Julia OGLEBY 169
William 169
BABCOCK
Dr. 146
Elsie 12
Francis M. 13
G.F. 125
Louisa 146
Lyman Frank 146
Mary V. 146
Mrs. 146
Parnel ELY 13
Priscilla A. 13
BABER
Alice SHERKEY 6
Annie RIGSBY 6
Eliza 124
Frank H. 6
Jane HOWELL 6
John 6
Mary M. HAMMOND 6
Richard T. 6
BABEY
Justin P. 36
BABEZE
Mary 125
BACH
Christian 148
BACHARD
Charlotta 110
BACHE
Anna K. 75
BACHME
Elisa 66
BACHUS
Mary A. 38
BACK
Helene 146
BACKEN
Henry 146
BACKHUUS
Christiana 69
Christina SIEL 69
Claus 69
Mary 69
BACKSTER
Susan 73
BACKSTROM
Carl L. 92
BACKUS
Nancie 83
Nancy 165
BACON
Benjamin 109
Josephine 12
Mary A. 112
Nancy Jane 109
Sylvia 109
BACSTORFF
Frena 22
BADGER
S.D., Rev. 124
BADGLY
Catherine GOGGIN 6
James 6
BAEDERLOW
Auguste 84
BAEMER
Herman 125
BAER
Amelia 68, 90
BAERWALDE
Johanna 170
Wilhelmine 170

BAEUMER
Mathilda 125
BAGDLY
Catherine GOGGIN 6
James 6
BAGG
C.L., Mrs. 59
BAGLEY
Ann MAHAR 6
Charles 39
Honora 165
Honora LOMAY 6
James 28, 165
John 6, 157
Margaret 39
Mary 124, 157
Mary DURELEY 39
Mary WREN 157
Michael 6
BAGLY
Ann MAHAR 6
Honora LOMAY 6
James 6
John 6
Michael 6
BAIER
Christian 6
Elizabeth HETTINGER 6
Frederich 6
Wilhelmina SCHULTZ 6
BAILES
Mary Ann 36
BAILEY
Alice I. HILL 6
Ann Emma HOLLAND 6
Anna CHRISTIAN 6
Catherine HALL 6
Clara KYLE 6
D.R. 6
Dora SUIT 6
Eaton 6
Elizabeth 27
Elizabeth FAVRE 6
Elizabeth MANNING 6
Ella A. 96
Emma 83
Emma BENNETTS 6
Emma J. McLAUGHLIN 6
Emma L. 7
Francis L. 6
Frank L. 6
Frederick 6
G.B. 6
G.B., Mr. and Mrs. 6
George M. 6
Gordon B. 7
Hannah HOPE 6
John 6, 27
John B. 6
John C. 6
Joseph 6
Joshua B. 6
Josphine VERMIRE 27
Lizzie HOGAN 6
Lizzie LOWE 6
Lucy BRADFORD 6
Maria BEER 6
Martha 31
Mary F. FLETCHER 6
Mary PIKE 6
Matilda HINES 6
Minerva BROWN 7

Peter 22
Rachel 78
Sarah A. 125
Stella 83
Thomas 6
Turner 6
William T. 6
BAILY
Anderson 6
Liddy 41
Mary F. FLETCHER 6
Mary PIERCE 6
William T. 6
BAIN
Helan 165
Rosalie 137
BAKER
A. 127
Alexander H. 6
Anna 170
Anthony 45
B.J. 29
Catharine SANFORT 69
Charles E. 6
Christina R., Mrs. 164
Clara RAMET 6
Conrad 27
Daniel W. 6
Eleanor 67
Eliza COOPER 142
Eliza SAINT CLAIR 6
Elizabeth 27
Elizabeth POPERT 27
Elmira BURNELL 6
Ernestine 73
Harriet 146
Hattie 146
Ina L. 105
J. 15, 24
Jacob L. 165
James 6, 133
James A. 6
James N. 142
John 6
Laura 45
Margaret 149
Margaret McKEOWN 6
Martha SCOTT 6
Mary DOLAN 6
Mary J. BERLIN 6
Mollie 60
Nelson 33, 91
Nettie 142
Phoebe 68
Rebecca FOX 6
Robert 45
Salome ELDRED 6
Samuel 6
Sarah P. BRANDON 60
Susan F. FAY 38
Thomas 143
W.I. 107
W.T. 88
William 6, 60
BALACH
Johann 129
Maria 129
Maria K. 129
BALCH
Edward E. 6
Lizzie STEWART 6
BALCOLM
Lorinda 133
BALCOMBE
A.D. 67
Anna FOX 67

Celma 67
BALDOCK
Mary 119
BALDWIN
Anna FLANAGAN 6
B.B. 6
C.A. 17, 24, 62, 87, 103, 126, 153, 164
Calistia KINGSBURRY 6
Caroline LETZIR 6
Charles A. 103, 159
Chas. A. 140
Cyrus 27
David 6
Ella F. 152
Esta WILLIS 6
Grove 6
Harriet H. 25
Henry 6
James H. 29
John C. 152
Lucy M. GARY 152
Margaret ROSE 6
Marion GRIDLEY 103
Marion L. 103
Mary 59, 93
Mary CHAMBERS 6
Runey 6
Sherman C. 6
Talitha 5
BALES
Mary A. 63
BALIMAN
Robert R. 165
BALIN
Oscar 116
BALINGER
---- WADE 66
Alvira 66
Watt 66
BALKWELL
Charles 6
Emily J. ADAMS 6
Susannah KNIGHT 6
BALL
Charlotte ADAIR 7
Daniel 6
Daniel B. 10
Elisha E. 6
Eliza 59
Esther WICKAM 6
Eva McCLARY 6
Fredericke 12
James 59
Jane E. SANFORD 59
Mary 6
Nate 6
Norman F. 7
Phoebe I. 123
Silas S. 7
BALLARD
Elizabeth GOODWIN 149
Hattie CAWEN 7
John L. 149
Louis 7
Margaret MULFORD 7
Mary Jane 148
Nancy P. BORAN 7
Osceola R. 7
Phillip 7
Sarah L. LORAH 7
Thom. 92
Thomas 7
Tom 55

Virginia 71
BALLIET
Charles H. 7
Hannah STARVER 7
John 7
Mary F. ATKINS 7
Saml. A. 7
BALLINGER
Elizabeth 161
Elizabeth WILLIAMS 29, 161
Mary 29
William 29, 161
BALLON
Hariet Marian 154
BALLOU
Otis H. 122
BALLOW
Everett G. 32, 128
Harriet C. 32, 149
Otis H. 35, 56
Susie P. 128
BALLUND
Charles G. 93
BALSON
J., Mrs. 33
BALTCH
Louisa 12, 21
Max 12, 21
BALTSCH
Louisa 12, 21
Max 12, 21
BALTZARSON
Christine ANDERSDOTTER 74
Jacob 74
BAMFORTH
Frederick F. 7
Maria STANSBY 7
Mary Ann CARR 7
S.O. Charles 7
BAND
Henry F. 156
BANDEY
Mary 113
BANDOLE
Frank 150
Mary 150
BANE
Rosena 161
BANER
Catharine 136
Chas. 92
BANES
Sarah 2
BANGET
Christine 108
BANGSTON
Elsa 95
Lena NELSON 24
Nels 24
BANIGER
Magdalena 20
BANKES
Charles 7
Christine HENSE 7
Emilie HUMSTEDT 7
Henry 7
BANKRUFT
Malvina 157
BANKS
Ann NELSON 7
Gain 7
J.W. 7
Jessie E. SNOWDEN 7

BANKS, cont.
John 104
Lucinda 60
Mahala 104
Margaret STUBENE 7
Mariah 104, 156
Orpha RUBY 7
Sarah 5
Thomas 7
BANKSSON
Elsie 113
BANNER
Carrie A. 71
George W. 71
Nancy A. HAGER 71
Thos. 143
BANNISTER
Johanna Matilda 109
Lucretia LILLY 132
Lucritia 132
Margureta 33
Nathan 132
BANSOHELLE
Egeligne 87
BANZA
Mary 84
BANZER
Catherine 150
Dorothea 149
BARAK
Elizabeth 161
John 161
Maria KRUDEL 161
BARAN
Martha A. 166
BARATA
L. 145
BARBA
Mary 70
BARBAN
Elina 110
Lewis 110
Margaret 110
BARBARA
Adaline 169
Catharine O'BRIEN 169
Louis 169
BARBARO
Eliza MEAD 7
Joseph 7
Orsula BRIGNONE 7
BARBER
Adella A. CLARK 7
Anna 43
Charles D. 7
Charles H. 7
Charles J. 7, 130
E.A., Miss 125
Emma L. BAILEY 7
Hannah A. 165
Ida BERRY 7
John 7
Joshua T. 7
Leonora E. OSTROM 7
Mary Ann O'DELL 7
R.W. 7, 32, 52
Rachael WASHBURN 7
Rachel WASHBURN 7
Reuben W. 7
Sarah 127
Sarah FOSTER 7
Sarah J. 137
Thomas 92
William 7
BARBOE
Sarah A. 13

BARBOUR
Mary A. 119
BARD
Ellen 40
BARDEN
Jane 61
BARDWELL
Susan 108
BAREN
Christena 167
BARET
Fanny 85
BARGAUSEN
Charles 7
Matilda C. PETERSON
7
BARGER
Susan 166
BARGHAUSON
Conrad 7
Henrietta HEKMAN 7
BARGSTEDT
Edward 35
Margaretha 35
Wiebke EHLERS 35
BARICALLA
Catharine 2
BARKALOW
Newton 64
BARKELOW
Newton E. 87
Richard 28
BARKER
Austin P. 7
Eliza E. PATRICK 7
Elizabeth BULLIS 7
Elizabeth M. BULLIS 7
Emily CLARK 7
Emily, Mrs. 7
Frances SALT 7
Frances SAULT 60
James 7, 98
James M. 7
John 117
Joseph 7, 60
Joseph, Jr. 7, 60
Joshua M. 7
Mary BURNS 7
Mary E. KETCHAM 9
Mary Jane 60
Mercy F__th 80
BARLEIGH
Frank 12
BARLOW
Alice OAKSON 7
Bluford 7
Dolly McCORMICK 7
Elizabeth 93, 97, 128
Elizabeth PILLING 7
George 7
Harlan 7
Harriet MERVIN 7
Harry 123
James H. 7
Mary HAYS 7
Milton T. 7
Richard 7
BARNACLE
Eliza T. JONES 7
Emily 25
James R. 7
Louisa SMITH 7, 25
Richard 7, 25
BARNARD
Jane C. 8
Mrs. 8

BARNES
Aaron T. 122
Annie HOWARD 7
Barbara 36
Calista 29
Caroline GRAY 7
Catharine 31
Edmund F. 7
Elizabeth KEITH 7
Ellen 54
Emma 111
Ezekia 36
James G. 7
John 48
John H. 7
John J. 7
Maggy 48
Malinda 147
Margaret 98
Margaret COTTER 7
Margaret HERMES 7
Margaretta 36
Martha A. 45
Martha WILSON 122
Mary 131
Mary J. 154
Melissie 122
Minerva 138, 147
Mrs. 143
Percy 70
Theordore B. 7
Thos. 143
William 154
BARNETT
Catharine Ann
SOMERVILLE 7
James 7
John 7
Julia SAUNDERS 1
Lucy L. 1
Randolph 1
Susan UNDERHILL 7
BARNEY
Augusta M. 119
Ella 29, 95
Ella N. 162
Ellen MYERS 110
Ellis 13
Frederick 119
Henry 162
Jennie V. 110
John M. 110
Lucy WERKES 162
Mrs. 170
BARNICH
Elizabeth 5
BARNICOAT
Elizabeth 131
BARNS
Mary 54
BARNUM
Altha E. 72
David 151
Edith G. 72
Ellen 151
Horace W. 141
Levina PALMER 151
Milo S. 72
BARON
Antoine 87
Brigite LAPRE 87
Edward P. 7
Leonore 87
BARR
Annie M. JOHNSON
114

Cynthia L. ANNIS 8
E. Estella 85
Elias A. 8
Elizabeth A. 114
Emily C. 85
Emily C. GUILD 85
Emmilie GILL 8
Galen 8
Jacob 8
John 8, 85, 114
Maria MARSHALL 8
Susanna 8
BARRATT
Ebenezer D. 8
Jesse W. 8
Lucy CHESBROW 8
Lucy CHESSBROW 8
Prudence
WADDINGTON 8
BARRBER
A., Mrs. 69
BARRET
Edmund 135
James A. 8
Jane C. BARNARD 8
Mary 135
BARRETT
Ann BROWN 8
Annie NAUGHTON 8
Daniel S. 8
Edward 48
Eliza 45
H.C. 70
Harriett 96
Honora LYNCH 48
James A. 5
James C. 8
John 8
Julia SHANAHAN 8
Margaret McCARTHY
8
Maria STRANG 8
Mary 48
Mary E. SMITH 8
Miss 109
Patrick 8
Peter 8
Sarah KING 8
William 8
BARRETTE
Edmond 8
BARRICKMAN
Mary 31
BARROFSKY
Erkmuth 79
BARROLL
Lousia 17
BARROT
Edmond 62
Mary 62
BARROWS
Benjamin H. 24
BARROWSKI
Irkmud 128
BARRY
Agnes RYAN 68
Albert 19
Annie 12
Bridget MURRAY 8
Hanora CUMINGS 8
John 8
Julia 40, 115
Kate 1
Lawrence 68
Lillie Esther 19
Mary 12, 20, 60, 68

Mary KELLEY 12
Mary KELLY 8
Mary MANEY 8
Michael 8
Michael J. 8
Mira 19
Silvia BUTTERFIELD
19
T.J. 8
Thomas 8, 12, 19, 20
Thomas J. 8
BARSBALLE
Joes 142
BARSHAN
Charles 7
Matilda C. PETERSON
7
BARSTON
Sarah E. LEWIS 8
Sumner 8
BARTAS
Barbara 118
Barbara LEDR 118
Charles 118
BARTEL
Annie E. 30
BARTELS
Christine PAHLMANN
8
Gustav 8
BARTH
Valentine 38
BARTHOLOMEW 113
A. 115
A.C 45
A.C. 118, 126
Arthur C. 8
Charlotte FLORKEE 8
James 8
L.M. 45, 118
Leonard B. 8
Lottie 126
Mary Ann LABAUGH 8
Mattie LINDSEY 8
Mr. 38
Ruth SMITH 8
William 8
William O. 27
Wm. 124
Wm. O. 148
BARTIG
Adelia A. 137
August 66, 137
Juliana ZELLMAR 137
Juliane ZELLMER 66
Mathilda 66
BARTIGKETT
Wilhelmine 118
BARTLE
Albert 8
Elizabeth TRUBL 8
Frank 8
John 8
Veronika J. KAVAN 8
BARTLET
E.G. 162
BARTLETT
Cora A. BUTTS 8
David 8
E.G. 32
Emma A. 6
George 6
J.P. 28, 143
John P. 95, 120
Phebe G. ELLSWORTH
8

BARTLETT, cont.
Rosaline M.O. WIESE 8
Sarah F. 107
Sarah R. TOWNE 8
V., Mrs. 47
W.R. 107
W.W. 8
Wallace R. 8
William H. 8
William Wallace 8
BARTOE
Cady 74
BARTON
Alice 155
Alice E. 97
Ava SAGE 8
Charles C.C. 97
Eliza RUSSELL 97
Hannah LOWE 8
Ida 162
James 162
Lucy A. 112
Rebba C. WHITE 162
Robert F. 8
Thomas 8
BARTOS
Anna ESPANDE 8
Anton 143
Barbara LEDER 8
Barbara LEDERER 138
Cady 74
Charles 8
Frantisa 143
Frantiska KRISMON
143
Joseph 8, 138
BARTOSCH
Katharina 56, 67
BARTOW
Amelia F. KREBS 81
BASALER
Willhelmina 82
BASCOM
Sarah 124
BASCOMB
Alice PICKORD 8
Anna 8
Hubert T. 8
John 8
BASFORD
Nancy G. 34
BASIL
Barbara 72
BASOM
Amos 65
Eva 65
Sarah L. McCURDY 65
BASS
Sigmond 144
BASSET
Ellen OPENSHAW 8
Geo. C. 24
George C. 58
James H. 8
Joshua H. 8
Maggie OPENSHAW 8
BASSETT
Geo. B. 47
Geo. C. 24
BATE
Winfred 71
BATEMAN
Ella H. 127
Hannah E. POPPLETON
127
R.P. 127

BATES
A.B. 35
Benjamin 59
Caroline 151
Dexter 8
Ellen 65
Emily VOSE 8
Eva WOODS 8
Fannie JOHNSON 82
Fred 8, 167
Hattie 55
Henry 82
J.E., Miss 35
Jane 32
John 65
Mary E. JUSTIN 8
Mary Jane 82
Selah 8
Susana 30
BATESON
John A. 34
BATHEIS
K. 71
BATRAN
Alice 128
BATSFORD
Ann KNIGHT 8
Caroline RADFORD 8
Matthew 8
Thomas 8
BATTE
Algernon 8
Medora S. CLARK 8
BATTLE
Minerva 14
BATTLES
Elizabeth 84
BATTON
Alice 41
Liddy BAILY 41
T. 41
BATY
Mary 124
Nancy J. 83
Nellie 124
Sarah BURGET 124
Sarah J. BURDICK 83
William 83, 124
BAUCHETTE
Emily C. 113
Joseph 113
Margery FRAZER 113
BAUDEN
Marion 89
BAUDER
George 89
Mary A. LYMAN 89
BAUER
Alfred 70
Anna Maria
OSTERTAG 9
Barbara GRUINER 9
Gotthilf 9
Karl 9
Margaretha WEBER 39
BAUERT
Mary A. 70
BAUGHMAN
Barbara 69
BAUMAN
Adam 9
Barbara BOSS 9
Christina 58
Jack 58
Jonas 9, 85
Louisa BOYER 9

BAUMANN
Johanne 74
Joseph 9
Lena ZEPF 9
Otto 9
Wilhelmina MERTENS
9
BAUMEISTER
Anton 9
Frank 113
Lorenz 9
Margaret 137
Marguerita CERTS 113
Mary K. 113
Theresa MAILANDER
9
Victoria STOETZEL 9
BAUMER
Adele Von WASMER 9
Adelia M.H., Mrs. 41
Bernhart 9
Clara WEIHE 9
Col. 27
Herman 9
Hermann 9
John 9, 86, 135, 137
Josephine
GRANACHER 9
Julius 9, 163
Matilda KOBS 9
Mr. 9
Pauline KUPPIG 9
Sophia MARTIN 9
Theodore 9, 41, 65, 103
BAUMESTER
Vichtor, Mrs. 136
BAUMGARDEN
Rachel 117
BAUPUM
Angeline 18
BAUSCH
Catharina P. 9
Helen WEINER 9
Jacob 9
Mathe 9
BAUTHE
Jane 81
BAUVAIS
Betsy 92
Louis 92
Mary A. RAMIA 92
BAVENZER
Jemima 120
BAVERMAN
Nellie 26
BAWEHN
Dorothea 136
BAWES
Cynthia 35
Margaret SMITH 9
Mary HIGGINS 9
Nicholas 9
Silas 35
Stephen 9
BAXTER
A.M. 78
Ann 60
Elizabeth 21
Irving F. 148
Mary A. 125
BAY
Alice 122
Christina McCALL 9
Christine McCALL 9,
122
Harry X. 31

John P. 9, 122
Lizzie H.
WHITEHOUSE 9
Mary BUSH 9
William H. 9
BAYELL
Jennie M.
SHELLINGLORE 90
BAYER
Anna Maria 41
Barbara URBAN 133
Joseph 133
Mary 133
BAYLES
Mary Ann 36
BAYLESS
Susannah 63
BAYLEY
Dora L. 1
Jefferson 1
Mary Jane ANDERSON
1
BAYRHOFFER
Charles Th. 154
Charlotte 154
Fanny J. 154
BEABER
A. Catharine WIETZEL
57
Ella N. 57
Jeremiah 57
BEACH
E.J. 140
George E. 9
Joseph 9
Lucy FISH 9
Mary E. KETCHAM 9
BEAL
Rudolph 12
Wm. T. 11
Wm., Mrs. 11
BEALES
Austin W. 9
Elizabeth AUSTIN 9
F.A. 144
Hannah HALL 9
Priscilla F. HALL 9
Robert 9
William B. 9
BEALL
Roger L. 9
Sarah Ellen HUGUS 9
BEALS
Charlotte 142
BEAM
Nellie 146
BEAMAN
Minerva 83
BEANS
E.A., Mrs. 90, 141
Ethel A., Mrs. 152
Lorenzo W. 144
W.K., Mrs. 68, 83, 94,
112, 115, 123, 131,
144, 165
BEAR
Agnes STIBEL 9
Catharine 51
Elizabeth SPRUHEM 9
Helen WALMER 99
John 9
John C. 99
Mary 140
Minnie 99
BEARBEEN
Caroline 121

BEARD
Camilla E. 42
Delas 88
Eva N. 140
Geo., Mr. and Mrs. 42
George W. 140
Jane 100, 132
Lillie 148
Martha REED 140
BEASON
E. 154
BEATTY
Mary 68
Sam. 155
BEATY
Annie 49
BEAUCHEY
Jennie 94
John 94
Margret
MALLET-DEVINE
94
BEAUMONT
Edward 138
L.E. 45
BEAUREGAURD
Hortense 89
BEAUSOLIEL
Angelique 87
BEAVERS
Adaline 102
Eugenie COURVISEE
102
Louis 102
BECHER
Gustavus 104
Josephine 104
Marie Elenore 84
Mr. 84
BECHTEL
Elizabeth HANN 9
Henry 9
Jacob 9
Julia O'NEIL 9
BECK
Alfred M. 9
Annie C. DUDLEY 9
August 123
Caroline 77
Doralty 167
Helena NELSON 77
Kate S. FRENZER 9
Martin 9
Mary SELINGER 9
MathildeK. 142
Nels Peter 77
Nick P. 94
Theodore 9, 65
Thilde C. 25
BECKER
Dorothea L. FONQUET
30
Edmund 152
Edward 30
Helen HAMMEL 9
Henrietta E.L. 30
John 9
Louisa 170
Margaret DOSE 9
Melinda STAPLES 152
Minnie 30
Phillip 9
Rosana 152
BECKET
Chloe A. 159

BETHGE
A.C. 12
Andrew F. 12
Catherine FOERSTER
12
Mary T. BURKLEY 12
BETLACH
Franz 12
Franziska BLASKA 12
Veronika HYNEK 12
BETSCHER
Henriette 32
BETTS
Caroline 165
Charles 12
Elizabeth WAND 12
G.C. 41, 88
George C. 94
James 12
Thos., Rev. 88
Weat ALBERTSON 12
BETZ
Elizabeth LISTLAND
13
Elizabeth, Mrs. 13
Rebecca 150
BETZELY
Fanny 50
BEUBAKER
Rebecca 150
BEUTEL
Caroline
UNGELFHENE 12
George 12
Jacob 12
Kate REYNOLDS 12
BEVERAGE
Ann WATT 12
Emma SMITH 12
Peter 12
Simpson 12
BEVINS
Andrew 8
George 12
BEWS
Henry 12
Kate METSKER 12
Mr. 22
BEYER
Christian 12
Elizabeth 40, 133
Margaretha
BRAUNLING 12
Maria NERN 12
Wilhelm 12
BEYERSTAN
Christine 92
BICE
Alice 37
Charles 37
Rebecca RICHMOND
37
BICHEL
Christian 12
John 12, 136
Margaretha THUN 12
Maria POHLMANN 12
BICKETT
Charles P. 12
BIDWELL
Angeline 15
BIEBER
Susanna 25
BIEDE
Frederick 12
Fredericke BALL 12

BIEL
Abel BOCK 12
Hans H. 12
Jacob 12
Maria D. PAULSON 12
BIELER
Fritz 12
Gertrude BUCHNER 12
Jacob 12
Salome ERHARDT 12
BIEN
Bernard 2
Burnett 2
Emily, Mrs. 2
Lizzie S. 2
Sophia HELM 2
BIENDORF
Charles 50
Charles, Mr. and Mrs. 66
BIENDORFF
Caroline TIMME 10
Catherine
FAHRENBACH 10
Charles 10
Louis C. 10
BIERBAUM
Elizabeth 73
Johann 73
Theresa
WUENSCHBERGER
73
BIERFOWER
Ellis L. 91
BIERMAN
Henry 12
Kate DEICKMAN 12
Minnie EMMERICH 12
William 12
BIERMANN
Catharine M. PICKMAN
43
Christian H. 43
Louisa W. 43
BIERS
Catherine 56
BIESENDORFER
Jos. 107
Joseph 12
Lizzie SMITH 12
Mary SEIRINGER 12
BIFFAR
Barbara SAILER 58
Catharine "Katy" 58
Francis 58
BIGALOW
Esther 29
BIGELOW
Frances E. 18
Harriett 21
Tamson 5
BIGIRMAN
Mary 156
BIGLAN
Ellen 87
BIGLOW
Lucy 28
BIKOVIS
Augustine 79
Wilhelmina MAKIES 79
William 79
BILETER
Mary E. 19
BILIMECK
Charles 83
Joseph 83

BILIMEK
Charles 83
Joseph 83
BILL(MILL?)MAN
Charles, Mrs. 104
BILLENGREGG
Margaret 132
BILLERBECK
Agnes HERRMANN 12
Ferdinand 12
Wilhelmine? 12
BILLETER
James 127
BILLINGRIN
Margaret 77
BILLINGS
Artie 129
Betsey N. 108
Harriet L. 118
Levi 108
Lizzie 68
Martha WORDMAN
129
Ruth SHERMAN 108
William 129
BILLINGSLY
Anna 22
BILLITER
Marks J. 12
Rebecca M. MORRIS
12
W.L. 110
BILLMAN
Bell S. 109
Bella D. 115, 130
Bella D., Mrs. 80
Bella L., Mrs. 3
Bella S., Mrs. 31
Bella, Mrs. 5
Belle D., Mrs. 34
Ira C., Mrs. 19, 20, 48,
60, 92
J.N. 19
Mrs. 13
BILLS
Albert 12
Elsa ELLYTHORP 12
Lyman 12
Rilla JONES 12
BILSTED
Gustina GRAT 96
Natalie Alida 96
Niels 96
BINCKLY
Nora 11
BINDER
Samuel 138
Thorothea 155
BING
R. 106
BINGAY
Benjamin B. 64
BINGER
Hedwig 20
BINGHAM
Caroline WINDSAY 55
Irene 50
Persis 110
BINGMAN
Cordelia 97
Mary 97
William 97
BINKE
Henry 115
BINKLEY
Charles 152

Nora 152
BINMAN
Margarethe 27
BINZENSHAM
Barbara ZODER 12
Frederick 12
Fredericka METZGER
12
Martin 12
BIRCH
Amelia 36
Emma 68
Mary Anna, Mrs. 12
Mary COMBS 68
Michael 68
BIRCHARD
M.A. 145
BIRD
Belle 4
Elizabeth THIRTLE 4
George 4, 41
John 4
Missouri E. 4
Nellie or Nettie 25
O., Mrs. 122
BIRDSALL
Rachel 168
BIRDSLEY
L.T. 89
BIRK
Alex. John 65
BIRKETT
C.P., Mr. and Mrs. 113
Charles 97
Charles P. 12, 26, 35,
69, 74
Charles P., Mr. and Mrs.
26, 84
Chas. P. 52
Mary Anna BIRCH 12
BIRLINMIER
Christopher 12
Dorothea KAUFMAN
12
George 12
Magdalena BENDER 12
BIRMINGHAM
Francis 12
Frank 12
Jane 101
Julia PENDERGEIST
12
Mary BERRY 12
Mary J. 122
BIRRELL
Margaret 30
BIRT
Lizzie DAVIS 12
Richard 12
BISBEE
Catherine S. 154
Clara A. 154
Hariet Marian BALLON
154
William H. 154
William O. 154
BISCHOFF
Marianne 137
BISHOP
Bell 115
C.L. WILSON 120
Fanny 29
James E. 120
Lucasey HIGGINS 115
Mary 46
Mary E. 120

Wesley 115
BISSELL
Betsey MUNCY 122
Eliza 122
Peter 122
BITHER
Almaretta WILKINS
165
Dean 165
Lillian 165
BITTELIE
Barbara 136
BITTEROFF
Fred 137
Rebekah 137
BITTEROLF
Frederick, Mr. and Mrs.
113
BITTING
Eliza 12
James 12
Louis 12
Lucy KENYON 12
BITTNER
Annie 103
William 103
BIUNKE
Henrietta 125
BIVEN
Charlott 127
BIVRY
Agnes 147
BIXBY
Alfred 12
Catharine MICHIGAN
12
Cleora OAKS 12
R.A. 12
BJEHAUNEK
Barbara 84
BJORKLAND
Fredrika 161
BJORKLUND
Alfred 13
Antonette ELMGREN
13
Margaret HANSEN 13
Peter 13
BJORKMAN
Anna S. NORSILGUS
13
Lawrence 13
Mari Margaretha 81
BJORSETH
Mary 86
BLAAK
Mary 91
BLACHLY
Elizabeth ROUGH 13
Elizabeth SNEATH 13
J.C. 88
Julius C. 13
Miller 13
BLACK
Alexander 13
Christine ANDERSON
13
Clara 40
D.D. 13
David 10
Davy Crockett 13
Elizabeth 93
Elizabeth DOUGLAS 13
Emma ARMAL 13
Georgia Idith
SAUNDERS 13

BLACK, cont.
Henry 119
James 13
Jane MOORE 13
John W. 13
Lyda McLAUGHLIN
 13
Margaret 10
Margaret, Mrs. 119
Mariah 167
Mariah RICE 119
Mary BROWN 13
Mathew 13
Mr. 68
Mrs. 167
Sarah WALLACE 13
William 13
Wm. 86, 119
Wm. H. 115
BLACKBURN
Margaret 70
BLACKFORD
Hannah M. 29
BLACKMER
Elizabeth LISTLAND
 13
Ephriam 13
Matthew 13
Tursey MORLEY 13
BLACKSON
---- 22
Sarah 22
BLACKWELL
Francis 46
Hattie 72
BLACKWOOD
Anna 103
Hannah COLLINS 103
Joseph 103
BLACKY
Elizabeth 52
BLAHA
Barbara 140
Katherine VLCK 140
Maria 85
Wenzel 140
BLAHOW
Barbara 24
BLAIK
Joseph 133
BLAIR
Electa 70
Elizabeth 142
Fannie A. 50
Jane 28
Mrs. 91, 115
Sarah 70
BLAKE
Ann 155
Eleanore DODANE 13
Eliza SPROLE 13
George 13
James 13
Jennie H. GREEN 13
Joseph E. 13
Josephine VAN
 HOUSEN 13
Kate CREIGHTON 13
Walter A. 13
William 13, 31, 139
Wm. 119
BLAKELY
Josephine 98
Margaret 98
Martin 98

BLAKEMAN
Eli 59
George 49
Ida J. 49
Mary E. 59
Mary Elizabeth 59
Melissa C., Mrs. 49
Melissa SCOTT 49
Polly COOK 59
BLAKESLEY
Albert 13
Harriet LEACH 13
BLAKESLY
Albert 57
BLAKSLEE
Charles H. 13
Harriet CARPENTER
 13
Melsena JONES 13
William T. 13
BLAMBERG
Andrew 13
Carrie ANDERSON 13
Jonas 13
BLANCHARD
Bridgett FITZGERALD
 13
Harriet 147
Kathrin HERMAN 13
Martin N. 13
W.S. 13
BLANGUEST
Christina PETERSON
 145
Eva 145
Johannes 145
BLAPOVA
Barbra 80
BLASKA
Franziska 12
BLATCHLEY
Elizabeth ROWE 95
Jenine L. 95
Miller 95
BLAXIM
Catherine GORMAN 13
George 13
Richard 13
BLAZEK
Anna RUZICKA 13
Anna SEMRAD 13
Anna SIMRAT 13
Anna SIMROTH 13
Frank 13
Joseph 13
Josephine NEMEC 13
Josephine NIEMETZ 13
BLEASDALE
Alice 118
Jane 85
Robert 85
BLEICK
Adolph 13
John, Mr. and Mrs. 104
Margaret PETERS 13
BLEIDOM
Caroline 90
BLEIK
Clara 40
Dorothea SCHROEDER
 40
Dorothea, Mrs. 40
John 40
BLESSINGTON
Margaret 126
Patrick 13

BLEWETT
Elizabeth 165
BLIER
Concordia 46
BLISECKER
Magdalena 63
BLISS
Beriah 13
Eliza 5
Ephram H. 13
George L. 13
Hannah GIBBS 13
John 157
Kate 45
Lucinda J. KINTZ 13
Malvina BANKRUFT
 157
Mary LEWELLYN 13
Moses H. 13
Priscilla A. BABCOCK
 13
Priscilla A. CROSBY 13
BLOCH
Ellen 107
BLOCK
Annie, Mrs. 37
BLODGETT
Jane P. 89
Mary A. 125
BLOEK
Mary 98
BLOHM
Christine BRINGE 13
Gustav 13
Theodore 13
Wilhelmina HACKER
 13
BLOIEN
Mary 37
BLOMBERG
Anna 116
Carrie 43
Hans Peter 13
Helena Sophie HYIEM
 13
Karen ERICKSON 13
Peter 43
BLOODGOOD
Sarah N. 71
BLOOM
August 13
Doras BUCHOLZ 13
Ferdinand 13
Fredericka
 LAMPRECHT 13
Simeon 52, 81
BLOOMAUER
Catharine 145
BLOOMHART
Geo. H. 151
BLOTZ
Anton 91
Bertha 91
Clara 91
BLOTZER
Anton 13
Magdalena PRICKEL
 13
Maria GLOCKNER 13
BLOUM
Agata 46
BLUBM
Louise 3
BLUCK
Maria 158

BLUHM
Maria 91
BLUM
Margaret 28
Maria 169
BLUMBE
Caroline BOWER 13
Joseph 13
Maglalena YALTER 13
Sebastian 13
BLUME
W.A. 65
BLUMELE
Sabastian 4
Sebastian 138
BLUMENAN
Catharina 120
BLUMENAUER
Catharine 145
BLUMENSTEIN
Carry 160
Elizabeth LUDWIG 160
Matheas 160
BLUMER
David 14
Henry 14
Lena SPECK 14
Sophie OSBORN 14
BLUTH
Minna 68
BOAND
Euphrosine 25
Francois 25
Harriet CHEVAUX 25
BOARDMAN
Abigal NORTH 14
Kate HOLMES 14
Maria J. 5
William 14
William F. 14
BOASEN
Christian 14
Maggie A. CORBID 14
Peter 14
Sedsel OLESEN 14
BOAZ
E.C. 14
J.M. 14
Mary A. FIELD 14
Mary J. WATTS 14
BOBBIN
Ernestene 79
BOBER
John 6
Rebecca J. 6
BOBIN
Ernestine 79
BOCK
Abel 12
Annie 73
Annie C. LUEDERS 14
Annie
 QUICKENSTEDT 14
Catherina DECKMANN
 14
Eggart 14
Eggert 14
Frederick 14
Hans 73
Henry 14
Jochim F. 14
Margaret KUHL 14
Margaretha EHLER 14
Margaretha KUHL 14
Margarita BUNDS 73
Marguert KUHL 14

Mary BOHMSEN 14
BOCKHOFF
John 149
BOCKOVER
Elizabeth E. 92
BODEN
Andrew 106
BODINE
Sarah 38
BODING
Andrew A. 114
Lina JOHNSON 114
BODINGER
F.W. 162
Frederick W. 158
BOE
F. 45
Louise SCHWARS 45
Meto 45
BOEGE
Katrina 68
Meto 45
BOEHL
Werner 23, 66
BOEHM
E.A. 68
Ella WHALAN 14
Frederick 14
Hafaer 70
Lizzie 68
Marie 70
Minna BLUTH 68
Minnie 68
Regina 70
BOEHME
Augusta 66
Charles 59
Charles H. 14
Elisa 66
Gussie 141
Gussie W. 26
Ida H. BENSON 14
Ida H., Mrs. 59
L. 14
Lewis 141
Louis 92
Mary 92
Mathilda MILLER 14
Mathilda MUELLER
 141
BOEKHOFF
Adeline MEYER 14
George A. 14
John 14, 92
L. 14
Sophia SMITH 14
BOELTER
Henrietta
 MIESENDALL 14
Jack 14
Jacob 14
John Henry 14
Juliette HANS 14
BOEMAN
Amanda J. 25
Jemima BRADLEY 25
John 25
Martha 25
BOESE
Catharina OLDEGS 67
Johann 67
Mary 67
BOETEL
Catharine 108
Catharine GOSCH 108
George 14

BRODERSEN
Brigitta 12
BRODERSON
Dietrich 75
Mrs. 75
BRODFUEHRER
Anna KRUSE 18
Barbara SCHUBARDT
18
Bernhard 18
Fernand 18
BRODFUEHUR
Ferdianand V. 52
BROF
Mary 92
BROFFE
Cordelia A. LACEY 107
James 107
Kitty 107
BROGLE
Mr. 8
Mrs. 8
BROMAAN
Ignatius 108
Rachel 108
BROMENN
Regina 108
BROMOL
Eva 47
BRONICK
Helena WESTERMAN
18
Kate HUGHES 18
Martin 18
William 18
BROOKINS
Belle 61
Jane BARDEN 61
Walter 61
BROOKS
Alice 105
Charles 18
D.C. 42
Datus C. 42
Emily PARKER 18
Florence 42
Harriette BRIER 42
Harvey 95
Martha 95
Mary Isabel SMITH 18
Sarah 21
Thornton 18
BROPHY
Catharine LANAGAN
18
Catharine LANAGARN
77
Ellen 77, 96
James 18, 124
Mary MULLEN 18
Patrick 18, 77
BROSH
Carolina JANETZKO
118
Ferdinand 118
Henriette 118
BROSINS
Augusta 144
Carolina HAELMAN
144
Daniel 144
BROSIONS
Caroline HEILMANN
43
Caroline, Mrs. 43
Carrie S. 43

Daniel 43
BROSIUS
Caroline HILEMAN 18
Daniel 18
Lizza HEOURTH 18
Martin C. 18
BROSLING
J.G. 13
BROTHERLINE
Sarah M. 27
BROUDER
Addriane J. 59
BROUGHTON
M. 122
BROW
Benjamin 133
BROWLEY
Rosa 22
BROWN
---- McCOY 120
A. 18
A.G. 28
A.V. 19
Abbie 129
Abby 81
Abraham 1
Abraham S. 18, 20
Adeline 144
Adeline G. 130
Alice K. 126
Amelia 18
Amelia CREYS 18
Amos 18
Amos H. 18
Angeline 15
Angeline BOUQUET 18
Ann 8
Ann STOVER 18
Anna 48, 112
Anna HINES 15
Anney JONES 18
Annie 19
Annie JONES 19
Arthur 18
Asa B. 18
Barbara 126
Caroline 9, 16
Catharine 1
Catharine EWING 19
Catharine JUDY 18
Charles 1, 18, 27
Charles H. 7, 15, 53, 56,
81, 93, 120, 143, 156,
162, 164
Charley 18
Chas. 18
Chas. F. 123
Chas. H. 79
Christine NELSON 89
Cornelia 69
D.F. 32
Dora RANDOLF 18
Dora S. 60
E.C. 46
Elias 119
Elisha W. 18
Eliza 132
Eliza G. 64
Elizabeth 29, 165
Elizabeth E. MITCHELL
18
Elizabeth M. 36
Ella 33
Ella L. 32
Ellen 54, 105, 141, 158
Emiline 144

Emily A. 100
Emma 32
Emma N. 101
Esther J. 17
Esther NEWMAN 18
Evangaline 1
F.M. 18
Floretta CLARK 18
Frances E. BIGELOW
18
Francis W. 18
Frank E., Mrs. 158
George 18
H.M. 1
Hanna 18
Hannah 69
Hannah E. 32
Hannah E. ANDERSON
32
Harrason 18
Harriet 17
Harrison 18, 120
Helen 158
Henrietta STEINBURG
18
Henry 18
Henry L. 18
Henry M. 119
Henry O. 18
Hester 19
Hiram 32
Ida M. COX 18
Isaac 18
Isabelle CAMERON 18
J.W. 20
James 29, 42, 48, 89
James A. 18
James B. 124
James J. 18, 45
James S. 20
James, Mr. and Mrs. 48
Jane 60
Jane DIXON 19
Jennie 26, 41, 90, 156
Jennie A. 48
Jennie L. BENNETT 18
Jennie REED 19
Johanna 94
John 60, 165
Joseph 18, 112
Julia 57
L. 18
Laura CAMPBELL 18
Lazar 112
Lazare 69
Lena 112
Lillias TORREY 18
Lizzie B. 1
Lizzie E., Mrs. 120
Louisa 166
Lucretia DAVIS 18
Lucy A. 44
M.B. 18
M.K., Mrs. 45
Maggie 35, 83
Mamie A. 120
Margaret 79, 116, 119,
122, 124
Margaret M. 119
Martha 42
Martha A. 75, 162
Martha A. PATTERSON
158
Martha Ann
PATTERSON 101
Mary 1, 13, 15, 25, 64,

105, 146, 165
Mary A. 45
Mary A. BRENT 18
Mary DUFREES 18
Mary E. 4
Mary E. BILETER 19
Mary E. BONE 19
Mary Ellen 130
Mary M. RYAN 18
Mary MERLATTE 33
Mary OSTROM 18
Mary STOVER 42
Mary W. 131
Matilda 49
Minerva 7
Missouri KENNEDY 18
Molly WARE 1
Myron 18
Nancy 69, 145
Nelson 18, 99
Oscar H. 19
Patrick 94
Peter J. 19, 111
Pliney E. 18
Randall A. 19, 162
Rebca Jane 99
Rebecca 51
Rebecca CHRISTIAN
32
Rebecca Jane 54
Rebecca WATTS 119
Robert 33
Romania 158
Romania GRAY 18
Rosa 112
Rudolph 112
Sarah BENNETT 124
Sarah M. VAN SYCLE
19
Sarah SINGLETON 60
Sarah, Mrs. 9
Scynthia 153
Sina B. 89
Solomon 19, 162
Sophia 32
Sophia O. 18
Susan 67, 84, 127
Susan C. 22
Susanna 33
Susannah 156
W.F. 151
W.H. 8, 108, 162
Walter 18
Will 22, 76, 82
William 15, 18, 19, 101
William F. 19
William H. 18, 19
William H.F. 19
William Young 11
Wm. 5, 67, 158
Wm. H. 21, 26
Wm. R., Mr. and Mrs.
91, 145
Wm. Young 132
BROWNE
Martha PATTERSON
146
Mary R. 146
W.D. 146
Will 22, 82, 94
BROWNING
Corinthia ATKINSON
18
Elizabeth 19
Jennie HANGER 18
John 19

Ruth MAYWEATHER
19
Walker 19
William D. 18
Woodson W. 18
BRUCE
Caroline 152
Eva 92
J.A. 92
Maria 22
Miner W. 105
Walace 125
BRUDER
Lizzie KELLY 19
Martin 19
Mary CALAN 19
Timothy 19
BRUDERMANN
Elizabeth 149
John 149
Mary BRECHBRIEHL
149
BRUDMAN
Bernard F. 19
Henry J. 19
Madaline DOSE 19
Marianna
HEBENSTREIT 19
BRUENING
William 96
BRUGH
Magdalene 86
BRUHN
Anna M. LUENEBURG
19
F. 137
Henry 12, 93
Joachim H. 19
Johann 19
Wiebke WENNINGES
19
BRULN
John 19
Wilhelmine
TIMMERMAN 19
BRUMM
L. 65
Susan 65
BRUNER
Bella E. 152
Charles E. 152
Elizabeth 164
T.C. 58
Uriah 152
BRUNING
Henry 96
Maragaret FOSTER 96
Margaret 96
BRUNNER
Chas. 66
Jas. B. 87
John G. 19
Judith ERDMAN 19
Maria 157
Nellie M. REED 19
T.E. 19
Thomas C. 19
BRUNO
Dennis 49
BRUNS
Threasea 135
BRUNTSON
Martha PETERSON
152
Swen 152

BURGOUN
Charity 83
BURGOYNE
Emma ROBERTS 20
Margaret DUNCAN 20
P.E. 20
W.M. 20
BURGSTROM
S. 28, 41
BURHAM
Nathan J. 168
BURHUS
A.P. 125
F.M. 125
BURIS
Maria 141
BURK
Alexander J. 20, 32
Christina PARSSON 11
Edward 20
Eliza RUSSELL 20
Emma Christina 11
Henry F. 20
John 11
Julia BERRY 20
Julia N. 20
Margaret 155
Mary 20, 82
Nancy 26
Phoebe 159
Sarah 159
William 20
BURKANSTOCK
Adolph 20
Caroline DONALDSON
20
Charles 20
Mary GIBSON 20
BURKE
Alexander L. 20
Ann DULING 20
Barton 37
Catherine BRIGGS 20
Christina ELGE 20
Daniel 22
Edward 137
Eliza 72, 107
Elizabeth 153
Elizabeth KELLY 23,
153
Ellen 125
G. 80
George 6
George B. 20
Gustavus 20
Henry F. 20
J.H. 108
John 20, 23, 40, 72, 141,
153
Justina M. 169
Lizzie 23
Margaret J. 23
Mary 22, 141
Mary Ellen 37
Mary HILL 72
Mary KENNEDY 20
Mary L. MURRAY 20
Mary McCARTHY 20
Mary O'CONNELL 37
Mary TIERNEY? 20
Matilda JOHNSON 20
Mrs. 6
Peter 20
Phoebe 40
Phoebe L. 158
Thomas 19, 20

William 20
BURKET
Ella M. HASKELL 20
Fred C. 20
Henry K. 20
Julia A. KENNEDY 20
Mary 94
BURKETT
C.P. 136
BURKHARD
A. 20
Catherine RIEDEL 20
Catherine RUDELL 20
Cecilie BURLKEY 20
Frank 20
Jennie V. PISCHKE 20
John 20, 58
Kate 169
Mary DORNALDT 20
Rosa SCHOFF 20
Sylvester 20
BURKHART
A. 150
Annie 92
Date 86
Mary 112
BURKLEY
Frank 12
Louisa 20, 89
Mary T. 12
Patrick 45
Theeresa STELTZER
12
Thersia STELTZER 89
Vincent 12, 89
BURLAGE
Henrietta, Mrs. 110, 149
BURLEY
D.E. 49, 114, 163
David E. 14, 129
John 33
BURLIN
Francis A. 96
BURLINGHAM
Ella E. 156
BURLKEY
Cecilie 20
BURMEISTER
Charles E. 20
Elizabeth GEITMANN
20
Frederick 68
J.F., Mr. 20
Mary E. MEYER 20
BURMESTER
Adolph 43, 163
Adolphus 20
C.E. 160
Charles 20
Emele 79
Mary R. WEHRER 20
BURNAP
Mary P. 145
BURNE
Margaret 95
BURNELL
Elizabeth HOLLAND
59
Elmira 6
Lida 59
Wm. 59
BURNES
Bridget 28
Ellen MAHAR 20
John 20
John G. 20

Mary 151
Mary FARLEY 30
Samuel 93
BURNET
Josephine 47
BURNETT
Charlotta M. 162
Harriet WILSON 20
John 20
Matilda WILSON 20
BURNEY
Gustave 21
Herman 21
John G. 21
John Willis 21
Josie JOHNSON 21
Mary H. DENTON 21
Mr. 18
Nancy J. HANEY 21
Sarah M. 18
Susanna SALHOLM 21
BURNHAM
A.M., M.D. 72
A.M., Mrs. 72
Annie 103
Col. 157
Eliza 90
Fannie Amelia 130
Harriet 105
Horace B. 21, 29, 103
Julia KNOWLAND 78
L. 167
Leavitt H. 36
Mary 29
Mary Clarke MORGAN
21
Mary E. 130
Mary M. 130
Mary MORSE 130
N.J. 15
Nathan J. 21
Noah 130
O.C. 93
Ruth A. JACKSON 21,
29, 103
BURNS
Alice 41
Ann 130
Annie 64
Bridget 21
Catharine 21
Daisy A. 89
Edward 2
Eliza 9
Elizabeth 65
Ellen 107
Emily COPELAND 21
Fannie 81
Fanny TRETLER 21
Francis 21
Frank 21
George 21
Harriet E. FOX 21
James 30, 80
John 7, 21
Joseph 21, 87
Lizzetta 19
Lizzie 133, 156
Maria 30
Mary 7, 29
Mary DORMER 21
Mary E. DENMAN 21
Mary MAHER 7
Mary WILLIAMS 21
Mirum 57
Patrick 21

Rosa 130
Rose 30
S. 8
Sallie McCORMICK 21
Sam'l. 157
Sam'l., Mrs. 157
Samuel 7, 21, 40, 68,
112
Sarah E. TRUEX 89
Sarah M. 160
Selina McKELL 21
Sylvester 149
William 21, 89
BURNUM
Mr. 72
Mrs. 72
BURR
David P. 21
George C. 21
Mary Jane YEOMANS
21
Nathaniel 21
Ruth M. 168
Stella N. SHAW 21
BURRAL
Maria 76
BURRILL
Arnold 21
J.W. 21
Lula J. KELLEY 21
Mary J. PHILLIPS 21
BURRIS
Christine HYDE 21
Jacob 21
Jennie SHAFER 21
O.P. 21
BURROUGHS
Chretia MERRILL 138
J.H. 44
Jennie 138
John H. 138
Louisa 91
BURROWS
Ellen J. 165
Ellen Jane 55
BURSELL
Oliver 9, 115, 138
Olivia 75
Sarah Elizabeth 115
BURSIC
Jacob 20
BURSIK
Albert 21
Katy KOFKA 21
Veronicka HASA 21
BURSKI
Edward 39
BURT
Lizzie DAVIS 12
Mary A. 144
Richard 12
BURTON
Elizabeth 69
Elizabeth A. 156
Henry 21
Isaac B. 21
Juliet C.
BRITTENDALL 21
Louisa JOHNSON 21
Margaret 57
Nancy
QUACKENBURKE
69
Phillip 69
BUSCH
Fr. 79

BUSEY
Amanda E. 81
Bell 30
Rebecca LUTZ 30, 81
William 30, 81
BUSH
Bridget 9
Frederiki 24
Hannah SMITH 55
Jennie 9
John 9, 62
Julia S. 55
Margaret A. 62
Mary 9
Mary E. 31
Mary STEVENS 62
Rosalia 62
William 55
BUSHEA
Joseph 159
Mary 159
Rosana 159
BUSHEL
Casper 79
Julia KALCH 114
Julia KELCH 79
Mary A. 79
BUSHEY
Alice BURNS 41
Bridget BURNES 28
Bridget BURNS 21
J. 28
John 21, 28, 41
Julia COLBERT 21
Kittie 41
Martha WAYBRIGHT
21
Michael 21, 114
Susie J. 28
BUSHIE
Catherine Able 132
BUSHNELL 21
Chester 21
Delia DAYTON 21
Lucinda M. WILLIAMS
21
Mary 43, 47
Mary J. 47
BUSING
Ger. 41
BUSKAT
Carl 21
Gustav 21
Louisa RINGAT 21
Minna STAGAN 21
BUSSE
Dorathea MARWIPS 14
John 14
Louise 14
Mary 129
BUSSEL
Jane TUCKER 155
John 155
Sarah J. 155
BUTE
Joseph 158
Mary SMITH 158
Sara Virginia 158
BUTLER
Alice 102
Amanda 147
Amanda CAREL 164
Amanda CARROLL 46
Amelia 119
Ann 142
Anna 164

CAMPBELL, cont.
Thomas 22
W. 74
Wesley Williams 22
William 22
Willson 22
CAMRON
Florilla 101
CANABEY
Alexander 88
Mary BRENARD 88
CANAN
Margaret 8
Sibby 122
CANAVAN
B. 103
Eliza 103
CANDEE
Helen M.K. 69
Mary LA
  TARUUETTEE 69
Wm. B. 69
CANDLISH
James 60
CANE
Catherine 143
John 125
CANFIELD
Geo., Mrs. 24
Mary 57
Mrs. 119
CANHORN
Rebecca 22
CANNARY
Charlotte BURCH 129
Marth 129
Robert W. 129
CANNELL 23
Catherine 23
Edward 91
Esther 91
Hannah RYAN 23
Margaret 11
Mary RECRAFT 91
Michael 23
Patrick 23
CANNER
Mary 91
CANNING
Catherine 115
George 23
Hannah HASELL 23
M.P. 23
May MORRIS 23
CANNIS
Margaret 90
CANNON
Anna McMANAMEY
  23
Charles 23
E.E., Miss 105
James L. 23
Martin 23
Mary 49
Mary GRIFFIN 23
CANOYER
Charles 29
CANTY
Ellen 35
Johanna 30
CANTZ
Ellen 54
Mary LAWLER 54
Timothy 54
CANTZEN
Angela 65

CANZETT
Andrew 23
Hans 23
Lizzie B. SCHITTRA
  23
Lucy MINCH 23
CAPELLE
Julia 39, 166
CAPPENHAN
Ludwig 105
Mollie 105
Wilhelmina KOKOLEES
  105
CAPPINS
Catharine 158
CAPPIUS
Catharine 158
CAPPOCK
M.C. 107
CAPRON
Hattie 151
CAPWELL
Lydia 27
CARDIN
Mary 89
CAREFOOT
Mary Agnes 81
CAREL
Amanda 164
CAREY
Andrew 23
Annie SHELTON 33
Augustus 23
Bridget 113
Catharine 7
Del CLEMONS 23
Dellia GOODWIN 23
Ellen 81
Ellen AUSTIN 23
Ellen SULLIVAN 105
Hannah 105
Henry 23
Justus 54
Mary 38, 51
Michael 105
Sarah 52
Simon 7
T.J. 23
CARHART
Mary 76
CARIMODY
Mary 35
CARLEN
Bridget SMITT 23
Margaret A. McATEE
  23
Michael 23
Patrick 23
CARLESON
Johanna 11
CARLILE
Jacob 23
Maggie KELLIHAN 23
Mary E. KIRK 23
Wm. 23
CARLISLE
---- 18
CARLSDOTTER
Clara JOHNSON 25
Martha 164
CARLSON
A.J. 75
A.P. 23
Alfred 23
Anders 3
Andrew F. 23

Anna C. 46
Anna JACOBSON 23
Anna PETERSON 23
Annie F. GRANSTRIM
  23
Annie HANSEN 23
Berta NELSON 23
Caren Elizabeth
  SODERLAND 23
Carl Gustav 88
Catharine 89
Charles 89, 151
Chas. 43
Christina FLINK 3
Christine 122
Clara 43
Gertrude HINRICKSON
  88
Hannah JOHNSON 23
Hannah RYDQUIST 43
James 23
Johanna JOHNSON 20
John 20
John F. 23
Louise 88
Louiza 145
Maria 3
Martha 114
Mary 159
Mary JACOBSEN 89
Ole 23
Sara Maria 135
Sarah Maria 111
CARLTON
Catherine MORRIS 23
Florence J. 83
George 83
George L. 165
Henry 30
James 23
Lizzie 165
Margaret 53
Maria CORDAN 23
Nancie BACKUS 83
Nancy B. 165
Nancy BACKUS 165
Sabins 35
Thomas 23
CARLYLE
Adam 146
Anna 146
Catherine E. COOK 146
Jennie 146
CARMEL
Ellen 69
CARMICHEL
Matilda 34
CARMICK
Ann 131
CARMODY
Catherine 94
Johanna 69
Kate 24
Mary 128
Mary RYAN 24
Stephen 24
CARNABY
Joseph 100
CARNAHAN
Catherine 29
CARNAN
Louisa BONNER 72
Robert N. 72
Sarah G. 72
CARNAY
Johanna 114

CARNES
Andrew 23
Edmond C. 23
Margaret J. BURKE 23
Mary E. MITCHELL 23
CARNEY
Anna LAWLER 23
Bridget CAMPBELL 23
Eliza PHELPS 23
John 23
John M. 23
William H. 23
CARPEHR
John W. 141
CARPENTER
Anna B. McCULLOCH
  32
Annie B.
  McCULLOUGH 155
Bridget 91
Camilla 21
Cynthia M. 159
Daniel W. 32
Francis M. MUNGER
  110
Harriet 13
Harry 110
Julia 127
Julia A. 116
Kate Z. 32
Minnetta J.W. SNOW
  23
Ophilia R. WHEELER
  23
Peter C. 23
Thomas W. 23
CARR
Adeline 1
Amanda E. COLE 23
Ann J. 52
Annie 130
Belle E., Mrs. 47
Benjamin 23
Catharine 28, 83
Christopher 99
Eliza Jane 99
Ellen 36
Emilie 102
George 23
James 115
June 8
Margaret 134
Margaret MAREN 7
Mary 99
Mary Ann 7
Mary E. OLEPHANT
  23
Roba 101
Stephen A. 23
Susanna DIXON 23
Timothy 7, 43, 134
CARRAGG
Margaret 126
CARRIDEN
Maggie 145
CARRIDOR
Mary 10
CARRIER
Richard 57, 71
CARRIGAN
David 30
Margaret LAFFERTY
  30
Mary 156
CARROL
Ellen 24

Julia 99
Margaret 69
CARROLL
Agnes TROY 30
Amanda 46
Anne HAWKINS 23
Bridget 55
Bridgett 165
Delia HENNESSEY 23
Denis 8
Eliza 45
Ester COLEMAN 23
Eunice Malisee BOWER
  23
Frances E. 64
Frank B. 23
George L. 23, 35
James 22
John 23, 37, 42
Julia 81, 151
Julia Ann PROPHET 23
Kate 39
Kate E. 100
Kate NERKIE 64
Louisa HEANY 23
Margaret 114
Margaret, Mrs. 32
Martin 23
Mary 30, 139
Mary ROONEY 23
Nora 165
P.J. 122
Patrick 23, 122
Peter 23
Thomas 30, 64
CARRY
Elizabeth 160
CARSEN
Jens F. 75
CARSON
Catharine 35
CARSTENS
August 23, 35
Bernard 23
Catharine 20
Christine 97
Dorothea KOBARK 23
Hans 23
Margaret KOCH 23
CARSTENSEN
Kathrina 61
CARTER
Alcinda PETTIS 24
Anna 90
Annie 147
E.V. 130
Elizabeth J. 39
Francis Mary 76
G.E. 12
J., Mr. and Mrs. 167
Jennie W., Mrs. 129
John 24, 119, 167
Judith W. 103
Julia 40
Lee 24
Mary 152
Mary E. LOCKRIDGE
  10
Mary Jane 24
R.G. 98
Sarah 107
Thursa JOHNSON 90
Wm. E. 90
CARTREL
Elizabeth 166

CARY
Ann McCANNON 24
Catharine WHEELER 23
George 23
Martin 23
Mary HUGHES 24
Nettie 162
Patrick 24
CASDELL
Charles 41
Emma WOODRUFF 41
Lucy A. 41
CASE
Bertha 157, 158
Bridget 115
Ellen 84
Ellen SLOAN 24
Flavious 24
Hannah PAGE 24
James A. 24
John 146, 158
Melinda COATES 24
Michael 84
Sarah CALDWELL 158
Sarah COLNELL 146
Susie H. PEASE 24
Tabitha 146
William Page 24
CASEY
Alice REGAN 29
Benjamine 24
Bridget 10, 17, 23, 30, 101, 134
Caroline DUMAN 24
Caroline DUMAR 24
Catharine REAL 30
Catherine 30, 59
Christopher 24
Ellen 109, 132, 164
Ellen CHASE 24
Ellen CHILTON 24
Henry 24
John 24
Kate CARMODY 24
Kate REALE 134
Maggie 134
Maggie SANNOT 24
Margaret 29, 83
Margaret McCANN 24
Margaret NOLAN 24
Margaret RYAN 37
Mary 28, 37, 43
Mary ELWOOD 83
Mary NALAN 24
Mary NOLAN 24
Michael 24, 29, 30, 134
Patrick 37
Peter 83
Rachael 162
Stephen 24
Susan ISAACS 24
Thomas 24
Thomas J. 24
CASHEN
Bridget 68
CASPER
Alice 168
Hannah 138
CASPERSON
Anna 26
CASSADY
Jane 85
Margaret PHELEN 85
Margret A. 98
Maria 85, 98

Philip 85
CASSEDY
Patrick 100
CASSELL
Fanny GREEN 131
John 131
Nettie 131
Sarah 131
CASSHIN
Ellen KENNEDY 64
Hugh 64
Jane 64
CASSIDY
Edward 22, 24, 96
Henry 24
Jane F. 96
Lara 66
Margaret 71
Margaret A. 100
Margaret PHALON 24
Mary Ann 6, 39
Philip 24
Phillip 96, 153
Rosey 100
Sarah 153
CASSLER
Abraham 85
Anna, Mrs. 85
CASSON
Margaret A. 19
CASTDORF
Joanne Christina Friederike 104
CASTILLO
Mary A. 46
CASTLE
Elizabeth 1
CASTLETON
Ellen MORRIS 24
Joseph 24
Mary SMITH 24
William 24
CASTNER
Barbara BLAHOW 24
Elizabeth CILIAM 110
Elizabeth CILIAN 24
John 24
Thomas 24
CASTON
Catherine 132
CASTONSON
Cary 75
CASY
Benjamine 24
CATAMER
Leah 21
CATHER
Rebecca 25
CATHERWOOD
Anna 27
Annie 10, 106, 112, 121, 160, 170
Annie B. 33
Elizabeth PATTERSON 48
James 48
Matilda 48
CATLIN
Charles F. 24
Elizabeth TRUMAN 24
Josephine HOMAN 24
Mary Jane CARTER 24
Philip 24
Robert 24
CATTLE
Charles 24

Eliza COY 24
Henry A. 24
Rebecca KULER 24
CAUDLE
Gervan 49
Martha DUNCAN 49
Sarah 49
CAULFIELD
John S. 47
CAVANA
Margaret 81
CAVANAGH
Mary 22
CAVANAUGH
Ellen 80
Hannah LEARY 24
Lizzie 81
Mary WILLIAMS 24
Patrick 24
CAVENAUGH
Henry 54
CAVEO
Edward 32
Louisa 32
CAVY
M. 122
CAWAN
Caroline McGUIRE 5
Edward 5
Mary 5
CAWEN
Hariett RASE 7
Harry 7
Hattie 7
CAYTON
Almeda CLARK 24
James G. 24
CEARY
Ellen CARROL 24
Hugh 24
Mary LEAHY 24
Thomas 24
CEDERBLOM
C. 9, 113
CEDERLIND
John A. 24
Louisa A. LEION 24
CELACHEK
Veronika 145
CEMMENSTEONE
Henry 102
Louise 102
Sarah N. RADAWAY 102
CEMPAL
Magdalene 69
CENNEBAUGH
H.W. 37
CENTER
Brozel 81
Jane BAUTHE 81
Maitland 24
Maria MORRIS 24
CERTS
Marguerita 113
CESSIN
Augusta LINDTSTED 24
Carl 24
F. 24
Lena MELCHER 24
CESSNE
Jane 146
CETTELMOYER
Mary Ann 62

CHAD
Ruth A. 156
CHADWICK
A.M. 6, 127, 152, 164
A.N. 28
Angie HOLMES 24
David 24
Fidelia PARISH 24
Rose 163
Willis T. 24
CHALFANT
John 24
Lena M. GANTT 24
CHALLMAN
John 116
CHALMAN
Henry 77
John 25
Maria 77
CHALMER
Mr. 8
CHALMERS
---- 8
Alice M. WALKER 24
Elvira J. MACKEY 24
Joseph Harvey 24
Wm. 24
CHALS
Rosa 92
CHAMBERLAIN
Adaline 21
H.A., Mrs. 54
H.H., Mrs. 54
Nancy 144
CHAMBERLIN
E.B. 24
Emma PARMLEY 24
Malinda RUSSELL 24
S.P. 24
CHAMBERS
Hannah 119
Jeannette KIDDER 78
John 6
Mary 6, 78
Mary VERKIER 6
Sarah GARVEY 24
William 24
Wm. 78
CHAMPLIN
Elizabeth 112
CHANDLER
C.H., Mrs. 47
Clara D. KENNEDY 24
Clarisa 97
E.B. 24
Elizabeth 57
Lydia 146
Phillis 19
CHANNEL
Samuel M. 44
CHAPIN
Mary 41
CHAPLIN
Edward H. 16
CHAPMAN
A.F. 84
A.Y.[G.] 25
Adelaide 40
Adeline 141
B.H., Mr. and Mrs. 40
Elizabeth 66
Elizabeth IRELAND 25
Emily BARNACLE 25
H.A. 3
Henry 141
Hugh 25

James 73
James J. 70
Jane 168
John 25
Margaret DONOVEN 25
Martha J. WILSON 25
Mary R. ARNOLD 17
Nellie BIRD 25
Nettie BIRD 25
Olufreer 117
Phoeba 114
Samantha 39
William 25
William Laub 25
CHARLES
Carrie 43
Henry 131
Lettie J. 131
Luida THOMAS 25
Main 25
Mary E. WHITING 25
Sadie E. REDMAN 131
Sara 71
Susan 132
Warry I. 25
CHARLESON
Anna 11
CHARLICOM
Sarah 32
CHARLTON
A.G. 41
J.B. 41
Lucy GOW 41
Mary Grace 41
CHARTERS
Annie 32
Eliza ALLEN 32
James 32
CHARTIER
Leonore BARON 87
CHARVOZ
Anna M. BOVIN 25
John 25
Louis "Lew" 25
CHASE
A.W. 103
C.S. 106, 149
C.S., Mrs. 149
Champion S. 103
Charles 25
E.J. READER 25
Ellen 24
Elmina ALLEN 78
Enoch M. 78
Herman 93
Isaac 24
J. 24
L.H. 55
Lathiel T. 33
Lucy E. 78
M.L. 25
Margareta RUNNER 93
Mary 55, 93
Mary J. GUARD 24
Mary J., Mrs. 94
Mary LUDLOW 24
Nancy R. 153
Rebecca CATHER 25
CHASTE
Eugene 25
Katie WALL 25
Mary SCHWABATA 25
CHATFIELD
Hannah A. 32

CIPERA
  Anna 69
  George 69
  Josephine TACHOVA 69
  Theresa 66
CISAR
  Anthony 99
  Franciska HVEZDA 156
  John 156
  Katharina 156
  Katie 99
CISEINER
  Franciska HVEZDA 156
  John 156
  Katharina 156
CLABBY
  Delia 162
CLABROUGH
  Jane 158
CLAIBORNE
  Charles B.E. 26
  Richard B. 26
  Rose THOMPSON 26
  Sarah WOODWORTH 26
CLAIR
  James 26, 160
  John 26
  Margaret FANNING 26
  Mary REDDEN 26
CLANCY
  Mr. 1
CLAP
  Julia 165
CLAPP
  Charles M. 26
  Emma L. GOERNER 26
  Flora GODING 26
  Moody 26
CLAPSHAW
  S.H. 81
CLARE
  Arena ALBEN 26
  Charles 26
  Elizabeth HOLT 26
  J. 44
  John 26, 109
CLAREY
  Michael 157
CLARK
  A.M. 21, 27, 73, 97
  Adella A. 7
  Agnes 57
  Albert M. 27, 140
  Alice 28
  Almeda 24
  Annie 139, 167
  Bridget E. 48
  Byron D. 166
  Carrie E., Mrs. 53
  Catharina 102
  Catharine LYNCH 48
  Catharine MURPHY 27
  Catherine 33, 40
  Catherine AULT 1
  Catherine, Mrs. 105
  Celestia M. 147
  Charles 167
  Charlotte E. 25
  Christena GUNTER 27
  Christopher 27
  D. 126
  D.B. 26
  D.R. 33
  David 115

Dora ROBINSON 105
E.V. 1
Edith E. 26, 47
Edward 26
Edward Mills 26
Edwin J. 26
Edwin K. 26
Elam 7, 26, 47
Elizabeth BAILEY 27
Elizabeth BAKER 27
Elizabeth E. STUBEN 26
Elizabeth M. RILEY 27
Ellen 126
Ellen McGUE 27
Ellen WILLIAMS 26
Emily 7
Esther JONES 26
Fannie CAMPBELL 27
Fannie COPBELL 27
Fannie GIBBS 27
Fanny HARPER 46
Floretta 18
Francis 64
Frank 78
George 50, 105
George J. 132
George W. 26
Gertrude 82
Grace 170
H. 27
H.H. 27, 56
Hannah 134
Hannah V. JACKSON 154
Harriet C. 154
Helena LEISGE 26
Henry S. 26
I.T., Mrs. 36
Imogene 8
Isabelle 90
J.H. 150
J.T. 3, 154
J.T., Mrs. 23, 89
James 26
Jane 50, 154
Jane GOLDSWORTH 27
Jean 168
Jennie 39
Jenny COE 7
Jno. T. 141
John 27, 126
John C. 26
John M. 129
John S. 8
John S., Mr. and Mrs. 8
Joseph 27
Josiah 27, 42
Justin S. 26
Kate J. DENNIS 26
L.B. 154
Libbie M. RILEY 27
Lida 155
Lily M. 1
Lizzie 46
Lizzie M. BOWLES 26
Lorenzo D. 39
Louisa 55
Lucinda 33
M.H. 144
M.H., Mr. and Mrs. 144
Margaret 28
Margaret LYNCH 26
Maria GARNER 27
Martha M. RISLEY 27

Mary 69, 95, 106, 112
Mary CRONAN 26
Mary E. 101
Mary E. TRUMBULL 26
Mary J. MILLER 26
Mary KNAPP 27
Mary O'BRIEN 33, 139
Mary, Mrs. 2
Medora 9
Medora S. 8
Miles J. 27
Minerva COLE 27
Minerva RIGGS 27
Minnie M. HAWES 27
Miranda BOWEN 50
Mitchell 27
Nancy M. 42
Nancy MAXFIELD 42
Noah S. 27
O.P. 24
Oscar 154
Patrick 33, 48, 139
Peter 90
Pierce 27
Priscilla Jane 47
Rebecca 51
Rebecca ---- 47
Rebecca HARMON 7
Rebecca JUDSON 26
Rhoda SWAN 27
Robert 28, 155
Roda SWAN 27
Rose ---- 39
S.E. 21, 97
S.F. 7
S.H.H. 44
S.H.H., Mrs. 35, 104
S.S. 24
Samuel R. 27
Sarah 28, 108, 110
Sarah Ann REED 50
Sarah E. FISHER 26
Sarah M.
  BROTHERLINE 27
Sarah SAGE 26
Simon B. 27
Steven 26
Susan McKENNA 26
Susan SEWARD 27
Thomas 27
Thomas H. 27
Virginia Harrison 129
W.F. 27
W.P. 155
William 26, 27, 46, 52
William H. 27
William R. 27, 53
Wm. H. 145
CLARKE
  Catherine 119
  Ella 128
  Gertrude 82
  Gertrude L. 57
  Hannah 49
  Henry H. 112
  Hugh G. 71
  Oscar 36
  William Thomas 21
  Wm. Thos. 131
CLARKSON
  Joseph R. 105
  Mary 8, 105
  Mary M. 60
  Meliora 34, 105

Meliora McPHERSON 34, 105
Melissa 60
Melissa McPHERSON 60
Nellie S. 34
R.H. 60
R.H., Mrs. 76, 103, 142
Robert 105
Robert H. 34
CLARY
  Mary 109
CLASSEN
  Amelia A. LOHMANN 27
  Metta LOHSE 27
  Peter 27
CLAUSEN
  Christine LOCKSTOER 27
  Engerburg 60
  Fred 27
  Hans 27
  Henry 27
  Lars 27
  Mary A.
    ANTHONESSEN 27
  Mattie M. PETERSON 27
  Michael ROVER 27
  Peter 27
  Rekena MUSSER 27
CLAUSIN
  Cathrina RORER 79
  Hans 79
  Sophie 79
CLAUSON
  Anna Maria 121
  Emory 28
  Henry, Mr. and Mrs. 34
CLAUSSEN
  Anna 73
  Claus Jens 27
  Geo. 70
  Hannah M. GREBE 27
  Heinrich 143
  Henry 94
  Hilda 143
  Jurgen 27, 70
  Paulina C. RODEWALD 27
  Pauline 134
  Perlina 90
  Reinhard 133
CLAVER
  Belle 7
CLAWSON
  Ann MARTINSON 27
  Erastus H. 27
  Henry 128
  John H. 27
  Margaret KENNEDY 27
  Martha GUILL 27
  Nellie BERGGREN 27
  W.H. 27
  William 27
CLAY
  Catherine, Mrs. 158
  Charlotte ALEXANDER 27
  Christian 56
  Giles 27
  Henry 27
  Laura 56
  Lydia CAPWELL 27

Maggie MORSE 27
Maria YATES 56
Seth H. 165
William 27
CLAYPOOLE
  Elizabeth 62
CLAYSEN
  R. 79
CLAYTON
  Henry 19
  Laura STRONG 19
  Mary L. 32
  Nannie B. 19
CLEAMAN
  C.A. 101
CLEAR
  John 53
  Mary Ann 53
CLEARY
  Ann 139
  Ann RUSSELL 27
  Edward 27
  Ellen HEGGERTY 27
  Honora MATHER 27
  James 27
  Joanna DONAHY 27
  John 27
  Margaret 30
  Margaret LYNCH 27
  Margaret McDONALD 27
  Mary KNOWLAN 27
  Michael 27, 91
  Nathan K. 27
  Nicholas 27
  Thomas 27, 30
CLEAVELAND
  E.L., Miss 35
  Edward 35
  H. 16, 47, 170
  Laura THOMPSON 35
  Mary 95
CLEBURN
  Eliza T., Mrs. 75
CLEBURNE
  Anna 140
  Wm. 143
  Wm., Mrs. 26, 143
CLECK
  Mary R. 83
CLEFNER
  George 110
CLEGG
  Columbia Helen 72
  Dorothea MAVIS 27
  Emma A. 108
  Ida 108
  Ida V. 155
  Isaac 72, 108, 155
  Isaac, Mrs. 155
  John 27
  Minnie BROCK 27
  Susan 155
  Susan C. RUSSELL 108
  William 27
CLELAND
  Bessie 29
  Lucretia SAVAGE 29
  T.H. 29
CLEMANT
  Dorothea M. 60
CLEMEAN
  Emmanuel 64

COLLINS
Albert 29
Alice 108
Anne MUMFORD 29
Annie 158
Belle STITT 29
Bridget 37, 39
Catherine LANG 29
Charles 29
Delia CUNNINGHAM
  29
Dennis 29
Ed 95
Edward 29
Ellen 37, 127
Hannah 103
Hannah M.
  BLACKFORD 29
Hanora 28
Hanorah GALVIN 29
Harriet N. HART 29
J. FITZSIMONS 29
J.S. 97
Jacob S. 29
James 29
James L. 29
Jeremia 39
Jeremiah 39
Jerry 29
Johanna MAHONEY
  158
John 6, 29, 158
John S. 29
Juda 113
Louisa 10
Margaret CASEY 29
Mary 58, 110, 115
Mary BALLINGER 29
Mary BURNHAM 29
Mary CALAGAN 29
Mary REDDY 29
Mary SMITH 29
Nellie 168
Patrick 29
Sylvia 40
Thomas 28, 29, 35
Winniford 115
COLLOPY
John 122
M. BROUGHTON 122
Mary 122
COLNELL
Sarah 146
COLNOW
James 43
COLSEN
Mary 34
COLSON
Annie SOLMERSON
  121
Helen 145
Mary 152
Petter 121
Thana COBURN 87
COLTON
Francis 104
COLVIN
Mr. 170
Mrs. 170
COLWAY
Bertha 141
COLYAR
Charles 29
Daniel 29
Julia HUMPHREY 29
Mary A. KING 29

COMBE
Mary Ann 16
COMBS
Mary 68
COMER
Mary Ann 10
COMES
Byron 29
H.T. 29
Liddie EASTWOOD 29
Lottie WRIGHT 29
COMIN
Rosa M. 24
COMNEY
Mary 2
COMONS
Robert 131
Sarah F. 131
Sophia BOYED 131
COMSTOCK
Margaret 45
CONAGHAN
Cecelia 13
CONCANNON
Hattie A. 149
Mary L. 53
Mrs. 149
Rhoda HATHAWAY
  149
Thomas 149
CONDON
Alice 36
Daisy 40
Hannah 40
John 40
Mary T. 40
CONERLY
Amanda 60
CONGDON
Isaac N. 153
CONGER
E., Mrs. 121
Mrs. 98
Rebecca 109
CONGLETON
Francisco E. WYMAN
  29
James R. 29
Jane GASS 29
John M. 29
CONKLIN
Ann FRANKS 29
Bessie CLELAND 29
D.J. 29
Elijah 29
Etta EWING 29
G.H. 29
Harriet WILSON 29
J.R. 140
William B. 29
CONKLING
J.R. 31, 132, 147
CONLEY
Wineford 70
CONNEL
Kate 16
CONNELL
George T. 99
Hannah RYAN 23
Hanora 20
Julia 45
Mary 71
P., Mrs. 80
Patrick 23, 80
W.J. 63, 67
William J. 165

Wm. J. 31, 107, 159,
  160
CONNELLEY
Celia O'HARA 20
Kate 139
Mary 20
Michael 139
Patrick 20
CONNELLY
Angelia 70
Annie 56
Catharine 164
Catherine
  BERMINGHAM 29
Delia MONAGHAN 56
Dennis 29
James 29
Julia CORCORAN 29
Mary COWIN 29
Mary O'HARA 29
Michael 29
Morris 29
Patrick 70
Rebecca 164
Thomas 56
CONNELS
Mary 101
CONNELY
Margaret 130
CONNER
Charles H. 29
Ellen 110
Jane 166
John 35
John W. 29
Julia WALSH 29
Maggie 148
Margaret HARKINSON
  29
Margaret O'NEIL 110
Margarett 38
Patrick 110
Sarah M. HURLEY 29
William 29
CONNERS
Alice 47
Catharine LANCE 109
CONNERY
Anna RYAN 29
Catherine 98, 150
John 29
Mary BURNS 29
CONNOLL
Wm. J. 49
CONNOLLY
Catharine 99
Jane 55
CONNOR
Bridget J. 162
Catharine 35
Elizabeth RECTOR 29
Henry 82
J.C.H. 29
John W. 29
Julia WALSH 29
Martha E. STUDLEY
  29
Mary Anne 93
Mary J. OVERLANDER
  29, 64
Mary TRUEAUX 82
Mattie 154
Sarah Ann 82
Susan WALTERS 29
William 29
William C. 29

William F. 29
CONNORS
Ann 108
Bridget 101
Ellen 28
CONNOYER
Charles M. 23
CONOYER
Charles 29
Charles M. 29
Chas. M. 161
Mary HANTING 29
Mary KOPPS 29
CONPROPST
T.M., Mr. and Mrs. 96
CONREY
James 60
Margaret 60
CONRY
Catherine 31
CONSIDEN_?_
Bridget 32
CONSIDINE
Mary 33, 49
CONSTINE
Sarah 68
CONVERSE
Sarah M. 144
CONVEY
Bridget WALSH 156
Mary 156
Patrick 156
CONWAY
Anastatia 66
Annie NEEDHAM 89
Annie O'NEILL 66
Catharine 60
Margaret 66
Mary 89
Patrick 89
Robert 66
CONYER
Charles M. 142
COOK
Aaron 29
Alice WARNER 29
Allan 29
Amanda 74
Anna SWEENEY 29
Catherine E. 146
Charles B. 29, 30
D.E. WILLIAMS 29
E.F. 116
E.F., Mrs. 116
Edward F., Mrs. 166
Eliza 22
Elizabeth BROWN 29
H.H. 29
H.H., Mrs. 110
Hannah WITTY 29
Hanora 128
Hattie MOORE 29
Henry 29
James 154
John 29
John P. 29
Julia C. 59
Katie SPAULDIN 76
Lydia A. CULAN 29
Maria 15
Maria MIDLER 29
Martha J. 11
Mary RICE 29
Nora 154
Polly 59
Simeon 29

Sophia 116
William 49
Z. 29
COOKE
Honora 128
COOKS
Bell BUSEY 30
Charles 30
Rebecca MASON 30
Samuel 30
COOKSON
Imogene 50
COOLEY
Abbie A. 120
Alice 17
Arthur H. 30
Clarissa 96
John 30
Laura J. LEHMER 30
Patrick 17
Susan HILLARD 17
Susanah PATTERSON
  30
W.P. 120
COON
A.F. 145
Amanda 21
Archibald F. 97, 119
Elizabeth 140
Fannie R. 145
Henrietta M. 97
Louisa C. 72
Rachel DAVIS 21
Rebecca MEREDITH
  145
Sarah K. 119
William 21
COONAY
Maria BURNS 30
Patrick 30
Rose BURNS 30
William 30
COONEY
Elizabeth SULLIVAN
  30
Eveline MORTIMER
  135
Hannah 137
John 30
Mary WELCH 30
Patrick 30
COONIHAN
Catharine 35
COONS
Almira SIMMONS 30
D.B. 28
Edward 30
Elmira SIMMONS 30
Jessie H. BULLOCK 30
L.L. 28
Lucy L. WILLIAMS 30
Philip 30
Thulia THOMAS 28
COOPER
Aaron 96
Anna C. CRUME 30
Carrie V. 17
Catherine 96
Daniel M. 17, 125
Diana MILLER 17, 134
Dianna MILLER 125
E.C. 158
Eliza 142
Elizabeth FLEUKEY 96
Emma 17
F.D. 118

COOPER, cont.
George H. 53
Henry 80
James 30
Lizzie 53
M. GANNAN 53
Mary 19, 32
Mary E. 59, 128
Mary L. 125
Mary MITCHELL 30
Mr. 12
Mrs. 12, 167
Rebecca P. 16
Robert E. 30
COOPS
Henry 30, 83
Iler 30
Maria KARBACH 30
Topla TAMLICK 30
COOTE
Anna PUMPHREY 30
Anna WARREN 30
O.W. 30
Thomas 30
COPBELL
Fannie 27
COPELAND
Alexabder 107
Anna ANDERSON 107
Emily 21
Kate E. 124
Mary L. 124
Mary L. ROBINSON
124
W.E., Mrs. 131
Williamina A. 107
Wm. W. 124
COPPOCK
Henry 163
Mary 82
N.W. 82
CORBID
John J. 14
Maggie A. 14
Maggie A. HIGGINS 14
CORBIN
Henrietta H. 96
Rosella 120
CORBY
Joseph D. 30
Lauretta LEWIS 30
CORCORAN
Catharine HOGAN 81
Cathrine 109
John 29
Julia 29
Julia LEARY 29
Maggie 167
Maria 24, 81
Martin 81
CORDAN
Honora HARRINGTON
23
Laurence 23
Maria 23
CORDES
Anna KREIGER 30
John Henry 30
Katharina M.
PETERSON 30
Peter Christoph 30
W. Margaretha 14
CORDIN
Johannah 19
COREDEN
Maria 27

COREL
Mary 157
COREY
Amey TILLINGHAST
30
Charles C. 30
Elmira A. 135
James B. 30
Minnie E. KENNEDY
30
CORKERELL
Abby TUNNISON 30
Jabez 30
Susana BATES 30
William 30
CORLEY
Annie 94
CORLISS
Eliza A. 110
CORMAN
Thomas 52
CORN
Isabel 78
Louisa C. 72
CORNEILLE
George 30
Henrietta E.L. BECKER
30
Maria PIPER 30
William 30
CORNELL
George T. 30
Jane KEYES 30
Jennie COILE 30
Thomas 30
CORNEY
Letia THORNTON 30
Peter 30
CORNIG
Letia THORNTON 30
Peter 30
CORNISH
Annie E. PALMER 30
Anora TURNER 119
Barnard 30
Bernard 30
Cordelia 62
Cordelia W. 72
Delos 30
Ebenezer 44
George T. 30
Isaac 30
Louisa
FREDENBURGH 30
Louisa VREDENBURG
30
Louisa
VREEDENBERG 30
Lucy HENSMAN 30
Marcus 30
Nancy PRATTS 44
Nora FERRIS 30
Phebe Ann 44
CORRELL
Catherine HARMON
114
Margaret 114
Margeet 114
Mrs. 114
Timothy 114
CORRICK
Elizabeth M. MARSHAL
30
Thomas 30
William E. 30

CORRIDON
Elizabeth LEARY 30
Mary RYLE 30
Richard 30
Timothy 30
CORRIE
Harriet V. ASH 68
CORRIGAN
Anna M. 68
David 30
Elizabeth NOLAN 49
Margaret 49, 58
Margaret LAFFERTY
30
Maria 39
Patrick 49
CORVIN
John 134
CORWELL
J.M. 26
CORWIN
Edmund 27
COSGRAVE
Catherine CASEY 30
James 15, 30, 95
Mary WELCH 30
Patrick 30
COSLILE
Jacob K. 130
COSON
Julia 119
COSSLEY
Howard, Mrs. 97, 164
COSTELLO
Mary 127
COSTILO
Mary 142
COSWELL
Carlotta E. WHITMORE
142
COTHRIL
ELizabeth F. 92
COTTER
Elizabeth 166
Ellen 90
Margaret 7
Nellie 89
COTTON
Elizabeth ALLISON 64
Elizabeth FISHER 64
Harriet E. 93
Libbie 64
Maria 64
T.D. 64
COUFAL
Fanny 153
COUFFER
Rebecca 22
COULIHAN
Nancy 96
Patrick 96
COULTER
Catherine GOSS 30
Christopher C. 30
Elizabeth MALONY 30
George A. 30, 128
George S. 30
Jerome 45
Jerome, Mrs. 45
M.J. WILSON 30
Sarah F. MAXWELL 30
Susie M. 128
Susie SIDNER 30
William 30
Wm. F. 30

COUNT
F. 102
COUNTRYMAN
Amanda DeLaMATER
30
Annie E. BARTEL 30
Charles K. 30
Isaac 30
COURT
Celia 36
COURTER
L.W. 123
COURTNEY
Elizabeth 139
COURVISEE
Eugenie 102
COURVOISIER
Eugenia 15
COUSINS
Benjamin 96
Jane 96
Love 96
COUTANT
Chas. V. 147
COVELL
Frances E. 145
Lemuel 145
Lorana CHURCHILL
145
COVEY
Wealthy 103
COVION
Mary 151
COWAN
Celia M. FAY 30
Hannah
FRANSWORTH 31
Hattie 59
John 30
Margaret BIRRELL 30
Mary E. GALLUP 31
Nancy 34
R.W. 59
Robert W. 31
Samuel 30
Sara Virginia BUTE
158
Thomas M. 31
COWDEN
Eliza NOTHERLAND
112
Harriett 133
Hattie 112, 118
William 112
COWIN
E.T 2
E.T. 60, 89, 154
J.C. 89
John H. 46
Margaret McQUILLAN
29
Mary, Mrs. 29
Robert 29
COWLES
James 134
John 31
Louisa P. CULLEY 31
Penelope JENKINS 31
Rosa 134
COX
Aphelon 31
Charles W. 31
Charles, Mrs. 90
Charlotte L. 163
David M. 18
Elizabeth CHRIST 31

Emelie Bell TUTTLE
31
Ermina A. KELLOGG
31
George 31
George P. 31
H.E. 31
Hannah C. 32
Ida M. 18
Irene 117
J.R. 115
Jeremiah 31
John R. 28
Lizzie G. McDONALD
31
Lucrecie L. LAMB 31
Mary 148
Mary Ann LANDER 31
Mary E. KEM 18
Mrs 68
Richard 163
T.J. 46
Thomas J. 31
W. 163
Zelda 96
COY
Eliza 24
Martha 103
Mary Jane 63
COYLE
Catherine CLARK 40
Hugh 40
James 36
Mary 38, 40
COYN
May 110
COZZENS
Rosa A. 152
Sarah 158
COZZOLO
Ferdinand 31
Frances K. 31
CRADY
Patrick 50
CRAFT
Jesse H. 20
CRAFTS
Sarah F. 130
CRAGG
Elizabeth 16
CRAIG
Almita 14
Arminter 14
Berry, Mrs. 18
Bridget GARAHAR 106
Elizabeth 106
Jane 91
John 106
Johnson 31
Maggie 105
Marie E. 42
Martha THOMPSON 31
Mary L. HAYNES 31
Moses H. 31
Sarah HUMBLE 31
Thomas A. 14
Thomas P. 31
William S. 31
CRAIGIE
Christian 22
CRAIN
Gracia 91
CRAMER
Wm. 130

CRANDAL
Catharine BARNES 31
James R. 31
CRANDALL
Albert 31
Alice O'BANNON 31
Harvey 31
Nellie HOLCOMB 31
CRANDELL
Abram 86
Almira 69
Ann Eliza H. LAKE 31
Ann Janette TAYLOR
31
Clara 86
George T. 31
Otis 31
Stratira EVERETT 86
CRANE
Abram 162
Electa 162
John T. 31
Julia 115
Margaret AYRES 162
Maria J. 5
Mary A. 31
Mary E. BUSH 31
Van Buren 31
CRANEY
Anna 5
James 5
Mary HAWS 5
CRAREN
Robert 31
CRARON
Ellen HAUGHEY 31
Ellen RILEY 31
James 31
William 31
CRARY
Anna A. 140
Anna A. LITTLEJOHN
140
B.D. 140
Chas. T. 159
Mary Ellen 140
CRASS
Ann 4
CRAUSE
Ernstine VOLZMANN
31
Frederick 31
Henrietta WENZENER
31
CRAVEN
Catharine 37
Miss 90
Sarah J. 90
Sarah McBRIDE 90
William 90
CRAVENS
America WYATT 31
Belle WILLS 31
James 31
Squire 31
CRAVER
Elizabeth NELSON 31
Mary D. NOBLE 31
Samuel P. 31
Theophilus B. 31
Thomas S. 31
CRAWFORD
Bryce 53
Daniel W. 31
David 153
Eliza A. 117

Eliza BEERS 31
Eliza E. 16
Emma 16
Emma M. LINK 31
Frances A. 158
Frank J. 31
Geo. 31
Hannah 62
Helen E. 56
Josephine JANNEY 31
Lida 153
Lida C. 129
Louisa 128
Mary 53
Mr. and Mrs. 56, 158
Nancy Jane McGREW
153
Sarah 157
CREBO
Joseph 54
CREIGHTON
Alice 102
Catharine Ann
McCALLUM 31
Catharine FURLONG
139
Catherine 99
Catherine FURLONG
31
Francis 100
Francis H. 73
James 31, 51, 54
Jennie 139
John 31, 127
John A. 31
John V. 90
Joseph 13, 31, 99, 139
Joseph, Mr. and Mrs. 92
Kate 13, 51, 100, 115
M., Miss 106
Martha 73
Martha Kate 73
Mary 139
Mary BARRICKMAN
31
Mary E. 99
Mary F. 100
Phoebe DRISCOLL 73,
100
Sarah E. WAREHAM
31
Sarah WALLS 54
Susan 54
CREMB
George E. 31
Mary HINES 31
Nathan L. 31
Susanna ETSON 31
CREMER
Mary 106
CRESAP
W.D. 119
CRESSER
Amos 123
CRESTEN
Catharine 31
Clarence 31
Emma HOOKER 31
CRETEN
Elin 45
CREW
Nellie 107
CREYS
Amelia 18
CRIGLER
Elizabeth LEACH 31

James R. 31
Jennie MASON 31
CRIPHTON
Catharine 153
CRISGANSEN
Mary M. 143
CRISS
Emma KENNEDY 31
George W. 31
Martha BAILEY 31
CRIST
Elizabeth SELLON 1
George 1
Mary 1
CRITCHFIELD
A.J. 1, 69
Absolam W. 31
Andrew J. 128
Delia 35
Delphine 1
Harriet BOWER 31
Isabella A. REEVES 31
Jacob 31
Sarah A. POLMANTIRE
1
CRITTENDEN
John 91
CROCKETT
Martha 101
CROFFORD
Cassandra 55
CROFT
Augusta Harriet 33
Eliza NICHOLS 33
John T. 33
Susan 89, 141
Susannah 141
T.T. 149
Thomas T. 116
CROLLUS
Johanna 50
CROMIE
Fanny MALLOY 31
Florence DALLY 31
James 31
William D. 31
CROMWELL
Ellen HYLAND 31
Ellena 77
Fritz 31
Herman 77
Herman Robert Otto 31
Mary MEYERS 31
CRONAN
Bridget RYAN 26
Jeremiah 107
John 26
Mary 26
CRONEMEYER
Emeline L. 168
CRONICHER
Josephine 71
CRONIN
Catherine MORIARTY
32
Jeremiah 32
John F. 53
Kate HANRAHAN 32
Margaret 48
Mary 9, 64
Mary CALLAHAN 32
Michael 32
CRONK
Albert 32
Emma BROWN 32
O.B. 32

Sophia BROWN 32
CRONLAND
John P. 95
Mary E. ALLEN 95
Mary Justiva 95
CRONYN
Anna HAWTHORNE
32
David 32
William W. 32
CROOK
Geo. H. 90
Hannah HOPPER 32
James D. 32
Jane BATES 32
Joseph 32
Joseph D. 128
Louisa L. 32
Mrs. 90
Olaf 32
Selina ANDERSON 32
Swen 32
CROOKS
A. 156
CROPENHOFF
Hannah 141
Henry 141
Minnie KRUIG 141
CROPSEY
Carrie M. 110
CROSBIEN
John 59
CROSBY
Emma 28
G.A. 13
Lucy BIGLOW 28
Mary 28
Mary A. 28
Priscilla A. BABCOCK
13
Thomas 28
CROSE
Mary 156
CROSEN
Mary 59
CROSMAN
Annie GRAVES 32
Fannie STOCKFORD
32
Henry 32
John 32
CROSS
Albert 163
Annie 163
Bertha MILLER 163
Charlotta MILLER 26
Elizabeth 38
Hannah 87
J.C. 69
Kate 26
Mary 168
Mary WANNS 168
Phillip 22
R.D. 168
Sarah Jane CHURCH 32
Simon 26
William 163
William R. 32
CROSSLE
Charlotte WALLER 32
Georgiana CHOULER
32
Georgina E. 127
Henry W. 32, 105
James 32

CROW
Gilbert C. 32
Manirva 138
Mary L. CLAYTON 32
Ruby R.
WANNEMAKER 32
Thomas G. 32
CROWDER
Ella L. BROWN 32
Hannah C. COX 32
James H. 32
Wm. M. 32
CROWE
Nealia 90
CROWELL
Ada 140
George W. 106
George W., Mr. and Mrs.
106
George, Mr. and Mrs. 56
Henry, Mrs. 106
Johannah LEWNWALL
32
Joseph W. 32
Levella M. 134
Mary 10
Mary HOEL 134
Wm. 134
Wm. B. 10
CROWLEY
Anastasia 99
Anastatia 95
Henriette B. 32
John W. 32
Statia 101
CROWNER
Mary HOLMES 32
Nathaniel 32
CROY
Annie G. CHARTERS
32
David 32
Henry 32
Jane ROBERTSON 32
CRUFFIER
James 32
Mary Jane CUTTING
32
CRUGAN
Charles E. 32
Daniel 32
Mary A. McKEE 32
Melissa A. WILLIAMS
32
CRUISE
Catharine CARSON 35
Jennie 22, 100
Jennie E. 35
Thomas 35
CRULEY
Charles 32
Louisa CAVEO 32
Michael 32
CRUM
Alex 16
Ellen J. 16
Mary A. HOWE 16
CRUME
Anna C. 30
Fannie 32
Hannah SEARS 30
James B. 30
John 32
Mary E. CHRISTIAN
32
Nicholas M. 32

DALGREN
C.M. 50
Mary C. LINDQUIST
50
DALL
Fred 33
Leopold 33
Minnie WALTHER 33
DALLAN
John F. 70
DALLBORN
Mary 2
DALLEY
John W. 33
DALLONE
Frederick, Mr. and Mrs.
25
DALLOW
Anna BRADLY 33
E. 73
Ebenezer 33, 165
Ebenizer 33
Elizabeth 73
Fanny 165
Hannah BRADLEY 33
Mary Anne 78
Samuel 33
Sophia AMOSS 33
DALLY
Florence 31
John W. 31, 33
Nancy L. 33
Ruth A. GOODRICH 31
DALMAS
Annie CARR 130
Elizabeth 130
William 130
DALTON
Bridget 126
Delia 109
Jane DOOLEY 33
Maggie 100
Margaret 109
Margaret BOOK 126
Mary MAXWELL 109
Maurice 126
R. Grand 56
William 33
Wm. 109
DALY
Elizabeth HUGHES 22
Hannah DENAN 48
John 33
Mary 22, 48, 110, 122
Peter 22
William 48
DAMAN
Phebe 71
DAMBROSKI
Elizabeth ROSS 137
Ludwig 137
Maria 137
DAME
Minnie 8
DAMON
Alex 161
Jeremiah H. 34
Mary Ann McCARTHY
34
Nancy G. BASFORD 34
Rosena 161
Seth G. 34
DANALSON
Henry 20
Maria ANDERSON 20

DANAMAN
Christina 168
DANE
Ellen 146
Joseph 146
DANECKER
Nicholas 104
DANEEDER
Annie 52
Crescentia 52
DANELSON
Albertina 121
Lisa 76
DANEN
Kate McMILLEN 137
DANESH
Mary 80
DANIEL
Christ 67
Christian 34, 168
JONES 135
Lucy RAMM 34
Wetha HIBBLER 34
DANIELS
Eliza 160
Esther M. 162
Henry 34
John M. 34
Margaret 2
Martha Jane
McDOWELL 34
Mary 51
Mary SIMONS 34
DANIELSEN
Christianna
JOHANNSON 104
Emelie 104
Peter 104
DANIELSON
Anna 76
Catherine GALESEN 34
Christine
CHRISTENSON 34
Esmus 34
John A. 34
Lena 135
Mary SWANSEN 89
Nels 89
DANIELSSON
Carl 145
Johanna NILSSON 145
DANKER
Engerburg CLAUSEN
60
Henry 60
Margaret 60
DANNELLY
Elizabeth GREEN 110
Margaret 46
Patrick 110
DANNEMANN
Catharina 67
Mary 131
DANNER
John 115
Martha TAYLOR 115
Mary 115
DANON
John 42
DANSLOW
Virginia 97
DANZHLER
Christina 150
DAPLY____?
Wesley 81

DARBOY
Mary 100
DARIMUR
J. Frank 96
DARLING 39
Amanda 62, 107
Benjamin 34
Cahterine MEEHAN 34
De 21, 22
Elisa D. 34
Elizabeth HEART 34
Elizabeth VAN ORDER
34
Hulda PERRY 34
J.A. 34
Joseph 34, 62
Mary GRIMSHAW 34
R. De 55, 121, 153
Richard 34, 82
Sarah 167
Stephen 34
Thomas 34
DARLTON
Catherine 94
DARRAH
Maria M. 44
Rachel 44
DARROW
George M. 10
DARSCHER
Bernhard 34
Catharine KRULL 34
Margretha E. STRUBE
34
Reimer 34
DART
Chloe 124
DASHER
Alsabiah JOHNSON 14
Amelia 14
B. 14
Benjamin 42
Lucy 42
Nancy DAVIS 42
DATTON
Mary 58
DAUB
Barbara ANTON 34
John A. 34
Lawrence 34
Mary or Maria HASSER
34
DAUBLE
Anthony 51
Mary 51
Mary HABER 51
DAUGHERTY
Theodore 169
DAUTH
Margarethe 5
DAVENPERT
B.M. 29
DAVEY
Ellen MORAN 108
John 108
Mary 108
DAVID
Adah B. 6
Adam 62
DAVIDSON
C.E. 67
D. 128
George 34
George S. 34
Jenette N. SMITH 34
M., Mrs. 101

Maggie MORGAN 34
Mary 47
Rebecca 46
Samantha A. 46
William 46
DAVIER
Rosalie V. 88
DAVIES
Dell O'NEIL 34
Eliza PIPE 34
James 34
James H. 34
DAVIS
Ada H. 70
Addie 96
Almira 115
Amanda 15
Amanda HENDRICKS
154
Amanda Jane WEST 34
Amos 35
Andrew 34
Andrew J. 34
Anna TWINE 130
Annie 17
Benjamin 61
Catharine MAACK 34
Catharine W. 144
Charles B. 34
Charles M. 34
Douglas A. 34
E.L. CLEAVELAND 35
Edwin 34
Eliza P. 44
Eliza Permela 71
Elizabeth 34, 85
Elizabeth BENYON 34
Elizabeth CLIFTON 34
Elizabeth GOFF 34
Elizabeth LEIDY 144
Ellen TOZER 34
Emma 140
Emma V. 147
Ephriam 144
Esther A. SHIVLEY 34
F.A. 70
Frances STONER 34
Frank 96
Frederick E. 34
Frederick H. 34, 103
George 34
George M. 34
H.C. BARRETT 70
H.L. 59, 129, 158
Harriet G. 11
Harriett BARRETT 96
Hattie L. BRIDGE 35
Helen 58
Henrietta GREEN 34
Henry 154
Ida 11
Ida GIFFORD 34
Isaac 34
J.W. 34, 77
J.W., Mrs. 90
Jacob 34
James 34, 152
Jane 42, 165
Jane J. TAYLOR 18
Jennie 130
Jesse T. 47
John 12, 17, 34, 59, 63,
125, 130, 156
John C. 144
John W. 34
John, Mrs. 63

Joseph 34
Julia 168
Julia HOSKINSON 47
Katie DIERKS 34
Kina, Mrs. 153
Lettie 47
Lizzie 12
Lorenzo K. 34
Lucretia 18
Lydia 151
Lydia WILSON 34
M.J., Miss 151
Margaret DAY 17
Maria ROSA 130
Maria ROSE 35
Marie FRANKLIN 34
Mary 8, 44, 52, 71, 133,
158
Mary A.
FETHERSTONE 34
Mary AMUNDSON 34
Mary B. LOWARY 34
Mary COLSEN 34
Mary COLSON 152
Mary I. 10
Mary J. 61
Mary M. HANEY 34
Mary OLESON 34
Mary RATLIFF 34
Mary TEEPLES 34
Mathilda J. PHELPS 34
Meldora 152
Melvina 129
Minnie 140
Moses T. 18
Nancy 42
Nancy COWAN 34
Nancy WHITING 48,
112
Nathaniel W. 34
Nellie S. CLARKSON
34
O.F. 104
O.F., Mrs. 87
O.H. 49
Ole S. 34
Oscar F. 21, 34, 82
Pamiliane WILLIAMS
61
Pearl 48
Rachel 21, 164
Rebecca E. SHARP 34
Rebecca, Mrs. 10
Rheumilla TILDEN 34
S.B. 83
S.J., Miss 31
Samuel 34
Sarah 56, 57, 94, 112,
130, 154
Sarah A. 22
Sarah E. 112
Sarah E. KEEFER 79
Sarah F. DICKINSON
34
Seward B. 104
Susan 79, 96, 163
Susan LEWIS 35
Thomas 34, 156
Thomas G. 34
Thos. 85
U. or N. W. 34
William 35, 130
William F. 35
William R. 35
Wm. 35, 48, 112
Zephania 35

DAVISAN
Minnie 96
DAWLEY
A.L. 35
D.V. 35
Ida A. WAGNER 35
Sabins CAROLTON 35
DAWSON
Ann BRADY 11, 122
Caroline 113
John 11, 122
Kate 122
Katharine 11
Margaret 122
Nancy 169
DAY
Anna OWENS 87
David 87
Elizabeth H. 50
Jane 12
Margaret 17
Martha 87
Mary Ann 67
Mary E. 130
Susan 145
DE LANGUELETTE
Fredericka 141
DE LANGUILLETTE
Fredericka 138
DE PIESE
Peter 154
DE VOL
P.C. 56
DEACON
Sarah 152
DEAHEK
F. 171
DEALEY
Mary 104
DEALY
Mary Ann 81
DEAMON
John 145
WIlhelmine 145
DEAMUD
Samuel 35
Sarah B. WILLETT 35
Sarah M. MOORE 35
William H. 35
DEAN
Caroline 16
Cynthia BAWES 35
Elizabeth THOMAS 35
Ellen 90
Henry 35
John D. 35
Nellie 115
DEANE
Ellen 52
DEAR
H.C. 158
DeARMON
Joanna 82
DEBELKA
Anna 86
DEBOLT
George, Mrs. 98
DEBORDE
Caroline 116
DEBRESSEN
Mrs. 20
DeCASTER
Nancy 17
DECATUR
George W. 163
Helen F. 163

Mary RICHARDS 163
DECH
Waldburga 103
DECK
Susin 46
DECKER
Catharine FORBES 35
Ellen 120
James 100, 120
James F. 35
Jennie E. CRUISE 35
John P. 35
Katey FORBES 120
Katie E. ANDERSON
35
Mary SMITH 35
Michael 35
S. 120
Simeon V. 35
Theodore 69
Timothea 69
DECKMAN
Magdalena 91
DECKMANN
Catherina 14
DECKNER
James 22
DEE
Catharine CONNOR 35
Catharine HARGAN 47
Elizabeth 37
Ellen 35, 47, 63, 124
Jeremiah 82, 119
Johanna 128
Johanna KERN 128
John 35
Julia COSON 119
Margaret 29
Mary 82
Mary ENWRIGHT 35
Mary LONG 35
Michael 35, 47
Nellie 119
Thomas 128
DEEMUN
Norah 142
DEERING
Lois 107
DEERSON
Hellen MILLER 35
Margaret GUTHARD
35
Peter N. 35, 137
DEETKIN
Albert 40
Clara BLEIK 40
Julia BENDER 40
Leanhard 40
DeFORREST
C.V. 35
Catherine RICE 35
Con E. 35
J.E. BATES 35
DEGNAN
Bridget 129
John 35
Martha F. MURPHY 35
Mary DIVINE 35
Matthew J. 35
DEGRAFFENRIED
W.F. 46, 121, 136, 147,
150
DEHL
Lena 98
DEHMST
Catherine MARTI 35

Christopher 35
Margareta YEGER 35
Peter 35
DEHN
Barbara JAKL 35
Catharine 35
Daniel 35
Markus 35
DEICKMAN
Kate 12
DEIRINGER
Theresa 117
DEIRKS
Augusta HANSON 118
Detleff 118
Sophia 118
DEISING
Annie HERNICK 35
Elizabeth SNYDER 35
Geo. 35
George 35
DEISSE
Wilhelmine 138
DeKAY
Edwin 35
Fannie I. FELLOWS 35
Sarah QUICK 35
Thomas 35
DELAHUNT
Michael 127
DeLaMATER
Amanda 30
DeLaMATYR
N.C. 139
N.O. 59, 72, 118, 170
Nettie O. 145
T.C. 125
DELAND
Ellen BUCKLEY 35
Ellen BUCKLY 35
Geneva REEVES 35
James 35
James H. 35, 116
James T. 35
Kate C. GUNDERSON
35
William Henry 35
DELANEY
Abby KELLEY 35
Alice 142
Ann BRIDGES 142
Cornelius 142
David E. 35
Dennis 35
Dora 110
Ellen 109
Ellen SCANLAN 35
Esther 143
Jeremiah 35
John 43, 147
Mary 102
Mary KELLEY 35
Patrick 35
Sophia NELSON 35
DELANY
Anne G. ROBERTS 35
Catharine 131
Dora 110
Dora M. 81
Esther 81
Henry A. 35
John 124
Mary 112
Patrick 35
DELAWARE
F.R. 88

Louisa N. 117
Mr. 117
DELBOR
Francisca 110
DELENY
Catharine 81
DELFEL
Christine LEIHGEBER
35
George 35
John 35
Lizzie ROSS 35
DELFS
Christina RAHN 35
Fritz 65
Henrietta 129
Johann C. 35
John 35
Katharina SCHMIDT 35
Margaretha
BARGSTEDT 35
Margaretha WRIEDT
35
Marx 35
Max 35
DELIGHT
Hattie 118
DELLAHAM
Ella 7
DELLAHUM
Ella BERRY 149
DELLER
Anna 138
DELLESTIN
James W. 35
Maria 35
Mary M. McKENZIE 35
Uriah 35
DELLON
Adile SAUNIER 36
Edward J. 36
DELLONE
---- 36
Alexander 36
F. 27
Frederick 36
Jennetta HEANEY 36
DELMAR
Mary 21
DELONG
Patrick 38
DELSMAN
Clara HEITKEMPER
36
Dina EIMERS 36
John B. 36
DEMAIN
Elizabeth 22
DEMAREST
Cornelia 47
Ida 92
DEMARIST
Ida F. 148
Mary COX 148
William R. 148
DEMEREST
Charles 3
DEMOREST
B. 2
Hannah M. STEWART
36
Peter A. 36
Sarah, Mrs. 2, 113
DEMORY
Mary A. 131

DeMOTT
Carrie V. 73
DEMPSEY
Joseph 56
Michael 21
DEN
Dr. 20
DENAN
Hannah 48
DeNAYER
Edward 36
John B. 36
Margaretta BARNES 36
Marie Antoine PERRIER
36
DENEHY
Caroline LASSER 36
Daniel 36
Elizabeth HANLON 36
James 36
DENEN
Hannah 131
DENILLE
Elisa 34
DENIN
Bridget 31
DENKER
Christina DUEHRKOP
36
Emma SEIDLER 36
H.C. 36
Wm. 36
DENMAN
Jacob S. 21
Mary E. 21
Selina LYON 21
DENNEMANN
Catharina 67
DENNER
C. 36
Louis 36
Mary 36
Nellie F. BOWMAN 36
DENNEY
John 141
Susan 79, 141
DENNING
M. 109
DENNIS
Abraham 36
Catherine 128
Elizabeth HARVEY 36
J.B. 26
James H. 36, 67, 88
Kate J. 26
Martha M. MILLER 36
Mr. 104
Mrs. 104
Susan E. 147
DENNY
Ellen HUGHES 36
John 36
Mary MENNEN 36
William 36
DENT
Florence E. 96
John 167
Lizzie VOGAN 96
Margaret 167
Mary A. HERD 167
William 96
DENTON
Ella 73
I. 18
J.W. 139
John W. 36

DOBRA
  Mary 47
  Mary HOFFEK 47
  Michael 47
DOBRY
  Mary 47
  Mary HOUFEK 47
  Michael 47
DOCHENY
  Bridget 148
DODA
  Barbara 49
  James 49
  Mary MORISH 49
DODANE
  Eleanore 13
DODD
  Cornelia SHEERS 10
  Hattie 10
  Stephen 10
DODGE
  Annie 18
  Clara Electa 151
  H.L. 169
  Irene A. BROCK 37
  M.M. CAIN 37
  Peter C. 37
  R.V., Rev. 63
  W.E. 37
DOEHARTY
  Mr. and Mrs. 46
DOELAR
  Charles 164
DOER
  Phil 30
DOFFEN
  Frederika RAUH 37
  Henry 37
  Powell 37
DOHENEY
  Ada 51
DOHERTEY
  Bridget 95
DOHERTY
  Anastasia 48
  E., Mrs. 5
  Emma WINDSOR 37
  Grace GARVEY 37
  Isabella HARMAN 37
  John 37
  Mary 7
  Robert 37
  Robert, Rev. 24, 170
DOHLE
  Helene SCHWEITER
    37
  Henry 37, 136
  Julia STOCKHAMMER
    37
DOHN
  Mary 105
DOHRMANN
  Christina EVAN 37
  Dora DOSE 37
  F. 37
  Henry 37
  Hinrick 37
DOHRNANN
  Frederick 82
DOLAK
  John 85
DOLAN
  Ann 55
  Annie 100
  Eliza Anna ALLEN 6
  H. 6

Honorah 101, 106
John 82, 100, 122
John R. 37
Lizzie 71
Lizzie ZACHARY 71
Margrett REILY 37
Mary 6, 55, 122
Mary DALY 122
Mary Frances 122
Mary GLYNN 100
Minnefred 66
Patrick 37
William 71
DOLAND
  Adelia 167
DOLEN
  Joseph 37
DOLID
  Tarrent 15
DOLIN
  Mary 8
DOLL
  Almira 118
  Annie 84
  August 37
  Caroline 132
  Caroline OSWALD 37
  Carrie 20
  Charley 37
  Eliabeth FRIER 37
  Elizabeth KROEGER 37
  Fred 37
  Friedrich 37
  John 37, 132
  Lisette 158
  Louisa 9
  Maggie BRANDLE 37
  Mr. and Mrs. 122
  Sina MILLER 37
  Wilhelm 106
  William 37, 104, 169
  Wm. 20
DONAGHUE
  Ellen 24
DONAHEY
  Fulton 37
DONAHO
  Thos. 162
DONAHOE
  Ann 95
  Margaret 54
DONAHOO
  Mollie 28
  Nancy M. DIBBLE 28
  Thomas J. 28
  Tom 28
DONAHUE
  Cornelius 93
  Helen 93
  James 22
  Mary McCAULIFF 93
DONAHY
  Joanna 27
  Mary SULLIVAN 27
  Timothy 27
DONALD
  Julia 129
  Rebecca 140
DONALDSON
  Adel HALL 37
  Caroline 20
  Caroline JONES 37
  Cyrus 37
  Ellen A. PANCOAST
    37
  Fielding 37

James W. 37
Lizzie LITTLE 37
N.F. 37
Sarah HALL 37
William A. 37
DONALLEY
  Brdiget 11
DONALSON
  Mary SWENSON 112
  Nels Otto 112
DONAVAN
  Annie 111
  Hannah 102
  Jane LYTLE 111
  John F. 111
  M. 115
  M., Mrs. 115
  Susan 111
  Wlliam 111
DONCASTER
  Emma 140
DONECKER
  Augustus 37
  Augustus H. 66
  Sarah 66
  Sarah BUCHANAN 37
DONEHUE
  Hanna 157
DONELLY
  John 37
  Kate AGAN 37
  Mary Ann 69
  Mary CASEY 37
  Thomas 37
  Wright 100
DONK
  Carl 37
  Charles 37, 102
  Hannah EICKHOFF 37
  Mary ASHFORD 37
  Mary F. ASHBURN 99
DONNALLY
  Mary 99
DONNAN
  Elizabeth 31
DONNELL
  Sarah A. LATHAM 115
  William G. 115
DONNELLEY
  Bridget 63, 109
  Bridget FALLON 109
  Rose 63
  William 109
DONNELLY
  Ann 24
  B.V. 116
  Delia McMAHAN 37
  Edward 37
  Ellen McCARTY 37
  Ellie 60
  Fanny McGOVERN 37
  G.G. 37
  James 37, 90
  John 37
  Julia A. GATES 37
  Margaret 96
  Mary Ellen BURKE 37
  Mary J. 116
  Mary J. WATSON 37
  Nancy MURPHY 37
  Patrick 101
  Samuel F. 37
  Susan WEED 37
  Terrence 37
  Thaddeus Henry 37
  William 37

DONNEMAN
  Catherena 65
  Maria 65
DONNOLLON
  Bridget 115
DONOGHUE
  James 109
DONOHOE
  Edward 20
  Mary Ann 56
DONOHUE
  Michl. 22
DONOLAN
  Bridget 18
DONOUGH
  Mary COLLINS 115
  Michael 115
DONOVAN
  Ann 148
  Ann McGUIRE 37
  Anne 15
  Annie 168
  Bridget 48
  Catharine 106
  Ellen ALLEN 37
  John F. 168
  John J. 37
  M. 100
  Mary 102
  Mary GALVIN 37
  Michael 15, 37, 67, 146
  Michiel 37
  Susan 168
DONOVEN
  Jane HICKEY 25
  John 25
  Margaret 25
DONSE
  Elizabeth 83
DOODY
  John 16
  Kate FINELY 38
  Maggie A. 16
  Maggie DOWNEY 16
  Mary CAREY 38
  Michael 38
DOOLAN
  Mary 17
DOOLEY
  Jane 33
  John 38
  Mary 10
DOOLING
  Bridget 47
DOOLITTLE
  Ida 47
  Jennie E. 43, 47
  Mary BUSHNELL 43,
    47
  Mary J. BUSHNELL 47
  W.V. 43
  William 47
  Wm. F. 2, 47
  Wm. V. 47
DOOLY
  John 38
  Maria REDLIG 38
DOON
  Ann Stina ANDERSEN
    38
  Rasmus Peterson 38
DOOSE
  John 126
DOOYER
  Johannah 114

DORAK
  Barbara 150
DORAN
  Mary HUGHES 24
  Annie 74
  Daniel 164
  Ellen 115
  Harriet 25
  Mary 71
  Mary HUGHES 38
  Patrick 38
  Rose 102
  Sarah 164
  Sarah ALLISON 164
  Sarah RUTNER 164
DORE
  Annie McGLINCHY 38
  Edmund 38
  Ellen 43
  Nora LEE 38
  Patrick 38
DORECKAN
  A.H. 99
DOREMUS
  Jane 106
  S.C. 3
DOREN
  Ellen J. 71
DORING
  Helen C., Mrs. 170
DORK
  Mary P. 104
DORKS
  Louisa J. 72
DORMANN
  August 38
  Bertha Juliana
    SANGENSEFREN 38
  Frederika KANENBLEY
    38
  Mary 43
DORMER
  Mary 21
DORN
  Annie YANDA 38
  Francis 38
  Francisca 38
  Francisca PROKOP 38
  Frank 38
  Mary NEWARK 38
  Mary NOVAK 38
  Wiebke 14
DORNACKER
  Augustus 37
  Sarah BUCHANAN 37
DORNALDT
  George 20
  Mary 20
  Sophia GEFF 20
DORNECKER
  Henrietta VALCHER 38
  Nicolas 38
DORR
  Elizabeth 38
  Frederick 38
  Joseph W. 38
  Margaret P. DURRITT
    38
  Marie POHLMANN 38
  Mary A.
    WHILHARBOR 38
  Philip G. 38
  Phillip G. 38
  Pilipp Gottfried 50
DORSCHER
  Anna 128

DORSEY
Anna 100
Elizabeth 36, 153
Mary 106
Mollie 127
DORT
A.C. 159
Alonzo C., Mrs. 31
Jane PARKS 159
May 159
Mittie, Miss 31
Mr. 134
Mrs. 134
DORVIS
Julia 27
DORWALD
Augustus SALZWELD 38
Frederick 38
DOSE
Dora 37
Madaline 19
Margaret 9
DOSIER
J.M. 115
DOSTAL
Mary 128
DOTSON
Mary 151
DOTTEREVEICH
Christiana ---- 69
Mary 69
Valentine 69
DOTY
Elizabeth CROSS 38
Ezra S. 38
George N. 38
John 38
John C. 38
Olive E. WALKER 38
Sarah J. ELLIS 38
Susan F. FAY 38
DOUGHERTY
---- 26
Betsey BUTLER 64
Bridget M. 109
Catharine 134
Charles 38
Elizabeth 108
Ellen McARDLE 22, 51, 134
Eneas 75
Francis 38
Frank 22
Grace GARVEY 37
Hugh 22, 51, 98, 134
Jane 22
John 37, 38, 109
Joseph 141
Kate 22
Maggie 51
Margaret CALL 38
Margaret COLL 109
Mary 100, 134
Mary A. 51
Mary BROADY 108
Mary DUFFY 38
Mr. 118
Pat. 51
Perry 108
Sarah 64
William 64
DOUGLAS
Adeline 68
David 38
Elizabeth 13, 128

Ellen 108
James M. 38
Jenny A. HANEY 38
Malinda 28
Maria 14
Mary A. 11
Mary B. 42, 161
Mary M. 94
May WARNICK 38
Melinda 168
Mrs. 14
Robert W. 38
DOUGLASS
Clara B. PRINTZ 38
Stephen M. 38
DOULAUGHTY
Elizabeth 107
DOUTHETT
E. 38
Eliza MONTGOMERY 38
Mary DEVLIN 38
R. 38
DOVE
Ellen 169
Joseph 169
Mary SHELTON 169
Mr. 29
Mrs. 29
DOW
Ann BENNETT 38
Emly LANE 60
Lizzy J. 60
Mary ---- 93
Mary Jane JARVIS 38
Nellie 93
Robert 60, 93
Robert M. 38
Willard W. 38
DOWD
Harriett 165
Mary 29, 119, 128, 151
DOWDALL
Catharine T. JUDGE 38
John 38
Peteer 38
Rose HALL 38
DOWLING
Hannah McCARDLE 38
Mary E. PURCELL 38
Michael 38
Nellie E. 118
Sarah J. 118
Sarah J. MILLER 118
William 118
DOWN
Ellen 102
Peter, Mrs. 150
DOWNES
Alice 65
Elizabeth SMITH 65
John 38
Joseph 65
Margarett CONNER 38
DOWNEY
C.E. 83
John 98
Kate Cora 98
Kitty Cora 98
Maggie 16
Mary MURRY 38
Mary O. MEARS 98
Patrick 38
S.E., Mrs. 15
DOWNS
Bridget 144

J., Mrs. 141
DOWNY
C.A. 49
DOYLE
Andrew 38
Ann 164
Benjamin N. 38
Bernard 102
Betty 109
Bridget 93, 98, 113
Carrie GERSBECK 38
Catharine 8, 50
Dellie WELSH 38
Edward F. 38
Elizabeth E. MARSH 38
Elizabeth FENODAH 81
Ellen Maria 52
Evaline 60
Frank D. 163
Hattie E. PALMER 38
James 38
Jane LANGDON 38
John N. 38
Joseph 81
Louisa 60
Martin 38
Mary 32, 48, 81
Mary A. BACHUS 38
Mary LESTER 52
Michael 52
Sarah 22
Sarah BODINE 38
William 38, 142
Winnie 33
DRAGE
N. 75
DRAKE
Anna M. STEWART 38
C. 31
E. 44
Electa DEPUE 38
Eliphalet 38
Fannie C. 44
Flemon 38
Frank E. 38, 44
Hellen M. INGALLS 38
Herman 78
Sarah M. KOON 38
DRAPER
Clara 33
Ellen 33, 79
DRAWAK
Anna 74
DRAWN
Mary 72
DREESSON
Anna 92
DREFHOLT
Henry 66
DREHER
Barbara MATHNER 39
Conrad 39
Margaretha WEBER 39
Victor 9, 39
DREIER
Carl 23
Wilhelmina JENSON 23
DREIN
William 30
DRELL
Louis 46
DRENNAN
Alice KEOWEN 39
Daniel 39
James W. 39

Mary WALLACE 39
DRENNEN
James W. 29
DRESON
Anna 92
DREW
---- GREENLEAF 52
Carrie M. SORENSON 39
Charles L. 39
Charlotte E. 52
Ella J. HOLLAND 39
Ezra 52
George T. 39
Hiram 39
Loraine J. 39
Louisa TYLER 39
Martha McNEAL 39
Rebecka PERKINS 39
S.H. 6
Sands P. 39
Sanuel H. 39
DREWN
Mary 148
DREWRY
Mrs. 92
William 92
DREWS
Lena 110
Magdalene 124
DREXEL
F. 135
Fred, Mr. and Mrs. 92
Fredk. 92
John C. 165
Katharina 157
Thomas 10
DRIEFHOLD
Auguste, Mrs. 137
H. 137
DRINES
Lena 110
DRINKHARD
Joshua 153
Martha 153
Polly GREGG 153
DRISCOL
Ellen 90
Ellen REIDY 90
James 90
DRISCOLE
Ellen 99
DRISCOLL
Catharine 28
Dennis 39
Eliza 24, 64
Elizabeth F. JENNINGS 39
Ella JONES 39
Ellen 114
George W. 39
John 39, 72
Mabel LEWIN 135
Martha E. ELLISON 39
Martha McGUIRE 39
Mary DRAWN 72
Mary Jane 72
Matilda J. 135
Phoebe 73, 100
Riley 135
William 39
DRISKELL
Mariam R. 45
Perry 45
Sarah Ann HOBBS 45

DRIVER
Rachael M., Mrs. 44
DROESSEL
Lena KLEIN 39
Paul 39
Ralph 39
Theodora SAUTER 39
DROHAN
Alice 47
DROLL
Maria 164
DROSSIN
Cecelia, Mrs. 121
R., Mr. 121
DROST
Bernard 78
Frederick 39
Louis C. 39
Mary E. McGEE 39, 71
Minna SONNE 39
DROSTE
August 39
Edward 39
Emilie 166
Emma HARTWIG 39
Ernestine ACKERMANN 39
Julia CAPELLE 39, 166
William 39, 166
DROUGHT
Diana 143
DROWLEY
Statia 27
DRUBA
Charles 84
Elizabeth 84
Elizabeth VOLTZS 84
DRUHENE
Margaret 77
DRUMMER
Eva 13
DRUMMOND
Elizabeth McINTYRE 39
Jennie CLARK 39
Melville J. 39
Pelton 39
DRURY
Elizabeth Mabell TUTTLE 39
William 39
DRYSDALE
Christina 45, 167
Christine 45
DuBOIS
Celista MOORE 140, 158
Eva C. 140
Jennie H. 158
P.B. 140, 158
P.B., Mrs. 140
Sarah 162
Sarah WILLIAMS 162
William 162
DUCE
Alice 63
Eliza 57
Esther 81
Esther ICKERSON 63
Henry 63
DUCHER
Rodney 123
DUCKER
Esther THOMAS 39
Lewis 39

DUCRO
  Susan 51
  Victor 51
DUCROS
  Amanda 144
  Ellen GETO 149
  Ellen GIBEAUX 144
  Susan 149
  Victor 144, 149
DUDLEY
  Annie C. 9
  E., Judge 62
  E.G. 101
DUEHOLM
  Christian P. 39
  Magdelina HOLST 39
DUEHRKOP
  Christina 36
DUEL
  Harry P. 147
DUEST
  Esther 141
DUFEK
  Margaret 69
  Wenzel 69
DUFF
  Dennis 39
  Emily BRODERICK 39
  James M. 39
  Mary 83
  Mary A. DUGAN 39
DUFFAK
  Barbara J. 39
  James 39
DUFFEY
  A.T. 52
  Bessy 137
  Catherine McCORMICK
    39
  Eliza MORAN 39
  Martin 39
  Mary 109
  Michael 39
  Patrick 39, 137
  Rose A. KIRCLAHAN
    39
  Rose Ann 39
DUFFIELD
  Harvey 93
DUFFY
  Annie McGARVIN 39
  Bernard J. 39
  Bridget 29
  Bridget EAGEN 39
  Bridget EGAN 29, 39
  James 38, 39, 156
  Margaret BAGLEY 39
  Mary 38, 90
  Mary McCORMICK 39
  Michael 29, 39
  Patrick J. 39
  Winnefred
    GALLAGHER 38
DUFREES
  Anna LUCAS 18
  Jacob 18
  Mary 18
DUFREND
  A.R. 19
DUFRENE
  Alfred R. 142
DUGAN
  Chatarine, Mrs. 52
  Mary 159
  Mary A. 39

DUGGAN
  Bart 1
  Catharine 22
  Johanna 47
  Rosana 115
DUGUID
  Annie NUSLEIN 39
  Eliabeth McDONALD
    39
  Robert 39
  Thomas 39
DUHRENDORFF
  Fred 155
  Lucie M. 155
  Lucy M. RIXEN 155
DUIGIN
  Emeline 123
DUKE
  Emma L. 1
  John James 39
  Nancy 129
DULANEY
  David E. 35
  Sophia NELSON 35
DULCHER
  Rodney 155
DULING
  Ann 20
DUMAN
  Caroline 24
DUMAR
  Caroline 24
DUMAS
  Marceline GOYETTE
    151
DUMMER
  Albertine 91
DUMPERTH
  Valentin 170
DUMPHY
  Anastasia McGRATH
    74
  Delia 74
  James 74
  M.P., Mr. 74
  P., Mrs. 74
DUMSER
  Lena 111
DUNBAR
  Margaret 58
DUNCAN
  Addie O. 119
  Alexander 39
  Alice May 161
  Charles 119, 161
  Chas. 119
  Elizabeth LICHKY 39
  Elvira 97
  Emma J. KELLEY 39
  Filure 97
  G.W., Mr. 143
  Hallie 19
  Hattie 117
  Henry 161
  John 99
  John W. 97
  Lemuel 39
  Margaret 4, 20
  Marie HAM 117
  Martha 49
  Mattie S. 117
  Odyssa SANDS 119,
    161
  Peter 117
  Sarah ALAWAY 39
  Wm. A. 39

  Woods 160
DUNDY
  Elmer S. 39
  Mary H. ROBINSON
    39
DUNGAN
  George W. 39
DUNHAM
  Benjamin 39
  Cornelius 39
  Emeline 39
  John 39
  M. 149
  Margaret SCOTT 39
  Martin 1, 39
  Rose Ann DUFFEY 39
  Rosetta 153
  Samuel 39
  Sarah 21
  Sarah J. WINSHIP 39
  Sophia ELLWOOD 153
  Sophrona ROBBINS 39
  William 153
DUNK
  Mary REEVES 40
  Richard 40
  William 40
  Winnie WICKS 40
DUNKER
  Dora 90
  Henry 83, 90
  Pauline CLAUSSEN
    134
  Perlina CLAUSSEN 90
  Sophia 134
  Steffen H. 134
DUNKLY
  Anna 47
  Lucy Ann 47
DUNLAP
  Charles 98
  Eliza 150
  Mary A. 98
DUNLOP
  Mary A. 27
DUNMORE
  Laura SIMMONS 40
  Louis 40
  Lucy NICHOLS 40
  Wm. H. 40
DUNN
  Anna S. STREETER 40
  Betsy E. PRATT 40
  Elijah 40, 63
  Eliza Jane 114
  Ellen BARD 40
  James T. 40
  Martin 40
  Mary 100
  Mary A. WALKER 40
  Mary BOYLE 40
  Michael 40, 98
  Mrs. 19
  R.H. 40
  T.E. 115
  William 40
DUNNE
  George B. 40
  John 40
  Mary BRADLEY 40
  Sarah J. GARDNER 40
DUNNIGAN
  Anne McGARRY 40
  Francis [Frank] 40
  Lizzie MASON 40
  Thomas 40

DUNNING
  Anna L. WINT 40
  Elizabeth CHORD 40
  Henry 40
  Hilliard S. 40
  Lucy HOLDING 40
  Mary T. CONDON 40
  Reuben 40
  William H. 40
DUNTHE
  Nancy 63
DUQUEMY
  Alfred F. 40
  J.B. 40
  Mary C. LOY 40
  Mary COLIN 40
DURALL
  R. Burns 156
DURANT
  Mary A.J. 168
DURDICK
  Sarah 48
DURELEY
  Mary 39
DURHAM
  Catherine M. 22, 114
  Louisa 50
DURKIN
  Mary A. 71
DURMANDY
  Catherine ISDELL 40
  Charles 40
  Mary COYLE 40
DURNALL
  Adelaide CHAPMAN
    40
  Eliza BOYD 40
  Ezekiel 40
  Frank 30
  Henry 40
  Jane LATEY 40
  Samuel 40
  Samuel, Jr. 40
DURR
  Katie 65
DURRER
  Frank 137
  Mena 137
  Theresa ANDERMAT
    137
DURRITT
  Henry 38
  Margaret P. 38
  Sarah H. ASCOTT 38
DUS
  Catherina 66
  Mary GROFECK 66
  Witelea 66
DUSEY
  Abbie 139
  Abbie KELLY 139
  John 139
DUTCHER
  Rodney 5, 27, 36, 41,
    83, 87, 123, 150, 168
DUTHCER
  Rodney 147
DUTKIN
  Albert 40
  Clara BLEIK 40
  Julia BENDER 40
  Leanhard 40
DUTTON
  Edward 40
  Maria BUTLER 40
  Mary 55

  Mary B. WALLACE 40
  Nathan C. 40
DUVALL
  Christine 104
DUVERNOY
  George 104
DWIER
  Joanna 106
  John 106
  Mary DEWIRE 106
DWORAK
  Anna 74
  Annie SHANKA 40
  Barbara 150
  Catherine HERPST 40
  George 40
  Joseph 40, 69, 84, 85,
    96, 123, 134
DWORAZ
  Andrew 94
DWORK
  Joseph 69, 84, 85, 96,
    151
DWYER
  Annie SULLIVAN 40
  Alice 117
  Belle 81
  Edmund 40
  Ellen 73
  Ellen BUTLER 40
  Fanny WILKESON 81
  Jeremiah 81
  John 40
  M.A., Mrs. 124
  Margaret 148
  Mary 81
  Mary RYAN 40
  Mary WHITE 40
  Michael 102
  Thomas O. 40
  William M. 40
DWYRE
  Belle 153
DYE
  Louise 68
  Saray 72
DYER
  Abigail GRENDALL
    108
  David 108
  Jennie 94
  John 94
  Malinda THORN 94
  Mary 156
  Mary E. 53
  Mary G. 108
  Olivia A. 155
DYKEMAN
  L. 93
DYKES
  Cynthia 22
  Mary 125
DYMOND
  Martha 73
EADEN
  Margaret 107
EADIE
  Sarah 139
EAGAN
  Ed 22
  Edward 120
EAGEN
  Bridget 39
EAK
  Archie 125

EAMES
Ann BERNANT 40
Anna ASTMAN 40
John 40
EARLE
Geo. G. 95
Melissa 33
EARLY
Mr. 54
Sarah Anne 124
EASLEY
Mary C. 166
W.D. 166
EASTER
John D. 110
Rev. 7
EASTON
Mary 16
EASTWOOD
Liddie 29
EATON
---- 167
David 40
E.L. 158
Edrick L. 40
Emma SLAVETER 40
Lanona 110
Mollie ADAMS 40
Mr. 140
Mrs. 158
EATOUGH
James 40
Sarah FOOT 40
EAVES
Mary 63
EAYERS
Edwin 131
Edwin, Mrs. 131
EAYRES
Della MURPHY 40
Edwin Wm. 40
Rachel MEEHAN 40
William 40
EAYRS
Mary J. 22
EBAUGH
Sarah Frances SMITH
63
EBBESON
J. 42
T. 42
EBBISSON
Anna OLSDOTTER 40
James 40
EBERHART
A.G. 31, 32
Alvin G. 40
Catharine GIESEY 40
Maggie GUERIN 40
Maggie T.G. GUERIN
106
Mary A. GREEN 40
Uriah 40
EBERT
Catharine KRULL 34
EBNER
Maria 67
EBOLD
Elizabeth MILLER 11
Frederick 11
Mary 11, 30, 112
EBREIGHT
David 40
Ezra 40
Hannah O'BRIEN 40

Mary LONGSBERRY
40
EBRIGHT
Jessie 156
ECKFORD
Jennie M. 72
ECKLUND
ECKLUND 59
Ella 59
Mary SCHROEDER 59
ECKMAN
Kate 60
ECKMANN
Magdalena 92
Martholina 110
EDDY
Alda Van CAMP 40
Jefferson 41
John M. 40
Lura 118
Maria A. MATNEY 41
Mary CHAPIN 41
Mary STEVENS 40
Ruben L. 41
S.A., Mrs. 11
Spaulding 40
EDELMAN
Catherine 52
EDEN
A.O. 41
Albert 83
Antge M. JANSSEN 41
Henriette MAUKE 41
Onne 41
EDGAR
A.J. 23
Adolf J. 76
Francis Russell SMITH
126
John 108
John T. 126
Mary 126
EDGERTEN
Chas. W. 119
EDGERTON
C. Wm. 4
Charles W. 13, 132
Chas. H. 146
Chas. U. 135
Chas. W. 12, 47, 55, 87,
165
EDHOLM
Benjamin 41
J.J. PETERSON 41
J.J., Mrs. 41
Johana J. PETERSEN
41
Johanna ANDERSON
41
Johannah J. PETERSON
41
Kittie BUSHEY 41
L.P. 41
Mary A. RICE 41
Mary Grace
CHARLTON 41
Nelson J. 41, 170
Osborn 41
P.L. 41
EDLER
Alice BATTON 41
Anna Maria BAYER 41
Q. Phil 41
T. Phil 41
EDLING
Adam 56

Brita JOHANSDOTTER
119
Brita JOHNSON 113
John 113, 119
Karin 119
Lizzie 113
Margaret 56
EDMANDS
Geo. W. 43
Josephine, Mrs. 43
EDMOLDS
Ceceilia 163
EDMONDS
Lucindia 62
EDMONDSON
Annie 144
Ephriam 41
Sarah Anna
PATTERSON 41
EDMONSON
Anne 171
Charles 78
Elizabeth PARKINSON
78, 171
William 78, 171
EDMUNDS
Charlotte JONES 125
Hannah 125
Nathaniel 125
EDMUNDSON
Eliza 110
Frank 125
James 105
Julia GREESON 125
Lethe 105
Luellia 125
Mary TUMBLESON
105
EDSALL
Hannah 5
EDSTROM
Andrew 60
Charlotte ANDERSON
60
Johanna 60
John P. 11
Louisa 11
Lousia M. 11
Maratin 60
EDWARDS
Ann M. COLES 41
Aster 100
Benjamin 60
Charlotte 60
Deana N. 137
Eliza 139
Eliza J. PLEAT, Mrs. 41
Elizabeth GLASS 41
Evaline DOYLE 60
F. 40
H.L., Mrs. 44
Harriet ENGLISH 129
Isaac 41, 170
Jane 118, 125
Jessie SAUNDERS 41
John E. 29
John W. 41
Lucy A. CASDELL 41
Lucy S. WALKER 41
M. Jonathan, Jr. 41
M.G. 93
Martha WILKINSON
129
Mary E. 129
Mathias G. 41
Nicholas Norway 41

P.T. 41, 93
Sarah A. 91
Sarah Ann RITCHIE 41
Sarah E. 170
Sarah J. PHELPS 170
Sarah PHELPS 41
Susan 101
William 41, 129
William J.F. 41
Wm. 129
EFFERS
Lena 87
EGALAND
Andres 41
EGAN
Bridget 29, 39, 40, 129
Ed 36
Edward 30, 38, 64, 73,
95
Florance McCARTHY
41
Lucy McCARTHY 41
Michael J. 82
Owen 23
Patrick 37
Peter 41
Peter F. 41
EGBERT
Augustus A. 41
James 41
Lutheria L. GRIFFIN 41
Marion 132
Mary VLIET 41
EGEN
John 73
Margaret 73
Mary 1, 73
EGENBERGER
Veronica 5
EGGE
Adolph 41
Anna RITTER 41
Otielie ROSENKRANZ
41
Peter 41
EGGER
Anna FICENS 41
Elizabeth 87
Joseph 41
Rosa BULAG 41
EGGERS
Caroline BOYE 41
Henry 41, 43, 137
EGLADDEN
Lodemia 163
EHLEN
Mrs. 131
EHLER
George 14
Katey BORNSON 14
Margaret BORNSON 14
Margaretha 14
EHLERS
Anna E. WARAGE 41
Carl 41
D.C 169
Damin KIESER 129
Dietrich C. 41
Kate 129
Katherina RUZER 41
Margaret 68
Margareta 94
Mary KUMPS 41
Nicholas 41
Richard 129
Wiebke 35

William 41
EHRENFFORT
Henry 12
Mary D. 12
EICHER
Anna NIMAND 62
Claus 62
Mary 62
EICHNER
Anna 155
Anna NIEMANN 41
Claus 41
Elsabe HARMSEN 41
Willmina 87
EICHORN
Francisca 5
EICKE
Cathrine RYMAN 41
Elizabeth 146
Elizabeth SOHL 41, 54
Emma 54
H. 63
Henry 41, 54, 63, 65,
110, 116, 120
Henry A. 41
Jacob 41
John 41
Mary SIEVERS 41
Solama RAMALA 41
EICKHOFF
Hannah 37
EICKHORN
Franziska 72
EIFFLER
Mary 84
Nicholaus 84
EIFFLIE
Mary 120
EIFLER
Maria 164
Maria
WELLENMLCHER
164
Nicholas 164
EIKEMAN
Caroline 153
EIMERS
Dina 36
EINBLEN
Geo. F. 64
EIRING
Elizabeth STROUP 41
Henry 41
Wilhelmine MILLER 41
William 41
EISELE
Catrine FRANK 41
Jacob 41
John C. 41
Katie REMINGTON 41
EISENHANER
Eliza 96
EITNER
Christian 41
Ernest 41
Mary HOPPE 41
Mary KASISMIR 41
EKBERG
Andos 41
Andrew S. 74
Karna PETERSON 41
Lizel NELSON 41
Nels 41
EKELEY
Inga Chri 94
John 76, 94

EKELUND
  A.A. 119
  Anna 119
EKERSON
  Catherine SIMSON 42
  Hannah PERSON 42
  O. 42
EKLUND
  A. 111
  Anton 42
  Carl 59
  Caroline 42
  Christian 42
  Mary JOHNSON 42
  Miss 59
  Mr. 59
EKSTROM
  Henrietta C. 55
EKWALL
  John 126
ELAESSER
  Jacobine WACKER 56
  Maria 56
  Peter 56
ELBERT
  H.C. 3
ELBING
  Anna KROVINEK 42
  George 42
  John 42
  Mary STOUGHTON 42
ELBLING
  Anna KROVINEK 42
  George 42
  Gerhard 74
ELBRING
  John 42
  Mary STOUGHTON 42
ELCOCK
  E.H., Mrs. 30, 36
  Emma C. 108
  Lizzie 126, 165
  Thomas 126
ELCORK
  Lizzie 14
ELDER
  Perry A. 152
  Samuel M. 152
ELDRED
  Olive 53
  Salome 6
ELDRIDGE
  Nancy 14
  W. 80
ELDRIEDGE
  Lucy N. 128
  Luna MECHEM 128
  Samuel S. 128
ELGE
  Christina 20
ELGUTTER
  Morris 139
ELHERT
  Anna 55
  Helena PETERS 55
  Jacob 55
ELIASON
  Christian 42
  Petennalla SWENSON
    42
ELICE
  J.W., Mrs. 3
ELIESON
  Inge ACKER 42
  Ingebright S. 42

Katherine C. DEVOLD
  42
  Ole 42
ELIKINS
  Fa____ 11
ELINGSON
  Josephine DAHLINE 42
  Peter 42
ELLEGAARD
  Christian 94
  Magdalena 94
  Maire KORKHOLM 94
ELLEN
  Carl 137
  Carolina ACKERMAN
    137
  Minnie 137
ELLENGWOOD
  Lydia 100
  Mary CLEMENTS 100
  Samuel 100
ELLENHUSEN
  Anna RUSCAMP 131
ELLERMANN
  Elisa 136
ELLERTH
  Annie PETERSON 42
  Peter 42
ELLEY
  Ann 50
ELLICKSON
  Beckey LUNDVALL 42
  John 42
ELLINGWOOD
  Lucy DASHER 42
  Mary CLEMENTS 42
  Samuel F. 42
  Thomas B. 42, 159
ELLIOT
  Mary 121
ELLIOTT
  Camilla E. BEARD 42
  Emma A. 145
  George 100, 145
  H.P. 168
  Isabella 45
  John 44
  Nathan 14, 38, 42, 84
  S.H. 168
  V.A. 56, 64
ELLIS
  Anna 101, 147
  Eva HANELINE 42
  Fanny MARKS 42
  J.D. 42
  J.F. 127
  John 46, 47
  Jonathan D. 38
  Joseph 165
  L.A. 71
  Lizzie C. 165
  Louise BOND 165
  Luella 110
  Martin 42
  Mary 165
  Mary E. 38
  Mary E. LUDDINGTON
    38, 42
  Mollie 62
  Moses or Moris 62
  Nancy M. CLARK 42
  Permelia STERET 62
  Rosanna 86
  Sarah J. 38
  William 42
  Wm. Henry 42

ELLISON
  Elizabeth J. CARTER
    39
  Elizabeth Jane 39
  Martha E. 39
  Mary 165
  Wm. E. 39
ELLSBORG
  Christian 79
  Margaret BROWN 79
  O. Lina 79
ELLSTON
  Laurinda 51
ELLSWORTH
  Annie E. HATHAWAY
    109
  Gyda THOBRO 42
  John 42
  Maria PROCTOR 42
  Phebe G. 8
  William 42
ELLWOOD
  Elizabeth FRY 89
  Sophia 153
ELLYTHORP
  Elsa 12
ELMGREN
  Antonette 13
  John P. 13
ELMGRIN
  I.P., Mrs. 120
ELROD
  Pauline 2
ELSAASER
  E., Mrs. 160
ELSAESSER
  Anna K. 146
  Emilie 129
  Emilie WALKER 129
  G.F. 129
ELSASSER
  Amelia WACKER 155
  Amelia WALKER 42
  Anna LORENZEN 42
  Anna WACKER 87
  Catharina 39, 42
  Catharine 12, 43
  Charles 42
  Christ 42
  Christian 42, 87
  E., Miss 42
  Elizabeth HENGEN 42
  Emilie 87
  Emilie WACKER 42
  G. Frederick 42
  G.F. 42, 110
  J.F. 42
  Jacob 42, 87
  Jacobine WACHER 42
  Jacobine WAKER 42
  Karl 42
  Katharina HUNT 42
  Maggie KNAUBER 42
  Peter 42
ELSEISSER
  F. 68
ELSESSER
  Fred 55
ELSSASER
  Catherine 171
  Fred 171
  Jacobine WALKER 171
ELSTON
  Elizabeth HENRY 76
  Linda 22
  Sarah A. 76

  William 76
ELWELL
  Addie GROSSE 42
  Edward W. 42
  Joseph 42
  Mary T. 7
  Merendie REDLON 42
ELWIN
  Ann 59
ELWOOD
  Mary 83
ELY
  Caroline 145
  Eliza MILLER 42
  Eliza PALMER 42
  Jerry 42
  Lucy PAYNE 42
  Parnel 13
  Thomas 42
  William H. 42
EMALD
  Celia 171
EMBKA
  Christina 138
EMERICK
  Elizabeth JOHNSON 42
  John 42
EMERSON
  Edwin 42
  Florence BROOKS 42
  Harrington 42
  Mary 82, 159
  Mary Louise INGHAM
    42
  Samuel D.J. 42
EMERY
  Aliance MAYO 42
  Arlena 42
  Charles 42
  E.L., Mrs. 42
  Elias L. 42
  Emeline 42
  Emma WALKER 42
  Frederick B. 42
  Joseph 42
  Maud 118
  Rachael Ann LOWMAN
    42
  Sarah 106
  Sarah WILLIAMS 42
EMEYER
  Mary Hak 93
EMMERICH
  Bernhardt 12
  Margareta MUNNING
    12
  Minnie 12
EMMERIK
  G. 148
  Johanna 148
  Mina 148
EMMERY
  E.L. 57
EMMICK
  Mary 139
EMMONS
  Amina 132
EMONDSON
  Alice 159
  Charles 159
  Elizabeth PARKINSON
    159
EMONS
  Anna Maria 92
EMPEY
  Albert T. 42

  Ellen 42
  Emma J. MOORE 42
  Thomas 42
EMRY
  E. 13
EMS
  Edward 42
  Jane DAVIS 42
  Martha BROWN 42
  Mary 152
  Richard 42, 152
  Rosa A. COZZENS 152
ENDER
  Christian 42
  Rebecca KASSELL 42
ENDFIELD
  Adam 43
  Henry 43
  Louisa 43
  Lucy Ann LOWER 43
  Peter 43
  Susanna ALHOUSE 43
ENDLY
  Anna M. 147
ENENBAG
  Elizabeth 103
ENEWALD
  Chas. 43
ENEWOLD
  Anna C. HENRICKSON
    43
  Christen R. 43
  Christian R. 43
  Karen M. JENSEN 43
  Lawrence 22
  Lawrence C. 43
  Maggie KLINDT 43
  Marie JENSEN 43
  Robert C. 43
ENGEL
  Anna HAMMEL 43
  Annie 11
  Caroline SCHLOUTZ
    95
  Charles 43
  Johanna 120
  Mary 57
  Mina TIMME 43
  Nathanel 43
  Nicholaus 43
  Poppatabea JOHNSEN
    43
  Sam'l. 11
  Tilly REINHART 11
  Wipke 92
ENGELKE
  Augusta 14
  Emilie 149
  Julius 14, 149
  Mathilda
    ZIMMERMANN 14
  Matilda ZIMMERMAN
    149
ENGLAND
  Chaplain 112
  Elizabeth 99
ENGLE
  Clarence M. 43
  George B. 43
  Lida A. ROGERS 43
  Mary 57
  O., Mrs. 161
  Permelia KELLOGG 43
ENGLEBRECKSEN
  Carl 23
  Eva LINDBORN 23

ENGLEMAN
Margareeta HANSEN 116
Ole 116
ENGLEMEIER
Johanna 155
ENGLER
Christoph 43
Ephriam 43
Maria M. BOYE 43
Sophia RICHTER 43
ENGLISH
Anna H. HEDLEY 162
Edward 162
Ella M. 162
George C. 43
Harriet 129
Jennie E. DOOLITTLE 43, 47
John 141
Margaret 123
Mary HOBBS 43
Nathan 43
ENGLUND
Charlotte 168
ENGSTROM
A. 43
Andres 43
Axel 10
Bertha 160
C.A. 160
Caroline KOHLER 43
Charles A. 43
E. SEIGEL 43
Elizabeth SIAGREN 43
F.E. 43
Francis Oscar 43
Hannah PEHRSON 43
Mathilda HAGLUNDH 160
V.A. 43
ENIS
Catharine 9
ENK
Dora 66
ENKEN
Johanna HOLZEGER 167
Wilhelmina 167
William 167
ENNIS
Jennie REED 19
ENOS
A.A. 43
A.C. HENRY 43
Flavel 43
Harriet STORER 43
ENRIGHT
David 43
Ellen D. 102
Ellen DILLON 43, 102
Jeremiah 35
Margaret 36, 48
Mary CARIMODY 35
Mary, Mrs. 35
Michael 43, 102
Nora LEINHAN 43
ENSIGN
Carrie F. HIGBY 43
Clarinda PRENTIS 43
Sidney 43
Theodore 43
ENTELKE
Mary 2
ENTRENSEN
Mary 67

ENYEART
Catharine 85
EPENETER
Henrietta RUDOESKY 43
John 43, 119, 163
EPPERSON
Green 43
Mary 100
Mary E. WHITE 43
Sidney C. 43
Thirza WOOD 43
ERASSHOF
Catharina 93
ERATH
Catharine SCHULTZ 43
Max 43
Sophie WAGNER 43
William 89
William H. 43
ERB
? ACHTE 43
Catharine METZGER 43
Elizabeth 104
Eugene W. 43, 115
Francis C. 43
ERBEN
Annie 171
Bridget GILL 43
Emanuel 43
Josef 171
Joseph 43
Kate S. 43
Katharina SAMELIK 171
ERCK
Henry 43
John H. 43
Louisa 12
Louisa W. BIERMANN 43
Mary DORMANN 43
ERDMAN
Judith 19
ERFLING
E.C. 48
Edward Charles 43
Frances 161
Francis M. SCHAEFER 43
Francis Meta 138
ERGGEN
Mary 107
ERHARDT
Salome 12
ERICKSEN
Charlotta Marie 57
Charlotta May 57
Elsie 3, 4
ERICKSON
A. 43
Ambrose 76, 117
Andus 26
Ann Marie 98
Anna 22
Auguste TYBELL 53
Carl 23
Caroline JOHNSON 43
Caroline OLSEN 111
Carrie OLESON 11
Carrie S. BROSIONS 43
Charles 43
Chris L. 43
Christ N. 43

Christiana Gusta JOHNSON 61
Christine 11
Christine CARLSON 122
Clara CARLSON 43
Elizabeth 133
Elizabeth FOX 43
Ellen 127
Ellen NEILSEN 61
Elna 89
Frederick 11
Gertrude 11
Hannah ERKBACH 43
Isobel 160
Johanna JENSEN 26
Johannes 116
John 43, 53, 61, 122
Kirsten NIELSDOTTER 88
Lars 88
Lena ANDERSON 23
Louisa BRADFORD 43
Maria 53
Maria SWENSON 43
Martha OLSON 116
Nels 43
Olaf F. 43
Peter 111
Pher 43
Sarah 55
Stina LARSON 43
Swen 61
ERICKSSON
Chas. 113
ERICSON
Christina NELSON 43
Fred 43
ERIKSEN
Hans P. 43
Hansena JOHANSON 43
ERIKSON
Caren JOHNSON 58
Carie 153
Caroline OLESEN 13
John 58
Karen 13
Oleg 13
ERKBACH
Hannah 43
ERKESON
Johanna ERLANSON 152
Swan 152
ERLANSON
Johanna 152
ERLENBORN
Alfred A. 44
Anton 44
Ernestine W. PITSCHNER 44
Rosa HAEFNER 44
ERLICKSON
Anna 76
ERN
Fredrica 136
ERNAY
Charlotte GARDNER 147
Ezra 147
Mary Anna 147
ERNST
Anna ROHWER 44
Catherine MUMM 44
George 44

Henry 44
ERP
V.P. 38
ERRICKSON
Amostine MAGNUSEN 44
Carolina Wilhelmina PETERSON 44
Carrie 50
S.H. 44
Sivert 44
ERSKINE
Jane WILLIAMS 44
Mary FULMER 44
Matilda 7
R.J. 44
Robert 44
ERWIN
Catharine 59
Elizabeth C. 155
Mary A. 155
ESBERG
Claus 55
Gerda Caroline 55
Sarah ERICKSON 55
ESCHLE
Constantine 44
Lena DIESCHLER 44
Lena RUDOLPH 44
William 44
ESDOHR
Albert 44
Henry 44
Matilda WENDT 44
Phebe Ann CORNISH 44
ESKELL
Rebecca 17
ESKELSON
Ellen 66
Eskel 66
Mila NILSEN 66
ESMAY
Francis 91
ESMER
Frederick 44
Frederick W. 44
Louisa KIEBING 44
Mary SAUER 44
ESPANDE
Anna 8
Anna FRIDRICH 8
John 8
ESSELLAMANN
Isabella 87
ESSMEY
F.A. 167
ESTABROOK
Caroline A. 28, 76
Caroline A. MAXWELL 44
Clara M. CAMPBELL 44
E. 129
E., Gen. 83
E., Gen. and Mrs. 98
Experience 44
General 147
H.D. 96, 118
Henry 61
Henry D. 44
ESTELL
Belle, Mrs. 50
ESTY
Sarah 33

ETSON
Susanna 31
ETTLEMAN
Anna BOWMAN 44
Daniel 44
Lillie May MORTON 44
W.R. 44
ETZENSPERGER
J.C., Mrs. 26
EUBANKS
Maria, Mrs. 91
EUKANY
William 58
EULER
Elizabeth 170
EVAN
Christina 37
EVANS
Anna PETERSON 37
Annie M. SNELL 44
C.A. 29
Catharine 154
Charity 18, 60
Charles 44
Charles E. 44
Charles T. 44
Chas. B., Mr. and Mrs. 29
Chester A. 44
E. Pearl 100
E.D. 127
Eliza P. DAVIS 44
Eliza Perla 71
Eliza Permela DAVIS 71
Elizabeth 52, 167
Elizabeth ASTMAN 44
Elizabeth FAULKNER 69
Elizabeth KELLEY 44
Elizabeth PARREY 71
Ellen MAGEE 44
Ellen McGEE 44
Emily 69
Evan 37
F. 29
Fannie C. DRAKE 44
George 69
John 44, 71
John B. 44
John E. 44
John, Mrs. 10
Julia F. 29
Leonard 19
Lillie C. 127
Lizzie 88
Lizzie H. 47
Lorinda PECKENPAW 127
Lucy L. 44, 120
Manda FRY 44
Margaret 154, 167
Mary 4, 19
Mary E. KINCAID 44
Mary Jane 160
Mary L. 71
Mary WILLIAMS 71
Mattie 19
Mr. and Mrs. 120
Patrick 44
Phoebe P. 71
Priscilla 19
Rachael M. DRIVER 44
Rachel 71
Robert 75

EVANS, cont.
Roger 71
Sarah ASHBURN 44,
137
Thomas 71
W. 94
Wm. 127
EVENS
Albert S. 44
Elizabeth TILLEY or
FILLEY 44
Hattie TWEED 44
Wm. T. 44
EVENSEN
Helene 76
Julia F. 12
Mary 138
EVENSON
Andrew 44
Henrekke L.C. MORK
44
EVEREST
Aaron S. 44
Belle L. RICHARDSON
44
David 44
Frank L. 44
Maria M. DARRAH 44
Myra H. WILLARD 44
EVERETT
Annie COLLINS 158
Stratira 86
EVERGREEN
Margaret 114
Robert 114
EVERS
Annie SENJAN 44
Dorothea ZIESENIS 44
Frank 83
Frederick 44
Henry 44
Ollie, Miss 37
EVERSON
Anna S. 84
Mary 66, 107
Mary PETERSON 122
Peter 122
EVERTON
Elizabeth 146
EVINGER
Elizabeth 79
EVISON
Geo. 119
Geo., Mrs. 119
EVLYN
Emmarilla 144
EVMER
Fredrick 44
Fredrick W. 44
Louisa KIEBING 44
Mary SAUER 44
EWELL
Sophronia 106
EWERS
Frank 44
Jonathan 44
Nancy TAVERNER 44
Rose J. WYLIE 44
EWING
Anna NEAL 44
Catharine 19
David 44
Emerson 44
Etta 29
Freddie LANGHOFF 44
George 156

James P. 44
John 29
Joseph 44
Maggie 54
Margaret 45
Susan BUTLER 29
EXTERMANN
Elizabeth 137
EYSTER
Margaret 165
EYTH
Joseph 44
Mary FEISER 44
FABER
Mary 129
FACKLER
Jacob, Mrs. 103
FADLUND
Mary 16
FAGAN
Bridget KENNEDY 44
James 44, 52
M., Miss 44
Mary 52, 115
Mary DAVIS 44, 52
May T. 52
Peter 44, 52
FAGERSTJERNA
Anna P. MARIA 45
Edna T. SNELL 45
Ole 45
Peter Wilhelm Pouleon
45
FAGIN
Ann HULE 53
Kate 53
Owen 53
FAGUE
Lizzie 108
FAHEY
Bridget 82, 83
FAHRENBACH
Catherine 10
FAIR
Adeline A. WELLS 45
David 45
James B. 45
Mary Jane 72
Rebecca McMONIGAIL
45
FAIRBANK
E. 142
FAIRFIELD
Eliza 108
Sarah 166
FAIRMAN
Martha A. BARNES 45
Richard 45
FAIST
Annie 57
Annie PLANE 45
Catharine HARRNER
45
Louis 45, 57
Wm. G. 45
FAIT
Albert 60
Alice 60
Mary BOWDEN 60
FAKE
Harriet C. 170
Mr. and Mrs. 170
FALCONER
Christina DRYSDALE
45, 167

Christine DRYSDALE
45
Eliza McKITTRICK 45
Ellen D. 167
James 45
Maggie ALLEN 45
Thomas 45, 167
Wm. T. 32
FALES
Mary 78
Mary E. 101
FALK
Caroline 152, 162
Charles 45
Christine PETERSON
45
Gust 159
Gustave 45
Maria S., Mrs. 4
Sohpia B. 70
Theresa S. 45
FALKNER
---- 21
ELiza 168
James 167
FALLER
Caroline KAFER 45
Herman 45
Josephine FLAK 45
Thomas 45
FALLIN
Mary POLAND 45
FALLIN,
David A. 45
FALLON
Ann 73
Annie 73
Bridget 109
George 168
Mary 109, 168
Nellie COLLINS 168
Thomas 115
FANERE
Louise 58
FANGER
Henry 32
FANGMANN
Anthony 30
FANING
Ellen 64
FANNELL
John 45
FANNING
Annie MASTERSON 45
Annie Maude SICKER
115
Bridget MURPHE 45
Margaret 26
Patrick 45
FANSHER
Nancy 1
FARDAN
Mary 62
FARINGTON
Martha 25
FARLEY
Ann 110
J.C. 129
Mary 30, 133
Mary A. 152
Mary Ann 152
FARLY
Ann 156
FARM
Christina JOHNSON 45
Ellen SWANSON 45

John 45
FARMAINE
G.F. 38
FARMER
Ann 10
FARNSWORTH
Hannah 31
Rosetta 148
Thomas 148
FARQUER
Elizabeth SMITH 45
Jeremiah W. 45
John 45
Rebecca R. FRENCH 45
FARR
Adeline 112
FARRAL
Martha 148
FARRAR
L.P. 150
Sarah Ann 127
Susan G. 119
FARREL
Julia 23
FARRELL
Bridget 156
Catharine SWEENEY
45
Cornelius 45
Dorothy 169
Dorthy 32
Eliza CARROLL 45
Ellen POWERS 45
Emma 164
Homer 164
John 45
Joseph 45
Margaret DIGNAM 156
Margaret RILEY 45
Maria SHANNON 45
Mary HANLON 45
Michael 45
Patrick 45
Phillip 156
FARREN
Martha 155
FARRER
Isabella ELLIOTT 45
Joseph 45
Margaret GARRIGAN
45
Samuel 29
Sysander P. 45
FARRINGTON
Permilia 162
FARRISH
Ellen A. 54
FARROW
Susan 47
FASE
Andreas 45
Henry 45
Mary UHE 45
FATE
Francis 130
Mary BELDEN 130
Rebecca 130
Sarah HULL 45
Thomas 45
William H.H. 45
FATH
Fred 86
Lavina 83
Mary 86
FAULKNER
Elizabeth 69

FAUST
Elizabeth F. 84
F.E., Mrs. 146
Fridericke 66
FAVRE
Elizabeth 6
FAWCETT
Eliza 105
Eliza RODGERS 105
Mary 105
Mrs. 105
William 105
FAXAN
Mary 48
FAXON
Mary 90
FAY
Anna 60
Annie E. 46
Catharine CALLIGAN
30
Catherine 46
Celia M. 30, 46
David 45
Edward 30, 46
Louisa 93
Mary A. BROWN 45
Susan F. 38
Warren 38
Wealthy Lucy 65
FAYHTENGER
Barbara NOWOK 45
Frank 45
FAYHTINGER
Frances WOSHEKER
45
Frank 45
FAYTINGER
Frank 45
FEAY
Alfred T. 45
Alfred Taylor 146
Carrie E. SMITH 45
Fanny TAYLOR 45
James 45
FECH
Charles H. 60
Eliza 88
Jacob 88
Johanna JEPPERSON
88
Johannah C. 60
Maria E.C.
JOHANNSEN 60
FECHNER
Augusta 68
Bertha 15, 104, 136
Carl 15, 68
Juliana SEILER 68
Juliane SEIDLER 15
Pauline 136
FEDDE
Christian 5, 45
Claus 45
John 5, 45, 72
Maggie GLANDT 45
Maggie MARTINS 45
Margareth MARTENS 5
Maria MULLER 45
Meto B. 45
Wiebke Catharine 5
FEDRLE
Frederick 45
Mary REIZ 45

FEE
  Bridget 47
  Charlotte McGUIRE 45
  Eliza J. 31
  John 45
  Maria 107
  Mariam R. DRISKELL
    45
  William F. 45
FEEDERLE
  Frederick 45
  Mary REIZ 45
FEENEY
  J.H. 28
FEHRLI
  Maria 51
FEISER
  Mary 44
FEISOBSEN
  Mrs. 150
FEKENSCHER
  Augustus 45
  Caroline VOGT 45
  Henry H. 45
  Mary K. HALDY 45
FELD
  Rebecca 81
FELDKAMP
  Anton 37
  Caroline SCHROEDER
    37
  Maria 37
FELICI
  Mailan 93
FELIX
  Henry 45
  Jane MOORE 45
FELL
  Emily 94
  Emily J. 94
  John B. 94
  Mary AUMOCK 45
  William H. 45
FELLIAN
  Fred 45
  Hannah O'MERA 45
  Kate BLISS 45
  Michael 45
FELLOWS
  Alice W. PERKINS 35
  Ephraim 35
  Fannie I. 35
FELMAR
  Louise 164
FELT
  Anna C. JOHNSON 46
  Carrie RASSMUSSEN 3
  Gustave 46
  John M. 46
  Mary PETERSON 46
  Nels 3
  Stina 3, 97
FELZMANN
  Auguste 98
  Ernest 98
  Nina 98
FENDRICH
  Anna WOBORIL 46
  Catharine NOWAK 46
  Frank 46
  Wenzel 46
FENELL
  Adalaide 88
FENKELL
  Annie E. FAY 46
  Eli B. 46

Ernest L. 46
  Hannah HOWELL 46
FENNELL
  Adalaide 88
FENODAH
  Elizabeth 81
FENSER
  Gertrude 154
FENTAN
  Annie 81
FENTON
  Abby 101
  C.S. 46
  Dan 46
  Ellen FITZGERALD 46
  Ethal CUSTER 46
  Jane 165
  Joan O'BRIEN 46
  Lucia M. 44
  Margaret SULLIVAN
    46
  Mary 152
  Mary Ann KEARNEY
    46
  Mary FOLEY 101
  Matilda 51
  Morris 46
  Norman C. 46
  Roger 101
  Susin CULBERTSON
    46
  Thadeus 46
  Thomas 46
  William 46, 126
  Wm. 75
FERGISON
  Elizabeth HOPKINS
    114
  John 114
  Madoria 114
FERGUSON
  A.N. 159
  A.W. 97
  Armstead O. 63
  Arthur N. 46
  Catharine E. 59
  Clara 34
  Clerinda 149
  Cynthia 78
  Delia L. SEARS 46
  Esther A. 100
  F., Mrs. 46
  Fenner 46
  George 59
  Helen E. UPJOHN 46
  Katie E. ANDERSON
    35
  Martha 63
  Mary 59, 144
  Nancy 63
  Sarah Jane 127
FERRIS
  J.W. 46
  Johanna CANTY 30
  Josephine WARNER 46
  Mary 70
  Nora 30
  Thomas 30
FERRY
  Anna E. 133
  Catherine 37, 69, 164
  Edward 46
  Eliza Jane, Mrs. 95
  James 46
  Kate 46, 115

Margaret DANNELLY
    46
  Mary Ann DONELLY
    69
  Mary BRITTON 46
  Matthew 69
FERTSCH
  Paul 137
FESSENDEN
  Ada E. 150
  Amanda NICHOLS 150
  John W. 150
  M.A., Mrs. 30
FEST
  Anna E. 148
  Augusta 150
  Fredricka 150
  Friederika 150
FESTNER
  F.C. 108
  Julius 5, 39, 88
FETHERSTONE
  Mary A. 34
  Matilda CARMICHEL
    34
  Thomas 34
FIALA
  Anton 46
  Kathrine SOUSEK 46
  Wenceslas 35
  Wenzel 46
FIALD
  Anton 46
  Barbara WAVRA 46
  Kathrine SOSKA 46
  Wenzel 46
FIBE
  Edward 102
  Martha 102
  Wilimine 102
FICENEC
  Anna 41
  Annie 80
  Barbara KOSCHEREK
    80
  Fanny 41
  George 80
  John 41, 123
FICENS
  Anna 41
  Fanny 41
  John 41
FICK
  Charles 169
  Christina VOIGHT 169
  John 16
  Lucy 16
  Malvina 16
  Mary Ann ALLEN 16
FICKLE
  Elizabeth 117
FIELD
  Aggie C., Mrs. 88
  B.R. 77
  H.W. 139
  John A. 149
  Mary A. 14
  Mrs. 139
  Susan 149
  Susie 139
  Thomas 14
FIELDING
  George 97
  Jane PHILLIPS 97
  John 46
  Kate MAHONEY 46

Mary MURRAY 46
  Nancy J. 97
  Patrick 46, 68
FIELDS
  Eliza 7
  Laura 55
  Lucy A. 54
FIELDSTED
  Sophia 1
FIEPEN
  Fred 131
FIKE
  Appolona 83
FIKES
  Elizabeth McELWAIN
    46
  Isabella SNELL 46
  Nelson 46
  William H. 46
FILDT
  K.R. 146
FILLEY
  Elizabeth 44
FILLMORE
  Sarah 141
FILSUF
  Catharine Marthe 26
FINCH
  Aaron 33
  Emily N. PORTER 46
  Geo. 46
  Geo. W. 46
  Hiram A. 46
  John 53
  John M. 46
  Louisa BRADLEY 46
  Margaret 33
  Mary CRAWFORD 53
  Mary MORROW 46
  Ora 53
FINDLEIGH
  Agnes S. 30
FINELY
  James 38
  Kate 38
  Mary O'DONNELL 38
FINEY
  Elizabeth NORTON 33
  Moses 33
FINKAN
  Catharine 92
  Catharine GANS 92
  Matthias 92
FINKE
  A., Mrs. 161
FINLAW
  Charlotte 105
FINLAY
  Martha F. 87
FINLEY
  Catharine 71
  Margaret 6, 94
FINLY
  E., Mrs. 38
FINMANT
  Jorgen 27
FINN
  Bridget MADDEN 130
  Catherine 130
  Eva 94
  John 130
  Julia 151
FINNEL
  Jennie 18
FINNELL
  Benjamin W. 46

Eliza C. WALL 46
  Mary Jane BUTLER 46
FINNEN
  Margaret 56
FINNEY
  Elizabeth NORTON 33
  Geo W. 46
  Geo. W., Mr. and Mrs.
    51
  Jennie MURPHY 46
  Moses 33
  Mrs. 71
FINNSTROM
  Augusta 114
FIRIENGA
  Emma 147
FIRTH
  Abram 46
  Clara E. BURDETTE
    46
  John 46
  Mary YARDLEY 46
  Nancy Jane TOOKER
    46
  Rowland 46
  Samuel 46
  Susan HAEGH 46
FISCHER
  A. 86
  Anna 72
  August 14, 15, 161
  Christine 155
  Mary E. 1
  Rosa 72
FISCHIE
  August 55
FISETTE
  Charles 46
  Charles H. 46
  Chas. 46
  Judith BERTHIOME 46
  Judith BERTHROME
    46
  Louisa M. YOKELE 46
  Louise M. YOKEL 46
FISH
  George L. 2
  Laura 114
  Lucy 9
  Lucy CALL 2
  Matilda 2
FISHER 105
  A.J. 46
  Albert 46
  Amanda RINGO 46
  Amy D. 96
  Andrew 47
  Anna 95, 131, 160
  Anna B. 73
  Anne 46
  Annie 84
  Annie B. 151
  Annie C. 123
  August 46
  Bazil 46
  Betsy MUCK 160
  C. 73
  C.G. 137
  Caspar 46
  Catharine 149
  Catharine AULTHAUS
    131
  Catharine HACKER 47
  Charles 104, 128, 131
  Christian 46
  Christiana, Mrs. 96

FOGG
  Benjamin S. 47
  Charles N. 47
  Jennie E. DOOLITTLE
    47
  Susan FARROW 47
FOHLER
  Anna 14
FOLBRE
  Clara 89
FOLEY
  Abby 152
  Alice CONNERS 47
  Bridget 88
  Catherine 93, 114
  Daniel 48
  Edmund 47
  Eliza 22, 48, 152
  Eliza DINAN 48
  Ellen 48
  Jeremiah 48
  Johanna 36, 60
  Johanna DUGGAN 47
  John 22, 39, 47, 48, 60
  Katharine 81
  Maggie 93
  Margaret CRONIN 48
  Margaret ENRIGHT 36,
    48
  Mary 22, 48, 81, 93,
    101, 108
  Mary BARRETT 48
  Mary DALY 48
  Patrick 23, 48, 94, 114,
    115
  Patrick D. 48
  Timothy 48, 81, 93
  Timothy T. 36
FOLGMAN
  Catharina STRBENOR
    48
  Ernst 48
  Friedrich 48
  Louisa SCHROEDER
    48
FOLHAN
  Catharine 102
FOLKES
  Fanny C. 13, 90
FOLL
  Albert 48
  Antoine 48
  Catharine SCHMEOR
    48
  Mary SHAFFER 48
FOLLETT
  Nancy F. 167
FOLLY
  Mary 139
FOLSOM
  Charles N. 48
  David W. 48
  Maria SEVER 48
  Pearl DAVIS 48
FOLTHIZER
  Barbara POL 163
  Caroline 163
  Frederick 163
FONQUET
  Dorothea 30
FONTS
  Elizabeth SMITH 48
  Ella MOATS 48
  N. 48
  W.N. 48
  Wm. A. 48

FOOT
  Catherine 154
  Lieut. 130
  Sarah 40, 140
  W.W. 3, 132, 150
FOOTE
  Delia S. 46
FORAN
  Bridget DONOVAN 48
  Phillip 48
  Sarah HILLAHAN 48
FORBES
  Catharine 35
  Ella E. KNIGHT 48
  Emma May 97
  Fanny 28
  George W. 21
  J. Walker 48
  J.B. 48
  James 48
  James W. 48
  Katey 120
  Lydia 112
  Maggie 144
  Matilda
    CATHERWOOD 48
  Sarah BURDETT 48
  Sarah DURDICK 48
FORD
  Adie R. HALL 48
  Ambrose 166
  Andrew 48
  Bridget A. GORMAN
    48
  Bridget E. CLARK 48
  Brigetta E. 102
  Delinda A. PRATT 48
  Elizabeth FLOYD 48
  Ellen 22, 114
  Ellen CALLAHAN 22
  Emma LONGFELLOW
    48
  Jacob 74
  James 48
  John 22, 48
  Lizzie ALLEN 74
  Louise 74
  Mary 105
  Mary DOYLE 48
  Mary LUCKEY 166
  Michael 48
  Olivia 166
  Pamelia STILLWELL
    48
  Samuel N. 1
  Sarah 59
  Stephen 48
  William W. 48
FORDYCE
  Aaron 48
  Amy M. JONES 48
  John A. 48
  Susan
    BRANDINGBURG
    48
FOREMAN
  E. JOHNSON 100
  Emma 100
  F. Lee 114
  Margaret 129
  Mason 129
  Peter 100
  Sarah ROGERS 129
FORGEY
  Margaret R. 82
  Mary 82

Samuel 82
FORNER
  Christine SCHNEIDER
    48
  Edward 48
  Eliza 114
  Eva KOOSER 48
  Frederick 48
FORNES
  Mary Ann 50
FORNING
  Adloph 55
FORRER
  J.M. 163
FORREST
  Ann O. 64
  Annie HALL 48
  James A. 48
  John 48
  Julius W. 48
  Sarah 48
  Sarah E. WILSON 48
  William H. 48
FORRISEY
  Catharine 95
FORSELL
  Anna Sophia
    GRONHOLM 48
  Gustavis 48
FORSEYTH
  Elizabeth 134
  Mary PETERS 134
  William 134
FORSLAND
  Louisa 170
FORSS
  Susan 16
FORST
  Anna BROWN 48
  Francis 48
  John 48
  Margaret Jane PECK 48
FORSYTH
  Agnes 168
  Elespoi 159
  James 48
  Jennie A. BROWN 48
  Louisa 63
  Mary Ann R. 74
FORT
  J.L. 72
  J.L., Rev. 72
  Jesse L., Rev. 24
  Mary A. 72
FOSS
  Mary A. 103
FOSTER
  ---- 18
  Betsy 18, 163
  Betsy TUCKER 89
  Catharine O'HEARN 48
  Charles 48
  Charles H. 13, 126
  Charlotte 44
  D.M. 16
  Ed 31
  Eliza 158
  Elizabeth J. KIRKLAND
    48
  Frankling P. 48
  Grace MYERS 48
  Henry 47
  J. Lemuel 48
  John 48
  Maragaret 96
  Marion FLEMING 48

Mary 17, 47
  Mattes 48
  McKager 89
  Nancy A. RANDALL
    48
  Romania BROWN 158
  Sally A. 168
  Sarah 7, 108
  Sarah GUY 48
  Susan B. 55
  Susan R. 62
  T.A., Mr. and Mrs. 136
  Virginia 66
  Waity Ellen 98
  Zelda 89
  Zerviah P. PORTER 48
FOULLER
  Elisa 156
FOUNTAIN
  Alfred 49
  Belle WILSON 49
  Isaac 49
  Mary GOODRO 49
  Susan CREIGHTON 54
FOURIE
  Emma WHITE 49
  Henry 49
FOUSEK
  Mary 51
FOUST
  George W. 49
  Lucy JOHNSON 49
FOUTS
  Edisey 63
  Eli 49
  Emeline YOUNG 49
  George W. 49
  James N. 49
  Lucy JOHNSON 49
  Rena ROUNDY 49
FOWLER
  Katarine MENNIX 49
  Katarine SCOW 49
  Margaret 76
  William 49
  William J. 49
FOX
  Anna 67
  Anna BARBER 43
  Charles 21
  Electa A. STONER 49
  Elizabeth 43, 81
  Ellen 66
  George 49
  Hannah CLARKE 49
  Harriet E. 21
  Henry 49
  Henry, Mr. and Mrs. 149
  Hepsabeth 159
  Joseph 33, 43, 46, 49,
    60, 91
  Joseph, Mr. and Mrs. 78
  Julia A. GRIGSBY 21
  Mary 27, 59
  Mary Catharine
    REDMAN 49
  Mr. 59
  Rebecca 6
  William C. 44
FOY
  Charlotte KEARN 49
  Elizabeth 54
  Hugh 49, 66
  Mary CANNON 49
FOYED
  Barbara 139

FRAHM
  Anna C. KURT 49
  Claus 49
  Dora ROHWER 49
  Henry 49, 136
  Ida THORNDORF 49
  John 49
  Juergen 49
  Margaret 49
FRAISSINET
  Pauline STANKE 49
FRAIZER
  Elizabeth 57
FRALICH
  Frederick 83
FRANA
  Josephine 106
FRANCE
  Agnes M. 157
  Annie MILL 157
  Hattie 164
  J. 164
  J.S. 157
  James 157
  Mary 122
  William 27
  Wm. 65, 157
FRANCER
  John 50
  Mary O'CONNOR 50
FRANCES
  Margaret 33
FRANCIS
  Calvin 49
  James R. 49
  Leona SNYDER 49
  Margaret 55
  Mary 144
  Mary LYNCH 55
  Milda SHARP 49
  Nancy 142
  Rebecca 51
  Robert 55
FRANDSEN
  A.E. 70
  Christine NELSON 104
  Michael 104
FRANK
  Augusta RUESS 85
  Catrine 41
  Charles 148
  Coelestine SEEMAN 49
  Emma 148
  Fanny ROSS 85
  J. 17, 142
  Jacob 45, 49
  James 85
  Johanna 165
  John 85, 133
  Mary 144, 148
  Nellie 133
  Sarah 12
  Sarah ROOT 133
FRANKE
  Carolina, Mrs. 52
  Charlotte 95
FRANKLIN
  Ann 28
  B.F. 104
  Clorenda THOMPSON
    49
  Edward B. 49
  Joannah McCARTY 49
  Joseph 49
  Margaret 19
  Maria PERKINSON 49

FRANKLIN, cont.
Marie 34
Mary J. PAINE 49
Minnie 129
Semantha 1
Warren B. 49
William 49
FRANKS
Ann 29
Hannah 21
FRANSON
Christina LENSEN 104
Lars 135
Mary NICHOLSON 135
Michal 104
FRANSWARTZ
Margaretta 13
FRANZ
Dora ENK 66
Eliza 66
Ferdinand 66
FRANZEL
Antone 49
Barbara DODA 49
Barbara SAVISCOSKA 49
FRANZEN
Emil 85
Ida 69
FRASER
Andrew 49
Ann 107
Anna ROSS 49
Donald 49
James A. 137
Jennett McKAY 49
Louzelia KELKER 49
Margaret CORRIGAN 49
Simon 49
FRASIER
---- 161
FRASSINET
Gustav 49
Hugo 49
FRAZELL
Ida J. BLAKEMAN 49
Jacob H. 49
Margaret PENCE 49
Moses A. 49
FRAZER
Addie PETER 49
Ann 118
Elmira WOOD 49
George 49
Margery 113
FRAZIER
A. 88
Flora 100
Jane 5
FREDENBURGH
Louisa 30
FREDERICK
Barnard 49
C.H. 21, 154
Eliza GENKS 49
George 49
Johanna MASSENHELTER 49
Julia 53
FREDERICKS
William 125
FREDERICKSON
---- 79

Andrew 79
Anna 110
C. 49
Catharine PETTERSON 49
Christena 75
Christina HENRICKSON 49
Claus 49
Dorothea NISSEN 49
Dorothea NISSON 75
Henry 49
Johann 98
Johanna JENSEN 98
John 49, 75
Karen LARSON 79
Louisa HINZ 49
Margaret 62, 98
Mary 98
Mary E. 105
Mette LAURSEN 43
Nicholas 49
Paul 43
FREDERIKSEN
H.P.C. 88
FREDERIKSON
Fred 88
FREDRICKSEN
Catherine NESENE 75
John 75
Nesine 75
FREDRICKSON
Anders 62
FREDRIKSON
Augusta P. 3
Carrie OLESON 3
Frederick 3
FREED
Elizabeth A. 19
Jane YOUNG 19
Samuel 19
FREEDMAN
Charlotte 81
Rebecca FELD 81
Samuel 81
FREEMAN
Alice 165
Alice SPELLMAN 50
Alice ULRIC 49
Alta 130
Andrew 49
Arebella ROW 49
Betsy HODGES 49
Charles 74
Edward C. 28
Ella F. BALDWIN 152
Emily M. SURDAN 50
Emily MASON 50
Emma 161
Francelia G. WEEKS 50
George A. 49
Gilbert G. 50
John M. 49
Joseph 49, 50, 161
Julia E. SHAW 28
Lewis N. 50
Lindsay 165
Louis W. 50
Lucinda PENNEY 49
Martha ASTHMAN 161
Mary 32
Mary A. PERKINS 49
Mary C. 28
Mary MOORE 165
Mr. 40
Mrs. 64

Patrick 50
S.J. 139
Sarah CAUDLE 49
Tina 76
William 49
FREES
Charles 50
Elizabeth HAMMER 50
Frederick 50
Madaline WICKERSHEIM 50
FREET
John 12
FREEZE
Amanda 107
Jane McMULLEN 107
Peter 107
FREICHELS
Elizabeth 160
FREID
Eva 145
FREIKE
M.F. 61
FRENCER
John 50
Mary O'CONNOR 50
FRENCH
Elizabeth W. 99
Emile 52
Mary 143
Nellie M. 64
Rebecca F. 45
FRENCHEN
Eliza 169
FRENCZER
John 50
FRENDSEN
Ingaborg ANDERSON 113
Nels 113
FRENZEL
Earnest A. 50
Johannah LIPPAH 50
FRENZER
Cath. 54
Catharine 36
Elizabeth BREMER 50
John 100
Joseph 50
Kate S. 9
Margaret SCHABBACH 9
Nicholas 9
Peter 126, 138
Phillip 13
FRESE
Adolph W. 50
Barbara KAMM 50
Henrietta SCHMERSAHL 50
Henriette 85
Henry 50
Mathilde 85
FRESLER
Matilda 121
FRETWELL
D.S.M. 18, 43
Mary A. 43
FREVOLT
Fredericka 148
FREZER
Sophie 80
FRICK
Anna Stina PETERSON 142
Eliza 142

I.M. 142
John 60
FRICKE
Caroline UHE 50
Dorothea 15
Elizabeth 53
Frederick 50
Friedrich 50
Julius 50
William 50
Wm. 103
FRIDAY
Catharine 18
FRIDRICH
Anna 8
FRIEDERICH
Anna 110
Francisca DELBOR 110
Matthias 110
FRIEDERIECHSON
Mary 111
FRIENGA
Emma 147
FRIER
Eliabeth 37
Elizabeth MOR 37
George 37
FRIES
Caroline 113
Mae MULLEN 98
Peter 98
FRIGELS
Elizabeth 154
John 154
Mary SIMON? 154
FRIK
Maria 39
FRILETZ
Mary 120
FRILL
Kate 99
FRINELL
Elnor 128
FRISBIE
Irene BINGHAM 50
William W. 50
FRISBY
W.W. 23
FRISE
Jane 28
FRISH
John 145
FRISHEDT
Christina 44, 117
Gustaf 44, 117
FRISHEY
Lucinda 140
FRISHOUER
Melinda 24
FRISONI
Louise YOUNG 50
Marie POEHLMANN 50
Otto 50
Phillip Julius 50
FRITSCHE
August 157
Henrietta WILDER 157
Julius 157
Katharina DREXEL, Mrs. 157
FRITSCHER
C.L. 164
Charles Lewis 50
Ernestine GERSENHEIMER 50

Mary M. SCHNEIDER 50
William 50
FRITZ
Catherine MANN 50
Israil L. 50
John 50
Mary E. MIDDLETON 50
Mary M. GRAYBILL 50
Miranda BOWEN 50
Nicholas 50
Thomas 50
William H. 50
FRODEL
Anna 107
FRODMAN
Charles Uldric 121
Emily C. 121
Sophia Fredericka PARSON 121
FROESIG
Maren 136
FROGE
Cynthia 146
FRONDEL
Anna 17
Landolin 17
Rosa HESS 17
FROSHLE
Anna SANSER 50
William G. 50
FROST
Abbie P. PICKERING 97
Becca LARSON 50
Caroline M. 97
Carrie ERRICKSON 50
Charlotte MEEHAN 50
Eva Charlotte ANDERSON 50
George 50
George W. 97
Harry 50
Herick 50
Jane CLARK 50
John V. 50
Lucy HOWLETT 50
Mary M. 73
Mats 50
William 50
FRUEHAUF
Fanny BETZELY 50
John J. 50
FRULLER
Sarah KLINE 105
FRY
Anna OSTLER 50
Elizabeth 55, 89
George W. 50
Joel 50
Jonas A. 50
Manda 44
Mary A. 97
Mary Ann FLORENCE 89
Mary Ann FORNES 50
Matilda 167
Samuel 50, 89, 97
Sarah PALMER 50
Sophrona PALMER 50
FUERST
Johanna 83
FUGERSON
Line 16

GIBBS, cont.
W.S. 13, 52
William 52
Wm. H. 52
GIBEAUX
Ellen 144
GIBERSON
Ardelia 126
GIBHART
Annie DINELIVE 15
Caroline 15
Johan 15
GIBNEY
Mary 142
GIBS
Mary 108
GIBSON
A.L. 158
Augusta A. KEYES 53
Catharine O. 88
Eliza JOHNSON 112
Ella H. 2
George L. 53, 115
Gunemaria HANSEN
121
Henry 53, 165
J.S. 31
James 53
James S. 26, 42
Jennie 72
John 2, 112
John D. 53
Juliette LUDINGTON
53
L.B. 53, 59, 149
Lizzie COOPER 53
Lydia SMITT 53
Margaret HENDERSON
2
Mary 20, 112, 150
Mary J. 115
Mary J., Mrs. 47
Mary McCURLEY 53
Mary, Mrs. 44, 81, 88
Matilda 112
Peter 121
Rosanna 22
S. 105
Sophia 127, 171
William E. 53
GIDDENFELD
Sophie 155
GIDDINGS
Mary C. 21
GIEBER
Caroline 71
William 71
GIELSER
Elizabeth 133
GIER
Anna 1
GIES
Teresa 132
GIESEY
Catharine 40
GIESLER
Mary 29
Mary, Mrs. 29
GIFFORD
Eliza J. 137
Francis LANG 34
George 34
Ida 34
Jane 85
Jane HERAS 85
Jane, Mrs. 69

Mary A. 148
Ruth Anna 85
Simon 85
GIFNER
Elizabeth 87
GILBERG
Annie ANDERSON 144
Beata 144
Nicholas 144
GILBERSON
Anne KEARNEY 31
Simon 31
GILBERT
Angeline 133
Annie CLIFFORD 53
Betsey E. 163
Champ 158
Clara 1
David 53
Emily JANES 1
Frank 53
G.I. 87
George J. 121
Ira D. 62
James 53
John 53
Joseph 23
Louisa 158
Maggie, Mrs. 53
Maria 62
Maria ERICKSON 53
Mary INGOLDSBY 53
Mary MORRIS 53
Morris 53
Nathan E. 53
Olive ELDRED 53
Sarah E. SPURGEON
53
William H. 1
GILE
Polly 151
GILES
Jane HAYES 53
Josephine GRIGSBY 53
Paul 53
Russell 53
GILHAM
Julia FREDERICK 53
William 53
GILL
Bridget 43
Emmilie 8
Harriet NEWHOUSE 53
Hattie 168
James 168
James M. 53
John 43
Maggie OATES 43
Mary APPLEGATE 53
Mason C. 53
GILLBANKS
Annie MATHEWS 53
John 53
GILLE
Andrew 53
Catharine SMITH 53
Elizabeth FRICKE 53
Frederic 58
Frederick 53
Kate 58
Kate SCHMIDT 53
GILLEGAN
Michael 32
GILLEHOUSER
G. 92

GILLELAND
Belinda PARKER 73
Caroline J. 73
Micajah 73
GILLEM
Emily 46
Michal 168
GILLEN 161
Kate FAGIN 53
Patrick 53
Sarah KELLEY 53
William F. 53
William Francis 171
GILLESPIE
Alexander 53
David W. 53
Hugh 53
J.S. 19, 49
John 53
Mary E. DYER 53
Mary MANERLY 53
Nellie HANIFINN 53
Ora FINCH 53
W.M. 53
GILLETT
Abagail 120
B. 38
Eliza 17
Flora 116
GILLHORN
Fred 38
GILLIGAN
Mary CURLEY 53
Mary KILLANAN 53
Michael 53
Michael T. 53
GILLISPIE
J.A. 84
Prof. 19
GILLMORE
Eliza 116
Elizabeth McCASCAY
153
Elizabeth McCASCEY
151
Elizabeth McKASKIA
70
James 70, 151, 153
Mary M. 70
Mrs. 91
Sophronia 151
GILMARTIN
Margaret 38
GILMORE
A.R. 161
A.R., Col. 161
Daniel 53
Eliza 2, 76, 83, 153
Elizabeth Leadbetter
BECKWITH 53
John R. 53
Kitty 150
Louisa 69, 118
M.L. 161
Mary L. CONCANNON
53
Mrs. 150
GILPIN
Maria 140
GIMBEL
Ad 83
Adam 126
Clara 83
GINSON
Morentze Sophia 122

GINTER
Louisa 11
GIPSON
Franklin 53
Laura PATTEN 53
Nelson 53
Rebecca Ann 53
Sarah BUNDY 53
Sarah STEVENSON 53
William 53
William H. 53
GIRLLY
Caroline 66
GISE
Jonas 21, 56
GISEKE
Henry 53
Hermann 53
Laura WESSEL 53
Mary TOHLE 53
GISH
Jacob 15, 16, 53, 165
Jennie E. HORNER 53
Maria HOLLINGER 53
GISIGER
George 128
Mary 128
Mary LEMMER 128
GISSLER
M., Miss 128
GIST
Christian 18
GITHENS
Sarah Jane 44
GIVENS
Belle NYSWANER 53
Daniel 53
Elizabeth TAYLOR 53
J.M. 53
GLADE
Henry 54
Louise MUELLER 54
Mary NOZISKA 54
William 54
GLADSTONE
Bernard 54
Hannah 54
Kitty LYTER 54
Sam 54
GLAE
Annie 95
Dora 95
Max 95
GLANDT
Lena LANDTAN 96
Maggie 45
Marcus 45
Mary 45, 96
Peter 96
GLASCOW
Nancy 26
GLASMAN
Augusta 55
Henry 55
John 55
Louise RONNAN 55
GLASS
Almira 37, 44, 99, 102
Elizabeth 5, 41
Elmira 54
Herman 54
Lucy Ann GOODWILL
54
Mira 137
GLAZE
Benjamin 54

Ellen CAMPBELL 54
Mr. 54
Sadie HARLAN 54
W.A. 54
GLEASON
Ann HAWKINS 100
Anne HAWKINS 23
E.M., Rev. 53
Ellen BROWN 54
Johanna 58, 108
Michael 54
Olive 26
Theresa 100
William 100
GLEESON
Teresa 124
GLESMANN
Anna GOETTSCH 54
Elizabaeth ROEURRAN
54
Elizabeth RONAN 54
Elizabeth RUNNER 54
Henry 54
John 54
John D.W. 54
GLINDT
Egert 149
GLINES
Augusta 163
GLISPIE
Mary 47
Mary THOMAS 47
Wm. 47
GLISSMAN
Augusta 55
Dorothea
KRENBZVELD 54
Emma EICKE 54
Hans. Chr. 54
James 54
John 55
Louise RONNAN 55
GLOCKNER
Andreas 13
Catharina PRICKEL 13
Maria 13
GLOVER
E.N. 94
Eliza CHILD 67
Gracie M. 67
John B. 67
Lottie 87
GLOYE
? 141
Mary 14, 141
GLUCK
Sone 81
GLYN
Patrick 32
GLYNN
Bridget NAUGHTON
54
Margaret O'CONNOR
54
Mary 100
Nicholas 54
Patrick 54
Robert 34
GOAL
Phidelia A. 15
GOARTIC
Rosa 71
GOARY
Mehitabel 52

GRAABE
Anna KAKEN 55
Claus 55
John 55
Minnie RABE 55
GRAACK
Henrietta 80
GRABBE
Claus 126
GRABBERT
Charles 169
GRABOW
Anna ELHERT 55
Heinrich 55
Johann 55
Maria SHRADER 55
GRACE
Alice 55
Allie 1
Bridget 68
Elizabeth McNALLY
100
Ellen KEARN 55
Helen RYAN 55
James 55
Jane 124
Katie 16
Martin 100
Mary 12
Mary D. 69
Mary EGEN 1
Mary NORTON 55
May 1
Philomena 100
Richard 1, 55
Samuel 55
Therese 100
Thomas 55
GRADDY
Dr. 37
L.B. 148
GRADY
Bridget MILLEY 55
Catherine 150
Charlotte O'CONNOR
55
Jane CONNOLLY 55
Lacky 55
Margaret F. 48
Margaret FRANCIS 55
Mary 96
Michael 55
Thomas 55
William 55
GRAF
M. 103
GRAFF
James W. 80
GRAFFORD
Triphenia 119
GRAHAM
Albert 150
Annie 62
Bertha SCHMID 55
Bessie 88
Charles H. 55
E.M. 116
Eliza M. 49
Elizabeth A. 65
Ellen DEVINE 55
Elmira Bell MITCHEL
55
George 55, 134
Guy 88
Henry 16
Henry R. 55

Kate CHRISTOPHER
55
Lottie 50
Margaret 55, 85
Mary 156
Mary Ann 150
Mary GRANT 55
Mary J. 88
Mary, Mrs. 16
Matilda 150
Melissa A. 109
Samuel 65
Thomas 55
William 55
GRAM
H.T. 55
Karn NEILSON 55
Kirsten Schmidt
BRANDRUP 55
U.T. 55
GRAN
Andrew 55
Emile 20
Peter J. 55
GRANACHER
Joseph 82
Joseph, Mr. and Mrs. 93
Josephine 9
GRANATH
Allthea E. 89
Carl Gustaf 89
Hedwig A. LAGER 89
Per G. 89
GRANCEY
Lucie 5
GRANDEN
Gerda Caroline ESBERG
55
John Arved 55
John P. 55
Ulirka MATTSEN 55
GRANDPRE
Carl 25
GRANDSBERRY
Edward L. 55
Julia S. BUSH 55
Louisa CLARK 55
William 55
GRANDY
Lauretta 139
Lucritia BANNISTER
132
GRANGER
Catharine 127
George 71
Mary DAVIS 71
Mary Jane 71
Melissa 133
Wm. 20
GRANICHER
Joseph 150
Josephine 150
GRANITH
Charles 55
Elizabeth LAGER 55
Gustave 55
Henrietta C. EKSTROM
55
GRANSTRIM
Annie F. 23
Charles 23
John 23
Sophia JOHNSON 23
GRANT
Caroline 94
Eliza 117

Ellen 150
Eva FINN 94
George H. 55
Hattie BATES 55
Mary, Mrs. 55
Mattie OLMSTEAD 55
Nannie E. FYE 81
Theodore 94
William 55
GRAPENGIEFSER
Charlotte 151
GRAPHOFF
Henry 90
Kate 90
GRAPP
Mary SCHULTZ 55
William 55
GRASSHOPPER
Katie 54
GRAT
Gustina 96
GRATH
Geo. W. 28
GRATIOT
Charlota 75
Charlotte 107
GRATTAN
George W. 85
GRATTON
Caroline WINDSAY 55
Emma WEBSTER 55
Frank 55
John 55
Wm. E. 140
GRAU
Rasalind 126
GRAVE
Anna Maria 25
GRAVER
G.C. 4
GRAVES
Amelia MURRAY 56
Annie 32
C.H. 56
Charles 56
Elizabeth RUPLE 56
Ella SPOOR 56
Emma E. HOMAN 57
Emmaline WETZEL 83
G.C. 135
Geo. A. 57
George 56
George C. 98
Ida 83
J.G. 78
Jane G. 9
Jennie TAYLOR 56
John 32, 137
Louisa 135
Martha A. McAFFEE
137
Mary 137
Mary Jane CARTER 24
S.E. 154
Sallie WALKER 32
T.H. 83
GRAWBOW
John 55
GRAY
Caroline 7
Catharine B. PRUCE 96
Eunice T. 166
F.W. 56
Frederick W. 56
Geo. 73
George W. 73

Georgia Maud 73
H.A. 155
Helen E. CRAWFORD
56
Henrietta 132
Henrietta F. 118
Henry 56, 117, 162
James 56
Jane 97
John 19, 156
Kate LITTLE 56
Lillie V. 96
Maggie ROTHHWETZ
56
Mr. and Mrs. 5
R. Wallace 56
Romania 18
Romania, Mrs. 18
Rose 162
Sarah MEREDITH 56
Susan BACKSTER 73
Theo 117
William L. 96
GRAYBILL
Mary M. 50
GRAYER
Lottie TUNNER 50
GREAR
James 57
Maggie 57
Sarah DAVIS 57
GREATHOUSE
Sarah 54
GREAUBAUM
Lena, Mrs. 106
Morris 106
GREB
Christoph 56
Frederick 56
Mary NOWAK 56
Rosa SHARR 56
GREBE
Christoph 56
Frederick 56
Hannah M. 27
Henry 56, 80, 142
L.J. 149
Louis 38
Mary NOVAK 56
Rosa SHARR 56
Theodor 38
GREEK
John 148
Mary M. BRYANT 148
GREELY
Louisa 119
GREEN
Agnes MEDLOCK 56
Annie CONNELLY 56
Bell 167
Bessie TAYLOR 56
Bethia 41
C.J. 91, 130
Caroline HOKENSEN
56
Catharine 170
Catherine HORSTMAN
56
Charles J. 73, 122
Docia 165
Duff 31
E.R. 69
Elizabeth 81, 110
Emily 54
Emma J. 151
Fanny 131

Fanny C. BRYAN 13
Fanny C. FOLKES 13,
90
Francis M. 56
G.L. 87
H.T. 68
Hannah NEILSON 56
Harriet E. D. 56
Harriet MONT__GUE
56
Harry 13
Harry W. 90
Henrietta 34
Isaac A. 56
J.C. 156
James 99, 100
James H. 56
Jane 100, 167
Jennie 16
Jennie H. 13
John 40, 47, 56, 79
John H. 56, 127
Joseph 16
Jude JOHNSON 56
Kate ANDERSON 56
Lucius C. 56
Margaret 31
Martha BROOKS 95
Mary 81, 114
Mary A. 40
Mary L. 90
Mr. 144
Mrs. 144
Oscar 56
Pear 56
Polly GILE 151
Presly H. 56
R.L. 13
Rosa 165
Sarah ATEROFT 16
Sarah E. TOMLINSON
56
Sarah WOODS 56
Thomas 165
W.E. 139
William 167
William N. 56
Zacheus 151
GREENBAUM
Morris 144
GREENBEC
Rosie 54
GREENE
Catharine O'DONNELL
56
John J. 56
Julia A. SANFORD 56
Robert 72
Thomas 56
Winslow A. 56
GREENFIELD
E. 56
Elijah 56
Ella L. ARTZ 56
Henry C. 56
Mary F. WINTERS 56
Mary F., Mrs. 56
GREENLEAF
---- 52
John 63
Lena SLATER 63
Minnie L. 63

GRUENEWALD
  Elizabeth 71
GRUENIG
  Annie PARKER 57
  Charles 57
  George 57
  Mary ENGEL 57
GRUENING
  Charles 146
  Enora DILLMONN 57
  George 57
  Hannah, Mrs. 57
  Mary ENGLE 57
GRUENWALD
  August 57
  Hattie YOUNG 57
  John 57
  Margaret BREWERS 57
GRUINER
  Anna Maria 9
  Barbara 9
  Franz 9
GRUMBAUGH
  Elizabeth RIBLET 57
  John 57
  Josephine ABNEY 57
  William J. 57
GRUNING
  C. 128
GSANDNER
  Anton 121
  Caroline 121
  John 121
  Magdalena HARTMAN
    121
GSANTER
  Lenah 86
GSANTNER
  Annie 86
  John 86
  Magdalina
    HARTMANN 86
GUAINE
  Edward 108
  Ella 108
  Johanna GLEASON 108
GUARD
  Mary J. 24
GUBRON
  Mary 9
GUDMAN
  Brendel 128
  Dina 128
GUE
  Anna B., Mrs. 8, 12
  Annie B. 70
GUELKER
  Christian 58
  Henry W. 58
  Louise LOHEIDE 58
  Mary DESBOIS 58
GUERIN
  Daniel 106
  Maggie 40
  Maggie O'BRIEN 106
  Maggie T.G. 106
GUES
  Joseph 73
  Joseph, Mrs. 73
GUGIN
  Grace 4
  Grace NOBLE 155
  James N. 155
  Sarah Ann 155
GUGLER
  Marie 146

Otto 146
GUHEEN
  John 48
GUIGAN
  Mary 60
GUILD
  David 58
  Elizabeth McFARLAND
    58
  Emily C. 85
  Jane Harriet 124
  John 58
  Laura A. READ 58
  Margaret DUNBAR 58
  Mr. 127
  Nellie LESLIE 58
  William 58
GUILFOYLE
  Catharine HANNON
    128
  Catherine 128
  Lawrence 128
GUILICK
  Anna 163
GUILKER
  Elizabeth 132
GUILL
  James 27
  Julia DORVIS 27
  M.C. 6
  Martha 27
  Parasetta 152
  Thomas 152
GUILTOR
  Ada 78
  Francis 78
  Mary MORGAN 78
GUINAN
  John 39
GUINANE
  Edward 58
  Johanna GLEASON 58
  Mary E. LOWRIE 58
  Patrick 58
GUINN
  Maggie F. 40
GUIO
  Lorenzo 142
GUIOU
  C.H. 113
GUITAN
  Adolph 58
  Anna HOAKERSON 58
  Francis 58
  Mary Ann MORGAN
    58
GULICKSON
  Sunnar SEVERSON
    138
GULK
  Mary 86
GUMP
  Ann 99
GUNAINE
  Johanana 108
GUNDERSON
  Adam 35, 113
  Ellen 155
  Gussie HANSON 35
  Julius 58
  Kate C. 35
  Mary 113
  Mary JOHNSON 58
GUNNERSON
  Carrie 92

GUNTER
  Charles S. 27
  Christena 27
GUNUP
  Ann 99
GURNEY
  Annie RIEDEL 103
  Elizabeth 103
  George 103
GURTCH
  Anna 62
  Margaret 62
GUS__GER
  Robert 87
GUSCH
  Friederika 169
GUSHORT
  Gustina 150
GUSHURST
  Bridget HUCK 58
  Frederick 58
  Mary STOCKMYRE 58
  William 58
GUSHWIST
  P.A. 119
GUSLEY
  M. 58
GUSTAFERSON
  Mary 92
GUSTAFSON
  Catharina JACOBSEN
    58
  Frank A. 58
GUSTAFSSON
  Anna M. PETERSON
    58
  Friederich 58
  Helma NEISTROM 58
  Leonard 58
GUSTAVESON
  Clara J. 73
GUSTHHORST
  Mrs. 52
  William 52
GUSTINE
  Catherine A. 158
GUSTOFSON
  Lina 135
GUTCHOW
  John Jacob 58
  Catharine "Katy"
    BIFFAR 58
  Christian 58
  Fredericka 58
GUTEHUNET
  Mary 169
GUTEKNUST
  Mary 99
GUTHARD
  Anna MORTH 58
  Annie 61
  Hans 35, 58, 61
  John 58
  Margaret 35
  Margaretha SMIDTH 58
GUTHRIE
  John 81
  Lucinda 124
  Telitha 123
GUTMAN
  Dina R. 136
GUTMANN
  Dina 139
GUTSCHOW
  Catharine BIFFAR 58
  Christian 58

Fredericka 58
  John Jacob 58
GUTTKUNST
  John G. 58
  Mary MAJO 58
GUTTMAN
  Dine 133
GUY
  Anna 117
  Elmer 58
  Frankie LAUGHLIN 58
  Geo. H. 71
  Jane 165
  Mary BRANDON 58
  Samuel G. 58
  Sarah 48
GUYER
  Idalyn H. 170
  Sarah HALL 170
  Wm. A. 170
GWIN
  Helen DAVIS 58
  John W. 58
GWINLIEN
  Charlotte 146
GUSLEY
  Idalyn H. 170
  Sarah HALL 170
  Wm. A. 170
GWYNN
  Daniel 58
  Eliza THOMAS 58
  Emily HALL 58
  William J. 58
GYDESEN
  M. 62
  M.C.E. 61
  P. 74
  W. 62, 74
  William 61
GYGER
  Elizabeth 52
HAAG
  Andew 58
  Catharine RUHL 58
  Christina THONS 58
  Clara W. BOLDT 58
  George 58
  Jacob 58
  Margaretha NEU 58
  Mary M. ALSCLOMAN
    58
  Mathias 58
  Peter 58
  Rebecca HATSELL 58
  Thomas 58
HAAS
  Christ 58
  Christina BAUMAN 58
  Christina MONSA 58
  George 58, 65
  John A. 125
  Marie 65
HAASE
  August 58
  Engeline
    WINKELMANN 58
  Henry 58
  Kate DERNRADY 58
HAASS
  Hanna KOBS 112
  John 112
  Matilda 112
HABBE
  Adolph Frederick 92
  Emma 76, 113

Lena Stna JOHNSON
    92
HABEL
  Margaret 75
HABER
  Mary 51
HABERCOM
  Louis W. 163
HACKER
  Catharine 47
  Johann 13
  Maria WENT 13
  Wilhelmina 13
HADE
  Anna 111
HADEN
  Catherine 105
  H.C. 2
HADLEY
  Alice H. 141
  Elizabeth HEELEY 58
  Emma 61
  Harriet C. ULTZ 58
  Hiram 58
  Hiram M. 58
  Huldy D. 167
  Jane 125
  John 61
  Mary JOHNSON 61
  William 58
HAEFNER
  Rosa 44
HAEGEN
  Henry J. 58
  John W. 58
  Mary A. McCAFFERY
    58
  Mary A. SEABENALER
    58
HAEGH
  Susan 46
HAELMAN
  Carolina 144
HAFFKE
  Carl 58
  Rosalia SCHEWELIER
    58
  Wilhelmine PREIKSCH
    58
  William 58
HAFNER
  Barbara 26
HAGAEDORN
  Caroline 80
  Henrich 12
  Wilhelmina 80
HAGAN
  Helen M. LIDDARD 58
  Isaac A., Rev. 58
  Mary 109
HAGAR
  Helen M. LIDDARD 58
  Isaac A., Rev. 58
HAGDEN
  Mary 91
HAGE
  August 58
  Charlotte
    STEINBRICKER 58
  Christian 58
  Wilhelmina SCHANER
    58

HAMILTON, cont.
John 60
Lizzy J. DOW 60
Louisa DOYLE 60
Marion LOUDON 60
Martha A. WALTERS
  60
Mary J. 119
Mary Jane BARKER 60
Robert 60
Sarah BRAIDEN 60
Thomas 60
Violat 157
Wm. R. 60
HAMILTTON
Mary CLARKSON 105
HAMLEN
Miles M. 73
HAMLET
Charles 60
John 60
Mary Ann ROSE 60
Mollie BAKER 60
HAMLIN
Phoebe 68
HAMM
Catharine 36
HAMMED
Conrad 60
Jens 60
Johanna EDSTROM 60
Mary HEDERSTEDT
  60
HAMMEL
Ann KING 43
Anna 43
Helen 9
Henry 9
Owen 43
HAMMER
Carl E. 60
Caroline JOHNSON 60
Elizabeth 50
John 60
Kathrine LILGA 60
Louis 10
HAMMERLOF
Britta HAGLAN 60
Conrad 60
Mathias 60
Sophie LINDSTROM
  60
HAMMETT
Anna CLINE 60
Dora S. BROWN 60
James H. 60
N.E., Mrs. 70
Nancy E. 129
William 60
Wm. 9
HAMMOND
A. WARFIELD 101
A.S. 140
A.S. WARFIELD 60
Achsah S. 60
Ann LOCKWOOD 6
Anna FAY 60
Anna N. 101
Annie M. OLESON 60
Aschsa WARFIELD 140
Charles H. 60
Eliza 141
Emily J. 68
George 60, 101
Harry 60
J.H. 50, 91, 154

John T. 6
Julius H. 60
Loren K. 60
Lucinda BANKS 60
Maria 166
Maria MERWIN 60
Mary M. 6
Mathias 140
Mathilda B. 140
Nannie 64
Olive A. HURLEY 60
T.P., Mrs. 123
HAMPLETON
Eliza E. WALKER 124
HAMPTON
Elizabeth W.
  HENDERSON 64
John 64
Minnie E. 64
HAN
Francisca EICHORN 5
Kate 5
Valentine 5
HANAVAN
Mary 167
Morris 167
HANCHETT
Carrie J. 146
HANCOCK
Esther 147
HANDBINE
Desire 152
HANDLEY
Mary H. 57
HANDRAHEN
Kate 95
HANDREHAN
Hanora 94
HANDRUKAT
Minna 21
HANDY
Deana 134
Elizabeth 161
HANE
John D. 104
HANELINE
Eva 42
HANEMAN
Christin F. 60
Dora WIESEMAN 60
Kate THODT 60
HANEY
Ann BAXTER 60
Berry 60
Catharine SHERRY 95
Clark B. 38
E.J. 21
Edward 60
Edward J. 21
Edwin 99
Hannah 21
Hannah FRANKS 21
Inez 126
Jenny A. 38
John 38, 60
Julia 95
Margaret 139
Margaret L. 139
Margaret Rose 62, 152
Mary M. 34
Mary Rose 62
May A. PORTER 60
Mollie 38
Mollie ELLIS 62
Nancy J. 21
Patrick 95

Samuel B. 38
Sarah BOLIN 38, 60
William 62, 139
William C. 62
Wm. 152
HANFORD
F.A., Col. 151
HANGER
Charity EVANS 18, 60
Jennie 18
John 18
John Preston 60
Mary Ann KEEFE 60
Peter 18, 60
HANIFFIN
Mr. 53
HANIFINN
Johanna LUCID 53
Morris 53
Nellie 53
HANIGAN
Anastasia 156
HANKE
Crezenia 113
Josephine 60
Lewis 60
HANKINS
Gilbert 145
Jane 132
Mary VIOLET 145
Rebecca S. 145
HANKINSON
Mary 107
HANLAN
Catherine 59
Frederick 60
Margaret CONREY 60
Michael 60
Nancy BULLYER 60
HANLEY
Charles 39
Chas. 18
Emilie 57
M. 16
Mary H. 119
HANLON
Elizabeth 36
F.P. 17, 29, 33, 34, 36,
  37, 39, 46, 52, 60, 61,
  66, 68, 77, 83, 84, 89,
  90, 113, 114, 116,
  132, 146, 148, 151,
  164, 167, 168
Frank P. 12, 35, 38, 60,
  69, 78, 83
H.P. 145
John 45
Julia CONNELL 45
Kate 45
Mary 45, 99
HANLONG
F.P. 136
T.P. 24
HANLOU
Frank 126
HANN
Ann MELBOURNE 124
C.B.W. 136
Elizabeth 9
Emma 124
James 124
HANNAH
Catharine 147
HANNAN
Alice 148

HANNER
Margaret 75
HANNIGAN
Cathrine CORCORAN
  109
Edward 109
Mary A. 109
HANNON
Andrew 14
Catharine 128
HANRAHAN
Elizabeth
  FITZMAURICE 32
Kate 32
Mary 94, 104
Thomas 32
W.J. 156
HANS
Christopher 14
Eda HOPE 36
Juliette 14
Justina STUTCKA 14
Lena 36
Peter 36
HANSCOM
Andrew J. 125
Catharine Ann YOUNG
  125
Harriet G. 125
Jacob 111
HANSDATAR
Olena 47
HANSEL
C.C. 128
George 101
Laura 101
Sarah 101
HANSEN
A. 66
Andras 61
Andres 25, 61
Andrew 61, 116
Ann Christine 25
Ann M. 157
Ann Marie 79
Ann NEILSON 61
Anna 61, 123
Anna ARNESON 61
Anna Christena 162
Anna CHRISTENSEN
  61
Anna M.M. 144
Anna Mary 145
Anna NICOLAI 61
Anne 76
Annie 23, 37
Annie GUTHARD 61
Annie M. SKERBEK 61
Astrid RISMER 61
August 61
Auk 61
Bertha Hanssine 74
Bertie OLESON 61
Betty Christiana
  LARSON 61
Biddy SWANSEN 61
Bodil 155
Bodil RASMUSSEN
  111
Brigita 76
Caroline 97
Caroline JOHNSON 61
Caroline PETERSON
  98
Carrie 76, 136
Carrie C. 66

Carrie M. MARQUIS
  116
Carsten 61, 97
Catharine 130
Catharine ANDERSON
  63
Catherina 76
Catherina M. 66
Catherine JORGENSON
  77
Cena 146
Chr. 25
Chresten 61
Christ 26, 80
Christian 25, 61
Christina 65, 113
Christina ANDERSON
  76
Christina GEIER 145
Christina HENSEN 61
Christina HOLMER 61
Christine CARSTENS
  97
Dora BERTELSON 61
Dora BERTHESEON
  66
Dorothea 4
Egidia 113
Ella HAGG 61
Ellen ERICKSON 127
Ellen TUPVE 145
Emma HADLEY 61
Emma PIERSON 61
Eric 43
Erick 43
Eve 61
Fred 77
George F.J. 61
Gertie 77
Gunemaria 121
Gunne Maria 121
H.C. 61
Hannah 76
Hannah NELSON 61
Hans 61, 76, 78
Hans Jacob 61
Hans N. 61
Hansena J. 155
Helene 92
Henrietta 164
Henrietta ANDERSON
  61
Henry 127
Inger W. 78
Ingwer 61
Jennie JOHNSON 43
Jens 25, 61
Johanna 64, 164
Johanna Katharina
  LUND 61
Johannes 76
John 25, 33, 61, 111,
  155
Julius 116
Jurgen M. 61
Karen 62
Karen Kirstine 75
Karen Margarethe
  PETERSON 61
Karoline 61
Kathrina CARSTENSEN
  61
Lar 138
Lars 61, 155
Laurs 61
Louisa THOMPSON 61

HANSEN, cont.
M. 26
Magdalena 10
Maggie 127
Maggie SIERKS 127
Maggie, Mrs. 10
Magnus C. 61
Maren 60, 157
Margareeta 116
Margaret 13, 15, 127
Margaret JOHNSON 43
Margaretta NELSON 33
Maria 61
Maria A. LARSEN 61
Maria ANDERSEN 61
Marian 77
Marie THROULSON 78
Mark 61, 73, 76, 155
Marrgie INGELS 61
Martha 80
Martin 61
Martina 155
Mary 3, 64, 76, 102,
  125, 127, 144, 155
Mary BRENGLESON
  111
Mary J. DAVIS 61
Mary NELSON 155
Mary NICKOR 61
Mary NILSON 61
Mary PAULSON 61
Mary POULSON 61
Mary RASMUSSEN 61
Mat 61
Mathias 98
Mathilda C. 33
Mattie M. 26
May 77
Meta M. 127
Michael 145
Minnie JOHNSON 61
Neils 77
Nels 61, 66, 111
Nils 61
Ole 116
Peter 61, 116, 145
Peter A. 61
Peter E. 61
Rasmus 127
Regine PETERSON 61
Robert 3
Sarah 155
Sene JOHNSON 61
Solomon 61
Sophia BENSON 61
Sophia Maria 70
Sophia NELSON 26
Sophie 80
Teresa KINGBEIL 61
William 27, 61
HANSER
Caroline 132
HANSOM
Isobel ERICKSN 160
Mrs. 86
Paul 160
Rachael 160
HANSON
A.E. 61
Amalia SWENSON 61
Ane K. JORGENSEN
  62
Anna 26, 117, 121
Anna JACOBSDOTTER
  11

Anna Sophia JENSEN
  111
Augusta 118
Belle BROOKINS 61
Benta LARS 117
Boeld 117
Christian 112
Christiana SWENSON
  61
Debara PRAY 61
Dorothea LARSON 62
E.B. 116
E.S. 61
Emma 108
Enger B. MICKELSON
  112
Georgine M. NELSON
  62
Gundil 113
Gussie 35
Gussie N. 116
H. 3
Hannah MORTENSEN
  62
Hans 61, 62
Hans C. 61
Hellen 121
Jacob 11, 61, 111
James P. 62
Jens 25, 62
Lars 117
M. 61
M.B. WILSON 116
Marcus 76
Maren 122
Marene K.
  RASMENSEN 62
Margaret 125
Marian 77
Maron 122
Mary 116
May 80
Metta JENSEN 61
Nils 111
Ola 117
Olaf 61
Peter 62, 121
Peter A. 25
S. 11
Sophia 112
HANSTON
Mary 116
HANTHER
Edith 50, 97
HANTING
Cecilia SATORIUS 62
Celia 154
John 62
Lilly 29
Mary 29
Mary FARDAN 62
William 62
HANTSCHKE
Louisa 85
HANY
Edwin 92
M. 141
William C. 62
HANZEL
Barbara 74
HANZER
Sarah 162
HAPEN
Anna M. 169
John 169
Selony CURTIS 169

HAPETTOR
Catherine 157
HAPS
Betsy 147
HARBACH
John A. 10
HARBIN
Ann A. GOFF 62
William 62
HARCOMBE
W. 167
HARDEN
Louisa M. 121
Sarah W. 121
William 121
HARDER
Anna 132
Claus 62
John 62
Lena WEHEDE 62
Margaret
  FREDERICKSON 62
HARDESTY
Ellen FLAHERTY 62
J. 83
John 62
Mary BELL 62
Samuel V. 62
HARDIE
Cynthis 82
John 82
Sallie SCOTT 82
HARDING
Edward 62
Estella GOLDSTEIN 62
Francis 139
James T. 166
Jane CONNER 166
Martha 166
Minnie HAROLD 62
Mrs. 40
Solomon 62
HARDY
Jennie L. 63
HARGADON
Bridget 35
HARGAN
Catharine 47
HARGREAVES
Thomas 53
HARING
David 164
Mary Ann 164
HARIVIORT
Frank 157
HARKINS
A., Mrs. 129
HARKINSON
Charles 4
Hannah S. 4
Margaret 29
Sarah TIBBEN 4
HARKNESS
David 62
Julia M. TOWNE 62
HARLAN
Ellen BARNES 54
N.A. 54
Sadie 54
HARMAN
Danis 8
Isaac 4
Isabella 37
P., Mrs. 167
Paul 25, 105

HARMANN
F.A. 27
HARMANS
P., Mrs. 167
HARMON
A.J. 62, 72, 120, 135
Abagail GILLETT 120
Abigal GELLETT 135
Andrew 14, 30, 62
Andrew J. 30
Arthur S. 62
Catherine 114
Chatharina PERSON 62
Christi Anna
  HOLLENBACH 62
Cordelia CORNISH 62
Cordelia W. CORNISH
  72
D.A. 151
Elizabeth 140
Eugene L. 62
H.M., Mrs. 8
Ida J. ATKINS 62
Johannah BRISNEE 62
Johannah GRIFFIN 62
John 62
John E. 62
L.A. 8, 12
Louisa A. 72
Lucinda H. STEARNS
  62
Luther A. 28
Luther H. 97
Mary H. 151
Mary M. 135
Otelea KJELSTROM 62
P. 135
Paul 17, 62, 72, 114,
  120, 135
Rebecca 7
Richard 62
Sarah G. 120
HARMSEN
Elsa B. THADE 62
Elsabe 41
Fred 155
John 62
Kate HAGGE 62
Kate PEPPER 62
Katrine Hawe PEPER
  41
Mary EICHER 62
Max 62
Rolf 41, 62
HARMSON
Fred. 41
HARNED
Anna R. 145
HARNER
Mat 142
HARNETTE
Katie 106
HARNISH
Amanda 81, 117
Anna KNICELY 62
Benjaman 81
Benjamin 62, 117
HAROLD
Minnie 62
HARPER
Caroline LUCK 62
Catharine CURLE 80
D.C. 5
Fanny 46
Jane HALLEY 62
John W. 62

Joseph L. 62
HARPSTER
Amanda L. REDMAN
  62
Barbara ALLEY 62
Charles M. 62
David 62, 65
John 62
Loretta SANDERS 62
HARPY
Alfred 114
HARR
Emilie JUNG 62
Louis 62
Minna FLYNN 62
Rudolph 62
HARRIGAN
Annora MURPHY 17
Josephine A. 17
Margaret 115
Mary QUINLAN 115
Morris 115
Patrick 17
Robert 137
HARRINGTON
Bridget 10, 17, 94, 120,
  139
Catherine 70
George A. 163
Honora 23
John 10, 139
Margaret 10
Mary 80
Mary CAARRIDOR 10
Mary CARROLL 139
HARRIS
Amanda 114
Angeline McCASLIN 62
Arabella 64
Benjamin 114
Diana 101
Edward E. 62
Eliza WALL 64
Elizabeth CLAYPOOLE
  62
Elizabeth KELLEY 62
Emma 105
Emma SEVEARE 62
George 156
Hannah A. RICHARDS
  62
Harriet M. 142
Hattie 62
J.W., Mrs. 152
James 62
John 19, 62
Lewis D. 62
Lucindia EDMONDS
  62
Martha 123
Mary B. 21
Mary CROSE 156
Mary E. 159
Mary L. 36
Mary W. 156
Mrs. 19
Nellie, Mrs. 102
Peter 62
Pierson 62
R.A., Mr. and Mrs. 140
R.A., Mrs. 61
Sarah A. 139
William 62, 64

HARRISON
Annie GRAHAM 62
Charles 62
Francis 62
Margaret A. BUSH 62
Maria DAKINS 62
Mary E. 107
Nannie McMAMOR 62
Robert 62
Sarah 101
William H. 165
Wm. H. 62
HARRNER
Catharine 45
HARROLD
John 61
HARSHA
N.J., Mrs. 57
W.J., Mrs. 12, 103, 144
Wm. J., Mrs. 56, 68, 163
Wm. Justin 99
HARSTIG
Caroline 84
HARSTMAN
Frank 127
Kate RICHTER 127
Sophia 127
HARSTON
Tarley M. 63
HART
Amos A. 63
Anna C. VIERS 63
Anna GOODWIN 63
Anton 63
Benjamin A. 63
Catharine 100, 124
Charles 21, 37, 63, 167
Dominic 63
Elizabeth CLEMISON
63
Ellen 106
George 63
Harriet N. 29
Henry 63
Henry A. 63
James 63
John 63
John R. 63
Julia FLYNN 63
M.E. 91
M.H. 91
Margaret McKALE 63
Mary 82
Mary EAVES 63
Mary H. 63
Mary JETTER 63
Mr. 113
Mrs. 113
Nancy FERGUSON 63
Nora BOYLE 63
Peter 79
Robert 63
Sada POWELL 63
Ursula HEILIG 63
HARTE
Fred 63
J.H. 14
Johanna ROESINK 63
John 63, 136
Magdalena 158
Mary H. BOLIVER 63
Nil F. 14
Wm . F. 63
HARTFORD
Elias 63, 77, 107

Elizabeth HAMILTON
77
Emily C. 77
Harrison 77
Jasper 63
Mary Jane COY 63
Rachel LAMB 107
Sarah 83, 107
Susannah BAYLESS 63
Thomas 63
HARTING
Anna 160
Elizabeth J.M. 10
John F.J. 10
Katharina PAULSON
160
Lina 136
Sophia M.M. 10
Thomas 160
William 88
HARTMAN
Anna M. 113
Annie MATTSON 113
Austo 63
Chris 133
Francisco BUCKEN 63
George 162
H.C. 34
Hannah HAGELIN 63
Joseph 122
Lydia 117
Magdalena 121
Margaret BROWN 122
Mary F. 122
Olof F. 113
Oscar 11, 63, 135, 148,
151
Sarah 71
T.G. 12
HARTMANN
Anna 65
Anna AMELING 63
Christian H. 63
Magdalina 86
Martha G. THOMAS 63
Nicholas 65
Trena SANN 65
Wilhelm 63
HARTNETT
Mary A. 100
HARTNEY
James 145
Margaret 145
Mary HERAGAN 145
HARTRY
Caroline SHEPARD 10
Caroline SHEPHERD
122
Edwin 10, 122
Harry C. 122
Lucy E. 7, 122
Matilda M. 10
HARTSHORN
Clarence E. 63
Jane SIMINGTON 63
Joshua P. 63
Minnie L. GREENLEAF
63
HARTSON
D. 40
Darius 63
J.D. 63
Louisa FORSYTH 63
Mary A. BALES 63
P.M. 40

HARTTE
Maria 24
HARTWIG
Catharine ANDERSON
63
Emma 39
Johann 61, 63, 97
Magdalena BLISECKER
63
Maria SCHMIDT 39
William 39
HARTY
F.H. 5
HARVAT
Annie JAHNAR 63
Catherine PAZDIRKA
63
Frank 63, 157
James 63
HARVEY
Andrew 63
Charlotte 44
Elizabeth 36
Ellen IRWIN 63
J.F. ROBERTS 63
J.T. 63
Margaret KIRKWOOD
63
Margaret RITCHIE 63
S.N. 63
HARZOG
George 43
HASA
Veronicka 21
HASCALL
---- 31
Etta 123
Henrietta 71, 101
Henry A. 63
I.S. 101
Isaac S. 101
Issac G. 46
J.S. 50
Jennie L. HARDY 63
Joseph 20
S.J. 52, 123
Sarah HARRISON 101
Sarah J. 71
Sylvia A. PIDGE 20
HASEBROCK
Albert 161
Christine 161
Christine BOLLN 161
HASELL
Hannah 23
HASERALTT
Charles 150
HASERODT
Charles 133
Chas. 162
Elizabeth R. 162
Frederica 133
Frederica ROTH 133
Fredicka MAUF 133
Helena 133
HASHSBURGER
Sarah C. 79
HASKALL
I. 53
HASKELL
Bell TRAPP 63
Della KETHAM 63
Ella M. 20
Henry A. 63
Jane NORRIS 63
Jennie L. HARDY 63

Joseph M. 20
Joseph W. 63
M.F. 63
M.M. 63
N.D. 63
Nancy DUNTHE 63
W. 63
HASKINS
Charles 107
Elizabeth 147
S.H. 26
HASOWI
Mathias 131
HASPAN
Christina 136
HASSEN
Joseph 137
HASSER
Frank 34
Mary or Maria 34
HASSETT
John E. 63
Sophia 99
Sophia QUINN 63
HASSON
Bridget DONNELLEY
63
John 63
Patrick 63
Rose DEVLIN 63
HASTINGS
Mary GALLAHAN 63
Michael 63
Patrick 63
Sarah Frances SMITH
63
HASTLETON
Civilah 52
HATCH
Almira 114
Betsey N. BILLINGS
108
Ira 63
Katie KELLEY 63
Louise 93
Malita, Mrs.? 133
Mary L. CHURCHILL
63
Mary VILAS 63
Mason C. 63
Sylvanus S. 63
HATELIN
Maria NELSON 63
HATHAWAY
A.L. 109
Alice DUCE 63
Annie E. ASHLEY 109
Annie E. 109
Christenia HUFMAND
63
Elizabeth 147
Rhoda 149
Samuel B. 63
Stephen B. 63
HATSEL
Rebbaca 124
HATSELL
Hilard 58
Nancy HOSKINS 58
Rebecca 58, 63
Rebecca Ann 140
HATT
Hugo 103
HATTEN
Agnes 86
Annie 92

Margaret 92
Michael 92
HATTEROTH
Emma 101
John 101
Mary E. CLARK 101
HATTON
Elizabeth 130
Margaret CONNELY
130
Thomas 130
HATZMENN
Annie M. 36
HAUAFAN
Johanna LUCID 168
Kate 168
Morris 168
HAUCK
Anna Maria MAHR 63
Clara 112
Franz Georg 63
Jacob 63, 153
Kate H. BUCHAN 63
HAUG
Agnes 117
HAUGHEY
Ellen 31
HAUN
W.J. 65
HAUPTMAN
Henry 63
Wilhelmina
MUHLENBROCK 63
HAUSE
Annie 40
Lizzie A. HONEY 75
HAUSHAELTER
Frederick 153
Henrietta SPENHART
153
Rosa 153
HAUSNER
Magdalena 136
HAVEL
Anna KUCERA 64
John 64
Maria KRUMER 64
Rollins 64
HAVENS
Mary 168
HAVLEK
Barbara KAVAN 64
Frank 64
Jacob 64
Mary PASHTA 64
HAVLINEK
Anna, Mrs. 46
HAWE
Axey 96
HAWES
A.M., Mrs. 86
A.W., Mrs. 84
Abraham 64
Abram 27, 64
Amelia M. 18
Amelia M., Mrs. 130,
141
Amelia, Miss 29
Mary W. NILE 64
Mathew M. 24
Minnie M. 27
P.O. 14
Patrick O. 57, 122
Sarah A. TURNER 27
Sarah TURNER 27, 64
W.F. 27, 68

HEINERSKVEN
Fred E. 70
HEINIECKE
Henry 107
HEINIKEL
Catharine 69
HEINRICHS
Catharine CARSTENS
20
Christine 20
John 20
HEINS
Ellen, Mrs. 145
Wm. F. 110
HEIRES
Katie KUHL 65
M.J. 65
Mary NOEL 65
Peter 65
HEIRLZLIN
Albert 26
HEIS
Minnie A. 138
Wilhellmine
KLEINSCHMIDT
138
HEISA
Frederick 65
Wilhelmina
WEDDENBERDER
65
HEISER
A., Miss 122
HEITKEMPER
Anna 36
Clara 36
Hermann 36
HEITMAN
Anna K. 65
Jeremiah 65
HEITMANN
Catharina 14
HEITOLD
Henry 135
HEJNY
Mary 40
HEKNAN
Henrietta 7
HELAN
Ellen TOBIN 101
Mary 101
Thomas 101
HELBIG
Wilhemine 133
HELBLUCK
Louisa 169
HELD
Angela CANTZEN 65
Herman 65
Herman C. 65
Marie VON WUSNER
65
HELDRETH
Jennie 170
HELDY
Mary 10
HELEBRANT
Frantiskr LYTVER 65
John 65
Josephine SLADOVNIK
65
HELFIN
Louis 14
Margaret ROGERS 14
Nettie 14

HELIN
Maria 7
HELLBORN
Augusta
SCHAUERHAMMER
65
Gottlieb 65
Louis 54, 58, 65
Mary SMITH 65
HELLEM
Amanda 117
HELLEN
John 14
Margaretta JOHNSON
14
Wilhelmina 14
HELLER
Hattie 32
John 32
Mary DOYLE 32
HELLM
Amanda 96
HELLMAN
M. 108
HELLWIG
Charles 65
Doris GRIMM 65
Mary KOVANDA 65
HELLY?
Mary 28
HELM
Amanda M. 120
Johan 110
Sophia 2
HELMBOLD
Franda Christine 166
HELMER
Julia 23
Mathew 23
HELMES
Henriette DEYNIKE 65
William 65
HELMKE
Engle 103
HELMS
Charles 65
Ellen BATES 65
Jane 66
John 65
HELQUIST
Annie 63
N.M. 63
HELVERSON
Gurnil 116
HEMENWAY
Charles 65
Charles E. 65
Elizabeth A. GRAHAM
65
Wealthy Lucy FAY 65
HEMPEL
Anna Katharina 61
Christian A. 65
Louisa MARR 65
Mary JOCUMSEN 65
HEMPHILL
Bell 101
Hester A. ROGERS 101
J.C. 101
HENBERG
E. 78
HENDEE
Alma Elizabeth 146
Mary E. MATHEWS
146
S.W. 146

HENDER
Cora 110
Hildreth 110
Lanona EATON 110
HENDERSON
Ann 96
Annie ROLLS 65
Cassie Ray LARKIN 65
Cornelius 65
Daniel 100
Elizabeth W. 64
George 84
Irene 84
James N. 65
James, Mrs. 65
John E. 65
K.A. BOURRET 65
M. 62, 152
Maggie 59
Margaret 2
Martha E. 100
Mary 80, 121
Mary MALONY 65
Mary MARSH 65
Melissa 77
Sam 156
Sara 26, 137
Sophia MALTHWAIDE
84
T. Marsh 65
Wm. 65
HENDRICK
Andrew 66
Mary MITCHELL 66
Robert 66
HENDRICKS
Amanda 154
Andrew 66
James 66
Robert 66
Virginia FOSTER 66
HENDRICKSON
Andrew 95
Anna JENSEN 151
Annie 150
Brita 11
Elizabeth 95
Enoch 66
George D. 66
Helena 130
James 89
Jane LANGLEY 89
John 66, 151
Julia A. CLUNGER 66
Lucinda MOORE 66
May J. POWELL 66
Rose BELVILLE 66
Sarah 89
Saul 39, 66
HENELY
Anastatia CONWAY 66
Lawrence 66
Minnefred DOLAN 66
HENESEY
Catharine 71
HENGEN
Elizabeth 42
Elizabeth FREICHELS
160
Elizabeth ROEBLING
42
Joseph H. 42, 160
Josephine 160
Morice 42
Morris 81

HENKEL
Maria B. 121
HENLEY
Charles 60
John 66
Lissie 68
HENN
Franziska EICKHORN
72
Ludwine 72
Valentin 72
HENNECK
Wm. 33
HENNESEY
Ellen KELLEY 159
John 159
Maggie 159
HENNESSEY
Caire WILLEFORD 66
Delia 23
Elizabeth ROBISON 66
James 66
John 23, 128
William P. 121
HENNESSY
Josephine 156
Mary MULVILLE 66
Rose McARDLE 66
William 66
William P. 66, 77
Wm. 56
HENNESY
William 57
HENNEY
C.L. 23
Catharine 102
E., Mrs. 21
Enoch 152
HENNING
Adeline FARR 112
Anna SCALPKOHL 66
Arthur Reinhard 66
Friedrich Gotthelf 66
John 112
Pauline SCHURIG 66
Susan A. 112
HENNINGS
Catharine GEHL 66
Claus 66
Henry 66
Louis 19
Rebecca LUEBECK 66
HENNINGSEN
Annie M. PAULSEN 66
Henning 66
Peter 66
Rose Clara SCHMIT 66
HENNISEY
Mary 23
HENRICKSEN
Ellen ESKELSON 66
Knud 66
HENRICKSON
Anna C. 43
Anna E. 89
Christina 49
Christina JANSEN 66
Dora 43
James 43
Louis 66
Louis, Mrs. 66
Peter 66
HENRIKSEN
Louis 89
HENRY
A.C. 43

A.M. 144
Alice BUCHANAN 66
Anna 100
Annie AYERS 66
Bridget O. KANE 25
Catherine SWARTZ 43
Christopher 66
Elizabeth 76, 102
Fred. 35
J.M. 58
James 66
John 66
John S. 66
Lissie A. 52
Martha McMASTER 66
Mary 25
Mary CAMPBELL 66
Ora B. 100
Orpha 170
Robert H. 25
Sarah 142
Wm. 10, 33, 43
Wm., Mrs. 10
HENSCHKE
Louise 86
HENSE
Christine 7
HENSEN
Annie RASMUSSEN 76
Bertha OLSEN 66
Caroline 88
Christina 61
Dorothea C.
ZACHARIASEN 66
H.C. 66
Hannah 61
Jens 76
Julius 66
HENSINGER
Augusta 147
Charles 42, 147
Christopher 49
HENSMAN
Elizabeth 148
Ellen FOX 66
George C. 102
James 66
Joseph 30
Lucy 30
Mary 102
Mary Ann
RICHARDSON 30
Mercy WILCOX 102
Mercy, Mrs. 102
HENSON
Buliah 140
Henrietta C. 127
Mary 65, 77
Rasmuss 127
HENTON
Sarah 161
HENZE
Lizzie 43
HENZIE
Catharine DELANY
131
Daniel 131
Mary 131
HENZL
Anna 96
HEOURTH
Catharine MUNTD 18
Lizza 18
Michael 18
HEPPLER
Dietrich 131

HERAGAN
Mary 145
HERAMAN
Johane 67
HERAS
Jane 85
HERBERT
L.M. 119
Mr. 138
HERBERTZ
Charles 112, 138
HERBST
D.F. 66
Lucia KAY 66
Sophia A.W. LAPTIN 66
William 66
HERD
Mary A. 167
HERDLICKE
Annie UNCAJTCH 66
Ferdinand 66
Jacob 66
HEREMANN
William 84
HERGERADER
Helena 52
HERHAHN
Theresa 154
HERIMAN
Alley 112
HERING
Frederike 87
HERLITZ
Carl Gabriel 133
HERMACH
Mary 140
HERMAN
Catherine KELLY 66
Eliza C. 123
John 11
Kathrin 13
Mary EVERSON 66
Mrs. 90
Richard 66
Sophie 90
William 66
Wm. 90
HERMANIDER
Johanna 15
HERMANN
Elizabeth 5
HERMEL
Edward 66
Margaret THOMAS 66
HERMES
Gracie MYERS 7
M. 7
Margaret 7
HERNICK
Annie 35
John 35
Mary SHULER 35
HEROLD
John 49
Josephine 154
HERON
Anne 88
Margaret E. 88
Mary HORRIGAN 88
Thomas 88
Wilson 3
HERPST
Catherine 40
HERR
Louis 37

HERRING
Alvira BALINGER 66
Augusta POHL 104
Bertha 104
Charles 66
Emily OWENS 66
Ferdianand 104
Wilson 66
HERRINGTON
Catherine 70
HERRLE
Caroline ROLAND 66
Frederick 66
Johann 66
Mathilda BARTIG 66
HERRMANN
Agnes 12
HERRON
Ellen 16
Francis G. 88
John 88
Margaret 143
Mary F. 143
Mary HORRIGAN 143
Mary HOURIGAN 88
Terresa 88
Thomas 143
HERRZ
Christance 75
HERSCH
Abraham 54
HERSCHFELD
Almina 129
Amelia 129
HERSCHFELDT
Almina 129
Amelia 129
HERSKE
Frederick 1
Wilhelmina, Mrs. 1
HERSMOND
Abeloni DACRIEF 66
Christian 66
Johanna SOULDER 66
Louis 66
HERTEN
Agnes 86
Eliza FRANZ 66
Frank 66
Margaret MYER 66
Margareta MEYER 86
Michael 66, 86
HERTZMANN
J.F.L.D. 59, 134
Jerome 38, 77
Jerome F.L.D. 43, 66, 85, 111, 117, 168
HERUM
Carrie C. HANSEN 66
Catherina M. HANSEN 66
Hans J. 66
John 66
HERZ
Adelaide 133
HERZBERG
Ernest 80
Fredericka JEISLER 80
Ida 80
HERZER
Catherine S. KESSLER 66
Franz 66
Sophia L. MANKE 66
HERZKE
Fred 45

Fredrick 67
HERZOG
George 18, 66
Hedwig L. 66
HESELTINE
Ellenor 167
HESS
Albert 67
Charlotte 51
Elizabeth MUSSLER 67
Elizabeth REEVES 67
George A. 67
J. Frank 124
Maggie 75
Rosa 17
HESSE
Helene 86
HESTADT
Wm. 66
HETER
Emily 151
HETRICK
Adam 67
Evanna MOCK 67
Maria J. 67
Phillip M. 67
HETTAND
Moses 167
HETTER
Annie 95
HETTINGER
Elizabeth 6
HEUBEL
Angelie REITZ 129
Annie C. 129
Valentine 129
HEUBOCK
Anna 80
HEUCK
Annie M.P. 72
George 72
HEUGSLER
Katharine 170
HEUNIG
A.R. 82
HEUSTON
Hattie KING 94
Josephine 94
L. 94
HEWELL
Feibie 57
HEWIT
Sarah A. 159
Sarah A. ROBESON 159
Wileus 159
HEWITT
C.S. 77
Carrie L. 125
Charles 67
Minnie REYNOLDS 67
Phebe 6
Susan KEYNER 67
W.I. 67
HEYBEAY
Ernest 80
Fredericka JEISLER 80
Ida 80
HEYDE
Adelle SAGO 91
Fred R.D. 91
Frederick 91
Helen E. 91
O.R.D. 91
HEYDEN
Lislie Sister Mary 25

Mary 20
HGORD
Casper 67
Emily GROND 67
HIBBELER
Annie 168
Catharina DANNEMANN 67
Catharina DENNEMANN 67
Christian 168
Christina DANAMAN 168
Christof 67
Christoffer 67
Dedreich 67
Detrick 65
Dietrich 67
Henry 65
Ludwig 67
Margaretha GOSCH 67
Mary BOESE 67
HIBBILER
Dedrich 168
HIBBLER
Henry 34
Kate RUSK 34
Wetha 34
HICKER
Anders 67
Balana SHATZ 67
Henrietta SHULTZ 67
Morton 67
HICKERHAAS
Dorathea 92
HICKEY
Ann 91
Bridget 105
Bridget MORAN 67
Eliza 109
James 65, 67, 95, 105
Jane 25
John 67
Margaraet KELLEY 67
Mary Ann 7
William P. 39
HICKMAN
Charity F. 16
Elizabeth THOMAS 67
Elvira PROUD 120
Erastus M. 67
Henry 16, 142, 168
Henry, Mr. and Mrs. 45
Henry, Mrs. 82, 142
Sallie V. 120
Wm. W. 120
HICKMON
Franie 137
HICKOX
G.W. 103
HICKS
Amelia A. HUNT 67
Ann RICHARDS 80
Benjamin C. 67
Eben 67
Eleanor BAKER 67
Libbie 80
Mary TURNER 162
Obediah 80
HICKSTEIN
Christ 67
Fred 67
Frederick 84, 117
Hennie 79
Henrietta WOHLFEIL 67

Mary RONNER 67
HIENT
Naomi A. 104
HIENTZE
Pauline, Mrs. 108
HIER
Amelia M. KLAUSCH 67
Catharine SCLEIFREDT 67
Gotlieb 67
HIES
Ludwig 138
HIGBY
Hellen McD 144
Aletta 81
Beecher 144
Caroline J. LANDON 67
Carrie F. 43
Francis A. PADDOCK 43, 67, 144
Ira P. 67
J.C. 43
John 33, 137
John C. 67, 144
John C., Mr. and Mrs. 67
Mrs. 129
Nettie M. 140
S.W. 16
HIGGEN
Gurt 113
HIGGINS
Annie O'CONNOR 67
Caroline McLEAN 102
Catharine 32
Chas. 119
Daniel 9
John 67
John G. 67
Lucasey 115
Maggie 102
Maggie A. 14
Mary 9, 29, 73
Mary CRONIN 9
Patrick 64
Theophilus 102
Thompsien MURPHY 67
HIGGINSON
A.G. 67
Anna TYNG 67
Celma BALCOMBE 67
George 67
HIGGS
Mrs. 158
HIGHNY
Mary 40
HIGINBOTHOM
Elizabeth 157, 158
HIGLEY
Mrs. 32, 129
HIKE
Emma 55
Henry 55
Minerva STONE 55
HILBER
Benedict 67
HILBERT
Alois 67
Andreas 67
Benedict 67
David 142
Lee A. 142
Marie POHL 67
Mary ATKINSON 142

HODKINSON
　Hannah 74
HODSON
　Emma 82
HOEFER
　Jacob 68
　Johannah STARK 68
HOEFT
　Wibke 160
HOEL
　A.R. 52, 95, 163
　A.R., Mr. and Mrs. 68
　Aaron R. 22, 114, 124,
　149
　Catherine M. DURHAM
　22, 114
　John 149
　Lucy B. 114
　Mary 134
　Mary C. 22
HOELL
　A.R. 74
　A.R., Mr. and Mrs. 74,
　119
　C.M., Mrs. 74
HOELM
　Albertina 14
HOESSLY
　Henry 68
HOEY
　Anna M. CORRIGAN
　68
　John M. 68
HOFELDT
　Anna WOMELSTROF
　69
　Claus 69
　Mary BACKHUUS 69
　Peter 69
HOFF
　Birgitt 108
HOFFACHTER
　Maurice 4
HOFFEK
　Mary 47
HOFFMAN
　Andrew 69
　Anna CIPERA 69
　Carl 69
　Caroline 163
　Caroline BUNS 69
　Conrad 69
　George 69
　J.F. ROBERTS 63
　John 84
　Kate 96
　Margaret 135
　Margaret DUFEK 69
　Mary 16
　Mary DOTTEREVEICH
　69
　Mary SMITH 69
　Mary, Mrs. 91
　Max 69
　Peter 163
　Rosa SCHMIDT 163
　Teresa 143
　Wilhelmina
　SALZWEDEL 69
HOFFMANN
　Annie LEONARD 69
　Christian 69
　Elizabeth 57
　George 112
　John 69
　Louise 69

Mary GROSSMAN 64
　Mr. 52
HOFFMEIER
　Charles 69
　Hannah KERMAR 69
　Mary KELLY 69
HOFFMEISTER
　Anna RICHELMANN
　69
　Emil 69
　Ernie 2
　H. 69
　Mary WUNSEH 69
HOFFNER
　Mary ANN 15
HOFICK
　Frances TUDOR 69
　Frank 69
　Frederick 69
　Magdalene CEMPAL 69
HOFKE
　Charlotta BACHARD
　110
　Elizabeth 110
　Friederich 110
HOFMANN
　Adam 69
　Catharine HEINIKEL
　69
　Elizabeth TROUTWINE
　69
　Emily ARMSLAN 69
　Margaretta GERHARD
　69
　Michael 69
　Peter 69
　Simon 69
HOFMEISTER
　Annie 85
　H. 85
HOFNEY
　Lizzie 168
HOFSTED
　John C. 73
HOGAN
　Bridget CALVERT 69
　Catharine 81, 114
　Catherine FERRY 69
　Cornelius 69
　Daniel 51, 69
　Dorah 19
　Elizabeth 6
　Ellen CARMEL 69
　Ellen FOGARTY 69
　Ellen FOGERTY 69
　Emily EVANS 69
　James 69
　John 69
　Lizzie 6
　Martin 69
　Mary TWOMEY 69
　Thomas 69
　Wm. 46
HOHLFELT
　Chas. 169
HOHMANN
　Cornelia BROWN 69
　F.W. 69
　Helen M.K. CANDEE
　69
　S.B. 69
HOHNER
　Sydney 71
HOILIEN
　Anna Gertrue S. 142

HOILT
　Mary 2
HOKANSON
　Ulricke 73
HOKE
　Andrew 69
　Catharine SANFORT 69
　Mary Eve THIERI 69
　Mathias 69
HOKENSEN
　Caroline 56
HOLBROOK
　Eliza Ann 96
　Polly P. 144
HOLCOMB
　Nellie 31
HOLDEN
　D.C. 150
　Delia E. 150
　Eliza I. SMITH 150
　Jane 78
　Jane P. 104
　John 78
　Louise A. 36
　Patience MILLER 78
HOLDER
　Margaret M. 87
HOLDERNESS
　Charles A. 69
　Emma E. LETNER 69
HOLDHIES
　Minnie 116
HOLDING
　Lucy 40
HOLDREGE
　Francis R. KIMBALL
　69
　George W. 69
　Henry 69
　Mary R. GRINNELL 69
HOLDSTDT
　Annie M. JOHNSON
　113
　John 113
HOLEN
　Amelia 169
HOLGIN
　Rebeckey WARNISS 69
　Vernavel 69
HOLIDAY
　Wm. 25
HOLLADAY
　A.S. 143
　Louisa PROUTZ 143
　Mary E. 143
HOLLAND
　Ann Emma 6
　Anna L. 167
　Bridget MARMION 69
　Elizabeth 59
　Ella J. 39
　J.E. 69
　James 6, 39, 69, 102
　Johanna CARMODY 69
　John 69, 167
　Margaret FINLEY 6
　Margaret RIORDAN 69
　Margaret WEBSTER 39
　Mary D. GRACE 69
　Michael 69
　Susan FLINN 69
　Thomas 69
HOLLEN
　Joanna 116
　Lars 116

Margaret ANDERSON
　116
HOLLENBACH
　Christi Anna 62
　D.A. 62
　Mary Ann
　CETTELMOYER 62
HOLLENBACK
　Daniel A. 69
　Mamie KERBY 69
　Mary ZETTLEMOYER
　69
　William 69
HOLLENBECK
　Alice HALL 69
　Hannah BROWN 69
　J.B. 69
　John 69
HOLLENS
　Richard 134
HOLLER
　Weibke 86
HOLLERT
　Elizabeth 66
HOLLIDAY
　Jane GIFFORD 69
　Nora 100
　William 69
HOLLING
　Annie 132
　Cecelia MARTENS 132
　Ekert 132
　Hans 120
HOLLINGER
　Maria 53
HOLLINGS
　Wm. J. 166
HOLLINGSWORTH
　E. 128
　Elam 69
　Martha KEETCH 69
HOLLINS
　G.N. 98
　Martha A. ALLIS 69
　William G. 72
　Wm. G., Capt. 69
HOLLISTER
　Elizabeth BURTON 69
　Henry H. 69
　Hiram 69
　Rody A. 21
HOLLMAN
　Mary 31
HOLLY
　Elizabeth 161
　Joh 161
HOLM
　Alma B. ANDERSON
　70
　Anna 11
　C. 88
　Carl 20, 169
　Detlef 70
　Dorothea ALBERS 70
　Heinke ROHDE 70
　Hillia C. 88
　Johanna ---- 70
　Johanna CARLESON
　11
　Johanna M. PETERSON
　169
　John 70
　S. 61
　Swen 11, 70
　T. 61

HOLMAN
　---- 78
　Angie 18
　Angie H. BRYANT 70
　Johanna ARNE 149
　Martha S. 149
　S.A. 149
　Samuel 70
HOLMBERG
　Lovisa 111
HOLMER
　Andrew J. 61
　Anna Katharina
　HEMPEL 61
　Christina 61
HOLMES
　A. 70
　A.E. FRANDSEN 70
　Angie 24
　Catherine H. 70
　George 70
　Hannah 24
　Hannah LAWLEY 24
　Joseph 70
　Joseph H. 96
　Joseph S. 70
　Kate 14
　Maren JENSEN 70
　Mary 32
　Mary GOODKNIGHT
　70
　Mrs. 159
　Myra HYDE 70
　Rebecca 166
　Susan WHITNEY 14
　Thomas 151, 155
　Thos. 21
　Walter R. 14
　William 24
HOLMQUIST
　Anna C. 152
HOLSIZER
　Wm. H. 164
HOLST
　Annie JENSEN 70
　Engal TIBKE 131
　Henry 131
　Ida Christine 141
　Jonas Frederic 141
　Katie 131
　Louise LINDEBORG
　141
　Magdelina 39
　Mary 169
　Mrs. 94
　N.P. 70
　Peter 169
　Sohpia B. FALK 70
　Sophus W. 70
　Wenzel 148
HOLT
　Eliza Jane 57
　Elizabeth 26
HOLTAM
　Thomas 70
HOLTEN
　Margaret 163
HOLTON
　Ellen 137
HOLTZ
　Margaret 19
HOLTZMAN
　Frank A. 70
　John T. 161
　Mary FERRIS 70

HOWLAND
Charles 132
Minnie 132
Sarah STRAIGHT 132
HOWLETT
Ann ELLEY 50
Emma 95
Lucy 50
William 50
HOWRAK
Barbara 13
HOWTEN
Harriet 153
HOXIE
Laura 100
HOYE
Amelia BIRCH 36
Gotleib 150
John 36
Laura 36
Mary S. INGOLDSLY
127
Nora F. 127
Patrick 127
HOYT
Abbie F. 16
Ruth C. HOPLINS 16
W.B. 16
HRDLICKA
Annie UNCAJTCH 66
Ferdinand 66
Jacob 66
HROMAS
John 20
Kate 20
Mary 20
HUBA
Catherine MARTIN 71
Elizabeth
GRUENEWALD 71
Jacob 71
John 71
HUBBARD
Anna W. 102
Annie LOVELADY 71
C.A., Mrs. 77
Carrie A. BANNER 71
Charles A. 71
E. 157
E.B., Mr. & Mrs. 110
Eliza Ann ROBERTSON
71
Emma ROE 157
Eva 157
George 98
George E. 71
Henry 71
Ira 71
Jennie HOVEY 87
Joanna 130
Joanna, Mrs. 16
Margaret McNAIRY 71
Mary Ann 98
HUBER
Caroline 85
Dora SORGE 71
Frederick 85
J. 71
Jeremias 71
Mary 71
Regina BOEHM 70
Sebastian 70
HUBERMAN
A.B. 86
Amelia 86

HUBERT
Catharine QUINN 95
Elizabeth SHAUDORF
71
John H. 71
Mary Jane GRANGER
71
HUBIA
Elizabeth TWEARY 30
John 30
Rebecca 30
HUCK
Bridget 58
Louis 26
HUCKFELDT
Hannah 58
John 58
HUDSON
J.A., Rev. 26
Mary 66, 169
Susan 98
William 142
HUDZ
Barbara JANAUSCHEK
71
John 71
Joseph 71
Lizzie CUHEL 71
HUERNER
Anna MOSER 136
Emma 136
Jacob 136
HUERTZ
Barbe 57
HUESTIS
Ann J. BRACKIN 71
Daniel 71
Eugene D. 71
Julia 148
Mary DIXON 71
Mrs. 148
HUFF
Alexis M. 71
Ellen J. DOREN 71
Melissa C. 154
HUFFMAN
Henry 71
Howe 71
Rachel EVANS 71
Sarah HARTMAN 71
HUFMAND
Christenia 63
HUGDEN
Lislie 63
Mary 63
HUGE
Fanny 162
J.T. 162
Mary MANDEHOUL
162
HUGEL
Joanna 46
HUGHES
Agnes 155
Agnes, Mrs. 97
Ann 50, 154
Anna 105, 106
Anne 63
Annie 109, 139, 153,
156
Bernard 71
Bride 142
Bridget DONOLAN 18
Catherine 36
Edward C. 93
Elizabeth 22

Ellen 36
Harriet ROSING 71
Ida 11
James 71
John 24, 28, 36, 57
John E. 71
Julianna FLEMING 71
Kate 18
Margaret 28, 50
Margaret G. BERLIN
71
Martha HEDGES 71
Martin 18, 71
Mary 24, 38
Mary BOOLEY 71
Mary DORAN 71
Mary HITE 153
Mary J. LAMBERT 71
Mary MAHONEY 71
Mary McCORMICK 24,
28
Mary PATTERSON
155
Mary RYAN 71
Michael 153
Michael E. 71
Mrs. 13
P.F. 71
Patrick 71
Peter 9
Phoebe P. EVANS 71
Rebecca C.A. SMILEY
71
Sarah Ellen 9
Sarah M. CHRISTMAN
71
Susan 153
Thomas 71
W.H., Mrs. 160
W.H.S. 72
W.H.S., Mrs. 111, 169
William 134, 155
William B. 71
William H.S. 71
Wm., Mrs. 3
HUGHFIELD
Francis, Mrs. 140
HUGHS
Sarah 36
HUGONIOT
Jules 71
Julia Constance BRAND
71
Peter 71
Susan MEJNIEN 71
HUGUS
Eliza McCORMACK 72
John W. 72
Peter 9, 72
Sarah Ellen 9
Sarah G. CARNAN 72
HUICK
Annie M.P. 72
George 72
HULA
John 51, 74
HULE
Ann 53
HULIN
Annie 166
HULL
Sarah 45
HULLMAN
Francis 143
Frank A. 25

HULT
C.L.A. 17
Esther J. BROWN 17
Ida L. 17
HULTMAN
Annette 116
Annie G. ANDERSON
72
Frank A. 116, 119
Frank Augustus 72
Jennie M. PALMGREN
72
Mrs. 150
Peter 72
HULTZINGER
Jennie 19
Mary HOUSEL 19
Peter 19
HUMBEL
Marie 135
HUMBELIN
Mollie, Mrs. 24
HUMBLE
Sarah 31
HUME
Arminta REDMAN 72
Elizabeth THOMAS 72
Ersiala 91
George 72
Richard 72
William 72
HUMMELL
John 75
Kate 75
Lena ---- 75
HUMPAL
Caroline STIBO 72
Jacob 72
Joseph 72
Mary SPINLER 72
HUMPERT
Regina STARKE 72
Casper 72
Franz 72
Ludwine HENN 72
HUMPHREY
Eliza BURKE 72
Emaline JOHNSON 72
H.N. 72
John 29
Julia 29
Watson 72
HUMPHRIES
Anna GORDON 72
Edmund 72
Emma SCHACK 72
Wm. H. 72
HUMSTEDT
Elizabeth BURGDORFF
7
Emilie 7
Henry D. 7
HUNDERLICK
Theresa 38
HUNDLEY
George 72
Julia SMITH 72
Nellie THOMAS 72
Thomas 72
HUNGER
Julia 149
HUNN
Emiline 12
Ferdinand 12
Margaret 48

HUNSACKER
Elizabeth 78
HUNT
A., Mrs. 154
A.S.A. 163
Adah 88
Adalaide FENELL 88
Amelia A. 67
Asa 72
Asa. Mrs. 72
Catharine 108
Charles 72, 122, 159
Flora 1
G., Mrs. 159
G.J. 100
Gennie M. 157
George 67
Gertrude H.
VANDENBURGH 72
Jane M. SEAMAN 72,
163
Jennie M. 154, 163
Johanna KERN 42
Johannis 42
Katharina 42
M., Mrs. 122
Marck 1
Margaret 11
Margaret BERRELL
159
Margaret, Mrs. 166
Maria 101
Mary A. 4, 73
Mary Jane BALLARD
148
Moses 88
Mrs. 32, 45, 129
Naomi MESNER 67
Phebe 143
Sarah M. 148
Wm. C. 148
HUNTER
Alexander 72
Anna 16
Anthony 72
Caroline DEAN 16
Charlotta L. BUNNELL
72
Deborahan 79
E.A., Mrs. 165
Elizabeth 72, 104
Ella A. 106
Frank 72
Harrison M. 72
J.R. 165
James 72
James H. 72
James M. 106
Jane McCAMON 72
Jennie M. ECKFORD
72
John 82
Laura TIBBALS 72
Len 16
Louisa A. HARMON 72
Margaret WEDDLE 104
Margaretta SILL 72
Mary A. FORT 72
Mary HORD 72
Mary STOUGHTON
106
Nettie 17
Robert 72
T.C. 72
William 104

HUNTINGTON
  L.C. 133
HUNTLEY
  Sarah J. 97
HUNTOON
  A.S., Mrs. 155
  Asa Sylvester 72
  Columbia Helen CLEGG
    72
HUNTZINGER
  Amanda KITCHEN 164
  Chas 164
  Mary S. 164
HUPERT
  John 72
  Julia WATSON 72
  Susan MALONEY 72
  Wilton M. 72
HUPP
  J.W. 151
HURBITT
  Elizabeth 130
HURD
  Byron 72
  Dave 72
  Esther Ann 162
  Isaac W. 72
  Louisia Jane, Mrs. 124
  Mary STETEN 72
  Saray DYE 72
HURFORD
  Louisa C.C. 72
  Mr. and Mrs. 145
  O.P. 126, 128, 161
  Oliver P. 72
  Thomas J. 72
HURKET
  Alice LESTER 101
HURLBERT
  Benjamin F. 72
  Edith G. BARNUM 72
  Elmira J. POOL 72
  Warren 72
HURLBUT
  Cordelia E. MUNGER
    72
  E.B. 169
  Everett B. 72
  O.P. 103
HURLEY
  A.A. 72
  Betsey 29
  Betsey WEBB 29
  Betsy WEBB 72
  Bridget 28, 115
  Catharine A. KANE 72
  Daniel 72
  David 29
  Dowd 72
  Ellen 72
  James C. 72
  Jeremiah 72
  John 60
  Julia COCHLIN 72
  Margaret BLUM 28
  Marth 157
  Martha 60
  Mary Jane DRISCOLL
    72
  Mary NOLAN 72
  Olive A. 60
  Patrick 28, 72
  Sarah M. 29
HURM
  Anton 72
  Louisa KENNER 72

Louisa STONESTREET
  72
  William 72
HURREA
  Alice 115
HURST
  James 72
  Mary 106
  Rebecca Jane FULTON
    72
HURT
  Amelia 120
  George 120
  Jane ROGERS 120
  Melher 109
  Susanna 109
HUSEN
  Antje 87
HUSON
  Abel 18
HUSS
  Anna 79
  Antonie TRAISSENETT
    73
  Catharine LOEB 73
  Elizabeth BIERBAUM
    73
  Franz 73
  Joseph 73
  Rudolf 73
  Rudolph 73
  Wilhelmina TRESCHER
    73
HUSSEY
  Brdiget 124
  Mary 107
  Rebecca 42
HUSTAD
  Anna STROM 73
  Charles 73
  John 73
  Mary EGEN 73
HUSTED
  Anna CLAUSSEN 73
  Christian C. 73
  E. 73
  Louisa JESSEN 73
  Mr. 78
HUSTES
  E.D. 108
HUSTON
  Martha JACKSON, Mrs.
    73
  Wade 73
HUTCHENSON
  Elizabeth PRICE 73
  Ellen 154
  Mary E. RIDER 73
  Nathan 73
  William H. 73
HUTCHINS
  A.M.L. FURBUSH 153
  Ellen MOWHINIA 73
  Henry 73
HUTCHINSON
  Ann 20
  D.S. 88
  Emeline 129
  Hariet L. 82
HUTESON
  Martha DYMOND 73
  Thomas J. 73
HUTH
  Ellen 63
  Frederick 170
  Ida 59

Louisa BECKER 170
  Minnie 170
  Minnie, Mrs. 44
HUTTON
  Lucy WILD 73
  Thomas H. 73
HVEZDA
  Franciska 156
HYCHCOX
  Mr. and Mrs. 16
HYDE
  C.D. 37, 69, 82, 93, 94,
    107, 117, 140
  Carrie V. DeMOTT 73
  Christine 21
  Cornelius D. 73
  DeMott 51, 129
  DeMotte 39, 61, 64, 81,
    120
  E.S. 73
  George W. 73
  J.R., Mrs. 2, 33, 81
  Judson R. 73
  Lou REED 73
  Lucy 31
  M.D. 33
  Mary M. REYNOLDS
    73
  Mollie MACKEY 73
  Mortimer 120, 129
  Myra 70
HYIEM
  Helena Sophie 13
HYLAND
  Ellen 31
  John 31
  Margaret KENNEY 31
HYMAS
  Catharine 133
  Catharine PERRY 73
  John 73
  William A. 73
HYNE
  Acena HODGE 16
  Adda 16
  Martin 16
HYNEK
  Anna MASEK 12
  Anna SIMON 68
  Annie MITATEK 98
  Anton 68, 98
  Barbara ROUBAL 68
  Franc 12
  Frank 68, 98
  Josie 98
  Veronika 12
HYNES
  Thomas N.J. 73
  Ann FALLON 73
  Annie FALLON 73
  Ellen DWYER 73
  John 29
  Mary 29
  Patrick 73
  Thomas N.J. 73
ICKERSON
  Esther 63
IDE
  Ella B. 19
  John 19
  Lydia RICHARDS 19
IECHELL
  Mary SCHWAB 107
IJAMS
  Mary 158

William H.  3, 7, 18, 80,
    118, 119, 153, 158,
    160
ILARS
  Annie OELARENG 136
  John 136
  Lena 136
ILER
  Conrad 73
  Georgia Maud GRAY
    73
  Joseph D. 73
  Julia STRINE 73
  P. 73
IMIKE
  Anna C. 2
ING
  Eliza 33
INGALLS
  Eliza 141
  Hellen M. 38
  Kate STARING 38
  Maggie 27, 28, 68
  Mary 27
  O.P. 68, 116
  O.P., Mrs. 129
  Oscar P. 38, 78
INGALS
  Maggie 68
INGEBREGTSEN
  Fredrik 13
INGELS
  Marrgie 61
INGERSOL
  Lucy 8
INGERSOLL
  Lucy 123
INGHAM
  Clara H. 167
  Harriet 155
  Mary Louise 42
INGHRAM
  Caroline J. GILLELAND
    73
  Eliza MORGAN 73
  HenryM. 73
  Thomas 73
INGLE
  Maggie 127
INGOLDSBY
  Mary NARIE 53
  Mary 53
  Owen 53
INGOLDSLY
  Mary S. 127
INGRAM
  E. May 15, 16
  Eva M. 102
  J.A. 16, 19, 163
  Julia A. 145
  L.J. 15
  Lettie J. 100, 163
  Mary 130
  Mary E. 20, 124
INTERHOLZINGER
  James 151
  Katy 151
  Maggie
    STANPERKOVA 151
IONGSTIN
  Ann Catherine
    PETERSON 79
  Nelsen 79
IRA
  George 73
  George W. 73

Mary A. HUNT 73
  Mary B. HOBBS 73
IRELAND
  Antonia Maria 119
  Elizabeth 17, 25
  Ellen LABADIE 119
  Thos. A. 119
  W.J. 105
IRISH
  Mary E. 92
IRVINE
  Ann K. JOHNSON 73
  Clarke 73
IRWIN
  Ellen 63
  Henriette H. 142
  Joseph 142
  Rebecca SMITH 142
ISAAC
  Clara J. GUSTAVESON
    73
  Ernestine KAHLER 73
  George 73
  John 73
  Joseph 73
  Regina MULLER 73
  William 73
ISAACS
  Bertha M. 99
  Chris 99
  Lizzie 99
  Maria D. WORDEN 99
  N.P. 99, 145
  Susan 24
  William 13
ISAAKSON
  August 73
  Christine PIERSON 73
ISAKSON
  Anna 134
  Aug. 90
ISBERG
  Carrie PEARSON 73
  Emilie ANDERSON 73
  J.N. 73
  Nils 73
ISDELL
  Catherine 40
ISHAM
  Daniel T. 73
  David T. 73
  Emeline J. CADY 73
  Maggie A. McNICHOL
    73
  Marilla 68
ISLAND
  Johnette 64
ISRAEL
  Mary 60
ISREAL
  A. 57
ISTLER
  K. 149
  Louise 149
  Marie KLEIN 149
ITNYER
  Hiram N. 73
  J. 73
  Martha J. CREIGHTON
    73
  Susan RHOADES 73
ITTNER
  Mr. 164
  Mrs. 164
  Nicholas 164

JOHANSON, cont.
Johanna 33
Johanna PETERSON 70
Johanna SEVANSEN 75
Lars 33
Louisa 158
Meta Alena
  ANDERSON 116
Rasmus 116
Swan 75
JOHANSSEN
Bankda 41
JOHN
Adelina 168
Anna 158
Carl 30
Charley 75
Frederika STRUKMAN
  75
Mary REINHART 75
Sarah COZZENS 158
Thomas 158
William 75
JOHNDATER
Sara Stina 92
JOHNS
Bettie 42
Catharine M. CAHILL
  75
John F. 75
John V. 75
Margaret HABEL 75
JOHNSDOTAR
Christina 48
JOHNSDOTTER
Christina 26
JOHNSEN
Poppatabea 43
Sven G. 11
JOHNSON
Louise BENSON 76
---- 66
---- HOLMAN 78
A. 59
A. ANDERSON 160
A.C. 75
A.M., Miss 160
A.S. 75
Abbie J. 109
Abel 158
Ablone 76
Adah H. 81
Agnes 154
Agusta ANDERSEN
  126
Albert 20
Ale 111
Alfred 75
Alfrid 76
Alsabiah 14
Amos 76
Anders 10
Anderson 98
Andreas 3
Andres 26
Andrew 3, 4, 42, 65, 76,
  112, 135
Andrew F. 76
Ane 136
Ann 77
Ann Catharine 156
Ann K. 73
Ann M. HANSEN 157
Anna 13, 15, 76, 77,
  108, 121, 122, 135

Anna ANDERSON 4,
  42
Anna Botelle 26
Anna C. 46
Anna CHRISTENSEN
  56
Anna
  CHRISTOPHERSON
  113
Anna DANIELSON 76
Anna ERLICKSON 76
Anna GERETTA 117
Anna JOHNSON 76
Anna Keiser 116
Anna LARSDOTTER
  88
Anna MATTSON 76
Anna NELSON 78
Anna PETERSON 3, 77
Anna S. ANDERSON
  76
Anna SAMPSON 111
Anna SMITH 76
Anna, Mrs. 149
Anne C. AUSTROM
  151
Annie 22, 33, 77, 89,
  106, 116, 118
Annie A. LINDBORG
  76
Annie B. 94
Annie C. 169
Annie E. OLESON 77
Annie LARSON 78, 117
Annie M. 113, 114
Annie M. ANDERSEN
  127
Annie MORRISON 97
Annie NELSON 77
Annie OLSON 78
Annie RASMUSSEN 76
Annie SMITH 78
Annie SWANSON 76
Annie, Mrs. 78
Anny LARSON 76
Anton 76
Arminda VINE 55
August 76
Augusta 155
Augusta PETERSON 78
B.F. 76
Bendta 11
Bengt 76
Bengta ANDERSON 86
Benjamin 78
Benson Emanuel 76
Beret Martha
  OLSDOTTER 77
Bertha M. 44
Betsey 14, 60, 111, 116
Betsy ANDERSON 121
Betta NEALSON 77
Bola BENGSTON 76
Boletta 111
Brigita HANSEN 76
Brita 113
Britti 77
C.F. 134
Caren 58
Carina MORTENSON
  146
Carl 23, 76, 111
Carl Peter 25
Caroline 43, 60, 61, 88
Caroline A.
  PONGELLEY 76

Caroline BECK 77
Carrie 50, 75, 77, 105,
  116
Carrie JOHNSON 77
Carrie NEILSON 78
Carrie RASSMUSSEN
  117
Carrie, Mrs. 40
Cary CASTONSON 75
Catharine 33, 93, 121,
  151
Catharine
  ANDUSDOTTER 25
Catharine E.
  ANDERSON 78
Catharine SEMONSON
  75
Catherina HANSEN 76
Catherine C. 22
Catherine COOPER 96
Cecilia 50
Celiea 92
Charles 23, 76, 77
Charles A. 76
Charles M. 76, 169
Charles P. 76
Charles S. 76
Chris 22
Christ 12, 76, 78, 117
Christene 67
Christian 76, 77
Christiana 92
Christiana Gusta 61
Christina 23, 45, 117
Christina GRINQUEST
  77
Christina
  JOHNSDOTAR 48
Christina
  JOHNSDOTTER 26
Christine 65
Christine LARSON 76
Christine M. 26
Christof 120
Christopher 75, 120
Clara 16, 25, 127
Dafnay 78
David H. 76
Detleff 78
Dora 117
Dora SCHWEEL 78
E. 100
Edna BERGQUIST 77
Edward 32, 76
Eleanor SWENSON 155
Eli 42, 49, 76, 128
Elin 120
Eliza 98, 112
Eliza Christina 89
Elizabeth 21, 42, 69, 70,
  156
Elizabeth A. WALKER
  77
Elizabeth GOOD 42
Elizabeth KEELER 21,
  137
Elizabeth KING 77
Elizabeth OCANDER
  77
Elizabeth RAUP 77
Elizabeth W. 87
Ellen 3, 77, 120, 152
Ellen BROPHY 77
Ellen JOHNSON 77
Ellen SWENSEN 155
Elmire METEER 77

Else
  LOUISDAUGHTER
  3
Elsse 77
Elsse JOHNSON 77
Emaline 72
Emily 77
Emily C. HARTFORD
  77
Emily JOHNSON 77
Emily SMITH 76
Emily Sophia 92
Emma 71, 75, 130
Emma C. PETERSON
  77
Emma JOHNSON 75
Emma M. 98
Engeback ANDERSON
  77
Engey STENI 4
Enos 76
Erasmus 76
Esther J. DIMAND 78
Eva C. 113
Eva NILSON 155
Evalina NELSON 76
Everlena PEERSON 155
F. 148, 160
Fannie 82
Fanny RICHARDSON
  78
Frank 76, 77
Frank B. 76
Frederik 77, 120
Frederikie 146
G.J. 108
G.J., Rev. 145
Geo. 61
Geo. W. 2
Georg 117
George 77
George Annie 127
Georgietta M., Mrs. 83
Gracie 90
Gusta 44
Gustava L. 155
H. 87
H., Mrs. 102
H.D. 83
Hadley 102
Hanna 3
Hanna C. 3
Hanna SWANS 42
Hannah 23, 32, 45, 50,
  77, 108, 121
Hannah HANSEN 76
Hannah JOHNSON 77
Hannah MESSEL 77
Hannah SWANSON 4
Hans 38, 76, 121, 125
Harrison 77, 90, 117,
  124, 132
Harrison, Mr. and Mrs.
  76
Harry 77
Hattie L. 167
Hedwig 133
Helsey PEARSON 76
Henrika 151
Henry 70, 76, 77, 108
Henry C. 77
Herrick 77
Humphrey 76
Ida M. 4
Ida SWENSEN 76
Inga L. NILSON 77

Ingeborg 126
Inger LARSON 76
Inger W. HANSEN 78
Ingre 108
Ingred JONASON 11
Ingrid 77
Ingrid JOHANSON 106
Isaac 41
J. 75
J.G. 81
J.P. 15
Jacob 77
James 40, 42, 50, 77,
  112
James C. 77
Jane 59
Jane E. KELLOY 76
Jans 50
Jennie 43, 121
Jennie M. ALLAN 78
Jenny 117
Jens 45, 76, 114
Johann 76, 88
Johanna 20, 148
Johanna C. 146
Johanna LARSDOTTER
  97
Johanna Maria JEPSEN
  108
Johanna Mary 3
Johanna OLSON 116
Johanna PEDERSEN 77
Johannah NELSON 76
John 3, 4, 11, 16, 28, 46,
  48, 55, 56, 59, 60,
  76-79, 89, 92, 94, 105,
  108, 111, 116, 117,
  121, 126, 155, 159,
  166
John A. 77
John C. 76
John E. 77
John P. 76
John Peter 94
John W. 77
John William 76
Johnathan 78
Jonas 88, 106
Joseph 77
Josephina NYSTET 76
Josephine "Josie" 112
Josie 21
Jude 56
Julia 68
Julia K. MARSH 123
Karen ANDERSON 77
Karen M. IVESON 77
Katie KOWISKA 112
Katie SPAULDIN 76
L. 87, 90, 117
Lars 77, 151
Laura 156
Lelzequiest 43
Lena 113
Lena Stna 92
Lena TRELSON 76
Leonora OLESON 76
Lewis 77
Lina 114
Lizzie 71, 89, 137
Lizzie B. ROWE 76
Lizzie KEALER 71
Lizzie NELSON 46
Lorence 26
Louis PIERSON 77
Louisa 21, 92

JONSON, cont.
  Hans 127
  Lars 89
  Matilda 154
JONSSON
  Hanna SKONBERG
    111
  Johana 111
  Nils 111
JORDAN
  Amantha 104
  Catherine CLARKE 119
  Daniel T. 79
  Eva 57
  Eva SCOTT 57
  Frank 57
  Hannah G. 2
  Mary 119
  Mary J. THOMPSON
    79
  Mr. 135
  Patrick 72
  R.C., Mrs. 138
  Susan DENNEY 79
  Walter 79
JORENSON
  Brita ALSDOTTER 4
  Swan 4
JORGANSON
  Christine ANDERSON
    121
  Peter 121
JORGENSEN
  Ane K. 62
  Anna 147
  Anna J. 112
  Anna Katrina LARSON
    79
  Anna Maria OLSEN 79
  Annie M. THOMPSON
    121
  Barmus 79
  C. 61
  Charlotte N. NIELSEN
    79
  Christian 79
  Christina 127
  Christina HORNSLETH
    112
  Cordy 166
  Eliza May JENSEN 79
  George (Jorgen) C. 62
  Helen THOMPSON 79
  Jens 77
  Jeppe 79
  John 112
  Jorgen 121
  Kari 104
  Lars 26, 79, 148
  Marian HANSON 77
  Micaeline C. 121
  Soren 79
JORGENSON
  Andrew 3
  Catherine 77
  Maren 4
  Maren ANDERSON 3
  Soren 88
JOROCEEK
  Anna 75
JOSEPH
  Amelia 36
JOY
  Caroline 108
  Zena 148

JOYCE
  Caroline 140
  Jacob 140
  Rebecca DONALD 140
JUDD
  Anna A. MEAD 79
  M.H. 79
  Mary A. BUSHEL 79
  Merritt 79
JUDGE
  Anthony 79
  Bridget PRICE 79
  Catharine T. 38
  Cisley 125
  John 79
  Margaret 79
  Margaret GILMARTIN
    38
  Margaret RUHANE 79
  Paul 38
JUDSON
  Charity BRADLEY 79
  H.C. 8
  Henry M. 79
  J.J. 6
  Mary A. WALLS 79
  Philo 79
  Rebecca 26
JUDY
  Catharine 18
  Catharine MIMAX 18
  James 18
JUKA
  Catharine 80
JUKES
  John 67
  Martha Ann 67
JULIAN
  Aurelia 71
  Elizabeth ALLEN 97
  Henrietta 97
  Jacob 97
JUMAN
  Hannah 59
  Hiram 59
  Mary YOUNG 59
JUMP
  Mary 124
JUNG
  Emilie 62
JUNGERS
  Eugenie 53
JUNGSTROM
  Louisa 162
  Nils or Nilson 162
JURGENSEN
  Doria, Mrs. 168
  Jurgen C. 74
  Mary NELSON 74
JUSTESEN
  Ellen K. ANDERSON
    79
  S. Peter 79
JUSTIN
  Mary E., Mrs. 8
KAASCH
  F.J. 79
  Fritz 79
  Maria LIPPKE 79
  Pollie JHANS 79
KACK
  Barbara 79
  John 79
  John C. 58, 79
  Lizzie SCHNELLER 79

KACY
  Mary 30
KADIS
  Annie 159
  Annie ULIHRACH 159
  Joseph 159
KADLECEK
  Caroline WASOWSKY
    79
  Vacslav [Vaclav] 79
KADLIK
  Anna 86
KAEBLER
  Christian 41
KAECHEL
  Mary 79
KAELBER
  Anna Clara PETZINE
    132
  Christian 132
  Sophia 132
KAERSTEN
  Charles 91
KAESEBIER
  Mary 56
KAESSNER
  Carl 79
  Gustav 79
  Mary KAECHEL 79
  Sophie CLAUSIN 79
KAFER
  Caroline 45
KAHLER
  Ernestine 73
  Ernestine BAKER 73
  Gottlieb 73
KAHN
  Babette 18
  Meyer 18
KAHOUN
  Frances 84
  John 84
  Katie REZEK 84
KAISER
  Anna HUSS 79
  Anna THANS 79
  Anton 79
  August 79, 90
  Augustine BIKOVIS 79
  C., Mrs. 35
  Caroline Margrolat 80
  Caroline SPRAKTES 79
  Clemens 79
  Dorthea 86
  Ernestine BOBBIN 79
  Ernestine BOBIN 79
  Ernestine RUBIN 90
  F. 80
  Ferdenand 79
  Ferdinand 90
  Frederick 79
  Henriette 90
  Ida, Mrs. 118
  Jacob 79
  John 79
  Lena MEYER 79
  Mary 79
  Mathias 79, 109
  O. KINGING 80
  O. Lina ELLSBORG 79
  Peter 79
  Sarah E. KEEFER 79
  Sophia GOTTSTEIN 79
  Victoria ALEXANDRIA
    79

KAKEN
  Anna 55
KALBE
  William 67
KALCH
  Joseph 114
  Julia 114
  Margaret SMITH 114
KALENBACH
  Christ 99
  Louise 99
  Mary GUTEKNUST 99
KALER
  Josephine 150
KALIK
  Anna 65
  Barbara 65
KALIKOWA
  Anna 65
  Barbara 65
KALLARY
  Mary 154
KALMAN
  A. 72
  A., Mrs. 72
KAMM
  Barbara 50
  Maria 50
  Maria VOLK 50
  Melchior 50
KAMMERLING
  Benjamin 79
  Frederick A. 79
  Margaret KECHELE 79
KAMPE
  Johanna 161
KAMPRECHT
  Riekie, Miss 62
KANE
  Anne 130
  Bridget O. 25
  Catharine A. 72
  Catharine ANDERSON
    80
  Catherine 9
  Catherine KELLEY 122
  Daniel 79
  Edward 80
  Ellen 47, 63
  Ellen CAVANAUGH 80
  Jermiah 79
  Kate 149
  Margaret GALLARY 80
  Margaret GALLERY 80
  Margaret SMITH 79
  Mary 57
  Mary C. LOWREY 80
  Mary CURRY 80
  Mary HARRINGTON
    80
  Mary RAFFERTY 72
  Michael 80
  Nicholas 80
  Patrick 80
  Peter 80
  Sarah C.
    HARSHBURGER 79
  Thomas 72, 80
KANEELY
  Margaret 78
KANENBLEY
  Anna 85
  Frederick 38
  Frederika 38
  Friederich 85
  Martha MEIER 85

  Metta MEYER 38
KANES
  Barbara 85
KANIMEYER
  Elizabeth 104
KANNEY
  Mary 110
KANSCHEIT
  Caroline Margrolat
    KAISER 80
  Charles A. 80
  G. 80
  Johannah NOUTSCH
    80
KAPP
  Sophia C. 132
KAPPENHORN
  Wilamina KUKLISS 82
KARBACH
  Charles 80, 83
  Charles J. 80
  Grete LAMP 80
  Joseph 80
  Maggie 69
  Margaretha 52
  Margaretha KESSLER
    52
  Maria 30
  Mary 80
  Peter 30, 52, 80
  Peter J. 80
  Wilhelmina H. 80
KARGA
  Rosalia 117
KARKAW
  Gustavis 135
KARLE
  George 36
KARLIK
  Anna 65
KARLIKOWA
  Anna 65
KARLL
  George 29, 80, 154
  Henrietta GRAACK 80
  Herman 80
  Ida WEST 80
KARR
  N.J., Miss 12
KARSCH
  David 80
  Elizabeth PRANCH 80
  Emil 80
  Emile 145
  Frederika
    KNOLLMILLER 80
KARSTEN
  Dorothea 14
KARSTENS
  Catharina 68
KASCHAN
  Julia 137
KASIMIR
  Mary 41
KASSELL
  Rebecca 42
KASSER
  Anna HEUBOCK 80
  Charles 80
  Christopher 80
  Ida H. 80
KASSON
  John A. 23
KASTEL
  Barbara 70
  Xavier 70

KASTNER
  Barbara TUPY 80
  Barbra BLAPOVA 80
  James 80
  Thomas 38, 80
KATCHUM
  Hopestie 96
KATES
  E. 68
KATZEMIRE
  Elizabeth 136
KAUCKY
  Catharine PALIK 80
  John 80
  Mary DANESH 80
KAUFAMANN
  Chas. 145
KAUFFMAN
  Augustus J. 16
KAUFMAN
  Doretha WINDER 12
  Dorothea 12
  George 12
KAUFMANN
  Agnes WEBBER 80
  Annie FICENEC 80
  Charles 80
  Chas. 9
  Elizabeth STRACK 80
  Gotfried 80
  Gottfred 80
  Gottfried 80
  H. 52
  Henry 80
  Julius 80
  Mary KARBACH 80
  Mary SHAWLICK 80
KAUFMEYER
  Christine FISCHER 155
  Johann 155
  Mary 155
KAUP
  Casy 57
  Joseph 80
  Mary 57
  Sophia 70
KAVAN
  Annie 126
  Barbara 64, 145
  Flora R. 126
  Frank 160
  Hensen 126
  James 64
  Joseph 138
  Mary 160
  Theresia VELEBA 160
  Vernika SEDLACEK 64
  Veronika J. 8
  Veronika SEDLACEK
    145
  Veronka SUCHY 8
  Wenceslas 152
  Wenser 126
  Wenzel 8, 145
  Wm. 160
KAVANAUGH
  Ellen 100
  John 100
  Mary 100
KAY
  Annie Elizabeth 97
  Catharine 101
  Fanny 124
  Lucia 66
  Mr. and Mrs. 124

KAYNOR
  Levina 126
KAYSER
  Constantine 80
  Frederick 80
  Martha HANSEN 80
  Mary 55
  Sophie FREZER 80
KEALER
  Lizzie 71
KEAN
  Mary LUCAS 80
  Michael S. 80
  P.H. 98
  Patrick H. 80
  Winifred KINSLA 80
KEANE
  Katharine 28
  Patrick H. 28
KEAR
  A.N. 65, 88
  Andrew N. 80
  Anna NELSON 80
  Christiana SMIDT 80
  Daniel 68
  Eliza A. 68
  Hans N. 80
  Phoebe HAMLIN 68
KEARN
  Charlotte 49
  Ellen 55
  Ellen ARTHUR 49
  Matt 49
  Nancy 55
KEARNEY
  Ann KELLEY 80
  Anne 31
  Catharine McEVOY 80
  Ellen 92
  Francis 80
  James 80
  John 46
  Joseph 80
  M.J. 80
  Margaret 46
  Mary 124
  Mary Ann 46
  Mary E. LYNCH 80
  Mary McCRISKAN 46
  Mary ROSSMAN 80
KEATING
  Edward 80
  James 80
  Mary ---- 80
  Owen 80
  Sarah E. ADAMS 80
KECHELE
  Anton 79
  Margaret 79
KECK
  Chr. 79
  Elizabeth 81
  Elizabeth SCHALLEN
    158
  John C. 158
  Lizzie B. 158
KEEF
  William 47
  William B. 168
KEEFE
  Bridget 108
  Daniel 60
  Jennie 162
  Johanna 109
  Maggie 26
  Margaret 108

Mary Ann 60
  Mary GUIGAN 60
  Mrs. 60
  P. 105
  Richard 48
  Timothy 60
KEEFER
  Caroline SEELY 79
  George 75, 79
  Katie 75
  Magdalena DILLMAN
    75
  Sarah E. 79
KEELER
  Elizabeth 21, 137
KEEN
  Anna 122
KEENE
  Augustus B. 80, 154
  Catharine CURLE 80
  Emily F. 154
  Eunice PATTERSON
    80
  James C. 80
  Libbie HICKS 80
  Prudence W. WOODS
    154
  Prudence WOODS 80
  Samuel 80
  William H. 154
  William W. 80
KEEP
  Amanda FREEZE 107
  William W. 80
KEEPS
  Amada 98
  Jennie 98
KEETCH
  Alfred G. 69
  Ann GREENWOOD
    149
  Ann Mariah 149
  Charles G. 80
  Emma 128
  Maria 39
  Martha 69
  William K. 149
KEETON
  Georgianna O. YOUNG
    80
  John 80
  Sarah BUCKLE 80
  Thomas F. 80
KEEVENS
  Ann RINNELS 100
  Katie 100
  Patrick 100
KEGAN
  Ellen 154
  John 154
  Mary KALLARY 154
KEGLER
  A. Minna LEY 80
  Charles 80
  Emily 80
  Emily PARTAL 80
  Julius 80
KEHEW
  Lois 21
KEHL
  Henry 81
  Julianna
    HILDERBRANDT
    81
  Margaret MOORE 81
  William 81

KEIL
  Barbara 83
  Jesse F. 39
KEILSON
  Mary KRYASKOW 110
KEILY
  John 109
KEIN
  Ellen 93
KEIRCH
  Catharine 103
KEISER
  Catharine 113
KEITH
  Charles 7
  Elizabeth 7
  Hannah 170
  Harriet 99, 138
  Jane 7
  Nellie 68
KELCH
  Julia 79
KELKER
  Elanor RANDOLPH 49
  Louzelia 49
  Rudolph 49
KELLEHER
  Dennis M. 81
  Francis J. 101, 128
  Jane McGRATH 81
KELLER
  Katrine 109
  Martin 71
KELLEY
  ---- 99
  Abby 35
  Adah H. JOHNSON 81
  Amanda E. BUSEY 81
  Ane 164
  Ann 80
  Ann NOWIKY 39
  Anna 147
  Anna WELLS 81
  B. 143
  Catharine 139
  Catherine 122
  Edmund 48
  Elizabeth 44, 62, 107
  Elizabeth, Mrs. 167
  Ellen 16, 114, 159
  Emma C., Mrs. 96
  Emma J. 39
  Esther DUCE 81
  Frances 31
  Frances A. 129
  Frank M. 81
  H.B. 81
  Hanora 128
  Harriet BLANCHARD
    147
  Hedwig Mathilda
    WENNGREN 81
  Honora 16
  Honora GANEY 128
  Ingred NILSON 81
  J. Emmet 81
  J.E., Mrs. 9, 52, 85
  J.P., Capt. 47
  James 16, 63, 122, 147
  Jan Jansen E. 81
  Jane 170
  John 21, 81, 143
  John E. 38, 81
  John H. 81
  Kate 12
  Katharine FOLEY 81

Katie 63
  Lolan 81
  Lula J. 21
  Margaraet 67
  Margaret 56
  Maria CORCORAN 81
  Martin 114
  Mary 8, 12, 35, 99, 114,
    143
  Mary Agnes
    CAREFOOD 81
  Mary Ann DEALY 81
  Mary MITCHELL 81
  Mrs. 31
  Nappy 107
  Patrick 37, 39, 128, 167
  Purden 142
  R.H.N. 96
  S.A. 142
  Sarah 53, 96
  Sarah DUNHAM 21
  Sibby CANAN 122
  Susan 143
  Timothy 81
  Timothy, Mr. and Mrs.
    49
  W.T. 82
  William A. 81
  Wm. Albert 81
KELLIHAN
  Maggie 23
KELLNER
  B. 145
  Bernhard 81
  Charlotte FREEDMAN
    81
  Moritz 81
  Sone GLUCK 81
KELLOGG
  Abby BROWN 81
  C.W. 42
  Ermina A. 31
  Fannie 28
  Frances 31
  Henry 64, 81
  Henry, Mrs. 64
  Judge 34, 39
  Mrs. 31
  Permelia 43
  Roxana 166
  W.C. 4, 69
  Wm. 4
KELLOM
  Clara 117
  Clara Eliza 1
  Harriet N. NEWELL 1
  Harriette N. 34
  J.H. 47, 87, 162
  J.H., Mrs. 87, 117
  John H. 1, 28, 34, 44,
    53, 159
KELLOY
  Jane E. 76
KELLY
  Abbie 139
  Amanda, Mrs. 30
  Ann GALLAGHER 165
  Bridget WELSH 69
  Catharine 83
  Catherine 66
  Charles 79
  Colam 81
  Daniel 81
  E. 128
  Edmund 81
  Elizabeth 23, 153

KEYES, cont.
Clarence E. 82
David L. 121
Edward 82
Emily 15, 150
Eugenia 53, 98
Hariet L.
HUTCHINSON 82
Isabella, Mrs. 138
Jane 30
Jennie 163
Lucine PRATT 82
Rachel M. MOORE 82
Sarah TOOLE 82
Thomas 82
KEYLER
Julius 106
KEYNER
Susan 67
KEYS
Carrie E. 59
KEZARTEE
N.K., Miss 36
KHILLIAN
Mary 126
KIANDER
Alexander 82
August 82
Maria 82
Wilamina KUKLISS 82
KIDD
D.T. 105, 128
J.D. 84
KIDDER
Clarisa CHANDLER 97
Emma L. 97
Geo. F. 97
George C. 137
Jeannette 78
Merick E. 82
KIEBING
---- 44
Elvina 44
Elvira 44
Herman 44
Herman G. 44
Hermania 44
Louisa 44
KIEFF
Bridget 47
Mary FLINN 47
Patrick 47
KIEFFE
Bridget 114
KIER
Claus 82
Joanna NELSON 82
Mary THOMPSON 82
Nels 82
KIESER
Damin 129
KILE
F.W. 8
KILFEATHER
Catharine GALLAGHER
82
John 82
Mary HART 82
Michael 82
KILGALLON
Ellen 63
Ellen MURPHY 63
Michael 63
KILKENNEY
Ellen 13

KILKENNY
Catharine MURPHY 82
James 82
Mary GROGHAN 82
Patrick 82
KILKER
Augustus F. 82
Elizabeth REED 82
John B. 82
Willhelmina BASALER
82
KILL
Hannah HIT 82
Peter 82, 161
KILLANAN
Bridget TUEY 53
Jeremiah 53
Jerry 53
Mary 53
KILLDON
Elizabeth 96
KILLIAN
Mary 126
KILLINGSWORTH
O.P. 114
Will B.R. 3, 41, 57
Willie R.B. 117
Wm. B.R. 100
KILLMER
Ella 53
Jane KNOWLES 53
John 53
KILMER
Emma HODSON 82
John H. 82
KIMBALL
Caleb 74, 114
Eliza 114
Fanny NIXON 114
Francis NIXTON 74
Francis R. 69
James 72
Margaret 74
Mary M. 76, 169
Mary MOWBRAY 72
Mary P. ROGERS 69
Nancy 28
Rebecca 123
Richard 15
Sarah 72
T.L. 69
Thomas L. 69
KIMBERLAND
Amanda MERRYMAN
82
Daniel 82
Henry 82
Mary LUCAS 82
KIMMELL
M., Miss 14
KINCAID
Mary E. 44
Mr. 44
KIND
Martha 165
KINDLE
Caley 82
Carey 82
Carr W. 82
Narcissa COE 82
Rosa G. ROBERTS 82
KINDMAN
Anna 134
KINDRED
Francena 123
M.R. 123

KINEL
Mary L. 103
KINELLY
Elisabeth 6
KING
? 151
A.L. 57
Addie 148
Albert L. 82
Alice 100
Ann 43, 159
Ann O'NIEL 83
Aster EDWARDS 100
C.A., Mrs. 120
Carrie SHEETS 83
Chloa 65
Chr. C. 74
Christene 125
Clara 71
Elizabeth 77
Elizabeth RILEY 17
Elizabeth SMITH 83
Elizabeth, Mrs. 22
Elsie 57
Florence A. 123
Florence J. CARLTON
83
Frank M. 82
George 63
Gertrude CLARK 82
Gertrude L. CLARKE
57
Gilmore 101
H.C. 11
Hannah MURPHY 77
Hannah REGAN 83
Hattie 94
Helen M. WILSON 83
Ida L., Mrs. 101
Jacob 11, 22, 76, 82,
125, 167
James 83
Jeremiah 77
Jerry 83
John 83
Joseph 83
Katy 87
Lavina FATH 83
Liberty 83
Lulu 117
Malinda 14
Margaret CANAN 8
Margaret R. FORGEY
82
Maria SIMPKINS 83
Martin 8
Mary 17
Mary A. 29
Mary M. 57
Mary McMULLIN 57
Matthew 57
Mrs. 100
Owen 83
Peter 17
Phillip 83
Richard H. 83
S.C. 129
Sarah 8
Susie E. 14
Thomas 96
Virginia 83
W.H. 117
William B. 38
William H. 83
Wm. 100

KINGBEIL
Charles 61
Dora SCHULTER 61
Teresa 61
KINGHAM
Annie SKINNER 83
Elizabeth DONSE 83
George 83
George H. 83
KINGING
O. 80
KINGLY
Bridget 95
KINGMAN
Eugenia 158
KINGSBURRY
Calistia 6
KINGSBURY
Daniel 83
May J. LOBDILL 83
Nancy J. BATY 83
T.B. 83
KINGSHOT
Sarah 107
KINKADE
A.C. 27
KINKEL
Minnie A. LUTHER 92
KINLEN
Mary 156
KINNEAR
Hattie TURNER 83
James 83
Maggie V. 123
KINNECUT
Helen 74
John 74
KINNEY
Bridget FAHEY 83
Catharine 22
Francis H. 83
Jerome 83
John 119
Kate 169
Kate BURKHARD 169
Lucy NEWELL 83
Lucy PICKARD 83
M.T. 72
Margaret BROWN 119
Margaret CASEY 83
Martin 83
Michael 83, 139
Michael T. 83
Peter 169
R.D. 134
R.H., Prof. 63
Rosa 89, 169
Sarah K. 119
Stella BAILEY 83
T.D. 82
Thomas 83
KINNICUT
David 74
KINSELLA
Ida GRAVES 83
James 83
Margaret 83
P. 83
Winifred 80
KINSEY
J. 72
Lizzie 13
KINSLA
Winifred 80

KINTZ
Cecelia CONAGHAN
13
George 13
Lucinda J. 13
KIP
William 167
Wm. 163
KIP (KIPP)
G.J. 117
KIPP
William 86
KIRBY
Ann 68
Mary Ann 157
KIRCH
Matthew 58
Mr. and Mrs. 122
KIRCHAFLE
Alfred 154
KIRCHL
---- 10
KIRCLAHAN
Rose A. 39
KIRK
Ada A. 130
Bridget 68
James F. 23
Lucy F. LOCKWOOD
23, 130
Mary E. 23
Robert 130
Robert F. 23
Wm. H. 130
KIRKHART
Joseph 83
Joseph F. 83
Kate C. McKENNA 83
Mary DUFF 83
KIRKLAN
W.M. 65
KIRKLAND
Elizabeth J. 48
Elizabeth J.
McCLELLAND 48
John 48
Wm. M. 12
KIRKWOOD
Margaret 63
KIRLEY
Catharine CARR 83
Peter 83
KIRLIN
George 83
Mary McSWIGGEN 83
KIRNER
Ellis 83
Joseph 83
Mary C. JOHNSON 83
Mary R. CLECK 83
KIRTLEY
Luella ADAMS 21
KIRVANEK
Therese WILLIMOVA
42
KIRWAN
Bridget HEAVER 83
Edward 83
Katharine CALNA 83
KISCINE
Bridget 100
KISLIN
George 83
Mary McSWIGGEN 83
KISLINGBURY
Fred 49, 167

KOBARK
  Dorothea 23
  Henry 23
  Sophia SIEVERS 23
KOBARY
  Augusta 147
  Henry 147
  Mattie REIF 147
KOBERG
  Johanna 92
KOBS
  Albert 84, 112, 170
  Dority STEIK 9
  Hanna 112
  Henrietta LOBS 84
  Johanna 125
  Leopold 9, 84
  Matilda 9
  Mrs. 112
KOCH
  Adam 36
  Allen 8
  Caroline HARSTIG 84
  Johanna 130
  Lena RICHTER 84
  Ludwig 84
  Margaret 23
  Paul 84
KOCHEN
  Margaretha ROEHRIG
    84
  Mary EIFFLER 84
  Paskall 84
  Peter 84
KOCHLER
  Charles 84
  John W. 84
KOCK
  Paul 84
KODSA
  Anna 125
  Anna KESERA 125
  Joseph 125
KOEHLER
  Amelia 52
  Anna 95
  Caroline 169
  Gothelf 52
  Willhelmina KRUHER
    52
KOENIG
  Charles W. 84
  Franz 87
  Henry 163
  Henry A. 65
  Marie Elenore BECHER
    84
KOENLER
  Caroline 80
KOESTERS
  Doress SHOULSE 84
  Frank 109
  Henry 84
  Jos. 122
  Joseph 9, 69
  Magrata WAGMAN 84
KOFAN
  Mary C. 149
KOFKA
  John 21
  Katy 21
  Katy THREAD 21
KOHLER
  Caroline 43
  Johan 43

Louisa SODERQUIST
    43
KOHLMEHER
  Eva, Mrs. 129
KOHLMEIER
  Carl 51
  Eva 51
KOHLMEYER
  Charles 73, 95, 103,
    129, 158
  Chas. 135
  Eva 73, 103, 158
  Mr. 161
  Mrs. 161
KOHN
  Maria M. 121
KOHOUT
  Annie 151
  Annie HONLEH 84
  Annie NEIHOUSE 84
  John 74
  Joseph 84
  Wenzel 84
KOHREGER
  Amelia CIEPFORT 84
  Dora LORGE 84
  Dora SORGE 71
  Gustavus 84
  Henry 84
KOHUT
  Annie SELIGECK 84
  Annie
    TEHALSCHENCH
    84
  James 84
  John 84
KOILE
  Mary GADOLA 28
  Patrick 28
KOKER
  Sadie 156
KOKOLEES
  Wilhelmina 105
KOLAR
  Anna 123, 138
KOLBE
  Carl Heinrich 84
  Carolina KUNTZE 84
  Catharine AYE 84
  William 84
KOLHE
  Catharine 169
  Wm. 169
KOLLNAKER
  Mary 158
KOLLS
  Gustavis 84
  Gustavus 112
  Korotheas MOSS 84
  Matilda ROEDER 84
KOLN
  Karen 77
KOLP
  John 72
KONDELE
  Annie PESHIKOVA 84
  Frances VANOUS 84
  Frank 84, 143
  Martin 84
KONDILE
  Frank 74
KONES
  Barbara 85
KONIG
  Frederick 136
  John 136

KONNAGER
  America 14, 141
KONVALIN
  Barbara BJEHAUNEK
    84
  Frank 46, 84
  John 84
  Lizzie K. 84
KONVALLEN
  Barbara B. 84
  Frank 84
  John 84
  Lizzie K. 84
KONWALIN
  Barbara BELOWS 146
  Frank 146
  Louisa 146
KOON
  E.M. 38
  Sarah ---- 38
  Sarah M. 38
KOONS
  Ann TANLENSON 84
  Emma L. ALLOWAY
    84
  George B. 84
  William 84
KOOSER
  Eva 48
  Margarett 57
  William 48
KOPP
  Flora I. MOON 84
  Mary Jane 97
  Stephen A. 84
KOPPER
  Anna, Mrs. 52
  Michael 52
KOPPES
  Michael 29, 129, 137
  Michael, Mrs. 129
KOPPS
  Mary 29
KOPS
  Frederica 145
KORHOUT
  Annie HONLEH 84
  Annie NEIHOUSE 84
  Joseph 84
  Wenzel 84
KORKHOLM
  Maire 94
KORNES
  Annie E. 141
  Josephen 135
KORSGREN
  Annie DOLL 84
  Clara PETERSON 84
  Jacob 84
  Jacob William 84
KORTEL
  Margaret 167
KORTING
  Charles 88
  Maggie LANGE 88
  Mary 88
KOSCHEREK
  Barbara 80
KOSENICK
  Anna 13
KOSENTKI
  Anna 85
  Gustave 85
  Katharina KOSUTKA
    85

KOSTERS
  Charles M. 85
  Emma LEWIS 85
  H.A. 85
  Lizzie 65
  Margaret WOLL 85
KOSUTKA
  Katharina 85
KOTHE
  Elizabeth 163
KOTREC
  A. 128
  Barbia 128
KOTTERMAN
  Anna KANENBLEY 85
  Charles 85
  Wilhelmine KRUEGER
    85
  William 85
KOTTRAS
  Barney 85
  Henry 85
  Kate LEWON 85
  Mary ONIG 85
KOTYZA
  Alvoisia POSPISEL 85
  Franciska KYSELA 85
  Frank 85
KOUGH
  Catharine ENYEART
    85
  E. Estella BARR 85
  E. Estella, Mrs. 119
  Jacob 85
  Jose S. 119
  Joseph F. 85
KOUNTZ
  Augustus 116
  Herman 34, 145
KOUNTZE
  Augustus 88, 134
  Augustus, Mr. and Mrs.
    85
  Christian 116
  Elizabeth DAVIS 85
  Herman 85, 156
  Kate, Mrs. 88
  Margaret ZERBE 116
  Mary D. 7
  Mary D. 116
KOUSKI
  Margaret O'BRIEN 85
  Maximillian Marcin 85
KOUTCERA
  Anton 85
  Fanny BARET 85
  Fred. 85
  Maggie LASCHANSKY
    85
KOUTNICK
  Antonia SVANDOVA
    85
  Frank 85
  Matias 85
  Victoria PENKOS 85
KOVANDA
  Anna SPIMVATSCKY
    65
  Joseph 65
  Mary 65
KOVAR
  Mary 63
KOVARIK
  Wenceslaus 74
KOWISKA
  Katie 112

KOZIC
  Joseph 96
KOZICH
  Joseph 96
KOZINEK
  Anna 13
KRAAK
  Elizabeth 16
KRACHT
  Sophie 138
KRACKE
  Elenore 138
KRAEMER
  Clara 65
KRAFFT
  Katharine 169
KRAFT
  Levi 56
KRAGCEKE
  Frank 74
KRAGSKOW
  Caroline KNUDSON 85
  Christine M. NELSON
    85
  Christine Maria
    NELSON 77
  Joseph 61
  Joseph S. 85
  Peter C. 85
  Peter C.S. 77
  Peter S.C. 77
  Sine Nicoline 77
KRAIL
  Caroline SYTHZ 85
  Drederick 85
  Fredrica
    KNOLL-MILLER 85
  William 85, 91
KRAJCIK
  Mary 151
KRAMARIC
  Anna KOSENTKI 85
  Barbara PETRIK 85
  Joseph 85
  Mattheas 85
KRAMBECK
  Christine KUEHL 85
  Claus F. 85
  Detlef 85
  Katharine A. 85
KRAMER
  Antje LEBBERT 116
  Baldac 85
  Catharine SCHITE 85
  Clara 83
  Claus 85
  Hannah LEBBERT 85
  Kate KLINE 85
  Peter 85
KRANK
  Augusta RUESS 85
  Fanny ROSS 85
  James 85
  John 85
KRAPEL
  James 75
KRASI
  Theresia 103
KRATKY
  F.V. 138
KRATOCHVIL
  Cady BARTOS 74
  Mary 74
  Wencel 74

KULGHER
D. 105
KULIK
Anna 163
KULP
Mary Ann 67
KUMP
Frederick 49
KUMPF
Frederick 33, 80, 83, 86
Kate E. ROHWER 86
Magdalena SCHULL 86
Michael 86
KUMPS
Mary 41
KUNAS
Christina CRISTINSIN
156
Louisa 156
Peter 156
KUNASH
Barbara SHAVLIK 84
Joseph 84
Lizzie 84
KUNCL
Matilda M. 168
KUNDE
August 86
Caroline LOSCH 86
Frederike L. KRELLE
86
Herman 86
KUNE
August 57
Harriett A. 57
KUNES
Barbara SHAVLIK 84
Barbara SMITH 129
Joseph 84
Katharine 65
Lizzie 84
KUNKL
Charles 51, 74
Mary FOUSEK 51
KUNTZE
Carolina 84
KUONIG
John B. 86
KUONY
Agatha SCHEIBEL 86
Christina MEHRING 86
Eugene 86
John 86
KUPPIG
Adeline MUHS 86
Caroline AUST 9
Caroline SCHULTZE
86
Charles 9
Edward 5, 86
Gottlieb 86
Pauline 9
KURE
Josephine 92
KURT
Anna C. 49
KURTZ
Catharine 14
M.A. 3
Mark 137
KUTCH
Charles G. 80
KUTELEK
Anna DEBELKA 86
Anna POLALECAK 86
Mike 86

KYELSBERG
Nils NILSON 97
KYLE
Benjamin 6
Charles 53
Clara 6
Clara BRADFORD 6
KYON
Adaline 9
Mary GUBRON 9
Michael 9
KYRESTON
Mary 56
KYSELA
Franciska 85
LA CHAFRELLE
D.C. 87
LA FOLLETT
Anna B. 94
C., Mrs. 94
LA FOLLETTE
Clarissa, Mrs. 49
LA TARUUETTEE
Mary 69
LABADIE
Ellen 119
LABAREE
Eliza 90
LABAUGH
Mary Ann 8, 12
LABBEDEE
Martha 15
LABS
Caroline 125
Ferdinand 125
Henriette KLABUNDE
125
Joh. 125
Johann 170
LACEY
Cordelia A. 107
J.H. 7, 145
James T. 87
Jesse 99
Jesse H, 153
Martha F. FINLAY 87
May RICE 87
Mr. 135
Thomas M. 87
LaCHAPELLE
Alexander 87
Angelique
BEAUSOLIEL 87
Charles 87
Egeligne
BANSOHELLE 87
Enseba 87
Eusedi 87
Hannah F. NIEDIECK
87
Leonore CHARTIER 87
LACHNER
Joseph 87
Polly Ann PUTNAM 87
Thana COBURN 145
William 87
LACHRER
Elizabeth EGGER 87
Ferdinand 87
John 87
Mina VOGT 87
LACHSE?
Bernhard 98
LACKERMAN
Henry W. 87
Lottie GLOVER 87

LACY
Ellen 13
H.T. 29
Mary 101, 106
LADD
Jno. A. 124
LADISCH
Theresa 135
LAFATRE
Susan F. 82
LAFEIN
Margaret 108
LAFERDY
John 10
LaFERRE
Nancy 33
LAFERTY
Catharine 164
·LaFESSE
Nancy 33
LAFETRE
Asher 168
Elizabeth 168
Susan F. 168
LAFFER
Elizabeth BOYD 87
H.B. 87
John 87
Susan MORGAN 87
LAFFERTY
Alzina 42
Elizabeth A. 155
James 155
Margaret 30
Mary A. ERWIN 155
LAFFIN
Ann FRANKLIN 28
Mary 28
Patrick 28
LAFFING
Bridget 108
LaFOLLETTE
Clarissa, Mrs. 7, 142
LaFOND
Harry 51
Mary, Mrs. 33, 86
LAFSTROM
Aug. 11
LAGE
Antje HUSEN 87
Celia 87
Henrik 87
Henry 127
Jennie HOVEY 87
Karen JOHANNSON 87
Maria JOHANNSON 87
P.R. 87
Peter 87
Peter Rasmus 87
Rasmus 87
Rasmuss 87
LAGEMAN
Wm. 93
LAGER
Anna 10
Elizabeth 55
Hedwig A. 89
LAGERGREN
J.T. 96
LAGERQUIST
John A. 146
LAGERSTROM
Petronella 153
Petronella V. 65
Petronelle 76
Wilhelmina P. 88

LAGGE
Celia 90
Eggert 90
Kate STOLLENBERG
90
LAGKJER
Carin 75
LAHAL
Chrine 166
LAHANAHA
Joseph 129
LAHNAN
Christina 70
LAIBLE
Emilie ELSASSER 87
George 87
Leonard 87
Margaret UNSELT 87
Mary UNSELT 87
LAING
Lena F. 100
R. 57, 100
Robert 35, 63
LAIRD
Amanda SAFFEL 47
Annie M. 47
J.A. 47
Mary Z. 14
LAKE
Abbie G. HAYS 87
Ann Eliza H. 31
Carrie J. 108
Geo. 20
Geo. B., Hon. 7
George B. 87, 108
Jane POPPLETON 108
LAKIN
Charles 87
James 87
Maria WHITEHEAD 87
Sarah BRINDLEY 87
LAKINS
Rachel 71
LALON
George 58
LAMANN
Amelia 136
Amelia MILLER 136
Fred 136
LAMASTER
H. 95
LAMB
Abel 88
Andrew 87
Charles W. 87
Eliza 88
Elizabeth 52
Elizabeth STRUTT 87
Katy KING 87
Lizzie EVANS 88
Lucrecie L. 31
Quirene 87
Rachel 107
Susie 160
LAMBERT
M.F. 71
Mary J. 71
Rebecca WALKEY 71
LAMM
Charles L. 87
Johanna STICH 87
Peter 87
Scholestick SECHMEN
87
LAMMERSDORF
Charles 20, 136, 143

LAMMERTSEN
Rikja 159
LaMONTAINE
Israel 87
John 87
Katie LESTER 87
Laura FULTON 87
LaMOTT
Alfred 11
Alice 11
Franklin SMITH 11
LAMOTTE
Caroline SLITTER 87
Frederick 87
Herman 87
Lena EFFERS 87
LAMP
Celia LAGE 87
Grete 80
Hans A. 87
Henry 54, 87
Lena 54
Margaret
SUVERKRUBBE 87
Sarah 44
Silke 142
LAMPHER
George 87
Lucia LANNING 87
LAMPHIRE
Esther WATKINS 22
Joshua M.E. 22
Mary A. 22
LAMPKIN
Jane 26
LAMPLEIGH
Quinby 87
Thomas 87
LAMPLUGH
Jane Hedden 91
John 91
Margaret WALKER 87
Martha DAY 87
Quinby 87
Thomas 87
LAMPRECHT
Dora 13, 98
Dorothea 13
Dorotheas 98
Fred 13, 98
Frederick 13, 98
Fredericka 13
Mary 98
LAMSON
Louise 161
LANAGAN
Catharine 18
LANAGARN
Catharine 77
LANCASTER
Mr. 28
LANCE
Catharine 109
Jacob 109
Mary WHEELER 109
LAND
Anna 57
Charles R. 87
Charlotte SMITH 87
Priscilla SIMS 87
Wm. P. 87
LANDECKER
Annie SMITH 87
Clay 87
Lawrence 87
Malinea SLAGO 87

LANDEN
J. 117
Maria 117
LANDER
Mary Ann 31
LANDERS
W.O. 101
LANDIN
Johanna 61
LANDON
Amanda VOGAL 67
Calvin 67
Caroline J. 67
Cynthias PIERCE 87
Elizabeth P. WATKINS 87
Luther 87
Maggie LEONARD 146
Milton A. 87
LANDROCK
Carl G. 87
Charles 87
Marion M. PAGE 87
Willmina EICHNER 87
LANDTAN
Lena 96
LANE
Betsy 55
Dennis D. 87
Dennis W. 87
Emeline 119
Emly 60
Jefferson 87
Jennie P. MORAN 87
Margaret M. HOLDER 87
Mary C. YOUNG 87
Mary E. McDEVITT 87
T.J. 166
Thomas J. 87
LANEBERT
Agnes RITTMAN 91
Frederick J. 91
LANER
Bridget FOLEY 88
Henry 157
Isaac 88
Leonard 88
LANERY
Margareta 109
Thomas 109
LANEY
Gospel 158
LANFER
Annie 137
LANG
Catherine 29
Chas., Mrs. 139
Emma R. 109
Francis 34
Fredericke 134
John 109
Mary WILEY 88
William 88
LANGDON
Anthony J. 88
Catharine THOMAS 88
Catherine THOMAS 88
Francis G. HERRON 88
Jane 38
John J. 88
Margaret E. HERON 88
Martin 88
Michael 38
P.J. 88
Patrick 88

LANGE
A.T. 19
Anne KITCEHGEL 88
August 88
B. 160
Emilie KNAPPE 88
Frederick 88
Gottlieb 88
Maggie 88
Mary KORTING 88
Otto 88
Wilhelmine HODEN 88
LANGHOFF
Freddie 44
Freddie WOLF 44
John 44
LANGLEY
Jane 89
LANGLOTZ
Frederica 159
H. 159
LANGON
Catherine GRADY 150
James 150
Mary 150
LANGRAN
Charlotte 64
LANGSTAFF
Sarah A. HEWIT 159
LANGUILLETTE
Fredericka de 138
LANIRSEN
Anna 75
LANKILDE
Mary 132
LANNING
Lucia 87
LANNSBERRY
Daniel W. 98
Emeline WOOD 98
Mary E. 98
LANPHER
Alonzo H. 88
Anna 75
Malinda POST 88
Mattie J. MARTIN 88
Orrin 88
LANPHERE
A.H. 78, 141
LANSENT
Henry 88
Margaret SLEMMER 88
LANSER
Peder 79
LANSING
Catharine O. GIBSON 88
Charles M. 88
Cornelius 88
Eliza GOODHUE 88
Eliza LAMB 88
Eliza M. ROGERS 88
Henry L. 88
Jno. B. 88
LANSON
Anna Marine 74
Nelson S. 74
LAPASH
Frederick 165
LaPOINT
Clara 129
LAPORT
Mary, Mrs. 128
LaPORTE
Exilda 135

LAPRE
Brigite 87
LAPTIN
D.M. ROHRBERG 66
J.P. 66
Sophia A.W. 66
LARAWAY
Adah HUNT 88
Peter B. 88
Susannah STARLINE 88
William F. 88
LARGE
Caroline, Mrs. 83
R. 10
Sarah 10
LARGEN
Elizabeth 135
LARGERQUIST
John A. 146
LARGEY
P.A. 106
LARIMUR
J. Frank 96
LARISON
Estella 62
LARK
S.H.H., Mrs. 35
LARKIN
Adelia B. McMILLEN 65
Anna M. McDONALD 96
Cassie Ray 65
Danford S. 88
Danforth 88
Mary A. 113
Melissa REED 88
Phelina 126
William 65
LARKINS
Catharine M. 110
Elizabeth GOVELIE 110
James 110
LARNED
James 64
LaROCHE
Charles 88
Mary J. GRAHAM 88
Robert 88
Rosalie V. DAVIER 88
LAROCK
Saloma 104
LAROSCHEL
Marie M. 134
LARRISON
Rachel 162
LARS
Benta 117
Gunhilda JANSDOTTER 65
Kari 117
Nelson 65
LARSDATER
Anne 26
LARSDATTER
Anna 26
LARSDOTTER
Anna 88
Inger 4
Johanna 97
LARSEN
Abraham 88
Ane 4

Ann M. RASMUSSEN 88
Anna 122
Anna C. 84
Anna Katharina PETERSON 97
Anthan C. 89
Caren 61
Christian 4
Christina 127
Christine CHRISTENSEN 88
Eliza FECH 88
Ellen 116, 127
Elsi Matine Frederika JENSEN 88
Emma 88
Engrid 151
Erik 88
Hannah 94
Hans 88
Helena 84
Hillia C. HOLM 88
Ingeborg JOHNSON 126
J. 87
Johanna 146
John Peter 88
Karen HANSEN 62
Lars 122
Louise CARLSON 88
Maria A. 61
Mary 3
Mathias 97
Morten 62
N.C. 88
Nils 88
Nils J. 113
Ole 126
P. 1
Sarah 152
Sophia CHRISTENSEN 88
Soren 89, 122
LARSON
A.M. 58
Abraham 88
Allthea E. GRANATH 89
Anders 4, 41
Andreas 152
Andrew G. 88
Anna 121
Anna BEHRENS 88
Anna Christina BENSON 88
Anna E. HENRICKSON 89
Anna Katrina 79
Anna L. NELSON 89
Anna OLSON 89
Anne 25
Annie 78, 117, 127
Annie JOHNSON 89
Annie PALSEN 88
Anny 76
Anton 88
August 4, 76, 88, 152
Axel 88
Becca 50
Becca ANDERSON 50
Bert GENSEN 122
Betty Christiana 61
Botilda 153
C.T. 11
Cagsa 11

Carolina 11
Caroline JOHNSON 88
Carrie 155
Carry NELSON 111
Catharine CARLSON 89
Catherine PETERSON 123
Cathrina SCHAFFLED 88
Charla S. 153
Chr. 117
Christena ANDERSON 3
Christian 88
Christian Peter 88
Christina 88
Christine 76, 153
Christopher 26
Dorothea 62, 127
Dorothia M. 104
Elizabeth AMMUNDSEN 89
Ella 130
Elna 164
Elna SVENSDOTTER 89
Else Christina JENSEN 89
Emma 161
Eric M. 76
Gurtie 38
Hannah JOHNSON 32
Hans 4, 43
Inger 76
Jacob 89
Jennie 65
Joanna 116
Johan F. 89
Johann JOHNSON 88
Johanna C. 65, 88, 116
Johanna C., Mrs. 2, 4, 15, 25, 60, 92, 135
Johanna. Mrs. 11
Johanna, Mrs. 135
John 4, 89, 116
Jossie 50
Karen 79
Karen ANDERSON 89
Karen M. 62
L.P. 89, 122
Lars 32, 50, 88, 116, 127, 134
Lars C. 89
Laurine M. 3
Lawrence 89
Lena SWENSON 41
Lewis 111
Lina C. PETERSON 135
Lizzie GADERBURG 89
Louis P. 89
Louisa 32
M.A. 33
Mads 89
Magt 113
Maren JORGENSON 4
Margaret 111
Maria 75
Marian 38
Marie NIELSEN 1
Marion Christina RASMUSSEN 89
Marren 26
Marren LARSON 26

LARSON, cont.
Marten 89
Martha ANDERSON
134
Martha C. 114
Mary 26, 116, 121, 155
Mary B., Mrs. 2
Mary CHRISTIANSEN
89
Mary JACOBSEN 116
Mary JOHNSON 89
Mary M. 117
Mathias 3
Matilda, Mrs. 4
Mena 50
Metty CHRISTIANSON
89
Michael 123
Minna 50
Minnie 5
Miristina MAGNUSSON
152
N. 157
Neils 4
Nels 76, 89, 111
Nelson 89
Nils 58, 88, 161
O. 72
Olean 42
Oliver 89
Peder 1
Pernila SWANSON 4
Peter 61, 89, 122, 135,
153
Peter Jensen 89
Rachel 7
S.J. 42, 121, 133
Sarah E. 53
Simon 89
Sina B. BROWN 89
Sophia C. JENSEN 88
Sophia, Mrs. 159
Stina 11, 43
Tilda 3
Turner 89
Velbor 77
Wilhelmina P.
LAGERSTROM 88
LARSSON
Peter 145
Sophia 115
LARY
Casper 83
LASBY
Essie RYAN 89
William 89
LASCHANSKY
Annie LANFER 137
August 85, 137
Catharine LEMPFER 85
Maggie 85
Maria 137
LaSEUR
Amasa 89
Pauline 89
Sarah HENDRICKSON
89
William 89
LASHANSKY
Angus 75
Anna 75
Anna LANPHER 75
LASHER
Catharine C. 54
LASKE
Hedwig 66

LASKI
Mr and Mrs. 66
LASSER
Amelia JOSEPH 36
Caroline 36
Jacob 36
LAST
Annie 129
LATEY
Henry 40
Henry L. 89
Henry, Mrs. 137
Jane 40
Jane WARREN 40, 89
Jennie 58
Mary E. SPOOR 89
Thomas H. 40, 89
Thomas, Mrs. 137
LATHAM
Sarah A. 115
LATHAN
Lizzy 80
LATHROP
Annie E. LECKENBY
89
Clara FOLBRE 89
Louis S. 89
N. 89
LATHRUM
Lucinda 49
LATTA
Louis 145
Mary J. 145
Rebecca SWINNEY 145
LATTON
Isabella 54
LATY
Carrie 139
H. 139
Henry, Mrs. 90
T., Mr. and Mrs. 139
LAUB
Anna Maria GRAVE 25
Philip 25
LAUBAUCH
H.M. 6
LAUGHLIN
Frankie 58
John C. 58
Olive Hannah THORN
58
Sarah A. 27
LAUMAN
Isabel 110
James 110
Reuben 110
Sally SUMNER 110
LAUNDAUER
Max 50
LAUNDRIGAN
Julia 54
LAURANCE
Louis 14
Sarah 14
Stena 14
LAURENCE
Silvia 159
LAURENT
Henry 93
LAURSEN
Anna 106
Mette 43
LAUSAN
Eliza 73
LAVELL
Sarah 164

LAVILLE
Bridget COLEMAN 148
Ella 148
Patrick 148
LAVINE
Cecelia 107
Isaac 107
LAVTEN
Christian 24
LAW
Daisy A. BURNS 89
Dr. 50
Eliza A. MILLINGTON
89
Franklin M. 89
Harriet 33
Joseph F. 89
LAWE
Antonie 85
Bernhardt 85
LAWLER
Anna 23
David 23
Mary 54
Mary HENNISEY 23
William H. 153
LAWLESS
James 165
LAWLEY
Hannah 24
LAWLOR
Annie 105
LAWN
Anna 95
LAWON
Eliza 92
LAWRANCE
George A. 89
Ida B. SHULL 89
Jane P. BLODGETT 89
Orrin 89
LAWRENCE
Dorthula CAMPBELL
153
E. 153
Fannie RUNYON 133
Kate M. SHULL 89
L., Mr. and Mrs. 36
Luch A. 153
R.E. 101
William 89
LAWS
Elizabeth FRY 89
John 89
L.T. BIRDSLEY 89
M. 89
LAWSON
A.G. 76
Albertha 1
Andrew 89
Anna 76
Augustus D. 89
Bengta 89
Brita ANDERSON 133
C.I. 132
Carna KNAPP 123
Carrie L. 116
Emeline 76
F.M. 97
H.B. 89
Helen 123
J.E. 89
Jens 133
John 123
John D. 89
Louisa 32

Lucius C. 89
Margaretha 89
Maria STEWART 89
Marion BAUDEN 89
Martin 89
Mary
FRIEDERIECHSON
111
Mathilda LINDBERG
89
Nels 111
Nettie NELSON 89
Nils 116
Paruna KNAPP 89
Sophia 125
Stena 76
Zelda FOSTER 89
LAWTON
Margaret 154
Mr. and Mrs. 48
W.H. 108
William 138
William H. 44
LAYET
Anna KITZENGER 89
Hortense
BEAUREGAURD 89
John E. 89
Paul E. 60, 89
LAYTON
C.D. 89, 131, 156
Frank 89
Maria PIKARD 89
Mary CONWAY 89
LEACH
Alice 11
Edward 130
Elizabeth 31
Harriet 13
Jane LEAKE 96
Martha 130
Mary Ann KEY 130
Mary E. 57
Mary J. 96
Samuel C. 96
Susan EDWARDS 101
LEADBETTER
Elizabeth 53
LEADER
Louis 144
LEADMAN
John 51
Mary DANIELS 51
Minnie 51
LEAHEY
Anna 107
Michael 107
LEAHY
Daniel 24
Ellen GAVEN 24
Mary 24
LEAKE
Jane 96
LEAKY
Michael 81
LEAM
Mary 23
LEARNED
Elvira M. 153
Mr. 68, 90
Mr. and Mrs. 68
Mrs. 90
LEARY
Ann SULLIVAN 90
Cornelius A. 89
Dennis 89, 90

Elizabeth 30
Ellen COTTER 90
Ellen CUTTER 90
Ellen McCARTY 37
Hannah 24
James 89, 90
Jennie M.
SHELLINGLORE 90
Jeremiah 90
Johanah MONDABLE
24
Johanna MANDEVILLE
90
Julia 29
Kate GRAPHOFF 90
Louisa BURKLEY 89
Margaret LINAHAN 90
Martin 90
Mary Ann 90
Mary CARDIN 89
Mary DUFFY 90
Mary MAHONEY 89
Mary MORAN 90
Mary MORRISEY 90
Michael 90
Mike 51
Nellie COTTER 89
P.H. 90
Patrick 24, 89, 90
Patrick H. 90
LEASE
Eliza BURNHAM 90
Gracie JOHNSON 90
Henry 90
R.W. 90
LEAVETT
Mary 92
LEAVITT
Florence N.
BUCHANAN 90
H.F. 90
H.T. 50, 168
Hannah WATERHOUSE
90
Herbert T. 66
M.B. 143
Thomas 90
LEBBERT
Anna E. OFT 85
Anna OFT 90, 116
Antje 116
Hannah 85
Hans 90, 116
Henriette KAISER 90
Johan 116
John J. 85
John Jacob 90
LEBENSKA
Josephine 112
LEBERDEE
Angeline BAUPUM 18
Michael 18
LEBMANN
Dorothea 134
LeBOURVEAN
Anna CARTER 90
Benjamin 90
Eliza LABAREE 90
LECKENBY
Addie 115
Annie E. 89
James 89, 115
Margaret BOYD 89
Margaret CLINTON
115

LEDEN
  Augusta ANDERSON 90
  Catharine ANDERSON 90
  Olaf 90
  Peter 90
LEDER
  Barbara 8
LEDERER
  Anna SLANINA 138
  Barbara 138
  Joseph 138
LEDR
  Barbara 118
LeDUC
  Mathilde 102
LEE
  Alice HOCANSON 90
  Alice OAKSON 7
  Alice, Mrs. 55
  Catharine MARIETTE 90
  Catherine MORIETTA 47
  Eliza M. NELSON 65
  F. Georgiana 38
  Hannah Jane 21
  Harry 90
  Ichabod 90
  Ira 170
  John 14, 15, 170
  John A. 90
  John G. 102
  Lillie 65
  Lonzo 90
  Margaret MANNAGAN 102
  Mary 15
  Mary A. SMITH 170
  Mary E. 47, 93
  Mary M. 102
  Michael 72
  Mrs. 22
  Nathan 47
  Nora 38
  Peter M. 90
  Phoebe E. CLOUGHS 90
  Rosa HOVEY 90
  Ruth PARKS 15
  Sadie M. 170
  Sarah J. CRAVEN 90
  Simon 21
  Warren F. 65
LEECH
  Jane 93
LEEDER
  Augustus 90
  Caroline BLEIDOM 90
  Caroline KLEEDUM 90
  Caroline PLEDUING 90
  Catharine BYERS 90
  Charles 90
  Christine CHRISTY 90
  Edward 90
  Elizabeth SMITH 90
  Henry 90
  Louis 90
  Thomas 90
LEEDS
  L.C. 159
LEEHY
  Bridget GRIFFIN 90
  Margaret CANNIS 90
  Morris 90

LEEKOTTER
  Mary MULHED 138
  William 138
LEEMAN
  Belle MEEKER 90
  John 90
  Minnie A. JOHNSON 90
  W.H. 90
LEEN
  Kate 165
LEEPER
  Chastina 168
LEFEVRE
  Hamilton 90
  Hamilton, Jr. 90
  Mary L. GREEN 90
  Sarah Jane STREETT 90
LEFFERT
  Frank 90, 108
  Frank, Mr. and Mrs. 108
  Herman, Mrs. 108
  Sophie HERMAN 90
LEFFINGWELL
  Andrew 28
  Fannie KELLOGG 28
  Harriet 28
LEFFLER
  Anna E. FEST 148
  August 148
  Wilhelmina H. 148
LEFHOLZ
  Fried 75
LeGEE
  A. 78
  A., Miss 78
LEGER
  Dorothea WANSCHEIDT 90
  Edward 90
  George 90
  Margaret IVERS 90
LEGRO
  Albina 165
  Henry 165
LEGROS
  Frank 90
  Josephine St. CLAIR 90
LEHER
  Katharine 56
LEHEY
  Daniel 90
  Ellen DRISCOL 90
  Honora GARVEN 90
  Mary 30, 90
  Michael 89, 90
LEHIGH
  Anna 101
  Annie 15
  Jane DACK 101
  John 101
LEHMAN
  Bertha 160
  Catharine ARP 160
  Celia LAGGE 90
  Henrietta 83
  Kate ARP 90
  Peter 90, 160
  William 90
LEHMANN
  Catharine ARP 90
  Catharine GROTMACK 90
  Catherine ARP 90
  Charles 160

Dora DUNKER 90
  Henry 55, 90
  John 90
  John C. 90
  Katharina ARP 160
  Peter 90, 160
  Wilhelmina 160
LEHMER
  Elizabeth STOKES 30, 108
  Emma R. 108
  F. 148
  Frank 28
  Frank L. 10
  G.F. 108
  George F. 30
  Joseph 95
  Laura J. 30
  William 30, 108
  Wm. 108
LEHNER
  Anna 135
LEHNERT
  Karolina 146
  Karolina PATSCH 146
  Leopold 146
LEHR
  Annie JETTER 90
  Barbara PRUISEN 90
  William 90
  Wm. 90
LEIBER
  Christina 119
LEIBERT
  John 90
LEIDY
  Elizabeth 144
  H. WYNCKOOP 165
  Hattie 165
  Samuel 165
LEIFFE
  Will 135
LEIGH
  Alice, Mrs. 146
LEIHGEBER
  Christine 35
LEIMBERT
  Agnes RITTMAN 91
  Frederick J. 91
  John E. 91
  Mary RASMUSSEN 91
LEIN
  Catharine VAUGHN 91
  James F. 91
LEINHAN
  Ellen DORE 43
  Nora 43
  Patrick 43
LEION
  Gustavus 24
  Henry 100
  Lena ANDERSON 24
  Louisa A. 24
  Rachel C. 100
  Sarah WILTZ 100
LEISGE
  Bertha BLOTZ 91
  Conrad 26, 37, 91
  Helena 26
  Henry 91
  Mary BLAAK 91
  Mary PLAACK 26
LEIST
  Caroline 10
LEITH
  Catharine 152

LELAND
  Elizabeth HILL 117
  George 117
  Mary 117
LEMING
  Anna POTTER 91
  C.C. 91
  Florence 118
  H.L. 91
  L.T. 91
  Mary T. MILLER 91
LEMKE
  John 5, 91, 160
  Margaret AIE 91
LEMME
  Anne 128
  Charles 91, 128
  Frederick 91
  Maria LUEHR 91
  Wilhelmina HAHN 91
LEMMEL
  George 5
  Katharine 5
LEMMER
  Mary 128
LEMON
  Christina M.D. BEITZEL 91
  Elizabeth PICKELS 91
  Frederick 91
  Henry 91
  John R. 91
  Loa 2
  M.B., Mrs. 72, 121
  Magdalena DECKMAN 91
  Margaret B., Mrs. 34
  Mr. 79
  Mr. and Mrs. 153
  Mrs. 79
  Nancy ROBINSON 91
  Samuel 91
  T.B., Jr. 45, 68
  T.B., Mrs. 70
  T.B.W. 21
  Thomas B., Rev. 50
  William 91
LEMONIES
  J.C. 138
LEMPFER
  Catharine 85
LEMPKE
  John 132
LEMSDOTTER
  Agnethe 25
LENAN
  Ellen 109
  Patrick 109
LENBURG
  Lena 25
LENDAIMER
  Jacob 91
  Mary HOFFMAN 91
LENDQUEST
  Anna PETERSON 91
  Olof 91
LENEHAN
  Michl. 115
LENIHAN
  Margaret 33
  Margaret FITZGERALD 91
  Thomas 91, 109
LENKOSE
  Wilhelmina 79

LENNEN
  Ellen 21
LENNING
  H. 118
LENSEN
  Christina 104
LENTELL
  J.V. 91
  Junius V. 91
  Louisa BURROUGHS 91
  Thaiza WILLIAMS 91
LENTS
  Lotte 94
LENZ
  Max 56
  Susannah 161
LEONARD
  Ann HICKEY 91
  Annie 69
  Annie McDONOUGH 69
  Bridget CARPENTER 91
  Ellen 170
  Esther CANNELL 91
  James 91
  John 69, 91
  Maggie 146
  Mary A. 91
  Mary BRENNING 146
  Mary CANNER 91
  Mary MADIGAN 27
  Patrick 91
  Peter 91
  Thomas 146
  William 91
LEOPOLD
  Anna 148
  Mary 148
LEPHOLZ
  Fred 92
LEPPEN
  Amelia DI ZRINY 91
  Harriet C. KRAUSE 91
  Joseph A. 91
LEPPER
  Ersiala HUME 91
  Helen E. HEYDE 91
  Henry G. 91
  William 91
LERCH
  Annie KRENEK 91
  Gustav 91
  Henrietta UTECH 91
  John 91
LERCHES
  Emelia 100
LERCHNER
  Augusta 95
  Justine 10
  Lina WESTPHAL 10
LERNED
  Elsie KENDALL 91
  Etta E. STOOKAY 91
  Frederick T. 91
  Thos. P. 91
LEROTH
  Augusta 86
LERWILL
  Betsey 157
LESCHANSKY
  Annie LANFER 137
  August 137
  Maria 137

LESIEND
  Louis 102
LESIR
  Bertha J. 26
LESKE
  Johanna C.W. 125
LESLEY
  Mary JARVIS 142
  Nancy E. 142
  Nicholas 142
LESLIE
  Margaret STURROCK
    58
  Nellie 58
  Peter 58
LESSENTIN
  Albertine DUMMER 91
  Ernst 91
LESSENTINE
  Frederick W. 91
  Jane Hedden
    LAMPLUGH 91
LESSMAN
  Charles 138
  Mary B. KREEN 138
LESSMANN
  Christ 68
  Emma 68
LESTER
  Alice 101
  George 101
  J.A. 123
  James 105
  Katie 87
  Martha CROCKETT
    101
  Mary 52
  Rebecca 87
  William 87
LESURE
  Margarett Ann 170
  N. 170
LETEL
  John 91
LETNER
  Emma E. 69
  John R. 33
  Lewis 33
  Lozania 33
  Rirama ADAMS 33
LETZIR
  Caroline 6
LEUCHS
  Mary 56
LEURS
  Henry 16
LEUTSCHER
  Bernerd 91
  Bouwdwina
    OSTERBANN 91
  Ida Matilda ANDERSEN
    91
  Jacob B. 91
LEVON
  Fritz 120
LEVY
  David 91
  Esther BEHRENDT 91
  M.H. 91
  Margaret WELLS 91
  Priscilla 10
LEWAN
  Fred 75
LEWARK
  John 91
  Lusetta 91

LEWCUS
  Eliza 155
  Y.R. 155
LEWELLEN
  Myra May 54
LEWELLYN
  Mary 13
LEWIN
  Eliza 166
  Eliza L. 17
  Gracia CRAIN 91
  Mabel 135
  Maria EUBANKS 91
  Nancy Elizabeth 145
  Washington 91, 145
LEWIS
  Abbie M., Mrs. 139
  Alfred 162
  Allen 91
  Ann PITMAN 91
  Anna Maria HAWKINS
    123
  Belle REICHARD 92
  C. 120
  Caroline CNARR 91
  Catharine 1
  Charity TURNER 91
  Cornelius 92
  Cynthe 119
  E. 155
  E.D., Mr. and Mrs. 163
  Eldora A. 150
  Elizabeth 105, 127
  Emlen 35, 127, 139, 170
  Emlin 34
  Emma 43, 85
  Enlen 75
  Ernest P. 145
  F. Stanton 8
  Hattie A. 82
  Hellen MEEKER 92
  J.F. 91
  J.R. 85
  James 91
  James H. 91
  John 91, 119, 162
  John, Mrs. 76
  Joseph 91
  Josephine KALER 150
  Lauretta 30
  Lizzie A. POTTER 91
  Lucinda 140
  Mahala SIMON 91
  Margaret GRAHAM 85
  Mary A. LEONARD 91
  Mr. 158
  Nellie 163
  Richard 92
  Samuel 91
  Sarah A. EDWARDS 91
  Sarah E. 8
  Sarah NEWBERRY 92
  Shelton 150
  Susan 35
  Walter 92
  Washington 34
LEWLESS
  Maria 33
LEWNWALL
  Andrew 32
  Johannah 32
  Rebecca 32
LEWON
  Elsabeth OTTE 92
  Fred 110
  Frederick 92

Henry 92
  John 85
  Magdalena ECKMANN
    92
  Wilhelm 92
  William 126
LEWORTHY
  Ann 96
LEWUHO
  Hannah 23
LEY
  A. Minna 80
  Anna GEHAL 92
  Anna Maria EMONS 92
  Caroline KOEHLER
    169
  Caroline KOENLER 80
  Charles 169
  John George 92
  Karl 80
  Minna 169
  William 92
LEYET
  Anne KITCENGEL 88
LEYFERTH
  Annie BURKHART 92
  Annie HATTEN 92
  Edward 92
  Thankmar 92
LIBBY
  Betsy BAUVAIS 92
  Josiah 92
  L.J. 92
  Mary LEAVETT 92
LIBENSKY
  Josephine 112
LIBERG
  Christina 151
LIBINSKA
  Barbara 144
LIBZELL
  Maria C. 148
LICET
  Josepha 104
LICHKY
  Elizabeth 39
LIDDARD
  Helen M. 58
LIDDEL
  James A. 16
  M. HANLEY 16
  Nannie M. 16
LIDDELL
  John Craig 92
  Kate PYPER 92
LIDDIARD
  Helen M. 58
LIDELL
  Thomas 45
LIDLY
  Thomas 14
LIEBER
  Adam 92
  Clara MANTEL 92
  Dr. 137
  Maggie 137
  Margaret 137
  Mary BOEHME 92
  Max 92
  P. 25
  Philip 137
  Philipp 113
LIEBLER
  Anthony 53
  Max 86

LIEFFERS
  Emma 108
  Johann 108
  Johanne Doris
    RODEMANN 108
LIENENGER
  Ada 148
LIES
  Joseph 160
  Teresa 39
LIEVER
  Catharine FINKAN 92
  Gertrude LOCH 92
  Matthias 92
  Nicholas 92
LIFRE
  Lizzie 169
LIGHTFOOT
  E.W. 160
LIGHTNER
  Charles H. 92
  Eva BRUCE 92
LILGA
  Kathrine 60
LILIENCRON
  Alexander N.C.G. 92
  Andreas 92
  Augusta STRUBE 92
  Yart Louisa Francisca
    PETERSEN 92
LILJA
  Anders 161
  Cajsa JOHNASON 161
  Carolina 161
LILLEY
  Hattie TINSLEY 92
  John 92
LILLIE
  Caroline PARMETER
    92
  J.A. 138
  Jerome A. 92
LILLY
  Lucretia 132
LIMKE
  John 84
LINAHAN
  Jerry 67
  Johanna 126
  Margaret 90
  Patrick 90
LINBERG
  Christian 113
LINBLAT
  Mary 142
LIND
  Edward 11
  J. 3
  John 88
LINDAL
  G. 146
LINDBERG
  Alexander 89
  Catherin PETERSEN 15
  Charles 88
  Clara 88
  Frane 25
  Frank 3, 105
  Gustava
    ABRAHAMSON 89
  Helene Marie 15
  Martha 105
  Martha, Mrs. 3
  Mathilda 89
  Peter 15

LINDBLAD
  John 89
  John, Mrs. 89
LINDBLOM
  Alexander 89
LINDBORG
  Annie A. 76
  Catharine PEARSSON
    76
  Peter 76
LINDBORN
  Eva 23
LINDE
  Eliza LAWON 92
  George 10, 92, 110
  Helene HANSEN 92
  Lena 10
  Magdalena HANSEN 10
  Max 92
  Minnie A. LUTHER 92
LINDEBORG
  Louise 141
LINDEMAN
  Effie D. HAZARD 92
  Elizabeth E.
    BOCKOVER 92
  Joseph P. 92
  M. 92
LINDEN
  Inga SWANSEN 75
  Johanna G. HEDLUND
    92
  Louisa 75
  Swans 75
  William 92
LINDGREN
  Mary Jane CLINE 92
  Ole 92
LINDLEY
  Wm. 138
LINDLOFF
  Amalia WENDELL 92
  John 92
  Mary SCHRODER 92
  William 92
LINDQUEST
  Anna 122
  Annie 89, 162
  Carry PAISKER 92
  G.A. 111
  Nils Peter 92
  O. 92
LINDQUIST
  Gunnar A. 121, 133
  Mary C. 50
LINDSAY
  Ellen KEARNEY 92
  John 92
  Wm. C., Mr. and Mrs.
    92
LINDSEY
  Mattie 8
  Nancy THOMPSON 8
  Wm. 8
LINDSTROM
  Betty 111
  Emma BORK 92
  Fanny A. GORDON 16
  John 92
  Lars 60, 92
  Mary BRAW 60
  Mary BROF 92
  Sophie 60
LINDTSTED
  Augusta 24

LINDVALL
Katie 34
LINGEL
John C., Mr. and Mrs.
138
LINGENFELDER
John 137
LINGNER
E. 122
J.C. 122
John C. 92, 122, 147
Mary E. IRISH 92
Mr. and Mrs. 147
LINGQUIST
Anna 50
LINGREN
Louisa JOHNSON 92
Peter M. 92
LINK
Anna 88
Emma M. 31
Harvey 31
Mary ABBOTT 31
LINN
Carrie 4
LINNEHAN
Betty COKE 109
Ellen 109
Jermiah 109
LINQUEST
Christiana JOHNSON
92
Christine BEYERSTAN
92
Gunnar A. 92
LINSTROM
Adolph Albert 92
Emily Sophia JOHNSON
92
LIPE
Addie W. 8
Eva 62
Eva J. 14, 76, 120
Lizzie 62, 64
Lizzie E. 8, 14, 26, 69,
72, 74-76, 92, 114,
123, 146
Lizzie E. BROWN 120
Lizzie E., Mrs. 120
Lizzie, Mrs. 50
W.A. 120
LIPFERT
Christian 16
Henry 16
LIPPACH
Johannah, Mrs. 50
LIPPAH
Johannah, Mrs. 50
LIPPE
Annie RAMM 92
Dennis 92
Mary MOLTINGER 92
Mathias 92
LIPPINCOTT
Lucretia 2
LIPPIRT
Anna DRESON 92
Katrina BEROT 92
Peter 92
Philip 92
LIPPKE
Maria 79
LIPROZ
Alice 126
Antony 126

LIPSEY
Ann M. JONES 92
Edwin 92
Sarah HAYNES 92
William M. 92
LIPSTREN
Josephine 70
LISH
Maria 78
LISK
Abigail 110
LISKA
Magdalaena 149
LISKE
Hedwig 66
LISTEN
Sarah 155
LISTER
Elizabeth 142
LISTLAND
Catharine HOP 13
Charles 13
Elizabeth 13
LITER
Hannah M. RAMSEY
93
John 93
LITKE
Charlotte 84
LITTLE
Annie ARMROD 103
Felecia WICK 37
Felicia WICK 56
Francis WICK 37
George 103
George L. 37, 56
Ida 144
Ida M. 93
Isaac 93, 144
James H. 56
Jane CUMMINGS 144
June CUMMINGS 93
Kate 56
Lizzie 37
Mary 103
LITTLEJOHN
Anna A. 140
LITTON
Ellen HYLAND 31
LITZEN
Caroline REHN 127
Jacob 127
Josephine 127
LIUTHECUM
Sarah 124
LIVESEY
Henry 160
LIVESY
Henry 168
LIVINGSTON
Frank R. 93
George H. 93
Martha RODGERS 93
Mary WILBURN 93
Phebe 166
Ruth 108
LIVINGSTONE
Ida May REEVES 93
Jane LEECH 93
Lucien 93
R.L. 93
LIVSEY
Henry 74
LIYPOLDT
Catharine OSWALD 93
Clara HOUCK 93

Jacob F. 93
John G. 93
LLEWELLYN
Ida M. LITTLE 93
Joseph 93
Louisa FAY 93
W.H.H. 93
LLITZ
Mary 147
LLOYD
Catharine 149
M.A., Mrs. 70
LLOYDE
Helen DONAHUE 93
Henry J. 93
Sarah TUBBS 93
Warren 93
LLOYDJOINS
Christiana Jane
ROGERS 100
LNYGG
J.P. 103
LOBDILL
May J. 83
LOBS
Henrietta 84
John 84
LOCH
Gertrude 92
Rozena 112
LOCHNER
Caroline 141
LOCKARD
Andrew J. 93
Mary E. JONES 93
Mary NASH 93
LOCKE
Julia M. 98
Sidney E. 5, 153
LOCKERMAN
Henry W. 87
Lottie GLOVER 87
LOCKLIN
Harriet E. ALLEN 118
Harriet E. COTTON 93
Henry F. 93
LOCKLING
Charlotte MAULE 93
Orson W. 93
LOCKNER
Adam 147
Caroline 106
Josephine FLICKER
147
Lena 147
LOCKRIDGE
Jennie 98
Mary E. 10
Robert 10, 98
Sarah E. WINTERS 10
Sarah WINTER 98
LOCKSTOER
Christine 27
LOCKWOOD
Ann 6
Ann Zuella 144
C.L. 144
Emmarilla 144
Emmarilla EVLYN 144
James B. 47
Judge 39
Lucy F. 23, 130
LOCUM
Anna 15
LODEL
Mary 16

LODL
Mary 16
LODZ
Mary 107
LOEB
Catharine 73
LOEPTIN
Magdalene ROHRBERG
148
Peter 148
Sophia 148
LOEWEL
Amaena 136
LOFTUS
Sarah 69
LOGAN
Eliza A. 147
Emma L. 166
Fannie 33
Hannah 82
Harmantha H. THOMAS
93
Jane 31
John 166
John H. 82, 93
Mary 73
Mr. 51, 112
Roxana KELLOGG 166
Sarah 158
Sarah J. 158
LOGEMAN
F. 93
Harry 93
Henry 93
Lizzie REX 93
Mary Hak EMEYER 93
LOGEMANN
Fred 62, 93
John W. 93
Lena MARTINS 93
Mary HOCKMEIER 93
LOGES
John 93
Kate SYLVESTER 93
Peter 93
LOHEIDE
Louise 58
LOHMANN
Amelia A. 27
Johanna C. MILLER 27
John G. 27
LOHRER
John 70
LOHSE
Carolina 113
Metta 27
LOMAY
Honora 6
LOMBARD
Horace, Mr. and Mrs.
120
LOMBARDY
B.C. 93
Mailan FELICI 93
Matilda C. TAYLOR 93
R.K. 93
LONERGAN
David 141
Dennia 136
Dennis 24
Ellen SUBY 93
John 161
Mary A. McCOY 93
Thomas 93
William 93

LONERGIN
Dennis 60
LONG
Amelia 99
Amelia POWALTZ 99
Amelia PROVISE 117
Anna Elizabeth 163
Bertie P. 117
E.K. 60
Elizabeth BLACK 93
Ella WHALEN 93
Ellen B. SWITZER 93
Eric 163, 166
George 168
John 99, 117
Lucretia 139
Mahoea 156
Martha JOHNSON 163,
166
Mary 35
Nancy 28
Nora 36
Patsy 168
Sarah 166
Stephen 93
Warren 93
William 93
LONGFELLOW
Emma 48
LONGHREN
Elizabeth A. MORROW
93
James R. 93
Maggie FOLEY 93
Thomas 93
LONGSBERRY
Mary 40
Mary McACARTHY 40
William 40
LONMON
E. 153
LONOMON
E. 151
LONSBERRY
Nancy 28
LONSDALE
Cecelia A. JAMES 1
LONVIN
Louisa 120
LOOKER
Henry 93
Louise HATCH 93
Nellie DOW 93
William H. 93
LOOMIS
L.B., Miss 70
S.B. 91
S.B., Miss 168
LORAH
Sarah L. 7
LORCHEN
Mary 139
LORD
John B. 80
Sarah A. 119
LORENSEN
Eliza Louisa R. 82
Mary 41
LORENSON
Mary 49
LORENTSEN
Niette 26
LORENZ
Hedwig 170

LORENZEN
Anna 42
Anna SCHNOOR 93
H. 42, 93
Lizzie JENSEN 42
Margurita 44
Mary JENSEN 93
William F. 93
LORGE
Dora 84
Elizabeth BATTLES 84
Henry 84
LORING
A.B., Mrs. 169
David R. 93
Eliza J. BRYANT 93
Mary POTTER 93
Nathan 93
LORZA
Leah 136
LOSCH
Caroline 86
LOTT
Ann Eliza 59
Charles J. 26
Elizabeth WILSON 26
Frances E. 26
LOTTEN
Frederika 153
LOUDA
Maria 161
LOUDON
Marion 60
LOUGHLIN
Mary 115
LOUIE
Anna 94
LOUIS
Annie 56
Fannie GASTNER 56
Walter (George?) 56
LOUISBERRY
J.W. 124
LOUISDAUGHTER
Else 3
LOUNT
Sarah 149
LOVE
James 65
James W. 4, 113
LOVEJOY
Bridget E. LUCEY 93
Charles 62
Eugene F. 93
Francis C. 93
Jerusha WHITMORE
93
LOVELACE
Catherine E. 94
George 94
LOVELADY
Annie 71
John 71
Mary E. McGEE 71
LOVELAND
Albert E. 93
Carrie 159
Edward 93
Edwin 93, 159
Flora C. GRIDLEY 59,
93
Harriet BENTON 93
Harriet C. BENTON
159

LOVELLY
Bridget DONNOLLON
115
Edward 115
Ellen 115
LOVELY
Edward 115
LOVETT
Henry 93
Madison 91
Mary E. LEE 93
LOVETTE
Madison 52
LOVEWELL
H.A. 40
LOW
Mary 82
Phoebe 102
LOWARY
Fannie MANN 34
James 34
Mary B. 34
LOWBER
Frederick 93
Louisa SCHMOLD 93
LOWE
Agnes 152
Belle CUSTER 93
Benjamin K. or R. 93
Celia WHEELER 93
Charlotte A. 145
Col. and Mrs. 93
Dr. 167
E., Dr. and Mrs. 94
Emily EVANS 69
Enos 145
Enos, Dr. and Mrs. 93
Hannah 8
Helen A. NEWHALL 93
James A. 93
Jesse 93, 145
Jesse, Mr. and Mrs. 93
Jesse, Mrs. 30
John 93
Lizzie 6
Mary VAUGHN 93
Mrs. Col. 93
Mrs. Dr. 93
Nelson 64
Sophia 145
Sophia HOPPIN 145
T.B. 145
Thomas 93
LOWEN
Sophia 91
LOWER
Anna E.
WICKERSHAM 93
Elizabeth 131
Elizabeth SORGER 86
Lucy Ann 43
William H. 93
LOWMAN
Rachael Ann 42
LOWREY
Ann CUSHION 80
Edmond 80
Mary C. 80
Mary E. 48
LOWRIE
Elizabeth MORRIS 58
Jane 155
Mary E. 58
Thomas 58
LOWRY
Elizabeth MORRIS 20

Ellen 80
Ellen L. 25
J. 25
Maggie 25
Margareta 109
Mary A. 20
Mary MURPHY 25
Patrick 25
Thomas 20, 80, 109
Winefer 39
LOWSLEY
I.W. 112
LOY
Jane RITTNER 21
John G. 21
Mary C. 21, 40
LOYD
Margaret Ellen 127
Mary 31
LOYDE
Catherine E.
LOVELACE 94
Fredrick M. 94
Jennie BEAUCHEY 94
Thomas 94
LOZIER
Anne E. 165
E.S. 165
LUBENS
Catherine ARPS 94
Hans 94
Martha GOSCH 94
LUCAN
Ringe 5
LUCAS
Anna 18
Anthony 94
Clara 22
E., Mrs. 21
Edward 40, 90
Ellen 143
Ellen BYRNE 80
H.F. 55
H.R. 159
Hary R. 143
Henry J. 134
Henry Joseph 102
J.C. 26
John 22, 80
John A. 94
Lavina J. 20
Maggie 22
Mary 80, 82
Mary M. DOUGLAS 94
Mr. and Mrs. 18
Olive 131
Priciller, Mrs. 49
Rachael A. TURNER 94
LUCEY
Bridget DOYLE 93
Bridget E. 93
Jeremiah 93
LUCHSINGER
Anna Sophie 57
Casper 57
Elizabeth 57
LUCI
Catherine DARLTON
94
Johanna BROWN 94
Michael 94
Patrick 94
LUCID
Johanna 53, 168
LUCK
Caroline 62

LUCKEY
Edward 94
Harriet 166
Mary 166
Mina KLINKE 94
LUCUS
A.K. 4
LUDA
Maria 161
LUDDEN
Mr. 8
LUDDINGTON
Catharine 118, 167
H.S. 166
Henry 118
Juliette TARPENNING
118
Julyett 166
Mary E. 38, 42
LUDINGHAM
Elspet 145
LUDINGTON
Eliza CULLER 53
H.L. 53
Juliette 53
Nancy 70
LUDLOW
Mary 24, 142
Mary J. CHASE 94
Oliver C. 94
LUDTENWARK
Caroline 161
LUDWIG
Elizabeth 160
George 66
LUDWIGSEN
Chaterina MUHS 110
Jens 110
Margaret 110
LUEBECK
Rebecca 66
LUEDERS
Annie C. 14
Mike 14
Wiebke DORN 14
LUEHR
Henry 91
Maria 91
Maria BLUHM 91
LUEHRMANN
Louisa 145
LUELLIN
Amanda, Mrs. 166
LUENEBURG
Anna M. 19
Christene STROEH 19
Johann F. 19
LUGSINGER
Anna ZOEPFE 18
Caspar 18
LUHENS
Anna RASMUNSEN 94
Henry 94
J.H. 94
Lotte LENTS 94
LUHER
Catharine 136
LUHSINGER
Anna ZOPFI 84
Caspar 84
Lena 84
LUKENS
Henry 123
LUMKINS
Elizabeth 117

LUMLEY
Arabella WILKINSON
94
Emily J. FELL 94
Geo. 94
James R. 94
LUMPKIN
Elizabeth 10
LUMPKINS
Elizabeth 137
LUND
Annie B. JOHNSON 94
Catharine 94
Catharine ANDERSON
94
Eunice R. 21
Ever Peter 105
Johanna Katharina 61
John A. 152
Julia 75
Julia Augusta 105
Larson 94
Lewis E. 94
Mary E.
FREDERICKSON
105
Mr. and Mrs. 89
Peter 94
LUNDBECK
Fritz 94
Lena JOERGENSEN 94
Magdalena
ELLEGAARD 94
LUNDBERG
Anna 61
Helena C. 4
J.A. 75
LUNDE
C. 70
LUNDQUIST
E.G. 11
Gunnar A. 3
LUNDVALL
Beckey 42
LUNDWALL
Hannah LARSEN 94
Martin 94
LUNE
Christine 56
LUNENBORG
Bernhard 94
Christine A. 94
Gertrud SURMANN 94
Henry 94
LUNGREN
Christina 150
Oli 150
LUNT
Andrew J. 94
C.J. 94
Louisa SORENSON 94
Mary JASPERSON 94
LUPKA
Mary 84
LUREY
Mary 68
LUSCHKAT
Carolina 136
Henrietta 136
LUST
Christine 169
LUTES
James 162
Jennie 162
Mary WILSON 162

MARCY
  Axey HAWE 96
  Catherine COOPER 96
  Marcia 25
  Stephen 96
  Stephen B. 96
MARE
  Eliza Jane FERRY 95
  Hannah 47
  Louis 95
MARECEK
  J.W. 72
MAREN
  Margaret 7, 134
MARES
  Charles 96, 138
  Francis 80, 96
  John 96
  Leona VODICKA 96
  Mack 96
  Mary 69
  Mary BORCK 96
  Mary BOWER 96
  Mary NEMECEK 96
MARESH
  Anna ROUBAL 123
  Francis 80
  Frank M. 47
  Magdalena 123
  Matthew 123
MARIA
  Anna P. 45
MARIETTE
  Catharine 90
MARK
  Peter J. 96
MARKEL
  Anna M. McDONALD
    96
  Elizabeth KILLDON 96
  Ettie 123
  Eunice SWEET 81, 99
  Hattie H. 123
  Henrietta H. CORBIN
    96
  Henry 96
  J. 81
  J.E. 81, 123
  Jacob 35, 81, 99
  Jacob E. 96
  Leah Caroline 81
  Mollie S. 99
  Solomon 96
MARKHAM
  Catherine 22
MARKIN
  Bridget QUINLAN 96
  John 96
  Michael 96
  Nancy COULIHAN 96
MARKKURSEN
  Darthe 61
MARKLE
  Alexander 96
  Elizabeth BUCKHAM
    96
  James W. 96
  Julia PERKINS 96
MARKS
  Anna 94
  Carrie J. 126
  Fanny 42
MARLEY
  Ann LEWORTHY 96
  Charles 96
  Mary J. LEACH 96

Thomas 96
MARMION
  Bridget 69
  Hugh 69
  Mary CLARK 69
MARQUETT
  H., Mrs. 122, 165
  Hulda 22
  Huldah 14
MARQUETTE
  David, Mrs. 1
MARQUIS
  Carrie M. 116
MARRINAN
  John 33
MARSH
  Eliza 110
  Elizabeth E. 38
  Julia K. 123
  Mary 65
  Phoebe I. BALL 123
  Washington 123
MARSHAL
  Elizabeth M. 30
MARSHALL
  A., Miss 8
  Agnes CLOW 16
  Allen 97
  Allen, Mr. and Mrs. 97
  Annie Elizabeth KAY 97
  Caroline M. FROST 97
  Catharine 19
  Elizabeth MUNSELL 97
  Elvira 34
  Elvira DUNCAN 97
  George W. 96
  John 8
  John L. 97
  Lewis K. 34, 97
  Maria 8
  Martin A. 97
  Mary B. 16
  Mary DAVIS 8
  Pardon 97
  R.M. 87
  R.P. 16
  Sarah 70
  Sarah J. THOMPSON
    96
  Wm. H. 138
MARSHOUW
  Issabella 19
MARSTEN
  J.M., Mrs. 58
MARSTON
  Bridget 37
  Elizabeth
    ABERCROMBIE 97
  J.M. 97
  John M. 51
MARTAR
  Mgar 122
MARTEN
  Claus 121
  Frederick 137
  Martha Ann YEAGER
    131
  Mary Eve 136
  N. 84, 122
MARTENS
  Bohne 97
  Caroline HANSEN 97
  Cecelia 132
  Christine
    CHRISTIANSON 97
  Dorothea 55, 84

J.F. 97
  Margareth 5
MARTENSDOTTER
  Elsa 89
MARTENSON
  Annie SWENSDOTTER
    97
  M. 155
  Olof 97
MARTERSON
  Ola 67
MARTI
  Catherine 35
  Elisa BRIEDERMAN
    103
  Elizabeth 65
  Elizabeth
    BRUDERMANN 149
  Peter 35
  Salome WUISTER 35
MARTIN
  Ann 90
  Annie 147
  Betsey PECK 97
  Bridget C. RILEY 64
  Catherine 71
  Charles 89
  Charles F. 97
  D.W.F. AUTTENSEN
    143
  Dorothea 64
  Edmund 97
  Eliza 169
  Elizabeth MERRILL 97
  Ellen STEVENS 97
  Emily 79
  F.S. 97
  Frank R. REED 97
  G.L. 50
  G.P. 26, 99
  Harry 44
  Henrietta JULIAN 97
  Henry S. 70
  Ida 104
  Jane 67, 119, 134
  Jas. M.K. 137
  John 97
  Kate 82
  Louisa 82
  Louvenia 44
  Margaret 56
  Margaret JOHNSON 79
  Martha 97
  Mary J. 163
  Mary J. WORLEY 105
  Mary OSTLER 97
  Mary T. 64
  Mattie J. 88
  Moses S. 97
  Nancy 44
  Peter 64, 71
  Presly 72
  Robert E. 97
  Salma 71
  Samuel P. 97
  Sophia 9
  Sophrona E. REEVES
    97
  Welcome 79
  William S. 97
MARTINEK
  Anna 85
MARTINELL 113
  Charles J. 119
MARTINS
  Anna SCHLOMER 97

Anna SIEMONSEN 97
  Fritz C. 97
  Gretta REIKEN 93
  Henning 97
  John 93
  Lena 93
  Maggie 45
MARTINSEN
  Anna 36
  Margaretha 142
MARTINSON
  Adolph 97
  Ann 27
  Annie MATSON 97
  Annie MORRISON 97
  Caroline PETERSON
    97
  Erick 126
  Gonela SWANSON 126
  Marsh 97
  Martin 97
  Morten 97
  Nels 3, 151
  Nelson 156
MARTIS
  John Peter 97
  Terissa DISH 97
MARUSAK
  MARUSAK 161
  Wenzel 161
MARWIPS
  Dorathea 14
MARYWEATHERS
  James N. 129
  Jane 129
  Lucy 129
MASANEK
  Mary 46
MASCRIPE
  Hattie 166
  Robert 166
  Sarah FAIRFIELD 166
MASEK
  Anna 12
MASEN
  Judide 116
MASER
  Alice E. BARTON 97
  Anna MAYFIELD 97
  Julius F. 97
  Theodore 97
MASON
  Alida 16
  Bennett F. 23, 98
  Bennett Fdr. 75
  Cora TALCOTT 97
  D.G. 22
  E. 157
  Elizabeth 87, 145
  Elizabeth DEMAIN 22
  Elizabeth WERNIAN 22
  Emily 50
  Emma B. 160
  Emma L. KIDDER 97
  Emma May FORBES 97
  H.E. 16, 31, 97
  H.P. 97
  Harriet RYAN 40
  Harry 97
  Henrietta RYEN 50
  Henry 133
  Henry C. 97
  Hezekiah 143
  Ira 97
  Jennie 31
  Joseph H. 97

Josephine 133
  Josephine KNIGHT 97
  Kate E. 22
  Lizzie 8, 40, 50
  Mary E. 140
  Mattie E. 28
  Michael 40, 50
  Milla S. BUTLER 97
  Mrs. 4
  Otis E. 97, 103
  Phebe 167
  Rachel WRIGHT 97
  Rebecca 30
  Ruth GARVAN 97
  Ruth GOWEN 97
  Ruth GOWIN 31
  Ruth GOWING 16, 143
  Sadie A. 97
  Sarah J. HUNTLEY 97
  Sophia 143
  W.P. 97
  William 97
MASSEN
  Karn 2
MASSENHELTER
  Johanna 49
MASSION
  Alfred 39
  Elizabeth 39
MASSON
  Mary 23
MASTERS
  Ann 118
  Catharine GARNETT
    97
  Cecelia A. 158
  George 97
  Maria BLUCK 158
  Rosalie 158
  Samuel 97
  Sarah FISHER 97
  W.L. 158
  William 158
MASTERSON
  Andrew 45
  Annie 45
  Bridget DIAL 45
  Margaret 162
MATA
  Catherine RILEY 97
  Lee 97
  Peter 97
MATCHA
  Wenceslaus 125
MATESEN
  Ivor 77
  Martha M. ANDERSEN
    77
MATHANER
  Barbara 39
MATHER
  Honora 27
  John 27
  Martha 87
  Mary A., Mrs. 78
  Mary FOX 27
MATHESEN
  Lucy 130
MATHESON
  Mary 144
MATHEWS
  Annie 53
  Archie 97
  Betsy 82
  C. VANCE 97
  Clark L. 97

MATHEWS, cont.
Cordelia BINGMAN 97
Doct., Mrs. 95
Elizabeth SPENCER 97
Ellen PRYOR 97
John M. 97
Mary 20
Mary E. 146
Nancy 119
Nancy J. FIELDING 97
Samuel 97
William 97
MATHEWSON
Anna Hansen
LYNGSTADT 97
Charles 97
Charles P. 97
Henrietta M. COON 97
Margaret S. McCURDY
97
Mary 102, 144
Mary G. GROSVENOR
97
Moses C. 97
Nels 97
Robert 97
Sadie A. MASON 97
MATHIS
Edwin R. 98
Enoch J. 98
Ester REEVE 98
Esther REEVES 98
Jennie LOCKRIDGE 98
Selina JONES 98
William R. 98
MATHISON
Ann Marie ERICKSON
98
Bertha OLSON 98
Chris 98
Matthew 98
MATIAS
Mary 20
MATISEN
Berti M. 113
MATLICK
D. 127
MATNEY
Bethia GREEN 41
Charles 41
Maria A. 41
MATS
Caroline 15
MATSEN
Anna JOHNSON 121
Christian 121
Marian 121
MATSON
Annie 97
B.J., Mr. and Mrs. 152
B.P. 1
Betsy 57
Carrie 76, 164
Christiana 92
Christina OLSEN 164
Christine 91
Emmarancy 169
Enish 104
Maria 150
Mary 101, 148
Mary DEALEY 104
Mats 164
Olof 113
Peter 98
Sophia PETERSON 98

MATTES
Anastasia 135
John 135
Mary 135
MATTESON
Emma ANDERSON 98
Mary 76
Max 121
Peter D. 98
MATTHEWS
Charles 70
Electa BLAIR 70
Harriet 70
Nancy 88
MATTHEWSON
Mary 3
R. 77
MATTHIER
Mary 10
Witke 10
MATTHIES
Claus 98
Margaretta SCHULTZ
98
Mary WAGNER 98
Thomas 98
MATTHIESEN
Juliane 64
MATTHIESON
Anna 56
Mary 3
MATTIES
Elizabeth 98
George 98
Henry 98
Josephine BLAKELY 98
MATTINGLY
Margret A. CASSADY
98
Peter 98
Samuel I. 98
MATTISON
Anna 112
MATTON
Mr. 142
MATTSEN
Annie 121
Ulirka 55
MATTSON
Andres 3
Anna 76, 162
Annie 113
Annie M. 66
Caroline NELSON 98
Elsie ERICKSEN 3
Ingra 3, 113
Ingri, Mrs. 13
Jens 66
John 96, 111
Kristina NIELSON 111
Mary 17, 111
Nels 98
Rulof 111
MATZA
Catharine PRANGAR
98
Josie HYNEK 98
Peter 98
Thomas 98
MAUF
Fredicka 133
MAUKE
Daniel 41
Henriette 41
Wilhelmina KNOR 41

MAUL
Margaret M. 51
MAULE
Charlotte 93
Wm. 93
MAURER
Edward 69
Mary 103
MAURETZEN
Theodor Alfr. 98
MAURITZEN
Alfred 98
John C. 98
Lena Marie ADAMS 98
Thora A.E. WIPPERT
98
Tillie ATZEN 98
MAUSHARK
Katarina 161
Wenzel 161
MAUSS
Catharina SCHEIDT 98
Johannes 98
Nina FELZMANN 98
Vic 98
MAUTTERNASH
Catherine 129
Mary FABER 129
Nicholas 129
MAVIS
Dorothea 27
MAWAS
Charles 98
Ludwig 98
Mary BLOEK 98
Mary LAMPRECHT 98
MAXFIELD
Abram W. 98
Clara CLINTON 98
J.B., Mrs. 14, 30, 70, 78,
126, 150
M., Mrs. 126
M.M., Mrs. 18, 36
Manne, Mrs, 168
Mary 165
Nancy 42
MAXON
Estina FULLER 52
Mary C. 52
Rufus 52
MAXTED
Levi 98
Levi, Mr. and Mrs. 77
Mary MESSEL 98
MAXWELL
Caroline A. 44
Charles A. 98
Fanny GANLY 33
Harriet 33
Johnston 33
Julia M. LOCKE 98
Mary 109
Sarah F. 30
MAY
Agnes LOWE 152
Britekeck 21
C., Mrs. 28
Carolina, Mrs. 59
Clara 123
James 21, 152
Jenny 21, 159
John 79, 108, 165
Margaret Ann 26, 52
Mary A.E. 127
Stella 152

MAYBURY
Frances TOPHAN 98
John 98
Nora O'SULLIVAN 98
Richard 98
MAYERS
James 69
MAYFIELD
Anna 97
MAYMARD
Mr. and Mrs. 165
MAYNARD
Elizabeth 86
T.E. 19
MAYNES
James G. 73
MAYO
Aliance 42
MAYOR
G.F. 162
MAYS
Amada KEEPS 98
Charles L. 98
Elizabeth WELCHER
98
Margaretha 41
Thomas 98
MAYWALD
Augusta 163
MAYWEATHER
Catharine 2
David 2
Jane YOUNG 19
Nicholas 19
Ruth 19
Violet 2
MAYWETHERS
Margaret 149
Nicholas 149
McACARTHY
Mary 40
McADAM
Mary 54
McAFFEE
Martha A. 137
McALARNEY
Catharine 128
McALBERTSON
Johanna 37
McALDIN
Sarah 150
McALISTER
Danl. 60
McALLEN
M., Miss 103
McALLISTER
Alfred 98
Elizbeth C. HOBBY 98
Mary 125
Ralph 98
Waity Ellen FOSTER
98
McALLROY
Rosanna 22
McANDRES
Julia 123
McANDREW
Mary 109
Mary HOOKS 109
Mike 109
McANDREWS
Briget 59
Mary 59
Tom 59
McANSLAND
Agnes RITCHIE 98

Alexander 98
Mary E. LANNSBERRY
98
Mrs. 98
Robert R. 98
McARDLE
Catharine BOURKE 98
Catherine CONNERY
98
Ellen 51, 134
Emma M. JOHNSON
98
James 67
James H. 12, 141
John 98, 159
Patrick 98
Rose 66
Rosy 35
McARRAGHER
Bessie 169
Jane NELSON 169
Joseph 169
McARTHUR
Archie 98
Catharine SMITH 98
James, Mrs. 160
Maria 31
Mary FREDERICKSON
98
McARTNEY
Lizzie 109
Lizzy F. 149
McATEE
Ellen GOODIN 23
Margaret A. 23
Patrick 23
McAUSLAND
A. 132
A.G. 21, 98
Agnes 48
Andrew 53, 163
Eugenia KEYES 98
Miss 29
McAVIN
Sarah 80
McAVOY
Mary 32
McBAY
G.M. 104
Geo. N., Mr. and Mrs.
139
George M. 125
George N. 98
Margaret BARNES 98
Mary 97
Mary Ann 104, 125
Mary Ann HUBBARD
98
Robert 98
McBRAY
George N. 98
Mary Ann HUBBARD
98
McBRIDE
Bridget DOYLE 98
John 98, 110
Kate Cora DOWNEY
98
Kitty Cora DOWNEY
98
Mary 40
Rebecca ROBINSON 98
Sarah 90
Thomas 98
McBRIDGE
M. 93

McCABE
Ann 156
John 54
Joseph W. 98
Joshua 98
Nancy Jane POPE 98
Susan HUDSON 98
McCAFFERY
Barney 58
Mary A. 58
Rosa CAMPBELL 58
McCAFFREY
Catherine 36
Elizabeth DORSEY 36, 153
Hugh 69, 99
James 89
Joseph 99
Mary A. 153
Owen 99
Patrick 36, 153
Susan McDERMOTT 99
Therese KENNEDY 99
McCAGUE
H.M. 48
H(enrietta) M(atilda), Mrs. 36
John 41
Matilda, Mrs. 114
Mrs. 95
McCAHILL
Bridget LYNCH 36
John 36
Susan 36
McCAIG
Catharine CONNOLLY 99
John K. 99
Sarah WISEMAN 99
William 99
McCALL
Christina 9
Christine 9, 122
Elizabeth 80
Hugh 80
Mary 116
Mary ---- 80
McCALLUM
A.M., Mrs. 150
Archibald 99
Carrie SIMONS 99
Catharine Ann 31
John 99
M.A., Mrs. 32, 124
Mary THOMPSON 99
McCAMLEY
James 99
Katie SERSION 99
William 99
McCAMON
Jane 72
McCAMPBELL
John 100
McCANDLESS
Alex. B. 71
Rachel, Mrs. 71
McCANDLISH
Isabella Sharp 10
M. 99
Maria 71
Maria H. HOWELLS 99
Marie HOWELLS 10
Mollie S. MARKEL 99
R.C. 99
W.N. 72

William 10, 99
McCANDRY
Bridget 125
Mary HOOKS 125
Michael 125
McCANN
David 99
George 144
John 32
John H. 99
Margaret 24
Mary 32, 47
Mary McAVOY 32
Minnie GODRIGE 99
Sarah DECKER 99
McCANNEY
Kate 103
McCANNON
Ann 24
McCANTZ
---- 110
McCARDLE
Ellen 22
Hannah 38
John 99
Patrick 71
McCARRAGHER
---- NELSON 163
Anna 163
Jennie 163
Joseph 163
McCART
J.O. 122
McCARTHEY
Johanna 30
McCARTHY
Catharine 142
Charles 99
Florance 41
Francis 41
James P. 41
Jane McGARVEY 99
John 34
Kate 74
Lucy 41
Maggie 72
Margaret 8, 99
Margaret BUCKLEY 99
Martha 68
Mary 75
Mary Ann 34
Mary BOWES 74
Mary COSTILO 142
Mary, Mrs. 20
Michael 46, 74
Michl. 20
Timothy 142
McCARTNEY
Elizabeth F. 22
M.F., Mrs. 9
Maria 8, 149
McCARTY
Amy SEXTON 99
Catharine CRAVEN 37
Catharine CURRAN 37
Catharine HOGAN 114
Charlotte Jane SEXTON 99
Dean 140
Delia 34
Eliza Jane CARR 99
Ellen 37
Ellen DRISCOLE 99
Enoch 99
Hannah 114
Hannoraha 99

Hannoraha McCARTY 99
Henry 99
J.T. 5
Jennie E. 99
Joannah 49
Johanna RYAN 99
John C. 119
John R. 99
Judy Ann REMER 99
Louise KALENBACH 99
Martin 99
Mary 114
Mary CARR 99
Michael 99
Robert 62, 99
Robert A. 99
Timothy 37, 114
William 68
McCASCAY
Elizabeth 153
McCASCEY
Elizabeth 151
McCASLIN
Angeline 62
Eliza J. GREY 62
George B. 62
McCAULIFF
Mary 93
McCAUSLAND
Andrew, Mr. and Mrs. 152
McCAW
Susan 167
McCAWLEY
Elizabeth MORROW 99
James 99
Patk. or Peter 99
McCHAENE
Jeremiah 123
McCHANE
J(eremiah) 60
Jeremiah 89
McCHEANE
J. 137
Jeremiah 16, 43, 55
Jerry 142
McCLAIN
Eliza 36
James 118
Mattie 118
Nancy J. 118
McCLAINE
Louisa 156
McCLANE
Anna 130
Thomas 130
McCLARY
Aaron 6
Alice WADKINS 6
Elizabeth 4
Eva 6
McCLASKY
Miss 167
McCLEAN
Bridget 114
Caroline 102
Hugh 114
McCLEES
Alexandre 57
Feibie HEWELL 57
Mary A. 57
McCLELLAN
Alexander 105
Bridget RAFTER 99

Elizabeth ENGLAND 99
Henry C. 99
J. 160
Uriah 99
McCLELLAND
Adam 99
Alexander 29
Anne HAMILTON 99
Elizabeth J. 48
Florence ROGERS 99
Robert 99
Susan N. 127
Susan RILEY 99
William, Dr. 99
Wm. 117
McCLINTON
Emma 21
McCLOUD
Harriet D. 162
Martha Ann REED 162
Mathew 162
McCLUNE
Patrick 103
McCLURE
Alvina S. 135
Annie E. 144
E.A. 1, 9, 55, 121, 153
George 132
Henrietta GRAY 132
J.A. 11
Jane 153
McCOFFREY
John 70
McCOLLIN
Rebecca 47
McCOLLUM
Ruhanna 160
Susie LAMB 160
William 160
McCONAUGHEY
B.G. 163
McCONNELL
Amea WARDELL 99
Amy SCIOIP 67
Anna L. WARDELL 99
Annie WARDELL 153
Bertha M. ISAACS 99
Fannie L. 153
Fred R. 99
Indiana 67
Mattie E. STORRS 99
Robert 67, 99, 153
Robert J. 99
McCORD
William 53
Wm. 53
McCORMACK
Eliza 72
John 134
M. 28
McCORMICK
Andrew 65
Ann PLUNKETT 99
Bridget 65, 127
Bridget FEE 47
Catharine 47
Catherine 39, 51, 99
Dolly 7
Elizabeth BERGADOLL 99
Elizabeth HAMILTON 99
John 99, 145
John, Mrs. 62
Josiah L. 99

Josie 145
Kate 65, 115
Margaret or Anna M.G. MILLS 99
Mary 24, 28, 39, 145
Mary C. MAXON 52
Mary O'BRIEN 99
Michial 47
Richard 21
Robert 99, 115
Sallie 21
Thomas 97, 99
Winnifred SHEA 99
McCOURT
Catherine GALLAGHER 99
Ellen McHUGH 99
Francis 99
John 99
McCOY
---- 120
Ada CROWELL 140
Ada V. 140
Alonzo A. 99
Anis Elizabe 18
Anna Laura PRUETT 99
Archie 28
Catherine 93
Delia 38
George A. 140
James 28
Jane 28
Jane FRISE 28
Jennie 61, 144
John 18
Mary A. 93
Prestin 99
Thomas 93
McCRACKEN
Martha 147
McCRANEY
Catherine COATS 78
McCRAREY
Jane 100
Lawrence 100
Mary DARBOY 100
McCRARY
Margaret 100
McCRAY
Eliza J. SCOTT 99
James 99
Mary F. ASHBURN 99
Samuel 99
McCREA
David 137
Mr. 84
Renhanna 84
McCREADY
Amelia LONG 99
George 99
John 99
Wilmina STEWARD 99
McCREARY
Ida 52
John 99
Mary E. CREIGHTON 99
McCRELLIS
Mary C. 64
McCRILLIS
Matilda 103
McCRISKAN
Mary 46

McCRISTAL
Catharine 134
Daniel 115, 134
Sadie E. 115
Susan LYNCH 115
Susannah LYNCH 134
McCRYSTAL
Bridget 51
McCUEN
Elizabeth HAYES 99
G.H. 99
J.R. 99
J.W. 114
John W. 22
Minnie BEAR 99
McCULLOCH
Anna B. 32
Elizabeth 123
McCULLOUGH
Annie B. 155
Annie Maria 28
Esther A. FERGUSON 100
James 38
John 100
Lucea B. SAUNDERS 100
Mary A. 38
Melvira PICKET 155
S.H. 100
Samuel 155
McCUNE
Anna DORSEY 100
Bridget L. 101
Ellen 101
John 101
John W. 100
Joseph M. 100
Julia A. WILSON 100
Lydia ELLENGWOOD 100
Mary 77
Seth R. 100
W.J. 5
McCURDY
Annie DOLAN 100
J.R. 100
Margaret S. 97
Mary EPPERSON 100
Samuel C. 100
Sarah L. 65
McCURLEY
Mary 53
McCUTCHEN
Emelia LERCHES 100
Fredericka ZAH 100
George 100
J.H. 100
McDAVITT
Kate 115
McDERMOT
Catharine 22
Catharine, Mrs. 32
McDERMOTT
Bridget 70
Catharine 82
Catherine 97
Catherine BRANNAN 100
Charles 100
Charles M. 100
Christiana Jane ROGERS 100
John 100
Katie KEEVENS 100
Luke 20

Mary 9, 139
Mary A. HARTNETT 100
Mary SMITH 100
Michael 47, 100
Mike 55
Norah RUSH 100
Patrick 100
Peter 12
Rosey CASSIDY 100
Susan 99
Tom 100
McDEVETT
Maggie 101
Mary BRADLEY 101
William 101
McDEVITT
Charles 87
Ellen BIGLAN 87
Mary 87
McDEVITTE
Molly 30
McDONAGH
Bridget 100
McDONALD
----, Miss 109
Alexander 100, 151
Alice KING 100
Allie, Mrs. 139
Anna M. 96
Annie 108, 115
Annie O'NEILL 115
Archibald 96
B.H. 149
Bridget 120
Catherine GIBBONS 108
Charles 100, 115
Chas. 131
Drusilla K. STEWART 100
Eliabeth 39
Elizabeth SMITH 83
Ellen 114
Eva NORRIS 100
Flora FRAZIER 100
Frank L. 100
Hellen FULLER 151
J.W. 70
James 100
Jane RUSSELL 31, 100
John 31, 100
John W. 100
Lena 151
Lizzie 114
Lizzie G. 31
M.E., Mrs. 70
Margaret 27, 76
Margaret E. MOORE 96
Martha E. HENDERSON 100
Mary 108, 134, 156
Mary KINLEN 156
Mary PAINTER 100
Mattie E. MORANE 5
Michael 29
Mills 120
Mrs. 88
Nellie 31
Ora B. HENRY 100
P. 115
Randall 108
Thomas 156
William 100
McDONAUGH
Mary 64

McDONELL
C.D. 100
Emma FOREMAN 100
Helen McLAREN 100
John 100
McDONNELL
Patrick 90
McDONOUGH
Annie 69
McDOUGALL
Archibald 100
Mary CURRY 100
McDOWD
Elizabeth 102
McDOWELL
Amanda 37
Elizabeth 102
Martha Jane 34
Mr. 34
Mrs. 34
McEDWARD
Nancy 22
McELAXANDER
Martha 59
McELHANY
Martha E. 103
McELLIGOTT
Patrick 24
McELROY
Catharine HART 100
F.A., Mrs. 168
John 100
Mary M. O'BRIEN 100
W.E. 115
William 100
McELWAIN
Elizabeth 46
Emily A. BROWN 100
James S. 100
McENEN
A.J. 146
Clara 146
McENTEE
Ellen RILEY 100
John 100
Mary DUNN 100
Rose 100
Rose McENTEE 100
Terrence 100
McEVOY
Bridget D. FITZPATRICK 100
Catharine 80
F. 122
James 24, 71, 100
Joanna KENELLEY 100
Mary PHALAN 100
Patrick 100
McEWEN
Mary 74
McFALL
Andrew J. 100
Eliza SPROUL 100
Ellen KAVANAUGH 100
James A. 100
McFARLAND
Andrew 105
Annie TIBBETT 52
Catharine 105
Daniel 57
Elizabeth 58
John 105
Johnna, Mrs. 165
Mary 47

McGARRY
Anne 40
McGARVEY
Hugh 99
Jane 99
Kate FRILL 99
Margaret McCRARY 100
Margaret McNALLY 100
Michael 100
Thomas 100
McGARVIN
Annie 39
Ella 39
Patrick 39
McGAVERN
Mr. 105
McGAVEY
Mary 118
McGAVOCK
Alexander 100
Mary F. ARNOLD 100
Patrick 134
Sarah DEVELIN 100
William J. 100
McGEE
Ann 108
D.K. 100
Daniel K. 108
Elizabeth 17
Ellen 44
Lizzie Ann 108
Mary E. 39, 71
Mary WETZEL 100
T.C. 149
Thomas C. 100
McGERTY
Alice 100
McGILL
Mary Ann 51
McGINN
Kate CREIGHTON 100
Mary DOUGHERTY 100
Mathew 100, 102
Mathew A. 100
McGINNIS
Ann FITZSIMONS 28
Julia 28
William 28
McGLEN
Bridget 96
William 96
McGLINCHY
Annie 38
Cornelius 38
Mary COYLE 38
McGLINCY
May 153
McGLINN
Bridget WALDREN 100
Catharine 161
William 100
McGLOPHIN
Louisa 145
McGLOUGHLIN
Ann 33
McGORK
Edward James 15
McGORMAN
Abby 115
McGOVERN
Alice McGERTY 100
Fanny 37
John 100

Julia REILEY 56
Mary 126
Nellie J. 56
Patrick 37, 100
Terence 56
Therese GRACE 100
McGRADY
Christine 111
McGRATH
Anastasia 74
Jane 81
Jane GREEN 100
Mary 109
Mary CLARY 109
Nellie 109
Owen 109
Roderick 100
Roger 100
Theresa GLEASON 100
McGRAW
Minerva 140
McGREGH
Mary 142
McGREGOR
Harry 80
McGRETCH
Margaret 164
McGREW
Esther J. 107
Jane 107
Nancy Jane 153
McGRIFF
Wm. 68
McGUE
Anna C. 143
Briget CURTIS 27
Ellen 27
Mary CURTIS 143
Tarrance 143
Terrance 27
McGUILEY
Charles 64
McGUINNESS
Catharine 129
McGUIRE
Ann 37
Caroline 5
Catharine 131, 161
Charles, Mr. and Mrs. 106
Charlotte 45
Martha 39
McGUIRK
Edward 24
McGURK
Edward 157
McHALE
Ann LYONS 100
David 100
John 100
Mary MULLONEY 100
Susan 103
McHEANE
J. 139
McHIRRON
Elizabeth 27
McHUGH
Ann WALKER 101
Elizabeth JAMES 101
Ellen 99
Ellen NELAN 101
Maggie McDEVETT 101
Maria BOHAN 101
Mary 103
Mary KELLEY 99

McHUGH, cont.
Michael 101
Patrick 101
Rosa K. WELCH 101
Thomas 99
Thomas P. 101
William 138
McILWREITH
Alice LESTER 101
Hamilton H. 101
Jesse H. HOWAT 101
John 101
McINERNEY
Delia 107
Eliza BURKE 107
Michael 107
McINERNY
Annce MEAS 59
Annie 59
Thomas 59
McINROE
Catharine KAY 101
Ellen O'CONNER 101
Owen 101
Patrick 101
McINTEE
Catharine, Mrs. 140
McINTIRE
Florilla CAMRON 101
Robert 101
McINTOSH
Ann DERGEN 101
Azelia ALBRO 101
Bridget CONNORS 101
Hellen Laura 119
James 101, 119
James J. 101
James R. 101
Laura RAWSON 119
Mary HELAN 101
McINTYRE
Ann RAMSEY 51
Anne 82
Bridget HALL 101
Darriel 51
Elizabeth 39
Elizabeth NICHOLS
101
Mary C. WHIPP 101
Mary E., Mrs. 51
Nancy 159
Owen 101
Richard P. 101
Sarah 82
Stephen F. 101
McKAHIL
Bridget LYNCH 95
Margaret 95
Thomas 95
McKAIG
Elizabeth WRIGHT 101
Hariffa NASH 101
Silas 101
Walter W. 101
McKAIN
James 106
Jas. 101
Mary LACY 101
McKALE
Margaret 63
McKANE
Jas. 101
Mary LACY 101
McKASKIA
Elizabeth 70

McKAY
Jennett 49
McKEE
A. 101
Eliza 170
Elizabeth ANDRE 101
Henry 101
Jane MERRIWEATHER
101
John A. 101
Mary A. 32
Mary MATSON 101
Nancy Jane MORRIS
101
Richman, Mr. and Mrs.
170
Sarah A. 170
Scipio P. 101
Thomas 101
McKELL
J.S. 21
Selina 21
McKELVEY
Angie 99, 150
Ann OSBURN 127
Anna OSBORN 22
Joseph 127
Joseph S. 22
Matilda 127
Nettie 127
Nettie B. 22
McKELVRY
Angelina 42
McKENNA
Charity BURGOUN 83
James 101
Kate C. 83
Lawrence 101
Mary Ann 102
Mary Elizabeth 157
Mary MONTAGUE 101
Susan 26
Susan EDWARDS 101
William 83
McKENNEY
Isabella C. 131
McKENNY
Martha 133
Nancy 133
Robert 133
McKENZEY
Mendice B. 101
McKENZIE
---- 92
Alexander 101
Clementine 101
Elizabeth 81
Emma N. BROWN 101
George 59
John 35
Mary M. 35
McKEOWN
Bridget 98
Hugh 6
Margaret 6
Mary SCHROWFORD
6
McKEU
Chas. P. 167
McKEVITT
Bridgett CARROLL 165
Mary 165
Timothy 165
McKEY
Anna LEHIGH 101
Garten H. 101

Grace 95
J.C., Mrs. 95
Lizzie JONES 95
Sarah GARTIN 101
Walter 101
Wm. Van M. 95
McKINLEY
Bridget CAREY 113
Edward 113
John 113
Mary Agnes 113
McKINNEY
Anna MONJOYE 101
James 101
Laura HANSEL 101
Peter 101
McKINNON
Sarah 2
McKINSTRY
Catherine M.
HODGSON 101
H.K. 101
Horace K. 101
McKINZEY
Mendice B. 101
McKINZIE
Mary 142
Murdock 130
McKITTRICK
Eliza 45
Eliza McPHERSON 45
Thomas 45
McKNABB
John W. 10
McKNIGHT
D.M. 116
Ellen TALCOTT 101
George E. 101
McKOON
Helen 128
J.M. 13
M.E. 81
M.G. 52, 107, 131
McKOY
Priscilla 26
McKUGH
Mandy 139
McLAIN
Alice 101
Alice J. 78
Charles F. 101
Eva 47
J.J. 15, 78, 101
Mary 105
Mary E. FALES 101
Mary FALES 78
Ora M. CHESWELL
101
McLANE
Mary 134
McLAREN
Helen 100
McLAUGHLIN
Daniel 101
E.D. 47, 108, 161
Edward D. 71, 110
Elizabeth 128
Ellen McCUNE 101
Emma J. 6
Ida McC. 52
James 52
Jane PATTERSON 128
Jas. 87
John 13, 128
Lizzie KINSEY 13
Luella 22

Lyda 13
Mary 106
Mollie 52
S., Miss 52
McLEAN
Alice 82
Ann 107
Barbara 107
Chas. 82
Laughlin 107
W.J. 107
McLUCAS
Abraham 101
Bell HEMPHILL 101
J.M. 101
Jane NAISON 101
McMAHAN
Ann LYNCH 37
Delia 37
John 29
Mary 164
Michael 37
McMAHON
Abby FENTON 101
Amelia 152
Emelia 113
Henrietta HASCALL
101
James 101
John 115
Juda COLLINS 113
Kate 62
Kate FOGERTY 101
Margaret TAYLOR 101
Mary 39, 55
Mary A. 141
Michael J. 101
Patrick 101
Peter 113
Philip 152
Phillip 113
Rosa 113
Susan 152
McMAMOR
Elizabeth STEVENSON
62
Nannie 62
P.J. 62
McMANAGAL
Catharine 147
McMANAMEY
Anna 23
McMANNERS
Ann 152
McMANNING
Anna 15
McMANNIS
Catharine 51
Catharine SLOWIE 101
James C. 101
John 101
Mary 80
McMANUS
John 54
Mary 80
McMASTER
Jane 165
Martha 66
McMASTERS
Sarah 134
McMCULLEN
Tillie M. 15
McMEANS
Martha LYBROOK 101
Mary Jane
WHITTLOCK 101

N.S. 101
Rollin L. 101
McMICHAEL
James 6
McMILLAN
Hattie 127
Mary 123
Sarah BARBER 127
McMILLEN
Adelia B. 65
Bridget L. McCUNE
101
Daniel 101
Duncan 101
Kate 137
Sarah J. BARBER 137
W.E. 65
William 137
McMILLIN
Margaret 134
McMONIGAIL
Rebecca 45
McMULLEN
Emma HATTEROTH
101
Ester HALL 101
Hugh 101
Jane 107
Margaret 113
Mary 143
William H. 101
McMULLIN
Mary 57
McMURPHY
John 73
McMURRAY
Eliza 143
Marietta JOHNSON
102
Richard M. 102
T.S. 19
McNABB
John W. 10
Maggie 10
Rachael HILLYER 10
McNAIRY
Margaret 71
McNALL
Mary E. JACKSON 102
Wilber 102
McNALLY
Ann 139
Bernard 165
Bridget WINTERS 165
Catharine 165
Elizabeth 100
Margaret 100
McNAMARA
Bridget 29, 63
Catherine 20
Daniel 29
Ellen SULLIVAN 102
Mary NOLAN 102
Mathew A. 129
Matthew A. 102
Patrick 102
McNAMARRA
Bridget 95
John 95
McNAMEE
Hannah DONAVAN
102
Joseph 102
Mary Ann McKENNA
102
William J. 102

McNANY
Hugh 102
Nellie TILLIE 102
Sarah JOHNSON 102
McNARRI
B. 52
McNAUGHTON
Eliza A., Mrs. 2
Eliza INGALLS 141
Jno. S. 141
John 2
John S. 141
Mattie 141
Nancy SMITH 2
McNAULTY
Eliza DEVINE 102
James 102
James S. 102
Kate NOLAN 102
McNEAL
Hellen Man 115
Martha 39
McNEELY
Emilie CARR 102
Francis M. 102
Hugh 102
James 5
Wilimine FIBE 102
McNEIL
A. 102, 167
Ann NOLAN 102
Benina MOOR 102
Bessie 163
Binina MOORE 163
James 102
Maggie HOWER 102
Margret 82
Patrick 102
R.F. 102
Samantha 99
Samantha ASHBURN
102
Sylvester 102, 163
McNELEIGH
Mary J. O'GRADY 102
Willis S. 102
McNERLEY
Jane 96
McNERLY
Jane 96
McNERNY
Daniel 102
Margret WALSH 102
McNICHOL
James 73
Maggie A. 73
Mary LOGAN 73
McNIECE
Margaret 153
McNIEL
Jennie 158
Nellie 158
McNULTRY
J.G. 145
McNULTY
Anna 82
Bridget HURLEY 115
Hugh 115
John 102
Mary 109
Nellie 115
McNUTT
Eliza HAWK 162
James 162
Nancy 162

McPHARLAN
Jemima 120
McPHERSON
Ada 107
Adaline BEAVERS 102
Damost 102
Eliza 45
J.P. 102
John 89
Marquis S. 107
Mary TIBBALLS 107
Mathilde LeDUC 102
Meliora 34, 105
Melissa 60
Susannah SHULL 102
William 102, 164
McQUADE
Catharine HOUGH 102
Felix 102
Patrick 102
Rosa TRANNOR 102
McQUARRIE
Charles 102
John 102
Maggie HIGGINS 102
Mary MATHEWSON
102
McQUILLAN
Bernard 22
Margaret 29
McREADY
Ida 52
McREYNOLDS
Jane 51
McSHANE
Alice CREIGHTON 102
Catharine 114
Edward C. 16, 46, 49
F.T. 102
John A. 102
Mary M. LEE 102
Thomas 102
McSHARE
Felix 153
McSWIGGEN
Mary 83
McTECKHAM
Helen 169
McWATERS
Charles H. 102
Louise
CEMMENSTEONE
102
Sarah ALBROW 102
William H. 102
McWHINNEY
Andrew 94
Elizabeth McDOWELL
102
William 102
McWINNIE
Frank 93, 102
Mary DELANEY 102
Michael 102
MEAD
Abigail W. WOOD 7
Anna A. 79
Augustus 102
Charles 65
Charlotte B. 59
D.B. 7
Eliza 7
J.W. 102
Mary J. MONAHAN
102

Phebe E. WILLIAMSON
102
MEADE
C.E. 144
Ella 144
Polly P. HOLBROOK
144
MEADER
Eliza E. 101
MEADIE
John C. 35
MEAGHER
J. 133
John 77
MEALIA
S.N. 52, 124
MEALIO
S.N. 67
Stephen N. 24
MEANEY
Alice 95
Alice BUTLER 102
Bridget GARVEY 102
Helen STANLEY 95
John 102
Mary HENSMAN 102
Michael 102
Patrick 95
Patrick B. 102
MEARS
Mary O. 98
MEAS
Annce 59
MECHEM
Luna 128
MECK
Theresa 9
MECKELSON
Claus 149
Margaret SCHWAGER
149
Mary 149
MECKGRAFF
Catharina CLARK 102
Lewis 102
MEDDEN
Bridget 37
MEDLOCK
Agnes 56
Charlotte SHAFTERR
102
Charlotte SHAFTON
144
Emma 144
Geo. W. 31
George 24, 102, 144
George W. 102
Mr. 144
Mr. and Mrs. 56
Mrs. 144
Susa GOLDEN 102
MEDSON
Frederick 102
Mary HANSEN 102
MEEHAN
Cahterine 34
Catharine O'GRADY
102
Charlotte 50
Ellen D. ENRIGHT 102
Honora 34
Margaret 102, 130
Mary 83, 102, 107, 138
Mary FLYNN 102
Mary MURRAY 34
Mary MURRY 102

Micahel 34
Michael M. 102
Patrick 34, 102
Rachel 40
MEEKER
Augustus 103
Belle 90
Hellen, Mrs. 92
Kitty TURNER 103
Mr. 156
MEEKS
Annie PFEIFFER 103
James 103
Thomas J. 103
MEEMES
Lotte 67
MEENEY
Elizabeth 108
MEERHOLZ
Bernard 103
Eliza CANAVAN 103
Eva MAINZ 103
Herman 103
MEERMANN
Anna 111
MEES
Gilbert 37
MEEWES
Sophia 169
MEGARY
Catherine 95
MEGEATH
E.V. CARTER 130
Elizabeth F. 130
J.G. 130
James G. 132
Jas. G., Mr. and Mrs.
144
Joseph 112
Judith W. CARTER 103
Samuel A. 103
MEGLEY
Olivia 3
MEHAN
Michael 131
MEHREN
Charles 103
Elizabeth GURNEY 103
Frederick 133
Henry 103
Mary Ann ROHRIG 103
MEHRING
Anna Mary PETERS 86
Bernhard M. 86
Christina 86
MEIDLINGER
Johann 103
John 57, 103
Julia BERTENLEHNER
103
Kate 57
Katharina SCHUSTER
103
Maria 103
Matthias 103
Paul 103
Theresia OSWALD 103
MEIER
Auguste 113
Dora 143
Louise 107
Maria 128
Martha 85
MEIERDIERKE
Maria 148

MEILHEDE
Peter 74
MEINHART
Elizabeth 119
MEIS
Elizabeth ENENBAG
103
Joseph 103
MEISEL
Henry 152
Johanna 152
Mathilda 96
MEJNIEN
Susan 71
MEJSTRICK
Joseph 85
MELACEK
Barbara 159
MELBOURNE
Ann 124
MELCHER
Frederick 24
Frederiki BUSH 24
Lena 24
MELCHIOR
Henriette 165
MELDRUM
Charles A. 46
Jenny H.P. FLEMING
103
Susan 123
Thomas 103
Thos. 170
MELENSON
John 86
MELIA
Brighet 164
Catherine 148
Kate McCANNEY 103
Mary Ann 164
Michael 103, 148, 164
S.N. 17
MELIUS
? 30
MELLBURNE
Mary E. 118
MELLEN
Ruth 155
MELLIS
S., Mrs. 30
MELLONE
Ellen RILEY 103
Mary MURRAY 103
Michael 103
Thomas 103
MELLUS
Anna BLACKWOOD
103
Emily AVERELL 103
John 103
Richart T. 103
Sarah 81
Sarah, Mrs. 103
MELONE
Peter 59
MELQUIST
Christine J. SANDBERG
103
John A. 103
MENDEL
Annie 84
MENDENAHAAM
Mary L. 82
MENDENHAAM
Isreal 82
Mary LOW 82

MOATS, cont.
  Ella 48
  Jennie 126
  Peter 48, 126
MOBAEK
  Catherine 94
MOBINE
  Elizabeth 94
MOBLEY
  John B. 106
  Lucy A. PRATT 106
  Maggie T.G. GUERIN
  106
  Seth P. 106
MOBURY
  Fanny E. STEHPENSON
  106
  William 106
MOCK
  Evanna 67
  John D. 33
  John W. 67
  Mollie 14, 94
  Molly 135
  Mrs. 67
  Sarah E. 33
  Susan BROWN 67
  Susanna BROWN 33
MOCKBEE
  Charles E. 106
  Delia A. WHITNEY
  106
  Joanna DWIER 106
  Richard 106
MOCKELMANN
  Andrew 106
  Barbara MILLER 106
  Maria HAGEMANN
  106
  Nicholas 106
MOCKLER
  Jos. 115
MOE
  Annie JOHNSON 106
  Annie NELSON 106
  Charles N. 106
  Ellen HART 106
  Gulbran 106
  Hans Andreas 106
  Henry A. 20
MOELLER
  Catharina BUELK 106
  Charles 106
  Christian 95
  Fred 106
  Fritz 106
  Henry 23
  Katharina SCHEEL 106
MOEYER
  Therklee 52
MOFFAT
  D.H. 170
  John D. 106
  Myra HILL 106
MOFFIT
  D.H. 56
MOGENSEN
  Anna LAURSEN 106
  Soren Peter 106
MOGNUS
  Ingren 76
MOHAN
  Honorah DOLAN 106
  Thomas 101, 106
MOHEN
  Fredericka 68

MOHR
  Annie TIEDERMANS
  106
  Bernard 106
  Charlotte 86
  Claus 68
  Dorothea J.L. 138
  Dorthea 58
  Elizabeth PRENZ 106
  Frederick 106
  Henry 106, 125
  Jacob 106, 138
  James 36
  John 43, 86, 137
  Katrina BOEGE 68
  Louisa C.M. MEYER
  106
  Magdalena 68
  Mathilda OLAND 106
  Matilda D.J. OLANDT
  138
MOIST
  Jennie R. 36
MOJEAN
  Oscar 63
MOLFINTER
  Catharine 80
MOLIBER
  John P. 34
MOLLER
  H. 61
  Nicholine 91
MOLLOTT
  Lilly M. 5
MOLONE
  Peter 124
MOLOY
  Margaret 45
MOLT
  Dorah 121
MOLTAN
  Charles 51
MOLTINGER
  Mary 92
MONAGHAN
  Delia 56
MONAHAN
  Bernard 102
  Catharine DONOVAN
  106
  Elizabeth CRAIG 106
  Hugh 106
  Margaret HOWE 102
  Mary J. 102
  Timothy 106
MONDABLE
  Johanah 24
MONELL
  Annie M. 68
  G.C. 11
  G.C., Dr. 72
MONER
  L.W. 153
MONFELDT
  H. 146
MONJOYE
  Anna 101
MONK
  Anna PETERSEN 26
  Annie PETERSON 106
  Catherine SHERWIN
  106
  Ella M. SANFORD 106
  Hugh 106
  Johanna Christina 26
  John S. 106

Kate Ann MOSSON 106
Peder 26
Peter C.F. 106
Sern 106
Soren 26
MONLEY
  Bridget 163
MONNELL
  G.C., Dr. 49
  Gilbert C., M.D. 58
MONRO
  John 106
  Marian STEVENSON
  106
  Mary E. MILLER 106
MONROE
  D. 25
  David 15
  Maggie 15
  Mary BROWN 15
MONSA
  Christina 58
MONSON
  G. PETERSON 76
  Karna 95
  Margaret 45
  Mary JOHNSON 152
  Nels 76
  Swan 152
MONT__GUE
  Harriet 56
MONTAGUE
  John 106
  Mary 101
  Mary DORSEY 106
MONTANA
  Jane 124
MONTGOMERY
  D.W. 32
  Eliza 38
  Susan 124
MONTIETH
  Annie 149
MONYHAN
  Daniel 16
MOODY
  O.L., Dr. 142
  Sarah Jane 37
MOOK
  Jane Ann 122
MOON
  Barney 95
  Edwin 106
  Flora I. 84
  George 106
  Hill 106
  Ira K. 84
  Margaret MORE 106
  Mary 95
  Sarah EMERY 106
MOONEY
  Ellen 107
  Mary 81, 107, 171
  Melinda C. 159
MOONY
  M. 63
MOOR
  Benina 102
MOORE
  Adell 41
  Alsina WHITTAKER
  29
  Alzina LAFFERTY 42
  Anna 106
  Anna L. RILEY 106
  Binina 163

C.A. 106
Caroline E. 146
Celista 140, 158
Clayton 106
D.S. 141
Daniel 146
Dr. 6
E.C. 100
E.M. 30
Edward C. 106
Elizabeth O'BRIEN 81
Elizabeth TONER 106
Ella 84
Ella A. HUNTER 106
Ellen 163
Ellen BURNS 107
Emma J. 42
Frank M. 29
Fred 84, 106
George P. 106
Grace M. BURGMAN
  107
Hannah WEBB 106
Hattie 29
Hattie J. 42
Helene WHITE 106
Hugh 106
J.B. 120
J.R. 107
James B. 107
Jane 13, 45, 144
Jane DOREMUS 106
John 107
Kate SEWARD 106
L.M. 42
Lavinia HAINSWORTH
  106
Linus 106
Louisa or Joanna 83
Lucinda 66
Lucy 98
Margaret 81
Margaret E. 96
Margaret SPRECHER
  107
Mary 165
Mary Ann 119
Mary CLARK 106
Mary McLAUGHLIN
  106
Mary TOYE 107
Mercia M. ROWE 146
Patrick 106
Rachel M. 82
Richard 40, 107
Robert 106
Russell 106
S.J., Mrs. 141
Samuel 29, 42
Sarah 28
Sarah M. 35
Susan 59, 95, 168
Thomas 81
Wm. 165
Wm. E. 132
Wm. E., Capt. 73
MOR
  Elizabeth 37
MORAN
  Ann 109
  Anna 11
  Annie 115
  Bridget 67
  Bridget BRADY 124
  Catharine 82

Catharine O'CONNELL
  90
Catharine O'CONNER
  39
Delia McINERNEY 107
E., Miss 90
Eliza 39
Ellen 108
James 107
James H. 87, 124
Jane 113
Jennie P. 87
Maggie 87, 124
Mary 90, 100
Michael 107
Nappy KELLEY 107
Patrick 39, 48, 90
MORANE
  Mattie E. 5
  Moses 5
  Nancy MILLER 5
MORANEY
  Helena 169
  Hellena 169
  Michael 169
MORAVEC
  Mary 70
  Solin 70
  Susy 70
MORE
  George 107
  Jacob 107
  Johanna 131
  Lydia THOMAS 107
  Margaret 106
  Samuel 159
MOREHEAD
  Louisa J. 54
MOREL
  Elise OBERT 129
  Mary 129
  Paul H. 129
  Paul Henri 129
MORELL
  John 82
  Mrs. 82
MOREY
  Ellen 47
  William R. 47
MORFORD
  A.T. 107
  Abner T. 28, 107
  Esther J. MAGREW 28
  Esther J. McGREW 107
  James H. 28, 107
  Jane McGREW 107
  Martha E. OGDEN 107
  Mary E. HARRISON
  107
  Norma S. 28
  William N. 107
MORGAN
  Albert C. 21
  Eliza 73
  Ellen MOONEY 107
  Hannah CROSS 87
  Lute E. 68
  Maggie 34
  Mary 78
  Mary Ann 58
  Mary Clarke 21
  Mary GEORGE 158
  Nancy 47, 105
  Nathan 87
  Patrick 133
  Patrick C. 107

MOYER
　Andrew 27
　Mary 27
MOYLAN
　Eliza CANAVAN 103
　Eliza, Mrs. 103
MOYNEHAN
　Daniel 115
MUCHTEY
　Emma 55
MUCK
　Betsy 160
MUCKLEY
　John 108
　Molly JOHNSON 108
　Sarah FOSTER 108
MUEHL
　Anna 131
MUELLELER
　E. 86
MUELLER
　Alois 113
　Anna 86
　Carl F.A. 108
　Caroline 113, 144
　Catharine BOETEL 108
　Christine BANGET 108
　Crezenia HANKE 113
　Elizabeth 104
　Emma LIEFFERS 108
　Fred 115
　Friedrich 108
　Jacob 104
　Johann 108
　Joseph F. 108
　Karl 86
　Lorenz 108
　Louise 54
　Maria NEVE 108
　Mary 150
　Mary STRASSER 104
　Mathilda 141
　Melvina KRIEBS 108
　Minnie SCHARTOW 86
　Sophie REINBOHT 108
MUELLHAGEN
　Charlotte 149
MUHES
　Ann 94
MUHL
　Anna 131
　Annie 130
MUHLENBROCK
　Wilhelmina 63
MUHR
　J.P.A. 161
MUHS
　Adeline 86
　Ann 94
　Anna SCHNEECLOTH
　　86
　Anna SCHNEKLOTH 5
　Chaterina 110
　Emma 5
　Peter 5, 86
MULBURN
　Robert J. 108
MULCAHEY
　Catherine 64
　Ellen 59
　Thos. 97
MULCAHY
　A.J. 108
　Bridget LAFFING 108
　Ella GUAINE 108
　John 108

Margaret LAFEIN 108
Mary McDONALD 108
Miss 139
Patrick B. 108
T.H. 108
Thomas 107, 108
W.H. 77
MULCHAY
　Thomas 24, 89, 97
MULDOON
　Ann 162
　George 123
MULFORD
　Margaret 7
MULHED
　Anna 138
　Mary 138
　Peter 138
MULHEDE
　Peter 61
MULL
　Ingre JOHNSON 108
　John 108
MULLADY
　Bridget 165
MULLAN
　Richard 8
MULLEGAN
　Susan, Mrs. 135
MULLEN
　Ann 156
　Anna MORAN 11
　Bridget 18
　Bridget KEEFE 108
　Ella NOONAN 18
　Ellen 34, 81
　Helen 11
　Jeremiah 108
　Jerry 108
　John 108
　Mae 98
　Mary 18, 56
　Mary DAVEY 108
　Patrick 11, 18
　Patrick M. 11, 23
　Richard 56
　Sarah JOHNSON 108
　William 108
　Wm. 108
MULLER
　Catharine 163
　Dinis 106
　George 11
　John 109
　Maria 45
　Melissa A. GRAHAM
　　109
　Regina 73
　Zilke 169
MULLHOLLAN
　Margaret 96
MULLIGAN
　John 109
　Mary DUFFEY 109
　Mary GALLAGHER
　　109
　Mary O'HARRA 109
　Michael 109
　Patrick 109
　Sarah STEPHENS 109
　William J. 109
MULLIN
　Ann MORAN 109
　Bridget DONNELLEY
　　109
　P.M. 109

Richard 83, 109
MULLINGER
　Elizabeth POWELL 109
　George 109
　Mary STANLEY 109
　William R. 109
MULLINIX
　Phoebe Jane 1
MULLIS
　Katrina 153
MULLONE
　Catherine 128
MULLONEY
　Bridget McDONAGH
　　100
　Mary 100
　Samuel 100
MULLOY
　Ann PHILLIPS 109
　Harriet ULAN 109
　James G. 109
　Mary E. NORRIS 109
　Thomas 109
　Thomas F. 109
MULVIHILL
　Delia DALTON 109
　Jeremiah 109
　Johanna MAHONEY
　　109
　John 109
MULVILLE
　Mary 66
MULVY
　Charles 10
　Louisa COLLINS 10
　Mary A. 10
MUMFORD
　Anne 29
MUMM
　Catherine 44
　Detlef 44
　Elsiba THOEMING 109
　Jorgen 109
　Karsten 109
　Margurita LORENZEN
　　44
　Wiebke SIEVERS 109
MUNCHNA
　Anna 160
MUNCY
　Betsey 122
MUNDELL
　Debby C. 60
　Hiram 60
　Jane BROWN 60
MUNDSCHENK
　Augustine J. BOUND
　　109
　Katrine KELLER 109
　Peter 109
MUNDT
　Claus H. 94
MUNDWEILER
　Alice NEED 145
　Christian 145
　Hattie May 145
MUNGER
　A.F. 2
　C.K. 110
　Cordelia E. 72
　Eliza MARSH 110
　Francis M. 110
　J.E., Miss 2
　Jennette 51
　Laura 8
　Maria, Mrs. 138

MUNHOVEN
　Anthony 109
　John 109
　Susan THILLEN 109
　Susanna HURT 109
MUNK
　Karen, Mrs. 66
　P.C.F. 66
　Peder C.T. 74
MUNN
　Anna BEHRENS 88
MUNNING
　Margareta 12
MUNSELL
　Elizabeth 97
MUNSEN
　Elsie 118
MUNSMAN
　Christiane 74
MUNSON
　Abbie J. JOHNSON 109
　Dorte 3
　Evelyn Grace
　　O'CONNELL 109
　John B. 109
　Julia A. WALKER 109
　M. DENNING 109
　Mary 4
　O.A. 109
　Samuel 109
　Sophia SPONEMAN 83
MUNSTER
　Annie DORAN 74
　Bertha 74
　John 74
MUNTD
　Catharine 18
MUPRHY
　William L., Jr. 109
MURBACH
　Lena OBERLE 109
　Maggie GESLER 109
　Simon 109
　Ulrich 109
MURDOCK
　Emily A. 165
　M.E. 67
　Robert 36
MURPHE
　Bridget 45
MURPHEY
　Annie 55
　Bridget SHERIDAN
　　139
　Bridgett 139
　Daniel 139
　David 109
　Ellen LINNEHAN 109
　Margaret 157
　Margaret RAGAN 109
　Mary McANDREW 109
　Patrick 109
MURPHY
　---- McCANTZ 110
　Almira 28
　Andrew 37, 109
　Ann 114
　Annie 95, 144
　Annora 17
　Anthony 109
　Barton 40
　Ben 94
　Betty DOYLE 109
　Bridget 82
　Bridget HARGADON
　　35

Bridget M.
　DOUGHERTY 109
Bridget SHERIDEN 109
Catharine 27, 82
Catharine LANCE 109
Catharine SHENEHAM
　109
Catherine 23, 114
Daniel 109
Della 40
Dennis 109
Edward 109
Eliza HICKEY 109
Eliza P. THOMAS 40
Elizabeth 52, 115
Ellen 33, 63, 115
Ellen DELANEY 109
Fannie 60
Francis 115
Frank 28, 103, 144, 156
Hannah 15, 77, 110
Hanora 151
Hugh 109
J.W. 19
James 109
Jennie, Mrs. 46
Johanna KEEFE 109
Johanna Matilda
　BANNISTER 109
John 10, 33, 45, 109,
　110
Kate 47, 143
Lizzie 64, 100
Luke 114
Maggie KENNEDY 109
Martha 28
Martha F. 35
Martin 82, 109
Martin D. 109
Mary 1, 16, 25, 130
Mary A. CALLAHAN
　109
Mary A. HANNIGAN
　109
Mary GARVEY 109
Mary MALONE 109
Mary SEWARD 114
Mary SWORDS 82
Michael 148, 162
Nancy 37
Nellie McGRATH 109
P. 78, 99
Patk. 109
Robert 109
Rose Ann PYNEN 115
Sarah E. 154
Thomas 36, 115
Thomas M. 154
Thompsien (sic) 67
William 109
William F. 109
William L. 109
William R. 35
Wm. S. 35
MURRAY
　Amelia 56
　Ann 132
　Ann FARLEY 110
　Bridget 8
　Bridget FITGERALD
　　103
　Bridget O'MALEY 8
　Catharine 27, 151
　Catherine 77
　Eliza 156
　Ellen CONNER 110

NEWCOMB
Christine 51
Emma 157
NEWELL
Harriet N. 1
Lida M. 138
Lucy 83
NEWHALL
Eliza 64
Helen A. 93
NEWHOUSE
Anna 136
Harriet 53
Lewis 53
Mary, Mrs. 129
NEWLAND
Joseph 154
Josephine 154
Mary KELLY 154
NEWMAN
August 112
David 112
Esther 18
Ferdinand 112
George 10, 112
George F.H. 112
H. 50
Hattie COWDEN 112
Henry 112
Horace C. 112
Jane Harriet GUILD 124
Jesse 112, 118
Jessie 167
Joseph 18
Julius 112
Lena BROWN 112
Lydia FORBES 112
M. 18
Matilda HAASS 112
Mine KLEUDER 112
Mr. and Mrs. 53
Peppi
  SCHOENWETTER
  18
Rose MOSS 112
Sadie 124
Stanley HAWKINS 112
William 124
NEWMEISTER
Edward 112
Frederick 112
Kate DIPPEL 112
Rozena LOCH 112
NEWSHAM
James 112
Maggie WHELAN 112
Nancy PARKINSON
  112
NEWSYNGER
Barbara 131
NEWTON
Adel 94
Flora 149
John 112
Mary CLARK 112
Michael 112
Nellie M. BURDEN 112
Ruth E. TURNER 131
NICHOLAS
Nancy 34
NICHOLS
Amanda 150
Anna 105
Anna MATTISON 112
C.H. 105, 159
Charles E. 112

Charles H. 101, 111
Charlotte MOSES 40
Debora BUTLER 17
E.B., Mrs. 168
Edmund 112
Eliza 33
Elizabeth 101, 113
Eloise B. POWELL 112
Eunice VINCENT 112
George 112
Helena KUERR 112
J.M. 112
Jeremiah V. 112
John 40
John M. 129
Joseph 159
Julia S. HOMAN 112
Julia, Mrs. 70
Louisa 40
Lucy 40
Mary 28
Mary NELSON 112
Maxilnili 17
Phebe 40
Robert 17
Sarah E. DAVIS 112
Stephen R. 112
T.A. 112
NICHOLSON
Caroline MUELLER
  113
Charles P. 113
Christine GREGERSON
  75
Ellen OLIVER 113
Frederick 75
Hannah G. 158
Hester 132
James 113
James Henry 113
John 113
Margaret McMULLEN
  113
Mary 75, 135
Mary A. LARKIN 113
NICK
John M. 17
NICKELS
Claus M. 113
Cynthia H. 123
Regina ROSE 113
NICKELSEN
Barbara 66
NICKENDECKER
J. 92
NICKERSON
Carrie L. 10
Hannah 64
Johanna HANSEN 64
John 64
Matilda PRESTON 10
Orson 10
NICKLES
Catharine ROWERT
  113
Claus M. 113
NICKOR
Mary 61
NICOLAI
Anna 61
Auk HANSEN 61
Soenke 61
NICTEL
Wenzel 10
NIEBER
Marie 137

NIEDERMEYER
Anna 169
Anthony 47
Anton 169
Carrie 169
Louisa HELBLUCK
  169
NIEDIECK
Hannah F. 87
Isabella
  ESSELLAMANN 87
John H. 87
NIEHAUS
Edward 147
NIELSDOTTER
Annie 97
Ingrid 124
Kirsten 88
NIELSEN
A.M. 1
August 127
Bodel C.N. TAUSEN
  113
Bodil Christine 4
Casper 113
Charlotte N. 79
Christen 1, 113
David H. 61
Egidia HANSEN 113
Ellen Marie SIMONSEN
  113
Erik 43
Frederik 26
Hans 111, 113
Inger Catharine 25
Inger POULSEN 43
Jens P. 113
Johan H. 113
Johanna 127
Johanna PETERSON
  136
Karin 121
Lars 66
Marie 1
Mary GUNDERSON
  113
Meta K. JOHANSEN
  113
Mette JENSEN 43
N. 25
Nicoline M. 4
Niels Christian 88
Niels S. 4, 113
P. 104
Peter 113
Sanne NILSEN 113
NIELSON
Andres 113
Ane Maria Sophia 26
Anna 146
Anna K. 79
Annie 162
Annie FLAHERTY 113
Bohl Christina JENSEN
  89
Caroline DAWSON 113
Caroline PRIES 113
Charles F.M. 113
Christian B. 113
Christina 117
Emily C. BAUCHETTE
  113
George 113
Inger 1
John 113

Kiersti ANDERSON
  113
Kristina 111
L. 3
Lars 89
Maran 156
Mary 1, 155
Mary CHRISTIANSEN
  113
Mary SYKES 113
Matilda 127
Niels 113
Peter 122
Prod 98
Rasmis 122
Thomas 113
NIEMANN
Anna 41
NIEMETZ
Barbara HOWRAK 13
Josephine 13
Mathias 13
NIESSENKEAR
Andrew 79
NIEWALD
Amalia 136
Minna WHITE 136
Toens 136
NIGLEY
Olivia PETERSON 3
NIKLAUSEN
Christina HANSEN 113
Gustave 113
NILADON
Anna PLATEKA 113
Frank 113
Joseph 113
NILE
Carrie E. WILSON 64
Mary W. 64
Wm. 64
NILES
A.G. 159
Arther G. 157
Arthur G. 157
Dencie A. 157
Dencil A. 157
Deuce A. 159
Emma R. 159
Sally WILMARTH 157
Sally WILMOOTH 157
Sarah WILMARTH 159
NILSDOTTER
Anna 4
Kestina 116
NILSEN
Aug. 85
E., Mrs. 78
Jacob 113
Lizzie EDLING 113
Mila 66
Mrs. 78
N.P. 24
Nette 15
Nils Kgelsberg 33
Sanne 113
NILSON
A.W. 11
Amelia 75
Anders 150
Anna 75
Anna M. HARTMAN
  113
Anna SVENSON 150
Caroline HENSEN 88

Caroline J. JACOBSON
  113
Carrie 133
Charlotte SWANSON
  170
Christian 113
Elna LARSON 164
Emiline 151
Eva 155
Halvren 77
Hans 3
Henry 45
Inga L. 77
Ingred 81
Ingrid 4
Jacob N. 113
Lars 75, 88
Magdaline 25
Mary 3, 61
Mary CHRISTIANSEN
  113
Mary PETERSON 148
Mats 148
Nils 113, 164
Peter 170
Sofa 111
NILSSON
Anna 11
Charstina PEARSON
  152
J. 3
Johanna 145
John 116
Kestina NILSDOTTER
  116
M. 3
Nils 152
NILSTOTTER
Christine 88
NIMAND
Anna 62
NIMICH
Katie 56
NINDEL
Carolina LOHSE 113
Christian N. Paul 113
F. Clara W. MILDNER
  113
Johann C. 113
NIRA
Andrew 33
Christina PERSON 33
NISLET
Wenzel 56
NISSEN
Dorothea 49
NISSON
Dorothea 75
NISTEL
Annie 12
W. 130
Wenzel 24, 83, 98, 128,
  150, 171
NIXON
Albert 162
Fanny 114
NIXTON
Francis 74
NJVARY
Elizabeth REIS 113
Juliana SCHNABLE
  113
Martin 113
Paul 113
NOBAUM
Caroline 139

O'CONNOR
Ann MURPHY 114
Annie 54, 67
Charles 131
Charlotte 55
Ebbie 54
Elisabeth 114
Eliza 22
Ellen 38
Ellen FORD 114
H. 55
Honoria 131
J.J. 19
Jeremiah 114
Johanna FLYNN 131
John 71, 114
Katie 71
Margaret 54, 114, 131
Margaret ROONEY 101
Mary 50, 126
Mary CAVANAGH 22
Mary CONNELL 71
Mary GREEN 114
Mary KELLY 114
Michael 101
Morris 114
Norah 131
Patrick 22
Thomas 54, 55, 114
O'DEA
Bridget CALLIVAN 54
John 114
Margaret 54
Patrick 54
O'DELL
Mary Ann 7
O'DERNAL
Ellen 51
O'DONAHUE
Eliza T. 115
Ellen J. FLEMINGS 114
James 114
Johannah DOOYER 114
Michael 114
Patrick 115
O'DONELL
Bridget HALEY 114
Margaret ROCHFORD 114
Thomas 114
O'DONNEL
Eliza T. 115
Ellen 59, 132
Patrick 115
O'DONNELL
Catharine 56
Cornelius 99
Daniel 115
Edward W. 115
James 115
Kate McDAVITT 115
Lavina ZEGRINO 115
Mary 38, 125, 149
Mary DANNER 115
Sarah A. LATHAM 115
Sarah BOYLE 115
William G. 115
O'DONOGHUE
Bridget BUTLER 115
Dennis 115
J.B. 115
Jannie E. STAFFORD 115
Julia CRANE 115
Mary A. SPILANE 115
Michael 115

Patrick 115
O'DONOHOE
James 115
John 115
Mary LOUGHLIN 115
Nellie McNULTY 115
O'DONOUGH
Mary COLLINS 115
Michael 115
O'FLANNIGAN
John 115
Julia Frances THOMAS 115
O'GORMAN
John 94
Julia WHALEN 137
Kate 137
Mary 94
Mary FITZ GIBBONS 94
Michael 137
O'GRADY
Catharine 102, 130
James 102
Jeremiah 115
Margaret HARRIGAN 115
Margaret MEEHAN 102
Mary J. 102
Mary SHEA 115
Thomas 115
O'HANLON
Mary 57
O'HARA
Bridget MONLEY 163
Celia 20
Mary 29, 163
Patrick 163
O'HARER
ELiza Ann 38
O'HARRA
John 109
Margrete MANT 109
Mary 109
O'HEARN
Bridget CODY 115
Catharine, Mrs. 48
Kate McCORMICK 115
Michael 115
O'HERN
Lizzie 114
O'KEEF
Mary 164
O'KEEFE
Kate 26
Maggie 11
Mary 60
O'KEEFFE
Bell BISHOP 115
Catherine CANNING 115
Ellen DORAN 115
Ellen MURPHY 115
James 115
John 115
William 115
O'LEARY
Andrew J. 93
Margaret 94
Mary E., Mrs. 93
O'MALEY
Bridget 8
O'MALLEY
Catharine M. LARKINS 110

Ellen GENTLEMAN 115
James 115
Peter 99, 115
Winnifred 115
O'MARA
Mary A. 28, 86
O'MERA
Eliza BARRETT 45
Hannah 45
Thomas 45
O'NEAL
Bridget 48
Henry 81, 115
Mary MAHER 115
Phoenix 115
Rachel SMITH 115
O'NEIL
Ann 2, 51, 134
Catharine WHALEN 115
Delia McCARTY 34
Dell 34
Eliza BURNS 9
Ellen LOVELLY 115
Hanora 134
Henry 122
Hugh 114
J.W. 115
James 34
John 9, 156
Julia 9
Lizzie O'HERN 114
Lucretia 115
Margaret 110, 114
Michael J. 11
Nora (Norah) 60
Patrick 115
Sarah 11
Thomas 115
William P. 115
Winniford COLLINS 115
Winniford GORMLEY 115
O'NEILL
Alice HURREA 115
Anastasia HANIGAN 156
Annie 66, 115
Annie McDONALD 115
Edward 115
Hellen Man McNEAL 115
Hugh 115
James 52
Julia PERCIL 52
Kate 156
Mary 52
Michael 6, 156
Michael J. 115
Patrick 115
Paul 115
Rosana DUGGAN 115
Sadie E. McCRISTAL 115
O'NIEL
Ann 83
Eillone 83
O'REILEY
Bartholomew 115
Ignataius 23
O'REILLY
Addie LECKENBY 115
Francis MURPHY 115
J. 65

John 115
Joseph 115
Mrs. 153
O'REILY
Ann 115
Mary HEALY 115
Michael 115
O'RILEY
Mary 101
Michael 115
O'ROURKE
Abby McGORMAN 115
Anna 108
Farron 115
John J. 156
Mary J. DEVIN 115
Michael 108
Peter 101, 115, 126
O'SHEA
Mary, Mrs. 37
Thomas 37
O'SULLIVAN
Ed 82
Ellen BRENNAN 115
James 115, 151
Margaret 107
Nora 98
OAK
Henry 103
OAKES
Elizabeth 153
OAKLEY
Lorena J. PETERSON 115
Lucinda COLBURN 115
Nelson A. 115
Robert 115
OAKS
Annie Maud SICKER 115
Cleora 12
Elsie BABCOCK 12
Geo. D. 13
George 115
John F. 115
Lucius 12
Mary RONGUEY 115
OAKSON
Alice 7
Anna ANDERSON 7
Martin 7
OATES
Maggie 43
OATHWAIT
Milton, Mr. and Mrs. 105
OATMAN
Mollie COATS 163
OATS
Margaret 140
OBERBURG
Margareta 58
OBERG
Eric L. 166
Frederica STIEGHORST 115
L.C. 81
Richard 115
OBERLE
Lena 109
Maggie 109
OBERLENDER
John 141
Mary FISHER 141
Rosa 141

OBERMAN
Mary 75
OBERMEITE
Augusta BEIL 95
OBERMILLER
Mary 17, 127
OBERMULLER
Hans 156
Helena 156
OBERST
Elizabeth ROLAND 115
Jacob 115
Martin 43, 115
Minna 43
Minna MEYER 115
OBERT
Elise 129
OBERUNDER
Annie 157
John 157
Mary YAGLER 157
Rosa 157
OCANDEL
Gabriel 25
Magdaline NILSON 25
Mary 25
OCANDER
Elizabeth 77
Emma 145
Emma OSTWALD 115
Gabreal 115
Gabriel 77
Lene NELSON 77
Oscar 115, 138, 145
Sophia LARSSON 115
OCHS
Margaret 79
OCHSE
Conrad 116
Wilhelmina STORDA 116
OCHSENBEIN
Betty ANDERSON 116
Elizabeth STIGER 116
George W. 116
Samuel 116
OCKANDER
Carl 89
ODEN
Anna BLOMBERG 116
Bertha 64
C.W.B. 77, 116, 170
Charles 116
E.G.B. 116
Eliza HODGES 116
Eva VINCENT 116
Laurence B. 116
Lawrence B. 92
Nellie NELSON 116
ODMAN
Dora OLESON 112
Josephina 112
Lars 112
OELARENG
Annie 136
OELKE
Margaret 68
OFFICER
M., Rev. 132
Thos. 37
OFMAN
Margaret 85
OFT
Anna 90, 116
Anna E. 85
Antje LEBBERT 116

ONHE
  Agnes HAUG 117
  Rachel BAUMGARDEN
    117
  William 117
ONIG
  Mary 85
ONTZEN
  Annie H. 15
  Jacob 15
OPENSHAW
  Ellen 8
  Henry 8
  Maggie 8
ORALL
  Alice 7
ORCHARD
  A.R. 117, 120, 125
  A.R., Mr. 120
  A.R., Mr. and Mrs. 157
  A.R., Mrs. 120
  Alice A. 96
  Amanda HELLEM 117
  Amanda HELLM 96
  Amanda M. HELM 120
  Amanda Z. 120
  Andres R. 96
  Anna GUY 117
  Eliza A. CRAWFORD
    117
  Emily Victoria 125
  John 88, 117
  Mabel G. 144
  Margery M. 157
  Mattie S. DUNCAN 117
  Mr. 110
  Mr. and Mrs. 117
  S.A. 125, 128
  Saml. 47
  Samuel A. 56, 117
ORD
  Catharine 134
  E.O.C. 131
ORRETSON
  Bolla JEPPERSON 61
  Swen 61
ORRICK
  Georgiana 170
ORRILL
  Alice 98
ORSBORN
  Eliabeth 107
ORTON
  L.L. 117
  Louisa N. DELAWARE
    117
ORTT
  Catharine 47
ORUM
  Catherine 91
  Hamlet 91
ORWIG
  Elizabeth R. WILBORN
    117
  George W. 117
  Lydia HARTMAN 117
  Samuel 117
OSBERG
  Christina 170
  Christina OLSON 170
  Nils M. 170
OSBORN
  Abraham 117
  Anna 22
  Elizabeth WYSEL 117
  Enoch B. 117

H. 50
Irene COX 117
John 117
Julia HEATH 117
Luther W. 117
Maggie A. ROGERS
  117
Mary A. SMITH 117
Mary E. WRIGHT 117
Mary LYON 117
Mrs. 50
Sally M. 56
Sophie 14
Troy C. 117
William 93, 117
OSBORNE
  Anne 143
  Christiana 107
  James 70
  Jefferson 117
  Jenny JOHNSON 117
  Rebecca
    BRECKENRIDGE 70
  Ruth E. 70
  William 20
OSBURN
  Ann 127
  Eliza GRANT 117
  Eliza MAGRUDER 117
  Ellenor MAGRUDER
    117
  George 117
  John L. 117
OSMUND
  Ellen 15, 37
OSTERBANN
  Bouwdwina 91
OSTERGAARD
  Ane Mary 42
OSTERHAUS
  Jessie 105
OSTERHAUT
  Jesse 138
OSTERHOUST
  Jessie 82
OSTERLUND
  ---- 108
OSTERMAN
  Charles 117
  Henry 117
  Tracie TEMBEL 117
OSTERTAG
  Anna Maria 9
OSTLER
  Anna 50
  Edith H. ADDER 162
  Edith HANTHER 50, 97
  Edith HODDER 110
  George 50, 97, 110, 162
  Jane 162
  Lottie 110
  Mary 97
OSTLY
  Mary 89
OSTON
  L.L. 117
  Louisa N. DELAWARE
    117
OSTRAM
  Albert 32
OSTROM
  A.S. 7, 22, 82, 107
  Adam S. 7
  Alice 57
  Annie M. 57
  Carrie F. 82

Christine 123
Florence 107
Henry 57
Hiram H. 57
Jennie L. 22
Lavina VALLEY 57
Leonora E. 7
Lois 7
Lois WALKER 7
Lois WEIBKE 107
Louise WALKER 22
Mary 18
OSTRUM
  Alice DWYER 117
  Harvey J. 117
OSTWALD
  Catharine
    MORTENSSON 115
  Emma 115
  Johan 115
OSWALD
  Caroline 37
  Caroline HOUSER 37
  Catharine 93
  Charles 37
  Mary 56, 120
  Theresia 103
OSWOLD
  Barbara 132
  Caroline HANSER 132
  John 132
OTIS
  Ada PERKINS 117
  Bloomey Jane 112
  Frank L. 117
  Rufus 117
  Therese M. SIX 117
OTT
  Elizabeth 156
  Mary S. 136
OTTAWAY
  Mr. and Mrs. 12
OTTE
  Claus 92
  Eggert 92, 156
  Elsabeth 92
  Kate 132
  Kate RUSHMAN 132
  Mary WIEBKE 92
  Nick 132
OTTEN
  Albert 117
  Bertie P. LONG 117
  Ellen PEAK 117
  John A. 117
OTTERBIEN
  Christof 137
  Elsie 137
  Louise 137
  Marie Catharine
    WESJOHANN 137
OTTHOLM
  Rachael 72
OTTO
  Friederike 134
  Gustav 9
OTTOWAY
  Charles R. 117
  E. Jane CHIVINGTON
    117
OTZEN
  Elsabe 155
  Mary 121
OUREDNIK
  Barbara 142
  Fanny JANDA 142

John 142
OVERAKER
  ---- RISBY 4
  Henry 4
  Susan 4
OVERALL
  Edwin 70
  Edwin R. 70
  Grace V. 70
  Margaret BLACKBURN
    70
OVERGARD
  Anders Christensen 117
  Anna CHRISTIANSEN
    117
  Christian A. 117
  Dorothea JENSEN 117
OVERKERGEN
  Peter 59
OVERLAND
  Mary J. 168
OVERLANDER
  Mary J. 29, 64
  Mary NEAL 29, 64
  William 29, 64
OVERMAN
  Flora D. 78
OVERMIRE
  Elizabeth FICKLE 117
  George B. 117
  Mary LELAND 117
  William H. 117
OVERMYER
  William H. 134
OVERTON
  Annie 65
  Annie KITE 65
  M.L. 127
  Margaret YANTS 168
  Mary 168
  Mr. 147
  Robert 168
  Samuel 65
  Thompson 94
  Wm. 147
OWEN
  John 81
  Mattie McCLAIN 118
  Otis 118
  Rachel SPEAR 118
  Samuel 118
OWENS
  Alberta 104, 118
  Ann Elizabeth
    TRIVILLA 104
  Anna 87
  Anna TRAVILLA 118
  Ella 118
  Emily 66
  Flora M. ROGERS 118
  Hannah 6
  Jane EDWARDS 118
  John 118
  John W. 118
  Loring 118
  Mary 11
  Mary E. MELLBURNE
    118
  Mary Ellen CURRENCE
    118
  May M. HAWLEY 118
  Phil B. 118
  Richard 118
  Sally 159
  William 118
  Young 104

OWNEY
  Bedford 118
  Mary M. ASHBURN
    118
OZIAH
  Mary 72
PAASCH
  Charles 118
  Frederick 118
  Henry 132
  Johanna 132
  Lena SCHNEIDER 118
  Lottie PETERSON 118
PABIAN
  Barbara BARTAS 118
  John 118
  Theresa SPEDL 118
PACE
  Edward 156
  Emily E. 156
  Mahoea LONG 156
  Sarah 167
PACKEISER
  Henriette BROSH 118
  Leopold 118
  Wilhelmine
    BARTIGKETT 118
PADDEN
  Thomas 139
PADDOCK
  A.S. 22, 152
  A.S., Mrs. 22, 136
  Algernon Sydney 118
  E.A., Miss 138
  Emma L. MACK 118
  Francis A. 43, 67, 144
  J.M. 118
  Nellie 47
  Susan 118
PADOCK
  S. Dwight 87
PAGAN
  Lena 68
PAGE
  ---- NASH 39
  Charles 124
  Charles W. 39
  Cordelia C. 39
  E. 28
  E.T. 82
  E.T., Mrs. 123
  Elizabeth C.
    WINCHESTER 118
  Elizabeth W. JOHNSON
    87
  Emma 152
  Ezekiel T. 87
  Ezekiel T., Mr. and Mrs.
    87
  Flora L. 124
  Geo. W. 124
  Hannah 24
  John E. 118
  John S. 118
  L.J., Mrs. 82
  Larane SEVENS 118
  Lizzie 105
  Marion M., Mrs. 87
  Martha J. GIBBS 124
PAGEL
  Christof 170
  J. 170
  Johanna 170
  Johanna BAERWALDE
    170
  John 126

PETERSON, cont.
Kirstene 75
Kirstina 73
L. 60, 122
Lars 4, 121
Lena SCHRODER 121
Lina C. 135
Lizzie ANDERSON 121
Lorena J. 115
Lorentz Christian 122
Lotte 119
Lottie 118
Louisa M. HARDEN
121
Louisa
YOUNGSTETLER
15
M. 157
Mads 98
Maggie 143
Maren NELSEN 61
Margaret 3
Margaret
FREDERICKSON 98
Margarethe BINMAN
27
Margrethe FULLARD
16
Maria Christena 131
Maria CHRISTIANSON
87
Maria E. 9
Maria JOHNSON 122
Marian 77
Marian MATSEN 121
Marie CHRISTENSON
121
Marsey 3
Martha 116, 152
Mary 1, 46, 76, 78, 117,
122, 131, 132, 148,
160, 166
Mary A. ALEXANDER
121
Mary DEWEY 143
Mary EVERSON 107
Mary HANSEN 3
Mary JOHNSON 122
Mary NELSON 77, 119
Mary OLESON 122
Mary OTZEN 121
Mary PETERSON 1,
122
Mary THISE 97
Mary WILSON 121
Matilda 116
Matilda C. 7
Mattie M. 27
Matz 148
Mette J.J. PLATZ 122
Morentze Sophia
GINSON 122
Mr. 17
Nancy M. 167
Nellie 56
Nellie JOHNSON 121
Nels 4, 97, 114, 122
Nelson 167
Nicolas 113
Niels 44, 89, 121
Nils 1, 61, 136
Nils C. 113
Olena 77
Olivia 3
P.E. 142
Patre 89

Paul 119
Pete 78
Peter 3, 13, 42, 61, 77,
80, 91, 121, 122, 143,
153
Peter C. 122
Petrina Maria 1
R. 142
Rasmus 23, 38, 55
Regine 61
S.M. 84
Samuel 115
Segra WAHLBERG 4
Severt 138
Sophia 98
Soren 146
Soren C. 122
Stenlesa 92
Stephen 148
Stina 77
Swan 77
Swen 121
Swen M. 122
Tinnie 76
Ulette CHRISTENSEN
74
Veldera KNUTSON 75
Wilhelmina 160
Wilhelmina K. 160
William 77, 122
William, Mrs. 77
PETIT
Ann 40
PETOT
Anna 5
PETRICEK
Anne 129
Joe 134
Katie 134
PETRIE
M.J., Miss 76, 114
PETRIK
Barbara 85
PETTEGREW
David A. 122
Lidie 122
Lydia SHAW 122
Melissie BARNES 122
PETTENGILL
Geo. W. 38
PETTER
Martin 103
PETTERSON
Anders 58
Catharine 49
Charl 39
Claus Frederick 122
Lotta 58
Margreet 141
Maria 25
Mary LORENSON 49
Thomas 49
PETTINGLEY
Benjamin F. 101
PETTIS
Alcinda 24
Harriet N. 28
PETTIT
Elizabeth 28
Malinda DOUGLAS 28
Mary E. 168
Melinda DOUGLAS
168
William 28
Wm. F. 168

PETTRE
Maria 86
PETTS
E.C., Miss 19
Eleverria C. 19
Levina 137
PETTY
John W. 122
Mary FRANCE 122
Mary Frances DOLAN
122
Solomon 122
PETZ
John 109
PETZINE
Anna Clara 132
PEYCKE
Arnold 166
Caroline M. REIFORT
122
Edw. 141
Ernest 122
John H. 122
Julia L. Von BORRIES
122
PEYTON
A. 139
Elizabeth COURTNEY
139
Etta 139
PFANNER
Anna B. PFYSTERER
70
Anton 70
Caroline 70
PFEFFERER
Augusta 130
Johanna KOCH 130
Joseph 130
PFEIFER
Barbara RADLER 122
Francisca WEISER 122
Frank 122
George 122
PFEIFFER
Annie 103
Augusta F. 59
Francis 103
Susan MADDOX 103
PFLEIDARER
Anna FRODEL 107
Jacob 107
Louise 107
PFLUG
Frederick 122
Grettchen BRANT 122
Jacob 9
Margaret 135
PFOUTZ
Ira 122
Jesse 122
Mary F. HARTMAN
122
Rebecca 94
Rebecca KENZIE 122
PFUFFER
August 148
Augusta 148
Fredericka FREVOLT
148
PFYSTERER
Anna B. 70
PHAAB
Hans P. 122
Kierstine M.
SORENSEN 122

Mary RASMUSSEN
122
Neils P. 122
PHALAN
Mary 100
PHALON
Margaret 24
PHEIFER
Mary Ann 149
PHELAN
Albert 122
John 26
Kate M. 26
M. CAVY 122
Mary COLLOPY 122
Mary DOLAN 122
Mary RAHER 26
Patrick 122
William 122
PHELEN
Margaret 85
PHELPS
A.W. 122
Alfred 122, 159
Alfred W. 159
Alfred, Mrs. 159
Alice BAY 122
Alice V. 119
Amanda WEBB 124
Amelia 98
Amelia J. 159
Anna HONSELL 160
Anna M. NELSON 122
C. 58
C.J. 122
Catherine KELLEY 122
D. 23
Eliza 23
Eliza MORRIS 122
Emily PRICHARD 122
Emily PRITCHARD
122, 159
Frank 122
George 160
George W. 122
Hannah GRINNELL
122
Hattie 36
Horace W. 119
Jennie KRIEBS 122
John 122
John C. 122
John E. 122
Margaret DAWSON
122
Maria J. 71
Mary E. 32
Mathilda J. 34
Mrs. 112
Nettie 98, 160
Nola 122
O.J. 122
Oliver J. 122
Sarah 41
Sarah J. 170
Sarah SEDELL 122
Sarah SIDELL 122
Sarah, Mrs. 23
Saray SEYDELL 122
Timothy G. 122
Viola M. 122
Walter 122
PHENIX
William, Mrs. 77
PHENNIG
Lena 123

PHILBROOK
B.F. 122
Lube 122
Lucinda SMITH 122
Lucy E. HARTRY 122
PHILIP
Maria 56
PHILLIP
Maria 56
PHILLIPS
Ann 109
Annie 63
Annie E. 133
Eliza BISSELL 122
Elizabeth STEVENS 51
Geo. S. 122
Hannah WILLIAMS
122
Haynes 51
J.N. 71, 157
James N. 141
Jane 97
Joseph 122
Linda Jane 46
Mary 16
Mary J. 21
Minerva E. 67
Sarah A. 51
Seth 122
Thomas 95
PHIPPS
Charles A. 122
Ilena 139
Nora VAN DEUSEN
122
PHOENIX
Anna KEEN 122
Jennie HOOD 122
Richard 122
PHOVE
Christine 139
PICKARD
Catharine BOYER 52,
57
Catie BOYER 24
Clara 163
Ellen A. BOWERS 123
Emma BROCK 123
Eugene 24, 123
Frank 123
J., Mrs. 123
James 123, 153
James W. 123, 163
Jane SCHOTT 163
Jane SCOTT 123
John 16, 83, 123, 146
Julia McANDRES 123
Juliaette SKINNER 146
Juliette SCINNER 123
Juliette SKINNER 16,
83
L.W. 146
Laomei W. 52
Laura BELL 123
Linda 123
Linda W. 16
Lonama W. 24
Lucy 83
Marion 24, 52
Mary 15
Nancy BOYER 123
Orin W. 123
Oscar J. 123
Philicia J. 27
R.H. 123
Reuben 123

PICKELS
Elizabeth 91
John 91
Mary WITHNELL 91
PICKERING
Abbie P. 97
PICKET
Melvira 155
PICKETT
Ann COLEMAN 123
William 123, 131
PICKMAN
Catharine M. 43
PICKORD
Alice 8
John 8
Julia Nette SKINNER 8
PIDGE
Sylvia A. 20
PIER
Mary A. HEFLIN 123
Mathew 123
Rebecca KIMBALL 123
William H. 123
PIERCE
Alice 123
Anna Maria HAWKINS
123
Cornelius 123
Cynthia H. NICKELS
123
Cynthias 87
Daniel 123
Darius, Mrs. 150
Darras 105
Doran 123
Elizabeth 123
Fannie M. 10
Frank 123
Hannah FLAG 5
Helen LAWSON 123
Helen N. KELSEY 123
Isaac N. 123
Jackson 6
James 123
Jennie 5
John 6
Joseph G. 123
Julia K. MARSH 123
Julia RICHARDS 123
Mary 6
Mary ROBINSON 123
Peter 123
Susan MELDRUM 123
Telitha 6
W.B. 123
William 5, 123
PIERCEY
Addie F. COLBY 123
Anna W. FLETCHER
123
M. James 123
Moses 123
PIERCY
Alexander 123
David A. 123
Elizabeth McCULLOCH
123
S. Libbie STOUT 123
PIERSON
Anders 73
Celia 159
Christine 73, 168
Ella NELSON 159
Emma 61
Gabrial 159

John 73
Kerstine SWENSEN 3
Louis 77
Maggie 3
Maria 107
Nellie 75
Paul 3
Stina JOHANNISON 73
PIGMAN
Charles 100
S.P. 9
PIHLKJER
Anna MICHAELSEN
123
Christine
JACOBSDOTTER
123
Jens 123
William 123
PIKARD
Maria 89
PIKE
Brigham 123
Lois H. 5
Martha WRIGHT 123
Mary 6
Moses 5
Rachel 57
PILES
Florence A. KING 123
Issac 123
James 123
Margaret ENGLISH 123
PILGRIM
James M. 123
PILLING
Elizabeth 7
PILLSTER
Bertha SMITH 123
Catherine RICHOUT
123
Charles F. 123
Joseph 123
PINE
James 123
James A. 123
Julia ASHTON 123
Mary J. PEARCE 123
PINNEY
Dr. 27
M.A. 20
PIPE
Eliza 34
PIPER
Ezetta 168
J.B. 129
Maria 30
PISCHKE
Albert 20
Jennie V. 20
PISKACKOVA
Maria 138
PITCHER
Mary 161
PITENGER
Rebecca 59
PITMAN
Ann, Mrs. 91
PITSCHNER
Ernestine W. 44
Ernst 44
PITTS
Charles 123
Joseph 123
Mary 123
Virginia WATSON 123

PITZ
John 80
PIVONKA
Anna KOLAR 123, 138
Frank 144
Frederick 123
James 123, 138
Magdalena MARESH
123
Mary 138
PJIRRON
Christine OSTROM 123
Emma C. 123
Esther ROBINSON 123
John F. 123
Magnus F. 123
PLAACK
Mary 26
PLACE
Cora M. 118
George W. 118
Harriet L. BILLINGS
118
PLAEHN
Christine 15
PLAIN
Mary, Mrs. 17
PLAMBECK
Anna Elizabeth
WAGEMANN 123
Annie M. 72
George 123, 150, 156
Jochim 123, 150
PLAN
Albert 25
Christina 15
PLANE
Annie 45, 81
James 45
M.J. SULLIVAN 166
Margaret SULLIVAN
45
PLANT
Lewis 17, 59
PLATEKA
Anna 113
PLATT
Araminta D. 1
PLATZ
Jens Hensen 122
Matte J.J. PAULSON
122
Mette J.J. 122
Paul 107
PLEASENT
Ettie MARKEL 123
J.H. 123
PLEAT
Eliza J., Mrs. 41
PLEDUING
Caroline 90
PLESTED
James 123
Judith PERRIN 123
PLEULER
Annie ANGLER 123
Frederick 123
George 123
Mary BOETTNER 123
PLOETZ
Catharine 16
PLUECKHAHN
Fritz 86
Gretchen PETERS 86
Sophie 86

PLUMBECK
Annie M. 72
George 72, 84
H. 72
PLUMELEY
Anna 138
PLUMLEIGH
Charles 123
Eliza C. HERMAN 123
Ella M. BRADFORD
123
Thos. 123
PLUMMER
J.B. 89
J.B., Dr. 19
Samuel 123
Sarah A. BEEZLEY 123
Susan GOLLADAY 123
Thomas G. 123
PLUNKETT
Ann 99
POEHLMANN
Henry 50
Margaret 135
Marie 50
Theresea
WANDERLICH 50
POHL
Augusta 104
Marie 67
POHLMAN
Henry 12
POHLMANN
Anna HAHN 12
Herr 38
Maria 12
Marie 38
Theresa HUNDERLICK
38
POINTS
Charles N. 123
Emma PRUETT 124
J.J. 17, 87
Jno. J. 16
John 124
John J. 123
Josie A. SOLOMON
123
Mary JUMP 124
T.R. 123
Telitha GUTHRIE 123
Zebdee 124
POL
Barbara 163
POLAK
Antonie 113
POLALECAK
Anna 86
Barbara TROGAN 86
James 86
POLAND
A. 50
B. 62
Clara M. BENNETT
155
John 47
L. 155
Luther, Jr. 155
Mary 45, 47
Mary Jane 47
Mary McCANN 47
Mattie L. 155
POLLACK
Emma, Mrs. 15
Johannah 124

POLLAND
Fanny KAY 124
James 124
POLLARD
Catharine BUENS 24
Charles 124
Frank 20, 124
Mary 24
Mary E. INGRAM 124
Myra 151
Sophia JONES 124
Thomas 24
POLLOCK
Emma Christina BURK
11
Emma KNIGHT 124
Mr. 124
Samuel S. 124
POLM
Christina 161
POLMANTIRE
Sarah A. 1
POLSEN
Gens 25
Mary 25
POLSON
Andrew 124
Hannah PETERSON
124
Swen 124
POLSTER
Magdalena 113
POMEROY
Catherine 162
Eveline 120
Mary D. 28
Sarah G. 120
POMROY
Eliza E. WALKER 124
Hiram 124
Mary BAGLEY 124
Sylvanus 124
Thomas 67
POND
W.W. 83
PONGELLEY
Caroline A. 76
Edward 76
Elizabeth SMITH 76
PONN
Frank 166
PONSFORD
Sallie B. 43
PONTS
J.J. 19
POOL
Charles H. 7
Elmira J. 72
Hattie 139
POOR
Mary 142
POPE
Lucy MOORE 98
Nancy Jane 98
Warrington Cary 98
POPERT
Elizabeth 27
POPPE
Elizabeth MORRIS 124
John 124
Sadie NEWMAN 124
William 124
POPPENBERGER
Barbara MERRITT 55
John 55

PROBST
  Catharine 110
PROCHASKA
  John 110
PROCHNOW
  August 125
  Caroline LABS 125
  Erstine HAKS 125
  Ferdinand 125
  Frederick 125
  Fredericka 125
  Fritz 125
  Henrietta BIUNKE 125
PROCTOR
  Alfred H. 125
  Doratty H. COCKFIELD
    125
  George Wesley 125
  Harriet M. HOOVER
    125
  Maggie JARVIS 125
  Maria 42
  Mary A. BLODGETT
    125
  Mary O'DONNELL 125
  Richard 125
  Richard A. 125
  Sarah MINETT 125
  Thomas 125
PROGER
  Lizzie CHIPLEY 104
  Mary 57, 104
  William 104
PROHASKA
  Josephine 74
PROKOP
  Catharina 9
  Francisca 38
PROPHET
  Julia Ann 23
PROPLESCH
  Augusta 131
  Charlotte REICH 131
  Christoff 131
PROPST
  Elizabeth A.
    CUNNINGHAM 125
  George F. 125
  Luellia EDMUNDSON
    125
  W.A. 125
PROTEAN
  Florence BOURGET 36
  Joseph 36
  Mary 85
  Mary M. 36
PROUD
  Elvira 120
PROUTZ
  Louisa 143
PROVAST
  Louisa 167
PROVISE
  Amelia 117
PROVOST
  Lieut. 162
PRUCE
  Catharine B. 96
PRUCHA
  Anna KODSA 125
  John 125
  Joseph 125
  Mary BABEZE 125
PRUESS
  Carolina LUSCHKAT
    136

PRUETT
  Anna Laura 99
  Eliza BABER 124
  Emma 124
  Marten 124
  Miss 99
  Mrs. 99
PRUICE
  Sol 139
PRUISEN
  Barbara 90
PRUSHA
  Joseph 152
PRYOR
  Ellen 97
  Lizzie 15
PUARTELL
  Patrick 109
PUGH
  Jane EDWARDS 125
  Mary L. COOPER 125
  Richard 125
PUGSLEY
  C.H. 149
  Charles H. 125
  G.L. 125
  Gidean L. 34, 125
  Joseph F. 125
  Julia E. CAMERON
    125
  Margaret WORDEN
    125
  Minnie STEVENSON
    125
PULS
  Albinie RASHKE 125
  Annie 137
  Augustus 137
  Carl 125
  Elisabeth 35
  Henry 35, 125
  Julia KASCHAN 137
  Julius A. 125
  Lucy STURL 125
  Luzia STUHL 125
  Mary 149
  Matthilde GROTHE 125
  Thomas 125
PULTIN
  Bridget 113
PUMPHREY
  Anna 30
  E.M. MOORE 30
  H. 30
PUNCHER
  Sarah Ann 128
PUNDT
  Henry 10
  Mr. and Mrs. 84
PURCELL
  ELiza Ann O'HARER
    38
  Mary E. 38
  Thomas 38
PURCHASE
  E.A. BARBER 125
  Emma BENTON 125
  Esther 142
  Evan 32
  Evlan 125
  M.W.E. 7, 125
  Mary 32
  Mary BOHEE 125
  Morris W.E. 7
  Thomas J. 125

PURCHETT
  Teresa 162
PURDY
  Elizabeth 57
PURINTON
  D.B. 125
  D.C. HOWE 125
  Emejean WALLACE
    125
  T.E. 125
PURLOCK
  Kasar 133
PURTELL
  Alvira SAUER 125
  Margaret FITZGERALD
    125
  Patrick 125
PUSSER
  Caroline SEIFFERT 125
  Charles 125
PUTMAN
  Elizabeth 109
  John S. 109
PUTNAM
  John 125
  Loiza, Mrs. 4
  Nancy SMITH 125
  Polly Ann 87
  Susanna Day MANGER
    125
  W.E. 125
PUTNUM
  Wm. E. 131
PYE
  Catharine 36
PYLE
  Aaron 126
  Hartwell 126
  Jennie MOATS 126
  Lydia A. WILLIAMSON
    126
PYNEN
  Rose Ann 115
PYPER
  A.C. 147
  Kate 92
  W.M., Mr. and Mrs. 92
QUAACK
  Eliza 68
  Fritz 68
  Margaret OELKE 68
QUACKENBURKE
  Nancy 69
QUADE
  Dora RUST 126
  Heinrich "Henry" 126
  Henry 126
  Louisa KEPPENHAHN
    126
QUALEY
  Bridget 91
  Patrick 91
QUANN
  Edmund 126
  John 126
  Mary QUINLAN 126
  Mary QUIRKE 126
QUEALEY
  P.J. 124
QUEEN
  Elizabeth 156
QUICK
  Andrew 2
  Elizabeth BELLIS 126
  John P. 126
  Lena OLSON 126

Libbie B. THAYER 126
  Martin 3, 126
  Mary 2
  Nora 155
  Sarah 35
  Tunis P. 126
QUICKENSTEDT
  Annie 14
  Willhelm 14
QUIGLEY
  Catharine FINLEY 71
  Anne 23
  Kate 71
  Mary 71
  Peter 71
QUIGLY
  Annia 15
  Mary RYAN 15
  William 15
QUINLAN
  Bridget 96
  Bridget RYAN 126
  Ellen 94
  Ellen LYONS 126
  J., Dr. 49
  Jas. 34, 70, 95, 153
  Johanna GOGGIN 94
  John 126, 167
  Jos. 21, 97
  Joseph 26, 132, 145
  Margaret HOWELL 126
  Mary 102, 115, 124,
    126
  Mary KEARNEY 124
  Michael 126
  Pat 71
  Patrick 46, 94, 124, 126
QUINLIN
  Daniel 2
  Mary 2
  Mary HALLEY 2
  Patrick 126
QUINLIVAN
  Eliza FLYNN 130
  Mary 130
  Patrick 130
QUINN
  Anna L. 67
  Bridget DALTON 126
  C.E. DAVIDSON 67
  Catharine 95
  Catharine MURREY
    126
  Catherine CALLAHAN
    126
  Daniel 126
  Edward 67
  Hanora 102
  Hanorah BOLAN 126
  Henry 126
  Honora 24, 102
  James 72, 126
  Johanna 99
  John 126
  John H. 126
  Maggie NAGLE 126
  Margaret CARRAGG
    126
  Mary 126
  Mary Q. KENNEDY 95
  Mary QUINN 126
  Michael 95
  Sophia 63
QUINTZ
  Antoinette 136

QUIRCK
  Nora 155
QUIRKE
  Mary 126
  Mary O'CONNOR 126
  Patrick 126
QUITSOW
  Sophia 169
QUOO
  Liddie 170
QVISTGARD
  A.J. 126
  Jens 126
  Maren CHRISTINSON
    126
  Minna PAGEL 126
QWARNSTROM
  A.T. 11
QWARNSTRON
  A. 126
  A.P. 126
  Annie PERSON 126
  Matilda J. JOHNSON
    126
RAABE
  Henry 126
  Margaretha SCHRAMM
    126
  Nellie STUHR 126
RAASCH
  Alice K. BROWN 126
  August 126
RABBESON
  Josephine A. 17
RABE
  Anna STICK 126
  Anna STICKEN 55
  Charles H. 126
  Dora RAGENDORF
    126
  Hans 55, 126
  Henry (Hinrich) 126
  Mary KNIGGE 126
  Minnie 55
  Sophia Dorothea
    Wilhelmina NIEKELL
    126
  William 126
RABELER
  Magdalene 136
RABOLD
  Louise 69
RACEK
  Annie KAVAN 126
  Annie SUCHE 126
  Mathew 126
  Matthew 126
RADAS
  Minna 135
RADAWAY
  Sarah N. 102
RADEMANN
  Marie 161
RADFORD
  Caroline 8
RADLER
  Barbara 122
RADMANN
  Margareth 5
RADNEY
  E. 49
RAFERT
  Anna Margaret 2
  Anthony F. 2
  Margaret DANIELS 2

REARDON
  Hannah 22
  Miles 9
REASONER
  Gustave 27
REAVIS
  Elizabeth LEWIS 127
  Isaac 127
  N.F. 122
REBHAUSEN
  Gertrude 44
  Gotfried 44
RECHELIEU
  Elizabeth 167
  Robert 167
RECORD
  Alexander 127
  Helen JACKSON 127
  Matilda McKELVEY 127
  William 127
RECRAFT
  Mary 91
RECTOR
  E.M. 29
  Edward 3, 14
  Elizabeth, Mrs. 29
REDD
  Alice BENNETT 127
  James A. 127
  Nathaniel 127
  Sarah Ann FARRAR 127
REDDEN
  Alice DINGLE 26
  Eliza J. 149
  John 26, 149
  Kate KANE 149
  Mary 26
REDDICK
  Jno., Mrs. 152
  John 152
REDDINGTON
  Elizabeth 141
  H.B. 141
REDDY
  Mary 29
REDEN
  Cassander 124
REDFIELD
  Frankie Rosella SMITH 127
  Josiah B. 71, 127
  Like C. 96
  M.H. 2, 3, 23, 33, 83, 114, 128, 164
  Margaret Ellen LOYD 127
  Melvin H. 127
  Phebe A., Mrs. 96
  Susan BROWN 127
REDICK
  Charles R. 34, 142
  John I. 1, 127, 132
  John T. 102, 130
  Mary A.E. MAY 127
  Mrs. 1
REDLIG
  Maria 38
REDLON
  Merendie 42
REDMAN
  Amanda L. 62
  Arminta 72
  Daniel 49
  David 72

David P. 168
George L. 127
Hannah 62
Joseph 42, 45, 49, 72, 127
Joseph. Mrs. 45
Martha Ann OLMSTED 127
Mary Catharine 49
Mary J. THAYER 127
Mary Jane FAIR 72
Porter D. 34
Sadie E. 131
REDMOND
  Bridget McCORMICK 127
  Catharine 17
  Hattie McMILLAN 127
  Henry 127
REEBER
  Dora 155
REECE
  Sophia 104
REED
  Aaron 82
  Annie WALKER 128
  Austin 82
  Austin W. 168
  Byron 5, 21, 74, 127
  Caroline 5
  Catharine McALARNEY 128
  Catherine GUILFOYLE 128
  Chancey W. 164
  Charles 19, 49
  Charlott BIVEN 127
  Ed 150
  Elizabeth 82, 154
  Emma KEETCH 128
  Frank R. 97
  Fred C. 1
  Fred I. 49
  H. Loretta 140
  Hannah L. 78, 166
  Henry 19
  Jennie 19
  Jeremiah 66
  John E. 127
  Jonathan 128
  Joseph 128
  Leander 73
  Lewis 7, 21, 67, 157
  Lewis S. 40
  Lillie C. EVANS 127
  Lou 5
  Louisa 156
  Martha 140
  Martha Ann 162
  Martha SCOTT 73
  Mary 23, 101, 166
  Mary Ann ROSS 19
  Mary E. COOPER 128
  Mary M. PERKINS 127
  Melissa 88
  Mrs. 5
  N.E. 16
  Nellie M. 19
  P.H. 19
  Parker 88
  Peter 128
  Philander H. 16, 38
  Robert 158
  Samuel G. 128
  Sarah Ann 50
  Sarah VANE 19

Susan F. LAFETRE 82, 168
Susan F., Mrs. 82
T.L. 128
Warren 101
Wm. E. 127
REEPER
  Christina 136
  Detlev 136
  Fritz 136
  Henrietta HAHN 136
REES
  Catharine 21
  Saml. 13
REESE
  Addie KNOX 128
  Almira Van TRESS 128
  Angeline BUTORFF 128
  Catherine 149
  Choxley 128
  Clara PANECKA 128
  Daniel 128
  Franklin Pierce 128
  J. 136
  John F. 128
  Laura FISHER 128
  Lucy N. ELDRIEDGE 128
  Mary 122
  William J.J. 128
  Wm. 128
REEVE
  Ester 98
REEVES
  Alice BATRAN 128
  Aranetta 166
  Cameron 167
  Cora B. 129
  Edward 128, 130
  Elizabeth (Bettie) SUMNER 128
  Elizabeth BARLOW 93, 97, 128
  Elizabeth EVANS 52, 167
  Elizabeth, Mrs. 30, 67
  Esther 98
  Geneva 35
  George 128
  George J. 128
  Henry 128
  Hulda M. RICKER 128
  Ida May 93
  Isabel R. 46
  Isabella A. 31
  J.C. 52
  Jane BRADDOCK 31, 46, 128
  Jesse 56, 93, 97, 124, 128
  John 40, 56, 128
  Josephine 167
  Louisa 46
  Mary 40
  Mary J. 166
  Mary KENNISTON 40
  Mary KYRESTON 56
  Mary M. 52
  Mary? Jane BRADDOCK 35
  P., Mrs. 67
  Permelia STERRITT 129
  Preston 56, 129
  Sophrona E. 97

Victoria WILBORN 128
William 31, 35, 40, 46, 128, 166
William N. 128
REFEL
  Elizabeth McLAUGHLIN 128
  Hersh 128
  Maurice 128
REGAN
  Alice 29
  Eliza Jane 170
  Hannah 83
  Hanora COOK 128
  Hanora KELLEY 128
  Honora COOKE 128
  Johanna DEE 128
  Michael 128
  Thomas 128
REGNISHECK
  Anna BUBEK 128
  John 128
  Joseph 128
REGTROP
  Mamie 41
REHN
  Caroline 127
REICH
  Annie ERBEN 171
  Charlotte 131
REICHARD
  Belle 92
  Catie 23
  Cillia HAWKIN 92
  John 23
  Swan 92
REICHENBERG
  Brendel GUDMAN 128
  Fanny 103
  Fanny ROSENDALE 128
  Lob 128
  Samuel 103, 128
REICHERN
  Catherine TEITGEN 128
  Nicholas 128
REICHMAN
  John P. 136
REID
  Elizabeth DOUGLAS 128
  Hugh 128
  Mary N. SMITH 128
  William J.I. 128
REIDY
  Ellen 90
  James 49
  John 28
  John L. 66
  Martin 69, 124
REIF
  Mattie 147
REIFORT
  Caroline M. 122
REIKEN
  Gretta 93
  Manerva 162
REILEY
  Julia 56
REILY
  Catherine MULLONE 128
  Helena 36
  Margrett 37

Patrick 128
REIMERS
  Botilde THOMPSON 128
  John 128
  Rebecca 90
REINBOHT
  Sophie 108
REINEKE
  Ernest 128
  Ernest H.L. 128
  Margaret RATGINS 128
  Mary 57
  Mary GISGER 128
REINEMAN
  Henrietta A. 84
REINES
  Cherry 168
REINHARDT
  Annie 125
REINHART
  Henry 75
  Julius 129
  Mary 75
  Mary OBERMAN 75
  Tilly 11
REINHARTS
  John 113
REINICKE
  Louise 160
REINING
  Louisa WINTER 128
  Paul 128
  Peter 128
  Theresa BOS 128
REIS
  Eli 113
  Elizabeth 113
REISS
  Caroline 74
REISTHER
  Francis 130
REITER
  Anna DORSCHER 128
  Anna MILLER 128
  John 128
  Simeon 128
REITZ
  Angelie 129
REITZE
  Henry 104
REIZ
  Mary 45
REKINGER
  John 128
  Lucy SMITH 128
REMANN
  Julia A. 28
REMELIA
  David 59
  Sarah GROVENOR 59
  Seloma 59
REMER
  Judy Ann 99
REMI
  Charles 128
  Eleonore RUHOFF 128
  Max 128
  Wilhelmine SPARKTIES 128
REMINGTON
  Catharine SULLIVAN 128
  D.E. WILLIAMS 29
  Eliza NORTON 128

REMMINGTON, cont.
  Hannah WILLIAMS
    128
  Ida 29
  Jane H. MORSE 128
  Joseph 41
  Katherine R. 28
  Katie 41
  Richard M. 128
  Sarah MALORY 41
  W. 128
  Wagar W. 15
  Wager H. 128
  Walter E. 128
REMMINGTON
  Catharine 138
RENAN
  Exilda LaPORTE 135
  Exilde 135
  Tusa 135
RENECKER
  Andrew J. 160
  Elizabeth B. SMITH
    160
  Huldah J. 160
RENFER
  Ann Elizabeth 163
RENNELS
  Elizabeth 20
RENNER
  Caroline 15
  Catherine 15
  Frank 15
  Joseph 15
  Tarrent DOLID 15
RENSCH
  Conrad 86
RENSCHLER
  Christian 50
RENSHAW
  Sarah A. 154
RENTSHLER
  Caroline BRACHT 128
  G. 128
  Jacob 128
  M. GISSLER 128
REPASS
  Ellis 128
  Jacob 128
  Mary JOHNSON 128
  Rebecca 128
REPEN
  Datlef 73
  Magdalene 95
REPROBLE
  George 129
  John 129
  Mary E. EDWARDS
    129
  Sarah F. GROSNICLE
    129
RESER
  Mary 151
RESLINGER
  Mary Ann 163
RETTY
  F., Mrs. 166
REULAND
  Annie LAST 129
  Catherine
    MAUTTERNASH
    129
  John 129
  Peter 129
REVER
  Alexander 129

Clara LaPOINT 129
Mary NEWHOUSE 129
REX
  Lizzie 93
  Turgen 93
REYNOLD
  Augusta 11
REYNOLDS
  Betsey 82
  Bridget DEGNAN 129
  Dock 53
  Elizabeth SULLIVAN
    129
  Francis C. KELLY 129
  James 129
  John 129
  Kate 12
  Mary 130
  Mary CAMERON 129
  Mary M. 73
  Minerva E. PHILLIPS
    67
  Minnie 67
  Nancy, Mrs. 160
  P.H. 67
  Taylor 167
  Zachariah Taylor 129
REZEK
  Katie 84
REZNICEK
  Anna BUBEK 128
  John 128
  Joseph 128
RHEIN
  Anna Maria STEIN 120
  Frederick 120
  Louise A. 120
RHOADES
  Mary Ellen 156
  Susan 73
RHODE
  Elsbeth 121
RHODES
  Artie BILLINGS 129
  Cora B. REEVES 129
  Edward 129
  Frederick 129
  Hannah 73
  Henry F. 129
  John S. 129
  Lorena A. GEORGIA
    129
  Mary C. 46
  Susan CULVER 129
RHULLIES
  Eugene 98
RIBLET
  Elizabeth 57
RIBONSON
  Andrew P. 5
RICCKLE
  Barbara 68
RICE
  A.M., Mrs. 41
  Abbie BROWN 129
  Adell MOORE 41
  Catherine 35
  Charles 129
  Chas. E. 54
  Ellen STEVENSON 87
  Emilie ELSAESSER
    129
  Hannah 34
  Harriet N. 123
  Henry 31
  James 129

James A. 87
John 129
Jorelian 159
Joseph T. 129
Maggie 52
Margaret FOREMAN
  129
Mariah 119
Mary 29, 106
Mary A. 41
Matilda 119
May 87
Melvina DAVIS 129
Minnie FRANKLIN 129
Nelson 41
Olivia P. ROSS 47
S.H. 83, 164
Valencia E. 47
William F. 129
Wm. P. 47
RICH
  Almina
    HERSCHFELDT 129
  Amelia HERSCHFELDT
    129
  Andrew 129
  Barbara SMITH 129
  Cecelia MYERS 129
  Elizabeth A. 156
  Fannie 15
  Jacob 129
  Jason 156
  Julius 129
  Kaufman 129
  Mary Ann AHLER 129
  Mary C. 170
  Susan COLERIDGE
    156
  Susan COLERIGE 170
  Thomas 156, 170
RICH----
  John 69
RICHARD
  Emiline 114
  Henry 36
  J., Mrs. 118
  John 36, 118
  Katie 36
  Katy 86
  Sophia SENKEL 36
RICHARDS
  A. 138
  A.J. HILL 1
  Alice E. 15
  Ann 80
  Burr H. 129
  Burr H., Mrs. 129
  Charles R. 73
  David 112
  David F. 129
  Eleanor JENKINS 129
  Eliza 141
  Fannie Ella TOWNES
    129
  Fidelia GOOLD 129
  Hannah A. 62
  Jesse 129
  John 1
  Joseph M. 158
  Julia 123
  Louisa C.T. 129
  Lydia 19
  Mary 163
  Mary MOREL 129
  Mrs. 45
  Phidelia A. GOAL 15

Phidelia A. GOULD 62
Sarah 149, 162
Sarah J. 1
T.W.T. 28
Thomas W.T. 129
William 15, 62
William H. 129
RICHARDSON
  Adeline HILL 129
  Adie 70
  Belle L. 44
  Benjamin 129
  Charles 78
  Cornelia 8, 162
  David 163
  Edwin P. 129
  Elizabeth, Mrs. 50
  Ellen, Mrs. 24
  Emeline HUTCHINSON
    129
  Emmeline, Mrs. 83
  Fannie 78
  Fanny 78
  Jennie W. CARTER 129
  John 129
  Julia Ann 163
  Lucy
    MARYWEATHERS
    129
  Lyman 78, 129, 157
  Mary 86
  Mary Ann 30
  Mary BURGESS 163
  Nancy DUKE 129
  O.D. 129
  Prescott V. 44
  Rachel DARRAH 44
  Theodore W. 129
  Trad 129
  Virginia Harrison
    CLARK 129
  Virginia, Mrs. 8
RICHELEU
  Edward 129
  Mary Ann WADHAM
    129
RICHELMANN
  Anna 69
RICHMOND
  Elizabeth BLEWETT
    165
  Rebecca 37
  Susie 165
  William 165
RICHOUT
  Catherine 123
RICHTER
  Christian 84
  Frances 50
  Fredericke 136
  Fredricka 36
  Henry 56, 119, 129, 150
  Joanna IVERSON 129
  John 13
  Kate 127
  Lena 84
  Maria A. 83
  Mrs. 150
  Ottilie 86
  Sophia 43
  Sophia KLEEBLATT
    84
RICKARD
  A.N. 129
  Adam 129

Amanda WOODWARD
  129
Catharine
  McGUINNESS 129
John 129
Marth CANNARY 129
Minnie ROLFER 129
Thomas 129
RICKER
  Abigail SPAULDING
    128
  Hilda 157
  Hubbard 157
  Hulda M. 128
  W.H. 128
RICKETS
  Lizzie C. 165
RICKETTS
  J.R. 163
RICKLEFSEN
  Henrietta DELFS 129
  Mary STISCOLA 129
  Oscar 129
RIDDIFORD
  Eliza PEARCE 129
  Erin 129
  Henry 129
  Kate EHLERS 129
RIDDLE
  Catherine 120
RIDER
  Fidelia RANDALL 73
  Mary E. 73
  Romain 73
RIDGWAY
  Geo. 4
RIDINGS
  Ginnie PATTERSON
    129
  Henry 129
RIDLE
  Sarah 150
RIEBER
  Frederick 155
RIECKEN
  N.C. 158
RIECKS
  Auguste 39
RIEDEL
  Annie 103
  Catherine 20
  George 129
  Lena PASCH 129
  Mary BUSSE 129
  William 129
RIEDT
  Annie C. HEUBEL 129
  Annie YOUNG 129
  Carl 129
  Christoph 129
RIEGE
  Wilhelmina 58
RIEKEN
  Carolina 104
  Charles N. 104
  Christian 104
RIEPEL
  Catharine
    NEWBERGER 129
  Johann 129
  Joseph 129
  Maria BALACH 129
RIEPEN
  Detlef 130
  Fredirick 130
  Fritz 78

ROBERTSON, cont.
Margarett I. 141
Margureta BANNISTER 33
Martha 153
Martha THOMPSON 131
Mary 5, 100, 123
Mary A. DEMORY 131
Mary A. TAYLOR 131
Mary E. MILLER 131
Mary GORDON 166
Mary H. 39
Mary KENNARD 17
Mary L. 124
Mary MAHER 131
Mary McMILLAN 123
Mary McMULLEN 143
Mary PETERSON 131
Mary URWIN 131
Mary W. 59
Mattie 11
Mattie AVERY 131
Mattie BUFFINGTON 131
Minerva 8
Moore 131
Mr. and Mrs. 55
Mrs. 5, 92
Nancy 91
Nellie 130
Olive LUCAS 131
Rebecca 98
Redick 131
Robert 131
Sarah BANKS 5
Sarah CASSELL 131
Sarah F. COMONS 131
Sarah HALE 131
Stephen 70
Steven 36
Susan C. 131
T.H. 131
Thomas 131
Thomas F. 131
Virginia BALLARD 71
W.G.T.H. 131
William 17, 131
William G. 131
William T. 131
ROBISON
A.L. 131
Alma V. NYMAN 131
Amy 105
Annie M. 165
Caroline BETTS 165
Davis 113
Elizabeth 66
Henriette H. IRWIN 142
Henry B. 165
Isabella C. McKENNEY 131
John K. 131
Mary 118
Mrs. 92
Rachel 58
ROBLANGEL
Manie or Morris 154
ROBLING
Elizabeth FRIGELS 154
Mich 9
ROCHE
Honoria O'CONNOR 131
Jeremiah J. 131
Lizzie 64

Margaret O'CONNOR 131
Maurice 131
ROCHFORD
Honora CLOON 114
John 114
Margaret 114
Thomas 114
ROCKMANN
Margareta 84
ROCKWELL
A.H. 67
Mary A. JENCKS 67
Nellie 163
Nellie E. 67
RODDY
Ann CARMICK 131
Mary HENZIE 131
Michael 131
Patrick 131
RODE
Elizabeth 120
RODEBANK
Emma M. SPRINGER 131
J.W. 131
RODEMANN
Johanne Doris 108
RODEN
Matilda Christine 135
Neils F. 135
Sarah C. JOHNSON 135
RODEWALD
Ann C. TIEDJE 27
John F. 27
Paulina C. 27
RODGER
Rebecca B. 169
RODGERS
Alexander B. 131
Eliza 105
Martha 93
Mary BARNES 131
Ruth E. TURNER 131
Thomas B. 131
RODNEY
James 100
RODWAY
C.L., Mr. and Mrs. 53
ROE
Emma 157
Henry 73, 131
J. Phipps 89
Maria WHALIN 131
Marie 73
Rosena FISHER 131
Thomas 54
William 131
ROEBLING
Elizabeth 42
ROEDER
A., Dr. 84
Augustus 84, 160
Clara 84
Julius 25, 31, 84
Matilda 84
Mrs. 67
Pauline 160
ROEDINK
Christina HASPAN 136
John 136
Maggie 136
ROEHRIG
Margaretha 84

ROEKGER
Betty SWANSON 131
H.P.C. Fredrickson 131
ROEMER
Augusta PROPLESCH 131
Charlotte 136
John 131
Simon 131
Victoria Essig KRUG 131
ROENFELD
Andrew 131
Anna MUEHL 131
Anna RUSCAMP 131
ROENFELDT
Andreas 131
Anna MUHL 131
Henry 131
Katie HOLST 131
ROESINK
Henricke 131
Henry 131
Johanna 63
John 131
Mary GROTMACK 131
ROEURRAN
Elizabaeth 54
ROGERS
Alexander 117
Alexander B. 131
Alexr. T. 131
Alice 132
Amelia BOYD 43
Anna KUHN 132
Anna M. 107
Bernard 132
Christiana Jane 100
Clara WHITMEN 131
Clarissa STOKES 132
Cornelia L. 18
Cornelia S. 160
Edwin J. 131, 169
Eliza M., Mrs. 88
Eliza SPENCER 131
Ella J. SPOOR 132
Ezekiel R. 132
Fanny KNIGHT 107, 118, 132
Flora M. 118
Florence 99
Francis 62
Geo. A. 131
Henry 43
Henry?, Mrs. 43
Hester A. 101
Isaac M. 132
Jane 120
Jane BEARD 100, 132
Jane S. SPOOR 132
John 132
John H. 131
John T. 28
John W. 100, 132
John William 100
Joshua P. 132
Lena BENSON 132
Lida A. 43
M., Mrs. 128
Maggie A. 117
Margaret 14
Marshia R. GENTRY 132
Mary 131
Mary P. 69
Milton 132

Milton, Mr. and Mrs. 152
Milton, Mrs. 90
Peter 117, 131
R. 22
Ruth E. TURNER 131
Samuel 9, 107, 118, 132
Sarah 129
Sarah Maria WYMAN 132
Sarah WRIGHT 117, 131
T.C. 43
T.J. 132
Theresa MEYERS 131
Thomas B. 131
Tirza BEDDIS 132
ROGGIN
Augusta 84
ROHDE
Heinke 70
ROHN
Catharine 164
ROHRBERG
D.M. 66
Magdalene 148
ROHRIG
Mary Ann 103
ROHVEDDER
Margreta 116
ROHWEDDER
Margaret 147
ROHWEDER
Lena 16
ROHWER
Ann HODERS 132
Anna 44, 88
Anna HARDER 132
Anna THOMPSON 132
Annie HOLLING 132
Carsten 132
Catherine 86
Cathrina 79
Charles 132
Christina 86
Christina E. SIMONSEN 86
Dora 49
Dorah 86, 110
Elizabeth BUESEL 132
Elsabe 119
Elsabe THODE 132
Elsabeth THODE 119
German 132
Hans 108, 132
Hans J. 49
Henry 132
Joergen 132
Jurgen 119, 132
Kate 127
Kate E. 86
Lena 16
Timothy 86
ROLAND
Caroline 66
Elizabeth 115
Emma 28
Maud 143
ROLD
Karen JENSEN 132
Peter C. 130, 132
ROLF
Catherine Able BUSHIE 132
Henry 132
James 132

Sophia KAELBER 132
ROLFEN
R. 85
ROLFER
Catharine LAFERTY 164
Henry 51, 129, 164
Josephine 51
Mary 164
Mary BERGENSTEIN 129
Minnie 129
ROLIG
Maria Chatharine 110
ROLL
Catherine CASTON 132
Dorothea KARSTEN 14
George 132
Johanna PAASCH 132
Katie 14
Nicholas 132
Nicholaus 14
ROLLA
Henry 106
ROLLI
Christian 132
Varene VAUTHRECH 132
ROLLINGSON
Ann 1
ROLLINS
E.F., Mrs. 168
Elizabeth 120
Nancy Jane 59
ROLLS
Anna 51
Annie 65
Elizabeth BURNS 65
Joseph 65
ROMANS
Elisha 132
Elizabeth KNIGHT 132
Lewis 132
Minnie HOWLAND 132
ROMASOVA
John 20
Kate 20
Mary 20
ROMBERG
Anna 144
ROMETSCH
John 12
RONAN
Catharina STEFFEN 54
Catharine 25
Christian 54
Elizabeth 54
Susan 101
RONFELDT
Andrew 130
Annie MUHL 130
Margaret 130
RONFIK
Marie 15
RONGUEY
Mary Ann 115
RONNAN
Louise 55
RONNER
Catharine STEVENS 67
John 67
Mary 67

RUDOLFF
Maria 85
RUDOLPH
George 44
Lena 44
Lena SPRESLER 44
RUDSTRUM
Caslin OLESON 133
John 133
Mary JOHNSON 133
RUDY
James 38
RUEDY
Andrew 133
Elizabeth GIELSER 133
John 133
Margaret MILLER 133
RUERICH
• Catharine 160
RUESS
Augusta 85
Blacka Maria 85
Jacob 85
Maria BLAHA 85
RUF
Emma WALKER 133
L. 30, 85
Louis F. 133, 161
RUFF
Annie E. PHILLIPS 133
Christina 82
Edward L. 133
John 133
John E. 133
Luis 130
Margaret 16
Sarah CUMMINGS 133
RUFFIN
Harriet 154
RUGENMEISS
John 52
Louise 52
Louise SUELWOLD 52
RUGGLES
Geo. D. 159
George D. 29, 59
RUHANE
Margaret 79
RUHL
Catharine 58
RUHLAND
Caroline VOGEL 133
Frank 133
Helena HASERODT
133
Morrice 133
RUHOFF
Eleonore 128
RULE
Joshua 6
RULKOWSKI
Adam 133
Bogmula
MAICZROWIC 133
Frank J. 133
Helena HASERODT
133
RUMEL
Amanda PATER 133
Louisa SYLVESTER
133
Mr. 133
Mrs. 133
Nicholas 133
William M. 133, 152

RUMMER
Emeline A. 5
RUMPH
Anna 133
RUNCEY
Rev. Dr. 30
RUNNELLS
H.J. 106
RUNNELS
Charlotte 40
Matilda 156
RUNNER
Elizabeth 54
Margareta 93
RUNNION
Emily, Mrs. 9
RUNOLDS
Martha 131
RUNYON
Alexander 78
Angeline GILBERT 133
Fannie 133
Mary Ann WILKIN 78
Mrs. 48
Sarah 78
Wm. 133
RUPERT
Catharine SHAFER 133
Henry 133
Menna UHLING 133
William 133
RUPLE
Elizabeth 56
RURSER
Celia 136
RUSCAMP
Anna 131
John 131
Mary DANNEMANN
131
RUSER
Henry 19, 62
RUSH
Anna E. FERRY 133
Annie 81
Grace 159
John 81, 107, 115, 133
Norah 100
RUSHLAU
Joseph 133
Mary A. SMITH 133
Mathilda JAMBOAH
133
P.J. 133
RUSHMAN
Kate 132
RUSKIN
Kate 34
RUSSELL
Amanda M. 80
Ann 27
Eliza 97
Eliza DRISCOLL 24, 64
Eliza, Mrs.? 20
Ellen 140
Esther L. HOWARD
134
Indiana McCONNELL
67
James 24, 64
Jane 31, 100, 154
Joseph B. 134
Kate 7
L.E. 64
Lydia A. COLE 134
Malinda 24

Margaret 78
Mary E. 164
Mary G. DYER 108
Mary, Mrs. 20
S.B. 1
Sarah 134
Sarah E. TRISSLER
134
Sarah J. 64
Susan C. 108
William 134
William H. 134
RUST
Dora 126
Esther 126
George 144
Mary E. ROYCE 137
Mary M. 137
Wm. E. 137
RUSTIN
C.B. 85
Harriet, Mrs. 59
RUTAN
Hannah CLARK 134
Medora WILEY 134
William 134
William H. 134
RUTH
Augusta D. SMILEY
134
L.J. 134
Laura M. 7
William 134
RUTHE
Barbara 141
RUTHENG
Maggie 161
RUTHER
C.D. 6
RUTHERFORD
Isabella MACKIE 134
James 134
John 134, 141
Sarah McMASTERS
134
RUTHUFF
Mary 85
RUTHVEN
Catherine 170
RUTTER
Ann L. 20
RUZER
Henry 41
Katherina 41
Kathrina SERK 41
RUZICKA
Anna 13
Anna K. 13
Anna TOMISKA 134
Catharine HORAK 134
John 84, 134
Joseph 13, 134, 159
Josephine NOHEJL 134
Katharina HORAK 159
Mary 86, 159
Mary SOLINKA 134
RUZICKER
John 134
RYAN
Agnes 68, 107, 156
Ann DOLAN 55
Ann McCABE 156
Ann O'NEIL 51, 134
Anna 29
Bridget 20, 26, 126
Bridget BRENNAN 134

Bridget DOCHENY 148
Bridget POWERS 134
Catharine 51, 134
Catharine McCRISTAL
134
Daniel 23, 35, 134
Denis 143
Denis, Mrs. 143
Dennis 36, 134
E. 124
Edward 143
Eliza 45, 51
Ellen 28, 143, 148
Essie 89
Hannah 23
Hanora O'NEIL 134
Harriet 40
Helen 55
J.P.J. 76
James 27, 81
James C. 134
James M. 134
Jane MARTIN 134
Johana FLOOD 134
Johanna 99, 165
Johanna LINAHAN 126
John 18, 55, 82, 134
John I. 134
Katharine 81
M.J. 63
Maggie CASEY 134
Margaret 37, 160
Margaret BOYLE 134
Margaret CARR 134
Margaret CAVANA 81
Margaret GAVEN 23
Margaret HALL 134
Margret 15
Mary 8, 15, 24, 39, 40,
51, 71, 82, 126, 134
Mary A. 139
Mary Alice RAND 134
Mary CALAHAN 134
Mary DEE 82
Mary DOLAN 55
Mary KERWAN 134
Mary M. 18
Mary McDONALD 134
Michael 126, 134
Olive B. 76
Olive B. OLESON 12
Olive B. OLSON 12
P. 24
Patrick 134
Rosa 34
T.C. 95
Thomas 39, 51, 134,
156
Timothy 55, 90
Timothy T. 134
William 33, 134, 148
Winefer LOWRY 39
Wm. 39, 125, 134
Wm. M. 32, 125
RYANT
Mary 149
RYBERG
Johanna ANDERSON
134
Johanna, Mrs. 23
Nels G. 134
Nels J. 23
RYBERT
Nils 152
RYDQUIST
Hannah 43

RYEN
Henrietta 50
RYLE
Mary 30
Mary KACY 30
Thomas 30
RYLEY
Edward G. 134
Fredricka C. KENZEL
134
RYMAN
Cathrine 41
RYNE
Catharine 114
RYPINSKI
Marx 83
S?CHICKETAINS
Catharine 163
John 163
SAALFELD
Christoph 134
Emme PERTUCH 134
W. 1
SAALFELDT
Friederike OTTO 134
Gustav 134
Sophia DUNKER 134
William 134
SAALFIELD
William 126
Wm. 84
SABATA
Elina 63
SABERMAN
Areker 59
SABIN
Arthur C. 134
Florence D. VAUGHN
134
Henry S. 134
Zadai VERNOL 134
SABLEMAN
Enich 75
Maria E. 75
SACHS
Elizabeth FORSEYTH
134
Fredericke LANG 134
John 134
John C. 134
SACKET
H.B., Mrs. 111
SACKETT
F.A. 159
SADERLUND
Andrew 134
Anna ISAKSON 134
SADLEE
Diana 17
Diana, Mrs. 17
SADLER
Diana MILLER 134
Levi 134
Sarah RUSSELL 134
William 134
SAFFEL
Amanda 47
SAFFELL
Nancy Jane 166
WIlliam 166
SAGE
Ava 8
E.H. 120
Harleight 8
Sarah 26
Sophia KNOX 8

SAGNER
  Christine PHOVE 139
  Fredk. 139
  Minnie 139
SAGO
  Adelle 91
SAGRE
  Mary 103
SAHLER
  J.H., Mrs. 91
  John H. 40
  Mary M. 42
SAIDE
  Catharine
    DOUGHERTY 134
  Jerry 134
  Margaret CALLAGHAN
    134
  Zepherino 134
SAILER
  Barbara 58
SAINT CLAIR
  Eliza 6
  Eliza BENNETT 134
  George H. 134
  Hattie NOBLE 134
  Samuel J. 134
SAINT FELIX
  Marie M. LAROSCHEL
    134
  Peter D. 134
  Prudens D. 134
  Sarah E. GROAT 134
SAISPAIR
  Mary 164
SALHOLM
  Charles 3
  Susanna 21
SALISBURY
  Mary Anne 148
SALLANDER
  Alexandra SWANSON
    134
  Arvid 134
  Gustaf 134
  Louise ASPELIN 134
SALLED
  Gertrude 154
SALLY
  Catharine COLLIN 135
  Elizabeth LYNCH 135
  Francis 135
  James 135
SALON
  Rosa 58
SALT
  Frances 7
SALTHER
  Matilda 77
SALVETER
  Emma 40
SALVY
  Fanny A. 5
  Sarah J. 5
  Thomas 5
SALZWEDEL
  Wilhelmina 69
SALZWELD
  Augustus, Miss 38
SAMELIK
  Katharina 171
SAMLER
  Jacob 86
SAMMER
  Nicholas 170
  Rosina 170

SAMOLOK
  Kate 43
SAMPLES
  Ellen 74
  James 74
  Mary Ann SIMPSON 74
SAMPSON
  Ann ROSE 135
  Anna 111
  Mary M. HARMON
    135
  Samuel 135
  Thomas 6
  William R. 135
SAMS
  Susanna 48
SAMSON
  Andrew 135
  Anna JOHNSON 135
  Caroline NYGREN 135
  Christine ANDERSON
    135
  Johannes 135
  Oscar 135
  Samuel 135
  Sessa PERSON 135
  Tilda 135
SAMUELSDOTER
  Mary 120
SAMUELSEN
  Anna JACOBSEN 113
  Nils 113
SAMUELSON
  Andrew 117
  Christina NIELSON 117
  Ingred 135
  John 26
  Sarah H. 75, 77
SAN
  Christina HANSEN 65
  Claus 65
  Sophia Margaritta 65
SANBERG
  Anna 127
  Gust 23
SANBY
  Lewis 144
SAND
  Aemilia 161
  Mary 161
SANDBERG
  Christine J. 103
  Helen 121
  Johanna C. 162
  Josephine 103
  P. 103
  P.A. 36
  P.G. 11
SANDEL
  Mary 11, 77
SANDELL
  Anna B. PETERSON
    162
  Carl Gustav 162
  Charlotte W. 162
  Mary 11
SANDER
  Julia 46
SANDERS
  Alvina S. McCLURE
    135
  B.C. 135
  G.P. 89
  Hannah REDMAN 62
  John 53
  Kate 167

Loretta 62
  Louisa GRAVES 135
  Lucinda TEMPLE 135
  Thomas H. 135
  William 62, 135, 171
  Wm. 62
SANDERSON
  John 135
SANDFUS
  Magrada K. 127
SANDMEYER
  Anna STRAUMANN
    135
  Jacob 135
  John Henry 135
  Marie HUMBEL 135
SANDS
  Abel J. 135
  Ellen ANDREWS 135
  George H. 135
  Odyssa 119, 161
SANDY
  Elizabeth 15
SANE
  Mr. 71
SANER
  Catharina BLUMENAN
    120
  Conrad 120
  Marie 120
SANFORD
  Ella M. 106
  Elliott B. 135
  Elmira A. COREY 135
  Jane E. 59
  Julia A. 56
  S.H., Mr. 106
  S.H., Mrs. 106
  T.S. 89, 93
SANFORT
  Catharine 69
  Maria STARK 69
  William 69
SANGENSEFREN
  Bertha Juliana 38
SANGSTER
  Francis 108
SANKY
  Kittie BUSHEY 41
SANN
  Trena 65
SANNOT
  Maggie 24
SANQUEST
  John 135
  Lena DANIELSON 135
SANSER
  Anna 50
SANTER
  Mr. 62
SAP
  Manda 68
  Retchel 68
SAPP
  Amanda 68
  F. 32
  Mr. and Mrs. 32
SARAN
  James 142
SARGENT
  Adie RICHARDSON 70
  Aggie 70
  John 70
SARP
  Anna GEHAL 92

SARSFIELD
  Ellen 47
SARTORIUS
  Agnes 154
  Gertrude SALLED 154
  Peter 154
SASS
  Dora 49
SASSE
  Dena 66
SASSTROM
  Frank 135, 141
  Lina GUSTOFSON 135
SATHER
  Anthony Olsen 135
  Matilda Christine
    RODEN 135
SATORIUS
  Anna 141
  Cecilia 62
  Peter 62
SATTERFIELD
  Rachel A. JONES 135
  Wm. M. 135
SATTLER
  Eva SIDEL 135
  George 135
  Johann 135
  Maria SPIELMANN
    135
SAUER
  A.K. 135
  Alice M. Van
    AEERNAM 135
  Alvira 125
  Annie REINHARDT
    125
  Elizabeth LARGEN 135
  Henry 135
  Jacob 135
  John 135
  John F. 125
  Lettie DAVIS 47
  Margaret PFLUG 135
  Mary 44
  Mary REAL 135
SAULPAUGH
  Eveline MORTIMER
    135
  Henry M. 135
  J.H. 51
  John A. 135
  Maria WEEKS 135
SAULSPAUGH
  Eveline 51
SAULT
  Frances 60
SAUNDERS
  Albern 135
  Albert P. 135
  Alvin 106
  Elizabeth AUSTIN 135
  Ellen BENNETT 135
  George 135
  Georgia Idith 13
  J.K. 13, 41
  Jessie 41
  John K. 41
  Julia 1
  L.M. 13
  Lucea B. 100
  Lucinda POWELL 135
  Marion B. VAN PLEW
    135
  Mary MURRAY 46
  P. 100

Perlia J. 166
  Platt 168
  Sarah PHELPS 41
  Thomas 135
SAUNIER
  Adile 36
SAUSE
  Ann MAGRAW 135
  Daniel A. 135
  Matilda J. DRISCOLL
    135
  Michael 135
SAUTER
  Theodora 39
SAUTTER
  Anna LEHNER 135
  Chris 58
  Christian 90, 170
  John 126, 135
SAVAGE
  Eliza 52
  Eliza BRYANT 52
  George 52, 140
  J.W. 38, 114
  J.W., Col. 43
  James W. 29, 118
  James W., Col. 32
  Jas. W. 105, 124
  John 77
  Lovey, Mrs. 77
  Lucretia 29
  Polly 67
  W.C. 67
SAVILLE
  Catharine 58
SAVISCOSKA
  Barbara 49
SAVLICK
  Anna HAJEK 135
  John 135
  Margaret HOFFMAN
    135
  Vaclav 135
SAWYER
  Harriet 144
  Mary Ann 157
SAYER
  Alfred 54
SCANALL
  Mary 102
SCANLAN
  Edward 35
  Ellen 35
  Honora WHELAN 35
SCANLON
  Lawrence 152
SCANNELL
  Mary 113
SCANTLIN
  Bran 3
  Brown 154
  Margaret 3
  Margaret LAWTON
    154
  Rosa 3
SCANTLING
  Brown 154
  Cecelia 10
  Emma 163
  Margaret, Mrs. 154
SCEELLY
  Mary 114
SCHAB
  Henry 161
  Mary 161
  Rosena BANE 161

SKLA
  Barbara 168
  Fanny BENZEL 168
  James 168
SKLENAR
  Anna KUBIK 142
  Barbara OUREDNIK
    142
  Joseph 142
SKLENER
  Joseph 46
SKOGLUND
  John P. 142
  Matilda SCOTMAN
    142
SKONBERG
  Hanna 111
SKONGAARD
  H., Mrs. 70
SKORGERSTROM
  Charles 111
  Mary 111
  Sophia 111
SKOUMAL
  Wenzel 80
SKOW
  Carrie JENSEN 142
  Hans J. 142
  Hans N. 142
  J. 146
  J.J. 142
  Martine C. JOHNSON
    142
  Mathilde K. BECK 142
  N. 142
  Sine MADSEN 142
SKRAYSKOW
  Mary 110
SKULLY
  Catherine 164
SLACK
  Jennie SHAFER 21
SLADOVNIK
  John 65
  Josephine 65
  Katharine KUNES 65
SLAGLE
  Emily 159
SLAGO
  Malinea 87
SLAMA
  Mary 151
SLANINA
  Anna 138
SLAPNICKE
  Barbara SKLA 168
SLATER
  Lena 63
  Levi 142
  Mary LUDLOW 142
  Nettie BAKER 142
  Thomas 142
SLATTER
  Anna C. McGUE 143
  Anne OSBORNE 143
  Charles 143
  Emma 143
  J.O. 143
  T.H. 170
SLATTERY
  Bridget MEDDEN 37
  C. 1
  Catharine 20
  Catherine 37, 40, 95,
    101
  Ellen RYAN 143

James 143
John 143
John B. 143
Mary 64
Mary F. HERRON 143
Michael 37
SLAUGHTER
  A.B. 8, 15, 100, 110
  A.B., Mrs. 1, 56, 102,
    167
  B.D. 150
  Carolina RITCHIE 143
  H.L. 100
  Hattie L. 49
  James 140
  Joseph 143
  Melinda MYERS 143
  W.B. 27
  Winfield S. 143
SLAVEN
  Felix 2
  Felix, Mrs. 2
  Michael 22
  Owen 31
  Rosanna McALLROY
    22
  S.B. 22
SLAW
  Elizabeth 64
SLAWSON
  Mary 131
SLEMMER
  Margaret 88
SLETRE
  Annie WOYLLACK
    143
  John 143
SLEZAK
  Joe 11
  Joseph 64, 96
SLIGHTAM
  Emma 108
  Emma C. ELCOCK 108
  William 108
SLIGHTARN
  Elizabeth WILBORN
    143
  Ellen SHANAHAN 143
  Henry 143
  James 143
SLIGHTEN
  James 81
SLIGHTHAM
  Elizabeth WILBORN
    143
  Ellen SHANAHAN 143
  Henry 143
  James 143
SLIGHTOM
  Mattie 10
SLINGLAND
  Harriet 159
SLIPE
  Sarah 35
SLITTER
  Caroline 87
  Christian 87
  Frederike HERING 87
SLOAN
  Catharine ROBINSON
    143
  Ellen 24
  Jane GREGG 143
  John B. 156
  Joseph 143
  Kate 156

William 143
SLOCKBOWER
  Elizabeth F. TURNER
    143
  Francis 143
  Maggie PETERSON
    143
  W.T. 143
SLOPER
  Frank 60
SLOSS
  John 143
  Susan KELLEY 143
SLOSSON
  Frank 152
SLOTHOWER
  E.B. 14
SLOVER
  Lottie 87
SLOWIE
  Catharine 101
SLY
  Ann 152
SMAHA
  Francis HULLMAN 143
  Frantisa BARTOS 143
  George 143
  Joseph 143
SMALL
  Rosa 161
SMART
  Hannah 137
SMIDT
  Andrew 80
  Christiana 80
  Gertrude 143
  John 143
  Mary 80
  Matilda JACOBS 143
  William 143
SMIDTH
  Cathrine 58
  Jacob 58
  Margaretha 58
SMILEY
  Agness 135
  Anna M.J. BOWEN 143
  Annie 20
  Augusta D. 134
  Carie 20
  Christina 107
  Diana DROUGHT 143
  Emily 163
  George 143
  Irene A. 20
  John A. 143
  John B. 143
  Libbie P. ANDERS 143
  Rebecca C.A. 71
SMIRSCH
  Francis MACA 45
  James 45
  Theresa 45
SMIRSH
  F.J. 159
  Francis 159
  Francis MACA 159
  Jacob 159
SMIT
  Catherine 163
SMITH
  A., Mrs. 160
  A.B. 87, 95
  Abidiah 16
  Adam 143
  Addison 154

Addison R. 143
Adeline BROWN 144
Adison 18
Agnes MOSLEY 83
Albert 143
Albin 144
Alfred B. 144
Aloizije NEMETZ 144
Amanda DUCROS 144
Amanda F. BULL 143
Angeline 106
Ann 144
Ann E. FURGESON
  144
Ann K. 76
Ann Zuella
  LOCKWOOD 144
Anna 3, 76
Anna GOSCH 144
Anna SIMON 129
Anna WIESE 144
Annie 51, 78, 87
Annie EDMONDSON
  144
Annie PHILLIPS 63
Arthur B.G. 143
Auguste STUPIED 143
B.W. 17
Barbara 129
Barnard 83
Beata GILBERG 144
Bertha 123
Bertha G. NOWAG 143
Bridget DOWNS 144
Bridget KNUDSEN 3
C.W. 101
Candis 83
Caroline 3, 116
Caroline ELY 145
Caroline L. WRIGLEY
  145
Carrie C. 116
Carrie E. 45
Carrie O. PATRICK
  144
Catharine 53, 98, 100
Catharine MILLER 143
Catharine W. DAVIS
  144
Catherine 163
Charles 143
Charles H. 143
Charles S. 21
Charlotte 87
Christian 3, 76
Christina M.C.
  SCHMIDT 144
Christine 75
Christopher 8
Claus 116
Cornelius 85, 143
D.W.F. AUTTENSEN
  143
Daniel 143
Daniel H. 143
Daniel W. 143
David G. 143
Delos S. 143
Dora 169
Dorcas S. 107
Douglas 51
E.P. 42
Edward 143, 145
Eli 143
Eliza 142
Eliza GILMORE 2, 76,

83
Eliza I. 150
Eliza McMURRAY 143
Elizabeth 45, 48, 65, 76,
  83, 90, 115, 123
Elizabeth ANDERSON
  144
Elizabeth B. 160
Elizabeth Bett
  SCHULTIS 143
Elizabeth BUCKLER
  144
Elizabeth MILLER 144
Ella 17
Ella MEADE 144
Ellen 152
Ellen J. MILLS 143
Ellen JONES 143
Elspet LUDINGHAM
  145
Emiline BROWN 144
Emily 76
Emma 12
Emma A. ELLIOTT 145
Emma MEDLOCK 144
Emma WRIGHT 87
Etta E. 28
Eugenie JUNGERS 53
F.E. 167
Fannie R. COON 145
Fanny GOULD 143
Frances E. COVELL
  145
Francis 5
Francis Russell 126
Frank 143
Frankie Rosella 127
Franklin 11
Franklin D. 143
Fred J. 142
Fred K. 16, 143
Fred W. 143
Frederick 144
Frederick W. 143
Fuller 144
G. 124
G., Dr. 125
Geo. H. 144
George 37, 64, 93, 129,
  143, 144, 170
George B. 50
George E. 144
George V. 144
George W. 143, 144
Gertrude 2
H.B. 144
H.F. 144
H.P. 127, 144
Hannah 55
Hannah NICKERSON
  64
Hannah TOMAU 145
Hans P. 3
Hariet ONEY 144
Harriet 108
Harriet SAWYER 144
Harvey 87
Hattie 32
Hattie E. 59
Hellen McD HIGBY
  144
Henry 143-145, 163
Herman 41, 144
Ida LITTLE 144
Ida M. LITTLE 93
Ira W. 144

SMITH, cont.
Irvine 144
J. 45
J.E. 144
J.H. 2, 108
J.J. 144
J.K. 144
J.L., Mrs. 163
J.M. 144
J.P. 12, 120
Jacob 53, 129, 144
Jacob J. 144
James 71, 144, 145
James C. 144
James E. 144
James H. 144
Jane HOBSON 18
Jane HOPSON 154
Jane R. 29
Jane STEVENS 144
Jarad J. 144
Jenette N. 34
Jennie R., Mrs. 152
Jennie S., Mrs. 54
Johanna VINTON 76
John 120, 143-145, 170
John B. 144
John Chr. 14
John E. 144
John J. 45
John K. 120
John L. 54
John L., Mrs. 78
John S. 144
John T. 18
Joseph 144
Judith E. SCOTT 144
Julia 72
Juliett 147
Justin 116
Kate 97, 137
Kate, Mrs. 119
Lena 108, 116
Lenah 90
Lizzie 12
Lotta BEDFORD 143
Louis 144
Louisa 7, 25
Lucinda 122
Lucy 128
Luella Mary JARMAN
144
M. Abbie 144
M.A. 144
M.A. BIRCHARD 145
M.A. SHEARER 144
M.A., Mrs. 144
M.C. 76
M.T. 83
Magdalena 158
Mahew 2
Margaret 9, 49, 79, 114
Margaret HARTNEY
145
Margaret KULENKAMP
144
Maria C. 3
Maria RINSKE 144
Maria STUPIED 144
Mariah GORMAN 144
Marie HAAS 65
Marietta 170
Marietta SHELDON 45
Martha 167
Martha A. 52
Martha Jane 16

Martha MATHER 87
Mary 18, 24, 29, 33, 35,
65, 69, 77, 96, 100,
110, 143, 158
Mary A. 117, 120, 133,
170
Mary A. BERCHORD
128
Mary A. BURT 144
Mary A. SHEARER 170
Mary ANDERSON 144
Mary C. JOHNSTON
144
Mary CLARKSON 8
Mary CNUDSON 144
Mary E. 8
Mary E. HOLLADAY
143
Mary FRANK 144
Mary GATHERWOOD
144
Mary HANSEN 144
Mary Isabel 18
Mary Isabella 154
Mary J. PEABODY 144
Mary KELLEY 143
Mary M. 144
Mary M. THOMAS 143
Mary N. 128
Mary T. 157
Mary URWIN 131
Mary WALDER 116
Mary WHITE 133
Mary, Mrs. 8
Matilda 144
Matilda SHRAY 143
Maud ROLAND 143
Melissa TISDALE 143
Melville 144
Michael 144
Mr. and Mrs. 140
Mrs. 166, 168
N.J. 67, 78, 120
N.P. 133
Nancy 2, 125
Nancy Belle STEWART
143
Nancy CHAMBERLAIN
144
Nancy Elizabeth LEWIN
145
Newton J. 28
Newton Jasper 127
Norman 86
P.S. 88
Patrick 143
Paul 144
Permelia SEBRING 144
Peter 144
Peter J. 144
Peter S. 144
Phebe HUNT 143
Philip 147
R.J.R. 57
Rachel 115
Rebecca 142, 155, 169
Rebecca F. 51
Rebecca FRANCIS 51
Rebecca S. HANKINS
145
Rollin C. 8, 128, 145
Ruth 8
S. 12, 51
S., Col. 21
S.P. 127
Samuel 144

Samuel C. 144
Samuel H. 144
Sarah E. CHILDER 16
Sarah Frances 63
Sarah Jane PRICE 144
Sarah M. CONVERSE
144
Sebastian 90, 123
Sophia 14
Sophia L. HAWKINS
144
Sophia MASON 143
Susan 36, 135
Susan A. STRAIGHT
144
Susan BENEDICT 28
Susan E. WILLIAMS
143
Susan FITZGEROLD
143
Susan S. 16
Susan SHARA 143
Susana BENEDICT 127
Susanna SCHERA 143
Theodore 65
Thomas A. 144
Thomas B. 132
Thomas H.F. 144
Thomas W.B. 144
Tillman 144
V.W., Mr. and Mrs. 91
Valentine 63
Volney W. 145
W. 168
W. Margaretha CORDES
14
W.B. 50, 64
W.H. 127, 131
W.P. 50
Watson B. 60, 97, 119,
145
Wenzel 159
William 144, 145
William H. 145
William L. 145
Wm. 105, 168
Wm. H. 10, 42, 124,
144
SMITHSON
Jane 52
SMITT
Bridget 23
Lydia 53
SMOLIK
Kate 43
SMRZ
Francis MACA 45
James 45
Theresa 45
SMYTH
Hattie May
MUNDWEILER 145
Nancy BROWN 145
William H. 145
Wm. 145
SMYTHE
Charlotte A. LOWE 145
E.F. 4, 104, 154
E.L. 148
Edwin F. 145
F. 43
Mary P. BURNAP 145
O.W. 145
SNEAD
John B. 145
Mary J. LATTA 145

Mumpford S. 145
Susan DAY 145
SNEATH
Catharine HAYMAKER
13
Elizabeth 13
Richard 13
SNEIDER
Susie 42
SNELL
Annie M. 44
Edna T. 45
Frederick 46
Isabella 46
Margaret COMSTOCK
45
Mary NEIDERAUR 46
Richard 45
SNOOK
Elizabeth 165
George G. 145
James 145
Mary GIBBS 145
Thana COBURN 145
SNOW
Albert 47
Anna R.H. 145
J.D. 145
Lydia C. ARBAUGH
145
Mercy W. ASHLEY 23
Minnetta J.W. 23
Solomon A. 145
Thatcher N. 23
SNOWDEN
A.B. 55
Jessie E. 7
Mar E. 162
Martha 87
Nancy 100
Nancy Jane 154
Rachel LARRISON 162
Rachel LARSON 7
W.P. 4, 7, 114, 127, 167
William P. 62, 162
Wm. 154
Wm. P. 7, 62, 101, 102
SNYDER
Adam 145
Anna CARTER 90
Annie 5
Azra 49
Christeen 121
Christine CUNSMAN
55
Elizabeth 35
Elizabeth EVINGER 79
Emily E. 79
Emma 55
John Adam 145
John F. 145
Leona 49
Louisa HILLMER 145
Margaret SMITH 49
Maria HORNING 145
Mary 49, 104
R. Annie RITCHIE 145
Sarah Ann SHILT 104
William 55, 79
SODERBERG
Martha 4
Mary C. 33
SODERGREN
Britta GOTPEMANN
145
Johan 145

Lars 145
Louiza CARLSON 145
SODERHOLM
L.P. 145
Matilda PETERSEN
145
SODERLAND
Caren Elizabeth 23
Christena SOLENG 23
Magnus 23
SODERLUND
A. 161
Andrew 168
SODERQUIST
Louisa 43
SOHILL
Gustave 79
SOHL
Annie E. 136
Aug 84
August 145
Casper 150
Catharine B. 145
Conrad 145
Elizabeth 41, 54
Maria HINE 150
Maria NEUHAUS 150
Nicholas 150
SOHRAUER
Amalie NEUMAN 145
Annie SINCERE 145
Ephriam 145
Jospeh 145
SOLAMAN
Julia 54
SOLENG
Christena 23
SOLHOLEN
Augusta
WALLINSTEIN 145
Charles 145
Eliza 145
SOLINKA
Catharine V. 134
Frank 134
Mary 134
SOLL
Christian P. 169
Elizabeth GOSCH 83
Friederika GUSCH 169
Fritz 83, 169
George 83
Lena 83
Lizzie 169
Peter 83
Peter F. 169
SOLLENGER
Caroline BURGHORT
145
Henry 145
John 145
Margaretha WISE 145
SOLMERSON
Annie 121
SOLOMAN
Jacob 145
Louisa McGLOPHIN
145
Simon 145
SOLOMON
Bertha 1
Emma 1
Jacob 1
Josie A. 123

SOLOMON, cont.
Maggie V. KINNEAR 123
N.I.D. 123
SOLTERBECK
Anna SIEH 145
Catharine GEHL 66
Catherine GEHL 145
Nicholas 145
SOMER
Barbara, Mrs. 95
SOMERVILLE
Catharine Ann 7
Margaret CURRY 7
William 7
SOMES
Betsey NUGENT 145
Carrie SHRATER 145
William 145
Wright E. 145
SOMMER
Anna Mary HANSEN 145
Barbara KAVAN 145
Bernhard 145
Charles 145
Frederick 38, 145
Mary HINE 145
Minnie SCHMIDT 145
Paul 145
SOMMERCAMP
Caspar H. 145
Josie McCORMICK 145
Louis H. 145
Louisa LUERMANN 145
SOMMERS
George 137
SOMR
Barbara, Mrs. 95
SONFRON
Susanne Maria 122
SONGUEST
Eva BLANGUEST 145
Eva FREID 145
Gustave 145
John 145
SONKEDNIK
Maria 85
SONNE
Minna 39
SORANSON
Annie M. 146
H.P., Mr. and Mrs. 146
Peter 146
SORENSDOTTER
Maria 25
SORENSEN
Andreas 146
Anna JENSEN 146
Anna JOHNSON 122
Anna K. NIELSON 79
Anna LANIRSEN 75
Caroline 112
Christian 75, 122, 146
Christina 75
Christine
JOHANNESDOTTER 146
Elsabe TOMSEN 146
Giss 146
Gotleib 128
Hanne M. 157
Hans P. 122
Jens 70, 146
Johannes 146

Just 79
Karran 25
Katrina BEIER 146
Kierstine M. 122
Lars 146
Lars Christian 146
Laurs 106
Lena NELSON 146
Mads 121
Marek JOHANSEN 106
Maren RASMUSSEN 106
Marguerite JOHNSON 146
Marianne
CHRISTENSEN 121
Mary A. 25
Mogens 106
Nils 146
Peter 113, 122
Peter M. 122
S. 142
Sophia 25
Sophia Maria HANSEN 70
Sophia PETERSEN 146
Soren 146
SORENSON
A. 88, 101
Alfred 146, 160
Anna K. BACHE 75
Anna LOUIE 94
Anna M. PETERSEN 146
Anna NIELSON 146
Annie JENSEN 146
C., Miss 1
Caren 26
Caroline GASMAN 146
Carrie M. 39
Catharine RASMUSSEN 146
Chris 94
Christina OLESON 146
Christine 89
H.P. 75
Hans 146
Joe 146
Johanna C. JOHNSON 146
Johanna ZIMMERMAN 39
John 39
John H. 146
Karin 78
Kirstene 75
Lars 89
Louisa 94
Martin F. 146
Mary R. BROWNE 146
Morten 146
Peter 146
Peter Christi 146
Thea MADSEN 146
SORGE
Dora 71
H. 71
K. BATHEIS 71
SORGER
Elizabeth 86
Elizabeth MAYNARD 86
Henry 86
SORRENSON
Johannes 25

SOSKA
Kathrine 46
SOUDERS
Elizabeth 57
SOULDER
Johanna 66
SOULEK
Frank J. 133
SOUSEK
Kathrine 46
SOUTHARD
J.P. 1, 114
SOUTHGATE
Alma Elizabeth
HENDEE 146
Henry W. 146
Mary Jane
CHITTENDEN 146
Walter 146
SOUTHWELL
Mary STEPHENSON 78
SOVORSON
Hellek 138
Ritel 138
SOVREN
Julia Ann 152
SOWLE
Hannah 155
SPAE
Christine 137
SPAETH
Charlotte GWINLIEN 146
Charlotte KROENLEIN 146
Daniel 146
David 146
Frank 146
Franz G. 146
Katharina D. SEHEER 146
Louisa KONWALIN 146
SPAGAK
Antonie 113
Antonie POLAK 113
John 113
SPAHR
Barbara 83
SPAN
Alice PICKORD 8
SPANGLER
Ella 154
George 146
Jacob 154
Jane CLARK 154
Jennie CARLYLE 146
Reuben 146
Susanne NOLAND 146
SPANN
Alice LEIGH 146
Henry 146
Henry V. 146
Jacob S. 28
Matilda BEITTER 146
SPANOGLE
James W. 146
Jane CESSNE 146
Joshua 146
Tabitha CASE 146
SPARKS
Stanton, Mrs. 168
SPARKTIES
Carl 128

Irkmud BARROWSKI 128
Lichnei 128
Wilhelmine 128
SPARROW
Caroline E. MOORE 146
Charles A. 146
Elizabeth EVERTON 146
Hannah 56
John 146
SPATZ
Anton 146
Josepha WOARTZEL 146
Lena HAZLE 146
Martin 146
SPAULDIN
Katie 76
Lucy WINSTON 76
William 76
SPAULDING
A., Mrs. 65
Abigail 128
Charles 125
Danial 146
L.B. 146
Lydia CHANDLER 146
Maggie LEONARD 146
Mary McALLISTER 125
Minnie P. 125
SPAUM
J.S. 107
SPAUN
J.S. 88
J.S., Mrs. 136
SPAWN
J.S. 94
SPEAR
Rachel 118
SPEARMAN
Charles 146
Cynthia FROGE 146
Harriet BAKER 146
J.D. 146
J.D., Mrs. 146
James D. 146
Josephine MEYERS 146
Sarah E. SIMONS 146
William T. 146
SPEARS
E.D. 26, 111
M.F. 158
SPECK
Jacob 14
Lena 14
Margaretta JETZ 14
SPEDL
Theresa 118
SPEER
Jane 10
SPEERS
Margaret E. 140
SPELLERBERG
Johann 146
Justine LUTTER 146
Karolina LEHNERT 146
Wilhelm 146
SPELLMAN
Alice 50
Catharine 28
Ella 28
Ellen 27

John 28
Mary HELLY? 28
SPENCER
Agnes BIVRY 147
Eliza 131
Elizabeth 97
Elizabeth C. 59
Ellen DANE 146
Ellen DOVE 169
Elmer E. 105
Emma 47
Emma V. 92
Emma V. DAVIS 147
Eugene 146
F.P. 78
Frank H. 146
George A. 147
Hannah CHAMBERS 119
Horace 29
J.D. 147
J.M. 27, 74
J.R. 78
James 146
James H. 147
Jane 32
John 147
Louisa BABCOCK 146
Lucy C. JACOBSON 147
Mary 113
Mary J. YOUNG 147
Mary ROTHWELL 147
Samuel 146
Sarah C. WOODS 146
William 140, 147
Wm. 47
SPENHART
Henrietta 153
SPENSER
Horace 152
SPERLING
Emeleia, Mrs. 168
John 168
Mary THOMAS 168
SPERRY
C.C. 9, 14, 16, 35, 55, 67, 159
John 147
Juliett SMITH 147
SPETMANN
Anna ELLIS 147
Augusta HENSINGER 147
Henry 147
Jochim H. 147
SPEVAK
Francis 112
Frank 85
SPICER
Elizabeth HATHAWAY 147
Ephriam R. 147
Lena LOCKNER 147
Richard 147
Thomas 33
SPIELMANN
Maria 135
Michael 135
Theresa LADISCH 135
SPIER
C.R. 5
SPIKER
Malinda BARNES 147
William M. 147

SPILANE
John 115
Mary 115
Mary A. 115
SPILLETT
Daniel 133
Sadie 133, 163
Sarah BRAMBLE 133
SPILMAN
Esther HANCOCK 147
Georgia B. GAYLORD
147
J. 147
J.H. 147
SPIMVATSCKY
Anna 65
SPINLER
Mary 72
SPINNER
Antonie 160
SPIVY
J.G. 146
SPOETLE
Marten 110
SPONEMAN
Christ 83
Sophia 83
SPONSAL
Adam 19
Lisetta 19
Lizzetta GRENNARD
19
SPOOR
Allen 147, 163
Allen M. 56
Ella 56
Ella J. 132
Eunice L. ROBBINS 89
Eunice ROBINS 132
Jane S. 132
Julia A. 163
Julia WICKS 56, 147
Mary E. 89
N.T. 132
Nelson O. 89
SPRAEL
Anna 155
SPRAGUE
Emma F. 147
G.L. 5
James K. 147
Maria 44
Sarah 57
SPRAKTES
Caroline 79
Erkmuth BARROFSKY
79
Wilhelm 79
SPRATLEN
Belle Francis
MURSINNA 147
Edward H. 147
Susan E. DENNIS 147
William H. 147
SPRATLIN
Martha E. 167
SPRAUWL
Samel 157
Sarah CRAWFORD 157
Susan 157
SPRECHER
George 154
Margaret 107
Mary R. 154
Sarah A. RENSHAW
154

SPRESLER
Lena 44
SPRIGG
Annie D. 28, 31
Belle 28
John C. 28
Julia A. REMANN 28
L.T. 28
SPRING
Jerimiah C. 147
SPRINGER
Anna M. ENDLY 147
Celestia M. CLARK 147
Elizabeth 136
Emma M. 131
John 147
William 147
SPRINGMEYER
G.H. 147
Hattie TURNER 147
SPROLE
Eliza 13
SPROUL
Cicilia A. STEMM 147
Eliza 100
James 147
Michael D. 147
Nancy SHOUP 147
SPRUHEM
Elizabeth 9
James 9
Mary McDERMOTT 9
SPURGANS
Edward 39
SPURGEON
Asa 53
E.T. 53
Sarah E. 53
Sarah E. LARSON 53
SQUIRES
Alfred 147
Catharine 147
Catharine
McMANAGAL 147
Charles E. 147
Eliza A. LOGAN 147
Elizabeth 140
Ella J. COLE 147
Emma 6
George G. 147
Jesse 147
Jesse T. 147
John 140
Lucinda FRISHEY 140
N. 147
Susan 21
ST. CLAIR
Vina KELSEY 147
Anna KELLEY 147
C.H. 147
George H. 117
Josephine 90
Mary LLITZ 147
Thomas 147
William H. 147
ST. GERMIN
Eliza GRIGWARE 147
Ella MILLER 147
Joseph 147
Nelson 147
ST. GEYER
Dominick 91
St. GYER
D., Mr. and Mrs. 35
STABENOW
Gustine 31

STACEY
Elizabeth B. STOUDER
147
Elizabeth HASKINS
147
George 147
Nathanial 147
STADE
Anna M. 127
George 147
John 147
Margaret
ROHWEDDER 147
Mary TIETJENS 147
STAENDER
Anna 78
STAFFORD
Elisha 147
Elizabeth SMITH 115
J.M. 147
Jannie E. 115
John 115
Lotta A. PARKINS 147
Nancy WHITE 147
STAGAN
Fritz 21
Minna 21
Minna HANDRUKAT
21
STAGE
Maria 118
STAGERSTROM
Emily 151
STAHL
Agatha M. 60
Hans H. 60
Henrietta 125
Henry 125
Maren HANSEN 60
Mary HANSEN 125
STALD
Rebecca C. 127
STALEY
David 59
Lillie 59
Rebecca 150
Susan ULLERY 59
STANARD
Catharine HANNAH
147
Catharine SQUIRES
147
James W. 147
William 147
STANBERG
Byron 147
STANDEN
Alfred 147
Betsy APPS 147
Betsy HAPS 147
Horace 147
John 147
Mary Anna ERNAY
147
Melissa 147
Richard 147
STANDER
Fredericke HINE 147
Frederick C. 147
Henry A. 147
John 85
Margaret B. 147
Martin J.F. 147
STANDISH
Clarisa L. 154

STANFIELD
Levi S. 147
Martha McCRACKEN
147
Mr. and Mrs. 48
STANG
Augusta KOBARY 147
C., Mrs. 56
Charles 147
Emma 160
Emma GROSS 147
Ernest 147
STANGE
Bertha 112
Catharina 14, 169
Charles 112
Emma GROSSE 112
STANGLAND
E.C. 119
E.C., Dr. 63
STANKE
Augusta 49
Michael 49
Pauline 49
STANLEY
A.A. 154
Helen 95
Mary 109
STANPERKOVA
Maggie 151
STANSBURY
Angeline 107
STANSBY
Maria 7
STANTON
Edwin 147
Margret VAN CICLE
147
W.G. 11
STAPENHORST
Fredericke BUEHLER
148
Henry 148
Josephine TIEMANN
148
Theodore 148
STAPLES
Melinda 152
STAPLETON
James 148
James H. 99
Jane O'BYRNE 148
Margaret DWYER 148
Mary JOHNSON 148
Peter 148
Richard 148
Samirah WARRACK
148
STAR
Annie 113
C.J. 113
Christine 113
Wm. 73
STARING
Kate 38
STARK
Ela JANSON 64
Eliza 59
Hermann 148
Johanna 126
Johannah 68
Maria 69
Mary Anne
SALISBURY 148
Person 64

Rachel HILGENKAMP
148
Sarah 137
W.H. 148
STARKE
Regina 72
STARKEY
A.H. 15
Ann McMANNERS 152
Anna McMANNING 15
Ellen RYAN 148
Jennie 15
John F. 148
Mary A. GIFFORD 148
Sarah A. 152
William 15, 148, 152
STARKIE
A.H. 148
Ann DONOVAN 148
Ella LAVILLE 148
STARKS
Mary 63
STARLINE
Susannah 88
STARRS
C.P., Mrs. 67
START
Alice E. 126
George G. 126
Phelina LARKIN 126
STARVER
Hannah 7
STATIN
James, Mr. and Mrs. 129
STEARNS
Lucinda H. 62
STEBBINS
Alice HANNAN 148
Alice U. SKINNER 148
Asa H. 148
Harry 148
Mary M. BRYANT 148
Mary WILSON 148
Monta John 148
Monte John 148
STECKLES
Polly 59
STEDELMEIER
Friedericka 110
STEEL
Hannah PERSSON 148
Ingrid NELSON 148
John 11, 83, 148
Magnus 148
Mary or Marie 116
STEELBERG
John 63
Maria NORDMAN 63
STEELE
Adaline 65
Adna 148
Elizabeth HENSMAN
148
Elizabeth HINKLEY
148
Hannah 119
James 148
John 119
L.A. 148
R.C. 131
Robert C. 153
Sarah M. HUNT 148
STEELL
Homer 167
STEEN
John 133

STUBEN, cont.
  Lucia Mary PAULSEN
    150
  Otto 125
  Peter Henry 150
STUBENE
  Margaret 7
STUBLES
  J.J. 10
STUCHLIKOWA
  Barbara PESIKOWA 74
  Josie 74
  Martin 74
STUCK
  Katrina 171
  R.J. 36, 63, 104, 141
STUDLEY
  Martha E. 29
STUELL
  Anna McG. 93
STUENKEL
  Sophia 105
STUFT
  Johanna 74
STUHL
  Luzia 125
STUHLMILLER
  Christina DANZHLER
    150
  Henry 150
  Jacob 150
STUHMILLER
  Emma SCHONBORN
    150
STUHR
  Anna SCHEEL 150
  Gretchen ARP 126
  James 150
  Jochim 126
  Marx 126
  Nellie 126
  Peter 150
  Trina SCHEEL 150
STUHT
  Ernest 150
  Maria MATSON 150
STULL
  H. 33
  Henry 88
  Home 4
  Homer 15, 162
STUMP
  Maria 162
STUPIED
  Auguste 143
  Caroline MUELLER
    144
  Dora MEIER 143
  Helena Magdalena 144
  Maria 144
  Marie 143
  William 143, 144
STURGER
  H.S. 143
STURGES
  H.A. 55
  Hiram A. 140
STURGESS
  H.A. 9, 39
  N.A. 6
STURGIS
  H.A. 112
STURL
  Lucy 125
STURMAN
  Moses H. 140

STURROCK
  Margaret 58
STUTCKA
  Justina 14
SUBY
  Ellen 93
SUCHE
  Annie 126
SUCHY
  Barbara 106
  Barbara D. 150
  Barbara J. 150
  Frank 150
  James 106
  John 150
  Mary Anna 106
  Veronka 8
SUDAN
  Adolph 150
  Agnes UNDEHOFER
    150
  Gustav Adolph 150
  Ottilia WINSKOWSKY
    150
SUDBOROUGH
  T. 102
SUELWOLD
  Louise 52
SUFHEN
  T., Mrs. 122
SUHENS
  Henry 123
SUHL
  Casper 150
  Maria HINE 150
  Maria NEUHAUS 150
  Nicholas 150
SUIT
  Dora 6
  Henry 6
  Mary 6
  Phebe HEWITT 6
SULIVAN
  Anna 81
  Johanna 89
SULLIVAN
  ---- POWERS 96
  Ann 90
  Annie 40, 129
  Bartholomew 150
  Bridget EGAN 40, 129
  Catharine 128
  Catharine BOWEN 102
  Catharine CUISICK 151
  Catharine POWER 22
  Catherine 94, 96
  Catherine CONNERY
    150
  Chrine LAHAL 166
  Edward O. 36
  Elizabeth 30, 129
  Ellen 102, 105, 114
  Ellen CURRAN 51, 151
  Elnor FRINELL 128
  Eugene 128, 151
  Hannah 102
  Hanora MURPHY 151
  Honora 51
  James 114
  James O. 151
  Jeremiah 51
  Johanna 52, 95
  Johanna McCARTHEY
    30
  John 40, 102, 129, 139,
    150

John M. 9, 17, 49, 71,
  91, 121, 151
  Joseph 46
  Julia 45
  Julia FINN 151
  Lydia C. 79
  M. 99
  M.J. 166
  Maggie 32
  Margaret 8, 45, 46
  Margaret DAILEY 46
  Margaret
    HARRINGTON 10
  Mary 10, 27
  Mary LANGON 150
  Mary, Mrs. 22, 52
  Maurice 151
  Melissa J. 153
  Nellie 87, 96
  Nora 139
  Patrick R. 102
  Richard 166
  Sarah KENNEDY 151
  Stephen 83
  Thomas 10, 30
  Timothy 151
SULLY
  Daniel 151
  Fanny VEAR 151
  Mary BURNES 151
  Thomas 151
SUMMER
  Hulda Van DEVER 151
  John 151
  Luther 151
  Mary WOLLEN 151
SUMMERS
  Barbara KAVAN 64
  Catherine RUTHVEN
    170
  John 170
  Samuel, Col. 54
SUMNER
  Annie B. FISHER 151
  Dolly 151
  Duby 153
  E.R. 151
  Ed. H. 151
  Elizabeth (Bettie) 128
  Ephrian 151
  Jerusha NASH 151
  John 151, 153
  John H. 151
  Lena McDONALD 151
  Mary DOTSON 151
  Mary RESER 151
  Sally 110
  Samuel 70, 151
  Samuel T. 151
  Sophronia GILLMORE
    151
SUMPTION
  Berilla WARD 158
  Josie 158
  Robert H. 158
SUNBLAD
  Augusta J. ANDERSON
    151
  Charles R. 151
  Sophia ARWIDSON
    151
  William 151
SUNDBORN
  Catharine JOHNSON
    151
  Catherine JENSEN 151

Charles 151
Charles G. 13, 151
Charlotte BOLIN 151
Edla Maria
  WENNGREN 151
G. 92
Peter W. 151, 161
SUNDEL
  Emily CAGERSTROM
    151
  Emily STAGERSTROM
    151
  Gust 151
SUNDERWALL
  Charles 151
  Charlotte
    GRAPENGIEFSER
    151
  Fred 151
  Sally GRIMSHAW 151
SUNDUN
  August 151
  Engrid LARSEN 151
SUNESSON
  Permilla 86
SURBER
  Sarah Ann 7
SURDAN
  Emily M. 50
SURMANN
  Gertrud 94
SURPRENENT
  Josette TROMBLE 151
  Marceline GOYETTE
    151
  Nacriss 151
  P.S. 151
SUSH
  August 167
SUSTERIC
  Joseph 68
SUTER
  Francis, Mr. and Mrs.
    138
  Jane K., Mrs. 28
SUTHER
  Joseph 4
SUTHERLAND
  T.M., Mrs. 51
SUTLEY
  Almeda 68
  Cornelia A. 68
  Emily J. HAMMOND
    68
  Malinda 163
  Wilson 68
SUTLIFF
  Clara E. 138
  Henry 138
  Lous E. WEBSTER 138
SUTPHEN
  Enoch W.N. 151
  James 151
  Maggie SKINNER 151
  Sarah SILCOZ 151
SUTTON
  A.M. BAXTER 78
  A.W. 151
  Catharine GEDDES 151
  Edna C. BURCHARD
    151
  Henry 42, 151
  Jacob 151
  John 151
  Joniah 78
  Josephine 78

Margaret M. HONEY
  151
Mary VERNON 151
Thomas L. 21, 123
Thos. L. 28, 110
SUVERKRUBBE
  Annie STEFFEN 87
  James P. 87
  Margaret 87
SVACINA
  Barbara HAJEK 151
  Jacob 151
  John 86, 151
  Katy
    INTERHOLZINGER
    151
  Martin 13, 106, 151
  Mary KRAJCIK 151
  Mary SLAMA 151
  Peter 151
SVANDOVA
  Antonia 85
SVANTNA
  Martin 13
SVATNA
  Martin 106
SVEHLA
  Mary 80
SVENSDOTTER
  Elna 89
SVENSON
  Anna 150
  Batilda SWANSON 152
  John 152
  Mary CHASE 93
  Ole 44
SVENSSON
  Annie 148
SVETASCH
  Barbara 157
SVITAK
  Barbara 157
SWACKHAMER
  Caroline BATES 151
  Clara Electa DODGE
    151
  Edgar 151
  Elija 151
  Ellen BARNUM 151
  Samuel Oscar 151
SWAFFORD
  Lucia E. 138
  M.D. 138
  Mary J. WILSON 138
SWAGER
  Matilda 160
SWAHA
  George 59
SWAIN
  Elmer P. 151
  Emma J. GREEN 151
  John F. 151
  Lydia DAVIS 151
  Nancy 160
SWAN
  A.F. 151
  Ande 151
  Anna 169
  Charlie P. 151
  Gust W. 134
  Henrika JOHNSON 151
  Lucy, Mrs. 161
  Martha NOBERG 151
  Rhoda 27
  Roda 27

SWANBERGER
Jacob 13
SWANEY
A.C. 152
Essie M. GROUNDS
152
Jane 154
Jerry 152
Ophy KETCHEL 152
SWANS
Hanna 42
SWANSEN
Anna MAGNUSON 135
Biddy 61
Christine PALLMER
152
Daniel 135
Inga 75
Mary 89, 95, 117
Nels 152
SWANSEY
Mary E. 139
SWANSON
Alexandra 134
Anders 4
Andrew 105, 152
Anna KINDMAN 134
Annie 43, 76
Augustus 48
Batilda 152
Betty 131
C., Mrs. 145
C.A. 134
Carrie 11
Charles Peter 151
Charlotte 170
Christine PETERSON
105
Clara 121, 152
Ella 151
Ellen 45
Gonela 126
Gustaf 89
Gustav 4
Hannah 4, 120
John 114, 152
Lena ANDERSON 152
Louis 2
Lucinda 2
Maggie 162
Margreet PETTERSON
141
Maria HELIN 7
Marie Catharina
JOHNSON 117
Mary MILLER 2
Mary MUNSON 4
Mattie R. 23
Nellie 111
Nels 121, 152
Niles 145
Olof 117
Origen S. 141
Paulene 138
Pernila 4
Peter 7
SWART
Charlotte GRATIOT
107
Isabella Wilhelmina 107
Thomas 107
SWARTS
Elizabeth FOY 54
Ella 54
Lewis 54

SWARTZ
Catharine LEITH 152
Catherine 43
George L. 152
L. 96
Richard 152
Sarah A. MANGER 152
SWARTZLANDER
A. 39, 55
Abigail RANKIN 152
Albert 9, 142, 147, 152
Bella E. BRUNER 152
Jacob 152
Joseph 152
Stella MAY 152
SWEATT
A.R. 152
Henry J. 152
J. TINSLEY 152
Lizzie E. CULVER 152
SWEDERS
A.N. 13
Andrew N. 152
Olia TROIL 152
Olivia, Mrs. 4
SWEENEY
Anna 29
Catharine 45, 46, 114
Elin CRETEN 45
Frank 13, 64
James 152
James A. 152
Johanna 90
John 29, 90, 152
Libbie BUTLER 152
Mary 43
Mary A., Mrs. 42
Mary Ann 29
Mary Ann EMS 152
Micah
VANDERVOORT
152
Pall 45
Rosana BECKER 152
William 152
SWEENY
Abby FOLEY 152
John 152
Mary 78, 94
Patrick 90
SWEESY
Charles C. 142
J.F. 46, 136
Mr. 19
SWEET
Antilla THOMPSON
152
Daniel 152
David 152
Eunice 36, 81, 99
Jennie R. SMITH 152
Marian T. 152
Mr. and Mrs. 35
SWEETMAN
Catharine 152
Thomas 152
Thoms 152
SWEEZY
Cazner W. 42
SWEINESON
Mary 142
SWENDLY
Andrew H. 152
Berke OLSEN 152
Hans 152
Randina VANWIG 152

SWENEY
James 152
Julia Ann SOVREN 152
SWENGEL
Samuel 39
SWENSDOTTER
Annie 97
Brita 4
Ellen 40
Engamyer 92
SWENSEN
Catharine MAGNUSON
76
Cesse 3
Daniel 76
Ellen 155
Elna ERICKSON 89
Gundhild OLSEN 166
Ida 76
Ida M. 135
Jorgen 166
Kerstine 3
Matt 98
Peter 124
Swen 89
SWENSON
Alner OLSEDOTTER
23
Amalia 61
Anna 131
Anton Ludwick 152
Bettie JOHNS 42
Brita OLSON 152
Carl G. 23
Caroline BRUCE 152
Carrie ANDERSON 116
Christiana 61
Christine 111
Eleanor 155
Elna PEERSON 96
Gustav 152
Ingre NELSON 89
Karna 164
Kate M. IVERSON 88
Lars 88
Lena 41
Lizzie 88
Margaret IVERSON 88
Maria 43
Mary 112
Mons 96
Nels 89
Ole 116
Petennalla 42
Swen 42
SWENSSON
Hanna JENSEN 3
Jens 3
Johana JONSSON 111
Johanes 111
SWESON
Johanna 116
SWETT
Hannah 40
SWICKARD
Albert F. 152
Elias 152
Elmira CAMP 152
Meldora DAVIS 152
SWIFT
Bridget DOOLING 47
John 47
Maggie 47
Mary 47
Thomas 47, 63, 75

SWIGART
Nancy M. 140
SWINDELL
Mary A. 148
SWINDLE
Mary A. 149
SWINN
Catharine 20
SWINNEY
Rebecca 145
SWITZER
Ellen B. 93
Lizzie 93
M.B., Mrs. 169
Mr. 93
SWITZLER
Warren 34, 59, 64, 72,
160
SWOBE
Alzina SCOTT 152
Emma J. 123
Thomas 9, 152, 161
Thos. 74, 157
SWOBODA
Amalie 152
Anton 155
Filipina 152
Frank Joseph 152
Joseph 152
Josephine DOBIAS 152
Kate 155
Kate ANDER 155
SWOPE
Thomas 39
SWORDS
Mary 82
SWORT
Charlota GRATIOT 75
Harriet A. 75
Lewis B. 75
Tunis 75
SYDENHAM
Wm., Mr. and Mrs. 41
SYDENKAM
---- 148
SYDNEY
Allen 50
SYKES
Mary 113
SYLVESTER
Catharine L.
MORRISON 152
Emma L. HILL 152
Ethan E. 152
George 133, 152
George, Jr. 152
Kate 93
Louisa 133, 152
Mary A. FARLEY 152
Mary Ann FARLEY 152
Mary FARLEY 133
Mr. 133
Mrs. 133
Samuel 152
Sarah A. STARKEY
152
SYMONDS
Charles 152
Ella F. BALDWIN 152
James J. 152
Jemina JOHNSTON
152
SYPHAX
Ennis 156
SYTHZ
Caroline 85

TABER
Albert H. 152
Parasetta GUILL 152
TABOR
Ann SLY 152
John 152
Joseph 152
Kate SISSON 152
TABS
E. 36
Willis 36
TACHNICKA
Anna 148
TACHOVA
Josephine 69
TAFFE
Clara A. RITCHIE 152
John 5, 152
TAFT
Lydia 153
M. 28
TAGGART
A. 153
Cecelia F. FURAY 153
Charley F. 153
James A. 153
M.C. COANJN 153
Malinda SCOTT 153
TAGGER
Caroline, Mrs. 75
H. 75
Henry 153
Laura HILL 153
Laurie 75
Miss 128
TAGGERT
Henry 151
Laura 151
TAIT
Frances 153
Lewis 81
TALCOTT
Cora 97
Ellen 101
Jane GRAY 97
Moses O. 97
TALLBEE
Mary T. 170
TALLENT
Anna 145
Annie D. 5
David 145
David G. 5
TALLINE
Carie ERIKSON 153
Ida PETERSON 153
John 153
Peter 153
TALLON
T. 68
Thomas 81
TALMAGE
J.O. 94
TALT
Annie HUGHES 153
John 153
Patrick 153
Susan HUGHES 153
TAMASDOTTE(R)
Bergette 88
TAMLICK
Topla 30
TANDEJSKOVA
Barbara 35

TIBBETT
Annie 52
Elizabeth LAMB 52
Thomas 52
TIBBITS
Abraham 155
Hannah SOWLE 155
TIBBKE
Anna 155
Johanna ENGLEMEIER 155
Martin 155
TIBBLES
L.H., Rev. 1
TIBKE
Dora REEBER 155
Engal 131
Engel MEYER 155
Martin 155
TICE
C.C. 115
J.A. 1
TICHACEK
Magdalaena LISKA 149
Mary 149
Vaclav 149
TIEDERMANS
Annie 106
TIEDJE
Ann C. 27
Anna 66
TIEHMANN
Henry 116
Louise 116
Sophia COOK 116
TIEMANN
Johanna 148
Josephine 148
TIERNEY
Ann BLAKE 155
Catherine 122
Luke D. 155
Mary 72
Mary, Mrs. 20
P.J. 32
TIETJENS
Anna JORGENSEN 147
Marx 147
Mary 147
TIETZ
Charles 125
TIETZE
Charles 167
Justine 167
TIFFANY
Wm. A. 41
TIFFEY
Julia 105
TIGHT
Winefred 139
TILDEN
Austin 155
Charles H. 155
Geo. 44
George 155
Ida V. CLEGG 155
Josiah 155
Julia GRIGGS 155
Mary B. WILLIAMS 155
Rheumilla 34
Roella E. POTWIN 155
TILESTON
Eliza 59
TILLEY
Elizabeth 44

TILLIE
Catharine HENNEY 102
John 102
Nellie 102
TILLINGHAST
Amey 30
TILLMAN
Flora 26
Jacob 26
Maria WESTBROOK 26
TILLOTSON
Francis 156
Margaret J. NASH 156
TILTON
Edward 49
TIMM
Geo. 156
Henry 136, 156
Louisa KUNAS 156
Mary BIGIRMAN 156
TIMME
Caroline 10
Hermann C. 58
Mina 43
TIMMERMAN
Ann M.E. 19
Annie 163
Joachim 163
John 19
Lean 163
Maria TODE 19
Mary TORD 19
Wilhelmine 19
TIMMONS
Ann MULLEN 156
James 156
Patrick 156
TIMPERLEY
John 139, 153
John, Jr. 139
Mary 153
Mr. 153
Sarah 139
TIMPERLY
Alice 156
Jennie B. 156
John 156
John P. 156
Mary 156
Rebecca A. WERTZ 156
TIMPKE
Heinrich 156
Helena OBERMULLER 156
TINKER
Almeda 16
Almeda S. 16
TINSLEY
Hattie 92
J. 152
TIPTON
James 156
Mary GRAHAM 156
TISDALE
Mary Ann 73
Melissa 143
TISHER
Christian 156
Leota Viella ROSS 156
Mary Ellen RHOADES 156
Zack 156

TITUS
Sarah KELLY 156
William 156
TIZARD
Edith BOW 156
Kate O'NEILL 156
Richard 156
TOBANA
Mary CAMERON 129
TOBANNAH
Joseph 156
Mary CARRIGAN 156
TOBIAS
Ann Catharine JOHNSON 156
Carston 156
James 11
Mattie J. 11
TOBIN
Ellen 101
James Charles 100
TOBY
Tho. 7
TODD
L.E. RUSSELL 64
Sarah 158
Thomas 64
TODE
Maria 19
TOENSFELDT
Elizabeth OTT 156
George 156
Henry 156
Margarret SCHOENER 156
TOFER
Henry 16
TOFT
John H. 156
M. 10, 26, 70, 147
Mary MILLER 156
TOHLE
Mary 53
TOLAND
Elizabeth WHELAN 156
William 156
TOLIVER
Dalton R. 156
Isam 156
Maggie MOSTILLER 156
Matilda RUNNELS 156
Sarah MOSTILLER 156
TOLLES
Mathis (Mattie) 169
TOMAU
Hannah 145
TOMBLESON
Henry 139
Louisa 139
Sarah M. GENTRY 139
TOMBLIN
E.S. 22
TOMBRINCK
Catharine HOCHS 156
Herman 156
Katharina C. 156
Martin 156
TOMEK
Franciska 70
TOMISKA
Anna 134
TOMLINSON
Cecelia 5
Mary 153

Sarah E. 56
TOMNEY
Elizabeth A. BURTON 156
Patrick 156
TOMPSETT
Elizabeth A. RICH 156
George 156
Isaac 156
Philadelphus POWELL 156
TOMPSON
John 156
Rachael STEWART 156
TOMSON
Henry 155
Mary LARSON 155
TONAR
Elizabeth QUEEN 156
Mary McDONALD 156
Redman 156
Terrence 156
TONCRAY
Anngenette 170
TONDER
Dorothea M. NELSON 156
Peter Peterson 156
TONEARY
Angenett 71
TONER
Anna HUGHES 106
Belle 150
Elizabeth 106
Francis 106
Jas. 135
Mary 89
Patrick 106
TOOKER
Hannah SIPPERLY 46
J. 38
J.A. 4, 104, 109
James A. 46
Nancy Jane 46
TOOLE
Sarah 82
TOOZER
A.R. 74
Caroline E. 74
Caroline HOBBS 74
TOPE
Eliza MURRAY 156
James 156
Jennie B. TIMPERLY 156
Sylvester P. 156
TOPHAM
D.B. 50, 108, 120, 124, 160, 168
T.P. 42
TOPHAN
Eva HAWKS 98
Frances 98
John R. 98
TOPPER
Ann 126
TORD
Mary 19
TORDSON
Sophia 16
TORDTE
Anna Katharina 104
TORGERSON
Karen JOHANNSEN 20
Lena 20
Mikkel 20

TORMEY
Barney 156
Mary CONVEY 156
Mary DYER 156
Thomas 156
TORRANCE
Ellen 82
TORREY
Clarissa 120
E.J. 65
F.J. 16
Isabella A. 65
Lillias 18
Mr. and Mrs. 64
T.J., Mrs. 52
TORREZ
Mr. and Mrs. 64
TORSON
Hans 61
Mary JOHNSON 61
TOSSEN
Henry 160
TOUHY
Kate SLOAN 156
Mary MALONEY 156
Michael 156
Patrick 156
TOULSEN
Fr. 43
TOUSLEY
Ella E. BURLINGHAM 156
J.W. 57, 128, 156
Jason W. 156
John H. 156
John W. 88
Samantha E. WELLS 156
TOVEY
Mariah BANKS 156
Thomas 156
TOWER
A.S. 5
TOWLE
Abraham 156
Albert L. 156
Mary W. HARRIS 156
Mary WILSON 156
TOWN
Elizabeth M. 158
Emily E. PACE 156
George S. 156
Julia M. 158
Louisa REED 156
Saylon 156
TOWNE
Julia M. 62
Sarah F. 8
TOWNES
Fannie Ella 129
John A. 129
Margaret UTTERBACK 129
TOWNSEND
C.F., Mrs. 101
Kezia 158
Keziah 166
Mary E. 1, 3
Mary E., Mrs. 19
Robert 50, 53, 77
TOWNSHEND
Mary Jane 65
TOWSLEY
Ellen M. CAMPBELL 156
Eunice S. WELLS 156

VAN PATTEN
S.E., Miss  103
VAN PLEW
Marion B., Mrs.  135
VAN SYCKLE
Elizabeth  87
VAN SYCLE
Sallie  162
Sarah M.  19
Van TRESS
Almira  128
VAN WITTERN
Augusta  85
VANASDAL
Ann  5
VANBALARICUM
Isabella  2
VanCAMP
Albert  159
Charles L.  159
Grace L. BRADLEY
159
Ham B.  159
I.  159
Ira  159
Levi  159
Maggie HENNESEY
159
Phoebe BURK  159
Sarah BURK  159
VANCE
C.  97
VANCHURA
V.  130
VANDANECKER
George  159
James B.  159
Mary DUGAN  159
VanDANIKER
Celia PIERSON  159
Geo. W.  159
James B.  159
Maggie S. BERNARD
159
VANDEFORD
Maggie  78
VANDENBAURGH
L.H.  159
VANDENBURG
G.  159
L.H.  159
Margaret BERRELL
159
Minnie  133
Rikja LAMMERTSEN
159
VANDENBURGH
Gertrude H.  72
Jane MILLER  72, 159
John A.  159
L.H.  72, 159
May DORT  159
VANDERBURG
L.H.  15
VANDERFORD
Alexander  159
Joseph  159
Nancy DIXON  159
Rosana BUSHEA  159
Tillie JOHNSON  159
William  159
VANDERVOORT
Micah  152
VANDUSEN
William  78

VANDYKE
Rebecca S. HANKINS
145
VANE
Sarah  19, 58, 127
VanKURAN
Amelia J. PHELPS  159
Arthur J.  159
Cynthia M.
CARPENTER  159
Isaac  159
Isaac, Mrs.  159
VANNER
Susana  133
VanORMAN
Chloe A. BECKET  159
Deuce A. NILES  159
Oliver O.  159
Oristen U.  159
VANOUR
Frances  40
VANOUS
Annie FISHER  84
Frances  40, 84
John  84
Joseph  86, 159
Joseph, Jr.  159
Mary  159
Mary RUZICKA  159
Mary WAVRIN  159
VANSCOY
Emily SLAGLE  159
John  159
Noah D.  159
Rose WEBSTER  159
VANSICKLE
Anna  152
VANSLAUS
C.  167
VANWIG
Caroline FALK  152
Peter  152
Randina  152
VARNA
Annie KADIS  159
Barbara MELACEK
159
Mathew  159
Thomas  159
VARNER
Ollavis  159
Sophia LARSON  159
VASAK
John  8
VASKU
Joseph  128, 150
Lotta  128
Mary DOSTAL  128
VAUCHMA
Anna URBANEK  159
Francis SMIRSH  159
John  159
W.  159
VAUGHAN
Sophrona  116
Thomas  116
VAUGHN
Ann  154
Catharine  91
Deana HANDY  134
Florence D.  134
John M.  134
Lucy  138
Mary  93
Mr.  134
Mrs.  134

VAUKURAN
Andrew  59
VAUN
A.M.  144
VAUTHRECH
Mayealona ZOUGH  132
Ulrach  132
Varene  132
VAVERKA
John  135
Mary  135
VAVRA
Barbara  46
Frank  138
John  46
Maria PISKACKOVA
138
Marie  46
Mary  138
VAVRIN
Katherine  86
VEACH
Elizabeth POWELL  109
VEAR
Fanny  151
VEDERSTROMER
John  77
Marian HANSEN  77
VEDESHAL
Antonie  156
VEIDLEIG
Frederica  148
VEIL
Joseph  159
Theresia BUNTRICK
159
VEIRS
Brice  159
Daniel  159
Ellen F. WEBBER  159
Helen  74
VELEBA
Theresia  160
VELETA
Albert  159
Mary  12, 159
Mary BOWER  159
Vencil  159
VELLEY
Ellen  114
VER BEIST
Cornelius  161
H.  161
VERKIER
Mary  6
VERMILLIAN
Ann KING  159
Charles  159
Sarah A. HEWIT  159
William P.  159
VERMIRE
Josphine  27
VERNOL
Zadai  134
VERNON
Catharine  166
Mary  151
VERPOORTEN
Hubert  55
VERR
Margrate  95
VESEY
Henry  83
VESS
Martha  166

VESSEL
Harriet C. CLARK  154
VESTEEG
Arie  159
VEZ
Josephine  26
VEZY
John  159
Minnie E. WIGHTMAN
159
Nancy McINTYRE  159
William  159
VICKERY
Anderson  160
John L.  160
Nancy SWAIN  160
Ruhanna McCOLLUM
160
VICKEY
Anderson  160
John L.  160
Nancy SWAIN  160
Ruhanna McCOLLUM
160
VICKROY
Ann HEANEY  155
Oliva B.  155
Orin  155
VICTOR
Alexander  160
C.C.  160
Elizabeth CARRY  160
Madalein HOMER  160
VIEHMANN
John  114
VIEN
John J.B.  151
VIEREGG
James  25
VIERS
Anna  63
Harriet SLINGLAND
159
Maria  63
Marie  63
Rachel  161
Thos. J.  63
VILAS
Mary  63
VILEM
Therese  42
VINCENT
Elizabeth  22, 143
Eunice  112
Eva  116
James  116
John  160
Mary E. ARNOLD  160
Mary Jane  124
Mary Jane EVANS  160
Mary McCALL  116
Thomas J.  160
VINCUC
Rosa  157
VINE
Arminda  55
VINEGAR
Hester  18
VINEMEL
Anson  57
VINTON
Camilla F. GOFF  21
Johanna  76
VIOLET
Mary  145

VIRTEL
Wenzel  154
VISHER
Mr. and Mrs.  19
VISSCHER
E.W. LIGHTFOOT  160
Emma B. MASON  160
F.  160
H.H.  13
Henry H.  160
Nancy REYNOLDS  160
Will L.  160
VITEK
Catharine  134
VITKOUVA
Catharine  134
VITTENBERG
Doras  19
VLACH
Katherine  140
VLCK
Katherine  140
VLIET
Almina  54
John  54
Mary  41
Pamelia BURGESS  54
VLNA
Frank  160
John  160
Mary KAVAN  160
Rosaria KLEKA  160
VOBORIL
Anna  46
John  46
Mary SKLENER  46
Mathew  74
VODDER
Ane JOHNSON  136
Mads  136
VODICKA
Anna HOLUB  96
Anna MUNCHNA  160
D.D.  95
Frank  43
Jacob  118, 160
Joseph  96
Josephine  118
Leona  96
Mary NEMETZ  160
U.L.  160
Vaclav L.  160
VOFR
Henry  107
VOGAL
Amanda  67
VOGAN
Jane MORTON  96
Lizzie  96
William  96
VOGEL
Caroline  133
Ernestine BERNDT  160
Herman  160
Louise REINICKE  160
William  160
VOGH
Elizabeth  10
VOGLE
Mary  126
VOGT
Caroline  45
Charles  87
Frederike MANGKY  87
Mina  87

VOIGHT
  Christina 169
VOIGHTLANDER
  Oscar 129
VOLK
  Anna FISHER 160
  Barnhard 160
  Grist 160
  Maria 50
VOLKMAN
  Jacob 160
VOLKNEIER
  Eliza DANIELS 160
  Ernst 160
  Gottfried 160
  Sarah CAMPBELL 160
VOLSTEDT
  Carsten 160
  Henry 160
  Teovile TRONOVSKA
    160
  Wibke HOEFT 160
VOLTZS
  Elizabeth 84
VOLZMANN
  Carl 31
  Ernstine 31
  Gustine STABENOW
    31
Von BORRIES
  Henry 122
  Julia L. 122
  Susanne Maria
    SONFRON 122
VON DER MARIVITZ
  Emma 160
VON DORN
  Abraham 160
  Huldah J. RENECKER
    160
  Sarah HEATH 160
  Theodore L. 160
Von GUNTER
  Barbara 104
VON KROSIGK
  A.M. JOHNSON 160
  Anton 160
  Emma VON DER
    MARIVITZ 160
  Heinrich G.F. 160
Von TROTT
  Albert 160
  Augustus 160
  Bertha ENGSTROM
    160
  Catharine STORK 160
Von WASMER
  Adele 9
  Charles S. 160
  Elizabeth B. SEXAUER
    160
  Mary WOLLER 160
  William 160
  Wm. 9
Von WINDHEIM
  Augustus 160
  Emma STANG 160
  George P. 160
  Josephine HENGEN
    160
  Philipp 160
  Sudnah JONES 160
VON WUSNER
  Marie 65
  Mary 65
  William H.L. 65

VONENG
  W.P. 153
VonMAKAROFF
  Olga 160
VonSTERNFELS
  Franz J. 160
  Jany JELINEK 160
  Olga VonMAKAROFF
    160
  Oskar N. 160
VOOHES
  Prudence 30
VOORHES
  Prudence 30
VOPEL
  Dorothea FRICKE 15
  Johann 15
  Maria 15
VORHEES
  Prudence 158
VORIS
  E.C. 160
  Julia TROXELL 160
  William A. 160
VOSE
  Emily 8
  Mary 142
VOSS
  Bertha LEHMAN 160
  Hans 20
  Henry 16, 20, 160, 170
  Henry, Jr. 160
  Jacob 20
  Louise 20
  Magdalena BANIGER
    20
  Margaret 137
  Wilhelmina K.
    PETERSON 160
  Wilhelmina LEHMANN
    160
  Wilhelmina PETERSON
    160
  Wilhelmine 160
  William 160
VOTICAKA
  Frank 43
VOUBEL
  Catherine 45
VOWINKLE
  Charles 160
  Pauline ROEDER 160
  Rosine GOETZ 160
VRANA
  Joseph 85, 118
VRBA
  Fr., Mr. 134
VREDENBURG
  Louisa 30
VREEDENBERG
  Louisa 30
VREELAND
  Geo. W. 160
  J.P. 160
  Rachael HANSOM 160
  Roxanna PARKER 160
VUTHRICH
  Varene 132
WAAK
  Paul 131
WACHER
  Jacobine 42
WACHTER
  Theresa 103
WACHTLER
  Elizabeth 57

WACKER
  Amelia 155
  Anna 87
  Annie 105
  Emilie 42
  Jacobine 56
  Johan 155
  Thorothea BINDER 155
WACKHAUS
  Carry BLUMENSTEIN
    160
  Catharine RUERICH
    160
  Conrad 160
  Martin 160
WADDINGTON
  Prudence 8
WADDLE
  Josiah 163
WADE
  ---- 66
  Amelia E. DeLes
    DERNIER 11
  David R. 11
  Eliza 69
  Emily A. RAND 160
  G.F. 18
  George F. 160
  M.L.B., Mrs. 18
  Mary L. BENNETT 160
  Rufus 160
WADHAM
  Mary Ann 129
WADKINS
  Alice 6
WADSWORTH
  Helen 124
WAEGERT
  Anna HARTING 160
  Christ 160
  Job 160
  Mary PETERSON 160
WAEGNER
  Henriette 85
WAGECK
  Frederick 161
  Jacob 161
  Margaaret MILLER 161
  Susannah LENZ 161
WAGEMAN
  Catherine BANZER 150
  John 150
  John H. 123
  Sophia 150
WAGEMANN
  Anna Elizabeth 123
WAGEY
  Ann 134
WAGGEY
  Ann 47
WAGMAN
  John H. 84
  Magrata 84
  Mary BANZA 84
  Peter 84
WAGNER
  Amanda WOODS 161
  Anna 20, 43
  Anna BUNDESMAN
    161
  Anna PATTERSON 161
  Anna SCHAEFER 161
  Cath. 84
  Charles 16, 27
  Charles S. 75, 116
  Christian 161

Christine HASEBROCK
  161
Eleanor PATTERSON
  161
Emeline J. BOWER 161
Ferdinand 35
Friedrich Wilhelm 161
George 161
Hattie S. 89
Henry 98, 161
Ida A. 35
Jacob 161
Johann 161
Joseph 43
Julius 161
M. HOWE 161
Magdalena 163
Magdelena 163
Marie RADEMANN
  161
Mary 98
Mary ---- 43
Mary SAND 161
Matthias 161
Minnie 16
Phil 20
Robert 161
Rosetta 161
Sophia 119
Sophie 43
Ursula
  WURTEMBERGER
  35
Wilhelmenia 148
WAGONER
  Geo. 128
  Hobert 161
  John 161
  Leeda HORST 161
  Margaret HAIR 161
WAGSTAFF
  John 32
  Mary 32
  Sarah HIRST 32
WAHL
  John 161
  Maria L. 161
WAHLBERG
  Annie ANDERSEN 161
  John 161
  Martha ANDERSEN
    161
  Segra 4
WAHLGREN
  Carl 161
  Christina POLM 161
  Eric 161
  Ulrica Charlotta
    TUDDEN 161
WAHLSTROM
  Anna O. BOHMAN 161
  Annie 43
  J. 161
  J.L. 43
  John L. 161
  Louise LAMSON 161
WAHTLER
  By 161
  Elizabeth BARAK 161
  George 161
  Theresa RIPPEL 161
WAISE
  Lizzie 167
WAKELY
  E. 112
  Judge 39

WAKEMAN
  Jane 44
WALBRIDGE
  Louisa C. 168
WALCH
  Joseph 161
  Mary PITCHER 161
  Mary SCHAB 161
  Michael 161
WALDER
  Mary 116
  Rosina 65
WALDREN
  Bridget 100
WALDRON
  Hester 138
  Lucy 2
WALDSON
  John G. 144
WALKER
  A.B. 42, 161
  A.J. 77
  Adam 161
  Alden B. 42
  Alice M. 24
  Amelia 42
  Andrew 161
  Ann 101
  Ann BENNETT 161
  Anna 39
  Annie 128
  Ara Ellen MAGRUDER
    161
  B.L., Mrs. 141
  B.S. 110, 131
  B.S., Mrs. 102
  Catharine McGUIRE
    161
  Catharine O'BOYLE
    161
  Catherine DENNIS 128
  Charlotte 161
  Chloe DART 124
  Edwin H. 161
  Elisabeth 158
  Eliza E. 124
  Elizabeth A. 77
  Elizabeth BALLINGER
    161
  Elizabeth HOLLY 161
  Emanuel 161
  Emilie 129
  Emma 42, 133
  Eunice BENNETT 161
  F.J. 23
  Frank 161
  G.T. 161
  George H. 124
  George M.P. 161
  George W., Mr. and Mrs.
    30
  Harry 133
  Hattie L. BENNER 77
  Henry 158, 161
  Jacobine 171
  James 161
  John 161
  Joseph 161
  Julia A. 109
  L.A., Mr. and Mrs. 41
  L.A., Mrs. 92
  Lanncelot 161
  Lois 7
  Louis, Mr. and Mrs. 135
  Louise 22
  Lucy S. 41

WALKER, cont.
Lutitia 70
Manda JAMES 161
Margaret 87
Margaret A. GORMAN
  161
Mary 19
Mary A. 40
Mary B. DOUGLAS 42,
  161
Mary Jane PATRICK
  161
Mary S. 161
Miss 72
Olive E. 38
Robert 161
Rosa COMIN 24
Sallie 32
Sarah HENTON 161
Thomas 24, 40
Thomas D. 161, 163
Thos. D. 133
Walter 161
William 128
William S. 161
Wm. N. 137
WALKEY
Rebecca 71
WALL
Andrew 161
D.B. 52
Eliza 64
Eliza C. 46
Emma FREEMAN 161
Francis 161
Katie 25
Mary HOPKINS 161
Patrick 161
Rosa SMALL 161
WALLACE
Hannah SWETT 40
Alice May DUNCAN
  161
Ann 169
Emejean 125
Fidelia M. STRAIGHT
  125
George 24
George Y. 161
H.C. 119
Inez C. BELDIN 161
John 40
Mary 39, 95
Mary B. 40
Miss 165
Sarah 13
Thomas 125, 161
W.L. 161
WALLANDER
Olof 14
WALLENBERG
Magnus 66
WALLER
Ann BECKLEY 161
Carrie TAYLOR 161
Charlotte 32
F.C.B. 161
George 161
Mary 17
WALLESCHEEK
Peter 148
WALLIN
Carolina LILJA 161
Johanna KAMPE 161
Lars 161
Olof J. 110

Victor 161
WALLINGTON
George 162
Mary TURNER 162
Rachel DIGGS 162
WALLINSTEIN
Augusta 145
S.P. 145
WALLS
Abram 79
Louisa WARNER 79
Mary A. 79
Sarah 54
WALLSTROM
Charles W. 162
Charlotte W. SANDELL
  162
WALMER
Helen 99
WALQUEST
Anna 3
Ingra MATTSON 3
John 3
WALRICH
Eliza 165
WALSER
Marie 10
WALSH
Ann MULDOON 162
Bridget 13, 156
Edward 162
Electa CRANE 162
Emilie SCHOLLE 162
Joseph 162
Julia 29
Katie 64
Margaret WHITE 162
Margret 102
Mary Jane DOAK 162
Stephen 162
Thomas 162
WALSLEBEN
E. 57
Elizabeth 57
WALSLEMM
Elizabeth 138
WALTAN
Francis LYANS 162
Francis LYONS 162
Mack 162
WALTER
Augustus 48
Barbara HALLET 48
Fanny HUGE 162
Frank 10, 33, 137, 162
George 162
Helen CUNIS 162
Isaac 162
Jesse 162
Joseph 69
Josephine 146
Louisa 128
Louisa JUNGSTROM
  162
Reeny WILLIAMS 162
Sanford 162
W.S. 123, 146
WALTERS
Charles 162
Frank 51
Henry 162
J.R. 41
Jennie LUTES 162
Marie 124
Martha A. 60
Mary FISHER 162

Susan 29
WALTHER
Jacob 33
Minnie 33
WALTHORN
C.H. 162
Eliza THOMPSON 162
Sarah DUBOIS 162
William 162
WALTMEYER
Edith 144
J.M. 144
WALTON
Carl 162
Charles 162
Emma ALTON 162
Mollie SEVENS 162
Rhoda 169
Susan WALTON, Mrs.
  91
WAMBAUGH
John M. 38, 40
WAMBSGANS
Louis, Mrs. 158
WAMPLER
Christopher W. 162
Mar E. SNOWDEN 162
Michael 162
Sarah GANTER 162
WAND
Elizabeth 12
WANDEL
Delia WELCH 162
George 162
Lizzie BERG 162
WANDERLICH
Theresea 50
WANG
Katey E. 59
WANGBERG
Anna Christena
  HANSEN 162
Annie PETERSON 162
Emely C. OLANDER
  162
John C. 162
Peter 162
WANICKE
Amalie SWOBODA 152
Filipina SWOBODA
  152
Frank 152
WANNEMAKER
Hannah A. CHATFIELD
  32
Ruby R. 32
W.L. 32
WANNS
Mary 168
WANSCHEIDT
Dorothea 90
WANTQUEST
Charles 162
Christina OLSON 162
WANVIG
Caroline FALK 162
John Peter 162
Jonas Peter 162
Selja NELSON 162
WARAGE
Anna E. 41
Anna E. SCHWENN 41
Henrich 41
WARBURTON
Lucy J. 131

WARD
Alexander 162
Ane KELLEY 164
Berilla 158
Bridget 100, 164
Eliza Ann 4
Elizabeth LISTER 142
Elizabeth R.
  HASERODT 162
Frances M. STEVENS
  170
Jesse 165
John 123
John L. 162
Kate 147
Louisa J. 142
Margaret M.
  MUSGROVE 162
Margaret MASTERSON
  162
Mary 47, 65
Michael 164
Mr. 21
Mrs. 133
Peter 142
Sarah 74
Susan 82
William M. 162
WARDELL
Amea 99
Anna L. 99
Annie L. 153
WARE
Betsey 73
Charlotta M. BURNETT
  162
Ella M. ENGLISH 162
Esther Ann HURD 162
Harriet D. McCLOUD
  162
Henry B. 162
James B. 162
Lyman Casy 162
Lyman Eugene 162
Molly 1
Myron 162
Nellie 159
Walter 162
WAREHAM
Emma 36
Sarah E. 31
WARFIELD
A. 101
A.S. 60
Aschsa 140
WARICKS
Caroline 83
WARING
Annie P. STEWART
  162
Joseph H. 162
Martha H. MINOR 162
WARKENER
Nicholas 162
Sally MISCHLER 162
WARNECKE
Heinr. F. 44
WARNER
Alexander 162
Alice 29
C. 105
E.H. 22
E.S. 90
Elizabeth W. 142
Ella N. BARNEY 162
Erastus H. 162

Frances E.M.
  SEYMORE 162
George 124
George A. 162
Hattie M.E. 168
Hyman 162
J.W., Mrs. 110
Josephine 3, 46
Louisa 79
Marie WALTERS 124
Marshall D. 168
Minnie, Mrs. 90
Mr. 29
Nancy McNUTT 162
Permilia FARRINGTON
  162
Sabina 124
Sally A. FOSTER 168
Sarah RICHARDS 162
WARNICK
May 38
WARNISS
Rebeckey 69
WARRACK
Amasa 148
Samirah 148
WARREN
Aaron 5
Anna 30
Annie M. 5
David 162
George E. 162
J.D. 127
Jane 40, 89
Jane OSTLER 162
Lucie GRANCEY 5
Mary E. 95
Nettie CARY 162
Oleg 151
Pernie 130
Sarah 111
Sarah HANZER 162
William 162
WARRINGTON
George 32
WARTNER
Wilheimne 137
WARWICK
Bessie McNEIL 163
Margaret HOLTEN 163
Robert 163
William 163
WASHBURN
Charles D.M. 163
Eliza 83
Eliza GILLMORE 163
Flora E. WIGHT 163
George 163
Mary J. MARTIN 163
Rachael 7
Rachel 7
Wm. G. 163
WASMER
Christian 163
Dora KUHL 163
William 163
Wm. 9
WASNER
E.H. 13
WASOWSKY
Caroline 79
WASSERMAN
Andrew 110
Crescenzia 31
Creszentia 110

WELLER, cont.
William 77
William W. 151
WELLING
James M. 164
Mary E. COFFEY 164
Rebecca CONNELLY 164
William H. 164
WELLINGHAM
Catharine SCHRODER 164
John B. 164
WELLINGTON
D.K. 142
WELLIVER
Sarah A. 153
WELLMAN
Charles K. 164
Irene WATKINS 164
Wm. H. 164
WELLS
Adeline A. 45
Amelia 168
Ann C. 1
Anna 81
Christina R. BAKER 164
Conrad 91
Eliza MILLER 164
Elizabeth 10, 17, 91, 112
Eunice S. 156
George G. 164
John B. 164
Louise SHAFER 164
Margaret 91
Margaret MONSON 45
Mary GREGG 164
Mary S. HUNTZINGER 164
Peter 45
Samantha E. 156
Samuel 164
Thomas 164
William 164
WELSH
Anastasia 55
Bridget 69
Dellie 38
Edward 164
Ellen GOULD 55
Isaac 164
John D. 164
Julia CHOAT 38
Kate 75
Mary 107, 164
Mary GOLDSBOROUGH 164
Mary ROLFER 164
W.E. 99
William 38, 55
William E. 164
WENBERG
Andrew 118
Christine 118
Mary 118
WENDELL
Amalia 92
Henry 92
WENDT
Catharine 75
Henry 164
Louise FELMAR 164

Margret SCHUMACHER 164
Matilda 44
William 164
WENHOLTZ
Alfred 164
Elizabeth BRUNER 164
Hattie FRANCE 164
William 164
WENNEMO
Sophia 33
WENNERMO
Caroline SHULTS 33
Hugo 33
WENNGREN
Amelia 166
Carl John 81
Charles 151, 166
Edla Maria 151
Hedwig M. 166
Hedwig Mathilda 81
Mari Margaretha BJORKMAN 81
Maria 151
Mary JENSEN 166
WENNINGES
Wiebke 19
WENT
Annie 123
Maria 13
WENTWORTH
Henni 88
WENZENER
Henrietta 31
WERKBACH
Gustav 5
Wm. 5
WERKES
Lucy 162
WERNAIN
Elizabeth 22
WERNARORKA
Catharine 86
WERNER
Mary Ann HARING 164
Sarah LAVELL 164
Theodore J. 164
Theodore W. 164
WERTHEIM
A. 137
WERTZ
Rebecca A. 156
WESHGREN
G.A. 95
WESJOHANN
Marie 137
WESSEL
Laura 53
WEST
Adelila A. JANVIRIN 164
Amanda Jane 34
Charles 164
Christina PETERSON 164
George 134
George W. 164
Ida 80
James 164
Johanna PERSERLER 164
John J. 164
Joseph B. 164
Lucinda N. RAMSEY 164

Marion E. BRIDGE 164
Martha A. 133
Mary A. 118, 164
Mary CULVER 80
Rachel DAVIS 164
Tehemia 80
WESTALL
Anna BUTLER 164
Mary TWITTY 164
William 164
William G. 164
WESTBERG
J., Mr. 151
J., Mrs. 151
WESTBROOK
Maria 26
WESTEN
Eva ANDERSON 164
Henry 164
WESTERBERG
Johanna SWESON 116
Olof 116
WESTERDAHL
B.C.E. 27
Berndt C.E. 164
C.J. 45, 86, 164
Charles 75
Charles J. 141
Hannah Carolina YUNGSTROM 164
Joanna SJOBERG 164
Ulof 164
WESTERGAARD
Anna 43
WESTERGARD
C.C. 130, 132
WESTERGREN
Carrie MATSON 164
Hans 164
Sicilia ANDRESEN 164
Swen A. 164
WESTERLIN
Kirstin NELSON 164
Nils P. 164
WESTERMAN
Catharine ROHN 164
Helena 18
Jacob 164
Joseph A. 164
Mary C. KLINCH 164
WESTFALL
B.C. 50
WESTGATE
Esther 2, 116
WESTON
Charles C. 43
Chas. C. 155
Christman 164
Ellen 168
Frank 30
George B. 168
James 100
John 22, 120, 162
Lucy STONE 120
Martha CARLSDOTTER 164
Mary M. 120
Milla 76
Mr. 31
Nellie 22
Rebecca CANHORN 22
WESTPHAL
Augusta KOBARY 147
Auguste KOBARG 165
Bertha JODET 10
George 165

Henriette MELCHIOR 165
Jacob 165
Johanna FRANK 165
Laura H. MICHELSON 165
Lina 10
Louis 10
Vilhelm Carl 165
WESTWOOD
H.C., Mrs. 50, 96
WETDERER
Christina 81
WETMORE
Frank K. 165
Geo. H. 165
Lizzie C. ELLIS 165
Mary ELLIS 165
WETTKOFF
John 71
WETTORFF
Otto 75
WETZEL
Carl E. 74
Emmaline 83
Johanne BAUMANN 74
Maria F. 74
Mary 100
WEYMULLER
Charles 147
WHALAN
Ella 14
WHALEN
Anna 82
Catharine 115
Catharine McNALLY 165
Catharine MORAN 82
Charles 81
Elizabeth, Mrs. 81
Ella 93
Ellen 22
Eugene 70
Hugh 93
James 165
Jeremiah A. 165
Johanna RYAN 165
John 82
Julia 70, 137
Maxilnili NICHOLS 17
Nora CARROLL 165
Patrick 165
Timothy 165
Wineford CONLEY 70
WHALEY
Charles H. 165
Joseph 66
Lizzie C. RICKETS 165
Nancy, Mrs. 66
WHALIN
Maria 131
WHAREHAM
Mary 89
WHEALEN
Mary Ann 57
WHEATON
Capt. 131
Harriet 152
WHEELER
A. 165
Adah WATE 165
Annie M. ROBISON 165
Candace THURBER 165
Catharine 23

Celia 93
Eliza WASHBURN 83
Emily A. MURDOCK 165
George H. 165
George R. 165
J.F., Miss 83
J.R. 103
James C. 165
James H. 165
Jane FENTON 165
John 163, 165
Johnna McFARLAND 165
Lois E. HORTON 165
Lottie 163
Maria WEBB 163
Mary 109
Mary A. 62
Mary SISCO 165
Monroe 83
Oley, Mrs. 7
Ophilia R. 23
Samuel S. 165
T.M. 165
WHELAN
Catharine 60
Elizabeth 156
Hanagh 83
Honora 35
John 157
Katharine RYAN 81
Maggie 112
Martin 112
Mary DELANY 112
Mary Ruth 60
Mr. 115
Mrs. 156
Murtagh 60
WHELEHAN
Edward 33
WHILHARBOR
Mary A. 38
WHINTHER
Louisa 138
WHIPP
Mary C. 101
WHIPPLE
Frances 82
Ira 82
Lucy HAZEN 82
WHITAKER
Charles 165
James 165
Margaret M. BURCKER 165
Sarah SCOTT 165
WHITCOMB
Burchard 165
Melissa M. JOHNSON 165
WHITCOME
Darras PIERCE 105
Seba 105
WHITE
Abraham C. 165
Aggie 40
Agnes STEVENSON 165
Albina LEGRO 165
Alexander 40
Alice FREEMAN 165
Alvina S. SIMMONS 150
Anna JONES 165
Arthur M. 165

WOLFER
Christian 169
Dora SMITH 169
Kate KINNEY 169
William 169
WOLFF
Alfred F. 169
Amelia HOLEN 169
August 169
Catherine
　BRETENSTEIN 169
Eliza FRENCHEN 169
Emma KLEFFNER 169
Emma M. LYON 169
Ferdinand 169
Fredericka SCHMIDT
　169
Henry 1
Ida 1
Joseph 169
Julius 169
Katharine KRAFFT 169
Otto 169
Victor 169
WOLGAMOTT
Albina BENNETT 169
John 169
Nancy DAWSON 169
Washginton 169
WOLL
Margaret 85
WOLLBURG
William 91
WOLLEN
Mary 151
Myra POLLARD 151
Truston 151
Truxton 151
W. 151
WOLLER
Mary 160
WOLLESEN
Catharina Maria
　KLINDER 169
Hans 169
Thomas 169
WOMELSTROF
Anna 69
WOOD
Abigail W. 7
Anna NIEDERMEYER
　169
Annie B. 4
Ben 125
Berry 169
C. 31, 53, 97
Carrie 155
Carrie M. 105
Charles 169
Charles L. 30
David 105
Eliza MARTIN 169
Elizabeth BABB 169
Elmira 49
Emeline 98
J.L. 129
James D., Mrs. 28
John 78
M.R., Mr. and Mrs. 165
Marion F. 35
Martha 2, 120
Martin 7
Mary 74, 105
Mattie 156
Mrs. 7
Nelson T. 76, 169

O.S. 27, 50, 64, 104,
　155
O.S., Mrs. 27
Rebecca SMITH 169
Sheldon L. 169
Thirza 43
WOODARD
James 87, 101
James I. 169
Rhoda WALTON 169
Sylvender 169
WOODFORD
May L. 134
WOODHAM
Joseph 6
WOODING
Elizabeth 28
WOODLAND
James 117
WOODMAN
Clark 130
WOODROW
Elizabeth 140
WOODRUFF
Emma 41
WOODS
Amanda 161
Anna M. HAPEN 169
Edward 101
Emmarancy MATSON
　169
Eva 8
Frank 8
George H. 169
H.T. 67
Laura MUNGER 8
Margaret 161
Mary 139
Mary A. 170
Mathis TOLLES 169
Mr. 156
Nathaniel 169
Prudence 80
Prudence W. 154
Sarah 56
Sarah C. 146
Willard 169
WOODSON
Elizabeth 142
WOODWARD
Amanda 129
WOODWORTH
C.D. 2
Esther NORTON 169
Fannie E. 106
Helena MORANEY 169
James 169
Latetia TANNER 106
Lyman 106
Perry 169
Sarah 26
WOOLEY
C.E. 107
F.R. 107
WOOLF
Samuel 90
WOOLFS
Annie 54
Edith 54
Louie 54
WOOLLEY
Celia E. BURGMAN
　169
Frederick R. 169
Mary Ann STEVENSON
　169

Stites 169
WOOLSEY
Ellen RUSSELL 140
Mary S. 140
Richard 140
WOOLWORTH
C.P. 89
J.M., Mrs. 142
WOOSTER
Emily 110
Rosalia 160
WOOTON
Caroline 83
WOPAREL
Mathew 74
WORDEN
Margaret 125
Maria D. 99
Maria E. 168
WORDMAN
Martha 129
WORKMAN
---- 169
WORKS
Harriet 17
WORLEY
Eliza H. BERLIN 169
H.A. 169
Justina M. BURKE 169
Mary J. 105
Philip H. 169
Preston 105
Sabina 139
Sarah CAMES 105
WORNER
Elizabeth 41
WORNES
Gurine 166
Mary PETERSON 166
Peter 166
WORTHINGTON
Callie WILLEFORD
　169
Caroline BREWER 169
Charles 169
Hortense 71
Irving 169
WORTMEN
Magdalena 70
WOSHEKER
Frances 45
WOTIZ
Catharine 169
WOYLLACK
Annie 143
WRAGE
Anna SWAN 169
Bessie McARRAGHER
　169
Henry 169
WRASSE
Albertine ZWEMCKE
　170
Carl 170
Johan 170
Johann 170
Johanna PAGEL 170
WREN
Catharine MALONE
　170
Hattie C. WILKINS 170
John 170
Mary 10, 157
Thadeus 170

WRIEDT
Elizabeth GRIMSMANN
　35
Margaretha 35
Peter 35
WRIGHT
Augustus S. 170
Betsey 73
Burril 73
Catherine 15
Charles A. Spencer 170
Charles H. 170
Elizabeth 101
Emma 87
Esther BIGALOW 29
Etta N. 32
F.P., Mrs. 15, 119
Fanny P. 168
Harriet 132
Harriet JONES 170
Hattie SMITH 32
Helen C. DORING 170
Hester 35
J.L. 84
J.S. 17, 51, 76, 133
James 32, 132
Jane 105, 117
Jane KELLEY 170
Jane KELLY 117
Joanna C. 117
Johanna E. 146
John 29
Joseph 78, 170
Josephine 11
L.R. 42
Lottie 29
M.H., Mrs. 51, 170
Martha 123
Martha Ann 142
Mary 20
Mary C. KETCHAM
　170
Mary E. 93, 117
Mary H. 9, 34, 119, 158
Mary H., Mrs. 15
Mimie 132
Mr. and Mrs. 11
Mr., Sr. 170
Rachel 97
S., Mrs. 87
Sadie M. LEE 170
Sarah 117, 131
Sarah E. ROBERTS 170
Silas 170
Sylvania 48, 88, 95,
　112, 117, 168
Sylvanus Mr. 6
Sylvanus, Mrs. 6, 112
Tho. K. 118
Thomas J. 117
Thomas K. 170
Thos. K. 117
WRIGLEY
Caroline L. 145
WROTH
A.B. 116
Ella 116
Martha M. UNVOCAY
　116
WUENSCHBERGER
Theresa 73
WUISTER
Salome 35
WULFF
Caroline 86
Charles 86

Sophie BRINKMAN 86
WULLBRANDT
D.E. FISHER 54
Emma 54
John 54
WUNSEH
Mary 69
Rurckhard 69
WURTEMBERGER
Ursula 35
WYATT
America 31
WYCOFF
Harriet 70
WYETH
Edward 170
Johan 170
WYHLEDADL
Fanny 153
Fanny COUFAL 153
John 153
WYLEY
Sarah 121
WYLIE
I.N. 44
Rose J. 44
Sarah Jane GITHENS
　44
WYLY
Sarah 121
WYMAN
Albert U. 170
Amelia Ann TUPPER
　29
Carrie E. 29
E. 40
Evan 149, 170
Francisco E. 29
Hannah KEITH 170
Harriet C. FAKE 170
Iantha C. 68
Ianthe C. 132
Joseph 170
Margaret 15
Minerva 149
Minervia C. NEIGHLY
　170
Mr. and Mrs. 170
Sarah Maria 132
Tesse 68
W.W. 29, 132
Wm. M. 40
WYNCKOOP
H. 165
WYNN
Susan 156
WYSEL
Elizabeth 117
YAGLER
Mary 157
YALE
Sarah A. 166
YALTER
Maglalena 13
YANDA
Annie 38
Joseph 38
YANSDOTER
Christina 120
YANTS
Margaret 168
YARDLEY
Mary 46
YARSTON
Selma, Mrs. 148

YATES
  Eliza J.D. 120
  Idalyn H. G. 170
  John C. 27
  Joseph I. 170
  Julia Ann NORRIS 170
  Maria 56
  Mary E. 64, 119
  W.J. 97
  Willis M. 119, 170
  Wm. J. 120
YAUBRA
  Henderson 161
YAW
  Eliza MILLINGTON
    170
  Franklin M. 170
  Joseph F. 170
  Mattie APPLEBY 170
YEAGER
  George W. 143
  Martha Ann 131
  Nancy Ann 131
  William 131
YEATES
  George 170
  Isophean BOULTON
    170
  Jane HALL 170
  William 170
YEATS
  Alexander 170
  Daniel 170
  Margaret CLUBB 170
  Mary C. RICH 170
YEGELEIN
  Mary Ann 104
YEGER
  Margareta 35
YENTZ
  Hannah 4
YEOMANS
  Mary Jane 21
YERGA
  David 170
  John M. 170
  S.E. 41
  Sarah E. EDWARDS
    170
  Susan SECHRIST 170
YETTER
  Balthas 170
  Bertha WINKLER 170
  John 170
  Katharine HEUGSLER
    170
YETZER
  Anthony 9
YING
  Charley 170
  Emma TRIPLETT 170
  Foo 170
  Liddie QUOO 170
YOGON
  Greta 92
YOKEL
  Louise M. 46
  Peter 46
  Rozella DHOHRDT 46
YOKELE
  Louisa M. 46
  Peter 46
  Rosella DHONDT 46
YONGA
  Annie 66

YONLEY
  Margarett Ann LESURE
    170
  Thomas D.W. 170
YORK
  Louisa 33
  Mary 105
  Melissa EARLE 33
  William 33
YOST
  C.E., Mrs. 16
YOSTE
  Frederick 170
  Gusta KETCHMIRE
    170
  Margareta WEBER 170
  Martin 170
YOUNG
  Andrew 170
  Ann MILLER 80
  Annie 129
  Auguste RANDON 170
  C.H. 170
  Catharine Ann 125
  Christina OSBERG 170
  Clara D. ALBERTSON
    170
  Cornelia 138
  Eliza Jane REGAN 170
  Elizabeth 15
  Elizabeth EULER 170
  Emeline 49
  Frances L. 24
  Frances M. STEVENS
    170
  Frank H. 170
  George 80, 170
  Georgiana ORRICK 170
  Georgianna O. 80
  Georgie A. 169
  H.W. 170
  Hannah 53
  Hans 170
  Hattie 57
  Ira 170
  J.F. 162
  J.H. 170
  James 15, 170
  Jane 19, 169
  Jennete MORRISON
    170
  Jennie 162
  John 147
  Kate WARD 147
  Louisa FORSLAND
    170
  Louise 50
  M.F. 170
  Maria PAULSEN 170
  Marietta SMITH 170
  Mary 37, 59
  Mary A. WOODS 170
  Mary C. 87
  Mary J. 147
  Mary KANE 57
  Mary T. TALLBEE 170
  Minnie HUTH 170
  Peter A. 170
  Shepard 170
  Stephen 57
  Thomas 169
  Toney 44, 170
YOUNGER
  Carrie E. 126
YOUNGSTEDT
  M. 15

YOUNGSTETLER
  Louisa 15
YOUNT
  Sarah 70
YOX
  Joseph 170
  Matilda C. PERRY 170
  Peter 170
YUKNESS
  Catharine 67
YUNGSTROM
  Hannah Carolina 164
  N. 164
  P. 164
ZACHARIASEN
  Dorothea C. 66
ZACHARY
  Lizzie 71
ZAEFFLER
  Joseph 164
ZAFF
  Phillipine 110
ZAH
  Catharine SMITH 100
  Fredericka 100
  John 100
ZAHRADNIK
  Franciska 138
ZEGRINO
  Lavina 115
ZEHNER
  Eliza McKEE 170
  John W. 170
ZELENA
  Barbara 138
ZELENKA
  Catharine V. 134
  Frank 134
  Mary 134
ZELLMAR
  Juliana 137
ZELLMER
  Juliane 66
ZENICEK
  Mary 8
ZEPF
  Lena 9
  Martina 9
ZERBE
  Margaret 116
ZERGER
  Josephine 84
ZERLER
  Joseph 20
ZETTLEMOYER
  Mary 69
ZIEGLER
  John 11
ZIEMAN
  H.J. 15
ZIEMANN
  H.J. 164
  Mary C. BERENDT
    125
  Mary L.C. 125
  Michael F. 125
ZIESENIS
  Dorothea 44
ZIMMERMAN
  Andrew 171
  Anne EDMONSON 171
  Catherine 155
  Catherine ELSSASER
    171
  Gotlieb 155
  Gottlieb 42, 171

Gottlob 95
Gratia 19
Johanna 39
John 13, 19, 171
Katrina STUCK 171
Katrina WEISS 171
Louise BUCHLER 171
Magdalena SMITH 158
Mary 158
Matilda 149
Powell 158
William F. 171
ZIMMERMANN
  Gottlob 87
  Helena 169
  Louise 136
  Mathilda 14
ZIMMIRMANSON
  Johanna 25
ZINK
  John 171
  Louisa BOWERS 171
  Rosa BERNARD 171
ZIPLIES
  Johann F. 54
  Maria TANTURATH
    54
  Rosalie 54
ZIPZ
  Fred 160
ZISKOVSKY
  Annie ERBEN 171
  Anton 171
  Josef 171
  Mary BRUSEK 171
ZOBEL
  Anna 150
  Augusta FEST 150
  Frederick 150
ZODER
  Barbara 12
ZOEPFE
  Anna 18
ZOPFI
  Anna 84
ZOTZMAN
  Charles 171
  Dorothea SEEGER 171
  Frederick 171
  Julia RASMUSSEN 171
ZOUGY
  Mayealona 132
ZWEIBEL
  Geo. 92
ZWEIFEL
  Fridolin 18
ZWEMCKE
  Albertine 170